The History of Science
in the United States

An Encyclopedia

The History of Science in the United States
An Encyclopedia

Edited by
Marc Rothenberg
Smithsonian Institution

GARLAND PUBLISHING, INC.
NEW YORK & LONDON
2001

Published in 2001 by
Garland Publishing, Inc.
29 West 35th Street
New York, NY 10001

Garland Publishing is an imprint of the Taylor & Francis Group.

10   9   8   7   6   5   4   3   2   1

Library of Congress Cataloging-in-Publication Data

The history of science in the United States : an encyclopedia / edited by Marc Rothenberg.
        p. cm. — (Garland reference library of the social sciences ; 0842. Special-reference)
    Includes bibliographical references and index.
    ISBN 0-8153-0762-4 (alk. paper)
    1. Science—United States—History—Encyclopedias.   I. Rothenberg, Marc, 1949–

    Q127.U6 H57 2000
    509.73 21—dc21   99-043757

Printed on acid-free, 250-year-life paper
Manufactured in the United States of America

To Nathan Reingold, my mentor and friend

Contents

Series Introduction

Since World War II, the historical study of science has grown enormously. Once the domain of a few scientists interested in their intellectual genealogy and a scattering of intellectual historians, philosophers of science, and sociologists of knowledge, it is now a mature and independent discipline. However, historians of science have not had a way until now to make the essentials of their subject accessible to high school and college students, scholars in other disciplines, and the general public. The encyclopedias in this series will furnish concise historical information and summarize the latest research in a form accessible to those without scientific or mathematical training.

Each volume in the series will be independent from the others. The focus of a particular volume may be a scientific discipline (e.g., astronomy), a topic that transcends disciplines (e.g., laboratories and instruments, science in the United States), or a relationship between the science and another aspect of culture (e.g., science and religion). The same entry title may appear in a number of volumes, perhaps with a different author, as individual volume editors/co-editors approach the subject from a different context.

What is common to each of the volumes is a concern for the historiography of the history of science. By historiography, I mean the recognition that there is never an undisputed explanation of past events. Instead, historians struggle to come to a consensus about the facts and significant issues, and argue over the most valid historical explanation(s). The authors of the entries in this and the other volumes in the series have been asked to provide entries which are accurate and balanced, but also cognizant of how historical interpretations have changed over time. Where historiographic debate has occurred, authors have been asked to address that debate. They have also been given the freedom to express their own positions on these issues.

The extent to which historiographic issues are prominent in the entries varies from entry to entry, and from volume to volume, according to the richness of the historical literature and the depth of the debate. Even for a subject with a rich historiographic literature, such as science in the United States, there are topics for which there is little scholarship. The one or two scholars working on a particular topic are still laboring to uncover the facts and get the chronology correct. For other fields, there have been too few active scholars for the development of a complex debate on almost any topic. The introductions to each of the individual volumes will clearly lay out the historiographic issues facing scholars in that particular area of the history of science.

Each entry also provides a concise, selected bibliography on the topic. Further bibliographic information can be obtained from the volumes in the Garland series "Bibliographies on the History of Science and Technology," edited by Robert Multhauf and Ellen Wells.

Marc Rothenberg
Smithsonian Institution

Introduction

Science is an essential element of American civilization. The historical study of American science—the study of the individuals, the institutions, the ideas, and the experiments that together constitute the rich fabric of science in the United States—is a lively and exciting field of scholarship. However, the knowledge and interpretations generated by this scholarship have not been easily accessible to the high school or college student or the interested general public.

This volume has been written to furnish that access. The entries in this encyclopedia provide factual information, identification and analysis of historiographic issues, and guidance to the most significant publications and most important manuscript collections. The primary focus of the volume is the history of science, but the reader will notice that topics in the history of invention, technology, engineering, and medicine are also included where the boundaries among the disciplines overlap.

Whenever possible, entries provide basic historical information, a review of the topic's significance for the history of science in the United States, and a discussion of historiographic issues, including controversies among historians. Not all entries, however, include the historiographic discussion. In some cases, there simply are not any historiographic issues. Historians are still struggling to ascertain the fundamental information.

The list of topics included in the encyclopedia is not exhaustive. Nonetheless, information on many individuals, institutions, and other topics not included among the list of entries can be found by referring to the index.

There are two major summary essays in the volume, covering science in the colonial era and science from 1789 to 1865. These essays demonstrate how rich the historical literature is for the history of American science until the Civil War. Although there are a wide range of topics, the emphasis has been placed on the history of institutions and scientific disciplines and subdisciplines. The individuals selected to be the subject of biographical entries were those deceased scientists whose primary contributions were in the development of the institutional infrastructure of American science or were key figures in the rise and growth of disciplines, as well the most important scientists as measured by history in terms of scientific discoveries. Patronage was also a very important topic, and an effort was made to include topics that highlighted the patronage system for science in the United States.

The length of entries is significant and does reflect, generally, but not always, the editor's perception of the significance of a particular topic in the history of science in the United States. Discerning readers will soon be aware that the same institutions, organizations, or individuals will appear in more than one entry, but from different perspectives and in different contexts. For example, Benjamin Silliman, Sr., is important as the editor of the *American Journal of Science,* a chemist and mineralogist, and a member of the Yale faculty. In some cases, the same author has written a number of entries and coordinated them to provide multiple and complementary contexts for a particular individual or institution. In other cases, different authors will provide somewhat dissimilar perspectives, reflecting historiographic differences. The index will guide the reader to the multiple entries dealing with the same topic.

Additional sources of information and bibliography that the reader may find useful are:

Elliott, Clark A. *History of Science in the United States: A Chronology and Research Guide.* New York: Garland Publishing, 1996.

Kohlstedt, Sally Gregory, and Margaret W. Rossiter. *Historical Writing on American Science.* Baltimore: Johns Hopkins University Press, 1986.

Rothenberg, Marc. *The History of Science and Technology in the United States: A Critical and Selective Bibliography.* 2 volumes. New York: Garland, 1982, 1993.

This encyclopedia was the idea of Clark A. Elliott. He had selected the topics, identified most of the contributors, and had begun editing the entries when circumstances forced him to give up the project. Having done most of the hard work, he then allowed me to take on and complete the project. Thanks, Clark.

Clark's editorial advisory board assisted him in the identification of authors, the most important step in the transformation of an encyclopedia from concept to reality. I want to thank Pnina G. Abir-Am, Robert Friedel, Patsy A. Gerstner, the late Stanley Goldberg, and Margaret W. Rossiter for their contributions.

This project has been in process for many years. I appreciate the support and tolerance of the many staff at Garland, past and present, who have worked with me, including Andrea Johnson and Richard Steins. I also want to thank Nancy Crompton and Ben McCanna at Stratford Publishing Services, who oversaw the copy-editimg. My family was tolerant of a project that occupied much of my free time and lots of floor space at home.

Finally, I want to express my appreciation of Nathan Reingold's many contributions to the history of American science and my own intellectual and professional development. My greatest regret as editor is that his health prevented him from contributing to this volume.

Marc Rothenberg
Smithsonian Institution

Contributors

David P. Adams, Jr.
Independent Scholar

Paul G. Anderson
Washington University

Rima D. Apple
University of Wisconsin, Madison

Adam Jared Apt
Independent Scholar

James W. Atkinson
Michigan State University

Anthony F. Aveni
Colgate University

Simon Baatz
National Library of Medicine

Mark V. Barrow, Jr.
Virginia Polytechnic Institute and State University

Silvio A. Bedini
Smithsonian Institution (emeritus)

James E. Beichler
Salem-Teikyo University

Roger E. Bilstein
University of Houston, Clear Lake

Stephen Bocking
Trent University

Charles Boewe
C.S. Rafinesque Correspondence

Marlene K. Bradford
Texas A&M University

Maynard Brichford
University of Illinois at Urbana-Champaign

Billie Broaddus
University of Cincinnati

Joan Lisa Bromberg
University of California, Davis (emeritus)

Robert V. Bruce
Boston University (emeritus)

Glenn E. Bugos
The Prologue Group

Vern L. Bullough
University of Southern California

Philip Cash
Emmanuel College (emeritus)

David C. Cassidy
Hofstra University

Peggy Champlin
Independent Scholar

Seymour S. Cohen
American Cancer Society (emeritus)

Mildred Cohn
University of Pennsylvania

S.R. Coleman
Cleveland State University

Martin J. Collins
Smithsonian Institution

Thomas D. Cornell
Rochester Institute of Technology

James W. Cortada
IBM

Janet L. Coryell
Western Michigan University

Hamilton Cravens
Iowa State University

Paul Jerome Croce
Stetson University

Stephen J. Cross
University of Texas, San Antonio

Tom Crouch
Smithsonian Institution

Barbara Ritter Dailey
Harvard University

Donald M. Davidson, Jr.
The Geological Society of America

Deborah C. Day
Scripps Institution of Oceanography

Steven J. Dick
United States Naval Observatory

Ronald E. Doel
Oregon State University

A. Hunter Dupree
Independent Scholar

Churchill Eisenhart
National Bureau of Standards (deceased)

Clark A. Elliott
Independent Scholar

Priscilla Jordan Elliott
Independent Scholar

Elizabeth W. Etheridge
Longwood College (emeritus)

Anne Fausto-Sterling
Brown University

J. Alan Feduccia
University of North Carolina

Elizabeth Fee
Johns Hopkins University

Mark R. Finlay
Armstrong State College

Donald C. Fisher
University of Mississippi

Donald Fleming
Harvard University

James Rodger Fleming
Colby College

Mike F. Foster
Independent Scholar

Oz Frankel
University of Michigan

Deborah Julie Franklin
University of Pennsylvania

Peter A. Fritzell
Lawrence University

Clifford Frondel
Harvard University (emeritus)

Robert C. Fuller
Bradley University

Laurel Furumoto
Wellesley College

W. Bruce Fye, M.D.
Marshfield Clinic

Elizabeth A. Garber
University at Stony Brook

Roger L. Geiger
Pennsylvania State University

Joel Genuth
American Institute of Physics

Patsy Gerstner
The Cleveland Medical Library Association

Carl-Henry Geschwind
George Washington University

Norman Gevitz
University of Illinois College of Medicine, Chicago

Douglas R. Givens
St. Louis Community College

Janice Goldblum
National Academy of Sciences

Daniel Goldstein
University of California, Davis

Gregory A. Good
West Virginia University

Judith R. Goodstein
California Institute of Technology

Michael H. Gorn
National Aeronautics and Space Administration

Patricia Gossel
Smithsonian Institution

John C. Greene
University of Connecticut (emeritus)

Ted Greenfield
Minnesota Public Interest Research Group

David H. Guston
Rutgers University

William J. Haas
Independent Scholar

Joel B. Hagen
Radford University

James R. Hansen
Auburn University

Victoria A. Harden
National Institutes of Health

Anne Harrington
Harvard University

Sidney Hart
Smithsonian Institution

Steve Joshua Heims
Independent Scholar

J. Douglas Helms
United States Department of Agriculture

Norriss S. Hetherington
University of California, Berkeley

Richard G. Hewlett
History Associates Incorporated

John Hildebidle
Massachusetts Institute of Technology

Lee R. Hiltzik
Rockefeller Archive Center

Peter B. Hirtle
Cornell University

Elizabeth Hodes
Santa Barbara City College

Edward R. Hogan
East Stroudsburg University

Reginald Horsman
University of Wisconsin, Milwaukee

B.F. Howell, Jr.
Pennsylvania State University

Margaret Humphreys
Duke University

Linda Hunt
Independent Scholar

R. Douglas Hurt
Iowa State University

Paul B. Israel
Thomas A. Edison Papers

Richard A. Jarrell
York University

Barry V. Johnston
Indiana University Northwest

George B. Kauffman
California State University, Fresno

Lily E. Kay
Massachusetts Institute of Technology

Elizabeth Keeney
Kenyon College

Nelson R. Kellogg
Sonoma State University

Clara Sue Kidwell
University of California, Berkeley

Peggy Kidwell
Smithsonian Institution

Barbara A. Kimmelman
Philadelphia University

Sharon Kingsland
Johns Hopkins University

Vernon N. Kisling, Jr.
University of Florida

William A. Koelsch
Clark University

Robert E. Kohler
University of Pennsylvania

Sally Gregory Kohlstedt
University of Minnesota

Phyllis D. Krasnick
Independent Scholar

Nancy Krieger
Kaiser Foundation Research Institute

John Lankford
Kansas State University (emeritus)

Léo Laporte
University of California, Santa Cruz (emeritus)

Edward J. Larson
University of Georgia

Roger D. Launius
National Aeronautics and Space Administration

Edwin T. Layton, Jr.
University of Minnesota (emeritus)

Susan E. Lederer
Pennsylvania State University College of Medicine

Muriel Lederman
Virginia Polytechnic Institute and State University

Stuart W. Leslie
Johns Hopkins University

Erwin Levold
Rockefeller Archive Center

Bruce V. Lewenstein
Cornell University

M. Susan Lindee
University of Pennsylvania

Rebecca S. Lowen
Metropolitan State University

Henry Lowood
Stanford University

Paul L. M. Lucier
Rensselaer Polytechnic Institute

Edward Lurie
University of Delaware (emeritus)

Stuart McCook
College of New Jersey

A. Michal McMahon
West Virginia University

Linda O. McMurry
North Carolina State University

David Magnus
University of Puget Sound

Leo J. Mahoney
Baskent Universitesi

Jane Maienschein
Arizona State University

Lynn Maloney
Independent Scholar

Kenneth R. Manning
Massachusetts Institute of Technology

Jordan D. Marché II
Independent Scholar

Geoffrey J. Martin
Southern Connecticut State University

Seymour H. Mauskopf
Duke University

George T. Mazuzan
National Science Foundation (emeritus)

Gordon Miller
Seattle University

Thomas J. Misa
Illinois Institute of Technology

Gregg Mitman
University of Oklahoma

Arthur P. Molella
Smithsonian Institution

James W. Montgomery, Jr.
Kenyon College

H. Wayne Morgan
University of Oklahoma

Edward T. Morman
New York Academy of Medicine

Peter J.T. Morris
Science Museum

Gary E. Moulton
University of Nebraska, Lincoln

Albert E. Moyer
*Virginia Polytechnic Institute and
State University*

Elizabeth A. Muenger
United States Air Force Academy

Clifford M. Nelson
United States Geological Survey

Julie R. Newell
Southern Polytechnic State University

Marilyn Bailey Ogilvie
University of Oklahoma

Therese O'Malley
National Gallery of Art

Donald E. Osterbrock
Lick Observatory

Richard A. Overfield
University of Nebraska

Larry Owens
University of Massachusetts, Amherst

John Parascandola
United States Public Health Service

Nancy Parezo
Arizona State Museum

Karen Parshall
University of Virginia

Linda Dugan Partridge
Marywood College

Philip J. Pauly
Rutgers University

Robert McCracken Peck
Academy of Natural Sciences of Philadelphia

John H. Perkins
Evergreen State College

Edward Pershey
Western Reserve Historical Society

Stuart Peterfreund
Northeastern University

Melba Phillips
American Physical Society (emeritus)

Andrew Pickering
University of Illinois

Harold T. Pinkett
National Archives and Records Administration (emeritus)

Cynthia DeHaven Pitcock
University of Arkansas for Medical Sciences

Howard Plotkin
University of Western Ontario

John A. Popplestone
Archives of the History of American Psychology

Laura Smith Porter
Independent Scholar

Michael L. Prendergast
University of California at Los Angeles

Carroll W. Pursell
Case Western Reserve University

Karen A. Rader
Sarah Lawrence College

Ronald Rainger
Texas Tech University

Wayne D. Rasmussen
Agricultural History Society (emeritus)

James W. Reed
Rutgers University

Martin Reuss
United States Army Corps of Engineers

Terry S. Reynolds
Michigan Technological University

Edward F. Rivinus
Smithsonian Institution (deceased)

Naomi Rogers
Yale University

Marc Rothenberg
Smithsonian Institution

Helen M. Rozwadowski
Independent Scholar

David P. Rubincam
NASA Goddard Space Flight Center

Michael Ruse
University of Guelph

Robert W. Rydell
Montana State University

Warren J. Samuels
Michigan State University

Clark T. Sawin, M.D.
Department of Veterans Affairs

Richard C. Sawyer
Newton (Iowa) High School

Sara Schechner
Gnomon Research

Martin W. Schein
Smithsonian Institution (deceased)

Londa Schiebinger
Pennsylvania State University

Judith Ann Schiff
Yale University Library

Robert E. Schofield
Iowa State University (emeritus)

Bruce E. Seely
Michigan Technological University

Robert W. Seidel
University of Minnesota

John W. Servos
Amherst College

Todd Shallat
Boise State University

Philip S. Shoemaker
Independent Scholar

Ana Simões
University of Lisbon

Nancy G. Slack
Russell Sage College

Hugh Richard Slotten
Harvard University

Edward H. Smith
Cornell University (emeritus)

John K. Smith
Lehigh University

Michael M. Sokal
Worcester Polytechnic Institute

Katherine R. Sopka
Four Corners Analytic Sciences

W. Conner Sorensen
Independent Scholar

Sarah Stage
Arizona State University West

Stephen C. Steacy
Independent Scholar

Kathryn Steen
University of Delaware

Carlene E. Stephens
Smithsonian Institution

Lester D. Stephens
University of Georgia

Keir B. Sterling
United States Army Combined Arms Support

Anthony N. Stranges
Texas A&M University

David Strauss
Kalamazoo College

Patricia Tyson Stroud
Independent Scholar

George Sweetnam
Princeton University (deceased)

Loyd S. Swenson, Jr.
University of Houston

D. Stanley Tarbell
Vanderbilt University (deceased)

Joseph N. Tatarewicz
University of Maryland, Baltimore County

Emily Thompson
University of Pennsylvania

Nancy Tomes
University at Stony Brook

Elisabeth Tooker
Temple University

Rodney G. Triplet
Northern State University

W. Peter Trower
World Physics Technology

Ton van Helvoort
University of Maastricht

David K. van Keuren
Naval Research Laboratory

Craig B. Waff
Encyclopedia Americana

J. Samuel Walker
National Regulatory Commission

Maila L. Walter
Harvard University

Jessica Wang
University of California at Los Angeles

Zuoyue Wang
California Polytechnic University, Pomona

Spencer R. Weart
American Institute of Physics

George E. Webb
Tennessee Technological University

John M. Weeks
University of Pennsylvania

Nadine M. Weidman
Harvard University

Margaret Welch
Maryland Historical Society

Dennis C. Williams
Southern Nazarene University

Dael Wolfle
University of Washington

William E. Worthington, Jr.
Smithsonian Institution

Charles D. Wrege
Cornell University

Ellis L. Yochelson
United States Geological Survey (emeritus)

Neil L. York
Brigham Young University

James Harvey Young
Emory University (emeritus)

John J. Zernal
Oregon State University

A

Abbe, Cleveland (1838–1916)

Astronomer and meteorologist. Born in New York City, Abbe was educated at The New York Free Academy (now The City College of New York), graduating in 1857, and the University of Michigan, where he studied astronomy with F.F.E. Brünnow from 1859 to 1860. He then worked for the United States Coast Survey until 1864. From January 1865 until November 1866, he was a research assistant to Otto Struve at Pulkova Observatory in Russia. In February 1868, he became director of the Cincinnati Observatory. He joined the United States Army Signal Corps storm-warning service, the predecessor of the Weather Bureau, in 1870, remaining with the bureau until his death.

Abbe had initially gathered meteorological data at the Cincinnati Observatory as part of an investigation of the impact of local atmospheric conditions on astronomical observations, an investigation necessitated by the poor observing conditions at Cincinnati and driven by his recognition of the poor understanding of atmospheric refraction among astronomers. It was this collecting of meteorological data which drew Abbe deeper and deeper into meteorology itself. On 1 September 1869, be began issuing a daily weather bulletin for Cincinnati.

Although he had over two hundred publications in the field of meteorology, he did not develop a reputation as a significant research scientist. Instead, he encouraged other researchers and disseminated information. He was a strong propagandist for the importance of basic research for weather forecasting. He was also an important figure in the development of standard time in the United States, a result of the need to standardize meteorological observations taken across the country.

In spite of his minor significance, Abbe has attracted more attention from historians than some more important researchers. According to the perspective of the historian, his career can be seen either in terms of success or failure. Reingold, for example, has described Abbe as "an exemplar of a particular vanished tradition" (p. 144). He saw Abbe as a practitioner of a form of applied astronomy which was going out of fashion at the time, but nonetheless was widely practiced in the United States and Europe. To him, Abbe's career was a continuum. In contrast, Hetherington viewed Abbe's early career as demonstrating the existence of serious barriers to a professional scientific career in the United States during the years 1856–1871, as compared to the opportunities in Europe. When Abbe joined the Signal Service, it was a transition which represented the end of his career as an astronomer.

Abbe's papers are in the Library of Congress.

BIBLIOGRAPHY

Abbe, Truman. *Professor Abbe . . . and the Isobars: The Story of Cleveland Abbe, America's First Weatherman.* New York: Vantage Press, 1955.

Bartky, Ian R. "The Adoption of Standard Time." *Technology and Culture* 30 (1989): 25–56.

Hetherington, Norriss S. "Cleveland Abbe and a View of Science in Mid-Nineteenth-Century America." *Annals of Science* 33 (1976): 31–49.

Humphreys, W.J. "Cleveland Abbe." *Biographical Memoirs of the National Academy of Sciences* 8 (1919): 469–508.

Reingold, Nathan. "Cleveland Abbe at Pulkowa: Theory and Practice in the Nineteenth Century Physical Sciences." *Archives internationales d'histoire des sciences* 17 (1964): 133–147.

A

———. "A Good Place to Study Astronomy." *Library of Congress Quarterly Journal of Current Acquisitions* 20 (1962–1963): 211–217.

Marc Rothenberg

SEE ALSO
Meteorology and Atmospheric Science

Academic Institutions

In the contemporary United States about one-half of basic research is conducted in academic institutions, making them the principal locus for the advancement of fundamental science. In fulfilling that mission, colleges or universities have established professional roles for scientists, provided for the education of new scientists, created a home for the scientific community, supplied facilities for scientific work, and acted as conduits for the resources that support scientific research. Historically, the different components of this mission have developed almost in sequence.

The first professional role for a scientist was created at Harvard College in 1727 by the Hollis Professorship of Mathematics and Natural Philosophy. John Winthrop, the second incumbent of that chair, used this opportunity to fashion a distinguished career as an astronomer. Later in the century, the colonial colleges were generally eager to create similar positions—if and when they could find funds and suitable candidates. Until well into the nineteenth century, however, the organization of American science lay outside of the colleges. It was based instead upon learned and scientific societies. The American Philosophical Society, organized in Philadelphia by Benjamin Franklin, was the first of these, but other locally based societies proliferated in the early Republic. Individual scientists in academic institutions at best were adjunct in this thickening, but essentially amateur, network.

American colleges were largely adventitious to the development of science. Between the end of the Revolutionary War and about 1820, they lost touch almost entirely with advancements being made in Europe. During the next generation, as the number of colleges mushroomed, the more substantial among them endeavored to keep abreast of scientific knowledge. They initiated courses in chemistry, zoology, botany, and geology, among others. This effort was soon frustrated by the fixed classical curriculum: there was little room for specialized subjects, and even those included

could only be taught at a superficial, introductory level. Active scientists were occasionally employed to teach these subjects, but no scientists were "trained" in academic institutions before midcentury. Preparation for a scientific career instead required crossing the Atlantic, initially to England and only later to Germany.

After 1840, scientific activity nevertheless quickened around and about the wealthier colleges without touching the classical course of study. A public subscription in 1843 paid to erect the Harvard Observatory. An observatory also became the focus of Henry Tappan's efforts to introduce serious scientific study at the University of Michigan. At these and other colleges, telescopes provided for research, but contributed little toward instruction. Academic museums occupied a similar role after 1860. More important, however, was the creation of separate scientific schools. The Lawrence School at Harvard and the Sheffield School at Yale both originated in 1847, but otherwise differed. Created by endowment, the Lawrence School emphasized pure science, but did little teaching of either college or advanced students. The Yale effort evolved in stages as a place for teaching practical science and advanced studies in scientific and literary subjects—both tasks eschewed by the classical college. It was subsequently solidified by the gifts of Joseph Sheffield. Both institutions were pioneers: the Lawrence School was an academic home for research, but Yale awarded the first American Ph.D.'s in 1861.

After midcentury, a nexus began to be forged between American science and higher education. Indeed, the Lazzaroni, science leaders of the day, increasingly sought strategic positions in the colleges for sympathizers in order to advance their cause. After the Civil War, the role of academic institutions was decisively transformed. Three separate developments brought science inside academic institutions, providing homes for scientists and means for the regular education of their successors.

First came success in establishing advanced schooling in practical subjects. Initially these undertakings were conceived as being separate from the colleges. Agricultural schools were founded in the 1850s on this basis, and the Massachusetts and Stevens Institutes of Technology replicated this pattern after the war. The utilitarian movement was decisively shaped, however, by the Morrill Land-Grant Act of 1862. It specified that agriculture and the mechanical arts would be taught alongside liberal subjects, a pattern that soon transcended the new land-grant colleges. The scientific component of these utilitarian "arts" was longer in coming. The creation of Agricultural Experiment Stations by the Hatch Act (1887) and the emergence of electrical engineering both stimulated the scientific dimension of their fields.

The replacement of the classical curriculum by the elective system was the second momentous innovation. Pressed most vigorously by Charles Eliot at Harvard (1869–1909), it was widely resisted until the mid-1880s. Afterward, though, acceptance quickly became nearly complete. From the standpoint of science, a professor's freedom to teach advanced subjects was more important than the student's right to elect courses of their own choosing. With the ascendancy of the elective system, colleges began to assemble large and specialized faculties. Harvard led the way, but in fact the largest institutions became preeminent by virtue of being able to support the most numerous faculty.

The third innovation was the institutionalization of graduate education and research, a development associated with the founding of Johns Hopkins University (1876). Inspired by the scientific achievements of German universities, Hopkins alone was consciously dedicated to this mission. Its salience and success quickly goaded other institutions to move in this direction. By the 1890s the American university had finally emerged. It did not conform to the mold of Johns Hopkins, however, nor that of the innovative University of Chicago, which opened in 1892, but rather was more like the reformed Harvard. That is, it harbored a growing and specialized faculty sustained largely by the teaching of undergraduates, but who were also given the resources for graduate education and the conduct of original research.

Between 1890 and World War I, the organizational base of American science shifted decisively into the universities. By 1905, all of the disciplines had formed associations and journals. The new universities, especially Johns Hopkins and Chicago, spearheaded this development. This superstructure, moreover, was controlled by the same university-based disciplinary elite that dominated research and graduate education. When James McKeen Cattell identified the 1,000 leading American men of science in 1906, 82 percent were in academic institutions, and two-thirds of those in the leading fourteen universities (Geiger, *To Advance Knowledge,* p. 39). Not even the endowment of independent research institutes (the Carnegie Institute of

Washington, the Rockefeller Institute of Medical Research) could deflect the ascendancy of the universities.

The academic research system of this era was primarily dependent upon the resources that the universities themselves could devote to science. Above all, the universities nurtured scientist-teachers and provided them with facilities. It was nevertheless assumed that the direct costs of research would have to come from endowed funds dedicated to this purpose. By World War I this was the limiting condition for academic science.

This constraint was lifted in the 1920s as universities became the beneficiaries of research funds from foundations and to a lesser extent industrial firms. The Carnegie Corporation and several of the Rockefeller trusts provided the bulk of the funds for a university research economy. Smaller foundations followed their lead, particularly in supporting medical research. Firms in communications, chemistry, and electricity supported university research in their respective fields. Academic research expanded greatly on the basis of private support, but by the 1930s the limits of these arrangements too had been reached.

The research needs of the military during World War II induced the federal government to support university-based science. Vannevar Bush wrote a manifesto for the new era—*Science—The Endless Frontier*—but in fact the postwar relationship was largely a continuation of wartime arrangements. The large laboratories at Massachusetts Institute of Technology, California Institute of Technology, Johns Hopkins, and others continued to operate; the Manhattan District Project was transmuted into the Atomic Energy Commission; and wartime medical research contracts were assumed by the Public Health Service, forming the basis of an extramural grants program. The most significant departure was the Office of Naval Research, which supported a broad spectrum of investigator-initiated academic research. The National Science Foundation was only created in 1950 and did not become a prominent patron of academic research until the end of that decade.

Another element of continuity was provided by the universities themselves. They had already become the home of scientists and conduits for research funds. Now they found it possible to expand research significantly with federal funds. The basic structure of American academic institutions greatly facilitated this development. Since their research role was driven by

A

external funding, it could fluctuate almost independently of the academic base. Indeed, in organized research units and federal contract research centers, universities fashioned an autonomous research role.

The sophistication and resource requirements of modern science make institutional factors highly consequential for its history. In the studies of Joseph Ben-David, the structure of academic institutions is the crucial factor in the relative scientific performance of modern nations. Indeed, the United States has been fortunate in this respect. The dimensions of its academic system accommodate professional positions for a large scientific community. The hierarchical, competitive structure of institutions has served to encourage the highest standards. And, the divided responsibilities of universities and external supporters of research have produced relatively ample support for academic research.

Given this interdependence, the history of American science and the history of universities share much common territory. Daniel Kevles's history of the physics community deals extensively with academic settings, as does Robert Kohler's account of the origins of biochemistry. Early developments in the social sciences are perhaps even more rooted in academic settings (Bulmer). The history of research universities, conversely, draws extensively from the history of science (Geiger, *To Advance Knowledge* and *Research and Relevant Knowledge*). Nevertheless, studies that attempt to relate institutional factors with the cognitive growth of scientific fields, such as those by John Heilbron, Robert Seidel, and Stuart Leslie, are rare. The postwar history of American science, in particular, has created ample opportunity for this kind of inquiry.

BIBLIOGRAPHY

Ben-David, Joseph. *The Scientist's Role in Society: A Comparative Study.* Chicago: University of Chicago Press, 1971, 1984.

Bruce, Robert V. *The Launching of Modern American Science, 1846–1876.* New York: Knopf, 1987.

Bulmer, Martin. *The Chicago School of Sociology: Institutionalization, Diversity, and the Rise of Sociological Research.* Chicago: University of Chicago Press, 1984.

Fleming, Donald. *Science and Technology in Providence, 1760–1914.* Providence: Brown University, 1952.

Geiger, Roger L. *To Advance Knowledge: The Growth of American Research Universities, 1900–1940.* New York: Oxford University Press, 1986.

———. "Science, Universities, and National Defense, 1945–1970." *Osiris,* 2d ser., 7 (1992): 94–116.

———. *Research and Relevant Knowledge: American Research Universities Since World War II.* New York: Oxford University Press, 1993.

Guralnick, Stanley M. *Science and the Ante-Bellum American College.* Philadelphia: American Philosophical Society, 1975.

Heilbron, John, and Robert Seidel. *Lawrence and His Laboratory.* Vol. 1 of *A History of the Lawrence Berkeley Laboratory.* Berkeley: University of California Press, 1990.

Kevles, Daniel J. *The Physicists: The History of a Scientific Community in Modern America.* New York: Knopf, 1978; reprint, Cambridge: Harvard University Press, 1995.

Kohler, Robert. *From Chemistry to Biochemistry: The Making of a Biomedical Discipline.* Cambridge, Eng.: Cambridge University Press, 1982.

Leslie, Stuart W. *The Cold War and American Science: The Military-Industrial-Academic Complex at MIT and Stanford.* New York: Columbia University Press, 1993.

Oleson, Alexandra, and Sanborn C. Brown, eds. *The Pursuit of Knowledge in the Early American Republic.* Baltimore: Johns Hopkins University Press, 1976.

Oleson, Alexandra, and John Voss, eds. *The Organization of Knowledge in Modern America, 1860–1920.* Baltimore: Johns Hopkins University Press, 1979.

Seidel, Robert. "Physics Research in California: The Rise of a Leading Sector in American Physics." Ph.D. diss., University of California, Berkeley, 1978.

Servos, John W. "The Industrial Relations of Science: Chemical Engineering at MIT, 1900–1939." *Isis* 71 (1980): 531–549.

Storr, Richard J. *The Beginnings of Graduate Education in America.* Chicago: University of Chicago Press, 1953.

Swann, John P. *Academic Scientists and the Pharmaceutical Industry: Cooperative Research in Twentieth-Century America.* Baltimore: Johns Hopkins University Press, 1988.

Veysey, Laurence. *The Emergence of the American University.* Chicago: University of Chicago Press, 1965.

Roger L. Geiger

SEE ALSO
Specific institutions

Academy of Natural Sciences of Philadelphia, The

Organized in 1812 by a small group of amateur naturalists dedicated to the "rational disposal of leisure moments" and "the advancement and diffusion of useful, liberal human knowledge" (Founders Document), the Academy of Natural Sciences of Philadelphia was one of the earliest institutions in the United States to devote its efforts exclusively to the study of natural history. Among its early members were many of the men whose names are synonymous with the first organized study of natural history in North America, including the entomologist and conchologist Thomas Say, one of seven founders; botanists William Bartram, Benjamin Smith Barton, and Thomas Nuttall; ornithologists Alexander Wilson, John Kirk Townsend, and later, John James Audubon; geologists Samuel G. Morton and William Maclure, who served as the president of the academy from 1817 to 1840; mammalogists John D. Godman, Richard Harlan, and Titian Ramsay Peale; and mineralogist Gerard Troost, another founder.

By April 1812, just three months after the academy's founding, its members secured the use of a permanent meeting place in the city and began to amass an institutional library and collection of natural artifacts, including some "very common insects & shells . . . some specimens of small birds stuffed, some foreign shells, a fine herbarium collected in the vicinity of Paris, and some artificial christals [sic]" (Barnes, quoted in Gerstner, p. 175). A few months later, its members pooled their resources to purchase an important collection of nearly 2,000 mineral specimens from Adam Seybert.

To fulfill its commitment to public education, in 1812 and 1813 the academy offered a series of lectures to its members and other interested parties, based on the newly acquired Seybert collection (then the largest mineral collection in North America). These were so well received that in subsequent years further lectures on mineralogy, chemistry, crystallography, and botany were offered for members and nonmembers alike.

Under the leadership and philanthropic patronage of William Maclure, the academy broadened its role from that of a regional center of scientific study to a national and international institution. An important step toward this end was the publication of a rigorously peer-reviewed scientific journal, beginning in 1817. Distributed to members and learned societies throughout the United States and Europe, this publication did much to attract attention to the young academy and its members.

As the academy grew in size and reputation during the early decades of the nineteenth century, its members reached westward into the continent and overseas to study the earth's unfamiliar flora and fauna. John Kirk Townsend and Thomas Nuttall were among the first to collect western American plants, birds, and other animals under the academy's aegis. Their specimens are still included in the academy's research collections. Academy members accompanied Major Stephen H. Long on his

western explorations in 1819 and 1823 and Lt. Charles Wilkes on the United States Exploring Expedition around the world (1838–1842).

To accommodate its growing collections and membership, the academy moved to new quarters in 1815 and to its own building in 1826. In 1840, the institution moved to an even larger building. With the completion of this new, fireproof building, the academy became the best-equipped institution in America for the study of the natural sciences. Among other things, the museum boasted the largest ornithological collection in the world (after 1856), and one of the finest natural history libraries in the country.

Membership figures were equally noteworthy. The original seven had grown to approximately 200 living members by 1850. There were an additional 450 corresponding members. Qualitative growth matched quantitative growth: of the fifty-five most prolific contributors to American scientific journals between 1815 and 1845, forty-four (80%) were affiliated with the academy (Bennett, p. 8).

The academy's fifth and final move came in 1876 when its members had a new building constructed at its present site on Logan Square (at the corner of Nineteenth and Race Streets).

Today the academy is still actively involved in scientific research around the world. Its collections rank among the most important in the United States, and include such historically significant materials as Lewis and Clark's plant specimens, Thomas Jefferson's fossil collection, more than 150 of John James Audubon's bird skins, and the Australian specimens collected by John Gould in preparation for his books on the birds and mammals of that continent.

Scientific collections and current areas of research at the academy include: botany (1.5 million specimens), entomology (3.5 million specimens), diatoms (160,000 lots), herpetology (37,000 specimens), ichthyology (2.5 million specimens), invertebrates other than insects and mollusks (23,000 specimens), invertebrate paleontology (1 million specimens), malacology (12 million specimens—second largest in the United States), mammalogy (22,000 specimens), mineralogy (32,000 specimens), ornithology (160,000 specimens), and vertebrate paleontology (22,000 specimens). There is also a natural history library with 200,000 volumes and 250,000 manuscripts. In addition to its center-city Philadelphia location, the academy has a permanent research facility and staff on the Chesapeake Bay in

A

Maryland. The academy's public museum and education programs in Philadelphia cover most fields of natural history and serve an audience of approximately 250,000 people per year.

BIBLIOGRAPHY

Barnes, John. "Rise and Progress of the Academy." 1816 (inserted in Minute Book of 1816), Academy of Natural Sciences Archives.

Bennett, Thomas Peter. "The History of The Academy of Natural Sciences of Philadelphia." In *Contributions to the History of North American Natural History*, edited by Alwyne Wheeler. London: Society for the History of Natural History, 1983, pp. 1–14.

Founders Document, Academy of Natural Sciences of Philadelphia, 1812. Academy of Natural Sciences Archives, Collection 527.

Gerstner, Patsy A. "The Academy of Natural Sciences of Philadelphia 1812–1850." In *The Pursuit of Knowledge in the Early American Republic*, edited by Alexandra Oleson and Sanborn C. Brown. Baltimore: Johns Hopkins University Press, 1976, pp. 174–193.

Linton, Morris Albert. *The Academy of Natural Sciences of Philadelphia, 150 Years of Distinguished Service*. New York: Newcomen Society of North America, 1962.

Meisel, Max. "Academy of Natural Sciences of Philadelphia." In *Bibliography of American Natural History, The Pioneer Century: 1769–1865*. 3 vols. New York: Premier Publishing, 1924–1929, 2:130–218.

Nolan, Edward J. *A Short History of the Academy of Natural Sciences*. Philadelphia: The Academy of Natural Sciences of Philadelphia, 1909.

Orosz, Joel J. *Curators and Culture: The Museum Movement in America 1740–1876*. Tuscaloosa: University of Alabama Press, 1990.

Peck, Robert McCracken. "The Academy of Natural Sciences of Philadelphia." *The Magazine Antiques* 128 (October 1985): 744–754.

Stroud, Patricia Tyson. *Thomas Say, New World Naturalist*. Philadelphia: University of Pennsylvania Press, 1992.

Robert McCracken Peck

SEE ALSO
Museums of Natural History and Science

Acoustical Society of America

An organization founded in 1929 by scientists and engineers who shared a professional interest in the science, technology and business of sound. The 1920s saw increasing numbers of investigators devote themselves to problems in acoustics. The use of acoustical technologies such as sound-ranging and submarine detection in World War I, the growth of the practice of architectural acoustics, and the development of new electroacoustic technologies such as public address systems, radio, and sound motion pictures at places like the Bell Telephone Laboratories and the Radio Corporation of America, all provided opportunities for workers in the growing field.

The applied science of acoustics was not, however, highly ranked in the hierarchy of early-twentieth-century physics, and those members of the American Physical Society who studied sound felt what one such member, Vern Knudsen, described as a "second-rate citizenship" within that organization (Knudsen and Mink, p. 313). In 1928, this perception motivated a small group of architectural acousticians to organize a professional society that would provide an independent intellectual forum for their work. The society would meet regularly to discuss current topics, and the *Journal of the Acoustical Society of America* would collect the various articles on acoustics that were then scattered about in physical journals, architectural periodicals, and other media. In order to increase the size and strength of the organization, all scientists and engineers interested in sound—not just those who pursued architectural problems—were invited to join.

The charter membership of approximately 450 had grown to about 6,500 by 1990. While the fields of expertise of this membership have changed over the years, they remain extremely diverse. In its early years, the society was dominated by individuals interested in architectural acoustics and the development of instruments of measurement; today, the most popular areas of investigation are underwater, psychological, and physiological acoustics. An early predominance of industrial scientists and engineers has given way to a growing number of academically situated members, indicating an "academic renaissance" in the field (Lindsay, p. 7).

Historians of science have devoted little attention to the subject of acoustics and subsequently to the Acoustical Society of America; thus the field remains open for future scholarship. The journal of the society has occasionally published articles of historical interest, but these tend to appear in anniversary issues, and are generally more celebratory than analytical. Future scholarship will be facilitated by the society's recently formed Committee on Archives and History.

BIBLIOGRAPHY

Fletcher, Harvey. "The Acoustical Society of America. Its Aims and Trends." *Journal of the Acoustical Society of America* 11 (July 1939): 13–14.

Knudsen, Vern Oliver, and James Mink. *Teacher, Researcher and Administrator: Vern O. Knudsen.* Los Angeles: UCLA Oral History Transcript, 1974.

Lindsay, R. Bruce. "Acoustics and the Acoustical Society of America in Historical Perspective." *Journal of the Acoustical Society of America* 68 (July 1980): 2–9.

Thompson, Emily. "'Mysteries of the Acoustic': Architectural Acoustics in America, 1800–1932." Ph.D. diss., Princeton University, 1992.

Waterfall, Wallace. "History of the Acoustical Society of America." *Journal of the Acoustical Society of America* 1 (October 1929): 5–9.

Watson, Floyd R. "The Journal of the Acoustical Society of America." *Journal of the Acoustical Society of America* 11 (July 1939): 15–20.

Emily Thompson

Acoustics

Little original inquiry into the scientific study of sound took place in the United States before the mid-nineteenth-century investigations of Joseph Henry into architectural and atmospheric acoustics. At the turn of the twentieth century, Wallace Sabine further developed the subject of architectural acoustics, but it was only after World War I that American scientists began a concerted, continuous effort to solve numerous intellectual and practical problems associated with sound phenomena. Then, as now, these efforts crossed and spanned disciplines, touching upon subjects as diverse as the production of human speech, the propagation of sound waves in liquids, and the design of concert halls.

During World War I, the development of sound-ranging and submarine detection technologies fostered general interest in the subject of sound. The continuation of Sabine's researches in architectural acoustics was sponsored by the booming building economy of the 1920s. Perhaps most importantly, the development of long-distance telephony and commercial radio stimulated fundamental researches into both the behavior of sound and its electroacoustic transduction. Indeed, the flourishing of the science of acoustics in the early twentieth century was dependent upon the utilization and improvement of the nineteenth-century technology of the telephone. Advances in this familiar electroacoustic technology, particularly the development of vacuum-tube amplifiers, condenser microphones, and dynamic loudspeakers, enabled scientists to measure the intensity of sound and analyze its harmonic content with a degree of accuracy and precision whose lack had impeded earlier investigators.

A 1922 National Research Council report "Certain Problems in Acoustics" emphasized the development of scientific tools of measurement, and the early meeting programs of the Acoustical Society of America (founded 1929) further attest to this initial preoccupation. The development of these new tools also affected acoustical theory, as scientists began to explain mechanical acoustical systems by utilizing electrical analogies, representing physical systems with circuit diagrams.

Any summary of the history of acoustics in the United States beyond this point of departure would have to be synthesized from the various trajectories of the diverse subdisciplines of the field. The development of underwater acoustics presents a case study of science and the military, while the history of the human physiological response to noise constitutes a very different kind of account, intersecting with phenomena such as the growth of industrial psychology and public health campaigns. The histories of these various subdisciplines remain, for the most part, unwritten, and consequently, the historiography of American science lacks any synthetic treatment of the science of acoustics. A small body of historical literature on the various subfields has been generated by practitioners, and their accounts, generally appearing in anniversary editions of the *Journal of the Acoustical Society of America,* will provide a starting point for historians who choose to explore these rich and neglected topics.

BIBLIOGRAPHY

Beyer, Robert T. *Sounds of Our Times: Two Hundred Years of Acoustics.* New York: Springer-Verlag, 1999.

"Certain Problems in Acoustics." *Bulletin of the National Research Council* 4 (November 1922).

Hunt, Frederick V. *Electroacoustics: The Analysis of Transduction, and Its Historical Background.* Cambridge, MA: Harvard University Press, 1954.

Journal of the Acoustical Society of America. Volumes 26 (1954), 61 (1977) and 68 (1980) contain numerous articles describing the development of numerous topics such as acoustical instrumentation, architectural acoustics, physiological acoustics, etc.

Lindsay, R. Bruce. "Acoustics and the Acoustical Society of America in Historical Perspective." *Journal of the Acoustical Society of America* 68 (July 1980): 2–9.

A

Miller, Dayton C. *Anecdotal History of the Science of Sound to the Beginning of the Twentieth Century.* New York: Macmillan, 1935.

Thompson, Emily. "'Mysteries of the Acoustic': Architectural Acoustics in America, 1800–1932." Ph.D. diss., Princeton University, 1992.

Emily Thompson

Acquired Immune Deficiency Syndrome
See AIDS

Adams, Roger (1889–1971)

Organic chemist, research worker on the structure of natural products and the stereochemistry of organic compounds; key figure in the development of graduate training in chemistry and growth of chemical industrial research; effective in many public service activities, for chemistry and science as a whole.

Adams spent a year in post doctorate study in Germany (1912–1913), after his formal education at Harvard (A.B. 1909, Ph.D. 1912). He taught at Harvard for three years, and then moved to the University of Illinois at Urbana in 1916 to join W.A. Noyes in the chemistry department. Adams remained at Illinois until his retirement in 1957, and was head of the chemistry department from 1926 to 1954.

His career was significant in the development of American science for many reasons. With able colleagues (C.S. Marvel, R.C. Fuson, W.H. Rodebush, W.C. Rose, and others), he made Illinois one of the largest and best departments in the country for graduate work in chemistry and related fields. A gifted trainer of researchers, he had 184 Ph.D.'s and about fifty postdoctorates who went on to responsible positions in academic and industrial research in this country and abroad. Among them were E.H. Volwiler (Abbott), W.H. Carothers (the inventor of nylon), T.L. Cairns and R.M. Joyce (DuPont), W.M. Stanley (Berkeley), R.C. Morris (Shell), Allene Jeanes (United States Department of Agriculture), N. Kornblum (Purdue), J.R. Johnson (Cornell), C.R. Noller (Stanford), W.H. Lycan (Johnson and Johnson), C.C. Price (Pennsylvania), and S.M. McElain (Wisconsin).

Adams consulted for DuPont and Abbott Laboratories, among others, and exercised a broad influence on the development of chemical research in industry, through his consulting and his students.

He was the moving spirit in founding the serial publications *Organic Syntheses* and *Organic Reactions,* which are still being issued and are invaluable for students and research workers in organic chemistry. Adams served his country in both world wars: in 1917–1918 in the Chemical Warfare Service, and in 1941–1945, with the National Defense Research Committee. He went to Berlin after World War II as scientific advisor to General Lucius B. Clay, and later served on two missions to Japan to survey Japanese science for General Douglas MacArthur's office.

Adams was president and later chairman of the board of the American Chemical Society, and was active in setting up the Petroleum Research Fund, which funds a wide variety of research projects related to petroleum, as broadly interpreted. Probably his most important project for American science was his design of the Sloan Foundation program, which makes unrestricted research grants for promising young researchers in the physical sciences.

He was internationally recognized as a research chemist and administrator. His own researches and those of his students were a significant factor in raising the quality of American chemistry to a position of world leadership by 1950.

Adams's own researches were structural and synthetic. He never became quite at home with the newer instrumental methods or with the developments in the reaction mechanism field.

The University of Illinois Archives holds Adams's papers. Other important depositories for understanding his life are the archives of the National Academy of Sciences and the National Archives.

BIBLIOGRAPHY

Tarbell, D. Stanley, and Ann T. Tarbell. *Roger Adams, Scientist and Statesman.* Washington, DC: American Chemical Society, 1981.

———. "Roger Adams." *Biographical Memoirs of the National Academy of Sciences* 53 (1982): 3–48.

———. *The History of Organic Chemistry in the United States, 1875–1955.* Nashville: Folio Press, 1986.

D. Stanley Tarbell

SEE ALSO
Chemistry

Aeronautics

The arrival of the twentieth century sharpened interest in a growing cornucopia of new advances in science and technology, including aviation. Significant aeronautical research originated with eighteenth-century ballooning, which yielded important understanding of temperature variations, oxygen levels, and wind velocities in the upper atmosphere. An important nineteenth-century tradition, aircraft research developed in Europe, where groups like Britain's Royal Aeronautical Society included many trained scientists and engineers who developed key research components such as wind tunnels; in Germany, Otto Lilienthal achieved glider flights in the 1890s and accumulated a significant body of data. All this collective work aided Orville and Wilbur Wright, creative and technically astute brothers in Dayton, Ohio, who had developed a successful business as designers and builders of bicycles. With logic and skill they fashioned improved test equipment and applied an impressive intuitive analysis in extrapolating practical designs from their test results. Success occurred above the windy sand dunes of Kitty Hawk, North Carolina, on 17 December 1903.

Between 1908 and 1910, a series of flight demonstrations in America for the United States Army and overseas for European governments marked public acceptance of flight. World War I led to accelerated development of airframes and engines for military operations in Europe, and the United States had to move purposefully in order to catch up after its entry into the conflict in 1917. Even before America's entry, an official commission to evaluate Europe's aeronautical status recommended federal action, resulting in the National Advisory Committee for Aeronautics (NACA), established in 1915. During the 1920s and 1930s, the NACA's wind tunnels and aeronautic research achieved worldwide recognition with such improvements as the NACA engine cowling, de-icing research, and a series of systematized airfoils that became standard in international designs. Pre–World War II expansion led to a powerplant research center in Ohio and a new center for advanced flight research in California.

Other organizations also made significant contributions in the prewar decades. A private philanthropy, the Guggenheim Fund for the Promotion of Aeronautics, supported experiments that led to successful "blind flights" using instruments only. During its activities from 1925 to 1930, the Fund also supported several university centers for aeronautical engineering and research, such as meteorology, giving crucial support to the development of an aeronautical infrastructure populated by trained professionals. Additional government research in The Bureau of Air Commerce (established

1925) led to improved radio; the military services laid the foundations of aerospace medicine and also promoted work in such diverse fields as metallurgy and fuels. For commercial aviation, the direction of these and other trends resulted in the pioneering over-ocean routes flown by Martin and Boeing four-engine flying boats and the trendsetting Boeing 247 and Douglas DC-3 twin-engine airliners.

At the start of World War II, most piston-engined frontline fighter planes achieved speeds of 300 MPH, while bombers reached 200 MPH. By 1945, they surpassed 400 MPH and 300 MPH, respectively. The improvement occurred by using high-octane fuels, a host of aerodynamic refinements, and supercharged engines that yielded greater speed at high altitudes. Advanced bombers like the Boeing B-29 also incorporated pressurized cockpits and crew compartments; the B-29's electronic, remotely controlled gun turrets marked a high level of sophistication in the development of complex weapon systems. Pioneered in Britain, the development of radar made air defense systems more effective; airborne radars raised bombing accuracy and evolved into compact units used by night fighters. Radar and similar electronic aids contributed to new levels of reliability for long-range navigation, not only for bombing missions, but also for regular transoceanic transport planes. Such trends underscored the reality of a "shrinking globe" and gave substance to wartime commentary about a new "air-age world" of radically different time-distance relationships. Hopes for a new era of global harmony were tempered by nuclear weapons and Cold War tensions.

Wartime research and development led to major advances in rocketry as well as jet propulsion. In England, Royal Air Force officer Frank Whittle successfully tested a centrifugal flow gas turbine aircraft engine in 1937, although the Germans were the first to fly a jet plane in 1939, using an axial flow engine designed independently by Hans von Ohain. During the war, Germany moved ahead in jet engine development and related high-speed aerodynamics. In a remarkable gesture of wartime cooperation, Britain shared its jet engine technology with the United States. After the war, America used this legacy, plus expertise commandeered from Germany and extensive funding from Cold War budgets, to assume world leadership in many areas of propulsion and aerodynamics. Germany's wartime development of the V-2 ballistic missile was another such legacy, as Wernher von Braun and

A

other rocket experts played key roles in America's post-war space programs.

Postwar military research continuously pushed the limits of high-speed flight. The rocket-engined Bell X-1 broke the sonic barrier in 1947, and production jet fighters regularly operated above the sonic barrier (Mach 1, after Austrian physicist Ernst Mach) during the 1960s. Bombers also appeared with jet engines, swept wings, and speeds of Mach 1. For some years after the war, 350–400 MPH passenger planes relied on piston engines as well as turbo-propeller designs. Britain's jet propelled Comet went into service during 1954, only to be surpassed by a new family of larger, faster jet airplanes produced by Douglas and Boeing. The size and 600 MPH speeds of the new airliners paralleled substantial advances in wing design, navigational aids, control systems, and other developments.

Whether civil or military, aircraft design represented a complex matrix of systems engineering, an approach that placed fundamental emphasis on electronic systems and computerized operations for research and development as well as global operation in an increasingly populated airspace. During the 1970s, the use of synthetic, composite materials in aircraft structures became more widespread. In military designs, these techniques led to "stealth" aircraft, like the Lockheed F-117 and Northrop B-2, with minimal radar signatures. Civil and military designs alike increasingly relied on computerized display systems that replaced intimidating ranks of dials and gauges in the cockpit.

Control systems were also computerized, using "fly-by-wire" circuitry to translate pilot inputs to the plane's control surfaces. Many such systems also used computerized programs to establish the most effective flying speeds and aircraft trim, depending on payload, altitude, fuel consumption, and other factors. For large, high-speed transports and advanced combat designs, computerized flight systems that reacted in a real-time environment were the only means of avoiding disaster.

BIBLIOGRAPHY

Bilstein, Roger E. *Flight in America: From the Wrights to the Astronauts.* Baltimore: Johns Hopkins University Press, 1991.

Ceruzzi, Paul. *Beyond the Limits: Flight Enters the Computer Age.* Cambridge, MA : MIT Press, 1989.

Hansen, James R. *Engineer in Charge: A History of the Langley Aeronautical Laboratory, 1917–1958.* Washington, DC: Government Printing Office, 1987.

Jakab, Peter L. *Visions of a Flying Machine: The Wright Brothers and the Process of Invention.* Washington, DC: Smithsonian Institution Press, 1990.

Miller, Ronald, and David Sawers. *The Technical Development of Modern Aviation.* New York: Praeger, 1970.

Roger E. Bilstein

Agassiz, Alexander (1835–1910)

Embryologist and oceanographer. The son of the zoologist Louis Agassiz, Alexander was born in Neuchâtel, Switzerland, and died on an ocean voyage returning to the United States, his adopted land. Alex came to America from Switzerland, where he joined his father after his mother's death in 1848. Alex attended Harvard College—where his father was professor of zoology and geology—from 1851 until 1862. Alex's Harvard education, which comprised the baccalaureate and two advanced degrees in engineering and natural history, blended with knowledge obtained from his father, made him exceptionally well versed in the natural sciences.

Agassiz administered the affairs of the Harvard Museum of Comparative Zoology founded by his father, and undertook fundamental research and publication in marine biology. In 1860, he married Anna Russell, daughter of an old Brahmin mercantile family, and, with his stepmother's patrician background, he was thus wedded to the Boston aristocracy. Theodore Lyman, Henry Lee Higginson, and Quincy Adams Shaw were his brothers-in-law, and this familial alliance determined Agassiz's immediate future.

Quincy Shaw persuaded Agassiz to manage the moribund Calumet and Hecla copper mines in Michigan's upper peninsula. These deposits became the richest in the world through Alex Agassiz's skillful management and dedication to planning, order, and control of affairs. Agassiz served as president of the mining company from 1871 to 1901, and his ability made his extended family and many Bostonians very wealthy. His fortune enabled Agassiz to complete the building of his father's museum, and gave him complete freedom to work and live in magnificent isolation and independence from the pressures of his times and his profession. At his death, he was one of the wealthiest men in the United States.

In 1873, a double tragedy severely impacted Alex Agassiz's life. In a two-week period in December of that year his father died, and two weeks later, his beloved

Anna succumbed to pneumonia. Alex felt as if a cloud had forever fallen over his life, and, indeed, a dour unhappiness always seemed to burden him thenceforth. He lived as much as possible in the quiet isolation of a splendid Newport, Rhode Island, home, that had a marine biological laboratory as an annex. Alex used the Newport laboratory to train selected students and write up the results of his marine researches. Newport was a refuge from the hurly-burly of running the large museum research establishment and the mines at Calumet, Michigan, upon which he lavished the close, almost obsessive attention to detail that marked his every activity. Alex Agassiz's wealth and power left him no need to toady to others, and he demonstrated a powerful self-imposed rectitude. The several careers that marked his life were pursued with single-minded effort and great energy. Business, science, administration, and exploration were intertwined occupations that sought control, in carefully planned ways, of large aspects of culture.

A friend of Charles Darwin, Agassiz at first opposed the evolution idea but never with the vehemence of his father. In 1872–1874, he published the monumental study *Revision of the Echini,* whose pages described the distribution, anatomy, paleontology, and embryology of most known European and American starfish, sea urchins, and related forms. In this and other works Agassiz now believed that evolution could be a useful idea in viewing problems of development, but he strongly opposed those radical mechanists who built "castles in the air" in their rush to embrace the new doctrine. He hoped to dampen his "wildest speculation," all the while affirming that "the theory of evolution has opened up new fields of observation in many departments of biology" (*Revision of the Echini,* pp. 753–754). He could not, however, be ranked as an adherent to the entire evolution doctrine.

In the late 1870s, Agassiz began a campaign to explore the oceans of the world. The new science of oceanography counted him as one of its founders as he pioneered new methods of dredging, plumbed the ocean depths for marine life, and mapped the sea bottoms. For over thirty years, Agassiz was wedded to this effort, traveling nearly 200,000 miles on his own ships, and government vessels that he provisioned. *Three Cruises of the Blake* was the outstanding example of this preoccupation, and, while he published over 150 books and articles on oceanography and marine studies, the single volume that would have given overall purpose to his mission never appeared.

That mission, inexorably and vexatiously, placed a dark cast on Agassiz's ultimate reputation. He became obsessed with the question of coral reef origins and structure, and this quest prefigured his oceanographic studies. His purpose ostensibly was to oppose and reinterpret the theory of reef origins pioneered by Darwin and the American geologist James Dwight Dana. These men saw the development of reefs and atolls as a continuous process; corals grew on the sides of slowly sinking volcanic islands, marching upward until the island subsided and disappeared, leaving an atoll or coral reef. For Agassiz, however, no single all embracing theory could explain reef building the world over, just as evolutionists should not raise untested "castles in the air." To Agassiz, the submerged banks from which atolls and reefs arose had been built up or leveled down through many different modes at many different times, with no universal explanation applicable except for the action of local chemical and biological forces. The work of Darwin he held was sheer "nonsense" and "twaddle," and though Agassiz had the support of Sir John Murray (of the famed *Challenger* expedition) all his work resulted in only local reports and one overall paper of weak character. It is reasonable to see Agassiz's efforts of later life as an effort to oppose Darwin on the comfortable ground of oceanography rather than the difficult one of evolutionary theory, perhaps once more showing fealty to father, loyalty to whom in death as in life was a constant struggle between filial piety and distaste of the pomp and excess he also associated with his father.

No single individual saw more coral reefs than Agassiz, but his work was often unreliable and his theoretical conclusions false. His great wealth and power enabled Agassiz to publish at will, without peer review. He could interpret oceanography with the same single-minded will with which the affairs of Calumet were directed. In the eyes of many Agassiz was the outstanding scientist of his time.

BIBLIOGRAPHY
Agassiz, Alexander. *Embryology of the Starfish.* Cambridge, MA: n.p., 1864.
———. *North American Acalephae.* Cambridge, MA: University Press, 1865.
———. *Revision of the Echini.* Cambridge, MA: University Press, 1872–1874.
———. *Three Cruises of the United States Coast and Geodetic Survey Steamer "Blake" in the Gulf of Mexico, in the Caribbean Sea, and Along the Atlantic Coast of the United*

States, from 1877 to 1880. Boston: Houghton Mifflin, 1888.

———. "On the Formation of Barrier Reefs of the Different Types of Atolls." *Proceedings of the Royal Society of London* 71 (1903): 412–414.

Agassiz, George Russell. *Letters and Recollections of Alexander Agassiz.* Boston and New York: Houghton Mifflin, 1913.

Mayer, Alfred G. "Alexander Agassiz, 1835–1910." *Popular Science Monthly* 77 (November 1910): 418–446.

Winsor, Mary P. *Reading the Shape of Nature: Comparative Zoology at the Agassiz Museum.* Chicago: University of Chicago Press, 1991.

Edward Lurie

Agassiz, Jean Louis Rodolphe (1807–1873)

Geologist, ichthyologist, and paleontologist. A Swiss by birth, Agassiz achieved scientific fame in Europe and, after 1846, employed his stature to advance nature study and organize scientific institutions in the United States. Agassiz died in Cambridge, Massachusetts, a professor of geology and zoology at Harvard College and Director of Harvard's Museum of Comparative Zoology. He left many students to carry forward the study of nature he inspired.

The son of Rose and Rodolphe Agassiz, Louis attended Swiss preparatory schools and then the universities of Zurich, Erlangen, Heidelberg, and Munich. His education and career as a naturalist took form during these years (1827–1832) aided by the instruction and advice of such luminaries as J.B. Spix, Ignaz Dollinger, Frederich Schelling, Lorenz Oken, Alexander von Humboldt, and Georges Curvier. Always romantically inspired to be the "first naturalist of his time" (Elizabeth C. Agassiz, 1:98), Agassiz, throughout his life, would dream great dreams of new and novel enterprises to advance natural history. He was never able fully to complete such grandiose projects, as newer goals always arose to challenge him.

Agassiz's first academic post as professor at the Collége de Neuchâtel in Switzerland, resulted from the support of von Humboldt. Two achievements at Neuchâtel became in fact the capstones of his fame before the age of forty. Between 1832 and 1843, Agassiz published six pathmarking volumes, the famous *Recherches sur les poissons fossiles,* a precise analysis and depiction of over 1,700 ancient fishes from museums and collections all over Europe. The work gained the high praise of naturalists in Europe and America. In 1837, Agassiz announced the theory of the Ice Age, namely that continental glaciation had marked a significant phase of Pleistocene history. This was a catastrophe willed by the creator that left in its wake the moraines and polished rocks now familiar. Agassiz's reputation now soared still higher, buttressed by the 1843 volume *Études sur les glaciers,* which gained him the admiration of English naturalists such as Charles Lyell and Richard Owen. The glacial concept had been enunciated previously by others and was not original with Agassiz, but he was able to give it a broad location in Europe and codify such ideas in published form. He would always be identified as the originator of the glacial concept.

At Neuchâtel Agassiz was aided by a score of assistants and a personal publishing establishment that brought out other works from his pen. This "scientific factory" spread his fame but cost him dearly in personal terms. He seemed to live only for science. But a life of virtual penury was not compatible with the desires of his wife, Cécile Braun, whom he had married in 1832, nor with the needs of his children, his eldest son Alexander and his daughters Pauline and Ida. By 1845, Agassiz had overextended himself monetarily, the printing establishment was forced to close, and his wife, ill and dispirited, left for her native Germany with the children. Now Agassiz's friendships with Lyell and von Humboldt won him a grant from the Prussian monarchy to fund a two-year research trip to the United States and to employ his extraordinary popularization talents as a lecturer at Boston's Lowell Institute.

Agassiz charmed all classes of Americans: scientists, an adoring public, and people of wealth and position. These influential folk soon made an offer to teach at Harvard possible for him. The death of his wife in 1848 and his second marriage in 1850 to a daughter of Boston Brahmin wealth—Elizabeth Cabot Cary—sealed his future as an American.

Agassiz's principal role in the United States was as an organizer of professional scientific activity, his penchant for grand projects melding perfectly with the optimistic, progressive, and romantic love of nature typical of his adopted land. The arrival of his children brought him great joy and solidified a new and promising family life. Affirming the need for European standards of excellence and distinction, Agassiz was instrumental in aiding the organization of the American Association for the Advancement of Science, the Smithsonian Institution, and the establishment of the National Academy of Sciences.

In natural science, Agassiz's contributions never matched those of his European days and in fact seemed to decline with increased public adulation. He extended the glacial theory to North America, made some important marine embryological investigations, and informed countless lecture audiences of the most recent discoveries and theories in geology and paleontology. Agassiz enjoyed the support of Boston's elite, and looked to them to foster his multifarious enterprises. Most notable were the establishment and support of Harvard's Museum of Comparative Zoology, the publication of the four volume *Contributions to the Natural History of the United States* (1857–1862), and the expedition to Brazil and the Amazon during 1865–1866. Such successes meant that Agassiz came more and more to rely on approval of the multitudes, a mode at variance with the larger currents of national scientific enterprise. Scientists who had greeted Agassiz as a "prince of naturalists" voiced increasing disappointment at his seemingly sterile defense of special creationism in a series of Boston debates surrounding the publication of Charles Darwin's *On the Origin of Species.* Vigorously opposed to a concept of the common origin and transmutation of species, Agassiz sought justification in assumptions of idealism stretching back to Aristotle and Cuvier. Each category of taxonomic existence represented an unchangeable and permanent hierarchy, unalterable "cateries of thought" given existence by the Creator. Each life form was separately and specially created, with catastrophes like the Agassizian glaciers appearing time and again to separate past life and present forms. Agassiz's colleagues and some of his students chafed at what seemed a tired and outworn idealism, heralded by him as the latest science in the *Essay on Classification* (1857) that comprised the first volume of the *Contributions.* But Agassiz never paused to look back or recast a life that had become a constant series of adventures in science, appealing to the public imagination but almost always half-realized in scientific actuality. But in the decades following his death former students were quick to claim affiliation with the man who had come to embody the romantic study of nature in America, and provided the means for the exacting study of its devotees. Recent study has given the pied piper more common feet of clay, but no opponent could topple Agassiz from his stature as a leading nineteenth-century student of nature and inspirer of many students, teachers, and researchers.

BIBLIOGRAPHY

Agassiz, Elizabeth Cary, *Louis Agassiz: His Life and Correspondence.* 2 vols. Boston: Houghton, Mifflin and Company, 1885.

Agassiz, Louis. *Recherches sur les poissons fossiles.* 6 vols. Neuchâtel: Imprimerie de Petitpierre, 1833–1843.

———. *Études sur les glaciers.* Neuchâtel: Jent et Gassmann, 1840.

———. *Introduction to the Study of Natural History.* New York: Tribune Natural Science, 1847.

———. *Contributions to the Natural History of the United States.* 4 vols. Boston: Little, Brown, 1857–1862.

Dupree, A. Hunter. *Asa Gray: American Botanist, Friend of Darwin.* Cambridge, MA: Harvard University Press, 1959; reprint, Baltimore: Johns Hopkins University Press, 1989.

Lurie, Edward. *Louis Agassiz: A Life in Science.* Chicago: University of Chicago Press, 1960; reprint, Baltimore: Johns Hopkins University Press, 1985.

———, ed. *An Essay on Classification.* Cambridge, MA: Harvard University Press, 1962.

Winsor, Mary P. *Reading the Shape of Nature: Comparative Zoology at the Agassiz Museum.* Chicago: University of Chicago Press, 1991.

Edward Lurie

SEE ALSO
Harvard University

Agricultural Chemistry

The science that deals primarily with the relationships between chemical compounds and soils, crops, and animals.

Agricultural chemistry first arose as an important concern among American farmers and scientists in the early nineteenth century. By the late 1830s, in response to declining yields and the emergence of professional chemists in Europe, agricultural journals like the *Cultivator* were promoting the application of chemical principles to agricultural problems. American enthusiasm for agricultural chemistry and soil analysis expanded dramatically following the publication of Justus von Liebig's *Organic Chemistry in Its Applications to Agriculture* in 1840. Numerous other European and American authors, including Humphry Davy, Jean-Baptiste Boussingault, Samuel Dana, Edmund Ruffin, John Pitkin Norton, and Samuel W. Johnson contributed to the expanding discussions of the nature of agricultural chemistry in the mid-nineteenth century. Though scientists debated, often heatedly, which

A

chemical elements and compounds were most vital to plant nutrition, their enthusiasm for chemical solutions to agricultural problems fostered a boom in the artificial fertilizer business. Countless theories justified myriad varieties of fertilizers, some effective but many worthless. To overcome farmers' resistance to the new science, agricultural chemists conducted soil analyses and investigations of fertilizer fraud, demonstrating chemists' value to the rural economy. The agricultural chemists who joined state payrolls and state university faculties from the 1850s to the 1880s were among the first regulatory scientists in American history. Since the nineteenth century, agricultural chemists have extended their interests beyond soils and fertilizers, turning their attention to food analysis, pest control, and other aspects of applied chemistry.

Historians of agricultural chemistry have generally focused on the emergence of the subdiscipline, which illustrates well the process of professionalization in the nineteenth-century history of American science. Despite conflicting theories and interest groups, agricultural chemists eventually won approval from the nonscientific public. Others have examined the ideas, including religious ones, that convinced some Americans to study agricultural chemistry in the nineteenth century. More recent developments have received less attention, though, largely because the notion that chemistry provides firm answers to agricultural questions has been replaced by more holistic analyses of agricultural phenomena. As greater understanding of physiology, nutrition, bacteriology, biochemistry, genetics, mycology, meteorology, mineralogy, and other sciences developed, the science of agricultural chemistry has waned in its significance and distinctiveness.

Some scholars have also looked at the brief emergence of the farm chemurgy movement in the 1930s, when some agricultural chemists articulated a vision of their science as a social solution. Many chemurgists argued that farm crops could become industrial raw materials, utilizing farm wastes and new crops in a way that could end the agricultural depression and reduce American dependence on imported raw materials. The chemurgists' program did not prevail, however, and most recent developments in agricultural chemistry have reinforced a system that supplies industrial chemicals to the farm rather the converse.

In sum, agricultural chemistry has contributed to the emergence of American research science, strengthened the state universities, hastened the growth of large, capital-intensive, and corporate farms, and increased the productivity of American farmers.

BIBLIOGRAPHY

Borth, Christy. *Pioneers of Plenty: The Story of Chemurgy.* Indianapolis: Bobbs-Merrill, 1939.

Browne, Charles A. *A Source Book of Agricultural Chemistry.* Waltham, MA: Chronica Botanica, 1944.

Marcus, Alan I. "Setting the Standard: Fertilizers, State Chemists, and Early National Commercial Regulation, 1880–1887." *Agricultural History* 61 (1987): 47–73.

Pursell, Carroll W. "The Farm Chemurgic Council and the United States Department of Agriculture." *Isis* 60 (1969): 307–317.

Rosenberg, Charles E. *No Other Gods: On Science and American Social Thought.* Baltimore: Johns Hopkins University Press, 1976.

Rossiter, Margaret W. *The Emergence of Agricultural Science: Justus von Liebig and the Americans, 1840–1880.* New Haven: Yale University Press, 1975.

Mark R. Finlay

SEE ALSO
Soil Science

Agricultural Experiment Stations

Institutions devoted to research in farm practice and the agricultural sciences, federally supported in the United States since 1887.

Since 1796, when George Washington asked Congress to establish a national board of agriculture, the government's role in agricultural research has been an important issue in the history of American science. Congress rejected Washington's suggestion, however, and agricultural scientific research remained outside the public domain for decades. By the middle third of the nineteenth century, though, a number of developments sparked increasing support for permanent, state-supported institutions for agricultural research. These included dramatic declines in the fertility of soils in New England and southern states, the emergence of agricultural chemistry in Europe, and the rise of an often fraudulent artificial fertilizer trade. Passage of the Morrill Land Grant Act in 1862, which funded agricultural colleges, further signaled the growing role of the federal government in agricultural policy.

By the 1870s, efforts to establish a state-supported experiment station became more vigorous, led particularly by the chemists Samuel W. Johnson and Wilbur

O. Atwater who had enthusiastically endorsed the earlier German experiment stations. After extensive negotiations among scientists, agriculturalists, politicians, and trustees of Wesleyan University, the first American state agricultural experiment station was founded at Middletown, Connecticut, in 1875. Within a decade, over a dozen states established kindred institutions for agricultural research. Under terms of the Hatch Act of 1887, the United States government allocated $15,000 for the establishment of an experiment station in each state and territory. Subsequent bills, including the Adams Act of 1906, the Smith-Lever Act of 1914, and the Purnell Act of 1925, insured that experiment station research would be well funded and that advances in scientific agriculture would be publicized among practicing farmers.

American agricultural experiment stations have made important contributions to virtually every branch of the life sciences. Stephen Babcock of the Wisconsin station developed an effective test for determining butterfat; E.V. McCollum, also of the Wisconsin station, was among the discoverers of vitamins; Selman Waksman of the New Jersey station established the principles of soil microbiology and isolated streptomycin, the antibiotic effective against tuberculosis; Raymond Pearl of the Maine station helped develop the foundations of statistical genetics. Experiment stations also sponsored research in eugenics, climatology, entomology, human and animal nutrition, agricultural technology, crop acclimatization, agricultural economics, rural sociology, and agricultural education. The stations' research achievements since the late nineteenth century certainly have contributed to the dramatic productivity increases of American agriculture.

Histories of the stations traditionally have been written by administrator / historians of the United States Department of Agriculture and the state experiment stations, and reflect an emphasis on institutional history. Such works typically stressed links between German experiment stations and similar institutions in the United States, and the primacy of research scientists in guiding the experiment stations' success. More recently, historians have questioned the assumption that the German and Connecticut stations were models for the future of publicly sponsored agricultural research in the United States. Recent studies also examine the complex social, political, and intellectual context in which the experiment stations were founded. Two opposing conceptions of the locus and agenda of American agricultural research emerged in the late nineteenth century. On one hand, many agricul-

turalists, politicians, and educators argued that only a greater knowledge of science could improve agricultural yields. Others, meanwhile, believed farmers could improve their operations through more efficient and rational management techniques. Some endorsed indoor laboratories where scientists could dominate the research agenda and uncover principles of scientific agriculture, while others favored model farms and outdoor plots where rational farm practices could be tested and demonstrated. Despite these differing visions, both sides saw agricultural experiment stations as valuable institutions that could solve agricultural problems, and both helped shape America's agricultural research.

Since the 1940s and 1950s, the experiment stations' position within the notion of "Big Science" has come under scrutiny. Federal agencies, agribusiness firms, and research universities now play powerful roles in shaping the experiment stations' agenda, while nonstation scientists have increasingly won fights for research dollars in the agricultural sciences. Consequently, the stations' preeminence in life science research has waned. Moreover, recent critics contend that experiment stations' research agendas generally support corporate clients and the agribusiness establishment at the expense of smaller farmers. The development of agricultural experiment stations illuminates a number of issues in the history of American science. Agricultural research policy has long been a battleground among politicians, scientists, and agriculturists, and the history of experiment stations demonstrates the negotiations that have shaped the applied sciences. In the nineteenth century, debates over experiment stations revealed deep rifts between an ascendant intellectual milieu that championed science and one that favored traditional farm practices. Recent trends in experiment station research that address the social, ethical, medical, environmental, and biotechnological consequences of agricultural research also reflect the changing cultural context of American science.

Future research may well focus on these intellectual and cultural issues. The impact of such stations on the daily lives of practicing (and displaced) farm families also deserves further scrutiny. Primary sources materials from the United States Department of Agriculture and many state experiment stations are available.

BIBLIOGRAPHY
Fitzgerald, Deborah. *The Business of Breeding: Hybrid Corn in Illinois, 1890–1940.* Ithaca: Cornell University Press, 1990.

Kerr, Norwood. *The Legacy: A Centennial History of the State Experiment Stations, 1887–1987.* Columbia: Missouri Agricultural Experiment Station, 1987.

Knoblauch, H.C., et al., *State Agricultural Experiment Stations: A History of Research Policy and Procedure.* Washington, DC: United States Department of Agriculture Miscellaneous Publication #904, 1962.

Marcus, Alan I. *Agricultural Science and the Quest for Legitimacy: Farmers, Agricultural Colleges, and Experiment Stations, 1870–1890.* Ames: Iowa State University Press, 1985.

Rosenberg, Charles E. "Science, Technology, and Economic Growth: The Case of the Agricultural Experiment Station Scientist, 1875–1914." *Agricultural History* 44 (1971): 1–20.

Rossiter, Margaret W. *The Emergence of Agricultural Science: Justus von Liebig and the Americans, 1840–1880.* New Haven: Yale University Press, 1975.

True, A.C., and V.A. Clark. *The Agricultural Experiment Stations of the United States.* United States Department of Agriculture, Office of Experiment Stations, Bulletin #80. Washington, DC: Government Printing Office, 1900.

Mark R. Finlay

Agricultural Societies

Agricultural societies and farm organizations are terms that are often used interchangeably, although "societies" usually refers to scholarly or social groups while "farm organizations" is used to refer to groups most interested in political or economic actions. Early in our nation's history, short-lived farmers' groups, mostly on the frontier, protested taxes, called for stronger actions against the Indians, demanded higher prices for their products and sought a greater voice in government. These groups, without any formal organization, took action in local movements such as Shays's Rebellion and the Whiskey Rebellion.

The Philadelphia Society for Promoting Agriculture was the first American society devoted to scientific agriculture. Organized in Philadelphia in 1785 by gentlemen farmers—distinguished intellectuals and political figures—the society, like the South Carolina Society for Promoting and Improving Agriculture organized later in the same year, numbered a few full-time farmers in its membership. Similar societies were organized in other cities. Members of these societies made contributions to agriculture, particularly in the application of scientific ideas to increasing farm production. For example, John Lorain of the Philadelphia Society purposefully experimented with crossbreeding flint and gourdseed corn and developed the more productive dent corn.

Local agricultural societies appealing to neighborhood farmers were first organized to sponsor agricultural fairs. The Berkshire Agricultural Society of Pittsfield, Massachusetts, organized by Elkanah Watson in 1811, was soon followed by many others. Some states made grants for paying premiums for products exhibited at fairs, but the local societies had no impact on such scientific research as might be carried on in the colleges of that time. Today's local farm societies are usually units of national farm organizations, primarily social and political in nature.

The United States Agricultural Society, organized in 1851 primarily to promote the establishment of a national department of agriculture, once again brought the need for scientific research to the fore. Agricultural activities, mainly the distribution of seeds and the collection of statistics, had been undertaken in the United States Patent Office as early as 1836. Many farm leaders and politicians felt that the effort, while useful, was inadequate. Under the leadership of the new agricultural society, combined with pledges of the Republican Party in 1860, Congress established the department in 1862.

The head of the new department was "to acquire and preserve in the Department of Agriculture all information concerning agriculture which he can obtain by means of books and correspondence and by practical and scientific experiments, (accurate records of which experiments shall be kept in his office,) . . ." (12 Statutes at Large 382) With the assignment of these duties to the new department, agricultural societies could urge the department to undertake particular research and the Congress to appropriate funds for such research. The organizations could also urge the newly established state agricultural colleges to concentrate on research related to particular regional or state problems. The organizations themselves could then emphasize economic and political problems. By 1900, the agricultural colleges and the Department of Agriculture were engaged in substantial research programs.

In 1867, Oliver Hudson Kelley and six associates organized a national secret society of farmers, the National Grange of the Patrons of Husbandry or the Grange. Kelley intended the organization to be fraternal and educational, but within a few years, because of a severe farm depression and obvious political corruption, it turned to economic and political action. While the Grange had some success, particularly in organizing cooperatives, many farmers considered it too conservative and joined the new Farmers' Alliance. The Alliance joined forces with the Populist Party and when that declined after the election of 1896 with the return of prosperity, so did the Alliance. The Grange became once more influential, generally avoiding political and economic questions. In 1995, it was the second largest farm organization in the nation, with some 500,000 members. It emphasizes family memberships and social and educational activities.

The National Farmers Union, founded in 1902 by Newt Gresham of Point, Texas, was the natural successor to the Alliance, emphasizing, as it did, economic issues. Its first success was in the cotton-growing states. However, it gradually moved into the wheat- and livestock-producing states of the west, where its base has remained since World War II. It supports research in the production of grain and livestock by the agricultural colleges and the Department of Agriculture. The Union has been a strong advocate of government intervention in agriculture, including price supports for surplus products, aid to low-income farmers, and, especially, actions to preserve family farms. In 1995, its membership was 250,000 farm families.

The American Farm Bureau Federation was organized in 1920 as an outgrowth of several farm bureaus or committees organized locally to support the new county agent and extension programs of the Department of Agriculture established to carry the results of scientific research to the farmers. While the national federation first sought to improve agriculture through more efficient farm practices resulting from research, the farm depression of the 1920s turned it to solving the problem of farm surpluses, through government controls if necessary. It supported the New Deal farm programs through World War II, but after the war urged the adoption of policies that would permit farming to respond to supply and demand. By the 1990s, the federation was asking for basic price supports with limited production controls. It is the largest farm organization with a membership of 2.5 million farm families.

Periods of farm depression have often led to the pulling together of new, more aggressive farm organizations. The National Farmers Organization, for example, began in Iowa in 1955 to protest low farm prices. It held product withholding actions, a march on Washington,

and other protest activities, but had little visible effect on the markets. Other similar groups have been no more successful.

Organizations devoted to the interests of a particular commodity or even to one strain of livestock have been established by interested producers. They are active in encouraging research by the agricultural colleges and the Department of Agriculture, with objectives ranging from maintaining the purity of lines of particular breeds of livestock to insuring that their particular commodity receives full attention in price-support legislation.

Farm organizations have appeared during periods of agricultural depression, with three surviving into periods of prosperity. However, as the farm population declines so must the farm organizations and their influence on national policies.

BIBLIOGRAPHY

Baatz, Simon. *"Venerate the Plough" A History of the Philadelphia Society for Promoting Agriculture.* Philadelphia: Philadelphia Society for Promoting Agriculture, 1985.

Campbell, Christiana McFadyen. *The Farm Bureau and the New Deal.* Urbana: University of Illinois Press, 1962.

Dyson, Lowell K. *Farmers' Organizations.* Westport, CT: Praeger Press, 1986.

Flamm, Michael W. "The National Farmers Union and the Evolution of Agrarian Liberalism, 1937–1946." *Agricultural History* 68 (Summer 1994): 54–80.

Howard, David H. *People, Pride and Progress: 125 Years of the Grange in America.* Washington, DC: National Grange, 1992.

Howard, Robert P. *James R. Howard and the Farm Bureau.* Ames: Iowa State University Press, 1983.

McMath, Robert C. *American Populism: A Social History, 1877–1898.* New York: Hill and Wang, 1993.

Nordin, D. Sven. *Rich Harvest: A History of the Grange, 1867–1900.* Jackson: University of Mississippi Press, 1974.

Rasmussen, Wayne D. *Farmers, Cooperatives, and USDA: A History of Agricultural Cooperative Service.* Washington, DC: Department of Agriculture, 1991.

———. *Taking the University to the People: Seventy-five Years of Cooperative Extension.* Ames: Iowa State University Press, 1989.

Schlebecker, John T. "The Great Holding Action: The NFO in September, 1962." *Agricultural History* 39 (1965): 204–213.

Schwieder, Dorothy. *75 Years of Service: Cooperative Extension in Iowa.* Ames: Iowa State University Press, 1993.

Wayne D. Rasmussen

A

Agriculture

See Agricultural Chemistry; Agricultural Experiment Stations; Agricultural Societies; Agriculture, Native American

Agriculture, Native American

Native Americans began farming in the area of the continental United States at least by 5000 B.C., when a native people in the area of present-day Illinois raised squash. Over the next several thousand years, Native Americans on the continent also domesticated and cultivated sunflowers, goosefoot, and sumpweed. By A.D. 1000, many cultural groups had developed important agricultural practices, and a variety of cultivated plants supplemented their traditional food supplies based on hunting and gathering. Although the Native Americans domesticated plants indigenous to their particular locations, archaeologists generally agree that the most important crops, corn, beans and squash, which became known as the "three sisters," diffused northward from Mesoamerica.

Among most Native American cultural groups, the women had the primary responsibility for farming. With several exceptions in the southwest, women controlled the use of the cultivated land. The women also cleared the land for agricultural plots, usually along the floodplains where they could till the soil relatively easily with stone or bone hoes, and where fertility and adequate moisture prevailed. In addition women farmers had the responsibility for domesticating and breeding plants to meet specific climatic locations. Native American women did not know about genetics, but they carefully used empirical evidence to achieve a desired result. They changed the corn plant, for example, to mature in as few as 60 days in the northern Great Plains compared to more than 200 days in Mesoamerica. They also bred corn to withstand hot and dry as well as cool and moist climates. Women bred new corn varieties by selecting the seed from the ears of the plants that exhibited the desired characteristics. Although twentieth-century geneticists proved this technique could not be relied on to improve crop production, the Native Americans achieved relatively pure corn varieties by planting certain seeds, such as blue, red, or yellow, at distances sufficient to prevent the cross pollination of their fields. Native American farmers made similar changes for beans, squash, and cotton.

The Native American farmers did not fertilize their fields with organic matter. By customarily burning the brush from a plot, however, they unknowingly added potassium, phosphorous, calcium, and magnesium to the soil, reduced soil acidity, and promoted bacterial activity and the formation of nitrogen. Although the scientific agricultural practices of the Native American farmers were rudimentary at best, they developed an agricultural system that made their food supplies more certain, enabled greater control of their environment and improved their nutrition. Prior to the development of the agricultural-experiment-station system at the land-grant universities during the late nineteenth century, Native American women remained unsurpassed as plant breeders, and white farmers would adopt many of their crops and agricultural techniques.

BIBLIOGRAPHY

Castetter, Edward F., and Willis H. Bell. *Pima and Papago Indian Agriculture.* Albuquerque: University of New Mexico Press, 1942.

———. *Yuman Indian Agriculture.* Albuquerque: University of New Mexico Press, 1951.

Ford, Richard I., ed. *Prehistoric Food Production in North America.* Museum of Anthropology, Anthropological Papers No. 75, University of Michigan, 1985.

Haury, Emil W. *The Hohokam: Desert Farmers and Craftsmen.* Tucson: University of Arizona Press, 1976.

Hurt, R. Douglas. *Indian Agriculture in America: Prehistory to the Present.* Lawrence: University Press of Kansas, 1987.

Smith, Bruce D. "Origins of Agriculture in Eastern North America." *Science* 246 (December 1989): 1566–1571.

Struever, Stuart. *Prehistoric Agriculture.* Garden City, NY: Natural History Press, 1971.

Trigger, Bruce G. *The Huron Farmers of the North.* New York: Holt, Rinehart & Winston, 1969.

Wessel, Thomas R. "Agriculture, Indians, and American History." *Agricultural History* 50 (1976): 9–20.

Will, George F., and George E. Hyde. *Corn Among the Indians of the Upper Missouri.* St. Louis: Wiliam H. Miner, 1917; reprint, Lincoln: University of Nebraska Press, 1964.

Wilson, Gilbert L. *Buffalo Bird Woman's Garden.* Originally published as *Agriculture of the Hidatsa Indians: An Indian Interpretation.* Minneapolis: University of Minnesota Press, 1917; reprint, St. Paul: Minnesota Historical Society Press, 1987.

Yarnell, Richard A. *Aboriginal Relationships between Culture and Plant Life in the Upper Great Lakes Region.* Museum of Anthropology, Anthropological Papers No. 23, University of Michigan, 1964.

R. Douglas Hurt

A

AIDS (Acquired Immune Deficiency Syndrome)

AIDS is a fatal chronic infectious disease that destroys the immune system, leaving persons vulnerable to a variety of opportunistic infections. It is a worldwide pandemic, and as of late 1992, an estimated 8 to 10 million people were infected by HIV (human immunodeficiency virus). Of this number, 1 to 1.5 million live in the United States. Although several palliative treatments have been developed to slow the progress of the disease, no cure or vaccine exists at present. The overwhelming majority of persons infected by HIV develop symptoms within ten years, and most die within two years of becoming ill.

First identified in 1981 among a few young gay men in New York and California, AIDS was initially termed "GRID," or gay-related immunodeficiency disease. Subsequent epidemiologic research demonstrated that AIDS was a blood-borne, sexually transmitted disease, with cases ascertained among hemophiliacs, intravenous drugs users, and the children and sexual partners of persons with the disease. It soon became clear that the initial association between AIDS and homosexuality in the United States was a historical contingency, as opposed to an intrinsic feature of the disease. In 1983, its name was therefore changed to AIDS, or acquired immunodeficiency syndrome. One year later, researchers in France and the United States announced the discovery of a retrovirus associated with AIDS. First termed "LAV" (lymphadenopatly associated virus) and "HTLV-III" (human T-cell leukemia virus, type III), the virus was later named, by international agreement, HIV (human immunodeficiency virus).

The controversy over the discovery of the virus is one of the most notable priority disputes in modern biomedical science. Mirko Grmek, in *History of AIDS,* clearly attributes priority to Luc Montagnier and his team at the Pasteur Institute in Paris. Contesting this claim, Robert Gallo, of the National Institutes of Health in Bethesda, Maryland, asserts his priority in *Virus Hunting.* This has not been a simple dispute between scientists, but has involved the governments of two countries and considerable international litigation. Besides the issue of scientific credit, the case concerns the financial income from patent rights. Identification of HIV permitted the development of a blood test for the presence of antibodies to the virus. This patented blood test has been the single most widely used method of diagnosing the disease and of screening blood supplies. By international agreement in 1987, France and the United States agreed to share the discovery and the patent income; as of 1992, however, this agreement has been called into question because of ongoing controversies.

The process of defining AIDS has been a continuing one, with the formal definitions being developed by the Centers for Disease Control in Atlanta, Georgia, and the World Health Organization in Geneva, Switzerland. Changes in the scientific understanding of AIDS have been extremely rapid, and have been presented and debated each year at the annual international AIDS conferences, first convened in 1985. Each year, thousands of scientific papers about AIDS are published in the fields of epidemiology, virology, clinical medicine, and the social sciences. The remarkably swift accumulation of biomedical knowledge about AIDS was made possible by earlier advances in basic research in immunology, virology, and cell biology. AIDS research in turn has stimulated interest in these fields, and has attracted considerable funding and scientific talent.

At almost every point, the scientific and medical understanding of AIDS has been challenged by AIDS activists and AIDS organizations. AIDS is perhaps the first disease in which the affected populations have played such a major role in defining the disease, influencing the research agenda, making health policy, organizing services, and establishing programs for education and prevention. Aware of social discrimination against people with AIDS, AIDS organizations have been particularly effective in counteracting political demands for mandatory testing and quarantines. In the field of prevention, community-based organizations have developed highly creative strategies for aiding the ill and coping with the crisis, from the "buddy system" to "safer sex" and needle-exchange campaigns.

AIDS was initially conceptualized as an infectious disease, a "gay plague," by analogy to the sudden, violent epidemics of the past. As such, it challenged the medical belief that the age of epidemics was safely over. AIDS seemed to hold the dire promise of resurrecting the true meaning of epidemic: a disease that spread like wildfire and raged out of control, killed tens of thousands, and then burned out, leaving devastation in its wake. Ten years into the epidemic, however, there is still no end in sight. AIDS is continuing to spread, albeit somewhat more slowly than the more pessimistic observers had first predicted. With the development of the HIV test and palliative treatments, such as AZT (azidothymidine), AIDS has come to be normalized as

A

a chronic disease, similar in many ways to conditions such as cancer. In the advanced industrial nations, the emphasis both for scientists and people living with AIDS is now placed on improving health services, including the testing of, and access to, appropriate pharmaceutical treatments. In many of the less wealthy nations, few resources are available to treat or prevent AIDS, and the epidemic rages virtually unchecked.

AIDS continues to challenge almost all of our social and scientific institutions. Transmitted sexually, it has variously reinforced and undermined notions of sexuality and morality in relation to disease and death. Spread through intravenous drug use, it has highlighted the massive international problem of drug addiction. Potentially passed on from an infected pregnant woman to her fetus, it has become entangled with the emotionally charged issues of abortion and reproductive rights. The difficult and costly necessity of providing health services for persons infected by HIV and people with AIDS adds to the already considerable strains on the welfare state in some countries, and in others, makes even more obvious the lack of equitable access to health care. Most dramatically of all, the failure to deal frankly with the ways in which we transmit AIDS and the refusal to allocate sufficient resources for explicit AIDS education continues to demonstrate the inadequacies of our disease prevention policies.

BIBLIOGRAPHY

Arno, Peter, and Karen L. Felden. *Against the Odds: The Story of AIDS Drug Development, Politics, and Profits.* New York: Harper Collins, 1992.

Bayer, Ronald. *Private Acts, Social Consequences: AIDS and the Politics of Public Health.* New York: Free Press, 1989; reprint, New Brunswick: Rutgers University Press, 1991.

Crimp, Douglas, ed. *AIDS: Cultural Analysis, Cultural Activism.* Cambridge, MA: MIT Press, 1988.

Fee, Elizabeth, and Daniel M. Fox, eds. *AIDS: The Burdens of History.* Berkeley: University of California Press, 1988.

———. *AIDS: The Making of a Chronic Disease.* Berkeley: University of California Press, 1996.

Gallo, Robert C. *Virus Hunting: Cancer, AIDS, and the Human Retrovirus: A Story of Scientific Discovery.* New York: Basic Books, 1991.

Grmek, Mirko D. *History of AIDS: Emergence and Origin of a Modern Pandemic.* Princeton: Princeton University Press, 1990.

Institute of Medicine, National Academy of Sciences. *Mobilizing Against AIDS: The Unfinished Story of a Virus.* Washington, DC: National Academy Press, 1986.

Kirp, David L., and Ronald Bayer, eds. *AIDS in the Industrialized Democracies: Passions, Politics, and Policies.* New Brunswick: Rutgers University Press, 1992.

Mann, Jonathan M., Daniel J.M. Tarantola, and Thomas W. Netter, eds. *AIDS in the World, 1992: A Global Report.* Cambridge, MA: Harvard University Press, 1992.

Shilts, Randy. *And the Band Played On: Politics, People and the AIDS Epidemic.* New York: St. Martin's Press, 1987.

United States Department of Health and Human Services, Public Health Service. *Surgeon General's Report on Acquired Immune Deficiency Syndrome.* Washington, DC: Government Printing Office, 1986.

Elizabeth Fee and Nancy Krieger

Air Force, United States, and Science

Two distinct periods characterize this subject. The first occurred before World War II, when the National Advisory Committee for Aeronautics (NACA), established by the United States Congress in 1915, served as the main research institution both for American airpower and for civilian aircraft research. The United States Army Air Corps also took steps in this direction. Two years after NACA's founding, the Army Signal Corps opened a complex of airplane design, fabrication, and test facilities at McCook Field in Dayton, Ohio. The McCook Field engineers made many contributions to the aviation art. They pressed manufacturers to satisfy the complex specifications of combat aircraft, modified industry prototypes, undertook extensive ground and air tests, and conducted research on such vital components as engines and propellers. But the more fundamental and far-reaching investigations occurred at the NACA's Langley Memorial Aeronautical Laboratory in Hampton, Virginia. Here, an impressive array of progressively larger wind tunnels rose on the marshy tidewater. More important, the laboratory assembled an impressive staff of scientists and engineers to research a wide variety of flight problems for the military and for the airplane manufacturers. Shortly after they began to appear in 1920, the famous NACA Technical Notes and Reports became the standard references for everyone working in the aeronautical sciences.

Parallel to the NACA's development, during the 1920s and 1930s the Guggenheim Fund for the Promotion of Aeronautics granted large gifts of money to several American universities to stimulate theoretical work on aviation. Until this time, the few aeronautics specialists were taught mainly in mechanical engineering departments. Perhaps the most productive center established by the Guggenheims materialized at the California Institute of Technology under the leadership of the brilliant Hungarian aerodynamicist Theodore von Kármán. Lured to the United States by Cal Tech President Robert A. Millikan, von Kármán quickly developed a thriving laboratory, in part the result of close links to the Army Air Corps and, after 1941, its successor, the United States Army Air Forces (USAAF).

The second period of collaboration between airpower and science began in 1936, when von Kármán met General Henry H. Arnold, then commander of nearby March Field, California, later commanding general of the USAAF. Until this personal connection, American airmen typically looked upon science and scientists with indifference or puzzlement. But once von Kármán and Arnold cemented their friendship, attitudes changed quickly, hastened by the onset of World War II. During the succession of crises which led to United States involvement in the war, Arnold increasingly enlisted Dr. von Kármán's advice on such pressing problems as rocket propulsion for aircraft, wind-tunnel development, and high-speed aerodynamics. This close tie between scientist and general, forged in the heat of wartime work, gradually weaned the USAAF from the NACA orbit.

By 1944, all doubts about the importance of in-house science to military aviation had vanished. Radar, ballistic and guided missiles, jet and rocket power, and highly explosive armament were but a few of the monumental advances wrought by basic and applied science. Arnold and others in the air high command now realized that to avert or deter sudden and devastating attack from above, a continuous research program needed to be pursued. Such knowledge could then be applied to American aerial offense and defense. Hence, in late summer 1944, General Arnold asked the ubiquitous von Kármán to undertake one last assignment: to assemble a scientific advisory group, travel to Europe, and gauge the aeronautical progress of all the combatants.

After selecting a number of eminent scientists, von Kármán and his team journeyed to Europe and Asia where they seized tons of captured data, crated much invaluable equipment, and interviewed dozens of enemy and allied researchers. The findings, presented to Arnold in a bold multivolume report entitled *Toward New Horizons,* laid the technical basis of United States air power throughout the Cold War. Indeed, it not only established the value of periodic, long-range aeronautical forecasts; it decided the manner in which they

should be undertaken and propagated the presumption that science itself should remain of crucial importance even in the distant future.

Von Kármán and his associates essentially recommended that the United States place itself on a footing of constant mobilization in order to ward off attack from hostile aerial forces. Since no means existed to block such threats by defensive measures, von Kármán suggested a powerful offensive capacity borne by airframes and systems at the leading edge of scientific knowledge. In the report, he not only foresaw a United States missile force; he also predicted aircraft of immense speed and range, equipped with advanced technologies to guide armament to targets, and to penetrate weather and darkness. Organizationally, he called for equally decisive measures: a permanent board of science advisors for the USAAF chief of staff, an in-house research and development establishment, new research and development centers, a recognized cadre of scientifically trained AAF officers, and special salary scales to attract the most able civilian scientists. By the early 1950s, these recommendations took shape in such forms as the massive air force wind-tunnel complex at Tullahoma, Tennessee, the United States Air Force (USAF) ballistic missile program, and the creation of the USAF Research and Development Command.

In the years since, the air force has essentially hewn to patterns drawn by Dr. von Kármán and General Arnold. Four long-range forecasts—the *Woods Hole Summer Studies, Project Forecast, New Horizons II,* and *Project Forecast II*—have followed with varying success the standards of influence and vision achieved by the first one. The fact that they continue to be undertaken at periodic intervals suggests the place accorded science in the present air force.

BIBLIOGRAPHY

Gorn, Michael H. *Harnessing the Genie: Science and Technology Forecasting for the Air Force, 1944–1986.* Washington, DC: Government Printing Office, 1988.

———. *The Universal Man: Theodore von Kármán's Life in Aeronautics.* Washington, DC and London: Smithsonian Institution Press, 1992.

Roland, Alex. *Model Research: The National Advisory Committee for Aeronautics.* Washington, DC: Government Printing Office, 1985.

Sturm, Thomas A. *The USAF Scientific Advisory Board: Its First Twenty Years.* Washington, DC: Government Printing Office, 1967; reprint, Washington, DC: Government Printing Office, 1988.

A

Von Kármán, Theodore. *Toward New Horizons: Science, the Key to Air Supremacy.* Washington, DC: U.S. Army Air Forces Scientific Advisory Group, 1945; reprint, Camp Springs, MD: Air Force Systems Command History Office, 1992.

Walker, Lois E., and Shelby Wickam. *From Huffman Prairie to the Moon: The History of Wright Patterson Air Force Base.* Dayton, OH: Government Printing Office, 1986.

Michael H. Gorn

SEE ALSO
National Advisory Committee for Aeronautics

Allee, Warder Clyde (1885–1955)

Prominent animal and behavioral ecologist. Trained at the University of Chicago under the direction of Victor Ernest Shelford, Allee obtained his Ph.D. in 1912 and returned to his alma mater as an assistant professor in zoology in 1921. Over the course of the next twenty-nine years, Allee, and his colleague Alfred Edwards Emerson, developed a program of animal ecology centered on studying the origins, development, and organization of animal societies. Through his research on the causes and significance of animal aggregations, Allee believed he had found experimental evidence opposing the doctrine of war and, also, the cornerstone to a theory of sociality centered not on the family but on the association of individuals for cooperative purposes found in the most primitive forms of life. He coauthored with Alfred Emerson, Orlando Park, Thomas Park, and Karl Schmidt the *Principles of Animal Ecology,* published in 1949, which represented the first synthetic animal ecology text structured around general ecological principles and organized according to increasing levels of integration. From 1917 to 1921, Allee served as secretary of the American Society of Zoologists, and he became president of the Ecological Society of America in 1929. He also served as editor of the journal *Physiological Zoology* and was elected to the American Academy of Arts and Sciences and the National Academy of Sciences.

A historical analysis of Allee and animal ecology at the University of Chicago reveals the extent to which American biologists saw their science contributing to discussions about the nature and government of human society during the period of and between World War I and World War II. Allee was himself influenced by a genre of biological literature that a number of American biologists appealed to during World War I, which stressed the importance of mutual aid and cooperation, rather than competition and individual survival, as the driving force behind evolutionary progress. The reliance of this literature on Herbert Spencer's ideas emphasizing specialization and cooperation as companion principles of progress, and the indebtedness of American ecology itself to the developmental philosophy of Spencer, raises important historiographic questions about the significance of Spencer for early-twentieth-century American biological and social thought. However, the use of social organism metaphors within biology declined as the Modern Synthesis refined the Darwinian theory of evolution by natural selection. In addition, scientists came to associate the organicist foundations of Chicago ecology with totalitarian ideologies abroad, suggesting that fears of communism and a renewed emphasis on individualism within 1950s American culture helped contribute to the shape of ecological and evolutionary theory after World War II.

BIBLIOGRAPHY
Allee, Warder Clyde. *Animal Aggregations: A Study in General Sociology.* Chicago: University of Chicago Press, 1931.

———. *The Social Life of Animals.* New York: W.W. Norton, 1938.

Allee, W.C., A.E. Emerson, O. Park, T. Park, and K.P. Schmidt. *The Principles of Animal Ecology.* Philadelphia: W.B. Saunders, 1949.

Banks, Edward M. "Warder Clyde Allee and the Chicago School of Animal Behavior." *Journal of the History of the Behavioral Sciences* 21 (1985): 345–353.

Caron, Joseph A. "La Théorie de la coopération animale dans l'écologie de W. C. Allee: Analyse du double registre d'un discours." Master's thesis, University of Montreal, 1977.

Mitman, Gregg. *The State of Nature: Ecology, Community, and American Social Thought, 1900–1950.* Chicago: University of Chicago Press, 1992.

Schmidt, Karl Patterson. "Warder Clyde Allee." *Biographical Memoirs of the National Academy of Sciences* 30 (1957): 3–40.

Gregg Mitman

SEE ALSO
Ecology

Allison Commission

Formally the Joint Commission to Consider the Present Organizations of the Signal Service, Geological Survey, Coast and Geodetic Survey and the Hydrographic Office of the Navy Department. The Allison

Commission, established in 1884, deliberated on the burgeoning scientific bureaucracy, heard testimony from prominent scientists, and established patterns for congressional scrutiny of research. It submitted its final report in 1886.

Senator William Boyd Allison, Republican from Iowa and chairman of the Senate Appropriations Committee, headed the Commission. The five other initial members were: Senator Eugene Hale, Republican of Maine; Senator George Pendleton, Democrat of Ohio; Representative Hilary Herbert, Democrat of Alabama; Representative Robert Lowry, Democrat of Indiana; and Representative Theodore Lyman, Independent of Massachusetts. Failing to be reelected in 1884, Pendleton and Lyman were later replaced with Senator John T. Morgan, Democrat of Alabama, and Representative John Wait, Republican of Connecticut, respectively. The substantive issue before the Commission was whether the government's scientific bureaus, particularly the surveys, should be consolidated. But the Commission was less interested in the rational organization of government science than in administrative details within the bureaus and how Congress—particularly Allison's Appropriations Committee—might exercise jurisdiction over them.

The Commission requested the National Academy of Sciences to study the question of consolidation. O.C. Marsh, president of the academy, appointed a controversial committee, led by General M.C. Meigs. Two committee members were subordinates in cabinet departments under examination, and its report was the first from the academy not to be approved by the entire membership. Alexander Agassiz resigned from the academy over the report, which recommended that the government's scientific work be consolidated into one department such as Interior or a new Department of Science.

The Allison Commission largely ignored the controversial report and began its own investigation, hearing testimony totaling more than 1,000 pages. Arguing against strict congressional scrutiny, John Wesley Powell of the Geological Survey testified that "it is impossible to directly restrict or control these scientific operations by law" and that "central bureaus engaged in research should be left free to prosecute such research in all its details without dictation from superior authority" (U.S. Congress, *Testimony*, pp. 23, 26). J.E. Hilgard, defending his Coast Survey, did "not like to have the work of the [Survey] considered in the light

of what you properly call scientific. . . . [I]t is economic, of practical value . . . , though some science comes of it" (U.S. Congress, *Testimony*, p. 54). Despite such differences, these scientist-administrators agreed that convincing the Commission to accept their vision of science would also convince the Commission to accept their prescriptions for its governance. But Lyman responded that there is no essential characteristic of research that limited congressional discretion over its organization.

The Commission heard testimony from less eminent sources about bureaucratic details: the food and discipline at Fort Myer; the reimbursement of expenses to Coast Survey employees; the publication practices of the Geological Survey and its payments to university scientists. As Powell was partially correct that science was beyond the ability of members of Congress to control in detail, they instead sought to control what details they could.

Dupree argues that "by taking no action at all [on the academy's recommendation], the Allison Commission both affirmed the worth of government science and denied the validity of a separate department for it" (p. 231). But the Commission did take action. Bills based on its inquiry—although never even debated on the floor—became law as committee amendments to appropriations bills passed through Allison's committee.

Although the implications for the scientific bureaus of these changes have not been fully explored, it seems that through them the Allison Commission limited and directed the authority of the bureaus in ways that later members of Congress seeking to control the practice of research would also find useful.

BIBLIOGRAPHY

Dupree, A. Hunter. *Science in the Federal Government: A History of Policies and Activities to 1940.* New York: Harper and Row, 1957.

Guston, David H. "Congressmen and Scientists in the Making of Science Policy: The Allison Commission, 1884–1886." *Minerva* 32 (1994): 25-53.

Kevles, Daniel J. *The Physicists: The History of a Scientific Community in Modern America.* New York: Knopf, 1978; reprint, Cambridge, MA: Harvard University Press, 1995.

Manning, Thomas G. *Government in Science: The U.S. Geological Survey, 1867–1894.* Lexington: University of Kentucky Press, 1967.

———. *U.S. Coast Survey vs. Naval Hydrographic Office: A 19th Century Rivalry in Science and Politics.* Tuscaloosa: University of Alabama Press, 1988.

A

Rabbit, Mary C. *A Brief History of the U.S. Geological Survey.* Washington, DC: U.S. Department of the Interior, 1979.

Sage, Leland L. *William Boyd Allison: A Study in Practical Politics.* Iowa City: Iowa State University Press, 1956.

U.S. Congress. *Report of the Joint Commission to Consider the Present Organizations of the Signal Service, Geological Survey, Coast and Geodetic Survey and the Hydrographic Office of the Navy Department.* Senate Report 1285 (Ser. 2361), 49th Congress, 1st session, 8 June 1886.

U.S. Congress. *Testimony Before the Joint Commission to Consider the Present Organizations of the Signal Service, Geological Survey, Coast and Geodetic Survey and the Hydrographic Office of the Navy Department.* Senate Miscellaneous Document 82, 49th Congress, 1st session, 1886; reprinted in I.B. Cohen, ed. *Three Centuries of Science in America.* New York: Arno Press, 1980.

David H. Guston

SEE ALSO
Federal Government, Science and

Almanacs

An almanac (or ephemeris) was an annual publication containing a calendar; astronomical data on the phases of the moon, times of sunrise and sunset, eclipses, and positions of the planets; reminders of ecclesiastical holidays; chronological lists of remarkable historical events; astrological and meteorological predictions; tide tables; and other useful information on science, health, farming, navigation, portents, politics, literature, art, and religion. Written by the educated for both high and low readers, these compendia were cheaply printed and widely purchased. They were frequently annotated by their owners, who recorded births and deaths, business transactions, and farming data in the margins and on blank leaves.

In the seventeenth and eighteenth centuries, almanac publications outnumbered all other books combined. Principal authors and printers included Nathaniel Ames, Benjamin Franklin, Benjamin West, and Benjamin Banneker. In the nineteenth century, however, almanacs with their astrometeorological overtones declined in favor among the learned, and today, specimens of the *Old Farmer's Almanac* are debased publications intended more to amuse than instruct.

Few comprehensive studies of American almanacs or almanac makers have been published, and only those by Sagendorph and Stowell aim to be more than anthologies. Stowell's book is the more scholarly, but does not approach the landmark study of English almanacs by Capp, whose work should not be neglected by Americanists. Other publications can be divided into checklists, bibliographies, and papers about particular series or printers. Written primarily by librarians of historical societies in the nineteenth and early twentieth centuries, these publications are not too analytical. Only recently have historians begun to move beyond debates about when the first almanac was published or what years Franklin prepared *Poor Richard's Almanack,* in order to use these ephemeral texts as a vehicle to analyze scientific beliefs, pedagogy, politics, and ideology.

Nevertheless, almanacs remain an underutilized resource for historians who wish to study popular scientific convictions, common utilitarian concerns, and regional differences. Since they frequently served as diaries or memoranda books, almanacs can offer insight into family life, daily chores, and home remedies as well.

BIBLIOGRAPHY

Capp, Bernard. *English Almanacs, 1500–1800: Astrology and the Popular Press.* Ithaca: Cornell University Press, 1979.

Drake, Milton. *Almanacs of the United States.* 2 vols. New York: Scarecrow Press, 1962.

Sagendorph, Robb. *America and Her Almanacs: Wit, Wisdom & Weather, 1639–1970.* Dublin, NH: Yankee, 1970; reprint, Boston: Little, Brown and Company, 1970.

Schechner Genuth, Sara. "From Heaven's Alarm to Public Appeal: Comets and the Rise of Astronomy at Harvard." In *Science at Harvard University: Historical Perspectives,* edited by Clark A. Elliott and Margaret W. Rossiter. Bethlehem: Lehigh University Press, 1992; London and Toronto: Associated University Presses, 1992, pp. 28–54.

Stowell, Marion Barber. *Early American Almanacs: The Colonial Weekday Bible.* New York: Burt Franklin, 1977.

Sara Schechner Genuth

SEE ALSO
Astronomy and Astrophysics; Popularization of Science

ALSOS Mission

Scientific intelligence arm of the War Department's Manhattan Project, the Office of Scientific Research and Development, and the Office of Naval Intelligence.

Established in September 1943, the ALSOS Mission's principal purpose was to determine the wartime condition of German atomic research with military applications. Under the military command of Colonel Boris T. Pash and the scientific leadership of Samuel A. Goudsmit, the mission proved an outstanding success. Following fruitless interrogatories in 1943 and early 1944, investigations in Paris, southern France, and the Low Countries led to the conclusion that German researches in atomic weapons were conducted on a small scale.

Despite the mission's discovery at Strasbourg, in December 1944, of clear evidence of German sluggishness in atomic bomb research, ALSOS's investigative activities grew in variety and pace. It added other missions, such as investigation of enemy development of proximity fuzes and biological warfare research. It acted to deprive French and Russian allies of access to prominent German atomic scientists. ALSOS's greatest triumph came in the spring of 1945, with its capture of ten enemy uranium scientists and their laboratories in three tiny villages near Stuttgart.

The War Department terminated the mission in October 1945. By then, ALSOS had become a model for Anglo-American scientific and technical intelligence missions in Europe, Japan, and Korea. ALSOS investigative techniques were employed by United Nations weapons inspectors in Iraq as late as 1992.

Documents dealing with the ALSOS Mission can be found in the Eisenhower Presidential Library (Devers Papers); the National Archives (Goudsmit Papers, Leslie R. Groves Papers, ALSOS Mission File); the Hoover Institution on War Revolution and Peace (Pash Papers); and the Naval Historical Center (Naval Technical Mission-Europe).

BIBLIOGRAPHY

Goudsmit, Samuel A. *ALSOS*. New York: Henry Schuman, 1947.

Groves, Leslie R. *Now It Can Be Told*. New York: Harper & Row, 1962.

Mahoney, Leo J. "A History of the War Department Scientific Intelligence Mission (ALSOS), 1943–1945." Ph.D. diss., Kent State University, 1981.

Pash, Boris T. *The ALSOS Mission*. New York: Award House, 1969.

Leo James Mahoney

SEE ALSO
World War II and Science

Alvarez, Luis Walter (1911–1988)

Physicist. Alvarez was born in San Francisco, grew up in Rochester, Minnesota, and attended the University of Chicago, obtaining his Ph.D. in physics in 1936. As an undergraduate Alvarez showed his promise as an experimentalist with his first paper, a measurement of the wavelength of light using a phonograph record and a parlor lamp. In his second, he and A.H. Compton used Alvarez's Geiger counters to discover the positive electric charge of the primary cosmic rays, the east-west effect. Alvarez's thesis in optics formed the basis for his later radar inventions.

Upon graduation Alvarez went to work with E.O. Lawrence at the University of California in Berkeley. There, while he prepared himself to become a nuclear physicist, he resolved to make important discoveries, not simply accomplish mundane measurements. His guide to important problems was the *Review of Modern Physics* compendium known as Bethe's Bible. In just four years, Alvarez discovered that some nuclei absorb their atomic electrons (K-Capture); the radioactivity of tritium and the stability of helium-3; the magnetic moment of the neutron; the spin dependence of nuclear forces; a new standard of length; the polarization of neutrons; and made the first heavy ion physics measurements.

Alvarez's career in nuclear physics was truncated by World War II. His war career began at the Massachusetts Institute of Technology Radiation Laboratory where he invented the linear phased array for the first radar bombing system, EAGLE; the VIXEN system to outfox German submarines; the Ground Control Approach system for landing airplanes in bad weather (winner of the 1946 Colliers Air Trophy); and the Microwave Early Warning which formed the basis for the postwar American air defense system.

In 1943, Alvarez spent six months with Fermi in Chicago, long enough to discover the long-range alpha particles from nuclear fission. He then proceeded to Los Alamos where he invented the exploding wire technique to simultaneously implode fissile bomb elements into a critical mass. Alvarez also developed the energy yield pressure gauges which he personally used on the Trinity test and the Hiroshima mission.

Back in Berkeley after the war Alvarez became an inventor of particle accelerators. Earlier he had suggested ideas from which the electron microtron evolved. Now he invented the proton linear accelerator, the so-called Tandem van de Graff, and the Materials Testing Accelerator.

A

When Alvarez returned to physics in 1953, he had to learn the new field of particle physics. When he heard that Don Glasser's ether-filled test tubes boiled with passing cosmic rays, Alvarez began a program to construct a gigantic liquid hydrogen bubble chamber to track particles from the Bevatron. The physics discoveries made with this technology earned Alvarez the 1968 Nobel Prize in physics.

Alvarez's interest soon strayed from the big science he helped to create and returned to cosmic-ray physics where he pioneered the use of superconducting magnets in balloon-borne studies and made a search for the magnetic monopole. He also used cosmic rays to search for undiscovered chambers in the Chephren pyramid.

The final scientific activity of Alvarez's life was motivated by a clay layer collected by his son, Walter, which exhibited a high concentration of iridium more characteristic of asteroids than of the earth's crust. The age of this clay coincided with the Cretaceous-Tertiary event in which many life forms, including the dinosaurs, vanished. From these data, Alvarez fashioned the Asteroid Extinction Hypothesis which has steadily gained acceptance.

Shortly before his death, Alvarez said that he should be remembered as an inventor more than a scientist. He was particularly proud of two companies he founded, Humphrey Instruments and Schwem Technology, which developed his optical inventions.

BIBLIOGRAPHY

Alvarez, Luis W. *Alvarez: Adventure of a Physicist.* New York: Basic Books, 1987.

Trower, W. Peter. "Luis Walter Alvarez (1911–1988)." In *Restructuring of Physical Sciences in Europe and the United States, 1945–60,* edited by Michelangelo DeMaria, Mario Grilli, and Fabio Sebastiani. Singapore: World Scientific Press, 1989, pp. 105–115.

———, ed. *Discovering Alvarez: Selected Works of Luis W. Alvarez with Commentary by His Students and Colleagues.* Chicago: University of Chicago Press, 1987.

W. Peter Trower

American Anthropological Association

The professionalization of anthropology was related to the growth of science and the rapid rise and expansion of universities as local college and university scholars and researchers replaced amateur enthusiasts. Scholarly societies, generally established in major cities, accompanied and aided the growth of anthropology from the nineteenth century onward. The first specifically anthropological society was the Ethnological Society of Paris (1839). Others followed in London (1843), Moscow (1863), Berlin (1869), Vienna (1870), and Tokyo (1884).

In the United States, the American Ethnological Society was founded in 1842 and the Anthropological Society of Washington in 1879. Founded in 1902, the American Anthropological Association is currently the largest anthropological society in the world. The goal is to advance the interests of anthropology and increase the use of anthropologists and anthropological knowledge in public debate and policymaking. Membership at the end of its first year was 175. In 1992, it includes 287 life members, 7,265 regular members, and 3,405 student members, totaling 10,957.

In addition to *American Anthropologist,* a quarterly journal published since 1888, the American Anthropological Association publication program includes several other quarterly journals, an annual guide to academic and research departments of anthropology, as well as the program and abstracts of its annual meeting.

Many specialized unit members have accompanied the growth of the American Anthropological Association. A number are small, informal, and have no publications. Some under the umbrella of the American Anthropological Association are: American Ethnological Society, Archaeology Division, Association for Feminist Anthropology, Association for Political and Legal Anthropology, Association of Black Anthropologists, Association of Latina and Latino Anthropologists, Association of Senior Anthropologists, Biological Anthropology Section, Central States Anthropological Society, Council for Museum Anthropology, Council on Anthropology and Education, Council on Nutritional Anthropology, Culture and Agriculture, General Anthropology Division, National Association for the Practice of Anthropology, National Association of Student Anthropologists, Northeastern Anthropological Association, Society for Anthropology in Community Colleges, Society for the Anthropology of Consciousness, Society for the Anthropology of Europe, Society for the Anthropology of Work, Society for Cultural Anthropology, Society for Humanistic Anthropology, Society for Latin American Anthropology, Society for Linguistic Anthropology, Society for Medical Anthropology, Society for Psychological Anthropology, Society for Urban Anthropology, and Society for Visual Anthropology.

BIBLIOGRAPHY
Stocking, George W., Jr. "Franz Boas and the Founding of the American Anthropological Association." *American Anthropologist* 62 (1960): 1–17.

John M. Weeks

American Association for the Advancement of Science, The

The nation's comprehensive scientific and technical society devoted to benefiting both scientists and the society in which scientists live and work. The American Association for the Advancement of Science (AAAS) was created by geologists, the best organized group of scientists in mid-nineteenth-century America. College faculties and state surveys provided opportunities for professional employment and reasons to meet periodically to discuss new finds and professional problems.

Inspired in part by the recently founded British Association for the Advancement of Science, geologists decided the United States needed a similar organization. Forming it all at once seemed too big a step, so in 1840 they formed the Association of American Geologists. Two years later, they added "and Naturalists" to the name. In 1847, they decided to convert the organization into the AAAS, which held its first meeting in 1848 with a program of some sixty papers presented to the AAAS Section on Natural History or the Section on General Physics.

The new organization was governed by a general committee—now called the council—and its executive committee—now called the board of directors. In 1850, those bodies decided the AAAS needed a paid permanent secretary, one not limited to an elected term of a few years. Initially a part-time position, in 1937 it became a full-time position with an office in Washington, D.C., and a staff that has gradually grown in size as activities have expanded and as membership has grown from 461 in 1848 to about 130,000 in 1970.

The first, and still a primary means of attaining the association's objectives was the holding of "periodical and migratory" meetings at which scientists could report new findings and discuss research and professional issues. Although there were often strains between professional and amateur scientists, membership has always been wide open to anyone who wished to join, amateur or professional, man or woman, interested in any field of science or technology.

Since 1848, the AAAS has met annually, or in some years has had two meetings. As membership has grown and as science has changed, the two original sections have grown to twenty-three serving all fields of pure and applied science and technology. Because of the travel time required of scientists in the western states who wished to attend annual meetings in eastern cities, in 1915 the AAAS formed a Pacific division, and later established the Southwestern and Rocky Mountain, Arctic, and Caribbean divisions, each of which holds its own annual meeting.

In addition to its individual members, the AAAS has accepted several hundred other societies as formal affiliates. Most of these are societies of specialized disciplines, but also included are state academies of science and other general scientific organizations.

The association's most widely known publication has been the weekly journal *Science.* Founded in 1880 by Thomas A. Edison, that journal lived a precarious life until its then owner and publisher James McKeen Cattell in 1900 agreed to mail copies of *Science* to all AAAS members and the AAAS agreed to give Cattell two dollars of each member's three-dollar annual dues. That agreement made *Science* the official journal of the AAAS, gave it a large assured circulation, and made it a success. In 1945, following Cattell's death and by prior agreement, the AAAS purchased the journal from Cattell's heirs.

During the twentieth century, the AAAS has expanded its activities in several directions. In 1938, it began sponsoring an annual series of week-long research conferences—the Gordon Research Conferences—each on a specialized research topic.

In seeking to improve education in science, the AAAS in the 1950s developed sets of materials for teaching science in the elementary school grades, and in 1985 became engaged in a long-term program of securing agreement on what elementary and secondary school pupils should know of science, and the development of curricula and material that will provide that education. In cooperation with the Girl Scouts of America and some church groups, the AAAS has sponsored other educational programs for young people. For adult education, the AAAS has welcomed opportunities to prepare radio and television programs on scientific topics, but has never had funds to support such programs on a permanent basis.

Increasing international interest led the AAAS, with help from the United Nations Educational, Scientific,

A

and Cultural Organization (UNESCO), to convene the first large international congress on oceanography, in 1959, and three international conferences on problems of arid lands, in 1955, 1969, and 1985. International interests have also included help and advice to counterpart organizations in developing countries; efforts to enhance the development and usefulness of science in sub-Saharan Africa; and cooperation with affiliated organizations in analyzing problems of global change and other problems of international concern.

In cooperation with some of its affiliates, the AAAS has worked with the United States Congress on matters of general scientific interest; has developed an annual analysis of the federal government budget for research and development; has developed fellowship programs that place scientists in temporary positions in congressional staff offices and in some federal executive agencies; has improved access of physically challenged persons to scientific meetings; and both in the United States and elsewhere, has worked to increase scientific freedom and responsibility and to safeguard human rights.

BIBLIOGRAPHY

American Association for the Advancement of Science. *Proceedings*. Published as separate volumes through 1948 and subsequently in *Science* and the annual handbook of officers, organization, and activities.

Kohlstedt, Sally Gregory. *The Formation of the American Scientific Community: The American Association for the Advancement of Science, 1848–1860*. Urbana: University of Illinois Press, 1976.

Wolfle, Dael. *Renewing a Scientific Society: The American Association for the Advancement of Science from World War II to 1970*. Washington, DC: American Association for the Advancement of Science, 1989.

Dael Wolfle

American Association of Engineering Societies

A federation of engineering societies created in 1979 to provide the American engineering profession with a strong, united voice. Initially, the American Association of Engineering Societies (AAES) represented forty-three engineering societies, but was seriously weakened by secessions of eighteen member societies in 1983 in disputes over who would speak for the profession in Washington, duplication of functions, rising costs, and clashing personalities. To prevent further secessions, remaining AAES members altered the constitution, significantly reducing the organization's power and scope. By 1993, AAES represented only twenty-two engineering societies, but still included the "Founder" societies.

The disintegration of the AAES paralleled earlier attempts to provide engineering with an umbrella organization similar in scope to the American Association for the Advancement of Science. During World War I, the pioneer, national American engineering societies representing civil, mechanical, mining, and electrical engineers (called the "Founder" societies) formed a joint committee, the Engineering Council, to deal with consensus issues. It was replaced in 1920 by the Federated American Engineering Societies (FAES), a unity organization created under pressure from progressive reformers who hoped such an organization would counter industrial influence in the profession. Under the leadership of mining engineer Herbert Hoover, the FAES initiated several controversial public interest studies. These studies antagonized segments of American industry and their supporters within important engineering societies. As a result, FAES's activism was quickly cooled. In 1924, it changed its name to the American Engineering Council and adopted a much more cautious and conservative agenda. Society withdrawals during the depression and growing apathy led to its dissolution in 1941.

To replace the American Engineering Council, the "Founder" societies created a Joint Conference Committee (JCC) to speak for the profession during World War II. After 1945, the "Founders" admitted other organizations, and the JCC grew into the Engineers Joint Council (EJC). In the 1960s, attempts to strengthen EJC's position as representative for the profession backfired, leading to the secession of several major societies in 1968.

In 1977, engineering leaders, desiring to replace the crippled EJC with a more effective organization, began the discussions that culminated in the formation of the AAES.

BIBLIOGRAPHY

Basta, Nicholas, and Wilma Price. "AAES Narrows Its Scope, Gives Up Unifying Role." *Chemical Engineering* 92 (27 May 1985): 27–31.

Calvert, Monte A. "The Search for Engineering Unity: The Professionalization of Special Interest." In *Building the Organizational Society*, edited by Jerry Israel. New York: Free Press, 1972, pp. 42–54.

Florman, Samuel C. "A United Voice for Engineers." *Technology Review* 86, no. 5 (July 1983): 8–10.

Layton, Edwin T. Jr. *The Revolt of the Engineers: Social Responsibility and the American Engineering Profession.* Cleveland: Case Western Reserve University Press, 1971; 2d ed. Baltimore: Johns Hopkins University Press, 1986.

———. "Past Attempts to Unify Engineering Professionals." In *Ethics, Professionalism and Maintaining Competence.* New York: American Society of Civil Engineers, 1977, pp. 132–146.

Rubinstein, Ellis. "IEEE and the Founder Societies." *IEEE Spectrum* 13, no. 5 (May 1976): 76–84.

———. "IEEE and the 'Founders'—II." *IEEE Spectrum* 13, no. 6 (June 1976): 67–72.

Zimmerman, Mark D. "A Setback for Engineering Unity." *Machine Design* 56 (8 March 1984): 36–37.

Terry S. Reynolds

American Association of Scientific Workers

Established by reform-minded scientists in 1938 to advocate that science be used in the public interest. The association was one of the earliest groups in the United States concerned with social responsibility of scientists. It was inspired by the British social responsibility movement, although distinct in that it was much less tied to Marxism or trade unionism. Its aim was to use scientific expertise for public service and education about science. Secondary aims were to safeguard the international community of science and protect academic freedom in America. The leadership included Bart Bok, Harry Grundfest, Kirtley Mather, Melba Phillips, and Harlow Shapley. Many others from almost everywhere on the political spectrum and from every branch of science were attracted by its idealistic aims, however, including Franz Boas, Anton J. Carlson, Walter B. Cannon, Robert Chambers, Arthur H. and Karl T. Compton, Watson Davis, Ralph Gerard, Hermann J. Muller, Robert Mulliken, J. Robert Oppenheimer, Glenn Seaborg, and Kenneth V. Thimann. Although the aims of the organization appealed to scientists on both the right and left, a small, but vocal Communist faction seemed influential in setting its agenda. By 1941, many of the scientists originally attracted by its goals had resigned, including most of its eminent members.

Historians find the association interesting both as a herald of growing social consciousness among American scientists and as evidence that scientists shared the radical sympathies of American intellectuals in the 1930s. Whether the association grew out of a true shift among scientists toward greater acceptance of social activism or an anomalous minority view is arguable.

Interpreting the significance of the organization is further complicated by questions about its having been a Communist front organization.

For those who see the history of American science as one of tension between democracy and elitism, the association strongly represents the democratic ideal. Unfortunately for the researcher, no attempt was made to preserve records of the association. Diligent searching through manuscript collections of its various members can provide pertinent documents.

BIBLIOGRAPHY

Hodes, Elizabeth. "Precedents for Social Responsibility among Scientists: The American Association of Scientific Workers and the Federation of American Scientists." Ph.D. diss., University of California, Santa Barbara, 1982.

Kuznick, Peter J. *Beyond the Laboratory: Scientists as Political Activists in 1930s America.* Chicago: University of Chicago Press, 1987.

Elizabeth Hodes

American Astronomical Society

The American Astronomical Society (AAS), then called the Astronomical and Astrophysical Society of America, came into existence in 1899, the same year as the American Physical Society. Several other American scientific societies were organized in that same decade. The AAS was only one of the many societies, congresses, and academies brought into existence by George Ellery Hale.

Hale was the founding director of Yerkes Observatory of the University of Chicago, and had organized a week of scientific congresses to celebrate its dedication in October 1897. Fifty-seven astronomers and physicists were present at the Williams Bay, Wisconsin, site, and twenty-nine papers were read. The visitors looked through the new forty-inch refracting telescope, the largest in the world, saw George Willis Ritchey grinding the sixty-inch mirror for what was to become the Mount Wilson reflector, and heard James E. Keeler deliver the main invited address, "The Importance of Astrophysical Research, and the Relation of Astrophysics to Other Physical Sciences." On the last day everyone went to Chicago, heard another address by Simon Newcomb, "Aspects of American Astronomy," and enjoyed a banquet as guests of Charles T. Yerkes, the donor of the telescope.

The meeting was such a success that a "Second Conference of Astronomers and Astrophysicists" was held the next year, at Harvard College Observatory in August 1898. Approximately 100 scientists attended, and the sessions were held in the drawing room of Director Edward C. Pickering's residence. Under Hale's prodding a committee was formed, with himself as secretary and Pickering as chairman, which recommended that a permanent society be formed. The committee prepared a first draft of a constitution within one day, and sixty-one of those present signed up as charter members. The Astronomical and Astrophysical Society of America then formally came into existence at the Third Conference, which was also its own first meeting, back at Yerkes Observatory in September 1899. Newcomb was its first president and George C. Comstock was its first secretary, but the young Hale was the main source of energy who kept the little society alive in its first few years. Newcomb stepped down as president in 1905 and was succeeded by Pickering, who served for fourteen years until his death in 1919. Presidents after him served single three-year terms, or, after 1952, two-year terms.

In 1914, the society abandoned its original name, which had been adopted to indicate that physicists and astrophysicists, as well as astronomers in the older dynamical, positional, statistical, and planetary fields were welcome as members. It published its *Publications*, which contained abstracts of papers given at meetings, observatory reports, and lists of officers and members, from 1910 to 1946. Since 1969, the same function has been fulfilled by the *Bulletin of the American Astronomical Society*. In 1941, the society took over publication of the *Astronomical Journal*, then devoted to positional and dynamical astronomy, from Dudley Observatory. Between 1944 and 1969, the society material was published in the *Astronomical Journal*. In 1971, the AAS acquired the *Astrophysical Journal* from the University of Chicago Press, so that it now controls the two main journals in American astronomy and astrophysics.

The society has continued to grow. In 1922, it had 370 members; in 1947, 625; and by the end of 1992, more than 5,000. It has a full-time executive officer and, in January 1993, had a staff at its Washington, D.C. office equivalent to ten full-time professionals. It has had one, two, or three scientific meetings each year from 1899, except for 1908 in which there was no meeting. All these meetings have followed essentially the format of the First Conference at the dedication of Yerkes Observatory, except that since Charles T. Yerkes's time the members have always paid for their own dinners. Approximately 1,700 members and guests attended the 181st meeting in Phoenix, Arizona, in January 1993, and presented some 1,000 invited and contributed papers, most of them as poster presentations.

BIBLIOGRAPHY

DeVorkin, David H. "The Pickering Years." In *The American Astronomical Society's First Century*, edited by David H. DeVorkin. Washington, DC: American Astronomical Society, 1999, pp. 20–36.

Osterbrock, Donald E. "The Minus First Meeting of the American Astronomical Society." *Wisconsin Magazine of History* 68 (1984) 108–118.

———. "AAS Meetings Before There Was an AAS: The Pre-History of the Society." In *The American Astronomical Society's First Century*, edited by David H. DeVorkin. Washington, DC: American Astronomical Society, 1999, pp. 3–19.

Stebbins, Joel. "The American Astronomical Society 1897–1947." *Popular Astronomy* 55 (1947) 404–413.

Donald E. Osterbrock

SEE ALSO
Astronomy and Astrophysics

American Geophysical Union

The American Geophysical Union (AGU) was founded in 1919 with the intent of establishing a professional organization for studies of the physics of the earth. Until 1972 an executive committee of the National Research Council of the National Academy of Sciences, the AGU is now an independent organization. Eschewing exploration geophysics, whose advocates sought to apply geophysical techniques to the discovery of petroleum deposits, leaders of the AGU focused on strengthening the "pure" sciences intermediate between physics, chemistry, and geology. They looked initially to European models. By the 1950s, the subject fields of the AGU included seismology, meteorology, oceanography, geodesy, terrestrial magnetism and electricity, volcanology, tectonophysics, and hydrology; space science was added in the 1960s. Its principal founders were Robert S. Woodward and William Bowie; through the 1930s and 1940s its permanent secretary was John Adams Fleming, director of the Division of Terrestrial Magnetism of the Carnegie

Institution of Washington. Other prominent members have included Maurice Ewing, Harry H. Hess, James B. Macelwane, and Charles Whitten. Membership in the AGU rose from a ceiling of 75 (1922–1928) to 4,600 (1950), 13,000 (1980), then 26,000 (1990).

The AGU played a major role in shaping the disciplinary structure of the broad confederation of fields which comprise geophysics. Its annual meetings (semiannual after 1952) offered an important forum for discussion of results in geophysics, and its *Transactions*—one of several publications—became a leading journal in the field. (The *Journal of Geophysical Research,* previously entitled *Terrestrial Magnetism and Atmospheric Electricity,* long served as an informal organ of the union.) The AGU has also sponsored geophysical expeditions, chiefly in oceanography and geodesy. Historians have noted the critical role played by AGU leaders in shaping American participation in the International Geophysical Year (IGY; 1957–1958). AGU officials also created a successful forum for reporting the results of rocket- and satellite-based investigations of the earth, moon, and solar system when space exploration burgeoned in the 1960s, making geophysics, rather than astronomy, the main disciplinary home for this research.

Because the union significantly influenced the development of American geophysics, a historical account of the AGU is warranted. Little is known about how the union contributed to the growth of academic geophysics, to the development of geophysical research programs including the IGY, or to the emergence of new geophysical fields. Early records of the AGU are available at the archives of the National Academy of Sciences in Washington, D.C.

BIBLIOGRAPHY

Fleming, John A. "Origin and Development of the American Geophysical Union." *Transactions of the American Geophysical Union* 35 (1954), 1:1–46.

Gillmor, C. Stewart, ed. *History of Geophysics.* 4 vols. Washington, DC: American Geophysical Union, 1984–1990.

Ronald E. Doel

SEE ALSO
Geophysics and Geodesy

American Institute of Chemical Engineers

One of the five most important American engineering disciplinary societies (collectively referred to as the "Founder" societies). The American Institute of Chemical Engineers (AIChE) was organized in 1908 under the leadership of chemists involved in industrial consultation, design, and management who hoped to use the organization to distance themselves from lower-status analytical chemists and discourage the use of mechanical engineers in chemical plant design. Until the 1930s, AIChE was an elitist organization, with a small membership and a clubby atmosphere.

The primary problem the new organization faced was securing recognition as a branch of engineering rather than simply an offshoot of chemistry. Recognizing that professional identities are established during the educational process, AIChE focused its slender resource base on education. In the late 1910s, at the instigation of Arthur D. Little, AIChE began a systematic study of the status of chemical engineering education. The results of this study led AIChE to adopt unit operations (operations like heating, pulverizing, distilling, evaporating, and so forth, used in different forms and orders in all industrial chemical operations) as the basis for defining chemical engineering and for distinguishing it from the concerns of chemistry. In 1922, the Institute authorized its committee on education to accredit schools whose curricula were built around unit operations, making it the first engineering society to accredit academic curricula.

AIChE remained a relatively small society until World War II, but it shared the very rapid growth of the chemical industry after 1941. In 1958, as a result of this growth, extended negotiations, and an agreement to contribute to the construction of a new United Engineering Societies Building, AIChE was, for the first time, formally recognized as a member of the "Founder" society group.

Generally, AIChE has remained a very technically oriented society, focusing heavily on publications and meetings. In the 1960s and 1970s, it resisted pressures to become heavily involved in lobbying efforts in Washington and to grade chemical companies as employers. In keeping with its traditional strength in education, however, AIChE developed a continuing education program much larger in proportion to its size than that of any other major engineering society.

BIBLIOGRAPHY

Basta, Nicholas. "Now Over 75, AIChE See No Major Shifts Ahead." *Chemical Engineering* 91 (9 January 1984): 27–31.

A

Guédon, Jean-Claude. "Il progett dell'ingegneria chimica: l'affermazione delle operazioni di base negli Stati Uniti." *Testi e contesti* 5 (1981): 5–27.

Olsen, John C. "Origin and Early Growth of the American Institute of Chemical Engineers." *AIChE Transactions* 28 (1932): 298–314.

Reynolds, Terry S. *75 Years of Progress: A History of the American Institute of Chemical Engineers.* New York: AIChE, 1983.

———. "Defining Professional Boundaries: Chemical Engineering in the Early 20th Century." *Technology and Culture* 27 (1986): 694–716.

Rubinstein, Ellis. "IEEE and the 'Founders'—II." *IEEE Spectrum* 13, no. 6 (June 1976): 67–72.

Van Antwerpen, F.J., and Sylvia Fourdrinier. *High Lights: The First Fifty Years of the American Institute of Chemical Engineers.* New York: AIChE, 1958.

Terry S. Reynolds

SEE ALSO
Engineering, Chemical

American Institute of Mining, Metallurgical, and Petroleum Engineers

Second oldest of the major American disciplinary engineering societies. In 1871, a number of American mining engineers, discontented with the highly professional standards of the American Society of Civil Engineers and wishing a more specialized forum, formed the American Institute of Mining Engineers (AIME). With this secession, the splintering of the American engineering profession into a host of specialized societies without a widely recognized unifying body began.

Placed on a spectrum ranging from the highly scientific and professional societies to loose, industrial trade associations, AIME has always inclined toward the latter. Its criteria for full membership were so lax in the late nineteenth century that it included "common miners, laborers, mine foremen, and people that cannot spell" as well as "captains of industry" who had few or no professional qualifications (Layton, p. 94). As a result, the society has traditionally followed a very conservative, industry-oriented agenda, rejecting an active role in broader professional issues like conservation, codes of ethics, and employment conditions.

Because of the diverse nature of the minerals extraction industry, AIME, earlier than most engineering societies, had to make radical organizational adjustments to avoid splintering into a host of minor technical societies.

AIME modified its original name by adding "Metallurgical" in 1919 and "Petroleum" in 1957. After World War II, to prevent its rapidly expanding petroleum engineering constituency from seceding, AIME began to decentralize, creating three broad, semiautonomous "branches" within the society. These branches evolved into "constituent societies" in the late 1950s and into separately incorporated societies in the mid-1980s. Today, AIME is an umbrella organization composed of four affiliated societies: the Society of Mining, Metallurgy and Exploration; the Minerals, Metals and Materials Society; the Iron and Steel Society; and the Society of Petroleum Engineers. The affiliated societies have their own headquarters, publications, and officers. They remain affiliated with AIME largely because of its prestige as one of the oldest American engineering societies and for joint functions, such as public relations and relations with other societies.

BIBLIOGRAPHY

Centennial Volume: American Institute of Mining, Metallurgical, and Petroleum Engineers, 1871–1970. New York: AIME, 1971.

Layton, Edwin T. Jr. *The Revolt of the Engineers: Social Responsibility and the American Engineering Profession.* Cleveland: Case Western Reserve University Press, 1971; 2d ed. Baltimore: Johns Hopkins University Press, 1986.

"Members to Decide AIME, SPE Incorporation." *Journal of Petroleum Technology* 36 (August 1984): 1294–1295.

Parsons, A.B. "History of the Institute." In *Seventy-Five Years of Progress in the Mineral Industry.* New York: AIME, 1948, pp. 403–529.

Rubinstein, Ellis. "IEEE and the Founder Societies," *IEEE Spectrum* 13, no. 5 (May 1976): 76–84.

"SPE Incorporation Has Deep Roots." *Journal of Petroleum Technology* 37 (January 1985): 62–63.

Weiss, Alfred, Andrew E. Nevin, and Thomas J. O'Neil. "AIME in Transition: Separate Society Incorporation." *Mining Engineering* 35 (October 1983): 1389–1390.

Terry S. Reynolds

American Institute of Physics

A membership corporation, founded in 1931, which provides services to the leading American societies in physics and allied areas.

The American Institute of Physics (AIP) was founded in response to funding problems brought on by the Great Depression. At the urging of the Chemical Foundation, which provided initial funding, leaders of

American physics formed a coalition to achieve economies in the publishing of journals and the maintenance of membership lists. Broader concerns also argued for cooperation: academic and industrial physics were drifting apart; the public was showing increasing skepticism about the value of scientific research. Thus, while publishing and membership services would always occupy the bulk of AIP's efforts, from the outset the institute also worked to foster cooperation among different segments of the physics community and to improve public understanding of science.

At the time of its formal incorporation in 1932, the AIP comprised five societies with a total membership of some 4,000 individuals: the American Physical Society, the Optical Society of America, the Acoustical Society of America, the Society of Rheology, and the American Association of Physics Teachers. A new set of members was added beginning in the mid-1960s: the American Crystallographic Association (1966), American Astronomical Society (1966), American Association of Physicists in Medicine (1973), American Vacuum Society (1976), and American Geophysical Union (1986). By 1999, the total nonoverlapping membership of the ten member-societies was over 100,000. Meanwhile AIP's staff had grown to over 500 people.

From the outset, the AIP published journals on behalf of its member societies, for example, the *Physical Review* for the American Physical Society. It also acquired or developed scientific journals of its own in fields where no single society had a mandate, notably the region between applied and academic physics. Almost from its foundation, AIP published the *Review of Scientific Instruments, Journal of Applied Physics,* and *The Journal of Chemical Physics*; starting in the late 1950s it added a number of others. Its most widely read publication, the general-interest magazine *Physics Today,* was inaugurated in 1948. In 1955, AIP began to publish English-language translations of Soviet physics journals. From the 1960s on, it increasingly developed other services, from book publication to computerized abstracts of journal articles.

As AIP's own publications grew, the revenue enabled the institute to hire staff dedicated to broader ways of serving the member societies, individual physicists, and the public at large: career placement services since 1947; in the mid-1950s, programs for public relations, the compilation of educational and employment statistics, and support of physics education; in the early 1960s, the Niels Bohr Library and Center for History

of Physics. Meanwhile the AIP continued to foster communication and common effort among physicists, for example, through meetings of its corporate associates. In 1993 it transferred its headquarters to College Park, Maryland to keep in better touch with the federal government as well as member societies.

General control is exercised by a governing board chosen by the member societies, apportioned according to the size of their memberships. Operations are overseen by a smaller executive committee of member society representatives, meeting with AIP's officers (ex officio). This confederate structure is unique among scientific organizations. The AIP has given physicists an unusual ability to coordinate their affairs and exert influence well beyond what would otherwise be possible for a community of such small size and great diversity.

The AIP's records are preserved in its archives, with manuscript histories and oral history interviews.

BIBLIOGRAPHY

Barton, Henry J. "The Story of AIP." *Physics Today* 9, no. 1 (January 1956): 56–66.

Weart, Spencer R. "The Physics Business in America: A Statistical Reconnaissance." In *The Sciences in the American Context: New Perspectives,* edited by Nathan Reingold. Washington, DC: Smithsonian Institution Press, 1979, pp. 295–358.

Spencer R. Weart

American Journal of Science and Arts

Oldest continuously published scientific journal in the United States, begun in 1818. The intended scope of the journal was accurately reflected in its original title: *The American Journal of Science, More Especially of Mineralogy and Geology, and the Other Branches of Natural History; including also Agriculture and the Ornamental as Well as Useful Arts.* It was more commonly referred to as *American Journal of Science* or *Silliman's Journal.* Its founder and first editor, Benjamin Silliman, intended his journal to contain primarily American work. In the early decades of its existence, Silliman was often forced to cover the costs of producing the journal out of his own funds when subscribers failed to pay. The "ornamental arts" never constituted much of the journal's content. The "useful arts" slowly disappeared from the journal's pages and ultimately from its title.

In keeping with his desire to promote and recognize the practice of science in America, Silliman kept his

A

pages open to a wide range of authors, topics, and approaches. He solicited scientific papers from friends and correspondents, printed excerpts from letters he received that discussed scientific issues, supplied notices and reviews of new scientific works both foreign and domestic, published the proceedings of miscellaneous scientific organizations, and reprinted material from European scientific journals. He also used his editorial voice to lobby for support of projects like state geological surveys and to try to mediate scientific disputes.

As the nineteenth century advanced, other avenues of scientific publication opened up in America and new editors assumed control of the journal, including Benjamin Silliman Jr., and the elder Silliman's son-in-law James Dwight Dana. Just as Silliman depended on eclecticism to fill his pages and attract subscribers, later editors working in a very different scientific climate strove to assure the journal's continued success by becoming increasingly selective with regard to the subject and quality of the material published. Nearly two centuries after its founding, the journal is now devoted to the earth sciences.

No extended historical study of the journal reaching beyond 1918 exists. Extensive collections of correspondence dealing with the founding and early history of the journal are to be found in the Silliman and Dana papers at Yale and the Hitchcock papers at Amherst.

BIBLIOGRAPHY

Bruce, Robert V. *The Launching of Modern American Science 1846–1876.* New York: Knopf, 1987.

Dana, Edward Salisbury. "The American Journal of Science from 1818 to 1918." In *A Century of Science in America with Special Reference to the American Journal of Science 1818–1918,* New Haven: Yale University Press, 1918, pp. 13–58.

Greene, John C. *American Science in the Age of Jefferson.* Ames: Iowa State University Press, 1984.

Julie R. Newell

SEE ALSO

Silliman, Benjamin, Sr.

American Mathematical Society

The principal professional society for the support of mathematical research. The New York Mathematical Society (NYMS) was founded in New York City in 1888 by Columbia College graduate student Thomas Scott Fiske, who modeled it loosely on the London Mathematical Society (begun in 1865). With only six Columbia students and faculty as members initially, the society's roster grew to over 200 by 1891 as a result of Fiske's campaign to secure subscriptions to the *Bulletin of the NYMS,* which was launched in 1891.

Holding monthly meetings in New York City during the academic year, the organization assumed more national proportions in 1894, spurred largely by the efforts of a core of mathematicians in the midwest. In 1893, E.H. Moore and his colleagues at the University of Chicago, together with Henry White of Northwestern, had staged a mathematical congress as part of the World's Columbian Exposition in Chicago. Their efforts to find a publisher for its proceedings had brought them before the NYMS in June of 1894, had garnered the society's financial support, and had "quickened the desire of the Society for a name indicative of its national or continental character" (Archibald, p. 7). One month later, the society became the American Mathematical Society (AMS), although it only slowly widened the restricted venue of its meetings. This motivated the formation of "sections" of the society, which held officially sanctioned meetings in other geographical locations and thereby provided increased opportunities for direct communication between mathematicians outside the northeast. The Chicago Section of the AMS first met officially in 1897, with the San Francisco and Southwestern Sections following in 1902 and 1906, respectively. These sections played a major role in increasing the society's membership from 770 in 1920 to 2,127 by 1938. At the time of its centenary, the AMS had more than 22,000 members.

The Chicagoans also worked to institute two other important features of the AMS. Complementing the 1893 congress, White had arranged for leading German mathematician Felix Klein to give a two-week-long series of high-level colloquia in Evanston. White ultimately pushed the idea of regular AMS-sponsored colloquia through the AMS Council; the first in the still ongoing series was delivered in 1896 with the express aim of introducing a wide audience to current topics of research. The AMS has published these lectures, delivered by leaders in the field, since 1905. An even greater activist than White, Moore lobbied the AMS to establish a research-oriented journal to supplement its more news-oriented *Bulletin.* In 1900, he became the first editor of the *Transactions of the AMS* and immediately established it as an outlet for the publication of first-rate work on American—as opposed to foreign—shores. Throughout the twentieth century, the AMS has continued to foster research of high quality by publishing, among many books, book series, and journals, its series of *Memoirs* starting in 1950 and its *Journal* beginning in 1988. It also underwrites a number of other periodicals and supports a major translation effort.

As the society's president from 1901 to 1902, Moore also tried to bring mathematics education at all levels into the society's purview. His efforts were unsuccessful, owing principally to the pronounced research focus that the AMS has largely retained to the present.

Throughout the final quarter of the nineteenth century, developments in American higher education had resulted in an emphasis at the university level on the production of original research and on the training of future researchers, while a generation of would-be American mathematicians had sought research training in Germany (the recognized leader in the field through the early 1930s). As the formation of the AMS reflected, the combined effects of these and other factors had brought about a self-sustaining community of research mathematicians in the United States by 1900. The AMS served as that community's focal point, providing a venue for both personal and published communication. It also set and maintained standards that helped establish the dominance of American mathematicians in the postwar era. A careful historical analysis of the society's history in the twentieth century—including studies of the principal society leaders—should shed much light on virtually all aspects of the history of mathematics in twentieth-century America, among them, the formation of American schools in certain research fields like point set topology and finite group theory and the dynamics involved in the professional splintering of the community initially defined by the AMS.

BIBLIOGRAPHY

Archibald, Raymond C. *A Semicentennial History of the American Mathematical Society: 1888–1938.* New York: American Mathematical Society, 1938.

Duren, Peter, et al., eds. *A Century of Mathematics in America.* 3 vols. Providence: American Mathematical Society, 1988–1989.

Fenster, Della Dumbaugh, and Karen Hunger Parshall. "A Profile of the American Mathematical Research Community: 1891–1906." In *A History of Modern Mathematics,* edited by Eberhard Knobloch and David E. Rowe. Boston: Academic Press, 1994, pp. 179–227.

———. "Women in the American Mathematical Community: 1891–1906." In *A History of Modern Mathematics,* edited by Eberhard Knobloch and David E. Rowe. Boston: Academic Press, 1994, pp. 229–261.

Parshall, Karen Hunger, and David E. Rowe. *The Emergence of the American Mathematical Research Community (1876–1900): J.J. Sylvester, Felix Klein, and E.H. Moore.* Providence: American Mathematical Society; London: London Mathematical Society, 1994.

Pitcher, Everett. *A History of the Second Fifty Years: American Mathematical Society 1939–1988.* Providence: American Mathematical Society, 1988.

Karen Hunger Parshall

American Medical Association

The oldest and largest national organization of physicians in the United States. It was founded in Philadelphia in 1847 through the efforts of Nathan Smith Davis with the stated intention "to promote the science and art of medicine and the betterment of the public health." At first, representation in the association was open to almost any group of physicians, but over the course of the nineteenth century, membership was restricted to those who belonged to constituent societies which excluded sectarian or irregular practitioners such as homeopathic, eclectic, or Thomsonian physicians. A reorganization of the association in 1900 established the association as a confederation of medical societies and greatly increased the influence of the national body as a result. Authority is vested in a representative House of Delegates supported by a professional staff. Today over 600,000 physicians, or slightly less than 50 percent of eligible doctors, belong to the association.

The impact of the association has been greatest in the areas of medical education, licensing of physicians and drugs, and compensation for medical services. The desire to reform medical education was the primary impetus for the creation of the association. At first medical schools which failed to meet its curriculum standards were excluded from representation in the society. Later the association's Council on Medical Education established standards against which it could judge medical schools; the association also worked to develop internships and residencies.

Early in its history the association encouraged its constituent societies to exclude sectarian and irregular physicians from its ranks. With the publication of the *Journal of the American Medical Society* (started on 14

A

July 1883), the association created a voice for the scientific investigation of medicine. In this century the association began to conduct scientific investigations into the content and efficacy of patent medicines and nostrums; Morris Fishbein, longtime editor of the *Journal*, effectively used the findings in his passionate attacks on all forms of medical quackery.

The other abiding interest of the association in this century has been the method by which physicians are compensated for their services. Until roughly World War I, many in the association favored some form of national health insurance, but shortly thereafter the association began to oppose any challenges to fee-for-service practice. The association initially opposed, for example, both the development of health maintenance organizations and Medicare.

Given the prominence of the association in American medical history, it is surprising that it has been little studied by historians. Employees of the association itself made the initial—and still essential—studies. Most of the best work on the association is found incorporated into general works on topics in which the association was active, such as medical education, quackery, or the regulation and compensation of medical practice.

BIBLIOGRAPHY

Burrow, James Gordon. *AMA: Voice of American Medicine.* Baltimore: Johns Hopkins University Press, 1963.

Campion, Frank D. *The AMA and U.S. Health Policy since 1940.* Chicago: Chicago Review Press, 1984.

Fishbein, Morris. *A History of the American Medical Association, 1847 to 1947.* Philadelphia: Saunders, 1947.

Starr, Paul. *The Social Transformation of American Medicine.* New York: Basic Books, 1982.

Stevens, Rosemary. *American Medicine and the Public Interest.* New Haven: Yale University Press, 1971.

Peter B. Hirtle

American Men of Science

This directory of American scientists first appeared in 1906 under the editorship of Columbia University psychologist James McKeen Cattell. Its title reflects Cattell's nineteenth-century predilections. Later editions appeared at irregular intervals; a seventeenth edition was published in 1989–1990. Since 1955, the directory has appeared in multiple volumes, and since 1971, it has been entitled *American Men and Women of Science.* (All earlier editions also included entries about women scientists.) Cattell began collecting in 1903 the data that appeared in the directory's first edition for his studies of the psychological basis of scientific eminence. He implemented "order-of-merit" procedures that had ten "leading representatives" in each of twelve fields rank order the "most eminent" scientists in their disciplines. Cattell conflated these ratings and, based on the number of workers in each science, identified (with a star at their entries in the directory) the 1,000 most eminent American scientists in 1903. He used the personal data on these 1,000 for his 1906 "Statistical Study of American Men of Science" and repeated these procedures (with various modifications) for all of the later *American Men of Science* editions he oversaw; that is, those published in 1910, 1921 (with Dean R. Brimhall), and in 1928, 1933, and 1938 (all with his son Jaques Cattell). In 1906, the American scientific community welcomed stars in *American Men of Science* as signs of distinction and many American scientists coveted them through the 1930s. But Cattell's star system also always attracted complaints. By the time the third edition was published in 1921, these focused on the too-few fields in which Cattell assigned stars, the too-few stars assigned, and the (apparent) biases of Cattell's judges. Their force became stronger as the American scientific community grew through the 1920s and 1930s, and as more interdisciplinary fields emerged, and the seventh edition, published in 1944 (edited by Jaques Cattell) was the last to include stars.

BIBLIOGRAPHY

Cattell, James McKeen. "A Statistical Study of American Men of Science." *Science* 24 (1906): 658–665, 699–707, 732–742.

———. "A Further Statistical Study of American Men of Science." *Science* 32 (1910): 633–648, 672–688.

———. "The Distribution of American Men of Science in 1932." *Science* 77 (1933): 264–270.

Rossiter, Margaret W. *Women Scientists in America: Struggles and Strategies to 1940.* Baltimore: Johns Hopkins University Press, 1982.

Sokal, Michael M. "Stargazing: James McKeen Cattell, American Men of Science, and the Reward Structure of the American Scientific Community, 1906–1944." In *Psychology, Science, and Human Affairs: Essays in Honor of William Bevan,* edited by Frank Kessel. Boulder, CO: Westview Press, 1995, pp. 64–86.

Visher, Stephen S. *Scientists Starred 1903–1942 in "American Men of Science": A Study of Collegiate and Doctoral Training, Birthplace, Distribution, Backgrounds, and Developmental*

Influences. Baltimore: Johns Hopkins University Press, 1947.

Michael M. Sokal

SEE ALSO
Cattell, James McKeen

American Mineralogical Journal

First independent scientific journal published in the United States. In 1810, Archibald Bruce, professor of mineralogy and materia medica at the College of Physicians and Surgeons in New York City, published the first issue of the *American Mineralogical Journal.* Four issues appeared and were published as a single volume in 1814; they contained descriptions of chemical analysis, the composition of minerals discovered in the United States, mining and manufacturing processes, and experimental techniques in addition to reprints of articles from European periodicals and news of the American scientific community. Mineralogy was becoming increasingly popular in the United States; scientists in New York, Philadelphia, and New Haven had established collections and were interested in problems of classification. Mineralogy was also taught as an ancillary discipline to geology and chemistry in the university curriculum. The journal was promoted as a patriotic endeavor and as a utilitarian enterprise but Bruce, who lost his teaching post in 1811 and who suffered ill health, failed to publish further issues after 1814. Benjamin Silliman Sr., at the bequest of several prominent geologists and mineralogists, began his *American Journal of Science and Arts* as a replacement for Bruce's journal in 1818.

BIBLIOGRAPHY

Baatz, Simon. "'Squinting at Silliman': Scientific Periodicals in the Early American Republic, 1810–1833." *Isis* 82 (1991): 223–244.

"Biographical Notice of the Late Archibald Bruce, M.D." *American Journal of Science and Arts* 1 (1818): 299–304.

Greene, John C. "Introduction." *The American Mineralogical Journal,* edited by Archibald Bruce. 1814. Reprint, New York: Haffner Publishing Co., 1968, pp. vii–xvii.

Simon Baatz

American Museum of Natural History

Begun in 1868, the museum became one of the largest institutions of its kind in the United States. Conceived by Albert Bickmore, it was originally dominated by businessmen and politicians interested in promoting civic pride, public education, and social welfare. With private donations and city funds, the museum moved into the New York Armory in 1869. In 1874, President Ulysses S. Grant dedicated the construction of a new building at 79th Street and Central Park West.

The museum experienced problems in its early years. While trustees purchased collections of mammals, birds, and shells, there existed no program for acquiring specimens and no means for displaying them. The museum, located outside the city center and closed on Sundays, attracted few visitors, had no well-defined objectives, and was deeply in debt by the late 1870s.

Changes occurred when Morris K. Jesup became the museum's third president in 1881. Jesup knew little about science but worked to create an institution with public appeal. He hired a taxidermist to create attractive and comprehensible displays and he supported Bickmore's plan to offer nature study lectures for school teachers. That program and Sunday admission increased the museum's popularity. In 1885, Jesup promoted scientific research by hiring Joel A. Allen as curator of mammalogy and ornithology, In 1891, Henry Fairfield Osborn launched a new program in vertebrate paleontology, and four years later Franz Boas joined the department of anthropology.

Jesup also defined new museum objectives. A devout Protestant, he wanted the institution to provide edifying and spiritually uplifting information about nature. For him, evolution was a law that confirmed progress and morality, and Jesup promoted programs in mammalogy, vertebrate paleontology, and anthropology that provided visible documentation of nature's productions and principles.

Osborn further implemented Jesup's objectives. In vertebrate paleontology he promoted expeditions, research, and an innovative program of exhibits. He succeeded Jesup as president in 1908, and over the next twenty-five years expanded the museum's size and scope. He launched such highly publicized expeditions as Roy Chapman Andrews's search for human origins in Mongolia and Carl Akeley's explorations of Africa. Through those endeavors new scientific departments and massive exhibit halls arose. Osborn succeeded in tripling the city's contribution to the museum, and a new wing was added in the 1930s. The museum likewise reflected his scientific interests and social values.

A

Money went to programs that documented evolution. Research remained important, but exhibits and public education became a priority. Expeditions and exhibits embodied his interest in preserving natural resources and traditional values. Osborn viewed outdoor studies and worldwide explorations as a bastion against the debilitating effects of modernization. The Hall of the Age of Man and the Akeley African Hall served not only to inform the public about science but to convey the social and political anxieties of Osborn and others among the upper class.

Subsequently, the museum moved out from under Osborn's shadow. In the 1940s, biologists Ernst Mayr and George Gaylord Simpson offered new interpretations of evolution. Through the influence of Margaret Mead, research in social and cultural anthropology flourished. In 1928, the museum added a department of experimental biology where G.K. Noble, Frank Beach, and Charles M. Bogert conducted important research on animal behavior. Albert E. Parr, appointed director in 1942, brought ecological and physiological topics to the fore. The creation of biological field stations in the 1950s reduced the need for worldwide expeditions. Astronomy expanded with the construction of the Hayden Planetarium in 1935. More recently, new interpretations have led to major renovations of fossil mammal and dinosaur exhibits.

The historiography of the museum has likewise undergone changes. Traditionally, museum-sponsored studies have emphasized achievements and one centennial history offered a fine analysis of the museum's institutional developments. New emphases in the history and sociology of science have yielded studies that examine the social and political dimensions of the museum's displays, expeditions, and research programs.

BIBLIOGRAPHY

Bal, Mieke. "Showing, Telling, Showing Off." *Critical Inquiry* 18 (1992): 556–596.

Haraway, Donna. "Teddy Bear Patriarchy: Taxidermy in the Garden of Eden, New York, 1909–1936." *Social Text* 4 (1983): 285–329.

Hellman, Geoffrey T. *Bankers, Bones and Beetles: The First Century of the American Museum of Natural History.* Garden City, NY: Natural History Press, 1968.

Kennedy, John Michael. "Philanthropy and Science in the City: The American Museum of Natural History, 1868–1968." Ph.D. diss., Yale University, 1968.

Rainger, Ronald. *An Agenda for Antiquity: Henry Fairfield Osborn and Vertebrate Paleontology at the American Museum of Natural History, 1890–1935.* Tuscaloosa: University of Alabama Press, 1991.

Ronald Rainger

American Physical Society

The American Physical Society (APS) was organized at a meeting held on 20 May 1899 at Columbia University, as the result of a call circulated by Arthur Gordon Webster of Clark University cosigned by six other prominent American physicists. They proposed a society meeting four or more times yearly for the reading and discussion of papers. Henry Augustus Rowland and Albert Abraham Michelson had agreed to serve as president and vice president; other officers and a representative governing council were selected at the meeting, and a draft constitution adopted. A *Bulletin,* set up to announce and report membership meetings, was supplanted in 1903 by the *Physical Review,* which had been founded by Edward Leamington Nichols of Cornell University in 1893, primarily for publishing research papers. The APS took over the *Physical Review* in 1913, and in 1925 publication of a *Bulletin* was resumed for announcing meeting programs and other APS news.

The only essential concern of the APS was the encouragement of pure physics, a view not fully in accord with the needs of all physicists. Eventually it was supplemented by other societies, the first in 1916 (the Optical Society of America) and others in 1929 and 1930. Meanwhile, publication, as important to APS members as meetings, had become a source of serious financial difficulties, particularly critical by 1930. The APS and four other physics societies formed the American Institute of Physics in 1931, and were then able to obtain financial relief. The institute not only took over publication production but also undertook activities concerned with industrial and public relations and later with aspects of physics participation in World War II, leaving the APS officially uninvolved.

As the physics community became larger and more diverse, APS divisions were created, the first in 1943, to facilitate communication within various research fields. (As of 1999 there are fourteen divisions and eight smaller topical groups.) To accommodate increased demand for publication, the *Physical Review* began in 1964 to appear in four parts; A. General Physics, B. Solid State, C. Nuclear Physics, and D. Particles and Fields. The weekly *Physical Review Letters* dates from 1

July 1958. The quarterly *Reviews of Modern Physics* began publication in 1929.

APS membership was initially reserved for research physicists, but in 1904 nonvoting associate members were admitted. In 1920, regular members were made fellows; the others were then simply members, who were given the vote in 1946. Regular members may become fellows if elected by the council. As of 1998, the membership is over 43,000, including approximately 7,000 foreign members. Of the total over 4000 are fellows.

Extensive membership discussion during the sixties led to significant policy changes by 1972: an ad hoc committee on the future of APS "faced decisions to address a much wider set of aims," (Minutes) and the first outreach committees were established, those on the status of women in physics and on minorities. A forum on science and society was set up (a forum differs from a division in that it concerns matters not exclusively in physics). In 1974, a panel on public affairs was created to help coordinate the outreach activities of the society; it is charged with making recommendations to the president, the executive board and the council of APS. There are now five outreach committees and five forums, including one on the history of physics. Sessions on outreach activities may be held at APS meetings; two general meetings are held each year, plus subunit meetings. These include meetings of the seven regional sections: Four Corners (Southwest), New England, New York State, Northwest Ohio, Southeastern, and Texas. In 1991, the society held or sponsored thirty-eight scientific meetings.

It should be noted that the APS has not only grown in size and prestige but has significantly broadened its stated purpose, the advancement and diffusion of the knowledge of physics, to include recognition of the interplay between science and society.

The minutes of the American Physical Society Council are in the society's office in College Park, Maryland.

BIBLIOGRAPHY

American Physical Society. *Bulletin,* 1899–1902, 1925–.

American Physical Society. *1998–1999 Centennial Membership Directory.* College Park: American Physical Society, 1998.

Phillips, Melba. "The American Physical Society: A Survey of Its First 50 Years." *American Journal of Physics* 58 (1990): 219–230.

Melba Phillips

American Psychological Association

The American Psychological Association (APA) began at Clark University on 8 July 1892 in a meeting called by Granville Stanley Hall, a psychologist and president of the university. There is ambiguity about who attended but thirty-one residents of the eastern United States, almost all academicians, have been identified. The program for the first annual meeting, 27–28 December 1892 at the University of Pennsylvania, included twelve papers, primarily research articles. Eighteen of the founders were present and eleven new members accepted invitations to join.

Growth soon emerged as one of the more outstanding characteristics of psychology. Its extent is apparent in changes in the association during its first hundred years. The Centennial Convention, 14–18 August 1992, Washington, D.C., attracted 17,900 registrants. Almost 2,000 people participated in the five-day program, no longer restricted to the reading of papers, but included such varied tasks as approving budgets, planning elections, monitoring legislative controls on the practice of psychology, reviewing techniques of assessing academic programs, and endorsing actions that serve the public interest. These conventioneers were international and were drawn from a roster of 114,000 members whose involvement with psychology ranged from student status through postdoctoral expertise.

Sporadically, the ever increasing size has induced the forming of new groups, some catering to particular specialties and others to geographic regions. Typically, the spin-offs either do not endure or they serve as supplements to, not replacements of, the association. APA has repeatedly tried to accommodate itself to this diversity. In 1945, it even restructured itself into a federation of nineteen quasi-independent interest groups, called divisions. By 1992, they totaled forty-seven. This transformation made APA both a learned society and a professional organization. It alleviated several complaints but did not resolve all of them. World War II was followed by an inflation in the number of psychologists in various service enterprises, such as hospitals, clinics, prisons, schools, factories, and offices. As a result, practitioners now dominate the academic-research segment that had historically controlled the association. During the 1980s, the resentment against this shift in power grew and an attempt to modulate the influence by a second restructuring failed. In response, in 1988, some members formed the American Psychological Society, a group that stresses science

A

rather than application. The association's administration reacted by modifying some programs, carrying out a membership drive, overcoming a financial crisis, and even acquiring a new headquarters building—all victories that keep the association in the forefront of modern pluralistic psychology.

The programs and services sponsored by the American Psychological Association are beyond the limited space of this description, but one example of success is encountered in the sustained facilitation of communication. The association has maintained professional journals, creates new ones (for a total of twenty-four), publishes books, and also supports a system of abstracting most psychological literature. The APA Website (*http://www.apa.org*) is a comprehensive information resource. The association has a creditable record of nurturing both applied and theoretical information.

BIBLIOGRAPHY

American Psychological Association. *75th Annual Convention Program Washington, D.C.* Washington, DC: American Psychological Association, 1967.

———. *Commemorative Program, Centennial Convention, August 14–18, 1992.* Washington, DC: American Psychological Association, 1992.

Cattell, J.M. *Proceedings of the American Psychological Association.* New York: Macmillan, 1894. (Reprinted in *American Psychologist* 28, no. 4 [April 1973]: 278–292.)

Fernberger, S. "The American Psychological Association, 1892–1943." *Psychological Review* 50 (1943): 33–60.

Fowler, Raymond D. "Report of the Chief Executive Officer: A Year of Building for the Future." *American Psychologist* 47 (1992): 876–883.

———. "The American Psychological Association: 1985 to 1992." In *The American Psychological Association: A Historical Perspective,* edited by R.B. Evans, V.S. Sexton, and T.C. Cadwallader. Washington, DC: American Psychological Association, 1992, pp. 263–299.

Hilgard, E.R. *Psychology in America: A Historical Survey.* San Diego: Harcourt Brace Jovanovich, 1987.

Ogden, R.M. "Proceedings of the Twenty-fifth Annual Meeting of the American Psychological Association, New York, December 27, 28, 29, 30, 1916." *Psychological Bulletin* 14 (1917): 33–80.

John A. Popplestone

American Public Health Association

The American Public Health Association (APHA) was founded in 1872 by reformers, most of them physicians, committed to upgrading municipal and state public health services. Inspired by the success of New York City's Metropolitan Health Board (founded 1866), they hoped to remove health boards from the realm of partisan politics and to make their practices more scientific. The APHA's first constitution defined the organization's goal as "the advancement of sanitary science and the promotion of organizations and measures for the practical application of public hygiene."

The organization grew slowly; as of 1890 it had only 500 members, but among them were the most influential doctors in public service, including George Sternberg and John Shaw Billings. The APHA held annual meetings and in 1879 began to publish a yearly volume, *Public Health Papers and Reports.* Its conventions and publications were primarily concerned with the prevention and control of infectious diseases, such as cholera, yellow fever, and tuberculosis.

As the germ theory of disease gained adherents in the 1880s, the APHA became an important force in the development of bacteriology. The first generation of European-trained bacteriologists worked almost exclusively in public health laboratories, and the APHA became an important forum for their work. In the early 1890s, the APHA's Committee on the Pollution of Water Supplies complained about the inconsistent results bacteriologists obtained by their varied laboratory methods, prompting an 1895 meeting at the New York Academy of Medicine to discuss standardizing methods, the first official gathering of American bacteriologists. Two years later, a committee appointed at that meeting published a standard protocol for diagnostic and sampling work. The Laboratory Committee, which was formed in 1898 and became the Section for Bacteriology and Chemistry in 1899, continued to play an important role in standardizing methods for detecting and identifying microorganisms present in the air, water, and milk supply.

As the technical sophistication of the various professions involved in public health work continued to grow, the APHA became increasingly organized around section work. In 1908, vital statistics and public health administration joined bacteriology and chemistry as permanent sections, followed in subsequent years by sociology, sanitary engineering, food and drug, and industrial hygiene. The APHA sought to act as an umbrella group for the varied professions involved in the public health movement. In place of the highly technical *Public Health Papers and Reports,* the association in 1911 began to publish the *Journal of the American Public Health*

A

Association, aimed at a wide audience of public health workers. The APHA had a membership of 1,600 on the eve of World War I; by the early 1920s, it had grown to over 3,000 members.

BIBLIOGRAPHY

Bernstein, Nancy, ed. *The First One Hundred Years: Essays on the History of the American Public Health Association.* Washington, DC: APHA, 1972.

Gossel, Patricia Peck. "A Need for Standard Methods: The Case of American Bacteriology." In *The Right Tools for the Job,* edited by Adele E. Clarke and Joan H. Fujimura. Princeton: Princeton University Press, 1992, pp. 287–311.

Ravenal, Mazyck, ed. *A Half Century of Public Health.* 1921. Reprint, New York: Arno Press, 1970.

Nancy Tomes

American Society of Civil Engineers

First national professional organization of engineers in the United States. Inspired by a similar society in England, the American Society of Civil Engineers (ASCE) dates its founding to 5 November 1852, when twelve engineers gathered in New York City at the Croton Aqueduct office. Although fifty-six members were listed on the rolls in late 1853 and meetings were held until 1855, the organization really began to function only after 1867. Almost at once, ASCE found its desire to represent all professional engineers challenged by increasing specialization. By 1890, several groups had split off, including the American Institute of Mining Engineers, the American Society of Mechanical Engineers, and the American Institute of Electrical Engineers. This pattern has continued to the present day, with one product being the absence of a single organizational voice for the engineering profession.

The ASCE, in its initial constitution, identified one of its purposes as "the advancement of science." In the nineteenth century, however, civil engineers drew little from science, relying instead on practical experience and rules of thumb. Not surprisingly, ASCE showed much concern for advancing the "art" of engineering practice through papers presented at annual meetings and publication of those papers. Volume I of the *Transactions of the American Society of Civil Engineers* appeared in 1872, and was followed by a *Proceedings* as a separate publication in 1896, and by a monthly publication for members, *Civil Engineering,* beginning in 1930. After World War II, the volume of papers,

increasing specialization, and the development of engineering science among academic engineers led to the division of the *Proceedings* into several specialized publications.

Yet the advancement of engineering practice has not been the main purpose served by ASCE. Almost alone among the engineering fields, civil engineering retained a traditional pattern of organization based on independent consulting, with the result that leading ASCE members have been more independent of large corporations. Accordingly, ASCE has been quite concerned with the professional, social, and status concerns of its members. Over the years, the society has devoted significant attention to professional registration, engineering education, codes of ethics, engineering salaries, and unionization of engineers. For this reason, much of the scholarly attention devoted to civil engineering has focused on the questions of professionalism and social status.

BIBLIOGRAPHY

Calhoun, Daniel H. *The American Civil Engineer: Origins and Conflict.* Cambridge, MA: MIT Press, 1960.

Hunt, Charles Warren. "The Activities of the American Society of Civil Engineering During the Past Twenty-Five Years." *Transactions of the American Society of Civil Engineers* 82 (December 1918): 1577–1652.

Layton, Edwin T. *Revolt of the Engineers: Social Responsibility and the American Engineering Profession.* Cleveland: Case Western Reserve University Press, 1971; 2d ed., Baltimore: Johns Hopkins University Press, 1986.

Wisely, William A. *The American Civil Engineer, 1852–1974: The History, Traditions and Development of the American Society of Civil Engineers.* New York: American Society of Civil Engineers, 1974.

Bruce E. Seely

American Society of Zoologists

Professional society for research scientists in the field of zoology. Although dating its origin at 1890, when the American Morphological Society was formed as an offshoot of the American Society of Naturalists, the American Society of Zoologists (ASZ), as such, was formed in 1902 when the American Morphological Society merged with another American Society of Naturalists's subgroup, The Central Naturalists (founded in 1899). The two founding groups remained as separate eastern and western branches of the ASZ, each with its own set of officers and a complex formula for

A

arranging joint meetings, until 1913, when the constitution was rewritten to form a single integrated society with a single set of officers and annual meeting. Growing in influence throughout the first half of the twentieth century, the ASZ served as the focal point for both the movement toward increasing specialization and the need for a general biological society, representing the interests of biologists nationally. The latter concern was manifest when members of the ASZ took a lead role in the formation of the American Institute of Biological Sciences in 1948. Starting in 1959, and based upon a 1955–1956 National Science Foundation supported study of the role of the society in biology, the ASZ members organized themselves into a series of divisions—developmental biology, comparative endocrinology, comparative physiology, animal behavior (1959), invertebrate zoology, vertebrate morphology (1962), ecology (1966), systematic zoology (1967), comparative immunology (1975), and history and philosophy of biology (1981). Despite these subdivisions, the society continued to meet as a single organization with a single set of national officers. In 1988, the ASZ adopted, as a part of its name, the phrase "Society for Integrative and Comparative Biology," as a recognition of the society's role of providing a forum where research themes, which may unite separate programs, can be discussed. Following the annual meeting in December of 1995 the American Society of Zoologists became the Society for Integrative and Comparative Biology (SICB) and has continued under the new name to the present.

In its early years, the ASZ published its business proceedings and meeting abstracts in *Science* (1890–1916) or *Anatomical Record* (1917–1960). In 1960, the society began to publish a newsletter containing news of the organization. The *American Zoologist* was founded in 1961 as the official journal of the ASZ, publishing abstracts of papers presented at the annual meeting and proceedings of symposia sponsored by the society and its divisions.

At its inception, the intent of the society's members was to provide a forum where research professionals could compare results and learn techniques from one another. Thus the ASZ restricted its membership to those who had published research articles and their students. Many of the most noted and influential of American biologists have served as president of the society: for example, C.O. Whitman, E.B. Wilson, T.H. Morgan, H.F. Osborn, E.G. Conklin, W.E. Castle, F.R. Lillie,

H.S. Jennings, R.G. Harrison, Sewall Wright, and Th. Dobzhansky. Despite the emphasis on research, the ASZ has been involved as well in influencing public science policy and has provided materials for teachers of biology.

Historical analysis of the ASZ has emphasized the way the society's history mirrors the tensions among American biologists between increasing professionalization and specialization, on the one hand, and the desire for a unifying organization, on the other.

The ASZ archives are housed at the Smithsonian Institution.

BIBLIOGRAPHY

Appel, Toby A. "Organizing Biology: The American Society of Naturalists and its 'Affiliated Societies,' 1883–1923." In *The American Development of Biology*, edited by Ronald Rainger, Keith Benson, and Jane Maienschein. Philadelphia: University of Pennsylvania Press, 1988, pp. 87–120.

Atkinson, James W. "The Importance of the History of Science to the American Society of Zoologists." *American Zoologist* 19 (1979): 1243–1246.

Benson, Keith R. "From Museum Research to Laboratory Research: The Transformation of Natural History into Academic Biology." In *The American Development of Biology*, edited by Ronald Rainger, Keith Benson, and Jane Maienschein. Philadelphia: University of Pennsylvania Press, 1988, pp. 49–83.

———. "Epilogue: The Development and Expansion of the American Society of Zoologists." In *The Expansion of American Biology*, edited by Keith R. Benson, Jane Maienschein, and Ronald Rainger. New Brunswick: Rutgers University Press, 1991, pp. 325–335.

Benson, Keith R., and Br. C. Edward Quinn. *The American Society of Zoologists, 1889–1989: A Century of Integrating the Biological Sciences*. Boston: American Society of Zoologists, 1989.

Grobstein, Clifford. "New Patterns in the Organization of Biology." *American Zoologist* 6 (1966): 621–626.

Quinn, Br. C. Edward. "The Beginnings of the American Society of Zoologists." *American Zoologist* 19 (1979): 1247–1249.

———. "Ancestry and Beginnings: the Early History of the American Society of Zoologists." *American Zoologist* 22 (1982): 735–748.

James W. Atkinson

American Sociological Association

Founded in 1905, as the American Sociological Society, to represent the interests of theoretical and academic sociologists, and those seeking practical solutions for social problems. The society participated in the founding of the American Council of Learned Societies (1919), the Social Science Research Council (1923), and became affiliated with the American Association for the Advancement of Science in 1931. In the early years, the *American Journal of Sociology* was the official journal, but was replaced in 1936 by the *American Sociological Review.* The society became the American Sociological Association in 1959. The executive office was moved from New York to Washington, D.C., in 1963 when the first full-time executive officer was appointed. The period of greatest growth was during the 1960s when membership more than doubled to 13,357. In 1999, the association again had over 13,500 members and offered participants thirty-nine specialty sections and nine official journals.

The specialty sections and journals reflect and incorporate the broad interest of members into the national structure. Recognized sections are given considerable latitude within the association and, depending on their size, varying amounts of program time at the annual meeting. The association also responds to membership's shifting interest with a procedure that gives emergent concerns a place on the annual program. Additionally, a flexible relationship is maintained with the major regional and specialized sociological organizations.

Historically the association has reflected the harmony and disagreements of its members. With the move away from domination by the University of Chicago, signaled by the founding of the *American Sociological Review,* sociologists have continued to battle over the proper identity for their enterprise and association. While the debate reflects a multitude of disciplinary perspectives, methodological preferences, and interests, the association remains committed to inclusiveness and diversity, rather than theoretical or methodological orthodoxy.

BIBLIOGRAPHY

Rhoades, Lawrence J. *A History of the American Sociological Association 1905–1980.* Washington, DC: American Sociological Association, 1981.

Barry V. Johnston

American Statistical Association

The world's largest statistical society, with more than 17,000 individual members. Founded in 1839 as the American Statistical Society, the "objects" of the society, as defined by its 1839 constitution, are "to collect, preserve and diffuse Statistical information in the different departments of human knowledge." The prime organizer of the American Statistical Association (ASA) was Lemuel Stattuck, a printer, bookseller, publisher, and public official with a strong interest in collecting reliable demographic data. Bylaws adopted at the 5 February 1840 meeting, when the society became the America Statistical Association, required each full member, or "fellow," to submit for publication at least one article a year on a statistical subject. The Massachusetts legislature granted the ASA a charter of incorporation in 1841.

The ASA was a regional organization for its first fifty years, with its quarterly meetings in Boston usually attracting no more than ten members, but Francis A. Walker, who became president in 1882, initiated a major change in orientation and scope. The Superintendent of the Censuses of 1870 and 1880 and president of Massachusetts Institute of Technology (1881–1897), Walker firmly believed that the ASA should be national in character. During Walker's tenure—through 1897—the ASA created an official journal (now called the *Journal of the American Statistical Association*). Membership grew from less than 75 in 1872 to 533 in 1897. Many of the new members came from New York City, where business analysts and economists were active users of statistical data, and Washington, D.C., home of a number of government bureaus concerned with statistical data, such as the Bureau of Statistics of the Treasury Department (1866), the Bureau of Labor (1885), the Interstate Commerce Commission (1887), and the Census Bureau (made permanent in 1902). The first "scientific meeting" of the ASA to be held outside of Boston was in Washington in 1896; twelve years later, the first annual meeting outside Boston occurred. In 1918, the ASA established a standing Census Advisory Committee, the first of its major panels serving as liaison to the federal government. Two years later, the ASA moved its headquarters from Boston to Columbia University.

In the 1920s, R.A. Fisher created the basic principals of, and the tools for, the statistical design of experiments. His small-sample theory and methodology had so affected agricultural, biological, and medical research that, during the 1930s, the federal government redefined statistical studies from clerical to professional tasks. This locus of activity led the ASA to

A

shift its headquarters from New York City to Washington, D.C., in 1934.

In the teens and early twenties, local groups met between the annual ASA meetings. The ASA chartered its first regional chapter (the original Los Angeles Chapter) in 1925. Eight years later, there were thirty-three chapters. In 1999, there were seventy-five in the United States and three more in Canada.

The ASA created its first section (biometrics) in 1938 to accommodate the practitioners of the new statistical methodology. By 1958, more than ninety percent of the members belonged to at least one of its five sections. In 1999, there were twenty-one sections.

The archives of the ASA are in the Department of Special Collections of The Parks Library, Iowa State University.

BIBLIOGRAPHY

American Statistical Association. "Historical Exhibits." *Journal of the American Statistical Association* 35 (1940): 298–308.

Anderson, Margo. "Expanding the Influence of the Statistical Association: ASA from 1880 to 1930." In *Proceedings of the American Statistical Association Sesquicentennial Invited Paper Sessions.* Alexandria, VA: American Statistical Association, 1989, pp. 561–572.

Bowman, Raymond T. "The American Statistical Association and Federal Statistics." *Journal of the American Statistical Association* 59 (1964): 1–17.

Duncan, Joseph W., and William C. Shelton. *Revolution in United States Government Statistics, 1926–1976.* Washington, DC: United States Department of Commerce Office of Federal Statistical Policy and Standards, 1978.

Mason, Robert L. "A Golden Era of Statistics in America." In *Proceedings of the American Statistical Association Sesquicentennial Invited Paper Sessions.* Alexandria, VA: American Statistical Association, 1989, pp. 486–496.

Ruberg, Stephen J., et al. "Statistical Science: 150 Years of Progress." Alexandria, VA: American Statistical Association, 1989. Videotape.

Churchill Eisenhart

Ames Research Center

When the Ames Research Center was founded in 1939 as Ames Aeronautical Laboratory, it became the second research laboratory under the direction of the National Advisory Committee for Aeronautics (NACA). With Langley Aeronautical Laboratory on the East Coast, the NACA hoped that Ames, located on the southeastern end of San Francisco Bay, would prove an important West Coast liaison with the growing aircraft industry, located primarily on the West Coast. Ames indeed became an important link in the process of government coordination of aeronautical research with industry's needs. As a major research institution, however, it has, over its fifty-five-year history, also identified and pursued unique fields of research not only in aeronautics, but also in astronautics, life sciences, and information sciences.

The increasing tension during 1940 and 1941 and the eventual involvement of the United States in World War II dictated the direction of Ames's early research from the beginning. The rapid building of a sophisticated assortment of wind tunnels meant that military and industrial need for extensive test data could be supplied by Ames engineers. For the duration of the war all research was directed toward the solving of war-connected aeronautical problems. Probably most noteworthy was the wing de-icing research that Ames conducted in support of the war effort, although wind-tunnel testing of military aircraft prototypes also played an important part in wartime research.

With the end of the war, Ames's research paths split into two divergent areas—low-speed aeronautical research, and the high-speed research that would eventually lead the laboratory into the astronautics field. Hypersonic research became increasingly crucial as aircraft attained high speed flight and as space exploration and research became a reality. By the mid-1950s, high-speed research via ballistics was creating a foundation for the design of transonic and supersonic aircraft and spacecraft, solving the reentry heating problems with revolutionary designs.

The formation of the National Aeronautics and Space Administration (NASA) in 1958 carried Ames and the rest of the old NACA laboratories into the space age, with obvious shifts in the directions of research. Because of NASA's defined goals of space exploration, research became much more goal-focused. In the early 1960s, the research center experienced two major transitions connected to the space effort—the addition of a life-sciences section and the development of project management responsibilities involving significant amounts of contracted research rather than internally conducted research efforts. Important among Ames's contributions were the pioneer projects sending exploratory spacecraft to Venus and Jupiter and the life-sciences experiments in support of the Viking mission to Mars.

Research in the late 1960s and the 1970s added a new alliance between NASA and the military—in efforts that included the Army's rotor research cooperation with Ames, the V/STOL (vertical/short take-off and landing) research of the 1970s, and the preliminary space-shuttle research, Ames and the Department of Defense cooperated closely. Computational fluid dynamics increased the versatility of wind-tunnel research and expanded research directions into new areas.

In the early 1980s, Ames and the Dryden Flight Research Center were linked administratively. Elements of their research were coordinated to maximize the various strengths of each facility. In 1992, the two centers separated administratively, and in 1994, complete separation of Ames and Dryden took place, a reflection of the centers' divergent areas of activity.

BIBLIOGRAPHY

Hartman, Edwin P. *Adventures in Research: A History of Ames Research Center, 1940–1965.* Washington, DC: Government Printing Office, 1970.

Levine, Arnold S. *Managing NASA in the Apollo Era.* Washington, DC: Government Printing Office, 1982.

Muenger, Elizabeth A. *Searching the Horizon: A History of Ames Research Center, 1940–1976.* Washington, DC: Government Printing Office, 1985.

Elizabeth A. Muenger

SEE ALSO

National Advisory Committee for Aeronautics; National Aeronautics and Space Administration

Animal Behavior Society

An organization established in 1964 to promote and encourage the biological study of animal behavior. The genealogy of the Animal Behavior Society can be traced back to the Committee for the Study of Animal Societies Under Natural Conditions (CSASUNC), formed in 1947. The meeting ground for the original CSASUNC members was a common interest in what and why animals do what they do, and a hope that an understanding of nonhuman social systems could be used to alleviate human social problems through the application of biological techniques and concepts to social behavior and social organization. By 1952, the CSASUNC had evolved into a standing committee on animal behavior and sociobiology within the Ecological Society of America, and the committee in turn

became a section of the society in 1956. Jointly with the British Association for the Study of Animal Behaviour, the section established the journal *Animal Behaviour* in 1958. In the same year, a Division of Animal Behavior was established within the American Society of Zoologists. The Animal Behavior Society resulted from a merger of these two groups.

The archives of the society are housed in the Smithsonian Institution Archives.

Martin W. Schein

BIBLIOGRAPHY

Collias, N.E. "The Role of American Zoologists and Behavioural Ecologists in the Development of Animal Sociology, 1934–1964." *Animal Behaviour* 41 (1991): 613–631.

Animal Experimentation

The use of animals in biomedical research, education, and product testing has been controversial since the late nineteenth century. Although the level of hostility to animal experimentation has fluctuated over the course of the twentieth century, lay critics of animal experimentation, known as antivivisectionists, influenced the biomedical research community even when their movement was in decline in the first four decades of the twentieth century. The intensification of opposition to animal experimentation in the 1970s and 1980s has renewed interest in the origins of animal protection and antivivisection, although the unresolved nature of the controversy has precluded a definitive history of animal experimentation and animal protection.

Some of the earliest American experiments involving live animals were undertaken by medical students in the late eighteenth and early nineteenth centuries. In the 1840s, the introduction of anesthesia and the influence of French physiologists François Magendie and Claude Bernard encouraged vivisectional research and the use of live animals in medical teaching. In 1854, physiologist John Call Dalton, on his return from France, was apparently the first to introduce vivisectional demonstrations in his medical lectures. Before the 1880s, most students did not observe such demonstrations, and the use of animals in research remained rare.

The rarity of animal experimentation did not prevent calls for laboratory animal protection. In 1866, philanthropist Henry Bergh founded the American Society for the Prevention of Cruelty to Animals

A

(ASPCA), and pressed unsuccessfully for laws to abolish experiments involving animals in the 1860s and 1870s. In 1883, Caroline Earle White established the first society to abolish vivisection, the American Anti-Vivisection Society, which continues to oppose the laboratory use of animals (1999. See their webpage: www.aavs.org)

Before World War II, scientific and institutional developments expanded the use of animals in research. Significant clinical advances, including the discovery of insulin and the development of antibiotics in the 1940s, resulted from animal research. Funding for war-related research and the growing budgets for the National Institutes of Health after the war dramatically increased the demand for laboratory animals. In the years 1959 to 1965, the number of rats, mice, and rabbits for laboratory use reportedly rose from 17 million to 60 million per year.

The postwar period also witnessed renewed opposition to animal experimentation. In the 1940s and 1950s, the American research community and animal protectionists engaged in a series of volatile battles for control of pound animals. Although the research community continued to insist on self-regulation of research involving animals, increasing demands for governmental oversight led to congressional passage of the Laboratory Animal Welfare Act in 1966. The act and its amendments now regulate all aspects of the acquisition, care, and use of laboratory animals. Regulations and investment in alternatives to animal research have not diminished opposition to animal experimentation. The animal rights movement grew enormously in the 1970s and 1980s. The popularity of the movement, and the increase of illegal activity, including destruction of laboratories, has mobilized the biomedical research community. The use of animals in research and teaching remains a highly charged issue.

BIBLIOGRAPHY

Atwater, Edward C. "'Squeezing Mother Nature': Experimental Physiology in the United States Before 1870." *Bulletin of the History of Medicine* 52 (1978): 313–335.

Benison, Saul, A. Clifford Barger, and Elin L. Wolfe. *Walter B. Cannon.* Cambridge, MA: Harvard University Press, 1987.

Blum, Deborah. *The Monkey Wars.* New York: Oxford University Press, 1994.

Garner, Robert. *Political Animals: Animal Protection Policies in Britain and the United States.* New York: St. Martin's Press, 1998.

Jasper, James M., and Dorothy Nelkin. *The Animal Rights Crusade.* New York: Free Press, 1992.

Lederer, Susan E. "The Controversy over Animal Experimentation in America, 1880–1914." In *Vivisection in Historical Perspective,* edited by Nicolaas A. Rupke. London: Croom Helm, 1987, pp. 236–258.

———. "Political Animals: The Shaping of Biomedical Research Literature in Twentieth-Century America." *Isis* 83 (1992): 61–79.

———. *Subjected to Science: Human Experimentation in America Before the Second World War.* Baltimore: Johns Hopkins University Press, 1995.

Orlans, F. Barbara. *In the Name of Science: Issues in Responsible Animal Experimentation.* New York: Oxford University Press, 1993.

Rowan, Andrew N. *Of Mice, Models, and Men.* Albany: State University of New York Press, 1984.

Sperling, Susan. *Animal Liberators.* Berkeley: University of California Press, 1988.

Turner, James. *Reckoning with the Beast.* Baltimore: Johns Hopkins University Press, 1980.

Susan E. Lederer

Antibiotics

Antimicrobial drugs. The field of bacteriology emerged in the late nineteenth century. The development of the germ theory of disease, growing out of the pioneering work of Koch in Germany and Pasteur in France, presented a new paradigm for medical science. Identification of specific microorganisms that caused specific diseases was but the first step. The next step was one of developing specific drugs to kill bacteria that produced disease in humans. Although medical scientists had begun to identify the organisms which caused diseases, they lacked therapies which could successfully treat them.

The sulfonamides were among the first antimicrobials developed. German researcher Gerhard Domagk demonstrated the effect of one of the first, prontosil, against streptococcal infections in the 1930s. Although the sulfa drugs could produce toxic reactions in some individuals, their use against streptococcal and gonococcal infections proved invaluable during the late 1930s and early 1940s.

American investigators demonstrated even further the efficacy of the sulfonamides. Following the initial German research, clinicians in the United States and Great Britain conducted trials with the sulfa drugs that followed in quick succession. By the early 1940s, researchers had shown that sulfadiazine was comparable in antimicrobial spectrum as sulfanilamide, sulfapyridine, and sulfathiazole but with relatively fewer adverse effects.

Penicillin, however, eclipsed the sulfonamides by the early years of the World War II. Although Alexander Fleming had noted the lytic effect of *P. notatum* on *Staphylococcus aureus,* an organism well known for its resistance to lysis, clinical researchers at Oxford did not evaluate penicillin fully until 1940. Penicillin greatly expanded the range of antimicrobial therapy. Producing far fewer toxic reactions than the sulfas, penicillin also provided an effective treatment for staphylococcal infections—against which the sulfonamides had proven useless.

The industrial production of penicillin proved a major hurdle. Manufacture of the drug, a tediously inefficient process during the early days of the war, increased to unexpected levels by 1944 as scientists and engineers in the Peoria, Illinois, United States Department of Agriculture facility improved production methods and technology.

Numerous drugs followed during the early postwar years. The first cephalosporins, streptomycin, the first tetracyclines, and chloramphenicol had all appeared by 1960. Each of these broadened the effective antimicrobial range of antibiotic therapy beyond the first sulfa drugs and penicillin. The development of newer antibiotics, however, has proven absolutely essential in the control of organisms resistant to existing antimicrobial drugs.

BIBLIOGRAPHY

Adams, David P. *"The Greatest Good to the Greatest Number": Penicillin Rationing on the American Home Front, 1940–1945.* New York: Peter Lang, 1991.

Clark, Ronald W. *The Life of Ernst Chain: Penicillin and Beyond.* New York: St. Martin's Press, 1986.

Hobby, Gladys L. *Penicillin: Meeting the Challenge.* New Haven: Yale University Press, 1985.

MacFarlane, Gwyn. *Alexander Fleming: The Man and the Myth.* Cambridge, MA: Harvard University Press, 1984.

Moberg, Carol L., and Zanvil A. Cohn. *Launching the Antibiotic Era: Personal Accounts of the Discovery and Use of the First Antibiotics.* New York: Rockefeller University Press, 1990.

Parascandola, John, ed. *The History of Antibiotics: A Symposium.* Madison: American Institute of the History of Pharmacy, 1980.

Sheehan, John C. *The Enchanted Ring: The Untold Story of Penicillin.* Cambridge, MA: MIT Press, 1982.

Spink, Wesley W. *Infectious Diseases: Prevention and Treatment in the Nineteenth and Twentieth Centuries.* Minneapolis: University of Minneapolis Press, 1978.

Swann, John Patrick. "The Search for Penicillin Synthesis during World War II." *British Journal for the History of Science* 16 (July 1983): 154-190.

Williams, Trevor I. *Howard Florey: Penicillin and After.* Oxford: Oxford University Press, 1984.

David P. Adams

Apollo Program

The name chosen for the American national endeavor, directed by its National Aeronautics and Space Administration (NASA), to send men to the moon, land them there, and retrieve them safely during the decade of the 1960s.

Apollo followed in the wake of NASA's Project Mercury (1959–1963) which used ballistic rockets to put test pilots into earth orbit, then Project Gemini (1962–1966), which developed manned spaceflight farther through orbital maneuvering, rendezvous, and docking. Sometimes called the "enterprise of the 1960s," the Apollo Program was an ambitious, awesome, and ultimately amazing adventure of manned spaceflight technology. It helped to convert the fearsome arms race between the Soviet Union and the United States into a benign space race. It was a manifestation of the geopolitical quest for pride and power during the Cold War. It also demonstrated and stimulated countless technological, scientific, military, industrial, and micrological-macrological capabilities during the era of superpower confrontation. President John F. Kennedy authorized the beginnings of a formal manned lunar landing program shortly after he took office in 1961. By the end of 1969, four American astronauts had walked on the moon and returned to earth safely. Mission accomplished . . . twice. By the end of 1973, twelve astronauts (the last one a bonafide geologist, Harrison Schmidt, Ph.D.) had explored in person various sites on the visible surface of the moon and seventeen others had circumnavigated it. Originally twenty Apollo-Saturn test flights and missions were planned, but funding cuts after 1970 reduced these to seventeen.

Project Mercury evolved from NASA's series of experimental guided-missile programs, especially those pioneered by Robert R. Gilruth and Max Faget in their Pilotless Aircraft Research Division of NASA at Langley, Virginia, and from NASA's supersonic aircraft, from the X-1 to the X-15, developed during the late 1940s and 1950s. Also basic were the ballistic-missile launch vehicle programs, especially those pushed by the German-American team led by Wernher von Braun, from the V-2's of World War II to the Saturn series of boosters in the 1960s. The Mercury spacecraft, a small, one-seat nose cone with a blunt-body ablative heatshield for reentry protection, was barely maneuverable, but it served valiantly on seven manned missions to demonstrate two suborbital flight capabilities and five manned satellite voyages of ever longer duration (up to seventeen earth orbits by 1963). The Redstone rocket developed by the von Braun team for the United States Army lofted the initial test flights, but then the Atlas ICBM (intercontinental ballistic missile) was the booster that made possible five subsequent Mercury-Atlas flights. Soviet achievements in spaceflight during the first half of the 1960s were always ahead of American accomplishments, but parity began to show as momentum built up, and safety and success was demonstrated mission by mission. Hardly any basic or pure science was even sought at first because all sciences were exploited for mission applications. But gradually the engineering sciences made possible all sorts of other scientific insights and investigations.

Project Gemini, NASA's intermediate manned spaceflight research and development effort, was specifically designed to fill the many gaps in engineering knowledge and spaceflight experience that faced American developers as soon as Congress endorsed President Kennedy's decision. The Gemini spacecraft was barely twice the size of the Mercury capsule yet more than five-times heavier, capable of carrying two men for two weeks in orbit, and designed to demonstrate rendezvous in space, docking, and "extra-vehicular activities" (tethered astronauts floating and working outside in their spacesuits). Designed after the same manner as Mercury but developed by a vastly enlarged team of engineers, now relocated at NASA's new Manned Spacecraft Center near Houston, Texas, the Gemini craft was equipped with ejection seats for launch escape if necessary. Otherwise the first and second generation craft looked similar outwardly but were inwardly very different. All Gemini missions were boosted into orbit *On the Shoulders of Titans* (as the title of B. Hacker's history commemorates), and that Titan II ICBM proved itself a most reliable launch vehicle. Because the Apollo-Saturn team had decided to go to and from the moon by a modular method called the Lunar Orbital Rendezvous (LOR),

the Gemini program was an integral part (although separately managed) of testing the feasibilities and main operational features for Apollo.

Perhaps the most "scientific" as opposed to technological parts of the Apollo Program before the world's first circumnavigation of the moon (by humans in *Apollo 8* at Christmastime 1968) were the series of three robotic projects (called Projects Ranger, Surveyor, and Lunar Orbiter) that probed the surface and the topography of lunar landscapes. These three sets of scouting expeditions began with many tribulations but ended in magnificent triumphs. Ranger was designed to send television pictures back to earth at ever smaller resolutions until impact and destruction. Surveyor was engineered to land softly at selected sites on the moon, test bearing strengths, sizes and shapes of rocks or boulders, lunar dust composition, lighting conditions, and so forth. Lunar Orbiter was designed to use radar and photography to map the entire lunar sphere topologically, for landing site selections. So well did the first three (out of five) Lunar Orbiter missions perform that the last two were devoted almost exclusively to more cartography.

The logical buildup of verified knowledge about the surface of the moon that these three programs provided by the end of 1968 vastly increased the confidence that Apollo design decisions (especially for the Lunar Module and for the astronauts' spacesuits) had been wise enough. Beyond Apollo's needs, however, these three programs provided solid selenography of permanent value.

Aside from the countless applications of scientific knowledge used to design, test, develop, and refine all the components of hardware and software needed to do the job of getting men to the moon and back safely within a decade, there were of course some discoveries about nature and human nature that may someday be recognized as more purely scientific than mission-oriented. NASA's sponsorship and subsidies for funding academic researchers, buildings, and laboratories for the space sciences, and grants for thousands of theoretical and experimental scientists, all this and more—mostly in the name of Apollo during the 1960s and its follow-up programs, Skylab and Apollo-Soyuz in the 1970s—must be credited as contributions to science. Two quite profound transitions may be seen as having begun during the decade characterized by Apollo: one, the astrophysical-cosmological-ecozoic beginnings of an appreciation for the ubiquity of biochemical building blocks in outer space; two, the biomedical and neuropsychical implications of space medicine (derived from military medicine) based on health rather than disease. Although the second is more closely tied directly to Apollo, the first is indirectly associated with its counterculture, with advances in astronomy, biochemistry, planetary sciences, instrumentation, microminiaturization, computer technology, and so on. Seeing what was necessary to construct Apollo spacecraft and space suits as artificial worlds certainly stimulated seeing earth itself as a spaceship.

Early in 1967, both the American and the Soviet manned spaceflight programs suffered tragic catastrophes that set back the clocks in the manned space-race to the moon. A disastrous fire in spacecraft 204 on the launch pad at Cape Kennedy killed astronauts Virgil I. Grissom, Edward H. White, and Roger B. Chaffee, who were later honored by calling this failed test the "Apollo One" mission. This tragedy prompted many changes for the sake of safety and reliability, chiefly a reduction of oxygen in cabin atmosphere composition. In April, cosmonaut Vladimir Komorov was killed in a crash after tumbling caused his parachute straps to twist and destroy all braking action for his spacecraft, *Soyuz One*. Agonized reappraisals of all systems by engineers and technicians in both nations undoubtedly vastly improved their equipment for both reliability and safety.

About this time in the American program alone more than 500,000 workers, whether in government or industry or academia, were directly associated with the Apollo Program. Congressionally appropriated funds for Apollo alone would eventually total more than $25 billion dollars.

Ultimately Apollo operations included two earth-orbiting missions (Apollo 7 and 9), two circumlunar missions (Apollo 8 and 10), one aborted mission (Apollo 13) that barely got to swing around the moon and return, hanging by a thread, and six ever more complex lunar landing missions (Apollo 11, 12, 14, 15, 16, and 17). Thus, there were eleven manned flights; twenty-seven Americans orbited the moon; twelve walked on its surface; six drove lunar vehicles on excursions around their landing sites.

The twelve men on the moon spent a total of 296 hours exploring its surface in six radically different areas facing the earth, bringing back 382 kilograms of lunar rocks and soil samples. All six lunar landings set up scientific instruments for various purposes, but the last five landing missions set up more elaborate equipment for science stations to operate by remote control.

About twenty-five different types of sensors or experiments were deployed on the moon's surface. More than 16,000 photographs of scientific interest were taken for the benefit of earthbound experts in such fields as geology, geophysics, geochemistry, petrology, petrography, and other similar disciplines.

On 20 July 1969, when Neil Armstrong took his first small step for man but giant leap for mankind upon the lunar dust, his teammate Edwin "Buzz" Aldrin became the photographic model of the man-on-the-moon because Armstrong held the camera. On 19 December 1972, when Ronald E. Evans, Eugene Cernan, and Jack Schmitt splashed down safely in the Pacific Ocean near Pago Pago, Apollo's ambitious and awesome adventure to explore the moon was over. But Apollo Applications took over for three Skylab missions, using Apollo spacecraft and Saturn launch vehicles in different configurations during 1973 and 1974. And finally in July 1975, the Apollo-Soyuz Test Project flew crews from the Soviet Union and the United States in space to rendezvous the superpowers symbolically, docking so that astronauts and cosmonauts could shake hands in orbit, toast each other, and share a meal and gifts in weightlessness. The scientific returns from the Skylab missions certainly were the greater, but the geopolitical and sociopsychological returns of Apollo-Soyuz may be adjudged as greater still, because cooperation has become recognized as being as important as competition.

Among spaceflight buffs, the Apollo 8 decision and mission, first to circumnavigate the moon at Christmastime in 1968 (manned by Frank Borman, James A. Lovell Jr., and William A. Anders) stands out sharply as a turning point in the space race. Popularly, the high drama and near-tragedy of Apollo 13 (manned by Lovell, John L. Swigert Jr., and Fred W. Haise Jr. in 1970) has captivated both literary and cinematic audiences. Apollo 15 in 1971, which moon-landed David R. Scott and James B. Irwin near Hadley Rille, saw the first use of the "Moon Buggy" for automotive transport. Televised to earth in real time, like all the Apollo missions, Apollo 15 made the sport seem more important than the science. Both quests obviously were central to the achievements of Apollo.

BIBLIOGRAPHY

Bilstein, Roger E. *Stages to Saturn: A Technological History of Apollo/Saturn Launch Vehicles*. Washington, DC: National Aeronautics and Space Administration, 1980.

A

Brooks, Courtney O. *Chariots for Apollo: A History of Manned Lunar Spacecraft.* Washington, DC: National Aeronautics and Space Administration, 1979.

Compton, William D. *Where No Man Has Gone Before: A History of Apollo Lunar Exploration Missions.* Washington, DC: National Aeronautics and Space Administration, 1989.

Ezell, Linda N. *NASA Historical Data Book.* Vols. 2, 3. Washington, DC: National Aeronautics and Space Administration, 1988.

Hacker, Barton C., et al. *On the Shoulders of Titans: A History of Project Gemini.* Washington, DC: National Aeronautics and Space Administration, 1977.

Hallion, Richard P., and Tom D. Crouch, eds. *Apollo: Ten Years Since Tranquility Base.* Washington, DC: National Air and Space Museum, 1979.

Levine, Arnold S. *Managing NASA in the Apollo Era.* Washington, DC: National Aeronautics and Space Administration, 1982.

MacDougall, Walter A. *The Heavens and the Earth: A Political History of the Space Age.* New York: Basic Books, 1985.

Murray, Charles, et al. *Apollo: The Race to the Moon.* New York: Simon & Schuster, 1989.

Newell, Homer E. *Beyond the Atmosphere: Early Years of Space Science.* Washington, DC: National Aeronautics and Space Administration, 1980.

Pitt, John A. *The Human Factor: Biomedicine in the Manned Space Program.* Washington, DC: National Aeronautics and Space Administration, 1985.

Swenson, Loyd S. Jr., et al. *This New Ocean: A History of Project Mercury.* Washington, DC: National Aeronautics and Space Administration, 1966.

Loyd S. Swenson Jr.

Aquariums
See Zoological Parks and Aquariums

Archaeoastronomy

Archaeoastronomy is the interdisciplinary study of the practice of astronomy by ancient cultures based upon a consideration of both the written and unwritten record. The latter includes archaeological and iconographic materials traditionally assigned to disciplines outside the domain of the history of science. To the former one could add the ethnohistoric record and the testimony of living people (anthropology). By broaching the social sciences, the interdiscipline attempts to expand the depth and scope of the traditional discipline of the history of astronomy, which, like its parent field the history of science, focuses upon the development of West European scientific astronomy and uses as its principal evidence the written legacy of the classical, ancient Middle Eastern, Renaissance, and post-Renaissance worlds.

First introduced formally in the literature in the early 1970s, the term seems to have derived from an inversion of the word astroarchaeology, which connoted the study of possible astronomical alignments of ancient architecture. This was largely a field-survey technique redeveloped by scientifically trained scholars of the 1960s as a means of explaining the alignments of Great Britain's Stonehenge and other megalithic monuments. Similar studies had already taken place in the 1890s at Stonehenge and among the Nilotic temples of Egypt.

By the early 1970s, alignment studies had expanded beyond the standing stones of northwest Europe to include the architecture of the cultures of Mesoamerica (e.g. the Aztecs, Maya, and Zapotecs), South America (most notably the Inca), the American Southwest (Hope-Anasazi-Pueblo) and, later, the Mediterranean basin (early mainland Italic cultures, Sardinia, Menorca, and the Canary Islands), China, and Eastern Europe. The investigative body also broadened to include historians of religion and art, ethnohistorians, linguists, and epigraphers. Such a development has resulted in a more even distribution of interest in astronomically related questions among the broad areas of science, social science, and the humanities.

Archaeoastronomical inquiries have since expanded beyond simple statistical considerations of the alignment of archaeological remains to incorporate the study of rock art, the development of prehistoric calendars and methods of timekeeping, mythology and folk astronomy, especially the practice of astronomy among contemporary non-Western peoples, a field that has come to merit its own designation: ethnoastronomy.

Archaeoastronomy claims two major journals, and more than two dozen edited books carrying the title have been published in the last quarter century (for example, Aveni, *World Archaeoastronomy*). About half the articles on the subject now appear in the disciplinary journals, thus implying the success with which archaeoastronomical material has been absorbed by traditional studies.

The principal goal of archaeoastronomy is to explore the interaction between culture and that segment of the natural world that includes the celestial sphere, regardless of whether the relationship between nature and the human condition be considered prescientific or scientific. Whether the technology applied by the culture one encounters be high or low, is no criterion for labeling studies as archaeoastronomical. For example, a study of the theonomy of celestially related gods, the role of the sky in a classic oral epic, or the designation of astronomical symbols in a picture-"codex" of a preliterate people all would fall under the domain of archaeoastronomy, even though none of these subjects would necessarily contribute directly to the body of knowledge comprising the history of Western astronomy. But by attempting to embrace all conceivable ways the human intellect has sought to understand the universe, archaeoastronomy can contribute indirectly to the history of scientific astronomy by offering comparisons between the scientific way of knowing and other modes of comprehending the cosmos.

BIBLIOGRAPHY

Aveni, Anthony F. "Archaeoastronomy." *Advances in Archaeological Method and Theory* 4 (1981): 1–77.

———, ed. *World Archaeoastronomy.* Cambridge, U.K.: Cambridge University Press, 1989.

Baity, Elizabeth C. "Archaeoastronomy and Ethnoastronomy So Far." *Current Anthropology* 14 (1973): 389–449.

Hawkins, Gerald S. "Astro-archaeology." *Research in Space Science.* Special Report No. 226. Cambridge, MA: Smithsonian Astrophysical Observatory, 1966.

Lockyer, J. Norman. *The Dawn of Astronomy.* London: Cassel, 1894.

Ruggles, C.L.N. and N. Saunders, eds. *Astronomies and Cultures.* Niwot: University Press of Colorado.

A. Aveni

Archaeology

Scientific archaeology in the United States may trace its origin to Europe, to that time when archaeological investigations turned away from antiquarianism to a more systematic study of prehistory involving new techniques for archaeological dating and the pioneering studies of the Paleolithic period in France and England which suggested a much greater antiquity of humankind. One of the earliest concerns for chronology and the establishment of the earth's age can be seen in the work of the Greek historian Herodotus (484–424 B.C.). He noted that thick sediments that were deposited over time were an indication or measure of the duration of prehistoric time. The Bible suggested that the earth was 6,000 years old while Rabbinical chronology indicated that the earth was as old as 3700 B.C. Roman Catholic chronology painted a picture of the planet as old as 5100 B.C. Nineteenth-century Scandinavian archaeologists like Christen Jürgenson Thomsen and Jens J.A. Worsaae developed the earliest concern for dating archaeological remains. Thomsen also first conceived of the idea of a controlled chronology of the development of cultures not based on written records. Their work was continued in France and England by Georges Cuvier (many consider Cuvier to be the first paleontologist), Jacques Crèvecoeur de Boucher de Perthes, and Charles Lyell. Lyell demonstrated the earth to be made up of a series of layers or strata. Boucher de Perthes demonstrated that ancient humankind lived during the Pleistocene (Ice Age) near Abbèville, France. His stratigraphic observations lead him to assume that the stone artifacts and extinct animals that he found there, in situ, were of equal age. Later, archaeologists in Europe and in the United States would take Lyell's idea of geological strata and develop the first method of relative dating in archaeology—stratigraphy. At about the same time, in France and England natural scientists were concerned with an ever-growing antiquity of humankind that exceeded the Bible's parameters. The work of Georges Louis de Buffon, Lyell, and Charles Darwin among others would shed light on the antiquity of humankind and the biological principles that govern change and variability from preexisting examples of life. Scientific archaeology in the United States owes a great deal to these European archaeologists and natural scientists.

Earlier scholars saw the ten "lost tribes" of Israel as ancestral to the Native American populations. Such an explanation was favored by Fray Diego Duran, who studied Aztec history, as well as by the American writer James Adair (1775). However, Fracastoro (1530) and Gonzalo Fernandez de Oviedo y Valdes (1534) saw Native American origins in Plato's Atlantis. In 1590, Fray José de Acosta suggested that the Americas might have been populated by a slow, overland process of migration. As early as 1637, the idea of humankind entering the New World via the Bering Strait was being seriously considered. In 1648, Thomas Gage suggested that the Bering Strait provided the linkage between ancestral Mongolia and the Americas. However, the intellectual climate of this period still favored a more romantic interpretation of the origins of peoples in the New World, an interpretation that fitted the socially stratified class system of Europe at the time.

A

Later, Thomas Jefferson (1790) and Caleb Atwater began to undertake archaeological excavations in Virginia and Ohio. The first major contribution to North American archaeology came with E.G. Squier and E.H. Davis's *Ancient Monuments of the Mississippi Valley* (1848). Squier and Davis described and partially excavated some of the mounds they studied. Both men suggested a "great race of Moundbuilders" were responsible for the construction of the mounds they discovered and that the American Indians and their descendants were not capable of such feats of construction. Many of the mounds described are no longer extant, their description being the only record of them. It was not until the work of Cyrus Thomas (1885, 1894) that Native American archaeological populations were given credit for the construction of the mounds.

Out of the work of James Hutton (the founder of "uniformatarian geology") and Lyell in England came the chronological revolution of stratigraphy in the United States. In 1914, stratigraphic dating was first applied to an archaeological site, San Cristobal Pueblo, New Mexico, by Nels C. Nelson. Later in 1915 (through 1924), Alfred Vincent Kidder (1855–1963) used stratigraphic dating on a massive scale at Pecos Pueblo, New Mexico. Kidder's use of stratigraphy not only brought the wide use of this relative dating method to archaeology but also a sense of the spatial distribution of territory under the control of a specific prehistoric culture. It was Kidder who also brought his "pan-scientific" approach to archaeology in the United States by pursuing a multidisciplinary approach to archaeological problems at Pecos Pueblo. There he involved the physical anthropologist, the ethnographer, as well as colleagues from other sciences—all coming together to bring expertise and mode of analysis to bear upon archaeological problems.

Kidder formulated the first "scientific" classification system of analysis and explanation of archaeological remains in the United States. His Pecos Classification (1927) arranged potsherds according to family (method of manufacture, decoration, form), much like the Linnean taxonomic system did for the sciences' botanical and animal world. Later, W.C. McKern's Midwestern Taxonomic System would continue the classificatory system of archaeological explanation. Today, Lewis Binford has argued, and still is arguing, for an "archaeological science" as the best means to enhance archaeological explanation of sites.

The single most important scientific development in the archaeology of the United States was the development of radiocarbon dating by Willard F. Libby at the University of Chicago. The discovery of cosmic radiation in 1911 by V.F. Hess was to give Libby, in 1947, a major beginning point for the discovery of radiocarbon (carbon 14) and its usefulness to other scientific disciplines. Radiocarbon dating was devised in the late 1940s and radiocarbon tests were made available to archaeologists in the United States during the 1950s. The method operates on the principle that radiocarbon in the earth's atmosphere is assimilated by all living organisms. This absorption ceases at the death of the organism, to be replaced by the decay of the carbon into nitrogen at a steady and predictable rate. Remains found in archaeological sites in association with cultural materials are also dated by their depositional relationship to the sample dated. Libby demonstrated that archaeological remains of wood, bone, and charcoal retain radiocarbon very well. Based on the data that living woods contain small amounts of radiocarbon, Libby and his collaborators first applied the technique to archaeological remains by determining the age of woods from the tombs of the Egyptian kings Zozer and Snefreu. Later, Andrew E. Douglass (University of Arizona, the inventor of dendrochronology, or "tree-ring dating") obtained dates from tree rings in wood samples from archaeological sites around the United States. Later, some of these wood samples with known ages would be used to complement Libby's technique by serving as a means to validate radiocarbon dates. Today, Libby's technique may be used not only to date ancient woods but also peat, bone shell, iron, and pottery—all items that may be found (with the exception of iron within the strata of prehistoric archaeological sites) in the United States. Radiocarbon had a tremendous influence on the archaeology of the United States, especially with the firm establishment of humankind's existence in North America to a time period older that 10,000 years.

Archaeology has in the past and continues today to incorporate other sciences into its tool kit to explain the archaeological record. Among some of the sciences drawn upon to more fully explain the archaeological record are chemistry, physics, biochemistry, medicine, and public health sciences.

BIBLIOGRAPHY

Adair, James. *The History of the American Indian, Particularly Those Nations Adjoining The Mississippi, East and West Florida, Georgia, South and North Carolina, and Virginia;*

Containing An Account of Their Origins, Language, Manners, . . . and Other Particulars Sufficient to Render It a Complete Indian System . . . Also an Appendix . . . With a New Map of the Country Referred to in the History. London: Dilly, 1775.

Binford, Lewis R. *An Archaeological Perspective.* New York: Seminar Press, 1972.

Buffon, George Louis de. *Natural History, General and Particular. . . . The History of Man and Quadrupeds.* 1749; W. Smellie, translation, edited by W. Wood. 20 vols. London: T. Cadell and W. Davies, 1812.

Gage, Thomas. *Travels in the New World.* Edited by J.E.S. Thompson. Norman: University of Oklahoma Press, 1958.

Givens, Douglas R. *Processual Papers in Archaeometric Dating: Potassium-Argon (K40/Ar40) and Radiocarbon Dating (C40).* Saint Louis: International Institute for Advanced Studies, 1980.

———. *Alfred Vincent Kidder and the Development of Americanist Archaeology.* Albuquerque: University of New Mexico Press, 1992.

Kidder, Alfred V. *An Introduction to Southwestern Archaeology with a Preliminary Account of the Excavations at Pecos.* New Haven: Yale University Press, 1924.

Libby, Willard F. *Radiocarbon Dating.* 2d ed. Chicago: University of Chicago Press, 1955.

Lyell, Charles. *Principles of Geology.* 3 vols. London: J. Murray, 1830–1833.

Suess, Hans E. "The Early Radiocarbon Years: Personal Reflections." In *Radiocarbon After Four Decades: An Interdisciplinary Perspective.* New York: Springer-Verlag (a copublication with Radiocarbon), 1992, pp. 3–11.

Thomas, Cyrus. "Who Were the Mound Builders?" *American Antiquarian and Oriental Journal* 2 (1885): 65–74.

———. *Report of the Mound Explorations of the Bureau of Ethnology.* Washington, DC: Smithsonian Institution, 1894.

Trigger, Bruce G. *A History of Archaeological Thought.* New York: Cambridge University Press, 1989.

Wauchope, Robert. *Lost Tribes and Sunken Continents.* Chicago: University of Chicago Press, 1962.

Willey, Gordon R., and Jeremy A. Sabloff. *A History of American Archaeology.* 2d ed., San Francisco: W.H. Freeman and Company, 1980.

Douglas R. Givens

Army, United States, Science and
See Engineers, United States Army

Art and Science

Although the complex relation between American art and science remains insufficiently studied, recent art historians have analyzed science-related artifacts, such as natural history illustration, and interpreted American art in the context of scientific theories.

The very discovery of the New World was a consequence of European empiricism. In the colonial period, Baconian explorers accumulated detailed evidence about the newly claimed land and its products. Visual records, such as Englishman John White's sixteenth-century drawings documenting natural resources and indigenous peoples in Virginia, were originally valued for their accuracy but today reveal the artists' cultural biases and artistic conventions. Later, Americans continued to invoke scientific inquiry and utility to justify national exploration and expansion, a practice which peaked with the nineteenth-century realization of Manifest Destiny. Both high art and popular imagery reflected, reinforced, and disseminated these precepts.

Lewis and Clark did not travel with an artist, but Samuel Seymour accompanied Colonel Stephen Long's expedition to the Rocky Mountains in 1819; and the illustrations in the published account of that trip set a standard for communicating subsequent data. In the same period, lavishly illustrated natural history volumes, many published through Philadelphia's Academy of Natural Sciences, satisfied chauvinism and curiosity about America's natural wonders. Robust images of flora and fauna countered the French Comte de Buffon's controversial theory that species degenerate in the American climate. Many of the specimens were arrayed according to a static, Linnaean classification system; others, like John James Audubon's *Birds of America,* 1828–1838, depicted philosophical and ethological concerns regarding animal intelligence, and even early evolutionary interests.

The arts and sciences were nurtured as not only compatible, but essential to the health of the young republic. The first public art exhibition in the United States, the 1795 Philadelphia Columbianum, exhibited technical engineering drawings beside oil paintings. Individuals were also lauded for productivity in both fields. Charles Willson Peale's 1806–1808 painting *Exhuming the First American Mastodon* is comprehensible both in Jeffersonian political terms and as celebration of Peale's own discovery of a lost link in the "great chain of being." The archetype of American Enlightenment, his 1822 self-portrait, *The Artist in His Museum,* further highlights his role as painter and founder of the nation's first important museum of science and art.

A

Samuel F.B. Morse's painting career was diverted by daguerreotypes, which he helped introduce to America from France in 1839, and by his invention of the telegraph. The artist/scientist role, to a more constrained degree, was also common among nineteenth-century women. Studying and drawing from nature, especially botany, was an acceptable female pursuit. On a different socioeconomic level of production were the anonymous women who laboriously hand colored the plates that illuminated natural history volumes.

Landscape, one of nineteenth-century America's defining national subjects, embraced religion and earth sciences. Frederic Edwin Church's biotic detail in paintings like *The Heart of the Andes,* 1859, reflected German scientist Baron von Humboldt's valuation of landscape painting as scientific aesthetic in the service of Christianity, and paid tribute to Humboldt's own fieldwork in South America. Landscape often was taken as literal evidence of God's handiwork, either through catastrophist or uniformitarian processes. Geologic debates shaped illustrations in midcentury western surveys sponsored by Congress as well as such popular, "operatic"-scaled paintings as Thomas Moran's 1872 *The Grand Cañon of the Yellowstone.* Art and science joined in serving national and corporate agencies, like railroads and land speculators, eager to identify, exploit, or more rarely (as in the case of Yellowstone), to preserve natural resources.

Representation of humans was also framed by "scientific" conceptions. Phrenology, which uncovered moral, intellectual, and personality traits through physiognomy, offered a useful vocabulary to portraitists and even to such celebrated sculptors as Hiram Powers. America's ubiquitous images of Native Americans, spanning every historical era, are especially problematic. They have functioned on multiple levels—as documents, metaphors, or fictional entertainment. George Catlin's anthropological catalog of native peoples in the 1830s was one of a number of collections intended to pictorially preserve a "vanishing" sector of American natural history; Frederic Remington and others in the early twentieth century perpetuated the elegiac Indian portrait. Only recently has such imagery been investigated within the larger framework of governmental Indian policies. More insidious regarding all racial representation is the existence of a body of "purer" scientific illustration, as Samuel Morton's 1839 *Crania Americana,* documenting the quantification of racial character and aptitudes.

The late nineteenth and early twentieth centuries were shaped by increasing industrialization and by revised intellectual concepts like evolution. The Darwinian paradigm informed biological representation, from flower painting to animal imagery; and, conjoined to Herbert Spencer's Social Darwinism, figural compositions as well. Moreover, increasing specialization began to distance professional from popular science. Perhaps one mark of this perspectival shift was the public's disapproval of Thomas Eakins's 1875 painting *The Gross Clinic* which, in its graphic depiction of surgery performed under anesthesia, was a pinnacle of scientific realism.

By the turn of the twentieth century, artists responded to science and technology in conflicting ways. The new Kodak (introduced by 1888) put the power of image making in the hands of the general public at the same time that photography was being championed as fine art. Photography provided some painters and sculptors with a tool for ensuring verisimilitude, and others a rationale for greater formal freedom. It is telling that photographer Alfred Stieglitz's New York photo gallery, "291," and his journal, *Camera Work,* were the sites of much avant-garde activity before World War I, sponsoring abstraction and challenging traditional aesthetic definitions.

Americans embraced the crisp, functional forms of a machine aesthetic in art—like Charles Sheeler's crystalline photographs and paintings of auto factories—and in manufactured, utilitarian objects. These latter were officially sanctioned with the 1934 "Machine Art" exhibition at the Museum of Modern Art. Theoretic concerns with both spatial and temporal interpretations of n-dimensional geometry impacted the development of much avant-garde art; and post-Einsteinian physics has continued to interest twentieth-century abstractionists.

Paradoxically, however, technological destabilizations of everyday life and world war laid the foundation for an artistic irony that would have been inconceivable only decades earlier. Nineteenth-century sciences that sought keys to God's creation, although fiercely debated, usually were illustrated with due reverence; the technological iconoclasm of some twentieth-century imagery was unprecedented. It is no coincidence that images which mocked cherished ideals, like Morton Schamberg's 1918 statue *God* (a plumbing drain trap), and that ultimately questioned the very premise of fine art, seized on the most blatantly functional or mechanized object. Yet movements such as "New York Dada" and "Precisionism" are often mistakenly viewed from this side of the twentieth-century divide as unconnected to the late-nineteenth-century art/science dialogue in which they are surely rooted.

Much recent art, heir to earlier twentieth-century movements like constructivism, has co-opted New Age technology. The 1960s saw art and engineering collaborations such as the international group, Experiments in Art and Technology (E.A.T.). In the 1980s, some interactive video projects evolved a heightened social/political awareness. Whether celebrating or criticizing progress, the technological media—video, computers, and even the equipment-intensive manipulations of earth art—became, self-consciously, part of the "message."

By the 1990s, contemporary art, criticism, and art-historical literature have finally begun to address science/art connections. The journal *Leonardo* regularly features theoretical and historical perspectives, including psychological and physiological studies on creation and perception. In a less speculative vein, the practices of art restoration, conservation, connoisseurship, cataloging, research, and even teaching are profoundly altered by their reliance on continually changing technologies.

Still, major lacunae and questions remain in art-historical research. Have American artistic responses to the sciences in fact substantially differed from European responses? How have they been mediated by American audiences, by scientific critiques, by popular publications and education? Should the modernist tradition in science and art be viewed as a mutual embrace of novelty as "progress"? How did art production parallel scientific developments after the intelligentsia exodus from Europe to the United States in the 1930s and 1940s?

The land, its products, and its indigenous inhabitants have formed one of the largest topoi for American art, reemerging forcefully in the 1970s–1990s with an environmentalist ethos. Can a proprietary agenda be identified at the base of all these endeavors, from the earliest documentation of new lands through electronic manipulation of information? Is ecological art an attempt to retake landscape from the positivist, empirical tradition and in fact use it to reshape scientific ideology? Have enough questions been raised by critics and contemporary artists themselves about the premises and values that are appropriated along with the media they use? Are these costly technologies elitist tools; and do certain social, economic, racial, and gender sectors control them?

More nuanced relationships will be articulated as historians of art and science apply parallel methodologies. Future research should seek theoretical perspectives and new historical models that can be useful in both fields. A historical overview of art's relation to science, in breadth and depth, remains to be written.

BIBLIOGRAPHY
Art Journal. Special edition, "Art and Ecology." 51 (Summer 1992).
Blum, Ann Shelby. *Picturing Nature: American Nineteenth-Century Zoological Illustration.* Princeton: Princeton University Press, 1993.
Brigham, David R. *Public Culture in the Early Republic: Peale's Museum and Its Audience.* Washington, DC: Smithsonian Institution Press, 1995.
Gould, Stephen Jay. "Church, Humboldt, and Darwin: The Tension and Harmony of Art and Science." In *Frederic Edwin Church,* edited by Franklin Kelly. Washington, DC: Smithsonian Institution Press, 1989, pp. 94–107.
Henderson, Linda Dalrymple. *The Fourth Dimension and Non-Euclidian Geometry in Modern Art.* Princeton: Princeton University Press, 1983.
Leonardo: Journal of the International Society for the Arts, Sciences and Technology.
Meyers, Amy R.W. *Art and Science in America: Issues of Representation.* San Marino, CA: Huntington Library, 1998.
Novak, Barbara. *Nature and Culture: American Landscape and Painting, 1825–1875.* Rev. ed. New York: Oxford University Press, 1995.
Pyne, Kathleen. *Art and the Higher Life: Painting and Evolutionary Thought in Late Nineteenth-Century America.* Austin: University of Texas Press, 1996.
Wilson, Richard Guy, Dianne H. Pilgrim, and Dickran Tashjian. *The Machine Age in America, 1918–1941.* New York: Brooklyn Museum, 1986.

Linda Dugan Partridge

Association for Women in Science

A national organization of women scientists formed in 1971 at a champagne mixer at a meeting of the Federation of American Societies for Experimental Biology (FASEB) in Chicago. The purpose of the Association for Women in Science (AWIS) was to improve the status of women in science through the support of an organized group. Discussions of the need for such an organization had occurred at previous social gatherings of the FASEB in Atlantic City, involving an exchange of information concerning the obstacles encountered by women scientists, as well as their achievements. From an original

A

membership of 40, the organization has grown to a 1992 membership of over 3,500, most of whom have Ph.D. or master's degrees. Local chapters are available in a number of states. The association's activities include publishing newsletters, grant information, career guides, employment and legislative information, and educational materials; participating in national coalitions and organizations to expand the role of women in science; monitoring the status of women working in science, and reporting the finding; providing advice and support to women involved in equal opportunity litigation; and establishing local AWIS chapters.

From its inception, the AWIS members have sought to increase the opportunities for women and end outright discrimination through changes in the law and enforcement of existing legislation. They stressed the importance of legal, professional, and dignified methods of action to elevate the professional role of women scientists and the necessity of taking a firm, public stand on matters of discrimination which involves the careers of professional women.

Marxist feminists, radical feminists, psychoanalytic feminists, and socialist feminists disagree over the sufficiency of legal approaches to right the inequalities of women in science. However, the AWIS stresses the liberal feminist view that when the state protects the civil liberties of all of its citizens equality of opportunity will be guaranteed and a climate conducive to scientific creativity by women will occur.

Central to understanding the AWIS is the recognition that, as conditions have changed, the goals of the organization have expanded and changed.

The archives of the AWIS are held by the organization in Washington, D.C.

BIBLIOGRAPHY
AWIS. Association for Women in Science, Inc. (Membership Brochure).
AWIS Magazine.
AWIS Newsletter 1 (Summer 1971): 1–8.

Marilyn B. Ogilvie

SEE ALSO
Gender—in Science

Astronomy and Astrophysics

European astronomy was brought to British North America by the first wave of settlers to New England and quickly took root. By the end of the seventeenth century, almanacs were published regularly in Massachusetts, and had appeared in other colonies, including Pennsylvania and New York. Readers could keep abreast of developments in European astronomy, in particular the displacement of the geocentric view by the Copernican heliocentric model of the solar system, and the subsequent refinement of Copernicus's theory by Kepler, through these almanacs, which often relied on British publications for their information. The first astronomical telescope to appear in the colonies, a refractor with a focal length of ten feet, was purchased by John Winthrop Jr., Fellow of the Royal Society and Governor of Connecticut. He was using it as early as 1660. In 1672, he donated a refracting telescope with a focal length of 3.5 feet to Harvard College. Neither Winthrop nor any subsequent observers in seventeenth-century British North America observed regularly, but some astronomically significant observations were made and transmitted to Britain. The most famous were of the comet of 1680 by Thomas Brattle. Brattle sent his observations to the astronomer royal, John Flamsteed, who in turn gave them to Isaac Newton. The observations were acknowledged in the *Principia.*

Colonial astronomy grew slowly during the eighteenth century, peaking with the observations of the transit of Venus of 1769. Thanks to an unprecedented outpouring of resources by colonial governments, institutions, and individuals, twenty-two sets of observations were obtained. These observations were made available to European astronomers through publication in the *Philosophical Transactions* of the Royal Society of London or the first volume of the *Transactions of the American Philosophical Society* (1771).

This level of activity could not be sustained after the outbreak of the Revolutionary War in 1775. A people engaged in war and subsequent nation-building were unable to provide its astronomical community sufficient resources to be competitive with Europe. For the next two generations American astronomers were, for all intents and purposes, peripheral to the international astronomical community, with astronomical practice in the United States frozen roughly at the level it had attained when the nation declared independence. The astronomical textbooks used in American colleges were usually adaptations or reprints of British texts, and reflected the state of British astronomy around 1750. Periodically, there were efforts to build an astronomical observatory, but none of these ever got beyond the design phase. The telescopes in use gave no hint of the great changes wrought in refracting telescopes by the Germans or in reflecting telescopes by William Herschel. Individuals interested in astronomy could earn a living as surveyors, through the publication of almanacs, or teaching, but not through research. As a result, what astronomical activity there was during the years from 1776 through 1830 was sporadic and inconsequential.

It took an infusion of money and what might be termed an intellectual revolution to transform this group of surveyors and almanac publishers into the independent astronomical community of international reputation that existed by 1875. Astronomy became one of the most generously supported sciences in nineteenth-century America. The money came from a variety of public and private sources. For example, the great refractor of Harvard College Observatory was paid for by the local gentry and business community in response to appeals to local pride. The view that the study of astronomy, within the context of natural theology, was a means of acquiring knowledge of the attributes of God, also played a role. The same sort of appeals (local pride and religious significance) to a much broader audience led to the raising of funds to build the Cincinnati Observatory. The establishment of the Naval Observatory was an acknowledgement by the federal government that astronomy was a utilitarian pursuit which should be supported by the taxpayer.

The concurrent intellectual revolution involved the recognition that there had been a massive transformation of astronomy in Europe during the two generations since the outbreak of the Revolutionary War. Nathaniel Bowditch issued what was perhaps the first call urging the revitalizing of astronomy in the United States and pointing to European advances in two articles in the *North American Review* (1820, 1822). Others soon took up the cause. From Europe, Americans obtained ideas, techniques, and instruments, as well as models for the organization of an observatory and training programs for astronomers. The first to be imported, from about 1820, were French analytical mathematical techniques. During the 1840s and 1850s, Americans adopted the German method of astronomy, characterized by mathematical rigor. Coinciding with this latter development was a switch from English to German instrument makers from whom Americans bought telescopes and other apparatus. Finally, in the 1860s, Americans recognized the significance of European advances in spectroscopy, setting

the stage for American participation in the development of astrophysics.

Americans used two techniques to transfer European astronomy to the Western Hemisphere. The first was through the printed page: reprints, translations, and adaptations of textbooks and articles. This transfer was facilitated by the lack of international copyright agreements. Two of the most significant publications were Bowditch's translation, annotation, and exposition of Laplace's *Méchanique Celeste* (1829–1839), which introduced Americans to the latest methods of analysis in celestial mechanics, and John Herschel's *Treatise on Astronomy* (first American edition, 1834), which alerted Americans to European developments in astronomy since the last quarter of the eighteenth century.

The second means of obtaining knowledge of European astronomy was through personal interaction. This took place in two ways. Thanks to the increasing availability of funds and improvements in transportation, the number of American astronomers touring Europe swelled during the nineteenth century. They visited observatories and instrument makers. Some attended university lectures or formally studied with European astronomers. Alternatively, the interaction took place in the United States. Especially after 1848, European astronomers were employed in American observatories and universities. Among the most notable were F.F.E. Brünnow at the University of Michigan and C.H.F. Peters at Hamilton College. These Europeans helped educate the next generation of American astronomers.

By 1875, the combination of money and knowledge had produced an American astronomical community able to offer educational, research, and employment opportunities. The growth of American astronomy was phenomenal. In 1835, there was only one observatory in the United States. Fifteen years later, only the German states collectively surpassed the United States in the number of observatories. By 1875, the United States had pulled ahead of Germany. Contributions to the *Astronomische Nachrichten,* the leading Continental research journal in astronomy, are another indicator of the growth and significance of the American astronomical community. Prior to 1840, Americans authored less than 1 percent of the papers in that journal. By 1875, Americans were annually contributing 15 percent of the papers, and the number was growing. By the 1880s, America probably had more astronomers than any other nation in the Western world.

A

Through the third quarter of the nineteenth century, celestial mechanics and astrometry were the dominant research concerns of American astronomers. Developing theories for the orbits of solar system objects, testing those models against observation, and the publication of ephemerides were the primary concerns of celestial mechanicians. Workers in astrometry compiled ever more accurate catalogs of stellar positions. These provided data to measure the proper motions of the stars and to help construct models of the sidereal universe. American astrometry also pioneered in the use of photography in determining stellar positions and parallax.

Unlike celestial mechanicians who relied primarily on pen and paper and observations made by others, researchers in astrometry used state-of-the-art instrumentation to collect data. Both fields were mathematically demanding and involved long-term projects, often stretching over a professional career. In neither celestial mechanics nor astrometry could an individual expect to make many dramatic discoveries.

Simon Newcomb, who became director of the Nautical Almanac Office in 1877, and his collaborator G.W. Hill earned international recognition for their work in celestial mechanics. They were followed in the next generation by E.W. Brown of Yale and F.R. Moulton of the University of Chicago. By the 1920s, however, celestial mechanics in America appeared to have reached a dead end. Events after 1950 would revitalize the field.

American astrometry came of age under the direction of Lewis Boss at the Dudley Observatory. Working with a large staff funded by the Carnegie Institution of Washington, the Dudley Observatory became one of the leading centers for astrometry in the world. Its work culminated in the *General Catalogue of 33,342 Stars* (1937). In the second generation, Frank Schlesinger, longtime director of the Yale Observatory, was the recognized leader of American astrometry. However, like celestial mechanics, interest in astrometry declined, only to revive as a consequence of the space age.

At first, astrophysics in the United States was the province of amateurs. L.M. Rutherfurd and Henry Draper were pioneers in the 1860s and 1870s, applying photography to solar and stellar spectroscopy and developing new forms of instrumentation that would become standard in astrophysical observatories by the end of the century. Professionals had such heavy career investments in existing problems and instrumentation

that the process of change in American astronomy was sluggish.

Astrophysics developed in several stages. E.C. Pickering, a physicist who became director of the Harvard College Observatory in 1877, instituted large-scale research programs in photometry and then spectroscopy. At first, observations were made visually, but soon Pickering introduced photography and data begin to accumulate at an astonishing rate. In the 1880s, Pickering organized the Harvard Observatory along the lines of a knowledge factory. Astronomers planned projects, supervised their execution, and interpreted the results. Semiskilled workers (generally male) spent long nights at the telescope exposing plates. An unskilled labor force composed of women analyzed the plates and reduced the data.

Soon the role of observatory director became similar to a chief executive officer in a major industrial corporation and research observatories became factories organized for the mass production of scientific knowledge, similar in organization to the United States Steel Corporation or other industrial giants.

Solar physics under C.A. Young at Dartmouth and then Princeton and in the second generation led by G.E. Hale, founder of the Yerkes and Mount Wilson observatories, quickly gained a foothold in America. Young was a pioneer in solar spectroscopy and Hale argued that the sun was the nearest star and that astronomers could learn much by carefully investigating its physical and chemical characteristics. Hale carried out important work in solar physics at Yerkes. He equipped Mount Wilson with special instruments designed for solar research and a large reflecting telescope (with a 60-inch mirror) to study stellar spectra. Astrophysics grew slowly through the 1890s, but by 1920 had come to dominate the American astronomical community.

It was Hale who defined the research agenda for American astrophysics from the 1890s through the 1920s. Influenced by European developments in experimental spectroscopy, he sought to apply the techniques and methods of physics to the sun and stars. Hale encouraged two generations of solar and stellar spectroscopists and made several important contributions to instrumentation and observational astrophysics, including the invention of the spectroheliograph and the discovery of solar magnetism.

At the Mount Wilson Observatory, Hale's large telescopes were soon used to study nebulae and galaxies. In time, this research, pioneered by Harlow Shapley and Edwin Hubble, produced data that redefined the size of the universe, the nature of the Milky Way galaxy, and the expansion of the universe. These investigations would lead to dramatic new conceptions in cosmology.

Astronomers working in stellar spectroscopy often believed that stars could be arranged in a sequence according to temperature. Before World War I, the Princeton astronomer H.N. Russell, working independently of E. Hertzsprung in Europe, developed a model relating absolute magnitude to spectral type and positing the existence of both giant and dwarf stars. These ideas remain an important part of the foundation on which theories of stellar evolution rest.

From the 1920s, a few American astronomers became interested in the physical processes that produced radiation in the sun and stars. Before World War II the physics on which these investigations rested came from Europe. In the late 1930s, Hans Bethe of Cornell proposed a mechanism to explain the production of stellar energy based on nuclear reactions in the interiors of stars. Physical processes in nebulae were under investigation at the same time, most notably by Donald Menzel and his team at Harvard.

Theoretical and observational astrophysics developed rapidly after World War II. Innovation in instrumentation, ranging from electronic computers to large telescopes, highly efficient auxiliary photon detectors, and close collaboration between physicists and astronomers resulted in greatly increased understanding of the physical processes operating in stars and nebulae. Indeed, by the 1960s, many practicing astronomers had earned a Ph.D. in physics before entering the field.

The coming of the space age rejuvenated celestial mechanics under the new label of dynamical astronomy. The success of space missions rested on the careful calculation of orbits for probes and later manned vehicles. This, in turn, stimulated renewed interest in theories of solar system objects, especially new methods of calculating models using Einstein's general theory of relativity, and the application of high-speed electronic computers to the process. Astrometry experienced a modest resurgence as space telescopes demanded new catalogs of faint stars in order to carry out their scientific missions.

Astronomy played an important role in the Cold War and benefited from federal patronage. Both the military and agencies such as the National Science Foundation (NSF) provided funds for the expansion of American astronomy. Especially important was a sys-

tem of national optical and radio observatories funded by the NSF. Solar physics was often supported by the military, who saw its potential for understanding long-term weather patterns as well as short-term effects on electronic communications.

Beginning in the 1970s, space-based telescopes and new ground-based telescopes observing in various portions of the electromagnetic spectrum (for example, X-ray, gamma-ray or infrared) provided exciting new information that greatly enhanced the knowledge of the physics of stars and galaxies. Of special importance were observations that confirmed the big bang origin of the universe and revealed its large-scale structure. Physics and astronomy merged in the study of the big bang and the very early universe.

Lankford and Edge have argued that astronomy was the first of the big sciences in America. By World War I, the scale and organization of astronomical research institutions, and the cost of astronomical research at observatories such as Mount Wilson, Lick, Dudley, and Yerkes were greater than any of the other sciences in America. The only competitors were the laboratories of industrial chemists and the Berkeley cyclotron project. American astronomy built on these foundations and enjoyed a period of remarkable growth in the postwar era. However, as is the case for all the physical sciences, the end of the Cold War means a new and uncertain future for American astronomy.

BIBLIOGRAPHY

DeVorkin, David H. "Stellar Evolution and the Origin of the Hertzsprung-Russell Diagram." In *Astrophysics and Twentieth-Century Astronomy to 1950,* edited by Owen Gingerich. Cambridge, U.K.: Cambridge University Press, 1984, 4A:90–108.

Jones, B.Z., and L.G. Boyd. *The Harvard College Observatory: The First Four Directorships, 1839–1919.* Cambridge, MA: Harvard University Press, 1971.

Lankford, John. "Amateurs and Astrophysics: A Neglected Aspect in the Development of a Scientific Specialty." *Social Studies of Science* 11 (1981): 275–303.

Lankford, John, and David Edge. "Astronomy 1850–1950: A Social-Historical Overview." In *Astrophysics and Twentieth-Century Astronomy to 1950,* edited by Owen Gingerich. Cambridge, U.K.: Cambridge University Press, 4B: forthcoming.

Lankford, John (with the assistance of R.L. Slavings). *Community, Careers and Power: The American Astronomical Community, 1859–1940.* Chicago: University of Chicago Press, 1997.

A

Loomis, Elias. *The Recent Progress of Astronomy, Especially in the United States.* 1856. Reprint, New York: Arno, 1980.

Rothenberg, Marc. "The Educational and Intellectual Background of American Astronomers, 1825–1875." Ph.D. diss., Bryn Mawr College, 1974.

———. "History of Astronomy." *Osiris,* 2d ser., 1 (1985): 117–131.

Struve, Otto, and V. Zebergs. *Astronomy of the Twentieth Century.* New York: Macmillian, 1962.

Warner, Deborah Jean. "Astronomy in Antebellum America." In *The Sciences in the American Context: New Perspectives,* edited by Nathan Reingold. Washington, DC: Smithsonian Institution Press, 1979, pp. 55–75.

Wright, Helen. *Explorer of the Universe: A Biography of George Ellery Hale.* New York, E.P. Dutton, 1966.

Yeomans, Donald K. "The Origin of North American Astronomy—Seventeenth Century." *Isis* 68 (1977): 414–425.

Marc Rothenberg and John Lankford

SEE ALSO
American Astronomical Society

Atomic Bomb Casualty Commission

An American agency created in 1946 to conduct epidemiological research on the estimated 300,000 survivors of the August 1945 atomic bombings at Hiroshima and Nagasaki. The Atomic Bomb Casualty Commission (ABCC) goal was to assess the long-term biomedical effects of the radiation released by the bombs. President Harry Truman approved the study; the Atomic Energy Commission paid for it; and the National Academy of Sciences managed it, through a National Research Council Committee on Atomic Casualties on which many leading biologists, physicians, and geneticists served. By 1948, the ABCC established research centers in Hiroshima and Nagasaki, and in a control city near Hiroshima, Kure.

The medical staff, predominantly Japanese physicians and nurses managed and directed by Americans, examined bomb survivors annually. Survivor participation in the study was voluntary, but shaped by the American military occupation of Japan until 1952, and by the wave of anti-American sentiment in the post-occupation period. ABCC researchers were looking for biological phenomena known to be associated with radiation exposure, such as cataracts, genetic effects, and cancers, and more generally for any pathologies that might be more frequent in bomb survivors than in control populations.

The most ambitious and high profile ABCC project in the early years was the genetics study. Genetic effects of radiation, demonstrated in H.J. Muller's Nobel Prize–winning research with Drosophila in 1926, were widely feared. Under the direction of University of Michigan geneticist James V. Neel, the ABCC staff examined more than 76,000 newborns in Japan in five years. A publication in 1953 suggested an effect on sex ratio, but not on malformation, stillbirth, or other indicators. By the time of the final analysis and publication in 1956, the sex ratio effect disappeared. The ABCC reported that no genetic effects could be demonstrated.

Meanwhile increases in rates of leukemia were documented in survivors in the early 1950s. Later the ABCC reported that survivors faced an increased risk of radiation cataract, delays in growth and development in children exposed to the bombings, microcephaly (small head-size and retardation) in those exposed in utero, as well as colon cancer, breast cancer, lung cancer, and multiple myeloma. More recently the ABCC's successor agency has reported an effect on cardiovascular disease.

The ABCC's study remains the most important source of information on the long-term effects of radiation exposure on human populations, and has been the basis of worker-exposure legislation around the world. It was, however, a complicated organization, subject to significant public scrutiny. Some Japanese critics argued that the survivors were "guinea pigs" for the American scientists and protested the ABCC's no-treatment policy which prohibited ABCC staff from providing medical care to those participating in the study.

The sociological and political problem of Americans studying persons who had been victimized by an American weapon has never entirely disappeared, despite significant changes in the organization and its program. In 1975, the ABCC was renamed the Radiation Effects Research Foundation (RERF), and funding and administrative control were divided evenly between the governments of the United States and Japan. The RERF, based on the laboratories that the ABCC built on Hijiyama Hill in Hiroshima in 1950, continues to study the survivors, their children, and their children's children.

BIBLIOGRAPHY
Atomic Bomb Casualty Commission. *Bibliography of Published Papers of the Atomic Bomb Casualty Commission,*

1947–1974. Hiroshima and Nagasaki: Atomic Bomb Casualty Commission, 1974.

Beatty, John. "Genetics in the Atomic Age." In *The Expansion of American Biology,* edited by Keith Benson, Jane Maienschein, and Ronald Rainger. New Brunswick: Rutgers University Press, 1991, pp. 284–324.

———. "Scientific Collaboration, Internationalism, and Diplomacy: The Case of the Atomic Bomb Casualty Commission." *Journal of the History of Biology* 26 (1993): 205–231.

Beebe, Gilbert W. "Reflections on the Work of the Atomic Bomb Casualty Commission in Japan." *Epidemiological Reviews* 1 (1979): 184–210.

Folley, J.H., W. Borge, and T. Yamawaki. "Incidence of Leukemia in Survivors of the Atomic Bomb in Hiroshima and Nagasaki." *American Journal of Medicine* 13 (1952): 311–321.

Lindee, M. Susan. "What Is a Mutation? The Problem of the Mutant Locus in the Genetics Project of the Atomic Bomb Casualty Commission." *Journal of the History of Biology* 25 (1992): 231–255.

———. *Suffering Made Real: American Science and the Survivors at Hiroshima.* Chicago: University of Chicago Press, 1994.

———. "The Repatriation of Atomic Bomb Victim Body Parts to Japan: Natural Objects and Diplomacy." *Osiris* 13 (1999): forthcoming.

National Academy of Sciences, Committee on the Biological Effects of Atomic Radiation. *A Report to the Public on the Biological Effects of Atomic Radiation.* Washington, DC: National Academy of Sciences, 1960.

Neel, James V. *Physician to the Gene Pool: Genetic Lessons and Other Stories.* New York: J. Wiley, 1994.

Neel, James V., and William J. Schull. *The Effect of Exposure to the Atomic Bombs on Pregnancy Termination in Hiroshima and Nagasaki.* National Academy of Sciences, National Research Council, publication no. 461. Washington, DC: National Academy of Sciences, 1956.

———, eds. *The Children of Atomic Bomb Survivors.* Washington, DC: National Academy of Sciences, 1991.

Schull, William J. *Song among the Ruins.* Cambridge, MA: Harvard University Press, 1990.

M. Susan Lindee

SEE ALSO
World War II and Science

Atomic Energy Commission

An independent agency of the federal government established in 1946 to promote and control the development of nuclear energy.

Although during most of the agency's history only one of the five members of the commission was a scientist, the commission commanded the support of many distinguished scientists, who served on its advisory committees, staffed its national laboratories, or conducted independent research in university or industrial laboratories.

Especially in the early years, most of the scientists in leadership positions were physicists and the commission's research programs centered on the physical sciences: the production of radioisotopes, the measurement of nuclear cross-sections, the identification and study of transplutonium elements, research in high-energy physics, and theoretical and design studies for a variety of power and research reactors.

As the Cold War intensified in the late 1940s, the commission devoted an ever increasing share of its funds, resources, and scientific talent to theoretical studies of new weapon designs, culminating in the successful testing of a thermonuclear device in late 1952. The rapid escalation of atmospheric weapon testing in the 1950s, with occasional incidents of significant fallout of radioactive fission products, prompted the commission to supplement research on the biological effects of radiation with intensive studies of the complex mechanisms of fallout. In the two years after 1950, the commission's annual budget for development and fabrication of weapons almost doubled to $278 million, while research in the physical sciences increased only 17 percent to $64 million and research in biology and medicine rose 38 percent to $25 million.

Although military requirements for weapons and nuclear propulsion plants consistently dominated the commission's budgets during the 1950s and 1960s, its scientific research and development programs profited indirectly from their association with defense needs. In comparison with the large expenditures for defense, those for research in the physical and biological sciences seemed smaller than they would have if they had had to stand alone.

During the Cold War, the commission supported basic research in other ways. In pursuit of the national policy to demonstrate the superiority of democratic capitalism over communism, the commission could justify large expenditures for projects beyond the leading edge of existing technology. Thus, competition with the Soviet Union pushed research on controlled thermonuclear reactions to a high priority in 1958, and

A

the western European threat to the nation's primacy in high-energy physics resulted in generous funding for new accelerators at the national laboratories.

The ten-year tenure of Glenn T. Seaborg as the commission chairman from 1961 until 1971 was the golden age for scientific research and development at the agency. Seaborg brought competent scientist-administrators to the headquarters staff to assure effective allocation of sharply increased funding for research in the national laboratories and universities. From 1961 to 1969, annual costs for physical research increased 115 percent to $332 million while total operating costs for all commission programs declined 2 percent to $2,566 million. Seaborg's announced goal was to bring expenditures for civilian projects in balance with those for military applications.

During the 1960s, the commission supported thousands of projects on a wide range of topics. Reactor development programs included component development, studies of new reactor systems, and a growing number of projects on reactor safety systems. Physical research continued to be dominated by high-energy physics, but there was extensive support of work on nuclear reactions at lower energies, on chemistry, metallurgy and materials, controlled thermonuclear reactions, mathematics, and computers. Isotope development, education and training, and space applications of nuclear power still commanded strong but declining support. Biomedical research included studies related to the somatic effects of radiation, environmental radiation, molecular and cellular effects of radiation, cancer research, radiation genetics, radiological and health physics, and chemical toxicity.

As public anxieties grew toward the end of the decade over the potential hazards of nuclear weapon testing and the possibility of a catastrophic accident as increasing numbers of nuclear power plants came on line, the commission's prestige and credibility began to decline. Although the commission had separated its regulatory staff from the rest of its operations in 1963, both the public and congressional leaders saw a continuing conflict of interest in an agency that was responsible for both the promotion and regulation of nuclear technology. The result was new legislation that replaced the Atomic Energy Commission in 1975 with the Energy Research and Development Administration and the Nuclear Regulatory Commission.

BIBLIOGRAPHY

Allardice, Corbin, and Edward R. Trapnell. *Atomic Energy Commission.* New York: Praeger, 1974.

Anders, Roger M., ed. *Forging the Atomic Shield: Excerpts from the Office Diary of Gordon E. Dean.* Chapel Hill: University of North Carolina Press, 1987.

Hewlett, Richard G., and Oscar E. Anderson Jr. *The New World, 1939–1946.* Vol. 1 of *A History of the United States Atomic Energy Commission.* University Park: Pennsylvania State University Press, 1962.

Hewlett, Richard G., and Francis Duncan. *Atomic Shield, 1947–1952.* Vol. 2 of *A History of the United States Atomic Energy Commission.* University Park: Pennsylvania State University Press, 1969.

Hewlett, Richard G., and Jack M. Holl. *Atoms for Peace and War, 1953–1961: Eisenhower and the Atomic Energy Commission.* Berkeley: University of California Press, 1989.

Lilienthal, David E. *The Atomic Energy Years, 1945–1950.* Vol. 2 of *The Journals of David E. Lilienthal.* New York: Harper & Row, 1964.

Mazuzan, George T., and J. Samuel Walker. *Controlling the Atom: The Beginnings of Nuclear Regulation, 1946–1962.* Berkeley: University of California Press, 1984.

Orlans, Harold. *Contracting for Atoms: A Study of Public Policy Issues Posed by the Atomic Energy Commission's Contracting for Research, Development, and Managerial Services.* Washington, DC: Brookings Insitution, 1967.

Seaborg, Glenn T. *The Journals of Glenn T. Seaborg, Chairman of the U. S. Atomic Energy Commission, 1961–1971.* 25 vols. Berkeley: Lawrence Berkley Laboratory, PUB-625, 1989.

Strauss, Lewis L. *Men and Decisions.* Garden City, NY: Doubleday, 1962.

Walker, J. Samuel. *Containing the Atom: Nuclear Regulation in a Changing Environment.* Berkeley: University of California Press, 1992.

Richard G. Hewlett

SEE ALSO
Joint Committee on Atomic Energy

Atwater, Wilbur Olin (1844–1907)

Nutritionist, agricultural scientist, physiologist, scientific administrator, and social reformer. Born in Johnsburg, New York, Atwater received his doctorate from Yale's Sheffield Scientific School as a student of Samuel W. Johnson, America's leading agricultural chemist of the day. Following postgraduate studies in the German states from 1869 to 1871, Atwater landed a post as chemistry professor at Wesleyan University in 1873. He held that position until his death, and also held simultaneous appointments as director of Connecticut's agricultural experiment stations at Middletown (1875–1877) and Storrs (1887–1901), and as director of the United States Department of Agriculture (USDA) Office of Experiment Stations (1888–1891).

In the early 1870s, Atwater and Johnson led efforts to establish an agricultural experiment station in Connecticut. Atwater's advocacy of the German experiment stations' fertilizer control activities was especially important in obtaining farmers' support for the new institutions. Atwater's work in agricultural chemistry included proof that legumes assimilate fixed nitrogen from the atmosphere.

As director of the USDA's Office of Experiment Stations, Atwater influenced much of the nation's research in the life sciences. His emphasis on scientific standards, cooperative research, and widespread dissemination of results strengthened support for the new institutions in both public and private sectors. In brief, Atwater helped establish the legitimacy of experiment stations and of agricultural scientists.

Atwater began his pioneering scientific studies of human nutrition in the 1880s. In alliance with economists, social reformers, and policymakers, Atwater and other nutritionists lobbied successfully for federally sponsored nutrition research. By the mid-1890s, Atwater had built a nutritional research empire, funded largely through the Office of Experiment Stations. Field workers conducted dietary surveys to record the foods purchased, consumed, and wasted in typical New England homes, while other researchers measured the nutritive value of thousands of American foodstuffs. Atwater's investigations of human metabolism extended the calorimetric research of the Munich physiologists Carl Voit and Max Rubner. Subjects were placed inside a respiration calorimeter chamber for periods up to several days, where measurements of all intake and outgo revealed the energy values of fats, proteins, and carbohydrates.

As a result, Atwater produced tables of nutritional guidelines. His recommendations proved of little value, however; convinced that a low-cost, high-calorie diet was most efficient, Atwater designed a diet that was laden with proteins, fats, and carbohydrates. Moreover, like all nutritional scientists of his era, Atwater was ignorant of the value of vitamins and amino acids. Not long after his death, subsequent research overturned his suggested daily intake of about 3,500 calories and his opinion that fruits and vegetables were wasted calories.

Agricultural chemists and nutrition scientists have long hailed Atwater as one of their founding fathers. More recently, scholars have turned attention to Atwater's significance in the social and cultural history of

science. In an era in which many Americans embraced notions of social engineering and the emerging progressive reforms, scientists like Atwater who had skills in the public arena were quite influential. Atwater participated in debates on urban reform, labor policy, temperance, and the role the federal government should play in scientific research. His cooperation with home economists was also important, opening opportunities in the sciences for a number of women.

Historians have also focused on the ideas that formed the foundation for Atwater's research. Atwater defined poor dietary habits as an important social problem, and enlisted nutritional science in the cause of humanitarian uplift. Convinced that low-income Americans spent more money than necessary on food, he argued that they should be taught to make more rational dietary decisions. By offering citizens clear professional direction, he assumed nutrition scientists could reduce the threat of labor and social unrest.

The Atwater papers are housed at Wesleyan University and are also available on microfilm. Although several historians have used these materials, to date no scholarly biography has appeared.

BIBLIOGRAPHY

Aronson, Naomi. "Nutrition as a Social Problem." *Social Problems* 29 (1982): 474–487.

Atwater, W.O. "Bibliography." *Wesleyan University Bulletin* 5 (1911): 31–40.

Carpenter, Kenneth J. *Protein and Energy: A Study in the Changing Ideas in Nutrition.* Cambridge, U.K.: Cambridge University Press, 1994.

Levenstein, Harvey A. *Revolution at the Table: The Transformation of the American Diet.* New York: Oxford University Press, 1988.

Maynard, Leonard A. "Wilbur O. Atwater—A Biographical Sketch." *Journal of Nutrition* 78 (1962): 2–9.

McCollum, Elmer V. *A History of Nutrition: The Sequence of Ideas in Nutritional Investigation.* Boston: Houghton Mifflin, 1957.

Pauly, Philip J. "The Struggle for Ignorance about Alcohol: American Physiologists, Wilbur Olin Atwater, and the Woman's Christian Temperance Union." *Bulletin for the History of Medicine* 64 (1990): 366–392.

Mark R. Finlay

Audubon, John James (1785–1851)

Naturalist and artist. The man who would be known as John James Audubon was born Jean Rabine on Sante-

A

Domingue (now Haiti) to Jean Audubon, a French sea captain, and his mistress, Jeanne Rabine. He was sent to France at the age of three, and adopted by his natural father and his wife in 1794. Audubon claimed that his lifelong fascination with the natural world grew during his boyhood wanderings around his parents' estate near Nantes. He received relatively little formal education in the sciences, languages, and drawing despite his later success as an artist-naturalist and writer. (He appears to have lied about studying under the French painter David.) A brief attempt at a naval career proved unsatisfactory so his father sent Audubon in 1803 to supervise a farm outside Philadelphia, "Mill Grove."

During his four years at Mill Grove (interrupted by a return to France), Audubon incessantly observed, hunted, and drew the American fauna new to him. He conducted perhaps the first bird-banding experiment when he tied a thread to a phoebe's leg and noted the bird's return to its nest the following year. He married a neighbor, Lucy Bakewell, who provided crucial support throughout his career.

From 1807 to 1819, Audubon undertook commercial ventures in Louisville and Henderson, Kentucky. Audubon declared bankruptcy in 1819 and acted briefly as a taxidermist for the new Western Museum in Cincinnati. In 1820, he and Lucy decided that Audubon should expand his portfolio of bird drawings for future publication. His 1810 meeting with Alexander Wilson, who was issuing *American Ornithology,* is often cited as one inspiration for this grandiose ambition.

With Lucy supporting his two sons, and aided by his talented assistant Joseph Mason, Audubon traveled through Mississippi and Alabama from 1820 to 1824, executing some of his best-known drawings. This largely self-taught artist, who began drawing birds and mammals as a teenager, developed a method of wiring fresh specimens into a variety of poses and outlining the exact proportions onto paper. His mature style united anatomical precision and aesthetically pleasing design. The life-size figures (often both sexes and young) move in characteristic fashion in their customary habitat. Previous natural history illustrators had sporadically depicted specimens in action against a background, but Audubon was the first to blend these elements consistently.

In 1826, Audubon sought a publisher in England for his drawings after failing to find one in America. His innovative drawings and knowledge of wildlife so impressed the scientific elite that he was quickly elected to societies and asked to write journal articles. Robert Havell Jr. undertook to produce the aquatint plates in "double elephant" size (the largest available). For twelve years, Audubon supervised production, solicited subscribers, and wrote the accompanying text, the *Ornithological Biography,* edited by William Macgillervay. Expeditions to Labrador, Florida, and Texas provided more specimens.

After the conclusion of *The Birds* in 1839, Audubon published its octavo edition and began *The Viviparous Quadrupeds of North America* with John Bachman as coauthor. He observed the large western mammals on an 1843 expedition to the upper Missouri. The extant drawings for this publication are among his most meticulously executed. Audubon's mental faculties deteriorated around 1847, and his son, John Woodhouse, completed the artwork. His other son, Victor Gifford, drew most of the backgrounds. Audubon died at his estate, "Minnie's Land," on the Hudson River in New York City.

His dramatic life and the continuing popularity of his images have overshadowed his contribution to nineteenth-century ornithology. The critics who discuss his scientific reputation often dismiss parts of his texts as sentimental and certain poses in the illustrations as exaggerated. However, Audubon figured the greatest number of American birds and wrote the most comprehensive text of any publication for the period roughly between 1830 and 1870. John Cassin and Daniel Giraud Elliot wrote continuations of *The Birds,* and Spencer Fullerton Baird's and Elliott Coues's works continuously refer to the Audubon publications.

His impact on zoological illustration is profound because most Western animal artists have known the works. His use of multiple figures, inclusion of habitat, and animated poses influenced his contemporaries such as the Englishman John Gould and the artists for Cassin's and Elliot's books. Louis Agassiz Fuertes, regarded as the next great American bird artist, closely studied Audubon in his formative years. Twentieth-century animal illustrators such as Roger Tory Peterson and Don Eckleberry acknowledge Audubon's impact on their styles.

BIBLIOGRAPHY

Audubon, John James. *The Birds of America.* 4 vols. London: J.J. Audubon, 1827–1838.

———. *Ornithological Biography, or an Account of the Habits of the Birds of the United States.* 5 vols. Edinburgh: A & C Black, 1831–1839.

———. *A Synopsis of the Birds of North America.* Edinburgh: A & C Black, 1839.

———. *The Birds of America.* 7 vols. Octavo edition. New York: J.J. Audubon, 1840–1844.

———. *The Original Water-Color Paintings by John James Audubon for the Birds of North America.* 2 vols. New York: American Heritage, 1966.

———. Writings and Drawings. Edited by Christoph Irmscher. New York: The Library of America, 1999.

Audubon, John James, and John Bachman. *The Viviparous Quadrupeds of North America.* 3 vols. Plates. New York: J.J. Audubon, 1845–1848.

———. *The Viviparous Quadrupeds of North America.* 3 vols. Text. New York: J.J. Audubon, 1846–1854.

Blaugrund, Annette, and Theodore E. Stebbins, Jr., eds. *John James Audubon: The Watercolors for The Birds of America.* New York: Villard and The New York Historical Society, 1993.

Ford, Alice. *John James Audubon.* 2d ed. New York: Abbeville Press, 1988.

Low, Susanne M. *An Index and Guide to Audobon's Birds of America.* New York: The American Museum of Natural History, Abbeville Press, 1988.

Margaret Welch

B

Bache, Alexander Dallas (1806–1867)

Geophysicist and science administrator. Bache was a great-grandson of Benjamin Franklin. Both his parents belonged to elite Philadelphia families with strong political connections. These connections would prove to be very important for his career as a scientist and public figure. Bache graduated first in his class from the United States Military Academy at West Point in 1825, where he received a specialized scientific education. After staying at the academy an additional year to teach mathematics and natural philosophy, he spent two years as a lieutenant in the Corps of Engineers assisting with the construction of Fort Adams in Newport, Rhode Island. In 1828, he returned to Philadelphia to become professor of natural philosophy and chemistry at the University of Pennsylvania. In his spare time, he also began to pursue physical and geophysical research, especially in meteorology and terrestrial magnetism. Perhaps more significant, however, were his activities as a key leader of scientific institutions in Philadelphia, notably the American Philosophical Society and the Franklin Institute, where he worked to raise the scientific standards of lectures and publications. At the Franklin Institute, he directed a federally sponsored effort to discover the causes of steam-boiler explosions on steamships. As one of the first large-scale, systematic uses of scientific experimentation by the federal government to solve public problems, this work set important precedents for science-government relations.

Bache resigned his position at the University of Pennsylvania in 1836 to accept an appointment as president of the newly established Girard College in Philadelphia. During the next two years he traveled to Europe to study educational systems in support of the organization of that school. The resulting *Report on Education in Europe*—which praised the Prussian educational system with its emphasis on science, modern languages, and practical training—became an influential document for educational reform. Because of a delay in the opening of Girard College, Bache assisted in the reorganization of Philadelphia public schools. His views on the importance of an advanced scientific and technical education were put into practice at the Central High School in Philadelphia, which he superintended from 1839 to 1842. During the late 1830s, he also continued to pursue scientific research, especially in the geophysical sciences. This work was increasingly inspired by some of the eminent scientists he had met during his European tour; the research also took advantage of his talents as an organizer. Beginning in 1839, for example, Bache organized American scientists to participate in the international effort to establish a global network of stations measuring terrestrial magnetism.

In 1842, Bache returned to the University of Pennsylvania; however, after the death of Ferdinand R. Hassler the following year, he accepted an appointment to succeed Hassler as the superintendent of the Coast Survey, a position he held until his own death in 1867. By the late 1830s, Bache and his close friend Joseph Henry had decided to do all they could to raise the status of science in the United States, which would involve finding sources of support and funding. Bache especially believed that government institutions such as the Coast Survey, controlled by first-rate scientists, would play a central role in this effort. By the 1850s, Bache had realized his ambitions by transforming the Coast Survey

B

into the preeminent science-supporting institution in the United States. The Coast Survey had a far larger budget than other institutions supporting science; it also employed more scientists, either as salaried employees or as outside consultants. Under Bache's direction, the survey pursued research in a wide variety of scientific fields from astronomy and geophysics to hydrography and natural history. The territorial expansion of the country provided a justification for expanding the scope of the survey, which operated on the Atlantic, Gulf, and Pacific Coasts. Bache successfully nurtured support for Coast Survey activities by forging political alliances and convincing the public that the scientific research was closely linked to commercial development.

Control of the Coast Survey and the Office of Weights and Measures, which he also inherited from Hassler, gave Bache an institutional base in the government from which he could extend his influence throughout the scientific community. He became the acknowledged "chief" of an exclusive group—which included Benjamin Peirce, Joseph Henry, and Louis Agassiz—who called themselves the Lazzaroni, or scientific beggars. The Lazzaroni supported Bache's efforts on the Coast Survey and Bache reciprocated by providing patronage. Bache and the Lazzaroni sought to raise the standards of science in the United States by, among other activities, cultivating government support and pursuing educational reform. Their influence extended to key institutions, such as the American Association for the Advancement of Science, which elected Bache president in 1851. Bache was also one of the most influential regents of the Smithsonian Institution. He helped guide the institution toward supporting the advancement rather than only the diffusion of knowledge, and he convinced Joseph Henry to become the first secretary. As the key leader of the antebellum American scientific community, Bache thus did much to establish patterns for science in the United States in the nineteenth century. His efforts to gain support helped define science as an elite occupation requiring professional, specialized training; as a government-supported enterprise conducted out of bureaus; and as a crucial ingredient of economic and commercial development. But although an elite pursuit, scientific practice would need to take into account democratic forces by acting to mold public opinion on the local level.

During the Civil War, Bache committed all his efforts to the war effort. He served as vice president of the sanitary commission, as a member of the permanent commission of the navy in charge of appraising new weapons, as a consultant to the army and navy counseling on battle plans, and as superintendent of the defense preparations for Philadelphia. But the Civil War also offered an opportunity for Bache and his friends to convince the remaining Northern members of Congress to pass legislation in 1863 creating the National Academy of Sciences. Bache served as the first president. Bache's activities after 1864 were limited by a series of strokes that impaired his abilities.

BIBLIOGRAPHY

Bruce, Robert V. *The Launching of Modern American Science, 1846–1876.* New York: Knopf, 1987.

Dupree, A. Hunter. *Science in the Federal Government: A History of Policies and Activities to 1940.* Cambridge, MA: Harvard University Press, 1957.

Odgers, M. *Alexander Dallas Bache: Scientist and Educator, 1806–1867.* Philadelphia: University of Pennsylvania Press, 1947.

Reingold, Nathan. *Science in Nineteenth-Century America: A Documentary History.* Chicago: University of Chicago Press, 1964.

Rothenberg, Marc, ed. *Princeton Years, 1844–1846.* Vol. 6 of *The Paper of Joseph Henry.* Washington, DC: Smithsonian Institution Press, 1992.

Slotten, Hugh R. "The Dilemmas of Science in the United States: Alexander Dallas Bache and the U. S. Coast Survey." *Isis* 84 (1993): 26–49.

———. *Patronage, Practice, and the Culture of American Science: Alexander Dallas Bache and the U. S. Coast Survey.* New York: Cambridge University Press, 1994.

Hugh Richard Slotten

Baird, Spencer Fullerton (1823–1887)

Naturalist, educator, and museum administrator. He was born in Reading, Pennsylvania, but after the death of his father, Samuel Baird, in 1830, the family moved to Carlisle, Pennsylvania, where he attended Dickinson College, graduating in 1840. Interested from an early age in natural history, he, together with his oldest brother, Will, actively collected and studied all forms of local vertebrata, with predominant emphasis on birds. The Baird brothers published articles in several scientific journals, and in the field identified two hitherto unrecorded flycatchers. Early on, Spencer communicated with virtually all of the naturalists of the day, including John James Audubon with whom he established a close association. In 1846, Baird became professor of natural science at Dickinson, and in 1850 was appointed by Joseph Henry to be assistant secretary of the Smithsonian Institution with duties as curator of its natural history museum, administrator of its publishing program, and organizer of international exchanges of scientific publications.

In 1846, he married Mary Helen Churchill, daughter of a senior officer who became Inspector General of the Army. With his father-in-law's support, Baird was able to assign selected naturalists to the many army topographic expeditions conducting explorations west of the Mississippi and to have all specimens which they collected sent to the Smithsonian. In 1857, he was made director of the United States National Museum, which Congress had newly created and placed under the management of the Smithsonian. In the late 1860s, his predominant interest turned to ichthyology and to the reported depletion of fish along the Atlantic Coast. At his urging, the Congress created the United States Commission of Fish and Fisheries, with Baird as commissioner in addition to his Smithsonian post. As commissioner, he founded America's first laboratory of marine biology at Woods Hole, Massachusetts, and also experimented widely in fish propagation and culture. In 1876, he was placed in charge of the United States Government exhibit at the Centennial Exposition in Philadelphia, at the end of which he obtained for the Smithsonian sixty carloads of objects from state and foreign exhibits, thus stimulating Congress to fund a new National Museum building for their care and exhibition. When Joseph Henry died in 1878, Baird was elected secretary of the Smithsonian Institution. Over the next nine years, he administered four separate agencies, the Smithsonian Institution, the United States National Museum, the United States Fish Commission, and the Bureau of American Ethnology, which had been attached to the Smithsonian in 1879. He died at Woods Hole.

Baird was a scientist in the Baconian tradition. He believed that general truths would emerge from detailed studies of many specimens. Essentially, he was a taxonomist, who devoted most of his many scientific publications to physical descriptions of species and their behavior, of value in the mid-nineteenth century when relatively little was known of the natural resources of the North American continent. He personally identified over 70 previously unknown mammals and 216 birds. He published over a thousand books and scientific papers, a few with the assistance of such respected associates as Thomas M. Brewer and John Cassin, and students such as Robert Ridgeway. Most important at the time were several volumes of the *Pacific Railroad Survey Report, The Mammals of North America, A Catalog of North American Birds,* and *The Reptiles and Amphibians of North America.* As fish commissioner he later published a number of important studies on coastal fish species. Baird never expressed a direct opinion on the Darwin controversy which was raging in midcentury, but his one effort in relatively theoretical analysis, a monograph entitled "The Distribution and Migrations of North American Birds," was fully Darwinian in its concept and conclusions, all of which continue to be valid. He did little fieldwork himself, but trained his collectors personally in an exactness of description which became known as "The Bairdian School of Ornithology." His breadth of knowledge of the natural resources of Alaska acquired from the reports of Robert Kennicott, William Healy Dall, and others enabled him to play an influential role in congressional consideration of the purchase of Alaska. This, together with his creation of the marine biological laboratory at Woods Hole, and his part in the design and funding of the oceanographic research vessel *Albatross* were major contributions to American science. But perhaps his most lasting contribution was his recruitment and training of many young scientists who subsequently became important leaders in the development of American natural history. Robert Kennicott, William H. Dall, David Starr Jordan, Elliott Coues, Addison E. Verrill, Robert Ridgeway, C. Hart Merriam, and George Brown Goode were all either students or proteges of Baird. Above all stands his establishment of the great natural history collections which propelled the Smithsonian Institution into the leadership of the American scientific museum world.

Baird was not respected by such prominent scientists as Louis Agassiz and Alexander Bache, in part because of personal conflicts, but also because they considered Baird only a "descriptive scientist" who contributed nothing to the development of scientific discovery. On this pretext, Agassiz excluded Baird in 1863 from membership in the National Academy of Sciences, although his election the following year had almost unanimous support from the members despite Agassiz's opposition.

Among most of his naturalist contemporaries, and among his former associates, trainees, and proteges for more than a quarter century after his death, Baird was

B

considered America's leading natural scientist, while his persuasive influence in Congress and Washington officialdom was legendary. He was internationally respected as well, and at the International Fisheries Exhibit in Berlin in 1880 received the First Honor Prize as "the first fish culturalist of the world" (Goode, pp. 188–189). Numerous tributes were written and published by respected scholars immediately after his death, and again in 1923 on the centennial of his birth, and in 1915 an affectionate and uncritical biography was written by his former associate William H. Dall. In tribute to him, many species of vertebrates and invertebrates were named *bairdii* by their discoverers.

Yet, by the middle of the twentieth century, the naturalist Baird had virtually dropped out of sight as a new crop of naturalists turned their attention away from taxonomy to more theoretical studies. And although the expansion of the Smithsonian Institution into a museum complex took place under Baird's direction, it is Joseph Henry who is popularly regarded as the father of the institution. Baird is better known for his creation of the marine biological station at Woods Hole, where he is commemorated by prominent memorials. Two analytical biographies describing his permanent contributions to American science and to the Smithsonian have been written in recent years, but today the name of Baird is little known to other than professionals, nor is it likely to be, given the unspectacularity of both his life and work styles.

BIBLIOGRAPHY

Allard, Dean C. *Spencer Fullerton Baird and the U.S. Fish Commission.* New York: Arno Press, 1978.

Goode, George Brown. "The Three Secretaries." In *The Smithsonian Institution, 1846–1896: The History of Its First Half Century.* Washington, DC: Devine Press, 1897, pp. 115–234.

Rivinus, E.F., and E.M. Youssef. *Spencer Baird of the Smithsonian.* Washington, DC: Smithsonian Institution Press, 1992.

Edward F. Rivinus

SEE ALSO
Smithsonian Institution

Ballooning and Science

While the notion of buoyancy dates to Aristotle (384–322 B.C.), the invention of the balloon was directly rooted in seventeenth- and eighteenth-century studies of pneumatic physics and chemistry. Father Laurenço de Gusmão may have flown a very small hot air balloon in Lisbon as early as 1709. Joseph (1740–1810) and Etienne (1745–1799) Montgolfier developed the idea independently, however, and staged the first public flight of a hot air balloon at Annonay, France, on 4 June 1783. Jacques Alexandre Cesare Charles (1746–1823) introduced the process for producing large quantities of hydrogen, and flew the world's first gas balloon in Paris on 27 August 1783. Pilatre de Rozier and the Marquis d'Arlandes were the first human beings to make a free flight, ascending from Paris on 21 November aboard a Montgolfier hot air balloon. Less than two weeks later, on 1 December, J.A.C. Charles and M.N. Robert made the first flight aboard a gas balloon.

Spectacular public ascents, long distance flights, and experiments in military aeronautics drew widespread attention and comment during the nineteenth century, but the potential of the balloon as a tool of science was also recognized at an early date. Etienne Robertson is credited with having made the first expressly scientific ascent from Hamburg on 18 July 1803. On 16 September 1804, J.L. Gay-Lussac reached a record altitude of almost 23,000 feet during the course of a flight dedicated to sampling the atmosphere, recording temperature and pressure, and conducting experiments in magnetism and electricity.

Scientific ballooning entered a new and more dangerous era on 5 September 1862, when the English balloonist Henry Coxwell and James Glaisher, a geophysicist and meteorologist, climbed above 30,000 feet for the first time. Suffering from intense cold and the lack of oxygen, both men fell unconscious. Momentarily regaining his senses, but unable to use his frostbitten hands, Coxwell pulled the gas release valve line with his teeth to begin the descent to safety. Theodore Sivel and Joseph Croce-Spinelli were less fortunate, perishing on 15 April 1875 during the course of a high-altitude ascent aboard the balloon *Zenith.* Gaston Tissandier, the pilot of the balloon, also lost consciousness but survived the flight. The introduction of instrumented balloon sondes in the late nineteenth century reduced the risk to human life, but the lure of extreme altitudes continued to attract the occasional aeronaut, including Captain H.C. Gray, USA, who died during an unpressurized ascent to 42,470 feet from Scott Field, Illinois, on 4 May 1927.

The development of the pressurized gondola by August Piccard, who climbed to 51,775 feet over Augsberg, Germany, on 27 May 1931, opened the era of stratosphere ballooning. Over the next four years, Swiss, Soviet, and American aeronauts would use the new technology in repeated efforts to push the world's altitude record ever higher. This international competition came to an effective end on 11 November 1935, when the crew of the U.S. Army Air Corps/National Geographic Society balloon *Explorer II* reached an altitude of 72,377 feet.

The introduction of lightweight plastic envelopes and other new materials and techniques following World War II resulted in a generation of balloons capable of carrying heavy payloads to the very roof of the atmosphere. Old records were shattered as United States Navy and Air Force balloonists reached altitudes in excess of 113,000 feet, conducting research and testing life-support systems and other items of equipment that would be required for spaceflight. New technology aerostats found application in defense and intelligence programs, and have served the needs of researchers in fields ranging from environmental studies to particle physics and x-ray astronomy. The free balloon, the first aircraft to carry scientific instruments and curious human beings aloft, remains an important tool for the study of the atmosphere, the earth, and the universe beyond.

BIBLIOGRAPHY

Crouch, Tom D. *The Eagle Aloft: Two Centuries of the Balloon in America.* Washington, DC: Smithsonian Institution Press, 1983.

DeVorkin, David H. *Race to the Stratosphere: Manned Scientific Ballooning in America.* New York: Springer-Verlag, 1989.

Tom Crouch

Banneker, Benjamin (1731–1806)

Tobacco grower, amateur astronomer and almanac maker, Banneker was the first black man of science. Born a free African-American in Baltimore County, Maryland, his father was a freed African slave and his mother was the daughter of a freed slave and an English indentured servant. Taught to read and write from a Bible by his white grandmother, Banneker's only formal education consisted of several weeks spent one winter in a one-room schoolroom. A voracious reader, he borrowed books when possible, favoring history, mathematics, and religion. From his youth, he demonstrated considerable mathematical ability. At about the

age of twenty-two, he made a wooden striking clock, it is said without ever having seen one. Approaching the project as a mathematical problem based on the ratio of wheels and gears, he cut each part from wood with a pocketknife. The clock continued to operate successfully over forty years later.

After witnessing astronomical observations made by a young neighbor, George Ellicott, in the evenings after work in 1789, Banneker became interested in astronomy. Ellicott loaned him a telescope and several books, including James Ferguson's *Astronomy Explained Upon Sir Isaac Newton's Principles, and Made Easy for Those Who Have Not Studied Mathematics* (London, 1756), Tobias Mayers's *Tabulae Motuum Solis et Lunae . . . Edited and Corrected by Nevil Maskelyne* (London, 1770), and Charles Leadbetter's two-volume *A Complete System of Astronomy . . .* (London, 1741). Without assistance, Banneker mastered the astronomical texts and taught himself to project eclipses and to calculate the ephemeris for an almanac. Now forced by rheumatism to retire from farming, he watched the skies nightly and made observations with his telescope, sleeping during the day. He completed calculations for the ephemeris for an almanac for the year 1791, but failed to sell it to several printers in Baltimore and elsewhere to whom he offered it.

In 1791, the surveyor Major Andrew Ellicott, a cousin of George Ellicott, was selected by President Washington to proceed immediately to Alexandria, Virginia, to begin a survey of a ten-mile square on which the national capital was to be situated. Lacking an interim field assistant sufficiently familiar with astronomical instruments, he hoped his cousin George could join him. The latter was unable to do so but recommended Banneker in his stead. Banneker worked on the survey in the field observatory tent for about three months, making nightly observations of transiting stars and daily observation each noon for correcting the field clock. In his leisure, he completed calculations for an ephemeris for the following year.

Upon the arrival of Ellicott's brothers in the spring to assist him, Banneker's services were no longer required. He was paid sixty dollars for his participation and returned home in April. He sold his ephemeris for 1792 to the Baltimore printers Goddard and Angell, who incorporated it in an almanac bearing Banneker's name in the title. Promoted by the abolition societies of Pennsylvania and Maryland, the almanac was an immediate success.

B

Banneker's ephemerides were published in almanacs for the years 1792 through 1797, in at least twenty-eight editions. The failure to market them thereafter was due chiefly to diminishing regional interest in the abolitionist movement. A computerized comparison made of Banneker's calculations with ephemerides of almanacs by other contemporary almanac makers for the same years has shown that Banneker's calculations were comparable and equal in accuracy to theirs.

Banneker never married, continuing to live with his mother on the 100-acre farm after his father's death in 1759. Following her death at some time after 1775, he lived alone, his needs attended to by two sisters living nearby. Upon his death, following his instructions, one of his nephews rode to Ellicott's Lower Mills (now Ellicott City, Maryland) to inform George Ellicott of his demise and to return the books and instruments he had borrowed. Included with them was his manuscript astronomical journal in which he had copied all his ephemerides. The borrowed books and his journal survive. While his burial was taking place in the graveyard on his farm, his house burst into flames and burned to the ground with all its contents, including his striking clock.

BIBLIOGRAPHY

Bedini, Silvio A. "Benjamin Banneker and the Survey of the District of Columbia." *Records of the Columbia Historical Society of Washington, D. C.*, 1969–1970, pp. 7–30.

————. *The Life of Benjamin Banneker.* New York: Charles Scribner's Sons, 1972; reprint, Rancho Cordova, CA: Landmark Enterprises, 1985.

————. *The Life of Benjamin Banneker.* Revised and Expanded Edition. Baltimore: Maryland Historical Society, 1999.

Latrobe, Jno. H.B. "Memoir of Benjamin Banneker, Read Before the Historical Society of Maryland." *Maryland Colonization Journal*, n.s. 2, no. 23 (May 1845): 353–364.

[McHenry, James]. "Account of a Negro Astronomer. A Letter from Mr. James McHenry to the Editors of the Pennsylvania, Delaware, Maryland and Virginia Almanack, Containing Particulars Respecting Benjamin Banneker, a Free Negro." *New York Magazine, or Literary Repository* 2 (1791): 557–558.

Tyson, Martha E. *Banneker, the Afric-American Astronomer. From the Posthumous Papers of Martha E. Tyson, Edited by Her Daughter.* Philadelphia: Friends' Book Association, 1884.

[Tyson, Martha E.]. *A Sketch of the Life of Benjamin Banneker, From Notes Taken in 1836. Read by J. Saurin Norris,*

Before the Maryland Historical Society, October 1854. Baltimore: John D. Toy, n.d.

Silvio A. Bedini

Bartram, William (1739–1823)

Naturalist, explorer, and writer. Bartram, third son of the Quaker botanist John Bartram and his second wife, Ann Mendenhall, was born at Kingsessing, Pennsylvania, now a part of Philadelphia. As a teenager, William began to accompany his father on botanical excursions and to sketch specimens for several British correspondents, including his father's principal advisor and patron, Peter Collinson. Because colonial America offered few opportunities to pursue natural history as a career, after four years at the Academy of Philadelphia (1752–1756), William was apprenticed to a local merchant. In 1761, he moved to Cape Fear, North Carolina, the home of his paternal uncle, where he attempted to establish his own trading business. Like most of his early ventures, the business proved an abysmal failure.

In 1765, John Bartram pressured his reluctant son to settle his affairs at Cape Fear and join him on a trip to East Florida, a newly acquired British territory. When they arrived later that year, William immediately fell in love with the place and convinced his father to outfit a rice and indigo plantation for him on the banks of the St. Johns River. Despite his initial enthusiasm, the attempt to grow unfamiliar crops on marginal land soon proved to be a fiasco, and after surviving a shipwreck off the coast of St. Augustine, a despondent William returned home. For the next several years he divided his time between Philadelphia and Cape Fear, where he did his best to eke out a living by various means.

In 1768, Collinson arranged for William to draw natural history specimens for the duchess of Portland and the Quaker physician John Fothergill, who soon became the Bartrams' most important patron. With Fothergill's financial support, William returned to the southeast in 1773 to begin a four-year exploring expedition. More often than not traveling alone in largely uncharted territory, the troubled young man collected specimens, made drawings, kept notes, and finally "found peace" (Bell, p. 489). His exuberant descriptions of Florida, Georgia, and the Carolinas are among the first to celebrate an American wilderness that others had viewed either as an evil, chaotic wasteland or a storehouse of economically valuable resources. He returned home in 1777 and never left again.

For the remainder of his long life, William Bartram labored at the family nursery business that his younger brother, John Jr., inherited after the death of their father. Even enticing offers to become professor of botany at the University of Pennsylvania (1782) and to join Freeman's Red River Expedition (1806) failed to lure him away from the family homestead. However, Bartram's Garden became a mecca for naturalists—including Thomas Nuttall, François A. Michaux, Thomas Say, Benjamin S. Barton, and Alexander Wilson—who ventured there regularly to seek out William's knowledge and advice.

After a long unexplained delay, in 1791 Bartram finally published an account of his southeastern expedition. Widely reprinted and translated into several languages, Bartram's *Travels* was generally praised for its authoritative treatment of southern flora and fauna (including a list of 215 native bird species) but condemned for its florid prose. Yet the book's enduring fame ultimately rests on its author's luxuriant descriptions of nature, which provided a source of inspiration and imagery for the nineteenth-century romantic movement. Coleridge, Wordsworth, Chateaubriand, and other romantics incorporated Bartram's strong sense of place and in some cases even his exact language into their own writing.

Because of his influence on other naturalists and the romantics, Bartram has continued to attract a great deal of scholarly attention (see the bibliography in Cutting, below). Harper has issued annotated editions of his *Travels* as well as the manuscript journal he kept during the first part of his southeastern expedition, while Ewan has edited an exquisite edition of surviving drawings. But as yet there is no adequate full-scale biography.

BIBLIOGRAPHY

Bartram, William. *Travels through North and South Carolina, Georgia, East and West Florida, the Cherokee Country, the Extensive Territory of the Muscogulges, or Creek Confederacy, and the Country of the Choctaws.* Philadelphia: James and Johnson, 1791. (See also, the "Naturalist Edition" edited by Francis Harper, New Haven: Yale University Press, 1958).

———. "Travels in Georgia and Florida, 1773—74: A Report to Dr. John Fothergill," edited by Francis Harper. *Transactions of the American Philosophical Society,* n.s. 33, part 2 (1943): 212–242.

Bell, Whitfield J. Jr. "Bartram, William." *Dictionary of Scientific Biography,* edited by Charles C. Gillispie. New York: Scribners, 1970, 1:488–490.

Cutting, Rose M. *John and William Bartram, William Byrd II, and St. John de Crevecoeur: A Reference Guide.* Boston: G.K. Hall, 1976.

Earnest, Ernest. *John and William Bartram: Botanists and Explorers.* Philadelphia: University of Pennsylvania Press, 1940.

Ewan, Joseph, ed. *William Bartram: Botanical and Zoological Drawings, 1756–1788.* Philadelphia: American Philosophical Society, 1968.

Fagin, Nathan B. *William Bartram: Interpreter of the American Landscape.* Baltimore: Johns Hopkins University Press, 1933.

Greene, John C. *American Science in the Age of Jefferson.* Ames: Iowa State University Press, 1984.

Porter, Charlotte M. "Philadelphia Story: Florida Gives William Bartram a Second Chance." *Florida Historical Quarterly* 71 (1992): 310–323.

Regis, Pamela. *Describing Early America: Bartram, Jefferson, Crevecoeur, and the Rhetoric of Natural History.* De Kalb: Northern Illinois University Press, 1992.

Slaughter, Thomas P. *The Natures of John and William Bartram.* New York: Alfred A. Knopf, 1996.

Mark V. Barrow Jr.

Beaumont, William (1785–1853)

One of the first Americans to achieve an international reputation in medical science. He accomplished this through the publication of *Experiments and Observations on the Gastric Juice and Digestion* in 1833. This work contributed significantly to the body of knowledge concerning the human digestive process; Beaumont's data were decisive in a prolonged controversy among leading physiologists concerning the existence and function of gastric fluid. His book was translated into French and German; it was included in text books in Scotland and used in England as well.

Born on a farm near Lebanon, Connecticut, presumably Beaumont was educated in the public school of the town. At age twenty-one, he left his home to become a schoolmaster in the village of Champlain, New York. While serving as schoolmaster, he arranged for a medical apprenticeship under Dr. Benjamin Chandler of St. Albans, Vermont. He had studied with Dr. Chandler for only one year when the War of 1812 began. Beaumont, a young Republican, now a pauper and in debt to his mentor, was swept by need and patriotic fervor into the army as a surgeon's mate. At the conclusion of the war, he attempted to practice medicine briefly in Plattsburgh, New York, but in 1819, he reenlisted in the newly organized Army Medical Corps. He was assigned to Fort Mackinac in the Great Lakes,

B

and there, a few years later, he encountered, quite by accident, his opportunity for important medical research.

Two aspects of Beaumont's career made it remarkable: First, his scientific experiments were conducted on the American frontier from 1822 to 1832. He was an army surgeon, stationed at Fort Mackinac, Fort Niagara, Fort Crawford, and finally, at Jefferson Barracks near St. Louis. He performed his research in the rude facilities of army hospitals; his equipment was primitive and homemade. Second, these experiments were carried out on a human being, a young French Canadian fur trapper, Alexis St. Martin, who received an accidental gunshot wound to the stomach in 1822. Beaumont treated the patient at Fort Mackinac, and after months of care and several attempts to close the gaping wound surgically, it was apparent that St. Martin's wound had healed in such a way as to produce a permanent opening or fistula into the stomach, a gastrostomy.

Beginning in 1825, Beaumont observed and experimented upon St. Martin's wound, treating him initially as a patient, and then, when he was ambulatory, hiring him as a household servant to serve his family in their army quarters. St. Martin found the routine of experimentation demanding and frustrating. He rebelled against Beaumont frequently in any way that he could, often escaping to the forests of Canada. The doctor was aware of the rarity of his opportunity with St. Martin to observe a healthy human stomach, but Beaumont was merely apprenticeship trained, almost self-taught in medicine, and he was not educated at all in physiology when his experiments began at Fort Mackinac.

With the guidance of the Surgeon General of the Army, Joseph Lovell, Beaumont began to read the various theories concerning human digestion which were held and vigorously defended by physicians in large medical centers. Surgeon General Lovell encouraged him and sent him books on digestive physiology. He arranged for Beaumont's first article on St. Martin to be published in the medical journal of the Territory of Michigan. Lovell always supported Beaumont's career in research, and in 1832, as Beaumont planned a European tour to various medical schools in order to exhibit St. Martin's gastrostomy, Lovell made arrangements for St. Martin to be paid a sergeant's wage by the army, to be stationed with a detachment of orderlies at the War Department in Washington, D.C., and to be assigned to Beaumont as an aide.

Before traveling to Washington with St. Martin, where the naive Canadian might be lured away from Beaumont by other scientists or institutions, Beaumont brought his subject before the county officials of Clinton County, New York. In attempting to safeguard his exclusive rights to St. Martin as an experimental human subject, Beaumont drew up a contract which is the first document in the field of human use for scientific research in the history of American medicine.

Lovell also arranged for Beaumont to meet with a distinguished physiologist from the University of Virginia, Robley Dunglison, in order to polish the manuscript and enlarge the experiments prior to publication. Beaumont hoped to obtain from Dunglison's laboratory a chemical analysis of gastric fluid which he was able to extract from St. Martin's stomach. The encounter with Dunglison was brief and unpleasant. It revealed to the professor Beaumont's obsessive fear of losing exclusive authorship of his book, and Dunglison's substantial contributions to the book were not acknowledged adequately by Beaumont.

As final arrangements for publication moved forward in Plattsburgh, New York, St. Martin took advantage of his proximity to the Canadian border and escaped from Beaumont to go home. Plans for the European tour of medical schools never materialized. Nevertheless, Beaumont refused to delay publication of his book, which appeared in December 1833, consisting of 280 pages. In title, format, and style, it was reminiscent of Benjamin Franklin's book on electricity, with a long introduction by Beaumont describing his years of work with St. Martin and ending with conclusions concerning gastric fluid. "My experiments confirm the doctrines . . . taught by Spallanzini," he asserted. He sought to demonstrate that gastric fluid contained solvent properties independent of the body, thus refuting the school of physiologists, based primarily at Philadelphia, known as Vitalists. The experiments described in the book involved the insertion into St. Martin's gastrostomy various items of food common in the human diet, and extracting them at intervals by a silk thread to chart the time required to digest each morsel.

Beaumont's book had been promoted vigorously prior to its publication. The story of the army doctor and the "man with a hole in his stomach" became a popular one in America of the 1830s, so the book initially sold briskly. Beaumont was pleased. In time, however, he was disillusioned by the scant recognition he received

B

from American physicians. He was the first to write about the effects upon digestion of emotional distress and the first to write of the injurious effects upon the stomach of tea and coffee as well as the pernicious influence of alcohol when taken in excess. All of these conclusions lend insight into the plight of St. Martin as he subjected himself year after year to Beaumont's experiments. Later in the century, Beaumont's book served as a resource for health food trends advocating vegetarianism and abstention from all stimulants.

As the brief notoriety which followed the publication of his book in 1833 embraced Beaumont, his hopes for greater fame were dashed when he was ordered to Jefferson Barracks near St. Louis. At the moment of his highest acclaim, Beaumont was sent by the army back to the frontier. His findings were never promoted, therefore, by the power of a practicing scientist in those circles where they would have made a difference.

Shorn of highest opportunity by his obligation to make a living in the army, Beaumont placed himself and his family in St. Louis, far from the Eastern establishment. He followed his military orders to St. Louis in a mood of anger and disappointment, and he spent the final twenty years of his life there. He became a prominent private physician after his resignation from the army in 1839. Beaumont was a charter member of the Medical Society of Missouri and a member of the first faculty of Washington University School of Medicine in St. Louis.

His papers are in the William Beaumont Collection, Washington University School of Medicine Library, St. Louis, Missouri.

BIBLIOGRAPHY
Beaumont, William. *Experiments and Observations of the Gastric Juice and the Physiology of Digestion.* Plattsburgh, NY: Allen, 1833.
Brodman, Estelle. "Scientific and Editorial Relationships between Joseph Lovell and William Beaumont." *Bulletin of the History of Medicine* 38 (March-April 1964): 127–132.
Miller, Genevieve, ed. *Wm. Beaumont's Formative Years: Two Early Notebooks, 1811–1821.* New York: Henry Schuman, 1945.
Myer, Jesse Shire. *Life and Letters of Dr. William Beaumont.* St. Louis: C.V. Mosby, 1939.
Numbers, Ronald L., and William J. Orr Jr. "William Beaumont's Reception at Home and Abroad." *Isis* 72 (1981): 590–612.
Rosen, George. *The Reception of William Beaumont's Discovery in Europe.* New York: Schumans, 1942.

Cynthia DeHaven Pitcock

Behaviorism

(1) A twentieth-century philosophy of the disciplinary status, subject matter, and methods of psychology; (2) an influential "school" of psychology that began after World War I in the United States; and (3) a theory of the conceptual status of words referring to mental activities, developed in Great Britain by Ludwig Wittgenstein and Gilbert Ryle and, in the United States, by philosophers, by psychologists such as B.F. Skinner, and by writers in the positivist tradition such as Gustav Bergmann and Kenneth Spence.

John B. Watson's 1913 *Psychological Review* article has often been regarded as a behaviorist manifesto that inspired a behaviorist revolution; it is customary to treat earlier epistemological formulations (e.g., Edgar A. Singer) and statements of such metatheoretical ideals as objectivism (Vladimir Bekhterev, Ivan Pavlov, Edward Thorndike), conceptual economy (Ernst Mach), and mechanism (Jacques Loeb) as intellectual background that paved the way for behaviorism.

The agenda of Watson's 1913 article were: to criticize introspective methods in human psychology and the method of analogy in animal psychology; to discredit competing "schools" of psychology (structuralism and functionalism); and to defend a definition of psychology as an objective, natural science of behavior, rather than as the science of conscious phenomena. To Watsonian behaviorism were later added, during the 1920s, the following: Pavlovian conditioning as the fundamental learning process; environmentalism; a "scientifically approved" program for raising children; and strident criticism of all reference to consciousness.

After Watson left Johns Hopkins University in 1920, behaviorism was developed along divergent lines by "neobehaviorists." Three major forms of neobehaviorism have been distinguished: methodological behaviorism (Clark Hull, Edward C. Tolman); radical behaviorism (B.F. Skinner); and neo-Hullian behaviorism (K.W. Spence, Neal Miller, etc.). Other, less influential versions splintered out from these three.

Behaviorism as a framework for theorizing in various research specialties and as a philosophy of science for psychology in general was most influential between the early 1930s and the early 1960s, particularly

B

among researchers in simple learning, conditioning, and motivation in animals (and, to a smaller extent, in humans). Those specialties were expected to provide a foundation of basic laws of learning that would permit the gradual, systematic extension—of methodology, extrapolation and theory, and genealizable laboratory findings—to successively more complex and typically human behavior, such as language, mental activities, and social behavior. Behaviorism was ambitious, reductionistic, and endorsed a bottom-up strategy of empirical and theoretical extension.

Most behaviorists believed: (a) behavior should be accounted for by causal explanation that specifies the relevant, particularly situational, factors upon which the performance depends; Skinner called this a "functional analysis"; (b) there are behavioral mechanisms, which operate pervasively and significantly, though often unnnoticed, in the daily life of all organisms, including humans, and psychology should study them; (c) there is a commonality of behavioral mechanisms in evolutionarily related species, including humans; (d) a proper scientific strategy is to tackle simple phenomena first, progressively moving on to more complex phenomena; and (e) theory development should be conservative, with a preference for concepts that can be linked to publicly observable (behavioral) phenomena.

Radical behaviorists insisted, in addition, that (a) the proper scientific ontology is materialistic monism, entailing a rejection of any form of dualism and of the existence of a mental realm having an ontological status distinct from the material organism; and that (b) the progress of behavioral psychology requires commitment of less effort to developing theory and more to establishing a factual foundation in the research specialties that behaviorism supported (i.e., learning and motivation).

Most of the debate that was inspired by behaviorism concerned the adequacy of the behaviorist research strategy, and especially the question whether behaviorist metatheory was too restrictive. At present, the most widely endorsed historical model holds (a) that the fragmentation of behaviorism increased during the 1950s, as it tried, unsuccessfully, to extend its bottom-up strategy to more complex, typically human, phenomena, that involve the higher mental [cognitive] processes; (b) that the downfall of positivism in Anglo-American philosophy of science in the 1950s and 1960s implied that the metatheoretical underpinnings of behaviorism had been invalidated; (c) that behaviorism's restrictive style and strategy were replaced, during the late 1960s and early 1970s, by a "top-down" approach legitimating the direct study of human complex performance independently of behaviorist guidelines; and (d) that a rival school called "cognitive psychology," with roots in computer science, linguistics, and other areas has now replaced behaviorism as the central metatheory for psychology. Presumably behaviorism survives in the form of isolated groups of holdouts, such as those following Skinner's banner. Currently, important historical questions concern whether this picture of contemporary psychology is adequate and whether the presumptive transition of twenty years ago involved a "paradigm shift" in the sense employed by the historian of science, T.S. Kuhn.

BIBLIOGRAPHY

Amsel, A. *Behaviorism, Neobehaviorism, and Cognitivism in Learning Theory.* Hillsdale, NJ: Erlbaum, 1989.

Boakes, Robert B. *From Darwin to Behaviourism: Psychology and the Minds of Animals.* Cambridge, U.K.: Cambridge University Press, 1984.

Hilgard, Ernest R. *Psychology in America.* New York: Harcourt Brace Jovanovich, 1988.

Hilgard, Ernest R., and Gordon H Bower. *Theories of Learning.* 5th ed. Englewood Cliffs, NJ: Prentice-Hall, 1980.

Kuhn, Thomas S. *The Structure of Scientific Revolutions.* Rev. ed. Chicago: University of Chicago Press, 1970.

Skinner, B.F. *Science and Human Behavior.* New York: Macmillan, 1953.

———. *About Behaviorism.* New York: Knopf, 1974.

Smith, Laurence D. *Behaviorism and Logical Positivism.* Stanford: Stanford University Press, 1986.

Watson, John B. "Psychology as the Behaviorist Views It." *Psychological Review* 20 (1913): 158–177.

———. *Behaviorism.* New York: Norton, 1925.

———. *Psychological Care of Infant and Child.* New York: Norton, 1928.

Zuriff, G.E. *Behaviorism: A Conceptual Reconstruction.* New York: Columbia University Press, 1985.

S.R. Coleman

Bell, Alexander Graham (1847–1922)

Inventor, teacher, and scientist. Born in Edinburgh, Scotland, he studied briefly at the University of Edinburgh and the University of London, but his intellectual interests were shaped by his father, a noted teacher of speech and deviser of a physiologically based system of phonetic notation. Both his father's system and his mother's severe deafness turned his mind to vocal physiology and the physics of sound. After teaching in boys' schools in Scotland and England, he emigrated with his parents to Ontario, Canada, in 1870. Shortly thereafter he took a job teaching speech at a Boston school for the deaf and later at Boston University. The technological and financial vigor of Boston stimulated him to work on a device for transmission of several messages at once over a single telegraph line. This line of research, along with his knowledge of sound and speech, led him to the concept of the telephone, which he patented in 1876. He successfully defended his patent against numerous infringers and claimants of priority. The comfortable, though not huge, fortune he reaped enabled him to devote the rest of his life to teaching and promoting lipreading and speech by the deaf (which he always listed as his primary occupation), dabbling in science, pioneering in the development of aviation, and producing a variety of inventions, including the photophone (which transmitted speech for short distances by light beams), space-frame construction using tetrahedral members, and significant improvements in phonographs and hydrofoil boats. During the last half of his life, he divided his time yearly between Washington, D.C., and Baddeck, Nova Scotia, but proudly retained his American citizenship.

From his childhood on, Bell aspired to scientific achievement. That he had talent as well as aspiration was demonstrated by a discovery he made at eighteen through systematic experiments in analyzing vowel sounds, unaware that the German physicist Hermann von Helmholtz had anticipated him a short time before. But physics was already beyond Bell's mathematical training and aptitude. In later years, his most notable scientific work dealt with deafness. He invented the telephonic audiometer, and his name entered the language in the decibel, the standard measure of sound intensity. He did significant work in the statistical study of inheritance, especially of deafness but also of longevity and of multiple births among sheep. After election to the National Academy of Sciences in 1883, he contributed five papers to its published memoirs, all but one related to his studies in heredity. He also published several scientific papers in respected journals, mostly related to speech, hearing, and his various inventions. In 1881, he devised a surgical probe that transmitted a telephonic click when it touched metal. It was widely used until superseded by X-rays. He belonged to several leading scientific societies and was appointed a regent of the Smithsonian Institution in 1898.

Bell explicitly disclaimed the status of professional scientist. After the 1880s, he settled for the role of spectator, patron, and promoter, reading widely though unsystematically in science, and hobnobbing regularly with eminent scientists, especially John Wesley Powell, Simon Newcomb, and Samuel P. Langley. In 1881, he financed a major phase of Albert Michelson's classic experiments establishing that direction had no effect on the speed of light. In 1882, he rescued the foundering journal *Science* and helped finance it for nearly a decade, after which the American Association for the Advancement of Science (of which he was a fellow) adopted it as its official journal. And not least, Bell advanced scientific exploration and communication as president of the National Geographic Society and as a shrewd advisor to the society's magazine.

BIBLIOGRAPHY

Bruce, Robert V. *Bell: Alexander Graham Bell and the Conquest of Solitude.* Ithaca: Cornell University Press, 1990.

Osborne, Harold S. "Alexander Graham Bell." *Biographical Memoirs of the National Academy of Sciences* 23 (1943): 20–29.

Robert V. Bruce

Bessey, Charles Edwin (1845–1915)

Botanist and educator. Born in Milton Township, Ohio, he received his formal botanical education at the Michigan Agricultural College. He later studied briefly under Asa Gray and William Farlow at Harvard during the winters of 1872–1873 and 1875–1876. He received an honorary Ph.D. from the University of Iowa in 1879. Most of Bessey's professional life was spent at land-grant colleges and universities. From 1870 to 1884, he taught horticulture and botany at the Iowa Agricultural College in Ames. There he gained a reputation as a radical educational innovator by emphasizing the necessity of scientific training in agricultural education. Agricultural programs would not be separated from scientific departments in the university, but would share a common core of basic science courses, faculty, and academic standards. For Bessey, the ideal land-grant university was to be a place where pure and applied science were harmoniously blended. He was unsuccessful in his attempt to have this educational model established in Iowa. More auspiciously, he

B

became an influential national spokesman for educational reform in the life sciences. Like several other newly professionalized plant scientists, Bessey championed the "new botany," an approach that emphasized laboratory training in college science courses. At a time when the microscope was often considered a novelty, Bessey required his undergraduate botany students to master the use of the instrument. His laboratory course in botany was the first offered to undergraduates in the United States. Bessey's educational approach was widely copied as a result of the success of his textbook *Botany for High Schools and Colleges* (1880). Although it was loosely modeled on Julius von Sach's *Lehrbuch der Botanik,* Bessey's book evinced a pragmatic approach to education that was typically American. Like John Dewey and William James, Bessey was committed to the idea of learning through practice rather than memorization.

In 1884, Bessey left Iowa to become professor of botany at the University of Nebraska. Here, too, he struggled, but failed in his attempts to keep agricultural programs within the regular university structure. By the end of his life, agricultural schools at the University of Nebraska, and elsewhere, had become semiautonomous institutions with their own courses, standards, and systems of academic rewards. Within the field of botany, however, Bessey was remarkably successful in building an influential program. The botany department at the University of Nebraska became a major center of research, and several of Bessey's students made important contributions, particularly to the new science of plant ecology.

Most historians have portrayed Bessey sympathetically as a leader in progressive science education and a visionary whose ideas played an important role in shaping the future of American botany. More recently, Elizabeth Keeney has argued that his "new botany" was also a driving wedge separating professional botanists from serious amateurs. By the end of the nineteenth century there was little communication between the two groups.

Bessey was raised in a deeply religious family, and he apparently never questioned the belief that the universe was God's creation. Nonetheless, his major scientific contribution was the development of the first explicitly phylogenetic classification of flowering plants. Bessey considered the angiosperms to be a monophyletic group derived from a single ancestral group. He provided a set of rules or "dicta" for distinguishing

between primitive and derived characteristics. The diagrammatic representation of the phylogenetic relationships among the orders of flowering plants, nicknamed "Bessey's cactus" because of its branching shape, was widely reprinted. Bessey spent twenty years developing his evolutionary ideas. The final version was published shortly before his death. His system was widely taught and has provided a starting point for several recent modifications. He was the first American botanist to make a major contribution to the theory of plant classification.

BIBLIOGRAPHY

Bessey, Charles E. *Botany for High Schools and Colleges.* New York: Henry Holt, 1880.

——. "Botany by the Experimental Method." *Science,* n.s. 35 (1912): 994–996.

——. "Phylogenetic Taxonomy of Flowering Plants." *Annals of the Missouri Botanical Garden* 2 (1915): 109–164.

Cittadino, Eugene. "Ecology and the Professionalization of Botany in America, 1890–1905." *Studies in History of Biology* 4 (1980): 171–198.

Keeney, Elizabeth. *The Botanizers: Amateur Scientists in Nineteenth-Century America.* Chapel Hill: University of North Carolina Press, 1992.

Overfield, Richard A. "Charles E. Bessey: The Impact of the 'New' Botany on American Agriculture, 1880–1910." *Technology and Culture* 16 (1975): 162–181.

——. *Science with Practice: Charles Bessey and the Maturing of American Botany.* Ames: Iowa State University Press, 1993.

Tobey, Ronald C. *Saving the Prairies: The Life Cycle of the Founding School of American Plant Ecology, 1895–1955.* Berkeley: University of California Press, 1981.

Walsh, Thomas R. "Charles E. Bessey: Land-Grant College Professor." Ph.D. diss., University of Nebraska, 1972.

Joel B. Hagen

SEE ALSO
Botany

Big Science

Coined in late the 1950s, this term describes what American scientists and policymakers regarded as a new set of social circumstances underlying scientific research. Most notably, in 1961, physicist and Oak Ridge National Laboratory Director Alvin Weinberg characterized Big Science as a mode of scientific inquiry, involving hierarchically organized team research and massive financial commitments. Weinberg suggested that the large-scale instruments of Big Science, such as particle accelerators, rockets, and space vehicles, could be seen as "symbols of our time" (Weinberg, "Impact," p. 161). Weinberg also warned that Big Science could lead to the decline of science itself, because it produced too many science administrators and it harnessed research to military interests.

Discussions of Big Science in American policy circles became widespread by the mid-1960s. This reflected an increasing awareness that growth in the scientific enterprise had impacted research practices, as well as the role of science in the American political and social agenda.

Many scientists and historians trace the origins of Big Science to the Manhattan Project during World War II. The building of the first atomic bombs mobilized financial and human resources on an unprecedented scale. Most of the contemporary American physics community worked on this government-sponsored scientific endeavor, which cost nearly $2 billion. The mission-oriented cooperation between academic scientists, the United States military, and American businesses that resulted from this technological project forged a new alliance between science, government, and industry that is now cited as a hallmark of Big Science.

Relatedly, the 1957 Russian launching of *Sputnik,* the world's first artificial satellite, is frequently identified as a major catalyst for the creation of postwar Big Science policy. For scientists and the American public, *Sputnik* precipitated Cold War fears about United States technological inferiority and led to a massive postwar infusion of federal funds for research. In 1958, the United States Congress established the National Aeronautics and Space Administration (NASA) in an effort to promote space-related research. NASA's hierarchical organization, its political entanglements, and its penchant for funding "mega-projects" such as the Hubble Space Telescope have led some to characterize it as the quintessential Big Science institution.

In 1963, the pioneering statistical work of physicist-turned-historian Derek J. de Solla Price provided an alternative, long-term view of Big Science as a historical phenomenon. Using data on the increasing number of scientists and scientific papers over the last 300 years, Price suggested that science had maintained a general exponential growth since its beginnings. Price defined Big Science as science at the saturation point of its logistic growth curve, that is, at the historical phase during which previously exponential growth begins to level off. Accordingly, Price argued that Big Science was a transitional phase of the scientific enterprise in between the previous era of "Little Science" and some future mode of "New Science."

Largely because of its quantitative methodology, Price's work on Big Science remains influential in policy circles even today. Interestingly, his historical approach to the problem of Big Science also provided impetus for an entire research specialty in science studies known as "scientometrics."

More recently, as historians have gained access to newly opened United States government archives, institutional case studies of postwar Big Science projects and laboratories have become a popular analytic genre. Yet scholars have also begun to address the broader role of Big Science as a predominant mode of experimental practice in twentieth-century American science. For example, a cross-national anthropological study of high-energy physics laboratories suggests that Big Science, as defined by Weinberg, might be a distinctly "American" form of scientific work. Also, a historical examination of postwar patronage for physics illustrates the difficulty of distinguishing between "basic" versus "applied" Big Science research.

The definition and history of Big Science continues to play a role in current science policy debates in the United States. In 1986, critics blamed NASA's Big Science-style management for the space shuttle *Challenger* explosion. More recently, advocates of several large physical science projects, such as the Superconducting Super Collider and the United States Space Station, have pointed to the many successes of past Big Science endeavors to justify a resource-intensive, centralized management approach to their research problems; these projects failed to persuade Congress. But in 1990, molecular biologists successfully argued that it would be more socially useful to apply some of Big Science's organizational methods and its massive resources towards a life-science research project, called the Human Genome Project. As a result, the contemporary study of Big Science remains connected to policy issues such as the role of commercial interests in science, the necessity of intellectual freedom in scientific problem choice, and the ethical and social responsibilities of modern scientists.

BIBLIOGRAPHY

Capshew, James H., and Karen A. Rader. "Big Science: Price to the Present." *Osiris* 2d ser., 7 (1992): 3–25.

B

Forman, Paul. "Behind Quantum Electronics: National Security as Basis for Physical Research in the United States, 1940–1960." *Historical Studies in the Physical and Biological Sciences* 18 (1987): 149–229.

Galison, Peter, and Bruce Hevly, eds. *Big Science: The Growth of Large-Scale Research*. Stanford: Stanford University Press, 1992.

Gilbert, G. Nigel. "Measuring the Size of Science: A Review of Indicators of Scientific Growth." *Scientometrics* 1 (1978): 9–34.

Heilbron, John L., and Daniel J. Kevles. "Finding a Policy for Mapping and Sequencing the Human Genome: Lessons from the History of Particle Physics." *Minerva* 27 (1989): 299–314.

Heilbron, John L., and Robert W. Seidel. *Lawrence and His Laboratory*. Vol. 1 of *A History of the Lawrence Berkeley Laboratory*. Berkeley: University of California Press, 1989.

Kevles, Daniel J. *The Physicists: The History of a Scientific Community in Modern America*. New York: Knopf, 1978; reprint, Cambridge, MA: Harvard University Press, 1995.

Kevles, Daniel J. "Big Science and Big Politics in the United States: Reflections on the Death of the SSC and the Life of the Human Genome Project." *Historical Studies in the Physical and Biological Sciences* 27 (1997): 269–297.

Kwa, Chunglin. "Modeling the Grasslands." *Historical Studies in the Physical and Biological Sciences* 24 (1993): 125–155.

Price, Derek J. de Solla. *Little Science, Big Science*. New York: Oxford University Press, 1963; republished with other essays as *Little Science, Big Science . . . And Beyond*. New York: Columbia University Press, 1986.

Remington, John A. "Beyond Big Science in America: The Binding of Inquiry." *Social Studies of Science* 18 (1988): 45–72.

Smith, Robert W. *The Space Telescope: A Study of NASA, Science, Technology and Politics*. New York: Cambridge University Press, 1989.

Traweek, Sharon. *Beamtimes and Lifetimes: The World of High Energy Physicists*. Cambridge, MA: Harvard University Press, 1988.

Weinberg, Alvin M. "Impact of Large-Scale Science." *Science* 134 (1961): 161–164.

———. *Reflections on Big Science*. Cambridge, MA: MIT Press, 1967.

Karen A. Rader

Biology

The term "biology" was invented at the beginning of the nineteenth century to designate the study of properties common to living organisms and specific to them. Through much of the century, however, it was a largely programmatic concept, of much greater interest to positivist philosophers such as August Comte and Herbert Spencer than to scientific practitioners. The first explicitly biological endeavor in the United States, the Philadelphia Biological Society, was established in 1857, but it dissolved within a few years due to lack of common interests to unite the naturalists and physicians who comprised it.

In the decades around midcentury, the major life-science rubrics included the broad term "natural history" (which also encompassed geological and geographic concerns) and the more specialized subjects of botany and zoology. Various health-related studies, such as anatomy, physiology, and hygiene, were loosely tied to botany and zoology, largely because many botanists and zoologists were physicians. Secondary school instruction was divided among botany, zoology, and physiology (including anatomy and hygiene), each of which was promoted and taught independently. At Harvard, the leading academic institution, the life sciences in 1871 included botany (Asa Gray), zoology (Louis Agassiz), comparative anatomy (Jeffries Wyman), and physiology (Henry P. Bowditch). Each was essentially independent.

Biology first became a substantive disciplinary unit in the United States between the 1870s and the 1910s. Americans drew on English rhetorical and conceptual resources, provided most notably by Spencer and T.H. Huxley, who united interest in protoplasm, the cell, and evolution with claims for a unified science of life. Yet they introduced two quite different programs, and soon transcended English efforts.

The broadest early American conception of biology was developed by federal scientists in the years around 1880. The U.S. National Museum, the Department of Agriculture, and a number of surveys and commissions supported a substantial community of individuals working on the taxonomy, geography, and behavior of a wide range of mostly North American organisms. These individuals included Spencer F. Baird, John Wesley Powell, Lester Ward, and Charles V. Riley. The Biological Society of Washington was created in 1880 as common ground for these bureaucratic specialists. For them, biology was the search for the general principles that underlay these disparate activities; it dealt with the "lifetime of nature:" how organisms evolved and grew.

A different conception of biology was arising in elite urban universities at the same time. In 1876, Daniel C. Gilman, president of the new Johns Hopkins University, accepted Huxley's argument that biology (composed of physiology and comparative anatomy, with evolution as its implied consequence) could function as a university discipline. Such a program jibed with Gilman's mandate to upgrade the status of medical education, and also with his desire to support higher education in life sciences without multiplying appointments or sinking capital into collections. The physiologist H. Newell Martin and zoologist William K. Brooks worked with some success over the next fifteen years to articulate biology as a science that would encompass undergraduate education, graduate training, and academic research. Their vision spread, in varying degrees, to the Massachusetts Institute of Technology, Bryn Mawr, Clark, Columbia, and the University of Chicago.

Charles O. Whitman, the first head of the Woods Hole Marine Biological Laboratory and both the Clark and Chicago biology programs, articulated the aims and structure of academic biology most fully around 1890. For Whitman, biology was an autonomous and unified subject, yet one that was so broad as to exist only as a community of more specialized endeavors; these were structured primarily, but not exclusively, on functional grounds into physiology, embryology, paleontology, ecology, and other similar specialties. This open-ended academic conception of biology was criticized in the mid-1890s by the groups whose standing was being negatively affected by its claims to intellectual and professional preeminence; these included botanists, medical scientists, and the naturalists and agriculturalists associated with the federal government. Besides asserting the importance of their own activities, representatives of these specialties questioned the presumption that professors who studied a few functions of marine invertebrates could claim to be at the center of the life sciences.

Academic biologists retreated, most notably through the reversion of the biology programs at Hopkins, Columbia, and Chicago to departments of zoology. Yet with some caveats, they maintained the importance of belief in biology, presented as a unified science comprised of a federation of formally equal functional units. This scientific community was centered around the Marine Biological Laboratory. The American Society of Naturalists functioned as an umbrella organization uniting a variety of more specialized groups. After World War I, the National Research Council's Division of Biology and Agriculture (in which agriculture was vestigial) coordinated more formal ventures.

Between the 1880s and the 1910s, the first generation of academic biologists—among the most notable of whom were E.B. Wilson, T.H. Morgan, Jacques Loeb, C.B. Davenport, H.S. Jennings, E.G. Conklin, R.G. Harrison, and Raymond Pearl—gradually expanded their interests beyond the study of invertebrate development. They built and populated the diverse subdisciplines Whitman foresaw, including general physiology, embryology, cytology, genetics, ecology, and animal behavior. After 1915, genetics was the most prominent of these, and through alliance with agriculture and eugenics it sometimes was on the verge of overwhelming other areas. Physiology and bacteriology, organized with biochemistry into the Federation of American Societies for Experimental Biology, were drawn toward identification with medical science. Yet there was a sense that all were federated enterprises, and that all were part of a real if not very fully articulated science.

Biology became an important unit in American high schools in the first decades of this century. In the 1910s, urban educators associated with academic biology constructed a course designed to introduce middle-class adolescents to the nature of life, and to build on that foundation injunctions regarding hygiene and the environment. Biology rapidly displaced the more specialized introductory subjects of botany and zoology, and became the most widely taught secondary-school science in the United States.

Beginning in the 1920s, and accelerating during the succeeding decades, physical scientists and foundation executives (the most prominent of whom was Warren Weaver, head of the Rockefeller Foundation's Natural Sciences Division from 1931 to 1955) pushed to make biology a more focused discipline with clearer intellectual hierarchies. From their perspective, the division of biology by functions was too diffuse, inefficient, small-scale, and egalitarian. They took for granted that an appropriately structured discipline of biology would comprise a basic science whose status would equal that of physics or chemistry; they interpreted the domain of biology primarily in terms of levels of structural complexity, a framework that linked the subject to chemistry and then to physics, while also displaying its distinctiveness. Weaver's program to foster work on "vital processes" involved the importation of both tools and concepts from physics and chemistry to analyze the simplest, most easily handled biological systems. The presumption was that basic knowledge would have important if as yet unknown benefits for medicine.

B

The biology program established at the California Institute of Technology in 1927 was the purest exemplification of this programmatic. Robert Millikan and Alfred Noyes, with the cooperation of the Rockefeller philanthropists, provided Thomas Hunt Morgan a mandate to build basic biology; yet Morgan's commitment to small-scale research, divided along functional lines, inhibited him from realizing their expectations. The physical chemist Linus Pauling, in alliance with George Beadle and others, ultimately gave substance to Weaver's hopes for a multidimensional assault on basic problems with major applications, most notably protein structure and chemical genetics.

The broader implications, and structural limits, of this reorganization of biology can be seen through examination of Harvard during the same period. Life sciences there had expanded substantially in the first three decades of this century, but they were still organized into taxonomically denominated units such as zoology and cryptogamic botany. The Rockefeller-funded International Education Board, guided by the comparative physiologist G.H. Parker and the astronomer Harlow Shapley, built biology laboratories at Harvard in the years around 1930 in order to bring the life sciences together and to modernize them. Further foundation and administration pressure led to the creation of a consolidated biology department in 1934–1935. Yet long-established taxonomically defined entities such as the Museum of Comparative Zoology and various herbaria continued to exist in conjunction with the consolidated program, and their leaders devoted considerable energy to maintain their units' autonomy.

The domination of the hierarchical structuring of biology increased in the two decades after World War II with the boom in molecular genetics and the broadly targeted support from the National Institutes of Health for investigations at the cellular level and below. Defenses of functional and taxonomic divisions were weak. The American Institute for Biological Sciences, established in 1947 to unite functionally defined units, was largely a failure. Its Biological Sciences Curriculum Study established three professedly coequal introductions to biology in the early 1960s, grounded in molecular, cellular, and ecological principles, respectively; but students and school boards soon recognized that these in fact formed a reductionist and meritocratic hierarchy.

It seems questionable, however, whether the hierarchical structuring is stable. When it was finally accepted at Harvard in the 1960s, it was as the basis for splitting the biology department into two programs: one in molecular and cellular biology, the other in organismal and evolutionary biology. In the last twenty years, cytology and embryology have become increasingly molecularized, and all these areas have become tied to industry and the production of standardized products. Organismal biologists, by contrast, have increasingly emphasized the importance of natural diversity. These developments would seem to presage the emergence of two different disciplines out of biology, but history indicates that such a change is not very likely. For more than a century "biology" has been an important intellectual talisman in the United States; as such, it is not easily divisible. On the contrary, the term's ability to connect disparate subjects has been highly strategic. This virtue continues.

BIBLIOGRAPHY

Appel, Toby A. *Shaping Biology: The National Science Foundation and Federal Support of Biology in the Cold War Era.* Baltimore: Johns Hopkins University Press, 2000.

Benson, Keith R., Ronald Rainger, and Jane Maienschein, eds. *The Expansion of American Biology.* New Brunswick: Rutgers University Press, 1991.

Kay, Lily E. *The Molecular Vision of Life.* New York: Oxford University Press, 1993.

Kohler, Robert E. *Lords of the Fly: Drosophila Genetics and the Experimental Life.* Chicago: University of Chicago Press, 1994.

Maienschein, Jane. *Transforming Traditions in American Biology.* Baltimore: Johns Hopkins University Press, 1991.

Pauly, Philip J. *Biologists and the Promise of American Life.* Princeton: Princeton University Press, 2000.

Rainger, Ron, Keith R. Benson, and Jane Maienschein, eds. *The American Development of Biology.* Philadelphia: University of Pennsylvania Press, 1988.

Smocovitis, Vassiliki Betty. *Unifying Biology: the Evolutionary Synthesis and Evolutionary Biology. Journal of the History of Biology.* Princeton: Princeton University Press, 1996.

Philip J. Pauly

SEE ALSO

Botany

Birkhoff, George David (1884–1944)

Perhaps the foremost American mathematician of the early twentieth century. He was one of the first mathematicians wholly trained in America and thus helped to usher in a new era in which American mathematics came of age. Before his day, the best mathematical students traveled to Europe for their formal educations.

Birkhoff was born in Overisel, Michigan, and received his education at the Lewis Institute, the University of Chicago, and Harvard, before returning to Chicago where he received his Ph.D. in 1907. He was introduced to abstract analysis by E.H. Moore at Chicago and studied the classical methods of analysis, which he favored, under Maxime Bôcher at Harvard. However, Birkhoff was more an intellectual disciple of Henri Poincaré from whose work he learned the dynamics which became the major focus of his professional mathematics career.

Birkhoff taught for short periods at the University of Wisconsin and Princeton before settling at Harvard for over three decades. At Harvard, he was responsible for training many of the important mathematicians of the next generation. In this capacity, his own significance as an American mathematician was enhanced.

Early in his career, Birkhoff established an international reputation by proving Poincaré's last theorem. This theorem of topology provided a basis for a more exact solution of the three-body problem in dynamics. In 1932, he formulated and proved his ergodic theorem, which has important applications in modern analysis, the kinetic theory of gases, and statistical mechanics.

These accomplishments alone were of great enough import to establish his position in the history of mathematics, but Birkhoff also completed work in other areas of thought. He was interested in aesthetics and applied his mathematical expertise to art and music. However, he also made fundamental contributions to modern physics in both quantum theory and relativity theory.

In 1936, he worked with J. von Neumann to demonstrate that the mathematical propositions of quantum mechanics were indistinguishable from the calculus of the linear subspaces known as Hilbert spaces. This work provided a deeper understanding of the mathematical structure of quantum mechanics and helped to initiate the axiomatic reconstruction of quantum theory. By the time that this work was accomplished Birkhoff was already known to physicists for his work in relativity theory.

In 1922, he had published his *Relativity and Modern Physics*. This was one of the first books which attempted to explain relativity in simpler terms for both the educated layman and the student of science. Birkhoff was one of a number of pure mathematicians who became interested in the new theories of relativity early on. He continued to work on relativity theory for the rest of his life. He attempted to reformulate relativity along the lines of a Minkowskian space-time framework which did not necessitate a curved space. He thought that his new formulation was more amenable to electrodynamical theory than the general theory of Einstein. This task was accomplished by hypothesizing a "perfect fluid." His theory duplicated Einstein's theoretical calculations for the advance in Mercury's perihelion and the bending of light, but gave testable results different from Einstein's predictions on other counts. In general, physicists respected Birkhoff's efforts, but never seriously considered adopting his theory in favor of Einstein's theory. Birkhoff worked on his theory until his death.

Although his role in the history of science is guaranteed by the fundamental nature of his mathematical researches, and his theoretical work in physics is well documented in existing publications, no major publications on Birkhoff have appeared. Historians have been relatively uninterested in him because his significance was due to his influence upon others rather than through direct contributions to science.

BIBLIOGRAPHY

Bell, E.T. *The Development of Mathematics.* New York: McGraw-Hill, 1945.

Berenda, Carlton W. "On Birkhoff's and Einstein's Relativity Theory." *Philosophy of Science* 12 (1945): 116–119.

Birkhoff, George David. "Newtonian and Other Forms of Gravitational Theory." *Scientific Monthly* 58 (1944): 49–57, 135–140.

Graef Fernandez, Carlos. "My Tilt with Albert Einstein." *American Scientist* 54 (1956): 204–211.

Jammer, Max. *The Conceptual Development of Quantum Mechanics.* New York: McGraw-Hill, 1966.

Jauch, Josef M. "The Mathematical Structure of Elementary Quantum Mechanics." In *The Physicists Conception of Nature,* edited by Jagdish Mehra. Dordrecht: D. Reidel, 1973, pp. 300–319.

Kaplan, James, and Aaron Strauss. "Dynamical Systems: Birkhoff and Smale." *Mathematics Teacher* 69 (1976): 495–501.

Langer, R.E. "George David Birkhoff." *Transactions of the American Mathematical Society* 60 (1946): 1–2.

Morse, Marston. "George David Birkhoff and His Mathematical Work." *Bulletin of the American Mathematical Society* 52 (1946): 357–391.

Veblen, Oswald. "George David Birkhoff." *Yearbook of the American Philosophical Society,* 1946, pp. 279–285.

B

Wilson, Edwin B. "George David Birkhoff." *Science* 102 (1945): 578–580.

James E. Beichler

Birth Control

An Americanism coined in 1914 by a radical male colleague of Margaret Sanger in an effort to articulate her vision of social liberation for women based upon reproductive autonomy. During the nineteenth century, pervasive concern over the declining fertility of the native-born white population had led to criminalization of contraception and abortion, and scientists, like other social leaders, did not regard the separation of sex from procreation as an appropriate subject for research.

In the 1920s, feminists and progressive physicians, who sought to decriminalize contraception and to make it more readily available, organized the first systematic efforts to conduct clinical evaluation of birth control methods and to translate advances in knowledge into new technology. This effort began in 1923 with the founding in New York of the Birth Control Clinical Research Bureau by Sanger and the Committee on Maternal Health by Robert Latou Dickinson, a prominent gynecologist. Over the next two decades, these organizations sponsored research that demonstrated the effectiveness of contraceptive practice and set the stage for the acceptance of contraceptive advice by the American Medical Association as a routine medical service in 1937. The Committee on Maternal Health published widely on the chemistry and physiology of contraception and successfully lobbied the Food and Drug Administration to impose standards on manufacturers of condoms. Sanger's systematic efforts to raise funds for contraceptive research led to the fundamental twentieth-century advance in technology: the use of synthetic hormones to prevent conception, primarily through the suppression of ovulation, first demonstrated by a research team led by Gregory Pincus of the Worcester Foundation for Experimental Biology in the 1950s, under the auspices of Sanger's financial angel Katharine Dexter McCormick. Pincus's technological innovation depended, however, upon the hormone concept and the systematic development of knowledge concerning the mammalian reproductive cycle, advances that were coordinated and heavily subsidized by the National Research Council's Committee for Research in Problems of Sex (1922), a prime beneficiary of John D. Rockefeller's Bureau of Social Hygiene and of the Rockefeller Foundation. Also essential were the availability of synthetic, and thus relatively inexpensive, analogues of the sex hormones. The first orally active analogue of progesterone was described by the steroid chemist Carl Djerassi in a 1951 patent application.

The rise of demography as an academic specialty and policy science reflected the concerns of social scientists and corporate philanthropists who did not share Sanger's desire to liberate all women from unwanted pregnancies but who did want to understand the declining fertility of the native-born white population of the United States and the differential fertility between social classes and ethnic groups. Concern over these vital trends led to the institutionalization of population study following World War I through the founding of the Scripps Foundation for Research in Population Problems (1922), the Research Division of the Milbank Memorial Fund (1928), the Population Association of America (1931), and the Office of Population Research at Princeton (1936). Frank Notestein and other social scientists associated with these organizations developed the theory of demographic transition which explained changing birthrates as a function of socioeconomic determinants. After World War II, Notestein served as a principal adviser to John D. Rockefeller III, whose concern over rapid population growth in the Third World led him to found the Population Council (1952) to promote both biomedical and demographic research in population control. The Population Council was the primary means through which government leaders and politicians were led to accept the importance of population research and the need for birth control programs. During the 1960s "the population problem" was redefined so that emphasis fell upon the carrying capacity of the earth rather than upon the dysgenic impact of differential fertility. Through the influence of corporate philanthropists, especially John D. Rockefeller Jr. and John D. Rockefeller III, the United States has been the world center of biomedical and social research, as well as technological innovation, concerning population control.

BIBLIOGRAPHY

Aberle, Sophie D., and George W. Corner. *Twenty-Five Years of Sex Research: History of the National Research Council Committee for Research in Problems of Sex, 1922–1947.* Philadelphia: Saunders, 1953.

Clarke, Adele E. *Disciplining Reproduction: Modernity, American Life Sciences, and "the Problem of Sex."* Berkeley: University of California Press, 1998.

Djerassi, Carl. *The Politics of Contraception.* New York: Norton, 1979.

Hodgson, Dennis G. "Demographic Transition Theory and the Family Planning Perspective: The Evolution of Theory within American Demography." Ph.D. diss., Cornell University, 1976.

Reed, James. *From Private Vice to Public Virtue: The Birth Control Movement and American Society since 1830.* New York: Basic, 1978.

James W. Reed

SEE ALSO
Sex and Sexuality

Bodley, Rachel Littler (1831–1888)

American chemist and botanist. Born in Cincinnati, Ohio, the third of five children of Rebecca (Talbott) and carpenter Anthony Bodley, she attended a private school in Cincinnati; Wesleyan Female College, Cincinnati (Classical diploma, 1849); and Polytechnic College, Philadelphia (1860). In 1862, Bodley returned to Cincinnati to teach at the Cincinnati Female Seminary, and in 1865 was appointed to the first chair of chemistry at the Female Medical College (later named the Woman's Medical College) in Philadelphia. In 1874, she became dean of the school. In addition to her work at the college, she was elected school director in Philadelphia's 29th School Section (1882–1885, 1887–1888) and was one of the women visitors appointed (1883) by the State Board of Public Charities to inspect local charitable institutions.

Bodley spent most of her time teaching chemistry and botany and in administrative duties. However, while teaching in Cincinnati, she classified and mounted an extensive collection of plants. At the Woman's Medical College, she continued to collect and classify plant materials, but made no theoretical scientific advances. Nevertheless, she was important in the history of women in science both for her teaching and because of a statistical study she conducted in 1881 concerning the careers of graduates of the Woman's Medical College. The study was published in pamphlet form as *The College Story,* and was one of the first collections of material about women and the professions. Two of her lectures have also been published.

Contemporaries of Bodley recognized her abilities by awarding her a number of honors. She was a member of the Academy of Natural Sciences of Philadelphia (1871), a corresponding member of the New York Academy of Sciences (1876), a charter member of the American Chemical Society (1876), and a member of the Franklin Institute (1880). She was awarded an honorary M.D. degree by the Woman's Medical College in 1879.

Bodley's honors, however, did not result from publications or theoretical breakthroughs, but were awarded for her competence in teaching chemistry and botany. As long as the history of science was concerned only with the history of ideas, Bodley was not included. H.J. Mozans, who incorporated a large number of women scientists into his *Women in Science* (1913), did not include Bodley. However, as the history of science began to take into account social history and feminist history, Bodley's importance has been recognized. Margaret Rossiter acknowledges her importance as the inspiration behind the formation of the American Chemical Society (p. 78); she is included in *Notable American Women* and in other works on American women scientists.

Bodley's special importance to the history of women in science was to establish an image of women in science. She did this through writing, teaching, participating in scientific societies, and delivering lectures.

BIBLIOGRAPHY
Alsop, Gulielma Fell. *History of the Woman's Medical College, Philadelphia, 1850–1950.* Philadelphia: Lippincott, 1950.

———. "Bodley, Rachel Littler." *Notable American Women,* edited by Edward T. James. Cambridge, MA: Harvard University Press, 1974, 1:186–187.

Bodley, Rachel Littler. *Catalogue of Plants Contained in Herbarium of Joseph Clark, Arranged According to the Natural System.* Cincinnati: R.P. Thompson, 1865.

———. *Introductory Lecture to the Class of the Woman's Medical College of Pennsylvania. Delivered at the Opening of the Nineteenth Annual Session, Oct. 15, 1868.* Philadelphia: Merrihew and Son, 1868.

———. *Valedictory Address to the 22nd Graduating Class of the Woman's Medical College of Pennsylvania, March 13, 1874.* Philadelphia: n.p., 1874.

Rossiter, Margaret. *Women Scientists in America: Struggles and Strategies to 1940.* Baltimore: Johns Hopkins University Press, 1982.

Marilyn B. Ogilvie

Bond, William Cranch (1789–1859)

Clockmaker and astronomer, born in Falmouth (now Portland), Maine, the son of Cornish immigrant

B

William Bond and his wife Hannah Cranch Bond. The elder Bond, a silversmith and watchmaker, set up a watch and jewelry business in Boston in 1793. The firm of William Bond & Son continued at different Boston locations until 1977.

William Cranch Bond is largely remembered as an astronomer, but he went to work at an early age for his father, and for most of his adult life, he earned a living in the family's business as a clock- and watchmaker. His astronomy was mostly self-taught, although he received some instruction as a teenager from Harvard's mathematics professor John Farrar and from New England's most famous self-taught astronomer Nathaniel Bowditch.

Bond married his cousin Selina Cranch in 1819, and they had four sons and two daughters. Selina died in 1831, and Bond married her sister Mary Roope Cranch.

About that time, the firm of William Bond & Son expanded from the watch and jewelry trade to include marine chronometers. Beginning in 1834, a series of contracts with the United States Navy gave Bond the opportunity to maintain ships' chronometers for the ports of Boston and Portsmouth. From 1838 to 1842, he received his first professional job as an astronomer, another contract with the navy to provide meteorological and astronomical observations for the United States Exploring Expedition under Charles Wilkes.

Late in 1839, Harvard's president Josiah Quincy convinced Bond to become the school's astronomer, but without a salary. When Bond's instruments proved inadequate for revealing the details of the dazzling comet of 1843, the wealthy citizens of Boston pooled their resources to build a formidable new observatory for the college and to equip it with a telescope equal to the world's largest at Pulkova Observatory, Russia. Bond received a professorship in astronomy, and both he and his son George, who worked closely with him, received modest salaries. Together they contributed new information about the physical features of planets, comets, and nebulae. The Bonds received international acclaim for their discoveries, which included a satellite of Saturn and the planet's "crepe" ring.

An emphasis on such discoveries ignores another more significant part of Bond's work during his twenty-year tenure as director of Harvard's Observatory. During that time, in the absence of an assertive fixed federal observatory, Harvard College Observatory helped meet the federal government's needs for basic positional astronomy. In addition to his early work with the navy, Bond worked with the United States Topographical Engineers on international boundary surveys and the Great Lakes Survey. For the United States Coast Survey he conducted numerous longitude campaigns, including transatlantic chronometer expeditions and the first international telegraphic determination between Halifax and Boston.

Also overlooked have been Bond's considerable successes in applying new technologies to astronomy. With his son George and Boston daguerreotypists John A. Whipple and William B. Jones, he helped pioneer celestial photography. The team took the first photograph ever made of a star in 1850. Under contract to the Coast Survey and under the supervision of the survey's Sears Cook Walker, Bond and his sons Richard and George improved devices for using the new American telegraph to determine longitude—a break-circuit device for attachment to the escapement of the clock and a drum chronograph for recording the instant of an astronomical event in a time scale. This technology made the everyday operations of longitude expeditions significantly easier, and for the first time, gave astronomers a way of recording observations with electricity. The Bonds promoted the apparatus they made for the Coast Survey at home and abroad, and at the London Crystal Palace Exhibition in 1851 they won a Council Medal, the exhibition's highest award. In December 1851, Bond started the world's first public time-service based on clock beats, telegraphed from Harvard's observatory. His principal clients for the service, which established a standard time in the region, were New England's railroads.

William Cranch Bond's papers relating to work at Harvard College Observatory are in the Harvard University Archives. Family memorabilia and papers relating to the firm of William Bond & Son are in the Collection of Historical Scientific Instruments, Harvard University. Two large collections of Bond artifacts survive at the Collection of Historical Scientific Instruments and at the National Museum of American History, Smithsonian Institution.

BIBLIOGRAPHY

Bailey, Solon I. *The History and Work of Harvard Observatory, 1839–1927.* New York: McGraw-Hill, 1931.

Bond, William Cranch. "History and Description of the Astronomical Observatory of Harvard College." *Annals of the Astronomical Observatory of Harvard College* 1, part 1 (1856).

———. "Observations of the Planet Saturn." *Annals of the Astronomical Observatory of Harvard College* 2, part 1 (1857).

Hoffleit, Dorrit. *Some Firsts in Astronomical Photography.* Cambridge, MA: Harvard College Observatory, 1950.

Holden, Edward S. *Memorials of William Cranch Bond and His Son George Phillips Bond.* New York, 1897.

Jones, Bessie Zaban, and Lyle Gifford Boyd. *The Harvard Observatory: The First Four Directorships, 1839–1919.* Cambridge, MA: Harvard University Press, 1971.

Stephens, Carlene E. "'The Most Reliable Time': William Bond, The New England Railroads, and Time Awareness in 19th-Century America." *Technology and Culture* 30 (1989): 1–24.

Carlene E. Stephens

Boston Philosophical Society

The first scientific society in America convened in Boston in the spring of 1683 and met fortnightly until perhaps 1688. Organized by Increase Mather, the Puritan divine and future president of Harvard College (1685–1701), the society was modeled after the Royal Society of London. Members hoped to lay the groundwork for improvements to natural history and natural philosophy. They collected specimens, shared observations of astronomical and physical phenomena, and likely cataloged cases of divine providence. It seems that meteorological observations made by the society were later incorporated into the *Curiosa Americana* that Cotton Mather sent to the Royal Society in 1712.

No records remain of its meetings. Information on membership and activities is inferred indirectly from diaries, letters, and published citations. In Boston, participants likely included Increase Mather, his sons Cotton and Nathaniel, Samuel Willard, William Avery, and Samuel Sewall. The society had at least one foreign correspondent, Wolferdus Senguerdius, a philosophy professor at the University of Leiden.

It is unknown why the society fizzled out. Cotton Mather blamed its decline on the tumultuous state of affairs in Boston when the colonial charter of Massachusetts was revoked by the crown. Preoccupied by politics and domestic necessities, few men had sufficient time and education to pursue scientific activities.

BIBLIOGRAPHY

Beall, Otho T. Jr. "Cotton Mather's Early 'Curiosa Americana' and the Boston Philosophical Society of 1683." *William and Mary Quarterly*, 3rd ser., 18 (1961): 360–372.

Mather, Cotton. *Parentator: Memoirs of Remarkables in the Life and Death of the Ever-Memorable Dr. Increase Mather.* Boston: Belknap, 1724.

Mather, Increase. "The Autobiography of Increase Mather." Edited by Michael G. Hall. *Proceedings of the American Antiquarian Society* 71 (1961): 271–360.

Senguerdius, Wolferdus. *Philosophia naturalis.* 2d ed. Leiden: Apud Danielem a Gaesbeeck, 1685.

Sara Schechner

Botanical Gardens

An ample area set aside for the growing and effective display of all the different kinds of worthy ornamental trees, shrubs, vines, and other plants which can be grown in a given area; with the responsibility for their maintenance, proper labeling, and study. The history of the modern botanic garden in America has shown that four main elements exist in greater or lesser degrees from the colonial period up to the present day: the utilitarian or economic; the aesthetic; the scientific; and the philanthropic.

From the earliest period of colonization, botanic gardens were founded in America under the auspices of various European courts and collectors interested in finding and cultivating new plants for food, medicine, and industry. The first botanical garden in America is often identified as that begun by John Bartram in Philadelphia in 1728; so-called because in addition to collecting and propagating, Bartram carried on early experimentation in plant breeding through cross-pollination. Bartram assembled a rich collection of native and imported plants and carried on extensive correspondence with botanists and collectors abroad. He was appointed the king's botanist in 1765. Through his efforts about 200 new species were brought into cultivation in America and abroad. Bartram's agent in England was Peter Collinson, who supplied the leading botanical collectors with plants sent from America. The fame of Bartram's garden grew and it became a popular site to visit when in the colonies.

Even after the Revolution, foreign botanists continued to come to the young republic in search of plants. For example, André Michaux on behalf of the French king, founded gardens in Charleston, South Carolina, and in Hoboken, New Jersey, from which he sent seeds and plants back to Europe.

Private gardens, such as The Woodlands and Lemon Hill in Philadelphia or Gore Place in Massachusetts,

B

belonged to proprietors with significant wealth, who established some of the early great botanical collections often coupled with a museum or collection of natural history objects. Thomas Jefferson sent much of the botanical material collected from the Lewis and Clark expedition of 1804–1806 to William Hamilton's The Woodlands. George Washington referred to a part of his garden at Mount Vernon where he experimented with new plants as his botanic garden.

The public botanic garden was promoted by Thomas Jefferson, George Washington, and John Quincy Adams at the founding of the new republic as an important government undertaking, requisite for the newly independent nation founded upon agrarian ideals. From the early national period, a succession of botanic gardens was established at the foot of Capitol Hill on the National Mall in Washington, D.C., where plants from all parts of the union were collected. In addition to the educational function of these botanic gardens, the naturalization and cultivation of useful plants underway there was recognized as essential to the welfare of the national economy.

The botanic garden has always served an important role in medical science. Throughout the eighteenth and early nineteenth centuries, when medical remedies derived from plants, botanic gardens were associated with medical institutions or universities such as the Elgin Gardens in New York City, founded in 1801 by David Hosack and affiliated with Columbia College. In 1805, Harvard University initiated a botanical garden in Cambridge. Also that year, the Medical Society of South Carolina announced its new botanic garden in Charleston. The Pennsylvania Hospital had one under the direction of Benjamin Smith Barton, who published the first botanic textbook in the United States, *Elements of Botany* (1803).

By the late nineteenth century, the botanic garden came to be seen as a tool of civic improvement, an essential urban ornament to a city and an integral part of the public park movement that was overtaking the country. It afforded orderly recreation and instruction of the public, while beautifying the cities. By the end of the century, there were approximately ten major public botanic gardens in America with international stature: the botanic garden of Harvard University; the Arnold Arboretum (also belonging to Harvard); the United States Department of Agriculture Gardens; the Missouri Botanical Garden; Michigan Agricultural College Gardens; the botanical gardens of the University of

California at Berkeley, the University of Pennsylvania, and Smith College; Buffalo Botanical Garden; and the New York Botanical Garden.

In the twentieth century, an increasing number of botanic gardens have been established, in different regions of the country, representing different climatic conditions where the plants hardy in any area may be grown. For example, the Fairchild Tropical Garden in Coconut Grove, Florida (1939) contains one of the largest palm and cycad collections in the world. The Huntington Botanical Garden in San Marino, California (1905) has given special attention to acclimatizing plants from arid and semiarid countries. Environmental awareness and ecological urgency have challenged late-twentieth-century botanic gardens to address issues of ecosystems studies, conservation, and sustainable economies in shaping the direction of their research and programs of education.

Two areas of scientific activity integrally related to the role of botanic gardens in America are botanical exploration and the dissemination of information through publication. The major botanic gardens support expeditions of trained botanists around the world in search of new plants. The tasks of describing and classifying the new plants depends upon access to living collections and herbaria and communication with the worldwide network of botanists.

There exists a sizeable primary and secondary literature on the history of botanic gardens in America, although in many cases it occurs in correspondence, journals, pamphlets, and periodicals. Recent monographs on the major botanical gardens such as the Arnold Arboretum, the Huntington, the New York, and the Missouri botanical gardens has contributed to the general literature on the subject. Because of the interdisciplinary nature of botanic gardens, scientific, aesthetic, and didactic in their mission, the scholarship is scattered in the literature of many fields and much of it is nonbotanical. Individual private gardens of architectural note, such as Shaw's garden in St. Louis or The Woodlands, have received attention from art historians. Gardens associated with important historical figures also have been investigated, such as David Hosack's Elgin Gardens, or John Quincy Adams's arboretum at the White House. An important resource for information about the history of American botanical gardens are the numerous serial publications, both domestic and foreign, founded in the nineteenth century. Botanical, gardening, and general science periodicals, such as

Silliman's *The American Journal of Science and Arts,* Downing's *The Horticulturalist,* or Charles Sprague Sargent's *Garden and Forest,* often contain invaluable material on botanical gardens and their activities.

BIBLIOGRAPHY

Britton, N.L. "Address on Botanical Gardens." *Bulletin of the New York Botanical Garden* 1 (1886–1900): 62–77.

Darlington, William. *Memorials of John Bartram and Humphrey Marshall. With Notices of their Botanical Contemporaries.* Philadelphia, 1849.

Hill, A.W. "The History and Functions of Botanic Gardens." *Annals of the Missouri Botanical Garden* 11 (1915): 185–240.

O'Malley, Therese. "'Your Garden Must be a museum to you': Early American Botanical Gardens." In *Art and Science in America: Issues of Representation,* edited by Amy R.W. Meyers. San Marino, CA: Huntington Library, 1998, pp. 35–59.

Punch, Walter, ed. *Keeping Eden: A History of Gardening in America.* Boston: Bulfinch Press, 1992.

Rafinesque, Constantine. "Notes on the Lecture on the Botanical Garden of Lexington Kentucky, Delivered on February, 1824." Manuscript in the American Philosophical Society, Philadelphia.

Reveal, James L. *Gently Conquest.* Washington, DC: Starwood Publishing, 1992.

Spongberg, Stephen A. *A Reunion of Trees.* Cambridge, MA: Harvard University Press, 1990.

Stannard, Jerry. "Early American Botany and Its Sources." In *Bibliography and Natural History: Essays Presented at a Conference Convened in June 1964,* edited by Thomas R. Buckman. Lawrence: University of Kansas Libraries, 1966, pp. 74–102.

Tanner, Ogden, and Adele Auchincloss. *The New York Botanical Garden.* New York: Walker and Company, 1991.

Waterhouse, Benjamin. *The Botanist.* Boston: Joseph T. Buckingham, 1811.

Wilbert, M.I. "Some Early Botanical and Herb Gardens." *American Journal of Pharmacy,* (September 1908): 412–427.

Wyman, Donald. "The Arboretums and Botanical Gardens of North America." *Chronica Botanica* 10 (1947): 395–482.

Therese O'Malley

SEE ALSO
Missouri Botanical Garden; New York Botanical Garden, The

Botanical Society of America

The professional organization of American botanists. The Botanical Society of America (BSA) originated from the Botany Club of the American Association for the Advancement of Science (AAAS). The original membership of the BSA was a group of twenty-five charter members elected at the 1893 meeting of the club to organize the society. The early leadership included such luminaries as Liberty Hyde Bailey, Charles E. Bessey, Charles Singer Sargent, and both Nathaniel and Elizabeth Britton. The group took as its mission "advancing research" and elected its membership accordingly, deliberately excluding prominent botanists who were not engaged in research at the time and setting strict expectations about continued research and attendance at meetings.

On 27 December 1906, at the annual meeting of the AAAS, the BSA merged with the Society for Plant Morphology and Physiology (founded in 1896) and the American Mycological Society (founded in 1903) combining memberships to yield a base of 119 members. The BSA grew slowly in its early years. By 1956, however, its membership approached 2,000 and today stands at 2,600. True to its early mission, the BSA has been active in promoting research. Its publications, especially the *American Journal of Botany* and the *Plant Science Bulletin,* have been major organs for the work of American botanists. *The American Journal of Botany,* created in 1914 to provide a journal that would publish both research and reviews, is America's leading botanical journal and one of the leading botanical journals in the world. *Plant Science Bulletin,* created in 1955, provides a monthly digest of brief research notes and botanical news of interest to professionals, amateurs, and teachers, allowing the *American Journal of Botany* to focus on research.

Regrettably, the Botanical Society of America awaits its historian.

BIBLIOGRAPHY

Overfield, Richard A. *Science with Practice: Charles E. Bessey and the Maturing of American Botany.* Ames: Iowa State University, 1993.

Tippo, Oswald. "The Early History of the Botanical Society of America." In *Fifty Years of Botany,* edited by William Campbell Steere. New York: McGraw-Hill, 1958, pp. 1–13.

Elizabeth Keeney

Botany

Following the European discovery of North America, there was great interest in collecting and cataloging its

B

flora (as well as other aspects of its natural history). Hope of discovering spices, medicines, food stuffs, timber sources, and other economically beneficial plant products coupled with scientific curiosity drove this movement. One result was a dramatic increase in the number of plant species known to European botanists, which threw plant systematics into crisis. Linneaus—who had received specimens and observations from both his own collector, Peter Kalm, and from colonists—developed his binomial nomenclature and his artificial method of classification as a direct result of this crisis. They were, arguably, the eighteenth century's greatest botanical accomplishments.

As colonists settled, they found that Europeans were interested in receiving both their botanical observations and plant specimens, whether live or preserved. A small circle of naturalists, many in contact with each other as well as with Europeans, emerged during the eighteenth century, spread up and down the Eastern seaboard. In Philadelphia, John Bartram established the continent's first botanic garden in 1728, filling it with specimens he and his son William collected locally and on expeditions to sights as far as Florida. As they cataloged the new land's flora, John and William Bartram, John Clayton, Cadwalleder Colden, and others laid the groundwork for the great synthetic works of the nineteenth century.

During the antebellum period, there emerged a new class of botanists, known derisively as "closet botanists," who, like their European predecessors, worked from the specimens collected by American naturalists rather than (or, in reality, more often in addition to) doing fieldwork of their own. John Torrey and Asa Gray in particular made huge strides in developing comprehensive floras of North America as they worked from specimens and observations contributed by vast networks of Americans spread throughout the country. In addition, they were able to draw upon the work being produced by explorations and surveys of the West and of many states being done by private interests (particularly railroad and canal companies) and by the state and federal governments. What their works lacked by being based largely on the work of others, they more than made up for in the comprehensiveness that resulted from a database no individual could possibly have amassed. As they worked, they faced a crisis not unlike that of Linneaus—that the system of classification in use was no longer equal to the task—and introduced de Jussieu's natural system of classification to America. This "big picture" enabled Gray to begin to draw conclusions about the geographical distribution of species, work which deserves to be considered the first great American contribution to botany.

In part driven by his desire to broaden the base of collectors and observers, Gray did more to popularize botany as a primary and secondary school subject and a recreational activity than any other American. While his scholarly publications alone earned him a place in the history of botany, so too would his textbooks and his vast correspondence with amateurs throughout the country, advising and encouraging them in their botanical pursuits. By the mid-nineteenth century, botany was a standard curriculum item in secondary education, and thousands of Americans, male and female, botanized for fun.

In the wake of the Civil War and of the publication of Charles Darwin's *The Origin of Species,* botany, like other scientific disciplines, began to become professionalized. Botanical societies that had happily included amateur and professional side by side were first joined and then supplanted by groups like the Botanical Society of America, whose membership was limited to those who were producing research of the highest quality. Similarly, journals that included contributions and news of both amateurs and professionals were replaced by scholarly works that editorialized about the necessity of maintaining "standards." At the same time, botany itself was undergoing a transformation from a branch of natural history to a branch of biology. Jobs for botanists with college and eventually university degrees began to emerge in higher education, in the government, and occasionally in business.

As the twentieth century dawned, understanding of plant science, especially physiology and genetics, began to revolutionize agriculture. At the land-grant universities, botanists like Charles Bessey were discovering and popularizing new techniques for breeding and growing crops that would make farming a science.

One of the first areas of botany to become professionalized had been ecology, in which the field became a laboratory. Suddenly the standards for observation changed and the notion of relying on an untrained amateur whose observations one might manipulate was unacceptable. In this area of botany, the transformation from natural history to biology was rapid and complete. In the post–World War II era, botany has been dramatically altered by computers and other technology. In the case of taxonomy, once a field in which

B

all one required was a hand lens or simple microscope, botanists now are dependent upon sophisticated systematic, biogeographic and ecological databases based on, among other things, molecular genetics. These databases promise to yield the same magnitude of revolution that emerged from the "closet botanists."

Molecular genetics, a field made possible by technological advances, illustrates another major trend in recent years; the tendency of biologists no longer to divide themselves into botanists and zoologists but rather into cellular and organismic biologists. Molecular botanists have more in common with other cellular biologists than with, for example, plant ecologists. In recent years, molecular botany has yielded new insights into the process of flowering and into the question of whether evolution occurs in a slow and uniform fashion or with periodic leaps and bounds.

Botanical education in America began as a happenstance, find-it-where-you-can mix of courses in medical schools and occasionally the liberal arts curriculum, mentoring relationships, and the school of experience. During the nineteenth century, botany became a popular school subject and as a result entered the college curriculum. In the wake of the Civil War, botany found a home in the land-grant colleges, with botanical research and education being touted as an adjunct to agriculture. Today, botany finds its academic homes under the wings of biology, ecology, molecular biology, agriculture, genetics, and a host of other fields, but rarely as a freestanding enterprise.

Over the years, botanists have developed professional societies and journals dedicated to botany and its subfields that serve as the major vehicles of communication. Comprehensive societies like the Botanical Society of America stand alongside groups with narrower scholarly or geographic focus. Their organs—for example the Botanical Society of America's *American Journal of Botany*—and some that are not affiliated with societies have and do serve the botanical community, the wider scientific community, and the dedicated layperson. Scientific research on plants has, of course, always had its share of space in general scientific journals, for example *Science,* and as the division between botany and zoology assumes less utility, that trend increases. In the past decade, electronic communication has added a host of new modes of communication—E-mail, electronic journals, bulletin boards, and discussion groups—that have dramatically increased the speed of communication.

BIBLIOGRAPHY

Bunch, Bryan. *Handbook of Current Science & Technology.* New York: Henry Holt, 1992.

Davis, Elisabeth B. *Guide to Information Sources in the Botanical Sciences.* Littleton, CO: Libraries Unlimited, 1987.

Dupree, A. Hunter. *Asa Gray: American Botanist, Friend of Darwin.* Cambridge, MA: Harvard University Press, 1959; reprint, Baltimore: Johns Hopkins University Press, 1989.

Keeney, Elizabeth B. *The Botanizers: Amateur Scientists in Nineteenth-Century America.* Chapel Hill: University of North Carolina Press, 1992.

Elizabeth Keeney

Bowditch, Henry Pickering (1840–1911)

Physiologist and medical educator. Henry Pickering Bowditch, the son of affluent Boston merchant Jonathan I. Bowditch, graduated from Harvard College in 1861. After serving in the Civil War, he entered the Harvard Medical School, where his interest in experimental medicine was kindled by the peripatetic physiologist Charles-Eduoard Brown-Sèquard. Following graduation in 1869, Bowditch went abroad, where he studied with Claude Bernard in Paris and Carl Ludwig at the new Leipzig Physiological Institute. Under Ludwig's supervision, Bowditch performed experiments in cardiac physiology that led to two important discoveries: the "treppe" phenomenon and the "all-or-none law" of muscular contraction.

While Bowditch was in Europe, Charles Eliot was elected president of Harvard and major curricular changes were introduced at the Harvard Medical School. Eliot invited Bowditch to return to Harvard "to take part in the good work of reforming medical education" (quoted in Bowditch to Eliot, 21 April 1871, Eliot Papers, Harvard University Archives). In 1872, the young physiologist returned to Boston imbued with the research ethic and committed to a career in medical science. He brought back sophisticated laboratory apparatus and inaugurated at Harvard a program of research and graduate education in advanced physiology.

Although Bowditch's laboratory was very modest at the outset—two attic rooms—his appointment represented the beginning of university support for the full-time medical scientist whose role was to combine research with teaching. Bowditch opened his laboratory to colleagues and advanced students who shared

B

his enthusiasm for experimental medicine. Papers based on their investigations began to appear regularly in the medical and scientific literature. Acknowledging the growing importance of research and laboratory teaching, Harvard constructed a spacious, well-equipped physiological laboratory building in 1883.

Bowditch's publications reflected his broad interests and included studies of neurophysiology, anthropometry, and medical education. He served as dean of the Harvard Medical School for a decade beginning in 1883. Due in large part to Bowditch and to H. Newell Martin of Johns Hopkins, physiology was emerging as a discipline in America at this time. Bowditch played a crucial role in founding the American Physiological Society in 1887 and served as its first president. His physiology department thrived during the final years of the nineteenth century. Many ambitious and productive investigators worked there and several assumed important positions at other institutions.

By 1900, Bowditch had withdrawn from teaching in the Department of Physiology. He remained active in the affairs of the university and helped secure a gift in excess of $1 million from J. Pierpont Morgan in 1901 to improve the facilities of the medical school. The closing years of Bowditch's life were marked by progressive disability from Parkinson's disease.

As a teacher, investigator, and educational reformer, Bowditch was among the most influential medical scientists of his generation. His career was a model for the introduction of the full-time faculty system into American medical education.

BIBLIOGRAPHY

Bowditch, Henry P. *The Life and Writings of Henry Pickering Bowditch.* 2 vols. New York: Arno Press, 1980.

Cannon, Walter B. "Henry Pickering Bowditch." *Biographical Memoirs of the National Academy of Sciences* 17 (1922): 181–196.

Fye, W. Bruce. "Why a Physiologist? The Case of Henry P. Bowditch." *Bulletin of the History of Medicine* 56 (1982): 19–29.

———. *The Development of American Physiology: Scientific Medicine in the Nineteenth Century.* Baltimore: Johns Hopkins University Press, 1987.

W. Bruce Fye

Bowditch, Nathaniel (1773–1838)

First American to master celestial mechanics. He grew up in a seafaring family in Salem, Massachusetts. After three years of schooling, he was apprenticed to a ship's chandler and served until he was twenty-one. He made five voyages as a mate, supercargo, and on the last, as part owner and captain. From 1804 until 1823, he was the president of the Essex Fire and Marine Insurance Company in Salem. From 1823 until his death in 1838, he was the actuary of the Massachusetts Hospital Life Insurance Company in Boston. He was a member of the Board of Overseers for Harvard University from 1810 until 1825, when he became a Fellow of the Corporation, serving to his death.

Bowditch devoted his leisure to the study of natural philosophy. He began studying Newton's *Principia* at age sixteen while still an apprentice in Salem. He continued his studies on the long sea voyages. On his last, from 1802 to 1803, he began working through Laplace's *Mécanique Céleste,* an effort he continued until 1814. In that year, he began preparing an English translation of the work with his commentary. It was finished in 1817, but he did not begin publishing it until 1828, when he could afford to do so at his own expense.

Bowditch was devoted to understanding how the world worked. He did it in isolation without colleagues, working through texts. Bowditch claimed no great originality, though he discovered Lissajou Patterns before Lissajou did. He did not wish to teach, turning down the Hollis Professorship at Harvard in 1806, a professorship at the University of Virginia in 1818 offered by Thomas Jefferson, and one at the United States Military Academy.

Bowditch published in *The Analyst* and *The Mathematical Diary* conducted by Robert Adrain. The publications in the latter journal were used by American mathematicians Robert Adrain, Henry James Anderson, Bowditch, Eugenius Nulty, and Theodore Strong for a discussion of Lagrangian dynamics in the late 1820s and early 1830s. Bowditch's more formal publications were mainly in the *Memoirs of the American Academy of Arts and Sciences* and in the *North American Review.*

After 1828, Bowditch devoted much of his leisure to the publication of the *Mécanique Céleste* translation. In those years, he encouraged younger men, such as Benjamin Peirce, who read proof for the translation, and Charles Francis McCay at the University of Georgia.

Bowditch's reputation was initially exaggerated after he died. He did not consider himself the "Laplace of America," though eulogies called him that. He was also highly respected as the author of *The New American*

B

Practical Navigator. The work was a commercial effort, one of his sources of income. He was subsequently denigrated as an amateur by the succeeding generation concerned with the professionalization of American science. In recent years, there has been interest in Bowditch's place as a Boston financier (Story).

Bowditch left no personal diaries of his inner thoughts. Before he died, he destroyed personal papers. The Boston Public Library collection of his manuscripts and scientific books contains mostly formal set pieces.

BIBLIOGRAPHY

Archibald, Raymond Clare. "Bowditch, Nathaniel."*Dictionary of American Biography.* Edited by Allen Johnson. New York: Scribners, 1929, 2:496–498.

Berry, Robert. *Yankee Stargazer.* New York: McGraw Hill, 1941.

Campbell, John F. *History and Bibliography of The New American Practical Navigator and The American Coastal Pilot.* Salem: Peabody Museum, 1964.

Greene, John C. *American Science in the Age of Jefferson.* Ames: The Iowa State University Press, 1984.

Montgomery, James W. Jr., and Laura V. Monti, eds. *The Papers of Nathaniel Bowditch in the Boston Public Library: Guide to the Microfilm Edition.* Boston: Boston Public Library, 1983.

Peabody Museum. *A Catalogue of a Special Exhibition of Manuscripts, Books, Portraits and Personal Relics of Nathaniel Bowditch (1773–1838): with a Sketch of the Life of Nathaniel Bowditch by Dr. Harold Bowditch, and an Essay on the Scientific Achievement of Nathaniel Bowditch, with a Bibliography of His Publications by Professor Raymond Clare Archibald.* Salem: Peabody Museum, 1937.

Rothenberg, Marc. "Bowditch, Nathaniel." *American National Biography,* edited by John A. Garraty and Mark C. Carnes. New York: Oxford University Press, 1999, 3:270–272.

Story, Ronald. *The Forging of an Aristocracy: Harvard & the Boston Upper Class, 1800–1870.* Wesleyan, CT: Wesleyan University Press, 1980.

James W. Montgomery Jr.

Bowman, Isaiah (1878–1950)

Geographer, born in the Canadian town of Berlin (later renamed Kitchener), Ontario. The family relocated in Brown City, Michigan, when Isaiah was eight weeks of age.

At the age of twenty-two, Bowman began a distinguished undergraduate career at Ypsilanti's Normal College. There he studied under Mark Jefferson in an institution later referred to as "the nursery of american geography." Jefferson recognized Bowman's abilities and sent him to Harvard, where he studied under William Morris Davis; there he was awarded a B.S. degree in 1905. He had taught at Ypsilanti's Normal College, and had undertaken work for the United States Geological Survey, when Herbert E. Gregory, himself a one-time student of Davis, invited Bowman to join the Geology-Geography Department at Yale University. Bowman accepted the invitation and remained there until 1915. At Yale, Bowman offered some of the earliest regional geography courses in North America, and began to specialize in the geography of Latin America. He made three field trips to South America in 1907, 1911, and 1913. This meant eighteen months in the field and 2,000 miles by muleback. During these ten years, he published twenty articles and four books, and received a Ph.D. degree in 1909 (from Yale University).

In the summer of 1915, he assumed the directorship of the American Geographical Society. His twenty years with the Geographical Society were significant ones for the cause of geography. He developed the library and map holdings, strengthened the society's publication (*The Geographical Review*), and housed "The Inquiry" (a euphemism for a host of activities preparatory to negotiating the peace following World War I). The three large research themes he initiated included commencement of a map of Hispanic America on the scale 1:1 million; research on the theme of pioneer settlement; and encouragement of polar research, especially the work of Louise Boyd, Richard E. Byrd, Robert A. Bartlett, Lincoln Ellsworth, Douglas Mawson, Fridtjof Nansen, Knud Rasmussen, Vilhjalmur Stefansson, and Hubert Wilkins. The results of his research program were, in part, published in a Research Series and Special Publications of the society. Their swath of excellence was noted by an international audience.

In July 1935, Bowman took office as the fifth president of Johns Hopkins University. He raised funds, created departments of geography and oceanography, published a considerable amount of geographical material, and gave numerous addresses to a variety of distinguished bodies.

His advice concerning the establishment of geography was sought by more than 100 colleges and universities. All this was done notwithstanding the three days a week he spent in the United States State Department

B

acting as special adviser to Secretary Cordell Hull, and his service on the political and policy committees of the department and as chairman of its Territorial Committee. He was a member of the Stettinius mission to London (1944), a member of the American delegation at the Dumbarton Oaks Conference on World Peace and Security (1944), and adviser to the secretary of state at the United Nations Conference on International Organization at San Francisco (1945). He also advised President Franklin D. Roosevelt on numerous occasions. Following the war, he sought retirement from both the university and government. He retired from the university in 1948, and although he reduced his work with government, he was an active adviser to the Economic Cooperation Administration at the time of his death.

Bowman was one of the more prolific American geographers of the twentieth century. He wrote 12 books, more than 180 articles, and numerous book reviews and notes, especially for *The Geographical Review.* (Of his books, perhaps the best known were *Forest Physiography* (1911), *The Andes of Southern Peru* (1916), *The New World* (1921), *The Pioneer Fringe* (1931), and *Geography in Relation to the Social Sciences* (1934). He received thirteen honorary degrees (he declined fifteen more), nine honorary fellowships, six medals, and the presidencies of the Association of American Geographers (1931), the International Geographical Union (1931–1934), and the American Association for the Advancement of Science (1943).

BIBLIOGRAPHY
Martin, Geoffrey J. *The Life and Thought of Isaiah Bowman.* Hamden, CT: Archon Books, 1980.
Wright, John K., and George F. Carter. "Isaiah Bowman." *Biographical Memoirs of the National Academy of Sciences* 33 (1959): 41–42.
Wrigley, Gladys M. "Isaiah Bowman." *The Geographical Review* 41 (1951): 7–65.

Geoffrey J. Martin

Bridgman, Percy Williams (1882–1961)

Physicist and philosopher of science. He was the founder of the field of high-pressure physics, for which he was awarded the Nobel Prize in 1946, and the the originator of the methodological interpretation of scientific concepts known as operationism or operationalism.

Educated at Harvard University, where he received his B.A. (1904), M.A. (1905), and Ph.D. (1908),

Bridgman spent his entire professional career there, becoming emeritus in 1954. Bridgman's practice of physics exemplified the experimental style characteristic of American science. His research program was directed toward measuring the physical properties of matter under high pressures. The success of Bridgman's program was the result of his ingenuity in designing equipment for the production and containment of high pressures and devising techniques for its measurement, together with advances in industrial materials technology.

Bridgman's career as a physicist spanned a period of great change in the theoretical content of physics and in the sociopolitical importance of pure research in the United States. Not only was he witness to the advent of Einstein's theory of relativity and the birth of quantum mechanics, both of which undermined the accepted Newtonian picture of physical reality, he also experienced the transformation of basic physics from a small scale, relatively autonomous individual activity to large-scale government-sponsored team research—big science.

Bridgman welcomed none of these changes. Indeed, his operational interpretation of physical reality—not without contradiction—was both an adjustment to and a defense against the revolutionary implications of relativity theory. It was a strategy intended to save the empirical and inductivist foundation of physics and, at the same time, accommodate what he perceived as the "anti-metaphysical" lesson of Einstein's discussion of measurement in the 1905 paper on special relativity. Bridgman believed that his operational method was an extension of Einstein's scientific epistemology, which if rigorously applied would purify science of metaphysics. Science would thus be protected against further revolution and the continuous progressive growth of scientific knowledge would be ensured.

Nevertheless, Bridgman was never able to accept Einstein's general theory of relativity, which he thought represented a betrayal of the empirical principles embodied in special relativity. Nor did he ever master quantum mechanics, which abruptly superseded his own attempt to formulate a theory of metallic conduction. Bridgman felt left behind by the rapid theoretical change in physics and conceded expertise to the next generation of American physicists, among which were his own students, J.R. Oppenheimer, J.C. Slater, and J.H. Van Vleck. Although disappointed, he rationalized this turn of events as evidence of scientific progress—of an increase in scientific genius.

Bridgman's attitude toward big science was not as generous. He regarded it not as the result of progress, but rather as an indication of the degradation of democracy. He believed that science should be done for its own sake—for the pursuit of truth. To subordinate science to economic and political goals was to compromise the intellectual integrity of the scientist and to sacrifice the very freedom upon which scientific progress depended. Accordingly, at the beginning of World War II (1939), he closed his laboratory to citizens of totalitarian states, on the grounds that such individuals were not free. Similarly, in 1943, he opposed the adoption of a formal national science policy, arguing that it would make science a servant of the state—that it invited control of science by government.

Bridgman's belief in the absolute moral worth of pure science—his belief that the search for scientific truth is in itself a service to humanity—was one often expressed by scientists before the two world wars demonstrated the strategic national utility of pure physics. If today this viewpoint is generally regarded as idealistic, even naive, the contrast serves to illustrate how much social attitudes toward science have changed throughout the course of the twentieth century.

BIBILOGRAPHY

Reingold, Nathan, and Ida H. Reingold. *Science in America: A Documentary History, 1900–1939.* Chicago: The University of Chicago Press, 1981.

Walter, Maila L. *Science and Cultural Crisis: An Intellectual Biography of Percy Williams Bridgman (1882–1961).* Stanford: Stanford University Press, 1990.

Maila L. Walter

Britton, Elizabeth Gertrude Knight (1858–1934)

Bryologist; first curator of mosses at the New York Botanical Garden, founder and editor of botanical journals. Elizabeth Britton spent much of her childhood in Cuba, where her family was in the sugar and furniture businesses. She was a graduate of Hunter College (then the New York Normal School) where she later taught. In 1879, she was the first woman admitted to membership in the Torrey Botanical Club, where she met her husband, botanist Nathaniel Lord Britton. They were married in 1885. Elizabeth Britton was the only woman among the twenty-five charter members of the American Botanical Society in 1893, elected on the basis of her many botanical publications. The majority of these were in bryology, the study of mosses, liverworts, and hornworts.

After her marriage, she became editor of the still extant *Bulletin of the Torrey Botanical Club* from 1886 to 1888. The Brittons visited the Royal Botanical Gardens at Kew in 1888, and on their return, Elizabeth Britton introduced the idea of a major botanical garden in New York to the Torrey Botanical Club. By 1891, the New York State Legislature chartered such a garden, Elizabeth Britton led a group of wealthy New York women to collect an endowment of $250,000 for the establishment of the New York Botanical Garden on 250 acres in Bronx Park. Her husband became director-in-chief in 1896. In 1899, she became curator of bryophytes at the garden; from 1912 until her death she held the official position honorary curator of mosses. She was unpaid, but it was an important and influential position, enabling her to carry on negotiations for the purchase of European herbaria, to travel widely to collect specimens for the garden's herbarium, and to supervise a doctoral student and garden employees. She was instrumental in founding the Sullivant Moss Society (now the American Bryological and Lichenological Society) and its journal, the *Bryologist,* of which she was an editor. She also edited the *Journal of the Torrey Botanical Club.* Altogether, she published 346 papers and reviews, largely on mosses.

During the winter months, Elizabeth Britton traveled to the Bahamas, Cuba, Puerto Rico, and elsewhere in the West Indies with her husband. He studied the flowering plants; she studied the bryophytes. She also traveled in Europe visiting herbaria, and collected extensively in the Adirondack Mountains of New York. She carried on a voluminous correspondence with bryologists and other botanists around the world. In her later years, Elizabeth Britton turned her energies to wildflower preservation and spoke and wrote articles on that subject.

Seventeen plants and one animal were named for Elizabeth Britton. Despite her many papers on mosses, the definitive books in the field were written by her graduate student, A. Joel Grout. Britton's correspondence, botanical collections, and her collected papers are at the New York Botanical Garden.

BIBLIOGRAPHY

Britton, Elizabeth G. Collected papers on mosses, 1887–1925. 1 vol., New York Botanical Garden.

B

———. Collected papers on wildflower preservation, 13 parts. 1 vol., New York Botanical Garden.

Howe, Marshall A. "Elizabeth Gertrude Britton." *Journal of the New York Botanical Garden* 35 (1934): 97–105.

Merrill, Elmer D. "Nathaniel Lord Britton." *Biographical Memoirs of the National Academy of Sciences* 19 (1938): 147–202.

Slack, Nancy G. "Nineteenth-Century American Women Botanists: Wives, Widows, and Work." In *Uneasy Careers and Intimate Lives; Women in Science 1789–1979,* edited by Pnina G. Abir-Am and Dorinda Outram. New Brunswick: Rutgers University Press, 1987, pp. 77–103.

Steers, William C. "Britton, Elizabeth Gertrude Knight." In *Notable American Women,* edited by Edward T. James, Janet Wilson, and Paul W. Boyer. Cambridge, MA: Harvard University Press, 1971, 3:243–244.

Tanner, Ogden, and Adele Auchincloss. *The New York Botanical Garden: An Illustrated Chronicle of Plants and People.* New York: Walker and Co., 1991.

Nancy G. Slack

Britton, Nathaniel Lord (1859–1934)

Botanist who led the establishment and development of the New York Botanical Garden, and author of important botanical works. Nathaniel Lord Britton was born in Staten Island, New York, and graduated from the School of Mines of Columbia College in 1879. He was a student of John Strong Newberry, professor of geology and mineralogy, but was largely self-taught in botany. Britton was an early member of the Torrey Botanical Club and coauthored a flora of Richmond County in 1879. He worked as botanist and assistant geologist for the New Jersey Geological Survey. In 1881, he received a doctorate from Columbia; his thesis was based on his "Preliminary Catalogue of the flora of New Jersey." In 1887, he was appointed instructor in botany and geology, and by 1891 was made professor of botany. At thirty-seven he became professor of botany emeritus at Columbia when he was named director-in-chief of the newly established New York Botanical Garden in 1896.

He married Elizabeth Gertrude Knight (Britton), also a botanist and first woman member of the Torrey Botanical Club, in 1885. Together they were instrumental in founding the New York Botanical Garden. A charter was granted in 1891 authorizing the setting aside of 250 acres of park land in the Bronx on the condition that $250,000 could be raised by private subscription. Britton himself had only a minor fortune, but his friendship with Vanderbilt, Carnegie, and Morgan, and others of New York's elite enabled him and his wife to raise the money. The garden was closely affiliated with Columbia University where Britton remained an ex-officio professor of botany. The university donated its herbarium and library to the garden in return for graduate instruction and research facilities. Britton made the garden into a research institution and a major American botanical center, supervising the construction of laboratories, hiring staff, and establishing journals for the publication of research findings.

Britton was the major champion of a new "Rochester" or "American" code of nomenclature in opposition to the current international code. Its main provision was a strict application of the principle of priority of publication. It was supported by the Torrey Botanical Club and the 1892 American Association for the Advancement of Science meeting in Rochester, but was opposed by Charles Sprague Sargent, director of the Arnold Arboretum and by western American botanists. Britton was at the center of often vitriolic controversy. The 1905 International Congress did not adopt the American (Rochester) code, but Britton and his colleagues continued to use it in their taxonomic publications.

Britton, together with Judge Addison Brown, who funded it, produced the first illustrated flora for any part of North America (*Illustrated Flora of the Northern United States and Canada.* 3 vols, 1896–1898, 2d ed. 1913). It was reissued six times until 1947, and a revised edition of this book by Henry A. Gleason (1952) is still in use. Other important Britton publications, in addition to several hundred published papers, are *North American Trees* with J.A. Shafer (1908), *Flora of Bermuda* (1918), *The Bahama Flora* (with C.F. Millspaugh, 1920), and *Botany of Porto Rico and the Virgin Islands* (with P. Wilson, 1923–1930). *The Cactaceae* (with J.N. Rose, 1919–1923), a four-volume illustrated monograph, is probably his most important taxonomic work.

Expeditions to the Philippines, the West Indies, and South America were carried out by the New York Botanical Garden under Britton's directorship. He and Elizabeth Britton made many botanical exploration trips themselves, to the West Indies, Cuba, and elsewhere. Also under his direction, floras were written for many parts of the United States and new journals were established including the *Journal, Bulletin,* and *Memoirs* of the garden and *Mycologia* and *Addisonia.* Seventy-four parts of the *North American Flora* were published. In the thirty-three years of Britton's directorship, the New York Botanical Garden grew from 250 acres of undeveloped land to 400 acres of specialized gardens, laboratories, museum, greenhouses, and offices. The library grew to 43,000 volumes and the herbarium to nearly 2 million specimens from all over the world. Fungi, mosses, and plant fossils were included in the collections; Britton developed paleobotany as a research specialty at the garden. He retired as director in 1929.

Britton received many honors, among them election to the National Academy of Sciences in 1914, the American Philosophical Society in 1928, and as a foreign member of the Linnean Society of London in 1925. He was a charter member of the American Botanical Society in 1893 and its president in 1898 and 1921. He was president of the New York Academy of Science in 1907. Mount Britton in Luquillo National Park in Puerto Rico was named for him, as were six genera and sixty-nine species and varieties of plants, including fossil plants. The garden's journal *Brittonia* was started in 1931. His major legacy, however, is the New York Botanical Garden itself, one of the most important American botanical institutions today.

BIBLIOGRAPHY

Britton, Nathaniel L. *Manual of the Flora of the Northern States and Canada.* New York: New York Botanical Garden, 1901; 2d ed., 1905.

———. Accounts of various families in *North American Flora.* New York: New York Botanical Garden, 1905–1930.

———. *Flora of Bermuda.* New York: New York Botanical Garden, 1918.

Britton, Nathaniel L., and Addison Brown. *Illustrated Flora of the Northern United States, Canada, and the British Possessions from Newfoundland to the Parallel of the Southern Boundary of Virginia and from the Atlantic Ocean Westward to the 102nd Meridian.* 3 vols. New York: New York Botanical Garden, 1896–1898; 2d ed., 1913.

Britton, Nathaniel L., and Charles F. Millspaugh. *The Bahama Flora.* New York: New York Botanical Garden, 1920.

Britton, Nathaniel L., and J.N. Rose. *The Cactaceae.* 4 vols. Washington, DC: Carnegie Institution of Washington, 1919–1923.

Britton, Nathaniel L., and John A. Shafer. *North American Trees.* New York: New York Botanical Garden, 1908.

Britton, Nathaniel L., and Percy Wilson. *Botany of Porto Rico and the Virgin Islands.* 2 vols. New York: New York Botanical Garden, 1923–1930.

Gleason, Henry A. "The Scientific Work of Nathaniel Lord Britton." *Proceedings of the American Philosophical Society* 104 (1960): 205–206.

Hove, M.A. "Nathaniel Lord Britton." *Journal of the New York Botanical Garden* 35 (1934): 169–180.

Merrill, Elmer D., and John H. Barnhart. "Nathaniel Lord Britton." *Biographical Memoirs of the National Academy of Sciences* 19 (1934): 147–202.

Slack, Nancy G. "Botanical and Ecological Couples; a Continuum of Relationships." In *Creative Couples in the Sciences,* edited by Helena M. Pycior, Nancy G. Slack, and Pnina G. Abir-Am. New Brunswick: Rutgers University Press, 1996, pp. 235–253.

Sloan, Douglas. "Science in New York City, 1867–1907." *Isis* 71 (1980): 35–76.

Stearn, William T. "Britton, Nathaniel Lord." *Dictionary of Scientific Biography.* Edited by Charles C. Gillispie. New York: Scribners, 1970, 2:476–477.

Tanner, Ogden, and Adele Auchincloss. *The New York Botanical Garden: An Illustrated Chronicle of Plants and People.* New York: Walker and Co., 1991.

Nancy G. Slack

SEE ALSO
New York Botanical Garden, The

Bulletin of the Atomic Scientists

Originally a newsletter to share information and concerns among scientists at different Manhattan Project sites about wartime use and postwar control of the atomic bomb. Under its first editor in chief, Eugene Rabinowitch, it became a magazine to educate the public about nuclear issues, public policy, and international affairs. In the 1970s, it enlarged its scope to include environmental issues. Lawyers, social scientists, theologians, and government officials have been among its contributors, but true to its origins, it retains scientists as its primary contributors.

Since 1946, the *Bulletin* has served as an important reference on scientific issues with national or international political implications. Among these are nuclear proliferation, radiation and health, nuclear energy, nonconventional weapons, the Cold War and the arms race, American defense spending, scientific advising to government, and the social responsibility of scientists. A special feature of the *Bulletin* is the Doomsday Clock, which has appeared on the cover of each issue since 1947. The number of minutes left before midnight on the clock face indicates the editors' assessment of the

B

level of international tensions and the danger of nuclear war. The *Bulletin* and its clock function as a gauge of international events and technological developments.

BIBLIOGRAPHY

Moore, Mike. "Midnight Never Came." *Bulletin of the Atomic Scientists* 51 (November/December 1995): 16–27.

"The *Bulletin* and the Scientists' Movement." *Bulletin of the Atomic Scientists* 41 (December 1985): 19–31.

Elizabeth Hodes

SEE ALSO
Federation of American Scientists

Bureau of American Ethnology

The Bureau of American Ethnology (BAE), originally the Bureau of Ethnology, was the first major government agency devoted to anthropological research. On 3 March 1879, Congress created it to complete the United States Geological Survey's *Contributions to North American Ethnology*. It was placed under the jurisdiction of the Smithsonian Institution, where it remained until it was folded into the Department of Anthropology, National Museum of Natural History, in 1965. The BAE was designed to serve government informational needs by comprehensively surveying North American Indian cultures so that effective and informed policies could be developed.

Noted geologist and explorer John Wesley Powell, the BAE's first director, wanted the research institution to undertake a "complete science of man." Under his leadership, the BAE staff systematically compiled ethnographic, linguistic, and historic information and developed classificatory paradigms using a natural history model. But Congress also wanted objects to fill the Smithsonian's halls. As a result early research expeditions often included collecting ethnographic and archaeological specimens for the United States National Museum and for government exhibitions at world's fairs. In 1882, BAE staff began archaeological research on mounds in the eastern and midwestern United States and ruins in the Southwest in order to understand and preserve America's past.

In general, the research focus of the BAE remained concentrated on North America and United States territories until the 1930s and stressed particularistic studies designed to elucidate our understanding of linguistic and cultural diversity in the past and present. Since then, the BAE staff has conducted research reflecting contemporary theoretical perspectives dominant in all four subfields of anthropology. During World War II, the Ethnogeographic Board and the Institute of Social Anthropology made significant contributions to the war effort and carried out cooperative training and research. After the war, Frank H.H. Roberts directed the extensive River Basin Surveys, one of the most ambitious and productive salvage archaeological programs that has ever been mounted in this country.

The list of men and women who worked under the auspices of the BAE reads like a who's who of anthropology: Homer Barnett, Franz Boas, Henry Collins, Frank Hamilton Cushing, Frances Densmore, Philip Drucker, William Fenton, Jessie Walter Fewkes, Alice Fletcher, George Foster, John Harrington, Frederick Hodge, William Holmes, Neil Judd, Frances La Flesche, WJ McGee, Truman Michelson, Victor and Cosmos Mindeleff, James Mooney, Paul Radin, Frank Russell, James and Matilda Coxe Stevenson, Julian Steward, William Strong, William Sturtevant, John Swanton, Cyrus Thomas, Harry Tschopik, and Gordon Willey, to name but a few. Their extensive contributions have been of immense theoretical, informational, and methodological importance to anthropology, and many of their works can be found in the BAE's series of *Annual Reports, Handbooks,* and *Bulletins*. These publications also offered outlets for the research of anthropologists in other institutions.

The BAE was crucial in the institutionalization, organization, and development of American anthropology. It profoundly influenced the content and direction of late-nineteenth- to mid-twentieth-century anthropology. The BAE's records are housed in the National Anthropological Archives at the Smithsonian Institution.

BIBLIOGRAPHY

Bureau of Ethnology and Bureau of American Ethnology. *Annual Reports*. 1879–1964.

Bureau of American Ethnology. *Bulletins* nos. 1-200 (1887–1965).

Hinsley, Curtis M. Jr. *Savages and Scientists: The Smithsonian Institution and the Development of American Anthropology, 1846–1910.* Washington, DC: Smithsonian Institution Press, 1981.

Judd, Neil M. *The Bureau of American Ethnology: A Partial History.* Norman: University of Oklahoma Press, 1967.

Nancy J. Parezo

Bush, Vannevar (1890–1974)

Prominent twentieth-century engineer who made important contributions to the development of the computer before going to Washington, where he played central roles in the mobilization of civilian science during World War II and in debates over national science policy afterward.

The descendant of New England sea captains and a father who was a Universalist minister, Bush's early career was spent at the Massachusetts Institute of Technology (MIT) and Tufts College, where, following his father's example, he enrolled as an undergraduate in 1909. Here Bush developed an interest in invention which eventually culminated in a series of pioneering analog computers during the 1920s and 1930s. Here also he acquired an affinity for graphical mathematics that became a distinctive feature of his mature work in engineering. Not least, the profoundly ethical context in which the professions were taught at Tufts combined with his father's pastoral commitment to shape his belief that engineering should be a ministry devoted to the public good. In 1913, he graduated with both bachelor's and master's degrees. After working briefly at General Electric and the New York Navy Yard, Bush earned his doctorate in electrical engineering at MIT in one year in 1916 before returning to Tufts as an assistant professor, where he taught for part of his time and consulted for the rest with a small radio company from which came the Raytheon Corporation in the early 1920s.

In 1919, he joined the electrical engineering department at MIT as an associate professor of electrical power transmission. There he helped Dugald Jackson modernize the curriculum, taking control of graduate training and coordinating the department's research activities. During his years at MIT, Bush's concerns ranged from engineering education to the larger role of the engineering professional in American society. In 1932, he became the institute's first vice president and dean of engineering under the new president Karl Compton.

Bush's most important inventive activities originated in his search for mechanical solutions to certain intractable equations arising from problems in power transmission. These interests led him to develop, between 1927 and 1943, a series of increasingly sophisticated electromechanical analog computers which proved useful far beyond these initial applications. In 1936, the Rockefeller Foundation awarded a major grant to MIT which led to the Rockefeller Differential Analyzer. While quickly superseded by faster digital computers, the analyzer clearly demonstrated the possibilities of machine computation for science and engineering. It also reflected, as Bush put it, the engineer's ability to "think straight in the midst of complexity" and thus symbolized that engineering rationality he believed would help remake American life.

In 1939, he moved to Washington to become president of the Carnegie Institution and, shortly thereafter, chairman of the National Advisory Committee for Aeronautics, where he planned to promote cooperative research of the sort that had characterized the previous decades. Within a year, however, the war in Europe forced his attention elsewhere. With the advantage of location and friendships with scientific and engineering leaders acquired over a decade and more, Bush quickly assumed command of scientific mobilization, as the head of the National Defense Research Committee and its successor, the Office of Scientific Research and Development. From these organizations and the laboratories they oversaw came radar, the proximity fuse, penicillin, and, of course, the atomic bomb. Such accomplishments brought fame to Bush and enormous public respect to the nation's scientists. They also lent his voice great authority in the public debates and legislative battles which followed the war and which eventually gave birth to the Atomic Energy Commission in 1947 and the National Science Foundation in 1950.

In November 1944, President Franklin D. Roosevelt asked Bush to report on how his experience in applying science to the problems of war might be turned to peacetime advantage, creating new jobs and enterprises, improving the standard of living, and fighting the war on disease. Bush's report, *Science—The Endless Frontier,* was delivered to President Truman in July 1945. It argued most importantly for the creation of a permanent federal agency to help subsidize basic science in the universities and institutes, oversee military and medical research, and support the training of new scientists. Made public shortly after its submission, the report became an influential best-seller, providing crucial impetus to public debates which led to the enactment of the National Science Foundation (NSF) in 1950. While the NSF never acquired the dominant central role envisioned in Bush's ambitious report, especially in the matter of military R&D and medical science, both the foundation and the report itself should be understood as the finally successful climax of a century-long struggle by scientist-entrepreneurs to gain national recognition and forge a partnership between the state and civilian science.

B

After the war, Bush returned to the Carnegie Institution, from which he retired in 1955. He nevertheless remained interested in the management of R&D and became a member of the boards of Merck and Company, AT&T, the Metals and Controls Corporation, and the MIT Corporation, where he became honorary chairman in 1959. Bush had become a respected figure on Capitol Hill, and he continued to testify afterward, particularly on matters of military research and development and patent reform. He wrote as well a number of best-selling books dealing with science, war, and public policy, of which the most famous were *Science—The Endless Frontier* and his 1949 *Modern Arms and Free Men*.

The latter was an early Cold War manifesto which entered the public arena at the same moment as the announcement of the first Soviet A-bomb test. *Modern Arms and Free Men* was both an accounting of the new technologies of war and an examination of their implications for modern government. Declaring his faith in the resilience of democracy at a time when, to many, the future seemed dangerous and uncertain, the author's populist faith touched a chord in the American public and made his book a best-seller. No, Bush wrote, science had not "doomed us all to die in a holocaust" and, yes, democracy could survive its struggle with a godless foe who had harnessed science with totalitarian efficiency to the ends of world domination. It could survive, he argued, if the nation remained true to the traditions of private enterprise that had made it strong, remembered that tolerant religious pluralism that gave science ultimate meaning, and refused to leave the complex issues of war and peace to "specialists" in government bureaucracies.

In short, Bush was an outstanding example of the early-twentieth-century engineer whose seemingly larger-than-life accomplishments in the service of an increasingly complex society captured the American imagination. If the dilemmas of Cold War life clouded this clear vision, Bush himself never lost faith, as he made plain in his last book, the autobiographical *Pieces of the Action* published in 1974.

BIBLIOGRAPHY

Bush, Vannevar. *Modern Arms and Free Men.* New York: Simon and Schuster, 1949.

———. *Pieces of the Action.* New York: William Morrow, 1970.

England, J. Merton. "Dr. Bush Writes a Report: 'Science—The Endless Frontier.'" *Science* 191 (9 January 1976): 41–47.

Goldberg, Stanley. "Inventing a Climate of Opinion: Vannevar Bush and the Decision to Build the Bomb." *Isis* 83 (1992): 429–452.

Kevles, Daniel. "The National Science Foundation and the Debate over Postwar Research Policy, 1942–1945: A Political Interpretation of *Science—The Endless Frontier.*" *Isis* 68 (1977): 5–26.

———. "Principles and Politics in Federal R&D Policy, 1945–1990: An Appreciation of the Bush Report." Preface to reprint of *Science—The Endless Frontier. A Report to the President on a Program for Postwar Scientific Research,* by Vannevar Bush. 1945. Reprint, Washington, DC: National Science Foundation, 1990.

Owens, Larry. "Vannevar Bush and the Differential Analyzer: The Text and Context of an Early Computer." *Technology and Culture* 27 (1986): 63–95.

———. "Bush, Vannevar." *Dictionary of Scientific Biography.* Edited by Frederic L. Holmes. New York: Scribners, 1990, 17, supplement II: 134–139.

Reingold, Nathan. "Vannevar Bush's New Deal for Research: Or the Triumph of the Old Order." *Historical Studies in the Physical and Biological Sciences* 17 (1987): 299–344.

Wiesner, Jerome. "Vannevar Bush." *Biographical Memoirs of the National Academy of Sciences* 50 (1979): 89–117.

Zachary, G. Pascal. "America's First Engineer—The Career of Vannevar Bush." *Upside* (June 1991): 94–103.

Larry Owens

SEE ALSO

Office of Scientific Research and Development

C

California Institute of Technology

A small, independent university of research and teaching in science and engineering, with 900 Ph.D.-level faculty, 900 undergraduates, and 1,000 graduate students. The beginnings of the history of the California Institute of Technology (Caltech) are rooted in a modest little college founded in Pasadena in 1891 by wealthy former abolitionist and Chicago politician Amos Throop. Initially named Throop University, the school changed its name to Throop Polytechnic Institute in 1893. In its first fifteen years, Throop served the local community, teaching a great variety of subjects, from arts and crafts to zoology, with considerable emphasis on vocational training. By 1906, Throop needed a fresh sense of purpose. The American astronomer George Ellery Hale, the first director of the nearby Mount Wilson Observatory and a newcomer to Pasadena, would provide it.

A scientist bubbling over with educational, architectural, and civic ideas, Hale was elected to the school's board of trustees in 1907 and promptly set about to transform it. He persuaded school officials to abandon Throop's high school and other programs and concentrate on expanding and developing the college along engineering lines; recruited James A.B. Scherer, who served as Throop's president between 1908 and 1920; and enticed Arthur A. Noyes, former president of the Massachusetts Institute of Technology (MIT) and the nation's leading physical chemist, to join him in Pasadena. In Noyes, Hale saw not only an opportunity to bring chemistry at Throop College (Throop officially changed its name to Throop College of Technology in 1913) up to a level with that at MIT but also to put Throop itself in the national limelight. The third member of Hale's scientific troika was the physicist Robert A. Millikan who began, in 1917, to spend several months a year at Throop as director of physical research.

The three of them spent the World War I years in Washington, organizing and recruiting scientists to work on military problems, but also building a superb network of contacts that would later serve the school well. Collectively ambitious for American science, eager to see their country play a larger role on the world's scientific stage, and determined to put Throop on the map, Hale, Millikan, and Noyes had become a formidable scientific triumvirate by 1918. By Armistice Day, they had set the stage to transform the engineering school into an institution that put pure science first.

Between 1919 and 1921, the school obtained a handsome endowment, drafted a new educational philosophy, took its present name, and selected a new man to guide its destiny for the next twenty-five years. Hale and Noyes wanted to use Caltech to reshape the education of scientists. Millikan wanted to make Caltech one of the physics capitals of the world. To do that, he needed research funds. The three men came to an agreement. Hale and Noyes promised Millikan the lion's share of the school's financial resources and minimal administrative duties as head of Caltech. In return, Millikan agreed to come, as director of the Norman Bridge Laboratory of Physics, and administrative head of Caltech. By then, Noyes had resigned from MIT and accepted a full-time appointment as director of chemical research in Pasadena.

C

In the early 1920s, Caltech was essentially an undergraduate and graduate school in the physical sciences. Indeed, until 1925, the institution offered graduate work leading to the doctorate only in physics, chemistry, and engineering. Geology joined the list of graduate studies in 1925, aeronautics in 1926, biology and mathematics in 1928. Physics was king from the very beginning. It had more students, more faculty, and more money than other departments had. Millikan initiated a visiting-scholars program shortly after his arrival in Pasadena. The list of scientists who accepted Millikan's invitation represented the cream of European physics, including Paul Dirac, Erwin Schrödinger, Werner Heisenberg, Hendrik Lorentz, and Niels Bohr. Albert Einstein's visits to the campus in 1931, 1932, and 1933 capped Millikan's plans to put physics on the map in southern California. If nothing else, Einstein's visits showed dramatically that the Caltech that Hale, Millikan, and Noyes had set out to build in the twenties had come of age in the thirties.

Millikan, who functioned as the school's president between the wars, was fiercely opposed to government funding of research. He relied on the major private foundations, especially the Rockefeller and the Carnegie, and a growing number of southern California philanthropists to provide the funds he needed. He believed that the modern world was basically a scientific invention, that science was the mainspring of the twentieth century, and that America's future rested on the promoting of basic science and its applications. Caltech, in Millikan's view, existed to provide America's scientific leadership.

The focus of scientific research at the institute under Millikan during the 1930s ranged from *Drosophila* genetics and the biochemistry of vitamins in biology, to the theory of turbulence and airplane wing design in aeronautics; from cancer therapy with radiation and the radioactivity of the light elements in nuclear physics, to soil erosion and the transmission of water from the Colorado River to Los Angeles in engineering; from the application of quantum mechanics to molecular structure in chemistry, to the introduction of the magnitude scale in seismology.

An educational institution in name only during the war, Caltech had a war arsenal that included rockets, proximity fuses, the Jet Propulsion Laboratory, and $80 million in federal funds for war-related research and development.

Caltech's history is divided into two distinct eras. The first Caltech era was created by Hale, Millikan, and Noyes. Thirty years later, after World War II, the physicists Lee Alvin DuBridge and Robert Bacher did the job all over again. DuBridge, the head of MIT's wartime radar project, became Caltech's new president in 1946. Bacher, the leader of the Los Alamos atomic bomb project's "G" Division (the "G" stood for "gadgets"), arrived in 1949 to head up the division of physics, mathematics, and astronomy and later became the institute's first provost.

During DuBridge's tenure (1946–1969), Caltech's teaching faculty doubled in number, the campus tripled in size, and new research fields blossomed, including chemical biology, planetary science, nuclear astrophysics, and geochemistry. In 1948, the 200-inch telescope on Palomar Mountain, the world's most powerful optical telescope for more than forty years, was dedicated. Unlike Millikan, DuBridge argued that the federal government had a responsibility to support scientific research.

As Caltech's new physics head, Bacher rebuilt the physics department, and he did so with a vengeance, starting with high-energy particle physics. Then a new field, particle physics hardly existed at Caltech in 1949, except for the work of Carl Anderson and his students, including Donald Glaser, a later Nobel Prize winner, who used cosmic rays from space as a natural source of high-energy particles to do particle physics. While chairman, Bacher initiated construction and use of a new electron accelerator, so that the Caltech group could make its own high-energy particles. The institute closed down its electron synchrotron in 1969, shortly after ground was broken for the national accelerator laboratory—Fermilab, in Batavia, Illinois. Theoretical physics, always a stepchild under Millikan, entered a golden age with the acquisition of Richard Feynman and Murray Gell-Mann. Feynman, then at Cornell, was Bacher's first acquisition.

Historical studies of the development of Caltech as a research university after the war are scarce. There are no biographies of key figures from George Beadle, Charles Richter, and William Fowler onward.

BIBLIOGRAPHY

Ajzenberg-Selove, Fay. *A Matter of Choices: Memoirs of a Female Physicist.* New Brunswick: Rutgers University Press, 1994.

Florence, Ronald. *The Perfect Machine: Building the Palomar Telescope.* New York: HarperCollins, 1994.

Geiger, Roger L. *Research and Relevant Knowledge: American Research Universities since World War II.* New York: Oxford University Press, 1993.

Goodstein, Judith R. *Millikan's School: A History of the California Institute of Technology.* New York: Norton, 1991.

————. "George Wells Beadle." *The Scribner Encyclopedia of American Lives.* Edited by K.T. Jackson, K. Markoe, and A. Markoe. *Notable Americans Who Died between 1986 and 1990.* New York: Charles Scribner's Sons, 1999, 2:74–76.

Gorn, Michael H. *The Universal Man: Theodore von Kármán's Life in Aeronautics.* Washington, DC: Smithsonian Institution Press, 1992.

Johnson, George. *Strange Beauty: Murray Gell-Mann and the Revolution in Twentieth Century Physics.* New York: Knopf, 1999.

Kargon, Robert. *The Rise of Robert Millikan: Portrait of a Life in American Science.* Ithaca: Cornell University Press, 1982.

Kevles, Daniel J. *The Physicists: The History of a Scientific Community in Modern America.* New York: Knopf, 1978; reprint, Cambridge, MA: Harvard University Press, 1995.

Murray, Bruce C. *Journey into Space: The First Three Decades of Space Exploration.* New York: Norton, 1989.

Reingold, Nathan. "Science and Government in the United States since 1945." *History of Science* 32 (1994): 361–386.

Servos, John W. *Physical Chemistry from Ostwald to Pauling: The Making of a Science in America.* Princeton: Princeton University Press, 1990.

Sinsheimer, Robert. *The Strands of a Life: The Science of DNA and the Art of Education.* Berkeley: University of California Press, 1994.

Judith R. Goodstein

Canada—Relations to Science in the United States

Given their proximity, shared language, similar cultures, and being each other's primary trading partners, it was inevitable that American and Canadian science would become closely linked. As early as the 1840s, relations were established to collect geophysical and natural history data. Prominent Canadian scientists were early members of the American Association for the Advancement of Science, which held its first meeting outside the United States in Montreal in 1857. During the nineteenth century, the strongest ties were among the practitioners of the inventory sciences: geology, meteorology, botany, entomology, zoology, and ethnology. Such ties were personal at first, but became institutional by the 1870s. These links were not without friction. The Geological Survey of Canada and, later, the Dominion Observatory, saw the Smithsonian Institution and the Carnegie Institution of Washington as competitors, if not poachers, in their national space.

The National Geographic Society, on the other hand, was less a problem, given that its president—Alexander Graham Bell—could be equally claimed by both nations.

Although some Canadian scientists looked to Britain for scientific leadership, the nature of the focus of the science undertaken, as well as the shared geology, flora, and fauna ensured that Canadian science would strongly resemble American. This was already evident by the 1890s, especially in applied science.

Science education in Canada generally followed American paradigms—though with some local variations—including the structure of departments and curricula. Canadian universities, like their American counterparts, adopted the B.Sc. and Ph.D. as research-oriented degrees. By the turn of the century, Canadians were more likely to undertake doctoral studies in the United States than anywhere else. Twentieth-century science teaching and curricula differed little in the two nations and graduates moved easily across the border in both directions. From the turn of the century, science education in Canadian elementary and secondary schools followed the American lead; the methods and controversies in the contemporary science curriculum are common to both communities.

As both Canada and the United States were developing nations, science quickly emerged as a tool of government, with Canadian federal and provincial governments paralleling (and often imitating) American efforts in agriculture, health, resource management, conservation, testing, and standards. Visits by officials of science-based departments across the border have been a common occurrence since at least the 1870s.

The scientific efforts of both nations were brought closer together during World War II and cooperation in many fields became the norm in the postwar years. Canada's early entry into nuclear technology and space science, along with mutual environmental concerns, allowed a free flow of people and information. Canada's participation in the North Atlantic Treaty Organization (NATO) and the North American Air Defense Command (NORAD) ensured that military science and technology moved in both directions.

Cooperative ventures, such as the International Polar Years (in the nineteenth and twentieth centuries) and the International Geophysical Year, provided natural opportunities for the exchange of scientific data. The CANUSA project, for example, undertaken in the

C

1970s and 1980s to study and control the spruce budworm, was the largest cooperative international forestry project in history. Canadian scientists became active participants in American scientific organizations, while American scientific periodicals have become the journals of choice in many fields. Given the relative transparency of the border for the movement of scientists, a significant number of American-born and trained scientists moved north to occupy important positions in Canada, while Canadians, from Simon Newcomb and William Osler to several living Nobel laureates have built American careers.

Increasingly, as the cost of Big-Science ventures surpasses the fiscal resources of individual nations, Canada and the United States are drawn together in joint international ventures in physics, astronomy, oceanography, geophysics, and biology with shared facilities and programs. This has accelerated since the late 1960s. Since the 1970s, the Canadian space program has begun to converge with the American, with Canadian astronauts participating in the space-shuttle program and the Canadian Space Agency with the space-station project. Canadians play a role in the Human Genome Project, building upon much earlier interaction in medical and pharmaceutical research. Environmental science naturally knows no border in dealing with transnational issues such as air and water pollution; this work is fostered by binational organizations and institutions.

Although we know little in detail of the history of industrial science, there are hints of sustained research links in hydroelectricity, pulp and paper, oil prospecting and extraction, food science and agriculture. A similar approach to industrial standards, food and drug regulation, and health ensured that links would be forged.

Despite the "undefended border," however, Canadian and American science do retain separate identities, for neither has quite the same community structure nor do their respective communities relate to government in the same way. Canadian scientists, though they participate in American organizations, maintain their own societies and journals. The French factor in Québec—even if most francophone scientists publish in English—does entail both challenges and tensions generally lacking in the United States.

BIBLIOGRAPHY

Berger, Carl. *Science, God and Nature in Victorian Canada.* Toronto: University of Toronto Press, 1983.

Chartrand, Luc, Raymond Duchesne, and Yves Gingras. *Histoire des sciences au Québec.* Montréal: Boréal, 1987.

Jarrell, Richard, and Yves Gingras, eds. *Building Canadian Science: The Role of the National Research Council.* Ottawa: Canadian Science and Technology Historical Association, 1982.

Jarrell, Richard, and James Hull, eds. *Science, Technology and Medicine in Canadian History.* Thornhill, ONT: Scientia Press, 1991.

Levere, Trevor H., and Richard A. Jarrell, eds. *A Curious Fieldbook: Science and Society in Canadian History.* Toronto: Oxford University Press, 1974.

Zeller, Suzanne. *Inventing Canada.* Toronto: University of Toronto Press, 1987.

Richard A. Jarrell

Carnegie Institution of Washington

A private organization pursuing research in the natural sciences. The Carnegie Institution of Washington (CIW) was established in January 1902 by Andrew Carnegie, who authorized the trustees to spend the income from his gift of $10 million (increased by $2 million in 1907 and $10 million in 1911) for a variety of purposes—the first two of which were as follows (CIW, *Yearbook,* No. 1, p. xiii):

1. To promote original research . . .
2. To discover the exceptional man in every department of study . . . and enable him to make the work for which he seems specially designed his life work.

Legal responsibility for the CIW lay with the trustees, who were represented between their annual meetings by an executive committee. In addition, a president—chosen by the trustees—administered the organization's ongoing affairs. The first president was Daniel Coit Gilman (1902–1904), who had recently retired from his long tenure as the first president of the Johns Hopkins University. But it was his successor, Robert Simpson Woodward (1904–1920), who gave the CIW its distinctive identity.

Just prior to Woodward's arrival, the CIW obtained a congressional charter that (among other things) weakened its mandate to support universities. Woodward favored this clear separation from academia. In his view, the CIW should concentrate on research, not education. Also under Woodward's leadership, primary responsibility for policymaking was shifted from the executive committee to the president. As the organization's chief policymaker, Woodward favored two ways of supporting "the exceptional man." One was to make direct grants to individuals. The other was for the CIW to establish its own research departments. By the time of America's entry into World War I, the emphasis lay on the work of the departments, and "the exceptional man" had come to mean "the proven specialist within an established discipline" (Reingold, p. 323).

Woodward's successor, John Campbell Merriam (1921–1938), held to the course that Woodward had established. He also kept the CIW in a central position among American research organizations. Thus, one historian has noted that under Merriam's leadership the CIW "served as the unofficial scientific embassy of the nation's researchers" (Pursell, p. 519).

After Vannevar Bush became CIW president in 1939, he led the efforts to mobilize the nation's scientists for wartime service. In June 1940, Franklin D. Roosevelt created the National Defense Research Committee, with Bush as its chairman, and a year later he created the Office of Scientific Research and Development, with Bush as its director. In both cases, Bush worked from offices in the CIW's Administration Building in Washington, D.C. Meanwhile, he "cleaned house" at the CIW by canceling several long-standing programs. He also encouraged CIW researchers to turn their attention to war-related projects.

Throughout the period from the end of World War II until his retirement in 1955, Bush advocated increasing the level of federal funding for scientific research. At the same time, however, he resisted accepting federal funds at the CIW. The overall result was a significant change in the role of CIW. Increasingly dwarfed by the new federally supported programs, the CIW found itself serving as "both refuge and symbol—a refuge for the untrammeled pursuit of fundamental science and a symbol of the vitality of private enterprise in the search for knowledge" (Owens, p. 138).

The presidents who followed Bush—Caryl P. Haskins (1956–1971), Philip H. Abelson (1971–1978), James D. Ebert (1978–1987), Edward E. David Jr. (1987–1988), and Maxine Singer (since 1988)—have faced the difficult challenge of supporting first-class scientific research at a private organization. The trend has been toward concentrating its resources on the work of its remaining departments, while at the same time preserving maximum flexibility for individual members of the departmental staffs. Greater emphasis

has been given to the program of postdoctoral fellowships, and Bush's stricture against accepting federal funds has been relaxed.

The CIW arose at a critical time in the history of the American scientific community. Despite increased societal support, there existed few opportunities at the turn of the century for long-term, cooperative research across organizational or disciplinary lines. The CIW was in no position to fund all such projects. Nevertheless, the scale of its early operations was unprecedented.

At first, much of the CIW's support went to individuals. Examples of these research associates (taken randomly from a long list) included Thomas H. Morgan and his study of fruit-fly genetics, Andrew E. Douglass and his study of tree-ring chronology, and Arthur H. Compton and his study of cosmic rays. Although the program of individual grants was later scaled back, during the first decade of its existence the CIW distributed (on the average) $100,000 per year in this way—making the program "the first significant experiment in large-scale sponsorship of academic science" (Kohler, p. 15).

Nevertheless, the primary work of the CIW has been accomplished through its research departments. Of the eleven established by the time of World War I, five remain today: the [Astronomical] Observatories (Pasadena, CA), the Department of Terrestrial Magnetism (Washington, D.C.), the Geophysical Laboratory (Washington, D.C.), the Department of Plant Biology (Stanford, California), and the Department of Embryology (Baltimore, MD).

In response to the news of Carnegie's original gift, George Ellery Hale began lobbying for an astrophysical observatory at Mount Wilson, near Pasadena. In 1904, the CIW trustees authorized the construction of a Solar Observatory, with Hale as its director. Installation of the Snow horizontal telescope (1905), the 60-foot tower telescope (1907), and the 150-foot tower telescope (1910) established Mount Wilson as a leading center for solar research. Meanwhile, funds from the CIW (as well as from other sources) enabled Hale to install a 60-inch reflecting telescope (1908) and then a 100-inch reflecting telescope (1917)—each being, at the time, the largest in the world.

Under the leadership of Hale and his successors (Walter S. Adams after 1923 and Ira S. Bowen after 1946), Mount Wilson dominated astronomy for more than a generation. Some researchers came as research associates (for example, Henry N. Russell, who regularly spent a

C

couple of months each summer at the observatory). Others (for example, Edwin P. Hubble) were full-time staff members. In the late 1920s, Hale arranged for the Rockefeller Foundation to fund a 200-inch reflecting telescope at Mount Palomar (northeast of San Diego), which was formally dedicated in 1948. Also by then, Mount Palomar was the site of a 48-inch Schmidt telescope. Although owned by the California Institute of Technology, these new facilities (along with those at Mount Wilson) were managed jointly with the CIW.

More recently, the CIW has founded an observatory and built major telescopes in South America. The first instrument completed at Las Campanas, Chile, was the 40-inch Swope telescope (1971). Next came the 100-inch DuPont telescope (1977). In cooperation with the University of Arizona, plans have been made to build a 6.5-meter telescope (the Magellan Project). Meanwhile, in 1980, the joint operation with Caltech ended. Thereafter, Caltech owned and operated the observatory at Mount Palomar, while the CIW owned the observatory at Mount Wilson (though operation of the facilities was transferred to others).

Another early CIW effort in astronomy involved the work of Lewis Boss. In 1903, the CIW began funding Boss's measurements of stellar positions at the Dudley Observatory in Albany, New York. A few years later, the support was expanded to include the creation of a Department of Meridian Astronomy, with Boss as its director. Along with further work in the Northern Hemisphere, Boss undertook similiar observations in the Southern Hemisphere, at an observatory he established in Argentina. After Boss's death in 1912, his son Benjamin served as director until the department was closed in 1936.

The Department of Terrestrial Magnetism was established in 1904 to conduct worldwide studies of earth magnetism and electricity. Its first director, Louis A. Bauer, emphasized surveys of earth magnetism, not only through land expeditions but also through ocean voyages (notably, the seven voyages that the *Carnegie*— a nonmagnetic sailing ship—made between the time it was launched in 1909 and the time of its accidental destruction in 1929). After World War I, the department established a pair of magnetic observatories, one in Peru and one in Australia, and under the leadership of Bauer's successor, John A. Fleming, it expanded its program of laboratory studies—including work in the new field of nuclear physics. During World War II, the department temporarily shifted its attention to developing proximity fuses for explosive shells. After Merle A. Tuve became director in 1946, the department transferred ownership of the magnetic observatories to others, scaled back its work in nuclear physics, and added work in seismology, radioactive-isotope geochemistry, astrophysics (including radio astronomy), and biophysics.

The Geophysical Laboratory emerged from discussions of how best to extend into geology the mathematical and experimental methods of physics and chemistry. In 1905, the CIW trustees authorized the creation of the new department, and Arthur L. Day was chosen to head it. Emphasis quickly focused on questions of geochemistry, including how various types of rocks are formed and how they behave under varying conditions of temperature and pressure. During World War I, researchers at the Geophysical Laboratory helped to increase domestic production of optical glass, and during World War II (by which time Leason H. Adams had succeeded Day) they gave attention to problems such as the internal corrosion of gun barrels. In 1990, the Geophysical Laboratory moved from its quarters on Upton Street to new quarters on Broad Branch Road, which it shares with the Department of Terrestrial Magnetism.

In 1926, the CIW and the California Institute of Technology jointly established a Seismological Laboratory in Pasadena, with Harry O. Wood as its head and, later, with Charles F. Richter as one of its staff members. In 1937, however, Caltech assumed full responsibility for the laboratory.

Early support for the study of plants included a series of grants to Luther Burbank. In addition, the CIW developed its own research facilities. In 1903, a Desert Laboratory was built on a hillside outside Tucson, Arizona, and in 1905 Daniel T. MacDougal was put in charge of the newly formed Department of Botanical Research there. Also established was a Coastal Laboratory at Carmel, California (to which MacDougal moved his offices in 1920), and in 1917 the CIW began supporting the Alpine Laboratory that Frederic E. Clements had established in Colorado.

In addition to its pioneering support for plant ecology, the CIW supported studies of plant physiology— notably, the work on photosynthesis conducted by Herman A. Spoehr. In 1927, the trustees decided to reorganize the CIW's botanical efforts, and the resulting Division of Plant Biology was placed under Spoehr's direction. By 1929, new quarters had been

C

built at Stanford University. Although its central concern continued to be the response of plants to their environment, during the 1930s the department shifted its focus from field studies to laboratory experimentation. In 1940, the Desert Laboratory (which, since 1928, had been headed by Forrest Shreve) was deeded to the U.S. Forest Service, and the property at Carmel was sold. Support for Clements's work ceased with his retirement in 1941.

Initially, the CIW gave serious consideration to acquiring the Marine Biological Laboratory at Woods Hole, but in 1904 it created new facilities. One of these was its own Marine Biological Laboratory, in the Dry Tortugas (west of Key West), which was directed by Alfred G. Mayor until his death in 1922 and finally closed in 1939 (largely because of problems associated with its location).

Also created in 1904 was a Station for Experimental Evolution at Cold Spring Harbor, Long Island. Under the leadership of Charles B. Davenport, research involved both plants and animals (including George H. Shull's studies of hybrid corn). Meanwhile, Davenport approached Mrs. E.H. Harriman for funds to establish a center for the study of human heredity. As a result, the Eugenics Record Office was created in 1910. In 1917, the CIW assumed responsibility for operating the office, which in 1921 was merged with the Station for Experimental Evolution to form the Department of Genetics—with Davenport as its director.

Headed by Harry H. Laughlin, the Eugenics Record Office trained field workers and collected field data on a wide range of human traits. During the 1920s, Laughlin advised Congress regarding the passage of restrictive immigration legislation. But rising criticism of the eugenics movement during the 1930s led the CIW to close the Eugenics Record Office in 1939.

Prior to taking the CIW post—and for many years thereafter—Davenport also served as director of the Brooklyn Institute of Arts and Sciences' summer biological laboratory at Cold Spring Harbor. In 1924, responsibility for this laboratory was assumed by the Long Island Biological Association, and in 1941 Milislav Demerec became its director. At about the same time, Demerec also became director of the CIW department (succeeding Albert F. Blakeslee). Unified under Demerec's leadership, the facilities at Cold Spring Harbor emerged as a major center for molecular genetics. In 1962, the CIW department was closed except for a small Genetics Research Unit, which supported the continued work of

Alfred D. Hershey and Barbara McClintock. Meanwhile, the other laboratory became what is today known as the Cold Spring Harbor Laboratory.

The Department of Embryology grew out of the work of Franklin P. Mall, who in 1893 became the first head of the anatomy department of the Johns Hopkins Medical School in Baltimore. During his earlier studies in Europe, Mall had begun collecting human embryos. Also as a result of his European travels, he had seen the value of organizations devoted to the study of particular problems. Convinced that such organizations served to raise the general level of research in their fields, Mall approached the CIW for the funds needed to house his collection of embryos and to undertake systematic studies of embryological development. Initial funding came in 1913 and formal establishment of the new department came the following year. After George W. Corner became director in 1940 (succeeding George L. Streeter), he shifted the department's emphasis from embryological form (morphology) to embryological physiology. Under Corner's successor, James D. Ebert, the emphasis was further shifted to developmental biology (involving molecular biology, genetics, and biochemistry)—and in 1973 the embryo collection was transferred to the University of California at Davis (and transferred again, in 1991, to Washington, D.C.).

From 1907 to 1937, Francis G. Benedict directed the CIW's Nutrition Laboratory at the Harvard Medical School in Boston. Topics of study included basal metabolism, heat production, and heat regulation in both human and animal subjects. After Benedict's retirement, Thorne M. Carpenter took over, serving as director until the department was closed in 1945.

Although the natural sciences quickly became its primary area of interest, the CIW initially supported research in a wider range of fields. At the department level, these included economics and sociology (1903–1916) and history (1903–1929).

Archaeology was another field in which the CIW was active. Early support went to Raphael Pumpelly, for his expeditions to Central Asia. But the CIW's main efforts lay in Central America. The first step came in 1914 with the appointment of Sylvanus G. Morley as a research associate. Focusing initially on a survey of Maya inscriptions, Morley turned his attention after World War I to the excavation and preservation of Maya cities—including Chichén Itzá and Uaxactun.

As the Maya project matured, Merriam enlisted the services of Alfred V. Kidder, first in 1926 as a research

C

associate and then in 1929 as head of a newly created Division of Historical Research (which included not only the archaeological work but also the work in American history and the history of science). Kidder brought to the project an interdisciplinary approach. Along with Morley's continued fieldwork, for example, the CIW project included Robert Redfield's studies of contemporary Maya descendents and Anna O. Shepard's technological analysis of ceramics.

When Kidder retired in 1950, Harry E.R. Pollock became head of the Department of Archaeology (by then the sole remnant of the former Division of Historical Research). After a final project—the excavation of the Maya city of Mayapan—the CIW's archaeological program was terminated in 1958.

Despite the availablility of extensive archival records, both at the CIW's main offices (located since 1909 at 1530 P Street, N.W., in Washington, D.C.) and elsewhere, no comprehensive history of the CIW has yet been published. Attention has tended to go to the earliest years of the CIW or to the work of particular departments or individual researchers. That leaves many topics largely unexplored: the administrative achievements of the presidents after Woodward, the responses of the departments over long spans of time to changing intellectual and societal developments, the changing relationships between the CIW and other science-related organizations in the United States, and the worldwide reputation and influence of the CIW.

BIBLIOGRAPHY

Allen, Garland E. "The Eugenics Record Office at Cold Spring Harbor, 1910–1940: An Essay in Institutional History." *Osiris,* 2d ser., 2 (1986): 225–264.

Bowers, Janice Emily. *A Sense of Place: The Life and Work of Forrest Shreve.* Tucson: University of Arizona Press, 1988.

Carnegie Institution of Washington. *Yearbooks.* Washington, DC: Carnegie Institution of Washington, 1903–.

Ebert, James D. "Carnegie Institution of Washington and Marine Biology: Naples, Woods Hole, and Tortugas." *Biological Bulletin* 168 (supplement; 1985): 172–182.

———. "Evolving Institutional Patterns for Excellence: A Brief Comparison of the Organization and Management of the Cold Spring Harbor Laboratory and the Marine Biological Laboratory." *Biological Bulletin* 168 (supplement; 1985): 183–186.

Givens, Douglas R. *Alfred Vincent Kidder and the Development of Americanist Archaeology.* Albuquerque: University of New Mexico Press, 1992.

Good, Gregory A. *The Earth, the Heavens, and the Carnegie Institution of Washington: Historical Perspectives after Ninety Years.* Washington, DC: American Geophysical Union, 1994.

Goodstein, Judith R. *Millikan's School: A History of the California Institute of Technology.* New York: Norton, 1991.

Hagen, Joel B. "Clementsian Ecologists: The Internal Dynamics of a Research Group." *Osiris,* 2d ser., 8 (1993): 178–195.

Haskins, Caryl P., ed. *The Search for Understanding: Selected Writings of Scientists of the Carnegie Institution, Published on the Sixty-Fifth Anniversary of the Institution's Founding.* Washington, DC: Carnegie Institution of Washington, 1967.

Kingsland, Sharon E. "The Battling Botanist: Daniel Trembly MacDougal, Mutation Theory, and the Rise of Experimental Evolutionary Biology in America, 1900–1912." *Isis* 82 (1991): 479–509.

Kohler, Robert E. *Partners in Science: Foundations and Natural Scientists, 1900–1945.* Chicago: University of Chicago Press, 1991.

Madsen, David. "Daniel Coit Gilman at the Carnegie Institution of Washington." *History of Education Quarterly* 9 (1969): 154–186.

Miller, Howard S. *Dollars for Research: Science and Its Patrons in Nineteenth-Century America.* Seattle: University of Washington Press, 1970.

Owens, Larry. "Bush, Vannevar." *Dictionary of Scientific Biography.* Edited by Frederic L. Holmes. New York: Scribner, 1990, 17:134–139.

Pursell, Carroll. "Merriam, John Campbell." *Dictionary of American Biography.* Edited by Edward T. James. New York: Scribner, 1973, supplement 3, pp. 519–520.

Reingold, Nathan. "National Science Policy in a Private Foundation: The Carnegie Institution of Washington." In *The Organization of Knowledge in Modern America, 1860–1920,* edited by Alexandra Oleson and John Voss. Baltimore: The Johns Hopkins University Press, 1979, pp. 313–341.

Servos, John W. "To Explore the Borderland: The Foundation of the Geophysical Laboratory of the Carnegie Institution of Washington." *Historical Studies in the Physical Sciences* 14 (1983): 147–185.

Thomas D. Cornell

Carothers, Wallace Hume (1896–1937)

Pioneer polymer chemist and discoverer of nylon. Born in Burlington, Iowa, he graduated from Tarkio College, Missouri, in 1920. He received an M.A. and Ph.D. from the University of Illinois in 1921 and 1924, respectively. At Illinois, he studied under the eminent organic chemist Roger Adams. During the 1921–1922 school year, he taught at the University of South Dakota. From

1924 to 1928, he served as instructor of organic chemistry at Illinois and Harvard for two years each. In 1928, Carothers left Harvard to accept a position as group leader in organic chemistry in the recently established fundamental research unit in the central research laboratory of the DuPont Company in Wilmington, Delaware. At DuPont, he did pioneering research in polymer chemistry and was largely responsible for the discoveries of neoprene synthetic rubber and nylon. His career ended tragically when he committed suicide in 1937. He had been elected to the National Academy of Sciences the previous year.

While attempting to convince Carothers to join DuPont, central research director Charles M.A. Stine listed polymers or long-chain molecules as one important field that he wanted to include in his new fundamental research program. Although Carothers had done no work in this area, he soon developed a research strategy to investigate these complicated molecules. At this time, the center of polymer research was in Germany where Hermann Staudinger several years earlier had made the assertion that polymers were long-chain covalently bonded organic molecules, differing from ordinary organic molecules only in size. This hypothesis contradicted the orthodox view held by Wolfgang Ostwald (son of the great Wilhelm Ostwald) and other physical chemists that polymers were colloids, aggregates of small molecules held together by weak bonds that were different from ordinary covalent bonds. To resolve this controversy, Carothers attempted to build up long-chain molecules using the simple standard organic reaction between an alcohol and acid to form an ester. By using alcohols and acids with reacting groups on *both ends* Carothers coupled together molecules into chains of polyesters with molecular weights over 10,000. In a number of important papers Carothers provided overwhelming evidence that polymers were just very large covalently bonded organic molecules. He also discovered that polymers could be formed by two different mechanisms which he called condensation and addition. The former were formed by condensation reactions such as that between alcohols and acids, and the latter by addition to double bonds. Importantly, Carothers's concepts and techniques allowed chemists to synthesize an enormous number of new polymers, many of which had commerical value.

For DuPont, the most important result of Carothers's research was the discovery of nylon, one of the most successful new products of the twentieth century. In April 1930, one of Carothers's Ph.D. assistants, Julian W. Hill, unexpectedly made a very strong fiber while attempting to make very high molecular weight polymers. This experiment demonstrated that synthetic fibers were feasible, but it was not until four years later that polyamide polymers—named nylon by DuPont—were found to have all the properties necessary to make a commercial fiber. In an unrelated experiment two weeks before Hill's discovery, another Carothers assistant, Arnold Collins, isolated a new liquid compound that, upon sitting, polymerized into a rubberlike solid. This new compound, named chloroprene, is an analogue of the basic building block of natural rubber, isoprene. The new polymer was the first one that was chemically related to natural rubber and was developed into a commercially successful specialty rubber, neoprene. Carothers's other major contribution to polymer science was in encouraging a young DuPont chemist, Paul Flory, to investigate the physical chemistry of polymers and polymerization. Flory then began his classical work, which won him a Nobel Prize in 1974.

In the post–World War II era, nylon appeared to be a dramatic example of pure science as the mainspring of technological innovation. This helped to raise the prestige of science generally and led DuPont and other corporations to invest heavily in basic research. More recent work has shown, however, that Carothers had almost no technological or commercial interests, and that the success of nylon was the result of many factors, including shrewd research management and the broad technological and market base of the DuPont Company. It has also been tempting to see Carothers's suicide as the product of conflict between a pure science and industry. Yet, a substantial body of Carothers's correspondence suggests that his suicide was not directly related to his relationship with his superiors. He had suffered from depression for many years and his mental health deteriorated after the discovery of nylon. He increasingly worried that he would never be able to duplicate the tremendous achievements he had made over the previous six years. This is a hard reality that many other scientists faced and grew to accept. If he was truly unhappy at DuPont, Carothers was one of the most renowned organic chemists in the United States and could have left DuPont for an excellent academic position. What precipated his suicide is not known, but personal factors, including the sudden death of a sister, may have been critical.

In addition to his scientific accomplishments, Carothers was an important figure in bridging what

C

had grown in the 1920s to be a wide gap between industrial and academic chemistry in America. His work demonstrated to industry that basic research could pay giant dividends and to academia that industrial researchers could do Nobel Prize caliber science.

BIBLIOGRAPHY

Adams, Roger. "Wallace Hume Carothers." *Biographical Memoirs of the National Academy of Sciences* 20 (1939): 293–309.

Hounshell, David A., and John Kenly Smith Jr. *Science and Corporate Strategy, DuPont R&D, 1902–1980.* New York: Cambridge University Press, 1988.

Mark, H., and G.S. Whitby, eds. *Collected Papers of Wallace Hume Carothers on High Polymeric Substances.* New York: Interscience, 1940.

John K. Smith

Carver, George Washington (c. 1865–1943)

African-American botanist, agricultural scientist, and educator. Orphaned and emancipated from slavery in infancy, Carver was raised by his mother's former owners in southwest Missouri. Unable to attend the local school because of his color, he left at an early age to seek an education. He encountered numerous obstacles but succeeded in obtaining a master's degree in agriculture from Iowa State College in 1896. The faculty of Iowa, including a number of leading botanists and two future secretaries of agriculture, was impressed by Carver's abilities. James Wilson claimed Carver was at least equal to the faculty in plant hybridization and propagation, and mycologist L.H. Pammel called Carver the best collector of fungi he had ever met. Because of his talents, Carver took charge of the greenhouses and taught freshman botany while a postgraduate student. He was thus the first black instructor at Iowa and was apparently asked to become a permanent faculty member there.

If Carver had remained at Iowa State, he would probably have gotten his doctorate and engaged in hybridization or mycological research. Believing he had a responsibility to aid other African Americans, he instead accepted an offer by Booker T. Washington to head the agricultural department at Tuskegee Normal and Industrial Institute in Macon County, Alabama, in 1896. Carver intended to remain only a few years before leaving to study for his doctorate but ended up spending the rest of his life there.

Tuskegee Institute was engaged in teaching basic survival skills to poor African Americans, and Washington did not encourage or support scientific research that did not have direct application to their problems. Naturally, the focus of Carver's research reflected Washington's priorities. Soon after his arrival, Carver established an agricultural experiment station—the only one entirely staffed by African Americans. Its low funding ($1,500 annually) helped ensure that Carver's research would be aimed at the problems of poor farmers. Carver also realized that the needs of poor, landless sharecroppers were different from those of Iowa farmers.

Many of the standard practices of scientific agriculture were theoretically sound but were too costly for impoverished sharecroppers and tenant farmers. Carver therefore focused his research on procedures that required few, if any, commercial products and could be easily duplicated. In several agricultural bulletins, he provided alternatives to expensive fertilizers. Bulletins on such crops as sweet potatoes, cow peas, and peanuts not only explained their cultivation but also suggested uses to replace goods bought from stores. Another bulletin told readers how to make paints from native clay deposits.

The closest Carver came to pure scientific research at Tuskegee was his continued work and contacts within the field of mycology. He collaborated with leading mycologists at other universities and the United States Department of Agriculture (USDA). He had a rare talent for discovering new or rare species of fungi, but lacked the equipment needed to identify all of them. Other scholars cited his findings in the *Journal of Mycology,* and the USDA retained a collection of his specimens.

Although Carver became the best-known African-American scientist of his era, he apparently made no significant scientific discoveries. His theoretical contributions were in the application of science to agricultural problems. He pioneered in the use of processes based upon available and renewable resources. A full evaluation of his scientific contributions is difficult because no records of his experiments have been found at Tuskegee. His only published formulae or processes are in three patents and in "recipes" in several of his forty-four agricultural bulletins. Scholars have debated the merit of his scientific work, but all agree that his fame encouraged other African Americans to pursue careers in science.

C

Carver's papers are in the Tuskegee University Archives.

BIBLIOGRAPHY

Elliott, Lawrence. *George Washington Carver: The Man Who Overcame.* Englewood Cliffs, NJ: Prentice-Hall, 1966.

Holt, Rackham. *George Washington Carver: An American Biography.* Garden City, NY: Doubleday, Doren, 1943.

Kremer, Gary R. *George Washington Carver in His Own Words.* Columbia: University of Missouri Press, 1987.

Makintosh, Barry. "George Washington Caver: The Making of a Myth." *Journal of Southern History* 42 (1976): 507–528.

McMurry, Linda O. *George Washington Carver: Scientist and Symbol.* New York: Oxford University Press, 1981.

Linda O. McMurry

Catesby, Mark (1682–1749)

Natural historian and botanist. Catesby was born of an aristocratic family in Essex, England, his father John being a lawyer and the magistrate of Sudbury in Suffolk. His grandfather was the Robert Catesby who had been involved in the failed Gunpowder Plot of 1605. Mark Catesby first traveled to Virginia in 1712, under the sponsorship of his brother-in-law, Dr. William Cocke, who would later become secretary of the colony. There he met influential people such as William Byrd II, and was entertained at Westover Plantation. Catesby gained recognition and money by sending valuable specimens, primarily botanical, back to England. In 1714, he traveled westward to the Appalachians, and during the same year to Jamaica. He remained in Virginia seven years, returning to England in 1719, where he was commissioned to produce a natural history of the New World. Catesby returned to Charlestown, South Carolina, in 1722, and in 1725 sailed for the Bahamas, where he remained for nearly a year; in 1726, he returned to England to begin the twenty-year task of producing *The Natural History of Carolina, Florida, and the Bahama Islands.*

Because of financial problems, Catesby learned the etching techniques himself and actually engraved the plates for the book. The text was issued in installments, beginning in 1729, bound into volumes of twenty plates each, with text in French and English. In all there were eleven volumes, for a total of 220 plates, with the last appearing in 1747. In May 1733, Catesby was elected a Fellow of the Royal Society.

In all, Catesby's monumental work illustrated 109 bird species, 33 amphibians and reptiles, 46 fish, 31 insects, 9 quadrupeds, and 171 species of plants; excluding duplicates, 75 North American and 3 Bahamian bird species were used by Linnaeus for modern taxonomic designations. After Catesby's death, George Edwards (1693–1773) took over the task of coloring the plates for a second edition of the *Natural History,* which appeared in 1754; a third edition appeared in 1771, and there were numerous other editions in other languages. Catesby's monumental *Natural History* was a celebrated work during the latter part of the eighteenth century, and was one of the primary means by which the Old World met the New; but with the advent of the Audubonian era (1827–1838), Catesby's work plummeted into obscurity.

BIBLIOGRAPHY

Allen, Elsa G. "The History of American Ornithology before Audubon." *Transactions of the American Philosophical Society,* n.s. 41, 3 (1951): 385–591.

Feduccia, Alan. *Catesby's Birds of Colonial America.* Chapel Hill: University of North Carolina Press, 1985.

Frick, George F., and Raymond P. Stearns. *Mark Catesby: The Colonial Audubon.* Urbana: University of Illinois Press, 1961.

Alan Feduccia

Cattell, James McKeen (1860–1944)

Experimental psychologist and scientific editor and publisher. Cattell developed an approach to science at Lafayette College (A.B., 1880) that combined a Comtean emphasis on quantification with a Baconian appreciation for the hypothesis-free collection of empirical "facts" and the usefulness of science. Throughout his career, he adopted methods that produced quantitative data about (potentially applicable) psychological phenomena, even if he often could not explain them. As a Johns Hopkins graduate student (1882–1883), he timed his subjects' reading of letters and words and claimed that people naturally read whole words, rather than syllables. (Many later reading teachers thus abandoned phonics for the "whole-word" approach.) At Leipzig (1883–1886), he became the first American to earn a German Ph.D. (in 1886) in the new experimental psychology with Wilhelm Wundt, and in England (1886–1888), he studied at St. Johns College, Cambridge, and adopted Francis Galton's interest in the differences between people, from which Galton developed his program of eugenics. By the mid 1880s, Cattell knew more about the new psychology than any other

C

American, and his father (longtime President of Lafayette College) used his connections to get his son a University of Pennsylvania professorship (1889–1891).

At this university, and especially at Columbia University (where he taught from 1891), Cattell developed a program of "mental tests" that used standard laboratory procedures—which measured (among other traits) reaction times and the sensitivity of the senses—to gather quantitative data on psychological differences. But he lacked a functional view of how these traits helped people live their lives, his tests produced no useful results, and by 1901 psychologists had abandoned them. Cattell then left the laboratory, but his address at the 1904 St. Louis Exposition—"On the Conceptions and Methods of Psychology," which called for the application of psychology—served to rally his students' generation, which proved eager to transcend its teachers' philosophical concerns. His later program for The Psychological Corporation tried to implement these interests.

From 1894 (when he founded *The Psychological Review* with Princeton colleague James Mark Baldwin), Cattell owned, edited, and (eventually) published five major scientific journals. Although his publications usually had professional goals—for example, *The Psychological Review* challenged G. Stanley Hall's leadership of the American psychological community—Cattell often seemed most interested in their profitability. In late 1894, he took control of the failing weekly *Science,* which soon became the country's most widely read general scientific periodical. In 1900, he took over another failing journal, *The Popular Science Monthly,* and used his editorship of *Science* to attract prominent contributors. (He sold the journal's name in 1915, but continued it as *The Scientific Monthly.*) In 1903, he began collecting data for what emerged (in 1906) as the first edition of *American Men of Science,* and in 1904, he sold his share of *The Psychological Review* and helped others start *The Journal of Philosophy, Psychology, and Scientific Method* (continued today as the *Journal of Philosophy*). In 1907, he took over *The American Naturalist* and planned to use it to promote his vision of a positive eugenics. (He implemented this vision by fathering seven children and by opposing in his journals eugenic sterilization and immigration-restriction efforts.) Soon afterward, however, he began following the editorial guidance of Columbia colleague Thomas H. Morgan, and the *Naturalist* began promoting Mendelian genetics. In 1915, he founded *School and Society* to serve educators as *Science*

served scientists. He edited these publications through the 1930s—and *Science* and *American Men of Science* through the early 1940s—and they largely defined his position in the American scientific community.

Cattell was always self-willed and always expected deference from those around him, and these traits often caused him trouble. In 1883, he lost his Johns Hopkins fellowship in part because he complained that the university president had "not taken as much interest in me as he might have." A Columbia colleague wrote in 1909 that "Cattell is chronically opposed nowadays to anything that anybody does," and in 1917 a friend complained that "it is too bad that Cattell is opposed to so many things." Cattell's opposition to others often emerged as a defense of academic freedom, and in 1913 he collected a series of *Science* articles in a volume, *University Control.* But these usually barely concealed ad hominem attacks on others that cost him friends. In 1913, when Columbia president Nicholas Murray Butler tried to force Cattell into retirement, these friends admitted his shortcomings but rushed to his defense. But he soon alienated most of them, and in 1917, when Butler finally fired him, ostensibly for opposing American conscription policy during World War I, Cattell found few supporters. He continued to edit his journals, established the Science Press to publish them, chaired the Executive Committee of the American Association for the Advancement of Science (AAAS, for which *Science* served as official journal, even while privately owned) for twenty years, and acted as psychology's grand old man. But he still alienated others, as the AAAS under his leadership hired and fired four permanent secretaries (i.e., executive officers) through the 1930s, and his public personal attack (as president of the 1929 International Congress of Psychology) on Duke University psychologist William McDougall scandalized American psychologists.

Past accounts—based primarily on Cattell's own reminiscences—emphasized his pioneering role in the development of psychological tests and his campaign (and personal sacrifice) for academic freedom. More recent analyses—often based on extensive manuscript research—attempt to place his action within the context of his personality.

BIBLIOGRAPHY

Cattell, James McKeen. "The Conceptions and Methods of Psychology." *Popular Science Monthly* 66 (1904): 176-186.

———. *University Control.* New York: The Science Press, 1913.

Gruber, Carol S. *Mars and Minerva: World War I and the Uses of Higher Learning in America.* Baton Rouge: Louisiana State University Press, 1976.

Poffenberger, A.T., ed. *James McKeen Cattell: Man of Science.* 2 vols. Lancaster, PA: The Science Press, 1947.

Sokal, Michael M. "The Unpublished Autobiography of James McKeen Cattell." *American Psychologist* 26 (1971): 626–635.

———. "James McKeen Cattell and the Failure of Anthropometric Mental Testing, 1890–1901." In *The Problematic Science: Psychology in Nineteenth-Century Thought,* edited by William R. Woodward and Mitchell G. Ash. New York: Praeger, 1982, pp. 322–345.

———. "Life-Span Developmental Psychology and the History of Science." In *Beyond History of Science: Essays in Honor of Robert E. Schofield,* edited by Elizabeth W. Garber. Bethlehem, PA: Lehigh University Press, 1990, pp. 67–80.

———. ed. *An Education in Psychology: James McKeen Cattell's Journal and Letters from Germany and England, 1880–1888.* Cambridge, MA: MIT Press, 1981.

Michael M. Sokal

SEE ALSO
American Men of Science; Psychological Corporation, The

Centers for Disease Control and Prevention

An agency of the United States Public Health Service (PHS) located in Atlanta, Georgia. Created in 1946, CDC, as it is usually called, grew out of a World War II organization, Malaria Control in War Areas, whose job it was to make the South safer for training troops and producing war materiel. After the war, the Communicable Disease Center, the first name for which the famous acronym has stood, continued work on malaria and other insect-borne diseases. It gradually added all diseases of zoological origin to its concerns, but this did not satisfy Dr. Joseph W. Mountin, the PHS officer largely responsible for its founding. He pushed CDC to live up to its name and embrace all communicable diseases. By 1960, this was accomplished. Even separate units of the PHS for sexually transmitted diseases and tuberculosis, previously located in Washington, had been transferred to Atlanta.

CDC was created to serve the states, to give practical application to scientific research. Even so, its laboratory division was soon internationally known for its authoritative work on salmonella and shigella and for its development of the fluorescent antibody technique by which disease organisms could be identified within minutes. The onset of the Cold War with its threat of biological warfare made a rapid response to disease outbreaks imperative. In 1951, CDC created the Epidemic Intelligence Service to answer any health emergency. The disease detectives quickly became famous for their ability to identify the cause of mysterious epidemics. To provide them with the data they needed, CDC began disease surveillance, first with malaria in 1950, then poliomyelitis in 1955, and influenza in 1957. Surveillance, now routinely done for hundreds of diseases, has revolutionized public health practice and is one of the initiatives for which CDC is best known.

By the 1960s, CDC had expanded its activities far beyond the control of communicable diseases. Nationally, it added programs in family planning and lead-based paint poisoning; internationally, it joined the campaign to eradicate smallpox; and, beyond the earth's orbit, it worked with the National Aeronautics and Space Administration to prevent the possible exchange of germs with the moon on lunar flights. CDC changed its name to better reflect its enlarged mission. In 1967, it became the National Communicable Disease Center; in 1970, the Center for Disease Control; and in 1980, the Centers for Disease Control. In 1992, the words "and Prevention" were added. Meanwhile, the institution's place in the PHS hierarchy changed as well. CDC began as a field station of the PHS's Bureau of State Services, and advanced by steps until 1973 when it became, like the National Institutes of Health, an agency of the PHS.

CDC played a leading role in the World Health Organization's campaign to eradicate smallpox. CDC staff worked in many countries but had sole responsibility in West Africa where the technique crucial to the success of the worldwide effort was developed. "Eradication escalation" used surveillance to diligently search for every smallpox victim and vaccinate their contacts. West Africa was declared free of smallpox in 1970, a year and a half ahead of schedule; surveillance subsequently became the key to eradicating smallpox everywhere. The last case in the world was in Somalia in 1977; two years later the world was declared smallpox free.

CDC was dramatically successful in the 1970s in identifying and helping to control three previously unknown and deadly diseases in Africa—Marburg, Lassa, and Ebola fevers. It also played a leading role in

C

understanding a mysterious epidemic that occurred in 1976 during the American Legion convention in Philadelphia. The cause of Legionnaires' Disease, as it was named, proved very elusive, but six months later a CDC laboratory scientist, Dr. Joseph McDade, identified it as a previously unknown though common bacterium.

CDC was sharply criticized in the 1970s for two ventures: its participation in the study of the long-term effects of untreated syphilis in black patients in Tuskegee, Alabama, and its nationwide immunization campaign in 1976 against swine flu, an epidemic that never materialized. The first study, often described as unethical, had been under way for a quarter century when CDC inherited it as part of the PHS venereal disease program in 1957, and was not one of its major thrusts. The swine flu campaign was a major initiative, launched to prevent a possible recurrence of the flu epidemic of 1918–1919 when a half million Americans died. Both projects, though strenuously defended by the staff, tarnished the institution's record.

In the early 1980s, CDC shifted its attention to lifestyle and disease prevention issues like the dangers of smoking and the necessity of exercise. It also began a study of violence as disease, something entirely new in public health. Any complacency that communicable diseases were under control, however, was shattered in 1981 when CDC epidemiologists discovered the AIDS epidemic. With fewer than a dozen cases, they identified a major threat to health, but several years passed before other public health agencies were convinced of the peril.

Activities of this complex institution stretch around the world. Most of the records are stored at the Atlanta Federal Records Center, East Point, Georgia.

BIBLIOGRAPHY

Etheridge, Elizabeth W. *Sentinel for Health: A History of the Centers for Disease Control.* Berkeley: University of California Press, 1992.

Hopkins, Donald R. *Princes and Peasants: Smallpox in History.* Chicago: University of Chicago Press, 1983.

Jones, James H. *Bad Blood: The Tuskegee Syphilis Experiment.* New York: Free Press, 1981.

Mullan, Fitzhugh. *Plagues and Politics: The Story of the United States Public Health Service.* New York: Basic Books, 1989.

Neustadt, Richard E., and Harvey V. Fineberg. *The Epidemic That Never Was: Policy Making and the Swine Flu Affair.* New York: Vintage Books, 1987.

Ogden, Horace G. *CDC and the Smallpox Crusade.* HHS Pub. No. (CDC) 87–8400. Washington, DC: CDC, 1987.

Reusché, Berton. *The Disease Detectives, I.* New York: Times Books, 1980.

———. *The Disease Detectives, II.* New York: E.P. Dutton, 1984.

Shilts, Randy. *And the Band Played On: Politics, People, and the AIDS Epidemic.* New York: St. Martin's Press, 1987.

Silverstein, Arthur M. *Pure Politics and Impure Science: The Swine Flu Affair.* Baltimore: Johns Hopkins University Press, 1981.

Thomas, Gordon, and Max Morgan-Witts. *Anatomy of an Epidemic.* Garden City, NY: Doubleday, 1982.

Williams, Ralph C. *The United States Public Health Service, 1798–1950.* Washington, DC: Commissioned Officers Association of United States Public Health Service, 1951.

Elizabeth W. Etheridge

SEE ALSO
National Institutes of Health

Chemistry

The history of chemistry in the United States may begin with John Winthrop Jr., son of the first governor of the Massachusetts Bay Colony. Within a year of his arrival in Boston in 1631, Winthrop brought chemicals, apparatus, and books from England and established the first chemical laboratory and scientific library within the present boundaries of the United States. His reading "Of the Manner of Making Tar and Pitch in New England" before the Royal Society in London in 1662 made him the first American colonial to present a scholarly paper to a scientific organization. Most colonists, however, paid little attention to the science of chemistry. Those interested studied with apothecaries or in medical schools and were mainly empirical and descriptive in approach. John Morgan at the University of Pennsylvania Medical School in Philadelphia was the first to present a complete course of chemical lectures, in 1765, and in 1767, James Smith at Columbia Medical School (King's College) in New York became the first professor to have the word "chemistry" in his title. At the College of Philadelphia, Benjamin Rush (1745–1813), one of the leading physicians of the time and a signer of the Declaration of Independence, held the first chair of chemistry in the colonies. His course, based on his textbook *A Syllabus of a Course of Lectures on Chemistry* (1770),

C

consisted of seven units: salts, earths, inflammables, metals, waters, vegetables, and animal substances.

The beginning of the American political revolution coincided with the chemical revolution, which emphasized the study of composition and thereby clarified the meaning of elements and compounds and of combustion. Its chief spokesman, Antoine Lavoisier of France, defined the chemical element and compound, stated the law of conservation of mass, introduced the system of nomenclature that formed the basis of today's chemical nomenclature, and after learning of Joseph Priestley's discovery of oxygen gas in 1774, correctly interpreted the results of Priestley's combustion experiments. Following Lavoisier's lead, chemistry moved from a speculative qualitative science to a quantitative analytical one. In the United States, chemists, such as Samuel L. Mitchill at Columbia and James Woodhouse at the University of Pennsylvania, overwhelmingly adopted Lavoisier's new chemistry. Woodhouse, who in 1792 founded the Chemical Society of Philadelphia, the first such society in the United States, had a ten-year debate on combustion with Priestley in Mitchill's journal *Medical Repository* after Priestley arrived in Pennsylvania in 1794 to escape political persecution in England.

The quantitative study of chemical identity and composition continued throughout the nineteenth century. In the United States, with its untouched vast mineral resources, the nineteenth century was the beginning of a long period of descriptive and analytical chemistry. The first published paper addressing chemical identity and composition, Dr. John de Normandie's "An Analysis of the Chalybeate Waters of Bristol in Pennsylvania," already had appeared in 1769 in Volume one of the *Transactions of the American Philosophical Society*. But the lack of apparatus, manpower, and public interest hindered additional work until President Thomas Jefferson appealed to chemists to apply themselves to the useful arts and sciences and encouraged the American public to support their study because the useful arts and sciences were important in promoting the country's prestige, power, and interests. Robert Hare at the University of Pennsylvania Medical School and Benjamin Silliman Sr. at Yale best exemplify the American outlook. In 1801, Hare invented the oxyhydrogen blowpipe, the first laboratory apparatus capable of fusing mineral samples; later he developed two types of electric batteries, the calorimotor in 1816 and the deflagrator in 1820. Visiting scientists

considered Hare's personally funded laboratory at the medical school unsurpassed in the world. His *Compendium of Chemistry* (1827), a textbook of plant and animal chemistry, inorganic chemistry, and physics contained more that 200 illustrations of his apparatus. Apparatus was in such short supply in the United States that when Silliman went to Europe to study in the early 1800s, he purchased $9,000 worth of apparatus and books. American chemists continued to have most apparatus made to order or imported from Europe until the 1840s, and only late in the century did demand support domestic production of laboratory apparatus and chemicals.

At the dawn of the nineteenth century, only six American universities (Pennsylvania, William and Mary, Harvard Medical School, Dartmouth, Columbia, and Princeton) offered separate courses of instruction in chemistry. During this period, chemistry made the transition from being one component of the college natural philosophy course, usually taught by clergymen, to a full-fledged academic subject offered in the third or fourth years. Silliman was instrumental in the transition. He regarded the importing of chemically based products from Europe an affront to the nation's independence and maintained that the United States would not achieve status as a world power until it produced its own chemists and became chemically self-sufficient. As professor of chemistry and natural history at Yale from 1802 to 1853, Silliman firmly established chemistry in the undergraduate curriculum through a combination of popular lectures filled with pyrotechnic demonstrations, pronouncements on chemistry's utility, and acknowledgement of God's omnipotence and the compatibility of science and religion. Eschewing European textbooks, he published *Elements of Chemistry* (1830), the most widely used American text of the antebellum period. His students, and Hare's, established chemistry departments in colleges from New England to Kentucky and Tennessee.

Although antebellum chemistry concentrated on data gathering, the period produced an exceptional theoretician, Josiah Cooke. Appointed chemistry professor at Harvard in 1850, Cooke established the college's chemistry laboratory with his own funds and used its facilities to determine precise atomic weights. His article "Numerical Relations Between the Atomic Weights and Some Thoughts on the Classification of the Elements" (1854) introduced a type of periodic table based on experimentally determined atomic

C

weights. Foreshadowing Dmitri Mendeleev's work, Cooke believed he could predict the properties of any undiscovered element and its compounds in any given series of elements.

The study of chemistry was not limited to college students, however. Popular lecturers strove to inform the public. Amos Eaton at Rensselaer Institute presented lectures and simple experiments to New England's and New York's farmers, mechanics, and housewives for over thirty years. In 1819, Dr. Russell offered lectures and experiments to the citizens of New Orleans, and the following year John Cullen, M.D., charged participants in Richmond, Virginia, ten dollars each for a series of lectures and demonstrations.

John Pitkin Norton at Yale was among the first of the new agricultural chemists to apply the principles of chemistry to improve farming in the United States. In the years after the Civil War, American science continued its applied research approach. Land-grant colleges established by the Morrill Act of 1862 stressed the practical aspects of chemistry and trained both agricultural and analytical chemists. Connecticut used Norton's ideas when it opened the country's first agricultural experiment station in 1875. Other prominent agricultural chemists included John Lawrence Smith, who taught at the University of Virginia (1852–1854) and the University of Louisville (1854–1866), and John William Mallett, who served as chemistry professor at the universities of Alabama, Louisiana (now Tulane), and Virginia, and in 1883 organized the chemistry department at the University of Texas. Smith carried out extensive analyses of soils and minerals; Mallett conducted an exhaustive chemical study of cotton, including the nutrients essential for its growth.

To pursue graduate degrees Americans had to go abroad, especially to Germany. Led by Harvard and Yale, American institutions began imitating the German universities in offering laboratory instruction and graduate degrees in science. Yale granted its first Ph.D. in science to Josiah Willard Gibbs, in 1863; in 1877, Harvard awarded Frank Gooch its first Ph.D. in chemistry. Universities excluded women and minorities from graduate study until much later. Ellen Swallow Richards, the first woman to enroll as a full-time science student at an American university, received a B.S. in chemistry from the Massachusetts Institute of Technology (MIT) in 1873, and though she later became the most prominent nineteenth-century American female chemist, no American university allowed her to pursue a graduate

degree. Twenty-one years elapsed before Fanny Rysan Mulford Hitchcock at the University of Pennsylvania and Charlotte Fitch Roberts at Yale, in 1894, became the first two of only thirteen women in the nineteenth century to receive doctorates in chemistry from American universities. African-Americans waited even longer. In 1916, the University of Illinois granted Saint Elmo Brady a Ph.D. in chemistry; thirty years later, in 1947, Columbia awarded Marie M. Daly her Ph.D. in chemistry.

By the 1880s, chemistry in the United States was moving toward parity with Europe. Credit for this achievement resulted from (1) professionalizing of the chemical community through the organization of the American Chemical Society in New York City in 1876; (2) the proliferation of journals such as *American Chemist* (1870), *American Chemical Journal* (1879), and *Journal of the American Chemical Society* (1879); (3) the great expansion of research into areas previously neglected, especially organic and physiological chemistry; and (4) the spread of scientific education including the founding of MIT (1861) and Johns Hopkins (1876). Gibbs best epitomized the stature American chemistry had achieved. His lengthy two-part paper "On the Equilibrium of Heterogeneous Substances," published in 1875 and 1878 in the *Transactions of the Connecticut Academy of Arts and Sciences*, introduced the phase rule and free energy to the study of chemical equilibrium in a complex system and inaugurated physical chemistry in the United States.

Whereas analytical, organic, and inorganic chemistry, much of it descriptive and empirical, dominated the nineteenth century, organic and physical chemistry dominated the first half of the twentieth century. With the discovery of subatomic particles, especially the electron in 1897 and the proton in 1911, chemists showed a new interest in theories of atomic bonding (valence) and molecular structure. In 1902, G.N. Lewis, then at MIT, proposed that an atom had its electrons arranged singly at the corners of a cube and that the sharing of one or more electron pairs by cubic atoms accounted for the bonds holding the atoms in a molecule. Lewis published his theory in 1916 after moving to the University of California at Berkeley, and though the cubic atom disappeared in 1923, his electron pair (represented by a pair of dots in a chemical formula) became the basis of modern bonding theory. Lewis summarized his ideas on valence in a 1923 monograph *Valence and the Structure of Atoms and Molecules* and at that

C

time introduced his well-known electron theory of acids and bases. Longtime rival Irving Langmuir, a General Electric research chemist who applied Lewis's theory to the elements following neon, in 1919 renamed the shared electron pair or nonpolar bond the covalent bond.

Lewis also was responsible for making Gibbs's thermodynamics intelligible to chemists. Gibbs's publications were highly mathematical and were lacking concrete examples to illustrate his thermodynamic principles; nor had Gibbs established a following of graduate students to continue his program. For over twenty years, Lewis and his coworkers provided the experimental evidence supporting thermodynamic functions such as entropy and free energy while introducing important new relations such as Lewis's fugacity. This work appeared in *Thermodynamics and the Free Energy of Chemical Substances,* another classic, published in 1923.

With the maturing of chemistry in the United States in the early twentieth century, international recognition followed. Harvard's Theodore W. Richards in 1914 became the first American chemist to receive the Nobel Prize for his precise atomic weight determinations of twenty-five elements. Langmuir received the Nobel Prize in 1932 for his research on monomolecular films and surface chemistry. He was the first American industrial scientist to win the prize. At Columbia, Harold Urey's spectroscopic discovery of deuterium (heavy hydrogen) by evaporation of liquid hydrogen, earned him the 1934 prize.

Linus Pauling at the California Institute of Technology was the most influential American chemist to emerge during this period. In a series of publications beginning in 1929, Pauling transformed Lewis's intuitive and qualitative electron-pair bond into a mathematical quantitative valence theory that was completely compatible with the new quantum theory of matter that had emerged in the mid 1920s. Pauling further developed the valence bond method or theory of chemical bonding in his highly influential *The Nature of the Chemical Bond and the Structure of Molecules and Crystals* (1939), which remains required reading for chemists to this day. In the 1940s and 1950s, Pauling's combination of theory—hybrid orbitals in the carbon atom—and crystallographic techniques enabled him to determine the structure of crystals and complex molecules such as the proteins. For this work he received the 1954 Nobel Prize. Although the valence bond method

dominated into the early 1960s, an alternative theory of chemical bonding had emerged during the period 1926–1932. The molecular orbital theory developed by Robert Mulliken at New York University and the University of Chicago (and independently by Friedrich Hund in Germany) offered less graphic descriptions though more satisfying explanations of molecular polarity, oxygen's paramagnetism, and molecular spectra. Mulliken received the Nobel Prize in 1966.

In organic chemistry (including biochemistry), research centered on discovering reaction pathways and on structual determinations of naturally occurring macromolecules in order to bring about their syntheses. Melvin Calvin at the Lawrence Radiation Laboratory, Berkeley, used radioactive carbon (C-14) to reveal the reactions occurring in photosynthesis, and for his work received the 1961 Nobel Prize. At the Glidden Company of Chicago, Percy Julian, the first African-American to achieve the rank of chief research chemist for a major corporation, received over 130 patents for synthetic hormones, steroids, and drugs. Harvard's Robert Woodward, the 1965 Nobel recipient, succeeded in synthesizing numerous biologically important compounds including quinine (1944), cholesterol (1951), cortisone (1951), chlorophyll-a, (1960) vitamin B_{12} (1976), and numerous antibiotics such as tetracycline (1954).

In the 1940s, the field of nuclear chemistry emerged. Enrico Fermi had tried in the mid-1930s to produce new elements with atomic numbers (number of protons) greater than ninety-two (uranium) by bombarding uranium with neutrons. His results were inconclusive, but in 1940 Edwin McMillan and Philip Abelson at the University of California, Berkeley, succeeded in their uranium-neutron bombardment experiments to produce neptunium, an element with ninety-three protons. Glenn Seaborg and his colleagues at Berkeley continued the search for other transuranium elements, and in December 1940, they identified and named plutonium, element ninety-four. Secret wartime research on plutonium showed that its isotope Pu-239 (like U-235) was fissionable, but the announcement of plutonium's discovery came five years later with the dropping of the second atomic bomb on Nagasaki. After the war, Seaborg identified and named americium, curium, berkelium, californium, einsteinium, fermium, mendelevium, and nobelium (elements 95–102). He and McMillan shared the 1952 Nobel Prize. Crucial to the wartime fission

C

research was the theoretical work of Yale chemist Lars Onsager which provided the basis for the gaseous diffusion method of separating uranium's isotopes. Onsager received the Nobel Prize in 1968.

Since World War II, chemistry and the chemistry profession in the United States have undergone dramatic changes. A blurring of the dividing lines between chemistry and the other sciences has occurred. Chemists bemoaned the loss of job opportunities as physics, geology, genetics, pharmacology, environmental science, and chemical engineering usurped various areas previously belonging to chemistry. Biochemistry emerged as a separate entity, and chemical physics rivaled physical chemistry. In spite of the apparent disruption, American chemists from 1955 to 1990 won outright or shared eighteen Nobel Prizes in chemistry for studies ranging from the structure, synthesis, and physical chemistry of macromolecules to carbon-14 dating, and inorganic and organic reaction mechanisms.

During the twentieth century, chemistry departments in American universities have consistently ranked among the world's best. Led by such notable chemists as William A. Noyes and Roger Adams at Illinois, Farrington Daniels at Wisconsin, Emma Perry Carr at Mount Holyoke, Joel Hildebrand at Berkeley, William Lipscomb at Harvard, Paul Flory at Cornell and Stanford, Henry Talbot at MIT, Henry Taube at Stanford, Roald Hoffman at Cornell, and Francis Cotton at Texas A&M, they remain in the forefront of chemical research. Since the early 1980s, the University of California at Berkeley has consistently granted the most chemistry Ph.D.'s while Iowa State, Cornell, and the Universities of Illinois, Texas, Michigan, North Carolina, and Washington have excelled in both undergraduate and graduate education. No other country can match that record.

Historians of science have not given adequate attention to American chemists and chemistry. Despite increasing membership in the American Chemical Society's History of Chemistry Division and financial support from the Chemical Heritage Foundation's Beckman Center for the History of Chemistry, historical research and writing on chemistry in the United States is in its infancy. No comprehensive history and few books on chemistry and chemists suitable for science and liberal arts students exist, although the bibliography contains several entries that deal with specialized periods and branches of chemistry in the United States.

Historians of science generally divide into two groups, those with scientific backgrounds and those from the humanities or social sciences. The first group tends to emphasize the historical development of scientific ideas whereas the second group deemphasizes scientific ideas in favor of sociological interpretations. Both approaches are necessary to give a fuller and richer history, and historians of science writing today incorporate the internal and external influences on the development of scientific ideas and the impact of these ideas on society. The history of chemistry has followed this pattern. Edgar F. Smith, the first historian of chemistry in the United States, and Aaron Ihde, the dean of history of chemistry in the United States, began their careers as chemists. Their books reflect this background, although Ihde's *Development of Modern Chemistry*, written fifty years after Smith's *Chemistry in America*, skillfully interweaves the development of chemical ideas and the impact of these ideas on society. More recent histories have been either topical or have downplayed much of the chemistry in favor of anecdotal and biographical information. The current trend is biographies and collective biographies of chemists including compilations of Nobel Prize winners, women, and minorities; topical and periodic histories; and histories of chemical industries and institutions. There are few general histories of chemistry.

Writing the history of chemistry in the United States somewhat parallels the position of chemistry within the sciences. Books on colonial and early Republic science included chemistry with the natural sciences or medicine. Smith's volume treated chemistry as a full-fledged, independent discipline. When chemistry splintered into several branches, so did its historical scholarship. The history of chemistry moved from straightforward, chronologically organized surveys to more specialized interpretive studies. The interconnectedness of chemistry with most scientific disciplines has hindered current historians of science from pinpointing successes in chemistry and has made the writing of comprehensive histories an increasingly formidable undertaking.

BIBLIOGRAPHY

Brock, William H. *The Norton History of Chemistry.* New York: W.W. Norton, 1992.

Browne, Charles Albert, and Mary Elvira Weeks. *A History of the American Chemical Society.* Washington, DC: American Chemical Society, 1952.

C

Bruce, Robert V. *The Launching of Modern American Science, 1846–1876.* Ithaca: Cornell University Press, 1987.

Greene, John C. *American Science in the Age of Jefferson.* Ames: Iowa State University Press, 1984.

Ihde, Aaron J. *The Development of Modern Chemistry.* New York: Harper and Row, 1964.

James, Laylin K., ed. *Nobel Laureates in Chemistry, 1901–1992.* Washington, DC: American Chemical Society, 1993.

Miles, Wyndham D., ed. *American Chemists and Chemical Engineers.* Washington, DC: American Chemical Society, 1976.

Rossiter, Margaret W. *Women Scientists in America: Struggles and Strategies to 1940.* Baltimore: Johns Hopkins University Press, 1982.

Servos, John W. *Physical Chemistry from Ostwald to Pauling: The Making of a Science in America.* Princeton: Princeton University Press, 1990.

Skolnik, Herman, and Kenneth M. Reese. *A Century of Chemistry: The Role of Chemists and the American Chemical Society.* Washington, DC: American Chemical Society, 1976.

Smith, Edgar F. *Chemistry in America: Chapters from the History of the Science in the United States.* New York: D. Appleton, 1914.

Stranges, Anthony N. *Electrons and Valence: Development of the Theory, 1900–1925.* College Station: Texas A&M University Press, 1982.

Tarbell, D. Stanley, and Ann T. Tarbell. *Essays on the History of Organic Chemistry in the United States.* Nashville: Folio Press, 1986.

Thackray, Arnold, Jeffrey L. Sturchio, P. Thomas Carroll, and Robert Bud. *Chemistry in America, 1876–1976: Historical Indicators.* Boston: Reidel, 1985.

Anthony N. Stranges
Marlene K. Bradford

SEE ALSO
Engineering, Chemical

Chicago School of Sociology

Chicago's sociological tradition originated through Albion Small in 1892, and the university became its academic center. This group of scholars under the leadership of W.I. Thomas, Robert Park, and Ernest W. Burgess enjoyed prominence and disciplinary hegemony for at least two decades. Prior to Chicago's ascendancy, sociological work was the enterprise of independent, philosophical, and historical scholars, working in libraries, often without the benefit of academic appointments or well-organized university programs. The Chicago school established a new pattern for doing sociological work. They combined an integrated body of empirical research with theory as the exemplar for artic-

ulating sociological understanding. This focus was nurtured by a supportive organization and an infrastructure that joined outside financial support with the sociologists' vision of science and progress. It was this confluence of ideas, methodology, and organization that gave the department a position of worldwide leadership and hegemony from 1915 to 1935.

The Chicago school has frequently been a topic of debate among historians of the social sciences. Some question the degree of control and direction that it exerted over the development of sociology. Others maintain that not only did it exert hegemony, but Chicago has never declined and continues as a dominant force in American sociology. Still others question to what degree it truly was a "school" rather than an aggregate of scholars using a variety of methods, and favoring an eclectic theoretical approach to society. Regardless of one's position, the Chicago school is widely accepted as a potent force in the shaping of American sociology.

BIBLIOGRAPHY
Abbott, Andrew. *Department and Discipline: Chicago Sociology at One Hundred.* Chicago: University of Chicago Press, 1999.

Bulmer, Martin. *The Chicago School of Sociology: Institutionalization, Diversity and the Rise of Sociological Research.* Chicago: University of Chicago Press, 1984.

Faris, Robert E.L. *Chicago Sociology: 1920–1932.* San Francisco: Chandler, 1967.

Fine, Gary Alan. *A Second Chicago School: The Development of a Postwar American Sociology.* Chicago: University of Chicago Press, 1995.

Kurtz, Lester R. *Evaluating Chicago Sociology: A Guide to the Literature with an Annotated Bibliography.* Chicago: University of Chicago Press, 1984.

Matthews, Fred H. *Quest for an American Sociology: Robert E. Park and the Chicago School.* Montreal: McGill-Queen, 1977.

Shils, Edward. "Tradition, Ecology, and Institution in the History of Sociology." In *The Calling of Sociology and Other Essays on the Pursuit of Learning, Selected Papers of Edward Shils.* Chicago: University of Chicago Press: 1980, 3:165–256.

Barry V. Johnston

SEE ALSO
Sociology

Child Development Studies

The scientific study of child development is a twentieth-century phenomenon. Although the systematic and naturalistic study of children can be traced back to

Child Development Studies 119

C

the later nineteenth century, as in the child study movement of G. Stanley Hall and certain women's groups, child development as a science and scientific profession did not exist until the 1920s in America. During the late nineteenth and early twentieth centuries, women's clubs and other organizations, local and national, sought to advance the cause of child welfare, or the amelioration of the circumstances of the lives of children, especially society's least fortunate children, often dubbed then the dependents, the delinquents, the degenerates—in other words, not middle-class children at all. If a child were normal it was not in need of ministration or the benisons of child welfare reform.

The first research center devoted to the scientific study of normal (e.g., middle-class) children was founded at the University of Iowa in 1917, the Iowa Child Welfare Research Station (ICWRS); it was singular among the first group of child development research institutes in owing its existence to reformist pressure groups, especially women's clubs and organizations. In the 1920s, the Laura Spelman Rockefeller Memorial (LSRM) spent about $3 million creating an entire professional subculture of child development, including new research institutes at Teachers College, Columbia University, at Minnesota, Toronto, and California, and vastly expanded ones at Iowa and Yale. The LSRM also created centers for parent education in the new science of child development at many other schools, especially land-grant colleges, such as Iowa State College of Agriculture and Mechanic Arts and Cornell University, or at women's colleges, such as Mills in California, a postdoctoral fellowship program, subventions for a professional society and technical journals, and even grants to a popular magazine, *Parents Magazine.*

By the mid-1930s, child development as a science had taken shape. It was fully a part of general evolutionary theory in the natural and social sciences. Its mainstream champions established the field as one in which growth was taken for granted as an automatic process. Its twin hypotheses were (1) the fixity of the intelligence quotient at birth, and (2) the relentless development of the individual, according to the limitations and advantages of the group (race, class, gender, etc.) to which that individual "belonged." Thus, child development was a science with highly conservative social policy implications, and at the same time, child and animal development studies were an integral part

of general evolutionary theory, for they purported to interpret how and why individuals took on the characteristics of the groups (or species) to which they belonged in nature. Put another way, the larger culture's notions of social class, caste, and hierarchy were encoded, so to speak, in the ideas and research programs of the child development scientists, just as larger notions of the development of social systems were contained within functionalist, liberal sociology and anthropology of the interwar years. Child developmentalists did not study or trace the development of individual children as individuals; rather they assessed the variations from the presumed mean for a trait in a group at a given point of time, a cross-sectional rather than a longitudinal perspective, common even among the major so-called longitudinal studies of the interwar years, as at the University of California, where there were open-ended studies of infants and adolescents, and at Stanford University, where the mental tester Lewis M. Terman headed up a study of California geniuses (i.e., schoolchildren in the early 1920s with IQs of more than 140), in which the progress of any individual child was always ignored for the study of group "portraits" of the children in the entire study. This group determinism had been attacked by other child developmentalists, especially at the ICWRS, but also by social workers outside the academy.

By the 1950s, however, child development as a field found a new orientation. At the California institute, the managers of the longitudinal studies began to trace the development of individual children in their data samples as a way of reconciling certain anomalies in work on the unstable IQ and on emotional maturation. Animal psychologists began to notice that when the developmental sequences of their infrahuman charges were interrupted, sometimes fortuitously, sometimes through experimental design, that maturation was not automatic or predetermined. Over the next two decades, the field's hypotheses of the fixed IQ and genetically predetermined maturation, were largely set aside by developmentalists, although not always by more traditional psychologists. The new perspective in child development was one that was echoed throughout the culture from the 1950s on: the system was oppressing or constraining all individuals and making them into victims. Life was not fair, nor were all individuals interchangeable (a vital assumption undergirding interwar-era group determinism in American thought). Hence developmentalists began to focus on children as individuals, and especially on those individual children at risk, who were usually poor, nonwhite, or both, and who lived in disadvantaged circumstances. The new guru of child development studies, in effect, became someone like Harvard child psychiatrist Robert Coles, who in numerous books under the general title *Children of Crisis,* rallied many in the crusade for the rescue of children and for the establishment of their "rights." Thus did the post-1950s public discourse of victimization come to reshape the field of child development, providing an object lesson in the way in which any science is formed or is changed in historical context.

BIBLIOGRAPHY

Cravens, Hamilton. *Before Head Start: The Iowa Station and America's Children.* Chapel Hill: University of North Carolina Press, 1993.

Hawes, Joseph M. *Children Between the Wars: American Childhood, 1920–1940.* New York: Twayne Publishers, 1997.

Hawes, Joseph M., and N. Ray Hiner. *American Childhood: A Research Guide and Historical Handbook.* Westport, CT: Greenwood Press, 1985.

Hunt, J. McVicker. *Intelligence and Experience.* New York: The Ronald Press, 1961.

Sears, Robert R. *Your Ancients Revisited: A History of Child Development.* Chicago: University of Chicago Press, 1975.

Senn, Milton J.E. *Insights on the Child Development Movement in the United States.* Chicago: University of Chicago Press, 1975.

Hamilton Cravens

Childbirth and Childrearing

In addition to their many economic, social, and cultural roles, the overwhelming proportion of American women through our history have also been mothers. In childbearing, childbirth, and childrearing, science has entered into women's lives in significant ways.

Before the late eighteenth century in the British colonies of North America, midwives commonly attended laboring women in their homes. Yet, by the second third of the twentieth century, virtually all laboring women birthed in hospitals attended by physicians. Concerned about extremely high maternal mortality rates throughout most of these decades, parturient women sought out the safest childbirthing situations they could identify. From the 1760s onward, the new obstetrics, medical education based on the newly developing scientific understanding of the process of parturition, offered hope for improved birthing outcomes. In addition, mid-nineteenth century obstetrics produced anesthesia, promising to alleviate pain in physician-assisted births. Continuing research created increasingly complex methods of anesthesiology which were not conducive to home births, and which, especially in the first half of the twentieth century, accelerated movement of childbirth into hospitals. With faith in the efficacy and comfort of scientifically designed childbirth procedures, women slowly turned first to physicians as scientifically trained attendants and then to hospitalized childbirth. Still, despite the supposed potential for safer childbirth, maternal mortality rates did not drop substantially and consistently until the late 1930s with the advent of sulfonamides, blood transfusions, and, later, antibiotics.

Since the late nineteenth century, scientific research has contributed increasing detail to our understanding of the process of reproduction. Some of the most dramatic results of these investigations were the development of contraceptives such as birth-control pills and intrauterine devices, which have had a profound impact on women's lives and on social mores. Today, in vitro fertilization, reproductive technology, and the human genome project introduce new considerations into preconception and prenatal aspects of childbearing and continue to shape women's reproductive lives and American society.

The belief in scientific motherhood exemplifies how science plays a major role in women's lives. Elaborated in the nineteenth and twentieth centuries by educators, social commentators, scientists, child psychologists, and mothers themselves, this ideology insisted that mothers need to learn about science in order to raise their children healthfully. Doctors, child-care manuals, and the articles and advertisements in mass-circulation magazines promoted scientific motherhood. For educators such as Catharine Beecher and Ellen Swallow Richards, home economics, most especially instruction in nutrition and mothercraft, provided science education for girls. Federal government pamphlets such as the very popular *Infant Care,* first published in 1914 by the Children's Bureau, much revised and still in print today, and books such as Benjamin Spock's *Baby and Child Care* continue to impress on women the need for scientific expertise in raising children.

In the mid-nineteenth century, proponents of scientific motherhood encouraged women to find and

C

evaluate scientific information for themselves. By the twentieth century, the ideology had been altered so that increasingly women were told not that they needed to learn from scientific expertise, but that they needed to follow the directions of experts. Reacting to this imposition model, in the late twentieth century, women's groups, such as the Boston Women's Health Book Collective and La Leche League, are once again seeking and evaluating for themselves the scientific information necessary to inform their childrearing, childbearing, and childbirth practices.

BIBLIOGRAPHY

Apple, Rima D. *Mothers and Medicine: A Social History of Infant Feeding, 1890–1950.* Madison: University of Wisconsin Press, 1987.

———. "Constructing Mothers: Scientific Motherhood in the Nineteenth and Twentieth Centuries." *Social Studies of Medicine* 8 (1995): 161–178.

———. "The Science of Homemaking: A History of Middle School Home Economics to 1970." In *The Education of Early Adolescents: Home Economics in the Middle School,* edited by Frances M. Smith and Cheryl O. Hausafus: Peoria, IL: American Home Economics Association, 39–48.

Beecher, Catharine. *A Treatise on Domestic Economy for the Use of Young Ladies at Home, at School.* New York: Harper & Brothers, 1848.

Boston Women's Health Book Collective. *Ourselves and Our Children.* New York: Random House, 1978.

Cowan, Ruth Schwartz. "Genetic Technology and Reproductive Choice: An Ethics for Autonomy." In *The Codes of Codes: Scientific and Social Issues in the Human Genome Project,* edited by Daniel Kevles and Leroy Hood. Cambridge, MA: Harvard University Press, 1992, pp. 244–264.

Gordon, Linda. *Woman's Body, Woman's Right: A Social History of Birth Control in America.* Rev. ed., New York: Penguin, 1990.

Leavitt, Judith Walzer. "'Science' Enters the Birthing Room: Obstetrics in America Since the Eighteenth Century." *Journal of American History* 70 (1983): 281–304.

———. *Brought to Bed: Childbearing in America, 1750–1950.* New York: Oxford University Press, 1986.

Weiss, Nancy. "Mother, the Invention of Necessity: Dr. Spock's *Baby and Child Care.*" *American Quarterly* 29 (1977): 519–546.

Rima D. Apple

China—Relations to Science in the United States

During the 1980s and 1990s, tens of thousands of scholars and students from the People's Republic of China came to American universities for advanced training. Among them were scientists who decided to remain here. Like scientists who came to the United States before the Chinese Communist takeover in 1949—one immediately thinks of the Nobel Prize–winning physicists Chen Ning Yang and Tsung Dao Lee—they were the cream of China's talent and have immeasurably enriched American science. The level of achievement of the recent group of intellectual émigrés is not explained by talent and the efficacy of American graduate education alone; in their homeland they received training from the first and second generations of China's scientists, which laid the basis for their subsequent work.

With foreign help, China's first generation of researchers and educators introduced modern science to China. The majority of Chinese students who enrolled in doctoral programs during the 1920s, 1930s, and 1940s did so in the United States. Unlike the recent group of the 1980s and 1990s, it was exceptional for this first generation of scientists to find permanent positions in America. Moreover, they seldom wanted to stay; they returned home to staff departments in colleges, universities, and research institutes, building the scientific establishment that made possible the preparation in China of the researchers who are now here.

Thus, there is balance to the story of China's relations with American science. Starting in the second half of the nineteenth century Westerners went to China and Chinese went to Europe and North America and then returned to their country with the knowledge and methods they studied in the great academic institutions of the West. This process was mediated by missions, philanthropies, governments, and academic institutions—predominantly American. Protestant institutions placed the greatest number of mission science educators in China; the New York State chartered Rockefeller Foundation was instrumental in funding science in China; the United States government's remissions of China's Boxer War indemnity payments were likewise crucial to science funding; and it was American universities and research institutions which became most involved with their counterpart institutions in China.

During the second half of the nineteenth century, Protestant missionaries promoted science by taking positions in Chinese government translation schools and starting schools of their own. By the turn of the century, there were mission colleges with science departments, and there were mission medical schools.

C

The Union Medical College, a cooperative effort of three mission societies, one British and two American, became the nucleus for the Peking Union Medical College, the Rockefeller Foundation's "Johns Hopkins" in China, which opened in 1921.

Obtaining students who were prepared to study at a world-class medical school was difficult given the existing level of basic science education, a situation ameliorated by the Rockefeller Foundation's program supporting biology, chemistry, and physics education in colleges and universities. In 1917, the foundation began funding professors' salaries, advanced training in the United States for professors, science buildings, and laboratory equipment. New teaching positions were often filled by Americans, but starting in the late 1910s, Chinese Ph.D.'s were taking positions in mission and Chinese institutions.

The majority of these "returned students" had received their training in America because the United States remitted to China portions of her Boxer War indemnity payments. The first remission in 1908 endowed the Tsinghua Fellowships and preparatory school. This program sent qualified students to the United States for advanced training; the preparatory school evolved into Tsinghua University, China's "MIT." The second remission in 1924 endowed the China Foundation for the Promotion of Education and Culture, an organization which funded science education and research in a way that complemented the Rockefeller Foundation's premedical education program; it was Rockefeller Foundation officials who provided the information the China Foundation trustees used to make their funding decisions.

Before modern science was established in China, Westerners studied China's geology, paleontology, zoology, and botany. Excluding northeastern China, where the research department of the Japanese South Manchurian Railway Company was preeminent, in the twentieth century, American institutions were most involved. As a general pattern, American researchers would commission Chinese or Westerners to collect small items which were shipped to the United States for study. For the study of large items or the physical environment itself, expeditions were undertaken, perhaps the largest being the American Museum of Natural History's Central Asiatic Expeditions which collected dinosaur bones and eggs under the leadership of Roy Chapman Andrews.

Even after the outbreak of war between China and Japan in 1937, institutions in China with American connections managed to continue operation until the bombing of Pearl Harbor in December 1941. At the end of the war in 1945, contact between Chinese and American researchers resumed but did not reach former levels because of the unsettled conditions due to the civil war between the Chinese Nationalists and Communists. After the Communist takeover in 1949, China turned toward the Soviet Union for scientific and technical aid. Exceptional circumstances aside, as when American neurophysiologist Robert Hodes sojourned in China from 1954 to 1959, China had no contact with American science until relations with the United States were normalized in 1979.

Of course, Chinese science students were coming to the United States during the entire post–world war period from the Republic of China on Taiwan, and some of them found positions which allowed them to stay in the United States. By sometime in the 1980s, opportunities for careers in research and teaching had so improved in Taiwan that staying in the United States was no longer seen as the goal it once had been. One imagines that as the People's Republic of China develops, Chinese from the mainland will be more inclined to return home to make their careers. The addition of significant numbers of mainland Chinese to America's corps of scientists has facilitated the resumption of ties between Chinese and American scientific institutions.

BIBLIOGRAPHY

Buck, Peter. *American Science and Modern China, 1876–1936.* New York: Cambridge University Press, 1980.

Bullock, Mary Brown. *An American Transplant: The Rockefeller Foundation & Peking Union Medical College.* Berkeley: University of California Press, 1980.

Haas, William J. *China Voyager: Gist Gee's Life in Science* Armonk, NY: M.E. Sharpe, 1996.

Reardon-Anderson, James. *The Study of Change: Chemistry in China, 1840–1949.* New York: Cambridge University Press, 1991.

Schneider, Laurence, ed. *Lysenkoism in China: Proceedings of the 1956 Qingdao Genetics Symposium.* Armonk, NY: M.E. Sharpe, 1986.

William J. Haas

Civil War and Science

The vast sums poured by government into scientific and technological development during World War II and the Cold War have led some to assume a similar stimulus

C

during the Civil War. Even at the time, some scientists, especially chemists, and many of the public hoped for one. But most scientists of the period feared the opposite, and they turned out to be better prophets. Even chemistry, much less other sciences, had not matured to the point of significant application to war making. In any case, the perennial expectation of an imminent peace seemed to make long-range research and development programs pointless. The same inhibition applied to military technology, in which government emphasis was on standardization and immediate production, to which private manufacturers necessarily acceded. In industrial capacity and technology, moreover, the Confederacy lacked the base and the Union consequently lacked the challenge. In the first two years of the war, President Abraham Lincoln personally involved himself in pressing innovation, but he was largely frustrated by the obstructionism of the army's chief of ordnance, General James W. Ripley. Although the Civil War is notable for the utilization of prewar innovations, it gave birth to few.

Far from helping American science, the war injured it. In the South, where science had been weakest before the war, military operations physically destroyed a significant proportion of scientific facilities, books, manuscripts, collections, and apparatus. The battle lines and blockade cut off the South from outside developments in science. Many Southern colleges were closed or drained of students by the military, and endowments were gutted by inflation or economic collapse. The South emerged from the war even further behind other regions in science than before.

Especially in the South but also in the North, the excitement and disruption of war suspended, slowed, or diverted the energies of scientists, civilian as well as those drawn into military service. Although Northern colleges suffered less than Southern, many of their students in the services never returned to science, while prospective students postponed their training. Currency inflation straitened scientists on fixed salaries and drew some to nonscientific pursuits. Inflation also affected institutions like the Smithsonian, while the diversion of philanthropy to war ends sapped support of science, at least until the Northern war boom of 1863–1865. Several scientific journals and periodicals suspended publication, and the demands of government printing crowded out publication of scientific books. The American Association for the Advancement of Science, the principal national scientific body, was suspended until after the war, and lesser societies, many of whose members joined the military, were weakened or permanently disbanded.

The only significant benefit incident to the war arose from the withdrawal of obstructionist Southern members from Congress and the war-inspired activist spirit of that body. Pressure from the potent farm vote led to the passage in 1862 of the Morrill Land-Grant College Act, which in later years subsidized a fruitful development of scientific and technological colleges, and of the act establishing the Department of Agriculture, which later in the century developed a program that made highly significant advances in agricultural science. And in 1863, a small group of scientists with the aid of an adroit supporter in the Senate slipped through, in the harried last day of the session, the act chartering the National Academy of Sciences, which like the other two acts paid off handsomely for American science in the fullness of time.

BIBLIOGRAPHY

Bruce, Robert V. *The Launching of Modern American Science 1846–1876.* New York: Knopf, 1987.

———. *Lincoln and the Tools of War.* Urbana and Chicago: University of Illinois Press, 1989.

Dupree, A. Hunter. *Science in the Federal Government: A History of Policies and Activities to 1940.* Cambridge, MA: Harvard University Press, 1957.

Robert V. Bruce

Clark University

Chartered in 1887 as a modern comprehensive university, Clark opened its doors on 4 October 1889 as "the first and only important all-graduate institution in the United States" (Veysey, p. 166). Until 1905, it offered only Ph.D. programs. Its initial mission was solely to advance science through research and the training of specialist investigators.

The strategy of beginning with graduate work in a small range of disciplines made possible the recruitment of a talented group of researchers. Of the fifty-two members of the Clark community (faculty, docents, assistants, fellows, scholars) present on opening day, nineteen had either taken the Ph.D. or studied in Europe, most in German universities, and fifteen had either studied, taught, or done both at Johns Hopkins.

Clark was initially organized into five comprehensive departments (mathematics, physics, chemistry, biology, and psychology, the last including neurology and anthropology). Mathematics, headed by William E. Story, was the second largest American source of Ph.D.'s in that field in its first decade. Research in physics, with special emphasis on measurement and light, was directed by Albert A. Michelson. Chemistry, first under Arthur Michael and then John U. Nef, gave priority to research in organic chemistry. Biology, the largest department, was headed by Charles O. Whitman, who was also head of the Marine Biological Laboratory and editor of the *Journal of Morphology.* Franz Boas in anthropology made pioneering and controversial physical measurements in Worcester schoolchildren. Early graduate students in these and other areas were frequently among the leaders of the next generation of American scientists.

Internal controversy, largely over president G. Stanley Hall's administrative methods, alienated significant numbers of faculty as well as Jonas Gilman Clark, the founder. In 1892, many faculty and graduate students moved to the new University of Chicago and other scientific institutions, and Clark University was reorganized around a dominant psychology and education group and a smaller mathematico-physical group that included Arthur Gordon Webster, principal founder of the American Physical Society. The doctorate in chemistry, suspended in 1894, was restored in 1907; between 1914 and 1924, under Charles A. Kraus, the chemistry program once again drew national recognition. After 1902, the scientists in the initially separately endowed and administered Clark College often taught single courses in their research specialties in Clark University, supplementing what were essentially one-man graduate departments. Yet one out of every two Clark scientists in 1910 was a member of the National Academy of Sciences.

A pioneer of science research and education in 1889, thirty years later Clark had clearly been surpassed by numerous larger and better-financed universities. After Hall's 1920 retirement, the university was reorganized around a new Graduate School of Geography and related disciplines. Ph.D. programs in mathematics and the natural sciences were closed out, though individual scientists, most notably the liquid-fuel rocket pioneer Robert H. Goddard, continued to be productive researchers and scientific role models for undergraduates, as later studies of the collegiate origins of American scientists showed.

Experimental psychology was revived in the 1920s and 1930s under Walter S. Hunter and others. In 1931,

Hudson Hoagland, newly appointed head of biology, began a doctoral program in general physiology and gradually assembled a research group of some fifteen people in neurology and endocrinology, including Gregory Pincus, later to develop the first practicable birth-control pill. Largely supported by external funding, the physiology laboratory separated from Clark in 1944 to become the Worcester Foundation for Experimental Biology. The doctorate in chemistry was also restored in the early 1930s.

In the years immediately following World War II, Clark science departments largely prepared undergraduates for medical school, graduate programs elsewhere, and science teaching positions. But in 1955, a science expansion program began, with chemistry as the bellwether department, and the 1960s saw the restoration of doctoral programs in biology, physics, and mathematics. These programs often rested on collaboration with the Worcester Foundation, the Worcester Polytechnic Institute, a new University of Massachusetts Medical School at Worcester, and other nearby research and training facilities. Although the graduate program in physics remains the smallest in the United States and the mathematics doctorate has again been discontinued, the rise of Worcester as a biotechnology center in the 1980s and substantial additional endowments and facilities helped move the biology and chemistry programs into the cutting edges of neuroscience, biochemistry, molecular biology, and environmental chemistry, among other current research developments.

Early writings about Clark University are largely either apologetic or dismissive. The Clark University segment of Hall's self-serving autobiography is frequently uncritically used as a source. More useful for early Clark science is a volume published for the decennial in 1899. A 1937 Carnegie Institution study, based partly on interviews with former Clark scientists, catches the spirit of the early years.

Most general histories of higher education and science present Clark as a failed experiment after 1892. In 1965, Lawrence Veysey showed the continuity of research ideals throughout the Hall period and even later, as did Dorothy Ross in a 1972 biography that both deflates and humanizes Hall. A narrative history prepared in anticipation of the Clark centennial in 1987 describes subsequent developments in science. In recent years, numerous books and articles in the history and biography of the special sciences have utilized materials in the Clark University Archives (established

C

in 1972), which also houses a collection of early scientific instruments constructed or used at Clark, as well as manuscript collections of former Clark scientists housed in other institutions.

BIBLIOGRAPHY

Hall, G. Stanley. *Life and Confessions of a Psychologist.* New York: Appleton, 1923.

Koelsch, William A. *Clark University, 1887–1987: A Narrative History.* Worcester: Clark University Press, 1987.

———. "The Michelson Era at Clark, 1889–1892." In *The Michelson Era in American Science, 1870–1930,* edited by Stanley Goldberg and Roger H. Stuewer. AIP Conference Proceedings, no. 179. New York: American Institute of Physics, 1988, pp. 133–151.

Ross, Dorothy. *G. Stanley Hall: The Psychologist as Prophet.* Chicago: University of Chicago Press, 1972.

Ryan, W. Carson. *Studies in Early Graduate Education: The Johns Hopkins, Clark University, The University of Chicago.* Carnegie Foundation for the Advancement of Teaching Bulletin, no. 30. New York: Carnegie Foundation, 1939.

Story, William E., and Louis N. Wilson, eds. *Clark University, 1889–1899: Decennial Celebration.* Worcester: Clark University, 1889.

Veysey, Lawrence R. *The Emergence of the American University.* Chicago: University of Chicago Press, 1965.

William A. Koelsch

Claude, Albert (1899–1983)

Belgian-born cytologist who was awarded the Nobel Prize for Physiology or Medicine in 1974 for his discoveries of the structural and functional organization of the cell. Claude entered the Medical School of the University of Liège at the age of twenty-three and graduated as an M.D. in 1928. In 1929, he became an associate of James B. Murphy at the Rockefeller Institute in New York. In 1941, he became an American citizen. After twenty years in the United States, he returned to his home country, where he became director of the Jules Bordet Institute.

In Murphy's laboratory, Claude joined in the study of agents of transmissible tumors of fowls, for example, Rous sarcoma virus (RSV). To that end, these agents were purified using the ultracentrifuge and their properties were studied by chemical and serological means. In a 1933 review, Claude and Murphy concluded that these agents did not have the characteristics of typical viruses and were better designated as "transmissible mutagens." In 1938, a control experiment surprisingly revealed that when the procedure of isolating the transmissible tumor agent was applied to normal chick embryo cells, the resulting preparation was similar to that isolated from tumor cells, although without the tumor-producing activity. This started his investigation of the particulate components of the protoplasm of tumor cells as well as of normal cells. He concentrated on liver cells because their cell membranes are easily broken, with the nucleus staying intact, so that the latter can subsequently be removed. But he also studied undifferentiated cells of certain tumors, such as neoplastic lymphoid cells of the rat.

Claude developed methods of mechanical fractionation of cells by means of differential centrifugation. His work was characterized by the combination of preparative and quantitative studies. He stressed the quantitative recovery of the activity of interest, which meant that all fractions had to be analyzed, whether certain of them were to be discarded or not. This resulted in balance sheets in which the summation of the activities of tissue fractions was compared with the activity of whole tissue. He combined this approach with extensive morphological studies using light and dark field microscopes and, starting in the mid-1940s, the pioneering use of the electron microscope.

Claude's fractionation studies (1946) resulted in four fractions, namely, the nucleus fraction, the "large granules" (secretion granules and mitochondria, the latter containing many components of the respiratory chain), the "small particles" or "microsomes," and the supernatant fraction. On the basis of electron microscope studies Keith R. Porter, Claude, and Edward F. Fullam, in 1945, claimed the existence in cells of a "lace-like reticulum." Two years later, Claude, Porter, and Edward G. Pickels concluded that this endoplasmic material of the electron micrograph was the "small particle" fraction of broken-up cells which had been described earlier by Claude. Since then, it has been established that Claude's "microsomes" consist of fragments of endoplasmic reticulum, Golgi membranes, ribosomes, and other cell components.

BIBLIOGRAPHY

Claude, Albert. "Concentration and Purification of Chicken Tumor I Agent." *Science* 87 (1938): 467–468.

———. "A Fraction from Normal Chick Embryo Similar to the Tumor Producing Fraction of Chicken Tumor I." *Proceedings of the Society for Experimental Biology and Medicine* 39 (1938): 398–403.

———. "The Constitution of Protoplasm." *Science* 97 (1943): 451–456.

———. "Fractionation of Mammalian Liver Cells by Differential Centrifugation. I. Problems, Methods, and Preparation of Extract. II. Experimental Procedures and Results." *Journal of Experimental Medicine* 84 (1946): 51–59, 61–89.

———. "Studies on Cells: Morphology, Chemical Constitution, and Distribution of Biochemical Functions [Lecture delivered 15 January 1948]." *Harvey Lectures* 43 (1950): 121–164.

Claude, Albert, and James B. Murphy. "Transmissible Tumors of the Fowl." *Physiological Reviews* 13 (1933): 246–275.

Claude, Albert, Keith R. Porter, and Edward G. Pickles. "Electron Microscope Studies of Chicken Tumor Cells." *Cancer Research* 7 (1947): 421–430.

Duve, Christian de. "Tissue Fractionation: Past and Present." *Journal of Cell Biology* 50 (1971): 20D–55D.

Duve, Christian de, and George Palade. "Obituary: Albert Claude, 1899–1983." *Nature* 304 (1983): 588.

Florkin, Marcel. "Pour Saluer Albert Claude." *Archives Internationales de Physiologie et de Biochimie* 80 (1972): 632–647.

Palade, George E. "Albert Claude and the Beginnings of Biological Electron Microscopy." *Journal of Cell Biology* 50 (1971): 5D–19D.

Rasmussen, Nicolas. *Picture Control: The Electron Microscope and The Transformation of Biology in America, 1940–1960.* Stanford: Stanford University Press, 1997.

Zamecnik, Paul C. "The Microsome." *Scientific American* 198 (March 1958): 118–124.

Ton van Helvoort

Coast and Geodetic Survey, United States

The United States Congress established the Coast Survey in 1807 to chart and map the country's coastline. It remains the oldest scientific institution of the federal government. The name was changed to the Coast and Geodetic Survey in 1878 when a decision was made to link the surveys on the Atlantic and Pacific coasts by a triangulation across the continent. In 1982, the Coast and Geodetic Survey was renamed the National Ocean Service. Nine years later, a separate office within the Ocean Service of the National Oceanic and Atmospheric Administration was retitled the Coast and Geodetic Survey. Finally, in 1994, government reorganization resulted in the reestablishment of an office with the title Coast Survey.

This entry will emphasize the important role of the Coast Survey for the history of science in the United States during the period when the connection was especially significant, from 1843 to 1867, when Alexander Dallas Bache was superintendent. Under Bache's leadership, the Coast Survey became the key scientific institution in the country. Bache used the survey to promote scientific research in the United States and to control other prominent institutions, notably the American Association for the Advancement of Science, the American Philosophical Society, and the National Academy of Sciences.

The routine fieldwork of the survey involved various activities, including hydrographic surveying, topographic operations, and triangulation measurements. Bache expanded operations to the Atlantic, Pacific, and Gulf coasts, But in order to complete the practical function of mapping with great accuracy and precision, the Coast Survey pursued wide-ranging scientific research, from astronomical and geophysical studies to observations of the Gulf Stream and studies of microscopic animals from the bottom of the ocean. Astronomical observations were needed to measure the shape of the earth and to fix the longitude and latitude of stations. The best university and private observatories in the country participated in the astronomical work of the survey.

The Coast Survey could undertake extensive scientific research because Bache successfully gained popular support and convinced politicians that the research was compatible with commercial interests, For example, since navigation relied on a thorough knowledge of the variation of magnetic north, Bache argued that any attempt to uncover lawlike behavior of terrestrial magnetism would serve the commerce of the country. By pursuing research in such fields as the study of terrestrial magnetism, the Coast Survey was also participating in international scientific collaborations organized by European savants. Major leaders of the American scientific community, including Louis Agassiz and Benjamin Peirce, actively participated in Coast Survey activities.

Compared to other federal agencies supporting science, Bache's Coast Survey had by far the largest budget. By the late 1850s, the expenditures had passed the half-million-dollar mark, an amount of support not surpassed until the mid-1880s by the U.S. Geological Survey. The Coast Survey also sponsored more scientists—either directly on the survey or indirectly through Bache's policy of using consultants. As the most significant institution in this period, the Coast Survey played a key role shaping a geographical style

C

for nineteenth-century American science. Bache's efforts to join the scientific resources of the country to the requirements of the survey also helped promote a major new trend in the history of American science: science as a large-scale endeavor comprising a hierarchy of scientific workers and elite theorists. Bache was one of the first scientist-entrepreneurs in the United States. These individuals helped transform modern science from a fundamentally individualistic activity to the highly ordered practices of Big Science.

BIBLIOGRAPHY

Bruce, Robert V. *The Launching of Modern American Science, 1846–1876.* New York: Knopf, 1987.

Cannon, S.F. *Science in Culture: The Early Victorian Period.* New York: Dawson and Science History Publications, 1978.

Dupree, A. Hunter. *Science in the Federal Government: A History of Policies and Activities to 1940.* Cambridge, MA: Harvard University Press, 1957.

Manning, Thomas G. *U.S. Coast Survey vs. Naval Hydrographic Office: A 19th Century Rivalry in Science and Politics.* Tuscaloosa: University of Alabama Press, 1988.

Reingold, Nathan. "Research Possibilities in the U.S. Coast and Geodetic Survey Records." *Archives Internationales d'Histoire des Sciences* 11 (1958): 337–346.

Slotten, Hugh R. "The Dilemmas of Science in the United States: Alexander Dallas Bache and the U.S. Coast Survey." *Isis* 84 (1993): 26–49.

———. *Patronage, Practice, and the Culture of American Science: Alexander Dallas Bache and the U.S. Coast Survey.* New York: Cambridge University Press, 1994.

Hugh Richard Slotten

Colden, Cadwallader (1688–1776)

Renaissance man and savant of colonial New York. Colden was born in Ireland. After graduating from the University of Edinburgh and studying medicine in London, Colden emigrated to Philadelphia in 1710. In 1718, he took up residence in New York City after accepting a governmental post offered him by Governor Robert Hunter.

Despite his long and often contentious political career, Colden is now primarily remembered for his scientific pursuits. In 1727, Colden moved from New York City to rural Orange County and established an estate which he called Coldengham. It was here that he began a concentrated three years of work in botany, the study of which garnered him his most favorable international recognition. In 1742, Colden encountered the Linnaean system of plant taxonomy. He immediately applied the new method to his own work, becoming the first American to utilize this new research tool. Despite his admiration for Linnaeus's work, Colden faulted what he believed to be the master's unnecessary multiplication of classes.

Although he never seriously pursued the practice of medicine, Colden retained a lifelong interest in the discipline. Early in his career, Colden was an advocate of the iatrophysical or iatromechanical school of physiology. The idea was that by utilizing a cooling regimen, bleeding, and giving medicines to dilute the blood, the physician could control the velocity of blood and hence the course of the disease. Gradually, however, Colden adopted the iatrochemical interpretation of physiology wherein the motion of the blood is controlled by fermentation.

Despite Colden's accomplishments in botany and his activities in eighteenth-century medicine, he always believed that his attempt to refine Newtonian cosmology should form the basis of his lasting renown. The task Colden set for himself was to establish a demonstrable principle to explain Newton's theory of universal gravitation. Colden did not doubt Newton's premise; he only sought to provide an explanation for this phenomenon.

Around the year 1743, Colden acquired copies of Newton's *Opticks* and *Principia*. In 1746, a few copies of Colden's manuscript, entitled *Explication of the Causes of Action in Matter and of the Cause of Gravitation* were printed in New York. The work was not meant to be sold to the general public; it was for dissemination to luminaries in natural philosophy, both in America and on the Continent. Unfortunately, a pirated copy ended up in the hands of a London printer, who published, in 1746, an unauthorized edition. Within five years, French and German editions of the work were also published.

Colden always claimed that he wanted constructive criticism from his peers before embarking on a full-fledged interpretation of natural philosophy. However, because the *Explication* was receiving a good bit of attention in Europe, he plunged ahead with an expanded work. This work, *Principles of Action in Matter,* was published in London in 1751.

The most interesting of Colden's speculations on matter was his idea of light as "moving matter." It is Colden's theory of light as moving matter which has led at least two scholars to credit him with "growing toward a modern conception of energy" (Lokken, p. 371).

Even if some of Colden's conceptions were rather ingenious, it must be stated that his work did not have the impact he had hoped for. Despite being a professed disciple of Newton, he had not read the master all that carefully. This is confirmed by his theory of light as a source of motion. In his *Principles of Action in Matter,* for example, he barely alludes to Newton's insights on centripetal and centrifugal force and their relationship to planetary motion, which are contained in the first two books of the *Principia.* Add to this Colden's distaste for empirical research and his lack of any grounding in calculus and conic sections and it is small wonder that his work was subjected to the scathing animadversions of his fellow scientists, especially on the Continent, who viewed his speculations as deductive, aphoristic, and inadequate.

BIBLIOGRAPHY

Colden, Cadwallader. *The Principles of Action in Matter, the Gravitation of Bodies, and the Motion of Planets Explained from those Principles.* London: n.p., 1746–1751.

———. "Observations on the Fever which prevailed in the City of New York in 1741 and 2, written in 1743. Communicated to Dr. David Husack by C. D. Colden, Esq." *American Medical and Philosophical Register* 1 (1811): 310–330.

———. "Observations on the Yellow Fever in Virginia with some Remarks on Dr. John Mitchell's Account of the Disease." *American Medical and Philosophical Register* 4 (1814): 378–383.

———. *The Letters and Papers of Cadwallader Colden.* 10 vols. New York: New-York Historical Society, 1917–1937.

Jarcho, Saul. "Cadwallader Colden as a Student of Infectious Diseases." *Bulletin of the History of Medicine* 29 (1955): 99–115.

——— "The Correspondence of Cadwallader Colden and Hugh Graham on Infectious Diseases." *Bulletin of the History of Medicine* 30 (1956): 195–212.

Lokken, Roy. "Cadwallader Colden's Attempt to Advance Natural Philosophy beyond the Eighteenth-Century Paradigm." *Proceedings of the American Philosophical Society* 122 (1978): 365–376.

Mitchell, John. "Account of the Yellow Fever which prevailed in Virginia in the years 1737, 1741, and 1742." *American Medical and Philosophical Register* 4 (1814): 181–215.

Purple, Edwin R. *Genealogical Notes of the Colden Family in America.* New York: Private Printing, 1873.

Silliman, Benjamin Jr., and Asa Gray, eds. "Selections from the Correspondence of Cadwallader Colden with Gronovius, Linnaeus, Collinson, Etc." *The American Journal of Science and the Arts* 14 (1843): 85–133.

Stephen C. Steacy

Colden, Jane (1724–1766)

A pioneering woman of science in America. Colden, the second daughter and sixth child of Cadwallader Colden, was born in New York City. As did all the Colden children, she benefited from the scholarly influence and love of learning evident in the Colden household. Early on, she developed a fondness for reading and the study of natural history, especially botany. When her father first became familiar with the work of the great Swedish taxonomist Linnaeus, he lost no time in teaching the new system to his eager young daughter. He translated the technical Latin terminology into simpler English equivalents to enable her to more rapidly apply the new knowledge. In a letter to his colleague Gronovius, dated 1 October 1755, Colden told of his daughter's rapid progress and made reference to her illustrated manuscript of the flora of New York, which contained impressions of the leaves of 300 plants along with their descriptions and uses. He indicated that his daughter had devised a method of taking the impression of the leaves on paper with printer's ink using a simple kind of rolling press. In addition to the stimulation of working with her father, Jane was also inspired by the periodic visits to the Colden family estate of other distinguished botanists, for example, John Bartram, Alexander Garden, and the noted Swedish scientist Peter Kalm. Both Garden and Bartram made frequent mention of Miss Colden in their writings. References to Jane's work were not confined to the epistles of Bartram and Garden. In April 1758, John Ellis, a noted English naturalist, wrote to Linnaeus that, "This young lady merits your esteem, and does honor to your system. She has drawn and described 400 plants in your method. Her father has a plant called after him *Coldenia;* suppose you should call this (referring to a new genus) *Coldenella,* or any other name that might distinguish her among your genera" (Purple, pp. 19–20). Also, Peter Collinson, a friend of Colden's and an assiduous collector and disseminator of scientific knowledge, also wrote Linnaeus: "I have lately heard from Mr. Colden. He is well, but what is marvelous his daughter is perhaps the first lady that has perfectly studied your system. She deserves to be celebrated" (Purple, p. 20).

C

Miss Colden's chief work, alluded to earlier, was her botanical manuscript of the flora of the province of New York, written in a close but very legible hand. The accompanying ink drawings, though not done in painstaking detail, add considerably to the value of the work. In addition to the drawings and the careful physical descriptions of 300 indigenous specimens, she includes medicinal uses for many of these plants; this knowledge was acquired from conversations with local settlers and Native Americans.

On 12 March 1759, at the relatively advanced age of thirty-five, Jane Colden married William Farquhar and abandoned her botanical studies. Although her career in science was not a long one, it certainly did not lack for achievement and recognition. Her skill in the new Linnaean taxonomy brought her to the attention of scientists in both America and Europe. She might even have contributed to Linnaeus's great synthesis, the *Species Plantarum* of 1753, as her father did. But her name is not specifically mentioned. Perhaps she was one of the anonymous *aliique,* or others, to whom Linnaeus gave thanks for their contributions to his great work.

BIBLIOGRAPHY

Colden, Cadwallader. *The Letters and Papers of Cadwallader Colden.* 10 vols. New York: New-York Historical Society, 1917–1937.

Colden, Jane. *The Botanical Manuscript of Jane Colden.* Edited by H.W. Rickett. New York: Garden Club of Orange and Dutchess Counties, 1963.

Purple, Edwin R. *Genealogical Notes of the Colden Family in America.* New York: Private Printing, 1873.

Stephen C. Steacy

Columbia University

A private university in New York City founded in October 1754 as King's College. In 1767, a medical school was added, but the college effectively stopped operating during the American Revolution when the building was used as a military hospital. In 1784, the state legislature rechartered the school as Columbia College and in 1787 returned control of the college to local trustees. John Kemp, professor of mathematics and natural philosophy in 1787, lectured to about 150 students in the college with the use of such apparatus as a reflecting telescope, a compound microscope, and a set of celestial globes; Samuel Latham Mitchill, professor of agriculture, chemistry, and natural history from 1792 to 1801, and David Hosack, professor of botany from 1795 to 1811, also lectured in the college. The progress of the medical school was hindered by faculty quarrels, a dilapidated building, and an inadequate library, and in 1813 it merged with the College of Physicians and Surgeons, an independent school established in 1807. The failure of the medical school at Columbia seriously crippled science at the university for the next fifty years; since science was then only viable as a part of the university medical curriculum, it had a significant presence only at those universities, most notably Harvard and the University of Pennsylvania, with a strong medical program. Robert Adrain, professor of mathematics and astronomy, and James Renwick, professor of chemistry, both appointed in 1813, gave Columbia some prestige but science at the college was otherwise undistinguished.

Not until 1864, when Frederick A.P. Barnard was appointed president, did science become a significant presence at the university. Barnard gave his support to the campaign to transform the School of Mines (established at Columbia in 1863) into a science and engineering school, and under the leadership of Charles Frederick Chandler, professor of chemistry, the School of Mines expanded to include the teaching of mathematics, surveying, physics, geology, and palaeontology. Chandler was also responsible for the eventual merger of the New York College of Pharmacy with the university in 1905. The College of Physicians and Surgeons had, in 1860, agreed to a connection with Columbia, but since the medical college had entire control of its own affairs, the connection existed in name only. Chandler, as professor of chemistry at Physicians and Surgeons, helped integrate the two institutions and in 1891, the medical college became part of the university.

Under Seth Low, president of Columbia from 1890 to 1901, the university moved uptown to Morningside Heights. Low raised more than $5 million for the university during his tenure and transformed Columbia into a major research university. In 1892, the university established the Faculty of Pure Science, with divisions of astronomy, biology, botany, chemistry, geology, mathematics, mineralogy, physics, and zoology. Columbia also signaled the importance of science at the university by the construction of six major groups of scientific and industrial laboratories. In addition, the resources of the American Museum of Natural History were made available to Columbia faculty and graduate students.

As a consequence, the university rapidly became the leading center of academic scientific research in the

United States. Thus, in anthropology Franz Boas joined Columbia in 1896 and reoriented the discipline to a relativistic and contextual approach with an emphasis on empirical fieldwork. At Barnard College, Margaret Mead, in such works as *Coming of Age in Samoa,* focused on the importance of adolescence, child-rearing, and sex roles while another of Boas's students, Ruth Benedict, studied Zuni culture and published *The Chrysanthemum and the Sword* (1946), a widely influential study of Japanese culture. Boas was also influential in the creation of ethnology and folklore as academic disciplines; the *Journal of American Folklore* was edited by both Boas (1908–1924) and Benedict (1925–1940). Psychology developed through the efforts of James McKeen Cattell, professor of psychology at Columbia from 1891 to 1917 and editor of *Science* and *Popular Science Monthly.* At Columbia, he was responsible for the appointment to the faculty of the philosopher John Dewey and had many students who became influential psychologists, most notably Edward L. Thorndike at Teachers College.

In 1885, Michael Pupin, inventor of the loading coil, established physics at Columbia, where he taught mathematical physics and electromechanics until 1931. A number of physicists connected with the Manhattan Project studied nuclear fission at Columbia until the project moved to Chicago in 1942, among them Enrico Fermi, I.I. Rabi, John R. Dunning, Harold C. Urey, and George B. Pegram (later head of the university's Division of War Research). Faculty and former students at Columbia who won the Nobel Prize include, inter alios, in chemistry, Urey in 1934 for his discovery of heavy hydrogen, and in physics, Fermi in 1938 for work on neutron bombardment, Rabi in 1944 for measuring the radio frequency spectra of atomic nuclei, Polykarp Kusch in 1955 for work in measuring electromagnetic properties of the electron, Tsung-Dao Lee in 1957 for showing that the conservation of parity was not applicable to weak interactions, James Rainwater and Aage Bohr in 1975 for a new theory of atomic nuclear structure, and Jack Steinberger, Melvin Schwartz, and Leon Ledermann in 1988 for their discovery of muon neutrinos and electron neutrinos.

Henry Fairfield Osborn, later to become president of the American Museum of Natural History, was appointed chairman of the new Department of Zoology at Columbia in 1891 and in 1904 recruited Thomas Hunt Morgan as professor of experimental zoology. Morgan's studies of *Drosophila melanogaster* demonstrated the mapping of genes on the chromosome and accounted for the Mendelian laws of inheritance of characters at the cytological level. Morgan won the Nobel Prize in 1933 for his work at Columbia; other Columbia faculty who have won the Nobel Prize in physiology or medicine include, inter alios, Hermann J. Muller in 1946 for the production of mutations by X-ray irradiation, Andre F. Cournand and Dickinson W. Richards in 1956 for their development of a technique of heart catheterization, Konrad E. Bloch in 1964 for cholesterol studies, Salvador E. Luria in 1969 for his studies of bacteria and viruses, and E. Donnall Thomas in 1990 for organ transplant operations.

In the social sciences, Columbia offered instruction in political economy as early as 1821, but it remained a peripheral subject until 1880 when the School of Political Science was established at Columbia to provide a training for public administration. The school rapidly expanded in the 1890s to include statistics and economics; members of the faculty established the American Economic Association and were conspicuous in the leadership of the American Statistical Association. The progressivist spirit of the period was reflected in a curriculum that emphasized the study of, inter alia, principles of tax reform, social ethics and the administration of poor relief, railroad regulation, and antimonopoly legislation. During the twentieth century, the professoriat has served the federal government in advisory roles, most notably on the War Industries Board, the National Bureau of Economic Research, and the National Resources Board. Sociology at Columbia was dominated in the early decades by Franklin Giddings who stressed the importance of its application to social problems and the central position of quantification and statistics in its elaboration. During the 1920s, the emphasis shifted to the examination of social structures, and subsequent appointments, most notably Robert Lynd in 1931 and Paul Lazarsfeld and Robert Merton in 1941, have followed this trend.

In 1921, the College of Physicians and Surgeons moved to Washington Heights to form an affiliation with Presbyterian Hospital, a medical complex now known as the Columbia Presbyterian Medical Center; other scientific sites outside the main campus include the Lamont-Doherty Geological Laboratory in Palisades, New York, and the Nevis Laboratories in Irvington, New York.

C

BIBLIOGRAPHY

A History of Columbia University, 1754–1904. New York: Columbia University Press. 1904.

Lamb, Albert R. *The Presbyterian Hospital and the Columbia-Presbyterian Medical Center, 1868–1943: A History of a Great Medical Adventure.* New York: Columbia University Press, 1955.

Sloan, Douglas. "Science in New York City." *Isis* 71 (1980): 35–76.

Simon Baatz

Committee on Science and Technology, United States House of Representatives

A standing congressional committee created in 1958 to oversee federal science, technology, and space programs. As a response to the Soviet launching of *Sputnik* in 1957, it was initially called the House Committee on Science and Astronautics and concentrated on the space program. Over the years, it acquired broader jurisdiction that included all nonmilitary research and development and oversight of the National Aeronautical and Space Administration, the National Science Foundation, the National Bureau of Standards (renamed the National Institute of Standards and Technology in 1988), and the National Weather Service. It changed its name to House Committee on Science and Technology in 1974, as national attention shifted from space to energy and environment; to House Committee on Science, Space, and Technology in 1987, when the space-shuttle program rekindled interest in space; and to House Science Committee in 1995, when the Republican majority in Congress strove to cut back federal involvement in applied research. Overton Brooks (Democrat of Louisiana) chaired the committee from 1959, when it first became operational, to 1961. He was succeeded by five other Democrats, George P. Miller of California (1961–1973), Olin E. Teague of Texas (1973–1979), Don Fuqua of Florida (1979–1987), Robert A. Roe of New Jersey (1987–1991), and George E. Brown Jr. of California (1991–1995), and two Republicans, Robert S. Walker of Pennsylvania (1995–1996), and F. James Sensenbrenner of Wisconsin (1996–). Among the committee's legislative achievements were the establishment of the congressional Office of Technology Assessment in 1972 and the passage of the National Science and Technology Policy, Organization and Priorities Act of 1976, which created the White House Office of Science and Technology Policy. The committee's fight against pork-barrel science funding has met, however, with limited success.

While official histories of the committee praised it for providing Congress a much-needed mechanism to deal with science and technology policy, others have criticized it for boosterism for the space program and other scientific and technological projects. Unfortunately, few detailed examinations and no full-length, critical history of the committee by historians of science and technology exist. The records of the committee are in the National Archives.

BIBLIOGRAPHY

Dickson, David. *The New Politics of Science.* New York: Pantheon Books, 1984.

Hechler, Ken. *Toward the Endless Frontier: History of the Committee on Science and Technology, 1959–1979.* Washington, DC: Government Printing Office, 1980.

McDougall, Walter A. *The Heavens and the Earth: A Political History of the Space Age.* New York: Basic Books, 1985.

Stine, Jeffrey K. *A History of Science Policy in the United States, 1940–1985.* Washington, DC: Government Printing Office, 1986.

Zuoyue Wang

SEE ALSO

Federal Government, Science and

Compton, Arthur Holly (1892–1962)

Experimental physicist and science administrator. The son of a college professor in Wooster, Ohio, Compton developed an early interest in astronomy and aviation, and built his own telescope and model airplanes, including a glider which could carry him several hundred feet. He was educated at Wooster College, where he did his first work with X-rays, discovered by Wilhelm Roentgen in 1895. His older brother, Karl T. Compton, was interested in physics, and preceded him to Princeton, where both pursued graduate studies in physics. He soon focused upon matter and radiation, and studied the properties of thermionic and photoelectric emission with O.W. Richardson. He collaborated with his brother in the design of a sensitive electrometer which was widely marketed. Compton began his career as an instructor at the University of Minnesota before accepting a position as an industrial research engineer at Westinghouse Lamp Company in 1917. The use of physicists in such positions expanded significantly during and after World War I, which brought new recognition of the importance of scientific research in the design of instruments of war.

After World War I, Compton became one of the first two fellows of the National Research Council and traveled to the Cavendish Laboratory at Cambridge University, where he worked with J.J. Thomson, Ernest Rutherford, and Sir William Bragg on X-ray scattering. Returning to the United States, he accepted a position at Washington University, St. Louis, where he discovered the scattering of X-ray photons by electrons, one of the clearest indications of the wave-particle nature of light, which is named after him. The Compton effect was one of the experimental discoveries which led to the formulation of quantum mechanics in the 1920s, and Compton received the Nobel Prize in Physics for this discovery in 1927.

Compton began the study of cosmic rays in the 1920s, using sensitive electrometers which he designed and distributed throughout the world. These instruments were used by approximately 100 physicists in a dozen scientific expeditions all over the world to map the intensity of cosmic radiation. The results showed that cosmic rays were less intense near the magnetic equator, indicating that they were deflected by the earth's magnetic field and, hence, were charged particles, rather than gamma ray photons, as Compton's principal rival in the field, Robert Andrews Millikan, maintained. Ironically, Compton had assumed Millikan's professorship at the University of Chicago in 1923 when the elder physicist left to preside over the development of the California Institute of Technology. *Compton's Scientific Papers,* which have been collected, reflect this period of his life.

At the beginning of World War II, a number of émigré physicists became concerned that the discovery of fission by Otto Hahn and Fritz Strassman in Germany might lead to a weapon of war using the energy released in a nuclear explosive. Although Albert Einstein wrote to President Franklin D. Roosevelt to warn him of this possibility and a small program was begun under the auspices of the National Bureau of Standards to explore this phenomenon, progress was slow until 1941, when a National Academy of Sciences committee was set up under Compton to review fission research. This committee recommended an accelerated effort to develop an atomic bomb, and Compton turned the resources of his laboratory at the University of Chicago to that effort. In the Metallurgical Laboratory at Chicago, the properties of the newly discovered fissionable element, plutonium, were explored and the first controlled chain reaction was achieved by Enrico Fermi in 1942. Work at the Metallurgical Laboratory led to the production reactors at Hanford, Washington, which produced the plutonium for the first atomic device exploded at Trinity Site near Alamogordo, New Mexico, in 1945. He recorded his memoirs of this time in *Atomic Quest.*

At the end of the war, Compton accepted the position of chancellor at Washington University, St. Louis, which he held from 1945 to 1961. In 1961, he became professor at large at Washington University and the University of California, Berkeley, where he died in 1962. The role he played as scientific statesman is reflected in a collection of his occasional writings, *The Cosmos of Arthur Holly Compton.*

BIBLIOGRAPHY

Compton, Arthur Holly. *Atomic Quest.* New York: Oxford, 1956.

Johnston, Marjorie, ed. *The Cosmos of Arthur Holly Compton.* New York: Knopf, 1967.

Shankland, Robert S., ed. *Scientific Papers of Arthur Holly Compton: X-Ray and Other Studies.* Chicago: University of Chicago Press, 1973.

Stuewer, Roger. *The Compton Effect: Turning Point in Physics.* New York: Science History Publications, 1975.

Robert W. Seidel

Compton, Karl Taylor (1887–1954)

Experimental physicist. He was educated at the College of Wooster in Ohio where his father, Elias Compton, was professor and president. Like his brother, Arthur Holly Compton, he was attracted to physics by the study of X-rays, and published his first scientific paper on the subject in 1910 in the *Physical Review.* He studied photoelectric emission under Owen W. Richardson at Princeton University, 1910–1912, and provided experimental evidence for Albert Einstein's quantum theory of the photoelectric effect. He taught at Reed College in Oregon from 1912 to 1915, and then returned to Princeton as an assistant professor of physics, where he studied electron collisions in ionized gases. During World War I, he helped the army develop artillery ranging devices. After the war, he returned to Princeton, eventually becoming chair of the physics department. In 1930, he was appointed president of the Massachusetts Institute of Technology

C

(MIT), which he transformed into a leading center of advanced training in the physical sciences.

As president of MIT, Compton introduced research in modern nuclear physics, especially the use of the electrostatic accelerator by his Princeton student, Robert J. Van de Graaff. MIT also pioneered in the elaboration of techniques for technology transfer from the laboratory to the marketplace, working with the Research Corporation of New York, which converted the proceeds of licensing patents of academic science to support of research in universities and colleges.

Compton became a leader in the interwar scientific community through his efforts to help the physics profession overcome the financial problems caused by the Great Depression. He helped to found, and became chairman of, the Board of the American Institute of Physics, which rationalized the production of journals in the field, and defended science against the condemnations of technocrats and other critics of the rapid growth of scientific knowledge.

In 1933, Compton became the chairman of the Science Advisory Board, the first presidential science advisory board appointed by President Franklin D. Roosevelt. In this role, he became an advocate of social planning and of a recovery program for science under the National Industrial Recovery Act. His proposal for a National Research Administration, similar to the National Recovery Administration, called for expenditures of $100 million for fellowships, contracts, and grants. This proposal of a "science fund" failed to win the approval of the Roosevelt Administration, but was reincarnated in Vannevar Bush's proposal for a National Science Foundation after World War II.

Compton recommended that Roosevelt establish a permanent science advisory board and allocate funds to the National Academy of Sciences and the National Research Council, but again failed to win the support of administration officials, who were loath to allow scientists to distribute their own funds. Despite these setbacks and the demise of the Science Advisory Board in 1935, Compton's proposals had considerable influence on his vice president at MIT, Vannevar Bush.

Compton helped Bush organize the National Defense Research Committee (NDRC) which mobilized American scientists to support preparedness in 1940. The NDRC division he headed helped develop radar at the MIT Radiation Laboratory during the war under the auspices of the Office of Scientific Research and Development (OSRD), which he and Bush also

organized. After the war, he succeeded Bush as head of the Defense Research and Development Board, the postwar successor to the NDRC and OSRD. There he sought to provide an integrated research and development program for the new Department of Defense, built up a staff of over 200, with advisory committees totaling some 2,500. The board provided to the Joint Chiefs of Staff a systematic plan for military research and development in late 1949.

Historians have only begun to evaluate Compton's contribution to the rise of the national scientific establishment before, during, and after World War II. In addition to his contributions to the Science Advisory Board and wartime mobilization, the development of defense-related research and development at MIT after World War II has begun to attract attention.

Compton's career spanned the vast expansion of his field in the twentieth century. Unlike his brother Arthur, he has not yet been favored by a biographer, despite the richness of materials pertaining to his career in the MIT archives.

BIBLIOGRAPHY

Bartlett, Eleanor R. "The Writings of Karl Taylor Compton." *Technology Review* 52 (December 1954), 89–92.

Compton, Karl. *A Scientist Speaks*. Cambridge, MA: MIT Press, 1955.

Hewlett, Richard. "Compton, Karl Taylor." *Dictionary of Scientific Biography*. Edited by Charles C. Gillispie. New York: Scribners, 1971, 4:370–372.

Kargon, Robert, and Elizabeth Hodes. "Karl Compton, Isaiah Bowman, and the Politics of Science in the Great Depression." *Isis* 76 (1985): 301–318.

Kevles, Daniel. "Cold War and Hot Physics: Science, Security, and the American State, 1945–1956." *Historical Studies in the Physical and Biological Sciences* 20 (1990): 239–264.

Leslie, Stuart. "Profit and Loss: The Military and MIT in the Postwar Era." *Historical Studies in the Physical and Biological Sciences* 21 (1990): 59–86.

Robert W. Seidel

Computer

A device that performs computations without the intervention of people while it is in progress. It sorts data, files away information, edits, and otherwise manipulates (processes) facts. It is made up of a central processing unit and various peripheral devices, such as printers and data storage units. The two most widely known types are analog and digital. The most important class of machines was digital. They became the technological basis for the rapid growth of the data processing industry. Digital machines became more widely used because they could perform a wide range of functions and hence were used for specific and varied applications in both business and science.

Historians categorize machines by one of four generations, marking the years they were built and upon what kind of technology. The first generation (1946–1959) was characterized by the use of vacuum tubes. Main memory involved use of delay lines, electrostatic tubes, and magnetic drums. These machines were quite slow and unreliable. By the early 1950s, primitive software began to emerge for programming them. Common examples of first-generation machines included the ENIAC, EDVAC, SEAC, SWAC, Mark III and IV, UNIVAC I, IBM 701, 702, and 650.

The earliest work on this class of machines was done by John V. Atanasoff at Iowa State University in the 1930s and then by John Mauchly and J. Presper Eckert at the University of Pennsylvania during World War II. The latter two built the first functioning digital computer (ENIAC). During the same period the British built a computer called COLOSSUS and later the EDSAC under the direction of Maurice V. Wilkes at Cambridge University.

All during the 1950s, work was done to improve reliability and capacity, especially of memory (data storage). This was also the golden age of programming when many software tools used for the next quarter century were initially developed: operating systems and programming languages such as Fortran and COBOL. Finally, the first generation established the agenda for digital computers for decades to come. Out of this generation emerged the standard configuration (known as the von Neumann machine). Terminals made their appearance and theories of information science were applied.

The second generation (1959–1964) was characterized by the replacement of vacuum tubes by transistors, and the improvement of memory quality and processing speeds. Fortran and COBOL came into full bloom. Many commercial machines appeared to do both scientific and business applications: Burroughs 5000, CDC 1604, IBM 1401, and PDP 1. Easier to run and less expensive than first-generation machines, thousands of second-generation machines were purchased. Many could run multiple programs or jobs simultaneously due to more advanced operating systems. Appli-

cations extended from accounting to manufacturing to military and scientific uses. Some machines were extraordinarily popular. For example IBM sold over 10,000 1401s; compare that to UNIVAC, which sold less than 70 of its popular UNIVAC I in the mid-1950s.

Historians mark the arrival of the IBM System 360 family of computers in 1964 as the start of the third generation, which ran to 1970. Components in these machines were made from monolithic integrated circuits and reflected the first of the medium- and large-scale integration that characterized the technology of later machines. Speeds and capacities continued to improve along with reliability. The S/360 was the most successful product introduction in the history of the data processing industry, propelling IBM's annual revenues from roughly $2.5 billion at announcement time to over $5 billion by the end of the decade. The product consisted of five computers (later more models) of different sizes, generally allowing software in one to operate on another, and with compatible peripheral equipment and an array of software: operating systems, utilities, and programming languages. All major vendors in this period evolved their products into families of compatible computer systems, many compatible technically with IBM's. Major third-generation machines included the Burroughs 5500, CDC 6000, UNIVAC 1108, RCA's Spectra 70, and NCR Century.

The impact of compatibility and other features was enormous. Prior to S/360, if a company wanted to move up to a bigger computer, it had to rewrite all of its programs, learn to operate new equipment and operating systems, and establish new managerial procedures. That process was traumatic and expensive. S/360 signaled the end of "conversions."

S/360 relied on what came to be known as solid logic technology (SLT), which in English meant that IBM had decided to base its computers on chip technology, departing from transistors. Other vendors soon followed suit. Chips offered the opportunity to make significant strides in speed, capacity, and reliability— the same reasons for earlier changes in the bedrock technologies of computers. Machines of the 1960s also rationalized and codified the use of various innovations that were evident in peripheral equipment (e.g., printers, disk storage, tape drives, etc.) into logical systems that as a whole provided more function and reliability than earlier configurations.

Fourth-generation equipment began to appear in 1970 and many have argued that we are still in that

C

generation. It was a generation less distinguishable from the third than were the first two periods. Throughout the 1970s and 1980s, product introductions came in a continuous stream with no radical innovations. In 1970, IBM introduced the S/370, which also relied on chips and the already available virtual storage capability. Throughout the 1970s and 1980s, other members of this line of computers, like its competitors, emerged with denser chips, larger memories, and declining costs of computing. Because of the fuzziness between what constituted late-third-generation and early-fourth-generation computers, historians have quibbled on how best to categorize technologies so close to their time. It was generally accepted that the IBM S/370 seemed to provide some sort of delineation between the two generations, if not so dramatic as between the second and third.

The important features of fourth-generation equipment were not necessarily technological, although their improved efficiencies and capacities could not be denied. Rather, the dintinguishing characteristic was the increased use of such equipment by people who had decreasing requirements to understand their inner workings.

During the 1970s and 1980s, three classes of computers emerged. First, there was the large mainframe, often a multimillion dollar system that did enterprisewide computing. A second class, called mini or midrange computers, were used either by one location (such as a factory) or by small companies to do either a specialized set of functions (manufacturing applications, for example) or to provide a range of general accounting functions. A third class of computers was the microcomputer or desktop computer. The minicomputer came into its own in the 1970s, led largely by the product introductions of the Digital Equipment Corporation.

The microcomputer (also known as the personal computer or PC) emerged in force during the 1980s. The two classes of personal computers most widely used during the 1980s were the Apple and the IBM PC. By the end of the decade, over 150 vendors had similar products. All three types were in wide use around the world. By the early 1980s, over a million copies of the personal computer were being sold annually and by the early 1990s, tens of millions of this class of machine were in use.

In the United States, by the early 1990s, over 30 percent of the population used computers directly each day at work. Almost all of the other 70 percent were indirectly affected by this technology. The information processing industry was approaching $1 trillion worldwide and occupied nearly 10 percent of the Gross National Product.

The analog computer has enjoyed less historical attention, largely because this class of machines was not used to the extent evident with the digital. They first emerged in embryonic form in the 1930s and became commercially viable products by the end of the 1940s, primarily for continuous processing applications such as those evident in oil refineries. These machines are used more to measure than to calculate. They have monitored voltage, pressure, and temperature. The earliest applications of this class of machines were astronomical observations and then navigation. Analog devices have been used for thousands of years; however, the analog computer, like its digital cousins, such as the S/360 and PCs, came in the mid-twentieth century and relied on similar electronic components—vacuum tubes, transistors, and chips. They used similar peripheral equipment (disk storage and printers) but also had other analoglike devices attached to them such as barometers and voltmeters.

Between the two world wars, analog devices were developed to help monitor electricity for utilities. An important developer of modern analog devices was George A. Philbrick, who, in the 1930s, applied operational amplifiers to computers making it possible for such a computer to model an electronic network. Centers of development in the 1930s and 1940s included the Massachusetts Institute of Technology, General Electric, and Bell Laboratories. In the late 1940s, J.B. Russell of Columbia University designed an early general-purpose analog computer. That development made it possible for a wide variety of commercially available analog computers to appear throughout the 1950s.

By the end of the 1960s, analog computers were appearing extensively in industries, first in laboratories and engineering departments and then on the shop floor, tracking the flow of events, materials, temperatures, and other environmental conditions. Because of the narrower set of possible applications, they never sold in the same quantity as digital devices. For example, during 1972 in the United States, $47 million in analog devices were shipped to customers as compared to $1.8 billion in digital. Specialized manufacturers appeared, such as Electronic Associates, Systron-Donner, Applied Dynamics Corporation, and Telefunken. Only

Hitachi was a major provider of both analog and digital devices in the 1970s and 1980s.

BIBLIOGRAPHY

Ceruzzi, Paul E. *A History of Modern Computing.* Cambridge, MA: MIT Press, 1998.

Cortada, James W. *Arrival of the Computer in the United States, 1930–1960.* Armonk, NY: M.E. Sharpe, 1993.

Lavington, Simon. *Early British Computers.* Bedford, MA: Digital Press, 1980.

Shurkin, Joel. *Engines of the Mind: A History of the Computer.* New York: W.W. Norton, 1984.

Stern, Nancy. *From ENIAC to UNIVAC: An Appraisal of the Eckert-Mauchly Computers.* Bedford, MA: Digital Press, 1981.

Williams, Michael R. *A History of Computing Technology.* Englewood Cliffs, NJ: Prentice-Hall, 1985.

James W. Cortada

SEE ALSO

International Business Machines Corporation

Condon, Edward Uhler (1902–1974)

Theoretical physicist and research administrator. Born in Alamogordo, New Mexico, the son of an itinerant railroad construction worker, he entered the University of California at Berkeley as a chemistry major in 1921. He switched to physics the following year, and received his bachelor's degree in 1924, and his Ph.D. in 1926. He traveled to Germany as a National Research Council fellow during the academic year 1926–1927, and studied under some of the leading lights of the new theory of quantum mechanics, including Max Born and Arnold Sommerfeld. He became a physics lecturer at Columbia University in the spring of 1928, and thereafter took a series of appointments at various universities, including Princeton, the University of Minnesota, and Stanford, returning to Princeton in 1930 and remaining there until 1937. He accepted an appointment as associate director of research at Westinghouse Electric in 1937 with responsibility to expand that company's fundamental physics investigations, especially in atomic and nuclear physics. In the fall of 1940, Condon's laboratory began work with the Massachusetts Institute of Technology Radiation Laboratory developing radar technology, and Condon also served briefly with Robert Oppenheimer in organizing the Los Alamos laboratory that would ultimately produce the atomic bomb.

Condon was a national science figure by the end of World War II. He was elected to the National Academy of Sciences in 1944, and became vice president and then president of the American Physical Society in 1945 and 1946, respectively. He was confirmed as director of the National Bureau of Standards (NBS) by the Senate in November 1945. His great ambitions for this national laboratory were only partially fulfilled when he came to the attention of the House UnAmerican Activities Committee in the late 1940s, and was brought to testify before the committee on several occasions, beginning in 1951. Although he was ultimately cleared of any charges of disloyalty, and his scientific colleagues voiced their support by voting him president of the American Association for the Advancement of Science (1953), his security clearance was summarily suspended by the secretary of the navy in 1954. The effects of these investigations proved highly disruptive to Condon's career, beginning with his decision to leave NBS in 1951 to protect the image and operations of that institution. Thereafter, he became a consultant to the Corning Glass Works, a part-time position he maintained until his death. Several offers in 1955 for university professorships failed final approval at the trustee level due to political pressure.

It was the intervention of Arthur Compton that returned Condon to academia as physics department chair at Washington University (St. Louis) in 1956. In 1963, Condon moved to the University of Colorado at Boulder and joined the Joint Institute for Laboratory Astrophysics there, cooperatively operated as a division of NBS. Between 1966 and 1968, Condon headed "Project Bluebook," the unofficial name for the investigation into reports of unidentified flying objects, or UFOs, by the Office of Scientific Research of the air force. Condon considered the entire matter to be pseudoscience, and was alarmed by the lack of critical scientific thinking in the public at large, writing sarcastically at one point that, perhaps "we need a National Magic Agency to make a large and expensive study of all these matters, including the further study of UFOs" (Barut, et al., *Popular Writings*, p. 308).

Condon made his first substantial contribution to quantum mechanics and spectroscopic theory with the elaboration, in his doctoral dissertation, of what became known as the Franck-Condon principle. His reputation as a leading figure in these fields was established between 1928 and 1938, with a series of important articles in leading scientific journals and two major books:

C

Quantum Mechanics (with P.M. Morse, 1929) and *The Theory of Atomic Spectra* (with G.H. Shortley, 1935). He was centrally important in helping develop the science of quantum physics and disseminating his expertise in this country during the interwar period. Yet he is equally significant for the development of Big Science in the decades after World War II as an influential leader, and as advisor to other scientists and politicians. He served but briefly on the Manhattan Project, but long enough to author an in-house technical handbook on the project, dubbed "The Los Alamos Primer." Early in 1945, he was asked to advise the office of Senator Brien McMahon, chairman of the joint House-Senate Committee on Atomic Energy on the future of atomic energy research and supervision in the United States. Condon's efforts were in no small part responsible for the passage of McMahon's bill, which established the civilian Atomic Energy Commission.

It was in part through this work, which put Condon in frequent contact with Commerce Secretary Henry Wallace, that Condon became the first director of NBS appointed from outside its standing research force. The bureau had become, shortly after its establishment in 1901, the largest and most vigorous laboratory for comprehensive investigation of the physical and engineering sciences in the world, but it had atrophied in the 1920s. Condon wished to restore preeminence to the venerable laboratory, and immediately began designing and sponsoring new projects and divisions. The most remarkable NBS addition was the Applied Mathematics Division, which designed and operated SEAC, the Standards Eastern Automatic Computer, which began operation in May 1950. This was, at the time, the most advanced scientific computer in the world, and incorporated hardware and architectural innovations that set it far apart from its famous predecessor ENIAC.

Condon, then, is significant as a touchstone to all that was happening in the development of wartime and postwar American physics, including the political and social battles that swirled around it. As one of his colleagues, I.I. Rabi, later wrote: "Wherever the action was thick, there was Condon" (Barut, et al., *Popular Writings*, p. 8). His personal papers, comprising 75,000 items, are located at the American Philosophical Society. To date, his published papers have been edited, along with various biographical essays, into two volumes, but no book length treatment of his life has been written.

BIBLIOGRAPHY

Barut, Asim O., Halis Odabasi, and Alwyn van der Merwe, eds. *Selected Popular Writings of E. U. Condon.* New York: Springer-Verlag, 1991.

———. *Selected Scientific Papers of E. U. Condon.* New York: Springer-Verlag, 1991.

Condon, Edward U., and Philip M. Morse. *Quantum Mechanics.* New York: McGraw-Hill, 1929; reprinted, 1964.

Condon, Edward U., and G.H. Shortley. *The Theory of Atomic Spectra.* New York: Cambridge University Press, 1935.

Morse, Philip M. "Edward Uhler Condon." *Biographical Memoirs of the National Academy of Sciences* 48 (1976): 125–151.

Nelson R. Kellogg

Congress, United States, and Science

See Allison Commission; Committee on Science and Technology, United States House of Representatives; Federal Government, Science and; Joint Committee on Atomic Energy

Conklin, Edwin Grant (1863–1952)

Cytologist, embryologist, and biology educator. Born in Waldo, Ohio, he received a B.S. degree in 1885 from Ohio Wesleyan University. From 1885 to 1888, he served as a professor of Latin and Greek at Rust University in Mississippi (organized by the Methodist Church for the education of Negroes). In 1888, he entered The Johns Hopkins University where he studied under W.K. Brooks, receiving a Ph.D. in 1891. He returned to Ohio Wesleyan as professor of biology in 1891, moved on to Northwestern University (1894), and the University of Pennsylvania (1896). In 1908, he became professor and chair of biology at Princeton University and served until his retirement in 1933. Although his summer research began at the United States Fish Commission Laboratory in Woods Hole, Massachusetts, in 1890, Conklin transferred to the Marine Biological Laboratory in 1892 and remained an active researcher there for sixty-two years. He served as president of the American Society of Zoologists (1899), the American Association for the Advancement of Science (1936), and the American Philosophical Society (1942–1945, 1948–1952). Conklin was elected to the National Academy of Sciences in 1908 and received the academy's gold medal in 1942.

C

Conklin's meticulous cell-lineage studies of the embryonic development of the gastropod mollusc *Crepidula* (Conklin, "Embryology") and the ascidian *Cynthia* (Conklin, "Organization"), along with his experimental analyses of ascidian development stand among the most important evidences for mosaic or determinant development. Comparisons of his mollusc work with E.B. Wilson's cell-lineage study of annelid development prompted Conklin to sort out the variations in cleavage pattern among the mosaic embryos, thereby clarifying the problems of determining embryonic homologies among these organisms (Conklin, "Cleavage"). He argued that the cytoplasm of the egg possesses patterns of symmetry and polarity and often specific determinants of embryonic structures. Although considering himself "a friend of the egg" in disputes over the role of the nucleus versus cytoplasm in development, he recognized as early as 1905 (Conklin, "Mutation") that the patterns of determinants in the cytoplasm may owe their origin to the action of the nucleus during formation of the ovum. He speculated that major evolutionary changes may more easily be accomplished through changes in the egg than in the adult.

Although not a geneticist, Conklin became an advocate for genetics, writing extensively on the evolutionary significance of studies in genetics. Many of his 150 published works are discussions of evolutionary, genetic, and eugenic topics written for a lay audience. Conklin was depicted on the cover of a 1939 issue of *Time* magazine in which he was described as one of the principle architects of the public understanding of biology.

Although there are several brief biographical sketches of Conklin and a "spiritual autobiography," there is no complete biography. Along with E.B. Wilson, T.H. Morgan, and Ross Harrison, Conklin is described as one of the students of W.K. Brooks who led a "revolt" against descriptive and speculative morphology in favor of experimental approaches to biological problems. Although there is disagreement as to whether the growth of experimental biology was truly a revolution, there is general agreement that Conklin played a significant role in that growth. He has been frequently cited as supporting the concept of cytoplasmic inheritance in disputes over the relative role of the nucleus and cytoplasm in embryonic development. His popular writings on evolution have been analyzed in the context of his belief in teleology, his apparent pantheism, his deep concern for Christian ethics, and his clear sense that science and religion have different yet compatible roles in society.

The Conklin papers are housed at Princeton University. A brief analysis of their contents indicates that they are a rich source not only for studies of Conklin's contributions to American biology, but also for an understanding of the changes taking place in biology in the early years of the twentieth century, as Conklin maintained correspondence with most of the major figures in American biology between 1890 and 1945.

BIBLIOGRAPHY

Allen, Garland. *Life Sciences in the Twentieth Century.* Cambridge, UK: Cambridge University Press, 1978.

Allen, Garland, and Dennis M. McCulloch. "Notes on Source Materials: The Edwin Grant Conklin Papers at Princeton University." *Journal of the History of Biology* 1 (1968): 325–331.

Atkinson, James W. "E. G. Conklin on Evolution: The Popular Writings of an Embryologist." *Journal of the History of Biology* 18 (1985): 31–50.

Conklin, Edwin G. "The Embryology of Crepidula." *Journal of Morphology* 13 (1897): 1–226.

———. "Cleavage and Differentiation." *Woods Hole Lectures for 1896–97.* 1898. Reprinted in *Defining Biology: Lectures from the 1890s,* edited by Jane Maienschein. Cambridge, MA: Harvard University Press, 1986.

———. "The Mutation Theory from the Standpoint of Cytology." *Science* 21 (1905): 525–529.

———. "The Organization and Cell-Lineage of the Ascidian Egg." *Journal of the Academy of Natural Sciences of Philadelphia* 13 (1905): 1–119.

———. "Edwin Grant Conklin." In *Thirteen Americans: Their Spiritual Biographies,* edited by Louis Finkelstein. Harper and Bros., 1953.

Cravens, Hamilton. *The Triumph of Evolution: American Scientists and the Heredity-Environment Controversy 1900–1941.* Philadelphia: University of Pennsylvania Press, 1978.

Maienschein, Jane. "Shifting Assumptions in American Biology: Embryology, 1890–1910." *Journal of the History of Biology* 14 (1981): 89–113.

Sapp, Jan. *Beyond the Gene: Cytoplasmic Inheritance and the Struggle for Authority in Genetics.* Oxford: Oxford University Press, 1987.

James W. Atkinson

Conservation

See Environmental and Conservation Concerns

C

Cooper, Thomas (1759–1839)

English chemist and emigrant to the United States. Schooled at Oxford University, Cooper became an industrial chemist and medical amateur in Manchester, and also served as a barrister in Lancashire. His attendance at the Inns of Court in London coincided in part with his membership and participation in the Chapter Coffee House Society, among whom were the leading English chemists of the time.

After a visit to the Jacobin Club in Paris in 1792, he was labeled a radical by Edmund Burke and felt compelled to emigrate to the United States in 1793. There he attempted to prepare an "asylum" for political and religious dissenters.

In 1794, Cooper brought his family to America to discover, as did his associate, Joseph Priestley, that the "asylum" site was not suitable. The expatriates then settled in Northumberland, Pennsylvania. As an American citizen, he became an outspoken supporter of Thomas Jefferson in the late 1790s. Tracts opposing the policies of President John Adams led to his arrest under the Sedition Act in 1800. He was fined and sentenced to six months in prison. His wife died during his imprisonment and his family was cared for largely by the Priestley family. After his release and the election of Jefferson, Cooper received positions in the Pennsylvania state government.

In 1804, he was appointed as a judge in Pennsylvania. This coincided with the death of Joseph Priestley, whose numerous activities in chemistry and other subjects Cooper was asked to summarize. This reawakened Cooper's interests in chemistry, which he then pursued in Priestley's laboratory and library in the intervals in which he did not serve as a traveling judge. During political change in Pennsylvania in 1811, he lost his position as judge, and accepted the professorship of chemistry at Dickinson College, in Carlisle, Pennsylvania. Cooper brought equipment from the Priestley laboratory. His published inaugural lecture established him as both informed chemist and historian of chemistry. He developed improved lecture courses in chemistry and new student experiments, and published annotated editions of English texts.

Convinced of the utility of chemistry and technology in a growing country, Cooper became the editor of the *Emporium of Arts and Sciences,* which published practical papers on science taken from foreign publications. Cooper wrote many essays himself on manufacturing processes. The obligatory military service of his publishing staff compelled him to cease publication in 1814.

In the years 1815–1818, Cooper became a professor of chemistry at the University of Pennsylvania in Philadelphia. He lectured on chemistry and mineralogy; Cooper also annotated several texts on chemistry and encyclopedias. These include *A System of Chemistry* by Thomas Thomson (fifth London edition), which introduced Dalton's Laws to an American audience, *Conversations on Chemistry* by Jane Marcet (fifth London edition), and the *Domestic Encyclopedia* by A.F.M. Willich. He also published a collection of *Tracts on Medical Jurisprudence* and several scientific papers in the *Transactions of the American Philosophical Society.* He had been elected to the society in 1802.

In 1818, Cooper was a candidate for the chair in the department of chemistry of the University of Pennsylvania School of Medicine. The chair was given to Robert Hare, who had agreed to release the students from examinations in chemistry. Cooper addressed a "Discourse on the Connexion between Chemistry and Medicine" to the Trustees at Pennsylvania. He presciently pointed to a developing relationship between the two disciplines in which chemistry could be described as in "the infancy of Hercules" (Cooper, *"Introductory Lecture"*).

From 1819, he taught chemistry and mineralogy as professor of chemistry at the College of South Carolina in Columbia. He was elected president of the college in 1821, but continued to teach. His opinions concerning his chemical assistants helped to place these men in scientific careers in the North. As president of the college, he proselytized in the state for a medical college, which was then formed in Charleston. He helped in the direction of a mental asylum in Columbia and contributed a mineralogical collection which became a major initiating component of the state geological survey. As his work in chemistry became less active, his interests in the nature of mental aberration grew, leading to his translation of F.J.V. Broussais's *On Irritation and Insanity* (1831). He followed geological advances closely, and taught that the Old Testament was not a satisfactory guide to the age of the earth. In the early 1830s, this teaching was attacked by fundamentalist clergy, who attempted to compel Cooper's discharge on the grounds of "infidelity." In 1832, Cooper fought these charges and was able to win the battle for his own freedom of speech. Nevertheless, he resigned from the presidency of the college in 1833 and began to seek new activities. Early in 1835, Cooper was appointed by the governor to compile the statute laws of the state, and five volumes of this important work appeared. Another five were completed by his successor.

Cooper was a significant teacher of chemistry and his annotated texts were useful in the development of the discipline in America. Cooper also achieved an early repetition of H. Davy's isolation of potassium. He was also an important teacher of mineralogy and geology in Dickinson College, the University of Pennsylvania, and in the South Carolina College.

His major laboratory discoveries have not received appropriate attention. In Manchester, Cooper, associated with a textile bleaching firm, was the first to achieve a commercially useful method of producing chlorine and hypochlorite for industrial bleaching. In developing the procedure, chlorine and hypochlorite were produced in closed barrels containing the cloth to be bleached. A rapid bleaching occurred, which is possibly attributable to the use of a reaction at a pressure greater than that existing in open vats. Actually, Cooper had explored the use of autoclaves to this end in collaboration with James Watt. In a second instance, Professor Cooper at Carlisle was provided with pieces of rockets discharged at Havre-de-Grace in Maryland in 1813. Cooper correctly analyzed and characterized the nature of this weapon, permitting its subsequent reconstruction.

The biographer Dumas Malone described Cooper as a man "ahead of his own age," and whose championing of freedom of mind were essential to scientific progress.

BIBLIOGRAPHY

Bell, Whitfield. "Thomas Cooper as Professor of Chemistry at Dickinson College 1811–1815." *Journal of the History of Medicine* 8 (1953): 70–87.

Cooper, Thomas. *Some Information Respecting America.* Dublin and London, 1794.

———. "Appendix No. I. An Account of Dr. Priestley's Discoveries in Chemistry, and of His Writings on That, and Other Scientific Subjects." In *Memoirs of Dr. Joseph Priestley.* Northumberland: John Binns, 1806.

———. *A Practical Treatise on Dyeing and Callicoe Printing.* Philadelphia: Thomas Dobson, 1815.

———. *Lectures on the Elements of Political Economy.* 2d ed., 1830. Reprint New York: Augustus M. Kelley, 1971.

———. *"The Introductory Lecture" (1811) and "A Discourse on the Connexion between Chemistry and Medicine" (1818).* New York: Arno Press, 1980.

Davenport, Derek A. "Reason and Relevance: The 1811–1813 Lectures of Professor Thomas Cooper." *Journal of Chemical Education* 53 (1976): 419–422.

Edelstein, Sidney M. "The Contributions of Thomas Cooper." *American Dyestuff Reporter* 43 (1954): 181–182.

Greene, John C. "The Development of Mineralogy in Philadelphia, 1780–1820." *Proceedings of the American Philosophical Society* 113 (1969): 283–295.

Jaffe, Bernard. "Thomas Cooper (1759–1839): Science Advances Slowly in the Newborn Republic." In *Men of Science in America.* New York: Simon and Schuster, 1944.

Klickstein, Herbert S. "An Early American Discourse on the Connexion between Chemistry and Medicine." *The Library Chronicle (University of Pennsylvania)* 16 (1950): 64–80.

———. "A Short History of the Professorship of Chemistry of the University of Pennsylvania School of Medicine 1765–1847." *Bulletin of the History of Medicine* 27 (1953): 43–68.

Malone, Dumas. *The Public Life of Thomas Cooper 1783–1839.* New Haven: Yale University Press, 1926.

———. "Thomas Cooper: Foe of Governmental Centralization." In *The Unforgettable Americans,* edited by John A. Garraty. Great Neck, NY: Channel Press, 1960.

Musson, A.E., and E. Robinson. *Science and Technology in the Industrial Revolution.* Manchester: Manchester University Press, 1969.

Smith, Edgar F. *Chemistry in America.* New York: D. Appleton, 1914.

Seymour S. Cohen

Cooper Union for the Advancement of Science and Art

Cooper Union, created for "honest mechanics and virtuous womanhood," opened in 1859 to provide the practical education Peter Cooper hoped to offer these groups. Cooper, who was himself very poorly educated, created his institution in the belief that he could offer the workingmen and women of New York vocational opportunities to improve their situations in a setting of "scientific" knowledge. By "science," Cooper meant not technological advances but, as he stated in his autobiographical manuscript, "the rule or law of God by which the movements of the material creation are rendered intelligible to man . . . science itself is nothing more than the knowledge of this law or rule, actually demonstrated by the experience of mankind." The conflict between pure science and technology did not exist in Cooper's mind. Natural science was an uncovering of God's natural law by the divine sense of comprehension that existed in

C

man's mind. Technical achievements, at which he himself had so excelled, he saw as the result of a fortuitous natural aptitude, rather like having an ear for music. The successful continuation of Cooper Union, however, was in large part to the credit of Abram Hewitt, Cooper's son-in-law. His was the practical force in the development of the institution into a prestigious school meeting newly expanded industrial needs in the post–Civil War period. Cooper, the philanthropist, and Hewitt, the practical administrator, both believed in the ability of education to stabilize society by offering workingmen an opportunity to change and improve their skills to keep up with a changing technology. Lyceums and workers' institutes that were much more important in size and offerings than Cooper Union disappeared in the course of the educational changes of the early twentieth century. Yet Cooper Union made a successful transition from Cooper's original hodgepodge of ideas about workers' education to a viable technical college and a continuing educational institution in New York City. This must be credited to the willingness of Cooper and Hewitt to accept changes in the economic and social makeup of the clientele Cooper Union served. The two men fitted de Tocqueville's description of Americans as "venturous conservatives."

BIBLIOGRAPHY

Cooper, Peter. "Autobiography of Peter Cooper 1791–1883." Manuscript. Cooper Union Archives.

Daniels, George H. *American Science in the Age of Jackson.* New York: Columbia University Press, 1968.

Krasnick, Phyllis D. "Peter Cooper and the Cooper Union for the Advancement of Science and Art." Ph.D. diss., New York University, 1985.

Kuritz, Hyman. "The Popularization of Science in Nineteenth Century America." *History of Education Quarterly* 21 (1981): 259–274.

Mack, Edward C. *Peter Cooper.* New York: Duell, Sloan and Pearce, 1949.

Phyllis D. Krasnick

Cope, Edward Drinker (1840–1897)

Zoologist and vertebrate paleontologist. Born in Philadelphia to a wealthy Quaker family, Cope's formal education included private training and one year at the University of Pennsylvania. At a young age, he developed an avid interest in natural history, and by the early 1860s was studying collections at museums throughout the United States and Europe. Much of his work pertained to collections at Philadelphia's Academy of Natural Sciences, and by the mid-1860s, he was a member and corresponding secretary of that institution. From 1864 to 1867, Cope taught zoology at Haverford College. In 1889, he became professor of geology and later zoology at the University of Pennsylvania. In 1896, he served as president of the American Association for the Advancement of Science.

While he wrote many studies of recent animals, Cope was most famous for his work in vertebrate paleontology. In 1866, he discovered dinosaur remains in New Jersey, and two years later helped mount the country's first dinosaur skeleton at the academy. Beginning in 1871, he undertook expeditions to western states and territories in search of extinct animals. In two major studies, he described over 1,000 new species and genera of fossil animals, including previously unknown fossil mammals, flying reptiles, and sauropod dinosaurs. He made some of the first American discoveries from the Eocene epoch and helped define the succession of faunas and geological horizons in the American West. Cope's descriptions were often brief and hasty, but he and his rival Othniel Charles Marsh brought America to the forefront in vertebrate paleontology.

Cope's work resulted in a serious controversy with Marsh. Both men, independently wealthy and ambitious, sought to dominate vertebrate paleontology. Overlapping explorations and competing claims for priority led Marsh in 1873 to accuse Cope of violating the canons of scientific practice. Their feud ended any personal relationship; it also limited Cope's opportunities for research. He and Marsh continued to compete for fossils, but by the late 1870s, Cope had squandered his fortune. In 1878, he purchased the *American Naturalist* as a vehicle for his publications, but it proved a costly venture. Marsh, conversely, became associated with new leaders in government science and isolated Cope from financial or institutional resources. As vertebrate paleontologist of the United States Geological Survey, he had access to fossil deposits, government outlets for publication, and a large budget and staff. In 1885–1886, Cope called on supporters to dislodge his rival, but the effort failed. In 1890, he published newspaper articles impugning Marsh's character and work, but Cope's actions did nothing to enhance his status and antagonized others in the scientific community.

Cope used the evidence of the fossil record to theorize about evolution and inheritance. Although a committed evolutionist, he rejected Darwin's theory and

C

became a leading proponent of neo-Lamarckism. Cope claimed that will or thought led organisms to make choices and to undertake motions, develop habits, and use bodily parts. The use or disuse of parts was passed on from an organism to its progeny and resulted in evolution. In *The Origin of the Fittest* (1887) and *The Primary Factors of Organic Evolution* (1896), he explained evolution as an additive process that yielded cumulative, linear patterns of change. In the 1880s, neo-Darwinians seriously challenged Cope's interpretation, yet his nonmaterial explanation of evolution appealed to many who did not accept Darwinism. His theory explained adaptation and provided a viable interpretation of the fossil record until the 1930s.

The literature on Cope emphasizes his feud with Marsh. Biographies and studies of the "bone wars" describe his brilliant insights but erratic temperament and excessive ambition. More recent studies analyze the institutional dimensions of the Cope-Marsh debate. Historians have examined Cope's neo-Lamarckian interpretations, and feminist scholars have analyzed his social and political views. There is no good biography of Cope nor extended study of his scientific work or his status as a transitional figure at a time of professionalization.

BIBLIOGRAPHY

Cope, Edward Drinker. "The Vertebrata of the Cretaceous Formations of the West." *Report of the United States Geological Survey of the Territories* 2 (1875): 1–302.

———. "The Vertebrata of the Tertiary Formations of the West." *Report of the United States Geological Survey of the Territories* 3 (1883): 1–1009.

———. *On the Origin of the Fittest: Essays in Evolution.* New York: Appleton, 1887.

———. *The Primary Factors of Organic Evolution.* Chicago: Open Court, 1896.

Lanham, Url. *The Bone Hunters.* New York: Columbia University Press, 1973.

Maline, Joseph M. "Edward Drinker Cope (1840–1897)." Master's thesis, University of Pennsylvania, 1974.

Osborn, Henry Fairfield. *Cope: Master Naturalist: The Life and Writings of Edward Drinker Cope.* Princeton: Princeton University Press, 1931.

Rainger, Ronald. "The Bone Wars: Cope, Marsh and American Vertebrate Paleontology, 1865–1900." In *The Ultimate Dinosaur,* edited by Robert Silverberg and Martin Greenberg. New York: Bantam Books, 1992, pp. 389–405.

———. "The Rise and Decline of a Science: Vertebrate Paleontology at Philadelphia's Academy of Natural Sciences, 1820–1900." *Proceedings of the American Philosophical Society* 136 (1992): 1–33.

Shor, Elizabeth Noble. *The Fossil Feud between E. D. Cope and O. C. Marsh.* Hicksville, NY: Exposition, 1974.

Ronald Rainger

SEE ALSO
Marsh, Othniel Charles; Paleontology

Cori, Carl Ferdinand (1896–1984)

Biochemist specializing in the investigation of carbohydrate metabolism. Although the pathway of glycolysis was elucidated mainly in Europe by Gustav G. Embden and Myerhof, Carl and Gerty Cori uncovered essential enzymatic steps in glycogenolysis and glycolysis. Their work convinced the scientific community that information gleaned from isolated enzyme systems was central to the understanding of physiological processes.

The major scientific contributions of Carl Cori resulted from joint research with his wife, Gerty. After finishing their medical education at the German University in Prague in 1920, the Coris decided to follow careers in research rather than practice medicine. Since living conditions and research facilities were decidedly substandard in postwar Austria, Carl accepted an offer from the State Institute for the Study of Malignant Diseases in Buffalo, New York, in 1922, where Gerty joined him. By jointly developing reliable and reproducible analytical methods for glycogen, lactate, and glucose, studying the fate of absorbed glucose in the rat and the effect of hormones thereon, the Coris made their first fundamental contribution to carbohydrate metabolism, known as the Cori cycle. They demonstrated that lactic acid in blood originating from muscle glycogen is transported to the liver to form glycogen; the carbohydrate cycles back from liver via blood glucose to form glycogen in muscle again.

A critical review on mammalian carbohydrate metabolism in 1931 established Coris' leadership in the field. In 1931, the Coris moved to Washington University and soon focused on enzymology. They discovered a new intermediate in the pathway from glycogen to lactate, glucose-1-phosphate and isolated the enzyme responsible for the phosphorolysis of glycogen to form glucose-1-phosphate. In the reverse reaction, a large, starchlike polysaccharide was formed. For the first time, a macromolecule had been produced in a test tube, a phenomenon that contradicted the accepted

C

concept that the biosynthesis of macromolecules required energy metabolism and could consequently only occur in intact cells. In 1947, the Coris were awarded the Nobel Prize for "their discovery of the catalytic conversion of glycogen."

The Cori laboratory became the outstanding enzymology center in the United States and produced a generation of future scientific leaders, American and foreign, including six future Nobel laureates.

In 1966, nine years after Gerty's death, Carl moved to Boston, and his research changed direction. In collaboration with the geneticist Salome Glueksohn-Waelsch, he investigated the regulation of enzyme synthesis at the level of gene expression. He continued to make contributions in this field until a year before his death.

BIBLIOGRAPHY

Cohn, Mildred. "Carl and Gerty Cori: A Personal Recollection." In *Creative Couples in the Sciences,* edited by Helena M. Pycior, Nancy G. Slack, and Pnina G. Abir-am. New Brunswick: Rutgers University Press, 1996, pp. 72–84.

Cori, C.F. "Mammalian Carbohydrate Metabolism." *Physiological Review* 11 (1931): 143–275.

Cori, C.F., S.P. Colowick, and G.T. Cori. "The Isolation and Synthesis of Glucose-1-phosphoric Acid." *Journal of Biological Chemistry* 121 (1937): 465–477.

Cori, G.T., and C.F. Cori. "The Enzymatic Conversion of Phosphorylase *a* to *b*." *Journal of Biological Chemistry* 158 (1945): 321–332.

Green, A.A., G.T. Cori, and C.F. Cori. "Crystalline Muscle Phosphorylase." *Journal of Biological Chemistry* 142 (1942): 447–448.

Mildred Cohn

Cori, Gerty Theresa Radnitz (1896–1957)

Biochemist, specializing in research in carbohydrate metabolism. The majority of Gerty Cori's research was pursued jointly with her husband, Carl, and is described in the entry on Carl Cori. Their first joint research project on complement was carried out while they were medical students and was published in 1920. Gerty Cori's experimental work was characterized by precise quantitative analytical methods which made their discoveries possible. Not only was this important for the "Cori cycle," but led to the identification of glucose-1-phosphate as an intermediate in glycogenolysis. In their paper on the analysis of hexose monophosphates, a large discrepancy between the determinations of phosphate and reducing power led them to postulate the existence of an unknown phosphorylated, nonreducing precursor of hexose-6-phosphate, which they later established to be glucose-l-phosphate.

When the Coris moved to Washington University in 1931, although they shared equally in planning and interpretation of experiments, Gerty could spend more time in the laboratory than Carl, since he had the responsibility of chairing a department, teaching, and so forth. In 1947, she shared the Nobel Prize in medicine and physiology for their work on the enzymatic conversion of glycogen. She was the first woman in the United States to be awarded the Nobel Prize in science and the third one in the world.

In the 1950s, Gerty Cori focused on three areas: (1) the 1,6 glucosyl bonds at the branch points of glycogen, (2) the conversion of phosphorylase *a* to *b*, and (3) glycogen storage diseases. Together with Joseph Larner, she discovered an enzyme, amylo-1,6-glucosidase which hydrolyzed glycogen at the 1,6 linkage. She used this enzyme to determine the structure of glycogens and amylopectins.

With Patricia Keller, Gerty found that, in the conversion of phosphorylase *a* to *b*, the molecule was halved. Subsequent work on the interconversion of the two forms of phosphorylase by Cori disciples ushered in the research era of regulation. The investigations of Earl Sutherland and coworkers led to the discovery of the regulator cyclic AMP, and Edwin Krebs's studies (with Edmond Fischer) led to the concept of regulation of enzyme activities by phosphorylation-dephosphorylation.

In the last decade of her life, in spite of debilitating ill health, Gerty Cori initiated studies on glycogen storage disease and revealed that there were at least four forms, each with its own enzymatic defect, as summarized in her Harvey lecture. Although the relationship of enzyme defects to genetic diseases is now commonplace, Gerty Cori was a pioneer in this area.

BIBLIOGRAPHY

Cohn, Mildred. "Carl and Gerty Cori: A Personal Recollection." In *Creative Couples in the Sciences,* edited by Helena M. Pycior, Nancy G. Slack, and Pnina G. Abir-am. New Brunswick: Rutgers University Press, 1996, pp. 72–84.

Cori, G.T. "Glycogen Structure and Enzyme Deficiencies in Glycogen Storage Disease." *Harvey Lecture Series* 48 (1953): 145–171.

Cori, G.T., and C.F. Cori. "A Method for the Determination of Hexose Monophosphate in Muscle." *Journal of Biological Chemistry* 94 (1931): 561–579.

Cori, G.T., and J. Larner. "Action of Amylo-1,6-glucosidase and Phosphorylase on Glycogen and Amylopectin." *Journal of Biological Chemistry* 188 (1951): 17–29.

Fruton, Joseph. "Cori, Gerty Theresa Radnitz." *Dictionary of Scientific Biography.* Edited by Charles C. Gillispie. New York: Scribner, 1971, 3:415–416.

Illingworth, B., J. Larner, and G.T. Cori. "Structure of Glycogens and Amylopectins. 1. Enzymatic Determination of Chain Length." *Journal of Biological Chemistry* 199 (1952): 631–640.

Mildred Cohn

Cosmology

The science, theory, or study of the universe as an orderly system, and of the laws which govern it; in particular, a branch of astronomy that deals with the structure and evolution of the universe. (The origin of the universe, as distinct from its structure and evolution, is the subject of cosmogony.)

Astronomical entrepreneurship in America's Gilded Age led to the construction of new observatories, larger telescopes, and accompanying astronomical instruments. With these developments came a shift of the center of observational astronomy from Europe to the United States at the end of the nineteenth century.

In 1918, Harlow Shapley at the Mount Wilson Observatory calibrated on a few nearby stars with known distances the period-luminosity relation for Cepheid variable stars (brighter variables have longer periods), utilizing the relation first noticed by Henrietta Leavitt at Harvard in 1908. Next, measuring periods of Cepheids in globular clusters, Shapley calculated their actual brightness, compared this to observed brightness, and inferred distances to the clusters (observed brightness decreases with distance). Then assuming that globular clusters define the skeleton of our galaxy, Shapley found the approximate size of our galaxy. His estimate was more than ten times larger than previously supposed.

During the 1920s, at Mount Wilson, Edwin Hubble discovered Cepheid stars in spiral nebulae, calculated their distances, and demonstrated that the "nebulae" are independent "island universes" beyond the boundary of our own galaxy. He also announced what quickly became the basic classification scheme for nebulae.

Beginning in 1912, Vesto M. Slipher at the Lowell Observatory had measured high radial velocities of spiral nebulae, and in 1917, a European astronomer had proposed a theoretical model of the universe with an apparent velocity of recession greater for objects at greater distances. In 1929, Hubble, with help from his colleague Milton Humason at Mount Wilson, established an empirical velocity-distance relation and ushered in a new age of thought, in which the universe is generally believed to be expanding rather than static.

As a rough generality, not until the 1930s were European theoretical developments combined with American observational work, resulting in the standard big bang cosmology.

A cosmic microwave background radiation, discovered serendipitously in 1964, is one of the observational foundations of big bang cosmology. In 1948 and 1949, George Gamow and Ralph Alpher at George Washington University and Robert Herman at Johns Hopkins had predicted the existence of a cosmic background radiation, but little attention was paid to their work. In 1963 and 1964, Arno Penzias and Robert Wilson at Bell Laboratories, studying what at first was thought to be noise in a radio antenna, found it to be excess radiation, apparently of a cosmic origin. For this work, they received the Nobel Prize in Physics in 1978. Robert Dicke and P.J.E. Peebles at Princeton had independently predicted a cosmic background radiation, and they explained the cosmological importance of Penzias and Wilson's discovery.

Recent cosmology has been driven importantly by particle theory, and considerably by American physicists. The universe is a relic of historical events that happened at energies far greater than can be achieved in particle accelerators. In the 1980s, Alan Guth, now at the Massachusetts Institute of Technology, proposed the inflationary universe model. Guth's theory of inflation applies to the first minuscule fraction of a second of the universe's evolution. In that tiny instant a huge inflation occurred. After that, the inflationary universe theory merges with the standard big bang theory. Physicists now run computer simulations of hypothetical universes, and astronomers try to reconcile their observations with theory.

Cosmology thrives late in the twentieth century, especially in the United States.

BIBLIOGRAPHY

Hetherington, Norriss S., ed. *Encyclopedia of Cosmology: Historical, Philosophical, and Scientific Foundations of Modern Cosmology.* New York: Garland, 1992.

C

———. *Cosmology: Historical, Literary, Philosophical, Religious, and Scientific Cosmology Perspectives.* New York: Garland, 1993.

Norriss S. Hetherington

Crystallography

Crystallography was formally established as a science in the eighteenth century chiefly through the work of two French mineralogists, Romé Delisle, who was the first to make systematic measurements of the interfacial angles of crystals, and Reneé Just Haüy, who proposed a theory of the internal structure of crystals that interpreted their systematic external morphology. Until the late nineteenth century, crystallography was primarily an aspect of mineralogy, especially in the United States. This was because crystallographic criteria were useful in the identification and classification of minerals.

Crystallography was introduced into the United States during the period 1780–1820 by immigrants who were familiar with the work of Haüy or had studied with him, and by Americans who went to Paris to study with him. The first American textbook to include a detailed study of crystallography was Parker Cleaveland's *Elementary Account of Mineralogy and Geology* (1816). A major factor in the development of crystallography in the United States and long the main avenue of entrance into this field were the six editions of the *System of Mineralogy* by James D. Dana and, in part, by Edward S. Dana of Yale University, together with the 1877 edition by E.S. Dana of the *Textbook of Mineralogy* and the 1850 edition by J.D. Dana of the *Manual of Mineralogy*. The first edition of the *System of Mineralogy* appeared in 1837; crystallographic material totalled 145 pages–about 40 percent of the book. The first American book devoted wholly to crystallography was G.H. Williams's *Elements of Crystallography for Students of Chemistry, Physics, and Mineralogy* (1890).

Crystal optics was the first field in physical crystallography to be extensively developed in this country. The impetus very largely came from the use of the polarizing microscope for the study of rocks in light transmitted through thin sections, beginning in the 1870s, and the identification of transparent minerals through their optical properties as seen in crushed grains immersed in liquids of known index of refraction.

By the end of the nineteenth century, a few aspects of pure crystallography had developed in this country. One was morphological crystallography, initially developed largely by Victor Goldschmidt of Heidelberg and imported into the United States by Charles Palache of Harvard, who studied briefly with Goldschmidt in 1895.

Following the discovery in Germany of X-rays and their diffraction by crystals, and the development of techniques for the recording and interpretation of X-ray diffraction effects, crystallography extended from essentially an adjunct to mineralogy into an independent science dealing with all of the solid state. These events are described by Ewald and, with particular reference to the United States, by McLachlan and Glusker.

Most crystallographic contributions in the United States appeared in either the *American Journal of Science* or the *American Mineralogist*. The literature on X-ray crystallography took a different course, with almost all early contributions appearing in American or European journals devoted to chemistry, physics, or metallurgy, or in the German journal *Zeitschrift für Kristallographie*.

The first successful effort to form a society inclusive of the various fields of crystallography was the organization of the Crystallographic Society of America in 1939. A second society, stressing X-ray crystal structure analysis, was the American Society for X-ray and Electron Diffraction, formed in 1941. These two societies merged in 1948 to form the American Crystallographic Association, with a charter membership of almost five hundred.

BIBLIOGRAPHY

Ewald, Paul P. *Fifty Years of X-ray Diffraction.* Utrecht: International Union of Crystallography, 1962.

McLachlan, Dan, Jr., and Jenny P. Glusker, eds. *Crystallography in North America.* New York: American Crystallographic Association, 1983.

Clifford Frondel

SEE ALSO
Mineralogy

Cutler, Manasseh (1742–1823)

Clergyman active in science, politics, and Western colonization. Born in Killingly, Connecticut, Cutler graduated from Yale (1765), where he pursued his studies in astronomy with great zeal. Somewhat later, he studied theology and, in 1771, was ordained pastor of the

Congregational church in Ipswich Hamlet (Hamilton), Massachusetts. There he began the study of medicine and botany, established a boarding school where students learned the elements of astronomy and navigation, and made contact with Harvard graduates with scientific interests in neighboring towns—men such as Joseph Willard, John Prince, William Bentley, and Joshua Fisher. He joined the Philosophical Club, formed originally to purchase that part of the Irish chemist Richard Kirwan's library which had been captured by privateers and, in 1781, was elected to the newly formed American Academy of Arts and Sciences. To their *Memoirs* he contributed astronomical observations and, in 1785, his "Account of Some of the Vegetable Productions, Naturally Growing in this Part of America, Botanically Arranged," which has been described as "the first serious study of New England plants" (Ewan, p. 36). The plants were arranged according to Linnaeus's sexual system, but without Linnaean binomials, the names being given in the local vernacular. In 1784, Cutler was elected to the American Philosophical Society.

Throughout a busy life, which included two terms in Congress (1801–1805) and a leading role in the Ohio Company's application to Congress for the purchase of lands in the Ohio territory, its contribution to the drafting of the Northwest Ordinance (1787), and its subsequent settlement at Marietta, Ohio, Cutler continued to study natural history as time permitted. He collaborated with Harvard botanist William Dandridge Peck in identifying and naming the plants and animals of New Hampshire for the third volume of Jeremy Belknap's history of that state (1792) and contributed substantially to the natural history section of Jedidiah Morse's *American Universal Geography* (1793). Hoping eventually to produce a comprehensive account of the botany of New England, he corresponded widely with American and European botanists, but his lifelong ambition was frustrated when, in January 1812, fire destroyed or damaged his manuscript volumes of plant descriptions.

Unfortunately, there is no modern biography of Cutler, but his *Life, Journals, and Correspondence* is a valuable source of information about the early history of the American Academy of Arts and Sciences, the scientific interests of Harvard graduates in eastern Massachusetts, the network of correspondence linking American and European botanists, and the state of scientific institutions in the cities Cutler visited in his travels. Northwestern University Library has seventy volumes of Cutler's diaries, correspondence, and other papers.

BIBLIOGRAPHY
Cutler, William P., and Julia P. Cutler. *Life, Journals and Correspondence of Rev. Manasseh Cutler, LL.D.* 2 vols. 1888. Athens, OH, and London: Ohio University Press, 1987.
Ewan, Joseph, ed. *A Short History of Botany in the United States.* New York and London: Hafner, 1969.
Greene, John C. *American Science in the Age of Jefferson.* Ames: Iowa State University Press, 1984.

John C. Greene

Cybernetics

"Cybernetics" is a term that was introduced into modern science in 1947 by the mathematician Norbert Wiener to name what promised to be a newly evolving branch of science: control and communication in the animal and the machine. The science of cybernetics encompassed both machines and organisms, but concerned itself especially with models and theories that could be transferred from the description of one to the other, thus linking biology, psychology, and social studies to engineering and mathematics.

A number of conceptual developments in the 1940s were at the core of the new science. The first was the notion of goal-directed action (by an organism or a machine) governed by continuous or intermittent information ("negative feedback") as to how near one is to reaching the goal. This type of circuit was identified as commonplace, exemplified equally by a person steering a ship as by an automatic pilot. The concept was developed, and its broad range or usefulness identified, jointly in 1943 by the Mexican physiologist Arturo Rosenblueth together with Norbert Wiener and the engineer Julian Bigelow. It spawned a series of conferences from 1946 to 1953 on the theme of circular causal and feedback mechanisms in biological and social systems, that came to be known as the cybernetics conferences, where the idea was explored in a cross-disciplinary way. The second conceptual development was the idea, worked out by neuropsychiatrist Warren McCulloch and polymath Walter Pitts in 1943, that human thought and the electrochemical patterns of the brain can be put into correspondence by means of a network of neurons describable by a mathematical-logical model. The Pitts-McCulloch model, although it made

C

use of a highly simplified picture of individual nerve cells, sufficed to demonstrate that anything that can be completely and unambiguously described, anything that can be completely and unambiguously put into words, is, ipso facto, realizable by a suitable finite neural network. The model offered a clear hypothesis concerning the relation of mind to brain. Moreover, in 1945, the mathematician John von Neumann discovered that the Pitts-McCulloch model of the nervous system is suited for describing the logical design of high-speed digital computers, another parallel between the organic and the machine. The first such computers were built in the following years. A third basic notion, derived from the statistical communication theory developed by Wiener and independently found by Claude Shannon, was a definition of "information" which resembled mathematically the definition of negative entropy in a physical system, and obeyed a variety of strict theorems.

All three of these powerful ideas proved to be seminal, and have influenced subsequent developments in science and technology enormously. The Rosenblueth-Wiener-Bigelow idea has found application so widely that it is often viewed as a matter of course, although biologists, especially Jacques L. Monod, have specifically called attention to "microscopic cybernetics" and feedback mechanisms in biological cells. Computers and information/communication technologies became the most rapidly developing technologies for several decades. The field of "artificial intelligence," that is, the design of artifacts displaying some form of "intelligent" behavior, grew out of cybernetic models. Information theory has been applied extensively to genetics, and the genes have come to be viewed as carriers of information. A field of investigation known as "cognitive science," dealing with how we know, learn, think, and perceive, also evolved from cybernetics, with its tendency to model minds on computerlike artifacts, or to describe them as information-processing devices. These mechanical or electronic models tend to foster not only a mechanistic philosophy of matter, but also of human behavior and even of minds.

In the field of social studies, Gregory Bateson became

the most astute proponent of ideas from cybernetics, but he insisted that any model describing humans or even many animals must contain various kinds of logical contradictions. These contradictions are essential so that ordinary everyday human communication, playfulness, and humor can be given their due. Thus, he broke the mechanistic spell. He used cybernetics to describe, for example, the stability of cultures studied by anthropologists, how people become schizophrenic, and how they can be cured from alcoholism. Ecologists, in particular, G. Evelyn Hutchinson and his students, have used cybernetics extensively to describe complex ecological systems. The Gaia hypothesis treats life on earth and the whole biosphere as one cybernetic system.

As early as 1947, Wiener stated that cybernetics "had unbounded possibilities for good and for evil" (Wiener, *Cybernetics,* p. 7). Indeed, as he feared, ideas from cybernetics have had a vast amount of application for military purposes, "smart bombs" and such; moreover, as he anticipated, robots, computers, and automation have resulted in much unemployment and downgrading of many kinds of skilled work.

BIBLIOGRAPHY

Ashby, Ross. *An Introduction to Cybernetics.* London: Chapman, 1958.

Bateson, Gregory. *Steps to an Ecology of Mind.* New York: Random House, 1972.

De Latil, Pierre. *Thinking by Machine: A Study of Cybernetics.* Boston: Houghton Mifflin, 1957.

Gardner, Howard. *The Mind's New Science.* New York: Basic Books, 1985.

Haraway, Donna J. "The High Cost of Information in Post World War II Evolutionary Biology." *The Philosophical Forum* 13, nos. 2–3 (1981–1982): 244–278.

Heims, Steve Joshua. *Constructing a Social Science for Postwar America: The Cybernetics Group 1946–53.* Cambridge, MA: MIT Press, 1993.

Wiener, Norbert. *Cybernetics or Control and Communication in the Animal and the Machine.* Cambridge, MA: MIT Press, 1948.

———. *The Human Use of Human Beings: Cybernetics and Society.* London: Free Association Press, 1989.

Steve Joshua Heims

D

Dalton, John Call, Jr. (1825–1889)

Physiologist, medical educator, leader in the fight against antivivisectionists. Born in Chelmsford, Massachusetts, Dalton received his undergraduate and medical education at Harvard (A.B., 1844; M.D., 1847) and studied in Paris with Claude Bernard. Imbued with Bernard's philosophy of experimentation, Dalton introduced into America the French style of physiology with its emphasis on vivisection. After briefly teaching in Boston, Buffalo, and Woodstock, Vermont, Dalton became professor of physiology at the College of Physicians and Surgeons in New York in 1855. There, he supplemented his lectures with vivisections, an innovation that proved popular with the students.

An avid researcher, Dalton made several discoveries in gastrointestinal physiology, neurophysiology, and reproductive physiology. He was a prolific author and published several books in addition to many papers detailing his experiments. Dalton's most influential publication was his textbook of physiology that first appeared in 1859. It reflected his knowledge of contemporary European physiology and included the results of his own observations and experiments. Equally popular was Dalton's elementary textbook on physiology and hygiene. First published in 1868, this book was aimed at high school and college students.

One of Dalton's most important contributions to the development of physiology and experimental medicine in America was his articulate, sustained, and effective response to the antivivisection movement. Dalton reacted immediately to Henry Bergh's first attacks on animal experimentation in 1866. For two decades, he was the chief spokesman for the American scientific community in their battle with the antivivisectionists. "Every important discovery in physiology has been directly due to experiments on living animals," claimed Dalton, who also maintained that many practical advances in medicine and surgery were the result of vivisection (Dalton, *Vivisection*).

In 1883, Dalton resigned as professor of physiology. The following year he became president of the College of Physicians and Surgeons. Dalton shared with others seeking to improve American medical education the conviction that curricular reform and the introduction of laboratory training required unprecedented endowment. He helped secure a half million dollar gift from William H. Vanderbilt for the construction of new clinical facilities and laboratories for teaching and research.

S. Weir Mitchell considered Dalton America's "first professional physiologist" (Mitchell, p. 177) because he earned his living by teaching and writing about the subject—he did not combine medical practice with these activities. Unlike Henry P. Bowditch at Harvard and H. Newell Martin at Johns Hopkins, Dalton did not establish a "school" of physiology. His impact was, nevertheless, significant. Through his lectures and publications, Dalton convinced many physicians and others of the essential role played by experimentation in the advance of medical science.

BIBLIOGRAPHY

Dalton, John C. [Jr.] *Vivisection*. New York: Balliere, 1867.
Fye, W. Bruce. "John Call Dalton, Jr., Pioneer Vivisector and America's 'first professional physiologist.'" In W. Bruce Fye, *The Development of American Physiology: Scientific*

D

Medicine in the Nineteenth Century. Baltimore: Johns Hopkins University Press, 1987, pp. 15–53.

Mitchell, S. Weir. "John Call Dalton." *Biographical Memoirs of the National Academy of Sciences* 3 (1890): 177–185.

W. Bruce Fye

Dana, James Dwight (1813–1895)

Geologist, mineralogist, and zoologist. Born in Utica, New York, Dana entered Yale College in 1830 to study natural science under Benjamin Silliman. Following graduation in 1833, he continued his studies with Silliman, particularly in mineralogy; Dana's *System of Mineralogy* (1837) became the definitive book on the subject in America.

From 1838 to 1842, Dana accompanied the United States Exploring Expedition on its around-the-world voyage of scientific exploration; his duties included mineralogy, geology, and zoology. During the thirteen years following the expedition's return, he wrote three of the expedition reports (*Zoophytes,* 1846; *Geology,* 1849; and *Crustacea,* 1854).

In 1844, Dana became co-editor with Silliman of the *American Journal of Science.* He was a member of the Association of American Geologists and Naturalists and of its successor, the American Association for the Advancement of Science, serving as president of the latter in 1854–1855. In 1855, he assumed the Silliman Professorship of Natural History at Yale. Dana supported the establishment of the Yale Sheffield Scientific School, which opened in 1860, and later the "young Yale" movement of the 1870s, which helped transform Yale from college to university.

In 1859, Dana suffered a breakdown in health, which limited social and professional activities for the rest of his life, but illness did little to interfere with fieldwork in New England or with publication. Continued ill health caused him to give up most of his teaching duties in 1890; he resigned his Yale professorship in 1894. Dana died in New Haven.

Dana's participation in the United States Exploring Expedition laid the foundation for much of his later work in geology and zoology. His fieldwork during the expedition, which provided him with a wider knowledge of geology than any other contemporary American scientist, stimulated his thinking about the processes involved in the geological history of the globe. Dana's expedition report on geology offered both a description of the landforms and geological processes of the Pacific region and a contractional theory of the origin and development of the earth's features. One conclusion from this theory was that the general form and position of the continents and oceans had become fixed and permanent during the earth's early history—a view that dominated American geological thought until the acceptance of continental drift and plate tectonics in the twentieth century.

While in Australia, Dana read of Darwin's subsidence theory of the formation of coral reefs, but his more extensive observations of Pacific coral islands allowed him to develop details of the theory concerned with reef structure, embayed shorelines, coral growth, and geographical distribution. He also demonstrated the importance of running water acting over long periods in carving the valleys of the Pacific islands and the coastal mountains of Australia, which contrasted with the marine erosion theory of Lyell and Darwin.

Dana's geological work culminated in the *Manual of Geology* (1862), which became the definitive geological text in late-nineteenth-century America. It surveyed geological knowledge from the perspective of North America, drawing its examples and illustrations as much as possible from this continent and from his own observations on the exploring expedition. Its overall theme was the history of the earth and the progress of life as revealed in the geological record. Perhaps Dana's greatest contribution to American science was helping to transform geology from a descriptive into a truly historical science.

Dana's deep-seated belief in evangelical Protestantism led him to view the development of life as requiring a number of divine acts of creation, each progressively leading to the human species. He believed that the species of each type of life possessed a vital force peculiar to itself, thereby insuring its immutability, and that each species had been created to fulfill a particular end in the economy of nature. The central concept of Dana's views on species was cephalization, the idea that the higher the animal class, the greater the concentration of body structure in the head—with the appearance of humans representing the ultimate expression of cephalization.

Not surprisingly, Dana initially opposed Darwin's *On the Origin of Species* (1859) on both religious and scientific grounds. But an openness to new evidence led him to accept a theistic version of evolution in the 1870s, although not until the late 1880s did he include the human species within the evolutionary process. As with many other scientists of his day, he accounted for the transmutation of species by neo-Lamarckian processes rather than by Darwin's theory of natural selection.

While Dana's early work focused on detailed description and classification in mineralogy and zoology, his intellectual and scientific tastes ran more to the generalizations and comprehensive theories that characterized his geological work. His broad views enabled him to synthesize the thinking of American and European geologists into many of the theoretical structures within which American geological work would be carried out into the early twentieth century.

BIBLIOGRAPHY

Appleman, Daniel E. "James Dwight Dana and Pacific Geology." In *Magnificent Voyagers: The U.S. Exploring Expedition, 1838–1842,* edited by Herman J. Viola and Carolyn Margolis. Washington, DC: Smithsonian Institution Press, 1985, pp. 89–117.

Dana, James D. *A System of Mineralogy; Descriptive Mineralogy, Comprising the Most Recent Discoveries.* 1837. 5th ed., Aided by George Jarvis Bush. New York: J. Wiley & Son, 1869.

———. *Zoophytes.* Vol. 6 of *United States Exploring Expedition. During the Years 1838, 1839, 1840, 1841, 1842. Under the Command of Charles Wilkes, U.S.N.* Philadelphia: C. Sherman, 1846.

———. *Geology.* Vol. 10 of *United States Exploring Expedition. During the Years 1838, 1839, 1840, 1841, 1842. Under the Command of Charles Wilkes, U.S.N.* New York: G. Putnam, 1849.

———. *Crustacea.* Vol. 13–14 of *United States Exploring Expedition. During the Years 1838, 1839, 1840, 1841, 1842. Under the Command of Charles Wilkes, U.S.N.* Philadelphia: C. Sherman, 1854.

———. *Manual of Geology: Treating of the Principles of the Science with Special Reference to American Geological History.* 1862. 4th ed. New York: American Book Company, 1895.

———. *On Coral Reefs and Islands.* 1872. 3rd. ed. New York: Dodd, Mead, and Co., 1890.

———. *Characteristics of Volcanoes, with Contributions of Facts and Principles from the Hawaiian Islands* New York: Dodd, Mead, and Co., 1890.

Dott, R.H., Jr. "The Geosyncline—First Major Geological Concept 'Made in America.'" In *Two Hundred Years of Geology in America,* edited by Cecil Schneer. Hanover, NH: University Press of New England, 1979, pp. 239–264.

———. "James Dwight Dana's Old Tectonics: Global Contraction under Divine Direction." *American Journal of Science* 297 (1997): 283–311.

Gilman, Daniel C. *The Life of James Dwight Dana: Scientific Explorer, Mineralogist, Geologist, Zoologist, Professor in Yale University.* New York: Harper & Brothers, 1899.

Natland, James H. "At Vulcan's Shoulder: James Dwight Dana and the Beginnings of Planetary Volcanology." *American Journal of Science* 297 (1997): 312–342.

Newell, Julie R. "James Dwight Dana and the Emergence of Professional Geology in the United States." *American Journal of Science* 297 (1997): 273–282.

Prendergast, Michael L. "James Dwight Dana: The Life and Thought of an American Scientist." Ph.D. diss., University of California, Los Angeles, 1978.

Rodgers, John. "James Dwight Dana and the Taconic Controversy." *American Journal of Science* 297 (1997): 343–358.

Rossiter, Margaret. "A Portrait of James Dwight Dana." In *Benjamin Silliman and His Circle: Studies on the Influence of Benjamin Silliman on Science in America,* edited by Leonard G. Wilson. New York: Science History Publications, 1979, pp. 105–127.

Sanford, William F., Jr. "Dana and Darwinism." *Journal of the History of Ideas* 26 (1965): 531–546.

Sherwood, Morgan B. "Genesis, Evolution and Geology in America before Darwin: The Dana-Lewis Controversy, 1856–1857." In *Towards a History of Geology,* edited by Cecil Schneer. Cambridge, MA: MIT Press, 1969, pp. 305–316.

Michael L. Prendergast

Darwinism
See Evolution and Darwinism

Davenport, Charles Benedict (1866–1944)
Experimental zoologist and leader in the eugenics movement. Born in Connecticut and raised in Brooklyn, New York, he was destined by his father for an engineering career. After receiving an engineering degree from Brooklyn Polytechnic Institute in 1886 and spending nine months on a survey crew, Davenport managed to enroll at Harvard, from which he obtained an A.B. in 1889 and a Ph.D. in zoology in 1892. He served as instructor at Harvard for the next seven years before becoming assistant professor at the University of Chicago. He remained at Chicago until 1904, being promoted to associate professor in 1901. From 1898 to 1923, Davenport also served as director of the summer school at the Brooklyn Institute of Arts and Sciences' Biological Laboratory at Cold Spring Harbor, on Long Island. An early advocate of experimentation in zoology,

D

Davenport convinced the Carnegie Institution of Washington in 1904 to establish a Station for Experimental Evolution at Cold Spring Harbor, which Davenport directed until his retirement in 1934. From 1910 to 1934, Davenport also directed the Eugenics Record Office at Cold Spring Harbor, supported at first by grants from Mrs. E.H. Harriman, the heir to the Harriman railroad fortune and, from 1918 on, by the Carnegie Institution.

Davenport was an early supporter of biometrical methods for studying biological populations and their variations and did much to introduce the work of the British biometrician Karl Pearson into the United States, publishing a book on statistical methods in 1899 and serving as American editor for Pearson's journal *Biometrika*. Interested in experimental morphology since his days at Harvard, Davenport also quickly became interested in experimental studies of heredity and evolution after the rediscovery of Mendel's work in 1900; by 1904, he had become fully converted to Mendelian principles. During his early days at Cold Spring Harbor, Davenport conducted breeding experiments on a number of different animals and published studies on heredity in chicken and canaries, but around 1907 Davenport's interest shifted to the application of Mendelian principles to human traits. Over the next several years, he and his wife, Gertrude C. Davenport, interpreted the inheritance of skin, hair, and eye color in humans in Mendelian terms. Davenport also sought to extend Mendelian principles to the inheritance of various diseases as well as such ill-defined traits as "feeble-mindedness" and even "lust for seafaring." He was aided in this work by the resources of the Eugenics Record Office, which collected pedigree charts on thousands of individuals. From his base in the Eugenics Record Office, Davenport also became a leader in the American eugenics movement.

Early discussions of Davenport's work concentrated on his scientific contributions, particularly his application of Mendelian principles to the study of human genetics, and viewed his eugenic commitments as an unfortunate, disturbing factor decreasing the scientific value of his work. With the growing interest amongst historians in eugenics during the 1970s and 1980s, historians of science have shifted their attention more fully to Davenport's eugenic activities. Historians of eugenics now place Davenport firmly in the vanguard of mainline eugenic agitation in America and cite the Eugenics Record Office as one of the most important institutional bases for eugenics in the United States. While this historiographic focus on Davenport's eugenics has led to a solid understanding of his work at the Eugenics Record Office, the scientific research conducted by Davenport and others at the Station for Experimental Evolution (later the Department of Genetics of the Carnegie Institution) still awaits detailed analysis and appraisal.

BIBLIOGRAPHY
Allen, Garland E. "The Eugenics Record Office at Cold Spring Harbor, 1910–1940: An Essay in Institutional History." *Osiris,* 2d ser., 2 (1986): 225–264.
Kevles, Daniel J. *In the Name of Eugenics: Genetics and the Uses of Human Heredity.* Berkeley: University of California Press, 1985.
MacDowell, E. Carleton. "Charles Benedict Davenport, 1866–1944: A Study of Conflicting Influences." *Bios* 17 (1946): 3–50.
Riddle, Oscar. "Charles Benedict Davenport." *Biographical Memoirs of the National Academy of Sciences* 25 (1948): 75–110.
Rosenberg, Charles E. "Charles Benedict Davenport and the Beginning of Human Genetics." *Bulletin of the History of Medicine* 35 (1961): 266–276.

Carl-Henry Geschwind

Davis, William Morris (1850–1934)

Geographer, geologist, and meteorologist. Born in Philadelphia, Davis graduated from Harvard's School of Mining in 1869 (S.B. magna cum laude) and took the degree of Mining Engineer (M.E.) the following year. He studied primarily with Raphael Pumpelly, Josiah Dwight Whitney, and Nathaniel Southgate Shaler.

After graduation, Davis worked in the Argentine National Observatory at Córdoba, and later assisted Pumpelly on his Northern Pacific survey and Shaler in summer field courses in the Appalachians. In 1876, Davis became Shaler's assistant in geology, and two years later was appointed instructor, responsible for his own course in physical geography and meteorology. In 1885, he was made assistant professor and, in 1890, professor of physical geography. His appointment eight years later as Sturgis-Hooper Professor of Geology relieved him of elementary teaching; he retired in 1912. Davis was a founding member and first secretary of the New England Meteorological Society, and founder and three times president of the Association of American Geographers.

Davis used his physical geography course as a base first to build a separate course in meteorology, and then, exploiting the resources of Boston-area institutions, created a teaching and research program in meteorology second to none in America for academic training in meteorology. In the decade 1884–1894, Davis published some forty articles and many additional notes in this area, capped in 1894 by a classic textbook, *Elementary Meteorology.*

Beginning with studies of rivers in the folded Appalachians of Pennsylvania and Virginia, Davis developed a method of landscape analysis around the concept of the erosional or "geographical" cycle. He vividly presented the notion that landscapes could be classified by origin and stage (youth, maturity, old age), proposing an ideal evolutionary model in which the scientific understanding of the contemporary landscape was dependent on knowledge both of its genesis and its present geometry. This deductive model provided both a systematic vocabulary and the promise of scientific explanation of otherwise disorderly empirical data. Davis's approach influenced geographers and geologists at home and abroad for half a century. Only in Germany and in the American Midwest was his cyclical formula initially contested as oversimplified and misleading.

Davis's greatest impact on geography came during the 1890s and the early years of the twentieth century. He viewed the discipline dualistically, dividing it into what he called "inorganic geography" or "physiography," and organic (including human) life and activity, which he called "ontography," insisting that the latter concerns were relevant to geography only if a physical "cause" or "control" could be shown for them.

During the 1890s, Davis attracted numerous able students to Harvard. Most emerged from his deterministic ideas and became leaders in human geography during the early twentieth century. At the secondary school level, the Committee of Ten recommended adoption of Davisian concepts in physical geography as the introductory high school science course, though within a decade "physical geography" was replaced in the secondary curriculum by "general science."

Davis founded the Association of American Geographers in 1904. Through his powerful and authoritarian personality, in its early years he exercised a veto power on membership and exercised a kind of intellectual control over the content of the field for a longer period. But his influence declined among geographers in the 1920s as a new functional human geography, particularly economic geography, became the dominant orientation in that discipline. The deductive, nonquantitative approach of his "geographical cycle" faded from fashion during the 1940s and 1950s as morphometric analysis succeeded cyclical notions in geomorphology. Now seldom read, Davis is remembered today primarily as an institution builder, influential teacher, and early practitioner of the use of models in landform studies.

Davis's lifetime bibliography runs to just over 500 items. The principal public collections of germane manuscripts are in the Harvard University Archives and in Houghton Library, Harvard University. Letters also survive in the papers of his many correspondents; others, quoted extensively in Chorley, Beckinsale, and Dunn, are still in family hands.

BIBLIOGRAPHY

Beckinsale, Robert P. "The International Influence of William Morris Davis." *Geographical Review* 66 (1976): 448–466.

———. "W. M. Davis and American Geography (1880–1934)." In *The Origins of Academic Geography in the United States,* edited by Brian W. Blouet. Hamden, CT: Archon Books, 1981.

Chorley, Richard J., Robert P. Beckinsale, and Antony J. Dunn. *The Life and Work of William Morris Davis.* Vol. 2 of *The History of the Study of Landforms.* London: Methuen, 1973.

Davis, William Morris. *Elementary Meteorology.* Boston: Ginn, 1894.

Davis, William Morris, and Reginald Aldworth Daly, "Geography and Geology, 1858–1928." In *The Development of Harvard University, 1869–1929,* edited by Samuel Eliot Morison. Cambridge, MA: Harvard University Press, 1930.

Hartshorne, Richard. "William Morris Davis—The Course of Development of His Concept of Geography." In *The Origins of Academic Geography in the United States,* edited by Brian W. Blouet. Hamden, CT: Archon Books, 1981.

Koelsch, William A. "The New England Meteorological Society, 1884–1892: A Study in Professionalization." In *The Origins of Academic Geography in the United States,* edited by Brian W. Blouet. Hamden, CT: Archon Books, 1981.

Tinkler, Keith. *A Short History of Geomorphology.* Totowa, NJ: Barnes and Noble, 1985.

William A. Koelsch

SEE ALSO
Geography

D

Delbrück, Max (1906–1981)

German-born physicist turned geneticist, microbiologist, and leader in molecular biology. Born in Berlin to a family of scholars and political leaders, Delbrück studied astronomy in Tubingen, Bonn, and Berlin. He then switched to theoretical physics under Max Born and Walter Heitler, receiving his doctorate in 1930. A Rockefeller Fellowship in 1931–1932 supported his studies with Niels Bohr in Copenhagen, an experience that sparked Delbrück's lifelong commitment to biology. He worked for five years in Berlin as an assistant in physics to Lise Meitner while pursuing his interests in biology at the Kaiser-Wilhelm Insitute for Biology. Between 1937 and 1939, as a Rockefeller Fellow, he initiated his research on bacteriophage at the California Institute of Technology, developing his phage project at Cold Spring Harbor and while teaching physics at Vanderbilt University from 1940 to 1947. In 1947, Delbrück returned to Caltech as professor of biology, remaining there until his death. He was a member of the National Academy of Sciences, Royal Danish Academy, Deutsche Akademie der Naturforscher Leopoldina, Royal Society of London, and American Academy of Arts and Sciences. In the 1960s, he participated in building molecular biology in Germany, and in 1969, he shared the Nobel Prize in Physiology and Medicine with Salvador E. Luria and Alfred D. Hershey for their contributions to molecular genetics.

Delbrück's projects in biology were shaped by the goal of establishing complemetarity as the guiding principle in biology. He aimed to show that fundamental knowledge of nature emerged out of uncertainty: just as in quantum physics, complete atomic accounts of organisms interfered with the essential properties of life. He began his quest by investigating the effect of X-ray radiation on mutations in Drosophila, providing explanations of genetic stablity and hereditary mechanisms in terms of a quantum mechanical model. In 1937, he turned to bacteriophage as a model system for studing mechanisms of genetic replication, substantially revising older concepts. His technically noninvasive approach, coupling mathematics with mapping genetic loci of viral recombinations, attracted many reseachers interested in genetics—biologists, chemists, and especially physicists. Delbrück's noted phage course, inaugurated at Cold Spring Harbor in 1945, served to recruit and promote a growing phage school as a subspecialty of the nascent field of molecular biology. Under Delbrück's remarkable intellectual and social leadership, phage workers by the late 1950s explained salient features of viral infection, organization of viral and bacterial genomes, their modes of replication, recombination, and mutation.

By that time, however, the elucidation of the double-helix structure of DNA by James D. Watson and Francis Crick (1953) underscored the explanatory power of biochemistry. This result effectively terminated Delbrück's personal quest to explain gene replication in terms of the complementarity principle. While continuing the management of phage genetics, his own intellectual efforts focused on neurophysiology, using phycomycetes as the simplest model system for studying sensory transduction of signals. Once again, he sought to reach a cognitive limit where, based on the complementarity principle, the observer's measurements interfered with observed signals. He pursued this project until his death. In addition to his broad scientific and philosophical vision, Delbrück had a deep interest in music, firm command of several languages, and wide-ranging knowledge of classical and modern literature. These attributes contributed to his stature as intellectual and eloquent spokesperson on critical issues in both science and the humanities.

Because of his immense popularity, intellectual leadership, and his large international phage network, Delbrück's researches have been viewed as "the origins of molecular biology" (Cairns et al.). His migration from physics to biology has been seen as daring, his applications of mathematical physics in biology have been touted as novel, and his choice of phage as pathbreaking. By the late 1960s, he became an icon of the new hybrid discipline focusing exclusively on microorganisms. As a German physicist, he has been credited with endowing biology with academic legitimacy that attracted researchers from the physical sciences, eventually altering the disciplinary character of biology. His theoretical vision of a pristine molecular genetics, uncontaminated by contingencies of the biochemical craft, have functioned as a historical indicator for the cognitive and disciplinary novelty of molecular biology. More recently, histories of molecular biology and biochemistry have undergone revisions, bringing new perspectives to the career of Delbrück. In rethinking the relation of institutions and disciplinary power to the production of scientific knowledge, the rise of molecular biology is no longer seen merely as the outcome of cognitive leaps and charismatic leaderships. Scholars have shown how the Rockefeller Foundation—the principal sponsor of the molecular biology program—has shaped the career of hundreds of life and physical scientists by investing vast institutional resources in physico-chemical biology (Kohler; Abir-Am). As long-term recipient of Rockefeller support, Delbrück's scientific trajectory appears as an element within a larger movement in American and European science. This explains why, despite his relatively low personal output, his collaborative and group projects carried so much weight within the molecular biology program. The enormous prestige of phage genetics has contributed also to the exclusion of biochemistry from historical reconstructions of molecular biology. Recent correctives (Cohen; Fruton, p. 195) have challenged the historiographic hegemony of the phage school, pointing to the pivotal role that biochemistry played in and outside phage research. Rethinking Delbrück's contributions has become an element in the reassessments of the history of molecular biology.

The Delbrück Papers (forty-four boxes) are housed at the California Institute of Technology, documenting in detail his professional life. Although there is a historical account of the phage school and a recent biography of Delbrück, they represent perspectives of participants. A critical biography based on these materials would greatly enrich the scholarship in the history of science in the twentieth century.

BIBLIOGRAPHY

Abir-Am, Pnina. "The Discourse of Physical Power and Biological Knowledge in the 1930s: A Reappraisal of the Rockefeller Foundation 'Policy' in Molecular Biology." *Social Studies of Science* 12 (1982): 123–143.

Cairns, John, Gunther S. Stent, and John D. Watson, eds. *Phage and the Origins of Molecular Biology.* New York: Cold Spring Harbor Laboratory of Quantitative Biology, 1966.

Cohen, Seymour. "The Biochemical Origins of Molecular Biology: Introduction." *Trends in Biochemical Sciences* 9 (1984): 334–336.

Fischer, Ernst P., and Carol Lipson. *Thinking About Science: Max Delbrück and the Origins of Molecular Biology.* New York: Norton, 1988.

Fruton, Joseph. *A Skeptical Biochemist.* Cambridge, MA: Harvard University Press, 1992.

Judson, Horace F. *The Eighth Day of Creation: The Makers of the Revolution in Biology.* New York: Simon and Schuster, 1979.

Kay, Lily E. "Conceptual Models and Analytical Tools: The Biology of Physicist Max Delbrück." *Journal of the History of Biology* 18 (1985): 207–247.

———. "The Secret of Life: Niels Bohr's Influence on the Biology Program of Max Delbrück." *Rivista di Storia della Scienza* 2 (1985): 485–510.

———. *The Molecular Vision of Life: Caltech, the Rockefeller Foundation, and the Rise of the New Biology.* New York: Oxford University Press, 1993.

Kohler, Robert E. "The Management of Science: The Experience of Warren Weaver and the Rockefeller Foundation Program in Molecular Biology." *Minerva* 14 (1976): 249–293.

Olby, Robert C. *The Path to the Double Helix.* London: Macmillan, 1974.

Lily E. Kay

Department of Agriculture, United States

Established on 15 May 1862, by a bill signed by President Abraham Lincoln, the United States Department of Agriculture (USDA) was one of the world's leading scientific research organizations from its establishment until World War II. After the war, it was still of major importance, although overshadowed by other establishments, particularly the military.

The head of the department (first called a commissioner), by law, was "by practical and scientific experiments (accurate records of which experiments shall be kept in his office), . . . to collect, as he may be able, new and valuable seeds and plants; to test, by cultivation, the value of such of them as may require such tests; to propagate such as may be worthy of propagation, and to distribute them among agriculturists." The commissioner was authorized to employ "chemists, botanists, entomologists, and other persons skilled in the natural sciences pertaining to agriculture."

The first commissioner established divisions of chemistry, entomology, botany, forestry, statistics, pomology, and vegetable physiology and pathology. A Bureau of Animal Industry was added in 1884, and, in 1890, the Weather Bureau was transferred from the War Department. The Forest Service became part of the department in 1905. Over the years, the names of many of the agencies were changed and a number were added, particularly since 1933 when the department was assigned responsibilities for supporting the prices of farm products and distributing surpluses to the poor.

Isaac Newton, a Pennsylvania dairy farmer, was appointed first commissioner. He immediately laid out experimental plots on what is now the Mall in Washington and began experiments with different varieties of grain.

D

Newton's immediate successors were, for the most part, content to carry out their assigned duties. However, a number of advances in agricultural science and technology were made before the turn of the century by scientists working for the department. These included such diverse achievements as determining the chemical composition of foods and establishing the science of human nutrition, introducing the vedalia beetle to control scale, breeding disease-resistant strains of plants, developing the serum-virus treatment against hog cholera, and identifying and finding a control for tick fever. Among the department's world-known scientists were W.O. Atwater, Theobald Smith, and William A. Orton.

The development of the department into the world's greatest research institution of its day came with the appointment of James ("Tama Jim") Wilson as secretary of agriculture in 1897, a post he occupied for sixteen years. Wilson had been a professor of agriculture at Iowa State College and a United States Congressman. During his tenure in office, employment in the department increased from 2,444 to 13,858 persons and expenditures from $3,535,000 to $21,103,000. Wilson consolidated a number of different divisions and offices into the Bureaus of Plant Industry, Soils, Statistics, Chemistry, Entomology, and Biological Survey. However, emphasis was on lines of work directed by individuals rather than on administrative units. The galaxy of scientists in plant research included Beverly T. Galloway, Seaman A. Knapp, W.J. Spillman, and Mark Carleton; in entomology, L.O. Howard; in chemistry, Harvey W. Wiley; in animals, Marion Dorset; in soils, Curtis F. Marbut and Milton Whitney; in nutrition, Wilbur O. Atwater; and in forestry, Gifford Pinchot. Of these scientists, Wiley became the best known to the public because of his efforts to insure consumers more wholesome foods.

The department inaugurated a unique educational program in 1914 when Congress approved the Smith-Lever Act. The act directed the department to work in cooperation with the states (usually the state agricultural colleges) and counties in establishing offices staffed by county agents to carry the results of research directly to farmers. This Cooperative Extension Service has been widely copied throughout the world.

During World War I, the department encouraged farmers to increase production to meet wartime needs. However, after the war, prices fell, and the department urged farmers to apply the results of research to cutting costs of production. It established the Bureau of Agricultural Economics in 1922, under the leadership of Henry C. Taylor, to help farmers cut costs and to better market their products.

The depression continued, resulting in the establishment, beginning in 1933, of a number of new agencies, geared toward action rather than research. These included the Agricultural Adjustment Administration (1933), Soil Conservation Service (1935), Federal Surplus Commodities Corporation (1935), Farm Security Administration (1937), Federal Crop Insurance Corporation (1938), Rural Electrification Admiministration (1939), Farm Credit Administration (1939), and Commodity Credit Corporation (1939). Some of these agencies were formerly independent, but all had been organized in 1933 or later. They, some with different names and with the Farm Credit Administration being independent, were still responsible for mainly the same programs some sixty-five years later.

In 1969, food distribution programs that had been carried out by the department on a somewhat erratic basis were formalized in the Food and Nutrition Service. The food stamp, school lunch, and related programs have been a substantial part of the department's programs so far as funds and personnel are concerned. The food programs have had more public and Congressional support than the more controversial farm production programs.

The department's major research programs in the physical sciences have been carried out in recent years in five regional utilization research laboratories and in cooperation with state agricultural colleges and experiment stations. Four laboratories were authorized by Congress in 1938 and a fifth in 1964. They are located in Wyndmoor, Pennsylvania; Peoria, Illinois; Albany, California; New Orleans, Louisiana; and Athens, Georgia. In addition to the five regional laboratories, the department maintains a major research station in Beltsville, Maryland. The Forest Service also maintains research facilities somewhat independent of the department.

Still, major research accomplishments are identified with individuals. For example, the control of insects through sterilization was developed by Edward F. Knipling, and home economics became recognized as an important area of research under the leadership of Louise Stanley.

Economic and statistical research has been carried on by agencies with varied titles—currently the Economic Research Service and the Statistical Reporting

Service. The Foreign Agricultural Service promotes exports of agricultural products. The National Agricultural Library, with some 1.4 million volumes, is used by researchers throughout the nation.

The Department of Agriculture has carried out problem solving rather than theoretical research. However, at times problem-solving research has contributed to scientific theory while theory has contributed to problem solving. Both are necessary to insure a continued adequate supply of food for the world.

BIBLIOGRAPHY

Baker, Gladys L., et al. *Century of Service: The First 100 Years of the United States Department of Agriculture.* Washington, DC: United States Department of Agriculture, 1963.

Moore, Ernest G. *The Agricultural Research Service.* New York: Frederick A. Praeger, 1967.

Rasmussen, Wayne D. *Taking the University to the People: Seventy-five Years of Cooperative Extension.* Ames: Iowa State University Press, 1989.

———. *Farmers, Cooperatives, and USDA: A History of the Agricultural Cooperative Service.* Washington, DC: United States Department of Agriculture, 1991.

Rasmussen, Wayne D., and Gladys L. Baker. *The Department of Agriculture.* New York: Praeger Publishers, 1972.

Simms, D. Harper. *The Soil Conservation Service.* New York: Praeger Publishers, 1970.

Steen, Harold K. *The U. S. Forest Service: A History.* Seattle: University of Washington Press, 1976.

Wayne D. Rasmussen

Drake, Daniel (1785–1852)

Pioneer physician, educator, and naturalist. Three years after he was born in Plainfield, New Jersey, Drake's family emigrated west. On this trip, his father met and formed a close personal friendship with Dr. William Goforth. When he was fifteen, in 1800, Daniel was sent to study physics, surgery, and midwifery with Dr. Goforth in Cincinnati, receiving the first medical diploma in the West. Subsequently, he received his medical degree from the University of Pennsylvania.

Drake's career as a medical educator began in 1817 when he joined the medical faculty of Transylvania University in Lexington, Kentucky. The next year, he returned to Cincinnati and petitioned the Ohio legislature to grant a charter to establish Cincinnati College and the Medical College of Ohio; it was granted in 1819. Drake's strong will, energy, and ambition often embroiled him in controversy. Dismissed from the school he founded, he went on to hold eleven faculty appointments in six different schools in Lexington, Louisville, and Philadelphia. He wrote and taught, and engaged in spirited debate until the end of his life.

Drake's concern with problems of medical education are outlined in his 1832 "Essays on Medical Education." He was one of the first to envision medical schools associated with universities and with public hospitals having extensive laboratories. He urged physicians to engage in lifelong learning, to publish in scientific journals, and to develop high professional qualities.

In addition to his work as a physician and teacher, Drake was also a naturalist. In 1810, he published "Notices Concerning Cincinnati," the first topographic description of any city in the West, including its flora and fauna, weather, population, and culture. For years, he collected data on geography and disease of the valley of North America and their relationship to the environment. In 1850, he published the first volume of his findings; the second volume was published posthumously.

Despite his disputes with his colleagues at Cincinnati, it was this city which claimed him. He created their medical and scientific societies, natural history museums, libraries, academies and colleges, botanical gardens, hospitals, and lunatic asylums, to serve the social, educational, and cultural need of the city. Sir William Osler observed that "everything good in the city comes from Daniel Drake" (p. 307). Raised in the woods of Kentucky, Daniel Drake took the opportunities given him to fulfill his own potential. His inherent ability, strong character, and great ambition lifted him beyond his humble beginnings to preeminence among American physicians.

BIBLIOGRAPHY

Drake, Daniel. *Doctor Drake on Medical Education and the Medical Profession in the United States.* Cincinnati: Roff & Young, 1832.

———. *Notices Concerning Cincinnati.* Cincinnati: Printed for the Author, at the Press of John W. Browne & Co., 1810.

Drury, A.G., "Drake, Daniel." *A Cyclopedia of American Medical Biography.* Edited by Howard A. Kelly and Walter L. Burrage. Philadelphia: W.B. Saunders, 1912, 1:328–329.

Flexner, Abraham. *Medical Education in the United States and Canada; a Report of the Carnegie Foundation for Advancement of Teaching.* New York: Carnegie Foundation for the Advancement of Teaching, 1910.

D

Flexner, James T. *Doctors on Horseback: Pioneers of American Medicine.* New York: Garden City Publishing, 1937.

Garrison, Fielding H. *An Introduction to the History of Medicine.* Philadelphia: W.B. Saunders, 1914.

Gross, Samuel D. *Discourse on the Life, Character and Services of Daniel Drake, M.D.* Louisville: Office of the Louisville Journal, 1853.

Horine, Emmet F. *Daniel Drake (1785–1852) Pioneer Physician of the Midwest.* Philadelphia: University of Pennsylvania, 1961.

Juettner, Otto. *Daniel Drake and His Followers.* Cincinnati: Harvey Publishing, 1909.

Major, Ralph H. *A History of Medicine.* 2 vols. Springfield: C.C. Thomas, 1954.

Meigs, Charles D. *A Biographical Notice of Daniel Drake, M.D. of Cincinnati.* Philadelphia: Lippincott, Grambo & Co., 1853.

Osler, Wiliam. *Aequanimitas.* 3d ed. Philadelphia: Blakiston, 1932.

Shapiro, Henry D., and Zale L. Miller. *Physician to the West: Selected Writings of Daniel Drake on Science and Society.* Lexington: University of Kentucky Press, 1970.

Billie Broaddus

Draper, Henry (1837–1882)

Astronomer. Born in Prince Edward County, Virginia, he lived in New York City from age two until his death. He graduated from the medical department of the University of the City of New York in 1858. After working for eighteen months at Bellevue Hospital, he was appointed professor of natural science at his alma mater. During the next twenty-two years, he held a number of academic and administrative positions there.

Draper's interest in astronomy was sparked by a visit to the famous six-foot telescope of the Earl of Rosse in Ireland in 1857. There, he conceived of the possibility of combining photography and astronomy.

The following year, he began construction of a telescope and observatory on land belonging to his father's estate at Hastings-on-Hudson. When his speculum mirror split in half one night due to the expansive force of freezing moisture, he began experimenting with silvered-glass mirrors on the advice of Sir John Herschel. By 1862, he succeeded in completing and mounting a 15½-inch glass mirror. This feat interested Joseph Henry, the secretary of the Smithsonian Institution, who persuaded Draper to write a monograph on it, which quickly became the standard reference on telescope making.

In 1872, Draper completed construction of a 28-inch glass mirror telescope. On 1 August 1872, he succeeded in obtaining with it the first photograph of a star (Vega) that showed distinct Fraunhofer lines, beating out William Huggins, his closest rival, by four years. He followed this pioneering work with further photographic studies of the spectra of Vega, Altair, the sun, Venus, and Jupiter. Within a short time, he succeeded in making photography—especially spectrum photography—the best means of studying the sky.

This research was interrupted by a laboratory study of the spectra of the elements. As a reference scale for the determination of their wavelengths, he took a diffraction-grating photograph of the solar spectrum in 1873 that far surpassed any available for several years.

Draper startled the scientific community in 1877 when he announced he had discovered the presence of bright oxygen lines in the solar spectrum. Spectroscopists were skeptical, however, even when he repeated his experiments at somewhat higher dispersion. Unfortunately for Draper, the low dispersion of his spectroscope and his apparent failure to understand Kirchhoff's law of radiation had caused him to make a significant scientific blunder.

Draper also achieved great success in photographing the Orion nebula. With an 11-inch Alvan Clark photographic refractor and the new dry photographic plates (suggested to him by Huggins), he obtained a 137-minute exposure of the nebula in 1882 that was by far the most brilliant success achieved by celestial photography up to that time.

After Draper's death in New York City, his widow established the Henry Draper Fund at the Harvard College Observatory, which enabled it to carry out fundamental research on the photography and classification of stellar spectra.

Although Draper was highly regarded in his day by his peers, he is "now often condescendingly characterized as [an] amateur" (Reingold, p. 253). Insofar as he neither had formal training in the subject nor taught it, used his own funds for his research, and worked in near-total isolation, this is a correct characterization. Moreover, he lacked the mathematical background necessary for any meaningful theoretical work in astrophysics. Nevertheless, his innovative research placed him on the cutting edge of the astronomy of his day.

The Henry and Ann Palmer Draper Papers in the New York Public Library contain five boxes of correspondence. There has not been a published full-length biography of him to date.

BIBLIOGRAPHY

Barker, George F. "On the Use of Carbon Bisulphide in Prisms; Being an Account of Experiments Made by the Late Dr. Henry Draper of New York." *American Journal of Science,* 3d ser. 29 (1885): 269–277.

———. "Henry Draper." *Biographical Memoirs of the National Academy of Sciences* 3 (1895): 81–139.

Draper, Henry. *On the Construction of a Silvered-Glass Telescope Fifteen and a Half Inches in Aperture and Its Use in Celestial Photography.* In *Smithsonian Contributions to Knowledge* 14 (1864).

Gingerich, Owen. "Henry Draper's Scientific Legacy." *Symposium on the Orion Nebula to Honor Henry Draper.* In *Annals of the New York Academy of Sciences* 395 (1982): 308–320.

Hoffleit, Dorrit. *Some Firsts in Astronomical Photography.* Cambridge, MA: Harvard College Observatory, 1950.

———. "The Evolution of the Henry Draper Memorial." *Vistas in Astronomy* 34 (1991): 107–162.

Plotkin, Howard. "Henry Draper: A Scientific Biography." Ph.D. diss., Johns Hopkins University, 1972.

———. "Henry Draper, the Discovery of Oxygen in the Sun, and the Dilemma of Interpreting the Solar Spectrum." *Journal for the History of Astronomy* 8 (1977): 44–51.

———. "Henry Draper, Edward C. Pickering, and the Birth of American Astrophysics." *Symposium on the Orion Nebula to Honor Henry Draper.* In *Annals of the New York Academy of Sciences* 395 (1982): 321–330.

Reingold, Nathan. *Science in Nineteenth Century America: A Documentary History.* New York: Hill & Wang, 1964.

Whitney, Charles A. "Draper, Henry." *Dictionary of Scientific Biography.* Edited by Charles C. Gillispie. New York: Scribners, 1971, 4:178–181.

Howard Plotkin

Draper, John William (1811–1882)

English-born American chemist and historian. Born in St. Helens, Lancashire, England, the son of a Methodist preacher, Draper as a child learned to use his father's Gregorian telescope. In 1829, Draper commenced premedical studies at the new University of London in what became University College. As the award of degrees in England was still confined to Oxford and Cambridge, Draper had to settle for a "certificate of honours" in chemistry. Relatives who had moved to Virginia before the American Revolution persuaded him to follow in 1832 with his mother, sisters, and new wife. From a farmhouse "laboratory," Draper published eight minor scientific papers (1834–1836). His sister Dorothy Catharine saved enough money from teaching to enable him to take his M.D. at the University of Pennsylvania in 1836. He was professor of chemistry and natural philosophy at Hampden-Sidney College in Virginia (1836–1839); professor of chemistry at New York University (1839–1882); a founding proprietor in 1841, and president (1850–1882), of the medical school nominally attached to the university. Under Draper's aegis, the university proper awarded the Ph.D. in chemistry five times (1867–1872)—though short-lived, one of the earliest American efforts to launch a Ph.D. program. Draper was not included in the initial membership of the National Academy of Sciences, probably with the connivance and certainly with the cognizance of the Lazzaroni, and his election was pointedly delayed until 1877. In 1875, he received the Rumford medals of the American Academy of Arts and Sciences for the sum total of his "Researches in Radiant Energy" and became first president of the American Chemical Society in 1876. He died in Hastings-on-Hudson, New York.

A classroom demonstration in London by the organic chemist Edward Turner triggered Draper's lifelong fascination with the chemical effects of light. The most spectacular of these was photography, and by December 1839 Draper had become one of the first three people known to have taken a photographic portrait. In the winter of 1839–1840, he became the first known astronomical photographer and announced in March 1840 his success in obtaining "distinct" representations of the lunar maria or dark spots. His son Henry (born in 1837) eventually became one of the greatest astronomical photographers. As a boy of thirteen, Henry took photographic slides through a microscope—thought to have been the first photomicrographs—at his father's behest. The elder Draper took, in 1844, the first known photograph of the diffraction spectrum. He was also the first to take a precise photograph of the infrared region and the first, in 1843, to describe three great Fraunhofer lines there. He and Edmond Becquerel independently photographed lines in the ultraviolet at about the same time.

On the theoretical front, Draper enunciated in 1841 the principle long known as Draper's law (subsequently renamed the Grotthuss or Grotthuss-Draper law from an earlier virtually forgotten statement by

D

C.J.D. Grotthuss)—that only absorbed rays produce chemical change. In 1843, Draper constructed a "tithonometer" for measuring the intensity of light on the basis of the discovery by Gay-Lussac and Thenard in 1809 that light causes hydrogen and chlorine to combine progressively. In this context, Draper demonstrated that chemical change is proportional to the *intensity* of the incident light. In the mid-1850s, Bunsen and Roscoe characterized the tithonometer as inaccurate and improved upon it in an "actinometer" based on the identical phenomenon. In his most important single memoir (1847), Draper proved that all solid substances become incandescent at the same temperature and thereafter with rising temperature emit rays of increasing refrangibility, and that incandescent solids produce a continuous spectrum. He implied in the mid-1840s and stated in 1857 that the maxima of luminosity and of heat in the spectrum coincide.

Draper owed his general celebrity to the historical writings—*A History of the Intellectual Development of Europe* (1863) and *History of the Conflict between Religion and Science* (1874)—that he perceived as a direct continuation of his earlier researches. He had been looking for "laws" in natural science and now professed to find their equivalent in social science. Without mentioning Auguste Comte, Draper embraced the Comtean "law" of three stages in historical development, from the theological through the metaphysical to the "positive," or scientific, modes of thought. But Draper grafted on to this an un-Comtean cyclical theory of history by which nations or cultures traversed the sequence only to expire from decrepitude analogous to old age in individuals. Draper's great moment in the limelight came at the Oxford meeting of the British Association for the Advancement of Science in 1860, when he (very problematically) treated Darwinism as another demonstration of lawfulness in nature as in history. His paper touched off the notorious exchange between Bishop Samuel Wilberforce and T.H. Huxley about descending from apes. The only lasting mark that Draper left as a historian was to lodge the dubious formula about "the conflict between religion and science" almost ineradicably in the popular mind. He was easily one of the half-dozen most notable physical scientists in America before 1870, surpassed only by Benjamin Franklin and Joseph Henry. But Henry and his fellow Lazzaroni never treated Draper as an equal and spoke contemptuously of him among themselves.

BIBLIOGRAPHY

Fleming, Donald. *John William Draper and the Religion of Science.* Philadelphia: University of Pennsylvania Press, 1950.

Donald Fleming

Drugs

The use of habit-forming or addictive substances which alter mood, physiology, or performance is probably as old as culture. Most societies have distinguished between medicinal use to treat physiological or psychological illness or distress, and recreational use for pleasure, escape, relaxation, or supposedly expanded sensation. The substances used, the profile of users, and societal responses vary greatly over time and place. But in general, modern western societies based on complex industrial and commercial systems have frowned on or prohibited the use of such substances for nonmedicinal reasons. This reflects fears of the loss of individuality through addiction to a drug or the sensations it produces; concern that such use will reduce productivity, which would harm the user and society; and fear of the effects of use or addiction on third parties such as family, community, or a larger economy. Drug use thus combines concerns for the safety, well-being, progress, and condition of both the individual and the larger society of which he/she is a part. This interrelation has generally provoked legal regulation as well as societal disapproval of recreational or habitual drug use which seems nonmedicinal.

Substances which produce these effects on individuals and responses from societies abound. People everywhere, in all times, including modern industrial societies, have employed plant alkaloids and extracts both for medicinal and recreational uses. The use of some of these, such as marijuana or hashish, has often been endemic in Eastern and Middle Eastern societies. But this alarmed Western cultures, who saw such use as a means to induce passive behavior or to separate the user from the demands of reality, and as a stepping-stone to more dangerous substances. Other plant products, especially opium, have had a complex history. Opiates in relatively weak forms, such as laudanum, opium dissolved in wine or another alcoholic medium, or powder or gum, were employed in the west to relieve pain. But society disapproved of this opiate use, and of opium smoking, for recreational reasons because opiates seemed to addict users and remove them from responsibilities. Morphine, the principal alkaloid of opium, was separated early in the nineteenth century, and became a widely used painkiller. Because of its power to relax the body, and to rearrange sensations processed in the brain, it became a fashionable drug for recreational use among some social groups. It was highly addictive, whether employed as a powder or in solution via the hypodermic syringe. A similar more potent product named heroin appeared at the end of the nineteenth century, touted as a nonaddictive painkiller. Its medicinal use was minimal, however, as studies quickly revealed addictive properties. In the century that followed, legal regulation at all jurisdictions paralleled the development and use of an apparently endless variety of chemicals and substances for nonmedicinal purposes. These included various preparations of cocaine; marijuana; hallucinogens such as LSD; tranquilizers like valium; barbiturates; and combinations of these and other substances. Whatever the merits or medicinal importance of such new substances, societies generally retained the inherited differentiation between recreational and medicinal usage. Modern chemistry has seemed to open the door to an endless chain of substances whose use society would have to confront, forbid, regulate, and challenge. Science was thus in the curious position of producing an array of products for medical usage, while being called on to develop treatments and cures for their nonmedicinal use.

BIBLIOGRAPHY

Courtwright, David T. *Dark Paradise: Opiate Addiction in America Before 1940.* Cambridge, MA: Harvard University Press, 1982.

McWilliams, John C. *The Protectors: Harry J. Anslinger and the Federal Bureau of Narcotics, 1930–1962.* Newark: University of Delaware Press, 1990.

Morgan, H. Wayne. *Drugs in America: A Social History 1800–1980.* Syracuse: Syracuse University Press, 1981.

———, ed. *Yesterday's Addicts: American Society and Drug Abuse 1865–1920.* Norman: University of Oklahoma Press, 1974.

Musto, David F. *The American Disease: Origins of Narcotic Control.* New Haven: Yale University Press, 1973.

Taylor, Arnold H. *American Diplomacy and the Narcotics Traffic, 1900–1939.* Durham, NC: Duke University Press, 1969.

H. Wayne Morgan

SEE ALSO
Pharmacology

D

Dryden, Hugh Latimer (1898–1965)

Leading contributor to aeronautical research and an administrator who helped to lay the foundation for the postwar success of American aviation and space-flight programs. The oldest of three sons born to Samuel Isaac Dryden and the former Zenovia Hill Culver, he grew up in Worcester County, Maryland, and in the city of Baltimore. Dryden graduated from high school at the age of fourteen and entered Johns Hopkins University, where he earned an honors degree in physics (1916), a master's degree (1918), and a Ph.D (1919).

While at Johns Hopkins, he came to the attention of Professor Joseph Ames, chairman of the Physics Department and a leader of the National Advisory Committee for Aeronautics (NACA). Ames helped Dryden to obtain a job with the National Bureau of Standards (NBS) in June 1918. He was named head of the Aeronautics Section of the NBS in 1919, and of the Division of Mechanics and Sound in 1934. During the years 1920–1940, Dryden earned an international reputation for his studies of turbulent and laminar flow, the boundary layer, and supersonic airflow around propeller blade tips (with Lyman Briggs).

Dryden took command of a guided missile program sponsored by the National Defense Research Committee (later the Office of Scientific Research and Development in 1940). Based at the NBS, Dryden's group was responsible for the development of the Bat, a radar equipped, self-guided bomb that sank several Japanese ships. He traveled to Europe in the spring of 1945 as a member of the Army Air Forces Scientific Group organized by Theodore von Kármán. Following his return to the United States, Dryden was a key participant in the preparation of two reports to the army air forces, *Where We Stand* and *Toward New Horizons,* focusing attention on the critically important role that technical research would play in the future defense of the nation. For his wartime efforts, President Truman awarded Dryden the National Medal of Freedom.

Dryden emerged from World War II as a seasoned administrator of research and development programs. He was named assistant director of the NBS in 1946, and associate director six months later. In 1947, he moved to the NACA, replacing Dr. George Lewis as director of aeronautical research. Two years later he was named director of the NACA. Dryden guided the agency during its final years, overseeing projects ranging from the cost-saving Unitary Wind Tunnel Plan to the development of the North American X-15 research

D

aircraft and early NACA plans for American entry into space. When NACA was replaced by the National Aeronautics and Space Administration (NASA) in 1958, Dryden became assistant director of the new agency, a position that he retained until his death.

The recipient of sixteen honorary degrees and dozens of professional awards, Dryden was especially proud of being named 1962 Methodist layman of the year. On March 26, 1976, NASA officials renamed their principal flight test facility in honor of Hugh Latimer Dryden.

BIBLIOGRAPHY

Gorn, Michael H. *Hugh L. Dryden's Career in Air and Space.* Washington, DC: National Aeronautics and Space Administration History Office, 1996.

Smith, Richard K. *The Hugh L. Dryden Papers, 1898–1965.* Baltimore: Milton S. Eisenhower Library, Johns Hopkins University, 1974.

Tom D. Crouch

Dubos, René Jules (1901–1982)

Biochemist, born in Saint-Brice-sous-Forêt, France, and educated at the Institut National Agronomique. He is best known for his isolation of gramicidin, which was the first antibiotic ever therapeutically applied. As a microbiologist, he adopted an ecological approach, and in his later career he became an environmentalist, always stressing the interaction between organisms and their biological surroundings. Dubos died in New York City.

Dubos started his career in 1922 as a member of the International Institute of Agriculture in Rome. Two years later, he was introduced in Rome to Dr. Selman Waksman, bacteriologist at Rutgers University. In October 1924, Dubos went to the United States to study with Waksman, taking a Ph.D. in agricultural chemistry and bacteriology. His thesis was on the decomposition of cellulose by soil bacteria. During a visit to Alexis Carrel at the Rockefeller Institute, Dubos met Oswald Avery, who introduced him to the problem of finding an enzyme that could degrade the polysaccharide capsule of the pneumococcus bacterium. Dubos found that pneumococci initially grew more abundantly when oxygen was removed from the culture than when this was added. This made Dubos realize that many of the ingredients used in the preparation of culture media had a toxic effect on bacteria. Thus, environmental factors which stimulated the initial growth of a culture were not necessarily those optimally suited to permitting that cell to attain its maximum development.

Dubos succeeded in isolating an enzyme which degraded the polysaccharide of pneumococcus by culturing a soil sample from cranberry soil from New Jersey with the polysaccharide as the only carbon source. This approach of selective culture distinguished Dubos from medical bacteriologists who added many different components (e.g., sugars, peptones, proteins) in order to obtain as many bacteria as possible. The bacterium that Dubos isolated only produced the degrading enzyme if the polysaccharide was the only carbon source. Dubos concluded that cells have many potentialities but that these potentialities usually become manifest only when the cells are compelled by their environment to make use of them.

The polysaccharide degrading enzyme was an example of an adaptive enzyme, unlike constitutive enzymes, which are always produced by the organism. Dubos concluded that the cell produces an adaptive enzyme only in response to the presence of a particular substance in the environment (probably during the production of new protoplasm). Dubos distinguished such a mechanism of adaptation from that by which a microbial culture produces a variant bacterial cell endowed with the new enzymatic property. This variant might then be favored because of its beneficial environment. Dubos concluded that the latter mechanism of adaptation or "training" is the result of natural selection of the variant form. Dubos suggested that the synthetic process of the adaptive enzyme was "oriented" by the chemical structure of the substrate, which thus determined the specificity of the enzyme.

In the late 1930s, Dubos set out to isolate a microorganism which could attack living cells (e.g., staphylococci). After two years of culturing soil samples supplied with the bacterium, Dubos isolated a spore-bearing bacillus, *Bacillus brevis,* which attacked and lysed the living cells of several species of gram-positive microorganisms. Dubos named the active substance tyrothricin, and obtained from it a crystalline substance, gramicidin. Thus, gramicidin is produced by a bacterium, unlike penicillin which is produced by a mold. Because of its toxicity, gramicidin was never used internally; it was only used as an antiseptic in medicated bandages and surgical dressings.

In 1942, Dubos's first wife, Marie Louis, died of tuberculosis (his second wife, Jean, also suffered from the disease). After two years at Harvard Medical School, Dubos returned to the Rockefeller Institute in 1944, to work on tuberculosis. The tubercle bacillus could only be cultured as thick pellicles on the surface of culture media. After an extensive study of the use of detergents in culturing tubercle bacilli, Dubos found Tween to be nontoxic and conducive to growth throughout the medium; quantitative studies of tubercle bacilli now became possible.

In the 1950s, Dubos developed his ideas on the importance of the natural history of microorganisms and their interactions with the environment. He emphasized the role of host-parasite relationship and concluded that one of the most neglected aspects of the germ theory of infectious disease was the fact that, under natural circumstances, infection rarely produces fatal disease. This is the more remarkable because the tissues of man and animals contain everything required for the existence of most microbes. Dubos argued that microbial infections (e.g., viruses) do not necessarily cause disease and that there are many instances of benign or even helpful microorganismal infections. He developed this idea even further by arguing that infection often constitutes a creative force, resulting in the appearance of characteristics and functions that neither the host nor the infective agent could manifest in the absence of the other.

BIBLIOGRAPHY

Benison, Saul. "René Jules Dubos and the Capsular Polysaccharide of Pneumococcus: An Oral History Memoir." *Bulletin of the History of Medicine* 50 (1976): 459–477.

Davis, Bernard D. "Two Perspectives: On René Dubos, and on Antibiotic Actions." In *Launching the Antibiotic Era: Personal Accounts of the Discovery and Use of the First Antibiotics,* edited by Carol L. Moberg, and Zanvil A. Cohn. New York: Rockefeller University Press, 1990, pp. 69–83; reprinted in *Perspectives in Biology and Medicine* 35 (1991): 37–48.

Dubos, René J. "Studies on a Bactericidal Agent Extracted from a Soil Bacillus: I. Preparation of the Agent: Its Activity in Vitro; II. Protective Effect of the Bactericidal Agent against Experimental Pneumococcus Infections in Mice." *Journal of Experimental Medicine* 70 (1939): 1–10, 11–17.

———. "The Adaptive Production of Enzymes by Bacteria." *Bacteriological Reviews* 4 (1940): 1–16.

———. *The Bacterial Cell in its Relation to Problems of Virulence, Immunity and Chemotherapy.* Cambridge, MA: Harvard University Press, 1945.

———. "Second Thoughts on the Germ Theory." *Scientific American* 192 (May 1955): 31-35.

———. "Integrative and Creative Aspects of Infection." In *Perspectives in Virology,* Vol. 2, edited by Morris Pollard. Minneapolis: Burgess, 1961, pp. 200–205.

———. "Infection into Disease." *Perspectives in Biology and Medicine* 1 (1958): 425–435; reprinted in *Life and Disease: New Perspectives in Biology and Medicine,* edited by Dwight J. Ingle. New York: Basic Books, 1963, pp. 100–110.

———. "Medicine's Living History: Dr. René Dubos." *Medical World News* 16 (1975): 77–87.

———. *The Professor, the Institute, and DNA.* New York: Rockefeller University Press, 1976.

———. *Pasteur and Modern Science.* Madison: Science Tech Publications, 1988.

———., ed. *Bacterial and Mycotic Infections of Man.* Philadelphia: Lippincott, 1948.

Hirsch, James G., and Carol L. Moberg. "René Jules Dubos." *Biographical Memoirs of the National Academy of Sciences* 58 (1989): 133–161.

Piel, Gerard, and Osborn Segerberg, Jr., eds. *The World of René Dubos: A Collection from His Writings.* New York: Henry Holt and Company, 1990.

Ton van Helvoort

Dudley Observatory

Astronomical observatory in Albany, New York. Incorporated in 1852, Dudley Observatory, named after a deceased United States Senator whose widow provided the initial funds, was formally inaugurated in 1856. Its early years were unsettled. The first director, Benjamin A. Gould, was removed in 1859 after numerous clashes with the trustees. His successor, O.M. Mitchel, died in 1862, having spent only about a year as resident director.

However, the appointment of George W. Hough, Mitchel's assistant, as director in 1865 initiated nearly a century of stability. Hough remained as director until 1874. Two years later, Lewis Boss was named director, and was succeeded upon his death in 1912 by his son, Benjamin Boss. In 1968, Dudley ceased operations as an astronomical observatory, although the institution remains in existence as an administrative entity.

Gould had envisioned the Dudley as a great center for positional astronomy. Lewis Boss made Gould's dream a reality. First, Boss participated in the Astronomische Gesellschaft international catalog of all stars in the northern sky of at least ninth magnitude. Then he initiated a research project, completed by his son, of observing all stars with acknowledged or suspected proper motion. To observe the stars of the southern sky, Boss

D

had the Olcott meridian circle, which Gould had acquired in 1856, shipped to an observing site in San Luis, Argentina. These observations of proper motions were incorporated into the *General Catalogue of 33,342 Stars for Epoch 1950* (five volumes, 1937).

The early history of the Dudley Observatory has held a prominent place in discussions of mid-nineteenth-century American science, with the ousting of Gould being viewed as a major blow to the hopes of the Lazzaroni to dominate American science. Olson (p. 265) has argued that the controversy was the result of "the disparity in attitudes toward the nature of science that existed between the public . . . and the small coterie of professional scientists." More recent scholarship has termed the clash between the trustees and Gould and his allies as one between two elites, each with its own sense of responsibility.

BIBLIOGRAPHY

Boss, Benjamin. *History of the Dudley Observatory, 1851–1968.* Albany: Dudley Observatory, 1968.

James, Mary Ann. *Elites in Conflict: The Antebellum Clash over the Dudley Observatory.* New Brunswick: Rutgers University Press, 1987.

Lankford, John. "Charting the Southern Sky." *Sky & Telescope* 74 (1987): 243–246.

Olson, Richard G. "The Gould Controversy at Dudley Observatory: Public and Professional Values in Conflict." *Annals of Science* 27 (1971): 265–276.

Marc Rothenberg

DuPont Company

American chemical company that was a pioneer in industrial research and has been a longtime supporter of in-house fundamental research. DuPont products include nylon, Dacron polyester fibers, Lycra spandex fibers, and Teflon. After being established in 1802 by the French émigré Eleuthère Irénée duPont, the company produced only black powder for almost eighty years. In 1880, a grandson of the founder, Lammot duPont, established a new business to manufacture dynamite, the new high explosive developed by Alfred Nobel in Sweden. Lammot had graduated from the University of Pennsylvania in 1849 and had done chemical experimentation for the company. His most important development was a blasting powder that substituted cheaper Chilean sodium nitrate for Indian potassium nitrate. The manufacture of dynamite involved reacting glycerine with nitric acid to make nitroglycerine, and the stabilization of this dangerous liquid by absorbing it in diatomaceous earth. Lammot was killed by a nitroglycerine explosion in 1884. This disaster led to the hiring of Oscar T. Jackson, a chemist who had done postgraduate work in Germany with Adolf von Baeyer and Emil Fischer. Under Jackson, the manufacture of dynamite improved significantly, prompting the company to open a full-time laboratory, the Eastern Laboratory, with its own director, Charles Lee Reese, in 1902. In this same year, the DuPont company was reorganized by three cousins who bought out the older generation. One of the cousins, Pierre S. duPont, who had graduated from the Massachusetts Institute of Technology in 1890, would become the driving force behind the expansion of the company into the chemical industry and the growth of the DuPont research program. In 1903, DuPont opened a second laboratory, the Experimental Station, to do research to improve relations with the federal government concerning the development of military smokeless powder and to evaluate outside inventions offered to the company.

The first major challenge for DuPont research came during World War I when the company entered the dyestuffs business. Before the war, German companies had dominated the American dyestuffs market. Learning the secrets of dyestuffs chemistry proved to be a difficult and expensive experience for DuPont, but after a decade of struggle, the company had a profitable business and, more importantly, an outstanding research capability in organic synthesis that would yield outstanding returns in the future. World War I also generated enormous profits for DuPont from the sale of explosives to the Allies. The company used some of this money to buy plastics and paint companies. To manage these diverse businesses, the company decentralized in 1921 into semiautonomous departments, each with its own manufacturing, sales, and research organization. The number and size of these research laboratories would grow in the 1920s as DuPont entered other chemical businesses through the acquisition of companies and technology. In the industrial departments, chemists were kept busy solving problems directly related to the new technologies.

The director of the central research laboratory, Charles M.A. Stine, in 1926, proposed to the company's executives that DuPont do more fundamental research. He pointed out that in many areas DuPont had little fundamental understanding of its products and processes. Stine argued that this research entailed very little risk because it would inevitably lead to significant technological improvements. He pointed out research topics such as polymers, chemical engineering, and catalysts that were critical to the company's existing technology and that were not receiving sufficient attention from academic researchers. These arguments won over the company's executives, who provided very generous funding including a new laboratory, which unofficially became known as Purity Hall. To staff it, Stine tried to hire prominent academic chemists. What he soon discovered was that a rather wide gulf had opened up between academic and industrial chemists. He found that he had difficulty persuading even junior faculty to leave academia and had to recruit mainly new Ph.D.'s. The major exception was Wallace H. Carothers, a Ph.D. organic chemist from the University of Illinois, who joined DuPont in 1928 after having taught at Illinois and Harvard for four years. While recruiting Carothers, Stine had pointed to polymers as a field ripe for research, especially since some of DuPont's most important products—Duco lacquers, cellophane, and rayon—were made from the natural polymer cellulose. After joining DuPont, Carothers began to do polymer research that soon yielded important scientific results, which were published. Just as Stine had hoped, fundamental research was raising the prestige of DuPont in the academic world. Carothers's work took on an added dimension in April 1930 when, only weeks apart, his associates discovered a synthetic rubber and fiber while doing more general studies of polymers. Eventually these discoveries would result in neoprene and nylon, two very successful products. Ironically, these breakthroughs were followed by a decreasing emphasis on fundamental research. A number of factors contributed to this trend but most important was Carothers's deteriorating mental health from 1934 until his suicide in 1937. Another factor was that the development of nylon took precedence over other research programs. Then, the outbreak of World War II diverted attention toward pressing wartime problems.

In the aftermath of World War II, DuPont renewed and expanded its commitment to fundamental research. There were many reasons for this shift in research strategy. Perhaps most important was the allure of discovering "new nylons." Another factor was research competition. The war effort was hailed as a triumph of modern scientific research; in the postwar era, many companies invested heavily in research. By doing twice as much fundamental research as its competitors, DuPont maintained its position as industry leader. The expansion of chemical research in both academia and industry led to increasing competition for Ph.D. chemists, the production of which remained constant during the 1950s. Under these conditions, research directors had to grant concessions concerning publication and other professional issues.

During the 1950s, most of the DuPont industrial department laboratories did considerable fundamental research or basic research, while the central research laboratory did so much of it that it began to resemble an academic institution. The central research laboratory took on the difficult mission of developing expertise across a broad spectrum of sciences with the expectation that scientific breakthroughs would open up new business areas for the company. With its near total commitment to academic-style science, the central research laboratory became increasingly isolated from the rest of the company. In the industrial departments, fundamental research thrived when it was integrated into the overall research programs and when it was performed by individuals who commanded the respect of their peers and superiors. Paul Morgan in the Pioneering Research Laboratory of the Textile Fibers Department made important contributions to polymer science and to several new products, including Lycra spandex and Kevlar fibers. Charles Pedersen of the Organic Chemicals Department laboratory won the Nobel Prize in chemistry in 1986 for his discovery of crown ethers, an unexpected outcome of a basic research investigation of the coordination chemistry of vanadium.

During the 1960s, DuPont executives became increasingly concerned that the large investment in basic research was not yielding "new nylons," and concluded that DuPont had made many important scientific breakthroughs but had failed to develop them into new products. Subsequently, the company launched a major initiative to commercialize new products, which it did in record number and at unprecedented cost in the 1960s. The profitability of these products, however, was at best mixed. This experience combined with the economic turmoil of the 1970s, including two oil embargoes that had dramatic effects on the chemical industry, to make DuPont executives skeptical about research, leading to a relative reduction in research effort. As a percentage of sales, research expenditures declined during the 1970s by 50 percent from their historical highs in the mid-1960s. Remarkably, during this period the central

D

research laboratory largely continued to do basic research. A major reorientation of central research would have done enormous damage to DuPont's reputation in the scientific community, which the company had done so much to establish over a long period of time. In the 1980s, CEO Edward Jefferson launched a new fundamental research initiative in the life sciences, hoping to establish a position for DuPont in this important field. Over the past seventy-five years, the DuPont company has been one of America's institutions that has maintained a symbiotic relationship between state of the art technology and scientific research.

BIBLIOGRAPHY

Chandler, Alfred D., Jr., and Stephen Salsbury. *Pierre S. duPont and the Making of the Modern Corporation.* New York: Harper & Row, 1971.

Hounshell, David A., and John Kenly Smith Jr. *Science and Corporate Strategy, DuPont R&D, 1902–1980.* New York: Cambridge University Press, 1988.

Wilkinson, Norman B. *Lammot duPont and the American Explosives Industry, 1850–1884.* Charlottesville: University of Virginia Press, 1984.

John K. Smith

Dye Industry

Commercial production of coloring materials, especially for textile manufacturing. Dye making in the United States, as in other industrialized countries, has become increasingly tied to the practice of scientific chemistry, particularly organic chemistry.

The American Revolution marked the end of a bustling mercantilist trade in natural dyes of the Americas, especially the export of indigo from South Carolina and Georgia plantations. Sources of natural dyes produced in the colonies and early Republic included the indigo plant, tree bark, roots, berries, and dried insects, among other things. Dyes from dyewood extracts became an industry staple between 1815 and the Civil War, although only black oak, source of the yellow dye quercitron, was native. Knowledge of chemistry expanded in the early nineteenth century, but organized science played little role in the natural dyes industry.

The synthetic dyes industry had its infancy in England when William Perkin synthesized mauve from coal tar in 1856, but Germany became the dominant producer by the 1870s. F.A. Kekule's theory of the benzene ring in 1865 contributed immensely to the development of the synthetic organic dyes industry in Germany, allowing chemists in the early industrial research laboratories to predict structures of new dyes. The United States contained only a small handful of synthetic dye manufacturers, most of whom depended on German supplies of intermediates. The underdeveloped state of graduate education in chemistry, the lack of tariff protection against strong German competition, and the use in the American steel industry of beehive ovens to produce coke rather than by-product ovens that captured coal tar, all influenced the slow development of the industry in the United States.

During World War I and the 1920s, the country developed its own successful synthetic dyes industry, partly because of the dyes' chemical relationship to some explosives and poison gases, as well as many pharmaceuticals. The industry developed new dyes to accommodate synthetic fibers in the 1930s and, after World War II, produced "fiber reactive" dyes that generated covalent bonds between the dye and fiber for improved fastness. Oil replaced coal tar as the source of synthetic dyes. After prosperous years in the 1950s and early 1960s, the American synthetic dye industry faced economic difficulties, and many major chemical companies sold their dyeworks, frequently to German companies, resulting once again in very few domestic producers.

Relatively little scholarly work has been written specifically about the American dyes industry.

BIBLIOGRAPHY

Haynes, Williams. *American Chemical Industry.* 6 vols. New York: D. Van Nostrand, 1945–1954.

Hounshell, David A., and John K. Smith Jr. *Science and Corporate Strategy, DuPont R&D, 1902–1980.* New York: Cambridge University Press, 1988.

Ihde, Aaron J. *The Development of Modern Chemistry.* New York: Harper and Row, 1964.

Reed, Germaine M. *Crusading for Chemistry: The Professional Career of Charles Holmes Hertz.* Athens: University of Georgia Press, 1995.

Servos, John. "History of Chemistry." *Osiris,* 2d ser., 1 (1985): 132–146.

Travis, Anthony S. "Synthetic Dyestuffs: Modern Colours for the Modern World." In *Milestones in 150 Years of the Chemical Industry,* edited by P.J.T. Morris, W.A. Campbell, and H.L. Roberts. Cambridge, U.K.: The Royal Society of Chemistry, 1991, pp. 144–157.

Kathryn Steen

SEE ALSO
Chemistry

E

Eaton, Amos (1776–1842)

Botanist, geologist, educator. Born on a farm in Chatham, Columbia County, New York, he graduated from Williams College (1799) and practiced law and land agency before contact with Samuel L. Mitchill and David Hosack led him to develop an interest in natural history. By 1810, he was offering a public course of lectures and publishing popular works on botany. In 1811, legal troubles resulting from land speculation ended his career as an attorney and he turned, upon his release from jail, to science full time. After studying with Benjamin Silliman and others at Yale, Eaton spent roughly a decade as a public lecturer on science and freelance naturalist with state and local surveys. During 1816–1817, for example, he lectured at Williams College and in surrounding towns, including Northampton and Amherst. In 1824, he relocated to Troy, New York, where he became a professor at the Rensselaer School (now Rensselaer Polytechnic Institute). In the remaining eighteen years of his life, he used Rensselaer as a base from which to transform American scientific education. At Rensselaer, he trained young men to do science and, perhaps more important, to teach it. Simultaneously he worked with Emma Willard and her sister, Almira Hart Lincoln Phelps, to introduce science to the students of Willard's Troy Female Seminary (now the Emma Willard School). Eaton and Lincoln Phelps initiated a pedagogical revolution that moved science instruction from an era of rote memorization to an era of direct observation. Their students from Rensselaer and Troy Female spread throughout the country taking this novel approach to science education with them.

While perhaps less important than his influence on others, Eaton's own scientific work deserves recognition. His geological work—done largely through the auspices of the various surveys of New York State—is credited with being one of the earliest attempts to link strata that are no longer contiguous through fossil analysis. His botanical work advanced the mapping of the flora of the American northeast. Eaton published prolifically, producing significant works on botany, zoology, geology, and chemistry. His *Manual of Botany for the Northern States* went through eight editions between 1817 and 1840. His work lobbying for science to the New York legislature resulted in the State Geological Survey, surveys of Albany and Rensselaer Counties, and a survey of the Erie Canal corridor.

Clearly Eaton's greatest influence came through his writings and through his students. His earliest student may have been the young John Torrey, whose father was the jailer charged with keeping Eaton. Young Torrey brought botanical specimens to Eaton to keep him busy and in return was treated to botanical lectures. Geologist James Hall, mineralogist Lewis Beck, and poet-novelist William Cullen Bryant all came under Eaton's influence later. While Eaton claimed his students numbered 7,000, there is no way to count those who heard his public lectures and became more scientifically literate in the process. His work at Rensselaer and at the Troy Female Seminary sent a generation of scientifically literate schoolteachers out across the nation. His voluminous written works—thirteen books on botany, chemistry, zoology, geology, and mineralogy—were his generation's best models of how to make science accessible.

E

Eaton's life was chronicled by McAllister and by Smallwood and Smallwood in the forties, but no recent, scholarly biography exists.

BIBLIOGRAPHY

McAllister, Ethel M. *Amos Eaton, Scientist and Educator.* Philadelphia: University of Pennsylvania Press, 1941.

Smallwood, William Martin. "Amos Eaton, Naturalist." *New York History* 18 (1937): 167–188.

Smallwood, William Martin, and Mabel Sarah Coon Smallwood. *Natural History and the American Mind.* New York: Columbia University Press, 1941.

Elizabeth Keeney

Ecology

The term "ecology" was coined by Ernst Haeckel in 1866, but it was rarely used either in Europe or the United States until the end of the nineteenth century. During the 1890s, a number of American biologists, particularly botanists, began using the term to describe a broad and sometimes ill-defined area of research dealing with the interactions between organisms and their physical and biological environments. In a general way, this research reflected the influence of Darwinism on late-nineteenth-century biology. It also reflected an important shift in research problems and methods that occurred at the end of the nineteenth century. During this period, a generation of professional botanists increasingly turned away from description and classification and towards studies in plant physiology, adaptation, and geographical distribution. This emphasis on process and function had occurred earlier in Europe, particularly in Germany. In style, if not always in substance, early ecology in America represented an extension of this physiological perspective to understanding organisms in their natural environments.

During the early decades of the twentieth century, ecology flourished in a number of institutional settings. A considerable amount of historical scholarship has been devoted to two university programs that did much to shape the intellectual landscape of ecology during the first half of the twentieth century. The students that gathered around Charles Bessey at the University of Nebraska formed a research school that was strongly oriented toward problems in plant ecology. Frederic Clements, the outstanding member of this group, did much to define the scope of ecology during the pre–World War II era. Equally influential was

Henry Chandler Cowles at the University of Chicago, whose pioneering study of succession on the sand dunes of Lake Michigan (1899) anticipated Clements's writings on this important problem. Cowles's many students at Chicago continued his tradition of detailed field studies in plant community ecology. More recently, historians have also emphasized the importance of the University of Chicago as an early center for the development of animal ecology, through the work of zoologists such as Victor Shelford and Warder Clyde Allee. Along with university research, ecology also flourished in nonacademic institutions. Private foundations, particularly the Carnegie Institution of Washington, played an important role in supporting ecological research. Ecological research in state and federal agencies was also important, although it has not received the detailed historical attention that it deserves. Several articles have documented the important roles that practical problems in agriculture and fisheries played in the growth of professional ecology. Some of the most suggestive studies have been done on limnology, with its diversity of institutional settings and rich interplay of theoretical and practical problems in the research of ecologists such as Shelford, Stephen Forbes, Jacob Reighard, Edward Birge, Chancey Juday, and G. Evelyn Hutchinson.

In 1915, the Ecological Society of America (ESA) was incorporated with 286 charter members. This number increased to approximately 500 by the early 1920s, but grew relatively little after that until the end of World War II. Although relatively small, this group was remarkably diverse. Zoologists and botanists each represented approximately a third of the original membership of the ESA, but the remainder was composed of an eclectic mix of foresters, agricultural scientists, marine biologists, plant physiologists and pathologists, climatologists, geologists and soil scientists, and parasitologists. This diversity continued to characterize professional ecology, and although it lends credence to the claim that ecology is an interdisciplinary and synthetic science, it may also partly explain the criticism that ecology lacks unifying principles.

Ecology was transformed after World War II. Membership in the ESA doubled almost every decade after 1950, reaching 6,000 in the late 1970s. Underlying this growth was the infusion of federal research funds from agencies such as the Office of Naval Research, Atomic Energy Commission, and National Science Foundation. The rise of environmentalism may also have played an important role in the growth of professional ecology, although historians have not explored this connection very deeply. Some historians (Kwa) have suggested that environmental concerns played an important role in generating support for American participation in the International Biological Program, a heavily funded study of ecosystems. Others (Nelkin) have emphasized the important differences between professional ecology and popular environmentalism. While these conclusions are not mutually exclusive, they suggest that the connection between ecology and popular environmental movements deserves greater attention.

The growth of ecology after World War II was also accompanied by increasing specialization and the emergence of competing subdisciplines. In particular, evolutionary population ecology and ecosystem ecology vied for intellectual authority and funding. These disputes have played an important part in shaping modern ecology.

Ecology, in general, was strongly influenced by the rise of mathematical modeling, systems thinking, and cybernetics after World War II. Mathematical models and ideas of self-regulation had been used even before the war, but ecologists such as G. Evelyn Hutchinson and his students did much to popularize these approaches during the 1950s and 1960s. Some historians (Kingsland, Hagen, Palladino) have emphasized the positive effect that this episode had on the growth of theoretical ecology. Other historians (Kwa, Mitman, Taylor) have been much more critical of the ideology underlying systems approaches in ecology.

BIBLIOGRAPHY

Bocking, Stephen. "Stephen Forbes, Jacob Reighard, and the Emergence of Aquatic Ecology in the Great Lakes Region." *Journal of the History of Biology* 23 (1990): 461–498.

———. *Ecologists and Environmental Politics: A History of Contemporary Ecology.* New Haven: Yale University Press, 1997.

Burgess, Robert L. "The Ecological Society of America." In *History of American Ecology.* New York: Arno Press, 1977, pp. 1–24.

Croker, Robert A. *Pioneer Ecologist: The Life and Works of Victor Ernest Shelford, 1877–1968.* Washington: Smithsonian Institution Press, 1991.

Golley, Frank Benjamin. *A History of the Ecosystem Concept in Ecology.* New Haven: Yale University Press, 1993.

Hagen, Joel B. *An Entangled Bank: The Origins of Ecosystem Ecology.* New Brunswick: Rutgers University Press, 1992.

Kingsland, Sharon E. *Modeling Nature: Episodes in the History of Population Ecology.* Chicago: University of Chicago Press, 1985.

Kwa, Chunglin. "Representations of Nature Mediating between Ecology and Science Policy: The Case of the International Biological Programme." *Social Studies of Science* 17 (1987): 413–442.

McIntosh, Robert P. *The Background of Ecology: Concept and Theory.* Cambridge, U.K.: Cambridge University Press, 1985.

Mitman, Gregg. *The State of Nature: Ecology, Community, and American Social Thought, 1900–1950.* Chicago: University of Chicago Press, 1992.

Nelkin, Dorothy. "Scientists and Professional Responsibility: The Experience of American Ecologists." *Social Studies of Science* 7 (1977): 75–95.

Palladino, Paola. "Ecological Theories, Mathematical Models, and Applied Biology in the 1960s and 1970s." *Journal of the History of Biology* 24 (1991): 223–244.

Taylor, Peter. "Technocratic Optimism, H. T. Odum, and the Partial Transformation of Ecological Metaphor after World War II." *Journal of the History of Biology* 21 (1988): 213–244.

Worster, Donald. *Nature's Economy: A History of Ecological Ideas.* Cambridge, U.K.: Cambridge University Press, 1977.

Joel B. Hagen

SEE ALSO
Environmental and Conservation Concerns

Economics

Modern economics commenced, in retrospect, with Adam Smith in the late eighteenth century but has always been heterogeneous, the differences centering on varying conceptions of how to do economics—what it means to be a science—and of what the economy is all about. Classical economics focused on several general axioms, such as supply and demand, the division of labor, the law of population, diminishing returns, and the labor theory of value to reach certain conclusions as to the distribution of income and conditions of economic growth, largely, though not entirely, as matters of deductive logic. The classical economists both promoted and assumed the hegemony of the market or business system then in the process of development and replacing an economy predominately agricultural and landed-interest dominated. One response was historical economics, which undertook to examine the details of institutional and cultural transformation

E

which led to commercial and industrial capitalism, that is, an analysis of the evaluation of the economic system as a whole. Marxian and other variants of socialist economics portrayed the new economic order as one of the exploitation of labor and projected the inevitable emergence of a labor- and not capital-oriented system. Neoclassical economics arose in the late nineteenth century and became dominant in the twentieth. It continued the classical focus on the market economy treated in a deductive manner but narrowed the scope of analysis to the allocation of resources. Among its leading rivals have been institutional economics and Keynesian economics. The former has focused on the institutional structure of the economy and its evolution, emphasizing the roles of technology, power, and the legal-economic nexus, the last in contrast to the neoclassical dichotomy of polity and economy. Keynesian economics has focused on the factors and forces determining the level of economic activity, and was profoundly influenced by both the Great Depression of the 1930s and the longer record of periodic recessions. Economics became a predominantly American, rather than European, even British, discipline in the twentieth century. This came about for several reasons, including the rising hegemony of American culture as a whole, the enormous growth of higher education (and its associated research and publications) in a country with a large and rapidly growing population, the increased emphasis on analytical technique and mathematics, and sociological forces within the discipline.

Both in the late nineteenth and throughout the twentieth centuries controversy over the nature of economics as a science has pervaded the discipline, although not always equally intensively. Periods of intense disagreement over whether and in what sense economics is and should be considered a science have existed in the late nineteenth century and recently (and currently) in the late twentieth century. Throughout the entire period, numerous publications dealt with the "nature and scope of economics," the relation of economics to other social science disciplines, methodology (epistemology and philosophy of science), and related topics. These controversies are derivative of a sociological or disciplinary quest for status, largely in the image of nineteenth-century science (or economists perceptions of that image), as well as the practice of the social control role of economics. But they are also and perhaps predominantly driven by differences of opinion as to what constitutes a science, what makes economics a

science, the scope of economics as a science, and the significance of economics being different from, say, physics, in that, for example (1) values seem inexorably to enter into economics, (2) economic agents make choices, and (3) the economy is an artifact, a matter of human construction.

The subsidiary elements of controversy are many and often exceedingly technical. They have been specified in different ways, including (1) explanation versus description, and what is meant by both; (2) induction versus deduction; (3) validity versus truth and the respective limits of deduction and empiricism; (4) tools versus truth (definition of reality); (5) apriorism versus empiricism; (6) rationalism/theory versus empiricism, especially measurement per se; (7) rigor versus realism and relevance; (8) philosophical and/or scientific realism versus some form of idealism; (9) technique-driven empiricism, generated by the combination of abstract, often conjectural models and econometric techniques and typically involving mathematical formalism, versus attention to the details of the actual economic system; (10) the nature and status of positivism (logical positivism, logical empiricism); (11) the role of falsificationism versus instrumentalism; (12) the possible role and significance of values and ideology—including precisely what constitutes values and ideology; (13) advocacy versus objectivity; (14) the significance of multiple substantive schools of economic thought; (15) methodological prescriptivism versus methodological pluralism and a more or less open-ended acceptance of alternative epistemological credentials; (16) science versus discipline; (17) the role of prediction (including prediction within the confines of a model versus prediction of actual economic futures, and prediction as the end of science versus predictive power as only one test of knowledge); (18) methodology (philosophy of science and epistemology) versus discourse analysis (rhetoric, hermeneutics, literary criticism, deconstruction, etc.); (19) the nature and criteria of theory choice; (20) the relevance of the sociology of science (and of knowledge in general), including the sociology of professionalization; and, inter alia, (21) the probative analytical significance of the limits of all epistemological, technical, and other positions.

The conflicts continue, notwithstanding, for example (1) that all economic research practice comprises combinations of seemingly mutually exclusive opposites, such as deduction and induction, although in varying and differently structured combinations; and

(2) over the possibility of "scientism," namely, that economists improperly apply to questions of economic policy and other areas the results of their putatively scientific practice, more or less unconscious of the practices of what may be called "economic politics."

A pervasive fundamental issue goes beyond the widespread recognition that all serious work requires abstraction (the making of *ceteris paribus*, limiting assumptions) and for that reason is necessarily unrealistic. The issue is whether the models, theories, and concepts of economics deal in some sense with reality (whatever that term might mean in a world subject to human social construction in either of two senses: one, human creation of the underlying economy; the other: human construction of attributed meaning to the economy as found, whether or not human socially constructed) or whether they merely tell selective stories dependent upon the use of technical tools, dominant paradigm, ideology, and so on.

Many, probably most, economists prefer to engage in their substantive work and not be distracted from methodological issues, confident that there is a legitimate epistemological or other warrant for that work, because that is the type of work that they were trained to do. These economists generally, when questioned, affirm some form of positivism, usually that advanced by Milton Friedman, although it has been subjected to severe, and possibly fatal, criticism.

The existence of so much controversy, strangely, itself conflicts with the high status achieved by economics among the social sciences. By the same token, this status has come into question. In response to the extension of economic modes of reasoning and analysis into other disciplines—so-called economics imperialism—there has developed (1) strong critiques of the probative value of what economics has to offer, (2) the conscious development and application of alternative modes of reasoning, and (3) renewed calls for and efforts at some form of integration of different disciplines, with the object being not narrow disciplinary affirmation but serious subject-matter and problem-solving research.

A further major issue of controversy is the status of the mainstream neoclassical practice of seeking unique determinate optimal equilibrium solutions to problems as a sine qua non of economics being scientific. This practice has been subjected to criticisms, such as (1) its necessarily having to make selective, ad hoc, and presumptuous assumptions, ultimately of a normative kind, so as to produce unique determinate results; (2) its neglect of reality as a state of disequilibrium and the processes of equilibration or adjustment, in order to concentrate on the existence and stability conditions of equilibrium; and, inter alia, (3) its neglect or presumptuous a priori treatment of the evolutionary nature of structural, psychological, technological, and resource variables. The mechanistic practices of rigorous formal abstract modeling which seem to some economists to either fulfill either the specific requirements of science or convey at least the image thereof, to others involves the foreclosure of actual economic processes and the substitution of economists practices, preferences, and conceptualizations for those of actual economic actors.

BIBLIOGRAPHY

Blaug, Mark. *The Methodology of Economics: Or How Economists Explain.* 2d ed. New York: Cambridge University Press, 1992.

Caldwell, Bruce J. *Beyond Positivism: Economic Methodology in the Twentieth Century.* Boston: George Allen & Unwin, 1982.

————. ed. *The Philosophy and Methodology of Economics.* 3 vols. Brookfield: Edward Elgar, 1993.

Eichner, Alfred S. ed. *Why Economics Is Not Yet a Science.* Armonk, NY: M. E. Sharpe, 1983.

Furner, Mary O. *Advocacy and Objectivity.* Lexington: University Press of Kentucky, 1975.

Himmelstrand, Ulf, ed. *Interfaces in Economic and Social Analysis.* New York: Routledge, 1992.

Hodgson, Geoffrey M. "On Methodology and Assumptions." In *Economics and Institutions.* Philadephia: University of Pennsylvania Press, 1988, pp. 27–50.

Johnson, Glenn L. *Research Methodology for Economists: Philosophy and Practice.* New York: Macmillan 1986.

Mayer, Thomas. *Truth versus Precision in Economics.* Brookfield: Edward Elgar, 1993.

Pheby, John. *Methodology and Economics: A Critical Introduction.* London: Macmaillan, 1988.

Rosenberg, Alexander. *Economics—Mathematical Politics or Science of Diminishing Returns?* Chicago: University of Chicago Press, 1992.

Samuels, Warren J., ed. *The Methodology of Economic Thought.* New Brunswick: Transaction, 1980; 2d ed., completely revised, with Marc R. Tool, 1989.

Warren J. Samuels

Edison, Thomas Alva (1849–1931)

Inventor and industrialist. Born in Milan, Ohio, Edison briefly attended school in Port Huron, Michigan,

E

after moving there in 1854, but he was largely taught at home by his mother and self-educated through his own reading. As a telegraph operator in the Midwest during the 1860s, Edison began to pursue invention, turning to it full-time after coming to Boston in 1868. In 1869, he moved to New Jersey and for several years operated telegraph manufacturing shops in Newark while working as a contract telegraph inventor. Between 1876 and 1881, Edison lived and worked in Menlo Park, New Jersey, where he established what was one of the largest private laboratories in the world and produced many of his most significant inventions, including the foundation for the incandescent electric light and power industry. In 1881, he moved to New York City to direct the operations of Edison electric light and manufacturing companies. From 1887 until his death, Edison worked at the laboratory he built in West Orange, New Jersey, and around which he established an extensive manufacturing operation.

Edison's relationship with science was complex and changed over time. Although he identified himself as an inventor, Edison sometimes referred to himself as a "scientific man." He also worked and corresponded with many of the leading scientists of his day, read widely in such subjects as electricity, chemistry, geology, and botany, and as he withdrew from active inventing around 1907, he turned his attention to what he called general scientific experiments. Because Edison and his laboratory staff often worked at the limits of scientific knowledge the technologies they developed were themselves important subjects of scientific investigation. The close connections between scientists and inventors experimenting with electrical technology led to his presentations before the National Academy of Sciences and the American Association for the Advancement of Science in the 1870s and in the early 1880s to his briefly publishing the journal *Science*. Although Edison's commercial interests certainly motivated him to cooperate with scientists interested in his technical work, he also saw himself as a participating member of this community. He often investigated natural phenomena that he encountered in his inventive work. Most notable were his 1875 investigations of what he termed "etheric force" and his 1883 vacuum lamp experiments with what was later known as the Edison Effect, both of which involved then-unknown electrical phenomena. He also experimented on and speculated about phenomena that had no clear commercial application, such as the electromagnetic char-

acteristics of the ether, gravity, and atomic structure. Edison's interest in scientific research led him to contribute such devices as his X-ray fluoroscope and his tasimeter, a sensitive heat-measuring device, to scientific and medical use. Perhaps his most singular contributions were his renowned laboratories, where he combined the talents of both self-taught and scientifically trained experimenters with those of skilled machinists to systematically produce a wide range of significant inventions. These laboratories served as models for other nineteenth-century inventors and also influenced some corporations to establish their own research laboratories.

During his life, Edison was popularly celebrated both as the great American inventor and as a man of science, but by the time of his death he was increasingly associated with his folk image as a self-educated inventive genius who relied on common sense and an empirical cut-and-try method, in contrast to the university-educated men of science working in industrial laboratories who turned fundamental scientific knowledge into technological advances. By midcentury, Edison the folk hero had been the subject of a number of hagiographic biographies, but the publication of Matthew Josephson's more critical, though still heroic, *Edison* in 1959 marked the beginning of a new evaluation of his work. In the last two decades, historians of technology, seeing science as only one important source of new technology, have begun to reveal an Edison who exhibited characteristics akin to those of the modern directors of industrial laboratories while remaining rooted in the machine-shop culture of nineteenth-century invention. They acknowledge that Edison was little concerned with producing fundamental scientific knowledge, but show him often approaching research projects in a systematic fashion, willingly employing university-educated scientists and engineers, and appreciating the utility of scientific knowledge. At the same time, they note that he often exhibited little patience with those interested in pursuing more fundamental knowledge in pursuit of technical solutions, was little interested in sophisticated mathematical analysis, and in later life, often promoted his folk-hero image as a practical experimenter in contrast to the esoteric man of science.

The Thomas A. Edison Papers Project (at Rutgers University and the Edison National Historic Site) is making available the most significant materials of an enormous manuscript collection that details Edison's work as well as that of his laboratories and companies. While the availability of these papers has encouraged new research, many important issues remain to be investigated, not the least of which are those concerning the relationships between science and technology.

BIBLIOGRAPHY

Dyer, Frank, and Thomas C. Martin, with William Meadowcroft. *Edison: His Life and Inventions.* New York: Harper & Brothers, 1910; rev. ed., 1929.

Friedel, Robert, and Paul Israel, with Bernard Finn. *Edison's Electric Light: Biography of an Invention.* New Brunswick: Rutgers University Press, 1986.

Hughes, Thomas P. "Edison's Method." In *Technology at the Turning Point,* edited by William B. Pickett. San Francisco: San Francisco Press, 1977, pp. 5–22.

Israel, Paul. *Edison: A Life of Invention.* New York: John Wiley & Sons, 1998.

Jeffrey, Thomas E., et al., eds. *Thomas A. Edison Papers: A Selective Microfilm Edition.* Frederick, MD: University Publications of America, 1985–.

Jenkins, Reese, et al., eds. *The Papers of Thomas A. Edison.* Baltimore: Johns Hopkins University Press, 1989–.

Josephson, Matthew. *Edison: A Biography.* New York: McGraw-Hill, 1959.

Millard, Andre. *Edison and the Business of Innovation.* Baltimore: Johns Hopkins University Press, 1990.

Pretzer, William S., ed. *Working at Inventing: Thomas A. Edison and the Menlo Park Experience.* Dearborn, MI: Henry Ford Museum and Greenfield Village, 1989.

Wachhorst, Wyn. *Thomas Alva Edison: An American Myth.* Cambridge, MA: MIT Press, 1981.

Paul B. Israel

SEE ALSO

Electric Lightbulb; Menlo Park Laboratory

Einstein, Albert (1879–1955)

European-American theoretical physicist. Born in Ulm, Germany, Einstein attended primary and secondary schools in Munich and Aarau, Switzerland, graduating from the Swiss Federal Polytechnic in Zurich in 1900. The University of Zurich awarded him a doctorate in 1906. From 1902 to 1909, Einstein served as a patent clerk in the Swiss Federal Patent Office in Bern, and from 1908 to 1914, he held university teaching positions in Bern, Prague, and Zurich. From 1914 until Hitler's rise to power in Germany, Einstein held a dual position with the Prussian Academy of Sciences and the Kaiser Wilhelm Society with the right to teach at the University of Berlin. He settled permanently in Princeton as a professor at the Institute for Advanced Study in October 1933. He became a citizen of the United States seven years later.

Einstein's research lay at the foundations of physics. He is best known for his special and general theories of relativity and for his contributions to quantum theory and statistical mechanics. He was also known for his outspoken views on social issues. He brought general relativity to the United States in 1921 while fundraising for the Zionist cause. Settling in the United States with his most famous work behind him, Einstein searched to the end of his life for a field theory uniting gravitation and electromagnetism. He believed that the solution would reveal a much deeper unity to the physical world and resolve the paradoxes inherent in quantum mechanics, which, though logically closed and widely accepted, he regarded as incomplete.

As America's most famous refugee scientist, Einstein paved the way for other refugees and ensured the success of the newly created Institute for Advanced Study. After Hitler's rise to power, Einstein renounced his prior pacifism, called upon the United States to end its isolation, and supported the creation of a binational Jewish homeland in Palestine. In 1939 and 1940, he signed letters to President Franklin D. Roosevelt, initiating American exploitation of nuclear fission, but, aside from minor work for the United States Navy, he did not engage in war-related research. After the war and the dropping of the atomic bombs, Einstein took on his most prominent public role. Together with other leading scientists, he called for creation of a world government to control conflicts and to enforce nuclear disarmament. During the Korean War, he again advocated pacifism and counseled civil disobedience in response to the McCarthy hearings.

Einstein has evoked such adulation, controversy, and puzzlement within and beyond scientific circles as to render him often much larger than life. With the passage of time and the application of historical methods to the many facets of his life and work, a fuller appreciation of Einstein as man and scientist is gradually emerging, but much remains to be known. Most serious historians have focused so far only on Einstein's early and most successful works. While they agree that he truly ranks among the greatest physicists, some have also examined Einstein as part of a generation in Europe that defined and institutionalized modern theoretical physics during the first third of the twentieth century.

E

The story is entirely different in America. Here Einstein felt and was very much treated as a stranger (Sayen, p. 125). By 1933, relativity, quantum mechanics, and theoretical physics had long since crossed the Atlantic. Einstein worked largely alone, had no students and few assistants, and did not join his colleagues in research. Nor did his colleagues pursue his proposals for unified theories. According to current judgment, "this work did not produce any results of physical interest" (Pais, p. 327). His opposition to quantum mechanics was often considered eccentric. Instead, Einstein's greatest influence in the United States seems to have occurred in the postwar social arena, where he helped to shape the public image and role of the theoretical physicist.

Einstein's influence on atomic bomb research is now considered slight. Often regarded as the "father of the atomic bomb" for signing the letters to Roosevelt, recent studies suggest that the Manhattan Project originated elsewhere. Thereafter, Einstein became an even greater stranger to American developments. FBI files indicate that he was denied a security clearance on the basis of political suspicions. As a leading exponent of the scientists' movement for the control of nuclear weapons after World War II and for the creation of the state of Israel, Einstein became a defining figure in issues of the social responsibility of the scientist and the Jewish intellectual, and the subject of intense public controversy and FBI scrutiny. While several authors have challenged popular perceptions of Einstein as a naive idealist by tracing his social engagement to sophisticated moral convictions, much more needs to be known about the origins, context, and impact of Einstein's social views.

The Albert Einstein Project at Boston University is collecting and publishing his complete papers. The project has identified over 30,000 manuscript items from, to, or about Einstein. Roughly half are in the Albert Einstein Archive at The Hebrew University of Jerusalem.

BIBLIOGRAPHY

Balazs, Nandor. "Einstein: Theory of Relativity." *Dictionary of Scientific Biography.* Edited by Charles C. Gillispie. New York: Scribners, 1972, 4:319–333.

Fölsing, Albrecht. *Albert Einstein: A Biography.* Translated by Ewald Osers. New York: Viking Press, 1997.

Frank, Philipp. *Einstein: Sein Leben und seine Zeit.* Braunschweig: Vieweg, 1979.

Holton, Gerald, and Yehuda Elkana, eds. *Albert Einstein: Historical and Cultural Perspectives, The Centennial Symposium in Jerusalem.* Princeton: Princeton University Press, 1982.

Jungnickel, Christa, and Russell McCormmach. *The Intellectual Mastery of Nature: Theoretical Physics from Ohm to Einstein.* 2 vols. Chicago: University of Chicago Press, 1986.

Klein, Martin J. "Einstein, Albert." *Dictionary of Scientific Biography.* Edited by Charles C. Gillispie. New York: Scribner, 1972, 4:312–319.

Moyer, Albert E. "History of Physics." *Osiris,* 2d ser. (1985) 1: 163–182.

Nathan, Otto, and Heinz Norden, eds. and trans. *Einstein on Peace.* New York: Schocken, 1960.

Pais, Abraham. *"Subtle is the Lord . . .": The Science and the Life of Albert Einstein.* Oxford: Oxford University Press, 1982.

Sayen, Jamie. *Einstein in America: The Scientist's Conscience in the Age of Hitler and Hiroshima.* New York: Crown, 1985.

Stachel, John, et al., eds. *The Collected Papers of Albert Einstein.* Princeton: Princeton University Press, 1987–.

David C. Cassidy

Electric Lightbulb

The incandescent electric lightbulb was commercialized in the early 1880s. Although Humphry Davy first demonstrated incandescence using a platinum wire in 1802, little significant research on incandescent lighting occurred until the 1840s. Over the next four decades, more than twenty researchers attempted to make practical incandescent lamps. Most used carbon, which was inexpensive but oxidized at incandescent temperatures. A few researchers turned to platinum because it did not oxidize and had a high melting point. However, platinum was expensive and difficult to make incandescent without heating beyond its melting point. Commercial development was also limited by inefficient power sources. Following the invention of the dynamo, the commercial introduction of arc lighting systems in the late 1870s to light streets and large indoor spaces spurred new research into "subdividing" the light into smaller units suitable for general indoor use. The first commercially successful incandescent lamp, using a thin, high-resistance filament of carbon in an evacuated glass globe, was developed by Thomas Edison at his Menlo Park laboratory in late 1879. Other researchers, notably British chemist Joseph Swan, also worked with carbon in a vacuum, but none used thin filaments or made high-resistance lamps until after Edison announced his invention. Like most researchers, Edison made use of chemical literature in his work on filament materials, but his research also produced new knowledge regarding occluded gases in metals, which he presented in a paper to the American Association for the

Advancement of Science. Edison's staff also used the new mercury vacuum pump technology developed by European chemists, notably Hermann Sprengel, but they greatly improved the pump's efficiency. Early lamps used vegetable-fiber filaments—Edison's was carbonized Japanese bamboo—but several chemists, including Swan, soon developed artificial, homogeneous, carbon filaments that increased lamp efficiency. Although chemical research on carbon filaments continued, little increase in efficiency was gained after the mid-1880s and attention turned to metals and metallic oxides as filament materials. Although the carbon-filament lamp was still dominant at the turn of the century, research by a number of European chemists in the 1890s produced lamps using metals and metal salts that threatened the future of the carbon lamp and General Electric's controlling position in the industry. General Electric responded by establishing a research laboratory under the direction of chemist Willis Whitney in 1901. Whitney hired a number of other chemists, including William Coolidge, who developed ductile tungsten, and Irving Langmuir, who conducted fundamental and Nobel Prize-winning research on the physical processes in incandescent lamps. Their work resulted in the development of the gas-filled, tungsten-filament lamp in 1912, which soon supplanted the carbon-filament vacuum lamp.

Historical research has focused on the initial invention of a commercial incandescent lamp and on General Electric's subsequent development of the tungsten lamp. Debate over whether the invention of the carbon lamp should be credited to Edison or Swan has continued since their initial public announcements. Of more significance is recent research that examines how Edison's design of an entire system of lighting helped him to establish the technical parameters of his lamp and allowed him to acquire the basic lamp patent. Little attention has been paid to subsequent carbon-lamp research or to early research on metal and metal-salt lamps. However, historians have established the crucial role played by General Electric's research laboratory and its use of university-educated chemists to successfully develop the gas-filled, tungsten-filament lamp in the rise of science-based industrial research.

BIBLIOGRAPHY

Bright, Arthur A., Jr. *The Electric-Lamp Industry: Technological Change and Economic Development from 1800 to 1947.* New York: MacMillan, 1949.

Friedel, Robert, and Paul Israel, with Bernard Finn. *Edison's Electric Light: Biography of an Invention.* New Brunswick: Rutgers University Press, 1986.

Reich, Leonard S. *The Making of American Industrial Research: Science and Business at GE and Bell, 1876–1926.* Cambridge, U.K.: Cambridge University Press, 1985.

Wise, George. "Swan's Way: A Study in Style." *IEEE Spectrum* 19 (1982): 66–70.

———. *Willis Whitney, General Electric, and the Origins of U.S. Industrial Research.* New York: Columbia University Press, 1985.

Paul B. Israel

SEE ALSO
Edison, Thomas Alva

Enders, John Franklin (1897–1985)

Virologist. Born in West Hartford, Connecticut, John Enders was educated in the humanities at Yale College (B.A., 1920) and in English at Harvard University (M.A., 1922) before his interests turned to bacteriology. He completed his Ph.D. at Harvard in 1930 working with Hans Zinsser. He served on the Harvard Medical School faculty in the Department of Bacteriology until he retired in 1967. In 1946, he became director of the new Infectious Disease Research Laboratory at the Harvard-affiliated Children's Hospital. There, Enders and two younger colleagues, Thomas H. Weller and Frederick C. Robbins, performed the research that won them the 1954 Nobel Prize in medicine for growing poliovirus in tissue culture.

Enders spent his entire career defining the procedures for growing and characterizing viruses of the childhood diseases mumps, poliomyelitis, and measles, research which made him the most respected virologist of his generation. In the 1940s, he developed diagnostic tests for mumps and succeeded in growing mumps virus in tissue culture. By refining these techniques, Enders, Weller, and Robbins succeeded in growing the Lansing strain of poliovirus in vitro in 1948. Their work eliminated the need for primates in virus production and made possible the successful polio vaccines of Jonas Salk and Albert Sabin. The "cytopathogenic effects" that Enders's group noted in poliovirus cultures enabled researchers to quantify the virus content, and type and identify the virus in culture. Their research overturned the accepted understanding of polioviruses as strictly neurotropic agents and confirmed the epidemiological evidence that suggested polio infections began in the intestine.

E

Beginning in 1954, Enders turned his attention to the measles virus. The attenuated strain of the virus he produced in his laboratory became the basis for a measles vaccine licensed in 1963. Toward the end of his career, he studied cancer viruses and the role of interferon in immune resistance to virus infection.

Historical accounts of Enders have been confined to his role in polio research and his Nobel Prize award. These accounts portray Enders as an exemplar of the model scientist, independent, yet genteel, humble, and patient. They praise his contribution to the understanding of viruses and consider his Nobel Prize richly deserved. At the time he received his Nobel Prize, some contemporaries had viewed its being awarded to him as a comment on the excesses of the campaign conducted by the National Foundation for Infantile Paralysis to lionize Jonas Salk. Enders own lack of interest in developing a polio vaccine has been attributed to his reluctance to be drawn away from "pure" research.

A large collection of Enders's personal papers is located at the Yale University Library, Division of Manuscripts and Archives. As yet, there is no full-length biography of Enders.

BIBLIOGRAPHY

Fox, Daniel M., Marcia Meldrum, and Ira Rezak, eds. *Nobel Laureates in Medicine or Physiology: A Biographical Dictionary.* New York and London: Garland, 1990, pp. 167–170.

Grafe, Alfred. *A History of Experimental Virology.* Berlin, Heidelberg, New York: Springer-Verlag, 1991.

Magill, Frank N., ed. *The Nobel Prize Winners. Physiology or Medicine.* Pasadena: Salem Press, 1991, 2:683–692.

Paul, John R. *A History of Poliomyelitis.* New Haven and London: Yale University Press, 1971.

Rogers, Naomi. *Dirt and Disease: Polio before FDR.* New Brunswick: Rutgers University Press, 1992.

Smith, Jane S. *Patenting the Sun: Polio and the Salk Vaccine.* New York: William Morrow, 1990.

Waterson, A.P., and Lise Wilkinson. *An Introduction to the History of Virology.* Cambridge, U.K.: Cambridge University Press, 1978.

Weller, Thomas H. "As It Was and As It Is: A Half-Century of Progress." *Journal of Infectious Diseases* 159, no. 3 (March 1989): 378–383.

Weller, Thomas H., and Frederick C. Robbins. "John Franklin Enders." *Biographical Memoirs of the National Academy of Sciences* 60 (1991): 47–65.

Williams, Greer. *Virus Hunters.* New York: Alfred A. Knopf, 1960.

Patricia Gossel

Engineering, Chemical

The branch of engineering affiliated with the chemical process industries and generally considered one of the four major branches of engineering.

Through much of the nineteenth century, chemical engineering did not exist. Scaling-up chemical processes from the test tubes and beakers of the laboratory to the pumps, pipes, and reaction towers of commercial plants was carried out by chemists or mechanical engineers or by a combination of both.

Around 1880, the British chemist George Davis popularized the term "chemical engineering" to describe the work of individuals combining chemical and engineering skills and involved in designing or managing industrial-scale chemical processes. But the concept did not immediately catch on. In Germany, where the chemical industry focused on batch production of a large number of low-volume, high value-added chemicals, the use of chemist-mechanical engineer teams worked well. The Germans and many influenced by their successes saw no need for a new "hybrid" field or for "combination men."

The United States, however, provided fertile ground for the emergence of "combination men" who focused on process more than product. Its industrial tradition had long emphasized volume production at low cost. Its chemical industry, unlike the German, produced only a few relatively simple chemicals, but those in large volumes. Thus, the world's first academic programs in chemical engineering emerged at the Massachusetts Institute of Technology (MIT) in 1888 and the University of Pennsylvania in 1892.

Early chemical engineering, however, faced serious problems of intellectual legitimacy. Its academic programs simply combined traditional engineering and chemistry courses. Its practitioners had difficulty convincing engineers that they were engineers and chemists that they were not simply chemists.

The key concept that permitted chemical engineering to stake out distinct intellectual boundaries was unit operations. Traditional industrial chemistry had centered on the manufacture of specific chemicals, with little recognition of the commonalities shared by the vast number of different chemical processes. Unit operations focused on these commonalities—a relatively small number of largely physical processes like heating, grinding, evaporating, dissolving, and distilling—into which any chemical manufacturing process could be resolved. These unit operations, suitably arranged or rearranged, could be used to produce any chemical. The

E

use of unit operations as a focus for chemical engineering had been latent in the writings of George Davis, but its explicit use to define chemical engineering and distinguish it from related fields was due to Arthur D. Little, working through the American Institute of Chemical Engineers and MIT between 1915 and 1925.

Because unit operations provided a strong focus for chemical engineering research and because this research had immediate industrial applicability, industrial and academic chemical engineering developed very close ties in the second quarter of the twentieth century. For example, academic and industrial chemical engineers, often working together, played a central role in scaling-up the American petroleum industry to meet demands sparked by the growing use of automobiles in the 1920s and 1930s. In addition, unit operations linked plant design and product in a manner unparalleled by any other engineering field. This link encouraged chemical engineers in the 1930s to closely study process efficiencies, to develop chemical thermodynamics, and to work out integrated, continuous, automated processes. Large-scale, continuous, automated production systems initially developed for the petroleum industry were then successfully adapted by chemical engineers to the emerging petrochemical industry from the 1930s on.

The central role of chemical engineering in the explosive expansion of the American chemical industry during and after World War II had a major impact on the field. The number of practitioners expanded rapidly. The American Institute of Chemical Engineers had only around 2,000 members in 1940. By 1960, it had almost 20,000 and by 1980, almost 50,000. Simultaneously, the American concept of chemical engineering was adopted worldwide, even in Germany.

Another impact of the rapid postwar expansion was the growing importance of specialized engineering firms (SEFs), which developed and installed "off-the-shelf" chemical plants for both domestic and foreign companies. Although such firms had originated earlier, after 1945 they became major employers of chemical engineers. By the late 1960s, nearly three-fourths of major new plants were the work of SEFs such as Universal Oil Products, M.W. Kellogg, and Lummus.

In the post–World War II era, chemical engineering began to shift away from unit operations, and academic and industrial chemical engineering began to part ways. After 1945, academic chemical engineering research focused on increasingly more sophisticated mathematical theories and models, often of little apparent relevance to industrial problems. The National Science Foundation's emergence as a leading funding source for university research and its preference for theoretical scientific studies encouraged this shift. Transport phenomena replaced unit operations as the discipline's unifying scheme in academia in the 1960s. Transport phenomena focused on more generalized theoretical concepts—the transport of energy, mass, and momentum—each of which embraced a number of unit operations but seemed further removed from actual industrial operations. Industrial research, although more empirical and less theoretical than academic research, also moved away from unit operations, concentrating more on such areas as reactor design and the economics of high-temperature processes.

Almost from its origins, chemical engineering diverged from its chemical parent. Unit operations, for example, were primarily physical rather than chemical phenomena. Attempts to draw the field back toward chemistry in the 1930s with Henry Shreve's concept of unit processes (i.e., chemical analogs to unit operations like oxidation, nitration, sulphonation, hydrolysis, etc.) did not attract widespread support. The more theoretical and mathematical emphasis of chemical engineering research after World War II accelerated the trend away from chemistry, leading some chemical engineers to caution that the field was moving too far from its original intellectual base. The chemical industry's shift in the 1980s to speciality chemicals has provided some corrective to this trend, but concerns remain.

The literature on the history of chemical engineering is sparse. Most is focused on chemical engineering in specific companies or academic institutions and is written by practitioners rather than professional historians.

BIBLIOGRAPHY

Aris, Rutherford. "Academic Chemical Engineering in an Historical Perspective." *Industrial and Engineering Chemistry—Fundamentals* 16, no. 1 (1977): 1–5.

"Chemical Engineering at DuPont: A Profession Comes of Age." *Chemical Engineering Progress* 85 (September 1989): 62–69.

Donnelly, J.F. "Chemical Engineering in England, 1880–1922." *Annals of Science* 45 (1988): 555–590.

Furter, W.F., ed. *History of Chemical Engineering.* ACS Advances in Chemistry Series, no. 190. Washington, DC: American Chemical Society, 1980.

———. *A Century of Chemical Engineering.* New York and London: Plenum, 1982.

E

Guédon, Jean-Claude. "Il progett dell'ingegneria chimica: l'affermazione delle operazioni di base negli Stati Uniti." *Testi e contesti* 5 (1981): 5–27.

———. "From Unit Operations to Unit Processes: Ambiguities of Success and Failure in Chemical Engineering." In *Chemistry and Modern Society: Historical Essays in Honor of Aaron J. Ihde,* edited by John Parascandola and James C. Whorton. ACS/Symposium Series 228. Washington, DC: American Chemical Society, 1983, pp. 43–60.

Hougen, Olaf A. "Seven Decades of Chemical Engineering." *Chemical Engineering Progress* 73 (January 1977): 89–104.

Landau, Ralph. "Chemical Engineering: Key to the Growth of the Chemical Process Industries." In *Competitiveness of the U.S. Chemical Industry in International Markets,* edited by Jaromir J. Ulbrecht. AIChE Symposium Series, 274. New York: AIChE, 1990, pp. 9–39.

Peppas, Nikolaos A., ed. *One Hundred Years of Chemical Engineering.* Dordrecht: Kluwer Academic Publishers, 1989.

Pigford, Robert L. "Chemical Technology: The Past 100 Years." *Chemical and Engineering News* 54 (6 April 1976): 190–203.

Reynolds, Terry S. "Defining Professional Boundaries: Chemical Engineering in the Early Twentieth Century." *Technology and Culture* 27 (1986): 694–716.

Servos, John. "The Industrial Relations of Science: Chemical Engineering at MIT, 1900–1939." *Isis* 71 (1980): 531–549.

Trescott, Martha M. *Rise of the American Electrochemical Industry, 1880–1910.* Westport, CT: Greenwood Press, 1981.

Terry S. Reynolds

SEE ALSO
Chemistry

Engineering, Civil and Military

Civil engineering is concerned with the design and construction of structures, transportation systems, bridges, tunnels, and water supply systems. Military engineering deals with similar problems in the military sphere, as well as with fortifications and such battlefield problems as sapping and trenching. The distinction between civil and military engineering appeared in Europe after 1600, as Renaissance engineers found royal patrons interested in such military problems as the fortifications, siege engines, armaments, bridges, and harbors. The term "civil engineering" emerged to identify engineering efforts divorced from these military needs. In England especially, by the late eighteenth century, private enterprise began to fund the design and construction of roads, bridges, canals, and water systems, while the French developed similar projects under state auspices, retaining a connection to military engineering in the quasi-military Corps of Bridges and Roads. This French bureaucracy first developed theoretical approaches and mathematical analysis to engineering problems such as bridge construction.

The earliest American engineering efforts were little connected to these developments, for craftsmen and millwrights with no formal schooling carried out most projects. Only the French military engineers associated with Washington's army were trained "engineers" in the European sense of the term. Even in the 1790s and early 1800s, expertise had to be imported. Examples include Englishmen such as William Weston, who designed the Middlesex Canal in New England, and Benjamin Latrobe, who oversaw the Philadelphia and New Orleans waterworks, the United States Capitol in Washington, D.C., and other projects.

American-trained engineers emerged from two sources. One was the United States Military Academy established at West Point in 1802. Superintendent Sylvanus Thayer, appointed in about 1815, turned West Point into the first engineering school in the country, introducing French texts and theoretical methods. For the next half-century, army engineers played important roles in American engineering. The Army Corps of Topographic Engineers not only mapped the West, but also were routinely detailed by Congress to design and construct private canal and railroad projects. In 1853, army survey teams plotted railroad routes through the mountains to the Pacific Coast, while other army engineers played key roles in the slow process of improving navigation on the Mississippi River system. Finally, West Point-trained engineers frequently left the military and, as civilian consulting engineers, played very significant roles in the development of the American railroad system.

The Erie Canal, begun in 1815, and other early canal and railroad projects, provided the other training ground for American civil engineers. The Erie Canal was designed by three prominent residents who knew how to survey and learned about engineering a canal as they went. In the process, they and a group of young assistants became engineers by the time the canal opened in 1824. During their "apprenticeship," these men progressed from cutting trees for surveying parties to carrying the chain, holding the stadium rod, using a transit, preparing drawings, overseeing small construction projects, and then designing small components like lock gates or culverts before they were entrusted with a division of the canal. Similar practical education on other canal and railroad projects offering the usual training for American engineers until after the Civil War.

For much of the nineteenth century, therefore, one can discuss American civil engineering without considering science, for engineering practice rested on empirical rules of thumb and experience, not theoretical criteria or mathematical calculations. American engineers never were completely empirical in their approach, and men like Herman Haupt developed methods of calculating stresses in bridges in the late 1840s. But American engineers were more like their British counterparts than the theoretically oriented French, and a mathematical and scientific approach appeared slowly in this country. The establishment of academic engineering schools beginning in the 1830s encouraged this development, although engineering colleges became the primary means of educating engineers only after 1875. Engineering educators, such as Robert Thurston at Stevens Institute and then at Cornell, were instrumental in developing curricula that shifted engineering away from practical orientation and toward a base in science, but the process was slow, and civil engineering lagged behind some other fields. A fundamental tension existed in the university between the need to prepare students to make immediate contributions to employers as engineers and the desire to provide a well-rounded education with a solid scientific base. Generally, the first goal took precedence. Within civil engineering, the study of strength of materials and structural design became more scientific and mathematical, but most civil engineering students, even in the 1930s, received a very practical education, symbolized by required courses in drafting and surveying and an extended summer camp in the field.

Only after World War II did civil engineering, at least in universities, embrace patterns of mathematical analysis, theoretical development, and engineering science adopted after 1890 in electrical, radio, aeronautical, and other engineering fields. In common with most fields of engineering, academic civil engineers enthusiastically moved toward research stressing mathematical analysis (funded primarily by the federal government), and the development of theory (published in new engineering science journals), steps that downplayed the traditional emphasis upon design and real world problems. Currently, civil engineering is more scientific in its approaches and methods than at the turn of the century, but one result has been the creation of divide between practice and academia.

BIBLIOGRAPHY

Armstrong, Ellis, Michael C. Robinson, and Suellen Hoy, eds. *History of Public Works in the United States, 1776–1976.* Chicago: American Public Works Association, 1976.

Calhoun, Daniel H. *The American Civil Engineer: Origins and Conflict.* Cambridge, MA: MIT Press, 1960.

Hill, Forest. *Roads, Rails, and Waterways: The Army Engineers and Early Transportation.* Norman: University of Oklahoma Press, 1957.

Kirby, Richard S., and F.G. Laurson. *The Early Years of Modern Civil Engineering.* New Haven: Yale University Press, 1932.

Latrobe, Benjamin Henry. *The Engineering Drawings of Benjamin Henry Latrobe.* Edited with an introduction by Darwin H. Stapleton. New Haven: Yale University Press, for the Maryland Historical Society, 1980.

Merritt, Raymond H. *Engineering in American Society, 1850–1875.* Lexington: University Press of Kentucky, 1969.

Stapleton, Darwin H., with assistance from Roger L. Schumaker. *The History of Civil Engineering since 1600: An Annotated Bibliography.* New York: Garland, 1986.

Bruce E. Seely

Engineering, Technology, and Science—Relations and Comparisons

"Science," "engineering," and "technology" may refer to either bodies of knowledge or to the communities of practitioners who use this knowledge. "Technology" is a catchall, in that it includes all who advance or apply the useful arts ("technology" in American English). This includes everything from self-educated tinkerers to Ph.D. scientists whose work has practical applications. Applied science is real and an important part of technology, perhaps more so in the United States than elsewhere because of this country's long-standing emphasis upon useful knowledge. Engineers fit somewhere in between, if we rank them either in terms of social prestige or in terms of the degree of abstraction and generality of their profession's esoteric knowledge. The United States has no national certification for engineers, so American engineers have accepted (rather reluctantly) the fact that their profession is a "vaguely bounded nucleus within a large body of technical workers" (Layton, *Revolt*, p. 26).

E

"Science" and "engineering" are useful, if ambiguous, categories for dealing with enormously complex aggregations of subcommunities, each with its corresponding body of knowledge, many of which overlap one another. Perhaps because the United States was born in the Age of Enlightenment, when the prestige of science was very high, American engineers from the start adopted the programmatic goal of making every aspect of engineering practice rest, as much as possible, upon solid foundations of scientific facts and scientific methods. The Enlightenment, and the United States's democratic tendencies, have equally placed a great emphasis upon the utility of science (e.g., in producing technological benefits). These complementary themes have encouraged convergence between science and engineering in the United States and produced many fruitful, mutually beneficial interactions between the two communities.

The efforts to found American engineering on science did not imply subservience to the scientific community. Most of the knowledge used by engineers has been generated by engineers (with help from physical scientists in the early stages) using methods that may differ significantly from those employed in the basic sciences. Engineers draw from (and contribute to) a scientific archive that includes experimental methods, mathematical theory, and instrumentation in the physical and mathematical sciences. This makes engineers applied physicists in exactly the same sense that physicists are applied mathematicians. That is, despite similarities and borrowings, they constitute distinct communities. Engineers also borrowed institutions and values from the community of basic science, in order to facilitate the generation, diffusion, and use of scientific knowledge in engineering.

Lacking state patronage for basic science, research American scientists sometimes justified such research by the theory that technology is no more than applied science. This is not totally false; applied science plays a large and growing role in technology. While the applied-science theory is not false, it certainly is misleading. It implies that scientists generate all the knowledge which engineers apply in a more or less mechanical way. It has been argued that it is impossible to draw a sharp line between scientists and engineers in the modern research system. This problem is like the birdwatcher who has difficulty in telling the gender of birds with little or no sexual dimorphism, say blue jays. This is not, however, a problem for the blue jays; they have

no difficulty determining the gender of other blue jays. Similarly, though social scientists cannot draw a sharp line, engineers and scientists can and do make sharp distinctions when they join professional societies and assimilate the values and orientations imbedded in these societies' reward systems and membership standards.

Engineers are not subordinate to the physical sciences, nor are they dependent upon the latter for all (or even most) of the new knowledge they use, as the applied-science theory claims or implies. On the contrary, science and engineering are autonomous, coequal communities. Each has creative methods for generating knowledge needed by practitioners. Engineers adapted to their own needs their borrowings from the scientific community, to which they made many additions in instrumentation, experimental methods, and mathematical theory. Although some of engineering knowledge is scientific, engineers have a distinct cognitive form, design, the critical act of synthesis which leads to the production, testing, manufacture, and use of engineering artifacts and systems. While design has become more scientific, it is not a science but an art, one involving visual and plastic imagination, a hierarchical structure, a distinct cognitive structure, and other attributes.

The scientific part of engineering is often (but not always) different in emphasis, form, and content from the basic sciences because its role is to assist in engineering design. Design requires large amounts of empirical data, much of it gathered by iterative experimental or test procedures. Sometimes these methods have been misleadingly called "cut-and-try." One such method has been named "parameter variation" by Walter Vincenti. Characteristically, its goal is to optimize a design, not to discover truth about nature. This rational experimental method is used extensively by engineers, but only rarely by physical physicists. As Vincenti has also pointed out, engineers developed mathematical theories or methods that are sometimes different than those used in the basic sciences; the method of control-volume analysis is almost universal in engineering courses on thermodynamics, and almost totally absent in physics textbooks on the same subject. Engineering research also is concerned with the use of an artifact, such information then shapes future design requirements, for example in determining flying quality specifications for aircraft. From the physicists point of view, heat transfer was largely complete by about the turn of the century. Engineers extended it, mainly in the twentieth century, developing new instruments and mathematical means of dealing with convective, often turbulent, heat transfer. These efforts enabled engineers to redesign virtually all heat-using or heat-dissipating artifacts, an enormously stimulating challenge for engineers, but one offering no Nobel Prizes for physicists.

In the United States, the efforts to create scientific foundations for engineering practice were shaped by cultural forces. The French engineering style favored mathematical theory, whose latent function was to favor the children of the rich who could afford the extensive private tutelage required for admission to elite engineering schools. American engineering long favored empirical methods which could be picked up by self-study and on-the-job experience, consistent with American ideals of an equal opportunity for all. Empiricism, for a time, represented a reaction against the materialism and atheism alleged to be part of mathematical science in France. In the long run, however, intrinsic needs have given theory greater stature in the United States, coequal with empirical procedures, particularly after World War II.

The United States drew both from British (and prior American) empiricism as well as the French theoretical engineering style. James B. Francis, who was British born and educated, relied upon experiments and admitted to a habit of doubting theoretical deduction. His experimental researches were published in 1855 as the *Lowell Hydraulic Experiments.* Included were design data and graphical methods for designing turbines, as well as new instruments and procedures for measuring the flow of water, both in testing turbine efficiency and in monitoring the water consumption of each of the ten large Lowell textile manufacturing corporations, both critical managerial tasks.

Most early American engineers were educated by self-training and on-the-job experience. Thus, major canal and other engineering projects were expected to and did produce practical and empirical engineers such as Benjamin Wright, who educated himself as an engineer while directing the construction of the Erie Canal. Mathematical theory usually requires a college education. West Point was the first engineering school in the United States; its program was modeled upon French engineering schools by Sylvanus Thayer after 1818. Dennis Hart Mahan, a former cadet, was sent to France to study engineering, and he taught two generations of West Point engineers a French-oriented style of engineering. His pupils were encouraged to become civil engineers, and they constituted an educated, mathematically literate elite among the mass of practically trained American engineers.

From whatever causes, American technology was, to a remarkable degree, self-consciously scientific. This was even true of many craftsmen inventors who got surprisingly good results by reasoning directly from Newton's laws of motion. Benjamin Franklin Isherwood, chief engineer of the United States Navy during the Civil War, continued the empiricism of Francis and gave it a philosophical rationale based on Hume and Scottish Common Sense Philosophy, a philosophy that sought to banish all "metaphysics" (and ungodly atheism) from engineering. Isherwood condemned many scientific idealizations, such as perfectly elastic fluids, thus denying the validity of many scientific laws, such as Boyle's law, which incorporated such idealizations. Immigrant engineers trained in mathematical theory played an important role in shifting American engineering science toward mathematical theory in the twentieth century. Included were Charles Proteus Steinmetz in electric power engineering, E.F.W. Alexanderson in radio engineering, Stephen Timoshenko in mechanics and the theory of structures, Theodore von Kármán in aerodynamics, and Max Jakob in heat transfer, to name only a few. This infusion of engineering theory was fortunate because theory was needed in dealing with new, advanced technologies in electricity, radio, large skyscrapers and bridges, aeronautics and rocketry, and more efficient thermal systems, including (for example) ablation cooling of the nose cones of rocket reentry vehicles.

Although the utilitarian and scientific biases of American culture (as well as intrinsic needs of advancing technology) led to a convergence between engineering and science, engineers in the United States (as elsewhere) resisted subordination within scientific professional and work organizations, and both engineers and scientists have repeatedly asserted the autonomy of their professions. In the case of the Franklin Institute, scientists, led by the young Alexander Dallas Bache, sought to control the institute and use it as a vehicle to professionalize and advance science, and further the scientist claim that engineering and applied science are the fruits of the undirected, basic research of scientists. Engineers resisted and won control of the institute, which, under the leadership of William Sellers, a distinguished mechanical engineer, became a vehicle for

E

professionalizing mechanical engineering in the middle years of the nineteenth century.

This story was repeated, in a win-win scenario, at General Electric (GE) after 1900. Charles Proteus Steinmetz, educated both as a mathematician (in Germany) and an engineer (in Switzerland), realized the need for scientific research to undergird the company's product line and assure its continued growth. He was instrumental in founding the General Electric Research Laboratory in 1901, with a physical chemist, Willis R. Whitney, as director. Whitney asserted his own autonomy and that of physical science from which he drew his star researchers; Steinmetz disagreed with Whitney and withdrew from the laboratory. Steinmetz was an engineering scientist, one of the leaders shaping the engineering science of electrical engineering. Steinmetz set up his own engineering research and development organization (with varying titles) at GE and recruited able young engineers such as E.F.W. Alexanderson, who did much to get GE into the radio field. Fortunately for GE, the scientists and engineers mutually supported one another, as in the struggle to control radio, much to the benefit of the corporation.

The scientification of engineering and the technologizing of science has proceeded at a breathtaking pace since World War II, aided by massive federal infusions of money for useful science and scientific engineering, much of which related to defense. Despite these converging trajectories, both scientists and engineers continue to show a stubborn determination to be autonomous. Now more than ever they share many of the same scientific values, but they rank order them differently: engineers value doing over knowing, practical achievement over theory, and they honor and reward successful "doers." Scientists value knowing over doing. They value general theories and they honor theorists such as Einstein and Newton. These differences in orientation are analogous to the subtle but persistent parity differences seen in left- and right-handed gloves or mirror images.

Frederick E. Terman, an electrical engineer and scientizer of legendary stature as the father of Silicon Valley, found that he had to rely upon physicists for the research he directed on radar countermeasures during World War II. Terman, while building bridges to physics after his return to Stanford, also upgraded electrical engineering research. "Never again," he wrote in reviewing the postwar upgrading of electrical engineering graduate curricula, "will electrical engineering have to turn to men trained in other scientific and technical disciplines when there is important work to be done" (quoted in McMahon, pp. 238–239).

BIBLIOGRAPHY

Calhoun, Daniel Hovey. *The American Civil Engineer: Origins and Conflict.* Cambridge, MA: MIT Press, 1960.

Calvert, Monte A. *The Mechanical Engineer in America, 1850–1910.* Baltimore; Johns Hopkins University Press, 1967.

Constant, Edward W. *The Origins of the Turbojet Revolution.* Baltimore: Johns Hopkins University Press, 1980.

Ferguson, Eugene S. *Engineering and the Mind's Eye.* Cambridge, MA: MIT Press, 1992.

Hill, Forest G. *Roads, Rails, and Waterways: The Army Engineers and Early Transportation.* Norman: University of Oklahoma Press, 1957.

Kranakis, Eda. "Social Determinants of Engineering Practice: A Comparative View of France and America in the Nineteenth Century." *Social Studies of Science* 19 (1989): 5–70.

Langrish, J., et al., *Wealth from Knowledge.* London: MacMillan, 1972.

Layton, Edwin T., Jr. "Technology as Knowledge." *Technology and Culture* 15 (1974): 31–40.

———. "American Ideologies of Science and Engineering." *Technology and Culture* 17 (1976) 688–701.

———. "Millwrights and Engineers, Science, Social Roles and the Evolution of the Turbine In America," in *The Dynamics of Science and Technology,* edited by Wolfgang Krohn, Edwin T. Layton Jr., and Peter Weingart. Dordrecht: D. Riedel, 1978, pp. 61–87.

———. "Science and Engineering Design." *Annals of the New York Academy of Sciences* 424 (1984): 173–181.

———. *The Revolt of the Engineers.* Baltimore: Johns Hopkins University Press, 1986.

———. *From Rule of Thumb to Scientific Engineering: James B. Francis and the Invention of the Francis Turbine.* Monograph Series of the New Liberal Arts Program. New York: State University of New York, Stony Brook, 1992.

Layton, Edwin T., Jr., and John Lienhard, eds. *History of Heat Transfer: Essays in Honor of the 50th Anniversary of the ASME Heat Transfer Division.* New York: American Society of Mechanical Engineers, 1988.

McMahon, A. Michal. *The Making of a Profession.* New York: IEEE Press, 1984.

Myers, Sumner, and D.G. Marquis. *Successful Industrial Innovations.* Washington, DC: National Science Foundation, 1969.

Sinclair, Bruce. *Philadelphia's Philosopher Mechanics: A History of the Franklin Institute, 1824–1865.* Baltimore: Johns Hopkins University Press, 1974.

Vincenti, Walter G. *What Engineers Know and How They Know It.* Baltimore: Johns Hopkins University Press, 1990.

Wise, George. *Willis R. Whitney, General Electric, and the Origins of U.S. Industrial Research.* New York: Columbia University Press, 1985.

Edwin T. Layton Jr.

Engineers, United States Army

Members of the United States armed forces trained in engineering who are responsible for diverse military and public projects. While the Corps of Engineers has military status, its workforce is largely civilian and its projects have been mainly in the public sector during peacetime. Design and construction of roads, bridges, buildings, lighthouses, docks, and water and navigation systems have all been within its purview.

The concept of army engineers is as old as the United States Army itself, dating to 16 July 1775, when Congress established an army and the position of chief engineer who would be responsible for fortifications. An ancillary engineering corps established by an act of Congress in March 1779 was disbanded at the conclusion of the Revolutionary War. But when war with Britain again threatened, Congress created a Corps of Artillerists and Engineers in May 1794 for the specific purpose of developing coastal defenses. At the same time, there were preliminary efforts to establish a school for training engineering officers at West Point, New York.

On 16 May 1802, Congress established a Corps of Engineers and directed that it also oversee a military academy to train engineers. Since there were no domestic schools of engineering, the first corps officers were sought from Europe and especially France, which had a tradition of formally trained engineers. Believing France to be the premier repository of military science, West Point's organization followed that of the École Polytechnique, where a heavily scientific course of study was prescribed for prospective military officers. As a result, mathematics, science, and engineering became the core of the new school's curriculum.

Topographical engineers from the corps surveyed, mapped, and compiled statistics about the nation's interior until 1863. The resulting routes for roads, canals, and railroads were vital to the nation's expanding commerce, and useful to the military during national emergencies. Following the Civil War, civilian scientists continued the work formerly done by the military engineers.

The primary point of contact between the corps and the public in general has been in the field of hydraulic engineering. In the nineteenth century, the corps began its program of waterway improvement and flood control with dams, levees, and canals. Since 1900, the vision limiting its hydraulic responsibilities strictly to matters of navigation has broadened to include control of water resource development. This includes regulating water usage involving dams and, beginning in the 1950s, responsibility for construction and operation of federal hydroelectric power facilities.

In order to better carry out its varied missions, the Corps of Engineers established three major research centers comprised of eight separate laboratories of applied science. The Waterways Experiment Station (WES) at Vicksburg, Mississippi, started in 1929 as a hydraulics laboratory, but today is the primary research, testing, and development facility of the corps. There is also research in geothermal, structural, environmental, and coastal engineering, and information technology. Among the staff is a broad range of scientists, including chemists, physicists, ecologists, botanists, and geologists, who study subjects as diverse as sail mechanics and computer applications. Work on corps projects is augmented by studies done under contract for other federal agencies, private industry, and state, local, and foreign governments. Research reports generated as a result of the facilities' work are widely distributed to colleges, universities, and professional organizations. These laboratories have an international reputation and stand at the forefront in their fields.

The purpose of the Construction Engineering Research Laboratory (CERL), established in 1968, is investigation and development in the area of vertical construction. It is charged with formulating long-range solutions to military needs, and includes laboratories studying energy systems and the environmental effects of army activities. CERL is unique in that it is a cooperative effort between the Corps of Engineers and the University of Illinois at Champaign-Urbana. This arrangement not only gives the corps direct access to the academic community, but scholars and students benefit from participation in the lab's many short-term projects. There is concerted effort to ensure that research results get widespread distribution in the construction industry.

Changes in world politics during the 1950s prompted the development of the Cold Regions Research and Engineering Laboratory (CRREL). With the possibility of military conflict in arctic regions

E

came the need to better understand design, construction, operation, and maintenace appropriate for sub-zero temperature conditions. Refrigeration units at the CRREL in Hanover, New Hampshire, provide the extreme temperatures needed for this research.

In its nearly two-hundred-year existence, the Corps of Engineers has suffered only minor public criticism for handling projects such as flood control and dredging. But in the late 1960s, it was seriously challenged on the civilian side for its overall policies in dealing with the nation's waterways—methods counter to those held by a growing environmental movement and changing public policy. In response the corps issued new guidelines and regulations dealing with issues of land, air, and water usage, and to study them it hired specialists in the environmental sciences. As a result of the National Environmental Policy Act of 1969, environmental impact became a consideration in all future Corps of Engineers projects.

BIBLIOGRAPHY

Ambrose, Stephen E. *Duty, Honor, Country: A History of West Point.* Baltimore: Johns Hopkins University Press, 1966.

Cotton, Gordon A. *A History of the Waterways Experiment Station, 1929–1979.* Vicksburg, MS: U. S. Waterways Experiment Station, 1979.

Hill, Forest G. *Roads, Rails, and Waterways: The Army Engineers and Early Transportation.* Norman: University of Oklahoma Press, 1957.

Morgan, Arthur E. *Dams and Other Disasters; A Century of the Army Corps of Engineers in Civil Works.* Boston: P. Sargent, 1971.

Parkman, Aubrey. *Army Engineers in New England.* Waltham, MA: U.S. Army Corps of Engineers, 1978.

Reuss, Martin. *Shaping Environmental Awareness; The United States Army Corps of Engineers Environmental Board 1970–1980.* Washington, DC: Historical Division, Office of Administrative Services, Office of the Chief of Engineers, 1983.

Schubert, Frank N. *The Nation Builders: A Sesquicentennial History of the Corps of Topographical Engineers, 1838–1863.* Fort Belvoir, VA: United States Army Corps of Engineers, 1988.

Shallat, Todd. *Structures in the Stream: Water, Science, and the U.S. Army Corps of Engineers, 1680–1880.* Austin: University of Texas Press, 1994.

Torres, Louis. *A History of the U.S. Army Construction Engineering Research Laboratory (CERL), 1964–1985.* Champaign, IL: U.S. Army Corps of Engineers, Construction Engineering Research Laboratory, 1987.

William E. Worthington Jr.

Environmental and Conservation Concerns

Conservation of natural resources and protection of environmental quality have been of variable but persistent concern to American society. To a greater extent than most social concerns, they have exhibited close ties to scientific research and advice.

Occasional concerns were expressed about the depletion of natural resources during the eighteenth and early nineteenth centuries. However, George Perkins Marsh, diplomat and scholar, provided the first extensive, and influential, treatment of environmental concerns, in *Man and Nature* (1864). He discussed the extinction of species, the consequences of forest cutting for streamflow and flooding, and other topics. The most significant organized response to these concerns was the progressive conservation movement of approximately 1890 to 1920. Stimulated by resource scarcities and waste, Gifford Pinchot of the United States Forest Service, and others, advocated efficient use of resources through professional management. Closely linked to the advocacy of scientific management in business and government, the conservation movement accelerated the application of expertise to the management of forests, water, and other resources. But, at about the same time, a contrasting perspective emphasizing the intrinsic, spiritual value of nature, independent of practical utility, was outlined by Henry David Thoreau, John Muir, and other writers. During this period, some ecologists also advocated preservation of nature, especially to ensure areas for field research. Largely separate from these initiatives concerning the use or protection of natural areas were efforts to improve urban and workplace environments to safeguard human health and well-being. Beginning in the 1890s, Alice Hamilton was the most prominent early exponent of these concerns. Overall, therefore, by the 1920s, the environment and conservation had become of concern from several perspectives within American society.

During the 1930s and 1940s, the assumptions of progressive-era resource conservation were challenged, but not overturned. Drought and dust-bowl conditions in the prairies, their impact magnified by the plowing up of natural plant communities, demonstrated the hazards of efforts to achieve efficiency through the control of nature. This experience stimulated interest, especially among plant ecologists like Frederick Clements and Paul Sears, in planning and integrated resource management, with the goal of a stable equilibrium for natural and human communities. Their perspective was grounded in their understanding of ecological succession, leading to a stable climax. Wildlife management practices, including predator control, were also debated during the 1930s and 1940s, with insights into the behavior of animal populations being provided by Aldo Leopold and other scientists and professional managers.

During the 1950s, certain environmental issues such as the impacts of pesticides and dam construction on wild rivers attracted scattered attention. However, professional resource conservation continued to dominate the management of the American environment. But, by the early 1960s, changes in American society, including economic prosperity and greater concern for noneconomic values and an improved quality of life, led to greater prominence for environmental issues. The state of the environment became accepted as a matter of public concern, and as a responsibility of governments. Scientists played important roles in this. For example, Rachel Carson provided in *Silent Spring* (1962) an accessible discussion of the risks of careless use of pesticides, while some ecologists and writers, including Eugene Odum, Barry Commoner, and Paul Ehrlich, explained the political implications of ecological insights. Leopold's *Sand County Almanac,* originally published in 1949, became appreciated as a prescient statement of environmental values. At the same time, many came to view science, because of its role in the development of nuclear power and other forms of technology, as potentially destructive. Thus, the position of science in environmental affairs became ambiguous, being viewed as both a source of knowledge about environmental problems and as a cause of these problems.

Since the 1970s, environmental concerns have exhibited several trends. Concern about more visible forms of environmental degradation, such as air and water pollution, has broadened to encompass more persistent, but less visible concerns, such as toxic chemicals. Greater concern for problems on larger scales, such as acid rain, depletion of the stratospheric ozone layer, and global climate change, has also become apparent. Evidence underpinning these concerns has most often been derived from scientific research; this reflects the significance of scientists' role in the identification of emerging environmental problems. Environmental regulatory agencies have also generated a greater demand for scientific expertise because of the importance of empirical evidence in the assessment of environmental risks, and in the weighing of the costs and benefits of environmental protection. The emergence of new environmental professions, development of large-scale research initiatives by government and industry, and the use of expertise by public interest groups all testify to the importance of scientific evidence in environmental politics.

Environmental and conservation concerns raise several issues of interest to historians of science. One is the impact of public priorities on science. While scientists have benefited from the increased funding that has resulted from environmental concerns, they have also had to negotiate between the sometimes conflicting priorities of the scientific community and of their patrons. Some scientists have welcomed public prominence and social relevance; others have retreated into the lab, because of perceived risks to scientific credibility and autonomy. The links between these responses and specific institutional or scientific contexts demands attention. The impact of the demands imposed by the frequently adversarial context of environmental politics would also repay further study.

Another area of interest are the values implicit in science and social ideologies. Scientific results have often been used to legitimate particular ethical assumptions regarding the exploitation or preservation of nature. One way to explore this is in terms of the common metaphors of science and society. For example, ecological science and technocratic approaches to managing human society have sometimes shared the metaphor of cybernetic systems, amenable to expert, outside control. Another approach to studying the relation of science to social values is to interpret science not in terms of the dominant values of society as a whole, but in terms of the values and priorities expressed within specific research or managerial institutions.

The disciplinary structure of environmental science is also of interest. Specific environmental and conservation concerns have led to development of specific professional disciplines, such as forestry and wildlife management, as well as scientific disciplines, such as toxicology and environmental chemistry. The structure of these disciplines—their central ideas, and the boundaries between them and political priorities—represents the outcome of interactions between public concerns and scientific ideas; these interactions would repay attention from historians. Has the structure of our knowledge about the natural world become defined in terms of public concerns, or scientific theo-

E

ries, or a combination of the two? Of particular interest is the disciplinary identity of ecology; it has been viewed as a specialized discipline, but also as a holistic, integrative perspective. Even the distinction between science and politics has blurred; for many, "ecology" signifies not a scientific discipline at all, but a specific ethical perspective, or political movement.

Finally, the implications of environmental and conservation concerns for the social role of science is of interest to historians. Resource conservation is based on the ideology of professional management: that scientific expertise can be relied on to define the problems, and solve them. Environmental concerns, being grounded in peoples' own values and experiences, constitute a challenge to this ideology; the implications for the conduct and organization of science are still unfolding.

BIBLIOGRAPHY

Carson, Rachel. *Silent Spring*. Boston: Houghton Mifffin, 1962.

Hays, Samuel P. *Beauty, Health, and Permanence: Environmental Politics in the United States, 1955–1985.* Cambridge, U.K.: Cambridge University Press, 1987.

Jasanoff, Sheila. "Science, Politics, and the Renegotiation of Expertise at EPA." *Osiris*, 2d ser., 7 (1992): 195–217.

Lacey, Michael J. *Government and Environmental Politics: Essays on Historical Developments Since World War Two.* Washington, DC: Woodrow Wilson Center Press, 1989.

Leopold, Aldo. *A Sand County Almanac*. New York: Oxford University Press, 1949.

Nelkin, Dorothy, ed. *Controversy: The Politics of Technical Decisions.* 3d ed. Newbury Park, CA: Sage, 1992.

Shortland, Michael, ed. *Science and Nature: Essays in the History of the Environmental Sciences.* Stanford in the Vale, Oxford: British Society for the History of Science, 1993.

Smith, Michael L. *Pacific Visions: California Scientists and the Environment, 1850–1915.* New Haven: Yale University Press, 1987.

Worster, Donald. *Nature's Economy: A History of Ecological Ideas.* 2d ed. Cambridge, U.K.: Cambridge University Press, 1994.

Stephen Bocking

SEE ALSO
Ecology

Environmental Protection Agency, United States
The federal agency responsible for enforcing laws designed to protect the environment and humans from both malicious and inadvertent environmental abuse.

In 1970, responding to the demands of the environmental movement, President Richard Nixon created the Environmental Protection Agency (EPA) by reorganizing various programs in the Departments of Agriculture, Health, Education and Welfare, and Interior, as well as other executive branch components, such as the Atomic Energy Commission, and consolidating them into one independent regulatory agency. Since that time, the agency has guarded public environmental health by enforcing laws such as the Clean Air Act, Clean Water Act, Toxic Substances Control Act, Superfund, and several others.

EPA's actions in this regard have been shaped by public priorities and contemporary scientific knowledge. In the early 1970s, when the environmental movement peaked, early EPA administrators, such as William Ruckelshaus and Russell Train, believed that the agency had a mandate from the people to swiftly improve the quality of American life by significantly reducing smog, noxious and toxic chemical effluents in rivers, lakes, and estuaries, and the potential health risks associated with pesticides and other chemical uses. During the 1960s, ecologists, such as Rachel Carson, had popularized the potentially devastating effects of pollution to the environment and ultimately to humans. Initially, EPA worked to clean up visible pollutants and chemicals identified as dangerous to human and environmental health. Ruckelshaus molded the staff he inherited from predecessor agencies into a functional organization and began tackling issues such as banning the use of DDT and requiring automakers to reduce the amount of smog-producing chemicals emitted from automobiles. Meanwhile, Congress passed laws that increased the scope and power of EPA's regulatory authority.

Under Russell Train, EPA continued to clean up the most visible pollutants, but as the staff worked toward that goal, they recognized the monumental complexity, ambiguity, and interconnectedness of environmental problems. Train, therefore, formed EPA's Science Advisory Board (SAB), composed of the United States' leading scientists, to assist agency policymakers to create scientifically sound regulations and also to direct them to environmental problems that EPA should address. By the mid-1970s, EPA faced opposition from various constituent groups who believed that EPA made policy without understanding the overall effects of its regulations. Thus, besides increasing the number of SAB committees, the agency also implemented public participation processes whereby everyone interested in a particular regulation could make their point heard by policymakers, and tasked the several laboratories that it inherited from predecessor agencies with research and testing projects to insure that EPA had the most comprehensive understanding of environmental problems and their potential solutions. These actions resulted in mixed feedback. Some said that EPA's goal of cleaning up the environment by the mid-1980s was too ambitious and too costly given the 1970s stagnant economy; others believed that EPA was addressing the wrong problems with the wrong solutions; still others believed EPA was not moving quickly enough to address issues such as toxic chemicals entering the environment.

President Jimmy Carter's EPA administrator, Douglas Costle, responded to these voices by continuing to enforce laws designed to clear the nation's air and water by setting regulations, but he encouraged greater flexibility in enforcing them to take into consideration experimental technology or regulatory approaches that might provide for a cleaner environment at less cost. However, in response to Congressional passage of the Toxic Substances Control Act (TSCA), EPA's emphasis began to change from visible pollution to protecting Americans' health from cancer-causing invisible chemicals. The agency's authority under TSCA made it responsible for regulating toxic substance production, handling, and disposal. Recognition of the historical sloppy handling of toxic substances, coupled with discoveries of toxic graveyards like that at Love Canal, New York, led Congress to pass the Comprehensive Environmental Response, Compensation, and Liability Act of 1980 (Superfund), which made the agency responsible for ensuring that the worst toxic waste dumps were cleaned up and that those responsible for creating them paid for their neglect. The emphasis on toxic substances forced EPA into an arena that lessened public enthusiasm for its efforts. By concentrating on removing carcinogenic chemicals measured in parts per million or smaller from the environment, EPA was forced to rely increasingly on the expertise of its scientists, who debated industry scientists over the validity of various studies. Conflicting newspaper reports about the likelihood of getting cancer from particular substances frightened, confused, and then made Americans apathetic toward environmental protection.

By the early 1980s, American public opinion wearied of government intervention in the economy and society, although opinion polls showed continued support for environmental protection. President Ronald Reagan's EPA administrator, Ann Gorsuch Burford, came to the agency as an outsider intent on making the agency's operations more efficient, consistent with the Reagan administration's deregulatory mood, and founded on stronger science. However, due to scandals regarding the administration of her new Superfund office, Burford was replaced by William Ruckelshaus, the agency's first administrator.

Ruckelshaus reoriented the agency's regulatory philosophy from command-and-control regulatory approaches that attempted to enforce every standard for every known threat to human health to using scientific risk assessment, as suggested by the agency's SAB. Risk assessment methodology became the preferred philosophical approach for agency operations during the late 1980s and 1990s as the agency's responsibilities, mandated by old and new laws, grew faster than its budgets. Risk assessment offered the agency a methodology for setting priorities. However, risk assessment conflicted with the way environmental activists believed the environment should be protected and with the regulatory strategy mandated by various laws. For instance, the Delaney Clause of the Pure Food and Drug Act required the government to enforce a zero tolerance standard for carcinogenic pesticides in the food supply. Using risk assessment, the agency preferred to balance the human and financial resources necessary to enforce the law's letter against the risk that carcinogenic chemical traces, detectable at far more minute levels in the 1990s than in the 1960s, would cause cancer and then decide whether agency resources might be better expended on other more important matters. Risk assessment also placed the agency into a far more esoteric realm of political debate with regulated-community scientists claiming that the agency's interpretation of scientific data, or the data itself, was flawed, or "bad science."

By the early 1990s, the agency ceased to be strictly an adversary to industry—in part because politically the adversarial role drew constant criticism from regulated groups who claimed that the agency was misguided in its approach. Instead, William Reilly, President George Bush's EPA administrator, and Carol Browner, President Bill Clinton's administrator, both encouraged industry to go beyond EPA standards and design strategies that would make EPA's traditional command-and-control regulations unnecessary by implementing new production processes that produced less pollution.

E

Meanwhile, EPA pushed Congress to write laws giving the agency more flexibility in its regulatory approach—especially with regard to prioritizing agency enforcement strategies based on risk. Congress responded with laws such as the Pollution Prevention Act.

Another thread that had run through the agency's history, but which had not been prominent until the 1990s, was the ecosystem approach to environmental regulation. EPA had long known that writing standards for single-media emissions, which are regulated at the end of the pipe, was the least complicated and quickest way to achieve measurable short-term cleanup of various pollutants. By the late 1980s, the agency had gathered significant amounts of data and largely exhausted the political and environmental benefits of single-media regulation alone. People in many regions questioned whether EPA's continued efforts would make a tangible difference in places that possessed cultural meaning to them, such as the Great Lakes or the Chesapeake Bay, and the antienvironmental-regulation groups questioned whether the agency's effectiveness was worth the effort. Further, some analysts suggested that the economic cost of end-of-pipe regulations would outweigh the potential benefits. Thus, the agency began to find ways to foster ecosystemwide health—a goal of ecology-inspired environmental groups since the 1960s. The agency focused on key geographical areas, such as the Great Lakes, Chesapeake Bay, and the Florida Everglades. It identified the most significant threats to those ecosystems, and then focused the agency's regulatory and scientific resources on improving the ecosystems' health in measurable and visible ways. This strategy allowed the agency to get around the difficult "good science, bad science" regulatory arguments and to draw public support by designing obvious and tangible objectives for environmental regulation programs.

As the federal agency responsible for environmental quality, EPA has set priorities and developed strategies for accomplishing its mission in response to national priorities. In the 1970s, the American people wanted a clean environment at any cost. EPA developed hard-hitting national standards that strove to achieve rapid and visible increases in environmental quality. By the 1980s, public priorities were more focused on economic facets of life than on environmental quality, which had improved visibly since the 1970s. EPA's challenges increased as the pollutants it regulated were no longer tangible and its objectives revolved around removing chemicals in the invisible realm of parts per million from the air, water, soil, and food supply. The agency responded to this challenge and the challenge of fulfilling its legally mandated responsibilities within allotted budgets and with an eye toward the total cost of regulation by building up its scientific support network with the SAB, utilizing its laboratories to evaluate environmental problems and technological solutions, using risk assessment methodology for priority setting, encouraging pollution prevention, and focusing attention on ecosystem management.

BIBLIOGRAPHY

Barnett, Harold C. *Toxic Debts and the Superfund Dilemma.* Chapel Hill: University of North Carolina Press, 1994.

Caldwell, Lynton. *Science and the National Environmental Policy Act: Redirecting Policy Through Procedural Reform.* University: University of Alabama Press, 1985.

Hays, Samuel P. *Beauty, Health and Permanence: Environmental Politics in the United States, 1955–1985.* Cambridge, U.K.: Cambridge University Press, 1987.

Landy, Marc, Marc J. Roberts, and Stephen R. Thomas. *The Environmental Protection Agency: Asking the Wrong Questions, From Nixon to Clinton.* New York: Oxford University Press, 1990; 2d ed. 1994.

Press, Daniel. *Democratic Dilemmas in the Age of Ecology: Trees and Toxics in the American West.* Durham, NC: Duke University Press, 1994.

Russell, Edmund P. "'Lost Among the Parts Per Billion': Ecological Protection at the United States Environmental Protection Agency, 1970–1993." Manuscript in author's possession.

Schnaiberg, Allan, and Kenneth Alan Gould. *Environment and Society: The Enduring Conflict.* New York: St. Martin's Press, 1994.

United States Environmental Protection Agency Press Release Collection. United States Environmental Protection Agency Historical Document Collection. Washington, DC.

United States Environmental Protection Agency Oral History Interview-1: William D. Ruckelshaus. Washington, DC: United States Environmental Protection Agency, 1993.

United States Environmental Protection Agency Oral History Interview-2: Russell E. Train. Washington, DC: United States Environmental Protection Agency, 1993.

United States Environmental Protection Agency Oral History Interview-1: Alvin L. Alm. Washington, DC: United States Environmental Protection Agency, 1994.

Williams, Dennis C. "EPA Laboratory Siting: A Historical Perspective." 1993 manuscript in United States Environmental Protection Agency Historical Document Collection. Washington, DC.

—. *The Guardian: EPA's Formative Years, 1970–1973.* Washington, DC: United States Environmental Protection Agency, 1993.

Dennis C. Williams

Erlanger, Joseph (1874–1965)

Physiologist and educator. Born in San Francisco, Joseph Erlanger studied at the University of California (B.S., 1895) and received his medical education at The Johns Hopkins University (M.D., 1899). He was an intern at the Johns Hopkins University Hospital under William Osler, 1899–1900. From 1900 to 1906, he was an assistant in physiology at the university under William H. Howell. He became professor of physiology at the University of Wisconsin Medical School in 1906. In 1910, he accepted an appointment as professor and head of physiology at Washington University in St. Louis. He retained this position until retirement in 1946, continuing in research at the university for several years afterward. In 1944, he and Herbert S. Gasser were awarded the Nobel Prize in physiology or medicine "for . . . discoveries relating to the highly differentiated functions of nerve fibres."

Erlanger's chief contributions to physiology can be divided into two distinct phases. Until 1921, he concentrated on problems relating to the cardiovascular system, developing an improved sphygmomanometer, and making important discoveries about the relation of blood pressure and the conduction of electrical impulses in the heart. During World War I, he led investigations of traumatic shock and developed an artificial serum for its treatment. The second phase of his research career began in collaboration with Gasser, a former student. The two adapted a cathode-ray oscillograph for the purpose of amplifying and recording electrical conduction, or action potentials, of the nervous system. Using this instrument, they analyzed and compared action potentials of different portions of the nervous system, determining that the speed of conduction is proportional to the diameter of the nerve fiber. Erlanger's later research built upon this key electrophysiological discovery, with studies of excitation and polarization of nerve fibers, among other investigations. His most important scientific publication is generally regarded to be the monograph *Electrical Signs of Nervous Activity* (1937), written in collaboration with Gasser.

Throughout his tenure at Washington University, Erlanger played an important role in the governance of the medical school through its "executive faculty" council. He also made important contributions to the American Physiological Society and other scientific organizations.

Erlanger's papers, fifteen linear feet, 1882–1965, are preserved in the Washington University School of Medicine Library.

BIBLIOGRAPHY

Davis, Hallowell. "Joseph Erlanger, 1874–1965." *Biographical Memoirs of the National Academy of Sciences* 41 (1970): 111–139.

Erlanger, Joseph. "Prefatory Chapter: A Physiologist Reminisces." *Annual Review of Physiology* 26 (1964): 1–14.

Frank, Robert G. "The J.H.B. Archive Report: The Joseph Erlanger Collection at Washington University School of Medicine, St. Louis." *Journal of the History of Biology* 12 (1979): 193–201.

Ludmerer, Kenneth M. "Erlanger, Joseph." In *Dictionary of American Biography,* supplement 7, 1961–1965. Edited by John A. Garraty. New York: Scribners, 1981, pp. 225–227.

Monnier, A.M. "Erlanger, Joseph." *Dictionary of Scientific Biography.* Edited by Charles C. Gillispie. New York: Scribners, 1971, 4:397–399.

Paul G. Anderson

Espy, James Pollard (1785–1860)

Educator and meteorologist. Born in Washington County, Pennsylvania, James Espy was the youngest of ten children of Josiah Espy, pioneer farmer, and Elizabeth Patterson. During his childhood, the family lived in Kentucky and Ohio. Espy graduated from Transylvania University in 1808. He taught grammar school in Lexington, Kentucky, and served as principal of an academy in Cumberland, Maryland. In 1812, he married Margaret Pollard and assumed her maiden name. The couple had no children. Espy practiced law in Xenia, Ohio. He moved to Philadelphia in 1817, where he taught mathematics and classics.

Espy's interest in meteorology developed in the 1830s. From 1834 to 1837, he served as the chairman of the Joint Committee on Meteorology of the American Philosophical Society and Franklin Institute. He gained support from the Pennsylvania legislature to establish a system of weather observers in each county. He also maintained a national network of volunteer observers. During this period, he invented a "nephelescope," an early cloud chamber. His theory of hail won the Magellenic Prize of the American Philosophical

E

Society in 1836. His theory of storms brought him into conflict with two other prominent scientists, William Redfield and Robert Hare.

Espy viewed the atmosphere as a giant heat engine. According to his thermal theory of storms, all atmospheric disturbances, from thunderstorms to winter storms, are driven by heated updrafts, inwardly rushing air currents, and the release of latent "caloric" (heat). He was a popular lecturer, and his book *The Philosophy of Storms* (1841) was well received by many scientists of his time.

In 1842, Espy moved to Washington, D.C., to pursue his storm studies. He served as professor of mathematics in the navy and as "national meteorologist" in the Army Medical Department. He issued several official reports, including *First Report on Meteorology to the Surgeon General of the United States Army* (1843) and *Fourth Meteorological Report* (1851). In 1848, he helped Joseph Henry establish a national meteorological project at the Smithsonian Institution. He died in Cincinnati.

Many retrospective evaluations of Espy echo the contemporary opinion of Alexander Dallas Bache that he was overly dogmatic and confrontational. His lack of a permanent position and his advocacy of impractical schemes for artificial rainmaking also cast a shadow over his work. Although later observations showed he was mistaken about centripetal wind patterns in hurricanes, he correctly emphasized the importance of thermally induced convection, the release of latent heat in moist air, and the convergence of winds in convective clouds and midlatitude storms.

Espy's basic physical insights were considered sound and his ideas were widely accepted by his contemporaries. Henry, James Coffin, Elias Loomis, and William Ferrel were all supporters, with modifications, of "Espian thermal processes." In 1893, Harvard geographer and meteorologist William Morris Davis wrote that Espy initiated the leading school of meteorological thought in America.

Espy was raised in the Presbyterian church. A series of his essays on religious issues was published posthumously.

There is no single collection of Espy's papers. Espy's brief autobiographical sketch (c. 1851) is at the American Philosophical Society Library.

BIBLIOGRAPHY

Bache, Alexander Dallas. *Annual Report of the Smithsonian Institution for 1859.* Washington, DC: Smithsonian Institution, 1860, pp. 108–111.

Dial (Cincinnati), February 1860, pp. 102, iii–vi.

Fleming, James Rodger. *Meteorology in America, 1800–1870.* Baltimore: Johns Hopkins University Press, 1990.

Kutzbach, Gisela. *The Thermal Theory of Cyclones: A History of Meteorological Thought in the Nineteenth Century.* Boston: American Meteorological Society, 1979.

Morehead, Mrs. L.M. *A Few Incidents in the Life of Professor James P. Espy.* Cincinnati: R. Clarke, 1888.

Reingold, Nathan. "Espy, James Pollard." *Dictionary of Scientific Biography.* Edited by Charles C. Gillispie. New York: Scribners, 1972, 4:410–411.

———, ed. *Science in Nineteenth-Century America: A Documentary History.* New York: Wang, 1964.

Reingold, Nathan, and Marc Rothenberg, eds. *The Papers of Joseph Henry.* Washington, DC: Smithsonian Institution Press, 1972– .

James Rodger Fleming

Ethics and Social Responsibility in Science

The notion that scientific ideas contribute to the betterment of humanity, whether through revelation of God's handiwork, stimulation of intellectual culture, service to the state, or the production of useful knowledge, has always been an underlying assumption of modern science. The ideology of progress—the Enlightenment notion that the expansion of knowledge inevitably contributes to the improvement of the human condition—has long provided a powerful, but uncomplicated, statement of the social good produced by science. But a more complex conception of social responsibility and the relationship between science and society, consisting of an understanding that science and technology might not always be beneficial, and that scientists have a special obligation to call attention to the harmful effects of scientific discoveries and ensure the beneficial application of knowledge, seems to be a more recent phenomenon. In the American context, social responsibility in science is primarily a twentieth-century concept. While individual scientists have always made decisions of conscience, it has usually been times of national crisis which have provoked groups of scientists to consider collective responses to the ethical dilemmas posed by scientific knowledge.

The social and economic dislocations associated with the industrialization of the United States led many intellectuals to consider the potential for expert knowledge to solve social problems. During the Progressive Era, recently professionalized social scientists and engineers tried to demonstrate that the scientific method could be used to reengineer society and solve urgent problems such as urban poverty and industrial inefficiency. But too often, Progressive Era reform tended to demean rather than uplift. As historian John M. Jordan has discussed at length, technocratic reform efforts usually reflected an ethos which was both simplistic and antidemocratic. Technocratic progressives promoted the concentration of power in the hands of experts as a way to subvert what they saw as the inefficiency and corruption which characterized political life. Operating within the confines of the ideology of progress, it rarely occurred to progressive reformers that their own interests and value-laden assumptions might belie the supposed objectivity of their proposals, and that their solutions might be unpopular for good reasons among those who would be affected by them. For example, engineers who advocated scientific management, or Taylorism, viewed workers more as inarticulate, mindless machines than as intelligent human beings with an intimate understanding of their labor. For the Taylorites, efficiency in the industrial workplace meant strict regimentation and managerial control. Not surprisingly, at Watertown Arsenal and elsewhere, whenever Taylorism was implemented, workers revolted (Noble, pp. 264–278).

It was not until the Great Depression that large numbers of scientists and engineers began to consider the possibility that expertise itself bore some of the responsibility for society's ills. According to historian Peter J. Kuznick, the economic chaos of the depression and severe unemployment among scientists led scientists themselves to question their assumptions about the inevitable benefits of scientific progress. In the late 1930s, the American Association for the Advancement of Science (AAAS) launched a series of symposia to consider the relationship between science and society and the possible negative consequences of science and technology, while the newly formed American Association of Scientific Workers (AASW) considered more radical approaches toward preventing the misuse of science.

The atomic bombings of Hiroshima and Nagasaki provoked another wave of organizing among scientists. Feeling a special sense of responsibility for the death and destruction wrought by the bomb, Manhattan Project scientists banded together as the Federation of American Scientists (FAS) and lobbied for legislation which they felt would ensure the development of atomic energy for peaceful purposes, avoid a ruinous arms race between the United States and the Soviet Union, and create a general political structure for science which would make basic research more responsive to social needs (Smith, Boyer). The rise of the Cold War and domestic anticommunism, however, meant that research instead became closely tied to the military needs of the Cold War state (Leslie).

The Vietnam War provoked the most recent case of widespread advocacy of social responsibility in science. Influenced by student protests at colleges and universities across the country, young scientists and engineers, primarily graduate students, led protests at the Massachusetts Institute of Technology, Stanford University, and elsewhere in the late 1960s and early 1970s. The students condemned what they saw as the destructive misuse of scientific research to serve a corrupt foreign policy, and they called for the redirection of military-funded university research toward medicine, clean energy, pollution control, and other more socially beneficial uses. Faculty members sometimes joined the students; at MIT in 1969, faculty members called for a daylong strike in which scientists would leave the concerns of the laboratory bench and devote themselves to discussing the "problems and dangers related to the present role of science and technology in the life of the nation" (quoted in Leslie, p. 233). Scientific societies also joined in the Vietnam-induced discussions. In 1972, the New York Academy of Sciences sponsored a conference on "The Social Responsibility of Scientists," while AAAS sponsored a committee which produced a 1975 report on "Scientific Freedom and Responsibility."

The protests at MIT and Stanford had some short-term effects. Both universities divested themselves from their laboratories which conducted secret research—Draper Laboratory at MIT, and Stanford Research Institute at Stanford, and military funding of university research declined for a brief period in the 1970s. But with the Reagan-era defense buildup in the 1980s, military research in the universities returned to the high levels of the early 1960s.

Throughout the twentieth century, scientists have attempted to exercise social responsibility in science in a wide variety of ways, both as individuals and in groups. Some individual scientists have tried conscientious objection, refusing to participate in any uses of science which they considered unethical or immoral. In 1947, MIT mathematician Norbert Wiener publicly announced that he would not supply information about his work to individuals or institutions engaged in research for military purposes of which he disapproved,

E

on the grounds that to do so would violate his moral responsibility as a scientist. Although his decision violated traditional scientific commitments to open communication, he felt it was necessary to demonstrate his duty as an individual not to cooperate in allowing his discoveries to be used in ways he deemed harmful. More recently, in 1990, a young plant biologist named Martha L. Crouch announced she would cease conducting experimental research. Writing in *The Plant Cell*, she contended that the discipline of plant science was embedded in a political and economic structure which inevitably tied research to applications which were harmful to the environment and devastating to indigenous peoples across the world. Since she could not abide such consequences, she decided it was best to end her research and direct herself toward redefining her discipline in such a way that it would reflect ecologically sound values.

Other scientists have felt they could stay within the system to ensure the socially responsible use of their work. For example, in the late 1950s, scientists at the University of Alaska at Fairbanks protested to the Atomic Energy Commission (AEC) regarding its plans to demonstrate in north Alaska the efficacy of atomic bombs as a means to dig harbors. The scientists objected that the AEC had failed to consider the threat fallout from Project Chariot posed to local inhabitants and the environment. In response, the AEC agreed to sponsor an environmental impact study, at a time when such studies were rare (O'Neill).

When the system itself fails, however, individual scientists are then faced with the difficult decision of whether or not to become whistle-blowers. Don Foote, William Pruitt, and Les Viereck, the biologists who conducted the study of the expected effects of Project Chariot, concluded that not only would the timing of the test disrupt the Eskimo population's short-term livelihood, but also that the radioactive fallout would have unpredictable, and potentially disastrous, consequences. Nevertheless, the AEC announced that, based on the study's results, Project Chariot was safe and would go ahead as planned. Feeling that their research had been unjustly ignored, the three biologists then decided to go public. They published their conclusions in the newsletter of the Alaska Conservation Society and sent copies all over the United States. The story became national news, and Project Chariot was ultimately cancelled. But Foote, Pruitt, and Viereck suffered from their insistence that the implications of their research be recognized. All three were blacklisted and had difficulty finding employment in the years afterward (O'Neill).

A few individual scientists have expanded the social role of the scientist by becoming public intellectuals. The publication of *Silent Spring* by the biologist Rachel Carson in 1962 sparked concerns about the adverse effects of pesticides nationwide and helped launch the environmental movement. In the 1980s, amid fears of growing instability in U.S.-Soviet relations during the early years of the Reagan presidency, astronomer Carl Sagan countered notions about the survivability of nuclear war by publicizing the nuclear winter hypothesis and the potential of nuclear war to foment environmental catastrophe.

Scientists have also tried a variety of collective responses, periodically organizing to rethink the responsibilities of scientific professionals and to discuss the prevention of what they perceived as actual or potential misuses of scientific knowledge. Sometimes they acted within existing organizations, such as the AAAS during the 1930s and 1970s. At other times, when existing organizations seemed inadequate, they created new organizations such as the AASW and FAS in the 1930s and 1940s, or in later years, the Union of Concerned Scientists and Scientists and Engineers for Social and Political Action (SESPA) in the late 1960s. Most scientists' organizations, in addressing the social and ethical implications of research, have emphasized studying particular instances of danger or abuse and providing information to the public. A few groups have emphasized individual behavior in addition to broader action—SESPA, for example, required its members to take a pledge not to participate in military research or weapons production and to urge other scientists to do the same (Chalk, pp. 64–65).

Self-policing at the disciplinary level is another approach to the exercise of social responsibility. Professional organizations have long reserved the right to enforce standards of professional conduct and to adjudicate over matters involving plagiarism or other types of professional misbehavior. In the 1970s, molecular biologists went beyond simple matters of professional conduct to propose regulations over experiments themselves. In 1973, concerns spread among molecular biologists that new recombinant DNA techniques might result in the unintentional creation of new infectious agents which would pose a serious danger to public health and safety. The following year, a committee of the National Academy of Sciences, chaired by Paul Berg of Stanford University, recommended that scientists voluntarily refrain from performing certain types of recombinant DNA experiments and called for the National Institutes of Health (NIH) to institute guidelines regulating recombinant DNA research. In May 1975, 150 molecular biologists met at the Asilomar Conference to discuss levels of risk and appropriate safeguards for different types of experiments, The summary statement produced at Asilomar formed the basis for guidelines established by the NIH in 1976.

The Asilomar Conference constituted a milestone in the regulation of experimentation, but its legacy as an exercise of social responsibility is mixed. The desire to forestall externally mandated regulation by nonscientists was at least as strong a motivation as health and safety concerns in the Asilomar conferees' deliberations. Discussion of the ethical implications of genetic engineering was also specifically excluded from Asilomar. Furthermore, the consensus reached at Asilomar masked divisions within the scientific community. Some biologists in other fields later contended that because the Asilomar Conference was attended primarily by molecular geneticists, its conclusions were biased and ignored the concerns of scientists with a better understanding of living organisms outside laboratory conditions.

Both individual and group attempts to define and express social responsibility in science have limits to their effectiveness. Individual statements of conscientious objection are powerful in their symbolic content, but they usually lack wider influence. Few scientists followed Norbert Wiener in withdrawing from Cold War research, for example. Furthermore, Wiener's published work remained available to anyone who took the trouble to track it down; Wiener readily admitted that his control over the dissemination of his research was far from complete. Individual scientists who become whistle-blowers, such as the biologists who opposed Project Chariot, run high risks of losing their jobs and being blacklisted. Protection for whistle-blowers by professional organizations remains ad hoc, and legal protections for whistle-blowers are still ill-defined. Well-known scientists with high visibility can command influence if they speak out about the potential harmful consequences of scientific research or specific cases of scientific misconduct, but most working scientists require support from the profession if they are to effect change.

Several problems impede the expression of social responsibility in science at the level of professional organizations as well. There is no consensus among scientists as to what constitutes their social and ethical responsibility. Scientists have no formal code of ethics, no Hippocratic oath that defines their moral obligations as practitioners of science. Questions about social responsibility have been relegated to the status of a periodically recurring discussion, but any codified statement has resisted definition.

The basic ethos of science remains committed to the generation of knowledge, while the creation of mechanisms to consider and regulate the consequences of new knowledge has remained elusive. Although scientists support the notion of social responsibility in theory, they are not generally sympathic if ethical considerations suggest the need for a slowdown or halt to research. As medical ethicist George Annas commented in 1989, "Ethics is taken seriously by physicians and scientists only when it either fosters their agenda or does not interfere with it. If it cautions a slower pace or a more deliberate consideration of science's darker side, it is dismissed as 'fearful of the future,' anti-intellectual, or simply uninformed" (quoted in Weiner, p. 49).

It has also been especially difficult for scientists' professional organizations to take concrete action to ensure the socially responsible use of science when such actions run counter to the direction of national priorities. For example, scientists who criticized the Cold War and what they saw as the development of science exclusively for destructive purposes made little headway in a political environment defined by U.S.-Soviet conflict. Similarly, scientists who currently advocate environmental protection as a national and global priority will have difficulty earning allies and achieving political success at a time when free market ideology and opposition to government regulation holds sway over American politics. Despite scientists' desire to ensure the responsible use of knowledge, social responsibility has been more a protest tradition than an integral part of science and its relationship to society.

BIBLIOGRAPHY

Boyer, Paul. *By the Bomb's Early Light: American Thought and Culture at the Dawn of the Atomic Age.* New York: Pantheon Books, 1985.

Chalk, Rosemary. "Drawing the Line: An Examination of Conscientious Objection in Science." *Ethical Issues Associated with Scientific and Technological Research for the*

E

Military. Annals of the New York Academy of Sciences 577 (1989): 61–74.

Johnson, Deborah G. *Ethical Issues in Engineering.* Englewood Cliffs, NJ: Prentice-Hall, 1991.

Jordan, John M. *Machine-Age Ideology: Social Engineering and American Liberalism, 1911–1939.* Chapel Hill: University of North Carolina Press, 1995.

Kuznick, Peter J. *Beyond the Laboratory: Scientists as Political Activists in 1930s America.* Chicago and London: University of Chicago Press, 1987.

Layton, Edwin T., Jr. *Revolt of the Engineers: Social Responsibility and the American Engineering Profession.* Cleveland and London: The Press of Case Western Reserve University, 1971.

Leslie, Stuart W. *The Cold War and American Science: The Military-Industrial-Academic Complex at MIT and Stanford.* New York; Columbia University Press, 1993.

Noble, David F. *America by Design: Science, Technology, and the Rise of Corporate Capitalism.* New York: Knopf, 1977.

O'Neill, Dan. *The Firecracker Boys.* New York: St. Martin's Press, 1994.

Primack, Joel, and Frank von Hippel. *Advice and Dissent: Scientists in the Political Arena.* New York: Basic Books, 1974.

Smith, Alice Kimball. *A Peril and a Hope: The Scientists' Movement in America, 1945–47.* Chicago and London: University of Chicago Press, 1965.

Weiner, Charles. "Anticipating the Consequences of Genetic Engineering: Past, Present, and Future." In *Are Genes Us? The Social Consequences of the New Genetics,* edited by Carl Cranor. New Brunswick: Rutgers University Press, 1994, pp. 31–51.

Jessica Wang

Ethnicity, Race, and Gender

Physicians, biologists, and anthropologists in the United States have tried for almost two centuries to clarify the biological underpinnings of race, gender, and ethnicity. The scientific debates about biological difference have always had a social viewpoint: women should/should not vote or get a higher education; slavery is/is not justified; blacks are/are not intellectually inferior and thus doomed to lives of poverty; Asians are/are not intellectually inferior (nineteenth century) or are/are not intellectually superior (late twentieth century). This field of scientific inquiry—perhaps more than any other—demonstrates the socially determined nature of scientific knowledge.

Louis Agassiz and Samuel Morton were the two most famous nineteenth-century American scientists to produce broadly acknowledged work on race. Agassiz, a professor at Harvard and founder of the Museum of Comparative Zoology, articulated and gained respectability for the concept of human polygeny—the idea that the different human races constituted different species. Although he did not advocate slavery, he did believe that the so-called Negro race was highly degenerate and that the superior Caucasian race should maintain a separate existence: intermarriage would only lead to the downfall of civilization. It was Agassiz's ideas about polygeny that first gained the respect of European intellectuals for American scientific endeavors. While Agassiz provided a theoretical framework for the idea of polygeny, Samuel Morton, a Philadelphia physician, provided the empirical data. During his lifetime, he amassed a collection of more than 600 human skulls and he used these to establish a racial ranking. Nineteenth-century biologists believed that brain size could be used to measure human intellectual abilities. Morton used BB shot to measure the cranial volume of his skulls and established a ranking in which Europeans came out on top and Africans on the bottom with Asians and Native Americans in between. Morton also used his ideas to justify complete separation of the races. Stephen Jay Gould recalculated Morton's original data and showed how he manipulated them—probably unconsciously—to support his preexisting prejudices.

The idea that larger brains came from smarter people developed in eighteenth-century Europe and was at first applied to male/female differences. European scientists went to great trouble to find some measure of brain size that "worked," that is, that showed that men's brains were larger than women's. If size alone mattered, then elephants should be smarter than humans. If one divided brain size by body weight, however, women came out "ahead." The great French naturalist Georges Cuvier tried to solve the problem by measuring the relative proportions of the cranial and facial bones. But this measure made birds appear to be smarter than humans. In the United States, the assumptions about brain size and intelligence derived from work on women were applied to people of color as well as to American women.

In the first part of the twentieth century, the hunt for gross structural differences in the brain faded away but was replaced by the development of intelligence testing. H.H. Goddard brought the IQ scale, developed in France as a method of identifying and aiding retarded children, to America, where he used it to devise a single measure of intelligence and applied it to normal as well as learning-impaired children. Louis Terman based his mass-marketed measures of IQ on his beliefs in racial differences in intelligence. Unlike the French originators of intelligence testing, Terman wished not so much to help the "feeble-minded" as he did to control them. His work fit well with an active eugenics movement, aimed at permitting only the mentally and morally fit to reproduce. Finally, Robert M. Yerkes gave IQ tests to large numbers of United States Army recruits and concluded that men of Nordic stock were intellectually superior to those from southern Europe; at the bottom of the scale lay people of color. Eventually, psychologists and civil rights activists attacked the racial and cultural biases of the IQ tests. New tests strive to eliminate questions favoring one ethnic group over another; but the success of such an endeavor always depends on prior belief: does one believe that all racial groups have similar average intelligences or does one expect to find different abilities?

The role of prior belief may also be noted in the application of intelligence testing to girls and women. Because in the original IQ tests girls outscored boys by a few points, Terman revised the test, eliminating questions on which girls did better. Similarly, until 1972, women did better than men on the verbal portion of the Scholastic Aptitude Tests taken for college entry but did not fare as well on the mathematical component. After 1972, the male/female differential in verbal ability began to disappear because the Educational Testing Service (ETS), which designs the exams, began to eliminate items on which women did better than men. In 1992, the male/female difference in mathematics, which the ETS was less vigorous in correcting, is still used to support the idea that women are less likely to succeed in careers which require strong mathematical skills, even though women get better grades in the mathematics classroom.

In 1992, the idea that there might be anatomical differences between men and women and blacks and whites is still very much alive. For women and men, the attempt has been to find structural differences in specific regions of the brain believed to be important for mathematical and spatial abilities. A minority of scientists have tried to revive the idea that blacks and women have smaller brains and that such size differences result in lowered performance on IQ tests. These ideas, however, remain deeply controversial and consti-

tute part of the scientific component of continued social debates about racial and sexual difference in America. Again, the lesson is that science is socially produced knowledge; when applied to race, gender, and ethnicity, it inevitably carries with it prior social beliefs which may, in turn, be reinforced by the findings of scientifically trained investigators.

In the early twentieth century, physical anthropologists devoted enormous efforts to finding scientific ways to measure racial difference. They devised charts of hair curliness, lip thickness, and shades of skin color, but none of the methods really worked. Biologists in the late twentieth century no longer believe in race as a biologically valid way to categorize humans. Instead they look at the frequency of genes in different human populations. Those groups which we have historically assigned to a different race are more genetically similar than they are different while those groups which we have historically assigned to the same race often have a wide degree of genetic variation. The concept of race remains with us as a social, historical, and geographical one, but it has no clear biological validity.

Similarly, biologists in the late twentieth century no longer view sex as a simple category. They acknowledge the existence of chromosomal sex, fetal gonadal sex, sex designated by external genitalia, hormonal sex (both fetal and pubertal), and socially assigned sex. Usually, these various aspects of biological sex are congruous and the individual assumes a gender role (a set of socially assigned behaviors) reflecting the underlying biological sex. But when the biological sex is mixed (e.g., in an individual with testes but whose external genitalia include a vagina and clitoris), gender role assignment may be more arbitrary. No single factor stands out as a biological hallmark of male or female and it seems clear that gender roles are culturally rather than biologically determined.

The history of scientific inquiry into the nature of sexual and racial difference has raised deep philosophical questions about the nature of scientific knowledge itself. Feminists, antiracists, and sociologists of knowledge no longer believe that scientists simply uncover truths about the natural world. Instead, they argue that scientists interpret natural phenomena with the social and political contexts in which they operate. In the nineteenth century, there was little disagreement among mainstream scientists with regard to race and gender: they all believed that sexual and racial inferiority was self-evident, a design of nature. In the late

E

twentieth century, the belief in such difference is far from unanimous. The conflicting views among the scientists themselves highlights the social conflict over racial equality and the roles of women and men in our culture. The socially contingent nature of scientific knowledge has been thrown into high relief. As a result, philosophers and sociologists of science are now actively engaged in attempts to redefine scientific objectivity so that its social component becomes recognizable.

BIBLIOGRAPHY

Fausto-Sterling, Anne. *Myths of Gender: Biological Theories About Women and Men.* 2d ed. New York: Basic Books, 1992.

———. *Sexing the Body: Gender politics and the construction of sexuality.* New York: Basic Books, 1999.

Gardner, Howard. *Frames of Mind: The Theory of Multiple Intelligences.* New York: Basic Books, 1983.

Gould, Stephen Jay. *The Mismeasure of Man.* New York: Norton, 1981.

Haraway, Donna. *Primate Visions: Gender, Race and Nature in the World of Modern Science.* New York: Routledge, 1989.

Harding, Sandra. *Whose Science? Whose Knowledge? Thinking from Women's Lives.* Ithaca, NY: Cornell University Press, 1991.

Kessler, Suzanne. *Lessons from the Intersexed.* New Brunswick: Rutgers University Press, 1998.

Kevles, Daniel J. *In the Name of Eugenics: Genetics and the Uses of Human Heredity.* New York: Knopf, 1985.

Marks, Jonathan. *Human Biodiversity: genes, race and history.* New York: Aldine de Gruyter, 1994.

Mensh, Elaine, and Harry Mensh. *The IQ Mythology: Class, Race, Gender, and Inequality.* Carbondale: Southern Illinois University, 1991.

Russett, Cynthia Eagle. *Sexual Science: The Victorian Construction of Womanhood.* Cambridge, MA: Harvard University Press, 1989.

Anne Fausto-Sterling

SEE ALSO
Gender—in Science; Women in Science

Eugenics

A social movement whose champions claim that controlled breeding can lead to the breeding of a better race. There were advocates of eugenics in nineteenth-century America, especially John Humphrey Noyes at his Oneida Community in New York State in the 1850s, who advocated plural marriage within his community (each man was married to every woman and vice versa) and selective breeding via the then-best-known methods of science, which meant assuming that Lamarckian notions of use inheritance would guarantee proper inheritance.

The English gentleman Francis Galton founded the modern eugenics movement. He published several studies, including *Hereditary Genius* (1869), in which he argued, by following pedigrees of famous men, that their mental abilities were inherited. Through use of then-available statistical concepts, he argued that mental abilities followed the Gaussian bell-shaped probability curve of distribution, with persons of average ability bunched in the middle, those with high abilities toward the top, and so on. If Galton believed that a man's social status or reputation indicated his innate merit, he also embraced the fundamental assumption of the Western social sciences—that there was no such thing as a free individual because all individuals existed only as members of predefined groups. Here were the underlying assumptions of the modern eugenics movement, whether in Britain or the United States or any other modern Western culture, including National Socialist Germany. By 1900, Galton's protégé, Karl Pearson, had founded the science of *biometrics,* or the study of the inheritance and variation of biological traits in species and individuals belonging to subgroups. The "rediscovery" of Mendel's laws of inheritance placed biometrics and the English eugenics movement in something of a shadow as compared with the American one, with its Mendelian scientific discourse, but both movements achieved common political and public policy objectives. Most eugenists were nationalistic, conservative, and racist, although some were not.

How significant or influential the American eugenics movement has been is arguable. Allegedly, its clearest success has been with encouraging enactment of sterilization laws, starting with Indiana in 1907, and including another fifteen Northern and Middle Western states by 1917; by 1931, thirty states, including many in the South, had enacted such laws, and the pioneering states had revised their earlier laws to be less punitive in character, and of these, twenty-seven kept their laws on the books. In the early 1930s, some 12,145 sterilizations had been performed in the United States, 7,548 in California alone; almost thirty years later, the total legal sterilizations had ballooned to 60,926, with the most in California, 20,011. And the enactment of the National Origins Act of 1925, with its racist quotas for United States immigration admissions, has often been seen by historians as another coup for the American eugenics movement. Even more problematic has been the assertion by some that the eugenics movement lives on the modern post–World War II population control movement. Historians of biology, in particular, have attributed these successes to the American eugenics movement, often without any real knowledge or understanding of the history of American politics and public policy. It remains unclear as to the eugenics movement's actual influence in getting sterilization and immigration laws enacted and enforced. What reliable secondary accounts we do have cast great doubt on such claims. And while there may be some individuals who were committed to eugenics before World War II and population control thereafter, that is not evidence that there was a relationship between the two movements. Indeed, it is unclear whether the modern American Mendelian-inspired eugenics movement was at all significant beyond its small circle of (chiefly) biologists and psychologists. It may be the case, however, that the idea of breeding a better race and a popular eugenics movement that included health educators and faddists, women's clubs activists, Sunday school teachers, and town sages had a more considerable influence, and that its leaders and followers appropriated the Mendelian scientific discourse away from the formal eugenics movement and used it for their own purposes. Only further investigation will determine that.

BIBLIOGRAPHY

Cravens, Hamilton. *The Triumph of Evolution: The Heredity-Environment Controversy, 1900–1941.* 1978. Reprint Baltimore: Johns Hopkins University Press, 1988.

Haller, Mark H. *Eugenics: Hereditarian Attitudes in American Thought.* 1963. Reprint New Brunswick: Rutgers University Press, 1984.

Kevles, Daniel J. *In the Name of Eugenics: Genetics and the Uses of Human Heredity.* New York: Knopf, 1985.

Ludmerer, Kenneth M. *Genetics and American Society: A Historical Appraisal.* Baltimore: Johns Hopkins University Press, 1972.

Hamilton Cravens

SEE ALSO
Heredity and Environment

Evolution and Darwinism

Charles Darwin's *The Origin of Species,* published in the fall of 1859, reached American readers in late December. Before this date, Americans had been debating whether human races had a single origin (monogenism) or were created separately (polygenism). Although Darwin did not address the evolution of humans in the *The Origin of Species,* the debate over monogenism versus polygenism influenced the response to Darwin's work.

Scientific debate was most vigorous in the Boston intellectual community. Asa Gray, botanist at Harvard University, was committed to serve as Darwin's champion even before the publication of *The Origin of Species.* His defense of Darwin focused on the compatibility of Darwinism with religious belief. Gray arranged for the publication of an American edition of the *Origin,* with a new historical preface, in the spring of 1860.

Leading the opposition was Louis Agassiz, whose scientific ideas had been used earlier to bolster the argument for polygenism. Agassiz ridiculed the idea of the bestial origins of humans. At the Boston Society of Natural History, he debated Darwinism with William Barton Rogers. Discussion focused on the interpretation of the fossil record; it was generally thought that Rogers emerged victorious. The crisis atmosphere in science soon dissipated, however; the controversy over Darwinism was overshadowed by the Civil War.

Apart from the Boston debates, American naturalists were at first indifferent to Darwinism, but in the 1860s and 1870s they began gradually to incorporate evolutionary arguments into their work. David Starr Jordan, a prominent Darwinian, explained his own conversion to evolution as resulting not so much from reading Darwin's book as from his growing recognition that the evidence in favor of evolution was compelling. He credited the influence of Louis Agassiz in facilitating this conversion, for Agassiz, despite his lifelong opposition to evolution, emphasized careful observation and taught his students to think for themselves. Most of Agassiz's students became evolutionists, as did his own son, Alexander Agassiz. By 1870, Darwin's theory was praised as one of the great intellectual achievements of the century, with ramifications in every area of study.

After Agassiz's death in 1873, Gray, following a long silence, returned to his defense of Darwinism. By this time, his arguments for the compatibility of science and religion did not speak to the main concerns of younger naturalists, who for the most part found no difficulty in marrying evolution to their Protestant beliefs. Their concerns were to work out the scientific

E

implications of Darwin's views and to gather further evidence of evolution from studies of fossils, geographical distribution, and ecology. Like Agassiz, Darwin's example inspired the younger generation to study biology.

Having arrived at an understanding of evolution through diverse areas of scientific research, these naturalists did not adopt Darwin's exact views about the mechanisms of evolution. They did not always agree that natural selection was the main mechanism of adaptive change. Other theories, notably the neo-Lamarckian theory of the inheritance of acquired characteristics, were explored as alternative mechanisms. Americans built on Darwin's later work, particularly his studies of variation, and also followed with interest the work of British and European naturalists such as Alfred Russel Wallace, Ernst Haeckel, and August Weismann. The evolutionary philosopher Herbert Spencer, in vogue during the 1870s and 1880s, also influenced how biologists thought about the natural world.

By the 1890s, Americans were wary of philosophical attempts to achieve a unified worldview through evolutionary theory, and questioned the more speculative features of neo-Darwinian science. They preferred to concentrate on specific problems that could be answered in experimental and field research. Research focused on the study of variation and inheritance and its connections to the study of regeneration and development, a connection that Darwin had recognized. Field naturalists concentrated on the nature of adaptation, the role of isolation in speciation, and the fossil record. A few naturalists grasped the radical significance of Darwin's work for biology. William Keith Brooks, for instance, understood that Darwin's work implied a new species concept. The idea that there was a real species "type" or essence was no longer valid; species were simply populations of individuals related to each other in certain ways. This new species concept was not universally recognized and would be reiterated as a foundation of Darwinism later in the 1940s.

Around 1900, two European theories cast doubt on the Darwinian concept of evolution by slow, gradual processes. The mutation theory of Hugo de Vries and the revival of Gregor Mendel's studies of heredity both focused scientists' attention on the abrupt appearance of new variations. According to de Vries, such mutations could explain the origin of new species in a single generation. Botanists were particularly attracted to the mutation theory and began intensive research investigations to probe the mechanisms behind these mutations. The

theory was attractive because it held out the promise of controlling the process of evolution by experimental means, if the causes of mutations could be discovered. Both botanists and zoologists also embraced the new Mendelism, which represented a major advance in the study of inheritance through breeding experiments.

In universities, agricultural stations, and in various research communities, experimental studies of evolution got underway. Two of the most active research communities were the Marine Biological Laboratory at Woods Hole, Massachusetts, and the Station for Experimental Evolution established by the Carnegie Institution of Washington at Cold Spring Harbor, New York. The traditional focus on morphology, the study of form, shifted as a result of the new emphasis on experiments. The two new sciences of genetics and ecology that emerged at this time represented different ways of synthesizing morphology and physiology in the study of evolutionary problems. American scientists made rapid advances in the understanding of genetic mechanisms, including identification of the X and Y chromosomes as sex determinants. Thomas Hunt Morgan's group of geneticists at Columbia University demonstrated the chromosomal basis of inheritance by the middle of the first decade of the twentieth century, successfully synthesizing Mendelian genetics and cytology. Concurrently with the spread of Mendelism, some biologists became involved in the eugenics movement, which sought to apply elementary genetic principles to humans, with the goal of improving the human stock in much the same way that animal breeders improved livestock.

By 1930, de Vries's mutation theory was long discredited, while Mendelian genetics revealed an increasingly more complex picture of the genome. Biologists argued that it was time to reassess Darwinian theory in the light of new research in genetics, including both experimental genetics and theoretical population genetics. The period between the mid-1930s and mid-1950s saw the publication of a number of Darwinian treatises that integrated field and experimental studies, and brought Darwinism into line with genetics. The first of these treatises was *Genetics and the Origin of Species* (1937) by Theodosius Dobzhansky. He was trained in Russia as a naturalist, came to the United States in 1927 to work with T.H. Morgan, and stayed in America for the rest of his life. He synthesized the field naturalist tradition and experimental genetics.

Dobzhansky was deeply influenced by Sewall Wright, a geneticist who pioneered the mathematical analysis of evolution at the population level. In addition to his mathematical contributions, Wright introduced the metaphor of the "adaptive landscape" as a way of depicting how natural selection caused populations to become better adapted or to go extinct. Wright's idea of visualizing evolution as a dynamic process of change across a shifting adaptive landscape caught on quickly and became a standard way of analyzing the evolutionary process.

Other important Darwinian treatises published in the United States included Ernst Mayr's *Systematics and the Origin of Species* (1942), George Gaylord Simpson's *Tempo and Mode in Evolution* (1944), and George Ledyard Stebbins's *Variation and Evolution in Plants* (1950). These works, along with European and British research, laid the basis for what came to be called the "modern synthesis" in evolutionary biology. This term stood for the synthesis of genetics and the natural history disciplines, a return to a stricter Darwinism than had prevailed in the early twentieth century, and the complete rejection of Lamarckian explanations or any explanation that postulated some form of inner directing force.

The modern synthesis helped to unify those branches of biology that were connected through genetics. The sense of unified purpose that evolutionary biologists felt by the 1950s was enhanced by the establishment of new scientific societies and new journals devoted to the causes of evolution. The status of the natural history disciplines was enhanced as a result of this synthesis, but naturalists also tried to ensure that their fields were not seen to be subservient to genetics. Some continuing tensions between experimental and field sciences were reflected in discussions about strategic alliances, for instance, whether paleontology should be included in the new Society for the Study of Evolution, founded in 1946.

Scientists saw the modern synthesis as defined by major conceptual breakthroughs. Ernst Mayr emphasized the importance of adopting a "population" concept of the species instead of the older "typological" view, which regarded species as uniform types rather than as populations of genetically unique individuals. Although the new species concept had been grasped by some earlier naturalists, it was not widely recognized until championed by the architects of the modern synthesis. Mayr also stressed the growing depth of scientific knowledge and the better definition of key concepts (such as mutation, genotype, and phenotype), which helped scientists to communicate across disciplines.

By the late 1950s, the synthesis was extending beyond the life sciences to include the human sciences and the inorganic sciences concerned with the origins of life. Scientists from these three areas were brought together for joint discussion at a symposium convened at the University of Chicago in 1959 to commemorate the centennial of the publication of *The Origin of Species*. The conference received wide coverage on radio and television. One of the main themes to emerge was the closer relationship that was developing between biology and anthropology, as biologists became interested in the study of social behavior and anthropologists became interested in evolution.

The postwar years also saw the expansion of mathematical approaches to the study of evolution, with population geneticists deriding descriptive and historical studies as examples of an outmoded style of research. At the same time molecular biology was emerging as a mixed blessing to Darwinian science. While the growth of molecular biology brought major advances in the study of the genetic mechanisms underlying evolution, the rapid rise of this new science had a negative impact on the natural history disciplines within American universities. Edward Osborne Wilson, evolutionary biologist at Harvard University, responded in the mid-1970s by drawing together the mathematical approaches of population genetics and population ecology and the field traditions in ethology to create a new synthesis, which he called "sociobiology." Wilson intended to inaugurate a new era of Darwinian science that focused on the evolution of social behavior and, in the process, challenged the autonomy of the social sciences. Sociobiology was controversial to the extent that it included human social behavior within its biological framework. But it boosted the study of the biological basis of behavior, with particular attention to behaviors associated with sex, aggression, altruism, and communication, and revived interest in sexual selection, a Darwinian idea that scientists had earlier rejected or neglected.

A series of controversies from the 1960s to the 1980s challenged some of the orthodoxies of the modern synthesis. Systematists had been arguing from the 1960s about how to depict revolutionary relations in a classification system. One new approach, dubbed "cladistics," attempted to base classification on the principle of phylogeny. When some American scientists, convinced of the logic and practicality of cladistics, started to use the new method in the 1970s,

E

intense controversy erupted. At issue was the reputation of taxonomy as a vibrant evolutionary science rather than a backwater of biology.

Related to the dispute over cladistics was the controversy caused by a new model of evolutionary change known as the "punctuational model" or theory of punctuated equilibrium. This model was proposed first by American paleontologist Niles Eldredge and then promoted and extended by other scientists. The punctuational view was that speciation most often involved not slow and gradual changes over a long period of time but rather rapid speciation events in small populations. Although the new model was compatible with ideas expressed by the architects of the modern synthesis, in general it was seen as a challenge to entrenched ideas about gradual evolution. The punctuational model was also controversial because it was applied to human evolution, suggesting the abrupt appearance of modern humans rather than gradual directional change. In general, the field of human evolution has been embroiled in perpetual controversy, in part because of the paucity of the fossil record.

Another debate involved the revival of catastrophism in the early 1980s, when physicist Luis Alvarez and a group of scientists in California suggested that mass extinctions, in particular the extinction of dinosaurs, could be the result of asteroid impacts and their effects. Alvarez's theory generated a tide of scientific publications and received enormous popular attention.

While these debates unfolded, a better understanding of the evolutionary significance of macromolecules was being gained and molecular biologists and evolutionists opened up lines of communication between their disciplines. In addition, new illustrations of evolutionary changes in the short term were coming to light, many of them consequences of human activities, such as pesticide use. Ecologists began to pay more attention to evolutionary processes and more readily incorporated genetics and molecular biology into their studies. But they also argued that environmental crises required more support for field research or the creation of a "new natural history," which would entail detailed studies of ecology and evolution in particular locations. The study of evolution acquired new urgency in the light of concerns about loss of biological diversity worldwide.

Darwinian science has had a long and vigorous history in the United States. Most historical research has focused on the immediate reception of *The Origin of Species,* the development of genetics and Mendelism,

and the emergence of the modern synthesis. Relatively little attention has been given to neo-Darwinism in the late nineteenth century and the eclectic research period in the early twentieth century, prior to the modern synthesis. In the mid-twentieth century, unorthodox individuals and lines of research that were not part of the modern synthesis have not received much attention. The recent developments in evolutionary science since the 1950s have not been given sustained historical analysis, although philosophers of science have analyzed various aspects of modern evolutionary biology in depth. A particularly rich collection of scientists' papers, with special strengths in the history of genetics and the history of molecular biology, is at the American Philosophical Society in Philadelphia.

BIBLIOGRAPHY

Bowler, Peter J. *The Eclipse of Darwinism: Anti-Darwinian Evolution Theories in the Decades around 1900.* Baltimore and London: Johns Hopkins University Press, 1983.

Dobzhansky, Theodosius. *Genetics and the Origin of Species.* New York: Columbia University Press, 1937; reprinted, 1982.

Glen, William, ed. *The Mass-Extinction Debates: How Science Works in a Crisis.* Stanford: Stanford University Press, 1994.

Kitcher, Philip. *Vaulting Ambition: Sociobiology and the Quest for Human Nature.* Cambridge, MA: MIT Press, 1985.

Lewin, Roger. *Bones of Contention: Controversies in the Search for Human Origins.* New York: Simon and Schuster, 1987.

Mayr, Ernst. *Systematics and the Origin of Species.* New York: Columbia University Press, 1942; reprinted, 1982.

Pfeiffer, Edward J. "United States." In *The Comparative Reception of Darwinism,* edited by Thomas F. Glick. Austin and London: University of Texas Press, 1972, pp. 168–206.

Simpson, George Gaylord. *Tempo and Mode in Evolution.* New York: Columbia University Press, 1944; rev. ed., 1984.

Smocovitis, Vassiliki Betty. *Unifying Biology: The Evolutionary Synthesis and Evolutionary Biology.* Princeton: Princeton University Press, 1996.

Somit, Albert, and Steven A. Peterson, eds. *The Dynamics of Evolution: The Punctuated Equilibrium Debate in the Natural and Social Sciences.* Ithaca, NY and London: Cornell University Press, 1989.

Stanton, William. *The Leopard's Spots: Scientific Attitudes toward Race in America, 1815–59.* Chicago and London: University of Chicago Press, 1960.

Stebbins, George Ledyard. *Variation and Evolution in Plants.* New York: Columbia University Press, 1950.

Tax, Sol, and Charles Callender, eds. *Evolution after Darwin: Issues in Evolution.* 3 vols. Chicago: University of Chicago Press, 1960.

Sharon Kingsland

SEE ALSO
Neo-Lamarckism; Social Darwinism

Exploring Expedition, United States, to the South Seas

See Wilkes Expedition

Extraterrestrial Life

Life beyond the earth, either in our own solar system or in planetary systems that may surround other stars. It is not known whether such life exists, but the concept has been the subject of intense speculation and study since the ancient Greeks. The idea reached new heights of speculation in the late nineteenth century when Percival Lowell claimed to have mapped canals on Mars, and argued they were constructed by intelligent beings for irrigation purposes. This controversy engaged many prominent scientists and was largely ended by 1909, when the French astronomer Eugene M. Antoniadi claimed to have resolved many of the canals into dark spots. Spacecraft later showed that the canals were largely illusory. After the downfall of the canals, it was widely believed, based on temperature conditions, seasonal variations in surface markings, and (by 1957) even spectroscopic evidence, that primitive forms of vegetation existed on Mars. The *Viking* spacecraft in 1976, however, showed the complete absence of organic molecules on Mars, thus precluding life. Twenty years later, National Aeronautics and Space Administration scientists announced possible fossil life in a Martian meteorite, a claim that still remains controversial. In the same year (1996), the Galileo spacecraft returned strong evidence of a possible ocean beneath the icy surface of the Jovian satellite Europa, further fueling speculation of life. At the end of the century, therefore, the possibility of life beyond Earth in our own planetary system still remains, although at a more primitive level.

With the revival of the nebular hypothesis in the mid-1940s, planetary systems were believed to be common, and a new phase of the debate began in the early 1960s when Peter van de Kamp announced that he had detected a planetary system around Barnard's star. Only in 1995, however, was a planet confirmed circling a Sun-like star, and more than twenty extrasolar planets are now known, all gas giants. Meanwhile, in 1960 Frank Drake began the first Search for Extraterrestrial Intelligence (SETI), using radio telescope technology to detect an intelligent signal from an extraterrestrial civilization. More than fifty such searches have been carried out in subsequent years; the largest today are projects Phoenix, SERENDIP and BETA, all centered in the United States. Such programs make many assumptions, from the frequency of planetary systems, to the origin and evolution of life, the evolution of intelligence and technology, and the lifetimes of civilizations. The subject of extraterrestrial life has been widely accepted in popular culture, where it is a prominent theme of science-fiction literature and film, and a favored hypothesis for the phenomenon of unidentified flying objects (UFOs).

Historians have only recently begun to deal with the myriads of issues involved in the extraterrestrial life debate. The central issues include the relative roles of philosophical ideas as opposed to more purely scientific components; the rise of a new discipline known as exobiology, bioastronomy, or astrobiology; the rules of evidence and inference when the observations are at the limits of science; and the role of the debate in the search for humanity's place in the universe. While philosophical and religious issues clearly play their part, the debate has also been shown to be closely tied to scientific and empirical traditions; any conclusions must take into account the evolving nature of science. The debate may also be seen as an evolution in cosmological ideas from the purely physical world to a biological universe.

BIBLIOGRAPHY
Crowe, Michael J. *The Extraterrestrial Life Debate 1750–1900: The Idea of a Plurality of Worlds from Kant to Lowell.* Cambridge U.K.: Cambridge University Press, 1986.
Dick, Steven J. *Plurality of Worlds: The Origins of the Extraterrestrial Life Debate from Democritus to Kant.* Cambridge, U.K.: Cambridge University Press, 1982.
———. *The Biological Universe: The Twentieth Century Extraterrestrial Life Debate and the Limits of Science.* Cambridge, U.K.: Cambridge University Press, 1996.
———. *Life on Other Worlds: The Twentieth Century Extraterrestrial Life Debate.* Cambridge, U.K.: Cambridge University Press, 1998.
Guthke, Karl S. *The Last Frontier: Imagining Other Worlds, from the Copernican Revolution to Modern Science Fiction.* Ithaca, NY: Cornell University Press, 1990.

Steven J. Dick

SEE ALSO
Unidentified Flying Objects

F

Fairchild, David Grandison (1869–1954)

Botanist, agricultural explorer and organizer of the United States Office of Plant Introduction, and author of books on tropical horticulture. David Fairchild was born in Lansing, Michigan, where his father was a professor of literature. His grandfather, Grandison Fairchild, was one of the founders of Oberlin College. His father became president of Kansas State College of Agriculture, where David Fairchild received his B.A. in 1888. He went on to do graduate work in botany at Iowa State College of Agriculture and at Rutgers University, studying mycology and plant pathology. He joined the United States Department of Agriculture (USDA), Department of Plant Pathology in 1889 in Washington, D.C. He worked at the Geneva, New York, State Agricultural Experiment Station in the summers of 1891 and 1892 studying grape diseases and helping to develop Bordeaux mixture. He received a master's degree from Kansas State in 1893.

Fairchild became a plant explorer after meeting Barbour Lathrop in 1893 on a ship en route to Naples Zoological Station. Fairchild was the first representative of the Smithsonian Institution to be awarded the use of a research table at Naples, where he worked on a marine alga. Lathrop financed Fairchild on a botanical expedition to Java and the Buitenzorg Botanical Gardens there in 1895 and 1896. Fairchild had studied tropical flora, bacteriology, and fungi for two years in Bonn, Berlin, and Breslau in preparation for this expedition. While at Bonn, he invented Fairchild's porcelain washing thimble, which was used for fifty years. Following his stay in Java, where his research showed that termites cultivate mushrooms, Fairchild traveled

with Lathrop in 1896 and 1897. They collected live plants and seeds throughout the tropics, including Australia, New Zealand, New Guinea, China, Japan, Africa, and South America. Fairchild was given an interim appointment at the USDA Department of Forestry in 1897 and appointed chief of the new Section of Seed and Plant Introduction, USDA, in 1898. He introduced many plants into the United States, starting with a small garden near Miami.

As special investigator (1898) and later as agricultural explorer (1903) for the USDA, he resumed his travels with Lathrop and sent out other plant explorers for the agency. Among the new plants he introduced were avocado, broccoli, pomegranates, dates, bamboo, Japanese cherry trees, and importantly, the soybean, which he introduced from Japan in 1898. Other examples he cited include an alfalfa variety from Peru (1899), a variety of sorghum introduced from the Sudan (1901), many varieties of dates from Egypt (1901), mangoes from India (1902), and the nectarine from Pakistan (1902). Agricultural and horticultural species and varieties were not only imported but rigorously tested for performance in various parts of the United States. Fairchild later headed the Office of Cereal Investigation.

Fairchild married Marian Bell, the daughter of Alexander Graham Bell, in 1905; she traveled with and assisted him. After World War I, Miami's Chapman Field, a desolate air-training field was transferred to the USDA. Fairchild transformed 200 acres into the United States Introduction Garden, introducing hundreds of tree species and varieties. Plant Introduction Gardens were later established under his direction in six states.

F

Fairchild made further expeditions as scientific leader of the Allison V. Armour expeditions on a former cargo vessel equipped with laboratory, library, and seed-drying equipment. Coastal regions of Africa, Norway, Mexico, the Canary and Balearic Islands were explored from 1925 to 1927 and in 1930 and 1932. In 1940, he carried out a Fairchild Garden scientific expedition to the Molukka Islands, the Celebes, and Bali, interrupted when the (then) Dutch East Indies ports were closed during World War II.

Fairchild Tropical Gardens outside Miami was named in his honor and formally dedicated in 1938. The garden became the largest botanical garden in the United States, with special collections of palms, cycads, and orchids and an important botanical library.

BIBLIOGRAPHY

Fairchild, David G. *Systematic Plant Introduction.* Washington, DC: Government Printing Office, 1898.
————. *Exploring for Plants.* New York: Macmillan, 1930.
————. *The World Was My Garden.* New York: Scribner's, 1938.
————. *Garden Islands of the Great East.* New York: Scribner's, 1944.
"Fairchild, Dr. David (Grandison)." *American Men of Science* (1944): 745.
"Fairchild, David (Grandison)." *Current Biography.* (1953): 190–193.
Huttleson, Donald G. "Eight Famous Plant Explorers." *Plants and Gardens* 8 (1952): 314.
Kay, Elizabeth D. "David Fairchild—A Recollection." *Huntia* 1 (1964): 71–78.
Lawrence, George H.N. "A Bibliography of the Writings of David Fairchild." *Huntia* 1 (1964): 79–102.
Obituary. *New York Times,* 7 August 1954.

Nancy G. Slack

Farrar, John (1779–1853)

Educator and physicist. A graduate of Harvard (1803), Farrar joined the faculty of Harvard in 1805. He became the Hollis Professor of natural philosophy and mathematics in 1807 after Nathaniel Bowditch turned down the chair vacated by Samuel Webber when Webber assumed the Harvard University presidency. He taught until 1836, when he resigned the post due to ill health.

Farrar made few contributions to the scientific literature. He is best known for his translations of French textbooks that introduced the Leibnitzian or Continental notation in mathematics to a generation of American students.

Farrar is typical of the American liberal arts college professor of the antebellum period. It was from a professor like Farrar that most students had their only formal science instruction. Their view of natural philosophy owes much to him.

BIBLIOGRAPHY

Greene, John C. *American Science in the Age of Jefferson.* Ames: Iowa State University Press, 1984.
Hindle, Brook. "Farrar, John." *Dictionary of Scientific Biography.* Edited by Charles C. Gillispie. New York: Scribners, 1971, 4:546–547.
Smith, David Eugene. "Farrar, John." *Dictionary of American Biography.* Edited by Allen Johnson and Dumas Malone. New York: Scribners, 1931, 6:292–293.

James W. Montgomery Jr.

Federal Government, Science and

Science and politics have been intertwined since the early days of the Republic. The history of science-government relations in the United States can be divided into three periods, each reflecting general trends in the American political economy. Between the 1780s and the late 1860s, federal support of science was generally ad hoc, with little in the way of permanent institutional arrangements. As long as the federal government itself was relatively small and weak, public sponsorship of science was similarly weak, although the growing complexity of the national economy by the 1830s and 1840s also spurred the beginnings of professionalization in science. From the 1870s to 1940, the creation of a federal science establishment in permanent government agencies accompanied the general growth of the federal government and the shift in state power away from Congress-based patronage to expanded executive power and the rise of an administrative state. These agencies conducted scientific research to meet a variety of economic and social needs, but federal support of science outside government departments was relatively rare. This situation changed radically as a result of World War II. The importance of science and technology to the war effort and the rise of the Cold War between the United States and the Soviet Union created a system of university-industry-military cooperation, a system which has only recently begun to break down due to the end of the Cold War.

The Constitution sanctioned a federal role for science through the patent clause, which called upon Congress "to promote the progress of science and the useful arts" by guaranteeing intellectual property rights to inventors; the power to coin money and establish standards for weights and measures; the power to expand the nation's territory; and the power to establish post roads, later interpreted as a general mandate to promote internal improvements. Given these priorities, federal support for science, not surprisingly, was generally linked directly to commerce, territorial expansion, and military needs. West Point, for example, was established in 1802 as an engineering school, following the French model of the École Polytechnique. In addition to training military officers, West Point also trained civilian engineers who provided critical expertise for the building of roads and canals in the early 1800s. Projects such as the Erie Canal, completed in 1825, provided the transportation infrastructure which aided the development of a national market economy in the United States. By the 1830s, army engineers also undertook surveying for the first railroads.

Exploration in the nineteenth century also served territorial expansion, commerce, and military needs. During his presidency, Thomas Jefferson envisioned the eventual control of all of North America by the United States. The 1803 Louisiana Purchase and subsequent expeditions such as the Lewis and Clark Expedition of 1804–1806 were meant to shore up the nation's military and diplomatic position, document available natural resources, and pave the way for future westward expansion. Later surveys, such as the United States Exploring Expedition, authorized in 1836; land surveys conducted by David Dale Owen under the auspices of the General Land Office during the 1830s and 1840s; and continued Army exploration of the trans-Mississippi west in the 1840s and 1850s, especially during the Mexican War, served similar needs. Scientific expertise in a wide range of fields, including geology, hydrography, meteorology, astronomy, botany, zoology, and anthropology, was an essential part of these expeditions.

Despite such activities, however, scientific research lacked a permanent institutional base in the first decades of the Republic. West Point notwithstanding, the failure to establish permanent bureaus underscored what historian A. Hunter Dupree once referred to as "the almost complete bankruptcy of science in the government in 1829" (Dupree, p. 43). A political order based on states' rights and decentralized government provided a counterweight against the growth of federal power fueled by the quest for empire. By the 1840s, however, a formalized structure for government science began to develop in the United States. In 1825, President Adams had called for the creation of a national observatory, and during the 1830s, the navy quietly began to gather material resources for astronomical observation to aid navigation. In 1842, Lieutenant James Gilliss convinced Congress to appropriate funds for the building of the Naval Observatory. In 1846, Congress established the Smithsonian Institution, and Joseph Henry, the nation's most eminent scientist, became its first director. The Coast Survey, originally established in 1807, had succumbed to congressional negligence and lack of leadership, but it was revived when Alexander Dallas Bache took over in 1843. Territorial expansion into Texas, California, and Oregon boosted the need for coastal studies, and the Coast Survey engaged in extensive studies in astronomy, topography, hydrography, terrestrial magnetism, and natural history in the Gulf and Pacific regions, as well as along the Atlantic seaboard. By the 1850s, the Coast Survey was by far the largest agency for scientific research in the nation, employing twice as many scientific personnel as the Naval Observatory and Smithsonian Institution put together, possessing annual budgets that approached a half million dollars.

Since World War II, people have tended to identify war with weapons development, but the Civil War resulted in little new weapons technology. As members of the Navy Department's Permanent Commission, Bache, Henry, and Charles Henry Davis evaluated inventors' proposals, fanciful and serious alike, but no significant technologies emerged. Several important organizational developments took place during the war, however. The passage of the Morrill Act in 1862 granted public land to endow colleges "for the benefit of agriculture and the mechanic arts" and encouraged the spread of scientific training in American universities. The creation of the Department of Agriculture, also in 1862, laid the groundwork for what would later replace the Coast Survey as the largest scientific enterprise in government. Although not very active in its early years, the chartering of the National Academy of Sciences in 1863 created an honorary scientific organization with a formally stated purpose to provide advice to the government.

The period between 1870 and 1920 was a time of significant change in which the federal government was

F

transformed from a system in which bureaucracies existed primarily as means for Congress to dispense patronage, to an administrative state with expanded executive power and professionalized government agencies. During this period, the federal scientific establishment grew rapidly. Individual states began to fund agricultural experiment stations in the 1870s; the 1887 Hatch Act added federal subsidies which constituted "the first significant federal research aid to states and universities" (Bruce, p. 317). Within the Department of Agriculture, research divisions gained power as scientific developments and increased regulatory functions on the part of the federal government proved mutually reinforcing. For example, the rise of the germ theory provided the Bureau of Animal Industry (created in 1884) the scientific capability to identify the causes of certain communicable animal diseases, such as pleuropneumonia and cattle fever in livestock, while the regulatory state gave the bureau the power to order the destruction of infected animals. In 1890 and 1891, Congress passed legislation granting the Bureau of Animal Industry the power to inspect meat for export in order to meet European objections and open foreign markets to American meat exports. During the Progressive Era, the regulatory function of the Department of Agriculture ballooned. In the early 1900s, the Bureau of Chemistry gained broad authority to inspect food imports. After the publication of *The Jungle*, by Upton Sinclair, Congress granted the secretary of agriculture both the authority and ample funds to inspect meat and meat-packing plants in the United States and to remove from the marketplace goods which did not meet quality standards. Similarly, passage of the 1906 Food and Drug Act gave the Bureau of Chemistry a mission to determine the purity of food and drugs in order to protect the public health and safety.

Public health concerns spurred the creation of other bureaus. The federal medical bureaucracy grew out of the Army Medical Corps, but by the 1890s, the Marine Hospital Service began to address civilian public health needs related to communicable diseases. In addition to research into the causes of disease and responsibility for the interstate control of the spread of disease during outbreaks, the Public Health Service, like the Department of Agriculture, also performed regulatory functions. The 1902 Biologics Control Act empowered the Public Health and Marine Hospital Service (reorganized as the Public Health Service a decade later) to inspect companies engaged in the manufacture of antitoxins and vaccines.

Additional bureaus were added to the federal science establishment in the early 1900s. The establishment of the National Bureau of Standards in 1901 created a powerful organization to set standards, test and calibrate precision instruments, solve problems related to standards, and conduct basic research concerning the determination of physical constants and properties of materials. Accurate standards were necessary to ensure the functioning of the increasingly complex system of commerce and industry in the twentieth century. Under Presidents McKinley and Theodore Roosevelt, conservation and scientific management of natural resources also became a federal responsibility. As head of the Division of Forestry in the Department of Agriculture (later renamed the Forest Service), Gifford Pinchot implemented a policy of business-government cooperation based on the application of scientific principles to promote the long-range development and use of forest resources.

Historian Robert V. Bruce has pointed out that in the nineteenth century, American science was strong in "data gathering, measuring, experimenting, and instrumentation" (Bruce, p. 352), but with a few exceptions such as Joseph Henry, and later, Josiah Willard Gibbs, American scientists contributed little compared to Europeans in terms of original theoretical discoveries or sophisticated experimentation. The federal science establishment created in the late nineteenth and early twentieth century was oriented toward solving problems related to economic, health, and public safety concerns and did not generally promote basic research or lend assistance to nongovernment laboratories. The primary impetus for fundamental scientific research in the late nineteenth and early twentieth century came not from the government science bureaucracy, but from research universities such as Johns Hopkins University, philanthropic support from organizations like the Rockefeller Foundation, and industrial laboratories at corporations like General Electric, DuPont, and Bell Telephone.

World War I posed organizational and technological challenges which led to the mobilization of science at unprecedented levels. Existing government agencies, the military, the newly created National Research Council (NRC) in the National Academy of Sciences, industry, and the universities cooperated on a wide variety of problems. At the outset of the war, the United States lacked sufficient sources of dyes, nitrates, and high-quality optical glass; by the end of the war, all could be manufactured in large quantities domestically. NRC, industry, navy, and academic scientists, in consultation with the Allies, worked on devices to detect German U-boats. The Bureau of Mines, and then the Army Chemical Warfare Service, conducted research in gas warfare with assistance from the universities, while industry put the deadly new weapon into production. Out in the field, the Gas Service, the Signal Corps, the Air Service, and the Corps of Engineers worked on flash- and sound-ranging systems and other technical problems. Although the United States demobilized quickly after World War I and a renewed conservatism insisting upon limited federal intervention in the economy prevailed in national politics, the blurring of lines between government, academia, and industry, and the coordination of research, development, and production during World War I provided a precedent for later developments in science-government relations.

The Great Depression hit American science hard. Between 1930 and 1933, industrial laboratories decreased their employment of scientific research personnel by over a third. At universities, senior faculty members took pay cuts, while junior faculty lost their jobs, and graduate students put off completing their degrees in order to hang on to their tenuous positions by culling together research assistantships, teaching assistantships, and any other work they could find. Nor did government scientists fare any better. In the Department of Agriculture, research funds fell almost 25 percent between 1932 and 1935. The National Bureau of Standards fared even worse, losing over half of its budget between 1931 and 1934.

Scientific leaders responded by appealing to the federal government to replace the failing system of support for research from the private sector. In July 1933, in response to contacts between NRC chairman Isaiah Bowman and Secretary of Agriculture Henry A. Wallace, President Franklin Roosevelt appointed a Science Advisory Board (SAB). Chaired by MIT president Karl T. Compton under the auspices of NRC, the SAB proposed a $16 million New Deal program, a "Recovery Program for Science Progress" to be administered under the National Industrial Recovery Act (NIRA). Compton attempted to link the program to NIRA's mandate for public works and unemployment relief by proposing to use the funds to directly employ scientists and engineers, and, through funding for fundamental scientific research, to improve public works and provide the foundation for new industries which would

help bring the nation out of the Depression. Compton's proposal quickly fell through when Secretary of the Interior Harold L. Ickes decided it lay outside NIRA's mandate. Federal funding for science rebounded somewhat by the mid-1930s, but the New Deal did not markedly change the relationship between science and government.

Major changes came with World War II. The war demanded even heavier mobilization of science than World War I had and resulted in permanent realignments in science-government relations. Taking new weapons technologies from the early stages of research to deployment in as little time as possible required extraordinary degrees of coordination between scientists, the military, and industry. Elite scientist administrators such as Vannevar Bush, director of the wartime Office of Scientific Research and Development (OSRD); James B. Conant and Karl Compton, members of the National Defense Research Committee; and J. Robert Oppenheimer, director of the atomic bomb project at Los Alamos dealt with military leaders on a regular basis and managed the application of research to wartime weapons and medical needs. The war ended the depression in American science, as scientists in all disciplines found jobs related to the war effort, and university departments engaged in military research enjoyed large research budgets won through government contracts. The Manhattan Project alone cost over $2.5 billion and employed about 10,000 scientists, engineers, and technicians, as well as thousands of other workers. Technologies such as radar and the proximity fuze proved crucial in the Allied victory, while the atomic bombings of Hiroshima and Nagasaki dramatically and tragically symbolized the destructive potential of science.

World War II set the tone for research in the physical sciences for the next forty-five years. The end of the war did not bring peace, but United States–Soviet conflict. Science as a means to military superiority was an integral part of both nations' Cold War strategy. In the United States by 1949, 96 percent of government-sponsored university research in the physical sciences came from defense dollars. The establishment of the National Science Foundation in 1950 barely made a dent in the proportion of military spending; in 1960, the Department of Defense and the Atomic Energy Commission (AEC) still accounted for 92 percent of federal support for physics research. Overall, by the late 1950s, 85 percent of federal R&D went to military

F

research—three-fourths of it to industry, and one-fourth to the universities.

The atomic bomb brought physicists and other scientists unprecedented political prominence. Before the war, they staffed and directed government laboratories, but they were not involved in high-level policy deliberations. After the war, scientists continued to serve on important government committees, such as the prestigious General Advisory Committee (GAC) of the AEC, and after *Sputnik,* the President's Science Advisory Committee, and they engaged in planning the application of science for defense needs. But prominence did not necessarily bring power. Scientists who opposed Cold War orthodoxy could find themselves frozen out of the policy process, especially in an era of red-baiting and loyalty investigations. In President Truman's decision to support crash development of the hydrogen bomb, for example, the General Advisory Committee, chaired by Oppenheimer, opposed the hydrogen bomb on both technical and ethical grounds. At a time when American military strategy was based on maintaining nuclear superiority above all else, the GAC position found little strong outside support, except from AEC chairman David E. Lilienthal. President Truman and other architects of the Cold War had no sympathy for the GAC's position, and in January 1950, Truman gave development of the hydrogen bomb top priority. The GAC never recovered its influence over high-level policy matters, and in 1954, after highly publicized hearings, Oppenheimer was stripped of his security clearance, primarily because of his opposition to the hydrogen bomb.

Oppenheimer's experience was exceptional. For the most part, scientists (including, to a great extent, Oppenheimer himself) reconciled themselves to and benefited from the postwar science-military alliance. The postwar influx of military funding in the physical sciences profoundly changed the social relations which governed research. Entire disciplines defined around military problems, students attending classified courses and writing classified research, and eminent scientists shuttling between their respective academic institutions and Washington all became an accepted part of American science in the postwar period.

The Vietnam War led some to challenge the prevailing military character of the postwar physical sciences. At universities across the nation, including the Masachusetts Institute of Technology (MIT) and Stanford University, two of the largest academic defense contractors in the nation, students protested on-campus military research and called for the creative redirection of research programs to civilian needs and pressing social problems. The protests led to the divestment of the Instrumentation Laboratory from MIT and the Stanford Research Institute from Stanford in 1970, but resulted in little long-term change. By the 1980s, under President Reagan's defense buildup, military R&D returned to pre–Vietnam War protest levels.

It took the end of the Cold War to provide what currently appears to be a long-term shift in the nature of federal support for science. By the early 1990s, both the defense industries and research universities felt the pinch of declining federal funds. By 1994, MIT feared defense cuts would lead to the halving of its basic research budget. What the post–Cold War organization of science will look like is not yet entirely clear. In 1994, President Clinton issued public statements calling for ample research funding as a means of building a robust high-technology economy, but he proposed no specific programs. The United States has never had a full-fledged, explicitly stated science and technology policy; from the beginning, federal support of science has been a manifestation of broader political trends. In the early Republic, a weak federal government meant relatively little government support for research. By the late nineteenth century, the growth of the administrative state led to the creation of a large federal infrastructure for science. World War II and the Cold War launched a half-century in which federal R&D meant military research. As America prepares for the twenty-first century, science-government relations will enter a new phase, perhaps tightly coupled to economic development. But at a time of strict budget control and lack of enthusiasm for expanded federal power, it is difficult to predict whether the United States will maintain large public expenditures for research in the absence of an overarching ideological rationale such as that provided by the Cold War.

BIBLIOGRAPHY

Bruce, Robert V. *The Launching of Modern American Science 1846–1876.* New York: Knopf, 1987.

Dupree, A. Hunter. *Science in the Federal Government: A History of Policies and Activities to 1940.* Cambridge, MA: Harvard University Press, 1957.

Greene, John C. *American Science in the Age of Jefferson.* Ames: Iowa State University Press, 1984.

Hays, Samuel P. *Conservation and the Gospel of Efficiency: The Progressive Conservation Movement 1890–1920.* Cambridge, MA: Harvard University Press, 1989.

Herken, Gregg. *Cardinal Choices: Presidential Science Advising from the Atomic Bomb to SDI.* New York and Oxford: Oxford University Press, 1992.

Kargon, Robert, and Elizabeth Hodes. "Karl Compton, Isaiah Bowman, and the Politics of Science in the Great Depression." *Isis* 76 (September 1985): 301–318.

Kevles, Daniel J. *The Physicists: The History of a Scientific Community in Modern America.* New York: Knopf, 1978; reprint Cambridge, MA: Harvard University Press, 1995.

Kuznick, Peter J. *Beyond the Laboratory: Scientists as Political Activists in 1930s America.* Chicago: University of Chicago Press, 1987.

Leslie, Stuart W. *The Cold War and American Science: The Military-Industrial-Academic Complex at MIT and Stanford.* New York: Columbia University Press, 1993.

Mendelsohn, Everett, Merritt Roe Smith, and Peter Weingart, eds. *Science, Technology, and the Military.* Vol. 1. Dordrecht: Kluwer Academic Publishers, 1988.

Sherwin, Martin J. *A World Destroyed: The Atomic Bomb and the Grand Alliance.* New York: Knopf, 1975.

Young, James Harvey. *Pure Food: Securing the Federal Food and Drugs Act of 1906.* Princeton: Princeton University Press, 1989.

Jessica Wang

Federation of American Scientists

Organization begun by some of the scientific participants in the Manhattan Project (the United States' World War II atomic bomb program) to lobby for civilian rather than military postwar control of atomic energy. These scientists feared that politicians, acting with a poor understanding of scientific fact and method, might make serious errors and commit the country to an unwise course. They formed first the Federation of Atomic Scientists and then the broader Federation of American Scientists to educate the public that there was no secret about and no defense against the atomic bomb. From late 1945 through 1947, the federation worked for international control of atomic weapons, sharing the fears of Niels Bohr and Albert Einstein of a disastrous arms race and the accompanying possibility of atomic warfare. Domestically, key members such as Eugene Rabinowitch, Leo Szilard, John A. Simpson, and William Higinbotham fought to secure passage of the 1946 McMahon Act establishing a civilian Atomic Energy Commission. Although less active after 1947, the organization has continued to speak out on public issues affecting scientists such as the Oppenheimer hearings and the 1968 debate over development of an antiballistic missile system.

The federation is an important case study of how government agencies are established and the ability of scientists to influence government policy. Historians differ in their assessment of the role the federation played in determining the postwar relationship between the federal government and science, but all agree it had a role. One aspect of this disagreement is whether the scientists acted as outsiders or insiders, as political naïfs or as shrewd assessors of the political situation. The attitude of the scientific community toward the federation raises another issue, the role in public affairs scientists see for themselves. The federation's position that scientists have a right, even an obligation, to speak out on public policy, but only where the scientific perspective is relevant, seems to exemplify the views of American scientists.

Historians interested in science and public affairs in the United States will find the Federation of American Scientists noteworthy. The standard reference by Smith treats with great sympathy the federation's efforts in the immediate postwar period, but no study exists of its subsequent activities.

BIBLIOGRAPHY

Smith, Alice Kimball. *A Peril and a Hope: The Scientists' Movement in America 1945–47.* Chicago: University of Chicago Press, 1965; reprint Cambridge, MA: MIT Press, 1971.

Strickland, Donald, *Scientists in Power; The Atomic Scientists' Movement 1945–1946.* Lafayette: Purdue University Studies, 1968.

Elizabeth Hodes

SEE ALSO
Bulletin of the Atomic Scientists

Fish and Wildlife Service, United States

Research and wildlife managment agency. The genesis of the present-day United States Fish and Wildlife Service properly begins with the appointment of Spencer Fullerton Baird (1823–1888) as assistant secretary of the Smithsonian Institution in 1846. From the beginning of his forty-two-year tenure with the Smithsonian, Baird championed federally sponsored research and collecting in natural history. From 1851, he attached young naturalists to the Pacific Railway Surveys, and, after the Civil War, to the various geological and geographic surveys of the terriories. In addition, a few men sent to Alaska under private auspices were given

F

support in the form of collecting equipment, supplies, publications, and encouragement, as were some employees of the Hudson's Bay Company in western Canada. Baird published massive compendia of available data concerning the species of North American birds, mammals, and other vertebrates beginning in the mid-1850s. In 1873, he persuaded Congress to establish the United States Fish Commission, and he became its first commissioner, an additional part-time duty which brought him no additional salary. He utilized the talents of university students and other young naturalists as he had previously, and in 1881, created a fisheries research facility at Woods Hole, Massachusetts, on land paid for by private universities and individuals. The Marine Biological Laboratory (1888) and the Woods Hole Oceanographic Institution (1930) are in some measure conceptual, but not direct descendants of Baird's earlier initiative. Baird favored pure research in ichthyology, but Congress soon pressed for fish culture and artificial propagation. The Fish Commission became an independent agency following Baird's death in 1888, and its commissioner, a political appointee, was salaried. This arrangement continued after 1903, when the agency was placed in the newly created Department of Commerce and Labor as the Bureau of Fisheries. There it remained until 1940.

In the summer of 1885, with the assistance of Baird, a committee, of the two-year-old American Ornithologists' Union (AOU) prevailed upon Congress to create an office of Economic Ornithology in the Agriculture Department. With an initial subvention of $5,000, the committee chair, a physician named C. Hart Merriam, began gathering data on the migration and distribution of birds, the task that had overwhelmed the resources of the AOU's volunteer group. Ostensibly, his work was supposed to aid farmers and ranchers, but he was primarily interested in ascertaining the nature and variety of the North American fauna, together with the biogeographical factors affecting their distribution. Within a year, Merriam had added mammals to his charge, and by 1891, he had largely abandoned the economic work. His agency became the Division of Biological Survey in 1896 and was made a bureau within the Department of Agriculture a decade later. Merriam became a dominant figure in his agency and in American vertebrate zoology, vastly expanding what was known about American mammals and birds. He trained people in his field methods when few university graduates were available to do this work.

In 1905, Congress stepped in, compelling Merriam and his modest staff to take on increasingly demanding management and regulatory chores for which he had little liking. An apolitical person who sometimes antagonized congressmen, Merriam delegated subordinates to make the most of the necessary appearances at budget hearings. His budget was a mere $62,000 when he resigned as bureau chief in 1910, at a time when the Bureau of Entomology, a comparable agency, had an appropriation of nearly $428,000, and the Bureau of Forestry almost $4 million. During the next thirty years, his six successors as chief, all but one of whom were professional biologists, adapted themselves to congressional priorities and secured much larger budgets. By 1926, annual appropriations exceeded $1.3 million. Later chiefs were also able to fulfill part of Merriam's dream of a continental survey of faunal resources. The survey did much work in predator and rodent control, which was highly controversial. For example, it drew much of the credit and blame, depending upon the point of view, for the extirpation of the wolf in the lower forty-eight states. At the same time, it maintained a low-key but steady program of research in the new and expanding field of wildlife management, and took on growing responsibility for the enforcement of federal game laws.

In 1940, The Biological Survey and the Fish Commission were both transferred to the Interior Department and combined to form the U.S. Fish and Wildlife Service. With better information concerning wildlife population management, the predator control programs were gradually deemphasized. There was continued stress upon management while the agency underwent several reconfigurations after 1945. In recent decades, increasing attention has been given to cooperation with other federal, state, private, and international wildlife agencies, to habitat preservation, and to the protection of endangered species. Research priorities have increasingly emphasized the relationship of wildlife to habitat, but have continued to play a secondary role in relation to the agency's increasingly demanding responsibilities. In 1993, the Secretary of the Interior, recalling some of the important objectives which prompted creation of the original Biological Survey, organized a new National Biological Survey (NBS) (later renamed the National Biological Service), drawing its personnel from various existing agencies within his department. During its brief life, the NBS took a fresh look at the nation's living resources, their condition, and their distribution. From its inception, however, some members of Congress objected that Secretary Babbitt had not secured their formal approval of his internal reorganization. This was prompted in part by growing resistance in certain quarters to the federal government's involvement in environmental policy-making, and because some lawmakers wanted to terminate NBS. Claims that NBS might "take" private property through eminent domain in pursuance of its environmental objectives was also a problem. NBS officials tried to allay these objections by pointing out that theirs was a research, analysis, and advisory function, and that NBS was not a regulatory agency. In the end, NBS avoided extinction. In 1996, it was instead transferred to the U.S. Geological Survey—also in the Interior Department—as the Biological Resources Division, with more limited responsibilities.

BIBLIOGRAPHY

Allard, Dean C. *Spencer F. Baird and the U.S. Fish Commission: A Study in the History of American Science.* New York: Arno Press, 1978.

Cameron, Jenks. *The Bureau of Biological Survey.* Baltimore: Johns Hopkins University Press, 1929.

Dunlap, Thomas R. *Saving America's Wildlife.* Princeton: Princeton University Press, 1988.

Durham, Megan, ed. *Fish and Wildlife News—Special Edition: Research.* April-May, 1981.

Lindsay, Debra. *Science in the Subarctic: Trappers, Traders, and the Smithsonian Institution.* Washington, DC: Smithsonian Institution Press, 1993.

Sterling, Keir B. *Last of the Naturalists: The Career of C. Hart Merriam.* Rev. ed. New York: Arno Press, 1977.

———. "Builders of the Biological Survey, 1885–1930." *Journal of Forest History* 30, no. 4 (October 1989): 180–187.

———. "Zoological Research, Wildlife Management, and the Federal Government." In *Forest and Wildlife Science in America,* edited by Harold K. Steen. [Durham, NC]: Forest History Society, 1999, pp. 19–65.

Keir B. Sterling

SEE ALSO
Baird, Spencer Fullerton

Food and Drug Administration, United States

In 1927, the Food and Drug Administration (FDA) replaced the Bureau of Chemistry within the Department of Agriculture as enforcer of the Federal Food and Drugs Act of 1906. Efforts to secure such a statute had begun in 1879 to protect an urbanizing public from increasing adulteration of the processed foods upon which their diet was ever more dependent. A coalition of chemists, physicians, journalists, elements of business, and congressmen from the agrarian West finally secured the law, which prohibited interstate commerce in spoiled, adulterated, and misbranded foods, drinks, and drugs.

Early enforcement cleaned up unprocessed foods, especially milk, eggs, poultry, and oysters, grappled with deleterious preservatives, and suppressed untrue proprietary medicine labeling claims. Pesticide residues began to be a problem in the 1920s. In 1938, the stronger Food, Drug, and Cosmetic Act—still the nation's governing statute—replaced the 1906 law, and in 1940, FDA moved from the Department of Agriculture to the Federal Security Agency, then to the Departments of Health, Education, and Welfare and Health and Human Services. The new law increased penalties for violation and added to the 1906 law's seizure and criminal sanctions the power of the injunction. FDA could now formulate food standards, akin to the drug standards of the *U.S. Pharmacopoeia* and *National Formulary* mandated in 1906. Cosmetics and therapeutic devices came under control. The 1938 law also originated the preventive principle, requiring that no new drug could be marketed until its sponsor had presented to FDA satisfactory evidence of its safety. The law came fortuitously at the start of a surge in industrial innovation that constituted both chemotherapeutic and chemogastric revolutions. Later laws applied the proof-of-safety-before-marketing concept to pesticides (1954), food additives (1958), color additives (1960), and medical devices (1976). The Kefauver amendments (1972) expanded premarket drug testing beyond safety to proof of efficacy for treating conditions listed in labeling. Other FDA responsibilities include radiation-emitting products, the blood transfusion supply, and feeds and drugs for animals.

At base, FDA's obligation has involved assessing risk, often balancing risks against benefits, involving complex scientific determinations. About two of five FDA employees are scientists, compared with one of ten in the remainder of government. From the small bureau of 1906, FDA has grown to an agency of nearly 9,000 employees who regulate products that account for over twenty-five cents of every dollar spent by American consumers. Foods and human drugs claim the largest share of FDA's budget, followed by devices

F

and radiological products, biologics, and veterinary medicines.

BIBLIOGRAPHY

Anderson, Oscar E., Jr. *The Health of a Nation: Harvey W. Wiley and the Fight for Pure Food.* Chicago: University of Chicago Press, 1958.

Food and Drug Administration. *FDA Almanac, Fiscal Year 1992.* Rockville, MD: Food and Drug Administration, 1992.

Temin, Peter. *Taking Your Medicine: Drug Regulation in the United States.* Cambridge, MA: Harvard University Press, 1980.

———. "Food and Drug Administration." In *Government Agencies,* edited by Donald R. Whitnah. Westport, CT: Greenwood Press, 1983, pp. 251–257.

Young, James Harvey. *The Medical Messiahs: A Social History of Health Quackery in Twentieth-Century America.* Princeton: Princeton University Press, 1992.

James Harvey Young

Forest Service, United States

An agency of the United States Government in the Department of Agriculture. It evolved from the passage of an act in 1876 authorizing the commissioner of agriculture to appoint a special agent to study forest conditions in the United States. In 1881, a division of forestry was established to function primarily as an investigative and information office. It was superseded in 1901 by a bureau of forestry, officially designated the Forest Service in 1905, after jurisdiction over the national forest reserves had been transferred from the Department of the Interior to the Department of Agriculture and vested in the Forest Service. In 1907, the forest reserves were redesignated national forests and placed under the supervision of six district offices, which established a pattern of agency regional decentralization.

The newly created Forest Service began systematic forestry on some 63 million acres of national forests in fifteen states and territories. This program accompanied a historic movement for conservation of forests and other natural resources led by Gifford Pinchot, first chief of the service, and strongly supported by President Theodore Roosevelt. Meanwhile, the agency in 1908 began to establish regional forest experiment stations to study forest and related range problems and, in 1910, established the Forest Products Laboratory at Madison, Wisconsin, which was to become the world's outstanding facility for the scientific study of wood and its uses.

The Weeks Act of 1911 stimulated the growth of the Forest Service by authorizing the purchase for national forests of private lands considered necessary to protect the flow of navigable streams. This legislation was expanded by the Clarke-McNary Act of 1924, which authorized the purchase of lands needed for the production of timber and agreements for cooperative fire control on state- and private-owned forest lands. Also in 1924, the service began to create an extensive wilderness and primitive area system.

The role of the agency expanded greatly during the 1930s when it became the principal technical cooperating agency with the Civilian Conservation Corps, a program which engaged more than a million young men in varied forest conservation work; and, in the Prairie States Forestry Project, cooperated with farmers to lessen drought conditions, protect crops and livestock, and reduce dust storms. Also during the 1930s, Secretary of the Interior Harold Ickes strove unsuccessfully to have the Forest Service transferred to his department, which was to be renamed Department of Conservation.

During World War II, the Forest Service made extensive surveys of war requirements and supplies of forest products and conducted numerous war-related scientific studies of wood at the Forest Products Laboratory. Also during the war years, Earle H. Clapp and Lyle F. Watts, heads of the service, failed in efforts to obtain federal government regulation of private timber cutting, but their efforts stimulated enactment of related regulatory measures in several states.

In recent years, the agency's activities have continued to expand in cooperative programs to provide technical assistance to private-forest owners and processors of forest products and in international forestry affairs. The Multiple Use-Sustained Yield Act of 1960 specifically sanctioned a long-standing Forest Service policy of administering national forest resources for multiple use and sustained yield. The Forest and Rangeland Renewable Resource Planning Act of 1974 stimulated greater agency long-range planning. With a continuing decentralized organization, the Forest Service now manages 154 national forests and 19 national grasslands (established since 1960) comprising 188 million acres in forty-one states and Puerto Rico.

BIBLIOGRAPHY

Dana, Samuel T. *Forest and Range Policy.* New York: McGraw-Hill, 1956.

Pinkett, Harold T. "Forest Service." In *Government Agencies, The Greenwood Encyclopedia of American Institutions,* edited by Donald R. Whitnah. Westport, CT: Greenwood Press, 1983.

Robinson, Glen O. *The Forest Service: A Study in Public Land Management.* Baltimore: Johns Hopkins University Press, 1975.

Smith, Frank E., ed. *Conservation in the United States: A Documentary History.* 5 vols. New York: Chelsea House, 1971.

Steen, Harold K. *The U.S. Forest Service: A History.* Seattle: University of Washington Press, 1976.

Harold T. Pinkett

Forestry

In its broadest sense, forestry is the scientific management of forests and forest lands for the continuous production of goods and services. The science emerged in Germany and France after 1800 with the growth of interest in the continuous management of forest lands for firewood and building materials. In North America, there was little interest in maintaining forest stands for the future, as long as the forests and other natural resources were thought to be inexhaustible. More interest, however, began to develop during the second half of the nineteenth century. In 1864, George P. Marsh, an American diplomat and pioneering ecologist, in a provocative book, *Man and Nature,* warned that continued reckless destruction of forests and other natural resources in the United States invited grave consequences. The American Forestry Association was organized in 1875 to protect existing forests of the United States and to promote the propagation and planting of useful trees. At the insistence of the American Association for the Advancement of Science, the United States Congress in 1876 authorized a study of means successfully used abroad to manage forests that might be applied in the United States to preserve and renew forests. The report resulting from this study, together with the warnings of Marsh and emerging organized groups, helped to create a climate for the practice of forestry in the United States by the end of the nineteenth century.

The first significant American demonstration of forestry came in 1892, when George Vanderbilt employed Gifford Pinchot to manage the forest land on his vast estate, Biltmore, in western North Carolina. Pinchot, who attended the French Forest School at Nancy and completed field studies in Germany, was the first native-born American to receive professional-level training in forestry. He further promoted forestry after his appointment in 1898 as the federal government's chief forester and his assumption of the administration of the national forest system in 1905. In 1900, he led in founding the Society of American Foresters, which became the nation's principal professional advocate of forestry, and encouraged his family to provide an endowment for establishing the Yale University Forest School, America's first graduate school of forestry. Within the next four decades, thirty universities in the country would establish four-year forestry programs.

During the early decades of the twentieth century, there was a rapid growth of the national forest systems, and increasing interest in forest preservation gave great impetus to a national conservation movement. After World War I, demand increased for improved protection and management of privately owned forests, which comprised approximately three-fourths of the country's commercial forests. There was debate concerning the need for federal government regulation of forest operations on private lands. Opponents of such regulation then and in later years were successful. Beginning in 1924, with the Clarke-McNary Act, measures were passed that provided government assistance in forest-fire protection and technical assistance to private forest owners and state governments, but without federal regulation. The establishment of the National Park Service in 1916 and the National Wilderness Preservation System in 1964 have provided greater protection and use of forests for recreational purposes.

The economic depression of the 1930s prompted government employment programs that advanced the practice of forestry. Projects of the Civilian Conservation Corps, Soil Conservation Service, and Tennessee Valley Authority in forest protection and reforestation brought improved forestry practices on public and private lands. The demand for forest resources during World War II produced more public awareness of the economic importance of forestry. After the war, there was increasing support for the principles of multiple use and sustained yield in public forest management. In recent years, environmentalists have complained that these principles have been ignored in many cases of extensive "clear cutting."

American forestry has directed much attention to three enemies: fire, disease, and insects. Extensive fire control facilities now guard public forest lands. Private forest lands have received increased protection by

F

government and private fire-control agencies. The control of diseases has emphasized the removal of infected trees and prevention of injury to young trees. Control measures against insects have centered on the maintenance of healthy growing stock and soil and of balanced biota.

Management and productivity of small private forest holdings in the United States tend to be relatively poor, because the owners often lack incentive and necessary operating capital or technical knowledge. Public and large commercial forests have made the greatest advances in management and productivity. In general, American forestry has become a major enterprise in the application of science to natural resource management.

BIBLIOGRAPHY

Argow, Keith A. "Forestry as a Profession." *Encyclopedia of American Forest and Conservation History.* Edited by Richard C. Davis. New York: Macmillan, 1983.

Clepper, Henry. *Professional Forestry in the United States.* Baltimore: Johns Hopkins University Press, 1971.

Dana, Samuel T. *Forest and Range Policy.* New York: McGraw-Hill, 1956.

Pinkett, Harold T. *Gifford Pinchot, Private and Public Forester.* Urbana: University of Illinois Press, 1970.

Harold T. Pinkett

Foundations

Private foundations have been an important source of funding for the natural, social, and medical sciences in the United States since the early 1900s. Prior to World War II and the vast proliferation of federal grants agencies, foundations were the largest source of extramural support for basic research in universities. Although a few private foundations also operated in European countries (especially Scandinavia and prerevolutionary Russia), nowhere was this institutional form so highly developed as in the United States. It is one of the hallmarks of American science.

There have been thousands of foundations, but the important ones for historians of science are the large, general-purpose foundations created in the first decades of this century by John D. Rockefeller, Andrew Carnegie, Olivia Sage, Mrs. Steven V. Harkness, and Henry Ford: the General Education Board (1902), Carnegie Institution of Washington (1902), Russell Sage Foundation (1907), Carnegie Corporation (1911), Rockefeller Foundation (1913), Commonwealth Fund (1918), Laura Spelman Rockefeller Memorial (1918–28), International Education Board (1923–28), Ford Foundation (1936), and Rockefeller Brothers Fund (1940). A dozen or so others have been significant sponsors of particular fields of science and medicine.

The large foundations were generally not operating organizations, but instead sponsored work in universities and other institutions. In this the foundations differed from endowed research institutes, which also proliferated between 1900 and the mid-1920s. (The Carnegie Institution, however, had both in-house research departments and an extramural grants program.) The general-purpose foundations also differed from traditional charitable organizations in their open-ended mandates, national or international scope, professional management, and self-conscious approach to social organization and public policy. They were meant by their founders to be agencies not just of charity and melioration but of active social engineering and reform.

There have been many explanations why business entrepreneurs created foundations. Once, the conventional wisdom was that foundations were the product of robber barons' guilt for ruthless business practices, or of their desire to improve their public image, avoid inheritance taxes, or shape public policy to favor their capitalist interests. However, these ideas have proved as simplistic as earlier appeals to simple altruism. Historians now look to the distinctive business culture of mass-production corporations, and to the experiences and ideals of the people who created the new social machinery for large-scale manufacturing and philanthropy.

The large foundations—philanthropic trusts—were distinctive creations of the era of trust-building and progressivism. The first modern foundations appeared during the great wave of trust-building around 1900. The money for most of them came from mass-production industries, especially oil refining, steel, and automobiles, in which capital was internally generated and reinvested in production, and in which business success depended most conspicuously upon innovative large-scale organization. (People who made money in more orthodox ways from merchandizing, finance, or real estate seemed to prefer more traditional forms of charity and cultural display.) Created by the same people, foundations shared with mass-production corporations an institutional culture that valued innovative social organization, efficiency and expertise ("scientific" methods), and production.

Protestant churches and charity organization societies had adopted systematic business methods in the 1870s and 1880s, and the large foundations did the same after 1900, as middle-class "progressive" reformers turned their attentions to new areas of economic, political, and social life. Foundations did not evolve out of "scientific" charity and religious institutions but rather were a parallel development. The large foundations, in short, were invented when modernizing corporate culture was extended to social reform within a national political culture that prevented the federal government from entering and co-opting these aspects of social life.

The historiography of foundations, not surprisingly, has paralleled the historiography of corporate capitalism. Foundations were highly controversial from the start, especially Carnegie's and Rockefeller's, and they have provoked a critical literature, the themes of which have changed little since the 1910s. Foundations' efforts to shape public policy and their partnership with universities raise issues of the political accountability of expert elites and of the proper balance between private and public power, business and government—issues central to American political culture generally. Foundations have generated the most controversy during episodes of political and cultural tension in the 1910s, 1930s, and 1960s, and historians are no less polarized today. Marxist and populist historians have applied a Gramscian analysis of cultural "hegemony," which depicts foundations as using patronage to co-opt intellectuals to corporate values and designs. Other historians see foundations as distinct from, and sometimes antagonistic to, big business.

Recently (a harbinger, perhaps, of a reviving interest in middle-class history) historians have begun to focus on foundation officers as a middle-class managerial elite with their own distinctive ideals and culture. While small foundations tend to be controlled by founders or their families, the middle managers of large foundations have determined their policies for most of their history. By the mid-1920s, these middle managers had largely succeeded in wresting control of program and policy from founders and their personal advisors, and from boards of businessmen trustees—a process that at times resembled bureaucratic warfare.

Foundation officers are a distinctive social group, different from founders and trustees. They have been drawn mainly from university bureaucracies—presidents or the lower echelons of administrators from whom presidents were recruited ("university handymen," they sometimes called themselves). Their experiences and values were those of middle-class professionals and intellectuals, not those of social and business elites. Their power, as with all middle managers, lay in a practical knowledge and control of day-to-day operations and of relations with their scientific clients. Foundation programs and policies were determined less by ideology than by practice; they were decided less in boardrooms than on the road and in the field, in the continuous practical interactions—designing grants, making projects—between officers and scientists. The patron-client relation was interactive, sometimes intense, and formative, and decisions about who and what to fund depended intimately on the social process of grant making.

Foundation patronage of the natural and social sciences has gone through a number of distinct periods. The 1900s and 1910s were a somewhat contentious period, in which grant givers and academic grant seekers adjusted their parochial expectations to the novel realities of large-scale patronage of individuals' research. In the 1920s, large-scale institutional grants dominated the scene, as foundation managers focused on developing academic infrastructure by means of capital grants to science departments or to organizations like the National Research Council and Social Science Research Council for national programs of postdoctoral fellowships. This style of community development was typified by the projects of the Rockefeller boards, led by Wickliffe Rose, Augustus Trowbridge, Halston J. Thorkelson, and Beardsley Ruml.

The 1930s saw an end to large, capital grants and a return to individual project grants, but now in a more strategic, programmatic mode. The Rockefeller Foundation's programs are exemplary of this style: Warren Weaver's program in physical-chemical or molecular biology, Alan Gregg's in bio-behavioral science, and Edmund Day's in the social sciences. In the 1950s, the entry of the federal government into research funding impelled foundations to more practical fields, and to areas in which public agencies feared to tread: for example, agricultural and scientific development in developing countries.

These periodic changes in foundations' policy mainly reflected the practical problems of finding significant and doable projects in a social system that was relentlessly outgrowing the fixed resources of even the largest endowments. In hindsight, the large foundations' love

F

affair with basic academic research between the wars was a passing interlude. The enduring role of foundations in American society seems to be practical research and demonstration in social and health services.

What effects foundation patronage has had on the practices and fortunes of the various sciences is an interesting and vexing question. In some special cases, cause and effect is clear. For example, foundation support was crucial to making fieldwork the sina qua non of cultural anthropology in the 1930s, when a majority of workers in the field were supported by the Rockefeller Foundation. Similarly, foundations funded the early development of cyclotrons and played an important role in the prehistory of molecular biology in the 1930s. The Ford and other foundations virtually created area-studies programs in the 1950s and 1960s.

In the behavioral and social sciences, foundations generally favored basic over applied sciences and physicochemical and mechanistic styles over social and observational styles. Some historians have criticized foundations for these preferences. However, since the applied and natural-history sciences had an array of different support systems (e.g., industries, museums, agricultural agencies, natural history societies), it is not clear that foundation preferences stunted their development. Generally, foundations avoided sciences that were supported by other institutions. Foundation officers also tended to follow rather than set trends. They depended on their scientific clients and advisors to identify who the "best" people were, that is, the most productive and innovative. Thus, foundations were generally amplifiers of developments within scientific disciplines.

It may be that foundations have had their most significant effects not within particular disciplines but on the institutional and social relations of science in general—as was, indeed, intended. Connections with foundations were crucial for the establishment of several generations of scientific politicians, who built national scientific institutions and professional networks: for example, George Ellery Hale, Robert A. Millikan, Frank R. Lillie, Karl J. Compton, Ernest O. Lawrence, and Vannevar Bush. In the 1920s and 1930s, foundations made postdoctoral training a routine feature of scientific careers, and helped create a new kind of scientific institution, in which research and teaching were more evenly balanced, to challenge the old elite of universities. The California Institute of Technology and the Massachusetts Institute of Technology exemplified this new style. Foundations were probably crucial in the creation of the Cold War generation of scientific intellectuals, the "best and the brightest," and in exporting American scientific culture to Latin America and elsewhere.

Most important, foundations virtually created the modern patron-client relationship. Foundation grants accustomed a whole generation of American scientists, large and small, to the peculiar practical and moral conditions of sponsored research, well before the era of large-scale federal sponsorship. Foundation grants helped to create a style of research in universities that looked forward to postwar Big Science, a style that was resource and management intensive, production oriented, programmatic, fast paced, and which could not be done without the participation of third-party sponsors. The institutional form of postwar federal granting agencies probably owed more to the ad hoc programs of World War II than to foundations. However, the expectations of academic scientists and the texture of their relations with federal patrons owed much to the prewar experience of foundation patronage.

Key respositories of published and archival sources for foundation history are the Rockefeller Archive Center and the Foundation Center.

BIBLIOGRAPHY

Abir-Am, Pnina. "The Discourse of Physical Power and Biological Knowlege in the 1930s: A Reappraisal of the Rockefeller Foundation's 'Policy' in Molecular Biology." *Social Studies in Science* 12 (1982): 341–382, and replies, ibid., 14 (1984): 341–364.

———. "The Assessment of Interdisciplinary Research in the 1930s: the Rockefeller Foundation and Physicochemical Morphology." *Minerva* 26 (1988): 153–176.

Arnove, Robert F., ed. *Philanthropy and Cultural Imperialism: The Foundations at Home and Abroad.* Boston: G.K. Hall, 1980.

Berman, Edward H. *The Influence of the Carnegie, Ford, and Rockefeller Foundations on American Foreign Policy.* Albany: State University of New York Press, 1983.

Bulmer, Martin. "Philanthropic Foundations and the Development of the Social Sciences in the Early Twentieth Century: A Reply to Donald Fischer." *Sociology* 18 (1984): 572–587.

Bulmer, Martin, and Joan Bulmer. "Philanthropy and Social Science in the 1920s: Beardsley Ruml and the Laura Spelman Rockefeller Memorial, 1922–1929." *Minerva* 19 (1981): 347–407.

Coben, Stanley. "American Foundations as Patrons of Science: The Commitment to Individual Research." In *The*

Sciences in the American Context: New Perspectives, edited by Nathan Reingold. Washington, DC: Smithsonian Institution Press, 1979, pp. 229–248.

Cuetos, Marcos. "The Rockefeller Foundation's Medical Policy and Scientific Research in Latin America: The Case of Physiology." *Social Studies of Science* 20 (1990): 229–254.

Ettling, John. *The Germ of Laziness: Rockefeller Philanthropy and Public Health in the New South.* Cambridge, MA: Harvard University Press, 1981.

Fisher, Donald. "The Role of Philanthropic Foundations in the Reproduction and Production of Hegemony: Rockefeller Foundations and the Social Sciences." *Sociology* 17 (1983): 206–233.

Fitzgerald, Deborah. "Exporting American Agriculture: The Rockefeller Foundation in Mexico, 1943–1953." *Social Studies of Science* 16 (1986): 457–483.

Fosdick, Raymond B. *The Story of the Rockefeller Foundation.* New York: Harper, 1952.

Geiger, Roger L. "American Foundations and Academic Social Science, 1945–1960." *Minerva* 26 (1988): 315–341.

Grossman, David. "American Foundations and Support of Economic Research, 1913–1929." *Minerva* 20 (1982): 59–82.

Karl, Barry D. "Philanthropy, Policy Planning and the Bureaucratization of the Democratic Ideal." *Daedalus* 105 (Fall 1976): 129–149.

Karl, Barry D., and Stanley N. Katz. "The American Private Philanthropic Foundation and the Public Sphere 1890–1930." *Minerva* 19 (1981): 236–270.

———. "Foundations and Ruling Class Elites." *Daedalus* 116 (Winter 1987): 1–40.

Kohler, Robert E. "Science, Foundations, and American Universities in the 1920s." *Osiris,* 2d ser., 3 (1987): 135–164.

———. *Partners in Science: Foundations and Natural Scientists 1900-1945.* Chicago: University of Chicago Press, 1991.

Lagemann, Ellen C. *The Politics of Knowledge: The Carnegie Corporation, Philanthropy, and Public Policy.* Middletown, CT: Wesleyan University Press, 1989.

Reingold, Nathan. "The Case of the Disappearing Laboratory." *American Quarterly* 29 (1977): 79–101.

Stocking, George W., Jr. "Philanthropoids and Vanishing Cultures: Rockefeller Funding and the End of the Museum Era in Anglo-American Anthropology." In *Objects and Others: Essays on Museums and Material Culture,* edited by George W. Stocking Jr. Madison: University of Wisconsin Press, 1985, pp. 112–145.

Wheatley, Steven C. *The Politics of Philanthropy: Abraham Flexner and Medical Education.* Madison: University of Wisconsin Press, 1989.

Robert E. Kohler

F

Fowler, Orson Squire (1809–1887)

Phrenologist and publisher. Orson Squire Fowler was born in Cohocton, New York, the son of Horace and Martha (Howe) Fowler. He was introduced to the subject of phrenology by his fellow student Henry Ward Beecher during his years at Amherst College, where he graduated in 1834. Phrenology is the science of the mind inaugurated by the European researchers Franz Josef Gall and Johann Gaspar Spurzheim. Gall, who was interested in cerebral physiology, proposed that each of our principal mental and characterological traits is controlled by a specific area or region of the brain. Gall further contended that, by examining the contour of a person's cranium, we can discern the size and relative strength of each of these regions of the brain. The science of phrenology, then, has to do with assessing a person's cranial characteristics in order to derive a precise index of his or her intellectual, moral, and emotional character. Spurzheim expanded upon Gall's phrenological science by emphasizing its practical benefits for education, government, and moral training. He maintained that rigorous forms of mental exercise, such as reading appropriate literature or memorizing specific kinds of information, could expand or strengthen the cranial areas responsible for our various character traits. Orson Fowler quickly grasped the utility of this new scientific theory and began studying how the various mental faculties could be scientifically gauged and regulated for the purpose of modifying human behavior.

With his brother, Lorenzo Niles Fowler, Orson published *Phrenology Proved, Illustrated, and Applied* in 1837 (and which eventually went through over thirty editions). In 1840, the two brothers established a publishing company and began the publication of the *Phrenological Almanac.* Two years later they assumed the editorship of the *American Phrenological Journal and Miscellany.* In 1844, they entered into partnership with S.R. Wells and changed the name of their publishing firm to Fowler and Wells until their retirement in 1863. Their firm's publications provided a public forum for books on a wide range of topics that might be designated as the "fringe" areas of medicine, science, and religious metaphysics.

Throughout this period, Fowler established himself as one of the nation's preeminent lecturers and writers on phrenology and such related topics as health, self-culture, education, sexuality, and social reform. He published widely, including such titles as *Phrenology*

F

Applied to the Cultivation of Memory (1842), *Phrenology Applied to the Selection of Companions* (1842), *The Christian Phrenologist* (1843), *Amativeness; or, Evils and Remedies of Excessive and Perverted Sexuality, including Warning and Advice to the Married and Single* (1849), and *Creative and Sexual Science* (1870). Fowler's exposition of these topics reveals his lack of formal training in science, medicine, or philosophy even as it reveals his eagerness to apply the "useful knowledge" ostensibly emerging from the science of his day to problems in education, religion, government, and sexuality.

Fowler's writings and publishing activity were instrumental in generating enthusiasm among the American reading public for areas of research that, by the 1880s, would give rise to establishment of academic departments of psychology in American universities. His wide-ranging interests, all under the banner of phrenological science, help remind us that sciences become popular not so much by their generation of verifiable facts as by promising solutions to problems that arise in the context of everyday life.

BIBLIOGRAPHY

Davies, John D. *Phrenology: Fad and Science.* New Haven: Yale University Press, 1955.

Wrobel, Arthur, ed. *Pseudo-Science and Society in Nineteenth-Century America.* Lexington: University of Kentucky Press, 1987.

Robert C. Fuller

SEE ALSO
Phrenology

Franklin Institute of the State of Pennsylvania

As the nation's premier mechanic's institute during the nineteenth century, the Franklin Institute served as the central repository of that most elusive of technology's key ingredients: knowledge. Things and processes were not alien to the Philadelphia organization. Begun in 1824 by a group of elite manufacturers and mechanics in the leading industrial city in the country, its founders intended the institute in part as a means of gathering information about new technologies in England and Europe. Primarily, the institute served the public by presenting technical knowledge through formal meetings and public lectures, maintaining a technical library, and publishing a journal and technical reports. The organization sponsored nearly thirty technical exhibitions before the Civil War and offered classes in drafting and other subjects for apprentice mechanics.

The institute's reach early moved beyond the local. The *Journal of the Franklin Institute,* launched in 1826, quickly became one of the nation's leading scientific and technical journals, distributed in cities ranging from New York, Boston, and Providence to Pittsburgh, Cincinnati, and New Orleans. As the Franklin Institute had followed the example of British mechanics' institutes, the Philadelphia organization was emulated throughout the settled parts of the United States. During the antebellum decades, in short, the Franklin Institute served as the chief purveyor of technical and industrial knowledge not only for the nation's largest city but for the nation itself.

In an era of empirical science, the institute established itself as one of the premier scientific institutions in the nation, sustaining a national role at least until the 1880s. These years were distinguished by a carefully devised investigation of waterwheels and waterpower initiated in 1829 by Samuel Vaughan Merrick, who also made the *Journal* a vehicle for "original matter." A London magazine asserted at the time that the waterpower experiments constituted one of the organization's "exclusive claims to the favor of the scientific public." During the next decade and a half, physical scientists like Alexander Dallas Bache and Joseph Henry, professors of natural philosophy at the University of Pennsylvania and Princeton University, joined Merrick to examine and report on new technologies for the Committee on Science and the Arts. Among the founders' aims was to use the committee to continue investigations similar to the waterpower experiments. Yet, except for an investigation of steam boiler explosions of the early 1830s, for which the sum of $2,000 constituted the federal government's first research grant, these hopes were not to be fulfilled. Merrick's death and Bache's move to Washington, D.C., in 1843 to head the United States Coast Survey were partly responsible. The claim of an institute president in 1863 was nonetheless accurate: that the institute pioneered "in the noble work of raising the labor of the mechanic and artisan to its true position as both handmaid and exemplar of science."

Certainly, the institute's national role did not end with the Civil War. The advent of a new generation of leaders at the end of the war led to continued achievements. President William Sellers, who was born in the year of the institute's founding, led the organization in responding to the new "extent of manufactures" in the nation by winning national acceptance for a standard screw thread. Tests on the efficiency of dynamos in 1877, led by a founder of the electrical industry, Elihu Thomson, continued in the older tradition of providing "reliable data" on fundamental technologies. The institute's period of greatest service was capped in 1884 when it staged an International Electrical Exhibition. Tests conducted at that time on a broad range of electrical machinery were led by William A. Anthony, a physics professor at Cornell University. As founder of one of the nation's first courses in electrical engineering, his presence pointed to a technological future that would render superfluous the Franklin Institute's scientific labors. A report of the Committee on Science and the Arts in the 1890s admitted as much when it described the committee's work as having become "annually more and more difficult in consequence of the great advance which is daily being made in all of the practical arts and sciences."

During the twentieth century, the institute has devolved into something quite different from its robust, nineteenth-century character. A bequest from a member led to the founding of a laboratory in nuclear physics after World War I and, following World War II, institute leaders established a research and development laboratory on the basis of newly available Cold War funds from the military and federal government. Yet, research would no longer win national prestige for the organization. A museum of science and industry founded in the 1930s provided a clearer picture of the future. During the twenty years after 1970, the institute's leaders not only dismantled its two twentieth-century research installations, but sold and dispersed the great technical library created during the previous century. Today, the halls of the Franklin Institute Science Museum resound chiefly with the noises of children playing with a large collection of interactive displays whose content is often only tangentially related to technological matters.

BIBLIOGRAPHY

McMahon, A. Michal. "'Bright Science' and the Mechanic Arts: The Franklin Institute and Science in Industrial America, 1824–1976." *Pennsylvania History* 46 (October 1980): 351–368.

McMahon, A. Michal, and Stephanie Morris. *A Guide to the Committee on Science and the Arts of the Franklin Institute.* Wilmington, DE: Scholarly Resources, 1977.

Sinclair, Bruce. *Early Research at the Franklin Institute: The Investigation into the Causes of Steam Boiler Explosions, 1830–1837.* Philadelphia: Franklin Institute, 1966.

———. *Philadelphia's Philosopher Mechanics: A History of the Franklin Institute, 1824–1865.* Baltimore: Johns Hopkins University Press, 1974.

A. Michal McMahon

Fusion Research

Physics and engineering studies directed toward the generation of electricity from the energy released during the fusion of light nuclei.

The idea of adapting fusion to the generation of electricity was widespread in the aftermath of World War II. Fusion reactions had been demonstrated in the 1930s using nuclei accelerated by Cockcroft-Walton machines. The significant energy released in these reactions had made it plausible to invoke fusion to explain the energy of stars. At the temperatures postulated for stellar interiors, atoms would be dissociated into electrons and nuclei, and the lightest nuclei in this "plasma" would have thermal velocities high enough to produce substantial numbers of (thermo)nuclear fusions.

The ensuing war brought hundreds of scientists into projects for applying both the newly discovered fission nuclear reaction and the older fusion to the generation of uncontrolled energy, that is, to bombs. It was natural that after the war, some should initiate work on controlled fusion energy.

The proximate cause of a sustained United States program was the announcement (later proved erroneous) by Argentine president Juan D. Peron on 24 March 1951 that his scientists had succeeded in producing thermonuclear fusions in the laboratory. The news inspired Lyman Spitzer Jr., a professor of astrophysics at Princeton University, to conceive a novel scheme that used magnetic fields to confine a high-temperature plasma. Spitzer secured research funds from the United States Atomic Energy Commission (AEC) in 1951. In 1952, the AEC laboratory at Los Alamos, New Mexico, started work on a second confinement scheme, and in the same year, Herbert York, then organizing a new AEC weapons laboratory at Livermore, California, built a small fusion project into his program. By mid-1953, thirty scientists worked on the secret program, and the AEC had spent $1 million.

In July 1953, Lewis L. Strauss became chair of the commission. Strauss passionately wanted to bring the

F

benefaction of fusion energy to mankind within his tenure. From fiscal year 1954 to fiscal year 1958, the annual fusion budget rose from $1.8 million to $29.2 million. Strauss ordered a display of thermonuclear neutrons for the Second International Conference on the Peaceful Uses of Atomic Energy, in August 1958, when the program would simultaneously be declassified. But the crash program failed to meet that goal, and rather succeeded in revealing that laboratory plasmas resisted confinement by any configuration of magnetic fields. During the 1960s, with Strauss gone and the Congress increasingly skeptical, fusion scientists struggled to understand the scientific laws of plasma behavior.

A window of opportunity opened in the early 1970s as the nation turned its attention to the twin problems of environmental degradation and energy shortages. Fusion appeared more benign than fission, since meltdowns would be impossible and, even in the worst case, its radioactive products would be shorter lived.

President Nixon was calling for a 60 percent rise in federal energy R&D. To qualify for a piece of the funding, the program leaders set out to show that fusion had graduated from the research to the development stage. The Soviet tokamak was selected as the front-runner among confinement schemes, with the Livermore "mirror" as backup. Research on alternate concepts was pared back. A massive Tokamak Fusion Test Reactor was ratified for Princeton and an equally costly Mirror Fusion Test Facility begun at Livermore. A deuterium-tritium mix was picked for the first fuel since it promised to lead to energy production in the shortest possible time. Magnetic fusion budgets soared from $28.4 million in fiscal year 1971 to $316.3 million in fiscal year 1977. Laser fusion had been pursued at Livermore since the early 1960s as a way of simulating the effects of hydrogen bombs; now projects were instituted to use it for energy.

The engineering reactor studies that had been commissioned in increasing numbers were beginning to show, however, that radioactivity from deuterium-tritium fuel would make reactors too costly to maintain, while the capital outlays for tokamak and mirror plants might be exorbitant. Energy leaders in the Carter administration called for a broad look at alternatives to the tokamak. This path was foreclosed, however, by a contraction in funding, in real dollars, which began in 1978 and continued through the 1980s. Even

the Mirror Fusion Test Facility, completed in 1986 at a cost of $372 million, was not put into operation for lack of funds. The Department of Energy began to promote a policy of combining a limited domestic program with a collaboration with Europe, Japan, and the Soviet Union on a scaled-up, billion-dollar tokamak, the International Thermonuclear Experimental Reactor.

Public interest revived in March 1989 when two University of Utah chemists claimed to have produced significant amounts of energy at room temperature from fusion reactions among deuterium atoms captured in the palladium electrode of an electrochemical cell. Utah hoped for a commercial bonanza. Within fifteen days the legislature appropriated $5 million for the research; within half a year, the state opened a National Cold Fusion Institute. As laboratories throughout the world entered the field, however, it soon became clear that no hitherto known fusion reaction was occurring. As of 1993, the significance of the Utah results and their bearing for energy were still in dispute.

Historians have used "hot" fusion as a case study of the way in which government science administrators preserve and augment their programs, often drastically affecting their technical content in the process. "Cold" fusion has received still more attention, because of controversies over the data, turf fights between physicists and chemists, the large role played by the media, and the bent of Utah and its university toward commercial exploitation of the findings. A Cornell Cold Fusion Archive has been organized under the aegis of the Division of Rare and Manuscript Collections at the Cornell University library, and comprises manuscripts, publications, media accounts, interviews, and cold fusion artifacts.

BIBLIOGRAPHY

Bromberg, Joan Lisa. *Fusion: Science, Politics, and the Invention of a New Energy Source.* Cambridge, MA: MIT Press, 1982.

Hendry, John. "The Scientific Origins of Controlled Fusion Technology." *Annals of Science* 44 (1987): 143–168.

Lewenstein, Bruce V. "Cold Fusion and Hot History." *Osiris,* 2d ser., 7 (1992): 135–163.

McAllister, James W. "Competition Among Scientific Disciplines in Cold Nuclear Fusion Research." *Science in Context* 5, 1 (1992): 17–49.

Joan Lisa Bromberg

G

Gamow, George (1904–1968)

Theoretical physicist and popularizer. Born and educated in Odessa, Russia, Gamow earned his Ph.D. at the University of Leningrad in 1928. On fellowships, he then studied at Göttingen, Copenhagen, and Cambridge, England, contributing to the application of quantum mechanics to nuclear theory. After a period of being refused permission to travel by Russian authorities, he emigrated to the United States in 1934. He served primarily on the faculties of George Washington University (1934–1956) and the University of Colorado (1956–1968). From the late 1930s, he was a prolific popularizer of science, writing many articles for news and scientific magazines, as well as publishing nearly thirty books.

Gamow contributed to a wide range of problems in theoretical nuclear physics and in astrophysics. He helped develop the concept of quantum mechanical "tunneling," contributed to the theory of thermonuclear reaction rates in stars, calculated the energies needed in proton accelerators, and collaborated with Edward Teller on the calculation of what became the Gamow-Teller selection rule for beta decay. In the 1940s, Gamow proposed the "big bang" model of the creation of the universe, and continued work in the area for many years. Demonstrating his remarkable intellectual range, shortly after the discovery of the DNA structure in 1954, he identified the process by which the DNA could code for proteins. During World War II, he was a consultant on explosives to the United States Navy, and after the war he worked on the hydrogen bomb.

Shortly after coming to the United States, Gamow began to write popular articles about science. He became one of the mainstays of the American popular science community, especially in *The Scientific Monthly* and *Scientific American.* As with his scientific research, his popular writings focused on nuclear physics and on cosmology, although with frequent excursions into other areas of science.

Gamow used humor frequently. His private papers are filled with witty doodlings, and he illustrated several of his own popular books. He was the architect of one of the most famous scientific jokes: a 1948 paper detailing the big bang theory published by "Alpher, Bethe, and Gamow," although Hans Bethe had not been involved in the work.

Although Gamow's significant contributions to nuclear physics in the mid-twentieth century are well recognized, he has not received much historical attention. He was neither a founder of quantum theory, nor a central member of the "atomic-bomb" scientists, two major areas of historical work. However, with increasing attention to the "national security state" of the postwar era, as well as to the history of big bang theory, he is likely to receive more attention.

BIBLIOGRAPHY

Stuewer, Roger H. "Gamow, George." *Dictionary of Scientific Biography.* Edited by Charles C. Gillispie. New York: Scribners, 1972, 5:271–272.

———. "Gamow's Theory of Alpha-Decay." In *The Kaleidoscope of Science: The Israel Colloquium,* edited by Edna Ullmann-Margalit. Dordrecht: Reidel, 1986, 1:147–186.

———. "Gamow, George." *Dictionary of American Biography.* New York: Scribners, 1988, supplement 8, pp. 198–199.

Bruce V. Lewenstein

G

Gasser, Herbert Spencer (1888–1963)

Physiologist and educator. Born in Platteville, Wisconsin, Gasser studied at the University of Wisconsin, Madison (A.B., 1910; A.M., 1911), and began medical training there. He completed medical studies at Johns Hopkins University in Baltimore (M.D., 1915). In 1916, he joined the department of physiology at Washington University in St. Louis under Joseph Erlanger. He collaborated with the latter in investigations on traumatic shock, before both turned to problems in neurophysiology. Gasser became professor and head of pharmacology at the university in 1921, with the provision that he could continue physiological research. In 1931, he was named professor of physiology at Cornell Medical College in New York. He became director of the Rockefeller Institute in New York in 1935. In 1944, he and Erlanger were awarded the Nobel Prize in physiology or medicine "for . . . discoveries relating to the highly differentiated functions of nerve fibres." Gasser retired in 1953, but remained active in research until nearly the end of his life.

Gasser played a key role in the early development of neurophysiology. At Washington University, he and physicist H. Sidney Newcomer connected a vacuum tube amplifier with a string galvanometer to record electrical activity, or action potentials, of nerves. Later Gasser and Erlanger adapted a cathode-ray oscillograph, by which potentials could be studied in detail and conduction through different portions of the nervous system compared. They classified nerve fibers in terms of a variety of electrophysiological properties. Gasser and Erlanger identified three groups (designated A, B, and C) based on the rate of conduction, and correlated this rate with fiber diameter ("A" fibers being the thickest and fastest). At Cornell, Gasser's investigations focused on means of differentiating functions of the central and peripheral nervous systems. Despite facing formidable administrative responsibilities at the Rockefeller Institute in the late 1930s, he made further important contributions to neurophysiology in those years, for example, by refining observations of action potentials through experiments on pain and tetany and differentiating properties of mammalian nerves from counterparts of other animal classes. He recruited several distinguished colleagues, thereby establishing the institute as a leading center of neurophysiological research. After interruptions imposed by World War II, Gasser resumed his specialty in the late 1940s, making use of the electron microscope in investigations of the properties of myelin and other substances in neuroanatomy.

Gasser's papers, 20 cubic feet, 1933–1961, are preserved in the Rockefeller Archive Center, Pocantico Hills, New York. A smaller collection, .4 cubic feet, 1886–1953, is in the State Historical Society of Wisconsin, Madison.

BIBLIOGRAPHY

Brandt, Allan M. "Gasser, Herbert Spencer." *Dictionary of American Biography.* Edited by John A. Garraty. New York: Scribners, 1961–1965, Supplement 7, pp. 279–281.

Chase, Merrill W., and Carlton C. Hunt. "Herbert Spencer Gasser." *Biographical Memoirs of the National Academy of Sciences* 67 (1995): 146–177.

Gasser, Herbert S. "Herbert Spencer Gasser, 1888–1963: Scholar, Administrator, Noble Laureate; an Autobiographical Memoir of a Distinguished Career in Medical Science." *Experimental Neurology,* Supplement 1, 1964, pp. 1–36.

Lloyd, David C.P. "Gasser, Herbert Spencer." *Dictionary of Scientific Biography.* Edited by Charles C. Gillispie. New York: Scribners, 1972, 5:290–291.

Paul G. Anderson

Gender—in Science

The study of both the real relations between the sexes and the representation of those relations in the institutions, subject matters, and methods of science.

As early as 1405, Christine de Pizan in her *Book of the City of Ladies* surveyed women's original contributions in the arts and the sciences. Despite scattered interest in this topic since the time of de Pizan, the role of women or gender in science did not become part of the modern discipline of the history of science founded in the 1920s and 1930s. Since the 1970s, with increasing numbers of women entering both science and the historical profession, interest in gender in science has grown steadily. The study of gender in science has five interrelated aspects.

The History of Women Scientists (in social and institutional contexts)

The first challenge historically was to prove that women have contributed to the development of science. Biographies of great women scientists (and more recently autobiographies) address questions about their lives: What sparked their interest in science? How did they obtain access to the tools and techniques of science? What barriers did they encounter? What recognition did these achievements receive in the broader community of scholars? More recently, historians of women have begun to steer away from the great-women-of-science model, where women's achievements are measured against men's, to examine more general patterns in women's work in science—how women have concentrated in particular fields (such as biology or medicine) and activities (such as observation in astronomy or illustration in botany). Historians also study differences among women; for example, how class and race has influenced women's access to science and the kind of science they do (Alic, Abir-Am, Rossiter, Schiebinger).

Sexual Science (women as the object of scientific inquiry)

The exclusion of women from science has traditionally been justified by scientific studies of sexual differences. Scientists (historically in the absence of women, although today some women also engage in these studies) teach that women simply cannot do science, that something in the constitution of their brains or bodies impedes progress in this field. Attempts to trace woman's social inferiority to her supposed biological inferiority date back at least to Aristotle, and has changed with leading theories of medicine and biology. While Aristotle argued that women are colder and weaker than men and simply do not have sufficient heat to cook the blood and purify the soul, late-eighteenth-century craniologists tried to account for sexual differences in intellectual achievement by measuring the skull. Social Darwinists in the nineteenth century invoked evolutionary biology to argue that woman was a man whose evolution—both physical and mental—had been arrested in a primitive stage. Since the 1920s and 1930s, arguments for women's different (and inferior) nature have been based in hormonal research. Today studies of brain lateralization try to persuade us that women do poorly in math because their brains are not as highly specialized as men's. Practioners of sexual science assume that biology is destiny, that something is wrong with women, not with the sciences that study them. Feminists have shown how, in many cases, sexual science is simply bad science. They have shown further how science has played a role in constructing sexual differences (Fausto-Sterling, Hubbard, Laqueur, Russet, Schiebinger).

Gendered Representations in Science

Gender also informs conceptions of nature and science. Most fundamentally, nature has been conceived as female (perhaps because the majority of scientists have been male). At the same time, scientists have claimed for science masculine traits—reason, objectivity, competitiveness. Notions of science, masculinity, and femininity vary wildly across centuries and cultures, yet in Europe and America, science has developed in opposition to something defined as "feminine." Not only women but the values they are thought to represent have been excluded from science (Keller, Merchant).

Women's Traditions in Science

Women have been active in sciences, such as astronomy, physics, and entomology, and yet, even under the best conditions, their participation in fields developed by men have remained marginal. But have women been leaders in others sciences—sciences developed primarily by women? Women have created and been the primary practioners of at least three science-related fields—midwifery, home economics, and nursing. These fields have generally been ignored by historians of science perhaps because they have not been considered science. Such a view may rest more on the fact that midwifery and nursing have been practiced by women than on the knowledge of nature involved or actual value of the service rendered.

Gendered Knowledge

There are two opposing views concerning how equality for women will effect science: (1) Many assume that men and women are essentially the same, and that women can become scientists through proper education. According to this view, science is value neutral; blacks and whites, men and women are interchangeable parts in the scientific machine. Increased numbers of women in science will enhance scientific production but not change its practices or findings; (2) a leading question in gender studies of science today is: In what ways might women do science differently? Animating this question is the notion that gender differences exist—most likely a product of nurture, not nature. Gender molds men's and women's behaviors and aspirations, and has also shaped the priorities and subject matters of science. According to this view, women entering science in significant numbers might bring significant changes to scientific institutions, research priorities, methods, and findings.

G

Studies have shown how particular sciences, such as anthropology and primatology, have changed with large influxes of women. Feminist studies have also begun to show how gender has shaped knowledge, from the naming of mammals *Mammalia,* to theories of generation, to studies of primates or cellular slime mold (Haraway, Harding, Keller, Schiebinger).

BIBLIOGRAPHY

Abir-Am, Pnina, and Dorinda Outram, eds. *Uneasy Careers and Intimate Lives: Women in Science, 1789–1979.* New Brunswick: Rutgers University Press, 1987.

Alic, Margaret. *Hypatia's Heritage: A History of Women in Science from Antiquity to the Late Nineteenth Century.* London: The Women's Press, 1986.

Fausto-Sterling, Anne. *Myths of Gender: Biological Theories about Women and Men.* New York: Basic Books, 1985.

Haraway, Donna. *Primate Visions: Gender, Race, and Nature in the World of Modern Science.* New York: Routledge, 1989.

Harding, Sandra. *Whose Science? Whose Knowledge? Thinking from Women's Lives.* Ithaca: Cornell University Press, 1991.

Hubbard, Ruth. *The Politics of Women's Biology.* New Brunswick: Rutgers University Press, 1990.

Keller, Evelyn Fox. *Reflections on Gender and Science.* New Haven: Yale University Press, 1985.

Laqueur, Thomas. *Making Sex: Body and Gender from the Greeks to Freud.* Cambridge, MA: Harvard University Press, 1990.

Merchant, Carolyn. *The Death of Nature: Women, Ecology, and the Scientific Revolution.* New York: Harper & Row, 1980.

Rossiter, Margaret. *Women Scientists in America: Struggles and Strategies to 1940.* Baltimore: Johns Hopkins University Press, 1982.

Russett, Cynthia. *Sexual Science: The Victorian Construction of Womanhood.* Cambridge, MA: Harvard University Press, 1989.

Schiebinger, Londa. *The Mind Has No Sex? Women in the Origins of Modern Science.* Cambridge, MA: Harvard University Press, 1989.

Londa Schiebinger

SEE ALSO
Ethnicity, Race, and Gender; Women in Science

General Motors Corporation

America's largest automobile manufacturer and long-time industry leader in research and development. Science and engineering were not always corporate priorities at General Motors. William C. Durant founded the company in 1908, and in just a few years built it into Henry Ford's only real competition by combining some twenty formerly independent firms, including Buick, Cadillac, Oldsmobile, and later Chevrolet. But research had no place in Durant's strategy of control through consolidation, for he believed that innovation could always be purchased more cheaply from the outside, in the form of patents or entire companies.

The DuPont Company, looking to invest its immense wartime profits and to diversify into new chemical markets, acquired controlling interest in General Motors (eventually totaling 36 percent of its common stock) during World War I. Pierre S. du Pont took over as president from Durant in 1920 with the aim of introducing into the automobile industry the managerial and organizational innovations that had made DuPont a leader in the chemical industry. As his executive vice president and protégé, du Pont selected Alfred Sloan, a brilliant young manager who had joined the General Motors family by selling his automotive parts company to Durant. Sloan and du Pont's corporate blueprint for General Motors included a central research laboratory modeled on DuPont's pioneering example. To head it, they appointed Charles Kettering, an electrical engineer, famous as the inventor of the electric self-starter and founder of Delco, which he had subseqently sold to General Motors. In 1920, Kettering became vice president and general manager of the General Motors Research Corporation, first in Dayton and, after 1925, in Detroit.

At the time, Ford was selling more than half the automobiles in the country, and General Motors less than a quarter. To catch up, Sloan, promoted to president in 1923, devised a new corporate strategy. Rather than compete directly at the bottom end of the market, General Motors would offer an escalator of style and status that could take car buyers as far as their aspirations (and their wallets) would allow, from the practical Chevrolet through the increasingly expensive Oldsmobile, Buick, and Cadillac—a car for every purse and purpose. Sloan's strategy depended in large measure on the research laboratory's ability to make each year's model more convenient, comfortable, and appealing than last year's. Kettering called it keeping the customer dissatisfied, the incremental innovations that kept the buyers coming back, and his laboratory mastered it, from such dramatic improvements as leaded gasoline and Duco, a fast-drying and durable colored lacquer, to better brakes, bearings, and crankshaft balancing. This unceasing campaign to upgrade the automobile, coupled with key innovations in marketing and sales, allowed General Motors to overtake Ford by 1927.

After 1930, with General Motors the predominant American carmaker and under some threat of antitrust action, the goal for research became diversifying into nonautomotive fields. For the Frigidaire division, Kettering's chemists developed Freon, a nontoxic, nonflammable refrigerant that immediately became the industry standard, and doubled sales to a quarter of the total home-refrigerator market. For the Electro-Motive division, Kettering's engineers developed an improved two-stroke diesel that ran steam locomotives off the rails, and gave General Motors a commanding position in that industry as well. Under Kettering, the laboratory grew from a total staff of 260 in 1925 to 500 in 1938, with a total annual budget of $2 million, divided among consulting work for the manufacturing divisions (40 percent), advanced engineering (40 percent), and fundamental research (20 percent). While small compared with the laboratories of science-based companies such as Bell Telephone, General Electric, and DuPont, General Motors' research division still dwarfed its automotive competition.

Following Kettering's retirement in 1947, the laboratory emphasized fundamental research. Convinced by the "physicists' war" that science was the key to the future, General Motors hired as research director Lawrence Hafstad, a prominent nuclear physicist and member of the Atomic Energy Commission. Under Hafstad, the laboratory focused less on production innovation and improvement and more on basic studies of materials, aerodynamics, electronics, and combustion. Symbolic of the new era was the opening in 1956 of the General Motors Technical Center, a $125 million campus in suburban Detroit, geographically and intellectually isolated from the rest of the corporation.

Federal safety, emissions, and milege regulations forced upon the laboratory a new set of priorities in the 1960s and 1970s, and a renewed coupling with the operating divisions. Paul Chenea, an academic engineer from MIT and Purdue, headed the laboratory from 1969 to 1982, devoting most of the laboratory's efforts to meeting increasingly stringent federal automotive standards. General Motors took a conservative approach (e.g., catalytic converters) compared with its foreign competitors, who preferred more radical alternatives (e.g., lean-burn and rotary engines). Like their counterparts at Ford and Chrysler, General Motors researchers frequently complained, with some justification, about the complexity, costs, and occasional contradictions of federal guidelines, and about antitrust laws that prevented the kind of pooling of corporate resources common among Japanese companies.

The General Motors laboratory, since 1983 under former defense scientist and NASA administrator Robert Frosch, remains the automotive industry's largest, with 525 professional staff (410 doctorates), including a sizable contingent of social scientists. Its basic mission, however, remains as Kettering once described it, a corporate life insurance policy, using research to anticipate and shape the automobile industry's future.

BIBLIOGRAPHY

Leslie, Stuart W. *Boss Kettering: Wizard of General Motors.* New York: Columbia University Press, 1983.

Rae, John B. *The American Automobile Industry.* Boston: Twayne, 1984.

Sloan, Alfred P. *My Years with General Motors.* New York: Doubleday, 1964.

Smith, John Kenly, Jr. "The Scientific Tradition in American Industrial Research." *Technology and Culture* 31 (1990): 121–131.

Stuart W. Leslie

Genetics

The science of inheritance. Genetics developed in the United States both as an academic discipline and as an applied science virtually from the moment Mendel's work captured the attention of American investigators in evolution and inheritance in 1902. A number of historical factors contributed to the rapid growth of the new science before 1920, as well as to its complex institutional development and varied uses. Publicly funded state universities, agricultural colleges and experiment stations, and newer private research universities took their places beside older elite institutions as centers of scientific research. Also, the budding philanthropic largesse of American industrial giants supported not only new academic institutions but also a number of private research ventures such as the Carnegie Institution's Station for Experimental Evolution. Genetics would find a home at all these institutions.

Each of the various kinds of research sites contributed its own legacy of theory and practice. At the older, more elite institutions and at the newer private universities, investigators joined in a reconstitution of

G

natural historical concerns to produce a more focused, intellectually unified biological enterprise that integrated the more experimental practices of physiological investigation with naturalists' concerns for morphology, development, and evolution. These researchers, among them C.O. Whitman, F.R. Lillie, Ross Harrison, E.G. Conklin, William Castle, and Herbert Spencer Jennings, as well as younger men like E.B. Wilson, T.H. Morgan, Raymond Pearl, and C.B. Davenport, were familiar with current critiques of Darwinian natural selection and with recent European research in development, inheritance, and cytology. In an entirely different context were agricultural breeders, particularly those working with plants, who investigated problems in plant pathology and physiology and introduced crossing and hybridizing to support their selectionist breeding programs. Furthermore, most American agricultural breeders, with their intense interest in artificial selection and variation as well as hybrids and sterility, were familiar with Darwin's discussions of those subjects.

By 1905, Mendel's researches and de Vries's mutation theory had been introduced to both groups of investigators in the United States, and each had developed its own characteristic response. International conferences on botanical hybridization, one held in 1899 at London and another in 1902 at New York (and retrospectively renamed the first and second International Congresses of Genetics), boasted delegates from American agricultural institutions, who learned there of the work of de Vries, William Bateson, and C.C. Hurst. In 1902, papers by both Bateson and Hurst urged an examination and elaboration of Mendel's work. Familiar with Mendel's techniques and motivated by practical concerns to apply new findings, many agricultural breeders obliged. The American Breeders' Association, founded in 1903 by agriculturalists at the federal and state levels, promoted both practical research and theoretical investigations of heredity, including Mendelian. The Departments of Plant Breeding at Cornell (founded 1907), of Experimental Breeding at the University of Wisconsin (founded 1910), and of Genetics at Berkeley (founded 1913), each dedicated to fundamental research on inheritance, were all established within state agricultural colleges. Their staffs, including H.J. Webber, R.A. Emerson, Leon Cole, and E.B. Babcock, cooperating with colleagues at other agricultural institutions—E.M. East, Raymond Pearl, and S.A. Beach, to name a few—pioneered genetics at academic agricultural institutions. And, as much civil servants as research scientists, academic breeders also were involved in a number of social movements with rural life as their focus, including the cooperative rural school movement and the Nature Study and Country Life Movements. Once engaged in Mendelian research, their adherence to rural nativism attracted many breeders to the eugenics movement, thanks in large part to Charles B. Davenport's efforts within the American Breeders' Association beginning in 1906. Thus, Mendelism became closely linked, in less than a decade, with both the practical and social concerns of the breeding research establishment.

From the viewpoint of developmental biologists, whose numbers were dominated by zoologically trained researchers, Mendel's work ignored developmental questions and seemed limited to specific kinds of alternating variation most easily examined in plant materials. From the perspective of evolutionary naturalists and experimentalists, de Vries's mutationism seemed of broader significance than Mendel's patterns. On the other hand, cytologists E.B. Wilson and Nettie Stevens supported Sutton's and Boveri's "chromosome theory" by confirming the resemblance between chromosomal behavior during meiosis and the inheritance patterns of alternating Mendelian characters. For at least a decade, cytologists and developmental and evolutionary biologists left Mendelian studies to the breeders, themselves pursuing connections between Mendelism and their own fields or assessing the evolutionary implications of the mutation theory.

One exception was William Castle, who at Harvard bred mice to explore the mechanism of coat color inheritance and who believed he had confirmed the power of natural selection when applied to "Mendelian" alternating characters. Another was Charles B. Davenport, director of the Cold Spring Harbor Station for Experimental Evolution, who maintained a strong allegiance to Darwinian evolutionary mechanisms while promoting new experimental investigations into evolutionary problems that included both Mendelism and biometry. These early American Mendelians thus did not reproduce the objections of British Mendelians to either Darwinian natural selection or biometry. Agricultural Mendelians displayed the same kind of tolerance. Raymond Pearl, until 1917 employed at the Maine Agricultural College and Experiment Station and interested in both practical and theoretcial issues, undertook simultaneous investigations in selection, Mendelian phenomena, and biometry, as did Harry Houser Love at the Cornell station.

Agriculturalists contributed significantly to both the practice and theory of genetics between 1900 and 1915. Working with a variety of economically significant organisms, they established that Mendel's findings had a wide applicability. They used the laws of dominance and independent assortment to explain troubling breeding phenomena that had puzzled breeders for centuries, thus providing an immediate context of use and illustrating Mendelism's explanatory power. Cornell's department under R.A. Emerson established corn as a crucial organism for genetic research. And E.M. East, in 1910, provided a crucial Mendelian explanation of continuously, or quantitatively, varying phenomena based on the physiological, even biochemical, interactions of multiple Mendelian factors.

At just this time, Thomas Hunt Morgan, whose early resistance to Mendel had been based on his mistrust of what he saw as "preformationist" notions surrounding the Mendelian "factors," undertook a series of experiments with *Drosophila melanogaster,* inspired by the cytological work of his colleague Wilson and by the possibility of identifying and investigating the kinds of mutations discussed by de Vries. With a group of graduate students, most notably A.H. Sturtevant, C.B. Bridges, and H.J. Muller, Morgan identified a series of mutations that resembled de Vriesian mutations—they were dramatic changes that appeared suddenly within a generation—and simultaneously behaved like one-half of a Mendelian alternating character when crossed with the original "wild" type. Recognizing the significance of these findings, Morgan and his students ultimately linked Mendelian patterns (and the increasingly notorious deviations from those patterns) with the chromosome theory of inheritance by identifying specific inheritance patterns with both "normal" and more unusual chromosomal behaviors, such as breakage and crossing over. Their efforts to provide gene maps of chromosomes transformed the genetics of the early Mendelians into what is known today as classical genetics. After 1915, when Morgan, Sturtevant, Bridges, and Muller published *The Mechanism of Mendelian Inheritance,* classical genetics came to dominate research in the discipline. In 1916, the journal *Genetics* was founded. Its editorial board included agriculturalists and experimental zoologists, and in its first decades, authorship was dominated by members or graduates of Morgan's laboratory and researchers at agricultural institutions.

A watershed in American genetics was reached between 1915 and 1920. Until then, most geneticists,

regardless of their training and institutional location, were self-made, having literally recruited themselves from the numbers of experimental and evolutionary naturalists and agricultural breeders of both plants and animals. While most breeding work addressed practical problems, investigators like E.M. East, Raymond Pearl, R.A. Emerson, and E.B. Babcock conducted fundamental studies in classical genetics while contributing to the practical functions of their home agricultural institutions. Some, like Pearl and East, left for more elite academic positions (at Johns Hopkins and Harvard, respectively), but others, like Emerson and Babcock, remained throughout their careers at agricultural institutions, recognized worldwide as geneticists. Of the group of zoologically trained, elite investigators, Jennings, Castle, Davenport, Morgan, and Shull ultimately made the transformation. But during the 1920s, the distinctions between breeders, embryologists, plant physiologists, agronomists, and zoologists, that earlier had been so fluid, hardened. Now, doing genetics required a Ph.D., available from both agricultural colleges and universities. Most of the next generation of geneticists—including Charles Metz, H.H. Plough, Sewall Wright, L.C. Dunn, Sterling Emerson, R.A. Brink, Barbara McClintock, George W. Beadle, E.G. Anderson, and E.W. Lindstrom—were trained either by members of Morgan's group, by the earliest Mendelian pioneers like Castle, or by the leading agricultural genetics programs at Cornell, Wisconsin, and Berkeley. Genetics was no longer an area of interest; it was an established discipline.

Also in this decade, the close association of eugenics and genetics culminated in testimony before congressional committees and in the 1924 Immigration Restriction Act. Perhaps because of this triumph for eugenicists, and the publicity it accorded both genetics and eugenics on the eve of even more notorious Nazi decrees, the explicit and highly visible association between them that had existed so strongly began to fade. This meant not that genetics would no longer be connected with a variety of social and political agendas (including eugenics), but rather that the kinds of social agendas, the kinds of publicity accorded them, and the theoretical and institutional links between them, would be different.

Both theoretical and practical investigations into the genetic makeup of populations, rather than of individuals, assumed a far more prominent place during the 1920s. Population studies of both domesticated and

G

natural populations had been undertaken earlier at agricultural institutions, chiefly by Pearl at Maine and by Love at Cornell. But the most important contributor in this area was Sewall Wright, who like Pearl was stimulated to undertake biometric analysis of the genetics of populations by his work at agricultural institutions. Between 1917 and 1930, Wright (for much of that time employed by the USDA's Bureau of Animal Industry) generated sophisticated statistical analyses of the effects of inbreeding, crossing, and selection on domestic breeding populations, subjects that had long been of interest to both practical breeders and evolutionary theorists. Wright's statistical exploration of the implications of Mendelian inheritance on gene frequencies within breeding populations when inbreeding and selection were present forged important links between Mendelian genetics and Darwinian evolutionary theory. His later elaboration of the crucial role in natural speciation of random genetic drift within small (rather than large) breeding populations was based directly on his statistical studies of artificial selection in domestic livestock herds.

Finally, in 1928, T.H. Morgan left Columbia to organize a department of biological research at the California Institute of Technology, to which Bridges and Sturtevant followed as colleagues and to which Morgan attracted a number of agriculturally trained geneticists, including Sterling Emerson and E.G. Anderson. A year later, Theodosius Dobzhansky, who had considered population questions in his native Soviet Union, joined Morgan's staff at Caltech. The removal of Morgan's group from East to West Coast as the core of a new biological department thus permitted its formal expansion and the inclusion of investigators with different training and different national backgrounds. In ensuing years, collaborations between Sturtevant and Dobzhansky and between Dobzhansky and Wright would further link Mendelian, population, and Darwinian studies.

During the 1930s and 1940s, two crucial developments dominated the disciplinary development of genetics in the United States. The first was continued attention to population genetics and its implications for evolutionary theory, culminating in Dobzhansky's 1937 book *Genetics and the Origin of Species*. The second was the rise to a dominant position of biochemical and ultimately molecular genetics. Like population studies by agricultural breeders, physiological investigation of problems in inheritance had been sustained in a number of contexts but had assumed a somewhat peripheral

role because of investigators' explicit antagonism to classical genetics. The 1930s and 1940s, however, witnessed a sustained focus on the physiological and biochemical basis of gene expression. New cooperative arrangements between leading universities and philanthropic institutions proved crucial in this shift. In particular, the Rockefeller Foundation's Division of Natural Sciences, headed by Warren Weaver, began an intensely focused funding of projects on the physiological and biochemical basis of more visible and socially significant factors, such as behavior. Genetics funded under this program—which included, among others, Tracy Sonneborn's demonstration of sexuality in paramecium and his then-controversial elaboration of a mechanism of cytoplasmic inheritance; serological and immunogenetic investigations by Sturtevant, and by M.R. Irwin and Leon J. Cole at Wisconsin; H.J. Muller's studies on structural and functional changes engendered by mutagenic agents; work on genetics and embryological development by H.H. Plough and Oscar Schotte; L.J. Stadler's work on cytological genetics; and G.W. Beadle's collaborations with Boris Ephrussi on *Drosophila* eye pigments and with the biochemist E.L. Tatum on the one-to-one ratio between gene and enzyme action in *Neurospora*—redirected attention directly to the biochemistry of gene expression and (less directly, perhaps) to the role of cytoplasmic substances in gene expression. While the Rockefeller funding policy could not directly determine the research agendas of individual scientists (most of whom had explored these areas for years), it could and did produce a discernible shift in disciplinary priorities.

Attention to genetically significant substances at the molecular level reached dramatic climax when, in 1953, American James Watson and Englishman Francis Crick proposed a double helical structure of DNA, in which the two helical strands were bonded to one another via biochemically complementary nucleic acids. They extended the theoretical underpinnings of the one-gene-one-enzyme model into the very structural elements of the genetic materal, thus accounting for the enzymatic specificity of both gene structure and action. And once theoretical and practical pathways had been cleared between expressed inherited characters and specific molecular structures on the chromosome and within the cytoplasm, a spate of intriguing and often controversial researches were undertaken, as often within a medical context as within research universities. The relationship between nuclear science, radioactivity, and genetics was cemented in the late 1940s and 1950s as the federal government's Atomic Energy Commission provided funds for medical research on the effects of radioactivity and for basic research employing radioactive materials. As mental health practitioners increasingly accepted biochemical as well as psychogenic bases for mental disturbances, the possibility of a genetic basis for the relevant biochemical disruptions were increasingly advanced. And interest in genetic manipulations with medical and commercial applications quickly evolved into a genetic engineering industry. Postwar genetics reminds historians to take very seriously the sociopolitical contexts within which disciplinary development occurs.

Other important themes emerge from this discussion. American genetics developed within a number of strikingly different institutional contexts. Some studies already have shown that certain kinds of institutions (e.g., agricultural, medical, commercial) provided unique opportunities and constraints that shaped the future development of the field. Historians may want to explore further the extent to which institutional location mattered in the development of genetics.

A large number of disciplines—physiology, cytology, developmental biology, evolutionary theory, heredity, ecology, and practical breeding and medical specialties —contributed to genetics and shaped its development. Studies of the extent to which, and why, these disciplines intersected with genetics at various times have produced (and will continue to produce) insights concerning the relationship between social and intellectual factors in disciplinary development.

Genetics is associated very closely with *Drosophila*, but many organisms have been the focus of genetic study. Research has been conducted on virtually all agricultural products (corn most prominently), and mice, guinea pigs, protozoa, bread mold, and human beings, not to mention plant and animal populations in the wild, have also been studied. Recent work has suggested that the choice of organism is indeed relevant for both theoretical and institutional development, exploring whether specific institutional contexts encourage or require work with particular organisms and whether different organisms encourage different approaches to genetic problems.

Sustained international relationships and collaborations have always been crucial for American genetics, from Bateson attending the 1902 conference on hybridization and early visits by Vilmorin, de Vries, and Johanssen to agricultural institutions as well as

Harvard and Cold Spring Harbor, to the permanent relocation of European scientists like Dobzhansky, Milislav Demerec, and Curt Stern; and from the interactions between Japanese geneticists and American population biologists to Wright's collaborations with Dobzhansky, Beadle's with Ephrussi, and Watson's with Crick. If we include the relationship of American agriculturalists with academic and commercial breeders in Latin America, Asia, and Africa, contacts often sustained by philanthropic, corporate, and government support, the range and nature of such interactions is extended even further. Historians may be interested in the nature and consequences of such contacts, in terms of comparative studies of national contexts, national research styles, and the implications of "imperial science." The history of genetics in the United States thus encompasses, and can illuminate, the global sociopolitics of science.

Finally, recent work in the history of agricultural, physiological, cytological, and medical genetics has issued the following challenge: that historians unravel the relationships between investigators in these often disparate areas and reconfigure notions of American genetics in given periods to include the entire range of genetic investigations, providing a series of cross sections as well as longitudinal accounts of change through time. Only in this way will a comprehensive account of genetics in the United States be developed, in which investigators conducting genetic research will be properly understood on their own terms within the intellectual and social context in which their work was originally conducted.

BIBLIOGRAPHY

Allen, Garland E. *Thomas Hunt Morgan: The Man and His Science.* Princeton: Princeton University Press, 1978.

Benson, Keith R., Jane Maienschein, and Ronald Rainger, eds. *The Expansion of American Biology.* New Brunswick: Rutgers University Press, 1991.

Fitzgerald, Deborah. *The Business of Breeding: Hybrid Corn in Illinois, 1890–1940.* Ithaca: Cornell University Press, 1990.

Kay, Lily. *The Molecular Vision of Life: Caltech, The Rockefeller Foundation, and the Rise of the New Biology.* New York: Oxford University Press, 1993.

Keller, Evelyn Fox. *A Feeling for the Organism: The Life and Work of Barbara McClintock.* New York: W.H. Freeman, 1983.

Kevles, Daniel J. *In the Name of Eugenics: Genetics and the Uses of Human Heredity.* New York: Knopf, 1985.

G

Kimmelman, Barbara A. "The American Breeders' Association: Genetics and Eugenics in an Agricultural Context." *Social Studies of Science* 13 (1983): 163–204.

———. "Organisms and Interests in Scientific Research: R.A. Emerson's Claims for the Unique Contributions of Agricultural Genetics." In *The Right Tools for the Job: At Work in Twentieth-Century Life Sciences,* edited by Adele E. Clarke and Joan H. Fujimura. Princeton: Princeton University Press, 1992, pp. 172–197.

Kohler, Robert E. *Lords of the Fly: Drosophila Genetics and the Experimental Life.* Chicago: University of Chicago Press, 1994.

Lindee, Susan. *Suffering Made Real: American Science and the Survivors at Hiroshima.* Chicago: University of Chicago Press, 1994.

Ludmerer, Kenneth L. *Genetics and American Society: A Historical Appraisal.* Baltimore: Johns Hopkins University Press, 1972.

Mitman, Gregg, and Anne Fausto-Sterling. "What Ever Happened to Planaria? C. M. Child and the Physiology of Inheritance." In *The Right Tools for the Job: At Work in Twentieth-Century Life Sciences,* edited by Adele E. Clarke and Joan H. Fujimura. Princeton: Princeton University Press, 1992, pp. 172–197.

Paul, Diane B., and B.A. Kimmelman. "Mendel in America: Theory and Practice." In *The American Development of Biology,* edited by R. Rainger, K.R. Benson, and J. Maienschein. Philadelphia: University of Pennsylvania Press, 1988, pp. 281–310.

Provine, William B. *Sewall Wright and Evolutionary Biology.* Chicago: University of Chicago Press, 1986.

Rosenberg, Charles E. "The Social Environment of Scientific Innovation: Factors in the Development of Genetics in the United States." In *No Other Gods: On American Science and Social Thought.* Baltimore: Johns Hopkins University Press, 1976, pp. 196–209.

Sapp, Jan. *Beyond the Gene: Cytoplasmic Inheritance and the Struggle for Authority in Genetics.* New York: Oxford University Press, 1987.

Barbara A. Kimmelman

SEE ALSO

Eugenics; Human Genome Project

Geographical Exploration

Organized expeditions of discovery were important sources of new scientific knowledge in nineteenth-century America. Their heyday coincided with the expansion of the United States from the Atlantic seaboard to the entire continent, roughly from 1790 to 1890. As the emphasis of the natural sciences shifted from description and classification to studies of form and function, geographical exploration began to play an increasingly peripheral role in the natural sciences in the United States. The golden age of scientific geographical exploration in the United States was the first two-thirds of the nineteenth century.

Long before the nineteenth century, however, British, French, Spanish, and American soldiers, priests, settlers, and travelers had explored large parts of what is now the continental United States. While the goals of these expeditions may have been primarily territorial, the early explorers also drew the first maps of the region and assembled some basic natural history collections. In the late eighteenth century, the search for new information about the natural world became a more important motive for exploration in what William H. Goetzmann characterizes as the "second great age of discovery." The United States was born at the beginning of this new age of discovery, and was profoundly shaped by it.

The Lewis and Clark Expedition, formed to explore Louisiana and the western half of the continent, was the first major odyssey of geographical exploration undertaken during the early Republic. The expedition was sponsored by Thomas Jefferson, president both of the United States and its then most important scientific institution, the Philadelphia-based American Philosophical Society. The maps that Lewis and Clark were charged with drawing and the botanical, geological, and ethnological collections they were to make had both scientific and commercial importance. By the time the mission began in 1804, the United States had purchased Louisiana from France. The expedition highlighted the strengths and weaknesses of science in the early republic. On the one hand Lewis and Clark did answer some pressing questions about American geography and drew attention to the resources of the American continent. But the scientific collections gathered by the expedition were dispersed over the United States and Europe, in part because of official indifference to the collections and in part because of the lack of an adequate institutional home for them.

The United States Exploring Expedition (also known as the Wilkes Expedition) of 1838–1842 was one of the most elaborate geographical expeditions mounted by the federal government. It included civilian scientists such as James Dwight Dana, who was later to become a prominent member of the American scientific establishment. The expedition spent four years sailing down the western coast of South America, around Antarctica, to Polynesia and Samoa, and Australia and New Zealand. They charted Pacific Islands, including Hawaii, and in 1841 explored the area around Puget Sound, what is now the coast of Washington. The collections assembled by the expedition were the base of the first federally sponsored scientific museum, the National Gallery of the Patent Office. Later, Joseph Henry, the secretary of the newly established Smithsonian Institution, had the collections moved to the Smithsonian, where they became the foundation of the new National Museum.

American scientific institutions sponsored many geographical expeditions, and then processed the information that the expeditions gathered. The remarkable growth of these institutions during the nineteenth century is in part a reflection of the scientific importance of the material discovered by the geographical expeditions. The Smithsonian Institution, founded in 1846, had established its role as the principal American repository and clearinghouse for geographical information of a scientific nature in the nineteenth century. Other institutions, such as the Boston Society of Natural History, the Academy of Natural Sciences of Philadelphia, the Albany Institute, the New York Lyceum of Natural History, and the Museum of Comparative Zoology at Harvard were also central in sponsoring expeditions and processing the collections of expeditions. These institutions were also important in processing natural history specimens collected by such prominent amateurs as the ornithologist and artist John James Audubon, and the more notorious gorilla hunter Paul Du Chaillu.

The middle third of the nineteenth century was the age of the great Army explorations of the western United States and the great civilian surveys which were the forerunners of the United States Geological Survey. The army explorations were largely by members of the army's Corps of Topographical Engineers. Under the leadership of men such as John C. Frémont, they mapped the West. By the 1870s, there were four competing surveys: the Geological Survey of the Fortieth Parallel, under the leadership of Clarence King; other surveys of adjoining (and sometimes overlapping) regions by George M. Wheeler and Ferdinand V. Hayden, and a civilian survey under John Wesley Powell. These surveys largely finished the job of mapping the continental United States.

Americans were also busy exploring overseas. The Wilkes Expedition was the first of several American expeditions to South America, the Pacific, and Africa. Matthew Fontaine Maury, for example, almost singlehandedly invented the science of oceanography while undertaking research about trade routes. Americans explored the Americas from the Amazon basin (as much with the end of forcing Brazil to open the river up to foreign navigation as to collect new scientific data) to the Northwest Passage.

In 1893, the historian Frederick Jackson Turner announced the closing of the American frontier. This date is also a convenient marker to indicate the end of scientific geographic exploration in the United States. This age had coincided with the settlement of the continent and the birth of the modern scientific community. At the beginning of the century, both the intellectual structure of natural history and the lack of knowledge of the continent made geographical exploration one of the most important sciences in the young Republic. Natural history emphasized the description and classification of new species. In the last two decades of the century, the center of scientific research in the United States shifted from the museums which emphasized natural history to the universities which emphasized the laboratory-based disciplinary sciences, such as anatomy and physiology. Natural history fell by the wayside. Geographical exploration became an activity largely divorced from the natural sciences as they had then come to be understood.

Much work remains to be done about the role of geographical exploration in the history of American science. Current history of exploration emphasizes the nineteenth century and afterward. There is considerable work to be done on the French, Spanish, and British explorers of what is now the continental United States, such as Sieur Robert Cavelier de La Salle, Cabeza de Vaca, and George Vancouver. These explorers were the first to map large areas of the current United States. We also need to know how the knowledge they assembled was incorporated into American geographical knowledge. Taking the long view would also highlight the transformations not only in the relationship between science and geography, but also the deep transformations within each field individually. These five centuries saw the Renaissance, the scientific revolution, the formation of scientific disciplines, and the emergence of the social sciences.

Historians of geography have suggested that expeditions of exploration be understood as part of a larger institutional process. This model is potentially very useful for historians of American science. For example, we can see the army surveys of the West as essential to

G

the growth of the great nineteenth-century scientific institutions such as the Smithsonian. Understanding voyages as part of the institutional process suggests that historians should look at the roles scientists had in planning the expeditions, what results they hoped to obtain from them, their relations with the people on the exploration, and the results of the exploration.

Some historians of science are beginning to look at how scientific knowledge is produced in settings other than laboratories. The nineteenth-century voyages are a potentially fruitful resource for the study of this problem. The archives of the Smithsonian Institution and the other natural history institutions mentioned above contain a wealth of untapped manuscripts that could help contribute to the emerging historiography of the field sciences. Recent work done on the history of scientific research schools suggests that research collectives in the field sciences were different from those in the laboratory sciences. The records of these voyages can help historians to identify some of the major research schools in American natural history.

The history of geographical exploration also has an important role to play in the emergent field of environmental history in the United States. Scientific explorers were important in assessing the natural potential of lands to be developed, and thus helped to shape the subsequent settlement and exploitation of those lands. In the later years of the nineteenth century, explorers such as John Muir became leaders in the conservation movement, founding organizations such as the Sierra Club.

Finally, there needs to be more research done into the causes and effects of the separation between geographical exploration and the natural sciences. For example, Robert Peary's voyages to Greenland and the North Pole at the turn of the century captured the public imagination but contributed little to either the life sciences or geological sciences. Voyages of scientific exploration, on the other hand, continue to this day, but their principal aim is not geographical discovery. Geology, ecology, and oceanography are three scientific fields related to geography in which exploration has remained important. If historians want to continue tracing the path of scientific exploration into the twentieth century, they need to look at these disciplines.

BIBLIOGRAPHY

Benson, Keith R. "From Museum Research to Laboratory Research: The Transformation of Natural History into Academic Biology." In *The American Development of Biology,* edited by Ronald Rainger, Keith R. Benson and Jane Maienschein. New Brunswick: Rutgers University Press, 1991, pp. 49–83.

Bowler, Peter J. *The Norton History of the Environmental Sciences.* New York: Norton, 1992.

Dupree, A. Hunter. *Science in the Federal Government: A History of Policies and Activities to 1940.* Cambridge, MA: Harvard University Press, 1957.

Goetzmann, William H. *Exploration and Empire: The Explorer and the Scientist in the Winning of the American West.* New York: Knopf, 1966.

———. *New Lands, New Men: America and the Second Great Age of Discovery.* New York: Viking, 1986.

Jackson, C. Ian. "Exploration as Science: Charles Wilkes and the U.S. Exploring Expedition, 1838–1842." *American Scientist* 73 (September–October 1985): 450–461.

Livingstone, David N. "The History of Science and the History of Geography: Interactions and Implications." *History of Science* 22 (1984): 271–302.

Overton, J.D. "A Theory of Exploration." *Journal of Historical Geography* 7 (1981): 53–70.

Smith, Michael. *Pacific Visions: California Scientists and the Environment, 1850–1915.* New Haven: Yale University Press, 1985.

Stuart McCook

SEE ALSO
Surveys, Federal Geological and Natural History

Geography

Prior to the 1880s, geography in the United States was a mix of geology, physiography, and exploratory observation. It was a subject matter in search of an organizing principle and a discipline.

It was not until 1883 that W.M. Davis seized on evolution as an organizing principle and established the cycle of erosion. This innovative idea provided a functioning model for physical geographers who wished to undertake fieldwork and comprehend what they saw. It also provided a model around which a literature could develop and that could be taught in the classroom, thereby giving birth to an embryonic discipline. Students of Davis became his disciples and spread his conception of geography across the United States and elsewhere. Davis himself took his system to Britain, France, and Germany.

In 1892, the Committee of Ten was formed and conferences were organized to study nine different academic subjects. It was in the subcommittee on geography that the Davisian viewpoint made its way into the majority report of the committee. Davisian geography was taught in many states, but the subject suffered from a lack of teacher preparedness.

Geographers then began turning their attention to forms of human geography. Davis offered his notion of ontography, an innovation that permitted a formal version of geographical determinism. Ontography constituted a study of life responses to the physical environment. This work ushered in the causal notion, and for the next twenty-five years, environmentalism dominated academic geography in the United States. Many extreme statements were advanced under this thesis, which brought the point of view into disrepute. Yet a lot of intelligent thought was also published on this matter. The largest problem confronting this tradition was the difficulty (and then virtually the impossibility) of measuring the impact of portions of a physical environment on an individual, a group, or society.

American geography essentially removed itself from environmentalism when many of the younger and more active members of the profession embraced Carl Sauer's article "The Morphology of Landscape" (1925), which argued that geographers could study the impress of humans on the land devoid of the necessity of "influences." Geographers began to study regions small enough to be traversed by foot, bicycle, or sometimes automobile. Sauer's statement had changed the scale at which geographers worked. Geographers in the United States now studied land use and the small-unit area. Fieldwork continued to be indispensable to geography.

During World War II, geographers worked in government in numbers as never before, and many offices were staffed to a considerable degree by them. As was the case in World War I, the map become very important, giving geography a standing it did not seem to enjoy in peacetime. It also encouraged geographers to realize that their regional specializations become very valuable assets in time of conflict. It also reaffirmed to geographers that no other discipline could produce such specialists.

Following the end of the war, the regional tradition continued but was joined by the innovation that was taking place at the University of Washington in Seattle. William Garrison and his (slightly) younger doctoral students were at work on a numerate and theoretical geography in the late 1950s; this genre spread across the United States and to other parts of the world. Certainly, it changed the face of American geography.

During the last twenty-five years, eclecticism has been the dominant mode. Fragmentation, typified by more than forty specialty groups in the Association of American Geographers, has been accompanied by a search for appropriate philosophy and methodology. The quest for comprehension of the nature of geography continues but seems ever more elusive.

The fact is that today's innovation becomes tomorrow's tradition. Traditions do not die easily and therefore are additive. In a study of the history of geography, these traditions have only theoretical significance. But in geography as a practicing field, geographers, encompassing many different ages and different traditions, perhaps all teaching in the same university department, tend to remind each other that there is no right way to comprehend humans on the land as our central mission. Innovations that become traditions are a vital part of the process by which the discipline advances.

BIBLIOGRAPHY

Blouet, Brian, ed. *The Origins of Academic Geography in the United States.* Hamden, CT: Archon Books, 1981.

Bowman, Isaiah. *Geography in Relationship to the Social Sciences.* New York: Charles Scribner's Sons, 1934.

Chorley, Richard J., R.P. Beckinsale, and A.J. Dunn. *The History of the Study of Landforms or the Development of Geomorphology, Vol. 2. The Life and Work of William Morris Davis.* London: Methuen, 1973.

Hartshorne, Richard. *The Nature of Geography: A Critical Survey of Current Thought in the Light of the Past.* Lancaster, PA: Association of American Geographers, 1939.

James, Preston E., and C.F. Jones. *American Geography: Inventory and Prospect.* Syracuse: Syracuse University Press, for the Association of American Geographers, 1954.

Martin, Geoffrey J., and Preston E. James. *All Possible Worlds: A History of Geographical Ideas.* 3d ed. New York: John Wiley & Sons, 1993.

Sauer, Carl O. "The Morphology of Landscape." *University of California Publications in Geography,* 2:19–53.

Stoddart, David R. *On Geography and Its History.* Oxford and New York: Blackwell, 1986.

Geoffrey J. Martin

Geological Society of America, The

A not-for-profit organization dedicated to advancing the scientific and professional growth of its members in ways that foster accelerated discovery of new knowledge in the geosciences, stimulate effective and creative teaching of the geosciences, generate innovative applications of geoscientific knowledge to the benefit of society, and stimulate informed public awareness of

G

critical scientific issues. The society was founded in 1888 by James Hall, James D. Dana, and Alexander Winchell as a descendant of the American Association for the Advancement of Science. Headquarters are located in Boulder, Colorado.

The Geological Society of America (GSA) is a membership society consisting of 14,500 fellows and members, as well as student and teacher associates. Primary activities of the society are the publication of scientific literature and the organization of scientific meetings and conferences. It also disburses student research grants, operates an employment matching and interview service, gives several medals and awards in recognition of outstanding scientific contributions, assists teachers in geoscience education, and fosters public awareness of geoscience issues. The society's elected officers (executive committee and council) control the management of its affairs.

Six regional GSA sections within North America have individual management boards, and each section conducts an annual meeting. The society holds a general annual meeting each year in a city in North America, featuring presentation of scientific papers in multiple sessions. GSA has twelve divisions for different specialty areas, such as archeological geology, hydrogeology, and geophysics. Any GSA member may join any division. The divisions generally meet at the annual meeting of the society, make awards to honor member contributions, and generate newsletters focused on member activities. Seventeen specialized associated societies also commonly hold their annual meetings in conjunction with the GSA annual meeting and assist in developing the scientific program, thereby ensuring breadth of program scope.

GSA received a substantial bequest in 1931 from geologist R.A.F. Penrose Jr. (Ph.D., Harvard, 1886). Income from this endowment makes possible the disbursement of research grants and supports some GSA publications. In 1980, the Geological Society of America Foundation was organized to support the Decade of North American Geology project, a multipublication synthesis, and to consolidate annual membership giving.

All GSA members receive *GSA Today,* the monthly membership newsletter. The society has published the technical journal *Geological Society of America Bulletin* continuously each month since 1890. In 1973, GSA introduced the monthly journal *Geology* in response to the need for rapid publication of short, topical scientific articles. All three publications are on *GSA Journals*

on Compact Disc, published twice a year. GSA also jointly publishes *Environmental & Engineering Geoscience* (with the Association of Engineering Geologists) and the *Journal of Applied Hydrogeology* (with the International Association of Hydrogeologists), both quarterly. Other GSA publications include several monograph series, a map and chart series, *Abstracts with Programs* for its meetings, and the Decade of North American Geology series, which includes books, maps, and transects.

BIBLIOGRAPHY

Eckel, Edwin B. *The Geological Society of America: Life History of a Learned Society.* Boulder, CO: Geological Society of America Memoir 155, 1982.

Donald M. Davidson Jr.

Geological Survey, United States

On 3 March 1879, the forty-fifth Congress and President Rutherford Hayes established the United States Geological Survey (USGS), as an agency of the Department of the Interior, for "the classification of the public lands and examination of the Geological Structure, mineral resources and products of the national domain" (*U.S. Statutes at Large,* 394). The politicians and scientists who shaped the USGS's legislation intended the new agency to aid the nation's struggling economy, by supporting its mining industry, and to improve the civil service by increasing economy, efficiency, harmony, and utility in federal geology. The statute discontinued the three competing federal geological and geographical surveys of the public domain in the West, a victory for civilian science, systematization, and retrenchment, but included some of these surveys' functions in the USGS. To protect the integrity and impartiality of the USGS's data and analyses, the law prohibited its employees from speculating in the lands or minerals under study or conducting outside consulting. The legislation also named the Smithsonian Institution's National Museum as the USGS's collections repository and detailed the nature of USGS publications. The reformers did not succeed in establishing within the Interior Department a separate mapping agency, for cadastral, geodetic, and topographic surveys, or in improving the department's administration of the public lands.

During the years 1820 to 1878, some twenty countries, and states and provinces within them, and one future nation established geological surveys to aid the scientific census and rational development of their national mineral resources for the public good. As they evolved into permanent agencies, some of these national surveys gained educational, topographic mapping, natural history, and museum functions, many of which now reside in other agencies, or they drew on older bureaus for this expertise. Because the USGS's founders eschewed activities in natural history and limited those in geology and topography that did not directly support the mandated principal mission in economic geology, some historians have seen the original vision as too narrow for good science and outside support. Clarence King, appointed the founding director by Hayes, drew on his experiences while serving (1863–1866) in the Geological Survey of California and leading the United States Geological Exploration of the Fortieth Parallel (1867–1879) in helping to shape and then conduct the USGS during 1879–1881. King intended USGS mineral-resource studies principally to yield immediate results of practical value for industry, currency, and scientific land-classification. King also expected results in economic geology to contribute to understanding the nature of ore deposits and, with related work in general geology, to advance knowledge of the earth and its history.

In 1882, Congress authorized USGS activities nationwide to support the production of the reliable national geologic map sought by King. Under this rubric, John Wesley Powell, the second director (1881–1894), remade the USGS as an agency for topographic mapping (by default and design the necessary national program) and basic research in geology, at the expense of economic geology. In 1888, Congress gave Powell an opportunity to pursue his long-standing goal of reforming land and water use in the West by authorizing the Irrigation Survey (IS) within the USGS. During 1890–1894, Congress repudiated Powell's policies and programs, principally because they did not yield the requested practical assessments of the nation's mineral and water resources. Congress first terminated the IS, then selectively slashed the USGS's staff and operating expenses, and finally encouraged Powell to resign by reducing his salary.

Under Charles Doolittle Walcott's leadership (1894–1907), the USGS became more useful to the nation by expanding its mission to include any practical objective that could be advanced by greater knowledge of the earth sciences. Walcott's balanced program

of applied and basic research restored Congress's confidence and increased appropriations beyond those granted Powell. Walcott restored the USGS's program in economic geology, reorganized its other geological work, professionalized its topographic mapping, and began successful studies of water resources and arid-land reclamation, native peoples' lands, forest reserves, and fuels- and structural-materials testing. Most of these and other functions later transferred to the USGS that did not develop or retain scientific components passed to other Interior Department bureaus—Reclamation (1907), Mines (1910), Land Management (1946), and Minerals Management (1982)—or to outside agencies (Forest Service and Bureau of Standards.)

The USGS's successes and failures in meeting societal needs, under its ten directors since 1907, have depended on both internal and external factors. Historians differ as to the value of directors' styles, techniques, and length-of-terms in managing scientific organizations, but the effectiveness and longevity of these agencies depend on successfully applying information obtained from basic research to evident or anticipated problems. Securing adequate funding for this work required the USGS and the Executive Branch to sustain Congress's belief that the agency could continue to aid the development and execution of informed policies regarding the national landmass, its natural resources, and its environmental quality. Congress expanded the USGS's geographical and intellectual frontiers in 1962, when it authorized operations outside the national domain. Since the 1960s, however, the USGS and other domestic science agencies have found basic research more difficult to justify and sell. Hard choices continue to face these agencies about how best to promote and fund their work (by direct appropriations or reimbursable monies), to plan and conduct balanced mission-oriented programs (with enough basic research to ensure having sufficient science to apply), and to accomplish their tasks (with staff or contract expertise).

To carry out its present investigative and advisory missions, the USGS is organized in six principal units—four program divisions (Biological Resources, Geologic, National Mapping, and Water Resources) and two sustaining offices (Director's and Program Support). The agency conducts geologic mapping, evaluates earthquake, landslide, and volcanic hazards, studies geologic processes, and assesses mineral and energy resources and offshore seabed areas, including

G

the Exclusive Economic Zone. The USGS prepares base, image, and thematic maps and atlases, produces digital cartographic and geographic data, and coordinates requirements for maps and map-related products from federal, state, and local governments. The agency also assesses the quality and quantity of, and the hazards associated with, the nation's ground- and surface-water resources. Adding the former National Biological Service in 1996 made the USGS responsible for understanding the status and trends of the nation's biological resources. The USGS draws on all these programs to provide information to address environmental issues, such as changes in global climate.

The most informed analysis of federal and USGS policies and activities in the earth sciences through 1939 is in the first three volumes of the agency's own history (Rabbitt, 1979–1986). This ongoing study, based almost entirely on the published record, is valuable as a reference and as a guide to further investigations. Only one printed study (Manning, 1967) has used significant unpublished sources in evaluating events during 1867–1894. Improved understanding of USGS history for use within the agency and by federal and other policy and decision makers must come from analyses based on unpublished sources in government and nongovernment archives. To aid future work, the USGS and the National Archives and Records Administration (NARA) have completed a detailed inventory (Jaussaud) of NARA's Record Group 57 (Geological Survey).

BIBLIOGRAPHY

Agnew, Allen F. *The U.S. Geological Survey.* Washington, DC: Government Printing Office, 1975 [U.S. Congress, 94th, 1st Session, Senate Committee on Interior and Insular Affairs, 59–715].

Dupree, A. Hunter. *Science in the Federal Government: A History of Policies and Activities to 1940.* Cambridge, MA: Harvard University Press, 1957.

Eaton, Gordon P., et al. "The New U.S. Geological Survey: Environment, Resources, and the Future." *Environmental Geosciences* 4 (1997): 3–10.

Jaussaud, Renée M., comp. "Inventory of the Records of the United States Geological Survey Record Group 57 in the National Archives." In *Records and History of the United States Geological Survey,* edited by Clifford M. Nelson. U.S. Geological Survey Circular 1179 (CD-ROM), 2000.

Manning, Thomas G. *Government in Science: The U.S. Geological Survey 1867–1894.* Lexington: University of Kentucky Press, 1967.

———. "United States Geological Survey (USGS)." In *Government Agencies,* edited by Donald R. Whitnah. Westport and London: Greenwood Press, 1983, pp. 548–553.

Mayers, Lewis, ed. *The U.S. Geological Survey. Its History, Activities and Organization.* New York: D. Appleton, 1918 [Institute for Government Research, Service Monographs of the United States Government No. 1].

Nolan, Thomas B., and Mary C. Rabbitt. "The USGS at 100 and the Advancement of Geology in the Public Service," In *Frontiers of Geological Exploration of Western North America,* edited by Alan E. Leviton et al. San Francisco: American Association for the Advancement of Science, Pacific Division, 1982, pp. 11–17.

Rabbitt, Mary C. *Minerals, Lands, and Geology for the Common Defence and General Welfare.* 3 vols. Washington, DC: Government Printing Office, 1979–1986.

Rizer, Henry C., transmitter. "The United States Geological Survey. Its Origin, Development, Organization, and Operation." *U.S. Geological Survey Bulletin* 227 (1904).

Smith, Charles H. "Geological Surveys in the Public Service," In "Earth Science in the Public Service." *U.S. Geological Survey Professional Paper* 921 (1974): 2–6.

Smith, George O. "A Century of Government Geological Surveys." In *A Century of Science in America,* edited by Edward S. Dana. New Haven: Yale University Press, 1918, pp. 193–216.

United States Congress, House of Representatives. *Report of National Academy of Sciences, Letter from O. C. Marsh, Acting President Transmitting Report of Operations . . . During the Past Year.* Washington, DC: Government Printing Office, 1879 [U.S. Congress, 46th, 1st Session, House Miscellaneous Document 7 (Serial 1861)].

Walcott, Charles D. *The United States Geological Survey.* Washington, DC: Judd & Detweiler, for the Geological Society of Washington, 1895.

Clifford M. Nelson

SEE ALSO
Surveys, Federal Geological and Natural History

Geology

The development of geology in the United States was to some extent determined by the physical features of the North American continent itself. Although in the early years Americans relied heavily on the work of geologists in England and Europe, the search for economic resources and attempts to explain the origin of unfamiliar landforms resulted in the production of new knowledge that soon made American geology widely admired abroad.

During the eighteenth century, geologists were attracted to various fanciful theories about the formation of the earth's crust that usually attributed its disturbed condition to the destructive force of a universal deluge. Such theories were soon abandoned by Americans, however, most of whom shared Thomas Jefferson's belief that they were useless speculation. Instead, some naturalists, both European and American, who traveled throughout the eastern United States, closely observed geological formations and collected specimens of rocks and minerals. Large mineralogical collections were acquired by Harvard, Yale, and other colleges and scientific institutions, providing valuable educational tools and forming the basis for geological museums.

Chief among the early field geologists was William Maclure, often called the father of American geology. Born in Scotland in 1763, he became a United States citizen in 1796, and in 1808 and 1809, he toured the regions east of the Mississippi, crossing the Alleghenies at least fifty times and collecting specimens every half mile. His report, published in 1809 by the American Philosophical Society, was accompanied by the first colored geological map of the United States. Maclure, like many other early American geologists, relied on the work of the Saxon mineralogist Abraham Gottlob Werner, whose rock classification system was widely used throughout the world. Maclure, however, did not accept Werner's Neptunist theory that the earth's crust was formed by sedimentation from primeval seas. On his map, which preceded William Smith's geological map of the British Isles by six years, Maclure indicated in different colors Werner's Primitive, Transition, and Secondary rocks and the unconsolidated alluvial deposits of the coastal plains. For its time, and considering the large area covered, the map was a good representation of the main geological formations of the eastern part of the United States. As president of the Academy of Natural Sciences of Philadelphia from 1817 to 1840, Maclure encouraged geological studies, and many articles on geology were published in the academy's *Journal*. George P. Merrill calls the period from 1785 to 1819 the "Maclurean era" of American geology.

Another important influence on early American geology was Benjamin Silliman Sr., who taught chemistry, mineralogy, and geology at Yale University from 1802 until his retirement in 1855. Silliman spent the winter of 1805–1806 in Edinburgh, where he became aware of the controversy between followers of Werner's Neptunist theories and proponents of James Hutton's

uniformitarian and Vulcanist views. With a new enthusiasm for geology, he returned to the United States, investigated the geology of the New Haven region, and soon made Yale an important center for geological studies. His students, who included Edward Hitchcock, James Dwight Dana, and Amos Eaton, went on to teach in colleges throughout the country and his *American Journal of Science* became an important forum for new geological ideas.

Amos Eaton was an early promoter of fieldwork, prompting Merrill to call the decade of the 1820s "the Eatonian era." Eaton used Werner's classification system for the rock formations but developed further subdivisions within Werner's Primitive, Transition and Secondary classes, which he published in his *Index to the Geology of the Northern States* in 1818. He tried to correlate American formations with those of England and Europe but, unlike William Smith in England and Georges Cuvier and Alexandre Brongniart in Paris, made little use of fossils to identify strata. Relying primarily on lithological characteristics, Eaton correctly determined the succession of the New York rocks and laid the groundwork for later studies of stratigraphy. In 1822, he surveyed the route of the Erie Canal for Stephen van Rensselaer, who chose him to head the science program at the newly established Rensselaer School (now Rensselaer Polytechnic Institute). Eaton taught many future high school and college teachers and members of state geological surveys, taking them on summer field trips during the construction of the Erie Canal.

The establishment of several state geological and natural history surveys in the 1830s and 1840s marked the beginning of true professionalism and a new maturity in the geological sciences in the United States. State geologists surveyed routes for roads, canals, and railroads and provided information about mineral and other economic resources. The Massachusetts survey, directed by Edward Hitchcock from 1830 to 1833, was the first to be completed at state expense. The final report of over 700 pages included a colored map of the state, geological sections, descriptions of rock formations and theories about their origin, as well as practical information. Surveys of New York and Pennsylvania were both begun in 1836. Pennsylvania's, directed by Henry D. Rogers, included evaluations of the state's extensive coal deposits and an important study of the structure of the Appalachians.

New York's survey was noted for the work done on paleontology by James Hall and others; it firmly

G

established the importance of fossils for determining age and for correlation of American and European formations. Using fossil criteria, New York's geologists worked out the order of the extensive undisturbed Paleozoic rocks of the state and found them to be the equivalent of the Cambrian, Silurian, and Devonian systems of the English geologists. Hall, who later served as state geologist of Iowa, determined that the strata, which were very thick and tilted in the Appalachians, thinned as they continued into the Midwest. Hall theorized that the thick strata near the mountains had originally been deposited by currents of a former Midwestern sea, and that the weight of the accumulating sediment had caused a sinking of the crust and a compensating uplift, with folding and faulting, of mountain ranges. Hall's theory was based on uniformitarian principles, in contrast to the "catastrophist" theories of William and Henry Rogers, who thought that earthquakes and other forces within the earth had pushed up mountains.

A rival theory, proposed by James Dwight Dana, was that mountains had been formed during the contraction brought about by the cooling of the earth, a process often compared to the wrinkling of a drying apple. Dana become established as one of America's leading theoretical geologists after serving from 1838 to 1842 as geologist with the United States Exploring Expedition. Contraction, according to Dana, had provided the lateral force that had deepened ocean basins and pushed up the mountains. Most American geologists accepted Dana's theory and, like him, remained convinced for most of the nineteenth century that the continents had been permanently in place. In 1873, Dana introduced the first comprehensive picture of the geosyncline, or downfold, a structure typical of the Appalachian region. As Silliman Professor of Geology and Mineralogy at Yale, as editor of *American Journal of Science,* and through his *System of Mineralogy* (1837) and *Manual of Geology* (1862), both textbooks being republished in many editions, Dana's strong influence on American geology was felt throughout the nineteenth century.

By the 1840s, British and European geologists recognized the importance of the work being done by Americans. In 1841–1842 and again in 1844–1845, Charles Lyell, proponent of uniformitarianism and author of the influential *Principles of Geology,* visited many interesting geological sites with Silliman, James Hall, and others, and published accounts of his American travels. The Swiss naturalist Louis Agassiz, who came to the United States in 1846, was also impressed with American accomplishments and stayed to teach at Harvard. Agassiz's *Etudes sur les Glaciers,* published in 1840, stirred up a controversy among American geologists. Silliman, Eaton, and Hitchcock had attributed erratic rocks and boulders deposited far from their original source to the work of the last Great Deluge, using their observations to show that geology supported the Bible. Agassiz proposed that such phenomena were the work of huge glaciers that had spread over the continents in former geological periods. Doubtful at first, Americans eventually accepted the glacial hypothesis, as the northern parts of the continent provided ample evidence to support it, in the form of glacial drift, moraines, and polished and grooved rock surfaces. By the late 1870s, Thomas C. Chamberlin of the Wisconsin state survey reported evidence of at least three glacial periods in North America, with interglacial warming periods.

Several antebellum federal surveys of the western territories demonstrated the usefulness of geology to the national economy. David Dale Owen surveyed the upper Mississippi Valley in 1839–1840 for the General Land Office and discovered that the region was rich in lead ores. Josiah Whitney and John W. Foster examined the copper lands of Upper Michigan, hoping to calm the excesses of the copper boom of the 1840s. In the 1850s, geologists accompanied the army Corps of Topographical Engineers as they surveyed possible routes for a transcontinental railroad, using the opportunity to study, describe, and map some of the unfamiliar formations of the West for the first time.

After the Civil War, four geological surveys of the West that included a number of well-trained geologists made notable contributions to both theoretical and practical geology. Ferdinand V. Hayden's Geological and Geographical Survey of the Territories made Hayden the "most powerful and most celebrated public scientist of the seventies" (Manning, p. 15). Hayden's survey was noted for its geological maps, for the work of its paleontologists Fielding B. Meek, Edward Cope, and Leo Lesquereux, and for Hayden's efforts in preserving the Yellowstone region as a national park, foreshadowing future conservation and preservation work by American geologists.

Clarence King and his assistants on the fortieth parallel survey, working from 1867 to 1877, identified the divisions of the geological column along the one-hundred-mile-wide cross section covered by the survey, and produced a thorough study of the Comstock Lode.

Volume six of King's final report, *Microscopical Petrography* (1876) by Ferdinand Zirkel, stimulated the adoption by Americans of German techniques in petrology. The Geographical Survey West of the 100th Meridian, led by Lieutenant G.M. Wheeler of the army engineers, was primarily a mapping expedition, but was important to geology because it shaped the future career of Grove Karl Gilbert, who joined the Wheeler survey as geologist in 1871. Gilbert's exposure to the western landscape inspired his later classic work on the Henry Mountains and Lake Bonneville, which was to make him one of the most admired of American geologists.

The Geological and Geographical Survey of the Territories was organized in the early 1870s by the one-armed John Wesley Powell, who had made a daring journey to explore the Colorado River in 1869. Members of the survey were especially impressed by the dramatic plateau and canyon regions of the West. From their studies of past erosion that had shaped the landscape, Powell, Clarence Dutton, and Gilbert, who joined Powell's survey in 1875, created a new, wholly American branch of geology, the study of the evolution of landforms. Their work was further developed by William Morris Davis of Harvard as the science now known as geomorphology. Powell introduced the concept of erosion to "base level" and the terms "consequent," "antecedent," and "superimposed" to describe streams at various stages in their evolution. Dutton's *Tertiary History of the Grand Canyon District* (1882) was a landmark study and the first monograph to be published by the United States Geological Survey (USGS). In 1889, Dutton coined the term "isostasy," a major concept in geology that was based partly on the work of English geologists but was further advanced by Gilbert and other Americans. The term refers to the tendency of the earth's crust to maintain equilibrium between blocks of different weight or density. The idea of a crust that adjusted itself challenged but did not immediately overthrow Dana's contractional hypothesis that had dominated theory in the United States up to that time.

In 1879, the four overlapping western surveys were consolidated by an act of Congress to create the USGS, with Clarence King as first director. Powell succeeded King in 1881, and under his direction the USGS became for a time the best funded and most powerful scientific agency in Washington, conducting research in many areas of geology, providing information useful to the mining industry, and making topographic maps.

With the founding of the survey, geology became a fully professionalized activity. In the last decades of the century, graduate departments of geology were created at universities, the Geological Society of America was organized (in 1888), and professional journals devoted solely to geology were founded.

With the growth of new knowledge, gained in part during what has been called the "heroic age" of the western surveys, new specialties developed, such as volcanology, hydrology, and geophysics. The invention of the internal combustion engine made new careers for petroleum geologists; the mining industry created a demand for economic geologists—those with a knowledge of the origin and location of ore deposits. The San Francisco Earthquake of 1906 stimulated the growth of seismology, providing an indispensable tool for the study of the earth's interior. Geoarchaeology became a subdiscipline because archaeologists realized the need to understand the past environment of a site undergoing excavation.

Nevertheless, by the end of the nineteenth century, theoretical geology was at a standstill, and remained so until after the middle of the twentieth century. The main outlines of the geological timescale had been filled in and the country was being mapped by a well-trained corps of workers, but there was no longer a satisfactory comprehensive explanation of mountain building. Structural geologists studied and mapped the features of mountains without agreeing on how they had risen. What stimulated the further growth of the earth sciences was the acceptance in the 1960s of the theory of continental drift, the most revolutionary development of twentieth-century geology. Originally proposed by the American Frank B. Taylor in 1910, but presented in the form of a more comprehensive hypothesis by Alfred Wegener in 1912, the idea that the continents had originally been joined in one large landmass and had drifted apart on a semifluid substrate was at first rejected at a symposium held in Washington, D.C., in 1926, by American geologists who were brought up on Dana's theory of contraction and the permanence of continents. In 1944, for example, Bailey Willis of Stanford called continental drift "Ein Märchen" (a fairy tale), and recommended geologists waste no further time on it.

While many scientists in many fields and countries contributed to the confirmation of drift theory, it was the American Harry Hess of Princeton who provided crucial evidence in 1962 that new crust was created by

G

magma rising at midoceanic ridges, spreading along the seafloor by means of convection currents, and plunging again into the mantle beneath the continents. Later, new paleomagnetic studies of oceanic rocks by geologists of the USGS, among others, provided dating methods and proof of seafloor spreading, and in April 1967, at a symposium of the American Geophysical Union, attendees enthusiastically endorsed Hess's concept. At the same conference, Jason Morgan of Princeton suggested that the earth's surface was composed of several large plates, on which the continents rode. In subsequent years, plate tectonics has become the unifying theory for research in all of the earth sciences, and its quick acceptance after 1967 has been cited as a paradigm shift illustrating Thomas Kuhn's model of scientific revolutions.

BIBLIOGRAPHY

Drake, Ellen T., and William M. Jordan, eds. *Geologists and Ideas. A History of North American Geology.* Boulder, CO: Geological Society of America, 1985.

Greene, John C. *American Science in the Age of Jefferson.* Ames: Iowa State University Press, 1984.

Manning, Thomas G. *Government in Science: The U.S. Geological Survey, 1867–1894.* Lexington: University of Kentucky Press, 1967.

Marvin, Ursula B. *Continental Drift: The Evolution of a Concept.* Washington, DC: Smithsonian Institution Press, 1973.

Merrill, George P. *The First One Hundred Years of American Geology.* New Haven: Yale University Press, 1924; reprinted, 1964.

———. *Contributions to a History of American State Geological and Natural History Surveys.* Washington, DC: United States National Museum, 1920; reprinted, 1978.

Pyne, Steve. "From the Grand Canyon to the Marianas Trench: The Earth Sciences after Darwin." In *The Sciences in the American Context: New Perspectives,* edited by Nathan Reingold. Washington, DC: Smithsonian Institution, 1979, pp. 165–192.

Rabbitt, Mary C. *Minerals, Lands, and Geology for the Common Defence and General Welfare.* 3 vols. Washington, DC: Government Printing Office, 1979–1986.

Schneer, Cecil J., ed. *Two Hundred Years of Geology in America: Proceedings of the New Hampshire Bicentennial Conference on the History of Geology.* Hanover, NH: University Press of New England, 1979.

Peggy Champlin

SEE ALSO

Crystallography; Mineralogy, Plate Tectonics

Geophysics and Geodesy

Respectively, the study of the earth's physical properties and of its shape. Both these sciences have been long practiced in the United States, and American scientists have contributed essentially to them. Early prominent researches included Benjamin Franklin's studies of lightning and the Gulf Stream in the eighteenth century and Elias Loomis's studies of geomagnetism and meteorology in the nineteenth. Throughout the nineteenth century, American researchers referred to these problem areas, as well as problems in tides, river flow, glacial geology, aurora, and more, as part of physical geography or terrestrial physics. The word "geophysics," although in use in the mid-nineteenth century, was not yet widely recognized.

The most important institutional support of geophysical and geodetic research in nineteenth-century America was provided by the federal government. The Coast Survey, the army's Corps of Topographic Engineers, the army's Corps of Engineers, and the United States Naval Observatory, each supported scientific research in addition to providing important public services: harbor and geodetic surveys, topographic surveys, river hydrography, and ocean-current studies. Some of these agencies gradually expanded the range of research problems promoted. The Coast Survey became the Coast and Geodetic Survey in 1878 and pursued rigorous geodetic and gravimetric investigations. Charles S. Peirce, John F. Hayford, and Seth Chandler all worked for the Coast Survey, making fundamental contributions, respectively, to gravimetry, geodesy, and geodynamics. The survey added a division for geomagnetic research in 1899 and later included seismology. Similarly, the Geological Survey (founded 1878) established a geophysical and geochemical laboratory in the 1880s.

While federal geophysics and geodesy continued, scientists active in these sciences began finding other sources of support. The first known instructor of geophysics in the United States was Louis Agricola Bauer at the University of Chicago in 1896. In 1904–1905, the privately endowed Carnegie Institution of Washington established three departments that either focused on or included geophysical topics: the Geophysical Laboratory, the Department of Terrestrial Magnetism, and the Mount Wilson Solar Observatory. In the 1920s, mining and petroleum companies began applying geophysical techniques to prospect for new resources. Texaco, Humble, and Gulf Oil were among the leaders, and researchers began terming themselves geophysical consultants. Professors such as Norman H. Ricker at Rice University and Max Mason at the University of Wisconsin began consulting firms on the side. A plethora of firms such as the Geophysical Research Corporation and Western Geophysical appeared in the 1920s and 1930s. Their roles in the development of new instruments and techniques, as well as of new understanding of the structure of the earth's crust, steadily grew in importance.

World Wars I and II changed geophysics and geodesy in the United States, just as they changed other sciences. Underwater acoustics and geomagnetic investigations were applied to submarine detection in World War I. By World War II, radio made knowledge of the ionosphere and of solar activity matters of national security. During the Cold War, seismic techniques and high-altitude air sampling were used to detect nuclear explosions. Oceanography greatly expanded. As a result, beginning in the 1930s, and particularly after 1945, progressively more military funding flowed into geophysics.

This increasing importance of geophysics to the nation-state was also reflected in the international relations of the science. Geophysics and geodesy, as global sciences, necessarily involved scientists from many countries. The first International Polar Year of the 1880s symbolized the beginning of international cooperation in geophysics. By World War I, international associations had formed for meteorology, seismology, geodesy, and so on, although there was none yet for geophysics as a whole. American scientists participated extensively in these fledgling efforts. Following World War I, all the old organizations were disbanded and new ones instituted, primarily to exclude German scientists and organizations. This also provided an opportunity to restructure the international organization of science. All the branches of geophysics were brought together in the International Union of Geodesy and Geophysics. The individual research areas became "sections" of the union. The American Geophysical Union (AGU) was founded as America's constituent part of the international union. While the AGU has done much to promote geophysical research, both nationally and internationally, it has also necessarily been a locus of political debate. A founder, George Ellery Hale, said it clearly when he argued to a secretary of state in 1920 that the AGU was intimately a part of the nation's relations with other countries. This became even more true after World War II, with the critical involvement of

American geophysicists in organizing the International Geophysical Year in the 1950s.

Another major institutional development in geophysics has been the dramatic increase in the number of university programs. Geophysics was being taught in a few American geology departments in the 1920s, and full departments were started at St. Louis University (1925) and at the Colorado School of Mines (1927). After World War II, institutes or departments of geophysics were founded at the University of California at Los Angeles (1944), the University of Alaska (1946), and Columbia University (1948). By 1950, eight geophysics departments and nine meteorology departments granted graduate degrees.

The advent of new electronic equipment, including computers, has drastically changed geophysics and geodesy since 1950. It became possible to detect stresses deep within the earth, or to describe complex seismic events quantitatively. Likewise, rocketry and high-altitude ballooning made study of the upper atmosphere and near-space possible. The discovery of the Van Allen radiation belts dramatized this new capability. The best known geophysical research of the late twentieth century, in America as elsewhere, was the success of plate tectonics in explaining numerous geological questions (see LeGrand).

In almost all of its aspects, geophysics in the United States offers rich opportunities for historical research. The most thoroughly examined topic is certainly the history of the plate-tectonic revolution. Very little has been written about the history of seismology, oceanography, or near-space physics. The relations of geophysics with better known sciences such as physics and geology are still not well understood. Lastly, the social and institutional development of geophysics and its branches are virtually unexamined.

BIBLIOGRAPHY

Bates, Charles C., Thomas F. Gaskell, and Robert B. Rice. *Geophysics in the Affairs of Man: A Personalized History of Exploration Geophysics and Its Allied Sciences of Seismology and Oceanography.* Oxford, U.K.: Pergamon, 1982.

Buntebarth, Gònter. "Geophysics: Disciplinary History." In *Sciences of the Earth: An Encyclopedia of Events, People, and Phenomena,* edited by Gregory A. Good. New York and London: Garland, 1998, pp. 377–380.

Doel, Ronald E. "Geophysics in Universities." In *Sciences of the Earth: An Encyclopedia of Events, People, and Phenomena,* edited by Gregory A. Good. New York and London: Garland, 1998, pp. 380–384.

G

Fleming, James Rodger. *Meteorology in America, 1800–1870*. Baltimore: Johns Hopkins University Press, 1990.

Good, Gregory A., ed. *The Earth, the Heavens, and the Carnegie Institution of Washington*. Washington, DC: American Geophysical Union, 1994.

Kertz, Walter. "Die Entwicklung der Geophysik zur eigenständigen Wissenschaft." *Mitteilungen der Gauss-Gesellschaft, E.V. Göttingen* no. 16 (1979): 41–54.

Le Grand, H.E. *Drifting Continents and Shifting Theories*. New York: Cambridge University Press, 1988.

Wood, Robert Muir. *The Dark Side of the Earth*. London: George Allen and Unwin, 1985.

Gregory A. Good

SEE ALSO
International Geophysical Year

Gibbs, Josiah Willard (1839–1903)

Mathematical physicist: thermodynamics, statistical mechanics, vector analysis. Gibbs was the only son of J.W. Gibbs, professor of sacred literature at Yale College. Gibbs's health was precarious and he lived a quiet, ordered existence with his two sisters and brother-in-law in New Haven. He entered Yale in 1854, received his degree four years later, then, unusual for this period, continued and obtained a Ph.D. in engineering in 1863. Gibbs worked at Yale as an unpaid tutor for three years before taking a grand, intellectual tour of Europe. For three years, he heard lectures by the leading mathematicians and mathematical and experimental physicists of Europe. At the same time, he carried out his own reading program in mathematical physics, completing the best education possible in that discipline for that era.

He returned to New Haven in the summer of 1869 and resumed his position at Yale. In 1871, Gibbs became professor of mathematical physics. However, it was not until Johns Hopkins offered Gibbs a paid position in 1880 that Yale gave him a salary. Gibbs rarely traveled to professional meetings and declined membership in the American Physical Society when it was organized in 1899. However, he sent his publications to all the important physicists of Europe and the United States.

Gibbs's research interests developed from engineering through mechanics to thermodynamics, vector analysis, the electromagnetic theory of light, and finally to statistical mechanics. The number of his publications was modest but all were important. While they range over a number of fields, they share common characteristics. The physical principles are clearly stated and are the most general possible, namely the Hamiltonian formulation of mechanics and the two laws of thermodynamics. He avoided any assumptions about the internal structure or the nature of the interactions of molecules in his mechanics, thermodynamics, and statistical mechanics. Thus, Gibbs redefined thermodynamics and defined statistical mechanics for later physicists. His mathematical development of basic physical principles was the most general possible while he focused on the physical implications of his assumptions, not mathematical results. Wherever possible the mathematics was geometrical, and even when algebraic are easily visualized. Simultaneously, Gibbs led the reader from the physically simplest to the most complex in a clearly defined series of steps. Finally, nothing superfluous appears in his prose or mathematics. Gibbs must be closely read.

Between 1873 and 1876, Gibbs transformed thermodynamics from a subject mired in conceptual muddle to one whose basic laws were clearly stated, understood, and seemed obvious as their geometrical expression made the implications of these laws so powerful. First, Gibbs guided the reader through the derivation of the known thermodynamic properties of homogeneous substances while simultaneously displaying those properties geometrically and incorporating entropy clearly as a state function into thermodynamics. In his next paper, the thermodynamic system was a substance in a mixture of physical states. Displaying these states graphically, Gibbs discussed the equilibrium states and the significance of the critical point where the three phases coexist. In his final paper, Gibbs considered a heterogeneous mixture of substances whose masses could vary. Gibbs wrote the first law as the change in energy as a function of the change in entropy, the work done, and the sum of the different masses multiplied by the "thermodynamic potential" for that mass. Thermodynamic potential could refer to the change of any physical property and Gibbs focused on mass, hence, on chemical change. Gibbs demonstrated the importance of thermodynamics in uncovering chemical equilibrium and the directions of chemical reactions through his phase rule.

His ideas on chemistry were important for the burgeoning chemical industries of Europe and the United States. However, Gibbs worked on a very abstract level. James Clerk Maxwell drew the attention of chemists to

G

the implications of Gibbs work. For Wilhelm Ostwald and J.H. van't Hoff, Gibbs's work became the foundation of their careers in a new field, physical chemistry. They also trained the first generations of graduate students who returned from Europe to establish that discipline in the United States.

Gibbs's attention then turned to vector analysis where he could again exploit his ability to express in mathematical form general solutions to classes of physical problems. In 1879, he taught one of the first courses in the subject and published his lectures in 1881. He derived his approach to vector analysis from William Rowan Hamilton on quaternions and William Kingdom Clifford's work in mechanics. However, his work was closer to that of Hermann G. Grassmann, and in the 1880s, Gibbs ran afoul of Peter Guthrie Tait, who defended the purity of Hamilton's quaternions against the rising tide of vectors. Gibbs countered by showing how useful vectors were for astronomy and indicating their use in electromagnetism.

In his final publication, Gibbs fused two earlier interests, thermodynamics and mechanics. He assumed nothing about the internal particulars of the mechanical systems, only that they obeyed Hamilton's equations. Gibbs considered collections in these systems and the distribution of energy and other characteristics among them, naming this approach to such ensembles statistical mechanics. In Gibbs's simplest case, his "microcanonical ensemble," the systems shared the same total energy but had different velocities and positions. Generalizing this, Gibbs defined the "canonical ensemble" where systems contained the same number of particles but had different total energies. Gibbs showed that this ensemble exhibited the same properties as thermodynamic systems. In his final generalization, his "grand ensemble," Gibbs examined the properties of systems with different numbers of particles as well as energies. To do this he needed to decide whether the particles in different systems, but identical in every respect, were distinguishable or not. If indistinguishable, then the entropy of a mixture of fluids was the same as the shift of the entropies of the fluids separately. If not, then the entropy changed as the fluids mixed. Gibbs was faced with other issues, that of equipartition, that all degrees of freedom of a mechanical system have the same average energy, and the ergodic hypothesis. The latter assumed that eventually every mechanical system of an ensemble passed through all possible configurations consistent with its

total energy. All three problems came under rigorous criticism with the development of quantum theory.

Gibbs's work was well known in Europe. He was elected to the major physical and mathematical societies of Europe and received honors from many. While he was a member of major scientific societies in the United States, Gibbs made less impression on a scientific community dedicated to accurate experiments and less aware than scientists in Europe of the power of physical theory.

BIBLIOGRAPHY

Donnan, F.G., and A. Haas, eds. *A Commentary on the Scientific Writings of J. Willard Gibbs.* 2 vols. New Haven: Yale University Press, 1936.

Gibbs, Josiah Willard. *Elementary Principles in Statistical Mechanics Developed with Special Reference to the Rational Foundations of Thermodynamics.* 1902. Reprint, New York: Dover, 1960.

———. *The Scientific Papers of J. Willard Gibbs.* Edited by Henry Andrews Bumstead and Ralph Gibbs Van Name. 2 vols. 1906. Reprint, New York: Dover, 1961.

Klein, Martin J. "Some Historical Remarks on the Statistical Physics of J.W. Gibbs." In *From Ancient Omens to Statistical Mechanics,* edited by J.L. Berggren and B.R. Goldstein. Copenhagen: Copenhagen University Library, 1987, pp. 281–289.

———. "The Physics of J. W. Gibbs." *Physics Today* 43 (1990): 40–48.

Knudsen, Ole. "The Influence of Gibbs's European Studies on His Later Work." In *From Ancient Omens to Statistical Mechanics,* edited by J.L. Berggren and B.R. Goldstein. Copenhagen: Copenhagen University Library, 1987, pp. 271–280.

Wheeler, Lynde Phelps. *Josiah Willard Gibbs: The History of a Great Mind.* New Haven: Yale University Press, 1952.

Elizabeth A. Garber

Gould, Benjamin Apthorp, Jr. (1824–1896)

Astronomer. Born in Boston, Gould graduated from Harvard in 1844, where he had become interested in mathematics and the physical sciences. From 1845 to 1848, he was in Europe learning the latest and best techniques in astronomical research. He spent approximately two years in Germany, and received a Ph.D. from Göttingen University in 1848, the first American to receive that degree in astronomy.

Initially unable to find a position as an astronomer, Gould taught modern languages and mathematics in Cambridge, Massachusetts. From 1852 until 1867, he

G

was with the United States Coast Survey, often working on a part-time basis. While with the Coast Survey, Gould also served as director of the Dudley Observatory in Albany, New York, from 1855 through January 1859. He ran the family mercantile business from 1859 to 1864. During the Civil War, he contracted to reduce the accumulated backlog of observations of the United States Naval Observatory. He was selected an original member of the National Academy of Sciences.

In 1869, the president of Argentina, Domingo Faustino Sarmiento, invited Gould to establish a national observatory for Argentina. Gould remained as director of the Córdoba Observatory until 1885.

Gould was one of the leading practitioners of astrometry—the determination of the positions of the stars and planets—in the United States. But his major contributions to astronomical research occurred in South America. Gould's staff determined the magnitudes and positions of all the naked-eye stars in the southern sky. Published as the "Uranometria Argentina" in Volume 1 of *Resultados del Observatorio Nacional Argentino en Córdoba* (1879), these observations established the existence of "Gould's belt" of bright stars intersecting the plane of the Milky Way at an angle of twenty degrees. An additional fourteen volumes of *Resultados* appeared before Gould's death.

Gould had also worked for the United States Sanitary Commission during the Civil War as an actuary, conducting an extensive series of observations on the physical characteristics of members of the Union forces. Published under the title *Investigations in the Military and Anthropological Statistics of American Soldiers* (1869), his study provided a unique opportunity to test theories correlating physical characteristics with nationality or ethnic group.

To Gould, his research was only a part of his larger program to model American astronomy upon German astronomy. Gould's one major success in this regard was his establishment of the *Astronomical Journal* in 1849, modeled after the *Astronomische Nachrichten*. Although Gould discontinued publication of the *Astronomical Journal* in 1861 because of the Civil War, he resurrected it in 1886 after his return to the United States from Argentina.

The pivotal event in Gould's life, however, was his dismissal by the trustees of the Dudley Observatory in 1859. Gould attempted to make Dudley the model research observatory. In doing so, he insisted that he, as director, not the trustees, had ultimate control over the observatory. The power struggle was fought out in pamphlets and newspaper articles before the trustees had Gould ejected from the observatory.

The clash between Gould and the trustees has attracted the attention of a number of historians. It has been seen as a rejection of the elitist values of science by antebellum America (Olson). James saw it as a clash between two elites—lay and scientific—each demanding deference from the other. Yet a third interpretation (Rothenberg) pointed to how the events at Dudley polarized the American astronomical community, and raised the issue of dominance within the astronomical community. James has also suggested that Gould's mood swings, apparent paranoia, and hostility to criticism, which was evident throughout his life, may have had their roots in mental illness.

There is no major collection of Gould manuscripts, nor is there a recent biography.

BIBLIOGRAPHY

Herrmann, D.B. "B. A. Gould and His *Astronomical Journal*." *Journal for the History of Astronomy* 2 (1971): 98–108.

Hodge, John E. "Benjamin Apthorp Gould and the Founding of the Argentine Observatory." *Americas* 28 (1972): 152–175.

James, Mary Ann. *Elites in Conflict: The Antebellum Clash over the Dudley Observatory*. New Brunswick: Rutgers University Press, 1987.

Montserrat, Marcelo. "La introdución de la ciencia moderna en Argentina: el caso Gould." *Criterio* 44, no. 1632 (25 November 1971): 726–729.

———. "Sarmiento y los fundamentos de su politica cientifica." *Sur: Revista semestral Sarmiento* 341 (July-December 1977): 98–109.

Olson, Richard G. "The Gould Controversy at Dudley Observatory: Public and Professional Values in Conflict." *Annals of Science* 27 (1971): 265–276.

Rothenberg, Marc. "Organization and Control: Professionals and Amateurs in American Astronomy, 1899–1918." *Social Studies of Science* 11 (1981): 305–325.

Marc Rothenberg

Gray, Asa (1810–1888)

Botanist. Born in Sauquoit, Oneida County, New York, Gray, the son of Moses Gray, farmer and tanner, and Roxana Howard, was educated in local schools, then the Fairfield (N.Y.) Academy, and, from 1829 to 1831, the Fairfield Medical School (also known as the Medical College of the Western District of New York).

In 1831, he received his medical degree, but his interest in botany, which had begun while a student at Fairfield Academy, won out. After several years of piecing together a living through teaching, he moved in 1834 to New York City to work with John Torrey. The two evolved rapidly from teacher and student to colleagues, collaborating on a number of projects, most notably the *Flora of North America.* In 1836–1838, Gray served as the botanist of the United States Exploring Expedition (known as the Wilkes Expedition) but delays caused him to resign before the expedition sailed. In 1842, he became the Fisher Professor of Natural History at Harvard University, a position he held until his death, in Cambridge.

Gray's contributions were twofold: scientific and institutional. With John Torrey, Gray introduced to America the new, natural systems of classification then in use in Europe to replace the artificial, Linnaean system of botanical classification. Both felt that adoption of the natural system and of type specimens for the classification of North American flora (which they also introduced) were crucial to bringing the United States into the world scientific community. Gray's synthetic works, most notably the *Manual of North American Botany* (1848, and five additional editions), provided America with its first comprehensive and natural flora. Correspondence with Charles Darwin led Gray to become interested in the geographical distribution of species. His work on the similarities of the floras of Japan and America, published in the memoirs of the *American Academy of Arts and Sciences,* stands as his most enduring work. In it, Gray argued that species and genera common to both eastern North America and Japan were not the result of separate creations but rather descendants of a common stock that moved south and separated during glaciation.

Gray maintained an extensive correspondence with collectors from throughout America. Amateurs and professionals alike sent Gray specimens and in return received specimens in trade, identification, information, collecting supplies, and sometimes cash. By greatly expanding the data base from which he was drawing conclusions, the specimens Gray received made his synthetic works possible.

Gray's impact on the teaching of botany was pivotal to the popularity of botany vis-à-vis other sciences among the lay public. His many textbooks for primary school to college level introduced thousands of Americans to botany, dominating the market for several generations. Gray was the first American to earn his living as a botanist. Few of his students became professional botanists, although he did train scores of collectors and did produce a great deal of research.

Long a trusted correspondent of Darwin, Gray was one of the small handful of people with whom Darwin had shared his ideas as they developed. In 1859, Gray championed the American reception of Charles Darwin's *The Origin of Species,* striving to ensure that the work received a fair reception based on the scientific merits of the work. His review in the *American Journal of Science,* his debates with Agassiz, and his later, more popular, essays in *Harpers* reprinted in *Darwiniana,* paved the way for the widespread acceptance of Darwin's work in America. Playing the role parallel to Thomas Huxley's role in Britain, Gray championed the American reception of Darwinian evolution.

Gray married in 1848, choosing Jane Lathrop Loring rather than any of Torrey's daughters as some had expected. His choice of a Loring, brought him into Boston society, a role he never really enjoyed. Quietly working in Cambridge, Gray was a shy man who preferred scholarship to politics. Because of this, Gray was not a leader in the emerging professional community of science, and hence he remained relatively unknown to historians until the publication in 1959 of A. Hunter Dupree's major biography. The largest collection of archival material is at the Gray Herbarium, Harvard University. Additional Gray material can be found in the letters of very nearly every American biological scientist and many amateurs of his era.

BIBLIOGRAPHY

Dupree, A. Hunter. *Asa Gray: American Botanist, Friend of Darwin.* Cambridge, MA: Harvard University Press, 1959; reprint, Baltimore: Johns Hopkins University Press, 1989.

Gray, Jane Loring, ed. *The Letters of Asa Gray.* 2 vols. Boston and New York: Houghton, Mifflin, 1894.

Sargent, Charles S., ed. *The Scientific Papers of Asa Gray.* 2 vols. Boston and New York: Houghton, Mifflin, 1894.

Watson, Serano, and G.L. Goodale. "List of the Writings of Dr. Asa Gray, Chronologically Arranged, with an Index." *American Journal of Science* 36 (1888): appendix, 3–67.

Elizabeth Keeney

Guyot, Arnold Henry (1808–1884)

Geographer, glacial geologist, the father of modern meteorology, and a kindly catalyst for much modern work in geology. Guyot's education comprised preparatory work

G

in classical studies at the University of Neuchâtel in his native Switzerland. From there he went to Germany and studied the natural sciences at the University of Berlin. He came under the influence of the German natural philosophers and scientists, most notably Alexander von Humboldt and Carl Ritter. The impress of Ritter's views of the world and its history informed Guyot's pietistic religion. To Ritter and Guyot, the world was like a great organism designed by an all-wise divine intelligence, comprising a structure whose parts were mutually interdependent. Earth history also provided the linkage between man and nature, a nation and its people. Guyot also spent much time in Carlshrue, Germany, where he met his Swiss compatriot Louis Agassiz, whose enthusiasm infected him with a curiosity about science and a love for untangling its mysteries.

Guyot soon became a colleague of Agassiz at the University of Neuchâtel, teaching geology and geography, and his associations with the dashing and brilliant Swiss ultimately made their careers—from early education to involvement with America—almost mirror images of each other. In 1837, Agassiz announced that an Ice Age had covered much of Europe in the past, setting the stage for modern creation. He urged Guyot to investigate aspects of glacial geology in need of explication. For the next decade, Guyot approached this task with the patience and painstaking care that marked all his work. He studied moraines, glacial movement, the nature of glaciers, and the so-called blue bands that formed the ribboned structure of the glacier.

Unfortunately for Guyot, these fundamental observations never saw current publisher's print, with the exception of an excerpt on the blue bands that Agassiz included in one of his works. Although Guyot communicated his findings orally, and Agassiz credited his research, as did other geologists, the fact is that Guyot's pathmarking work was largely unknown, due to a combination of illnesses, his reticence to go before the public in print, and a promise he had made to Agassiz to publish jointly in a volume that never materialized. His original glacier paper was published in 1883.

The European political turmoil of 1848 prompted Agassiz to plead with Guyot to try his future in the New World. Guyot accepted, and in a new world, much of his old country reticence seemed to disappear. Well established in Boston and at Harvard, Agassiz arranged for a series of Lowell Institute lectures for Guyot. Speaking in French before large audiences, Guyot's special ability comfortably to intermix science and religion was very pleasant to conservative audiences. Published and widely circulated in English translation in 1849, *The Earth and Man* was an ecological approach to geography based upon the interrelations that marked all nature. By this one stroke, Guyot placed geography on a modern footing, and, through his subsequent influence with state boards of education, was responsible for abolishing the old schoolbook geographies with their endless inventories of physiography. Guyot's book was an immediate success, and went through many editions in subsequent years. In many lectures, articles, and in the 1884 volume *Creation: Or the Biblical Cosmogony in the Light of Modern Science,* Guyot's words appealed to Americans desirous of always looking forward toward the future, and those public men and scientists alike who yearned for an accommodation between science and religion. For Guyot, all historical progress was development of some kind, comparable to the progress of the developing germ. Unity, diversity, beauty, goodness, utility, and truth were to be found in history as revealed in its admixture with geography. Although James Dwight Dana professed to see a meaningful embracing of the evolution doctrine in this last work, Guyot held man to be exempted from the evolutionary process and rejected man's development through natural forces alone.

With these beliefs, it was understandable that Guyot became a close intellectual and personal friend to American scientists eager to reconcile the claims of science with those of religion. Asa Gray, Chauncy Wright, and Dana were foremost among these scientists. But it was Dana who was the most impressed by Guyot's deep religious piety, his strong belief in the deity as prime mover, and the inability of Darwinian evolution to explain change mechanistically. Each man embraced the argument from design as the exemplar of an all-powerful deity, and each tried to fit the facts of change into a system posited on order, stability, and permanence.

Guyot's almost immediate American success, and his personal attributes, struck a responsive chord in Joseph Henry, secretary of the Smithsonian Institution. In 1850, Henry asked Guyot to employ his knowledge of mountains, terrain, and measurements to undertake and complete a survey of these early characteristics and make related meteorological observations. From an initial request, the project grew as large as the United States itself, and continued for over twenty-five years. So much of Guyot's time was devoted to this effort that he was, in effect, chief meteorologist of the Smithsonian during these years. His first work of 1850 was later revised, and the third edition, published in 1859, was a volume of 634 pages with 200 tables, praised by Henry as a novel work which would save other researchers considerable labor. Thereafter, Guyot became involved in many projects of this nature wherein he surveyed—with the aid of volunteers, the telegraph, and federal and state support—mountain chains in Massachusetts, North Carolina, Virgina, the Great Smoky Mountains, the Appalachian chain, and the Catskills, California, Rockies, and Coastal ranges. Guyot's studies were the first accurate barometric readings; in addition he studied wind velocities and air temperature. To Dana, Guyot, in his work, represented a microsmic "harmonic unity" of earth and man.

The wide reputation that came to Guyot caught the attention of James McCosh, president of Princeton University, strong advocate of science, and a philosopher equally determined to keep Princeton afloat between the seemingly godless claims of evolutionists and the comfortable strains of Christian piety. In 1854, Guyot became professor of physical geography and geology at the university, a professorship that was established for him by a benefactor who admired him as a Christian philosopher.

The work Guyot did at Princeton was of first importance. As an educator, he trained several generations of students in paleontological fieldwork. Among these were William B. Scott and Henry Fairfield Osborn, whose efforts convinced McCosh that two bright young men as these did not have to embrace evolution, and that science study had not undermined their faith. Both Osborn and Scott became distinguished paleontologists, believing, in the case of Osborn, that the evolution of fossil mammals was caused by non-material agents following plan and purpose. With the aid of a subsidy by William Libbey, the Princeton museum became a distinguished center of natural history. Based on Guyot's personal collection of over 5,000 rock specimens gathered in the European Alps, the museum was rich in paleontology and theology as well as European materials displayed in synoptic fashion in a background of true-to-life paintings. Fossil vertebrates were a special strength of what became known as the "E and M" museum, one that attracted many outstanding graduate students.

BIBLIOGRAPHY

Dana, James Dwight. "Arnold Guyot." *Biographical Memoirs of the National Academy of Sciences* 2 (1886): 309–347.

Guyot, Arnold. *Earth and Man, or Lectures on Comparative Physical Geography.* Translated by Cornelius C. Felton. Boston, 1849.

———. "On the Topography of the State of New York." *American Journal of Science,* 2d ser., 8 (1852): 272–276.

———. "On the Applachian Mountain System." *American Journal of Science* 2d ser., 31 (1861), 157–187.

———. *Cosmogony and the Bible, or the Biblical Account of Creation in the Light of Modern Science.* New York, 1873.

———. "Observations sur les glaciers." *Bulletin de la Société des sciences naturelles de Neuchâtel* 13 (1883): 151–159.

———. *Creation, or the Biblical Cosmogony in the Light of Modern Science.* New York, 1884.

Jones, Leonard C. *Arnold Guyot et Princeton.* Neuchâtel, 1925.

Libbey, William, Jr. "The Life and Scientific Work of Arnold Guyot." *Contributions of the E and M Museum of Geology and Archaeology* 2 (1884).

Livingstone, David N. *Darwin's Forgotten Defenders: The Encounter Between Evangelical Theology and Evolutionary Thought.* Grand Rapids, MI: Eerdmans, 1987.

Edward Lurie

H

Haldeman, Samuel Steman (1812–1880)

Naturalist and linguist. Born at Locust Grove, Pennsylvania; the eldest son of Henry and Frances (Steman) Haldeman. As a youth, Haldeman assembled natural objects and mounted specimens into a cabinet or museum. From 1826 to 1828, he attended the "classical academy" of Dr. John M. Keagy of Harrisburg. Two more years were spent at Dickinson College, in Carlisle, Pennsylvania, but Haldeman did not graduate, saying, "I cannot learn from others. I must see for myself" (Lesley, p. 145). But at Dickinson, he was influenced by Henry D. Rogers, who later appointed him assistant to the New Jersey and Pennsylvania Geological Surveys (1836–1842). In 1835, Haldeman married Mary A. Hough of Bainbridge, Pennsylvania, and settled near Columbia, Pennsylvania. He held a number of academic appointments, teaching zoology at the Franklin Institute (1842–1843), natural history at the University of Pennsylvania (c. 1850–1855), chemistry and geology at Delaware College (1855–1858), and comparative philology at the University of Pennsylvania (1869–1880). He received honorary degrees from Gettysburg College (A.M., 1844) and the University of Pennsylvania (LL.D., 1876). Haldeman was elected to the National Academy of Sciences (1876) and became president of both the American Philological Society (1876–1877), and the American Association for the Advancement of Science (1880).

Haldeman's scientific achievements were as diverse as they were extensive. As Rogers's assistant on the Pennsylvania Geological Survey, he was responsible for mapping Dauphin and Lancaster Counties. But Haldeman preferred examining the anatomical features of animals to unraveling the complexities of strata. Perceiving the intellectual vacuum created by Thomas Say's death, he extended that scientist's work in conchology and entomology. Between 1840 and 1845, Haldeman issued an eight-volume *Monograph of the . . . Fresh-water Univalve Shells.* An 1844 paper critically evaluated the "[L]amarckian hypothesis" and was cited by Charles Darwin in his *The Origin of Species.* A founding member of the Entomological Society of Pennsylvania, Haldeman promoted systematic over applied entomology by describing dozens of new American insects, principally among the order Coleoptera or beetles, including specimens collected by the Stansbury Expedition to Utah. Yet his observations superseded taxonomic purposes to uncover life histories and ecological relationships of specimens.

Haldeman was a "silent partner" in the iron smelting business conducted by his brothers, who were among the first (in the 1840s) to use anthracite as fuel. He described the construction of blast furnaces in the *American Journal of Science.* An acute sense of hearing enabled him to explore the full range of human vocal sounds, and he sought opportunities to examine Native American dialects. Haldeman proposed that a universal alphabet be devised, employing a minimum number of symbols. Continued research in classical philology and etymology produced analyses of Indo-European and Asian languages. His proficiency therein was demonstrated by winning the Trevelyan Prize Essay of 1858 with his work "Analytic Orthography." These linguistic labors came full circle with the interpretation of archaeological remains. Toward the end of his life, he excavated a prehistoric rock shelter located on his property and described its contents to the American Philosophical Society.

H

Geologist J. Peter Lesley characterized Haldeman's approach to knowledge as follows: His prevailing mental attitude was one of skepticism and refusal "to learn of others what they desired to teach" (Lesley, p. 147). For Haldeman, "laws were tiresome except as mere running commentary upon the glorious text of facts." He staunchly preferred analysis to synthesis, and was "never happy" until something was reduced to "mere description" (Lesley, p. 146). This so-called Baconian philosophy became less viable as American science grew more specialized, leaving Haldeman as something of an iconoclast. A taxonomist of both living forms and the scientific terms which described them, Haldeman nonetheless opened significant pathways in American zoology and linguistics.

Two important collections of his papers are housed at the Academy of Natural Sciences in Philadelphia. No complete biography of Haldeman exists.

BIBLIOGRAPHY

Ellis, Franklin, and Samuel Evans. *History of Lancaster County, Pennsylvania, with Biographical Sketches of Many of Its Pioneers and Prominent Men.* Philadelphia: Everts & Peck, 1883.

Gerstner, Patsy. *Henry Darwin Rogers, 1808–1866: American Geologist.* Tuscaloosa: University of Alabama Press, 1994.

Hart, Charles Henry. "Samuel Steman Haldeman." *Penn Monthly* 12 (1881): 584–601.

Lesley, J.P. "Samuel Steman Haldeman." *Biographical Memoirs of the National Academy of Sciences* 2 (1886): 139–172.

Livingston, John. *Portraits of Eminent Americans Now Living: With Biographical and Historical Memoirs of Their Lives and Actions.* New York: Cornish, Lamport, 1854, 4:88–103.

Rathvon, Simon S. "Tribute of Respect." *Lancaster Farmer* (November, 1880): 172.

Sorensen, W. Conner. *Brethren of the Net: American Entomology, 1840–1880.* Tuscaloosa: University of Alabama Press, 1995.

Jordan D. Marché II

Hale, George Ellery (1868–1938)

Astronomer, science administrator and statesman of science. The centrality of George Ellery Hale in the development of American astronomy and astrophysics from the 1890s through the 1930s can not be overestimated. As a research scientist, designer of instrumentation, founder and director of observatories, and statesman of science, Hale gave direction to the research activities of two generations of astronomers, provided them with a wide range of new instrumentation, established and administered three major research observatories, and created a number of institutions in the American astronomical community, the larger national scientific community, and, indeed, the international scientific community.

Key to understanding Hale is his complex character and personality. Tenacious to a fault, driven by curiosity about the natural world, and burning with ambition to succeed in science, Hale was endowed with tremendous physical and mental energy and a remarkable gift for friendship. Unfortunately, these traits were locked in a body that was at best frail, and often Hale drove himself far beyond his physical and psychological limits.

Hale's interest in science appeared early and by age fourteen his father, a wealthy Chicago businessman, had provided the boy with various scientific instruments including a four-inch refracting telescope, a shop, and laboratory. In 1886, Hale entered the Massachusetts Institute of Technology (MIT) from which he earned an undergraduate degree in physics in 1890. Far more important than course work at MIT were the hours spent reading physics and astronomy in the Boston Public Library. Hale's training in observational astronomy was gained as a volunteer assistant at the Harvard College Observatory.

In the decade following his twenty-first birthday, Hale demonstrated all the major attributes that were to characterize his scientific career. Fascinated by physics research in experimental spectroscopy, Hale longed to discover new ways of applying spectroscopy to the study of the sun. The result (developed during the summer between his junior and senior years at MIT) was the spectroheliograph, an instrument that permits observations in monochromatic light and lets the observer photograph the sun at various wavelengths. This, in turn, permits astronomers to study activity at different levels in the sun's atmosphere. Hale experimented with a prototype of the spectroheliograph using the facilities of the Harvard Observatory and the results became the basis for his senior thesis.

After a semester of graduate work in Germany, Hale returned to Chicago and concentrated on research at the Kenwood Observatory, financed by his father and dedicated to solar spectroscopy. Important results quickly ensued. The discovery of bright calcium clouds at various levels in the solar atmosphere was followed a few years later by the identification of dark clouds of hydrogen. These discoveries helped astronomers map the composition and circulation of the solar atmosphere.

From the beginning, Hale was an institution builder as well as a research scientist. He was cofounder (1891) of *Astronomy and Astro-Physics,* which became the *Astrophysical Journal* in 1895. In 1892, Hale joined the faculty of the new University of Chicago and soon was involved in raising funds for and then constructing the Yerkes Observatory, which opened in 1897. With its forty-inch refracting telescope, Yerkes boasted the largest instrument of its kind in the world. During these years, Hale also traveled extensively and by the mid-1890s could count as personal acquaintances virtually all the leading astrophysical researchers in Europe and America.

By age thirty, Hale had demonstrated remarkable skill as a research scientist as well as the ability to create new institutions and had developed a network of professional contacts on whom he could rely for support. In 1899, Hale would be a cofounder of the American Astronomical Society. Further, prestigious honors were already accruing: the French Academy of Sciences bestowed its Janssen Medal on Hale (1894) and the University of Pittsburgh awarded him an honorary doctor of science degree (1897).

Recently some writers (Osterbrock) have argued that Hale does not deserve to be ranked as a first-class scientist. This view is mistaken. His manifold administrative and fund-raising activities must not obscure Hale's status as an extremely successful scientist. His contemporaries certainly thought as much since they honored Hale with some of the most prestigious awards available to an astronomer. In addition to discoveries made with the spectroheliograph which provided an understanding of the complex nature of the solar atmosphere, Hale investigated low-temperature red stars whose spectra resembled sunspots. He also carried out important laboratory investigations. Between 1905 and 1923, using instrumentation especially devised for the work, Hale concentrated on the study of sunspots, deducing important information about their temperature and magnetic properties. Hale revitalized the study of solar physics. But he did more than that. Arguing that the sun was a typical star and that knowledge of its physical characteristics would help astronomers understand other stars, Hale infused new vitality into stellar spectroscopy.

In 1904, Hale succeeded in gaining support from the Carnegie Institution of Washington to establish the Mount Wilson Observatory in California. In addition

to a new generation of powerful solar telescopes that provided large, stable solar images for spectroscopic analysis, Hale constructed a sixty-inch (1908) and then a one-hundred-inch reflecting telescope (1917). For many years, these instruments had no rivals. Mount Wilson telescopes provided information on the physical nature and evolution of stars as well as the structure and distance of galaxies and furnished the observational foundations for the theory of the expanding universe.

Through his writings and speeches and, above all, activities at Yerkes and Mount Wilson observatories, Hale developed a research agenda that would guide the activities of two generations of American astrophysicists. Hale was deeply influenced by developments in experimental spectroscopy in the 1880s and 1890s. It comes as no surprise that physics was central to the Hale research program. By employing the tools and theories of physics, Hale believed that astronomy could move beyond the traditional fields of investigation (celestial mechanics and astrometry) and understand the physical and chemical composition of the universe. Following this line of reasoning, Hale suggested that astrophysics was, in fact, an interdisciplinary enterprise and that it owed as much to physics as it did to traditional astronomy.

Hale argued that astrophysical observatories should be equipped with powerful telescopes and state-of-the-art spectroscopic laboratories that would provide experimental data to help interpret solar and stellar spectra. As indicated earlier, he reasoned that the sun was a typical star and that careful study of this nearest stellar object would provide information useful to students of stellar spectroscopy. The Hale research program was not driven by theory, but rather represented a large-scale data collection program. As long as astrophysicists produced novel discoveries, the program remained vital. Once the rate of discovery declined, the Hale program degenerated into data collecting for its own sake.

If the Hale research program was rendered obsolete by new developments in theoretical physics led by N. Bohr, M.N. Saha, A.S. Eddington, and others, it nonetheless produced important results including the use of spectroscopic data to estimate the distance of stars and a deeper understanding of the composition of stellar atmospheres. Further, spectroscopy helped refine models of stellar evolution. Research in solar and stellar spectroscopy also set the stage for the discovery of the source of stellar energy by physicists in the late 1930s.

H

Hale suffered from physical and psychological maladies, apparently triggered by overwork, and increasingly found that scientific investigations taxed his intellectual and physical powers beyond endurance. He shifted his focus to institution building and concentrated on activities associated with the role of statesman in the national and international scientific communities.

Hale's institution-building activities took many forms. Elected to the National Academy of Sciences in 1902, he devoted considerable time and energy to the modernization of the academy. Hale sought to expand its membership and give the academy a more central place in American scientific and political life. After World War I, Hale led the drive to construct a permanent home for the academy in Washington. In 1904, he was the driving force behind the creation of the International Union for Cooperation in Solar Research, an organization which formed the nucleus of the International Astronomical Union after World War I. In 1916, as the general European war threatened to engulf the United States, Hale led a movement to make scientific expertise available to the federal government through the creation of the National Research Council (NRC). After the war, the NRC became the operating arm of the National Academy. Following the 1918 armistice, Hale worked for the creation of an International Research Council, which later (1931) became the International Council of Scientific Unions. In the 1920s, Hale was the father of the National Research Fund, a plan that would have drawn on contributions from business and industry to create an endowment for scientific research. Hale also played a central role in the creation of the California Institute of Technology and the Huntington Library and Art Gallery.

All these activities were punctuated by long periods of ill health during which Hale traveled in Europe or underwent treatment in various sanitoriums. In 1923, he retired as director of the Mount Wilson Observatory, but did not abandon astronomy. Hale ardently publicized the possibility of a very large reflecting telescope and by the end of the decade had secured funding from the Rockefeller Foundation to build a 200-inch reflector. He did not live to see his last great project come to fruition. The 200-inch Hale telescope was not completed until after World War II.

The bulk of Hale's papers are at the California Institute of Technology. There is a microfilm edition. The archives of the Yerkes Observatory at Williams Bay, Wisconsin, house a large collection of Hale manuscripts covering the period to about 1900. There are important Hale materials in the papers of the Allegheny Observatory, deposited in the Archives of Industrial America at the University of Pittsburgh Library, that throw light on the founding of the *Astrophysical Journal*. The W.S. Adams papers in the Huntington Library provide an invaluable resource for understanding Hale's career at Mount Wilson. The Wright biography was authorized and offers little more than a chronological narrative. While aspects of Hale's career have been examined in scholarly depth (e.g., by Kevles), there remain many facets of his life which would repay careful investigation. These range from an understanding of Hale's use of evolution as a controlling metaphor for organizing scientific research through his activities as a science ambassador to both government and industry.

BIBLIOGRAPHY

Adams, W.S. "George Ellery Hale." *Biographical Memoirs of the National Academy of Sciences* 21 (1940): 181–241.

Babcock, H.D. "George Ellery Hale." *Publications of the Astronomical Society of the Pacific* 50 (1938): 156–165.

DeVorkin, D.H. "Astrophysics," in *The History of Astronomy: An Encyclopedia,* edited by John Lankford. New York: Garland Publishing, 1996, pp. 72–80.

Hale, G.E. *The Study of Stellar Evolution.* Chicago: University of Chicago Press, 1908.

Hufbauer, K. *Exploring the Sun: Solar Science Since Galileo.* Baltimore: Johns Hopkins University Press, 1991.

Kevles, D.J. "George Ellery Hale, the First World War, and the Advancement of Science in America." *Isis* 59 (1968): 427–37.

———. "'Into Hostile Political Camps': The Reorganization of International Science in World War I." *Isis* 62 (1970): 47–60.

———. *The Physicists: The History of a Scientific Community in Modern America.* New York: Knopf, 1978; reprint, Cambridge, MA: Harvard University Press, 1995.

Lankford, J. *American Astronomy, 1859–1940: Community, Careers and Power.* Chicago: University of Chicago Press, 1997.

Osterbrock, D.E. *Pauper and Prince: Ritchey, Hale and Big American Telescopes.* Tucson: University of Arizona Press, 1993.

Wright. H. *Explorer of the Universe: A Biography of George Ellery Hale.* New York: E.P. Dutton, 1966.

Wright, H., J.N. Warnow, and C. Weiner, eds. *The Legacy of George Ellery Hale: Evolution of Astronomy and Scientific Institutions in Pictures and Documents.* Cambridge: Massachusetts Institute of Technology Press, 1971.

John Lankford

Hall, Asaph (1829–1907)

Astronomer at the United States Naval Observatory and discoverer of the two Martian satellites. Born in Goshen, Connecticut, Hall was a successful carpenter before enrolling in Central College in McGrawsville, New York, in 1854. Although the curriculum proved disappointing, Hall studied mathematics under a young teacher, Chloe Angeline Stickney, whom he married in March 1856. The couple soon moved to Ann Arbor, Michigan, where Hall studied for three months with astronomer Franz Brünnow. After a year of teaching at Shalersville Institute in Ohio, during which time his wife tutored him in German and continued to encourage him to pursue astronomy as a profession, Hall accepted a poorly paid position at Harvard College Observatory in 1857.

Hall's career advanced significantly when he joined the Naval Observatory five years later. In 1863, unknown to Hall, his wife proposed his name to the observatory superintendent for the recently announced position of professor of mathematics. Quickly promoted to this position, he directed asteroid and comet observations and led observatory expeditions to Siberia (1869), Sicily (1870), Vladivostok (1874), Colorado (1878), and Texas (1882). In 1875, Hall assumed direction of the Clark twenty-six-inch refractor, at that time the world's largest telescope. He used this instrument to discover the two satellites of Mars during the planet's 1877 opposition. Guided by theoretical considerations which suggested that Martian moons would orbit near the planet, Hall located the two satellites by mid-August, later naming them Phobos and Deimos.

Hall devoted the rest of his professional life to various endeavors, ultimately publishing nearly 500 articles and papers. He analyzed the orbits of the satellites of Saturn, Uranus, and Neptune, while continuing his measurements of the Martian moons. Also active in stellar research, Hall observed numerous double stars, calculated various parallaxes, and determined the positions of faint stars in the Pleiades cluster. During the 1880s, he also assisted in planning the observatory's move to its present site. Although he reached mandatory retirement age in 1891, Hall volunteered his services on the twenty-six-inch refractor until 1894. After teaching mathematics at Harvard from 1896 to 1901, he retired to his rural home in Connecticut. Hall died while visiting his son in Annapolis, Maryland.

Hall's various contributions to astronomy led to many honors. Elected to the National Academy of Sciences in 1875, he also received the Gold Medal of the Royal Astronomical Society (1879), the LaLande Prize (1877), and the Arago Medal (1893) of the French Academy of Sciences, and was made a knight of the French Legion of Honor in 1896. Hall served as president of the American Association for the Advancement of Science in 1902 and was associate editor of the *Astronomical Journal* between 1897 and 1907.

BIBLIOGRAPHY

Gingerich, Owen. "The Satellites of Mars: Prediction and Discovery." *Journal for the History of Astronomy* 1 (1970): 109–115.

———. "Hall, Asaph." *Dictionary of Scientific Biography.* Edited by Charles C. Gillispie. New York: Scribner's, 1972, 6:48–50.

Hill, George William. "Asaph Hall." *Biographical Memoirs of the National Academy of Sciences* 6 (1909): 240–275.

Horigan, William D. "Published Writings of Asaph Hall." *Biographical Memoirs of the National Academy of Sciences* 6 (1909): 276–309.

Webb, George Ernest. "The Planet Mars and Science in Victorian America." *Journal of American Culture* 3 (1980): 573–580.

George E. Webb

Hall, Edwin Herbert (1855–1938)

Physicist and educator. Born into a farming family in Great Falls (later North Gorham), Maine, young Hall attended local schools until enrolling in Bowdoin College. Earning his A.B. degree in 1875, he spent the next two years as a principal, first of an academy and then a high school. In 1877, he left Maine, becoming a physics graduate student at the recently opened Johns Hopkins University. Working closely with professor Henry Rowland, he earned his Ph.D. in 1880. After a European trip that included time spent at Hermann von Helmholtz's laboratory, he took up a lifelong teaching post at Harvard. Beginning as an instructor in 1881, he rose through the ranks to assume the Rumford chair, which he held from 1914 until becoming professor emeritus in 1921. Earlier, in 1904, he served as vice president in charge of the physics section of the American Association for the Advancement of Science, and in 1911, he was elected to the National Academy of Sciences. In 1924, he accepted an invitation to participate in the Solvay Congress in Brussels, and in 1937, he garnered the Oersted Medal of the American Association of Physics Teachers.

While engaged in his doctoral studies at Johns Hopkins, he made his most celebrated discovery: the 1879

H

experimental detection of an electrical property of conductors soon to be called the "Hall effect." A subtle property of metals, the effect shows itself as a transverse potential difference that is set up across a current-carrying conductor when a magnetic field acts perpendicular to the current. James Clerk Maxwell's earlier theoretical denial of the effect motivated Hall's experimental search, which Rowland encouraged and guided. Although he would return repeatedly during his career to the experimental and theoretical details of this transverse effect, Hall concentrated on an alternative research program during the two decades bracketing 1900. He investigated a variety of thermal phenomena, especially thermoelectric effects. In his later years, he sought a unified electrical theory of metals that would subsume thermoelectric and Hall-type transverse effects. Few of his colleagues, however, built on his theoretical insights, which typically lacked mathematical refinement and involved rather idiosyncratic uses of simple mechanical analogies. Nevertheless, the Hall effect itself played central roles in the elaboration of Maxwellian electrodynamics and, later, in the development of condensed matter physics.

Whereas Hall was best known among research physicists for his electrical studies, he was most recognized among educators for introducing into American secondary schools the laboratory method of teaching physics. Joining a movement begun by progressive educators and prodded into action by Harvard president Charles W. Eliot, Hall designed and popularized during the late 1880s a course of experiments for use in secondary schools. The course, structured around the "Harvard Descriptive List of Elementary Physical Experiments" and sanctioned by the National Educational Association, came to dominate secondary-school programs and college admissions criteria by about 1900. While Hall's primary intention had been to introduce the laboratory method, an additional impact was to enhance the professional status of physics teachers.

The Houghton Library of Harvard University holds a modest collection of Hall's private papers and letters.

BIBLIOGRAPHY

Bridgman, Percy W. "Edwin Herbert Hall." *Biographical Memoirs of the National Academy of Sciences* 21 (1941): 73–94.

Buchwald, Jed Z. "The Hall Effect and Maxwellian Electrodynamics in the 1880s." *Centaurus* 23 (1979–1980): 51–99, 118–162.

Moyer, Albert E. "Edwin Hall and the Emergence of the Laboratory in Teaching Physics." *The Physics Teacher* 14 (1976): 96–103.

———. *American Physics in Transition: A History of Conceptual Change in the Late Nineteenth Century.* Los Angeles: Tomash Publishers, 1983.

Rosen, Sidney. "A History of the Physics Laboratory in the American Public High School (to 1910)." *American Journal of Physics* 22 (1954): 194–204.

Sopka, Katherine R. "The Discovery of the Hall Effect: Edwin Hall's Hitherto Unpublished Account." In *The Hall Effect and Its Applications,* edited by C.L. Chien and C.R. Westgate. New York: Plenum, 1980, pp. 523–545. (In this volume, see also brief historical articles by O. Hannaway and B.R. Judd.)

Albert E. Moyer

Hall, James (1811–1898)

Paleontologist and geologist. Born in Hingham, Massachusetts, Hall moved from an early interest in science to study at Rensselaer Polytechnic Institute (B.N.S., 1832; M.A., 1833). He continued his association with Rensselaer as librarian (1832), professor of chemistry (1835–1841), and later professor of mineralogy and geology. His association with Amos Eaton and Ebenezer Emmons at Rensselaer led to a position as Emmons's assistant on the New York Natural History Survey in 1836–1837 and his appointment as geologist for the fourth district in 1837. When the survey concluded in 1843, he continued in state employment as state paleontologist (1843–1898), curator and then director of the state museum (1865–1898), and state geologist (1893–1898). In addition, he served as state geologist on the surveys of Iowa (1855–1858) and Wisconsin (1857–1860). He was one of the original members of the Association of American Geologists and of the American Association for the Advancement of Science (AAAS), which evolved from it in 1848. He served as president of the AAAS in 1856 and as the first president of the Geological Society of America in 1889. He was also a charter member of the National Academy of Science in 1863.

Hall's assertive, sometimes caustic, confidence in himself and his work carried him through periods when the state legislature resisted authorizing further work or failed to deliver adequate funds for work already authorized. The volumes he produced, beginning with the final report for the fourth geological district and continuing through eight volumes of paleontology, became the standard references for North American paleontology, and he was widely recognized as nineteenth-century America's foremost invertebrate paleontologist. He contributed material to several other state and federal surveys and published widely in scientific journals.

Hall devoted a great deal of attention to delineating the stratigraphy of North America. He was an ardent proponent of the New York System, a uniquely American system of stratigraphic nomenclature developed by the geologists of the New York survey and taking the New York rocks as its types. Despite his beginnings as student of and then assistant to Emmons, Hall became an outspoken opponent of Emmons's Taconic System as a subset of the New York rocks and nomenclature.

In his 1857 address as outgoing president of the AAAS, Hall elucidated a theory of sedimentation and mountain building that has attracted much attention for its similarities to later geological understanding. At the time, even Hall recognized his ideas as incomplete and speculative and the address remained unpublished for nearly thirty years.

Hall was often involved in acrimonious disputes with former friends and students. A period working as Hall's assistant was recognized to be one of the best courses of study available for training in paleontology, but such relationships often ended with the assistant feeling sorely used. He had a strong propensity to extend proprietary claims to results and collections of anyone who worked for or with him. He was, however, outspokenly protective of his own work and interests. During Charles Lyell's first visit to the United States (1841–1842), Hall publicly but anonymously accused him of intending to plagiarize the geological results of his American colleagues. In the 1850s, Hall was forced to defend himself in court as a result of his attempts to prevent the distribution of James T. Foster's geological chart of the New York rocks.

The only monographic biography of Hall is an early-twentieth-century life-and-letters volume written by his friend and student John Clarke. An extended biography of Hall grounded in the more recent historiography of American science is long overdue. The New York State Library at Albany houses the extensive James Hall Papers.

BIBLIOGRAPHY
Aldrich, Michele Alexis LaClergue. "New York Natural History Survey, 1836–1845." Ph.D. diss., University of Texas at Austin, 1974.

Bruce, Robert V. *The Launching of Modern American Science, 1846–1876.* New York: Knopf, 1987.
Clarke, John M. *James Hall of Albany: Geologist and Paleontologist, 1811–1898.* 1923. Reprint, New York: Arno, 1978.
Dott, Robert H., Jr. "The Geosyncline—First Major Geological Concept 'Made in America.'" In *Two Hundred Years of Geology in America: Proceedings of the New Hampshire Bicentennial Conference on the History of Geology,* edited by Cecil J. Schneer. Hanover, NH: University Press of New England, 1979, pp. 239–264.
Hall, James. *Geology of New York: Part IV, Comprising the Survey of the Fourth Geological District.* Albany, NY: 1843.
———. *Palaeontology of New York.* 8 vols. Albany, NY: 1847–1894.
———. "Contributions to the History of the American Continent." *Proceedings of the American Association for the Advancement of Science* 31 (1883): 29–71 [1857 AAAS Presidential Address].
Newell, Julie R. "American Geologists and Their Geology: The Formation of the American Geological Community, 1780–1865." Ph.D. diss., University of Wisconsin-Madison, 1993.

Julie R. Newell

Harris, Thaddeus William (1795–1856)

Credited with founding practical entomology in the United States. Harris graduated from Harvard College in 1815 and from the medical school in 1820. He was a physician in Milton and Dorchester, Massachusetts, from 1820 to 1831, when he became Harvard University librarian, a post he retained for the remainder of his life. Harris also lectured in natural history at Harvard from 1837 to 1842, and sought an appointment as professor, but in the latter year he was passed over in favor of Asa Gray.

The origin of Harris's interest in insects is uncertain, but one early influence was William Dandridge Peck, the first professor of natural history at Harvard, who had an interest in the relations of insects to agriculture. During his years in medical practice, Harris began an entomological collection which he later claimed was the best in the country. Like many others during that time period, however, he suffered from a lack of books and established collections for identification of his insect specimens. His first paper, on the salt-marsh caterpillar and its relations to hay, appeared in 1823, and in many ways this publication characterized his work. He was a broadly based entomologist, engaged in the naming and description of insects; he also promoted the necessity of knowing life histories as an aid to classification and a

H

concern for the harmful effects that some insects had on agriculture.

Harris contributed a list of Massachusetts insects to Edward Hitchcock's 1833 report on the geology and natural history of the state. Later in the decade, he was made one of the commissioners on the Zoological and Botanical Survey of Massachusetts, and in 1842 reissued his resulting report, at his own expense, under the title *Treatise on Some of the Insects of New England Which Are Injurious to Vegetation.* Although he was engaged in various entomological studies, especially of the moths (Lepidoptera), which he undertook with the encouragement of English entomologist Edward Doubleday, the failure to achieve a Harvard professorship and increasing responsibilities in the university library, effectively ended his active pursuit of entomology in the early 1840s. He is remembered especially for his *Treatise,* the foundation of American economic entomology. Significantly, Harris's integrated interests in the agricultural relations of insects, and in description and taxonomy, tended to become separate concerns for the entomologists who followed him. One consequence is that, in retrospect, he sometimes is seen as too scientific for the applied entomologists, too practical for the systematists.

Harris's entomological collection and his correspondence and other papers are in the Museum of Comparative Zoology at Harvard.

BIBLIOGRAPHY

Harris, Edward D. "Memoir." *Proceedings of the Massachusetts Historical Society* 19 (1881–1882): 313–322.

Harris, T.W. "Insects." In *Report on the Geology, Mineralogy, Botany and Zoology of Massachusetts,* by Edward Hitchcock. Amherst: J.S. & C. Adams, 1833. 2d ed., 1835, pp. 566–595.

Mallis, Arnold. *American Entomologists.* New Brunswick: Rutgers University Press, 1971.

Scudder, Samuel H., ed. *Entomological Correspondence of Thaddeus William Harris. Occasional Papers of the Boston Society of Natural History.* Boston: Boston Society of Natural History, 1869. Included is a memoir by Thomas Wentworth Higginson and bibliography of Harris's works. A supplement to the bibliography is in *Proceedings of the Boston Society of Natural History* 21 (1881): 150–152.

Sorensen, W. Conner. *Brethren of the Net: American Entomology 1840–1880.* Tuscaloosa: University of Alabama Press, 1995.

Clark A. Elliott

Harvard University

The oldest American university, located in Cambridge, Massachusetts, was founded in 1636. The early history of the sciences at Harvard, as for other colonial colleges, is largely the story of teaching and the development of physical resources. The course of study in 1642 included physics, arithmetic, geometry, and astronomy. Although botany appeared at that time, it soon disappeared from the curriculum until late in the eighteenth century. The facilities for science started with Connecticut Governor John Winthrop's gift of a telescope in 1672. Thomas Brattle used it to observe the comet of 1680 and Isaac Newton recognized the results in his *Principia Mathematica.*

If the scientific mission of the early college was modest, it was part of a larger stream of learning that ran both out of and into the institution. Graduates such as Cotton Mather made small contributions to knowledge, while persons of wealth and interest helped to direct the scientific development. A notable event in the colonial period was the establishment, in 1726, of a professorship of mathematics and natural philosophy; founded by London Baptist Thomas Hollis, the chair was filled from 1738–1779 by the college's major colonial scientist, John Winthrop. Until late in the eighteenth century, mathematics, physics, and astronomy continued as the focus of science teaching, but the beginnings of a medical school in 1782 led to expansion in the undergraduate college as well, notably in chemistry and natural history.

A collective involvement of community and economic interests (including agriculture) came together in the first decade of the nineteenth century to establish a professorship of natural history and a botanical garden. During these early years of the new century, small steps in curricular development were taken through Professor John Farrar's introduction of modern mathematics, and efforts were made to expand the place in the curriculum for chemistry, mineralogy, and geology. By the early 1840s, establishment of a new professorship of natural history brought the important presence of Asa Gray, and with him a personal research agenda as well as national and international connections.

Viewed historically, astronomy holds first place in Harvard science. Although its roots were in the seventeenth century, the appointment of William Cranch Bond as observer in 1839, construction of an observatory, and installation in 1847 of what was (with another in Russia) the largest telescope in the world, made Cambridge an astronomical center. Significantly, until the twentieth century, the observatory had little part in teaching; it was a research facility in an institution whose historic role had been largely to instruct. As such, the observatory (and the botanical garden to a lesser extent) led the way in developing a wider mission for science and scientific research in the university. By the end of the nineteenth century, the research activities at the observatory began to employ a number of women, one of the few opportunities for women in science at Harvard at that time.

During the period when the observatory and the new natural history professorship were established, pressures were felt—in part from the growing business and industrial sector—for a more practical education. The institutional answer was a separate school rather than a reform or redirection of Harvard College. The university's Lawrence Scientific School was established in 1847 and continued until 1906. The establishment of the scientific school coincided with the arrival and appointment of Louis Agassiz as its professor of geology and zoology. Agassiz's pure science interests diluted if they did not dissolve the practical mission of the school. He also forged independent links with sources of public support, and created the Museum of Comparative Zoology. In the 1860s, special donations founded a school of mining (soon terminated as a separate entity) and the Peabody Museum of American Archaeology and Ethnology; both these enterprises represented essentially external interests.

The election of chemist Charles W. Eliot to the presidency of the university in 1869 was an event of major importance. With Eliot, there developed a sense of leadership from within that was not so apparent in earlier years. His curricular reforms, and particularly promotion of the elective system, opened the way for many changes, including a more vital place for science in the college. He attempted unsuccessfully on several occasions to merge the Massachusetts Institute of Technology and the Lawrence Scientific School and in the end dissolved the latter. (Eliot's successor, A. Lawrence Lowell, effected a union of Harvard engineering with MIT between 1914–1917, but the arrangement was reversed by court decision.) Graduate education was begun in 1871. Also under Eliot, the Bussey Institution of agriculture and horticulture was established (1870) with a bequest left to the university in 1842. Only moderately successful and largely an institutional appendage, in the early decades of the twentieth century and until its termination in 1931, the Bussey was a center of university research in genetics.

From the mid-nineteenth century, the overall history of the sciences at Harvard was characterized by growth of facilities, development of research alongside instructional functions (the new Jefferson Physical Laboratory in 1884 designated separate sections of the building for these purposes), increasing specialization, and attempts to coordinate related interests separated by geography, funding sources, historical loyalties, differing research approaches, as well as different external focus groups. The institutional history of botany at Harvard is a particularly fractionated one that includes the botanical garden, the herbarium (derived from Gray's collecting), the Arnold Arboretum, Farlow Library and Herbarium, Botanical Museum, Harvard Forest, and a botanical garden in Cuba. Attempts to resolve the apparent problem in the mid-1940s resulted in an acrimonious legal battle over the status of the Arnold Arboretum that took twenty years to settle. A further example of institutional complexity was the development of the biological and medical sciences in the twentieth century, characterized by parallel research activities in the Faculty of Arts and Sciences and the medical school (since 1810, physically located in Boston).

Harvard, as other academic institutions, was transformed as well as aided by the growth of foundation funds in the years between the world wars. Rockefeller money helped establish an astronomical station in South Africa (1926) that replaced one in Peru, as well as new laboratories for chemistry (1928), physics (1931), and biology (1931), the latter to coordinate biological work in the university. World War II further changed the character of Harvard and other universities. Wartime federally funded facilities such as the Radio Research Laboratory (to develop measures to counter radar) helped prove that academic institutions could carry out a governmental research agenda. In the postwar period, however, Harvard benefited especially from the available funds for individual faculty research projects. Unlike some universities, Harvard did not become an institutional administrator of large government facilities. It did plan and operate the Cambridge Electron Accelerator jointly with MIT, and with funds from the Atomic Energy Commission, during the years 1956–1973.

An important function of Harvard in the historiography of American science is its place as the oldest scientific institution. Harvard's specific scientific history, and the university's long association with a geographical region having social, political, economic, and religious features not necessarily general to the American character, limit

H

the use of Harvard as a model. In all periods, however, Harvard faculty and students have been leaders in American science and their personal influence was widespread. A theme suggested in the historical account above is the interplay of internal institutional dynamics and outside sources of influence and money. The way in which these characterized but changed progressively from period to period is an important feature to be investigated for Harvard and comparatively with other institutions. The questions about engineering, agriculture, and other applied sciences in an institution whose dominant culture is liberal studies is worth pursuing as a means of understanding the tensions between these spheres of orientation in American society at large.

The Harvard University Archives is a rich source for Harvard's science history. Some recent research papers and an introduction to sources and topics are given in Elliott and Rossiter (below).

BIBLIOGRAPHY

Beecher, Henry K., and Mark D. Altschule. *Medicine at Harvard: The First 300 Years.* Hanover, NH: University Press of New England, 1977.

Bethell, John T. *Harvard Observed: An Illustrated History of the University in the Twentieth Century.* Cambridge, MA: Harvard University Press, 1998.

Cohen, I. Bernard. *Some Early Tools of American Science: An Account of the Early Scientific Instruments and Mineralogical and Biological Collections in Harvard University.* Cambridge, MA: Harvard University Press, 1950.

Elliott, Clark A., and Margaret W. Rossiter, eds. *Science at Harvard University: Historical Perspectives.* Bethlehem, PA: Lehigh University Press; London and Toronto: Associated University Presses, 1992.

Hawkins, Hugh. *Between Harvard and America: The Educational Leadership of Charles W. Eliot.* New York: Oxford University Press, 1972.

Jones, Bessie Zaban, and Lyle Gifford Boyd. *The Harvard College Observatory: The First Four Directorships, 1839–1919.* Cambridge, MA: Harvard University Press, 1971.

Morison, Samuel Eliot, ed. *The Development of Harvard University Since the Inauguration of President Eliot 1869–1929.* Cambridge, MA: Harvard University Press, 1930.

———. *Harvard College in the Seventeenth Century.* 2 vols. Cambridge, MA: Harvard University Press, 1936.

———. *Three Centuries of Harvard 1636–1936.* Cambridge, MA: Harvard University Press, 1936.

Winsor, Mary P. *Reading the Shape of Nature: Comparative Zoology at the Agassiz Museum.* Chicago and London: University of Chicago Press, 1991.

Clark A. Elliott

Hayden, Ferdinand Vandeveer (1828–1887)

Naturalist and geologist. Hayden was born in Westfield, Massachusetts, probably out of wedlock. Because of an alcoholic father and a neglectful mother, he experienced poverty and humiliation in his early life. His experience at Oberlin College (1845–1850) changed his life; he emerged an ardent naturalist. In 1871 he married Emma Woodruff of Philadelphia; the couple had no children.

Between 1853 and 1860, Hayden explored western territories that are now parts of modern Kansas, Nebraska, North and South Dakota, Montana, Idaho, Utah, Wyoming, and Colorado. Displaying energy and ingenuity, he gained patronage for his expeditions from the American Fur Company, the Smithsonian Institution, and the Corps of Topographical Engineers, as well as from individual sponsors, including the New York geologist James Hall. By the outbreak of the Civil War, Hayden had established a reputation as the most versatile collector of natural history specimens in America, and the country's foremost exploring geologist. In collaboration with Fielding Bradford Meek, he outlined for the first time the geologic structure of the entire Upper Missouri Basin. He and Meek were early leaders in pointing out the uniqueness of American geology.

Hayden authored 140 publications of his own, and he discovered and named many geologic formations. He was the first to suggest the Rocky Mountains resulted from a massive uplift. He found and described laccoliths, long before others named them and formalized their understanding. He helped lay the foundations of modern geomorphology by pointing out the vast powers of erosion; for example, he noticed antecedent streams well before John Wesley Powell described them. He was an early proponent of the once influential idea that all the great Tertiary basins of the West were lacustrine. His particular interest was the Cretaceous-Tertiary boundary, and his ideas on the Great Lignite (later the Laramie) Formation influenced periodization until the early twentieth century. His *Geology and Natural History of the Upper Missouri* (1862) best epitomizes his style as a collector and naturalist. Written before he had read Charles Darwin's *The Origin of Species* (1859), the book is one of the earliest in America to anticipate evolutionary thinking.

After the Civil War, during which he served as a volunteer surgeon and later a medical administrator, Hayden was a popular lecturer on geology in the Auxiliary Department of Medicine at the University of Pennsylvania (1865–1872). Working for the Department of the Interior from 1867 through 1878, Hayden directed an ambitious series of geologic and natural history surveys, whose scope and purpose he himself largely determined. During that time he persuaded the federal government to grant increasing funds to scientific research and exploration, especially to his Geological and Geographical Survey of the Territories, which became the model for the United States Geological Survey (founded in 1879). His survey's most influential publication was the *Atlas of Colorado* (1877 and 1881), a classic compilation of geology, topography, and landscape delineation.

Hayden solicited numerous monographic studies from a variety of naturalists, which he then published through his survey (see Schmeckebier). His patronage encouraged important works by scores of specialists, especially Meek, Joseph Leidy, Edward Drinker Cope, Leo Lesquereux, Cyrus Thomas, Samuel Hubbard Scudder, Thomas C. Porter, John Merle Coulter, Elliott Coues, Alpheus Spring Packard, Joel Asaph Allen, Charles Abiathar White, and Albert Charles Peale.

By distributing numerous photographs and reports, especially of Colorado and the Yellowstone region of Wyoming, Hayden profoundly influenced the way Americans saw and understood the West. He was ahead of his colleagues in recognizing and promoting the scenic values of Western topography. A genuine enthusiast for science, Hayden wanted laymen to appreciate both the erudite monographs and the more appealing annual reports of his survey. In these ways he pioneered the popularization of science.

Although he was an influential naturalist, a creative geologist, and a masterful entrepreneur, Hayden's place in history has been obscured by controversy. Largely due to his work in Yellowstone (beginning in 1871), he earned a popular reputation as the glamorizer of natural wonders and scenery. Colleagues who knew him better elected him to the National Academy of Sciences (in 1873) because of the important research he engendered. Both views of him persist.

Hayden possessed great ability, but his ruthless ambition, impatience, and combative style earned him widespread enmity. The creation of the U.S. Geological Survey gave his leading rivals (J.W. Powell and Clarence King) and his strongest enemies (John Strong Newberry and Othniel Charles Marsh) the opportunity to unseat him from his preponderant position in exploratory science. Hayden died in Philadelphia in 1887 after a long battle with syphilis, a condition that carried a strong stigma and was uncurable at the time.

The disease affected his conduct during the dramatic struggle for the directorship of the USGS in 1879, though none of his contemporaries were aware of it.

Hayden's opponents outlived him and deliberately besmirched his reputation—so successfully that their biased views continue to influence the literature on Hayden. In the only full and critical study of Hayden, Foster (1994) reviews the historiography of his life and career.

BIBLIOGRAPHY

Bartlett, Richard A. *Great Surveys of the American West.* Norman: University of Oklahoma Press, 1962.

Foster, Mike. "Ferdinand Vandeveer Hayden as Naturalist." *American Zoologist* 26 (1986): 343–349.

———. "The Permian Controversy of 1858: An Affair of the Heart." *Proceedings of the American Philosophical Society* 133:3 (September 1989): 370–390.

———. *Strange Genius: A Life of Ferdinand Vandeveer Hayden.* Niwot, CO: Roberts Rinehart, 1994.

Goetzmann, William H. *Exploration and Empire: The Explorer and the Scientist in the Winning of the American West.* New York: Norton, 1966.

Keyes, Charles Rollin. "Last of the Geological Pioneers: Ferdinand Vandeveer Hayden." *Pan American Geologist* 41 (March 1924): 80–96.

Merrill, George P. *The First One Hundred Years of American Geology.* New Haven: Yale University Press, 1924.

Nelson, Clifford M., and Fritiof M. Fryxell. "The Ante-Bellum Collaboration of Meek and Hayden in Stratigraphy." In *Two Hundred Years of Geology in America,* edited by Cecil J. Schneer. Hanover, NH: University Press of New England, 1979, pp. 187–200.

Nelson, Clifford M., Mary C. Rabbit, and F.M. Fryxell. "Ferdinand Vandeveer Hayden: The U.S. Geological Survey Years, 1879–1886." *Proceedings of the American Philosophical Society* 125:3 (June 1981): 238–243.

Peale, Albert Charles. "Ferdinand Vandeveer Hayden." *Bulletin of the Philosophical Society of Washington* 11 (1892): 476–478.

Schmeckebier, Laurence Frederick. *Catalogue and Index of the Publications of the Hayden, King, Powell and Wheeler Surveys.* United States Geological Survey Bulletin No. 222. Washington, DC: Government Printing Office, 1904.

White, Charles A. "Ferdinand Vandeveer Hayden." *Biographical Memoirs of the National Academy of Sciences* 3 (1895): 394–413.

Mike F. Foster

SEE ALSO

Geological Survey, United States; Surveys, Federal Geological and Natural History

H

Henderson, Lawrence Joseph (1878–1942)

Biochemist and physiologist. Born in Lynn, Massachusetts, Henderson attended Harvard University from 1894 to 1898. Interested in pursuing a career in biomedical research, he entered the Harvard Medical School, from which he graduated in 1902. After spending two postdoctoral years in the Strassburg laboratory of Franz Hofmeister, a pioneer in the application of physical chemistry to biochemistry, Henderson joined the Harvard faculty in 1904, and was soon teaching biochemistry courses in the chemistry department and in the medical school. He remained at Harvard until his death in 1942, achieving the rank of full professor in 1920.

In an age of increasing specialization, Henderson managed to remain very much a generalist. His interdisciplinary interests spanned such diverse fields as chemistry, medicine, history and philosophy of science, and sociology. His influence on Harvard University and its students and faculty was broad and substantial. Henderson was primarily responsible for establishing history of science as a discipline at the university, and for recruiting George Sarton to the Harvard faculty. He played an instrumental role in the creation of such institutions and programs as the Department of Physical Chemistry in the medical school, the Fatigue Laboratory in the business school, and the Society of Fellows.

In spite of the diversity of Henderson's interests, in retrospect one can observe a fundamental unity in his work. Throughout his career, he was interested in the organization of systems, whether physicochemical, biological, or social. He stressed the need to take a holistic view of such systems, and to recognize the mutual dependence of variables within a system. This apparent unity of approach was not the result of some preconceived plan, but rather his methodology and philosophic outlook evolved and became explicit during the course of his researches. This holistic, organismic approach was not unique to Henderson, but reflects an important trend in the science and philosophy of his time.

Henderson's early researches on the body's acid-base balance impressed him with the efficiency of the physiological mechanisms involved in the regulation of neutrality in the organism. He also concluded that the chemical elements and their compounds critical for life possessed unique (i.e., minimum, maximum, or anomalous) values for many important properties. The actual environment, in his view, was really the best of all possible environments for life. Cosmic and biological evolution seemed to be linked in a single, orderly process, and matter and energy apparently have an original property which organizes the universe in space and time. These philosophical speculations led to the publication of two books, *The Fitness of the Environment* (1913) and *The Order of Nature* (1917). Henderson's work on fitness and order influenced, among others, the Harvard philosophers Josiah Royce, R.F.A. Hoernlé, and Alfred North Whitehead.

The work on neutrality regulation also led to the equation for the mathematical treatment of buffer solutions for which Henderson's name is perhaps best known among students of science and medicine, the Henderson-Hasselbalch equation. This research also ultimately led Henderson to his study of blood as a physicochemical system, summarized in his classic book *Blood: A Study in General Physiology* (1928). Henderson's study of the interaction of the variables in the blood, and of the interaction of blood with other body systems, provided an excellent example of biological organization, and of what Claude Bernard called the constancy of the internal environment.

Having investigated the organization of living organisms and of the complex inorganic systems that make life possible, Henderson next turned to an examination of the order of social systems, stimulated by his reading of the work of the Italian engineer-turned-sociologist, Vilfredo Pareto. Pareto emphasized the equilibrium of social systems and compared this equilibrium to that of the organism, views which struck a responsive chord with Henderson. Through several seminars which he offered at Harvard, Henderson helped spread the concept of social equilibrium to colleagues and students in sociology and related fields. Among those influenced by his ideas were the Harvard sociologists George Homans and Talcott Parsons.

Perhaps because of the breadth of Henderson's activities, no full-length biography of him exists. Aspects of his work have been discussed, however, by historians of biology and medicine, social science, and philosophy. Henderson's influence extended beyond his actual scientific contributions, and his life and work are deserving of further study by historians of American science.

BIBLIOGRAPHY

Cannon, Walter. "Lawrence Joseph Henderson." *Biographical Memoirs of the National Academy of Sciences* 23 (1943): 31–58.

Henderson, L.J. *The Fitness of the Environment.* New York: Macmillan, 1913.

———. *The Order of Nature.* Cambridge, MA: Harvard University Press, 1917.

———. *Blood: A Study in General Physiology.* New Haven: Yale University Press, 1928.

———. *On the Social System: Selected Writings.* Edited by Bernard Barber. Chicago: University of Chicago Press, 1970.

Heyl, Barbara. "The Harvard 'Pareto Circle.'" *Journal of the History of Behavioral Sciences* 4 (1968): 316–334.

Parascandola, John. "L. J. Henderson and the Theory of Buffer Action." *Medizinhistorisches Journal* 6 (1971): 297–309.

———. "Organismic and Holistic Concepts in the Thought of L. J. Henderson." *Journal of the History of Biology* 4 (1971): 63–113.

———. "Henderson, Lawrence Joseph." *Dictionary of Scientific Biography.* Edited by Charles C. Gillispie. New York: Scribner, 1972, 6:260–262.

———. "L. J. Henderson and the Mutual Dependence of Variables: From Physical Chemistry to Pareto." In *Science at Harvard University: Historical Perspectives,* edited by Clark A. Elliot and Margaret W. Rossiter. Bethlehem, PA: Lehigh University Press, 1992, pp. 167–190.

Russett, Cynthia. *The Concept of Equilibrium in American Social Thought.* New Haven: Yale University Press, 1966.

John Parascandola

Henry, Joseph (1797–1878)

Experimental physicist and science administrator. Born in Albany, New York, Henry attended the Albany Academy between 1819 and 1822, although he afterward viewed himself as self-educated. After working as a tutor and surveyor, he returned to the Albany Academy in 1826 as professor of mathematics and natural philosophy. In 1832, he was named professor of natural philosophy at the College of New Jersey (Princeton University). He was chosen as the first secretary of the Smithsonian Institution in 1846, and remained secretary until his death. From 1868 until his death, he served as president of the National Academy of Sciences. He also served as president of the American Association for the Advancement of Science (1849–1850), member of the Light-House Board (1852–1871), and chair of the Light-House Board (1871–1878).

Henry wanted to understand the nature of the "imponderables"—electricity, magnetism, light, and heat, as well as their interrelationships. During his years at the Albany Academy, he produced his great electromagnet, which gained him initial recognition by the scientific community, devised a telegraph, invented the first electric motor, and discovered (independently of Michael Faraday in England) electromagnetic self-induction and mutual electromagnetic induction. While at Princeton, he explored the phenomenon of lightning and developed more effective ways of protecting buildings from lightning strikes, examined electromagnetic screening, discovered the concept of the transformer and the oscillatory nature of the discharge of a capacitor, experimented with ultraviolet light, used soap bubbles to explore molecular cohesion, and took the first empirical measurements of the temperature differences between the solar surface and sunspots by utilizing thermoelectric apparatus. While secretary of the Smithsonian, he set aside his personal research program to become an administrator and spokesperson for the value and necessity of basic scientific research, utilizing the Smithsonian to support research, scholarly publication, and international exchange. However, he did conduct investigations of fog-signals and illuminants for the Light-House Board. His research was characterized by short, intense bursts of activity, with frequent changes among topics. In part, this was a result of his institutional settings, which did not allow for full-time research; in part, it was a result of his intense and wide-ranging curiosity.

Contemporaries often compared Henry to Benjamin Franklin. Like Franklin, Henry became a larger-than-life symbol of American accomplishment in science. At the end of the nineteenth century, Henry was enshrined as one of the sixteen representatives of human development and civilization memorialized in the Main Reading Room of the Library of Congress, along with, for example, Isaac Newton, Herodotus, Michelangelo, Plato, and William Shakespeare. His name was given to the standard unit of inductance. There arose a hagiographic literature written by scientists and engineers which treated Henry as the father of modern electrical technology and an isolated example of American excellence.

By the mid-twentieth century, Henry had become symbolic of how little Americans achieved in the physical sciences in the century after Franklin. Historians agreed that he was the foremost American physicist

H

during the first half of the nineteenth century, with an international reputation. However, now they saw him as only the best of a mediocre group of American physical scientists. They argued that even he was not in the same class as the giants of European science, such as Faraday or James C. Maxwell. His relatively modest achievements were presented as evidence of the slow progress of science in the United States.

More recently, changing attitudes towards nineteenth-century American science have resulted in changing views of the significance of Henry. The focus of historians has shifted from the alleged lack of world-class scientists to an appreciation of the institutional evolution of American science during that century and the need to understand that evolution. Many historians feel that the infrastructure for the modern American scientific community was established during the middle third of the nineteenth century. Henry has been seen as one of the "leaders in the shaping of American science" (Bruce, p. 15) and as an institution builder. His success as an experimenter was important not only because of the discoveries he made, but because these discoveries gave him the prestige and respect necessary for success as a science administrator and spokesperson. Along with his friends Alexander Dallas Bache and Louis Agassiz, he was one of the major figures in the Lazzaroni, a group of scientists and science administrators who attempted to establish standards for the American scientific community and increase the level of public support for research. The study of Henry has become part of the wider study of the range and interconnections of American science and government during mid-nineteenth century.

The Joseph Henry Papers Project at the Smithsonian Institution has identified almost 100,000 extant Henry manuscripts. It maintains an automated database of this material, as well as of Henry's personal library. Moyer's biography is the first to be based on this material.

BIBLIOGRAPHY

Bruce, Robert V. *The Launching of Modern American Science 1846–1876*. New York: Knopf, 1987.

Cohen, I. Bernard. *Science and American Society in the First Century of the Republic*. Columbus: Ohio State University, 1961.

Coulson, Thomas. *Joseph Henry: His Life and Work*. Princeton: Princeton University Press, 1950.

Fleming, James Rodger. *Meteorology in America, 1800–1870*. Baltimore: Johns Hopkins University Press, 1990.

Henry, Joseph. *The Scientific Writings of Joseph Henry*. 2 vols. Washington, DC: Smithsonian Institution.

Hinsley, Curtis M., Jr. *Savages and Scientists: The Smithsonian Institution and the Development of American Anthropology, 1846–1910*. Washington, DC: Smithsonian Institution Press, 1981.

Molella, Arthur P., and Nathan Reingold. "Theorists and Ingenious Mechanics: Joseph Henry Defines Science." *Science Studies* 3 (1973): 323–351.

Moyer, Albert E. *Joseph Henry: The Rise of an American Scientist*. Washington, DC: Smithsonian Institution Press, 1997.

Reingold, Nathan. "Henry, Joseph." *Dictionary of Scientific Biography*. Edited by Charles C. Gillispie. New York: Scribners, 1972, 6:277–281.

———. "The New York State Roots of Joseph Henry's National Career." *New York History* 54 (1973): 133–144.

Reingold, Nathan, et al., eds. *The Papers of Joseph Henry*. Vols. 1–5. Washington, DC: Smithsonian Institution Press, 1972–1985.

Rothenberg, Marc, et al., eds. *The Papers of Joseph Henry*. Vols. 6–8. Washington, DC: Smithsonian Institution Press, 1992–1998.

Marc Rothenberg

SEE ALSO

Smithsonian Institution

Heredity and Environment

A hallmark of modern culture since about 1800 has been the belief in change in nature and society, usually thought of as the idea of progress. This progressivist thinking has been characteristic of American culture, even more than in European national cultures. American scientists, like other Americans, have sought to explain the development of things, animate and inanimate, and they have invoked two general categories of forces, heredity and environment, or those forces within and without the phenomenon to be explained. Especially in modern times, heredity and environment have allowed the developmentalist or evolutionary thinker to reconcile change and continuity. How can there be change without chaos? is perhaps the developmentalist's most difficult question. Of course, in each successive era scientists have always had to reconstruct these notions afresh, as their contemporaries' notions of the organization of natural and social reality have themselves changed.

American scientists first articulated developmentalist thinking in the eighteenth century. In his *Notes on the State of Virginia* (1781), Thomas Jefferson cast heredity and environment into an American scientific discourse. As part of a larger debate between Americans and Europeans over the nature of the New World, Jefferson asked, How has the New World's beneficent environment affected its flora, fauna, and peoples? He argued that the New World's environment was essentially good and that America provided Europe with the possibilities of a fresh beginning. The oft-cited universal human nature of Jefferson's *philosophe* colleagues assumed that the world's different environments accounted for its different peoples; yet the tension they cited between *civilization* (white European peoples) and *nature* (dark-skinned indigenous peoples) suggested the importance of biological inheritance as well. Yet Jefferson's contemporaries no less than Jefferson were biblical literalists for whom there was only a short history of the earth.

All this was to change in the nineteenth century, when American scientific discussion of heredity and environment proceeded along two tracks, one obscure to contemporary historians, the other not. Throughout the century, animal and plant breeders attempted to create better species, usually for economic reasons. They operated with little more intellectual guidance than the phrase, "like begets like," and the sense that they could, through directed breeding, combine desirable characteristics of different individuals of the same species in succeeding generations. There was also considerable interest, among plant breeders, in grafting plants, almost in the manner of Mary Shelley's Dr. Frankenstein, with the hope that a new life-form would breed true from this amalgam. The breeders thus believed that characters or traits acquired during the organism's lifetime would become a part of its permanent inheritance. This use-disuse formula had a long history before the French scientist Jean Baptiste Lamarck cast it in an evolutionary framework in his *Philosophical Zoology* (1809). There were three formulations of Lamarckian evolutionism in this century, all related to notions of heredity, environment, and speciation. In Lamarck's own formulation, to the late 1830s, a species was constituted of individuals, each of which adapted to changes in the environment and passed those adaptations onto its progeny; if the environmental changes were sufficiently forceful and general, then all individuals in a given species would "evolve." From the 1830s to the 1870s, Lamarckian evolutionism cast heredity and environment in a different mold. Now, the starting

point was the group, not the individual; it was a culture, an aggregate of individuals who did not exist apart from the group, rather than a mere population. The second version of Lamarckian evolutionism (and other varieties of developmentalism followed suit) emphasized the importance of a common material experience that made the group or the population what it was. This second Lamarckianism also stressed the importance of the mental or conscious life of the group coming from that common material experience, which in turn depended on the inheritance of acquired characters. The third version of Lamarckian evolutionism, often referred to in the relevant history of science literature as "Neo-Lamarckism," lasted from the 1870s to the 1920s. Its champions were reductionists who discounted the spiritual forces of their mid-century predecessors. They were determinists too: they assumed that whatever adaptations the group or species or race made to the environment was passed on as a biological inheritance, not a social one, to the next or succeeding generations, so that evolutionary progress continued in a straight line. Lamarckian ideas of heredity, environment, and evolution were so pervasive in American science (and among English and German scientists also) that even Charles Darwin modified the later editions of his epochal *The Origin of Species* (1859) to accept Lamarckian ideas of the inheritance of acquired characters at various points in his argument. In this late-nineteenth-century formulation of the inheritance of acquired characters, heredity mattered far more than environment, for it was literally the mechanism of transmission of all evolutionary change, and environment meant little or nothing. This was quite in contrast with mid-century Lamarckism, in which the common material experience caused environmental pressure that led over time to permanent alterations in the evolved species or group.

Between the late 1890s and the early 1900s, new descriptions of heredity and environment emerged. The German cytologist August Weismann challenged the Neo-Lamarckian principle of inheritance of acquired characters. Weismann was no hereditarian determinist, as most historians have consistently misread him to have been; he merely argued that changes in the body cells could not be biologically inherited, for the only mechanism of biological inheritance was through the germ plasm, literally the semen and the egg when united in fertilization. Such events were remote indeed from the kinds of environmental circumstances contemporary champions of Neo-Lamarckism had in mind.

H

The early-twentieth-century scientific discourse on heredity and environment included both Mendelian and biometric formulations. The former incorporated charts of dominance and recessiveness of "unit characters" through generations, as if they were blueprints, whereas the latter used measures of statistical correlation and regression, as if organic traits could be so depicted. Both techniques assumed a reductionist and mechanistic world in which traits were unique, segregated, and bred true, and in which organisms were nothing more than the aggregate of their individual parts, and species were likewise the mere sum of their aggregate data. The breeding of a better species or race, then, was merely a matter of the proper arithmetic, whether one deployed the qualitative Mendelian or the quantitative biometric discourse. Yet, ironically, neither approach stated, let alone proved, that heredity was more important than environment, although most Mendelians and biometricians believed that heredity determined almost all of the physical and mental traits of any organism, including humans. So powerful were the cultural notions of that age of American (and European) culture that scientists simply assumed that a Mendelian or biometrical explanation of inheritance allowed them to assert the power of heredity over environment. A more spectacular example of how the general cultural notions of an age drive any technical discourse, including that of science, is difficult to imagine.

In the interwar years—between the 1920s and the 1950s—a new holistic conception of heredity and environment took shape in American science and culture. In this new model, the whole was assumed to be greater than or different from the sum of the parts; each part was a distinct yet interrelated part of the larger whole. Thus, heredity and environment were considered interactive, in a fluctuating network, or system of systems. Thus, linear regression formulations yielded to multiple regression analyses; Mendelian heredity was said to involve the interaction of many genes in the creation of traits and patterns of behavior; and nature and culture were understood to be cooperative, as in the evolutionary synthesis of Sewall Wright, Theodosius Dobzhansky, and other American architects of that synthesis.

What occasioned the emergence of that new paradigm was the controversy over the relative contributions of heredity and environment in the making of mental and physical traits, especially of humans, in the natural and social sciences. This controversy involved evolutionary theory, psychology, anthropology, and sociology; it also helped shape child development, a field new in the interwar years. The battle over heredity versus environment functioned on two levels. One was the struggle over the notion of natural and social reality of the new age, in which holistic models of the interaction of a network of different yet interrelated elements or even whole systems was assumed to be superior in explanatory power to those of the 1870–1920 era, which took for granted the truth of reductionist, hierarchical models of reality. The other was purely the stuff of conflict among champions of the natural and social sciences over the turf—academic, institutional, and intellectual—that their disciplines could claim. Once the emerging social scientists won from the longer-established biological and natural scientists the grudging concession that social and cultural explanations were best left to the social sciences, just as biological and natural explanations were left to the biological and natural scientists, the controversy over heredity versus environment was essentially over. Many historians do not understand that this interactive model was still progressive, linear, and profoundly deterministic. An individual could not exist "outside" its group—species, race, family, clan, and so forth; this was the distinctive contribution of developmental science, as in comparative zoology and psychology and child and human development.

Since the 1950s, there has been a reformulation of heredity and environment. In our contemporary age, many have come to question the linear, progressivist, and evolutionary models that American scientists had used since Lamarck's time, as in the champions of cladistics, punctuated evolution, and other such challenges to progressivist thinking. Generally speaking, the advocates of nature have triumphed over the defenders of nurture; the individual, not the group or species, is the unit of analysis, and usually a genetic or hereditarian argument will win out over an environmentalist or indeterminist one, as, for example, in genetic engineering, in debates over race, class, and gender, or even over whether homosexuality is inborn or a "lifestyle" choice.

BIBLIOGRAPHY

Allen, Garland E. *Life Sciences in the Twentieth Century.* New York: Wiley, 1975.

Cravens, Hamilton. *The Triumph of Evolution: The Heredity-Environment Controversy 1900–1941.* 1978. Reprint, Baltimore: Johns Hopkins University Press, 1988.

———. *Before Head Start. The Iowa Station and America's Children.* Chapel Hill: University of North Carolina Press, 1993.

Gerbi, Antonello. *The Dispute of the New World: The History of a Polemic, 1750–1900.* Rev. and enlarged ed. Translated by Jeremy Moyle. Pittsburgh: University of Pittsburgh Press, 1973.

Hunt, J. McVicker. *Intelligence and Experience.* New York: Ronald Press, 1961.

Packard, Alpheus S. *Lamarck: The Founder of Evolution.* New York: Longmans, Green, 1901.

Provine, William B. *Sewall Wright and Evolutionary Biology.* Chicago: University of Chicago Press, 1986.

Hamilton Cravens

SEE ALSO
Neo-Lamarckism

Hitchcock, Edward (1793–1864)

Geologist, clergyman, and educator. Born in Deerfield, Massachusetts, Hitchcock attended Deerfield Academy and briefly studied theology at Yale. He served as pastor to a Congregational church in Conway, Massachusetts, from 1821 to 1825, abandoning the position due to ill health. In the fall and winter of 1825–1826, he studied with Benjamin Silliman Sr. at Yale. In 1825, he began a long association with Amherst College during which he served as professor of chemistry and natural history (1825–1845) and professor of geology and natural theology (1845–1864), taking on the additional duties of the college presidency for a decade (1845–1854). He conducted both the first (1830–1833) and second (1837–1841) Massachusetts state surveys and also served as state geologist of Vermont (1856–1861). His advice influenced the design of the New York Natural History Survey, but he ultimately declined to serve as a geologist in that project.

Hitchcock was greatly concerned with the relationship between science, especially geology, and religion. Early in his own natural history studies, he sought to reconcile his attraction to such studies with his intense religious sensibilities. Determining that both subjects could, and indeed ought to, be pursued by a single individual, he devoted much attention in subsequent years to the reconciliation of the biblical and geological accounts of earth history. In this endeavor, he joined his old mentor, Silliman, but came into public conflict with Moses Stuart, a biblical scholar at Andover Theological Seminary. Hitchcock's ideas were widely circulated during and after the 1850s in his *Religion of Geology.* His geological ideas—and religious perspective—were also available in his *Elementary Geology,* a text so popular it went through thirty-one editions in only two decades.

Motivated by his conviction that the geologists of the various state surveys should coordinate their efforts and by a sense of physical isolation from his colleagues, Hitchcock provided a strong force in the creation of the Association of American Geologists in 1840 and served as the organization's first president. Despite his prominent role in the organization of the American geological community, Hitchcock believed that Americans should defer to European geologists, especially in matters of nomenclature and stratigraphic correlation.

Hitchcock nurtured his relationship with the Massachusetts legislature by giving early and extensive attention to economic geology in the state survey. Thereafter, he was able to maintain financial support for less overtly utilitarian aspects of geological work. Beginning with the very first volume in 1818 and continuing for forty-five years, Hitchcock produced a steady stream of geological contributions for Silliman's *American Journal of Science.* His interest in the fossil footprints found in the sandstones of the Connecticut River valley gave rise to a protracted dispute with James Deane over priority and due credit. He also devoted considerable attention to the understanding of "diluvial" or "drift" phenomena and to the possible application of Louis Agassiz's glacial theory in America.

No monographic biography of Hitchcock is available. An extensive collection of the correspondence exchanged by Silliman and Hitchcock constitutes only a part of the President Edward Hitchcock Papers at Amherst College. Rodney L. Stiling has traced the development of Hitchcock's thought with regard to the relationship between the biblical and geological accounts of earth history.

BIBLIOGRAPHY
Guralnick, Stanley M. "Geology and Religion in America before Darwin: The Case of Edward Hitchcock, Theologian and Geologist (1793–1864)." *Isis* 63 (1972): 529–543.

Hitchcock, C.H. "Edward Hitchcock." *American Geologist* 16 (1895): 133–149.

H

Hitchcock, Edward. *Elementary Geology.* Amherst, MA: J.S. and C. Adams, 1840.

———. *Religion of Geology and Its Connected Sciences.* Boston: Phillips, Samson, and Company, 1852. New ed., Boston: Phillips, Samson, and Company, 1859.

Hithcock, Edward. *Reminiscences of Amherst College.* Northampton, MA: Bridgeman and Childs, 1863.

Hitchcock, Edward, and Charles H. Hitchcock. *Elementary Geology.* New [31st] ed. New York: Ivison, Phinney, and Company, 1860.

Newell, Julie R. "American Geologists and Their Geology: The Formation of the American Geological Community, 1780–1865." Ph.D. diss., University of Wisconsin-Madison, 1993.

Robinson, Gloria. "Edward Hitchcock." In *Benjamin Silliman and His Circle: Studies on the Influence of Benjamin Silliman on Science in America,* edited by Leonard G. Wilson. New York: Science History Press, 1979, pp. 49–83.

Stiling, Rodney L. "The Diminishing Deluge: Noah's Flood in Nineteenth-Century American Thought." Ph.D. diss., University of Wisconsin-Madison, 1991.

Julie R. Newell

Hollow-Earth, Theory of

A habitable world beneath the earth's surface figures in the mythology of the ancient Greeks and in that of some Amerindian tribes; it also has been imaginatively depicted in Dante's *Inferno*. A more literal hollow earth was envisioned in the hypotheses of Edmund Halley, Cotton Mather, and Leonhard Euler—as a way to explain the shifting of the earth's magnetic poles. The astronomer Halley conjectured that the earth might consist of an outer shell revolving around a many-layered rotating nucleus, each independent of the other.

The most notorious theory was developed by Captain John Cleves Symmes (1780–1829), an American who denied any knowledge of his predecessors. In 1818, after retiring from military service, Symmes issued a printed circular declaring the earth to be hollow, with vast openings in both polar regions. He pledged his life in support of this theory and invited the world to assist him in exploring the earth's interior. Needless to say, the announcement was greeted with derision. Amateur cosmographers rushed to print newspaper refutations of Symmes, and the term "Symmes Hole" became a code word for scorn. A novel, *Symzonia,* written under a pseudonym, explained that dwellers in the interior salute each other by placing a thumb at the end of the nose and waggling their fingers.

Surprisingly, as Symmes lectured from city to city, ridicule was replaced by healthy skepticism. More and more of his audience came away—if not convinced—at least with a willingness to see the theory tested by exploration. Two things help account for this change in public opinion. Symmes himself, although not a spell-binding orator, came across as wholly sincere and, in the course of time, collected wide-ranging bits of information that might bolster his theory. The other was his taking on the assistance of Jeremiah N. Reynolds (1799–1858), who developed visual aids such as a model of the hollow earth and was also an engaging lecturer. As early as 1826, one supportive book had appeared, written anonymously by James McBride.

Like Halley, Symmes first proposed a series of concentric spheres beneath the earth's surface. He dispensed with the interior spheres, however, as he got more deeply into the question of how the interior could be lighted through the northern opening 2,000 miles in diameter and the southern even larger. The verges of these openings were so gradual that, in the south at least, it was alleged a ship might pass through to the interior without its passengers being aware of the fact. Because the geography of the Antarctic region was still so much a mystery, exploration in that direction seemed best to Reynolds. Symmes, on the other hand, preferred overland exploration in the north, following herds of migrating reindeer, which he believed were fattened on interior pastures. It was this issue which split the two in 1826.

After each went his own way, there were many disappointments for both, although each also contributed to the accomplishments of others. Symmes believed for a time the czar of Russia was going to finance his expedition. Reynolds, who gradually moved away from the idea that the earth is hollow, continued to agitate for Antarctic exploration and thought he had obtained federal sponsorship, which failed to materialize. With others, he did make a sealing voyage into southern waters in 1829 with the brigs *Seraph* and *Annawan*. This expedition, under the command of Captain Edmund Fanning, resulted in the opportunity for James Eights (1798–1882), a member of the expedition, to become the first American to publish scientific papers on Antarctic islands. And, although Reynolds personally profited in no way, his continued work as a publicist surely contributed in some measure to federal sponsorship of the 1838–1842 Wilkes Expedition. Symmes's theory, as filtered through Reynolds, gave Edgar Allan

Poe the crux of his novel *A. Gordon Pym,* and a magazine article by Reynolds about a white whale, "Mocha Dick," gave Herman Melville the germ of his masterpiece. In two of the novels comprising his *voyages extraordinaires,* Jules Verne alluded with approval to Symmes, even though he spelled the name wrong.

The drug manufacturer John Uri Lloyd, who wrote fiction for his own amusement, carried the Symmes premise a step further in his highly successful 1895 novel *Etidorhpa* (read it backwards) that went through eleven editions. In the 1901 edition Lloyd made the device of a journey to the center of the earth a vehicle for serious speculation about the future, as science fiction writers often have done since. Although Lloyd was not taken in by Symmes's conjectures, a physician named Cyrus Reed Teed discovered in them the basis for a religious community. Teed added Koresh (the Hebrew equivalent of Cyrus) to his name; with a handful of disciples who helped him build the Koreshan Unity Settlement in Florida, he carried out a "great experiment" in 1896 on the Gulf shore with an instrument he had invented called a "rectilineator." His measurements proved, at least to his own satisfaction, that it is an optical illusion when a ship appears to sink below the horizon; rather, the earth is concave and we are living inside it.

In the first half of the nineteenth century, there were still enough unexplored regions to lend a degree of plausibility to the hollow-earth theory. When resurrected later it usually has been a literary device as with Lloyd, or a dogma or religion as with Koresh. Yet the concept was revived as sound cosmology as late as 1920 by Marshall B. Gardner, who asked in the subtitle of his book, "Have the Poles Really Been Discovered?" George Sarton (*Isis* 34 [1942]: p. 30) considered Gardner's book, *A Journey to the Earth's Interior,* "proof of the the melancholy fact that when an error is introduced, it can never be completely eradicated."

BIBLIOGRAPHY

Almy, Robert F. "J. N. Reynolds: A Brief Biography with Particular Reference to Poe and Symmes." *The Colophon,* n.s. 2 (1937): 227–245.

Clark, P. "The Symmes Theory of the Earth." *Atlantic Monthly* 31 (1873): 471–480.

Gardner, Marshall B. *A Journey to the Earth's Interior.* Aurora, IL: the author, 1920.

Lloyd, John Uri. *Etidorhpa; or The End of Earth; the Strange History of a Mysterious Being and the Account of a Remarkable Journey.* New York: Dodd, Mead & Company, 1901.

[McBride, James]. *Symmes' Theory of Concentric Spheres.* Cincinnati: Morgan, Lodge and Fisher, 1826.

Miller, William Marion. "The Theory of Concentric Spheres." *Isis* 33 (1941): 507–514.

Mitterling, Philip I. *America in the Antarctic to 1840.* Urbana: University of Illinois Press, 1959.

Peck, John Wells. "Symmes Theory." *Ohio Archaeological and Historical Publications* 18 (1909): 29–42.

Seaborn, Adam [pseud.]. *Symzonia, A Voyage of Discovery.* New York: J. Seymour, 1820.

Symmes, Americus, comp. *The Symmes Theory of Concentric Spheres.* Louisville: Bradley & Gilbert, 1878.

Symmes, Elmore. "John Cleves Symmes, the Theorist." *Southern Bivouac,* n.s. 2 (1887): 555–566, 621–631, 682–693.

Teed [Koresh], Cyrus Reed. *The Cellular Cosmology; or, The Earth a Concave Sphere.* Estero, FL: Guiding Star Publishing House, 1922.

Zirkle, Conway. "The Theory of Concentric Spheres: Edmund Halley, Cotton Mather, & John Cleves Symmes." *Isis* 37 (1947): 155–159.

Charles Boewe

SEE ALSO
Wilkes Expedition

Holmes, William Henry (1846–1935)

Anthropologist, archaeologist, and geologist. Holmes, a farmboy from near Cadiz, Ohio, began his career in a specialized field of art: scientific illustration. Visiting Washington in 1871, he came to the Smithsonian "Castle" and shortly began drawing pictures of fossils for F.B. Meek and recent shells for W.H. Dall. A year later, his skill led to his appointment as an artist of the United State Geological Survey of the Territories; in that capcity he accompanied the F.V. Hayden expedition to Yellowstone National Park. In that area, Holmes mastered field geology, and subsequently spent two years in Colorado, and next headed a division of the Hayden Survey in New Mexico and Arizona Territories. In 1876, he returned to Colorado to help establish a primary triangulation net, during the course of which he climbed thirty peaks, each over 14,000 feet high. In 1878, Holmes returned to Yellowstone, where he studied and illustrated a series of fossil forests which were successively killed and buried by volcanic ash. His most famous work of the Hayden period were his illustrations for the Atlas of Colorado, unequalled pen-and-ink renderings of the dramatic landscape. In the scientific field, G.K. Gilbert credited Holmes with

H

independently discovering the concept of lacoliths, wherein the intrusion of a thick mass of igneous rocks causes sedimentary strata to bend upward in mountain masses.

Following a year's study of art in Europe, Holmes joined the newly founded United States Geological Survey. His first assignment was with C.E. Dutton to the Grand Canyon. His panoramas of the canyon are unequalled and even more dramatic than those he made of the Colorado landscape. In 1889, Holmes transferred to the Bureau of Ethnology, headed by John Wesley Powell. His field experience among abandoned cave dwellings and pueblos in the Southwest had whetted his interest in Native Americans. Melding art and science, Holmes by now had become a master of display technique, for he had prepared public exhibits shown at the Philadelphia Centennial Exposition and the subsequent New Orleans, Louisville, and Cincinnati expositions. At the 1893, Chicago World's Fair, Holmes's habitat groups of Indians, shown life-size, set a new standard for both temporary and permanent museum displays.

His efforts at the Chicago exposition resulted in his appointment to the new Field Museum. A positive aspect of this venue was a trip to Yucatán, where Holmes used his skills in surveying and sketching to help clarify the abandoned Mayan cities. However, the Field Museum was unsatisfactory, and in 1897, Holmes returned to Washington to become the first head curator of anthropology in the reorganized United States National Museum. Holmes was responsible for expanding the department to include physical anthropology. Holmes continued his studies in Mexico and began archaeological investigations in Cuba and in the Midwest. Throughout this period, he supervised displays sent to various national expositions by the Smithsonian Institution.

Following the death of Powell in 1902, Holmes became director of the Bureau of American Ethnology. If Powell laid the groundwork for the science of ethnology, Holmes is to be credited with refining its practice. His most significant research for the bureau investigated native methods of the quarrying and manufacture of stone tools. Holmes was able to demonstrate that the supposed neolithic stone tools were the residue from manufacturing and did not indicate an earlier stage in development of stone instruments. Even though arguments as to the antiquity of man in America continue to this day, the prevailing view supports Holmes's argument that man arrived relatively late, bringing sophisticated stone tools with him.

In 1910, Holmes rejoined the United States National Museum as head curator of anthropology, simultaneously becoming head of the National Gallery of Art, although it was not for another decade that the gallery became a separate administrative unit of the government. Holmes judged that his single greatest accomplishment was the arrangement for continued research of the archaeological collections in the "new" National Museum and the installation of public displays in archaeology. In 1916, he conducted his final field investigation in Central America. During the 1920s, Holmes continued research in archaeology. Simultaneously, he devoted considerable effort to raising public support in an attempt to fund a National Gallery of Art building. He had a reputation as a water colorist and was an important figure in the Washington community of artists. Holmes finally retired in 1933 and died shortly thereafter.

The Department of Anthropology continues today as the single largest scientific unit of the National Museum of Natural History. Although his efforts to found a distinct National Gallery failed, they did lead ultimately to the National Museum of American Art and the National Portrait Gallery.

There are seventeen bound volumes assembled by Holmes to document various events in his life, including letters, certificates, newspaper clippings, and photographs in the library of the National Museum of American Art/National Portrait Gallery.

BIBLIOGRAPHY
Hough, Walter. "William Henry Holmes." *American Anthropologist*, n.s. 33 (1933): 752–755.
Swanton, John R. "William Henry Holmes." *Biographical Memoirs of the National Academy of Sciences* 17 (1935): 223–252.

Ellis L. Yochelson

Howard, Leland Ossian (1857–1950)

Applied entomologist and federal bureau chief. Howard was born in Rockford, Illinois, and raised in Ithaca, New York. As a boy, he encountered Cornell University entomology professor John Henry Comstock, who became Howard's mentor. An appointment as assistant to new United States Department of Agriculture (USDA) entomologist Charles Valentine Riley in 1878 diverted Howard from a medical career. While Riley resigned, was replaced briefly by Comstock, and then returned, Howard remained in the office. He rose to chief entomologist upon Riley's second resignation in 1894. Howard became the leading employer of entomologists, and a well-connected, outspoken champion of his discipline.

Howard specialized in the taxonomy of parasitic wasps, particularly those attacking scale insects, when first Comstock and then Riley made the latter group a major focus of USDA entomology. Howard advocated the use of such parasites in the biological control of pests after USDA agents, under Riley's direction, introduced Australian insects that controlled cottony-cushion scale in California in 1889. Howard inherited Riley's rivalry with California officials over credit for that achievement.

Howard witnessed, and later chronicled, four events between 1889 and 1898 that shaped the history of applied entomology (often called "economic entomology"). The gypsy moth, San Jose scale, and boll weevil, all foreign to the United States, became serious pests, and insects were proven for the first time to transmit human disease. The corps Howard established in the South largely failed to persuade farmers to adopt cultural methods against the boll weevil. The San Jose scale spurred other nations to restrict American produce, leading eventually to the first federal plant quarantine legislation in 1912. Howard's grandest project was a long-term, concerted effort in biological control, beginning in 1905, against gypsy moth in New England. Many parasites were introduced from Europe; none controlled the moth. In connection with the gypsy moth work, Howard and William F. Fiske articulated what came to be called density-dependent mortality, a concept ecologists debated hotly in later years.

Howard became a spokesman for medical entomology after insects were found to transmit malaria and other diseases. He wrote books on the dangers of mosquitoes and houseflies, and made "Swat the Fly" a nationwide slogan.

The small office Howard took over in 1894 became the Bureau of Entomology in 1904. He organized it into divisions on the basis of crop groups. In his thirty-three years at the helm, Howard oversaw rapid growth and professionalization of economic entomology. Preaching that insects threatened to doom civilization as both agricultural and public health pests, Howard constantly lobbied politicians and the general public for support.

Through his USDA position, his ties to leading entomologists around the world, and his founding role in national entomological organizations, Howard became the leading international figure in his field. In 1920, the American Association for the Advancement of Science elected him president, rewarding his twenty-two years as permanent secretary.

After stepping down as bureau chief in 1927, Howard continued to warn the public against "the insect menace." His history of entomology and his autobiography remain the principal works on the field during his time, casting a long historiographical shadow.

Howard's importance lies in his work as administrator and spokesman for entomology. Although a student of Comstock, he did not contribute to Comstock's school of evolutionary systematics. Howard's taxonomic papers were of the typological style that went out of fashion during his lifetime. He did little original research in medical entomology, but greatly publicized that field. The biological control projects begun under his administration accomplished little of practical value. His bureau's organizational structure retarded progress in biological control, scattering the few experts in that specialty among various crop divisions. Howard meanwhile worked to prevent state organizations from following the lead of California and introducing parasites and predators from abroad themselves. Despite his advocacy of this use of beneficial insects, Howard did more than anyone else to convince the public that insects in general were a menace to be vigorously fought. He thus contributed to the insecticidal orientation of American entomology.

BIBLIOGRAPHY

Graf, John E., and Dorothy W. Graf. "Leland Ossian Howard." *Biographical Memoirs of the National Academy of Sciences* 33 (1959): 87–124. (Includes bibliography of Howard's works.)

Howard, Leland O. *A History of Applied Entomology (Somewhat Anecdotal).* Washington, DC: Smithsonian Institution, 1930.

———. *Fighting the Insects: The Story of an Entomologist.* New York: Macmillan, 1933.

Howard, Leland O., and William F. Fiske. "The Importation into the United States of the Parasites of the Gipsy Moth and the Brown-tail Moth." *U.S. Bureau of Entomology Bulletin* 91 (1911).

Sawyer, Richard C. "Monopolizing the Insect Trade: Biological Control in the USDA, 1888–1951" *Agricultural History* 64 (1990): 271–285.

Richard C. Sawyer

H

Howard University

A predominantly black educational institution located in Washington, D.C. Established on 2 March 1867, the university came into existence as part of a larger post–Civil War campaign to provide African Americans with educational opportunities essential to their new station in society. Eight similar institutions were founded in Southern or border states around the same time. The uniqueness of Howard's early program lay in its effort to build an interracial student body. This experiment was short-lived, however, the victim of growing racial segregation following Reconstruction and, finally, the 1896 separate-but-equal decision in the case of *Plessy* v. *Ferguson*.

A primary goal identified in Howard's original charter was "the education of youth in the liberal arts and sciences." Yet, for half a century, the sciences remained a relatively low priority in the curriculum. In part, this was because the largely white administration and faculty envisioned blacks primarily as teachers and preachers among their own people; partly because, in conformity with the prevailing opinion of the day, they doubted that blacks could either reason rigorously or exercise adequate conceptual or quantitative skills; and partly because the market for black scientists or black science teachers was almost nonexistent. Nevertheless, science was a part of the curriculum almost from the start.

The first science courses were offered in the medical department, which opened in November 1868, a year and a half after the opening of the normal (teacher training) department. These courses included clinical, applied, and "pure" subjects. One faculty member, Silas L. Loomis, taught medicine, toxicology, and chemistry, and was appointed university-wide professor of chemistry in 1871 as the science curriculum was extended to the collegiate department (which had opened in September 1868). When Loomis resigned in 1872, William C. Tilden held the chair in chemistry for a year, after which the teaching of science in the collegiate and medical departments remained more or less separate. Of the five collegiate department faculty members in 1873–1874, one—Frank W. Clarke—taught science full-time. Clarke, an 1867 graduate of Lawrence Scientific School, Harvard University, served as "acting" professor of chemistry and physics. He left in 1874, and later became chief chemist of the United States Geological Survey.

Although the Howard administration expressed a commitment to providing "suitable prominence to the several branches of physical science" (*Catalogue*,

1873–1874, p. 41), the number of science courses offered grew slowly. Thomas Robinson, principal of the normal department, taught in Clarke's place until 1887, when Robert B. Warder was appointed professor of physics and chemistry. Horace B. Patton and Richard Foster lectured on "natural science," the umbrella designation for botany, zoology, astronomy, geology, physiology, and hygiene. Warder helped organize a faculty resolution, approved by the trustees on 19 January 1892, to develop a Bachelor of Science program. The first B.S. was awarded in 1896, to W. Edward Robinson. Few students, however, enrolled for the program in its early years—perhaps discouraged by the low demand for black scientists in industry and academe. The number of B.S. graduates averaged about one per year; two degrees were awarded in 1902, none in 1901 and 1903.

A name change in 1903—from the College Department to the College of Arts and Sciences—signified an enhanced level of recognition for the university's science program. In 1910, a major milestone was reached in the development of the science curriculum. Wilbur P. Thirkield, the university president, had successfully petitioned Congress for funds to construct a science center. Science Hall, as the new facility was called, comprised a separate floor for each of the major disciplines—biology, physics, and chemistry—with a multipurpose lecture hall on the third floor, and storage space and additional laboratories in the basement. At the dedication ceremony on 13 December 1910, Henry S. Pritchett, president of the Carnegie Foundation for the Advancement of Teaching, remarked on the facility's significance: "This is the most complete modern building ever prepared for the instruction of the Negro race in the sciences. . . . The Negro race of the United States is fast waking up to the idea that progress for it lies in the adoption of the scientific attitude of mind and of scientific methods. . . ." (*Catalogue*, 1911–1912, p. 251). Other dignitaries in attendance included President Taft, ex-President Theodore Roosevelt, and William H. Welch of Johns Hopkins University.

Science Hall served as a symbolic rejection of Booker T. Washington's belief that black educational institutions should concentrate on vocational or manual training. The science faculty at Howard came to include a new generation of African-American academics, men with advanced degrees—Ernest Everett Just (zoology), Thomas W. Turner (botany), St. Elmo Brady (chemistry), Elbert F. Cox (mathematics), and Frank Coleman (physics), to name a few—who gradually supplanted the white faculty as heads of academic divisions and departments. In 1914, the number of students earning the B.S. degree increased several fold (none in 1912, four in 1913, eighteen in 1914) and grew steadily thereafter. The first M.S. degrees were awarded in 1923, to Marcelle B. Brown (chemistry) and Clarence F. Holmes (mathematics). A doctoral program was established in 1955. The chemistry department was the first to offer the Ph.D. degree, followed by the physics department. On 6 June 1958, the first Howard Ph.D.'s were awarded to chemists Harold Delaney and Bibhuti R. Mazumder.

BIBLIOGRAPHY

Catalogue of the Officers and Students of Howard University, Washington, District of Columbia [title varies]. Washington, DC, 1869–.

Dyson, Walter. *Howard University, the Capstone of Negro Education. A History: 1867–1940.* Washington, DC: The Graduate School, Howard University, 1941.

Lamb, Daniel Smith, comp. *Howard University Medical Department, Washington, D.C.: A Historical, Biographical and Statistical Souvenir.* Washington, DC: R. Beresford, 1900.

Logan, Rayford W. *Howard University: The First Hundred Years, 1867–1968.* New York: New York University Press, 1969.

Manning, Kenneth R. *Black Apollo of Science: The Life of Ernest Everett Just.* New York: Oxford University Press, 1983.

Porter, Dorothy B., comp. *Howard University Masters' Theses Submitted in Partial Fulfillment of the Requirements for the Master's Degree at Howard University, 1918–1945.* Washington, DC: The Graduate School, Howard University, 1946.

Kenneth R. Manning

Hubble, Edwin Powell (1889–1953)

Observational astronomer and cosmologist. Hubble attended the University of Chicago, then Oxford University on a Rhodes Scholarship, and took his Ph.D. in astronomy from Chicago and the Yerkes Observatory in 1917. After serving in World War I (reaching the rank of major in the infantry), Hubble joined the Mount Wilson Observatory. There he worked for the rest of his life, except for service during World War II at the Army Proving Grounds in Aberdeen, Maryland, as chief of ballistics and director of the Supersonic Wind Tunnels Laboratory (work for which he received the

Medal for Merit). One of the foremost astronomers of the twentieth century, Hubble changed our understanding of the universe in several significant ways.

In the 1920s, Hubble announced what quickly became the basic classification scheme for nebulae (contemporaneously with his demonstration that the "nebulae" are independent "island universes" beyond the boundary of our own galaxy). His diagram of the sequence of nebular types was famous by the 1930s. And *The Hubble Atlas of Galaxies* by Alan Sandage, Hubble's student, appeared in 1961.

With the new 100-inch telescope at Mount Wilson, Hubble discovered, during the 1920s, Cepheid variable stars in spiral nebulae. Using the period-luminosity relation for Cepheids (established by Harlow Shapley, who had moved from Mount Wilson to Harvard), Hubble calculated the luminosities of such stars from their observed periods (the length of time for such a star to go from maximum luminosity to minimum and back to maximum). Then he compared these estimated intrinsic luminosities to the observed luminosities (diminished due to the distances of the nebulae in which the Cepheid stars were embedded), and derived distances that placed the spiral nebulae far beyond the boundary of our galaxy. Hubble settled centuries of speculation over the possible existence of island universes similar to our galaxy.

Vesto M. Slipher at the Lowell Observatory had measured high-radial velocities for spiral nebulae as early as 1912, and the Dutch astronomer Willem de Sitter had proposed in 1917 a static model of the universe with an apparent velocity of recession greater for objects at greater distances. (A general demise of static models of the universe occurred in 1929, but not before de Sitter's theory helped stimulate searches for a velocity-distance relation.) Using Slipher's data and more measurements collected by his colleague Milton Humason at Mount Wilson in the late 1920s, Hubble estimated distances to increasingly more-distant galaxies, and he established an empirical velocity-distance relationship in 1929. (Actually, the observed relation was between magnitude and spectral shift. Differences in observed brightness were readily attributed to differences in distance. Red shifts in the spectra of light from spiral nebulae were generally interpreted as Doppler shifts indicative of real motions in an expanding universe.) While some controversy remained over the interpretation of the velocity-distance relation, Hubble had established the relation empirically. In doing so, he

H

ushered in a new age of thought in which the universe is generally believed to be dynamic rather than static.

With the velocity-distance relation firmly established, Hubble turned to a theoretical interpretation of the empirical relationship. In addition to a relativistic, expanding, homogeneous universe, other models were possible. Hubble was joined by Richard Tolman, a theoretical physicist at the California Institute of Technology, who had developed the mathematical foundations of relativistic cosmology. They formulated methods for interpreting their evidence, but given the many observational problems, any conclusion could only be tentative. Nonetheless, Hubble had brought together observers and theorists, and thus had made cosmology—for centuries consisting of speculation based on a minimum of observational evidence and a maximum of philosophical predilection—an observational science.

Despite contradictory observations that arose (and were only much later resolved) and despite his often-stated scientific allegiance to observations on which it was possible to obtain universal agreement rather than to human values, Hubble continued to champion the relativistic, expanding, homogeneous model of the universe. Ostensibly, Hubble had taken up the problem of discriminating between possible models of the universe on the basis of observations. But before recourse to observation, the number of logically consistent systems to be compared against observations could be reduced by the application of fundamental principles. For Hubble, there were two fundamental principles: the General Theory of Relativity and the Cosmological Principle. The former gave both an unstable universe, either expanding or contracting, and a universe whose space was curved in the vicinity of matter. The latter, acknowledged by Hubble to be "pure assumption," stated that, on a grand scale, the universe will appear the same from any position, homogeneous and isotropic, with neither center nor boundaries. Such considerations caused Hubble to refuse to accept the apparent falsification of a relativistic, expanding, homogeneous universe, and instead to pursue unrelentingly his scientific vision, barring neither himself nor his science from the great world of values.

For following generations of astronomers, Hubble set major questions and outlined procedures for answering them. Results from the 200-inch telescope on Palomar Mountain completed in 1948 have removed much of the question surrounding Hubble's choice of cosmological model. His work, though, should be appreciated more for the assumptions it overthrew, for the vistas it opened, and as one of the great accomplishments of the human intellect.

BIBLIOGRAPHY

Christianson, G.E. *Edwin Hubble: Mariner of the Nebulae.* New York: Farrar, Straus and Giroux, 1995.

Hetherington, N.S. "Edwin Hubble's Cosmology." *American Scientist* 78 (1990): 142–151.

———. *The Edwin Hubble Papers: Previously Unpublished Manuscripts on the Extragalactic Nature of Spiral Nebulae, Edited, Annotated, and with an Historical Introduction.* Tucson: Pachart, 1990.

———. *Hubble's Cosmology: A Guided Study of Selected Texts.* Tucson: Pachart, 1996.

Hubble, E.P. *The Realm of the Nebulae.* New Haven: Yale University Press, 1936.

Mayall, N.U. "Edwin Powell Hubble." *Biographical Memoirs of the National Academy of Sciences* 41 (1970): 175–214.

Osterbrock, D.E., R.S. Brashear, and J.A. Gwinn. "Self-Made Cosmologist: The Education of Edwin Hubble." In *Evolution of the Universe of Galaxies, Edwin Hubble Centennial Symposium,* edited by R.G. Kron. San Francisco: Astronomical Society of the Pacific, 1991, pp. 1–18.

Robertson, H.P. "Edwin Powell Hubble, 1889–1953." *Publications of the Astronomical Society of the Pacific* 66 (1954): 120–125.

Norriss S. Hetherington

Human Genome Project

The international scientific effort to map and sequence the entire human genome—that is, all the genetic material in the twenty-four human chromosomes—by 2005. Gene mapping originated with T.H. Morgan and his *Drosophila* group at Columbia University in the second decade of the twentieth century. Later, the genomes of model organisms such as mice and highly manipulable experimental organisms such as *e. coli* and yeast were partially or completely mapped. But mapping the large and complex human genome did not seem to be technologically feasible until around 1985. Nobel laureate Walter Gilbert, a professor of biology at Harvard, began promoting the need for a large-scale mapping and sequencing effort in the late summer and fall of 1986. At the same time, the Department of Energy (DOE), still wrestling with the difficulties of detecting radiation mutation in human populations, began to take an interest in the construction of a map of the human genome. The DOE Human Genome

Initiative was the first government program of human genome research, but it led to participation by other scientists in the United States and around the world. The United States Human Genome Project (HGP)—now funded through both DOE and the National Institutes of Health (NIH)—is only one part of a large international effort. Important human genomics work is underway in Europe, the United Kingdom, Japan, Australia, Canada, Latin America, Russia, and South Africa. The proliferation of mapping and sequencing efforts worldwide led to the creation of the Human Genome Organization (HUGO) in 1989 to serve, in the words of Norton Zinder, as a "U.N. for the human genome."

In its relatively brief existence, the HGP has gone through several transformations—an early emphasis on sequencing (establishing the order of the estimated 3 billion nucleotide base pairs in the human genome) was abandoned; technologies for mapping improved dramatically; and the first director of HGP, Nobelist James Watson, resigned after the NIH raised questions about his ties to the biotechnology industry. The project has been controversial from at least three perspectives. Participants have disagreed about strategies for mapping and sequencing; scientists not involved have criticized the crash program as an unnecessary diversion of funds from more worthy research; and other critics outside the scientific community have questioned its ethical and social impact, suggesting that a map of the human genome will be used in ways that threaten individual rights. For historians, HGP provides a useful case study of big science in biology, of international collaboration, of the role of the biotechnology industry in contemporary academic science, of the increasing importance of electronic records and computational biology in genetics, and of the intellectual processes by which bits of DNA become points on a map. Both the NIH and the DOE have sponsored independent research into the uses of genetic information, privacy questions, genetic discrimination, and the social organization of genomics research. The HGP is unique in this respect. It is the first scientific project to also support critical social inquiry into the implications of new knowledge. The project has been the focus of several enthusiastic popular accounts and one critical insider's history. It is voluminously documented, extremely important, and controversial. It promises to be a rich subject of scholarly research for many years to come.

BIBLIOGRAPHY

Bishop, Jerry E., and Michael Waldholz. *Genome: The Story of the Most Astonishing Scientific Adventure of Our Time—The Attempt to Map All the Genes in the Human Body.* New York: Simon & Schuster, 1990.

Cook-Deegan, Robert Mullan. *The Gene Wars: Science, Politics, and the Human Genome.* New York: W.W. Norton, 1994.

Hall, Stephen S. *Invisible Frontiers: The Race to Synthesize a Human Gene.* New York: Atlantic Monthly Press, 1987.

Judson, Horace Freeland. *The Eighth Day of Creation: Makers of the Revolution in Biology.* New York: Simon & Schuster, 1979.

McKusick, V.A., and F.H. Ruddle. "Toward a Complete Map of the Human Genome." *Genomics* 1 (1987): 103–106.

National Center for Human Genome Research, National Institutes of Health. *Report of the Working Group on Ethical, Legal and Social Issues Related to Mapping and Sequencing the Human Genome.* Bethesda, MD: National Center for Human Genome Research, National Institutes of Health, 1989.

Nelkin, Dorothy, and Laurence Tancredi. *Dangerous Diagnostics: The Social Power of Biological Information.* New York: Basic Books, 1989.

Rechsteiner, Martin. "The Folly of the Human Genome Project." *New Scientist* 127 (15 September 1990): 20.

Roberts, Leslie. "Genome Backlash Going Full Force." *Science* 248 (1990): 804.

United States Congress, Office of Technology Assessment. *Mapping Our Genes—Genome Projects: How Big, How Fast?* Washington, DC: Government Printing Office, 1988.

Wills, Christopher. *Exons, Introns, and Talking Genes.* New York: Basic Books, 1991.

M. Susan Lindee

Huntington, Ellsworth (1876–1947)

Geographer, born in Galesburg, Illinois. Huntington's family moved to Gorham, Maine, the following year and Ellsworth spent the rest of his life as a resident of New England.

He graduated from Beloit College, Wisconsin (B.A.), in 1897, and then spent time as a missionary in Harput, Turkey. There he began informal studies of a geographic nature. In 1901, he entered Harvard University and began a lifetime association with William Morris Davis. He received an M.A. degree in 1902. In 1907, he accepted a post with Yale University (geology and geography department) and remained associated with Yale for the remainder of his life.

H

There was a design to Huntington's scholarship, although it remained obscure to many readers. He wished to study civilization—which for him was essentially the history of human progress. Refusing to countenance the march of civilization as chance, he posited climate, the quality of people, and culture as a triadic causation of human progress. He held that climatic circumstance brought about migration, hastened the processes of selection, and facilitated or denied the advance of culture.

The early years of his academic life were given essentially to the study of climate and more particularly to the quest for evidence (and later causation) of climatic change in postglacial time. Studies of climatic change and the relative merits of earth's climates appear and reappear throughout his lifetime, but are announced particularly in *The Pulse of Asia* (1907), *Palestine and Its Transformation* (1911), *Civilization and Climate* (1915), *World Power and Evolution* (1919), the very much revised *Civilization and Climate* (1924), and the mature summation "Climatic Pulsations" (*Geografiska Annaler* [1935], pp. 571–607). His interest in climate never did pass, but to it were addded the study of eugenics and culture.

Emerging in the teens of the century was Huntington's concern with the quality of people. He was concerned that democracy itself was threatened by the rapid multiplication of what he perceived to be the less able members of the species. He opted for restrictive American immigration; believed that measures should be taken to change the relative birth rates of the old Nordic population as compared with the new Mediterranean and Alpine population; associated with Roland Dixon, Lothrop Stoddard, and Madison Grant; became a significant force in the American Eugenics Society for a quarter of a century (president 1934–1938); and announced his interest in the quality of people in works including *The Character of Races* (1924), *The Builders of America* (with Leon Whitney, 1927), *Tomorrow's Children: The Goal of Eugenics* (1935), *After Three Centuries* (1935), and *Season of Birth: Its Relation to Human Abilities* (1938).

Huntington regarded culture as the field of recorded history. He enjoyed reading history and histories, but deplored the historian's omission of a due consideration to the role of environment and biological inheritance. He was especially thoughtful of the role of ideas and inventions in human progress; he gave attention to the role of the horseshoe in ninth-century Turkey, the glass window in fifteenth-century England, and the development of the boat throughout recorded history. Huntington accepted the role of culture as a moving force, expressing his ideas in such works as "Climate and the Evolution of Civilization," a chapter in the book *The Evolution of the Earth and Its Inhabitants*, edited by Richard S. Lull (1918), and "The March of Civilization," a chapter in *Europe* by S. Van Valkenburg and E. Huntington (1935).

Huntington attempted to summarize his life's work in *Mainsprings of Civilization* (1945) and the incomplete *The Pace of History*.

BIBLIOGRAPHY

Martin, Geoffrey J. *Ellsworth Huntington: His Life and Thought.* Hamden, CT: Archon Books, 1973.
Valkenburg, S. Van. "Ellsworth Huntington." *Geographical Review,* 38 (1948): 153–155.
Visher, S.S. "Ellsworth Huntington." *Annals of the Association of American Geographers,* 38 (1948): 38–50.

Geoffrey J. Martin

Hydrology

A multidisciplinary earth science that deals with the occurrence, circulation, distribution, and, to a lesser extent, chemical and physical properties of surface and subsurface water. Central to this science is the hydrologic cycle, a term that describes the circulation of water from the sea, to the atmosphere, to land, and eventually back to the sea through surface and subterranean routes.

Although hydrology can be traced back to the civilizations of the ancient world, both oriental and occidental, the modern science dates from the seventeenth century. Its principal progenitors were the Frenchmen Pierre Perrault and Edme Mariotte and the English astronomer Edmund Halley. These pioneers were followed in the eighteenth century by Bernard Forest de Belidor and, in particular, Antoine De Chézy, who devised a formula to measure the relationship between slope and velocity of a river that is still used today.

More than most sciences, hydrology developed in response to practical needs, and nowhere was this more so than in the United States. DeWitt Clinton stimulated public interest in hydrology when studying problems of water loss (1817–1820) along the Erie Canal. The United States Coast Survey, established in 1807, and the United States Exploring Expedition (Wilkes Expedition) of 1838–1842 contributed to the related science of hydrography. American army engineers and topographical officers prepared some of the earliest hydrologic studies of American rivers. Certainly, the most significant of these studies was the 500-plus-page report on the Mississippi River completed in 1861. The coauthors, topographical officers Captain Andrew A. Humphreys and Lieutenant Henry L. Abbot, studied and *tested* almost all previous theories dealing with channel resistance and river flow and developed their own formula for computing discharge. Although flawed in places, it was an impressive study that garnered praise around the world.

Meanwhile, several New England engineers performed experiments to measure discharge, motivated partly by the necessity of finding ways to allocate water to power the growing industries along the Merrimack River. These mid-nineteenth-century engineers included Charles S. Storrow, Uriah Boyden, and James B. Francis. The last two are better known for their contributions to early turbine technology. Finally, in 1857, Lorin Blodget published his *Climatology of the United States,* which presented a remarkable series of rainfall maps covering the United States.

The federal government's significant role in hydrological research continued after the Civil War. The United States Geological Survey (USGS), established in 1879, collected hydrographic information, concentrating initially on the arid West. Beginning in Embudo, New Mexico, in 1888, the survey established a series of stream-gauging stations that eventually covered the entire country. Under the leadership of Grove Karl Gilbert, it made important contributions to understanding sediment transport. Oscar E. Meinzer, who headed the USGS ground water group from 1912 to 1946, and Charles S. Slichter essentially established the field of groundwater studies. Eminent hydrologists Luna B. Leopold and Walter B. Langbein successfully impressed upon the USGS the importance of basic hydrological research and of applying the findings to problems faced in the construction of large-scale water projects. Both men made important contributions to flood hydrology, river morphology, and sedimentation problems.

Other federal agencies complemented the efforts of the USGS. The Weather Service, created in 1891, maintained precipitation records for the country. The Bureau of Reclamation, established as the United States Reclamation Service in 1902, developed numerous hydraulic laboratories, generally in response to specific project concerns. Its principal hydraulic laboratory eventually found a home at the Denver Federal Center in 1946. With the establishment of the Waterways Experiment Station in Vicksburg, Mississippi, in 1929, the army's Corps of Engineers began a series of three-dimensional model studies that advanced knowledge of river behavior. This was somewhat ironic since the corps had originally questioned the necessity for such a facility. In 1930, Congress authorized the development of a National Hydraulic Laboratory within the National Bureau of Standards, but professional rifts and a failure of leadership kept the laboratory from prospering. The Tennessee Valley Authority constructed a hydraulics laboratory in the 1930s. The Department of Agriculture analyzed soil moisture at its agricultural experiment stations. Eugene W. Hilgard and Lyman J. Briggs were leaders in this field.

The federal lead in the development of hydrology continued until the mid-1960s. By that time, state water offices began taking over some work formerly done by federal agencies, most large federal water projects had been completed, the environmental movement dampened enthusiasm for river basin development, and universities became centers of expertise in large-scale hydrology, often with the aid of federal funds. However, even before this shift occurred, academicians and private consultants had made important contributions. Daniel Mead wrote the first English language textbook on hydrology in 1904. By around 1900, a number of universities had established small hydraulic laboratories. These included Worcester Polytechnic Institute, the Massachusetts Institute of Technology, the University of Iowa, and Cornell University. However, unlike the federal laboratories that were eventually established, these laboratories were not large enough to address major river and harbor problems.

Of the private consultants, Robert E. Horton and Hans Albert Einstein were perhaps the most influential. Horton is sometimes called the father of American hydrology because of the breadth of his contributions. He promoted mathematical and quantitative approaches to the study of the hydrological cycle and developed a theory that relates the infiltration capacity of soils to the generation of surface runoff. Einstein (the son of Albert) made significant contributions to the study of sediment transport and river mechanics, applying the strict mathematical analysis that had often been lacking in earlier studies. The work of university professors Boris A. Bakhmeteff, Lorenz G. Straub, and

H

Theodore von Kármán in fluid mechanics also influenced hydrologic study.

Beginning in the 1950s, hydrologists used computers to measure complicated hydrologic systems and to test and formulate hydrologic theories. The computer stimulated the growth of what is called operational or synthetic hydrology, in which computers employ massive amounts of data to simulate stream flows for large river systems over very long periods of time.

The increasing emphasis on rational analysis rather than empiricism to solve hydrologic problems paralleled a growing effort on the part of hydrologists to gain recognition of their field as an independent geoscience. An important step occurred in 1922, when the International Association of Hydrological Sciences was formed as a branch of the International Union of Geodesy and Geophysics. Seven years later—and after several years of lobbying by hydrologists—the American Geophysical Union created a section on hydrology. Meinzer and Horton became chairman and vice chairman, respectively.

Despite its increasing sophistication, hydrology has not gained a totally separate identity as an earth science. There are several reasons for this. Going back to the beginning of the twentieth century, formal university education in hydrology was primarily descriptive, focused exclusively on *engineering* hydrology, and was generally taught within civil engineering departments. Partly in response to the increase of water projects throughout the country, textbooks and courses emphasized problem solving, often focusing on specific projects; the emphasis on rational analysis came later. Also, early hydrologists concentrated on water quantity and almost completely ignored increasingly important water quality problems. Finally, hydrologists'

increasing dependence on computers may actually have discouraged critical analysis and creativity and led to underestimating the importance of field and laboratory experience. While it seems clear that hydrologists in the future will continue to apply their knowledge to specific problems, it also is likely that hydrology will gain more recognition as a separate science as hydrologists develop macroscale theories to explain both continental and global water processes.

BIBLIOGRAPHY

Biswas, Asit K. *History of Hydrology.* Amsterdam and London: North-Holland Publishing, 1970.

Blodget, Lorin. *Climatology of the United States, and of the Temperate Latitudes of the North American Continent, Embracing a Full Comparison of These with the Climatology of the Temperate Latitudes of Europe and Asia, and Especially in Regard to Agriculture, Sanitary Investigations, and Engineering.* Philadelphia: J.B. Lippincott, 1857.

Humphreys, A.A., and H.L. Abbot. *Report upon the Physics and Hydraulics of the Mississippi River; upon the Protection of the Alluvial Region against Overflow; and upon the Directing of the Topographical and Hydrographical Survey of the Delta of the Mississippi River, with Such Investigations as Might Lead to Determine the Most Practicable Plan for Securing It from Inundation, and the Best Mode of Deepening the Channels at the Mouths of the River.* Professional Papers of the Corps of Topographical Engineers, U.S. Army, No. 4. Philadelphia: J.B. Lippincott, 1861.

Meinzer, Oscar E., ed. *Hydrology.* New York: Dover, 1942.

National Research Council, Water Science and Technology Board. *Opportunities in the Hydrologic Sciences.* Washington, DC: National Academy Press, 1991.

Rouse, Hunter. *Hydraulics in the United States, 1776–1976.* Iowa City: The University of Iowa Institute of Hydraulic Research, 1976.

Martin Reuss

I

Illinois, University of

Founded as a state land-grant institution, Illinois Industrial University opened in March 1868. Under the guidance of its first regent, John M. Gregory, the university placed a major emphasis on scientific instruction and research. Thomas J. Burrill joined the faculty in 1868 and became a leading researcher in plant pathology. In 1879, the university built a new chemistry laboratory. In 1885, Stephen A. Forbes brought to Urbana the State Natural History Survey and his interests in entomology and ecology. In 1887, the trustees established the Agricultural Experiment Station. By 1896, the College of Agriculture was engaged in an extensive research program. Beginning in 1893, the university experienced a period of rapid growth, especially in the sciences. In an eight-year period, an engineering hall, natural history building, library and an agricultural building were built. In the generation before World War I, presidents Andrew S. Draper and Edmund J. James recruited chemist William A. Noyes, parasitologist Henry B. Ward, physicist Jacob Kunz, astronomer Joel Stebbins, mathematician George A. Miller, and ecologist Victor Shelford and built new laboratories for chemistry (1902) and physics (1909) research. In 1905, the trustees established the Engineering Experiment Station for the scientific investigation of engineering problems. After World War I, chemist Roger Adams, electrical engineer Joseph Tykociner, animal scientist Harold H. Mitchell, physicists F. Wheeler Loomis and Donald Kerst, and civil engineer Nathan Newmark began work in a period characterized by stronger relationships between the university and corporate research interests. During World War II, many university scientists moved to military projects in Los Alamos, Boston, and Chicago. After the war, the university established ties with federal agencies for the sponsorship of research and development contracts. Physicists Louis Ridenour, Frederick Seitz, and John Bardeen, geologists George White and Ralph Grim, anthropologists Julian Steward and Oscar Lewis, animal scientist Orville Bentley, electrical engineers William L. Everitt and Heinz von Foerster, entomologist Gottfried Fraenkel, plant scientist Jack Harlan, botanists Eugene Rabinowitch and Lindsay Black, and psychologists J. McVicker Hunt and Raymond Cattell contributed to the development of the modern research university.

With the growth of the university, a need for coordination of interdisciplinary research arose. In 1932, the president appointed a Graduate School Research Board. In 1951, the trustees established the Control Systems Laboratory for pure and applied research in engineering, electronics, communications, and aerospace studies. Renamed the Coordinated Science Laboratory in 1959, it promoted cooperative research. In 1985, the Beckman Institute for Advanced Science and Technology was created to advance interdisciplinary research in the biological and physical sciences.

Scientists' personal papers have long been regarded as a primary source for the history of science. They consist of correspondence, proposals, grant and contract records, photographs, laboratory notebooks, publications, reports, consulting files, and committee records. Official administrative records of departments, colleges, laboratories, and institutes provide the institutional context for personal information systems. Established in 1963, the university archives contains the papers of the thirty faculty mentioned above (424

I

cubic feet) and another 218 scientific researchers. The archives also holds official records of the university (8,073 cubic feet), copies of 2,296 series of university publications, and the archives of the Argonne Universities Association relating to nuclear physics (seventy cubic feet), the National Association of State Universities and Land Grant Colleges (fifty-six cubic feet), the Paleontological Society (twenty-eight cubic feet) and the American Society for Quality Control (eighty-seven cubic feet). Recent holdings reflect the university's strengths in chemistry, engineering, solid state physics, supercomputing, and biotechnology.

Science is a cooperative enterprise based on shared information. Illinois is a research university with a strong tradition of departmental autonomy. Each administrative unit provides research facilities and opportunities for collaboration with colleagues in other departments and institutions. Archival holdings document programs that support scientific research, such as indirect contract costs, institutional research board grants, and patent files. Corporate or governmental funding is an essential ingredient in academic research, but the effectiveness of the product is due to the freedom of the researcher to carry out the investigation. Simplistic schemes for regulatory control and preconceived history probes of information systems often fail to comprehend the dynamic spirit of academic independence.

BIBLIOGRAPHY

Brichford, Maynard, and William J. Maher. *Guide to the University of Illinois Archives.* Urbana: University of Illinois Press, 1986.

Kingery, R. Alan, Rudy D. Berg, and E.H. Schillinger. *Men and Ideas in Engineering: Twelve Histories.* Urbana: University of Illinois Press, 1967.

Moores, Richard G. *Fields of Rich Toil: The Development of the University of Illinois College of Agriculture.* Urbana: University of Illinois Press, 1970.

Solberg, Winton U. *The University of Illinois, 1867–1894: An Intellectual and Cultural History.* Urbana: University of Illinois Press, 1968.

Tarbell, D. Stanley, and Ann Tracy Tarbell. *Roger Adams: Scientist and Statesman.* Washington, DC: American Chemical Society, 1981.

Maynard Brichford

Index Medicus

A printed monthly index by author and subject to the literature of the biomedical sciences. *Index Medicus* was started in 1879 by John Shaw Billings, a physician and director of the army's Library of the Surgeon General's Office (now the National Library of Medicine), as a supplement to the published *Index-Catalogue* of the library. From 1879 to 1899, it was published by commercial publishers; after a short hiatus it resumed publication in 1903 under the auspices of the Carnegie Institution of Washington. In 1927, *Index Medicus* merged with a publication of the American Medical Association and became the *Quarterly Cumulative Index Medicus.* In 1960, editorial responsibility reverted to the National Library of Medicine, which has continued to publish the index under the title *Index Medicus.* Experiments to automate the production of *Index Medicus* began in the 1950s and culminated in the development of MEDLINE, an expanded on-line version of the printed index.

The scope of *Index Medicus* has almost always been defined as the biomedical sciences in the broadest sense. Hence, it can serve as a valuable guide to the contemporary literature of the last century for historians of biology, biochemistry, and related fields.

BIBLIOGRAPHY

Blake, John B., ed. *Centenary of Index Medicus.* Bethesda, MD: National Library of Medicine, 1980.

Miles, Wyndham D. *A History of the National Library of Medicine.* Bethesda, MD: National Library of Medicine, 1982.

Moore, M.H. "Quarterly Cumulative Index Medicus." In *A History of the American Medical Association, 1847–1947,* edited by Morris Fishbein. Philadelphia: Saunders, 1947, pp. 1165–1169.

Peter B. Hirtle

Institute for Advanced Study

A research institution in Princeton, New Jersey, devoted to the pursuit of advanced scholarship in the fields of natural science, mathematics, history, and the social sciences. Since its founding in 1930, the institute has permitted a select group of scholars to conduct research in a secluded environment, free from teaching or administrative obligations. The faculty consists of approximately twenty professors, appointed for life. Each year, approximately 160 postdoctoral scholars, called members, come to the institute as fellows. Although the institute has always preserved its independence from Princeton University, the intellectual atmosphere of each institution has been enriched by regular contact between its faculties.

The institute was created by Abraham Flexner, who had been influential in the foundation-sponsored reform of American medical and higher education during the early twentieth century, and businessman and philanthropist Louis Bamberger who, with his sister, Caroline Bamberger Frank Fuld, provided the initial endowment. Taking as his models the German university and its most direct American representation, the Johns Hopkins University, Flexner hoped that the development of the institute would define scholarship as the principal purpose of the American university. During his directorship (1930–1939) and that of his successor, Frank Aydelotte (1939–1947), the institute consisted of Schools of Mathematics, Humanistic Studies, and Economics and Politics; its scholars shared offices at Princeton University until the institute's first building, Fuld Hall, was completed on its own campus in 1939.

Since 1930, the institute has established its strongest intellectual reputation in the sciences. In the 1930s and 1940s, scholars in the School of Mathematics helped to develop such new fields as mathematical logic, topology, and mathematical statistics, and made important contributions in differential geometry and theoretical physics. The presence of physicist Albert Einstein and mathematicians John von Neumann, Hermann Weyl, Oswald Veblen, and Marston Morse on the faculty drew scholars from all over the world. From 1933 until 1945, with Nazism dominant in Europe, the commitment of the institute's administration and faculty—several of whom were themselves émigrés from Hitler—to offer at least temporary refuge to European scientists, as well as to young American scientists facing unemployment during the Great Depression, helped to salvage a scientific generation.

In 1947, the appointment of theoretical physicist J. Robert Oppenheimer as director confirmed the institutional emphasis on scientific research. During his nineteen-year tenure, Oppenheimer combined economics and the humanities into the School of Historical Studies (1948) and added the School of Natural Sciences (1966). Under Oppenheimer, work in theoretical physics expanded with the appointment of Freeman Dyson, Abraham Pais, C.N. Yang, and Tullio Regge as professors and the regular association of physicists such as Niels Bohr, P.A.M. Dirac, Res Jost, George Placzek, Wolfgang Pauli, and L.C. Van Hove. John von Neumann's interest in the electronic computer, first realized with the formation of the Electronic Computer Project at the institute in 1946, came to fruition in 1952 with the completion of one of the first electronic stored-program computers. The institute's Meteorology Project successfully exploited the computer to carry out critical studies in the problem of weather prediction.

In the early 1970s, Oppenheimer's successor, economist Carl Kaysen (1966–1976), developed the School of Social Science and expanded the institute's work in astrophysics, particle physics, and plasma physics with the appointments of Marshall Rosenbluth, Stephen Adler, Roger Dashen, and John Bahcall to the School of Natural Sciences. Recent directors have included historian of science Harry Woolf (1976–1987), physicist Marvin L. Goldberger (1987–1991), and mathematician Phillip A. Griffiths (1991–).

The Institute for Advanced Study has consistently brought together scientists who rank among the best in the world. Most significant, however, has been its institutionalization of the concept—now imitated in programs, universities, and research institutes throughout the world—that scholars in a variety of disciplines require regular intervals of seclusion to ensure their continued productivity.

BIBLIOGRAPHY

A Community of Scholars: The Institute for Advanced Study, Faculty and Members, 1930–1980. Princeton: The Institute for Advanced Study, 1980.

Aspray, William. *John von Neumann and the Origins of Modern Computing.* Cambridge, MA: MIT Press, 1990.

Flexner, Abraham. *Universities: American, English, German.* New York: Oxford University Press, 1930.

———. *I Remember: The Autobiography of Abraham Flexner.* New York: Simon & Schuster, 1940.

The Institute for Advanced Study: Publications of Members, 1930–1954. Princeton: The Institute for Advanced Study, 1955.

"The Institute for Advanced Study: Some Introductory Information." Princeton: The Institute for Advanced Study, 1976–1991.

Kaysen, Carl. "Report of the Director, 1966–1976." Princeton: The Institute for Advanced Study, 1976.

Oppenheimer, J. Robert. "Report of the Director, 1948–1953." Princeton: The Institute for Advanced Study, 1954.

Porter, Laura Smith. "From Intellectual Sanctuary to Social Responsibility: The Founding of the Institute for Advanced Study, 1930–1933." Ph.D. diss., Princeton University, 1988.

Laura Smith Porter

I

Institute of Electrical and Electronic Engineers

The history of organized electrical engineering closely replicates the intellectual development of a field that came into being with the move from a shop-based activity to scientific engineering at the end of the nineteenth century. From electric-power engineering came the founding organization in 1884, the American Institute of Electrical Engineering. The advent of radio, first as wireless telegraphy on the basis of innovations by Guglielmo Marconi and others at the turn of the century, then as wireless telephony with Reginald Fessenden's alternator and Lee deForest's vacuum tube, led to the founding of the Institute of Radio Engineers in 1912. During the next half-century, major changes in physics and chemistry and the development of general systems theory produced an electronics revolution. Beginning in the 1930s, vacuum-tube applications expanded far beyond radio broadcasting, a trend that increased after World War II as new forms of electronic valves, specifically transistors and the integrated circuit, emerged from physics and engineering laboratories.

This "great growth," as Stanford University electronics engineer Frederick E. Terman described it, accompanied initiatives by professors to transform graduate training in an attempt to move beyond the reliance on physics for advances in the field. The growth in electronics transformed the electrical engineering landscape so that, in 1962, the two older societies merged to form the Institute of Electrical and Electronic Engineers. Within this dynamic organizational framework, the electrical engineering societies have constructed a professional base for the field's practitioners and the corporate and governmental interests gathered around it. Technical groups were early devised to contain the unrelenting stream of specialized areas that issued from the scientific and technical substrata of the field which began with areas like electroplating and accrued, by the end of the twentieth century, specialized areas associated with electronic computers and information theory. Conferences and publications have constituted the fundamental activities of the institute. Concern for the ethics of the engineers and their employers' desire to control the fruits of engineering innovation led to the first code of professional conduct in 1912.

Yet, a history of engineering societies does not constitute a history of engineers. For the great mass of working engineers, their issues have been the right to possess the patented results of their training and creativity, job security, and the existence of technical as well as managerial ladders for advancement within the large organizations that generally employ them. Engineering societies like the institute have served rather the needs of employers in the areas of technical standards and the dissemination of technical information.

BIBLIOGRAPHY

Kline, Ronald. *Steinmetz: Engineer and Socialist.* Baltimore: Johns Hopkins University Press, 1992.

Leslie, Stuart W. *The Cold War and American Science: The Military-Industrial-Academic Complex at MIT and Stanford.* New York: Columbia University Press, 1993.

McMahon, A. Michal. *The Making of a Profession: A Century of Electrical Engineering in America.* New York: IEEE Press, 1984.

Noble, David. *America by Design: Science, Technology, and the Rise of Corporate Capitalism.* New York: Knopf, 1977.

A. Michal McMahon

International Business Machines Corporation

This firm has been a major supplier of information technology throughout the twentieth century. It was formed in 1911 to sell punched-card technology, clocks, scales, and other mechanical products. By the end of World War II, it was the largest office appliance company in the United States and, by the end of the 1950s, the dominant supplier of digital computers. Its computer architectures were the industry standards between the 1950s and the 1980s. It was a major conduit of computer technology from laboratory to market and its operating systems the most widely used in the world of information processing.

While the International Business Machines Corporation (IBM) had long been interested in mechanization and, later, electrification of information-handling equipment, it was during World War II, while building electronic equipment for the United States government, that the company was exposed to advanced electronics. During World War II, IBM also sponsored research at Harvard University on the Mark I, a large calculator. By the end of the 1940s, IBM was actively pursuing development of digital electronic computers. The Selective Sequence Electronic Calculator (SSEC), announced in 1948, was the first commercially available stored computer. During the Korean War, under contract to the United States government, IBM built more-advanced machines (initially called the Defense Calculator) and in 1953, a commercial version, known as the IBM 701 became the first mass-produced computer within the company. From this experience emerged a generation of packaging and manufacturing techniques that made it possible for IBM to produce large numbers of profitable computers into the 1970s. In 1954, it shipped the IBM 650, and sold a massive number—over 1,800—making it the most popular digital computer of the decade.

Through each machine, technologies developed at universities and often under government contract, were applied. Memory systems, for example, evolved from tube technology through diodes to transistors by the end of the decade and then, in the 1960s, to the integrated circuit. Most development was done either at the Endicott or Poughkeepsie, New York, plants, each with its own laboratory. Most computer research was done at Poughkeepsie while Endicott, for decades home of IBM's punched-card manufacturing, had responsibility for peripheral equipment.

By the end of the 1950s and into the early 1960s, a stream of technological developments came from IBM. Programming languages (such as FORTRAN) became standards in the industry. Project Stretch, intended to create a raft of new hardware technologies for future systems in the late 1950s, led to important innovations in packaging techniques for second- and third-generation components, printing of circuit boards and cards, and better wiring methods. By-products included the IBM 7090 computers and the IBM 1401, which alone resulted in orders for some 20,000 systems. Like the 650, it was a low cost, reliable general processor.

In April 1964, IBM announced the S/360, initially a family of five processors, over 100 peripheral products, and new operating systems, making it the largest, most dramatic computer introduction up to that point. By the end of the decade, this product drove overall company sales upward by over 100 percent. The computer's architecture dominated the majority of the industry's computer products for the next two decades. Disk drives for direct access storage, while initially introduced by IBM in the mid-1950s, became standard issue with the S/360. Between 1953 and 1964, IBM had increased the speed of computers by 40 times and of memory by 6.5 times, while keeping costs the same as with older machines. In June 1970, IBM announced the S/370 family, which was an evolution out of the S/360, with more capacity and internal components all developed within IBM's laboratories. In the late 1960s, IBM's disk drives were also improved, increasing their data transfer rates by 250 percent over older devices.

All through the 1970s and 1980s, faster components, increased reliability, and more efficient manufacturing characterized designs of thousands of products. Miniaturization ultimately led both the industry and IBM to announce personal computers. IBM's first appeared in 1981 and, along with over 150 rivals, IBM introduced many personal computer products in the 1980s which ultimately had greater speeds and capacities than the S/360s.

IBM conducted most of its research in laboratories that, by the end of the 1960s, were located around the world. Most of its pure research, however, was housed at the Watson Research Center at Yorktown Heights, New York, home of several Nobel Prize winners. Their most recent contributions included development of the micron microscope and superconductors—both in the 1980s. IBM historically was also a leading developer of integrated circuits and, by the early 1970s, manufactured for internal use over 25 percent of the world's supply.

Historically, IBM's interest in science and technology focused on the faster, more efficient movement of information, first mechanically and then electronically. It funded much of this research through government contracts and often worked with university laboratories to develop key technologies—such as memory systems. By the 1960s, it had a growing family of its own research laboratories that continue to operate at the frontiers of information science both for pure and applied research. Its researchers are also active members of the scientific community, members of such leading organizations as the IEEE, and work in such varied fields as information science, mathematics, astronomy, physics, engineering, biology, psychology, education, chemistry, and space sciences.

BIBLIOGRAPHY

Bashe, Charles J., et al. *IBM's Early Computers: A Technical History.* Cambridge, MA: MIT Press, 1986.

Chposky, James, and Ted Leonsis. *Blue Magic.* New York: Facts on File, 1988.

Hazen, Robert M. *The Breakthrough: The Race for the Superconductor.* New York: Summit Books, 1988.

Killen, Michael. *IBM: The Making of the Common View.* Boston: Harcourt Brace Jovanovich, 1988.

Pugh, Emerson W. *Memories That Shaped an Industry.* Cambridge, MA: MIT Press, 1984.

———. *Building IBM: Shaping an Industry and Its Technology.* Cambridge, MA: MIT Press, 1995.

I

Pugh, Emerson W., et al. *IBM's 360 and Early 370 Systems.* Cambridge, MA: MIT Press, 1991.

James W. Cortada

SEE ALSO
Computer

International Geophysical Year

The International Geophysical Year (IGY) was a multinational effort to study geophysical phenomena from June 1957 to December 1958. Contributing scientists investigated solar-terrestrial relations, geomagnetics, meteorology, ionospheric physics, glaciology, oceanography, the upper atmosphere, geodesy, aurora and airglow, and cosmic rays. Leaders of the IGY looked to previous International Polar Years in 1882–1883 and 1932–1933 as models, where international cooperation made possible synoptic, coordinated geophysical measurements. Funding for American participation in the IGY came from the National Science Foundation, with logistical support provided by military agencies. The United States National Committee of the IGY was led by Joseph Kaplan of the University of California at Los Angeles. Other prominent American scientists involved in the IGY included Lloyd Berkner, Fred L. Whipple, Athelstan Spilhaus, and James Van Allen.

Until recent years, the IGY has been seen as an example of an international scientific organization that transcended the hostile political climate of the Cold War. In this view, the IGY provided a vehicle for international cooperation in research. Virtually all writers have emphasized the IGY's role in stimulating American and Soviet space efforts. Recent historical studies have focused on the political currents that influenced the participation and goals of American scientists who took part in the IGY. These include the role that overflight access to Soviet territory played in President Dwight D. Eisenhower's decision to develop the United States' satellite program and the perceived importance of maintaining access to Soviet scientific results for reasons of national security, in which the IGY served as a means of intelligence-gathering.

The IGY produced large quantities of data that informed and influenced geophysical work through the 1960s and strengthened existing university departments and institutes of geophysics, and helped initiate an international system of science-based organizations and treaties. Regrettably few historical studies of research generated during the IGY excepting solar physics are available, and few historical works have analyzed the IGY within an intellectual or institutional context.

BIBLIOGRAPHY
Bulkeley, Rip. *The Sputniks Crisis and Early U.S. Space Policy.* Bloomington: Indiana University Press, 1991.
Greenaway, Frank. *Science International: A History of the International Council of Unions.* New York: Cambridge University Press, 1996.
Hufbauer, Karl. *Exploring the Sun: Solar Science Since Galileo.* Baltimore: Johns Hopkins University Press, 1991.
MacDougall, Walter. . . . *The Heaven and the Earth: A Political History of the Space Age.* New York: Basic Books, 1985.
Pyne, Stephen J. *The Ice: A Journey to Antarctica.* New York: Ballantine Books, 1986.
Spencer-Jones, Harold. "Inception and Development of the International Geophysical Year." In *Annals of the International Geophysical Year.* Vol. 1, Pt. 3. London: Pergamon Press, 1959, pp. 383–412.
Sullivan, Walter. *Assault on the Unknown: The International Geophysical Year.* New York: McGraw-Hill, 1961.

Ronald E. Doel

SEE ALSO
Geophysics and Geodesy

Iowa Child Welfare Research Station

The first research institute in North America, and probably the world, devoted entirely to scientific research on the normal child. Founded by the Iowa General Assembly in 1917 and made a unit of the State University of Iowa, in Iowa City, the Iowa Child Welfare Research Station invented the field of child development, itself an adjunct of both developmental psychology and biology and of evolutionary theory. In the 1920s, its researchers plucked known information about the normal child from various fields—pediatrics, psychology, education, anatomy, and so forth—reconstituted it as child development, and added to it much new empirical work on the character and conduct of normal children. Such normative research became the field's mainstream dogmas at other centers, such as Stanford, Yale, Minnesota, and Berkeley.

In the 1930s and 1940s, under the leadership of directors George D. Stoddard (1928–1942) and Robert R.

Sears (1942–1949) the Iowa station's researchers did pathbreaking work in IQ measurement and in social psychology. The IQ work suggested that 40 percent of all preschool-age children (i.e., under six years) could and did dramatically change their IQ scores upon retesting by enough to change their mental classification. This work became highly controversial, and the Iowa scientists were discredited, even though their work foreshadowed the post-1960s work on IQ which justified Head Start programs. The work on social psychology, both on individual and group psychology, emphasized the importance of Freudian psychodynamics (individual) and of the mental constructs that members of a group held about the world around them. It marked the founding of modern individual and group social psychology, and was absolutely seminal. The German refugee Gestalt psychologist Kurt Lewin did his most important work at Iowa.

In the 1950s and 1960s, powerful figures in the university's psychology department controlled the Iowa station and changed its research agenda toward rigid behaviorist work, something the station earlier had powerfully criticized. In 1964, it was tellingly renamed the Institute of Child Behavior and Development and was closed in 1974, in reality because it had become a second-rate copy of a first-rate behaviorist psychology program. Its creativity and leadership in the field of child development had long since evaporated.

It was historically significant in several ways. Its history lays bare the institutional and intellectual processes by which any modern science is constructed in modern times. Its intellectual challenges to the dominant ideas of the innate IQ and automatic development presaged the reigning orthodoxy of the post-1950 individualistic era. Encoded within the science of child development were all significant scientific ideas (and cultural notions) about the meaning of group identity for the individual—that is, Can the leopard change its spots?

BIBLIOGRAPHY

Cravens, Hamilton. "Child-Saving in the Age of Professionalism, 1915–1930." In *American Childhood*, edited by Joseph M. Hawes and N. Ray Hinder. Westport, CT: Greenwood Press, 1985, pp. 415–488.

———. "The Wandering I.Q.: Mental Testing and American Culture." *Human Development* 28 (1985): 113–130.

———. "Recent Controversy on Human Development: A Historical View." *Human Development* 30 (1987): 325–335.

———. "A Scientific Project Locked in Time: The Terman Genetic Genius Study, 1920s–1950s." *The American Psychologist* 47 (1992): 183–190.

———. *Before Head Start. The Iowa Station and America's Children*. Chapel Hill: University of North Carolina Press, 1993.

———. "Child-Saving in Modern America, 1870s–1990s." In *Children at Risk in Modern America: History, Concepts, and Public Policy*, edited by Robert Wollons. Albany: State University of New York, 1993, pp. 3–31.

Sears, Robert R. *Your Ancients Revisited. A History of Child Development*. Chicago; University of Chicago Press, 1975.

Senn, Milton. *Insights on the Child Development Movement in the United States*. Chicago: University of Chicago Press, 1975.

Spiker, Charles. *The Institute of Child Behavior and Development: Fifty Years of Research, 1917–1967*. Iowa City: University of Iowa, 1967.

Hamilton Cravens

Iowa State University of Science and Technology

Chartered by the state in 1858 as the State Agricultural College and Model Farm, it was renamed the Iowa State College of Agriculture and Mechanic Arts in 1896 and received its present name, Iowa State University of Science and Technology, in 1959. The founding act of 1858 was not funded until 1862, when Iowa's State Agricultural College became the first qualifier in the United States under the Morrill Land-Grant Act. Students were first admitted in 1869–1870; registration the first year was ninety-three, seventy-seven men and sixteen women. Iowa Agicultural College was the first of the land-grant colleges to be coeducational from the beginning.

All students were at first required to work at least two hours per day in winter and three in summer. Women satisfied the requirement (and a curriculum in mechanic arts) by work in the college kitchen, dining room, and laundry. By 1884, the work system was replaced, for men, with laboratory work, field observations, and museum collections and, for women, with creation of a two-year program in domestic economy.

The primary curricula of the new college were agriculture and mechanic arts (engineering), with identical programs for the first one and one-half years. Women were permitted to enter either of the two courses and take any of the subjects they chose until that was replaced by the newly developed academic field of domestic economy, which became a four-year collegiate course in 1898.

I

Agriculture was the slowest to become academically structured. In 1879, agriculture and veterinary science were separated in departments, with the first state program leading to a degree in veterinary science. Farm mechanics grew into a supplemental engineering year with a bachelor of agricultural engineering degree and, by 1908, this had become a full four-year curriculum. In 1878, engineering was split into mechanical and civil engineering. A Department of Electrical Engineering was founded in 1891, of Mining Engineering in 1894, of Ceramic Engineering in 1906, and of Architectural Engineering in 1914. Chemical engineering, which was to become one of the major programs by 1925, was not recognized as separate until 1913, although industrial chemistry is listed as early as 1909.

Determination of a curriculum and method of teaching was initially hampered by lack of agreement as to what the college was for and for whom it existed. The conflict, which dominated attitudes toward most land-grant colleges as late as the 1900s, was between the advocates of systematic (businesslike) farmers, scientific (rationalized) farming, and agricultural science. Another early complaint was that professors of engineering and the sciences had a professional rather than a teaching outlook and that much of their instruction went beyond the students needs.

The turning point in internal and external relations of the college came in 1891, during a transition period resulting from the increased research endowment of the Hatch Act of 1887, and the influence of the Association of Agricultural Colleges and Experiment Stations. Iowa established its agricultural experiment station in 1888, and continuing the college's farmers' institutes of the 1870s, an agricultural extension service was begun with local short courses and, by 1900, agricultural demonstrations. The engineering experiment station was founded in 1904 to be of equivalent aid to the state's manufacturers, farms, and municipal activities and an engineering extension service followed in 1913, with its short courses and demonstrations.

In 1912, it was agreed that the principal lines of the college were to be agriculture, engineering, and veterinary science, supported by such literary subjects and fundamental sciences as were necessary. These peripheral subjects (for which only an occasional aberrant B.S. degree had been given) were grouped in a Division of Industrial Science which incorporated all the fundamental sciences, mathematics, economics, and those general subjects "not leading to undergraduate degrees" such as English, history, library, modern languages, music, psychology, and so on. Not until 1946 was a liberal arts degree again awarded, and not until 1959, with the organization of a Division of Sciences and Humanities, was the awarding of such degrees regularized. Forestry had achieved professional status in 1904 and bacteriology had been added to the general sciences in 1908. Establishment of the graduate college awaited educational reorganization and expansion following World War I, but by 1928 Iowa State College had the largest graduate enrollment of any of the separate land-grant colleges.

With the college's traditional emphasis on service to the state, research tended to focus on practical concerns. The college contributed to each of the major discoveries in agriculture cited by *Wallace's Farmer* in 1929. The work of researchers like Charles E. Bessey, L.H. Pammel, P.G. Holden, G.W. Carver, Jay Lush, and Wise Burroughs attest to the continuing importance of agricultural investigations at Iowa State. Nor has engineering and basic sciences research been neglected. Anson Marston and structural analysis, G.W. Snedecor and population genetics, John Vincent Atanasoff and digital computers, F.H. Spedding, rare-earth uranium chemistry—these are but a few of the specific names and topics involved in researches at Iowa State. More generally, engineer research focused on highways and railroads; sanitary, construction, and structural engineering; soils and other engineering materials. Similarly, research in chemical engineering was directed to research of value to the state: water softening, coals, agricultural by-product use.

The university is now a full-service undergraduate and selective graduate educational institution, with emphasis on agriculture and engineering. Its research pillars continue to be the extension services for agriculture, business, and industry, and the Institute for Physical Research and Technology, but there are also organizations in cooperation with the United States government: the Ames Laboratory of the Department of Energy and the Department of Agriculture soil, plant and animal health, and agricultural products laboratories.

BIBLIOGRAPHY

Arnold, Lionel K. *History of the Department of Chemical Engineering at Iowa State University.* Ames: Department of Chemical Engineering, 1970.

Fuller, Almon H. *A History of Civil Engineering at Iowa State College.* Ames: Alumni Achievement Fund, Iowa State College, 1959.

Marcus, Alan I. *Agricultural Science and the Quest for Legitimacy: Farmers, Agricultural Colleges, and Experiment Stations, 1870–1890.* Ames: Iowa State University Press, 1985.

Ross, Earle D. *A History of the Iowa State College of Agriculture and Mechanic Arts.* Ames: Iowa State College Press, 1942.

Robert E. Schofield

Iron and Steel Industry

An early consumer and later producer of applied scientific knowledge. With the rise of chemical metallurgy in the mid-nineteenth century, the industry became an important source of employment, especially for chemists. Philadelphia was the center of these activities. A pioneering analytical laboratory was organized there in 1836 by the German-trained James Curtis Booth; his notable students included Joseph Wharton, the business-school philanthropist, and Robert W. Hunt. In 1860, Hunt established at Cambria Iron in Johnstown, Pennsylvania, the first analytical laboratory at an iron and steel firm. Also in Philadelphia was the Ironmasters' Laboratory of J. Blodgett Britton, organized in 1866 by the American Iron and Steel Association to "encourage the development of workable bodies of iron ore and to inform producers of the quantity and quality of the metal they would yield" (Bartlett, p. 27). Subsequently, chemistry departments as far away as Columbus, Ohio, flourished by providing graduates for Pennsylvania iron and steel firms. Chemistry helped standardize raw material inputs and regularize production processes, two especially critical tasks with the Bessemer steel process which grew rapidly from the 1870s.

With the shift from Bessemer to open-hearth steel around 1900, the industry's unmet needs for knowledge spurred the development of structure-oriented metallurgy (metallography). Developed first by the English amateur scientist Henry C. Sorby, metallography came to the United States after chemical metallurgists proved incapable of addressing a series of pressing problems in the manufacture and treatment of steel for heavy rails and high-speed cutting tools. To address these problems, metallographers, including Albert Sauveur and Henry M. Howe, theorized that a metal's properties depended not solely on its chemical composition but also on its temperature history and heat treatment. The metal's resulting microstructure was visualized with a microscope. At Harvard, Sauveur showed experimentally that lowering the final rolling temperatures for heavy steel rails from the standard 1,000°C to *below* 700°C yielded a stronger microstructure. Similar investigations were done by the Carnegie, Maryland, and Illinois steel companies, and by the New York Central and the Philadelphia & Reading Railroads. At the Massachusetts Institute of Technology, and later at Columbia University, Howe made internationally recognized contributions to metallography and trained many of the next generation of metallurgists.

In the new century, the industrial research model never became the industry's chief mode of organizing knowledge; engineering laboratories were more important for product development, and universities for fundamental research. In 1928, United States Steel Corporation founded its central research laboratory. In charge of physical metallurgy was Edgar Bain, who suggested practical heat treatment processes and quantitatively investigated hardenability. His studies established the "S-curve" correlating time, temperature, and transformation during the hardening process. His colleague E.S. Davenport extended this analysis to alloy steels, used extensively in the automobile, electrical, and chemical industries. From the 1930s, professionally oriented metallurgists increasingly worked on such general scientific problems as the electron theory of metals and dislocation theory.

Much work remains to be done on the industry's subsequent decline—for that matter on its ascent as well—to evaluate whether the lack of industrial research had any effect on the industry's performance. The record is difficult to evaluate. The chief steelmaking process used after World War II (basic oxygen furnace) was an Austrian invention, spurred by cost-cautious American executives; yet, all of the fundamental steelmaking processes used with fabulous success in the American industry's rapid expansion after the Civil War were European inventions, too. Hampering this investigation is a dearth of satisfactory studies of the pioneering analytical laboratories, the later university consultants to industry, and the twentieth-century research and engineering laboratories in the steel industry.

BIBLIOGRAPHY

Bartlett, Howard R. "The Development of Industrial Research in the United States." In *Research—A Natural*

I

Resource: Part II: *Industrial Research: Report of the National Research Council to the National Resources Planning Board.* Washington, DC: National Research Council, 1941.

Mehl, Robert F. *A Brief History of the Science of Metals.* New York: American Institute of Mining and Metallurgical Engineers, 1948.

Misa, Thomas J. *A Nation of Steel: The Making of Modern America, 1865–1925.* Baltimore: Johns Hopkins University Press, 1995.

Thomas J. Misa

J

Jackson, Charles Thomas (1805–1880)

Chemist, geologist, and physician. Born in Plymouth, Massachusetts, Jackson obtained an M.D. from Harvard in 1829. In 1829–1832, Jackson pursued medical, geological, and mineralogical studies in Paris and Vienna. A practicing physician until the mid-1860s, he devoted much of his time to nonmedical endeavors, establishing an analytical chemical laboratory at Boston in 1836. He served as geological surveyor of Maine and Massachusetts and state geologist of Maine (1837–1839), as head of the Rhode Island survey (1839–1840), as head of the New Hampshire survey (1839–1844), and as head of Lake Superior Land District Survey for the General Land Office (1847–1849). He claimed to have invented guncotton, derived the basic principles of the electric telegraph, and discovered the anesthetic effects of ether, in each case after another individual had introduced the product publicly. His obsession with establishing his various priority claims contributed to his forced resignation from the Lake Superior Survey and clouded the rest of his life. In 1873, he was committed to an asylum, where he died several years later.

Jackson's chemical laboratory prospered as both a commercial and educational venture. Benjamin Silliman Jr. and Josiah Dwight Whitney were among the students who spent time under his tutelage. Jackson's laboratory conducted the mineralogical and soil analyses required in his survey undertakings, and his laboratory students served as survey assistants.

Jackson and Francis Alger undertook recreational geological investigations in Nova Scotia in 1827 and 1829. In these explorations, as in his later professional survey activities, Jackson focused on mineralogy and economic geology. Much of his published work comprised the results of chemical analyses of soils, mineralogical samples, and other geological products of economic value. Jackson devoted much attention to observational and analytical detail but avoided synthetic theorization. After 1850, he conducted numerous investigations and analyses for private mining concerns and individuals.

Although he made no single significant contribution to nineteenth-century chemistry or geology, Jackson's contemporaries saw him as both a valuable and a problematic participant in the American scientific community. His active involvement in the American Academy of Arts and Sciences, the Boston Society of Natural History, the Association of American Geologists and Naturalists, and the American Association for the Advancement of Science created an extensive published record of his opinions and his interactions with colleagues. Archival records relating to his life and work are minimal and scattered, and no extended biographical treatment exists.

BIBLIOGRAPHY

Aldrich, Michele L. "Charles Thomas Jackson's Geological Surveys in New England, 1836–1844." *Northeastern Geology* 1 (January 1981): 5–10.

Full Exposure of the Conduct of Dr. Charles T. Jackson, Leading to His Discharge from the Government Service, and Justice to Messrs. Foster and Whitney, U. S. Geologists. [Washington, DC: United States Department of the Interior, 1850.]

Gifford, George Edmund, Jr. "Jackson, Charles Thomas." *Dictionary of Scientific Biography.* Edited by Charles C. Gillispie. New York: Scribners, 1973, 7:44–46.

Woodworth, J.B. "Charles Thomas Jackson." *American Geologist* 20 (1897): 69–110.

Julie R. Newell

James, William (1842–1910)

Psychologist, religious thinker, and philosopher. James was the first of five children in a wealthy family of great intellectual vitality. His brother, Henry, became the great novelist; his sister, Alice, was an astute social commentator; his father, the elder Henry James, was an iconoclastic writer for religious and political reform.

Henry James raised his children with a Swedenborgian faith in the spiritual correspondences lurking within the natural world and with a bewildering array of schools, teachers, and international travel in a constant search for ideal instruction. For William, the father's spiritual ambitions took the form of strong incentives to study science, which the father interpreted as a path of inquiry for understanding nature's hidden meanings.

William at first resisted his father's prods, taking up the study of painting at William Morris Hunt's Newport studio. But in the fall of 1861, William enrolled at Harvard University's Lawrence Scientific School. Louis Agassiz, whose teaching of zoology and geology was infused with a transcendental idealism, gave the father every reason to believe that William's scientific training would have spiritual guidance, but the rest of his scientific education led him far from the orbit of his father's thoughts.

William James began the study of chemistry less than two years after Darwin's publication of *The Origin of Species* (1859), and the debates of Harvard scientists over the religious and scientific merits of natural selection shaped James's ambivalence about the intellectual authority of science. His chemistry teacher was Charles Eliot, who as president of the university from 1869 to 1909, would implement rigorous professional training in the graduate school based on the authority of science. James soon switched to the study of anatomy and physiology with Jeffries Wyman, who took an experimental posture in cautious support of Darwinism. James kept working with Wyman when he took on the study of medicine with Oliver Wendell Holmes Sr., who had strong literary connections to the elder James's circle, but who accepted Darwinism with an ironic detachment. Before receiving his M.D. in 1869, James spent a year with Agassiz on a natural history expedition to Brazil designed to find evidence to disprove Darwinism, but the trip had the opposite effect on James's scientific thinking.

After his formal education, James took a long time to choose his career. While still in his twenties, James's vocational indecision was complicated by confusion over his own philosophical orientation. While he spiralled into a period of depression and invalidism, James kept reading and discussing the implications of the new sciences such as Darwinism with friends in the Metaphysical Club, who included Chauncey Wright, Charles Sanders Peirce, and Oliver Wendell Holmes Jr., from whom he learned about the probabilistic bases of Darwinian science and about hypothesis formation in theories and beliefs generally. Still with shades of his father's vicarious hopes, James was particularly irked by the deterministic and antireligious implications of naturalistic science. He finally emerged from his personal crisis in 1872 with a conviction that he could rightly assert free will and the legitimacy of religious beliefs and moral actions, not despite science, but through an understanding of science in probabilistic and hypothetical terms.

James's intellectual resolutions coincided with the first steps in his career. In 1872, he became an instructor in physiology at Harvard; in 1876, he was promoted to assistant professor and then moved to philosophy in the same rank in 1880; he rose to professor rank in 1885 and retired in that position in 1907; during the years 1889 to 1897, James served as professor of psychology.

His academic migrations reflected his intellectual development. In 1876, using physiological equipment, he developed the first psychological laboratory in America. In the 1880s, while working on a psychology text for publisher Henry Holt, James produced theories of habit formation, consciousness, and emotion that earned him an international reputation. His essays became chapters in his widely influential, two-volume *Principles of Psychology*, which he soon abbreviated as *Psychology, the Briefer Course*.

Despite his fame in the emerging discipline of psychology, James grew impatient with empirical investigations and was drawn to more speculative questions about the nature of the human mind. These impulses culminated in his *Varieties of Religious Experience*, in which he proposed a "science of religions" to explore the psychological features of religious experience. In the last decade of his life, James turned to philosophy proper, but still showed the impress of the way he learned science in his youth. He developed the theory of radical empiricism, which expanded conventional empiricism to include mental relations not physically sensed. James is perhaps most famous for his pragmatism, which popularized Peirce's logical theory by defining truth based on an idea's utility rather than on abstract categories. In addition, James challenged America's politics of imperialism, kept a skeptical interest in psychical research, and earned great popularity as a speaker on philosophical, moral, and cultural issues (most notably, with the essay "The Will to Believe" [1895]). Throughout his work, James struggled to formulate theories based on his conviction that science rightly understood can be compatible with religion, morality, and free will.

BIBLIOGRAPHY

Croce, Paul Jerome. *Eclipse of Certainty, 1820–1880.* Vol. 1 of *Science and Religion in the Era of William James.* Chapel Hill: University of North Carolina Press, 1995.

James, William. *The Principles of Psychology.* 2 vols. 1890. Collected edition, Cambridge, MA: Harvard University Press, 1983.

———. *Psychology: Briefer Course.* 1892. Collected edition, Cambridge, MA: Harvard University Press, 1984.

———. *The Varieties of Religious Experience: A Study in Human Nature.* 1902. Collected edition, Cambridge, MA: Harvard University Press, 1985.

———. *Pragmatism: A New Name for Some Old Ways of Thinking.* 1907. Cambridge, MA: Harvard University Press, 1975.

———. *Essays in Radical Empiricism.* 1912. Edited by Frederick H. Burkhardt et al. Cambridge, MA: Harvard University Press, 1976.

———. *The Letters of William James.* Edited by Henry James. 2 vols. Boston: Atlantic Monthly Press, 1920.

———. *The Correspondence of William James.* Edited by Ignask Skrupskelis and Elizabeth M. Berkeley. Charlottesville: University Press of Virginia, 1992.

Myers, Gerald E. *William James: His Life and Thought.* New Haven: Yale University Press, 1986.

Perry, Ralph Barton. *The Thought and Character of William James.* 2 vols. Boston: Little, Brown, and Company, 1935.

Ruf, Frederick J. *The Creation of Chaos: William James and the Stylistic Making of a Disorderly World.* Albany: State University of New York Press, 1991.

Seigfried, Charlene Haddock. *William James's Radical Reconstruction of Philosophy.* Albany: State University of New York Press, 1990.

Simon, Linda. *Genuine Reality: A Life of William James.* New York: Harcourt Brace and Co., 1998.

Taylor, Eugene. *William James on Exceptional Mental States: The 1896 Lowell Lectures.* New York: Charles Scribner's Sons, 1983.

———. *William James on Consciousness Beyond the Margin.* Princeton: Princeton University Press, 1996.

Paul Jerome Croce

Jefferson, Mark (1863–1949)

Geographer, born in Melrose, Massachusetts. Jefferson's father, Daniel Jefferson, a bibliophile and worker for Wiley and Putnam, and then Little, Brown & Company, exerted a literary influence on him.

Jefferson graduated from Boston University in 1884. He spent the years 1883–1889 in Argentina, initially with the National Observatory at Córdoba, then, in 1887, as submanager and treasurer of a sugar plantation in the foothills of the Andes. In 1889, he returned to the United States, taught school in Massachusetts, and took a summer course at Harvard (1892) in earth science that inspired him. He returned to Harvard to study particularly with William Morris Davis from 1896 to 1898, and received the degrees A.B. and A.M.

In September 1901, Jefferson began teaching at the Michigan State Normal College in Ypsilanti. It was to be a remarkable career, which brought to this small teaching institution the appellation "Nursery of American Geography."

During the next thirty-eight years, he taught more than sixty different courses, which he designed himself and illustrated with slides that he made from his remarkable collection of photographs taken in the field. His reputation as an excellent teacher spread quickly, although Jefferson insisted that any "excellence" he inspired in the classroom derived solely from his knowledge of the subject, and was not the product of any supposed pedagogic skill.

During his Ypsilanti years, he published a number of articles that were read widely, reprinted, and became known in the literature. *Teachers' Geography* (ten editions, 1906–1923), *Man in Europe* (1924), and *Peopling the Argentine Pampa* (1926) were his most successful books. Among the most noted of his articles were "The Distribution of People in South America" (1907), "Where Men Live in North America" (1908), "The Culture of the Nations" (1911), "The Anthropography of North America" (1913), "The Civilizing Rails" (1928), "The Six-Six World Map; Giving Larger, Better, Continents" (1930), "Distribution of the

J

World's City Folks" (1913), and "The Law of the Primate City" (1939).

Jefferson's mentor at Harvard, William Morris Davis, was responsible for the emergence of geography as a professional field in the United States. Davis's geography was of a physiographic nature. However, he urged those of his disciples who felt inclined to study life responses to the physical environment to do so. This study of organic response was known at the time as ontographic study. Of Davis's students, it was undertaken by Jefferson, I. Bowman, and E. Huntington; each made his own unique contribution to the study. The study of "human geography" spread more widely and more quickly than Davisian physical geography.

It must be said that Jefferson was additionally a skilled and innovative cartographer. His work was invariably illustrated by his own maps, and he was frequently consulted by others as to how best to illustrate matters cartographically. Especial mention must be made of his work with The Inquiry and The Commission to Negotiate Peace at Paris at the end of World War I. Here, he was chief cartographer: he made maps for members of the American Delegation, and on occasion, for the Allies.

Jefferson's work was recognized in 1916 by election to the presidency of the Association of American Geographers. In 1931, he received gold medals from both the American Geographical Society and the Geographical Society of Chicago. And in 1939, he received the Distinguished Service Award of the National Council of Geography Teachers, in recognition of "Outstanding Contributions to Educational Geography."

BIBLIOGRAPHY

Martin, Geoffrey J. *Mark Jefferson: Geographer.* Ypsilanti: Eastern Michigan University Press, 1968.

Geoffrey J. Martin

Jefferson, Thomas (1743–1826)

Lawyer, governor of Virginia, minister to France, secretary of state, vice president, third president of the United States, and man of science. Jefferson was born in Virginia, the son of a land developer, cartographer, and surveyor. From him, young Thomas probably learned the principles of surveying which he utilized often during his lifetime. He matriculated at the College of William and Mary in 1760, receiving the B.A. in 1762. After studying law for five years in Williams-burg, he passed the Virginia bar and established himself with a practice in Williamsburg.

It was while in college, as a result of his studies with his professor William Small, that he became interested in the sciences. By the time he left the college, his knowledge of the physical sciences and higher mathematics was probably unrivaled by that of any American of his time. More than any other American, he epitomized the Renaissance man with the range of his interests and endeavors. His greatest scientific achievement was the promotion of the sciences in America, utilizing his public station to urge the application of the sciences as a most certain means of national advancement. He was adamant in his conviction that Americans must and should profit from scientific accomplishments, whether achieved abroad or at home, in order to produce a true democracy, for in his view, science was the common ground for engendering fraternal relations among men. While minister to France, he served as an information center on science and technology, informing Americans of new, useful European achievements, and promoting American accomplishments in Europe. As president of the United States, he initiated the first government-sponsored scientific enterprise, the Lewis and Clark Expedition, to explore and define the western lands. He specified that only the practical sciences were deserving of consideration, and advocated, although he did not always practice, the precept that in science there should be absolute freedom of inquiry, and that the only legitimate conclusions were those based on careful observation and experiment.

From his student days, Jefferson developed an idiosyncracy for collecting and recording statistical data relating primarily to measurement, which he later found occasion to apply for practical purposes. Throughout his travels, he noted methods of construction, details of devices, tools, furniture, and other items that he believed improved the quality of living. This practice led him to the investigation, acquisition, and occasionally to the invention of a variety of devices to achieve a practical purpose. Few of the inventions attributed to Jefferson are in fact original with him; most of them were modifications of or improvements on existing devices that he adapted to his own needs. Among his more important inventions were the portable desk on which he drafted the Declaration of Independence, a portable copying press, his wheel cipher device for secret communication, and his design of the moldboard plow.

Jefferson remained a practical farmer throughout more than three decades of public life, considering agriculture to be one of the sciences. The record of his farming activities, his *Farm Book,* reveals he was an agricultural engineer as well, engaged in building fencing, roads, and bridges and related activities as well as planting. He converted Monticello and his other lands into progressive experimental farms, testing new farm machinery and equipment, some of which he devised, and introducing new crops and new agricultural methods. Concerned with the inefficiency of the traditional wooden plow, in 1788, he applied mathematical principles to produce a design for a moldboard that was more efficient and that could be readily duplicated.

Jefferson was among the first in the American colonies to conduct systematic meteorological studies, maintaining records of temperature, rainfall, winds, and other climatological data throughout his life. He believed that only by means of simultaneous observations made at considerable distances could knowledge of the weather be successfully derived. He urged others to maintain similar records, and by this means he developed a veritable weather service of his own. In 1824, he proposed a plan for weather recording on a national scale.

Jefferson owned and used a large collection of mathematical instruments, some of which were made to his own specifications. Among his lifelong interests was astronomy, and he observed eclipses and other celestial phenomena and established latitudes and longitudes of his properties.

He constantly sought plants both useful and decorative for his own gardens and useful for the country. He exchanged plants and seeds at home and abroad, and introduced dry rice, the olive, and the caper from Europe. He was the first to identify the pecan, and in his *Notes on the State of Virginia,* he compiled a list of 129 plants—medical, esculent, ornamental, and useful for fabrication—that were native to Virginia.

Jefferson had an absorbing curiosity about the Native Americans and their origins and customs, and assembled many of their artifacts for the private "museum" he maintained in the White House and at Monticello. He eventually concluded that the best record of Indian origins was to be derived from their languages, and contemplated the compilation of a great Indian vocabulary. For this endeavor, he distributed printed forms to Indian agents and others for recording tribal vocabularies. Between 1780 and 1781, he undertook the excavation of an Indian burial mound, not in an endeavor to collect artifacts, but in an effort to resolve conjectures concerning the structure and purpose of these aboriginal burial places. Without precedents to guide him, he proceeded methodically with his excavation, recording stratigraphy as well as every detail of evidence encountered in a remarkable professional manner that anticipated the techniques of modern archaeology by almost a century.

Closely related to his interest in the Indians were Jefferson's speculations on the origins of the universe, and the formation of rocks, crystals, and fossil shells. He felt that it was too early to venture theories. Thoroughly familiar with published works of the living European scientists, and more fully informed about animal life in America than any of his contemporaries, he was in advance of the best specialists of his time in his conclusions on paleontology. He discarded existing classifications and proved that certain fossils found on the American continent were neither of the hippopotamus or elephant as claimed, but of the mastodon. He collected great numbers of fossil remains from various sources and identified bones found in Green Briar County as those of the Great Claw or *Megalonyx,* later named in his honor. He donated his extensive fossil collection to the American Philosophical Society, of which he served as president for seventeen years.

In about 1780, while governor of Virginia, Jefferson began to compile data about his native state, which he eventually published privately as *Notes on the State of Virginia,* often considered to be the most important scientific work produced in America in the eighteenth century. In his *Notes,* he disputed contentions of the comte de Buffon that animals on the American continent were smaller and fewer than those in Europe.

Later in life, Jefferson wrote, "Science is my passion, politics my duty." His dedication to the sciences won him no praise in his time, and instead brought him ridicule and vituperations from political opponents. His perception of the importance of science, which in his time included also technology, and his belief that it should be supported by government, has received greater recognition in modern times, however, as well as acknowledgement of his vision.

BIBLIOGRAPHY

Bedini, Silvio A. "Jefferson, Thomas." *Dictionary of Scientific Biography.* Edited by Charles C. Gillispie. New York: Scribners, 1973, 8:88–90.

———. "Godfather of American Invention." In *The Smithsonian Book of Invention,* edited by Robert C. Post.

J

Washington, DC: Smithsonian Exposition Books, 1977, pp. 96–103.

————. *Thomas Jefferson and His Copying Machines*. Charlottesville: University Press of Virginia, 1984.

————. *Thomas Jefferson and American Vertebrate Paleontology*. Publication 61. Charlottesville: Virginia Division of Mineral Resources, 1985.

————. "Man of Science." In *Thomas Jefferson. A Reference Biography*, edited by Merrill D. Peterson. New York: Scribners, 1986, pp. 253–276.

————. *Thomas Jefferson Statesman of Science*. New York: Macmillan, 1990.

Betts, Edwin Morris, ed. *Thomas Jefferson's Garden Book*. Philadelphia: American Philosophical Society, 1944.

————, ed. *Thomas Jefferson's Farm Book*. Princeton: Princeton University Press, 1953.

Jefferson, Thomas. "The Description of a Mould-Board of the Least Resistance and the Easiest and Most Certain Construction." *Transactions of the American Philosophical Society* 4 (1799): 313–322.

————. "A Memoir on the Discovery of Certain Bones of a Quadruped of the Clawed Kind in the Western Parts of Virginia." *Transactions of the American Philosophical Society* 4 (1799): 246–322.

————. *Notes on the State of Virginia*. Edited with Notes by William Peden. Chapel Hill: University of North Carolina Press, 1955.

Martin, Edwin T. *Thomas Jefferson: Scientist*. New York: Henry Schuman, 1952.

McAdie, Alexander. "A Colonial Weather Service." *Popular Science Monthly* 7 July, 1894, pp. 39–45.

Silvio A. Bedini

Jet Propulsion Laboratory

The Jet Propulsion Laboratory (JPL), in Pasadena, California, is a federally funded research and development center operated by the California Institute of Technology (Cal Tech) under a sole-source contract (renewed every five years) from the National Aeronautics and Space Administration (NASA). JPL began as an off-campus facility used by several Cal Tech graduate students in the late 1930s to conduct early rocket-propulsion experiments. As a United States Army Ordnance facility in the 1940s and 1950s, it developed a jet-assisted takeoff (JATO) engine for airplanes during World War II and the Corporal and Sergeant surface-to-surface missiles during the early Cold War years. Working with Wernher von Braun's rocket team at the army's Redstone Arsenal in Huntsville, Alabama, JPL engineers developed the upper stages and payload for the first United States satellite (*Explorer 1,* launched on 31 January 1958) and the first United States space probe (*Pioneer 4,* launched on 3 March 1959) to escape the earth's gravity.

After the Department of Defense agreed to transfer JPL to NASA in late 1958, it became the space agency's chief facility for designing, constructing, and operating unmanned solar-system exploration spacecraft. JPL-built spacecraft *(Ranger, Surveyor, Mariner, Viking, Voyager, Magellan,* and *Galileo)* have flown by and/or orbited every planet in the solar system except Pluto, as well as numerous planetary satellites and ring systems and several asteroids.

The JPL-managed Deep Space Network (DSN) is comprised of paraboloid antennas grouped at Goldstone Dry Lake in the Mojave Desert of California; Tidbinbila (near Canberra), Australia; and Robledo de Chavela (near Madrid), Spain. The primary mission of the antennas (currently thirty-four meters and seventy meters in diameter) is to support the space probes and high-altitude satellites of JPL and other institutions (such as other NASA centers and the European, Japanese, and Russian space agencies). This support includes the transmission of commands, the reception of engineering and scientific data, and the determination of the distance and direction of the probes from earth.

On a noninterference basis, however, various investigators have conducted radio astronomy and planetary radar investigations with the DSN antennas. The radio astronomy work has included collaborative very long baseline interferometry (VLBI) experiments conducted with other institutions around the world. The DSN first became involved in planetary radar because of the navigational needs of NASA's space-probe program. Planetary radar astronomers now generally agree that a DSN team (in anticipation of two planned *Mariner* missions to Venus in 1962) made the first definite radar contact with Venus on 10 March 1961. JPL staff subsequently made numerous radar contacts with the terrestrial planets (Mercury, Venus, and Mars), the major satellites of Jupiter and Saturn, the Saturnian ring system, and numerous comets and asteroids. Since the 1980s, planetary radar investigations have been conducted only at Goldstone and the National Radio and Ionospheric Center in Arecibo, Puerto Rico.

Difficulties with the *Ranger* spacecraft in the early 1960s led some to question JPL's unique insider-outsider status within NASA (its staff are Cal Tech employees); others in the 1990s, however, saw the

J

institution as a model for restructuring some of NASA's civil service centers.

BIBLIOGRAPHY
Burrows, William E. *Exploring Space: Voyages in the Solar System and Beyond.* New York: Random House, 1990.
Ezell, Edward Clinton, and Linda Neuman Ezell. *On Mars: Exploration of the Red Planet 1958–1978.* Washington, DC: Government Printing Office, 1984.
Ferster, Warren. "JPL Seeks Better Harmony with Industry." *Space News* 6, no. 37 (25 September–1 October 1995): 16.
Hall, R. Cargill. *Lunar Impact: A History of Project Ranger.* Washington, DC: Government Printing Office, 1977.
Koppes, Clayton R. *JPL and the American Space Program: A History of the Jet Propulsion Laboratory.* New Haven and London: Yale University Press, 1982.
Morrison, David. *Voyages to Saturn.* Washington, DC: Government Printing Office, 1982.
Morrison, David, and Jane Samz. *Voyage to Jupiter.* Washington, DC: Government Printing Office, 1980.
Murray, Bruce. *Journey into Space: The First Thirty Years of Space Exploration.* New York and London: Norton, 1989.
Waff, Craig B. "The Road to the Deep Space Network." *IEEE Spectrum* 30, no. 4 (April 1993): 50–57.
———. "A History of Project Galileo. Part 1: The Evolution of NASA's Early Outer-planet Exploration Strategy, 1959–1972." *Quest: The Magazine of Spaceflight* 5, no. 1 (1996): 4–19.

Craig B. Waff

Joint Committee on Atomic Energy

A committee of the United States Congress established in 1946 to monitor the development, use, and control of nuclear energy and the activities of the Atomic Energy Commission.

The Atomic Energy Act of 1946 specified that all bills related to atomic energy were to be referred to the committee, and the commission was required under the act to keep the committee "fully and currently informed" of all its activities. These statutory requirements, plus the high secrecy classification of atomic energy information during the early years, gave the committee almost exclusive legislative authority over the course of nuclear development. The committee regularly held extensive hearings, both in open and executive sessions, on commission programs and budgets. The Atomic Energy Act of 1954 gave the committee additional authority to hold annual hearings on the development of peaceful uses of atomic energy. The

new act also required the commission to submit to the committee proposed legislation authorizing the agency's appropriations. Thus, during the darkest days of the Cold War, when the commission was forced to expand both its plants for producing nuclear materials and weapons and its research and development efforts, the committee was able to exert substantial influence over commission programs.

Although committee chairmen frequently used public hearings to criticize commission policy and decisions on a broad range of issues in both the military and civilian spheres, the committee gradually came to associate its prominence and influence with that of the commission. Ultimately the committee's prestige and credibility declined with the commission's as fear of radiation exposure and disenchantment with nuclear power captured the public mind in the late 1960s. The Energy Reorganization Act of 1974 abolished both the Atomic Energy Commission and the joint committee.

BIBLIOGRAPHY
Green, Harold P., and Alan Rosenthal. *Government of the Atom: The Integration of Powers.* New York: Atherton, 1963.
Hewlett, Richard G., and Oscar E. Anderson Jr. *The New World, 1939–1946.* Vol. 1 of *A History of the United States Atomic Energy Commission.* University Park: Pennsylvania State University Press, 1962.
Hewlett, Richard G., and Francis Duncan. *Atomic Shield, 1947–1952.* Vol. 2 of *A History of the United States Atomic Energy Commission.* University Park: Pennsylvania State University Press, 1969.
Hewlett, Richard G., and Jack M. Holl. *Atoms for Peace and War, 1953–1961: Eisenhower and the Atomic Energy Commission.* Berkeley: University of California Press, 1989.
Thomas, Morgan. *Atomic Energy and Congress.* Ann Arbor: University of Michigan Press, 1956.

Richard G. Hewlett

SEE ALSO
Atomic Energy Commission

Jordan, David Starr (1851–1931)

Ichthyologist, evolutionary biologist, and university president. In his autobiography, Jordan described himself as "a naturalist, teacher and minor prophet of democracy." He was a leader in the movements to reform education, to promote peace, and to encourage "good breeding" (eugenics). His biological work centered on ichthyology

Jordan, David Starr 293

J

and evolution. Born in Gainesville, New York, Jordan attended Cornell University, receiving an M.S. rather than a B.S. because of the advanced work he did. He spent the summer of 1873 studying with Louis Agassiz at Penikesee Island, and always considered himself a student of Agassiz. He joined the faculty at Indiana University in 1879, and by 1885 was president. He introduced the modern "major" system of education there and became a leader in education reform. In 1891, he became the first president of Stanford University, which he remained affiliated with until his death. Jordan was a well-known and active pacifist, a leader in the eugenics movement, and a defender of evolution against creationism. He was involved in many of the leading political controversies of his time, and was a highly visible and important national figure.

Much of Jordan's work concerned the taxonomy and distribution of fishes. His works included *A Synopsis of the Fishes of North America* (with his student Charles H. Gilbert), and the massive four-volume work *The Fishes of North and Middle America* (with Barton Evermann), which remains the classic work on American fish. Jordan and Evermann's *The Shore Fishes of the Hawaiian Islands,* originally published in 1905, was still in print in 1995. He also made systematic studies of the fishes of the South Seas and Japan. Of the 12,000–13,000 species of fish accepted in the 1920s, Jordan and his students had discovered over 2,500. Of the 7,000 genera named at the time, 1,085 were named by Jordan and his students. In addition to being taxonomically important, this work made a significant contribution to the development of ecology. This research was sponsored by the United States Fish Commission, which was concerned with describing and understanding the underlying causes of the biogeographical distribution of fish species.

At the theoretical level, Jordan's principal contributions were concerned with speciation. In 1905, Jordan published the first comprehensive synthesis of the evidence in favor of the view that isolation is a necessary first step in the process of speciation. This view was called into doubt by the development and popularity of Hugo de Vries's mutation theory. Jordan continued to promote the concept of geographical speciation throughout his career, and his work is cited by many of the architects of the synthesis, including Sewell Wright, and Theodosius Dobzhansky.

In arguing for the role that geographical isolation plays in speciation, Jordan made use of a regularity he found, namely that the closest related species will usually not be found in the same region, but in neighboring regions, separated by a barrier of some sort. Joel A. Allen later termed this biogeographical regularity, "Jordan's Law" and it is still referred to in textbooks. He was the first to discuss the development of "geminate" species (sibling species) that often first result from speciation.

For a figure who at one time loomed large in American culture, there is surprisingly little historical work which has been done on Jordan. There have been a few treatments of his political, social, and educational ideas, but very little on his scientific writing. This is partly due to the decline in prestige of systematics. In addition, historians of biology who work on early-twentieth-century evolutionary biology have tended to focus on the contributions of geneticists and more experimentally oriented biologists, referring to Jordan only in passing. Thus, while Jordan is often referred to, particularly in the history of evolutionary biology, ecology, and eugenics, a great deal more work needs to be done. A great help in this regard is the collection of Jordan's papers and correspondence at the Stanford University Archives.

BIBLIOGRAPHY

Allen, Garland. "The Reception of the Mutation Theory." *Journal of the History of Biology* 3 (1979): 179–209.

Burns, Edward. *David Starr Jordan: Prophet of Freedom.* Stanford: Stanford University Press, 1953.

Hays, Alice Newman. *David Starr Jordan, a Bibliography of His Writings, 1871–1931.* Stanford: Stanford University Press, 1952.

Jordan, David Starr. "The Origin of Species Through Isolation." *Science* 22 (1905): 545–562.

———. *Days of a Man.* 2 vols. New York: World Book, 1922.

Jordan, David Starr, and Barton Evermann. *The Fishes of North and Middle America.* 4 vols. Washington, DC: Smithsonian, 1896–1900.

———. *The Shore Fishes of Hawaii.* Rutland, VT: Tuttle, 1986.

Jordan, David Starr, and Charles H. Gilbert. *Synopsis of the Fishes of North America.* Washington, DC: Smithsonian, 1882.

David Magnus

Just, Ernest Everett (1883–1941)

African-American zoologist and educator. Born in Charleston, South Carolina, Just attended the Colored Normal, Industrial, Agricultural and Mechanical College (South Carolina State College), Orangeburg,

South Carolina. After graduating in 1899, he attended Kimball Union Academy in Meriden, New Hampshire (1900–1903), before proceeding to Dartmouth College. At Dartmouth, he majored in biology and minored in Greek and history, graduating A.B. magna cum laude in 1907. He earned the Ph.D. in zoology at the University of Chicago in 1916.

Essentially, there were two professional options available to an African American with this academic background: teaching in a black institution or preaching in a black church. Just chose the former, beginning his career in the fall of 1907 as instructor in English and rhetoric at Howard University. In 1909, he taught English and biology, and a year later assumed a permanent full-time commitment in zoology as part of a general revitalization of the science curriculum at Howard. He also taught physiology in the medical school. A devoted teacher, he served as faculty advisor to a group trying to establish a nationwide fraternity of black students. The Alpha chapter of Omega Psi Phi was organized at Howard in 1911, and Just became its first honorary member.

Meanwhile, he laid plans to pursue scientific research. In 1909, he started studying at the Marine Biological Laboratory (MBL), Woods Hole, Massachusetts, under Frank Rattray Lillie, MBL director and head of the zoology department at the University of Chicago. He also served as Lillie's research assistant. Their relationship quickly blossomed into a full and equal scientific collaboration. By the time Just earned his Ph.D., he had already coauthored a paper with Lillie and written several on his own.

The two worked on fertilization in marine annelid worms. Just's first paper, "The Relation of the First Cleavage Plane to the Entrance Point of the Sperm," appeared in *Biological Bulletin* in 1912, and was cited frequently, by Thomas Hunt Morgan and others, as a classic and authoritative study. Just went on to champion the so-called fertilizin theory that Lillie had proposed to explain certain physiological processes underlying fertilization. The theory held that fertilizin was an essential biochemical catalyst or combinant in the key reactions between egg and sperm. Although aspects of the theory were challenged by subsequent advances in knowledge of molecular structure, its basic assumptions about the importance of interactions between molecules on the sperm surface and egg cortex remained influential.

Science was for Just a deeply felt avocation, an activity which he looked forward to doing each summer at the MBL as a welcome respite from heavy teaching and administrative responsibilities at Howard. Under the circumstances, his productivity was extraordinary. Within ten years (1919–1928), he published thirty-five articles, mostly relating to his studies on fertilization. He yearned, however, for a position in which he could pursue his research full-time. Largely for racial reasons, such a position was never offered to him.

In 1928, Just received a substantial grant from the Julius Rosenwald Fund which allowed him a change of environment and longer stretches of time for his research. His first excursion, in 1929, took him to Italy, where he worked for seven months at the Stazione Zoologica in Naples, Italy. He traveled to Europe ten times over the course of the next decade, staying for periods ranging from three weeks to two years. He worked primarily at the Stazione Zoologica; the Kaiser-Wilhelm Institut für Biologie, Berlin; and the Station Biologique, Roscoff, France. As the political turmoil in Europe grew during the 1930s, Just continued to be productive. Ironically, he felt more comfortable there, amidst the rise of Nazism and fascism, than in America.

In Europe, Just wrote a book, *The Biology of the Cell Surface* (1939), synthesizing many of the scientific theories, philosophical ideas, and experimental results of his career. Its thesis, that the ectoplasm or cell surface has a fundamental role in development, did not receive much attention at the time but later became a major focus of scientific investigation. Decades later, some biologists suggested that Just's work may have been prophetic, in light of "recent great advances in recognizing the role of the cell surface in regulating all ingress and egress of substances, and in revealing its astonishing biochemical mosaicism" (Glass, p. 45).

Also in 1939, in response to the urging of scientists who considered him a foremost authority on experimental techniques in marine embryology, Just published a compendium of experimental advice under the title *Basic Methods for Experiments on Eggs of Marine Animals*. In 1940, he was interned briefly in France following the German invasion and then released to return to America, where he died of pancreatic cancer a year later.

BIBLIOGRAPHY

Gilbert, Scott F. "Cellular Politics: Ernest Everett Just, Richard B. Goldschmidt, and the Attempt to Reconcile Embryology and Genetics." In *The American Development of Biology*, edited by Ronald Rainger, Keith R. Benson,

J

and Jane Maienschein. Philadelphia: University of Pennsylvania Press, 1988, pp. 311–346.

Glass, Bentley. "A Man Before His Time." *Quarterly Review of Biology* 59 (December 1984): 443–445.

Gould, Stephen Jay. "Just in the Middle: A Solution to the Mechanist-Vitalist Controversy." *Natural History* (January 1984): 24–33.

Lillie, Frank R. "Ernest Everett Just: August 14, 1883, to October 27, 1941." *Science* 95 (2 January 1942): 10–11.

Manning, Kenneth R. *Black Apollo of Science: The Life of Ernest Everett Just.* New York: Oxford University Press, 1983.

Kenneth R. Manning

K

Kármán, Theodore von (1881–1963)

One of the greatest achievements of twentieth-century science has been the discovery of the principles governing sustained, controlled flight. The Hungarian-American polymath Theodore von Kármán–a seminal figure in this revolution–deserves a position of preeminence among modern scientists. A brilliant applied physicist and mathematician, he helped found the disciplines of aerodynamics and aeronautical engineering, erected several famous aerospace institutions, forged international scientific cooperation, became a businessman, apprenticed and nurtured hundreds of students, and advised military leaders the world over. He also gained fame as a dedicated partygiver; indeed, his notably warm and energetic personality contributed materially to his many successes.

Born in Budapest, Hungary, Kármán grew up in a middle-class Jewish family, the son of Maurice von Kármán, a distinguished professor of education at the University of Budapest. After several years of home tutoring and matriculation at an elite gymnasium, Kármán studied at the Budapest Royal Technical Institute, and in 1902 took a degree with honors in mechanical engineering.

The young graduate then pursued the study of aerodynamics under one of the discipline's founding giants, Professor Ludwig Prandtl of Göttingen University, Germany, and received the doctor of philosophy degree there in 1908. His research at Göttingen led to a fundamental discovery in fluid mechanics: the so-called Kármán Vortices, or parallel trails of turbulence which flow beyond blunt objects in streams of air or water. This insight forever altered engineering approaches to aircraft, ship, and bridge design. With a reputation second only to his mentor's, Kármán accepted the position of director of the Aachen Aerodynamics Institute and taught there until 1929 (except for 1914 to 1918, when he served as chief aircraft designer for the Austrian Air Service). He quickly raised the Aachen Institute to prominence, and by the end of the 1920s, it rivaled Prandtl's Göttingen establishment.

Kármán's fame spread to America, where basic aeronautical research lagged far behind that of Europe. To remedy the situation, the Guggenheim Fund for the Promotion of Aeronautics provided a large grant to establish the Guggenheim Aeronautical Laboratory at the California Institute of Technology (GALCIT). Cal Tech's President Robert A. Millikan, anxious to persuade Kármán to become GALCIT's first director, invited him to lecture in Pasadena, which he did with great success in 1926. Kármán accepted the Cal Tech offer in October 1929 for two reasons: the rising tide of Nazi influence in Aachen, and Millikan's offer of a handsome salary and wide autonomy as GALCIT director. During the 1930s, Kármán exercised a powerful influence over aeronautical research and development in the United States. Due in part to his efforts, southern California became the hub of the nation's aircraft industry, the beneficiary of the faculty, students, and laboratory assembled by him in Pasadena.

When war threatened Europe during the late 1930s, Commanding General of the Army Air Forces Henry H. Arnold asked Kármán and his staff to investigate small rocket engines to augment aircraft performance. The motors proved so successful that, in 1942, the Kármán group formed the Aerojet Engineering Company to fabricate rocket canisters. Two years later, Cal Tech

K

received a contract from the army's Ordnance Department to develop tactical ballistic missiles. In response, the Jet Propulsion Laboratory, formed by Kármán from the sinews of GALCIT, began to research the fundamental problems of rocketry.

During the later years of his life, Kármán assumed the role of advisor to military leaders and senior statesman of the international aeronautics community. In 1944, General Arnold asked him to initiate the Army Air Forces Scientific Advisory Group, later the Air Force Scientific Advisory Board. He served as its chairman for a decade. In this capacity, he and a few colleagues wrote a prescient forecast for Arnold on postwar aeronautics entitled *Toward New Horizons* (1945). Meantime, having moved his household to Paris, Kármán laid the groundwork for and put in motion his last institutional creation—the NATO Advisory Group for Aeronautical Research and Development (AGARD), founded in February 1952. Composed like the Air Force Scientific Advisory Board of panels of subject-area experts, both institutions survive to the present day, long outliving their creator, who died at Aachen.

The impact of Theodore von Kármán is difficult to calculate exactly. His success rested not only on technical genius, but on personal magnetism and keen institutional instincts. Yet, the extraordinary diversity of his contributions to air and space render him perhaps the most influential twentieth-century practitioner of the science of flight.

BIBLIOGRAPHY

Gorn, Michael H. *Harnessing the Genie: Science and Technology Forecasting for the Air Force, 1944–1986.* Washington, DC: Government Printing Office, 1988.

———. *The Universal Man: Theodore von Kármán's Life in Aeronautics.* Washington, DC and London: Smithsonian Institution Press, 1992.

———, ed. *Prophecy Fulfilled: Toward New Horizons and Its Legacy.* Washington, DC: Government Printing Office, 1994.

Hall, R. Cargill. "Shaping the Course of Aeronautics, Rocketry, and Astronautics: Theodore von Karman, 1881–1963." *Journal of the Astronautical Sciences* (October-December 1978).

Hanle, Paul A. *Bringing Aerodynamics to America.* Cambridge, MA: MIT Press, 1982.

Von Kármán, Theodore, and Lee Edson. *The Wind and Beyond: Theodore von Kármán, Pioneer in Aviation and Pathfinder in Space.* Boston: Little, Brown, 1967.

Michael H. Gorn

SEE ALSO
Air Force, United States, and Science

Killian, James R., Jr. (1904–1988)

University administrator and science advisor. Born in Blacksburg, South Carolina, Killian attended Trinity College (now Duke University) from 1921 to 1923 before transferring to the Massachusetts Institute of Technology (MIT), where he graduated with a B.S. in business and engineering administration in 1926. He then went to work on the editorial board of *Technology Review,* where he became editor in 1930. In 1939, Killian joined the MIT administration as executive assistant to MIT president Karl T. Compton. He was appointed executive vice president in 1943, and he rose to the vice presidency of MIT in 1945. In 1948, Killian was chosen to be president-designate of MIT, and he was inaugurated as president the next year. In the 1950s, he served on several important government committees, including the Science Advisory Committee of the Office of Defense Mobilization (1951–1957), and he chaired the Army Science Advisory Panel (1951–1956), the Technological Capabilities Panel (1954–1955), the President's Board of Consultants on Foreign Intelligence Activities (1956–1957), and the President's Foreign Intelligence Advisory Board (1961–1963). In November 1957, President Dwight D. Eisenhower appointed Killian the first Special Assistant to the President for Science and Technology and chairman of the President's Science Advisory Committee (PSAC), a post he filled until July 1959. In early 1959, he resigned from the MIT presidency to become chairman of the MIT Corporation, a position he held until 1971. In the 1960s and 1970s, Killian continued to fill a public service role as a member of several committees which studied various aspects of science education, science-government relations, and arms control. He was also an early promoter of public television. He chaired the Carnegie Commission on Educational Television (1965–1967), which issued a report leading to the establishment of the Public Broadcasting Service, and he served as first director of the Corporation for Public Broadcasting (1968–1975).

As a nonscientist, Killian followed an unusual path to becoming president of MIT and science advisor to the White House. But his fund-raising activities as secretary of the MIT Alumni Association from 1928–1929 and his editorial work on *Technology Review* in the 1920s and 1930s brought him into contact with high-level MIT administrators. He developed a close relationship with then MIT vice president Vannevar Bush, who recommended Killian to incoming MIT president Karl Compton for a position on the president's staff. Compton appointed him executive assistant to the president, and from there he gradually rose to prominence in academic and government circles.

As vice president and president of MIT during the post–World War II years, Killian presided over a premiere research institution at a time when the influx of Cold War defense funding transformed American research universities. In his 1977 memoir on PSAC, Killian warmly embraced the "benign partnership of government and science" in the 1940s and 1950s (Killian, *Sputnik,* p. 264), and in his 1985 memoirs, he praised federal support of postwar science for allowing MIT and other universities "to make great strides ahead in their education and research." (Killian, *Education,* p. 265) In recent years, however, some historians of American science have contended that the Cold War university-government relationship was far more complex and problematic, arguing that military support of basic research subtly compromised universities' dedication to the open-ended pursuit of knowledge and shunted scientific research off to narrowly defined problems of military interest.

As a science advisor to the federal government, Killian played a direct role in formulating the relationship of science and technology to the Cold War. The Eisenhower administration deliberated over the military implications of the space age long before the October 1957 launch of *Sputnik* by the Soviet Union. As chairman of the Technological Capabilities Panel, Killian delivered a report to the National Security Council in February 1955 which recommended that the development of an intercontinental ballistic missile be given highest priority, a recommendation which President Eisenhower quickly implemented. The panel also stressed the need for better intelligence-gathering capabilities, which later led to the development of the U-2 spy plane and reconnaissance satellites.

Killian is best known as the first Special Assistant to the President for Science and Technology and chairman of PSAC. Appointed in the aftermath of *Sputnik,* amidst public perceptions that the technological and military might of the United States was falling dangerously behind that of the Soviet Union, Killian reported directly to the president on matters of science and technology policy. PSAC's recommendations contributed to Cold War missile development; the creation of a civilian space agency, the National Aeronautics and Space Administration; increased federal support of science education under the National Defense Education Act of 1958; and early discussions of the technical feasibility of a nuclear test-ban treaty.

Killian opposed the crash program mentality of the post-*Sputnik* era. Although he approved of the increased federal support for science education which followed *Sputnik,* he warned against engaging in an education race with the Soviet Union. He was also unenthusiastic about manned spaceflight, especially the Apollo program, and its role as part of a competition for international prestige. Historians of the space age have pointed out that *Sputnik* opened a new phase of the Cold War, one in which image, prestige, and technological display became as important as tactical military advantage. As first science advisor, Killian helped usher in the space age, but like Eisenhower, he thought about missile and space technology in concrete military terms and disdained the psychological dimension of Cold War politics, which grew increasingly powerful in the years after *Sputnik.*

A scholarly biography of Killian has yet to be written. A large collection of his personal papers (over eighty linear feet), as well as official records relating to his administrative role at MIT, are available at the MIT Institute Archives and Special Collections. On his advisory role in the Eisenhower administration, consult the Dwight D. Eisenhower Presidential Library in Abilene, Kansas.

BIBLIOGRAPHY

Divine, Robert A. *The Sputnik Challenge.* New York: Oxford University Press, 1993.

Killian, James R., Jr. *The Education of a College President: A Memoir.* Cambridge, MA: MIT Press, 1985.

———. *Sputnik, Scientists, and Eisenhower: A Memoir of the First Special Assistant to the President for Science and Technology.* Cambridge, MA: MIT Press, 1985.

Leslie, Stuart W. *The Cold War and American Science: The Military-Industrial-Academic Complex at MIT and Stanford.* New York: Columbia University Press, 1993.

Lester, Robert, ed. *The Papers of the President's Science Advisory Committee, 1957–1961.* Frederick, MD: University Publications of America, 1986. Microfilm.

McDougall, Walter A. . . . *the Heavens and the Earth: A Political History of the Space Age.* New York: Basic Books, 1985.

Schweber, S.S. "Big Science in Context: Cornell and MIT." In *Big Science: The Growth of Large-Scale Research,* edited

K

by Peter Galison and Bruce Hevly. Stanford, CA: Stanford University Press, 1992, pp. 149–183.

Smith, Michael L. "Selling the Moon: The U.S. Manned Space Program and the Triumph of Commodity Scientism." In *The Culture of Consumption: Critical Essays in American History 1880–1980,* edited by Richard Wightman Fox and T.J. Jackson Lears. New York: Pantheon Books, 1983, pp. 175–209.

Jessica Wang

SEE ALSO
President, Scientific Advice to

King, Clarence Rivers (1842–1901)

Geologist, science administrator, mining consultant, writer, and art collector. King's mother, Florence, the widow of a Newport merchant in the China trade, encouraged her son's early interests in natural history and art. Educated formally in Connecticut, King earned, in 1862, a Ph.B. in chemistry with honors from Yale's Sheffield Scientific School. He served as a geologist (1863–1866) with Josiah Dwight Whitney's Geological Survey of California. For the Corps of Engineers, King planned and led the civilian-staffed United States Geological Exploration of the Fortieth Parallel (1867–1879). As the Department of the Interior's principal geologist (1879–1881), King directed the new United States Geological Survey (USGS), supervised a nationwide study of mineral and mining statistics for the tenth census (1880), and served on the Public Lands Commission. After 1881, as a consulting geologist and expert witness, King served investors and his own interests in Mexico, the United States, Canada, and Britain, continued ranching in Wyoming, and began a bank in Texas. Recurring illness, the Panic of 1893, and financing his twice-widowed mother's family and his own left King hopelessly in debt to his friend John Milton Hay and ended attempts to reappoint King as USGS director.

King's experiences in California underlay his major contributions to science, its administration, and literature in America. The stories in his *Mountaineering in the Sierra Nevada* (1872) made some readers regret that King had chosen geology over literature, but King's early field work there fueled his intention to understand the nature and causes of geological processes and their products. King's own survey mapped the topography, geology, and natural resources of the lands flanking the route of the transcontinental railroad between the Sierras and the Great Plains. The Fortieth Parallel Exploration's organization, field methods, and scientific standards and publications served as models for the Hayden, Powell, and Wheeler surveys of the western territories in the 1870s. When King and his staff exposed as fraudulent the diamond deposits of an American "Kimberley" in Colorado in 1872, they more than repaid the whole cost of their survey. King, thanked by the investors and their geologists, gained a nationwide reputation for honesty. He also became known for his "catastrophist" interpretation of physical change and organic evolution. Convinced that major geologic events of short duration produced rapid changes in landscapes and climates (his "evolution of the environment"), King believed they caused quick biological modifications in the form of increased speciation (his "evolution of life"). In *Systematic Geology* (1878), King synthesized the stratigraphy, paleontology, tectonics, and geologic and mineral history of the Fortieth Parallel's West.

In 1878–1879, King helped the National Academy of Sciences and the federal government to shape the USGS. The founders intended the new agency to advance the nation's economy, by aiding its mineral industry, and to improve its civil service, but they failed to form a separate agency to conduct geodetic, cadastral, and topographic surveys, or to reform the administration of the public lands. As USGS director, King set the USGS on much of its future course. He established high standards for competence and probity in employment and work. To carry out Congress' mandate, King planned a scientific classification of the national domain, a comprehensive examination of the extent, nature, and geologic relations of its mineral resources, and other wide-ranging applied and basic studies. He also intended these investigations to advance the understanding of the nature and origin of ore deposits. King's own studies of the nation's precious metals appeared during 1881–1885. He aimed USGS work in general geology toward the completion of a reliable geologic map of the United States. King's failure to reach funding goals, personal financial requirements, struggles to avoid ethical compromises, and the resignation of Interior Secretary Carl Schurz confirmed King's original decision not to serve long as director. After 1881, King continued to promote the inventory and conservation (then "wise use") of natural resources and other political and social causes in the United States and in Cuba. He also supported and participated in USGS-academic experimental studies of the earth's age and its internal composition and dynamics.

John Wesley Powell was King's choice to lead the USGS. Powell reversed King's policies, making them seem a failure, when he emphasized basic far more than applied studies and nearly excluded economic work by the agency in favor of topography and general geology. In the early 1890s, Congress repudiated Powell and his choices. The legislators encouraged Powell to resign by selectively slashing USGS appropriations and staff, and then Powell's salary. Charles Doolittle Walcott, whom King had hired in 1879 as an entry-level geologist, succeeded Powell in 1894. As director, Walcott returned the agency to a balanced (but expanded) mission-oriented program. In the twentieth century, many historians and novelists increasingly came to see Powell, not King, as the founder of the USGS—a role they linked to Powell's guise as the unheeded prophet of the conservation (now often "preservation") movement. The inversion that stressed King's "failures"—his search for wealth and his personal eccentricities—persisted even after some historians rediscovered portions of King's vital role during 1867–1881 in advancing geology in the public service. In 1958 and 1988, Thurman Wilkins's biography analyzed King's successes and failures, and placed them in more accurate perspective within politics and science in America's Gilded Age.

King, the paleontologist "George Strong" of Henry Adams's *Esther* (1884), appeared as himself in four subsequent literary works. Wallace Stegner based a scene in his novel *Angle of Repose* (1971) on King's concern for integrity in the USGS. Gore Vidal's novel *Empire* (1987) and Patricia O'Toole's evaluation of the Adams-Hay-King friendship in her *Five of Hearts* (1990) emphasized the deceptions they saw in King's secret miscegenous marriage in 1888. In Sarah Conroy's *Refinements of Love: A Novel About Clover and Henry Adams* (1993), the three men murder Marian Adams to protect their sexual bond. Wilkins's revised and expanded biography (1988) remains the most impartial and meaningful evaluation of King and his career.

King's surviving papers are scattered. The largest collections are in Record Group 57 (Geological Survey) and 77 (Office of the Chief of Engineers) at the National Archives and Records Administration, and the Clarence King portion of the James Duncan Hague Papers at the Huntington Library in San Marino, California. Wilkins's biography cites all of the manuscript sources he used in his analysis.

BIBLIOGRAPHY

Aldrich, Michele L. "King, Clarence Rivers." *Dictionary of Scientific Biography.* Edited by Charles C. Gillispie. New York: Scribners, 1973, 7:370–371.

Bartlett, Richard A. *Great Surveys of the American West.* Norman: University of Oklahoma Press, 1962.

———. "Clarence King." *The Reader's Encyclopedia of the American West.* Edited by Howard R. Lamar. New York: Crowell, 1977, p. 622.

Crosby, Harry H. "So Deep a Trail: A Biography of Clarence King." Ph.D. diss., Stanford University, 1953.

Dupree, A. Hunter. *Science in the Federal Government: A History of Policies and Activities to 1940.* Cambridge, MA: Harvard University Press, 1957.

Goetzmann, William H. *Exploration and Empire: The Explorer and the Scientist in the Winning of the American West.* New York: Knopf, 1966.

Hague, James D., ed. *Clarence King Memoirs: The Helmet of Mambrino.* New York: Putnam/Century Association, 1904.

Manning, Thomas G. *Government in Science: The U.S. Geological Survey 1867–1894.* Lexington: University of Kentucky Press, 1967.

Nelson, Clifford M. "Toward a Reliable Geologic Map of the United States, 1803–1893." In *Surveying the Record: North American Scientific Exploration to 1930,* edited by Edward C. Carter II. *Memoirs of the American Philosophical Society* 231 (1999):54–71.

Nelson, Clifford M., and Mary C. Rabbitt. "The Role of Clarence King in the Advancement of Geology in the Public Service, 1867–1881." In *Frontiers of Geological Exploration of Western North America,* edited by Alan E. Leviton et al. San Francisco: American Association for the Advancement of Science, Pacific Division, 1982, pp. 19–35.

Rabbit, Mary C. *Minerals, Lands, and Geology for the Common Defense and General Welfare: Volume I, Before 1879; Volume 2, 1879–1904.* Washington, DC: Government Printing Office, 1979–1980.

Smith, Michael L. *Pacific Visions: California Scientists and the Environment 1850–1915.* New Haven: Yale University Press, 1987.

Wilkins, Thurman, with the assistance of Caroline L. Hinkley. *Clarence King: A Biography.* 1958. Rev. and enlarged ed. Albuquerque: University of New Mexico Press, 1988.

Wilkins, Thurman. "King, Clarence Rivers." *American National Biography,* edited by John A. Garraty and Mark C. Carnes. New York: Oxford University Press, 1999, 12:691–693.

Clifford M. Nelson

SEE ALSO

Geological Survey, United States

K

Kirkwood, Daniel (1814–1895)

Educator and astronomer. Daniel Kirkwood's biography validated the hope, common in the early Republic, that humble origins posed no obstacle to those who were willing to work hard to succeed. Born in Hartford County, Maryland, Kirkwood attended his local county school. Upon graduation, he took a post teaching in a small school in Hopewell, Pennsylvania, where, when one of his students requested that they study algebra, they worked through a textbook together. Fascinated by the subject, he entered York County Academy. He was soon appointed instructor of mathematics there. Prior to turning thirty, he accepted the post of principal of Lancaster High School. Two years later, he married Sarah A. McNair. He became principal of Pottsville Academy in 1849, but was soon on the move again, this time to accept a post as professor of mathematics at Delaware College, where, after 1854, he served as president. Kirkwood's interests lay in teaching and research, so he accepted the chairmanship of the department of mathematics at Indiana University in 1857. Except for a two year interval, 1865–1867, he remained at Indiana until 1886. He then moved to California, and at the age of seventy-seven, became a nonresident lecturer on astronomy at Stanford. He died in California.

While at York County Academy, Kirkwood became fascinated with the prospect of finding relationships between the rotational periods of the planets, which, he felt, would indicate that both the orbital and rotational movements had been impressed by the same impulse. He spent countless hours calculating and comparing masses, volumes, densities, and distances of the planets in a trial-and-error effort to determine any conceivable correlation. In 1846, he ran across the nebular hypothesis, which stated that the solar system evolved from a rotating mass of dust and gas. He immediately revised his search for relationships of the planets. He imagined that the planets had developed from rings of matter left behind as the sun coalesced, and that each planet had accreted from a ring or "sphere of attraction." Kirkwood found that the diameter of this ring bore a relationship to the number of rotations of the planet during the course of a year. He approached Sears Cook Walker, at the United States Coast Survey, concerning his discovery. Walker realized the significance of Kirkwood's work, and made it public at the 1849 meeting of the American Association for the Advancement of Science. Kirkwood's discovery soon became "Kirkwood's Analogy," which thrust him into the public spotlight as a scientific folk hero.

The scientific impact was to provide a firmer foundation for the nebular hypothesis, the credibility of which had remained problematic for a number of astronomers. Lord Rosse, for example, believed that the nebulae were composed of unresolved stars. The nebular hypothesis, however, required the existence of gaseous nebulae. Kirkwood's analogy appeared to bolster the case for Laplace's hypothesis. William Huggins resolved the issue fifteen years later when his spectral analysis of nebulae revealed some to be distended spheres of gas. Ironically, Kirkwood later came to doubt the validity of the nebular hypothesis, because he realized that the planets would have to have been formed cold, whereas the nebular hypothesis posited a hot origin of the planets.

Kirkwood's investigations fit into the general thrust of positional astronomy of the nineteenth century. Although astrophysics soon predominated research programs, Kirkwood continued to pursue positional topics. He remained focused on how the solar system evolved, and in particular, how the lesser members of the solar system—asteroids, comets, and meteoric bodies—fit into the explanation of the development of the system. As he turned his attention to the asteroids, he realized that they were not evenly distributed, but that "gaps," similar to the Cassini division in Saturn's rings, separated them into groups. These "chasms" became known as the "Kirkwood Gaps." He was the first to suggest that the passage of the earth through the orbit of comets produced meteor showers. His name was attached to asteroid number 1578.

BIBLIOGRAPHY

Marsden, Brian G. "Kirkwood, Daniel." *Dictionary of Scientific Biography.* Edited by Charles C. Gillispie. New York: Scribners, 1973:384–387.

Numbers, Ronald L. *Creation by Natural Law: Laplace's Nebular Hypothesis in American Thought.* Seattle: University of Washington Press, 1977.

Philip S. Shoemaker

Kitt Peak National Observatory

The Kitt Peak National Observatory (KPNO) near Tucson, Arizona, was the first federally funded astronomical observatory open to use by any qualified researcher. Developed by The Association of Universities for Research in Astronomy, Inc. (AURA) under contract to the National Science Foundation (NSF) 1958–1960, Kitt Peak maintains a suite of telescopes and support facilities as part of the National Optical Astronomical Observatories.

The creation of KPNO reflected federal government patronage as a new force in astronomy after the World War II. While private foundations and individual organizations had developed the larger astronomical observatories, and the United States Naval Observatory was dedicated to specific research programs, many astronomers at smaller institutions had no access to large telescopes or expensive instrumentation. After several proposals from individuals for cooperation in astronomical facilities, the NSF became interested in developing a new national observatory but did not have legal authority to operate it. During 1955–1956, NSF worked with many of the leaders of American astronomy to create a new organization to receive the NSF funding, and to develop and manage the observatory. In 1957, representatives of seven universities worked with NSF and the National Science Board to create AURA, which in March 1958 selected Kitt Peak, near Tucson, as the site for a new national observatory.

At Kitt Peak the initial 0.9-meter telescope went into operation in 1960, followed by a 2.1-meter (1964), and a 4-meter (1973). In addition, a variety of other optical telescopes, a large solar tower telescope, associated focal instrumentation, shops and support facilities, and other resources were provided on the mountain or in Tucson. Kitt Peak and other national observatories allowed astronomers access to instruments and facilities far beyond their individual means and thus served as a significant stimulant and facilitator of American astronomical research.

BIBLIOGRAPHY

Edmonson, Frank K. "Observatory at Kitt Peak." *Journal for the History of Astronomy* 15 (1984): 139–41.

———. "AURA and KPNO: The Evolution of an Idea, 1952–58." *Journal for the History of Astronomy* 22 (1991): 69–86.

———. *AURA and Its U.S. National Observatories.* New York: Cambridge University Press, 1997.

Goldberg, Leo. "The Founding of Kitt Peak." *Sky and Telescope* 65 (March 1983): 228–230.

Kloeppel, James E. *Realm of the Long Eyes: A Brief History of Kitt Peak National Observatory.* San Diego: Univelt, 1983.

Needell, Allan A. "The Carnegie Institution of Washington and Radio Astronomy: Prelude to an American National Observatory." *Journal for the History of Astronomy* 22 (February 1991): 55–67.

Joseph N. Tatarewicz

SEE ALSO
Observatory

Köhler, Wolfgang (1887–1967)

German-American experimental psychologist. Born of German parents in Reval, Estonia, Köhler grew up in Germany, and attended the universities of Tübingen (1905–1906), Bonn (1906–1907), and Berlin (1907–1909, Ph.D., 1909). While a Privatdozent at the Akademie für Socialwissenschaft, Frankfurt am Main (1909–1913), he met Max Wertheimer, who introduced him and Kurt Koffka to the concepts (and experimental results) that the three men soon developed into Gestalt psychology. In 1913, Köhler became director of the Prussian Academy of Sciences' Anthropoid Research Station on Tenerife, in the Canary Islands. The outbreak of World War I confined him to the island, where he continued to experiment with chimpanzees through 1920. Returning to Berlin in that year, Köhler served briefly as professor at the University of Göttingen (1921–1922), and then became professor and director of the Psychological Institute at the University of Berlin, where he stayed through 1935. He first visited the United States (as Powell Lecturer and Visiting Professor at Clark University) in 1925–1926 and later held visiting positions at the University of Chicago and at Harvard University (as William James Lecturer, 1934–1935). During his last years in Germany, he actively opposed Nazi educational policies and migrated to America in 1935 to become professor of psychology (later research professor of philosophy and psychology) at Swarthmore College. Köhler was elected to the National Academy of Science in 1947 (almost immediately after becoming a United States citizen) and retired from Swarthmore in 1958. He died on Enfield, New Hampshire, near Dartmouth College, where he worked after his 1958 retirement from Swarthmore.

Köhler and other Gestalt psychologists challenged earlier psychological theories that emphasized atomistic "sensory elements" and argued instead that humans perceive wholes, or configurations, or Gestalten in a "perceptual field." On Tenerife, Köhler developed the view that chimpanzees (and humans) learn by recognizing

K

the interrelationships of objects in—that is, by gaining "insight" into—their perceptual fields. His first reports of his work with apes attracted much attention in America, were soon translated into English, and (when coupled with general American interest in Gestalt psychology) led to his visiting appointments. In the early 1920s, however, Köhler began addressing theoretical implications of his work and developed hypotheses about "physical Gestalten" and the actions of the brain. At the same time, Köhler and his colleagues began campaigning for the primacy of their perspective over all other psychologies, and by the late 1920s many American psychologists began to decry (what they called) the Gestalt movement, even as they still respected the Gestalt psychologists' experimental work and overall approach to their science. This negative response influenced the course of Köhler's career in America, and he never achieved the Harvard professorship he sought, and that many of his followers believed he deserved. The earliest historical analyses of his work emphasized the unquestioned richness of Köhler's psychological ideas and thus argued (or at least implied) that American psychologists slighted him and his work. But this attitude well illustrates the aspects of his career that others depreciated, and later historians have emphasized their importance, and that of the interplay of the personalities involved.

BIBLIOGRAPHY

Asch, Solomon E. "Wolfgang Köhler: 1887–1967." *American Journal of Psychology* 81 (1968): 110–119.

Ash, Mitchell G. "Gestalt Psychology: Origins in Germany and Reception in the United States." In *Points of View in the Modern History of Psychology,* edited by Claude Buxton. San Diego: Academic Press, 1985, pp. 295–344.

———. *Gestalt Psychology in German Culture, 1890–1967: Holism and the Quest for Objectivity.* New York: Cambridge University Press, 1995.

Henle, Mary. "Wolfgang Köhler (1887–1967)." *Yearbook of the American Philosophical Society* 1968: 139–145.

———. "One Man Against the Nazis: Wolfgang Köhler." *American Psychologist* 33 (1978): 939–944.

———, ed. *The Selected Papers of Wolfgang Köhler.* New York: Liveright, 1971.

Köhler, Wolfgang. *Intelligenzprüfungen an Anthropoiden.* Berlin: Königlich Preussischen Akademie der Wissenschaft, 1917.

———. *Die physischen Gestalten in Ruhe und im stationaren Zustand: Eine naturphilosophsche Unterschung.* Braunschweig: Vieweg, 1920.

———. *Intelligenzprüfungen an Menschenaffen.* Berlin: Springer, 1921.

———. "Zur Psychologie des Schimpansen." *Psychologische Forschung* 1 (1921): 2–46.

———. *The Mentality of Apes.* Translated by Ella Winter. New York: Harcourt Brace, 1925.

———. "Intelligence of Apes." In *Psychologies of 1925,* edited by Carl Murchison. Worcester: Clark University Press, 1926, pp.145–161.

Mandler, Jean Matter, and George Mandler. "The Diaspora of Experimental Psychology: The Gestaltists and Others." In *The Intellectual Migration: Europe and America, 1930–1960,* edited by Donald Fleming and Bernard Bailyn. Cambridge, MA: Harvard University Press, 1969, pp. 371–419.

Sokal, Michael M. "The Gestalt Psychologists in Behaviorist America." *American Historical Review* 89 (1984): 1240–1263.

Michael M. Sokal

L

Ladd-Franklin, Christine (1847–1930)

Psychologist and logician. Born in Windsor, Connecticut, Ladd-Franklin graduated from Welshing Academy in Wilbraham, Massachusetts, in 1865 and from Vassar College in 1869. From 1878 to 1882, she studied mathematics and logic at Johns Hopkins University completing all the requirements for the Ph.D. Because Johns Hopkins was reluctant to award degrees to women at that time, she did not receive the degree; it was eventually awarded when Hopkins celebrated its fiftieth anniversary in 1926. In 1882, Ladd-Franklin, then Ladd, married one of her Hopkins mathematics instructors, Fabian Franklin. The couple had two children, a son who died shortly after birth, and a daughter. Ladd-Franklin was affiliated with Johns Hopkins from 1904–1909 where she taught courses in logic and psychology. After the family relocated to New York City in 1909, where Fabian Franklin had accepted a new position, Ladd-Franklin had an appointment at Columbia University from 1914 to 1929 also teaching courses in logic and psychology.

The dissertation which Ladd-Franklin completed at Johns Hopkins is credited with having made "contributions to the relatively new field of symbolic logic" (Green and Laduke, p. 121) and was published in 1883 as part of a collection of works by students of her advisor, Charles Sanders Peirce. Although she would retain a lifelong interest in logic, by 1887 Ladd-Franklin was producing work in psychology on the topic of vision, the focus of most of her subsequent research and writing.

In 1892, after spending a year in Germany working on color vision, first in G.E. Müller's laboratory in Göttingen and then in Hermann von Helmholtz's laboratory in Berlin, Ladd-Franklin announced her own theory of color-sensation. Building on the two major rival color-vision theories of the day, the Young-Helmholtz and the Hering theory, Ladd-Franklin argued that they were not, in fact, contradictory; rather, each pertained to a different stage of the visual process. What she viewed as her original theoretical contribution was the idea of the evolutionary development of color sensation from achromatic (black and white) to dichromatic (yellow and blue) to tetrachromatic (yellow, blue, red, and green).

Promoting her color theory in lecture series, at scientific meetings, and in numerous publications was to occupy Ladd-Franklin for the remainder of her life. This effort culminated in 1929 when a collection of her articles on vision published between 1892 and 1926 was reprinted as a book, *Colour and Colour Theories*. During her lifetime Ladd-Franklin's theory gained international recognition and came to rank in importance directly behind the Young-Helmholtz and Hering theories (Cadwallader and Cadwallader, p. 223). Current texts discussing the history of color theories rarely mention it, however (Green, p. 123).

The Rare Book and Manuscript Library of Columbia University contains the papers of Christine Ladd-Franklin and Fabian Franklin. The collection is extensive but largely unprocessed and consists of ninety-eight boxes estimated to contain more than 7,000 items, including correspondence, publications, and other documents. To date, no book-length biography based on this collection has been published.

L

BIBLIOGRAPHY

Cadwallader, Thomas C., and Joyce V. Cadwallader. "Christine Ladd-Franklin (1847–1930)." In *Women in Psychology: A Bio-Bibliographic Sourcebook,* edited by Agnes N. O'Connell and Nancy Felipe Russo. New York: Greenwood Press, 1990, pp. 220–229.

Furumoto, Laurel. "Joining Separate Spheres—Christine Ladd-Franklin, Woman-Scientist (1847–1930)." *American Psychologist* 47 (1992): 175–182.

———. "Christine Ladd-Franklin's Color Theory: Strategy for Claiming Scientific Authority?" *Annals of the New York Academy of Sciences* 727 (1994): 91–100.

Green, Judy. "Christine Ladd-Franklin (1847–1930)." In *Women of Mathematics: A Biobibliographic Sourcebook,* edited by Louise S. Grinstein and Paul J. Campbell. New York: Greenwood Press, 1987, pp. 121–128.

Green, Judy, and Jeanne Laduke. "Contributors to American Mathematics: An Overview and Selection." In *Women of Science: Righting the Record,* edited by G. Kass-Simon and Patricia Farnes. Bloomington: Indiana University Press, 1990, pp. 117–146.

Ladd-Franklin, Christine. *Colour and Colour Theories.* New York: Harcourt, Brace, 1929.

Laurel Furumoto

Langley Research Center

America's oldest civilian aeronautics laboratory, established in Hampton, Virginia, in the spring of 1917. At its foundation, the installation was known as the Langley Memorial Aeronautical Laboratory, named in honor of Samuel Pierpont Langley, aeronautical pioneer and head of the Smithsonian Institution. From 1917 to 1958, the laboratory belonged to the National Advisory Committee for Aeronautics (NACA). In 1958, it was transferred to the new National Aeronautics and Space Administration (NASA), and was renamed NASA Langley Research Center.

Langley Research Center has played an influential role in the development of the flying machine from a largely useless gadget into one of the most vital and pervasive technologies of the modern world. Although some flight-testing began at NACA Langley in 1919, the laboratory did not begin routine operations until 1920 when the first wind tunnel came on line. By the end of the 1920s, with its ingeniously designed Variable-Density Tunnel, Propeller Research Tunnel, and Full-Scale Tunnel, which outperformed any other single collection of facilities anywhere in the world, NACA Langley was generally acknowledged to be the world's premier aeronautical research establishment.

Thanks to the reliable data resulting from the intelligent use of Langley's unique complex of experimental equipment, American aircraft began to dominate the world's airways. During World War II, Langley tested virtually all types of Allied aircraft that saw combat.

After the war, NACA researchers turned their attention to the high-speed frontier and solved many of the basic problems blocking the flight of aircraft beyond the mythical "sound barrier" into supersonic speeds. They played essential roles in the development of several experimental high-speed research airplanes including Bell's X-1, the first plane to fly faster than the speed of sound, and North American's X-15, the first winged aircraft to fly into space.

In the early 1960s, Langley helped give birth to the space age. Project Mercury, the nation's inaugural man-in-space program, was conceived and managed initially from Langley. Spearheading this effort was the center's Space Task Group, a special force of NASA employees that later expanded and moved on to become the Manned Spacecraft Center (now Johnson Space Center) in Houston. NASA Langley went on to make several essential contributions to the Mercury, Gemini, Apollo, and Skylab manned programs, including proving the feasibility of lunar-orbit rendezvous, a concept essential to the manned moon landings.

Early unmanned space projects involving considerable creative effort by NASA Langley researchers included the *Echo, Explorer,* and *PAGEOS* satellites, all of which gave outstanding service as instruments for scientific research and global communications. A solid-fuel rocket developed at the center, the Scout, first launched in July 1960, provided NASA with its lowest-cost, multipurpose booster.

In the wake of Apollo came Viking. NASA Langley helped to send two orbiters and two landers in the mid-1970s to the planet Mars. Although the probes did not result in any definitive answer to the question of whether life exists (or has ever existed) on Mars, Viking nonetheless provided a wealth of valuable scientific information.

In response to a growing concern in the late 1960s for protection of the global environment, Langley researchers began to develop effective means by which to detect from space the presence of dangerous pollutants on earth. This effort in environmental space science quickly became a major research thrust at the center. In the 1980s, this undertaking was part of what former NASA astronaut Sally Ride called "Mission to Planet Earth."

Langley researchers had thought about "space planes" since the early 1950s. They had pioneered the concept of the boost glider and provided basic concepts for the development of the X-15. So it was natural for them to become deeply involved in the development and testing of NASA's Space Shuttle. Even before it could be test flown in 1977 (its first orbital flight took place in 1981), the Shuttle had to be put through thousands of hours of wind-tunnel testing and other rigorous experiments. Much of this was done at Langley. Langley was also responsible for optimizing the design of the Shuttle's thermal protection system.

Visions of space stations orbiting the earth had captured the imaginations of many Langley researchers as well. Long before plans for the International Space Station got under way in the 1990s, NASA scientists and engineers at the center had understood the advantages of a manned laboratory in space for scientific experiments, for communications, for astronomical observations, for manufacturing, and as a relay base for lunar and planetary missions. In the 1960s, they began to explore the problems of designing such a facility and operating it in earth orbit.

Although its achievements in aeronautics were sometimes overlooked in favor of the glories and wonders of spaceflight, NASA Langley not only maintained its historic position as a world leader in aeronautical research, it actually built and improved upon it. Langley has participated in too many significant aeronautical programs in support of too many civilian and military development programs to describe them all in detail. The following list of selected programs illustrate the center's wide-ranging aeronautical studies: hypersonics; lifting bodies; supersonic cruise aircraft research; quiet engine research; vertical/short takeoff and landing (V/STOL) research; aircraft energy efficiency; advanced turboprop; composite materials; crash dynamics; forward swept wing; automated pilot advisory system; stall spin research; advanced controls; rotor inflow research.

BIBLIOGRAPHY

Bilstein, Roger E. *Orders of Magnitude: A History of NACA and NASA, 1915–1990.* Washington, DC: Government Printing Office, 1989.

Hansen, James R. *Engineer in Charge: A History of the Langley Aeronautical Laboratory, 1917–1958.* Washington, DC: Government Printing Office, 1987.

———. *Spaceflight Revolution: NASA Langley from Sputnik to Apollo.* Washington, DC: Government Printing Office, 1995.

James R. Hansen

SEE ALSO
National Advisory Committee for Aeronautics: National Aeronautics and Space Administration

Laser

A family of devices producing light that, like radio waves, is highly coherent, and hence fit for a wide range of technological applications.

Charles H. Townes, whose Columbia University group operated the world's first maser, the progenitor of the laser, in 1954, had worked on radar at Bell Telephone Laboratories from 1941 through 1945. After his war work, he became a pioneer in microwave molecular spectroscopy using war-surplus radar equipment. He was also attentive to the uses of molecular quantum transitions in electronics.

Townes moved to the Columbia University physics department in 1948. Here he became associated with the Columbia Radiation Laboratory, funded by the military and largely dedicated to pushing radar components to higher frequencies. He also became a consultant to the National Bureau of Standards' atomic clock program and chair of the Office of Naval Research's Advisory Committee on Millimeter-Wave Generation. This set of interpenetrating scientific and technological interests was the context within which, in the spring of 1951, Townes conceived the idea of using molecular emission, stimulated by ambient radiation, as a novel way of generating (and, as was later realized, amplifying) microwaves. Thus, the acronym MASER, for Microwave Amplification by Stimulated Emission of Radiation. (Soviet scientists N.G. Basov and A.M. Prokhorov independently worked out the theory of the laser.)

From fall 1957 through 1958, both Townes, in collaboration with Arthur L. Schawlow of Bell Telephone Laboratories, and Columbia University graduate student R. Gordon Gould, carried out theoretical studies to extend the maser principle to infrared and optical frequencies. Schawlow and Townes's work was by far the more influential. By 1959, nearly a dozen teams at American industrial and university laboratories had initiated experiments. Theodore H. Maiman succeeded first, in spring 1960, with a pulsed laser made of synthetic ruby. Ali Javan and his collaborators at Bell Laboratories operated the first continuous laser, using noble gases, that December.

These first functioning lasers triggered an explosion of research. Dozens of new lasers were invented, with

L

new working substances and new methods of energizing them, providing a gamut of frequencies and power outputs. Fragile laboratory devices were developed into reliable and long-lived components. Applications of all sorts were assayed, from eye surgery and welding to surveying and the separation of isotopes.

In the United States, military dollars funded more than half this research and development during the 1960s and 1970s. As a corollary, the first systems deployed in significant numbers were military ones, like laser range finders for battle tanks in the early 1970s.

The most talked-of application, high-volume optical communications, only became possible in the 1970s, with the development of low-loss optical fibers and substantial improvement of the semiconductor laser that had been invented in 1962. Experimental American optical communication links were first built in the mid-1970s; by the end of the 1980s, the nation's long-distance lines had been converted to optical fibers. By that time, too, coherent light had become a standard part of the engineers' armamentarium, and the laser had been folded into a new technology, "photonics," with worldwide sales of roughly $15–20 billion a year.

Recent scholarship has made American research on the laser and the maser a paradigm of the interpenetration of physics and the military in the decades after World War II.

BIBLIOGRAPHY

Bromberg, Joan Lisa. *The Laser in America, 1950–1970.* Cambridge, MA: MIT Press, 1991.

Forman, Paul. "Behind Quantum Electronics: National Security as Basis for Physical Research in the United States, 1940–1960." *Historical Studies in the Physical and Biological Sciences* 18, pt. 1 (1987): 149–229.

———. "Inventing the Maser in Postwar America." *Osiris,* 2d ser., 7 (1992): 238–267.

———. "Into Quantum Electronics: The Maser as Artifact of American Cold War Culture." In *National Military Establishments and the Advancement of Science and Technology: Studies in Twentieth Century History,* edited by Paul Forman and J.M. Sánchez-Ron. Dordrecht: Kluwer, 1996, pp. 261–326.

Seidel, Robert W. "From Glow to Flow: A History of Military Laser Research and Development." *Historical Studies in the Physical and Biological Sciences* 18, pt. 1 (1987): 111–147.

Sternberg, Ernest. *Photonic Technology and Industrial Policy: U.S. Responses to Technological Change.* Albany: State University of New York Press, 1992.

Joan Lisa Bromberg

Lashley, Karl Spencer (1890–1958)

Psychologist and neurophysiologist who spent his career searching for the neurological basis of learning and memory. Lashley received a Ph.D. in genetics at Johns Hopkins under Herbert Spencer Jennings in 1914, but by then had already decided that his interests lay in psychology. As a postdoctoral fellow at Hopkins he worked closely with John B. Watson, the founder of behaviorism, but never accepted Watson's dismissal of the mind. Instead, he believed that the principal task of psychology was to explain the brain mechanisms that underlay mental functions, including the most complex abstract thought processes. During his Hopkins years, Lashley also worked closely with the clinical psychologist Shepherd Ivory Franz. From Franz, Lashley learned both his technique of cortical ablation and his opposition to the doctrine of localization of mental functions in discrete areas of the brain.

Lashley's first teaching job was at the University of Minnesota, where he continued his brain ablation work. There, he did the series of experiments on rats which made his reputation as a meticulous researcher. Lashley trained the rats to perform a variety of tasks, such as threading a maze, removed a portion of their brains, and then tested their ability to relearn the tasks. He found that reduction in efficiency of learning was proportional only to the amount of cortical tissue removed, and not to the locus of the lesion. He codified these results in two principles which have become synonymous with his name, equipotentiality and mass action. These principles stated that the whole brain was responsible for all its functions, there was no localization of function in discrete brain areas, and that as long as a critical amount of cortex was present, functions were normal.

From 1926 to 1929, Lashley was a research psychologist with the Behavior Research Fund at the Institute for Juvenile Research in Chicago. In 1929, he published his sole book, *Brain Mechanisms and Intelligence,* which described his brain ablation work.

From 1929 to 1935, he was professor of psychology at the University of Chicago, where he worked closely with the neurologist and psychobiologist C. Judson Herrick. At this time, he also began experiments on vision in rats, testing their ability to discriminate between different patterns. He concluded that the visual cortex showed equipotentiality for vision, just as did the cortex for learning.

In 1935, Lashley accepted an appointment as professor of psychology at Harvard University, where he encouraged the work of the Gestalt neurologist Kurt

Goldstein. In 1942, he also became director of the Yerkes Laboratories of Primate Biology in Orange Park, Florida, until his retirement in 1955.

Lashley was associated throughout his career with three trends central to American psychology in the first half of the twentieth century: behaviorism, psychobiology, and the Gestalt school. He was not, however, an ardent follower of any one of these movements, preferring to demonstrate how their theoretical positions conflicted with what he thought were the facts of brain function. He firmly believed that intelligence could ultimately only be explained by the biology of the brain, and not by analogies to machines, such as telephone switchboards or computers. He was vehemently opposed to the attempts of the psychologist Clark Hull to develop a machine that would display genuine intelligence. A determined hereditarian, Lashley rejected the behaviorists' emphasis on the power of the environment to shape behavior. His unitary conception of brain function made him sympathize with the notion of intelligence as a single, measurable factor, a notion made popular by some proponents of the mental-testing movement, in particular Charles Spearman.

Lashley himself said that his contribution to science was entirely negative, in that all he did was to destroy the theories of others with a barrage of facts, and that he had no theoretical presuppositions of his own. Recent historical work has begun to question his long-standing self-assessment, examining Lashley's science in its cultural, political, and institutional contexts.

BIBLIOGRAPHY

Beach, Frank A., Donald O. Hebb, Clifford T. Morgan, and Henry W. Nissen, eds. *The Neuropsychology of Lashley: Selected Papers of K. S. Lashley.* New York: McGraw Hill, 1960.

Bruce, Darryl. "Lashley's Shift from Bacteriology to Neuropsychology, 1910–1917, and the Influence of Jennings, Watson and Franz." *Journal of the History of the Behavioral Sciences* 22 (1986): 27–44.

———. "Integrations of Lashley." In *Portraits of Pioneers in Psychology,* edited by Gregory A. Kimble, Michael Wertheimer, and Charlotte White. Hillsdale, NJ: L. Erlbaum Associates, 1991, pp. 307–323.

Lashley, Karl S. *Brain Mechanisms and Intelligence: Quantitative Study of Injuries to the Brain.* Chicago: University of Chicago Press, 1929.

Weidman, Nadine M. *Constructing Scientific Psychology: Karl Lashley's Mind-Brain Debates.* New York: Cambridge University Press, 1999.

Nadine Weidman

Laura Spelman Rockefeller Memorial

A philanthropic foundation influential in the development of social science. Created by John D. Rockefeller in 1918 to promote women's and children's welfare, the memorial was reoriented in 1922 toward the advancement of basic research in academic social science. Under the direction of Beardlsey Ruml and his deputy, Lawrence K. Frank, programs were devised in social science and "social technology" (social work and public administration), child study and parent education, and interracial relations; the officers favored interdisciplinary research focused on concrete social problems. In a general reorganization of Rockefeller boards in 1929, the memorial was discontinued and its programs absorbed.

The total of almost $50 million appropriated since 1923 was strategically given; concentrating on a cluster of elite institutions and utilizing the intermediary services of the Social Science Research Council, the memorial significantly boosted the movement in American social science after World War I toward empirical and cooperative research.

The memorial has been the subject of debate over whether foundation patronage of social science reflected class interests. Whatever its merits, this and more topically focused research in memorial records at the Rockefeller Archive Center (Sleepy Hollow, N.Y.) has greatly enlarged understanding of the entrepreneurial role of activist foundation officers. Broad recognition of the memorial's pioneering and exemplary roles in the development of American science, however, is hampered by the lingering mutual exclusiveness of natural and social science history.

BIBLIOGRAPHY

Ahmad, Salma. "American Foundations and the Development of the Social Sciences Between the Wars: Comment on the Debate Between Martin Bulmer and Donald Fisher." *Sociology* 25 (1991): 511–520.

Alchon, Guy. *The Invisible Hand of Planning: Capitalism, Social Science, and the State in the 1920s.* Princeton: Princeton University Press, 1985.

Bulmer, Martin. *The Chicago School of Sociology: Institutionalization, Diversity, and the Rise of Sociological Research.* Chicago: University of Chicago Press, 1984.

———, and Joan Bulmer. "Philanthropy and Social Science in the 1920s: Beardsley Ruml and the Laura Spelman Rockefeller Memorial, 1922–1929." *Minerva* 19 (1981): 347–407.

Cravens, Hamilton. "Child-Saving in the Age of Professionalism, 1915–1930." In *American Childhood: A Research*

L

Guide and Historical Handbook, edited by Joseph M. Hawes and N. Ray Hiner. Westport, CT: Greenwood, 1985.

———. Before Head Start: America's Children and the Iowa Station. Chapel Hill: University of North Carolina Press, 1993.

Cross, Stephen J. "Designs for Living: Lawrence K. Frank and the Progressive Legacy in American Social Science." Ph.D. diss., Johns Hopkins University, 1994.

Fisher, Donald. Fundamental Development of the Social Sciences: Rockefeller Philanthropy and the United States Social Science Research Council. Ann Arbor: University of Michigan Press, 1993.

Fosdick, Raymond B. The Story of the Rockefeller Foundation. New York: Harper & Brothers, 1952.

Laura Spelman Rockefeller Memorial. Annual Reports and Final Report. New York: Laura Spelman Rockefeller Memorial, 1923–1933.

Schlossman, Steven L. "Philanthropy and the Gospel of Child Development." History of Education Quarterly 21 (1981): 275–299.

Stanfield, John H. Philanthropy and Jim Crow in American Social Science. Westport, CT: Greenwood, 1985.

Stephen J. Cross

Lazzaroni

A mid-nineteenth-century informal group of research scientists and science administrators who shared a common agenda for American science. Through control of major scientific institutions and the encouragement of public support for research, its members hoped to improve the quality and quantity of American scientific research. Members encouraged professionalization and specialization. They looked toward European models. The leader of the Lazzaroni was Alexander Dallas Bache, director of the United States Coast Survey. Other significant members were Joseph Henry, Louis Agassiz, and Benjamin Peirce.

Historians have debated whether the Lazzaroni constituted a clique attempting to implement an explicit program or a social grouping of scientists who shared interests, values, and ultimate objectives. Underlying this debate are disagreements over what constitutes evidence for the existence of a group program and the weight to be given to the sharp disagreements the members of the Lazzaroni had on specific strategies and tactics. Central to understanding the Lazzaroni is understanding the agenda of Bache.

BIBLIOGRAPHY

Beach, Mark. "Was There a Scientific Lazzaroni?" In Nineteenth-Century American Science: A Reappraisal, edited by George H. Daniels. Evanston: Northwestern University Press, 1972, pp. 115–132.

Bruce, Robert V. The Launching of Modern American Science, 1846–1876. New York: Knopf, 1987.

James, Mary Ann. Elites in Conflict: The Antebellum Clash over the Dudley Observatory. New Brunswick: Rutgers University Press, 1987.

Miller, Lillian, et al. The Lazzaroni: Science and Scientists in Mid-nineteenth Century America. Washington, DC: Smithsonian Institution Press, 1972.

Slotten, Hugh R. Patronage, Practice, and the Culture of American Science: Alexander Dallas Bache and the U. S. Coast Survey. New York: Cambridge University Press, 1994.

Marc Rothenberg

SEE ALSO
Bache, Alexander Dallas

LeConte, John Lawrence (1825–1883)

Entomologist, specializing in the Coleoptera (beetles) of North America. The son of John Eatton and Mary Anne H. (Lawrence) LeConte, John Lawrence was raised and taught by his father, the mother having died shortly after his birth. They lived in New York until 1852 when they moved to Philadelphia, at that time the center of entomological activity in America. The LeContes were wealthy Huguenots with scientific interests. John Eatton LeConte, an army engineer and naturalist, published on American Coleoptera and Lepidoptera. Joseph LeConte, geologist, and John LeConte, physicist, were first cousins of John Lawrence.

LeConte graduated from Mount St. Mary's College, Maryland (1842), and received an M.D. from the New York College of Physicians and Surgeons (1846). Independent wealth allowed him to devote his time to entomology, although he served as army surgeon and medical inspector (1861–1866) and as chief inspector for the United States Mint in Philadelphia (1878–1883). He lived in Europe from 1869 to 1872.

LeConte's most important systematic works were the "Classification of the Coleoptera of North America" (1861–1862; 1873), "The *Rhynchophora* of America, North of Mexico" (1876), and the "Classification of the Coleoptera of North America" (1883). The latter two were written with his student and coworker George H. Horn. Their revisions established groups according to more natural criteria, confirming or modifying almost every previously named species. LeConte named 4,739 species, nearly half of the North America Coleoptera then known to science. He edited Friedrich Ernst Melsheimer's catalogue of Coleoptera (1853) and the writings of Thomas Say (1859). He also authored the first study of faunal geographical distribution of the American West, and wrote on geology, mineralogy, and ethnology.

The LeConte collection, enriched through LeConte's collecting explorations in the West, constituted the standard reference for North American Coleoptera. It was deposited in the Museum of Comparative Zoology.

LeConte was the first president of the American Entomological Society (1859) and of the Entomological Club of the American Association for the Advancement of Science (1875). In 1874, he was president of the American Association for the Advancement of Science. He was active in the reform of federal science, particularly in the Department of Agriculture.

At a time when Americans were struggling to establish their science within national and international contexts, LeConte brought order to the complex field of North American beetles and won acceptance for his systematic revisions. He was regarded as America's leading entomologist.

BIBLIOGRAPHY

Haldeman, S.S., and John L. LeConte, eds. "Catalogue of the Described *Coleoptera* of the U.S. by Frederick E. Melsheimer, M.D." *Smithsonian Miscellaneous Collections* 15 (1853): 16–174.

Henshaw, Samuel. "Index to the Coleoptera Described by J.L. LeConte, M.D." *Transactions of the American Entomological Society* 9 (1881–1882): 197–272.

———. "Bibliography of the Writings of John L. LeConte." *Bulletin of the Brooklyn Entomological Society* 6 (1883): iii–ix.

LeConte, John L. "Classification of the Coleoptera of North America, Part 1." *Smithsonian Miscellaneous Collections* 3 (1862): 1–286.

———. "Classification of the Coleoptera of North America, Part 2." *Smithsonian Miscellaneous Collections* 11 (1873): 179–348.

———. ed. *The Complete Writings of Thomas Say on the Entomology of North America.* New York: Bailiere Brothers, 1859.

LeConte, John L., with George H. Horn. "Classification of the Coleoptera of North America." *Smithsonian Miscellaneous Collections* 26 (1883): i–xxxviii, 1–567.

LeConte, John L., assisted by George H. Horn. "The *Rhynchophora* of America, North of Mexico." *Proceedings of the American Philosophical Society* 15 (1876): iii–xvi, 1–455.

Mallis, Arnold. *American Entomologists.* New Brunswick, Rutgers University Press, 1971, pp. 242–248.

Riley, Charles Valentine. "Tribute to the Memory of John Lawrence LeConte." *Psyche* 4 (November–December 1883): 107–110.

Scudder, Samuel H. "A Biographical Sketch of Dr. John Lawrence LeConte." *Transactions of the American Entomological Society* 11 (1884): i–xxvii.

Sorensen, W. Conner. *Brethren of the Net: American Entomology, 1840–1880.* Tuscaloosa: University of Alabama Press, 1995.

W. Conner Sorensen

LeConte, Joseph (1823–1901)

Professor of natural history, geology, and physiology and author of numerous publications on geology and the theory of evolution. LeConte was born and reared in Liberty County, Georgia, on a large cotton and rice plantation owned by his father, Louis LeConte, an able naturalist. In 1838, he enrolled as a student at the University of Georgia, from which he received the A.B. degree in 1841. Two years later, he moved to New York and enrolled in the College of Physicians and Surgeons, from which he graduated with the M.D. degree in 1845. From 1848 until 1850, LeConte practiced medicine in Macon, Georgia, but he did not enjoy his work as a physician. He decided to give up his practice in order to study with Louis Agassiz in the newly formed Lawrence Scientific School of Harvard University.

In 1851, LeConte completed his work with Agassiz, returned to Georgia, and accepted the professorship of natural history and chemistry at Oglethorpe College. One year later, he was appointed to the same position at the University of Georgia, where he remained until a dispute with the president of that institution led to the termination of his appointment in December 1856. Soon thereafter, LeConte joined the faculty of South Carolina College (later, the University of South Carolina). When the southern states decided to secede from the Union in 1861, LeConte, who had inherited a large plantation and sixty slaves from his father's estate, opted to support the movement. During the Civil War, he aided the Confederacy by serving first in an agency to produce medicines for the army and later in a bureau for the production of gunpowder. As federal forces advanced into South Carolina in February

L

1865, LeConte and his brother John, also a professor at South Carolina College, attempted to remove the equipment of the Confederacy's Nitre and Mining Bureau from Columbia, but Union soldiers captured their wagons, looted their personal valuables, and burned their manuscripts.

LeConte resumed his duties with the college when it reopened late in 1865, but, like his brother John, he was pessimistic about his future in the South. In 1869, following his brother, he accepted appointment to the faculty of the newly established University of California. During the next thirty-two years, LeConte endeared himself to the hundreds of students who enrolled for his courses in geology and in physiology. He also added to the list of twenty-three works he had published before 1869 another 170 articles, and seven books. His autobiography was published soon after his death, and the journal of his experiences during the Civil War was published in 1937.

The most successful of LeConte's books were *Sight: An Exposition of the Principles of Monocular and Binocular Vision* (1881), *Elements of Geology* (1877), and *Evolution and Its Relation to Religious Thought* (1888). The work of LeConte on the physiology of vision was the first of its kind published in America, and his textbook on geology was widely used in classrooms throughout the nation for four decades. By 1873, LeConte had become a proponent of the Neo-Lamarckian theory of evolution and a dedicated advocate of the reconciliation of the theory with Christian beliefs, a view that he articulated in his book on the subject and in dozens of articles and addresses. He was elected to membership in the National Academy of Sciences in 1875, and he served as the president of the American Association for the Advancement of Science in 1891 and as the president of the Geological Society of America in 1896. An ardent camper and student of the Sierra Mountains, LeConte was a friend of John Muir and a founding member of the Sierra Club. He died in Yosemite Valley during his eleventh trip there.

BIBLIOGRAPHY

LeConte, Emma. *When the World Ended: The Diary of Emma LeConte.* Edited by Earl Schenck Miers. New York: Oxford University Press, 1957. Reissued, with a foreword by Anne Firor Scott; Lincoln: University of Nebraska Press, 1987.

LeConte, Joseph. *The Autobiography of Joseph LeConte.* Edited by William D. Armes. New York: D. Appleton, 1903.

Stephens, Lester D. *Joseph LeConte, Gentle Prophet of Evolution.* Baton Rouge: Louisiana State University Press, 1982.

Lester D. Stephens

Leidy, Joseph (1823–1891)

Paleontologist, biologist, and anatomist. Born in Philadelphia, Leidy was educated in a private school. His stepmother encouraged him to become a physician, and he graduated from the University of Pennsylvania School of Medicine in 1844. He was immediately appointed prosector to William Edmonds Horner, Chair of Anatomy, with whom he had studied. He succeeded Horner as professor of anatomy in 1853 and remained in this position until his death. Leidy served as surgeon to the Satterlee Military Hospital during the Civil War, where his primary responsibility was for pathological studies. In addition to his medical positions, Leidy was professor of biology at the University of Pennsylvania and head of the Department of Biology from 1885. From 1871 to 1885, he was professor of biology at Swarthmore College. He was also an active member of the Academy of Natural Sciences of Philadelphia from 1845, serving as chairman of its Board of Curators from 1847 until his death and as president from 1881.

Leidy published several papers and books on human anatomy but his most important contribution to human medicine was his discovery in 1846 that the nematode *Trichinella spiralis* was found in pork. This parasite was known to be associated with the disease trichinosis in man, but the origin of the disease was unknown until Leidy's discovery.

In spite of his dedicated work in anatomy, Leidy's greatest achievements were in the field of paleontology. He earned his reputation in this field in the late 1840s through his studies of the fossil horse in America, which proved for the first time that the horse was a native of this continent. He was soon acknowledged by his peers as an expert on fossil vertebrates, and he is considered one of the first professional paleontologists in the United States and one of those who developed the discipline into a true science. His growing reputation led to an invitation in 1852 to join an expedition to the Nebraska Badlands. Since he was unable to go because of his pending appointment as professor of anatomy, an appointment occasioned by Horner's sudden illness and death, the fossils were sent to him for study. The result was an extensive study, *The Ancient Fauna of Nebraska.*

Leidy was the first to identify the remains of dinosaurs in the United States. When his friend Ferdinand H. Hayden, who was also a paleontologist, sent him several fossils from Cretaceous formations in what is now Montana, in 1855, Leidy recognized them as similar to remains in Europe identified as dinosaurs. In 1858, he identified bones from New Jersey as a dinosaur which he christened the *Hadrosaurus foulkii.*

Leidy's most important work in paleontology was published in 1869, "The Extinct Mammalian Fauna of Dakota and Nebraska."

Leidy was a quiet and gentle individual, not given to argument. Growing controversies among paleontologists in the 1860s and 1870s caused Leidy to back away from his researches on fossil animals, and in the 1870s, he turned his attention to modern animals, particularly to microscopic studies of freshwater protozoa. A longtime interest in this subject was encouraged when Hayden asked him to study the microscopic life of the western waters as part of his (Hayden's) explorations. This resulted in an extensive and important contribution to knowledge about freshwater rhizopods.

Leidy was a greatly admired and highly respected scientist, praised for his tact, dedication, discretion, and integrity.

Several biographical sketches of Leidy were published at the time of his death. Ones by Ruschenberger and Chapman include useful listings of Leidy's lectures and publications as well as his written and verbal communications before the Academy of Natural Sciences of Philadelphia. The first comprehensive biography of Leidy was published in 1998. The principal collections of Leidy's correspondence and papers are at the Academy of Natural Sciences of Philadelphia and the College of Physicians of Philadelphia.

BIBLIOGRAPHY

Chapman, Henry C. "Memoir of Joseph Leidy, M. D., LL.D." *Proceedings of the Academy of Natural Sciences of Philadelphia* (1891): 342–388.

Leidy, Joseph. *The Ancient Fauna of Nebraska, or a Description of Remains of Extinct Mammalia and Chelonia, from the Mauvaises Terres of Nebraska.* Smithsonian Contributions to Knowledge. Vol. 6. 1853.

———. "The Extinct Mammalian Fauna of Dakota and Nebraska, including an Account of Some Allied Forms from Other Localities, Together with a Synopsis of the Mammalian Remains of North America." *Journal of the Academy of Natural Sciences of Philadelphia,* 2d ser., 7 (1869).

———. *Fresh-Water Rhizopods of North America.* Issued as a volume of the *Report of the United States Geological Survey of the Territories* by F. V. Hayden. Washington, DC: Government Printing Office, 1879.

Ruschenberger, W.S.W. "A Sketch of the Life of Joseph Leidy, M. D., LL.D." *Proceedings of the American Philosophical Society* (1892): 135–184.

Warren, Leonard. *Joseph Leidy: The Last Man Who Knew Everything.* New Haven: Yale University Press, 1998.

Patsy Gerstner

Lesley, J. Peter (1819–1903)

Geologist. Born in Philadelphia, Lesley attended the University of Pennsylvania (1834–1838), and planned to continue his studies in a theological seminary, but poor health prevented him from doing so. At the suggestion of Alexander Dallas Bache, Lesley became an assistant to Henry Darwin Rogers on the first geological survey of Pennsylvania (1839–1842). When the survey ended, Lesley returned to theology, graduating from the Princeton Seminary in 1844, and that year became a licensed preacher of the Philadelphia Presbytery. Between 1846 and 1848, Lesley worked as a paid assistant of Rogers, who was trying to finish the Pennsylvania survey, but then in 1848 Lesley became pastor of a Congregationalist Church in Milton, Massachusetts. By 1850, Lesley had decided that science and religion could not coexist in harmony, and once again he returned to assist Rogers. Two years later, Lesley and Rogers had an acrimonious separation, and Lesley became an independent consulting geologist and worked for a variety of Pennsylvania coal, iron, petroleum, and railroad companies. In 1859, Lesley was appointed professor of mining at the University of Pennsylvania, then dean of the science department (1872), and dean of the Towne Scientific School (1875). Lesley achieved his life's ambition in 1873 when he became the director of the second geological survey of Pennsylvania (1873–1887). He also served in numerous roles at the American Philosophical Society, including librarian (1859–1885) and secretary (1859–1887).

Lesley wanted to apply whatever he had studied or researched. Whether survey geologist or mining consultant, he attempted to combine practical and theoretical geology. This approach was clearly revealed in his first book, *A Manual of Coal and Its Topography* (1856) and in his second work, *The Iron Manufacturer's Guide* (1859). In a similar vein, Lesley served as secretary of

L

the American Iron Association (1856–1864) and editor of the weekly newspaper *The United States Railroad and Mining Register* (1869–1873). Lesley developed theories of the origin of coal and petroleum. He was one of the first geologists to delineate the structure of the Appalachian coal formations and to correlate them with formations in Britain and Europe. Lesley also explained the folding and subsequent erosion of the Appalachian mountains. His most important methodological contribution was his introduction of contour lines to denote elevation on geological maps.

Contemporaries respected Lesley for his work on coal and the structure of the Appalachians. Lesley thought his greatest contribution were the multiple volumes and maps of the second Pennsylvania survey, but historians have not agreed, principally because the focus of attention by the late nineteenth century had turned to the trans-Mississippi west. Recent historians have emphasized Lesley's consulting practice because of his contributions to the development of industry and, more important, because consulting represents one of the earliest examples of industrial support of science.

BIBLIOGRAPHY

Ames, Mary Lesley. *Life and Letters of Peter and Susan Lesley.* New York: G.P. Putnam's Sons, 1909.

Chance, H.M. "A Biographical Notice of J. Peter Lesley." *Proceedings of the American Philosophical Society* 45 (1906): 1–14.

Davis, W.M. "J. Peter Lesley." *Biographical Memoirs of the National Academy of Sciences* 8 (1915): 152–240.

Geilde, A. "Notice of J.P. Lesley." *Quarterly Journal of the Geological Society of London* 60 (1904): xlix–lv.

Lucier, Paul. "Commercial Interests and Scientific Disinterestedness: Consulting Geologists in Antebellum America." *Isis* (June 1995): 245–267.

Lyman, B.S. "Biographical Sketch of J. Peter Lesley." *Transactions of the American Institute of Mining Engineers* 34 (1903): 726–739.

Stevenson, J.J. "Memoir of J. Peter Lesley." *Bulletin of the Geological Society of America* 15 (1904): 532–541.

Paul Lucier

Lewis, Gilbert Newton (1875–1946)

Physical chemist. Born in West Newton, Massachusetts, Lewis attended the University of Nebraska and Harvard University, from which he received his B.Sc. in 1896, and his Ph.D. in 1899 with a dissertation on electrochemical potentials supervised by the physical chemist Theodore William Richards. He stayed at Harvard until 1905, although he spent a one-year period in the research laboratories of Walter Nernst at Göttingen and Wilhelm Ostwald at Leipzig, and worked for another year at the Bureau of Weights and Measures in Manila. He left Harvard for the Massachusetts Institute of Technology to join Arthur Amos Noyes and his team of physical chemists. In 1912, he became dean of the College of Chemistry at the University of California at Berkeley, and was responsible for the creation of one of the strongest departments of chemistry in the United States, where physical chemistry blossomed. He remained in Berkeley until his death in the laboratory. Lewis received many awards and was nominated several times for the Nobel Prize.

Lewis's scientific interests were wide-ranging. Beside his main contributions to thermodynamics and valence theory, he attempted to devise a new chemistry of deuterium compounds, was quick to understand the importance of quantum theory and relativity, was the first to postulate the existence of light pressure, named light corpuscles as photons, and became one of the few early American advocates of Einstein's relativity theory. He also delved into the field of American prehistory, geology, and economics.

Lewis's work on thermodynamics was crucial in convincing chemists of the utility of thermodynamics to the study of chemical systems. In the first decade of the twentieth century, Gibbs thermodynamic potentials were mainly known to physicists. Lewis realized that an exact chemical thermodynamics should be built upon the concepts of free energy and entropy, and immediately started an extensive compilation of data on the free energy of formation of inorganic and organic compounds. Then, he worked toward showing chemists how thermodynamics could be extended to deal with complex real chemical systems. With this purpose, he introduced new concepts such as fugacity, a function with the dimensions of pressure which measured the tendency of a substance to change from one chemical phase to another, and activity, a function with the dimensions of concentration which measured the tendency of substances to induce change in chemical systems. Although these concepts never played the central unifying role Lewis had envisioned, they proved fundamental to the study of deviations from the behavior of ideal systems. Lewis's textbook *Thermodynamics and the Free Energy of Chemical Substances* (1923), written with Merle Randall, was to shape the next generation of chemists.

Lewis conceived a static atomic model in an attempt to provide an explanation for the chemical bond. In this model, known as the cubical model, the electrons were distributed at the corners of concentric cubes. The formation of molecules aimed at the complete filling of the outer cubic layer. As accepted already, in the polar compounds of inorganic chemistry, the molecule resulted from the transfer of electrons from one atom to the other. In the nonpolar compounds of organic chemistry, Lewis suggested that the molecule could result from the sharing of electron pairs between the atoms. These two possibilities were different in degree but not in kind. The sharing of electron pairs was thus responsible for the unification of the two former theories of chemical union. Although the physical origin of such pairing was unknown, Lewis believed that quantum theory would eventually explain it. As an outcome of Lewis's ideas on chemical bonding a new theory of acids and bases was proposed, in which bases were defined as electron pair donors, and acids as molecules that could accept electron pairs. In 1919, Irving Langmuir took up and elaborated Lewis's theory of the shared pair bond. He made such a good job in popularizing it that the Lewis-Langmuir theory, as it came to be known, became widely accepted. In 1923, Lewis's ideas on valence were wrapped up in *Valence and the Structure of Atoms and Molecules,* a book in which Lewis showed how his static atomic model could be reconciled with the dynamical model of the physicists suggested by Niels Bohr.

There is no disagreement on the importance of Lewis on the history of twentieth-century chemistry, and especially on his role in raising American chemistry to prominence. A series of papers by Kohler has analyzed thoroughly Lewis's ideas on the chemical bond. Lewis's influence in the work of Linus Pauling and Robert Sanderson Mulliken, the American founders of quantum chemistry has been addressed recently in a paper by Gavroglu and Simões. Lewis's contributions to thermodynamics, which have been assessed in the context of Servos's analysis of the making of physical chemistry in America, still deserve much reflection. There is no recent scientific biography of Lewis. The G.N. Lewis Archives are at the Bancroft Library, University of California at Berkeley.

BIBLIOGRAPHY

Gavroglu, K., and A. Simões. "The Americans, the Germans and the Beginnings of Quantum Chemistry: The Confluence of Diverging Traditions." *Historical Studies in the Physical and Biological Sciences* 25 (1994): 47–110.

"Gilbert Newton Lewis, 1875–1946." *Journal of Chemical Education* 61 (1984): 3–21, 93–116, 185–215.

Hildebrand, J.H. "Gilbert Newton Lewis." *Biographical Memoirs of the National Academy of Science* 31 (1958): 209–235.

Kohler, R.E. "The Origin of G. N. Lewis's Theory of the Shared Pair Bond." *Historical Studies in the Physical and Biological Sciences* 3 (1971): 343–376.

———. "Lewis, Gilbert Newton." *Dictionary of Scientific Biography.* Edited by Charles C. Gillispie. New York: Scribner, 1973, 8:289–294.

———. "G.N. Lewis's Views on Bond Theory 1900–1916." *British Journal for the History of Science* 8 (1975): 233–239.

———. "The Lewis-Langmuir Theory of Valence and the Chemical Community, 1920–1928." *Historical Studies in the Physical and Biological Sciences* 6 (1975): 431–468.

Lewis, G.N. *Valence and the Structure of Atoms and Molecules.* New York: The Chemical Catalog Company, 1923; reprint, New York: Dover, 1966.

Lewis, G.N., and M. Randall. *Thermodynamics and the Free Energy of Chemical Substances.* New York: McGraw-Hill, 1923.

Servos, J.W. *Physical Chemistry from Ostwald to Pauling: The Making of a Science in America.* Princeton: Princeton University Press, 1990.

Stranges, A.N. *Electrons and Valence, Development of the Theory.* College Station: Texas A & M University Press, 1982.

Ana Simões

Lewis and Clark Expedition

As planned by President Thomas Jefferson, the Lewis and Clark expedition, 1804–1806, led by army officer Meriwether Lewis (1774–1809), Jefferson's private secretary, and former army officer William Clark (1770–1838), embodied the scientific heritage of the Enlightenment. Remembered today mostly for its great adventures and heroic nature, which are true enough, the real purpose of the undertaking was scientific inquiry.

Geographic discovery formed the most important aspect of the men's efforts. The captains hoped to find a relatively easy passage across the Rocky Mountains from the headwaters of the Missouri River to a stream flowing into the Columbia River. Lewis and Clark proved that such a pathway did not exist and that crossing the mountains was a difficult task. They dashed all hopes for the long-sought Northwest Passage, but in their scientific work of taking observations of longitude

L

and latitude, noting significant geographic features, and making detailed route maps, they made important contributions to knowledge of the West. While Lewis performed most of the astronomical duties, Clark charted the course and drafted expedition maps.

Investigations in ecology constituted another part of their work. Lewis and Clark took careful notice of the land's prospects for future agricultural use, while also studying plant and animal life, noting mineral deposits, and recording the country's climate. The leaders' accomplishments in the biological sciences are particularly noteworthy. They were the first to describe in detail a host of plant and animal species that were new to science and to provide better understanding of the range, habits, and physical characteristics of many known species. They wrote at length of the seasonal changes and range of plant life, of the extent and habits of animals, and of the migrations of birds and mammals.

Lewis and Clark also carried out ethnological and linguistic studies. They brought back the first detailed reports of three major Indian groups: the village Indians of the upper Missouri River; the intermountain tribes of the Rocky Mountains; and the riverine peoples of the Columbia valley and Northwest Coast. Handicapped as they were by the preconceptions and prejudices of their day, the men nonetheless displayed a degree of detachment unusual for the time. Working among a diversity of tribes, linguistic groups, and cultural settings, the captains found it nearly impossible to catalog, study, and understand this multitude of humanity. If they could not penetrate deeply into the culture of these people, hampered as they were by language and lack of time, they did rise above the cultural relativism of their age and presented a view of Native Americans that has been praised for its objectivity.

A final scientific legacy of the expedition are the journals which were so meticulously written and carefully preserved during the expedition. Most are now deposited in the archives of the American Philosophical Society, Philadelphia, and the Missouri Historical Society, St. Louis. Besides describing the daily events of the epic journey, the diaries contain the men's myriad scientific observations. The journals of Lewis and Clark are a national treasure.

BIBLIOGRAPHY

Allen, John Logan. *Passage through the Garden: Lewis and Clark and the Image of the American Northwest.* Urbana: University of Illinois Press, 1975.

Burroughs, Raymond Darwin. *The Natural History of the Lewis and Clark Expedition.* East Lansing: Michigan State University Press, 1961.

Chuinard, Eldon G. *Only One Man Died: The Medical Aspects of the Lewis and Clark Expedition.* Glendale, CA: Arthur H. Clark, 1979.

Cutright, Paul Russell. *Lewis and Clark: Pioneering Naturalists.* Urbana: University of Illinois Press, 1969.

Jackson, Donald, ed. *Letters of the Lewis and Clark Expedition with Related Documents, 1783–1854.* 2d ed. 2 vols. Urbana: University of Illinois Press, 1978.

Lavender, David. *The Way to the Western Sea: Lewis and Clark Across the Continent.* New York: Harper and Row, 1988.

Moulton, Gary E., ed. *The Journals of the Lewis and Clark Expedition.* 12 vols. Lincoln: University of Nebraska Press, 1983– .

Ronda, James P. *Lewis and Clark Among the Indians.* Lincoln: University of Nebraska, 1984.

Gary E. Moulton

SEE ALSO
Geographical Exploration

Libby, Willard Frank (1908–1980)

Chemist. Born in Grand Valley, Colorado, the son of farmer Ora Edward Libby and his wife, Eva May Libby (née Rivers), Willard Libby attended the University of California, Berkeley, from which he received his B.S. (1931) and Ph.D. (1933) degrees. He was instructor (1933–1938), assistant professor (1938–1945), and associate professor (1945) at Berkeley. His Guggenheim Fellowship was interrupted by World War II, and he was sent on leave to Columbia University on the Manhattan District Project to develop, under Harold C. Urey, methods of separating uranium isotopes by gaseous diffusion for production of the atomic bomb, which led to his interest in nuclear science. After the war, he became professor of chemistry at the Institute for Nuclear Studies and Department of Chemistry, University of Chicago (1945–1954), where he carried out the work for which he was awarded the 1960 Nobel Prize in chemistry "for his method to use carbon-14 for age determination in archaeology, geology, geophysics, and other branches of science" (Nobel, p. 587). He was appointed by President Dwight D. Eisenhower to the United States Atomic Energy Commission (1954–1959). He was professor of chemistry at the University of California, Los Angeles (1959–1980) and director of the Institute of Geophysics and

Planetary Physics (1962–1980). Ideologically committed to the Cold War, he and Edward Teller opposed 1954 Nobel in chemistry and 1962 Nobel Peace laureate Linus Pauling's petition that nuclear testing be banned. To prove that nuclear war was survivable, Libby, with great fanfare, built a fallout shelter at his home. After a fire burned the shelter, nuclear physicist and nuclear-testing critic Leo Szilard remarked, "This proves not only that there is a God but that he has a sense of humor" (Seymour and Fisher, p. 288).

In 1939, physicist Serge Alexander Korff at New York University had discovered that cosmic rays create showers of neutrons when they strike atoms in the atmosphere. Since nitrogen, which constitutes about 80 percent of the atmosphere, easily absorbs neutrons and then decays into the radioactive isotope carbon-14, Libby theorized that traces of carbon-14 should always occur in atmospheric carbon dioxide and that, since carbon dioxide is continuously being incorporated into plant tissues, plants should also contain traces of carbon-14. Because animal life is dependent on plant life, animals should also contain traces of carbon-14. After an organism died, no further carbon-14 would be incorporated into its tissues and that which was already present would begin to decay at a constant rate. (Martin D. Kamen, the codiscoverer of carbon-14, had found its half-life to be 5,730 years—a short time compared to the age of the earth but long enough for an equilibrium to be established between the production and decay of carbon-14). According to Arne Westgren, in his Nobel presentation speech to Libby, "it should be possible, by measuring the remaining activity, to determine the time elapsed since death, if this occurred during the period between approximately 500 and 30,000 years ago" (Nobel, p. 590).

To check the accuracy of this radiocarbon dating technique, Libby applied it to samples of redwood and fir trees whose exact ages had been determined by counting the annual rings and to historical artifacts whose ages were known, such as a piece of timber from Egyptian Pharaoh Sesostris's funerary boat. He established the fact that there was little variation of carbon-14 production due to the variation of cosmic rays with latitude by determining the radioactivity of animal and plant material obtained worldwide from the North Pole to the South Pole, and by 1947 he had perfected his technique. Among archaeological objects that he accurately dated were linen wrappings from the Dead Sea Scrolls, bread from a house in Pompeii buried by volcanic ashes in the eruption of Vesuvius in A.D. 79, charcoal from a campsite at Stonehenge, and corncobs from a cave in New Mexico. He also showed that the last Ice Age in North America ended 10,000 years ago rather than the 25,000 years previously estimated by geologists. Radiochemical dating was quickly recognized as a basic technique for determining dates within the last 70,000 years. Its most publicized recent use has been in dating the Shroud of Turin. In the words of one of the nominators of Libby for the Nobel Prize, "seldom has a single discovery in chemistry had such an impact on the thinking in so many fields of human endeavour. Seldom has a single discovery generated such wide public interest" (Nobel, pp. 591–592).

In 1946, Libby demonstrated that cosmic rays in the upper atmosphere produce traces of tritium (hydrogen-3), which could be used as a tracer of atmospheric water. He devised a technique involving the measurement of tritium concentrations for dating well water and wine and for determining water-circulation patterns and the mixing of ocean waters.

BIBLIOGRAPHY

Asimov, Isaac. *Asimov's Biographical Encyclopedia of Science & Technology.* Rev. ed. Garden City, NY: Doubleday, 1978, pp. 725–726.

Farber, Eduard. *Nobel Prize Winners in Chemistry 1901–1961.* Rev. ed. New York: Abelard-Schuman, 1963, pp. 296–300.

Libby, Willard F. *Radiocarbon Dating.* Chicago: University of Chicago Press, 1952; 2d ed., 1955.

Libby, Willard F. *Tritium and Radiocarbon.* Edited by R. Berger and L.M. Libby. Santa Monica, CA: Geo Science Analytical, 1981.

Millar, David, et al. *Chambers Concise Dictionary of Science.* Edinburgh: W & R Chambers, 1989, p. 246.

Nobel Foundation. *Nobel Lectures Including Presentation Speeches and Laureates' Biographies.* Amsterdam, London, and New York: Elsevier Publishing, 1964, pp. 587–612.

Seymour, Raymond B., and Charles H. Fisher. *Profiles of Eminent American Chemists.* Sydney, Australia: Litarvan Enterprises, 1988, pp. 287–289.

Wasson, T., ed. *Nobel Prize Winners.* New York: W.H. Wilson, 1987, pp. 632–634.

George B. Kauffman

Lick Observatory

America's first permanent mountaintop observatory. Lick Observatory went into operation on 1 June 1888 with the largest refracting telescope in the world, the

L

36-inch objective by Alvan Clark and Sons, and the mounting by Warner and Swasey. The observatory was built with funds provided by the San Francisco real estate magnate James Lick and turned over to the University of California on completion.

Edward S. Holden was the first director of Lick, but he was forced out in 1897 by a staff revolt, supported by the University of California regents he had antagonized and by other important figures in the West Coast educational world.

His successor was James E. Keeler, a member of the original staff, who had left Lick to go to the Allegheny Observatory. Keeler pioneered in nebular photography with Lick's 36-inch Crossley reflector and recognized, for the first time, the great number of spiral nebulae in the sky, but he died in 1900.

He was succeeded as director by William Wallace Campbell, who first came to Lick as Keeler's summer volunteer assistant in 1890, and had replaced him in 1891. Campbell focused Lick's research in two areas: the measurement of radial-velocity and solar eclipses. One of his first moves was to raise the money to establish a southern-hemisphere station at Santiago, Chile for radial-velocity observations. He also led eight solar eclipse expeditions from 1898 to 1922. The data was used by Donald H. Menzel to developed the modern theory of the chromosphere. Campbell was also concerned with testing Albert Einstein's theory of relativity. In 1922, at Wallal, Australia, Campbell and Robert J. Trumpler confirmed the general theory prediction to a very high level of accuracy.

After Campbell, the next three Lick directors were his former assistants Robert G. Aitken (1930–1935), William H. Wright (1935–1942), and Joseph H. Moore (1942–1945), and after them came his former student C. Donald Shane (1945–1958).

The Lick astronomers had long wanted a telescope larger than thirty-six inches in aperture, but funding was not procured until after World War II. Work on the 120-inch reflector began under Shane's directorship and was completed by his successor, Albert E. Whitford, the first director since Holden from outside the Lick staff.

The Mary Lea Shane Archives of the Lick Observatory, located in the University Library, University of California, Santa Cruz, contains 375 linear feet of holdings.

BIBLIOGRAPHY

Crelinsten, Jeffrey. "William Wallace Campbell and the Einstein Problem: An Observational Astronomer Confronts the Theory of Relativity." *Historical Studies in the Physical Sciences* 14 (1984): 1–91.

Lick, Rosemary. *The Generous Miser: The Story of James Lick of California.* Menlo Park, CA: Ward Ritchie Press, 1967.

Osterbrock, Donald E. "Lick Observatory Solar Eclipse Expeditions." *Astronomy Quarterly* 3 (1980): 67–79.

———. *James E. Keeler, Pioneer American Astrophysicist: And the Early Development of American Astrophysics.* Cambridge: Cambridge University Press, 1984.

———. "The Rise and Fall of Edward S. Holden." *Journal for the History of Astronomy* 15 (1984): 81–127, 151–176.

Osterbrock, Donald E., John R. Gustafson, and W.J. Shiloh Unruh. *Eye on the Sky: Lick Observatory's First Century.* Berkeley: University of California Press, 1988.

Wright, Helen. *James Lick's Monument: The Saga of Captain Richard Floyd and the Building of Lick Observatory.* Cambridge: Cambridge University Press, 1987.

Wright, William H. "William Wallace Campbell." *Biographical Memoirs of the National Academy of Sciences* 25 (1949): 35–74.

Marc Rothenberg

Limnology

The study of the physics, chemistry, and biology of lakes. In the United States, it developed as a distinct scientific discipline after 1890, following, and inspired by, its emergence in Europe.

The universities, state natural history surveys, and small lakes of the Midwest provided early opportunities for American limnologists. In Illinois, Stephen Forbes led studies of lakes and rivers between 1880 and 1930. In the 1890s, Edward Birge of Wisconsin began study of the physical and chemical conditions controlling plankton distribution. He was joined in 1900 by Chancey Juday. Jacob Reighard of the University of Michigan coordinated studies of Lake St. Clair in 1893, Lake Michigan the following year, and Lake Erie between 1898 and 1902. He also promoted, unsuccessfully, a Great Lakes biological station, to be modeled after marine stations. Other, smaller research programs began in Ohio and Indiana.

Limnology subsequently expanded throughout the nation, especially after the 1930s. Its growth was reflected in the establishment of the Limnological Society of America (now the American Society of Limnology and Oceanography) in 1936. Field stations have been important; early stations included one on the Illinois River in 1894, the Douglas Lake station of the University of Michigan (1909), and the Trout Lake station of the University of Wisconsin (1925).

L

A few schools have been especially influential in American limnology. One was at the University of Wisconsin, led by Birge and Juday until the 1940s, and by Arthur Hasler through the 1970s. A second was the Yale school, initiated in the late 1930s by G. Evelyn Hutchinson. Research and teaching at Wisconsin and Yale epitomized contrasting perspectives concerning method and theory. Birge and Juday stressed comparative survey of many lakes, and cautious induction of general principles. Hutchinson and colleagues studied individual lakes (including Linsley Pond in Connecticut) in detail, and used theory as a guide for field study, collecting data with specific hypotheses in mind. Such differences led in the early 1940s to a well-known dispute concerning publication in *Ecology* of a theoretical account of lake trophic-dynamics by Raymond Lindeman, a young associate of Hutchinson.

Early limnological theory emphasized dependency of lake biology on physical and chemical conditions, and a unitary view of lakes. This view was in part borrowed from European limnologists. Birge's studies of the heat budget of lakes illustrated its application. Forbes's conception of the lake as a "microcosm" was also influential; while viewing a lake as a single entity, it also considered interactions among its parts. By the 1930s the biological productivity of lakes had become a dominant theme. Since the 1940s, much research has emphasized dynamic processes, including the cycling of materials, and flows of energy. Such studies have also contributed to development of the ecosystem concept in ecology.

The impact of the ecosystem concept reflects limnology's ties with neighboring disciplines. Limnologists have also applied theoretical population ecology to plankton dynamics, and have used oceanographic methods and approaches. They have often viewed their work as synthetic, combining the perspectives of other, more specialized disciplines.

Limnological methods developed greatly in the 1940s. Wisconsin limnologists, under Hasler's leadership, applied experimental methods, eventually manipulating entire lakes. Experimental limnology subsequently developed elsewhere, particularly in Ontario, Canada. Radiotracers were applied to study of the movement of elements in lakes. Paleolimnological research—the use of pollen or microfossils deposited in sediments to study the biological history of lakes and their surrounding landscapes—also began, at Linsley Pond and elsewhere.

Limnology has often exhibited close ties to practical concerns. State natural history surveys in Wisconsin and Illinois provided early support because of the relevance of lake studies to natural resource surveys. Great Lakes studies contributed to debates concerning their declining fisheries. By midcentury, the significance of phosphorus to lake productivity had been identified; by 1970, this had led to controls on phosphorus entering the Great Lakes, Lake Washington, and other water bodies. Studies of the impact of acid deposition on lakes have helped place this issue on the political agenda.

Limnology raises numerous issues of historical interest, such as links between neighboring disciplines, development of field methods, and the significance of practical concerns. It has not yet, however, attracted sustained interest among historians.

BIBLIOGRAPHY

Beckel, Annamarie L., and Frank Egerton. "Breaking New Waters: A Century of Limnology at the University of Wisconsin." *Transactions of the Wisconsin Academy of Sciences, Arts and Letters.* Special Issue, 1987.

Bocking, Stephen A. "Stephen Forbes, Jacob Reighard and the Emergence of Aquatic Ecology in the Great Lakes Region." *Journal of the History of Biology* 23 (1990): 461–498.

Cook, Robert E. "Raymond Lindeman and the Trophic-Dynamic Concept in Ecology." *Science* 198 (1977): 22–26.

Egerton, Frank N. "Missed Opportunities: U.S. Fishery Biologists and Productivity of Fish in Green Bay, Saginaw Bay and Western Lake Erie." *Environmental Review* 13 (1989): 33–63.

Frey, David G., ed. *Limnology in North America.* Madison: University of Wisconsin Press, 1963.

Robertson, Carol Kelly. "Limnology in Michigan: An Historical Account." *Michigan Academician* 9 (1976): 185–202.

Stephen Bocking

Lipmann, Fritz (1899–1986)

Fritz Lipmann was awarded the 1953 Nobel Prize in physiology or medicine for the discovery of coenzyme A (CoA), an important catalyst in the cellular conversion of food into energy. Lipmann was born Königsberg, Germany (now Kaliningrad, Russia). He was educated during the years 1917–1922 at the Universities of Königsberg, Berlin, and Münich, where he studied medicine. He took his M.D. degree in 1924 in Berlin and took some additional courses in chemistry. In 1926, he became an assistant at Otto Meyerhof's laboratory at the Kaiser Wilhelm Institute in Berlin, where he obtained

L

his Ph.D. in 1927. In 1930, Lipmann became an assistant at the laboratory of Albert Fischer, and starting in 1931, he spent a year at the Rockefeller Institute working in the laboratory of Phoebus A. Levene.

From 1932 to 1939, Lipmann worked in Fischer's newly built laboratory in Copenhagen. Here he started the study of the Pasteur effect, which is the depression of wasteful fermentation in the respiring cell. He made a study of pyruvic acid oxidation because it is at the pyruvic stage that respiration branches off from fermentation. Through his work for Meyerhof, Lipmann had become familiar with the practice of using bacterial systems when mammalian tissues appeared to be too complex. When he chose a certain strain of *Lactobacillus detbrueckii* and substituted bicarbonate buffer for a phosphate buffer, he found that pyruvic oxidation depended on the presence of inorganic phosphate. He concluded that electron transfer potential is transformed into phosphate energy and hence to a wide range of biosynthetic reactions.

In 1939, Vincent du Vigneaud at Cornell Medical School invited Lipmann to return to the United States. After this fellowship, Lipmann became associated with the Massachusetts General Hospital, where he became a "biochemist among surgeons" and with Harvard Medical School. In 1941, he published his now classical essay "Metabolic generation and utilization of phosphate bond energy," in which he proposed a general function of the metabolic generation of ATP. He proposed that phosphorylated intermediaries such as acetyl phosphate (phosphoryl acetate, AcP) were precursors in biosynthetic events.

Lipmann studied the model system of acetylation of sulfanilamide in a cell-free pigeon liver preparation. In 1945, he became aware of the necessity of a heat-stable cofactor, designated as coenzyme A (for acetylation), which was also found to be necessary for the synthesis of acetylcholine from ATP, acetate and choline. By 1951, the general pattern of group transfer became recognizable, with donor and acceptor enzymes being connected through the CoA<->acetyl CoA shuttle. This is an example of the concept of "group transfer" proposed by Lipmann in 1941, which guided his later research on CoA, sulfate transfer, protein synthesis, and protein kinase. The idea of "group transfer" made him conclude that in the field of biosynthesis a rare example of progress leading to simplification had occurred. In 1957, Lipmann became professor of biochemistry at the Rockefeller Institute.

BIBLIOGRAPHY

Kleinkauf, Horst, Hans von Döhren, and Lothar Jaenicke, eds. *The Roots of Modern Biochemistry—Fritz Lipmann's Squiggle and Its Consequences.* Berlin: Walter de Gruyter, 1988.

Lipmann, Fritz. "Metabolic Generation and Utilization of Phosphate Bond Energy." In *Advances in Enzymology,* edited by Friedrich F. Nord and Chester H. Werkman. New York: Interscience, 1941, pp. 99–162.

———. "Biosynthetic Mechanisms [lecture delivered 16 December, 1948]." *Harvey Lectures* 44 (1950): 99–123.

———. "Development of the Acetylation Problem: A Personal Account [Nobel Lecture]." *Science* 120 (1954): 855–865; reprinted in *Nobel Lectures Physiology or Medicine, 1942–1962.* Amsterdam: Elsevier, 1964, pp. 413–438.

———. "Polypeptide Chain Elongation in Protein Biosynthesis." *Science* 164 (1969): 1024–1031.

———. *Wanderings of a Biochemist.* New York: Wiley, 1971.

———. "Discovery of the Adenylic Acid System in Animal Tissues." *Trends in Biochemical Sciences* 4 (1979): 22–24.

———. "Analysis of Phosphoprotein and Development in Protein Phosphorylation." *Trends in Biochemical Sciences* 8 (1983): 334–336.

———. "A Long Life in Times of Great Upheaval." *Annual Review of Biochemistry* 35 (1984): 1–33.

Novelli, G. "Personal Recollections on Fritz Lipmann During the Early Years of Coenzyme A Research." *Molecular Biology, Biochemisty and Biophysics* 32 (1980): 415–430.

Richter, Dietmar, and Helmuth Hilz. "Fritz Lipmann at 80." *Trends in Biochemical Sciences* 4 (1979): N123–N124.

Ton van Helvoort

Literature—Relations to Science and Technology

We have not always had "literature," "science," and "technology," much less relations between the first and the last two of these. Prior to the middle of the nineteenth century, it was difficult to distinguish between literature on the one hand and science and technology on the other. In the United States (and elsewhere, notably England), the knowledge to be found in the traditional preparatory and college curricula was ordered according to the seven *artes liberales,* divided into the more basic *trivium* of grammar, rhetoric, and logic, and the more advanced *quadrivium* of arithmetic, geometry, astronomy, and music. What we now call science was then called natural philosophy, and bore a relationship to philosophy, while what we now know as literature bore a relationship to rhetoric.

For the most part, natural philosophy depended on argumentation (rhetoric), not computation (arithmetic) or mathematics (geometry), to make its point, so quantitative reasoning had little bearing on most scientific discourse early on. Granted, there was, from the middle of the sixteenth century on, a flourishing literature of technical and trade manuals (Zilsel, pp. 544–562) which made use of computation and mathematics—the latter especially after the translation of Euclid's *Elements* in the middle of the sixteenth century. And granted, the likes of Galileo, Huygens, and Newton were exceptions in this regard. Nevertheless, it was not until the mathematization of nature begun by Galileo was widely accepted in the late-eighteenth and early-nineteenth centuries—that moment at which "the (more mathematical) American Philosophical Society [was] joining the (more Baconian) American Society for Promoting Useful Knowledge" (Limon, p. 21)—that the separation of literature from science and technology in the sphere of arts and letters (or higher education) began in serious earnest.

Prior to the period under discussion, nobody saw a need to view literature and science as mutually exclusive discourses. The Puritans who came to believe in America as the type of a new Eden understood the potential significance of such a place both on the authority of scientific apologists such as Bacon and on the authority of poets such as Milton. Moreover, Americans living before the mid-nineteenth century made no sharp distinction between texts that thereafter would have been labeled as "literary" or "scientific." Texts of both sorts derived their value from the presentation of useful knowledge. Thus it is that the Newtonianism that pervades Jonathan Edwards's journals also finds its way into his sermons, and the utilitarianism that pervades Franklin's scientific experimentation also pervades both *Poor Richard's Almanac* and the *Autobiography*.

With the mathematization of nature completed, there followed a quantum improvement of scientific and technical practice in the nineteenth century. This improvement was heralded by the rise of established scientific laboratories, the improvement of experimental method and instrumentation, and the proliferation of inventors and technologists able to harness elemental phenomena such as fire, light, steam, and electricity to specific purposes. This new quantitative and methodological precision, and the resultant data waiting to be put to use, made it apparent to virtually all concerned that scientific knowledge tended to be the sort of knowledge that gave rise to ready applications, whereas literary knowledge was knowledge either of broad social significance or for its own artistic sake. On the one hand, the Bessemer converter, the Fresnel lens, the Fulton steamboat, and the Morse telegraph bore witness to the proposition that science admitted no distinction between knowledge and use (Bronowski, p. 7) and was, accordingly, the knowledge of choice for the upwardly mobile and practical minded. On the other hand, the fiction of Hawthorne ("The Birth Mark" and "Rappacini's Daughter" in *Mosses from an Old Manse*) and the poetry of Poe (*Eureka*), at best critical of science and technology, at worst downright hostile to them, bore witness to the proposition that literary knowledge had no practical use and was accordingly the vehicle of intellectual recreation for the idle middle and upper classes possessed of sufficient leisure time to read it. The growing distinction between the way that educated people viewed and valorized science and technology, and the way that these same people viewed and valorized literature is reflected by the publications of the period. Exceptions such as the British chemist Humphry Davy, who wrote poetry as well as doing science, were celebrated as polymaths in such popular publications as *Mechanics Magazine*. Poetry appeared in middle-brow journals such as *Scientific American,* especially in the volumes published before the Civil War. But the poetry appeared as a "break" from the scientific matter, not in competition with it. Benjamin Silliman's *American Journal of Science and the Arts* "offered Americans an American sense of what it was like to be an American scientist for the first time" (Limon, p. 125).

The gulf between literature and science as social and intellectual practices, already fully developed by the mid-nineteenth century, although admitting of exceptions such as the one to be observed on the Cambridge-Concord axis (see Harding), has given rise to what was characterized by C.P. Snow in the mid-twentieth century as "the two cultures." It is a gulf that continues to exist today, notwithstanding efforts by philosophers such as Max Black and Mary Hesse to show that metaphor is the basis of scientific inquiry no less than it is of literature, and notwithstanding the literary efforts of scientists such as Roald Hoffman (*The Metamict State*), physicians such as Lewis Thomas (*The Lives of a Cell*), and engineers such as Henry Petrosky (*The Pencil*) to bridge this gulf. Nevertheless, efforts to describe—and thereby to preserve—the relations of literature and science and technology, especially literature

L

and science, have been ongoing for nearly three-quarters of a century. Not surprisingly, these efforts have focused within the domain of the seven liberal arts—where that gulf was opened, at "the scene of the crime," as it were—and especially on the *trivium* and the humanities to which the *trivium* has given rise.

Early studies in the area of literature and science proceeded on the assumption that science was something that literature took as a subject among other subjects. Thus Walter Clyde Curry's *Chaucer and the Medieval Sciences* (1926) explains the significance of Chaucer's physiognomical and astrological references in a manner that differs little from the manner in which E.F. Shannon's *Chaucer and the Roman Poets* (1929) explains the significance of Chaucer's references to Ovid and Virgil. Alternatively, scholars writing slightly later—E.A. Burtt and A.O. Lovejoy are notable examples—inscribed both literature and science within the frame of the history of ideas. Accordingly, when Marjorie Hope Nicolson, writing in *Newton Demands the Muse* (1946), deals with the use that writers in the eighteenth century made of contemporary accounts of light and vision in their work, she produces a special case of a general approach to the history of ideas that is epitomized by Lovejoy's *The Great Chain of Being* (1936), in which he deals with the use that commentators in the Renaissance and thereafter made of the neoplatonic doctrine of plenitude.

Lacking a canon, a period, a nation, a topos, a genre, or even a coherent methodological approach, the study of literature and science in the United States languished in the postwar, Cold War, and Vietnam eras, albeit with some notable exceptions such as Nicolson, her student and then younger collaborator G.S. Rousseau, and others such as Leo Marx. However, with the growth of interest in critical and cultural theory that blossomed in the mid- and late seventies, and with the growing realization that the history and philosophy of science and technology, when appropriated through the intermediation of theory, could serve a useful contextualizing and/or heuristic function, the study of literature and science experienced a surge of new interest. That interest was given an organizational basis in 1985 when, at the seventeenth International Congress of History of Science, held at the University of California, Berkeley, the Society for Literature and Science (SLS) was founded. What made this event truly remarkable is the fact that less than a decade earlier, within the organizational frame of the Modern Language Association (MLA), prominent scholars seeking the abolition of the MLA's Division on Literature and Science had nearly carried the day, with the result that the division convened at the 1978 MLA convention to debate what future, if any, the study of literature and science might hold.

The debate that took place in 1978 has, in the long run, reinvigorated the field. Since that time, the MLA Division on Literature and Science has presented provocative, high-quality sessions at the annual meeting, despite MLA's less than wholehearted support. (In 1987, for example, there was not one session in honor of the tercentenary of Newton's *Principia,* despite the fact that at least one such session was duly proposed.) In the 1990s, literature and science is a thriving field. SLS has held an annual fall meeting every year since 1987. Its original newsletter, *PSLS,* has given way to a new learned journal, *Configurations.*

The work currently being done in the field of literature and science is as diverse as it is sophisticated. Some of the best builds bridges from traditional areas of literary study to scientific inquiry by extending the methods of the former to the latter. For example, Charles Bazerman, writing in *Shaping Written Knowledge: The Genre and Activity of the Experimental Article in Science* (1988), extends genre theory to the analysis of the development of the scientific article in the seventeenth century and its final establishment in a position of intellectual authority in the twentieth. Gillian Beer, writing in *Darwin's Plots: Evolutionary Narrative in Darwin, George Eliot, and Nineteenth-Century Fiction* (1983), focuses on Darwin's characteristic uses of language and emplotment to show the almost atmospheric influence these exerted on nineteenth-century British fiction. Alan G. Gross, writing in *The Rhetoric of Science* (1990), subjects scientific prose to rhetorical analysis, studying rhetoric's role in the formation of scientific analogy, the creation of taxonomies, and such matters as the style and arrangement of the scientific article.

Other exemplary work makes a start out of a given intellectual milieu to show how both literature and science are conditioned by or responsive to that milieu. For example, N. Katherine Hayles, writing in *Chaos Bound: Orderly Disorder in Contemporary Literature and Science* (1990), brings together information theory, chaos theory, and critical theory to show how the insights of science regarding communication and its disruption have operated within the domain of contemporary fiction. And David Porush, writing in *The Soft Machine: Cybernetic Fiction* (1985), has been both a principal and one of the most talented exponents of bringing contemporary critical theory and information theory to bear in the study of the full range of modern and contemporary science fiction.

Looking back to the crisis addressed by students of literature and science at the 1978 MLA meeting, one may fairly state that reports of its death were greatly exaggerated. In proclaiming the demise of traditional ways of approaching literature and science, Rousseau invoked the French theorists—Barthes, Derrida, and above all, Foucault—as pointing the way beyond traditional approaches to the text, be it "literary" or "scientific," as the repository either of established authority or established meaning (Rousseau, p. 590). Those who attended that session or who have been influenced by it, whether directly or indirectly, are those who are responsible for making literature and science the exciting area of inquiry that it is today.

Stuart Peterfreund

BIBLIOGRAPHY

Bazerman, Charles. *Shaping Written Knowledge: The Genre and Activity of the Experimental Article in Science.* Madison: University of Wisconsin Press, 1988.

Beer, Gillian. *Darwin's Plots: Evolutionary Narrative in Darwin, George Eliot, and Nineteenth-Century Fiction.* Boston: Routledge & Kegan Paul, 1983.

Black, Max. *Models and Metaphors.* Ithaca: Cornell University Press, 1962.

Bronowski, Jacob. *Science and Human Values.* Rev. ed. 1965. Reprint, New York: Harper & Row, 1972.

Curry, Walter Clyde. *Chaucer and the Medieval Sciences.* Oxford: Oxford University Press, 1926.

Gross, Alan G. *The Rhetoric of Science.* Cambridge, MA: Harvard University Press, 1990.

Harding, Walter. "Walden's Man of Science." *Victorian Poetry* 57 (1981): 45–61.

Hayles, N. Katherine. *Chaos Bound: Orderly Disorder in Contemporary Literature and Science.* Chicago: University of Chicago Press, 1990.

Hesse, Mary. *Models and Analogies in Science.* Notre Dame: Notre Dame University Press, 1966.

Limon, John. *The Place of Fiction in the Time of Science: A Disciplinary History of American Writing.* New York: Cambridge University Press, 1990.

Lovejoy, A.O. *The Great Chain of Being: A Study in the History of an Idea.* Cambridge, MA: Harvard University Press, 1936.

Nicolson, Marjorie Hope. *Newton Demands the Muse: Newton's "Opticks" and the Eighteenth-Century Poets.* Princeton: Princeton University Press, 1946.

Porush, David. *The Soft Machine: Cybernetic Fiction.* New York: Methuen, 1985.

Rousseau, G.S. "Literature and Science: The State of the Field." *Isis* 69 (1978): 583–591.

Shannon, E.F. *Chaucer and the Roman Poets.* Cambridge, MA: Harvard University Press, 1929.

Zilsel, Edgar. "The Sociological Roots of Science." *American Journal of Sociology* 47 (1942): 544–562.

SEE ALSO
Nature Writing

Locke, John (1792–1856)

Chemist, physicist, geologist, educator, and inventor of several scientific instruments. Born in Lempster, New Hampshire, Locke exhibited early interests in machinery and in botany. He studied briefly with Benjamin Silliman Sr. at Yale in 1815–1816 and earned an M.D. at Yale in 1819. Unsuccessful in establishing a medical practice, he taught at or conducted a number of female academies in the 1820s and early 1830s and again in the last years of his life. He served as professor of chemistry at Medical College of Ohio in Cincinnati (1835–1853), spending the first two years of his tenure in Europe. While on the faculty, he also served as an assistant on the state geological survey of Ohio (1837–1838) and on surveys of federal mineral lands under David Dale Owen (1839–1840) and Charles Thomas Jackson (1847–1848). An active member of the Association of American Geologists and Naturalists, he served as president of that organization in 1844.

Locke's most important contributions to science comprised the development and application of scientific instruments. He invented a number of mechanical devices useful in scientific endeavors, including the electrochronograph. This instrument took advantage of telegraphic technology to simply and accurately record the times of astronomical observations at distant points and thus contributed to the accurate determination of longitudes. The electrochronograph earned Locke the praises of the heads of the Naval Observatory and the United States Coast Survey as well as a $10,000 award from the United States Congress.

Locke's early interest in botany led to his publication of an elementary botany manual (1819), but botany was not the focus of his professional scientific work. Locke devoted much attention in his geological survey work to barometrical determinations of altitude and to deviations of the magnetic compass. He also published

L

papers on the trilobites, glacial phenomena, and general geology of the West (Ohio) in the early 1840s. The balance of his scientific career was devoted to the study of electrical and magnetic effects and to the relationship between electrical and magnetic effects.

No extended or recent study of Locke is available. No deposit or archival material related to Locke or his work has been identified.

BIBLIOGRAPHY

Locke, John. *Outlines of Botany.* Boston: Cummings and Hilliard, 1819.

Waller, Adolph E. "Dr. John Locke, Early Ohio Scientist (1792–1856)." *Ohio State Archaeological and Historical Quarterly* 44 (1946): 346–373.

Winchell, N.H. "Sketch of Dr. John Locke." *American Geologists* 14 (1894): 341–356.

Wright, M.B. *An Address on the Life and Character of the Late Professor John Locke, Delivered at the Request of the Cincinnati Medical Society.* Cincinnati: Moore, Wilstach, Keys and Company [1857].

Julie R. Newell

Loeb, Jacques (1859–1924)

German-Jewish immigrant biologist. Born in the Prussian Rhineland, Loeb studied brain physiology at the University of Strassburg (M.D., 1884). For the next seven years, he pursued physiological research at the Berlin Agricultural College, the Universities of Wurzburg and Strassburg, and the Naples Zoological Station. In 1890, he married Anne Louise Leonard, an American studying in Zurich, and a year later, he came to the United States, working for a year at Bryn Mawr College, and then joining the new University of Chicago, where he rose to professor of physiology. In 1902, he became professor of physiology at the University of California, Berkeley, and eight years later became a member of the Rockefeller Institute for Medical Research in New York City, where he remained until his death. With the exception of his years in California, Loeb worked during summers at the Marine Biological Laboratory, Woods Hole, Massachusetts.

Loeb was a radical experimentalist who sought to transform biology from the study of the diversity of organisms into an engineering science. Influenced by the plant physiologist Julius Sachs and the physicist-philosopher Ernst Mach, Loeb used tools from physical chemistry to transform the functions and structures of animals. He explored ways to manipulate animal behavior (most notably in investigations of animal tropisms), to alter the forms of invertebrates, and to control the development of embryos. He believed that his greatest innovation was artificial parthenogenesis—the demonstration, in 1899, that by changing the chemical medium of an unfertilized egg, development could be initiated. He contrasted this activist experimentation with other biologists' concern to understand normal development. Loeb was an important influence on the biologists H.J. Muller and Gregory Pincus, and on the psychologists John B. Watson and B.F. Skinner.

The success of genetics, a shift from an academic to a medical research setting, and the ideological conflicts surrounding World War I combined in the second decade of the twentieth century to induce Loeb to adopt a more traditional reductionist position. After 1916, he largely abandoned his earlier wide-ranging biological concerns to focus on protein chemistry; his aim was to show, in opposition to the tenets of colloid chemistry, that gelatin obeyed the laws of solution theory.

As a secularized Jew, passionate about discovery but sardonic about human failings, Loeb was an exotic personality among American academic biologists, an intellectual community dominated by placidly optimistic investigators and institution builders. Most interpreted him in terms of long-standing stereotypes about German Jews and scientists—as a materialist and an adherent of pure science. This image of Loeb was fixed in the fictional character created by Sinclair Lewis—the bacteriologist Max Gottlieb—in *Arrowsmith* (1925). Holistic biologists and philosophers used Loeb's popular book *The Mechanistic Conception of Life* (1912), as an exemplar of the simplistic mechanistic reductionism they considered prevalent in the nineteenth century. More recent emphasis has been on his catalytic role in the development of experimental biology in the United States, and on his work as a prophet of biotechnology.

Loeb's research extended over many biological domains, including the psychology of perception, animal behavior, embryology, fertilization, cell membrane properties, regeneration, and physical biochemistry. His significance within a number of these areas is not well understood. A substantial collection of his papers is located in the Library of Congress.

BIBLIOGRAPHY

Allen, Garland E. *Life Science in the Twentieth Century.* New York: John Wiley, 1975.

Fleming, Donald. Introduction to *The Mechanistic Conception of Life,* by Jacques Loeb. Cambridge, MA: Harvard University Press, 1964, pp. vii–xlii.

Manning, Kenneth R. *Black Apollo of Science: The Life of Ernest Everett Just.* New York: Oxford University Press, 1983.

Osterhout, W.J.V. "Jacques Loeb." *Biographical Memoirs of the National Academy of Sciences* 13 (1930): 318–410.

Pauly, Philip J. *Controlling Life: Jacques Loeb and the Engineering Ideal in Biology.* New York: Oxford University Press, 1987.

Rasmussen, Charles, and Rick Tilman. *Jacques Loeb: His Science and Social Activism and Their Philosophical Foundations.* Memoirs of the American Philosophical Society 229 (1998).

Reingold, Nathan. "Jacques Loeb, the Scientist: His Papers and His Era." *Library of Congress Quarterly Journal of Acquisitions* 19 (1962): 119–130.

Rosenberg, Charles E. *No Other Gods: On Science and American Social Thought.* Baltimore: Johns Hopkins University Press, 1976.

Philip J. Pauly

Long, Stephen Harriman (1784–1864)

Explorer, inventor, and topographical engineer. Born in Hopkinton, New Hampshire, Long was a graduate of Dartmouth College. He worked as a school principal and civil engineer before joining the United States Army Corps of Engineers in 1814. When the War Department reorganized in 1818, Long was transferred into the new U.S. Topographical Engineers. As one of the bureau's most accomplished explorers, Long led a series of expeditions across the Great Plains as far west as the Rockies and from Lake Winnipeg in Canada to the Mexican borderlands—in all, about 26,000 miles of western reconnaissance, more territory than had been explored by Lewis and Clark. Long also designed steamboats, surveyed railroads, and pioneered applications of physics and mathematics to the construction of truss bridges and dams.

Long's place in the history of science rests primarily on his fame as the first army explorer to organize and lead parties of naturalists into the trans-Mississippi West. His most dangerous assignment was also the most controversial—a journey up the Missouri and Platte Rivers to the Rocky Mountains, part of Colonel Henry Atkinson's ill-fated Yellowstone expedition. On 4 May 1819, Long and a party of soldiers and scientists left Pittsburgh in an unusual shallow-draft steamboat, *The Western Engineer.* Designed by the explorer himself, it was the prototype of the western sternwheeler and the first steamboat to ascend the Missouri as far as the mouth of the Platte. The twenty-four man crew included zoologist Thomas Say, naturalist Titian Peale, artist Samuel Seymour, and two young topographical engineers from West Point. Long's botanist, William Baldwin, died en route and was replaced by surgeon and scientist Edwin James, the chronicler of the expedition.

After a disastrous winter of fever and scurvy near present-day Omaha, the War Department aborted the Yellowstone expedition, but Long's party soon reorganized for an overland expedition to the headwaters of the Red River of the South, a vaguely understood international boundary line. On 6 June 1820, Long headed west with twenty-one men. Following the Platte to the base of the Rocky Mountains, the explorers sighted a jagged summit, naming it Long's Peak. Turning south, they stopped to scale Pike's Peak (renaming it James's Peak) then moved along the base of the mountains across arid grasslands, and down the Canadian River to the Arkansas River and Fort Smith. The expedition had crossed from what is now Nebraska to the Colorado Rockies then back through Kansas, the Texas Panhandle, and Oklahoma. Echoing the explorer Zebulon Pike, whose 1810 report had called the region a desert, Long characterized the Great Plains as a sandy wasteland "almost wholly unfit for cultivation and, of course, uninhabitable by a people depending upon agriculture for their subsistence" (James, 2:361). Long's map labeled the region "Great Desert," which later became "Great American Desert" in a popular atlas. Treeless and cut off from navigable rivers, the arid country, said Long, was valuable to the United States only as "a barrier" to contain settlement and discourage a foreign invasion (James, 2:388).

Historians disagree over the value of Long's contribution. Fur trade historian Hiram M. Chittenden called the Long expedition "an unqualified failure" (2:570) while others have criticized the explorer for reviving the "myth" of the western desert that deterred western migration. Long's many defenders, however, say the explorer was true to a conceptual science that worked backward from theories to facts. Long expected to find a desert. He assumed, rightly perhaps, that an arid region far from the Mississippi-Missouri system would be difficult to farm and defend. Although the expedition failed to survey the headwaters of any major river, Long produced an important map that was the first to delineate the Arkansas-Canadian system. The

L

expedition also brought back samples and at least 270 drawings of indigenous alpine flora, new species of wolf and coyote, fossils, insects, and what the *North American Review* generally considered "highly important additions" to geography and natural history.

The War Department thought the achievement impressive enough to order Long back to the West for a second scientific expedition: a trek up the St. Peter's River (later renamed the Minnesota River) into the disputed Sioux and Chippewa country about Lake Superior. Leaving Philadelphia on 30 April 1823, Long eventually reached Lake Winnipeg, Canada, with a party of soldiers and scientists that included mineralogist William H. Keating, astronomer James E. Calhoun, and two veterans of the 1820 expedition—Seymour and Say. Again the explorers dismissed the mysterious land as a barrier to civilization—dreary, bug-infested, an impassible waste.

In the summer of 1824, as Keating edited journals of the Lake Winnipeg expedition, Long moved from water surveying to water construction at the army's wing-dam experiment in the Ohio River, the first federal dam. Long's subsequent career as builder and railroad consultant pioneered new applications of construction mathematics. As chief of surveys for the Baltimore and Ohio Railroad, he authored a widely used construction manual, published in 1829. He also built and patented a remarkable timber-frame railroad truss that historians have hailed as "the first truss where mathematical calculations entered into the construction of the bridge" (Wood, p. 167). As the army's senior topographer in the Ohio Valley during the 1840s and 1850s, Long invented dredging equipment, planned marine hospitals, and supervised the federal snag-boat program. Called back to Washington for his last assignment during the Civil War, Long, age seventy-six, was promoted to colonel and chief of the Corps of Topographical Engineers. He retired in 1863.

BIBLIOGRAPHY

"Account of an Expedition." *North American Review*, n.s., 7 (1823): 242.

Chittenden, Hiram M. *A History of the American Fur Trade.* 2 vols. Stanford, CA: Academic Reprints, 1954.

Goetzmann, William H. *Exploration and Empire: The Explorer and the Scientist in the Winning of the American West.* New York: Alfred A. Knopf, 1966.

James, Edwin. *Account of an Expedition from Pittsburgh to the Rocky Mountains. . . .* 2 vols. Philadelphia: H.C. Carey and I. Lea, 1823.

Kane, Lucille M., June D. Holmquist, and Carolyn Gilman, eds. *The Northern Expeditions of Stephen H. Long: The Journals of 1817 and 1823 and Related Documents.* St. Paul: Minnesota Historical Society Press, 1978.

Livingston, John. "Col. Stephen H. Long of the U. S. Army." In *Portraits of Eminent Americans Now Living with Biographical and Historical Memoir of Their Lives and Actions.* 4 vols. New York: Cornish, Lamport & Co., 1853–54, 4:477–89.

Nichols, Roger L. "Stephen Long and Scientific Exploration on the Plains." *Nebraska History* 52 (Spring 1971): 59–62.

Nichols, Roger L., and Patrick L. Halley. *Stephen Long and American Frontier Exploration.* Newark: University of Delaware Press, 1980.

Shallat, Todd. *Structures in the Stream: Water, Science, and the Rise of the U. S. Army Corps of Engineers.* Austin: University of Texas, 1994.

Wood, Richard G. *Stephen Harriman Long, 1784–1864.* Glendale, CA: Arthur H. Clark, 1966.

Todd Shallat

SEE ALSO
Geographical Exploration

Los Alamos National Laboratory

Sometimes called the "birthplace of the atomic age," Los Alamos National Laboratory is one of ten multipurpose laboratories of the Department of Energy. Since its founding by the Manhattan Engineer District as a nuclear weapons design laboratory in 1943, it has been operated by the University of California. Los Alamos developed both the fission and the thermonuclear weapons which form the basis of the American nuclear stockpile. Approximately two-thirds of all the weapons in that stockpile were designed at Los Alamos. Today, it employs over 7,000 scientists, engineers, technicians and support staff in a variety of research and development programs related to defense, energy, basic research, and technological development.

There is a rich popular historical literature concerning the work of the Los Alamos National Laboratory which has begun to be supplemented by more serious historical studies. The continuing controversy over the use of nuclear weapons in World War II and the nuclear arms race that arose in the 1950s has tended to color historical writing about Los Alamos and to obscure other issues, such as the rise of big science there. The multidisiplinary, mission-oriented research and development characteristic of the nuclear weapons program has, however, spread into many other areas of scientific activity, aided by the development of supercomputers at Los Alamos and other applied research institutions. For example, the human genome project takes advantage of both the world's largest scientific computing center and the skills of theoretical physicists, life scientists, and mathematicians working together at Los Alamos.

Among the many accomplishments of the laboratory have been the first detection of the neutrino by Frederick Reines and Clyde Cowan in 1956, the development of the first homogeneous uranium reactors, the first plutonium reactors, nuclear rocket engines, and dry geothermal energy technologies. Los Alamos also contributed the sensors used on satellites to detect atomic explosions on the earth, in the atmosphere or in space.

BIBLIOGRAPHY
Hoddeson, Lillian, et al. *Critical Assembly.* New York: Cambridge University Press, 1993.
Kunetka, James W. *City of Fire.* Albuquerque: University of New Mexico Press, 1979.
Rhodes, Richard. *The Making of the Atomic Bomb.* New York: Simon and Schuster, 1986.
Seidel, Robert W. "Books on the Bomb." *Isis* 81 (1990): 519–537.

Robert W. Seidel

Lowell, Percival (1855–1916)

The founder of the Lowell Observatory in Flagstaff, Arizona. Lowell descended from an eminent Boston family. Following graduation from Harvard College (1876), he managed family funds, then traveled to and wrote about East Asia before establishing the observatory in 1894. From then until his death, he focused his attention entirely on astronomy. Lowell was best known for his pursuit of evidence for the existence of life on Mars. He also searched in vain for a ninth planet. His planetary research was part of a larger scheme to explain the origins and development of the solar system. Indeed, three of his five books on astronomical subjects dealt with questions of cosmogony.

Lowell's work on Mars attracted widespread attention in the wake of his 1894 observations. Leading figures in the astronomical community disputed the existence of the canals on Mars and Lowell's contention that the Martian atmosphere could support life. By 1909, virtually all professional astronomers were convinced that the canals did not exist. Nonetheless, while diverting professional astronomers from other important work, the controversy called attention to research on the solar system which had been somewhat neglected. In addition, Lowell helped to pioneer the exploration of good seeing in remote areas. Following the lead of E.C. and W.H. Pickering at Harvard College Observatory, he was among the first to systematically test atmospheric conditions at potential observatory sites. Accordingly, the conditions at Flagstaff were an important factor in locating and maintaining the observatory there.

Lowell's work is documented in the collections at the Lowell Observatory Archives, which include his papers as well as those of his collaborators Vesto Melvin Slipher, Andrew E. Douglass, and Carl O. Lampland. A fuller understanding of his role in early-twentieth-century astronomy may be gained by reference to materials in the Harvard University and Lick Observatory Archives. While his work on Mars and Planet X has been the subject of a number of books and articles in recent years, further attention needs to be given to Lowell's research on other planets, his studies in cosmogony, the relationship between the early life and his astronomical career, and his role in promoting the work of various assistants at Flagstaff, notably V.M. Slipher.

BIBLIOGRAPHY
Hoyt, William Graves. *Lowell and Mars.* Tucson: University of Arizona Press, 1976.
———. *Planet X and Pluto.* Tucson: University of Arizona Press, 1980.
Lowell, A. Lawrence. *A Biography of Percival Lowell.* New York: Macmillan, 1935.
Lowell, Percival. *Mars and Its Canals.* New York: Macmillan, 1906.
———. *The Evolution of Worlds.* New York: Macmillan, 1909.
———. "Memoir on a Trans-Neptunian Planet." *Memoirs of the Lowell Observatory* 1 (1914): 3–105.

David Strauss

Lowell Observatory

Founded in 1894 in Flagstaff, Arizona, to explore the solar system. Percival Lowell supplied the funds for a project largely designed by W.H. Pickering. In the early years and during Martian oppositions, the staff amassed evidence for the existence of life on Mars, while investigating Venus, Saturn, and other planets. V.M. Slipher's discovery of the radial velocity of spiral nebulae in 1914

L

contributed to an understanding of the size of the universe. Following Lowell's death in 1916, Slipher became observatory director. Among notable achievements by Lowell astronomers since then have been Clyde Tombaugh's discovery in 1930 of the ninth planet which Lowell had sought unsuccessfully; Arthur Adel's identification of elements in the atmospheres of earth and other planets in the 1930s; and the codiscovery in 1977 by Robert Millis, with James Elliot of Cornell, of Uranus's ring system.

Discussion of the significance of work at the Lowell Observatory has largely been confined to the debate on the canals of Mars and the search for Planet X. Historians agree that the former focused attention on the solar system, but may also have distracted astronomers from stellar research projects. Other significant issues have been ignored. Too little attention has been paid to the work of Lowell's assistants before 1916, to the size and character of the observatory, which may have provided a more supportive environment than larger units for certain kinds of research, and, with the exception of the discovery of Pluto, to the important work which has been done at the observatory since 1916.

The focus on the history of the observatory's first years, partly due to the sensational character of the Mars research, also reflects the availability on microfilm of the early correspondence (1894–1916), including the papers of A.E. Douglass, V.M. Slipher, and C.O. Lampland. Subsequent work by these men, as well as by Clyde Tombaugh and Arthur Adel, can be documented in their papers in the Lowell Observatory Archives.

BIBLIOGRAPHY

Annals of the Lowell Observatory. 1–3 (1898–1905).
Bulletins of the Lowell Observatory. 1–167 (1903–1981).
Hoyt, William Graves. *Lowell and Mars.* Tucson: University of Arizona Press, 1976.
———. *Planets X and Pluto.* Tucson: University of Arizona Press, 1980.
———, ed. *Early Correspondence of the Lowell Observatory, 1894–1916.* Flagstaff: The Lowell Observatory, 1973. Microfilm.

David Strauss

M

Maclure, William (1763–1840)

Scottish-born geologist and philanthropist. Educated by private tutors, Maclure pursued a very successful career in business in Europe and America. After moving to America in 1796, he retired from business as a man of independent means in 1797 and subsequently became an American citizen. He traveled extensively in Europe and America both before and after his retirement. As an active participant in the scientific community of Philadelphia, his financial and geological contributions helped to shape the fledgling Academy of Natural Sciences, of which he served as president from 1817 to 1840. He also provided significant encouragement and monetary support for the American Geological Society founded in New Haven, Connecticut, in 1819, and for Robert Owen's utopian community founded at New Harmony, Indiana, in 1825. An ardent advocate of educational reform, he funded the introduction of the Pestalozzian educational system in America. Moving to Mexico in 1827 as a result of poor health, he pursued both his reform efforts and his scientific interests in that country until his death.

In 1809, Maclure issued a geologically colored map of the United States based on his own travels and including all the area between the Atlantic and the Mississippi. Although he used only a few formations and applied them to the continent in broad strokes, he produced a map of enduring utility and reasonable accuracy. In the accompanying text, he employed Wernerian classification and nomenclature, but did not bind himself to Wernerian theory. Maclure's second edition included a longer explanatory text, more accurate geographical details in the base map, numerous corrections in geological coloring, and a second plate with five extensive sections using the same colors as the map. Parker Cleaveland used Maclure's maps in both editions of his *Elementary Treatise on Mineralogy and Geology* (1816 and 1822), assuring that they were well known among American students of the earth sciences. The first-edition map was also republished in France, thus becoming the foundation of much European knowledge of American geology. "Mr. Maclure may be considered as the father of American geology," concluded Benjamin Silliman Sr. in 1844, "and was a most efficient patron of all other branches of science" (Morton, p. 1).

No extensive biography of Maclure is available. Archival materials exist at the University of Illinois (Illinois Historical Survey Collection) in Urbana, Illinois, and at the Working Men's Institute in New Harmony, Indiana. John S. Doskey has published several of the journals from the New Harmony collections, along with a biographical introduction.

BIBLIOGRAPHY

Dean, Dennis R. "New Light on William Maclure." *Annals of Science* 46 (1989): 549–574.

Gerstner, Patsy A. "The Academy of Natural Sciences of Philadelphia 1812–1850." In *The Pursuit of Knowledge in the Early American Republic: American Scientific Societies from Colonial Times to the Civil War,* edited by Alexandra Oleson and Sanborn E. Brown. Baltimore: Johns Hopkins University Press, 1976, pp. 174–193.

Maclure, William. "Observations on the Geology of the United States, Explanatory of a Geological Map." *Transactions of the American Philosophical Society* 6, pt. 2 (1809): 411–428.

————. *Observations on the Geology of the United States of America.* 1817. Reprint (Historiae Scientarum Elementa, 1), Munich: Werner Fritsch, 1966. Also published as "On the Geology of the United States of North America." *Transactions of the American Philosophical Society,* n.s., 1 (1818): 1–92.

————. *The European Journals of William Maclure.* Edited by John S. Doskey. *Memoirs of the American Philosophical Society* 171. Philadelphia: American Philosophical Society, 1988.

Morton, Samuel George. "A Memoir of William Maclure, Esq., Late President of the Academy of Natural Sciences of Philadelphia, (Read before the Academy, July 1, 1841)." *American Journal of Science* 47 (1844): 1–17.

Newell, Julie R. "American Geologists and Their Geology: The Formation of the American Geological Community, 1780–1865." Ph.D. diss., University of Wisconsin-Madison, 1993.

Julie R. Newell

Mammalogy

The study of mammals. The fauna and flora of North America were of considerable interest to the naturalists, travelers, colonists, and other visitors who arrived in this hemisphere beginning in the late fifteenth century. The animals encountered were either eaten or had their fur or hides utilized for clothing, decoration, or other purposes. Generally, only those species whose presence was most obvious or whose structure or habits were unusual had attention called to them.

The first descriptions of North American mammals were made by Spanish, French, and English explorers and date from the sixteenth century, and most published descriptions which appeared over the next 200 years consisted of accounts written by explorers, travelers, and those promoting settlement in the colonies. Pehr (Peter) Kalm, a Swedish protégé of Linnaeus, traveled in the colonies between 1748 and 1751. His notes and book *En Resa til Norra America* (1753–1761) contributed much to his mentor's understanding of North American wildlife for successive editions of the *Systema Naturae.*

The first detailed and illustrated, but non-Linnaean description of the mammals was provided by Mark Catesby, whose *Natural History of Carolina, Florida, and the Bahama Islands* (1729–1747) was perhaps the best colonial account.

Philadelphia was the first important center of research in mammalogy in the postrevolutionary United States, and it maintained its dominance from the 1790s until the late 1830s. The specimen collections of Peale's Museum (1784), the Academy of Natural Sciences of Philadelphia (1812), and several medical colleges were the largest in the nation before the establishment of the Smithsonian Institution in 1846.

The earliest American publication on mammals was probably an American edition of Thomas Bewick's *General History of Quadrupeds* (1804), with a few uniquely American species contributed anonymously, either by Samuel Latham Mitchill or George Ord. Ord was responsible for a section describing known American mammals in the second American edition of William Guthrie's *Geographical . . . Grammar,* published in 1815, although his name does not appear in the book.

Art and medicine were the two major avenues through which the study of mammals was approached during the first half of the nineteenth century. Charles Willson Peale, a self-taught artist, housed his museum first in his home and then on the second floor of Independence Hall. In 1799–1800, he presented what was probably the first popular American lecture series on mammals and birds of the world, based in part on his specimen collections. Peale's Museum was in operation for sixty years, and was the first to feature painted backgrounds suggestive of habitat for many mounted specimens. *The American Natural History* (1826–1828) was a three-volume work by Peale's physician son-in-law John Godman. Based in part on specimens in Peale's Museum, it was the first original monographic work describing all known American species. Courses in anatomy and other medical subjects constituted the only postgraduate training available to aspiring zoologists until the mid-nineteenth century.

Early collections of mammals of the American West were made by army explorers Captains Meriwether Lewis and William Clark (1804–1806); Lieutenant Zebulon Pike (1805–1807), and Major Stephen Long (1817, 1820, 1823). Artists, surgeons, and naturalists, most of them in the early stages of their careers, accompanied these and later expeditions. Canadian species first received monographic attention in the first volume of Sir John Richardson's *Fauna Boreali Americana* (1829), which remained standard for many decades.

The famous collaboration of the artist John James Audubon and the Lutheran clergyman John Bachman resulted in the three-volume *Viviparous Quadrupeds of North America* (1845–1854), a brilliantly illustrated account of the 155 American species then known.

Spencer F. Baird was a seminal figure in American zoology whose *Mammals of North America* (1859), a model of accuracy for its time, provided scientific descriptions of 273 forms. Baird, long assistant secretary (1850–1878) and secretary (1878–1887) of the Smithsonian, brilliantly synthesized data brought back by a number of young civilian naturalists attached to the Pacific Railroad Surveys of the mid-1850s and the later geological and geographic surveys of the territories. Much the same was accomplished in Canada by both native and Canadian collectors working for the Hudson's Bay Company.

Work in mammalian paleontology was pioneered in the United States in the 1820s and 1830s by Richard Harlan and John Godman, both trained as physicians at the University of Pennsylvania. Later giants in this field included Joseph Leidy and Edward Drinker Cope of the University of Pennsylvania, and Othniel Charles Marsh at Yale.

In the 1840s, state geological and natural history surveys began contributing much new information in works such as Ebenezer Emmons's *Report on the Quadrupeds of Massachusetts* (1840) and James E. De Kay's *Mammalia* (1842), the first volume in his *Zoology of New York*.

Recent mammalogy as a distinctive field emerged in the 1870s and 1880s with the work of such men as Joel A. Allen at the American Museum of Natural History in New York and Clinton Hart Merriam at the Biological Survey in Washington. The occasional monographs and reports appearing in the Biological Survey's *North American Fauna* series beginning in 1889 included some of the first modern studies of American mammals and the mammal fauna of various regions of the North American continent. These publications continue today under the aegis of the U.S. Department of the Interior.

By 1900, the number of known forms had reached 1,450, owing to better methods of collecting specimens and field observation largely devised by Merriam and a small group of his colleagues. His theories of geographic distribution dominated American mammalogy until the 1920s. From the late 1920s on, work in this field became increasingly sophisticated. A number of Spencer Baird's protégés, such as as Elliot Coues, Frederick True, and others were among the first of a small but distinguished group of mammalogists working for the federal government.

Graduate programs in mammalogy were not developed until after 1900—the first doctorate was awarded by the University of California, Berkeley, in 1914.

During the first quarter of the twentieth century, however, the conclusions reached by independent and government mammalogists, most of them self-taught or trained on the job, were increasingly being supplemented and in some cases challenged by younger, university-trained specialists.

Work in speciation was dominated after the Civil War by "splitters," who distinguished between species on the basis of very fine anatomical distinctions. Sub-specific differences were given increasing emphasis beginning in the 1890s. By the 1920s, the splitters were increasingly being challenged by "lumpers," who recognized fewer species but greater numbers of subspecific forms based on their examination of the growing number of available specimens. The aggregate number of recognized American forms had risen to about 3,200 by the 1970s.

The American Society of Mammalogists was founded in 1919, in large part because mammalogy had finally achieved recognition as a distinct biological discipline. The society's members have for eighty years made vital professional contributions to the field in this country and abroad. American mammalogists have compiled an impressive record of research and publication in the past century. They have also become increasingly involved in a variety of domestic and international management and conservation initiatives. By the mid-twentieth century, the National Museum in Washington, the American Museum of Natural History in New York, and the Field Museum in Chicago, among others, had developed world class specimen collections.

Until the 1940s, work in American mammalogy was dominated by research in taxonomic, distributional, and natural history studies. In the past half century, increasing emphasis has been placed on physiology, population dynamics, behavior, and ecology, and sophisticated new methodologies have revolutionized the discipline. Mammalian paleontology has also made great strides.

Interdisciplinary research projects, as for example efforts involving mammalogists, psychologists, and anthropologists in fields such as primatology, have been very productive. International cooperation between American researchers and those working in various other parts of the world have been among a number of other important recent developments. Most mammalogists have traditionally been employed by federal and state wildlife agencies, by museums, and by college and university zoology departments.

BIBLIOGRAPHY

Gunderson, Harvey L. "The Evolution of Mammalogy: A History of the Science." In *Mammalogy*. New York: McGraw Hill, 1976, pp. 3–39.

Hamilton, William J. Jr. "Mammalogy in North America." In *A Century of Progress in the Natural Sciences* [edited by Edward L. Kessel]. San Francisco: California Academy of Natural Sciences, 1955, pp. 661–668.

Hoffmeister, Donald, and Keir B. Sterling, "Origin." In *Seventy-Five Years of Mammalogy, 1919–1994*, edited by Elmer C. Birney and Jerry R. Choate. Special Publication of the American Society of Mammalogists, no. 11. Lawrence, KS: Allen Press, 1994, pp. 1–21.

Sterling, Keir B., "Builders of the Biological Survey, 1885–1930." *Journal of Forest History* 30 (1989): 180–187.

Keir B. Sterling

Management, Scientific

Refers to a system of management created by engineer Frederick W. Taylor (1856–1915) designed to control the operations of organizations on the basis of demonstrated facts and the results of scientific investigation.

Taylor said scientific management was the practical result of a long evolution which began when he was an engineer at Midvale Steel in 1880. Historical research by John Hoagland has revealed many of the methods attributed to Taylor were already practiced in Europe in 1699, 1781, and 1822. To improve output, Taylor decided to take control of the machine shop from the workmen and placed it in the hands of management, replacing rule-of-thumb methods by scientific control. To accomplish this, he replaced traditional foremen with experts, or "functional foremen," who were responsible for supplying tools and work to the workmen, insuring tools were run at correct speed, keeping machines in good repair, analyzing the elementary movements of workers by time study, and enforcing discipline.

In 1898, Taylor was hired by Bethlehem Steel to improve the output in their huge machine shop. To do this, he not only planned to take control from the workers, but increase the cutting speed of tool steel. Prior to 1898, many blacksmiths treated tool steel under high heat to improve cutting speed, but kept the process a secret to keep their jobs secure. Taylor began his own experiments on tool steel in 1898. In the process, his assistant, Edmund Lewis, accidently discovered the value of high-heat treatment in increasing tool steel cutting speeds. Taylor, along with Maunsel

White, saw the economic value of this discovery, and together they secured patents on the process by 1901. Lewis, however, at Taylor's urging left Bethlehem in 1899, became an assistant to Thomas Edison, and did not share in the patents. To insure scientific control over high-speed steel, Taylor installed four functional foremen in the machine shop and four functional foremen in a planning department: route clerk, planning the route of the work; order-of-work clerk, planning the sequence of work; rate-fixing clerk, responsible for time studies, and an analyst. The use of high-speed steel and management's control of the shop increased output 500 percent by 1901. Taylor became famous for phenomenal increases in pig iron loading from 12.8 long tons to 45.0 long tons a day, supposedly achieved in 1899. Subsequent research, however, has revealed the scientific pig iron loading methods described by Taylor were a myth.

By 1901, high-speed steel and his management methods made Taylor famous, and he used this fame to publicize his ideas through books and factory installations. In factories, Carl Barth used the Bethlehem experience as the basis for the procedures to follow in installing scientific management that became standard for forty years: an outline of all necessary operations; analysis, experimentation, and measurement of each operation; integrating operations into individual tasks; establishing a sequence of material supply and operations insuring an economic flow of work, including charts of information flow anticipating system analysis by fifty years.

Additional contributions were made by several of Taylor's followers: Henry Gantt developed the Gantt Chart depicting how work was generated and scheduled through various operations. Frank Gilbreth created motion study, as an adjunct to time study, to study motions and reduce fatigue in factories and improve surgical procedures in hospitals. Richard Feiss introduced the behavioral sciences by developing workers through personnel counseling. Morris Cooke extended scientific management into municipal operations and universities.

The Eastern Rate Case Hearings in 1910–1911 and Justice Louis Brandeis coining of the term "Scientific Management," and the publication of Taylor's *Principles of Scientific Management* and its translation into a dozen languages created worldwide interest in a management system based on science. From 1911, scientific management became a powerful force in America.

Businessmen and workers both realized that the methods of scientific analysis could be used to increase production and wages. It was used in World War I to improve productivity in Europe and America, and in the years after the war, scientific management became so integrated into industry that by 1940 it disappeared as a separate identity in industry.

Historical research has revealed that many portions of Taylor's books and experiments were prepared by his assistants Sanford Thompson and Morris Cooke. We need more information on both the early studies of human work prior to 1880, and the development of scientific management after 1901. Closer study of the literature on the science of human work and mechanics published before 1880, wills, deeds, and other public records in Pennsylvania, New Jersey, New York, and Massachusetts, and Taylor Archives at Stevens Institute of Technology, and the National Canal Museum Archives in Easton, Pennsylvania, may yield new knowledge.

BIBLIOGRAPHY

Hoagland, John H. "Management before Frederick Taylor." *Academy of Management Proceedings,* 1955, pp. 15–24.
Taylor, Frederick W. *The Principles of Scientific Management.* New York: Harpers, 1911.
Wrege, Charles D. "Medical Men and Scientific Management: A Forgotten Chapter in Management History." *Review of Business and Economics* 18 (1983): 32–47.
Wrege, Charles D., and Regina Greenwood. "Frederick W. Taylor's 'Pig Iron Loading Observations' at Bethlehem, March 10, 1899–May 31, 1899; The Real Story." *Canal History and Technology Proceedings* 17 (1998): 159–201.
Wrege, Charles D., and Ronald G. Greenwood. *Frederick W. Taylor: The Father of Scientific Management; Myth and Reality.* Homewood, IL: Business One Irwin, 1991.
———. "The Early History of Midvale Steel and the Work of Frederick W. Taylor: 1865–1890." *Canal History and Technology Proceedings* 11 (1992): 145–176.
———. "Frederick W. Taylor's Work at Bethlehem Steel: Phase II, The Discovery of High-Speed Tool Steel; Was It an Accident?" *Canal History and Technology Proceedings* 14 (1994): 115–163.
Wrege, Charles D., and Anne Marie Stotka. "Cooke Creates a Classic: The Story Behind Frederick W. Taylor's: Principles of Scientific Management." *Academy of Management Review* 4 (1978): 736–749.
Wren, Daniel. *The Evolution of Management Thought.* 3d ed. New York: Wiley, 1987.

Charles D. Wrege

Marine Biological Laboratory

The Marine Biological Laboratory's (MBL) charter explains that it was founded in 1888 "for the purpose of establishing and maintaining a laboratory or station for scientific study and investigation, and a school for instruction in biology and natural history" (MBL Annual Report, 1888, p. 38). This combination of research laboratory and natural history school was new, and in setting the dual purpose, the trustees had resolved to try an experiment. Perhaps they would have lost their resolve and veered off track toward one function or the other when the two became at times difficult to balance. Yet, they also decided in the first year to make Charles Otis Whitman director of the new laboratory. Whitman was committed to the dual function, and he was a very dedicated and even rather stubborn proponent of what he believed was best. Whitman guaranteed that the MBL would be new and different. From the first, the laboratory was defined by three strong themes: innovation, independence, and the combination of instruction and investigation together.

Innovation appeared in the original mission, of course, but also in other actions. Whitman experimented with new courses and areas of research, including general physiology—a new field in the United States. He enthusiastically selected Jacques Loeb to direct his effort because he felt that Loeb was the best—even though Loeb was German and Jewish at a time when neither was very popular. Whitman introduced neurobiology with a course beginning in 1896—even though this brought in interests normally thought to belong to psychology or medicine. The second director, Whitman's protégé Frank Rattray Lillie, carried on the tradition by working to bring oceanography to Woods Hole through the Woods Hole Oceanographic Institution. Other examples abound, but the general theme is clear. Innovation has remained central to the MBL.

It is perhaps easier to be innovative because the bureaucracy remains small and less constraining than at universities and more "normal" year-round laboratories. The fact that until recently the MBL was only a summer lab helped allow people to come, try new things, and return home to the old and familiar if the innovations had not worked. Young researchers and students could try things without their department chairs or senior colleagues watching them. When people had good ideas which stretched beyond the available budget, Whitman, then Lillie, and then other directors worked to attract the funds to facilitate the work.

Although sometimes risky and sometimes resulting in failure, this spirit of innovation has produced a continuing sense of excitement and vitality for the laboratory.

Independence has allowed the innovation to work. Because no other institution oversees the MBL—no university or government agency or private foundation—the scientists run the place. Since 1897, scientists who work at the MBL become eligible to become corporation members who oversee the general decision making, while a board of trustees and administration carry out the policies.

As with any institution, financial pressures have, on occasion, pushed the laboratory to the brink of losing its independence. In the 1890s, a group of individuals connected with the University of Chicago offered to pay the bills in exchange for some oversight of the MBL. The trustees objected and fended off what they saw as the threat to their independence. In 1902, the situation became even more dire, and the recently established Carnegie Institution almost took over the MBL as a department of its larger operation. Fortunately for the cause of independence, the Carnegie Institution was not ready to take on such a project and agreed to offer temporary financial support rather than seeking permanent control. The generosity of the Carnegie Institution, Carnegie Foundation, Rockefeller Foundation, the General Education Board, Lillie's brother-in-law Charles Crane, many other benefactors, and eventually the government in the form of the National Institutes of Health and the National Science Foundation have made it possible over the years to maintain independence. The cost is in restricted funds and the inability to do everything that a larger endowment or greater operating budget might make possible, but the advantages have appeared to MBL scientists well worth the costs.

From the beginning, Whitman insisted on the complementary combination of research and teaching, saying:

> The research department should furnish just the elements required for the organization of a thoroughly efficient department of instruction. Other things being equal, the investigator is always the best instructor. The highest grade of instruction in any science can only be furnished by one who is thoroughly imbued with the scientific spirit, and who is actually engaged in original work. Hence the propriety—and, I may say, the necessity—of linking the function of instruction with that of investigation. (Whitman, Director's Report, 1888, p. 16)

The intention has always been to offer courses that complement rather than duplicate those "back home" and to take advantage of the available materials and questions raised by marine life. Course directors have limited terms, and they are given the resources to attract a diverse team of other instructors, so that the courses can remain fresh and responsive to scientific innovation.

The MBL faces a number of challenges. As costs escalate, it suffers from an insufficient endowment to secure the library and all activities comfortably. The MBL and Woods Hole are too small to allow as much expansion as some advocate. It is not possible to explore all aspects of biological research and teaching, and choices become more difficult as more options become available. It becomes more difficult—and more important—to hold on to the ideals of innovation, independence, instruction, and investigation that have defined the laboratory for over a century.

BIBLIOGRAPHY

Lillie, Frank R. *The Woods Hole Marine Biological Laboratory.* Chicago: University of Chicago Press, 1944.

Maienschein, Jane. *One Hundred Years Exploring Life, 1888–1988.* Boston: Jones and Bartlett, 1989.

Marine Biological Laboratory. *Annual Reports.* [In the Marine Biological Laboratory Archives.]

The Naples Zoological Station and the Marine Biological Laboratory: One Hundred Years of Biology. Symposium Supplement to *Biological Bulletin* 168 (1985).

Jane Maienschein

Marsh, George Perkins (1801–1882)

Physical geographer and environmental theorist. Born in Woodstock, Vermont, Marsh was educated at Dartmouth College. For a time, he worked as a teacher, businessman, and lawyer. He was largely unsuccessful in these occupations, finding greater satisfaction in scholarship. During his lifetime, he wrote widely on art, philology, religion, politics, and conservation. In 1843, he was elected to Congress as a Whig. Neither a great statesman nor a scientist, he was, nonetheless, influential at the interface of science and politics, being one of the strongest congressional supporters of the newly established Smithsonian Institution. In 1849, Marsh left Congress to become minister to Turkey. He briefly returned to private life in the United States in 1854, but spent the final twenty-one years of his life (1861–1882) as minister to Italy.

M

In his early writings, Marsh espoused a strident environmental determinism. Northern climates bred strength and virtue, while warmer climates bred indolence and corruption. Extolling New England Puritans as the last vestige of the ideal Gothic type, he denounced Roman Catholicism and the influx of unassimilated immigrants from southern Europe. This parochial identification of America with New England also led him to strongly oppose the western expansion of the United States.

In his mature writings, Marsh reversed this environmental determinism. In *Man and Nature* (1864), his most influential work, he emphasized the pervasive influence that human activities have on the environment. Rather than nature shaping human character, as he had earlier claimed, the theme of his later book was that humans shape nature. Although not denying the benefits of industrial technology, Marsh was more impressed by the destructiveness of human activity. Through greed and thoughtlessness, humans degrade local environments. Rejecting both unrestrained development and Henry David Thoreau's return to nature, Marsh called for a rational management of the environment.

Marsh staked out a subtle middle ground between the poles of preservationism and utilitarianism in environmental thought. In contrast to Thoreau and John Muir, he rejected transcendentalism and was quite unsentimental about nature: humanity and nature are separate. Far more than Gifford Pinchot, however, he was willing to place esthetics on an equal footing with economics in environmental decision making. *Man and Nature* was perhaps the most important book on physical geography written during the nineteenth century. It was widely read, and it continued to influence environmental theory during the twentieth century, particularly through the writings of Lewis Mumford and Stewart Udall. More recently, some ecologists (Botkin) have criticized Marsh for perpetuating a misguided belief in the "balance of nature." Like many other naturalists of the period, Botkin argues, Marsh incorrectly assumed that undisturbed nature would remain indefinitely in a state of constancy and stability.

BIBLIOGRAPHY

Botkin, Daniel B. *Discordant Harmonies: A New Ecology for the Twenty-first Century.* New York: Oxford University Press, 1990.

Curtis, Jane, Will Curtis, and Frank Lieberman. *The World of George Perkins Marsh, America's First Conservationist and Environmentalist.* Woodstock, VT: Countryman Press, 1982.

Lowenthal, David. *George Perkins Marsh: Versatile Vermonter.* New York: Columbia University Press, 1958.

Marsh, George Perkins. *Man and Nature.* 1864. Edited by David Lowenthal. Cambridge, MA: Harvard University Press, 1965.

Nash, Roderick. *Wilderness and the American Mind.* 3d ed. New Haven: Yale University Press, 1982.

Russell, Franklin. "The Vermont Prophet: George Perkins Marsh." *Horizon* 10 (1968): 16–23.

Udall, Stewart L. *The Quiet Crisis.* New York: Holt, Rinehart and Winston, 1963.

Joel B. Hagen

Marsh, Othniel Charles (1831–1899)

Vertebrate paleontologist. Born in Lockport, New York, Marsh attended Phillips Academy in the early 1850s and later Yale College. Graduating from Yale in 1860, he entered the Sheffield Scientific School and completed his M.A. in 1862. Intent on pursuing an academic career, Marsh embarked for Germany for additional coursework. In 1863, his uncle George Peabody, eager to promote education and Marsh's career, donated $150,000 to Yale for a museum. The gift secured Marsh's future, and in 1866, he became professor of paleontology at Yale and director of the Peabody Museum of Natural History. From 1882 until 1899, he was vertebrate paleontologist of the United States Geological Survey. He was president of the American Association for the Advancement of Science in 1878 and president of the National Academy of Sciences from 1883 to 1895.

Marsh worked primarily in vertebrate paleontology. His early interests lay in mineralogy and chemical geology, but existing appointments at Yale led him to turn his attention to vertebrate paleontology. Following fieldwork in Connecticut and New Jersey in the late 1860s, Marsh became convinced of the significance of western deposits, and in 1870, he outfitted the first of several fossil hunting expeditions. Those explorations, financed by Marsh and manned by Yale College students, yielded magnificent discoveries. Remains of fossil horses, birds with teeth, and flying reptiles captured the attention of the scientific community and provided important confirmation of evolution. Marsh abandoned fieldwork in 1875 but continued to employ students and collectors, and by the early 1880s, his collection rivaled any in Europe. Those materials were the basis for Marsh's many technical papers as well as his monographs *Odontornithes* (1880), *Dinocerata* (1886), and "The Dinosaurs of North America" (1896).

Marsh's work in paleontology fueled a serious controversy with Edward Drinker Cope. Although they had worked together in the 1860s, Marsh in 1873 accused Cope of violating established scientific rules and regulations. Both men were highly ambitious, but Marsh initiated the accusations against Cope. The result was a bitter personal feud that led Marsh to seek retribution against Cope and Ferdinand V. Hayden, for whom Cope worked. In the mid-1870s, Marsh became part of an informal group of scientists who sought to gain control of government science. In 1878, as president of the National Academy, he played a crucial role in creating a new geological survey and appointing Clarence King its director. In 1882, John Wesley Powell, King's successor, appointed Marsh government vertebrate paleontologist. For the next ten years, Marsh maintained large operations in both the laboratory and the field. Cope complained that Marsh exploited his assistants and restricted access to his collections, but Marsh fended off such criticism and effectively isolated Cope from obtaining the necessary resources to continue his work. In 1890, Cope repeated the accusations in newspaper articles and several of Marsh's assistants promptly quit. A congressional investigation of Powell's survey in 1892 resulted in major budgetary and personnel reductions and had serious consequences for Marsh. He retained a position as honorary government paleontologist but with a much reduced budget and staff. His personal fortune was also depleted, and in 1896 Marsh, for the first time, taught classes at Yale. He continued to publish and promote collecting, but efforts in later years paled in comparison to his scientific activities of the 1880s.

Marsh, like Cope, has been the subject of many studies. Most biographies describe his notable achievements. Studies of the fossil feud discuss his discoveries and personality, describing Marsh as an intense, selfish, and ambitious man who sought to monopolize vertebrate paleontology. Recent work examines Marsh in light of social and political changes in American science. His interest in developing a more professional, specialized science influenced his actions against Cope in the 1870s (Rainger). Institutional factors explain his success in isolating Cope (Maline). To date, there is no good biography that examines Marsh in light of the changes occurring in late-nineteenth-century American science.

BIBLIOGRAPHY

Lanhan, Url. *The Bone Hunters.* New York: Columbia University Press, 1973.

Maline, Joseph M. "Edward Drinker Cope (1840–1897)." Master's thesis, University of Pennsylvania, 1974.

Marsh, Othniel Charles. *Odontornithes: A Monograph of the Extinct Toothed Birds of North America.* Washington, DC: Government Printing Office, 1880.

———. *Dinocerata: A Monograph of an Extinct Order of Gigantic Mammals.* Washington, DC: Government Printing Office, 1886.

———. "The Dinosaurs of North America." *Annual Report of the United States Geological Survey* 16, pt. 1 (1896): 133–244.

Rainger, Ronald. "The Bone Wars: Cope, Marsh, and American Vertebrate Paleontology, 1865–1900." In *The Ultimate Dinosaur*, edited by Robert Silverberg and Martin Greenberg. New York: Bantam Books, 1992, pp. 389–405.

Schuchert, Charles, and Clara Mae LeVene. *O.C. Marsh: Pioneer in Paleontology.* New Haven: Yale University Press, 1940.

Shor, Elizabeth Noble. *The Fossil Feud between E.D. Cope and O.C. Marsh.* Hicksville, NY: Exposition, 1974.

Ronald Rainger

SEE ALSO

Cope, Edward Drinker

Martin, Henry Newell (1848–1896)

Irish-born physiologist, biologist, and educator. Martin was educated at University College, London, where he studied under physiologists William Sharpey and Michael Foster, and Cambridge University. He served as Foster's demonstrator at both institutions and assisted biologist and educational reformer Thomas Huxley at the Royal College of Science, London. Huxley encouraged Daniel Gilman, president of Johns Hopkins University, to offer Martin the chair of biology at the new Baltimore institution. Martin accepted because the opportunities for research and advanced teaching at the well-endowed university seemed ideal. In 1876, Martin moved to Baltimore, where, three years later, he married Hetty Cary.

By the early 1880s, Martin had assembled at Hopkins an outstanding group of young scientists including William K. Brooks, William T. Sedgwick, Henry Sewall, and William H. Howell. Reflecting Foster's influence, circulatory physiology was the predominant theme of Martin's research. In the early 1880s, he and his colleagues developed the first isolated mammalian heart preparation with which they studied a wide range of physiological and pharmacological problems. Subsequently, many European and American investigators used Martin's preparation or variations of it in their circulatory experiments. Martin's contributions resulted in his election to fellowship in the Royal Society of London in 1883. The same year, he became the target of a malicious and sustained attack by antivivisectionists who objected to the animal experiments performed in his laboratory. He later was a cofounder of the American Physiological Society (1887), and, with Henry P. Bowditch and S. Weir Mitchell, was influential in defining its character.

Like his mentor Huxley, Martin tried to popularize science. Besides his formal university courses, Martin lectured to Baltimore physicians, spoke before public audiences, and organized a biology course for schoolteachers. With his wife, Martin wrote a popular college textbook, *The Human Body* (1881).

Martin's remarkable career came to a premature end, however. A sensitive and temperamental man, he was, by 1891, an alcoholic suffering from painful peripheral neuritis that resulted in morphine addiction. He was forced to resign from Johns Hopkins as these problems led to more frequent and prolonged absences. Martin returned to England in the spring of 1894. He died at Burley-in-Wharfdale, Yorkshire.

During his short career, Martin made important scientific discoveries and played a major role in the professionalization of physiology in America.

BIBLIOGRAPHY

Breathnach, C.S. "Henry Newell Martin (1848–1893) [sic]. A Pioneer Physiologist." *Medical History* 13 (1969): 271–279.

Fye, W. Bruce. "H. Newell Martin: A Remarkable Career Destroyed by Neurasthenia and Alcoholism." *Journal of the History of Medicine and Allied Sciences* 40 (1985): 133–160.

———. "H. Newell Martin and the Isolated Heart Preparation: The Link between the Frog and Open Heart Surgery." *Circulation* 73 (1986): 857–864.

Martin, H. Newell. *Physiological Papers*. Baltimore: Johns Hopkins Press, 1895.

W. Bruce Fye

Maury, Matthew Fontaine (1806–1873)

American oceanographer, meteorologist, astronomer, and naval officer. Born near Fredericksburg, Virginia, and raised in Tennessee, Maury had limited formal education, concluding with his graduation from Harpeth Academy in 1825. He entered the navy as a midshipman in 1825 and attained the rank of lieutenant in 1836. In 1837, he was appointed astronomer for the proposed exploring expedition to the South Seas (the Wilkes Expedition), but resigned in the extended quarrels that preceded the expedition's departure. Injury in a stagecoach accident in 1839 left him permanently unfit for sea duty, but appointment as superintendent of the Depot of Charts and Instruments in 1842 and head of the Naval Observatory at its creation in 1844 provided him with prestigious land duty and considerable influence and scientific resources. He resigned in 1861, joining the Confederate navy and serving the Confederacy in a number of roles until 1865. After the Civil War, he lived abroad, returning to the United States in 1868 to take a professorship at the Virginia Military Institute and remaining there until his death.

Maury's primary scientific interests lay in gathering and collating data on winds and currents to produce documents of use in military and commercial navigation. His contributions in astronomy were minimal and primarily observational, despite his control of the Naval Observatory. His utilization of information contained in numerous ships' logs stored at the Depot of Charts and Instruments and solicited from naval and civilian captains allowed him to produce navigational charts and instructions that saved time, money, and lives (Goetzmann, p. 314). He combined his various papers presented before the scientific associations of America with the data from his navigational works to produce *The Physical Geography of the Sea* (1855), a work often hailed as the beginning of the science of oceanography and equally often criticized as having little content of real value.

Maury often found himself at the center of contention and controversy. His position as head of the Naval Observatory generated animosity on two fronts. Other naval officers, especially those opposed to his outspoken views promoting naval reform, saw it as an undeserved and especially choice shore duty. The elite of American science, particularly Alexander Dallas Bache and the Lazzaroni, resented his control over the scientific resources represented by the observatory and his attempts to extend his authority and influence to issues and questions beyond his training and expertise. His status as a self-taught Southerner, as well as his willingness to generate seemingly outlandish theory and unwillingness to modify his ideas in the face of criticism, led to his condemnation as a scientific charlatan (Burstyn, p. 197).

Whatever his excesses of theory, Maury's contributions to navigation and to the understanding of the physical characteristics of the sea were recognized by his contemporaries at home and abroad and brought him numerous awards and honors. That the scientific elite of his day did not share this high opinion of Maury can be understood partly in their concern with setting and defending standards of professionalism, partly in their recognition that Maury's work and control of scientific resources represented potential competition to key projects such as Bache's Coast Survey and Joseph Henry's meteorological network, and partly in Maury's taste for theory and dispute.

BIBLIOGRAPHY

Bruce, Robert V. *The Launching of Modern American Science, 1846–1878.* New York: Knopf, 1987.

Burstyn, Harold L. "Maury, Matthew Fontaine." *Dictionary of Scientific Biography.* Edited by Charles C. Gillispie. New York: Scribner, 1974, 9:195–197.

Corbin, Diana Fontaine Maury. *A Life of Matthew Fontaine Maury.* London: S. Low, Marston, Searle & Revington, 1888.

Goetzmann, William H. *New Lands New Men: America and the Second Great Age of Discovery.* New York: Viking, 1986.

Maury, Matthew Fontaine. *Physical Geography of the Sea.* New York: Harper and Brothers, 1855.

Slotten, Hugh Richard. *Patronage, Practice and the Culture of American Science: Alexander Dallas Bache and the U.S. Coast Survey.* Cambridge, U.K.: Cambridge University Press, 1994.

Williams, Francis L. *Matthew Fontaine Maury, Scientist of the Sea.* New Brunswick: Rutgers University Press, 1963.

Julie R. Newell

McCarthyism and Science

One of the most significant periods in American history as it related to scientific freedom was the era of McCarthyism—the late 1940s and early 1950s—named after the anti-Communist crusade of Senator Joseph R. McCarthy. During periods of crisis, powerful government officials, such as J. Edgar Hoover, director of the Federal Bureau of Investigation (FBI) in the McCarthy era, can formulate a concept of academic freedom and free expression that makes scientists vulnerable to outside influences, particularly to government interference and to the pressures of public opinion.

The McCarthy era targeted many scientists as being subversive. A number of government scientists were employed by universities while working on military projects. These scientists were subject to loyalty-security checks by Hoover and the FBI.

Scientists were frequently suspected by Hoover of "subversive associations" and caught between political pressures and the demands of honest scientific research. A considerable number of scientists were suspended from government-funded research during this era.

Many scientists at that time argued that a policy of secrecy regarding atomic research would not prevent the Russians from gaining access to the atomic bomb. It was believed by scientists that secrecy would hinder the progress of the United States in atomic research because non-American scientists on an international level could not join together and share their ideas and research findings regarding atomic energy. Many congressional leaders argued the opposite and there was a call for tighter FBI controls in the area of government-sponsored scientific research.

Hoover's involvement in FBI investigations of many leading scientists during the McCarthy era produced government intrusion upon their intellectual freedom. Hoover's fear of internal subversion, his fear of a Communist takeover of America's atomic secrets, and his fear that intellectual talent of this country would subvert our academic institutions produced much turmoil within the intellectual community. The McCarthy era gave Hoover an opportunity to act on his concern over subversives and Communists within American society and to have a major impact on scientific research and free thought.

BIBLIOGRAPHY

Fisher, Donald C. "J. Edgar Hoover's Concept of Academic Freedom and Its Impact on Scientists during the McCarthy Era, 1950–1954." Ph.D. diss., University of Mississippi, 1986.

Donald C. Fisher

Measurement

John Quincy Adams defined measures and weights as "the instruments used by man for the comparison of quantities, and proportions of things" (Adams, p. 6). The Native American tribes of North America had adapted measuring systems built into their material culture. The ships bearing the first English colony to

Roanoke in 1584 navigated by the coordinates of latitude and longitude that in principle provided a grid for the whole new continent as well as the ocean. The mathematician Thomas Harlot, who accompanied the first settlement, described the fields of the inhabitants in terms of the English customary measure, the rod, thus imprinting on the landscape the length measure still in use in the United States.

By the eve of the American Revolution, all of the colonies had developed extensive bodies of statute law defining and regulating the use of measurement systems. The commissioners of customs sent over from England used standards and units common to the British mercantile system rather than to English or Scottish local custom. The colonies collectively thus had less diversity in their measurement systems than any country in Europe. The worldwide effort of scientists to observe the transits of Venus in 1761 and 1769 for the purpose of measuring the distance from the earth to the sun gave North Americans such as David Rittenhouse experience in making instruments and cooperative arrangements that met the highest standards of the time.

With peace in 1783, a pressing national problem was the measuring of western lands. Thomas Jefferson suggested a rectilinear grid based on the geographic mile, with units using customary names but bearing decimal relations to one another. A committee of the Confederation Congress retained the general frame but substituted the English statute mile. This choice made the area of a square mile of land, a section, comprise exactly 640 acres, and preserved the uniformity of proportion of the various length measures dividing the mile. The Land Ordinance of 1785 set the land grid for most of the country from Ohio westward.

The Constitution gave the Congress power to fix the standard of weights and measures, but the accumulated body of state legislation was left in place. Secretary of State John Quincy Adams's *Report upon Weights and Measures* of 1821 examined the whole question of policy for weights and measures on historical principles. He carefully examined the French metric system, at that time not working well in France, but concluded that the uniformity of the American system could best be preserved by authorizing the manufacture of new sets of standards according to existing units and by distributing them to the states and to customs houses. The office set up in 1831 to carry out this task was administered by the United States Coast Survey for the rest of the nineteenth century.

With the creation of the National Academy of Sciences in 1863, the scientific community began to take an active interest in reform of weights and measures. In 1866, Congress passed a law formally legalizing the metric system, and President F.A.P. Barnard of Columbia University became the leading proponent of the French system. He organized the United States participation in the international conferences leading to the Treaty of the Meter in 1875. He was also aware that, through the action of journal editors and scientific societies, most American chemists and physicists were using the metric system extensively by the 1880s. He did not feel, however, that in a democracy a decision to convert the language of the whole country should be imposed on the people from above, and his organizations concentrated instead on educational campaigns. Hence the evolution of the United States system of measurement continued, based on the units already in use.

During the 1890s, rapid industrial development and the need for standards in new fields such as electricity forced the federal government into action. The National Bureau of Standards, created in 1900, moved beyond the passive custody of standards of length and mass to the active comparison of standards used in science, engineering, manufacturing, commerce, and education. The bureau undertook to determine physical constants and the properties of materials. It also had the power to solve problems that arise in connection with standards, a very broad mandate to engage in research in many disciplines.

The adaptation of standards to the mainstream of American material life achieved under the guidance of the National Bureau of Standards has carried through into the electronic, nuclear, and computer ages. After World War II, for example, bureau scientists had a prominent role in developing an atomic clock.

Shifting to the metric system is an option considered in every age. In the twentieth century, the scientific community has provided the main advocates for the change. After British and Canadian conversion, the proposal reached the status of law in the Metric Conversion Act of 1975. Under it action remained voluntary, and the evolution of American measurement has been scarcely deflected. The place of measurement in American culture is unique because of the total historical experience of the people.

BIBLIOGRAPHY

Adams, John Quincy. *Report of the Secretary of State upon Weights and Measures.* 1821. Reprint, edited by A. Hunter Dupree, New York: Arno Press, 1980.

Barnard, Frederick A.P. *The Metric System of Weights and Measures; An Address Delivered before the Convocation of the University of the State of New York, At Albany, August 1, 1871.* New York: Board of Trustees of Columbia College, 1872.

Cochrane, Rexmond C. *Measures for Progress: A History of the National Bureau of Standards.* Washington, DC: National Bureau of Standards/United States Department of Commerce, 1966.

Comptroller General of the United States. *Report to the Congress: Getting a Better Understanding of the Metric System—Implications if Adopted by the United States.* Washington, DC: General Accounting Office, 1978.

Dupree, A. Hunter. "Metrication as Cultural Adaptation." *Science* 185 (19 July 1974): 208.

———. "The Measuring Behavior of Americans." In *Nineteenth-Century American Science: A Reappraisal,* edited by George H. Daniels. Evanston: Northwestern University Press, 1986, pp. 22–37.

Treat, Charles F. *History of the Metric System Controversy in the United States.* Washington, DC: National Bureau of Standards/United States Department of Commerce, 1971.

A. Hunter Dupree

Medicine, Native American

Medical practices among Native American tribes comprised the use of herbs, physical manipulation, and ritual acts designed to restore an individual to a state of well-being generally defined by perceptions of appropriate and harmonious relationship with both the natural and the social environment. Medicine was based in beliefs about the spiritual forces that manifested themselves in physical phenomena. It was thus concerned with balances of power. Healers were individuals who had control over certain kinds of spiritual powers or had the ability to enlist their aid in restoring an individual to health.

Illness was thought to be caused by human or spiritual agency. Human sorcery or spiritual malevolence could cause foreign objects to enter a person's body. Contact with a spirit, even a disinterested or benevolent one, could affect an individual.

Treatments followed an internal cultural logic. Humans, through ritual knowledge, could protect themselves from the dangers inherent in contact with spiritual powers. Plants, as living, spiritual beings in the environment, had power to effect changes in the human body. Rituals, which established relationships between human practitioners and spiritual forces, could right imbalances of power that affected a person's health. Physical manipulation was used in cases of broken bones, dislocated joints, or fetuses in difficult births.

Native American uses of plants and physical treatments did much to inform the medical practices of early European settlers in North America. Trillium, a widely used aid for childbirth among Plains Indians, was adopted by white settlers under the name "squaw root." The *ephedra* used by many tribes in the desert Southwest and Great Basin area was adopted by whites under the names "Indian Tea," "Mexican Tea," and "Mormon Tea."

Native medicine came to be a symbol of the credulity of ordinary Americans, attracted by the mystique of Indian-snake-oil salesmen, as "scientific" medicine emerged with the advent of such medical practices as pasteurization, vaccination, and anesthesia. Still, the medical practices of rural communities even by the late nineteenth century incorporated elements of native medicine. Almost 200 plants used by American Indian tribes appeared at some time in the *United States Pharmacopeia.*

Although settlers in the rural regions of America from the sixteenth through the nineteenth centuries rejected the religious basis of Native American medicine because of their own religious beliefs, they certainly found comfort in the relief that native knowledge of herbs could provide them.

BIBLIOGRAPHY

Moerman, Daniel E. *Medicinal Plants of Native America.* Technical reports, University of Michigan. Museum of Anthropology, no. 19. Research reports in ethnobotany; contribution 2. Ann Arbor: University of Michigan, Museum of Anthropology, c1986.

Vogel, Virgil J. *American Indian Medicine.* 2d ed. Norman: University of Oklahoma Press, 1990.

Clara Sue Kidwell

SEE ALSO

Native Americans—Relations to Natural World

Medicine, Unorthodox

All forms of health care practices not accepted as correct, proper, or appropriate, or that are not in conformity with the beliefs or standards of the dominant group of medical practitioners in a society, may be considered unorthodox medicine.

Various types of unorthodox medicine have arisen in America, including medical sects (homeopathy, eclecticism, hydropathy, and physio-medicalism in the nineteenth century, osteopathy and chiropractic in the twentieth century), folk medical practices (i.e., pow-wow, cuaranderismo), popular health movements (Thomsonism, Grahamism, physical culture, holistic health), medico-religious movements (Christian Science, Unity, Pentecostalism), as well as drug and device quackery.

Historically, all forms of unorthodox medicine have usually been viewed by scholars as representing the antithesis of science by embracing closed, narrow, and dogmatic systems of health and disease, unwilling to test assumptions, and fighting medical progress and needed public health reforms. Its exponents were often characterized as either scheming manipulators who knew of the hoaxes they were perpetuating upon the populace or else they were self-deluded. In either case, the consequence was that their patients/victims were being denied or otherwise kept away from scientific management which alone could convey true health benefits.

While some elements of this characterization are still considered valid, modern historical scholarship has moved away from this essentially orthodox medical perspective to also consider in historical and social context the claims of unorthodox practitioners with respect to what constitutes medical science, the failures of orthodox treatment, their motivation, and the data supporting their own successes. Furthermore, scholars have independently looked at the variety of reasons why patients seek out alternative forms of care and lay evaluation of such care. As a consequence, recent scholarly studies have been, on the whole, more balanced and objective, and have added considerably to our fund of knowledge about this range of phenomena.

Although doctrinally rigid at their inception, some forms of unorthodox medicine quickly manifest internal diversity of views and practices and undergo considerable evolutionary growth. Both sectarian and popular health movements have historically begun by justifying their existence through already existing scientific studies, although selectively incorporating only works which support their basic premises. However, new, significant lines of scientific investigation and discovery (such as bacteriology and immunology with the development of new biological tools such as vaccines and serum therapy) have posed intellectual and practical dilemmas, particularly to sectarian physicians, who have had to choose between dogma and powerful empirical data which does not find direct backing from original sectarian tenets. As sectarian groups have come closer to orthodox medicine with respect to both their principles and practices, the unity necessary to maintain a separate existence is weakened, particularly as orthodox medicine's barriers to interaction with their competitors is lowered. On the other hand, religious movements, whose beliefs in the superiority of divine or spiritual healing do not rely on scientific studies, can remain relatively stable, although the case of Christian Science at the turn of the twentieth century shows how political and legal challenges from without can lead to practical accommodations in a movement to ensure survival.

BIBLIOGRAPHY

Cayleff, Susan. *"Wash and Be Healed": The Water-Cure Movement and Women's Health.* Philadephia: Temple University Press, 1987.

Donegan, Jane. *"Hydropathic Highway to Health": Women and Water-Cure in Antebellum America.* Westport: Greenwood Press, 1986.

Gevitz, Norman. *The D.O.'s: Osteopathic Medicine in America.* Baltimore: Johns Hopkins University Press, 1982.

———, ed. *Other Healers: Unorthodox Medicine in America.* Baltimore: Johns Hopkins University Press, 1988.

Hand, Wayland, ed. *American Folk Medicine: A Symposium.* Berkeley: University of California Press, 1976.

Harrell, David. *All Things Are Possible: The Healing and Charismatic Revivals in Modern America.* Bloomington: Indiana University Press, 1975.

Kaufman, Martin. *Homeopathy in America: The Rise and Fall of a Medical Heresy.* Baltimore: Johns Hopkins University Press, 1971.

Rothstein, William. *American Physicians in the Nineteenth Century: From Sects to Science.* Baltimore: Johns Hopkins University Press, 1972.

Whorton, James. *Crusaders for Fitness: The History of American Health Reformers.* Princeton: Princeton University Press, 1982.

Young, James Harvey. *American Health Quackery.* Princeton: Princeton University Press, 1992.

Norman Gevitz

Medicine, Weather and

In the eighteenth century, a revival of Hippocratic medicine popularized the notion that atmospheric conditions were related to the outbreak and spread of disease. Dr. John Lining in Charleston, South Carolina, kept weather records throughout the 1740s and studied the influence of the weather and the seasons on his own body in an attempt to understand the cause of epidemic diseases. Numerous other physicians, including Lining's associate Lionel Chalmers, Edward Holyoke in Massachusetts, and William Currie and Benjamin Rush in Pennsylvania continued and extended these studies. In 1799, Noah Webster published a two-volume review of the relationships between "pestilential epidemics and sundry other phenomena of the physical world." He thought that weather conditions, comets, volcanic eruptions, earthquakes, and meteors were all epidemiological factors.

In the nineteenth century, before the development of the germ theory of disease, yellow fever was believed to be caused by hot temperatures, excess moisture, poor ventilation, and filth; mumps by exposure to severe cold weather, and storms of snow and rain. Even the ill effects of compounds such as sugar of lead as a treatment for chronic diarrhea (it paralyzed and killed patients) were blamed not on the medicine itself but on its unsupervised use in a fickle climate. The opinion of surgeon Henry Huntt, quoted by James Mann, in *Medical Sketches of the Campaigns of 1812, 13, 14* (1816), p. vii, was the dominant one: "A knowledge of geography in general, and topography [and climate], are particularly important to the physician and surgeon."

From 1814 to 1882, the surgeons general actively supported the collection of meteorological records by medical officers of the United States Army. Post physicians were instructed to "keep a diary of the weather" and "to make from time to time such remarks on meteorological phenomena, and the appearance of epidemicks, as may be deemed useful in promoting medical science" (*Military Laws* [1814], pp. 227–228, quoted in Fleming, p. 14). The result was a massive compilation of data on weather and health extending from the settled East Coast into the frontier and spanning most of the nineteenth century. Reports such as Samuel Forry's *The Climate of the United States and Its Endemic Influences* (1842) related a variety of climatic and weather conditions to the medical records of the troops. The surgeon general also supported the work of James Espy, who served as the "national meteorologist" in the 1840s.

In the 1850s, Edward Barton, a leading physician in New Orleans, argued that "the connection between mortality and meteorology is so intimate, that nowhere can they be independent of each other" (E.H. Barton et al., *Annual Report of the Board of Health of the City of New Orleans for 1849*, p. 3). He urged physicians and public health officials to compile both weather records and vital statistics so that miasmas could be avoided. Such compilations could be used to create maps of the fatal diseases of a community or region just as the collection of meteorological observations were employed to create weather maps.

Travel to remote areas for health reasons became popular in the 1830s, especially as a treatment for tuberculosis. This trend in medical therapy boomed with the development of health spas and with the settlement of the sunny and arid West. Late in the century, biometeorology and bioclimatology developed into scholarly subspecialties.

In the early twentieth century, the physical geographer and environmental determinist Ellsworth Huntington compiled statistics on factory workers output and correlated mortality rates with average temperature and humidity. He defined what he considered optimum climates for health and productivity: a temperature of sixty-four degrees Fahrenheit and a relative humidity of 80 percent for manual labor, and a temperature of forty degrees for optimal thinking.

There is still a considerable amount of work being done on medical and biological influences in meteorology and climatology. Recent publications include *Proceedings of the International Biometeorological Congress* (1960–) and *Advances in Bioclimatology* (Berlin, 1992). A "Weather and Health Workshop" was held in Canada in 1992. In 1994, the United States National Weather Service and the Environmental Protection Agency began to issue daily forecasts of potential health risks from exposure to ultraviolet radiation.

BIBLIOGRAPHY

Austin, Robert B. *Early American Medical Imprints: A Guide to Works Printed in the United States, 1668–1820.* Washington, DC: United States Department of Health, Education and Welfare, Public Health Service, 1961.

Bolton, Conevery A. "The Health of the Country: Body and Environment in the Making of the American West, 1800–1960." Ph.D. diss., Harvard University, 1998.

Cassedy, James H. "Meteorology and Medicine in Colonial America: Beginnings of the Experimental Approach." *Journal of the History of Medicine and Allied Sciences* 24 (1969): 193–204.

———. *Medicine and American Growth, 1800–1860.* Madison: University of Wisconsin Press, 1986.

Crosby, Alfred W. *The Columbian Exchange: Biological and Cultural Consequences of 1492.* Westport, CT: Greenwood, 1972.

Duffy, John. *From Humors to Medical Science: A History of American Medicine.* 2d ed. Urbana: University of Illinois Press, 1993.

Fleming, James R. *Meteorology in America, 1800–1870.* Baltimore: Johns Hopkins University Press, 1990.

Glacken, Clarence J. *Traces on the Rhodian Shore: Nature and Culture in Western Thought from Ancient Times to the End of the Eighteenth Century.* Berkeley: University of California Press, 1967.

Hippocrates. *Airs, Waters, Places.*

Hippocrates. *Of the Epidemics.*

Hume, Edgar Erskine. "The Foundation of American Meteorology by the United States Army Medical Department." *Bulletin of the History of Medicine* 8 (1940): 202–238.

King, Lester S. *Transformations in American Medicine: From Benjamin Rush to William Osler.* Baltimore: Johns Hopkins University Press, 1991.

Sargent, Frederick, II. *Hippocratic Heritage: A History of Ideas about Weather and Human Health.* New York: Pergamon, 1982.

James Rodger Fleming

Mellon Institute of Industrial Research

A nonprofit center for applied science that was founded in Pittsburgh in 1913 and merged with the Carnegie Institute of Technology in 1967 to become part of Carnegie Mellon University (CMU). Organized by the chemist and journalist Robert Kennedy Duncan, the Mellon Institute was among the first and most influential nonprofit vendors of research to American industry. Although the institution was housed and endowed by the Mellons, Pittsburgh's preeminent banking family, it performed research for hundreds of clients from across North America. Under the Mellon Institute's system, sponsors proposed topics of investigation and paid salaries and overhead for research fellows in return for access to the institute's facilities and exclusive rights to the results of research. By the late 1920s, the Mellon Institute handled nearly $1 million a year in contracts and employed over 140 research fellows, mostly chemists. These scientists were instrumental in developing scores of industrial products (e.g., adhesives, building materials, and oil-drilling muds) and enhancing the efficiency of industrial operations (e.g., removing benzene and sulfur from coking coals). Such firms as Kalgon, Plaskon, and Dow-Corning had their origins in products developed by the Mellon Institute, as did the chemical division of the Union Carbide Corporation and the research laboratories of the Gulf Oil Company.

The Mellon Institute's success helped prompt universities to establish agencies for sponsored research during the 1920s. The Mellon Institute also served as a model for such independent research institutes as the Battelle Memorial Institute of Cleveland and the Stanford Research Institute of Menlo Park. It ultimately forfeited its leadership as a vendor of research services to these rivals, however; some would argue because of its effort to shift emphasis from applied to basic research in the 1950s. Following its merger with Carnegie Tech, Duncan's fellowship system was discontinued and the Mellon Institute's property and endowment were absorbed by the educational divisions of CMU. A new Mellon Institute was later established by CMU to perform contract work for industry, although it lacked continuity with its namesake in personnel, facilities, and research emphasis.

The Mellon Institute may be seen as one among many twentieth-century experiments in the organization of industrial research; its little-explored history offers perspective on other such experiments (e.g., the in-house industrial research laboratory) and insight, as well, into the changing needs and expectations of scientists and businessmen in twentieth-century America.

BIBLIOGRAPHY

Mowery, David C., and Nathan Rosenberg. *Technology and the Pursuit of Economic Growth.* Cambridge, U.K.: Cambridge University Press, 1989.

Servos, John W. "Changing Partners: The Mellon Institute, Private Industry, and the Federal Patron." *Technology and Culture* 35 (1994): 221–257.

Thackray, Arnold. "University-Industry Connections and Chemical Research: An Historical Perspective." In *University-Industry Research Relationships: Selected Studies. Report of the National Science Board of the National Science Foundation.* Washington, DC: National Science Board, National Science Foundation, 1982.

John W. Servos

Menard, Henry William (1920–1986)

Marine geologist and science administrator. Menard's degrees in geology from the California Institute of Technology (B.A., 1942; M.S., 1947) were interrupted by naval service in the South Pacific. He completed his Ph.D. in marine geology at Harvard University in 1949, and in the same year joined the Sea Floor Studies Section of the Navy Electronics Laboratory in San Diego. In 1955, Menard joined the University of California's Scripps Institution of Oceanography (SIO) as associate professor of geology, where he was affiliated for the rest of his life. In 1965–1966, he was a technical advisor in the Office of Science and Technology and became director of the University of California's Institute of Marine Resources. Elected to the National Academy of Sciences in 1968, he served on several academy committees reviewing environmental issues from 1969 to 1974. Menard was director of the United States Geological Survey from 1978 to 1981.

Menard's research focused on the topography of the Pacific basin. By 1955, he had discovered and published his findings concerning a new class of geological structure: fracture zones. Fracture zones are faults which intersect midocean ridges at approximately right angles and on either side of which the ocean bottom has different depths. Menard discovered several parallel fracture zones in the Pacific. Others have been discovered in all of the earth's ocean basins.

The great size of fracture zones suggested that they were part of a global phenomenon. The examination of these zones by Menard and others led to the refinement of the seafloor spreading hypothesis. The increased acceptance of seafloor spreading has been recognized as a vital step in the development of the theory of plate tectonics. This theory states that the earth's outer shell is composed of several interdependent plates and includes principles for understanding the mechanisms that move these plates. This is the most widely accepted theory of continental drift.

During the ferment of what is commonly known as the "plate tectonic revolution," Menard published *Marine Geology of the Pacific* (1964), the most extensive discussion of the ocean floor in relation to tectonic ideas of that time.

Menard shared data and ideas with many of the scientists who made critical impacts on the revolution, including Harry H. Hess, Robert Sinclair Dietz, and Bruce Charles Heezen. His own account of the events that led up to the revolution are published in his *Ocean of Truth* (1986). Menard published a sociological study of science, *Science: Growth and Change* (1971), which was reviewed favorably by historians of science.

BIBLIOGRAPHY

Flanigan, Carol Lynn. *Guide to the Henry William Menard Papers.* SIO Technical Reference Number 92–27. San Diego: University of California, 1992.

Menard, H. William. "Deformation of the Northeastern Pacific and the West Coast of North America." *Bulletin of the Geological Society of America* 66 (1955): 1149–1198.

———. *Marine Geology of the Pacific.* New York: McGraw-Hill, 1964.

———. *Science: Growth and Change.* Cambridge, MA: Harvard University Press, 1971.

———. *Ocean of Truth: A Personal History of Global Tectonics.* Princeton: Princeton University Press, 1986.

Lynn Maloney

Menlo Park Laboratory

Thomas Edison's Menlo Park Laboratory, in West Orange, New Jersey, established in 1876, was the site of some of the most significant inventions of the nineteenth century—the carbon-transmitter telephone, the phonograph, and the incandescent electric light and power system. The laboratory was also important in its own right as a new location for inventive activity; it was the first research laboratory in which invention became an industrial process directed to corporate interests. At Menlo Park, Edison completed the process of separating his experimental machine shop from its manufacturing context and combining it with an electrical and chemical laboratory that was the envy of many scientists as well as other inventors. Initially, Edison directed his laboratory to research in telecommunications for Western Union Telegraph Company, which provided direct support for the laboratory. More significant for the laboratory's place in the history of industrial research, however, was its role as a research and development laboratory for the Edison Electric Light Company, formed in late 1878 by Western Union investors. By March 1881, the investors had spent nearly $130,000 on work that ranged from basic research into the problems of electric lighting to the development of components necessary for the commercialization of the new system. The laboratory itself was enlarged and Edison expanded its staff, hiring university-educated engineers and chemists as well as more of the machinists and self-educated experimenters he had relied on previously. In 1882, as Edison's new electrical factories established their own testing and research laboratories to solve problems specific to their products, he abandoned the laboratory.

During its brief existence, the Menlo Park Laboratory became a "celebrated" model for others and was visited by many of the leading scientists and technologists of the day. Historians have differed over how modern Menlo Park was, the relative place of science in the research process, and the extent of its influence in the rise of corporate industrial research laboratories. Nonetheless, there is general agreement that it was an important institution in the history of industrial research.

BIBLIOGRAPHY

Friedel, Robert, and Paul Israel, with Bernard Finn. *Edison's Electric Light: Biography of an Invention.* New Brunswick: Rutgers University Press, 1986.

Hughes, Thomas P. "Edison's Method." In *Technology at the Turning Point,* edited by William B. Pickett. San Francisco: San Francisco Press, 1977, pp. 5–22.

Israel, Paul. *Edison: A Life of Invention.* New York: John Wiley & Sons, 1998.

Israel, Paul, et al. *The Wizard of Menlo Park (1878).* Vol. 4 of *The Papers of Thomas A. Edison.* Baltimore: Johns Hopkins University Press, 1998.

Pretzer, William S., ed. *Working at Inventing: Thomas A. Edison and the Menlo Park Experience.* Dearborn, MI: Henry Ford Museum and Greenfield Village, 1989.

Rosenberg, Robert, et al. *Menlo Park: The Early Years (1876–1877).* Vol. 3 of *The Papers of Thomas A. Edison.* Baltimore: Johns Hopkins University Press, 1994.

Paul B. Israel

SEE ALSO
Edison, Thomas Alva; Electric Light Bulb

Mesmerism

A medical and psychological theory, often referred to as the science of animal magnetism. Mesmerism originated with the medical discoveries of the German physician Franz Anton Mesmer (1734–1815), who claimed to have detected the existence of a superfine energy or fluid which had somehow managed to elude scientific notice. Mesmer named this invisible energy "animal magnetism" and explained that it constituted the etheric medium through which sensations of every kind—light, heat, magnetism, electricity—are able to pass from one physical object to another. He reasoned that, when evenly distributed throughout the body, this vital energy imparts health to the human system. If, however, an individual's supply of animal magnetism is thrown out of equilibrium, bodily health begins to falter. Mesmer's science of animal magnetism aimed at recharging a patient's nervous system with this mysterious, yet life-giving energy by holding magnets in his hands and making manual "passes" along their spinal columns. One of Mesmer's disciples, the Marquis de Puysegur, found that many "mesmerized" patients fell into a hypnoticlike trance which contributed to their therapeutic recovery and frequently gave rise to such extraordinary mental feats as clairvoyance and telepathy. The adherents of mesmerism were confident that they had come upon not only the secret to medical science but also the means for exploring the untapped potentials of the unconscious mind.

Beginning in the 1830s, a number of spokespersons for the science of animal magnetism began making lecture tours of the eastern portion of the United States. Their demonstrations of mesmerism's healing powers captured the imagination of many middle-class Americans. Far more interesting, however, were the mesmerists' alleged ability to put volunteers into the mesmeric trance state and enable the subjects to spontaneously gain the ability to form telepathic communication with the mesmerist, gain clairvoyant knowledge of distant events, or diagnose and prescribe remedies for the illnesses of other members of the audience. Scores of books on the science of animal magnetism were written during the 1840s and 1850s, each heralding both mesmerism's medical value and its ability to shed light on "the psychological constitution of man." In particular, the American mesmerists proclaimed that humans possess a sixth sense or latent psychological power for receiving directly the information and vital healing energy transmitted via the spiritual medium of animal magnetism. Because mesmerism sought to study humanity's highest mental potentials, it was more than simply a medical or psychological theory. It also provided the framework for a metaphysical philosophy that promised to combine humanity's scientific and spiritual aspirations.

Few American investigators even attempted much in the way of rigorous experimentation with the medical and psychological phenomena surrounding mesmerism. Instead, they sought to connect mesmerism with the more innovative and unorthodox religious and metaphysical issues of the day, such as transcendentalism, Swedenborgianism, and spiritualism. By the mid-1860s, mesmerism all but disappeared as a distinct medical or psychological theory. Its major ideas, however, were by this time incorporated into any number of newly emerging medical, psychological, and religious theories. The mesmerist Phineas P. Quimby, for example, helped transform the science of animal magnetism into the popular philosophy known as the mind-cure or New Thought movement. The mind-cure movement can be accredited with developing wide-spread interest in early psychological ideas among the American reading public prior to the creation of academic departments in the 1880s. One of Quimby's students, Mary Baker Eddy, reworked mesmerist principles into Christian Science. Andrew Taylor Still and Daniel D. Palmer, the founders of osteopathic and chiropractic medicine, both practiced mesmerist healing and incorporated many of its principles into the early formulations of their innovative medical theories. And, finally, individuals such as Madame Blavatsky adapted mesmerist teachings into theosophy and other nineteenth-century metaphysical movements that were to lay the foundation for the many New Age medical and psychological theories popular in the late twentieth century.

BIBLIOGRAPHY

Ellenberger, Henri. *The Discovery of the Unconscious.* New York: Basic Books, 1970.

Fuller, Robert C. *Mesmerism and the American Cure of Souls.* Philadelphia: University of Pennsylvania Press, 1982.

Pomore, Frank. *From Mesmer to Christian Science.* New York: University Books, 1963.

Robert C. Fuller

Meteorology and Atmospheric Science

Early settlers in the New World found the climate harsher and the meteorological phenomena more violent than in the Old World. Many colonial Americans kept weather journals but, compared to European standards, few had adequate instruments. The first prolonged instrumental meteorological observations were taken by Dr. John Lining in Charleston, South Carolina, beginning in 1740 and were related to his medical concerns. Benjamin Franklin's famous lightning studies and Thomas Jefferson's support for wide-spread and comparative observations are worthy of note.

Early in the nineteenth century, the army Medical Department, the General Land Office, and the academies of the state of New York established large-scale climatological observing programs. The information was used in a variety of ways: physicians studied the relationship between weather and health, farmers and settlers needed temperature and rainfall statistics, and educators brought meteorological observations into the classroom. Of general interest were potential effects of the moon on the weather and of clearing and cultivation on the climate.

For over two decades, William Redfield, James Espy, and Robert Hare argued over the nature and causes of storms and the proper way to investigate them. Redfield focused on hurricanes as circular whirlwinds, Espy on the release of latent "caloric" in updrafts, and Hare on the role of electricity in storms. While it came to no clear intellectual resolution, the "American storm controversy" of the 1830s and 1840s stimulated the development of observational projects at the American Philosophical Society, the Franklin Institute, and the Smithsonian Institution.

The Smithsonian meteorological project, begun in 1848 under the direction of Joseph Henry, was America's "grand meteorological crusade," providing a uniform set of procedures and some standardized instruments to observers across the continent. Up to 600 volunteer observers filed their reports monthly. Experiments with telegraphy began in 1849. In addition, the Smithsonian established cooperative observing programs with the Navy Department, the states of New York and Massachusetts, the Canadian Government, the United States Coast Survey, the army's Corps of Engineers, the Patent Office, and the Department of Agriculture. The Smithsonian sponsored original research on storms, climatic change, and phenology; it also published and distributed meteorological reports, maps, and translations. James Coffin mapped the winds of the northern hemisphere and the winds of the globe using data collected through Smithsonian exchanges. William Ferrel used this information to develop his theory of the general circulation of the atmosphere.

In 1870, Congress established a national weather service in the War Department to provide "telegrams and reports" for the benefit of commerce and agriculture. Colonel Albert J. Myer, founder of the United States Army Signal Corps, became its first director. The well-funded service provided daily weather and crop reports, forecasts, and warnings. It employed upward of 500 college-educated observers and several civilian scientists, notably Increase Lapham and Cleveland Abbe. The Yale scientist Elias Loomis conducted extensive studies of the national weather maps. Under the leadership of Brigadier General William B. Hazen (1880–1887) the Signal Office established a scientific study room, published an international *Bibliography of Meteorology,* and responded to its critics on the issue of whether the military should be supporting a national weather service.

The United States Weather Bureau was established in the Department of Agriculture in 1891 and moved to the Department of Commerce in 1940. Early innovations included observation of the upper atmosphere by kites and balloons, data transmission by telephone and two-way radio, and regular marine and aviation weather forecasts. The most successful administrator, Francis W. Reichelderfer (1938–1963), standardized the acquisition of upper-air data by the use of balloon-borne radio-meteorographs and encouraged the use of the Bergen school's techniques of air-mass and frontal analysis. Jacob Bjerknes and Carl G. Rossby, both exponents of the Bergen school, were the leading meteorologists of their time.

During World War I, the Signal Corps and Weather Bureau cooperated in issuing military forecasts and studied the trajectories of artillery shells and weather conditions affecting gas warfare. During World War II, the army and navy trained approximately 8,000 weather officers and the Weather Bureau established a worldwide system of weather reports in support of military operations, especially aviation.

New tools and instruments became available to meteorologists after World War II. Surplus RADAR equipment and airplanes were used in storm studies, radioactive fallout from atmospheric nuclear tests provided worldwide tracers of upper-air wind patterns, and weather modification on both small and large scales was attempted using silver iodide and other cloud-seeding agents. At the Institute for Advanced Study, John von Neumann and Jule Charney experimented with electronic computers for weather analysis and prediction. The nation's first meteorological satellite program, Tiros, was established in 1960.

The development of meteorology as a "discipline" began rather late compared to parallel developments in other sciences. The *American Meteorological Journal* was published from 1884 to 1896. The American Meteorological Society was founded in 1920. The first meteorology departments were those at the Massachusetts Institute of Technology (1929) and the Pennsylvania State College (1935). There were only seventeen Ph.D. degrees in meteorology granted at four institutions in 1950. In 1958, the Committee on Meteorology of the National Academy of Sciences observed in an 1958 report that, "the percentage of meteorologists with doctor's degrees was the lowest of any major scientific group, while the percentage of persons with no degree at all who were designated as meteorologists was the highest of any major scientific group."

New interdisciplinary problems, approaches, techniques, and instruments characterize the modern subdisciplines of the atmospheric sciences. Specialties in cloud physics, atmospheric chemistry, satellite meteorology, and climate dynamics are found along with more traditional programs in weather analysis and prediction. The National Center for Atmospheric Research and many new departments of atmospheric science date from the 1960s.

In 1965, the Weather Bureau was consolidated with the Coast and Geodetic Survey and other agencies to form the Environmental Science Services Administration. Five years later, a National Weather Service was established within the newly reorganized National Oceanic and Atmospheric Administration. Since the late 1960s, American scientists have been increasingly involved in international projects such as the Global Atmospheric Research Program and, since the 1980s, in "global change" studies driven by environmental concerns such as stratospheric ozone depletion and climate change.

BIBLIOGRAPHY

Bates, Charles C., and John F. Fuller. *America's Weather Warriors, 1814–1985.* College Station: Texas A&M Press, 1986.

Brush, Steven G., and Helmut E. Landsberg. *The History of Geophysics and Meteorology: An Annotated Bibliography.* New York: Garland Publishing, 1985.

Eisenstadt, Peter. "Weather and Weather Forecasting in Colonial America." Ph.D. diss., New York University, 1990.

Fleming, James Rodger. *Guide to Historical Resources in the Atmospheric Sciences: Archives, Manuscripts, and Special Collections in the Washington, D.C. Area.* Boulder, CO: National Center for Atmospheric Research, 1989.

———. *Meteorology in America, 1800–1870.* Baltimore: Johns Hopkins University Press, 1990.

———, ed. *Historical Essays on Meteorology, 1919–1995: The Diamond Anniversary History Volume of the American Meteorological Society.* Boston: American Meteorological Society, 1996.

Nebeker, Frederik. *Calculating the Weather: Meteorology in the 20th Century.* San Diego: Academic Press, 1995.

Whitnah, Donald R. *A History of the United States Weather Bureau.* Urbana: University of Illinois Press, 1961.

James Rodger Fleming

Michelson, Albert Abraham (1852–1931)

Physicist, optical scientist, inventor; first citizen of the United States to win a Nobel Prize in science (1907). Michelson became a naval officer before he became a famous physicist. This fact affected his lifelong interest in relative motion. He also began his scientific career while at the United States Naval Academy, first as a cadet then as an instructor. This fact affected his lifelong efforts to perfect his measurements of the velocity of light. Michelson was meticulous in attention to detail, officious in his dealings with peers and underlings, and fastidious toward experimental optics as the bedrock for all scientific studies of the infinite and the infinitesimal.

Born in Poland, Albert was brought to the United States as a child, first to New York then to California in 1856. After attending Annapolis from 1869 to 1874, Ensign Michelson became an instructor in the academy's Department of Natural and Experimental Philosophy, where he taught from 1875 to 1879. Attending seminars in and around Washington and Baltimore by visiting British scientists, Michelson was inspired to delve deeper into wave theory, optical dynamics, and rational mechanics.

Thanks largely to Simon Newcomb's encouragement and needs for assistance in improving measurements of the velocity of light, Michelson found several ways to improve upon Lèon Foucault's method. After two years of tests, Michelson finished his determination during the summer of 1879. Soon published in the *American Journal of Science* as Michelson's first scientific paper, the value of the speed of light and the need to improve it became the initial stimulus and the lifelong goal of Michelson's half-century career in optical physics.

It was also in 1879 that James Clerk Maxwell raised the question whether some sort of second-order (that is, round-trip) measurement of the velocity of light might be possible to see whether light speed varies in different directions due to the various motions of the earth as it hurtles through space. Maxwell expressed serious doubts that such a tiny second-order difference (on the order of one part in 100,000,000 parts) could be detectable by terrestrial means but maybe celestial measurements could do it. Michelson was intrigued by this challenge and thought he might devise an instrument to compare the velocity of light beams from a single source traveling over equal distances at right angles to each other.

Michelson obtained a leave of absence to go to Europe for consultations with optical and spectoscopical experts. They were mildly encouraging. Various kinds of "interferential refractometers" had been designed, but Michelson's notion of using a half-silvered mirror as a beam splitter was new. He hoped that two light-pencils at right angles could be made to interfere with each other, thus producing measurable flanges of light and dark bands. In effect, Michelson was hoping to produce an optical current-meter that might measure the speed and direction of earth and the solar system against the background of the fixed stars by checking the velocity of light in all directions. In Berlin and the Potsdam Observatory during the winter and spring 1880–1881, his new optical interferometer was put through various tests, found to be marvelously sensitive, yet data reduction showed null results.

Michelson resigned from the navy in 1882 upon receiving an appointment to teach physics at the new Case School of Applied Science being established in Cleveland, Ohio. There he met Edward W. Morley, a senior chemist at Western Reserve College. They decided to collaborate on optical experiments to try to settle the issue of the relative motions of the velocity of light.

Michelson and Morley published their classic ether-drift results in 1887 and quickly began to exploit other uses for their aether-drift interferometer. Michelson became preoccupied by the potential of using it to measure lengths in terms of light waves, especially the relatively arbitrary length of the standard meter-bar in Paris. In 1889, Michelson moved to the new Clark University, where he learned to adapt his interferometer to astronomical telescopes in order to measure the diameters of satellites of Jupiter. In 1893, he spent a year at the International Bureau of Weights and Measures near Paris measuring the meter in terms of cadmium vapor.

The following year, Michelson left Clark to go to the new University of Chicago, chair its physics department, and help design its Ryerson Hall for experimental physics. Here, he created an extremely accurate ruling engine for the engraving of diffraction gratings, invented an echelon spectroscope, and produced with E.W. Stratton a complicated mechanical harmonic analyzer. Many publications and much more fame derived from these works.

In December 1907, Michelson was awarded the Nobel Prize in physics, only the seventh such prize in history and the first to be awarded to an American citizen for scientific attainment. Michelson's obligatory address was titled "Recent Advances in Spectroscopy," and his prize exhibit was a diffraction grating with a theoretical resolving power of 220,000.

During World War I, Michelson was recommissioned in the Naval Reserve as a lieutenant commander and spent a year in Washington at the Bureau of Ordnance, where he redesigned a range finder of his own invention (1890) for submarine use. Periscopes, optical gunsights, and binoculars were all improved as a result of his efforts to minimize imperfections.

Michelson was elected president of the National Academy of Sciences in 1923 and began a campaign to raise more governmental funds for pure research. At the height of his power and prestige and on the verge of retirement from academia, Michelson undertook several large-scale experimental enterprises. After improving his stellar interferometer for measuring diameters of various stars, he laid a set of horizontal pipes in a rectangular raceway, in effect a 5,200-foot vacuum-tube system, at a field on the outskirts of Chicago in order to measure the effects of the earth's rotation on the velocity of light. The results of this expensive and elaborate test of Einstein's theory of gravitational and inertial equivalence were equivocal. Meanwhile, Michelson returned to some major efforts to improve his aether-drift interferometer in order to confirm or deny Dayton C. Miller's recent challenges to the null results of earlier tests of the earth's orbital velocity on the speed of light. These works at the Mount Wilson Observatory shops in the mid-1920s were also inconclusive, much to Michelson's chagrin. But they were overshadowed by a major achievement in measuring the velocity of light over a carefully surveyed baseline of twenty-two miles between Mount Wilson and Mount San Antonio (or "Baldy"), mountain peaks north and east of Los Angeles. Using a carbon-arc lamp, an eight-sided prism as a rotating mirror, and the U.S. Coast and Geodetic Survey to determine with unprecedented accuracy his baseline, Michelson published results in 1926 as $299,796 \pm 4$ kilometers per second. Michelson's calculations of *in vacuo* values for this series of determinations remained the best available for several decades. Although Michelson tried to extend his open-air baselines to fifty or even eighty-two miles between other mountain peaks, atmospheric conditions were so poor that Michelson turned his attention toward constructing a mile-long vacuum. The Carnegie and Rockefeller Foundations furnished almost $70,000 for this purpose. From 1929 to 1931, Michelson worked with a team of colleagues to try to perfect the determination of the velocity of light in an actual vacuum. But many technical and technological problems were encoun-

tered in this ambitious attempt, and the partial vacuum was never achieved well enough to suit Michelson's standards.

As an experimental physicist of the "old school," Michelson was a genteel artist in the laboratory or observatory who avoided talk about the theoretical implications of his work. Knowing full well the resolving powers of his various optical instruments, he constantly tried to improve them toward advances to the next decimal place. He only met Albert Einstein personally once, within months of his death. But he was deeply aware that the constancy of the speed of light was a value that would outlive them both.

Michelson's papers and memorabilia are widely scattered, but the best collection was originally gathered by the Michelson Laboratory, Naval Weapons Center, China Lake, California, and is now held at the U.S. Naval Academy. See also the holdings of the Bohr Library, American Institute of Physics, Center for History of Physics, College Park, Maryland.

BIBLIOGRAPHY

Albert Abraham Michelson: The Man Who Taught a World to Measure. China Lake: Michelson Museum, 1970.

Holten, Gerald. "Einstein, Michelson, and the Crucial Experiment." *Isis* 60 (1969): 133–197.

Lemon, Harvey B. "Albert Abraham Michelson: The Man and the Man of Science." *American Physics Teacher* 4 (February 1936): 1–11.

Livingston, Dorothy Michelson. *The Master of Light: A Biography of Albert A. Michelson.* New York: Scribners, 1973.

Millikan, Robert A. "Albert A. Michelson." *Biographical Memoirs of the National Academy of Sciences* 19 (1938): 120–147.

"Proceedings of the Michelson Meeting of the Optical Society of America." *Journal of the Optical Society of America* 18, no. 3 (March 1929): 143–286.

Shankland, Robert S. "Albert A. Michelson at Case." *American Journal of Physics* 17 (1949) 487–490.

Swenson, Loyd S., Jr. "The Michelson-Morley-Miller Experiments Before and After 1905." *Journal for the History of Astronomy* 1 (1970): 56–78.

———. *Genesis of Relativity: Einstein in Context.* New York: Burt Franklin, 1979.

———. "Measuring the Immeasurable." *American Heritage of Invention and Technology* 3, no. 2 (Fall 1987): 42–49.

———. "Michelson and Measurement." *Physics Today* 40 (1987): 24–30.

———. "Michelson-Morley, Einstein, and Interferometry." In *The Michelson Era in American Science, 1870–1930,* edited by Stanley Goldberg and Roger H. Stuewer. AIP Conference Proceedings 179. New York: American Institute of Physics, 1988, pp. 235–245.

Loyd S. Swenson Jr.

Michelson-Morley Experiment

An attempt in physical optics to measure the relative motion of the earth against the luminiferous ether by means of right-angled interferometry, the failure of which is presumed to have caused the advent of relativistic physics. Often called a "crucial experiment."

Albert A. Michelson, having recently improved terrestrial measurements of the velocity of light, V, first conceived in 1880 of a potential method for the measurement of the earth's motion through all space, supposed to be filled with a medium called the *luminiferous ether*. Michelson was first stimulated by a challenge that James Clerk Maxwell had made about the time of his death in 1879 to devise an apparatus for a second-order (a squared ratio of two velocities) measurement of the velocity of light over two paths at right angles to each other. On academic leave in Europe from the U.S. Navy, young Michelson studied and sought advice for his design from some of the world's leading optical scientists: A. Cornu and E. Mascart in Paris; G.H. Quincke in Heidelberg; and Hermann Helmholtz in Berlin. He was encouraged to proceed, and so with subsidies from Alexander Graham Bell's Volta Fund, he designed and commissioned the construction of the world's first optical interferometer. This instrument was built by Schmidt and Haensch in the winter of 1891, tested in Berlin in March and at the Postdam Observatory in April.

The cruciform instrument on a turnstile consisted primarily of a half-silvered beam-splitting mirror at the center of two brass arms, each about a meter in length, with adjustable plane parallel mirrors at each end. It performed exquisitely well in providing interference fringes which could easily be measured to one-tenth of their width. But the aether-drift experiment itself gave only null results and, therefore, was very disappointing. Furthermore, theoretical critiques, one by M.A. Potier of Paris and another by the Dutch physicist Hendrik A. Lorentz, led Michelson to worry about his experimental design. Hence, after many consultations with experts, Michelson was anxious to try again with a bigger and better aether-drift interferometer. It should be a virtual speedometer, or better yet, a current meter, for the earth as it hurtles through space. But instead of "all space" or Isaac Newton's absolute space, Michelson would be satisfied to measure this time the velocity of the earth in orbit around the sun.

Hence began a half-century of intermittent optical experimentation to try various hypotheses, theories, and conjectures about the nature of light, space, and time, all based directly on Michelson's interferometer and its capacities for extremely precise second-order ($v^2 V^2$) measurements.

Edward W. Morley, a chemist in Cleveland, Ohio, became involved with Michelson in 1884 when the two found themselves at neighboring colleges and collaborated to improve and extend Michelson's instrument, originally called an "interferential refractometer." For five years, Michelson and Morley worked closely together, performing their classic aether-drift tests in 1887. Their preliminary null results published that year in a paper entitled "On the Relative Motion of the Earth and the Luminiferous Ether" (*American Journal of Science* 34 (1887): 333–345; and *Philosophical Magazine* 24 (1887): 449–463) gradually became a notorious theoretical issue.

During the 1890s and early 1900s, after Michelson and Morley had separated, the Michelson-Morley experiment gained a reputation which outstripped its historical character. And so Morley, together with Michelson's successor at Case in Cleveland, Dayton C. Miller, developed greatly improved aether-drift interferometers. Their null results were equally disappointing. Meanwhile, Albert L. Einstein simply assumed that no news was good news from these and other such experiments.

In 1905, Einstein declared the whole notion of an electromagnetic or luminiferous aether to be unnecessary. Accepting both the wave (or undulatory) and the particle (or emission) theory of light as equally valid under different experimental conditions, Einstein postulated the constancy of the velocity of light and the relativity principle with respect to measurements of the electrodynamics of moving bodies. Thus, he relied indirectly on Michelson's lifelong work to perfect his determinations of the fundamental physical constant V (now symbolized merely as c) for the velocity of light *in vacuo* and on Michelson and Morley's preliminary experiment in 1886 to refine and verify Fizeau's aether-drag or moving-water experiment.

As the rise of relativity theory in the first two decades of the twentieth century accelerated the fall of aether theory, many scientists, for pedagogical reasons, celebrated the Michelson-Morley experiment as the direct cause for the replacement of the aether by relativity. Things were not so simple. During the 1920s, more elaborate optical experiments and more expensive instruments on the Michelson-Morley paradigm were conducted around the world. All except D.C. Miller's retests seemed to corroborate Einstein's new views rather than Michelson, Morley, and Miller's old ones. Thus the Michelson-Morley-Miller experiment by 1930 (when the last tests at visible wavelengths on the old model were performed) had become a symbol for the failure of classical Newtonian physics and a talisman for the success of modern Einsteinian worldviews.

BIBLIOGRAPHY

Goldberg, Stanley, and Roger H. Stuewer, eds. *The Michelson Era in American Science, 1870–1930.* A.I.P. Conference Proceedings 179. New York: American Institute of Physics, 1988.

Haubold, Hans J., and R.W. John. "100 Jahre Michelsonsche Aether-drift Experiment." *Astronomische Nachrichten* 303, Part 1 (1982).

Holton, Gerald. "Einstein, Michelson, and the Crucial Experiment." *Isis* 60 (1969): 133–197.

Livingston, Dorothy Michelson. *The Master of Light: A Biography of Albert A. Michelson.* New York: Scribners, 1973.

Miller, Arthur I. *Albert Einstein's Special Theory of Relativity.* Reading, MA: Addison-Wesley, 1981.

Swenson, Loyd S., Jr. *The Ethereal Aether: A History of the Michelson-Morley-Miller Aether-Drift Experiments, 1880–1930.* Austin: University of Texas Press, 1972.

———. *Genesis of Relativity: Einstein in Context.* New York: Burt Franklin, 1979.

———. "Michelson and Measurement." *Physics Today* 40 (1987): 24–30.

Loyd S. Swenson Jr.

Miller, Samuel (1769–1850)

Presbyterian clergyman and educator interested in the progress of science and letters with special reference to religion. As a pastor in New York City (1793 ff.), Miller came to public attention early with his *A Brief Retrospect of the Eighteenth Century* (1803), an erudite survey of the progress of science, literature, and practical and fine arts in that century, aimed especially at showing the harmony of science and religion. The first volume concerned the sciences of nature and their applications in navigation, agriculture, and the mechanic arts; the second, the philosophy of the human mind, educational theory, literature, and the growth of scientific and literary institutions and publications, American and European. These volumes were notable not only for the range and general adequacy of Miller's account of scientific developments and applications but also as testimony to the widespread conviction among the educated Protestant clergy that science and Christian faith were compatible. Miller's book is still a useful source of information about American scientific and educational institutions, contributions to science and learning, and knowledge of eighteenth-century developments in science and its applications.

Miller became professor of church history and government at Princeton Theological Seminary in 1813 and continued to publish on a wide variety of topics until his death.

BIBLIOGRAPHY

Faris, Paul P. "Samuel Miller." *Dictionary of American Biography.* Edited by Dumas Malone. New York: Charles Scribner's Sons, 1928–1937, 12:636–637.

Greene, John C. *American Science in the Age of Jefferson.* Ames: Iowa State University Press, 1984.

Miller, Samuel. *A Brief Retrospect of the Eighteenth Century . . . Containing a Sketch of the Revolutions and Improvements in Science, Arts, and Literature During That Period.* 2 vols. 1803. Reprint, New York: Burt Franklin, 1970.

John C. Greene

Mineralogy

American mineralogy from its beginning until well into the twentieth century has been essentially a descriptive science responding to the question, more urgent in colonial times, "What is that mineral and what is it good for?" The mineralogical activity in the English colonies in North America was then virtually restricted to the building of mineral collections that recorded the useful products of a newly explored land. Mineralogy in the United States became established in the period 1780 to 1820, in Cambridge, Philadelphia, New York City, and New Haven.

Formal course instruction in mineralogy, with some reference to geology, had begun at Harvard in 1784 through the interest of Benjamin Waterhouse, who had been appointed to the Harvard Medical School in 1782. More significant was the appointment of Benjamin Silliman to the professorship of chemistry at Yale in 1802. He became the leading figure in the field.

Among his students were James D. Dana and Edward S. Dana, who kept Yale in a leading position in mineralogy for much of the nineteenth century through their publication of the *System of Mineralogy*, a world recognized reference work on descriptive mineralogy that appeared in six editions from 1837 to 1892, and other works in mineralogy and geology.

Descriptive mineralogy is a specimen science, and instruction therein must be sustained by detailed reference to collections of minerals and crystals. Harvard's collection started in about 1784 through the gift of European material by an English friend of Waterhouse. The initial growth of mineralogy in the Philadelphia area was supported largely by specimen material brought from Europe. Yale's collection began in 1810 with the gift of a fine private collection.

The practice and teaching of mineralogy expanded greatly after the Civil War, attending the marked growth of the mineral industry. In 1916, the Mineralogical Society of America was organized.

Around the turn of the twentieth century, mineralogy became a composite science, with numerous subfields. Its concern extended from mineral descriptions toward an understanding in chemical and physical terms of the formation of minerals and mineral assemblages. Crystallography from its beginning long remained a descriptive subfield of mineralogy. Not until the advent of crystal structure analysis by X-rays in the early 1900s did crystallography become a separate science interpretive of the solid state in general.

Two important factors in determining the nature of modern research in mineralogy were the research centering in the then-called Division of Chemistry and Physics in the Washington laboratories of the United States Geological Survey, beginning in 1883 under the direction of the geochemist F. W. Clarke, and the founding of the Geophysical Laboratory of the Carnegie Institution of Washington in 1902. The latter laboratory initiated the systematic experimental study of the physical chemistry of igneous rocks, with later experimental work extending to other matters, such as hydrothermal and high-pressure systems.

There is a close connection between mineralogy and metallurgy and mining. The United States early suffered from a lack of skilled practitioners in the latter fields. Even as late as 1854, a commentator stated that "we are in our infancy in anything appertaining to mines and the mineral resources of our country. . . . We are a nation destitute of mining men, Professors and mining engineers" (quoted in Frondel, "The Geological Sciences," p. 7). However, this general shortage began to be corrected by the middle of the century, with the establishments of the Sheffield Scientific School at Yale (1846) and the Lawrence Scientific School of Harvard (1847). By the second half of the century, there were numerous specialized colleges offering training in mining, metallurgy, and mining geology. These include the Columbia School of Mines, founded in 1864 and the Colorado School of Mines, founded in 1874. Travel abroad to study at European mining schools was also a common practice.

Among the most important applications of scientific research to problems in mining and metallurgy were the application of geophysical and geochemical techniques to ore prospecting, the development of flotation techniques for the concentration of ore minerals, and the application of optical microscopy to the study of opaque ore minerals as seen in light reflected from polished surfaces.

BIBLIOGRAPHY

Frondel, Clifford. "Early Mineral Specimens from New England." *Mineralogical Record* 2 (1971): 232–234.
———. "An Overview of Crystallography in North America." In *Crystallography in North America,* edited by Dan McLachlan Jr. and Jenny P. Glusker. New York: American Crystallographic Association, 1983, pp. 1–24.
———. "The Geological Sciences at Harvard University from 1788 to 1850." *Earth Sciences History* 7 (1988): 1–22.
Greene, John C. "The Development of Mineralogy in Philadelphia." *Proceedings of the American Philosophical Society* 113, no. 4 (1969): 283–295.
Greene, John C., and John G. Burke. "The Science of Mineralogy in the Age of Jefferson." *Transactions of the American Philosophical Society* 68, Part 4 (1978): 1–113.
Grew, Nehemiah. *A Catalogue and Description of the Natural and Artificial Rarities Belonging to the Royal Society and Preserved at Gresham College.* London: Privately printed, 1681.
Stearnes, R.P. "John Winthrop (1681–1747) and His Gifts to the Royal Society." *Transactions of the Colonial Society of Massachusetts* 42 (1964): 206–232.
Woodward, John. *An Attempt towards a Natural History of the Fossils of England.* London: Privately printed, 1724.

Clifford Frondel

SEE ALSO
Crystallography

Missouri Botanical Garden

The Missouri Botanical Garden, St. Louis, Missouri (also known as Shaw's Garden), was created in the mid-1850s by Henry Shaw (1800–1889) at his country estate, Tower Grove, with George Englemann as chief horticulturalist. By 1859, Shaw's botanical garden was open to the public and the Museum Building, holding the library, natural history collection, and herbarium, was available for researchers. With advice from Sir William Jackson Hooker, director at the Royal Botanical Gardens at Kew, and Asa Gray of Harvard University, Shaw established an important collection of live and dried specimens, books, and other scientific materials. He remained director of the garden until his death.

In his last will and testament of 1889, Henry Shaw made the botanical garden a charitable trust in the care of a self-perpetuating board of trustees. The garden was to be "easily accessible which should forever be kept up and maintained for the cultivation and propagation of plants, flowers, fruit and forest trees, and other productions of the vegetable kingdom; and a museum and library connected therewith, and devoted to the same and to the science of botany, horticulture, and allied objects."

The garden began to participate in collecting expeditions in 1890. At the same time, its herbarium and library collections were expanded, and it quickly became an international leader in botanical research. The garden's principal scientific activities are in taxonomy, systematics, and experimental botany, and it is known for exceptional collections of water lilies and orchids. It comprises seventy-five acres in the suburbs of St. Louis and contains a Japanese garden, English woodland rose gardens, and several greenhouses. Although the garden has developed a focus on plants of the tropics, it is not limited to any geographical area. For example, it is the organizational center for a multi-institutional effort to publish a *Flora of North America.*

As the edification of the public was always a high priority with Shaw, the grounds and architecture have been designed with great care and expense. The architecturally acclaimed Climatron, built in 1960, is a geodesic dome made originally of Plexiglas and aluminum that has the capacity of sustaining several different climates. The Plexiglas has been replaced with "low E glass" to conserve solar energy. In 1971, the garden was designated a National Historic Landmark.

The Missouri Botanical Garden is closely affiliated with the Henry Shaw School of Botany at Washington University, Saint Louis University, Southern Illinois University, and University of Missouri. It also administers the Shaw or Gray Summit Arboretum, 2,400 acres of woods and prairies located about thirty-five miles outside St. Louis.

BIBLIOGRAPHY

Britton, N.L. "Address on Botanical Gardens." *Bulletin of The New York Botanical Garden* 1 (1896–1900): 75–76.

Bry, Charlene. *A World of Plants: The Missouri Botanical Garden.* New York: Abrams, 1989.

Faherty, William Barnaby. *Henry Shaw: His Life and Legacies.* Columbia: University of Missouri Press, 1987.

"Henry Shaw's Will Establishing the Missouri Botanical Garden." St. Louis, 1889.

Hyams, Edward, and William MacQuinty. *Great Botanical Gardens of the World.* London: Nelson, 1969.

Wyman, Donald. "The Arboretums and Botanical Gardens of North America." *Chronica Botanica* 10 (1947): 437–439.

Therese O'Malley

Mitchel, Ormsby Macknight (1809–1862)

Astronomer, engineer, and scientific popularizer. Born in Morganfield, Kentucky, Mitchel enrolled in the United States Military Academy at age fifteen. Following graduation in 1829, he taught mathematics at the academy for two years, then served out his commission. He moved to Cincinnati in 1832, where he studied law and opened a practice in 1833. When the Cincinnati College reopened in 1836, Mitchel returned to academics, teaching mathematics, civil engineering, and mechanics. Six years later, he presented a series of public lectures on astronomy that catalyzed the formation of the Cincinnati Astronomical Society and led to the development of the Cincinnati Observatory.

Just as Mitchel was finishing the observatory a fire leveled the Cincinnati College, destroying Mitchel's source of income. Since Mitchel had agreed to direct the observatory gratis for ten years, he found himself searching for employment. Turning adversity to advantage, Mitchel undertook an expanded series of lectures, based on those delivered in Cincinnati. His circuit ran from Boston to New Orleans, usually during winter, when observing conditions in Cincinnati were marginal. He quickly established his reputation as one of the most erudite and inspirational speakers of the antebellum period. In addition to providing him a substantial income, the lectures introduced to the public astronomical concepts and connected those ideas to a growing body of natural theology. His lectures further permitted him the time to transform his observatory into a research institution.

With his observatory functional, Mitchel associated himself with Alexander Dallas Bache's network of researchers, who were based in the United States Coast Survey Office in Washington, D.C. He also linked himself to George Airy's group at the Royal Observatory in Greenwich, England. The Cincinnati Observatory was equipped with one of the largest refractors of the time, which Mitchel employed in the resolution of double stars. He also participated in the development of the "American System," which consisted of two related inventions. One, the automation of transit observations, which employed an automatic time register (known as the "electro-chronograph"), and the second, the telegraphing of time signals for longitude, which found immediate application in the work of the survey. The two inventions involved similar apparatus, proceeded simultaneously, and, from inception, involved Mitchel in a dispute over the priority of their invention.

Off and on, Mitchel served as an engineer for local railroad companies, an activity that interrupted his astronomical research. In August 1861, he received a commission as general in the Union Army. He took charge of the Department of the South in Beaufort, South Carolina, in September 1862 and died of yellow fever the following month.

Between his lectures and his success as an agent of railroads, he moved into the ranks of the wealthy in the early 1850s. But his financial success exacted its toll through diminishing involvement with his scientific peers. The diversity of his interests produces problems for modern historians as well. In our era of specialization we find it difficult to categorize one who could move from one career to another so conveniently. But to view his life as leading up to, and reaching an apex in a career in astronomy misses the mark. His first love was the stage. Applause motivated him more than income.

During the past century and a half, the record of his accomplishments has served several purposes. Twenty years after his death, the Reverend Phineas C. Headley, a Protestant divine, recognized the inspirational value of Mitchel's life story. Headley depicted Mitchel as an ideal Christian scientist, one who might inspire youth. Unfortunately, Headley's hagiography reduced Mitchel to caricature. Five years later, one of Mitchel's sons, Frederick Augustus Mitchel, wrote an excellent biography, largely employing autobiographical documents and his own experiences as one of his father's lieutenants during the Civil War. While undeniably an improvement over Headley's proselytizing work, it suffered from an absence of scientific context and an understandable reluctance critically to view the actions of a family member.

More recently, the story of the founding of the Cincinnati Observatory, and Mitchel's role therein, has (1) provided background and motivation for renewed interest in the observatory and astronomy in general; (2) illustrated the difficulties of funding antebellum scientific projects; and (3) served as an example of the linkage of scientific and religious ideas.

Most historians who have looked into the financial operations of the Cincinnati Astronomical Society have found a continuing monetary crisis that choked off productive astronomical research. But when one evaluates Mitchel's personal financial position in conjunction with the observatory, one finds that those problems are somewhat illusionary—despite Mitchel's claims of poverty, he made a comfortable living lecturing after 1847, and by 1853, he had achieved financial independence. Other assessments of Mitchel have found fault with his research program, concluding that his inexperience and uncertain patronage frustrated him, and that he failed "to use this superb instrument [the 'great refractor'] for any important scientific work" (Goldfarb, p. 178).

Yet some historians investigating the institutional development of science during the period have come up with a more positive interpretation of Mitchel. A study of the formation of the American Association for the Advancement of Science puts Mitchel in a group of 337 leaders within the AAAS, and an examination of the growth of science during the period 1815 to 1845, selects Mitchel as one of the fifty-six "leading scientists." (Kohlstedt, Appendix; Daniels). He promised more than he delivered, on occasion, straining credulity. But an analysis of his research reveals that his election to the Royal Astronomical Society proceeded from a solid contribution to astronomy, and a careful definition of his objectives shows that Mitchel exceeded all that was originally expected of him.

BIBLIOGRAPHY

Bruce, Robert V. *The Launching of Modern American Science 1846–1876*. New York: Knopf, 1987.

Daniels, George H. *American Science in the Age of Jackson*. New York: Columbia University Press, 1968.

Goldfarb, Stephen. "Science and Democracy: A History of the Cincinnati Observatory, 1842–1872." *Ohio History* 78 (1969): 172–178.

Henley, Phineas C. *Old Stars, The Life and Military Career of Major General Ormsby M. Mitchel.* Boston: Lee and Shepard, 1883.

Kohlstedt, Sally G. *The Formation of the American Scientific Community: The American Association for the Advancement of Science, 1848–1860.* Urbana: University of Illinois Press, 1976.

McCormmach, Russell. "Ormsby Macknight Mitchel's *Sidereal Messenger*, 1846–1848." *Proceedings of the American Philosophical Society* 10 (1966): 35–37.

Miller, Howard S. *Dollars for Research.* Seattle: University of Washington Press, 1970.

Mitchel, Frederick Augustus. *Ormsby Macknight Mitchel, Astronomer and General.* Boston: Houghton Mifflin and Co., 1886.

Musto, David. "The Development of American Astronomy During the Early 19th Century." *Proceedings of the Tenth International Congress of the History of Science.* Paris: Hermann, 1964, pp. 733–736.

Shoemaker, Philip S. "Stellar Impact: Ormsby Macknight Mitchel and Astronomy in Antebellum America." Ph.D. diss., University of Wisconsin, 1991.

Philip S. Shoemaker

Mitchell, Maria (1818–1889)

Astronomer and educator. Born in Nantucket, Massachusetts, Mitchell attended local dame schools, her amateur-astronomer father William's school, and spent a year in the school of Cyrus Peirce. In 1835, she operated a school for girls; from 1836 until 1856 she worked as the librarian for the Nantucket Atheneum, where she taught herself mathematics, astronomy, and science. In 1847, she discovered the first telescopic comet and was awarded a gold medal by the king of Denmark for the same. In 1849, she became a computer for the *American Ephemeris and Nautical Almanac,* and, in 1865, became professor of astronomy at the newly founded Vassar College, where she served until her retirement in 1888. Her honors include election to the American Academy of Arts and Sciences (first woman, in 1848), the American Association for the Advancement of Science (1850), founder (1873) and president (1875–1876) of the Association for the Advancement of Women, election to the American Philosophical Society (first woman, in 1869), and vice president of the American Social Science Association (1873).

Mitchell's discovery of the first telescopic comet and her plotting of its orbit using her self-taught mathematical training brought her international notice and acclaim. A close association with Louis Agassiz of Harvard and George and William Bond of the Harvard College Observatory gave her entrée to the American and international astronomical worlds. Her friends included her contemporary women scientists of Europe, such as Mary Somerville, as well as numbers of leading men scientists. Her own work focused primarily on observations of Saturn, sunspot and faculae activity and photography. While her true research interest lay in the plodding work of developing a definitive orbit for a specific asteroid, she responded to the demands of college teaching and the constraints of little research funding or assistance at Vassar by following a research plan of smaller and more numerous projects, despite her opinion that the work on the orbit would have a more lasting effect in the scientific community.

Her projects, constructed with her students in mind, included observations of double stars, comets, sunspots and faculae, planets (particularly Saturn), solar eclipses, and variable stars. Color was a particular interest of hers, and she focused her work there on observations and spectroscopic analyses of the planetary markings of Mars, Saturn, and Jupiter. Her examination and description of Jupiter in 1870 contained no reference to the Great Red Spot, and for a scientist so concerned with color, the lack of mention can be construed to mean that any color must not have been visible at that time. Mitchell's most valuable contributions to astronomical science were establishing the practice of daily photography of sunspots and faculae, as well as arguing that the latter were not clouds above the sun's surface, but vertical cavities.

As the first professional woman astronomer in the country and among the first professors of astronomy at women's colleges, Mitchell's career reflected the difficulties of being a pathbreaker. Her upbringing on Nantucket in a whaling community, where the men of the town were often gone for year-long voyages, embued her with a sense of individualism denied most middle-class women in the nineteenth century. While she practiced the domesticity that was the path of most women of the time adequately, her desire was to participate in the intellectual and scientific community. Her work at the Atheneum for twenty years brought her into contact with leading scholars and thinkers, including Ralph Waldo Emerson, as well as common sailors, for whom her expertise and lessons in celestial knowledge and navigation were crucial for success. She argued

M

against restricting women to domesticity throughout her life, and pointed out that the painstaking nature of astronomical calculations were ones women, trained in fine needlepoint and other domestic skills, could do far more easily than men. In an era where science was still the province of the amateur, Mitchell provided a role model for women wishing to pursue their scientific interests.

As the second half of the nineteenth century began to see the increasing professionalization of science, Mitchell's most valuable, long-lasting, and important contribution to the field of astronomy was her work with students. Mitchell taught astronomy first and foremost from a base in mathematics, turning away students who wished to study descriptive astronomy in favor of those who withstood the demands of mathematical rigor. During her tenure at Vassar, the college was the top producer of majors who went on to earn the doctorate in astronomy. Twenty-five of Mitchell's students became prominent enough in their fields to be documented in *Who's Who in America,* including scientists such as chemist Ellen Swallow Richards, mathematician Christine Ladd-Franklin, and astronomer Mary Whitney, who succeeded Mitchell at Vassar. These women went on to continue the long-standing tradition of women in science in American colleges, and serve as the most lasting legacy of Maria Mitchell.

BIBLIOGRAPHY

Arnold, Lois Barber. *Four Lives in Science: Women's Education in the Nineteenth Century.* New York: Schocken Books, 1984.

Belserene, Emilia Pisani. "Maria Mitchell: Nineteenth Century Astonomer." *Astronomy Quarterly* 5 (1986): 133–150.

Gormley, Beatrice. *Maria Mitchell: The Soul of an Astronomer.* Grand Rapids, MI: Wm. B. Eerdmans, 1995.

Kendall, Phebe Mitchell, comp. *Maria Mitchell: Life, Letters, and Journals.* Boston: Lee & Shepard, 1896.

Kohlstedt, Sally Gregory. "Maria Mitchell and the Advancement of Women in Science." In *Uneasy Careers and Intimate Lives: Women in Science, 1789–1979,* edited by Pnina G. Abir-Am and Dorinda Outram. New Brunswick: Rutgers University Press, 1987, pp. 129–146.

Lankford, John, and Rickey L. Slavings. "Gender and Science: Women in American Astronomy, 1859–1940." *Physics Today* (March 1990): 58–65.

Rossiter, Margaret. *Women Scientists in America: Struggles and Strategies to 1940.* Baltimore: Johns Hopkins University Press, 1982.

Wright, Helen. *Sweeper in the Sky: The Life of Maria Mitchell, First Woman Astronomer in America.* New York: MacMillan, 1949.

Janet L. Coryell

Mitchill, Samuel Latham (1764–1831)

Naturalist. Born on Long Island, Mitchill served a medical apprenticeship under Samuel Bard in New York City from 1780 to 1783. He studied medicine at the University of Edinburgh until 1786, and on receiving his degree, Mitchill returned to New York where he was licensed to practice medicine. From 1792 to 1801, he was professor of natural history, chemistry, and agriculture at Columbia College; during his tenure he established the first American medical journal, *The Medical Repository,* in 1797. Mitchill taught botany for two years (1793–1795) at the university, was a founder of the Society for the Promotion of Agriculture, Arts, and Manufactures in 1796, and served one term (1798) in the state legislature. From 1801 to 1813, Mitchill served intermittently in the United States Congress, promoting such issues as the exploration of the Louisiana Purchase and the enforcement of quarantine laws. In 1807, in New York, Mitchill helped establish the College of Physicians and Surgeons, where he held the chairs of chemistry (1807–1808), natural history (1808–1820), and botany and materia medica (1820–1826). In 1826, after losing a long battle for control of the college to a rival group of physicians, the college professoriat followed David Hosack in establishing Rutgers Medical College—Mitchill was vice president and professor of medicine at the new school until 1830. Mitchill's scientific contributions were on a par with his medical career. He helped organize the New York Literary and Philosophical Society in 1814 and three years later established the Lyceum of Natural History with the support of the medical students at the College of Physicians and Surgeons. Mitchill's scientific work encompassed a vast variety of subjects, most noticeably, geology, ichthyology, mineralogy, botany, meteorology, and chemistry; his catholicity was appropriate to the late eighteenth century but seemed suspect to the specialists in the Lyceum of Natural History. His influence among the New York scientific community was substantial on account of his role in creating a variety of institutions that remained significant on the local and national scene for decades.

BIBLIOGRAPHY

Aberbach, Alan David. *In Search of an American Identity: Samuel Latham Mitchill: Jeffersonian Naturalist.* Peter Lang, 1988.

Hall, Courtney Robert. *A Scientist in the Early Republic: Samuel Latham Mitchill, 1764–1831.* New York: Columbia University Press, 1934.

Simon Baatz

Morgan, Lewis Henry (1818–1881)

Anthropologist. A few years after he was born on a farm outside of Aurora, New York, Morgan's family moved into the village of Aurora, where he attended Cayuga Academy. After graduating from Union College, he returned to Aurora where he read law and was admitted to the bar. He moved to Rochester in 1844 to establish a law practice there. In the 1850s, he joined a group of Rochester men investing in railroads, mining, and iron smelting in the Upper Michigan Peninsula. The success of these ventures allowed him to give up his law practice in 1862 and, until his death in Rochester, to devote much of his time to scientific pursuits. He was elected to the National Academy of Sciences in 1875 and served as president of the American Association for the Advancement of Science (1879–1880).

After returning to Aurora in 1840, Morgan became interested in Iroquois society and culture, publishing in 1851 *League of the Ho-dé-no-sau-nee, or Iroquois* based on his fieldwork. He first visited Marquette, Michigan, in 1855 on business, and on subsequent trips became interested in the beaver and its behavior. The results of this research were published in 1868 in *The American Beaver and His Works.* At the same time, he undertook a worldwide comparative study of kinship terminology and clan organization based on information provided by others through correspondence and data he himself had collected, including that which he obtained on four western field trips (1859–1862). His study of kinship terminology was published in 1871 under the title *Systems of Consanguinity and Affinity of the Human Family* and that of clan organization in 1877 under the title *Ancient Society.* His *Houses and House-Life of the American Aborigines,* originally intended to be part of *Ancient Society,* was published shortly before his death in 1881.

Although there is a unity to Morgan's scientific work—among other things, an interest in the "mind"—this unity has not been preserved in its subsequent use by others. For all the considerable research on Iroquois society and culture done since Morgan's day, *League of the Iroquois* remains the best single ethnographic account of these people. *Systems of Consanguinity and Affinity* is now generally credited with establishing that most esoteric of all anthropological subjects of inquiry: kinship. *Ancient Society,* one of the most important nineteenth-century studies of cultural evolution, achieved added fame as a consequence of Karl Marx's and Friedrich Engel's interest in it that resulted in the publication of Engel's widely read *The Origin of the Family, Private Property, and the State* (1884). For many decades, Morgan's *The American Beaver and His Works* was the most important book on these animals. Yet, for all the work done since the publication of these volumes, they are not merely of historical interest. There is much still to be learned from a perusal of them.

BIBLIOGRAPHY

Engels, Friederich. *The Origin of the Family, Private Property, and the State in the Light of the Researches of Lewis H. Morgan.* (Printed in a number of editions.)

Morgan, Lewis H. *League of the Ho-dé-no-sau-nee, or Iroquois.* Rochester: Sage and Brother, 1851.

———. *The American Beaver and His Works.* Philadelphia: J.B. Lippincott, 1868.

———. *Systems of Consanguinity and Affinity of the Human Family.* Smithsonian Contributions to Knowledge 17. Washington, DC: Smithsonian Institution, 1871.

———. *Ancient Society.* New York: Henry Holt, 1877.

———. *Houses and House-Life of the American Aborigines.* United States Geological Survey, Contributions to North American Ethnology 4. Washington, DC: Government Printing Office, 1881.

Resek, Carl. *Lewis Henry Morgan, American Scholar.* Chicago: University of Chicago Press, 1960.

Trautmann, Thomas R. *Lewis Henry Morgan and the Invention of Kinship.* Berkeley: University of California Press, 1987.

Elisabeth Tooker

Morgan, Thomas Hunt (1866–1945)

Embryologist and geneticist, born at his family home "Hopemont," in Lexington, Kentucky. Morgan's family was gentry; his paternal uncle had been a brigadier general in the Confederate Army and his mother was the granddaughter of Francis Scott Key. Morgan grew up with an interest in natural history. At fourteen, he enrolled in the preparatory division of the newly established State College of Kentucky; his undergraduate training was there as well. For the baccalaureate, he

M

studied natural history and was graduated in 1886 as valedictorian of his class of three students.

Morgan pursued graduate work at Johns Hopkins University. His research for the Ph.D. degree, awarded in 1890, was on the embryology of the Pycnogonids (sea spiders). He followed the tradition of his mentor William Keith Brooks, using developmental anatomy to confirm evolutionary relationships among organisms. His first academic position, beginning in 1891, was at Bryn Mawr College, replacing another Hopkins graduate, the cytologist E.B. Wilson, who had moved to Columbia University. He remained at Bryn Mawr for thirteen years, carrying out research there, at the Marine Biological Laboratory at Woods Hole, and at the Stazione Zoologica in Naples, Italy. During this period, his work became more experimental, emphasizing manipulations to study fertilization, regeneration, and the localization of morphological determinants. This mode of investigation reflected a shift in the field, influenced by German and American physiologists, including Hans Dreisch, with whom Morgan worked at Naples, and Henry Newell Martin, Morgan's instructor at Hopkins. In 1904, he was recruited to Columbia by Wilson as professor of experimental zoology. Just before going to New York, he married Lillian Vaughan Sampson, a graduate student in biology at Bryn Mawr.

During the period 1900–1910, Morgan was one of the most outspoken in the debate resulting from the rediscovery of the data of Gregor Mendel. He adamantly opposed the notion that genes were located on chromosomes, postulated by W.S. Sutton in 1903 on the basis of cytological data alone. Morgan's opposition stemmed from his vantage point as an embryologist. In his view, it would be necessary to explain how "particles" in the chromosomes, which appeared to him (but not to Wilson) to be static and chemically identical, could affect the dynamic processes observable during development without resuscitating the discredited theory of "preformation."

As a result of the pattern of transmission of the traits of "white eyes" and "short wings" in the fruit fly *Drosophila*, by the end of 1910, Morgan was converted to the belief that genes indeed were on chromosomes. The segregation of these traits was "limited" by the sex of the progeny and could best be explained by the location of the alleles on the sex chromosome and recombination between them. Several previous lines of investigation—the patterns of Mendelian inheritance,

the mechanism of sex determination, and cytological studies showing that chromosome morphology differed with sex, some of which Morgan had studied—converged in this explanation.

Once converted, Morgan organized the "Fly Room," working with three extraordinary undergraduates, Alfred H. Sturtevant, Hermann Muller, and Calvin B. Bridges, who were to make an indelible imprint on this discipline. Morgan established a research program, (including Sturtevant and Bridges as his lifelong colleagues) that ignored his previous resistance to genes on chromosomes because that postulate could not explain the role of genes in development. In 1911, still short of his bachelor's degree, Sturtevant realized that the relative positions of genes on chromosomes could be mapped by the frequency with which they recombined. By 1916, Bridges published proof of the chromosomal location of genes by combining genetic and cytological evidence. Morgan was awarded the Nobel Prize, the first for research in genetics, in 1933.

Morgan himself worked intensively with *Drosophila* only for a relatively short time. By 1923, his publications again included studies of the experimental embryology of invertebrates, and he continued these studies even after his professional life took a different turn. In 1928, Morgan accepted the headship of the Division of Biology at the California Institute of Technology, even though he had previously been disparaging of administration. He was selected for this position because of his belief in the unity of chemistry, physics, and biology. He was responsible for appointing the first faculty members in biology, not all of whom proved to be distinguished. In spite of this, many of the premier researchers of the next generation of biologists passed through Cal Tech. Morgan's philosophy as leader of the division was that it should concentrate on research in cutting-edge, emerging areas, rather than trying to cover all areas of biology in a descriptive fashion. This goal has been maintained and helps account for the division's reputation. He retired in 1942 at the age of seventy-six.

Various "portraits" of Morgan describe him as having a wry sense of humor, being apolitical and nonreligious, overtly parsimonious, especially with research funds, but secretly extremely generous. There are reports of antisemitism, such as his declining to appoint enzymologist Leonor Michaelis as a faculty member, which are rejected by some colleagues. His professional life was the focus of his attention; by all accounts he was a somewhat distant but affectionate parent of four children, one of whom, Isabel Morgan Mountain, became a virologist. Morgan was a patrician in many respects: he was insulated from the inconveniences of life by the efforts of his wife (marginalizing her career), a leader of a research group, rather than a constantly active bench scientist, and supremely confident of his abilities. He took extreme positions, which he had the grace to recant publicly when they proved incorrect. Maienschein characterizes Morgan as an "American entrepreneur, following opportunity when resources are abundant and productive and abandoning projects with diminishing returns" (p. 260). This strategy is exemplified by his disparate research programs between 1890 and 1910, his temporarily discontinuing embryological research for genetics, and his having worked, according to Sturtevant, on at least fifty different organisms. Once he devoted his energies to *Drosophila*, he, as much as anyone, could be considered the founder of the American school of genetics.

BIBLIOGRAPHY

Allen, Garland E. *Thomas Hunt Morgan: The Man and His Science.* Princeton: Princeton University Press, 1978.

Bridges, Calvin C. "Non-Disjunction as Proof of the Chromosome Theory of Heredity." *Genetics* 1 (1916): 1–52, 107–163.

Gilbert, Scott F. "The Embryological Origins of the Gene Theory." *Journal of the History of Biology* 11 (1978): 307–351.

Goodstein, Judith R. *Millikan's School: A History of the California Institute of Technology.* New York and London: W.W. Norton, 1991.

Lederman, Muriel. "Genes on Chromosomes: The Conversion of Thomas Hunt Morgan." *Journal of the History of Biology* 22 (1989): 163–176.

Maienschein, Jane. *Transforming Traditions in American Biology, 1880-1915.* Baltimore: Johns Hopkins University Press, 1991.

Moore, John A. "Thomas Hunt Morgan—The Geneticist." *American Zoologist* 23 (1983): 855–865.

Morgan, Thomas H. "The Method of Inheritance of Two Sex-Limited Characters in the Same Animal." *Proceedings of the Society of Experimental Biology and Medicine* 8 (1910): 17–19.

Shine, Ian, and Sylvia Wrobel. *Thomas Hunt Morgan: Pioneer of Genetics.* Lexington: University of Kentucky Press, 1976.

Sturtevant, Alfred H. "The Linear Arrangement of Six Sex-Linked Factors in *Drosophila* as Shown by the Mode of

Association." *Journal of Experimental Zoology* 14 (1913): 43–59.

———. "Thomas Hunt Morgan." *Biographical Memoirs of the National Academy of Sciences* 33 (1959): 283–325.

Sutton, William S. "The Chromosomes in Heredity." *Biological Bulletin* 4 (1903): 231–251.

Muriel Lederman

SEE ALSO
Genetics

Morley, Edward Williams (1838–1923)

Chemist and educator, most famous for collaboration with Albert A. Michelson and later Dayton C. Miller in developing optical interferometers for luminiferous aether-drift experiments. Born into a family of old-line New England Congregationalists and educated at Williams College and Andover Theological Seminary, Morley served as a war-relief agent during the Civil War, then taught natural history and chemistry at several academies before being called to his first pastorate in Ohio. He found that he loved teaching more than preaching, and that he had a talent for research into astronomical and meteorological problems. So he became chaplain and chemist at Western Reserve College in Hudson, Ohio, in 1869. He established a library and launched a program in gas analyses of atmospheric air collected from hundreds of samples at different altitudes and latitudes and under different weather conditions. His techniques for handling so many atomic weight determinations accurately and precisely made his reputation compare favorably with that of Ira Remsen at the newly established Johns Hopkins University. When Western Reserve College moved to Cleveland in 1882 to become the core for the new Western Reserve University, Morley was well known as an analytic chemist and in much demand as a consultant.

Morley was profoundly interested in fundamental physical constants throughout his professional life. So when a talented young physicist moved nearby to the brand new Case School of Applied Science, Morley naturally became interested in Albert A. Michelson's efforts to perfect his terrestrial measurements of the velocity of light. The forty-five-year-old chemist and the thirty-one-year-old physicist began collaborating.

Morley and Michelson first repeated Fizeau's famous "water drag" experiment and found that the velocity of

M

light was indeed slightly increased or (decreased) when flowing with (or against) a current of distilled water. Then they designed and built an "aether-drift" interferometer about ten times more accurate than Michelson's original 1881 instrument. Many troubles, both personal and professional, attended these effects in 1886 and 1887, but Morley was steadfast through the "classic" tests in June 1887, and so they published their null results later in that year.

Their instrument in principle was extraordinary, capable of more accurate measurements of lengths, angles, and dimensions than any apparatus heretofore developed. But the aether-drift experiment seemed an abject failure.

Morley did his most significant chemical research after his work with Michelson. It was made possible by his design and construction of several new instruments, especially a precision eudiometer and a differential manometer. The Smithsonian Institution loaned him an exceptionally accurate Ruprecht balance, and so Morley was able to measure more exactly than ever before the combination and proportions of hydrogen and oxygen in water. Focusing his attention on the reaction by which these two gases form pure water, Morley gathered data over a decade to ascertain precisely what their relative atomic weights are. Using two independent calculations, one based on direct weighing of the gases and their product, the other based on volumetric and density analyses, Morley was able to assert in 1895 that the relative atomic weight of oxygen (within one part in 10,000) is 15.879. This result convinced Morley that he had at last shown Prout's hypothesis (regarding atomic hydrogen as the fundamental unit and multiple) to be incorrect. For such achievements, Morley was honored by election to the presidencies of the American Association for the Advancement of Science (1895) and the American Chemical Society (1899), and membership in the National Academy of Sciences (1897).

At the turn of the twentieth century, after Lord Kelvin, Rayleigh, Henri Poincaré, Hendrik A. Lorentz, and other physicists had made the Michelson-Morley aether-drift tests world famous, Morley began collaborating with Michelson's successor at Case, Dayton C. Miller, to try to improve the apparatus and to remove a number of embarrassing faults in the performance of that experiment. Intensively from 1902 to 1905, and intermittently after his retirement in 1906, encouraging Miller, Morley continued to be disappointed. After

Albert Einstein declared, in developing his theory of special relativity in 1905, the ether to be a superfluous idea, the Morley-Miller experiments were gradually taken to be definitive. But none of the three principal scientists involved in those tests ever accepted them as such.

Morley wrote no books, but produced a total of sixty-four papers (forty-eight with coauthors). Today, his fame derives mainly from his linkages, but his name remains important to the early development of physical chemistry in the United States.

Morley's papers are in the Library of Congress, Case Western Reserve University, and Williams College.

BIBLIOGRAPHY

Clarke, Frank W. "Edward Williams Morley." *Biographical Memoirs of the National Academy of Sciences* 21 (1927): 1–8.

Sokol, Michael. "Morley, Edward Williams." *American National Biography.* Edited by John A. Garraty and Mark C. Carnes. New York: Oxford University Press, 1999, 15: 874–875.

Spitter, Ernest G. "Morley, Edward Williams." *Dictionary of Scientific Biography.* Edited by Charles C. Gillispie. New York: Scribners, 1974, 9:530–531.

Swenson, Loyd S., Jr. *The Ethereal Aether: A History of the Michelson-Morley-Miller Aether-Drift Experiments, 1880–1930.* Austin: University of Texas Press, 1972.

Tower, Olin F. "Edward William Morley." *Science* 57 (13 April 1923): 431–434.

———. "Edward William Morley, 1838–1923." *Journal of the American Chemical Society* 45 (1923): 93–98.

Williams, Howard R. *Edward Williams Morley: His Influence on Science in America.* Easton, PA: Chemical Education Publishing, 1957.

Loyd S. Swenson Jr.

SEE ALSO
Michelson-Morley Experiment

Morrill Land-Grant College Act

Federal legislation providing for agricultural education. The need for agricultural education was pointed out in the early 1800s by agricultural societies and farm journals, and a few agricultural schools and academies were founded in the first half of the nineteenth century. These early efforts were limited, and the advocates of making agricultural education available to all citizens urged state governments to act. State agricultural colleges were established on a permanent basis in Pennsylvania and Michigan in 1855, in Maryland in 1856, and in Iowa in 1858.

In 1841, Alden Partridge, president of Norwich University, proposed to Congress that it appropriate funds from the sale of public lands, to be distributed among the states for the endowment of institutions which would teach the natural and applied sciences as applied to agriculture, engineering, manufactures, and commerce. Congress took no action.

Some ten years after Partridge's proposal, Jonathan B. Turner of Illinois gained national attention with a plan urging the establishment of state-supported industrial universities. In 1852, he proposed that Congress grant public lands to each state for establishment of such universities.

On 14 December 1857, Justin S. Morrill, representative in Congress from Vermont, introduced a bill for donating United States public lands to the states for colleges of agriculture and the mechanic arts. The bill was passed in 1859 but was vetoed by President Buchanan. Reintroduced in 1861, the bill became law with President Lincoln's signature on 1 July 1862.

Basically, the law granted each state unclaimed western lands for the support of one or more institutions of higher learning to teach agriculture and the mechanical arts. Eventually, every state and the District of Columbia adopted its provisions, with those adopting it after land was no longer available receiving cash payments. In 1890, Congress passed the Second Morrill Act providing for continuing funding. These colleges of agriculture and mechanical arts became an integral part of the nation's education system.

BIBLIOGRAPHY

Eddy, Edward Danforth. *Colleges for Our Land and Time: The Land-Grant Idea in American Education.* New York: Harper & Row, 1957.

Kellogg, Charles E., and David C. Knapp. *The College of Agriculture: Science in the Public Service.* New York: McGraw-Hill, 1966.

Marcus, Alan I. *Agricultural Science and the Quest for Legitimacy.* Ames: Iowa State University Press, 1985.

Neyland, Leedell W. *Historically Black Land-Grant Institutions and the Development of Agriculture and Home Economics, 1890–1990.* Tallahassee: Florida A&M University Foundation, 1990.

Rasmussen, Wayne D. *Taking the University to the People: Seventy-five Years of Cooperative Extension.* Ames: Iowa State University Press, 1989.

Schwieder, Dorothy. *75 Years of Service: Cooperative Extension in Iowa.* Ames: Iowa State University Press, 1990.

Simon, John Y. "The Politics of the Morrill Act." *Agricultural History* 37 (1963): 103–111.

Wayne D. Rasmussen

Morton, Samuel George (1798–1851)

Geologist, physician, and craniologist. Morton was born in Philadelphia where he attended Quaker schools. Following the wishes of his mother, he decided on a career in medicine. He studied with Dr. Joseph Parrish of Philadelphia and attended the University of Pennsylvania Medical School, from which he graduated in 1820. After a short visit to his father's relatives in Ireland, he was convinced that he should also study medicine at the University of Edinburgh, from which he received a second medical degree in 1823. Before leaving Europe, he traveled to the Continent, attending medical lectures in France. He returned to Philadelphia in 1824.

Immediately after his return from Europe, Morton started a medical practice which he continued throughout his life. He also taught anatomy from 1839 until 1843 at the Pennsylvania Medical College, and authored several works on medicine, including a treatise on pulmonary consumption and one on human anatomy.

As a child, Morton was interested in natural history and joined the Academy of Natural Sciences of Philadelphia in 1820. He was especially interested in geology and devoted his energies to the identification and analysis of the Cretaceous formation in the United States. Between 1828 and 1834, he published several papers and a final monograph on this subject entitled *Synopsis of the Organic Remains of the Cretaceous Group of the United States.* Based on his own observations and those of others, he traced the formation along the east coast and westward. Morton identified the Cretaceous on the basis of fossils, showing that it was the equivalent of the European Cretaceous. He was the first American to make extensive use of fossils as stratigraphic guides, and he influenced and assisted many of his contemporaries to do the same.

About 1830, Morton's interest began to turn toward the study of human crania. When he was asked to give a lecture on the five races into which mankind was believed to be divided, he wanted to illustrate his lecture with skulls of each race, but he could not locate one of each type. Thus, he began to amass his own collections which,

M

by the time of his death, numbered about 1,000 specimens from around the world, the largest in the United States at the time. He acquired the specimens through correspondence and rarely, if ever, collected in person.

Races were almost always distinguished by color. Morton devised means of measuring crania and principally on that basis concluded that the races were also distinct from each other by brain size. In contrast to the common belief that races had diverged from a single origin because of external environmental factors, Morton believed that the races were distinct in their origin. Morton published two major works on crania, the *Crania Americana* (1839) and *Crania Aegyptica* (1844), that earned him a reputation as the foremost craniologist of the time.

Morton divided all people into twenty-two families within the five races in accordance with cranial size. Morton did not make an overt effort to use his findings in support of the superiority of one race over another, although a certain prejudice in this direction may be apparent in his work (Gould, pp. 54–66). Nevertheless, his work was used in that fashion by others, notably Josiah C. Nott of Mobile, Alabama, who used it to support slavery in the South by arguing that cranial size showed that slaves were inferior and incapable of any other kind of life. Morton's arguments were used repeatedly in the nineteenth century to support slavery.

Important collections of Morton's correspondence are at the Pennsylvania Historical Society, the American Philosophical Society, and the Alexander Turnbull Library in Wellington, New Zealand. There is no modern biography or critical assessment of Morton's work as a whole, although he is frequently mentioned in works dealing with nineteenth-century American geology and racist attitudes.

BIBLIOGRAPHY

Gerstner, Patsy A. "The Influence of Samuel George Morton on American Geology." In *Beyond History of Science. Essays in Honor of Robert E. Schofield,* edited by Elizabeth Garber. Bethlehem, PA: Lehigh University Press; London and Toronto: Associated University Presses, 1990, pp. 126–136.

Gould, Stephen Jay. *The Mismanagement of Man.* New York: W.W. Norton, 1981.

Meigs, Charles D. *A Memoir of Samuel George Morton, M.D.* Philadelphia: T.K. and P.G. Collins, 1851.

Morton, Samuel George. *Synopsis of the Organic Remains of the Cretaceous Group of the United States.* Philadelphia: Key and Biddle, 1834.

————. *Crania Americana; or, a Comparative View of the Skulls of Various Aboriginal Nations of North and South America; to Which Is Prefixed an Essay on the Varieties of the Human Species.* Philadelphia: J. Dobson; London: Simpkin, Marshall and Co., 1839.

————. *Crania Aegyptica; or, Observations on Egyptian Ethonography, Derived from Anatomy, History and the Monuments.* Philadelphia: John Penington; London: Madden and Co., 1844.

Patterson, Henry S. "Memoir of the Life and Scientific Labors of Samuel George Morton." In *Types of Mankind,* edited by J.C. Nott and George R. Gliddon. Philadelphia: J.B. Lippincott & Co., 1865, pp. xvii–lvii.

Stanton, William. *The Leopard's Spots. Scientific Attitudes Toward Race in America 1815–1859.* Chicago: University of Chicago Press, 1960.

Wilson, Leonard, "The Emergence of Geology as a Science in the United States." *Journal of World History* 10 (1967): 416–437.

Wood, George C. "A Biographical Memoir of Samuel George Morton, M. D." *Transactions of the College of Physicians of Philadelphia,* n.s. (1853): 372–388.

Patsy Gerstner

Mulliken, Robert Sanderson (1896–1986)

Chemical physicist. Mulliken was born in Newburyport, Massachusetts, and was the son of Samuel Parsons Mulliken, an organic chemist at the Massachusetts Institute of Technology (MIT). In 1917, Mulliken received an undergraduate degree in chemistry from MIT, and then went on to the University of Chicago to work with the physical chemist William Draper Harkins. In 1921, he earned his Ph.D. in chemistry with a dissertation on the partial separation of mercury isotopes. After having accepted appointments at Harvard University and at New York University, he moved to the University of Chicago, where he stayed from 1928 until his death, with a dual appointment at Florida State University from 1964 to 1971. Mulliken was elected a member of the National Academy of Sciences in 1936, collaborated during World War II in the Manhattan Project as director of the Information Division, and was scientific attaché of the United States Embassy in London during 1955. In 1966, he was awarded the Nobel Prize in chemistry. Mulliken was instrumental in the definition of the basic concepts and methods used to study molecular structure and spectra, in developing its notation and shaping its language.

M

In 1923, when Mulliken turned to spectroscopy, a topic at the cutting edge of American physics, he looked for an isotope effect in molecular spectra. In the process, Mulliken identified a new compound and predicted the existence of what was later called the zero point energy, a phenomenon which was to be properly understood in the context of quantum mechanics. This line of research was soon to give way to the classification of the electronic states of diatomic molecules.

In the meantime, the German physicist Friedrich Hund, who became Mulliken's friend, introduced quantum mechanics in spectroscopy, and showed how the electronic states of molecules could be interpolated between two limiting cases: the situation in which the two atoms are separated, and the opposite situation in which the two nuclei are thought to be united into one. This work gave theoretical support to Mulliken's hint at what he later called "electron promotion," was used in Mulliken's "correlation diagrams," which relate the state of a molecule to the separated atoms and the united atom descriptions, and paved the way for Mulliken's subsequent assignment of individual quantum numbers to electrons in diatomic and polyatomic molecules, as well as for the consideration of the conditions which favored or inhibited the formation of molecules. Molecule formation was seen as a result of the motions of each electron in the field of the nuclei and the other electrons, in what Mulliken called "molecular orbitals."

The molecular orbital theory was at odds with the valence bond method developed by the Nobel Prize winner Linus Pauling and based on the quantum mechanical explanation of the formation of the hydrogen molecule given by the German physicists Walter Heitler and Fritz London. Although Pauling's approach was readily accepted by the chemical community, Mulliken's molecular orbitals proved later to be more useful in the study of highly symmetrical molecules, and more readily adaptable to computer calculations, which Mulliken and his research group used to move away from semiempirical toward wholly theoretical (ab initio) calculations.

The history of chemistry in the twentieth century, and of quantum chemistry in particular, is largely to be done. Recently, Servos addressed the rise of physical chemistry in the United States and Nye the development of theoretical chemistry, but both treated quantum chemistry as a concluding chapter. More recently, Mulliken's contributions to quantum chemistry have been addressed in Gavroglu and Simões's paper, whereas his role as a spokesman for science in the interwar era has been addressed in Butler's paper. Still, there is much room for work on Mulliken. His papers are at the University of Chicago.

BIBLIOGRAPHY

Butler, L. "Robert S. Mulliken and the Politics of Science and Scientists, 1939–1946." *Historical Studies in the Physical and Biological Sciences* 25 (1994): 25–45.

Gavroglu, K., and A. Simões. "The Americans, the Germans and the Beginnings of Quantum Chemistry: The Confluence of Diverging Traditions." *Historical Studies in the Physical and Biological Sciences* 25 (1994): 47–110.

Lowdin, P.-O., and B. Pullman, eds. *Molecular Orbitals in Chemistry, Physics and Biology: A Tribute to Robert S. Mulliken.* New York: Academic Press, 1964.

Mulliken, R.S. "Molecular Scientists and Molecular Science: Some Reminiscences." *Journal of Chemical Physics* 43 (1965): S2–S11.

———. "Spectroscopy, Quantum Chemistry and Molecular Physics." *Physics Today* 21 (1968): 52–57.

———. "The Path to Molecular Orbital Theory." *Pure and Applied Chemisty* 24 (1970): 203–215.

———. "Spectroscopy, Molecular Orbitals, and Chemical Bonding." *Nobel Lectures in Chemistry 1963–1970.* Amsterdam: Elsevier, 1972, pp. 131–160.

———. *Robert S. Mulliken: Life of a Scientist, An Autobiographical Account of the Development of Molecular Orbital Theory with an Introductory Memoir by Friedrich Hund.* Edited by Bernard J. Ransil. Berlin: Springer Verlag, 1989.

Ramsay, D.A., and J. Hinze eds. *Selected Papers of Robert S Mulliken.* Chicago: Chicago University Press, 1975.

Ana Simões

Mumford, Lewis (1895–1990)

Cultural historian and social critic. Lewis Mumford was one of the creators of the history of technology as a field of study. A philosophical interest in scientific thought informed this seminal work. Born in New York, Mumford attended Stuyvesant High School with an intention of becoming an engineer. Although he soon decided instead on the life of a writer, he never lost his boyhood fascination with invention and science. After writing books of literary and cultural criticism, Mumford made his first venture into the history of technology in 1930 with an article for *Scribner's Magazine,* entitled "The Drama of the Machines." Four years later, he published his masterpiece *Technics and Civilization,* a pioneering exploration of the

M

relationship between the machine and western civilization. In later writings on architecture, cities, and technology, Mumford returned repeatedly to the themes of this work.

While books on the history of invention had appeared as early as the fifteenth century, Mumford's work is distinguished by its insistent social and moral perspective. He was one of the first scholars to present technology within what he called social ecology, as much a mental as material construct and, as such, powerfully influenced by scientific and other ideas.

Technics and Civilization was a product of contemporary debates about the machine's role in society and the uses of technology in World War I. Although fascinated by the automobile, airplane, radio, and other inventions, Mumford was worried about the dehumanizing effects of automation and other modern technologies. He brought into question conventional assumptions about the relationships among science, technology, and social progress. He turned to the past, seeking the roots of the Machine Age and its moral dilemmas.

Technics and Civilization presented the past one thousand years as three great overlapping phases, each associated with a particular material basis: the eotechnic (wind, water, and wood) from 1000 to 1750; the paleotechnic (coal, iron, and steam) from 1700 to 1900; the neotechnic (electricity, alloys, and light metals) from 1820. In effect, he had moved the birth of the Industrial Revolution from the eighteenth century to the Middle Ages. Like most thinkers of his day, Mumford regarded science as the mother of invention and, hence, a major factor in these shifts. In general, he viewed the eotechnic phase as a harmonious preparatory period of quasi-magical scientific ideas and symbiosis between humans, science, and technology. In contrast, he traced the problems of the Machine Age directly to scientific ideas developed in the brutal paleotechnic phase. Mumford denounced Galileo, Descartes, Newton, and other scientists for creating the mechanical worldview, reducing the world to matter and motion, and eliminating organic and human qualities. He described the resulting depopulated world as a wasteland in which human beings were reduced to machines serving the needs of mills and factories.

Technics and Civilization was not ultimately a negative work, however. Along with other intellectuals shaped by World War I, he sought reconciliation of the rational and emotional sides of human nature. Mumford saw hope in a new dispensation of the neotechnic phase, based on the revolutions of relativity and quantum mechanics which seemed to signal the demise of the mechanical worldview. The twin revolutions had the effect, in Mumford's view, of reuniting the observer and the observed, reinstituting harmony, holism, and organicism. In these ideas, Mumford reflected the growing popularity of organic metaphors among contemporary thinkers, such as Edmund Wilson and Alfred North Whitehead. He was especially influenced by his Scots "master," Patrick Geddes, whose writings interwove technology, evolutionary biology, and the new physics in one grand synthesis.

Thirty years later, Mumford reexamined these views in a darker work, *The Pentagon of Power,* a book which reflected his horror at the Vietnam War. He repeated his indictment of Galileo and his brethren, while losing faith in neotechnic electricity, no longer viewed as a force for unifying human beings but as an intrusive, controlling presence in the form of the computer.

BIBLIOGRAPHY

Miller, Donald L. *Lewis Mumford, A Life.* Pittsburgh: Pittsburgh University Press, 1989.

———, ed. *The Lewis Mumford Reader.* New York: Pantheon, 1986.

Molella, Arthur P. "Mumford in Historiographical Context." In *Lewis Mumford, Public Intellectual,* edited by Thomas P. Hughes and Agatha C. Hughes. New York: Oxford University Press, 1990.

Mumford, Lewis. "The Drama of the Machines," *Scribner's Magazine,* August 1930, pp. 150–161.

———. *Technics and Civilization.* New York: Harcourt, Brace, 1934.

———. *The Myth of the Machine: I. Technics and Human Development.* New York: Harcourt, Brace and World, 1967.

———. *The Myth of the Machine: II. The Pentagon of Power.* New York: Harcourt, Brace, Jovanovich, 1970.

Arthur P. Molella

Museums of Natural History and Science

Museums for natural objects, while dating back to Alexandria and the Greeks, received fresh impetus from the dramatic expansion of known plants and animals following worldwide European explorations that included discovery of the Americas. Responding to requests from English collectors such as Peter Collinson and the Swedish taxonomist Carl Linnaeus, eighteenth-century colonists in North America sent specimens of plants, animals, and minerals back across the Atlantic Ocean and, in turn, earned books, status, and occasionally a small income. By then, some wealthy and well-educated individuals in the colonies also collected natural objects for study and display. Their cabinets of curiosity were symbols of learned achievement and signified as well the importance of physical objects in the learning of the moderns. Particularly after the Revolution, the American Philosophical Society, the American Antiquarian Society, and similar learned societies in other expanding cities such as Charleston acquired unusual and typical natural objects, sometimes organized in personal cabinets, from members and from correspondents beginning to explore their own environs as well as the western boundaries of the new nation.

The pioneering efforts of Swiss émigré Pierre Eugene Du Simietere to open a public display in Philadelphia about the time of the Revolution and to charge a fee was a significant step in public museum activity. His failure as proprietor did not deter the most well known museum proprietor of the period, Charles Willson Peale. For Peale, the artist turned naturalist, his ambitious "school of nature" in Philadelphia was to be a national establishment, and for nearly three decades he unsuccessfully sought government subsidies for a truly national museum like those of London and Paris. Although he was granted space in what became known as Independence Hall and the loan of specimens from the Lewis and Clark Expedition, Peale and his sons (who also established museums in New York and Baltimore) struggled throughout the period. Their extensive collections, which had attracted foreign as well as local visitors by the early decades of the nineteenth century, were sold in the 1840s and eventually displayed by P.T. Barnum until they burned in a fire. Peale's model of a museum for natural history was emulated by entrepreneurs, naturalists, and artists in Boston, New York, Cincinnati, and St. Louis, and by several itinerant showmen in the first half of the century.

During the same period, more systematic collections were gathered by members of learned societies seeking to identify local plants and animals and to document the diversity of the Americas. The most impressive in terms of membership and holdings in the middle of the nineteenth century was the Academy of Natural Sciences of Philadelphia. Provided with a building designed for use as a museum, the members established

important botanical and ornithological series. College and universities also created study cabinets whose sometimes spare holdings were enlarged by the systematic collecting and donations of students and faculty. Open to the local public when a museum acquired sufficient objects and display space, by the 1870s such facilities were considered standard teaching aids at well-respected colleges and their establishment a goal of emerging state universities. The largest developed by purchase, exchange, and expeditions was the specialized Museum of Comparative Zoology founded by Louis Agassiz at Harvard University. Many of the college museums relied on natural history dealers like Henry Ward, whose Scientific Establishment at Rochester, New York, supplied a generation of museums with skeletons, mounted specimens, minerals, fossils, and other natural history items. The Smithsonian Institution in Washington, D.C., built its collection during the 1850s into the 1880s under Spencer F. Baird, who worked in conjunction with federal agencies to acquire an extraordinary set of North American specimens and to publish ongoing bulletins and contributions to knowledge that set the standard in American natural history. Baird's exchange program also helped foster activities and interest in state academies of science and city museums across the country.

Cultural historians note that philanthropy in the late nineteenth century undergird such large facilities as the American Museum of Natural History on Central Park West in New York City and the Field Museum along Lake Michigan in Chicago. These urban museums developed, as well, novel approaches to public display and education including the highly detailed habitat groups and outreach courses for teachers. The pioneering museum curator George Brown Goode of the National Museum of the Smithsonian articulated a comprehensive theory of museum responsibility, while others like Charles Akeley in his Hall of Africa at the American Museum utilized display techniques that revolutionized the cabinet mentality of a century earlier.

By the late nineteenth century natural history museums were evident everywhere but their research functions were being challenged by other developments in science and public culture. Taxonomy lost status and support as another generation of researchers turned to experimental biology and ecology. Growing public interest in educational programs created demands that further constrained the human and financial resources

M

available for research within museums. While natural history museums maintained their public audiences, they also experienced competition from zoological parks and nature centers. Natural history museums remained important for some specialties, such as paleontology, and, more controversially, for the materials of human production acquired in anthropology.

In the twentieth century, reflecting American successes in technology, a new style of museum was developed, often with the support of industrialists. Building in part on collections acquired earlier as part of history and on the example of the Deutsches Museum in Munich, the Chicago Museum of Science and Industry became a prototype that relied on corporate as well as philanthropic sponsorship. Encouraging audience participation in a manner similar to that developed at world's fair exhibitions, the new museums of science and, particularly after World War II, the children's museums which appeared in major cities relied on changing exhibitions, planetariums, and omnitheaters to attract repeating local audiences. The Smithsonian Institution, with its traditional National Museum of Natural History now joined by the National Museum of Science and Technology (today the National Museum of American History) and the extraordinarily popular National Air and Space Museum, had staff and programs that played leadership roles in the American Association of Museums and in the museology more generally. By the end of the twentieth century, the *Official Museum Directory* (1994) reported that the United States had 7,892 museums of all types with an annual attendance of over 500 million.

BIBLIOGRAPHY

Alderson, William T., ed. *Mermaids, Mummies, and Mastodons: The Emergence of the American Museum.* Baltimore: Baltimore City Life Museums, 1992.

Alexander, Edward P. *Museum Masters: Their Museums and Their Influence.* Nashville: American Association for State and Local History, 1983.

Coleman, Laurence Vail. *The Museum in America: A Critical Study.* Washington, DC: American Association of Museums, 1939.

Findlen, Paula. *Possessing Nature: Museums, Collecting, and Scientific Culture in Early Modern Italy.* Berkeley: University of California Press, 1987.

Kohlstedt, Sally Gregory. "Museums: Revisiting Sites in the History of the Natural Sciences." *Journal of the History of Biology* 28 (1995): 151–166.

———, ed. *The Origins of Natural Science in America: The Essays of George Brown Goode.* Washington, DC: Smithsonian Institution Press, 1991.

Official Museum Directory. 24th edition. Washington, DC: American Association of Museums, 1994.

Orosz, Joel J. *Curators and Culture: The Museum Movement in America, 1740–1870.* Tuscaloosa: University of Alabama Press, 1990.

Sellers, Charles Coleman. *Mr. Peale's Museum: Charles Willson Peale and the First Popular Museum of Natural Sciences and Art.* New York: Norton, 1980.

Winsor, Mary P. *Reading the Shape of Nature: Comparative Zoology at the Agassiz Museum.* Chicago: University of Chicago Press, 1991.

Sally Gregory Kohlstedt

SEE ALSO
American Museum of Natural History; Smithsonian Institution

N

National Academy of Engineering

The leading engineering society in the United States. The National Academy of Engineers was organized on 10 December 1964, as a constituent part of the National Academy of Sciences (NAS). The NAS, since its establishment in 1863, had engineers among its membership, but they were few in number and scattered among sections identified by scientific discipline. As early as 1886, there had been calls for a separate academy for engineers, and during World War I, legislation to found such an academy was introduced into the Congress. Perhaps in part to discourage this attempt, the NAS in 1916 decided to set up its own section on engineering, to which engineering members might transfer and new members would be elected. Working also through its new (1915) National Research Council (NRC), the academy was now able to recruit, honor, and utilize engineers of unusual prominence while still keeping the power and prestige of science in a dominant position.

In the late 1950s, however, the question of a separate academy was again raised publicly and the interest of the Engineers Joint Council (EJC) was enlisted. The feeling was that, in an age of technological marvels and large government initiatives, engineers had neither the influence nor the credit they deserved in national forums. Still fearful of any effort to create a rival organization, the NAS joined with the EJC to study the matter in 1960. The result was a decision to form a separate but closely held National Academy of Engineering (NAE) under the authorization of the original 1863 congressional character of the NAS. The organizing meeting was held in December of 1964, and the first annual meeting on 28 April 1965.

By its tenth anniversary, the NAE had grown from its original 44 to 503 members and considered itself an operating agency in the public service. Differences between engineering and scientific cultures and procedures had made for some problems (especially with regard to the NAS-controlled NRC), but the link between the two academies had survived.

BIBLIOGRAPHY

National Academy of Engineers. *The National Academy of Engineering: The First Ten Years.* Washington, DC: NAE, 1976.

Pursell, Carroll W. "'What the Senate is to the American Commonwealth': A National Academy of Engineers." In *New Perspectives on Technology and American Culture,* edited by Bruce Sinclair. Philadelphia: American Philosophical Society, 1986, pp. 19–29.

Carroll W. Pursell

National Academy of Sciences

The National Academy of Sciences (NAS) is a private, nonprofit, self-perpetuating corporation engaged in scientific and engineering research, dedicated to the furtherance of science and technology and to their use for the general welfare. The NAS was established by an act of Congress and signed into law on 3 March 1863 by President Abraham Lincoln. Under the charter granted to it by the Congress, the NAS is required to advise the government on scientific and technical matters. In addition to its advisory role, the NAS is a membership organization whose members are elected for their original contributions to science and engineering. NAS membership is considered among the highest

N

recognition an American scientist can receive. The NAS elects its membership, officers, and set its rules, bylaws, and organization. The charter, also known as the Act of Corporation, authorizes that "the Academy shall, whenever called upon by any department of the Government, investigate, examine, experiment, and report upon any subject of science or art, the actual expense of such investigations to be paid from appropriations which may be made for the purpose but the Academy shall receive no compensation whatever for any services to the Government of the United States."

A small group of scientists in academia, the government, and the military were instrumental in pressing for the legislation that created the NAS. Known as the "Lazzaroni," this group included Louis Agassiz, Benjamin Peirce, Alexander Dallas Bache (who became the first president), B.A. Gould, and Charles Henry Davis. Joseph Henry, arguably America's most prominent scientist, was not in favor of the NAS as drafted, but joined to "give it direction." He was its second president and active in defining its early role and organization.

During its first fifty years, the academy received approximately fifty requests from American agencies and departments, many concerned with the organization and mission of governmental scientific bureaus and programs. But its advisory function was largely inactive by its 1913 semicentennial. In 1916, the academy's purpose and stature were expanded with the creation of the National Research Council (NRC). At the request of President Woodrow Wilson, the NAS created the NRC to coordinate the nation's scientific personnel and projects for war efforts during World War I. NAS Foreign Secretary George Ellery Hale was instrumental in the creation of the NRC. He was concerned with the lack of American preparedness for World War I as well as an enlarged mission and role for the NAS. Other contemporary scientists active in the NRC's early program were William H. Welch, Robert A. Millikan, Albert Noyes, and Robert M. Yerkes. In 1918, President Wilson issued an executive order perpetuating the NRC for peacetime organization under the academy charter. The NRC's wartime organization established standing committees to receive and respond to questions for advice and services; a similar organization of technical and programmatic units continues to the present day, although the NRC has been restructured to respond to changing scientific disciplines and national policy needs.

In 1924, again due to the efforts and vision of Hale, the NAS dedicated its headquarters building in Washington, D.C. (The headquarters building was entered on the register of National Landmarks in 1974.) In addition to this and other locations in Washington, the institution operates study centers in Massachusetts and California.

During World War II, the institution operated a wide range of activities for the federal scientific establishment, including over forty military medical committees to advise the Committee on Medical Research of the United States Office of Scientific Research and Development. A Committee on Atomic Fission determined that atomic fission was feasible for military purposes, leading to the Manhattan Project. In the postwar period, notable activities included the direction of the American scientific program for the International Geophysical Year and the administrative and scientific operation from 1947 to 1975 of the Atomic Bomb Casualty Commission in Japan, which studied the effects of the atomic bomb on successive generations of Japanese citizens.

The NAS marked its centennial in October 1963 with an extensive program of meetings and symposia. A centennial highlight was the convocation attended by thousands of scientists representing societies, universities, and research councils and academies of other nations. President John F. Kennedy delivered the centennial address, one of his last major appearances before his death.

In 1964 and in 1970, the NAS, under its corporate charter, created the National Academy of Engineering and the Institute of Medicine. Like the NAS, these groups elect members in recognition of distinguished achievement, and they share in the governance of the NRC through which the greatest part of the institution's advisory services are carried out. Collectively the four institutions are known as "The National Academies." In addition to oversight of the NRC, the academies and institute conduct fraternal activities, awarding medals for achievement and holding regular meetings and symposia.

Together they operate the National Academy Press, which publishes most study reports. The press is also a national leader in on-line publishing. Today, more than 1,000 institutional studies are available online. The academy has issued the scholarly journal, *The Proceedings of the National Academy of Sciences,* since 1915, and, with the NAE, publishes the quarterly policy journal *Issues in Science and Technology.* To recognize their deceased members, the academy has published

Biographical Memoirs of the National Academy of Sciences, starting in 1864. NAE Memorial Tributes have been issued since 1976.

Each year, the NRC releases approximately 200 study reports. In a typical year, more than 1,000 study units are active, with approximately 10,000 professionals volunteering their service on them. For the fiscal year ending 30 June 1998, the National Academies received $153,389,800 in federal funds and $28,136,600 in private and nonfederal grants, contracts, and contributions.

In addition to government advisory activities, the National Academies also direct self-initiated studies and science policy and dissemination activities, including the Office for the Public Understanding of Science and the Center for Science, Mathematics, and Engineering Education. The NRC also advises the government in the selection of fellows for various national laboratory and agency programs. In addition, the institution is the mechanism by which American scientists affiliate with most international unions and commissions in the sciences. The NAS is the United States' adhering national member to the International Council for Science, formerly the International Council of Scientific Unions.

BIBLIOGRAPHY

Berkowitz, Edward D. To Improve Human Health: A History of the Institute of Medicine. Washington, DC: National Academy Press, 1998.

Cochrane, Rexmond C. The National Academy of Sciences: The First Hundred Years, 1863–1963. Washington, DC: National Academy of Sciences, 1978.

Dupree, A. Hunter. "The Founding of the National Academy of Sciences—A Reinterpretation." Proceedings of the American Philosophical Society, 101, no. 5 (1957): 434–440.

———. Science in the Federal Government: A History of Policies and Activities to 1940. Cambridge, MA: Harvard University Press, 1957.

———. "The National Academy of Sciences and the American Definition of Science." In The Organization of Science in Modern America, edited by Alexandra Oleson and John Voss. Baltimore: Johns Hopkins University Press, 1979, pp. 342–363.

Halpern, Jack. "The U.S. National Academy of Sciences—In Service to Science and Society." Proceedings of the National Academy of Sciences 94 (1977): 1606–1608.

http://www.nas.edu/history/ (1999): About the National Academies' History from The National Academies' homepage. Historical pieces written by Daniel Barbiero, Archivist, National Academies.

True, Frederick W., ed. A History of the First Half-Century of the National Academy of Sciences. Washington, DC: National Academy of Sciences, 1913.

Wright, Helen. Explorer of the Universe: A Biography of George Ellery Hale. New York: E.P. Dutton, 1966.

Janice Goldblum

National Advisory Committee for Aeronautics

Forerunner of the National Aeronautics and Space Administration (NASA), created by the United States Congress in 1915. In 1915, the airplane was still largely a useless freak. Much had to be done to transform it into a practical and versatile vehicle. The mission of the National Advisory Committee for Aeronautics (NACA) was "to supervise and direct the scientific study of the problems of flight with a view to their practical solution" (Public Law 271, 63d Congress, approved 3 March 1915). This meant that the NACA was to treat aeronautics not so much as a scientific discipline, but as an area for engineering research and development. In practice, this turned out to mean that the NACA found solutions to serious problems facing the aircraft industry and military air services.

Although established in 1915, the NACA did not have operational laboratory facilities until 1920, when the Langley Memorial Aeronautical Laboratory, near Hampton, Virginia, came on line with its first primitive wind tunnel. Construction of Langley Field actually began in 1917, but the chaos of mobilizing for war in Europe delayed completion of the NACA's facilities for three years.

Once in possession of effective experimental equipment, however, the NACA pursued its mission with distinction. Already by the end of the 1920s, with its ingeniously designed Variable-Density Tunnel, Propeller Research Tunnel, and Full-Scale Tunnel, which outperformed any other single collection of facilities anywhere in the world, the NACA was generally acknowledged to be the world's premier aeronautical research establishment. Thanks to the reliable data resulting from intelligent use of the NACA's unique complex of experimental equipment, American aircraft began to dominate the world's airways.

Through systematic aerodynamic testing, NACA researchers found practical ways to improve the performance of many different varieties of aircraft. During World War II, they tested virtually all types of American

N

aircraft that saw combat. By pointing out ways for these aircraft to gain a few miles per hour or a few extra miles of range, their effort in many cases made the difference between Allied victory and defeat in the air.

During World War II, the size and scope of the NACA's operation expanded greatly. The "Committee," as it was known to insiders, opened large new research centers in California—the Ames Aeronautical Laboratory and the High-Speed Flight Research Station (later named NASA Dryden)—and in Ohio (the Lewis Flight Propulsion Laboratory).

After the war, NACA researchers turned their attention to the high-speed frontier and solved many of the basic problems blocking the flight of aircraft to supersonic speeds. They played essential roles in the development of several experimental high-speed research airplanes including Bell's X-1, the first plane to break the sound barrier, and North American's X-15, the first winged aircraft to fly into space.

The NACA flourished as a federal agency until 1 October 1958, when it was formally abolished, a victim of the hysteria triggered by the orbits of the Soviet *Sputnik*s the previous autumn. Congress dissolved the NACA and created in its place NASA. Much about the NACA, however, did live on. Its laboratories and their staffs, although reorganized and refocused, formed the nucleus of the new space agency.

BIBLIOGRAPHY

Bilstein, Roger. *Orders of Magnitude: A History of NACA and NASA, 1915–1990.* Washington, DC: Government Printing Office, 1989.

Dawson, Virginia P. *Engines and Innovation: Lewis Laboratory and American Propulsion Technology.* Washington, DC: Government Printing Office, 1991.

Hansen, James P. *Engineer in Charge: A History of the Langley Aeronautical Laboratory, 1917–1958.* Washington, DC: Government Printing Office, 1987.

Roland, Alex. *Model Research: The National Advisory Committee for Aeronautics, 1915–1958.* Washington, DC: Government Printing Office, 1985.

James R. Hansen

SEE ALSO

Ames Research Center; Langley Research Center; National Aeronautics and Space Administration

National Aeronautics and Space Administration

Government agency which conducts aeronautical and spaceflight research. The National Aeronautics and Space Administration (NASA) emerged in 1958 out of the Cold War rivalries of the United States and the Soviet Union. Engaged in a broad contest over the ideologies and allegiances of the nonaligned nations of the world, space exploration was one major area contested. The Soviets gained the upper hand in this competition on 4 October 1957 when they launched *Sputnik I,* the first artificial satellite to orbit the earth, as part of a larger scientific effort associated with the International Geophysical Year.

While American officials congratulated the Soviet Union for this accomplishment, clearly many Americans thought that the Soviet Union had staged a tremendous coup for the Communist system at the expense of the United States. Because of this perception, Congress passed and President Dwight D. Eisenhower signed the National Aeronautics and Space Act of 1958 establishing the new agency with a broad mandate to explore and use space for the benefit "of all mankind." NASA began operations on 1 October 1958, absorbing into it the earlier National Advisory Committee for Aeronautics intact; its 8,000 employees, an annual budget of $100 million, three major research laboratories—Langley Aeronautical Laboratory, Ames Aeronautical Laboratory, and Lewis Flight Propulsion Laboratory—and two small test facilities.

Within a short time after NASA's formal organization, the new organization also took over management of space exploration projects from other federal agencies, notably the Viking program from the Naval Research Laboratory and the rocket development effort at the Army Ballistic Missile Agency located at Huntsville, Alabama. It also acquired control of the Jet Propulsion Laboratory, a contractor facility operated by the California Institute of Technology in Pasadena, and created the Goddard Space Flight Center in Greenbelt, Maryland, specifically to conduct space science.

NASA began to conduct space science missions within months of its creation, especially Project Ranger to send probes to the Moon, Project Echo to test the possibility of satellite communications, and Project Mercury to ascertain the possibilities of human spaceflight. Even so, these activities were constrained by a modest budget and a measured pace on the part of NASA leadership.

Those constraints were suddenly lifted in 1961 when President John F. Kennedy, responding to perceived challenges to American leadership in science and technology, announced a lunar landing effort that would place an American on the moon before the end of the decade. Kennedy unveiled this commitment, called Project Apollo, before Congress on 25 May 1961 in a speech on urgent national needs, billed as a second State of the Union message. In the speech, he asked for support to accomplish four basic goals in space exploration, but only the lunar landing is usually remembered. In addition, he asked for congressional appropriations for weather satellites, communications satellites, and the Rover nuclear propulsion rocket. Congress agreed to all of them with barely any comment.

For the next eleven years, NASA was consumed with carrying out the Kennedy mandate. This effort required tremendous expenditure, more than $20 billion over the life of the program, to make it a reality by 1969. Only the building of the Panama Canal rivaled the Apollo program's size as the largest nonmilitary technological endeavor ever undertaken by the United States; only the Manhattan Project was comparable in a wartime setting. The human spaceflight imperative was a direct outgrowth of it; Projects Mercury (at least in its later stages), Gemini, and Apollo were each designed to execute it.

NASA eventually landed six sets of astronauts on the moon between 1969 and 1972. The first landing mission, Apollo 11, landed on 20 July 1969, when astronaut Neil Armstrong first set foot on the surface, telling the millions of listeners that it was "one small step for [a] man—one giant leap for mankind." The astronauts collected lunar rock samples and set up several experiments before safely returning to earth.

Five more landing missions followed Apollo 11 at approximately six-month intervals through December 1972, each of them increasing the time spent on the moon. Three of the later Apollo missions used a lunar rover vehicle to travel in the vicinity of the landing site. The scientific experiments placed on the moon and the lunar soil samples returned through Project Apollo have provided grist for scientists' investigations of the solar system ever since.

The scientific return was significant, but the Apollo program did not answer conclusively the age-old questions of lunar origins and evolution. Instead, the new information fueled the debate between scientists over these important questions. The data helped theorists to develop new ideas on the distribution of angular momentum between the sun and the planets, on whether planets formed directly by condensation of gaseous protoplanets or by accretion of solid planetesimals, on whether the "solar nebula" was ever hot and turbulent enough to vaporize and completely mix its components, and on whether an external cause such as a supernova explosion set in motion the gas cloud's collapse.

The lunar rock and soil samples returned by Apollo missions to the moon have been enormously significant in this ongoing scientific debate. Geologists conducted all manner of investigations using these samples, finding that, while the basalts and breccias were similar to those found on earth, they also were sufficiently different to question their origins on this planet. These lunar rocks and soil samples remain in a pristine condition in a nitrogen environment at the Lunar Receiving Laboratory at the Johnson Space Center in Houston, Texas, available for study by scientists worldwide.

NASA went into something of a holding pattern after the completion of Project Apollo. The major program for the 1970s was the development of a reusable Space Shuttle that was supposed to be able to travel back and forth between earth and space more routinely and economically than had ever been the case before. In 1981, the first operational orbiter, *Columbia*, took off from the Kennedy Space Center, Florida. By 28 January 1986, there had been twenty-four shuttle flights, but during the launch of *Challenger*, a leak in the joints of one of two solid rocket boosters detonated the main liquid fuel tank. Seven astronauts died in this accident, the worst in the history of space flight. The explosion became one of the most significant events of the 1980s, as billions around the world saw the accident on television and empathized with the crewmembers killed.

With the accident, the shuttle program went into a two-year hiatus while NASA worked to redesign the system and revamp its management structure. The Space Shuttle finally returned to flight without further incident on 29 September 1988. Through July 1995, NASA had launched more than forty follow-on Shuttle missions without an accident. Each undertook scientific and technological experiments ranging from the deployment of important space probes like the Magellan Venus radar mapper in 1989 and the Hubble Space Telescope in 1990, through the continued flight of

N

"Spacelab" in 1991, to a dramatic Hubble servicing mission in December 1993. Through all of these activities, a good deal of realism about what the shuttle could and could not do began to emerge.

In addition to those major human spaceflight programs, there have been significant scientific probes sent to the moon and planets, as well as earth observing systems placed in orbit. Among the most significant have been the Viking missions to Mars, the culmination of a series of missions to explore the planet that had begun in 1964 with *Mariner 4,* and continued with other missions. Viking consisted of two spacecraft designed to orbit Mars and to land and operate on the planet's surface. Launched in 1975, the probes spent nearly a year cruising to Mars. The project's primary mission ended on 15 November 1976, eleven days before Mars's superior conjunction (its passage behind the sun), although the Viking spacecraft continued to operate for six years after first reaching Mars. The last transmission reached earth on 11 November 1982. One of the important scientific activities of this project was the attempt to determine whether there was life on Mars, since the planet had long been thought of as having sufficient similarity to the earth that life might exist there. While the three biology experiments discovered unexpected and enigmatic chemical activity in the Martian soil, they provided no clear evidence for the presence of living microorganisms in soil near the landing sites. They concluded that the combination of solar ultraviolet radiation that saturates the surface, the extreme dryness of the soil, and the oxidizing nature of the soil chemistry had prevented the formation of living organisms in the Martian soil.

Another important probe was the Voyager mission to the outer solar system. During the later 1960s, scientists discovered that once every 176 years both the earth and all the giant planets of the solar system gather on one side of the sun. This geometric lineup made possible close-up observation of all the planets in the outer solar system (with the exception of Pluto) in a single flight, the "Grand Tour." The flyby of each planet would bend the spacecraft's flight path and increase its velocity enough to deliver it to the next destination. This would occur through a complicated process known as "gravity assist," something like a slingshot effect, whereby the flight time to Neptune could be reduced from thirty to twelve years. NASA launched these missions from Cape Canaveral, Florida: *Voyager 2* lifting off on 20 August 1977 and *Voyager 1*

entering space on a faster, shorter trajectory on 5 September 1977.

With the successful achievement of its objectives at Jupiter and Saturn, eventually the two probes explored all the giant outer planets, forty-eight of their moons, and the unique systems of rings and magnetic fields those planets possess. The two spacecraft returned to earth information that revolutionized the science of planetary astronomy, helping to resolve some key questions while raising intriguing new ones about the origin and evolution of the planets in this solar system. The two *Voyagers* took well over 100,000 images of the outer planets, rings, and satellites, as well as millions of magnetic, chemical spectra, and radiation measurements. They discovered rings around Jupiter, volcanoes on Io, shepherding satellites in Saturn's rings, new moons around Uranus and Neptune, and geysers on Triton. The last imaging sequence was *Voyager 1*'s portrait of most of the Solar System, showing earth and six other planets as sparks in a dark sky lit by a single bright star, the sun.

More recently the Hubble Space Telescope, initially impaired, has returned exceptional scientific data about the origins and development of the universe; the Magellan mission radar imaged Venus; and the Galileo probe to Jupiter, while having some problems with its communication system, returned important data on asteroids en route to its primary target. At the same time, because of budgetary and other constraints, NASA leaders have moved toward the building of a large number and variety of small, inexpensive satellites rather than a few large, expensive spacecraft. In the 1990s, the NASA administrator began to urge a new philosophy of "smaller, cheaper, faster" for the agency's space probes, and advocated a mixture of large and small spacecraft to avoid the long hiatus that came if a mission failed.

BIBLIOGRAPHY

Bulkeley, Rip. *The Sputniks Crisis and Early United States Space Policy: A Critique of the Historiography of Space.* Bloomington: Indiana University Press, 1991.

Burrows, William E. *Exploring Space.* New York: Random House, 1990.

Chaiken, Andrew. *A Man on the Moon: The Voyages of the Apollo Astronauts.* New York: Viking, 1994.

Chaisson, Eric J. *The Hubble Wars: Astrophysics Meets Astropolitics in the Two-Billion Dollar Struggle Over the Hubble Space Telescope.* New York: HarperCollins Publishers, 1994.

Compton, W. David. *Where No Man Has Gone Before: A History of Apollo Lunar Exploration Missions.* Washington, DC: NASA SP-4214, 1989.

Divine, Robert A. *The Sputnik Challenge: Eisenhower's Response to the Soviet Satellite.* New York: Oxford University Press, 1993.

Ezell, Edward Clinton, and Linda Neuman Ezell. *On Mars: Exploration of the Red Planet, 1958–1978.* Washington, DC: NASA SP-4212, 1984.

Hufbauer, Karl. *Exploring the Sun: Solar Science Since Galileo.* Baltimore: Johns Hopkins University Press, 1991.

Krug, Linda T. *Presidential Perspectives on Space Exploration: Guiding Metaphors from Eisenhower to Bush.* New York: Praeger, 1991.

Lambright, W. Henry. *Powering Apollo: James E. Webb of NASA.* Baltimore: Johns Hopkins University Press, 1995.

Launius, Roger D. *NASA: A History of the U.S. Civil Space Program.* Malabar, FL: Krieger Publishing, 1994.

Levine, Alan J. *The Missile and Space Race.* New York: Praeger, 1994.

McCurdy, Howard E. *Inside NASA: High Technology and Organizational Change in the U.S. Space Program.* Baltimore: Johns Hopkins University Press, 1993.

McDougall, Walter A. . . . *The Heavens and the Earth: A Political History of the Space Age.* New York: Basic Books, 1985.

Naugle, John E. *First Among Equals: The Selection of NASA Space Science Experiments.* Washington, DC: NASA SP-4215, 1991.

Newell, Homer E. *Beyond the Atmosphere: Early Years of Space Science.* Washington, DC: NASA SP-4211, 1980.

Tatarewicz, Joseph N. *Space Technology and Planetary Astronomy.* Bloomington: Indiana University Press, 1990.

Wilhelms, Don E. *To a Rocky Moon: A Geologist's History of Lunar Exploration.* Tucson: University of Arizona Press, 1993.

Winter, Frank H. *Rockets into Space.* Cambridge, MA: Harvard University Press, 1990.

Roger D. Launius

SEE ALSO
Apollo Program

National Audubon Society

One of the oldest, largest, and most influential environmental organizations in the United States. Until recently the National Audubon Society has focused primarily on bird protection.

Along with sportsmen, scientists were among the first to call attention to the growing threat that industrialization and economic growth posed to American wildlife by the end of the nineteenth century. In 1884, the newly organized American Ornithologists' Union (AOU) voted to create a Bird Protection Committee. Two years later, George Bird Grinnell, a Yale-trained paleontologist, patrician sportsman, and Bird Protection Committee member, launched the first Audubon Society from his popular sporting periodical, *Forest and Stream.* Named for the famed American naturalist and bird artist John James Audubon, the new society quickly grew to nearly 50,000 members before Grinnell abandoned the project in 1888. The idea was revived in 1896 when a group of wealthy New Englanders established the Massachusetts Audubon Society, the first of thirty-six state Audubon societies organized over the next fifteen years. At the urging of AOU Bird Protection Committee Chairman William Dutcher, most state societies joined together in a loose federation in 1901 and a more tightly knit group, the National Association of Audubon Societies, four years later. This organization became the National Audubon Society (NAS) in 1940.

Like its predecessors, the NAS has been active on a number of fronts: increasing public awareness about the plight of American bird species, promoting state and federal legislation to protect wildlife, hiring wardens to patrol important wildfowl nesting colonies, and establishing an extensive system of private sanctuaries. The organization has also promoted scientific research by sponsoring studies on endangered birds and an annual Christmas Bird Count (begun in 1901), which has provided important data on long-term avian population trends.

In the 1960s and 1970s, the NAS experienced a tremendous growth in membership and began expanding its agenda to include a broader spectrum of wildlife and environmental issues. By 1990, it boasted nearly 600,000 members. Discussion of the NAS appears in most standard histories of the American conservation movement, but the only comprehensive study is by Graham, who has long been affiliated with the organization. Ornithologists' central involvement in the Audubon movement challenges the pervasive notion that scientists first became politically active in the wake of the atomic bomb.

BIBLIOGRAPHY
Barrow, Mark V., Jr. *A Passion for Birds: American Ornithology after Audubon.* Princeton: Princeton University Press, 1998.

N

Doughty, Robin W. *Feather Fashions and Bird Preservation: A Study in Nature Protection*. Berkeley and Los Angeles: University of California Press, 1975.

Fox, Stephen. *John Muir and His Legacy: The American Conservation Movement*. Boston: Little, Brown and Co., 1981.

Graham, Frank, Jr. *The Audubon Ark: A History of the National Audubon Society*. New York: Alfred A. Knopf, 1990.

Orr, Oliver H., Jr. *Saving American Birds: T. Gilbert Pearson and the Founding of the Audubon Movement*. Gainesville: University Press of Florida, 1992.

Pearson, T. Gilbert. *Adventures in Bird Protection: An Autobiography*. New York: D. Appleton-Century, 1937.

                                              Mark V. Barrow Jr.

SEE ALSO
Ornithology

National Bureau of Standards
See National Institute of Standards and Technology

National Geographic Society

The largest popular science organization in twentieth-century America. Federal scientists, including A.W. Greely, John Wesley Powell, and Henry Gannett, established the society in 1888 to improve intragovernmental communication on geographical issues, and also to inform people who were influential in Washington society and politics. The society changed direction in 1900, when Gilbert H. Grosvenor, son-in-law of society president Alexander Graham Bell, transformed the *National Geographic Magazine* from a professional journal into a vehicle for mass education and entertainment. He combined the new technology of photoreproduction and techniques of national marketing with the traditional appeal of membership in a learned society and support for the advancement of learning. The magazine's circulation grew from 2,200 in 1900 to 600,000 in 1920, and 10 million by 1980.

Under Grosvenor's editorship, extending from 1900 to 1954, the *National Geographic* blended articles on natural history, natural disasters, and new technologies, with travelogues, accounts of heroic exploration, and depictions of primitive peoples. Its technologically advanced, carefully selected photographs provided middle-class Americans their primary images of the world. The magazine romanticized nature and non-Western peoples while affirming the beneficence of the United States and other colonial powers.

Through membership in the society, Americans supported exploring adventures and some scientific research. The society contributed, for example, to the polar expeditions of Robert E. Peary and Richard E. Byrd, the archaeologist Hiram Bingham's investigation of Machu Picchu, William Beebe's development of the bathysphere, and Jane Goodall's early studies of chimpanzee behavior. The magazine also promoted military aviation, aerospace pioneering, and, later, all aspects of space exploration. The society's grants generally led to first-person articles in the *Geographic*.

Grosvenor's son Melville, and his associates, maintained these policies. In the 1970s, under Gilbert M. Grosvenor (son of Melville), the magazine's viewpoints became more modern, and the society made a more systematic effort to link its activities with those of professional scientific communities. Yet, in both leadership and outlook, the society continues the Victorian era's tradition of popular natural history.

Celebrations of the National Geographic Society's history have been countered by some criticisms for conservatism and conflict of interest. The more prominent attitude among scholars, however, has been dismissal of its significance. As a pervasive force in American culture and a long-standing presence in science policy, the society warrants serious historical investigation. Its records, however, have not been open to outside researchers.

BIBLIOGRAPHY

Abramson, Howard S. *National Geographic: Behind America's Lens on the World*. New York: Crown, 1987.

Bryan, C.B.D. *The National Geographic Society: 100 Years of Adventure and Discovery*. New York: Abrams, 1987.

Grosvenor, Gilbert H. *The National Geographic Society and Its Magazine: A History*. Washington, DC: National Geographic Society, 1957.

Pauly, Philip J. "The World and All That Is in It: The National Geographic Society, 1888–1918." *American Quarterly* 31 (1979): 517–532.

Rothenberg, Tamar Yosefa. "*National Geographic*'s World: Politics of Popular Geography, 1888–1945 (National Geographic)." Ph.D. diss., Rutgers, the State University of New Jersey–New Brunswick, 1998.

                                               Philip J. Pauly

National Institute of Standards and Technology

Successor to the National Bureau of Standards (NBS). The NBS was established by act of Congress in 1901 as a successor to the tiny Office of Standard Weights and Measures of the Treasury Department. It had been the responsibility of that predecessor organization to maintain copies of standard measures of length, capacity, and weight, and to certify measuring instruments such as tape measures, thermometers, and scales as accurate within certain tolerances of accepted references. These services were significant for the nation's economy, both domestic and international commerce. However, at the dawn of the twentieth century, it was the new science-based industries that were in ascendance, notably electrical power and equipment manufacturing, and synthetic chemical industries.

Electricity and optics were leading-edge sciences at this time. Spectroscopy and the nature and measurement of fundamental electrical quantities constituted the primary agendas of most leading physics laboratories. It was clear to many individuals at the forefront of academic science and industrial research that a national laboratory for the investigation of the physical sciences, beginning with electricity, optics, and analytical chemistry, must supersede the nineteenth-century certification office if the United States were to seriously compete with Germany and Great Britain in the high technology industries of the twentieth century. Both these countries had established their own comprehensive laboratories before the turn of the century, namely the famed Physikalisch-Technische Reichsanstalt (established 1887), and England's National Physical Laboratory (established 1899).

Physicist Albert A. Michelson of the University of Chicago wanted a world-class physical laboratory established in this country. In 1899, he granted a temporary leave to one of his faculty, Samuel Wesley Stratton, to accept an appointment as "inspector of standards" at the Office of Weights and Measures. Michelson, and the treasury secretary (Lyman Gage) and assistant secretary (Frank Vanderlip) understood that Stratton's primary work would be to draw up plans and lobby support for establishing a major government laboratory. Stratton proved equal to the task, and in two years' time had developed a national consensus among academic researchers, industrialists, and government officials for the undertaking. When congressional hearings were held, Stratton was the most recognized and respected figure on the subject, and was appointed first director of the NBS by President William McKinley in March 1901. He served in that position until 1922.

The cautiously worded NBS charter, however, gave no indication of the scale and scope of the agency's agenda during that first administration. Already by 1912, NBS had become, by any measure, the world's largest comprehensive facility for research in the physical and engineering sciences. During World War I, NBS was given emergency powers that accelerated its growth, and the bureau was the most important focus of military research in this country. At the close of the war, the primary NBS facility, in Washington, D.C., was home to the country's most advanced radio laboratory, as well as leading design facilities and test beds for aeronautics, optics and photography, and research projects in X-ray metrology and radiatioactivity, and a massive program in materials science including synthetic chemistry for strategic products.

Stratton, along with his chief physicist, Edward Rosa, also moved the bureau into scientific investigation of the nation's utilities, including electric power, telephony, and heating and illuminating gas. The results of these multiyear projects produced seminal studies of safety and service performance standards, as well as useful pricing guidelines. These technical studies made feasible the regulation of utilities industries by their respective regional utilities commissions. It also tested the boundaries of federal interventionist research in the new regulatory state, and established the bureau as a model agency of the Progressive Era.

The bureau had become the central location for investigations in the laboratory physical sciences before the war. The NBS had more "starred" entries in American Men of Science during Stratton's tenure than any other institution. Already in 1904, more than half of the twenty papers presented at the American Physical Society (APS) conference were presented by bureau scientists, and the APS was holding all meetings of its annual conference on the NBS campus from 1914 until 1941.

The bureau also developed a remarkable laboratory culture during its first two decades, unlike that of any other government agency. It hosted regular scientific symposia, based on the European graduate school model, in which staff reviewed research from other institutions and made presentations of their individual investigations. There was also a visiting lecture series,

N

which brought renowned scientists from American and foreign laboratories. Several younger scientists, with the approval of Stratton, began a graduate studies program in 1908, before anything similar had appeared at other federal bureaus. Under this program, working scientists could take courses given at NBS by senior staff and leading scientists from universities such as Johns Hopkins, and, applying their bureau laboratory investigations as research projects, could secure advanced degrees up to the Ph.D. from the cooperating university. Degrees were granted by the leading universities of the day, including Harvard, Princeton, Johns Hopkins, Wisconsin, Michigan, and others.

Stratton attempted a great organizational experiment beginning in 1918. The bureau had moved to the forefront of research, both pure and applied, working intimately at the boundaries of industry, academia, and government. During the war it had even become a national inventions laboratory. Stratton urged Congress to allow the massive facilities accrued during the war to become converted to a concentrated program for civilian technology, whose innovations could be applied wherever useful in science-based industry, free to the public. Stratton secured his program of industrial research, but after the last of the military wartime contracts expired, the funding was insufficient to fulfill the goals.

After Stratton left, in 1922, to become president of the Massachusetts Institute of Technology, he was succeeded by a series of men who were competent scientists but far less imaginative and energetic administrators. In addition, the Great Depression took a terrible toll on NBS statutory funding and, consequently, on the ranks of bureau scientists and technicians. NBS had lost much of its luster by the time the United States began mobilizing for World War II. The original "uranium project" (later, Manhattan Project) was given to the NBS director, Lyman Briggs, to administrate, but he proved unequal to the urgency of the mission.

The bureau's primary contribution to the war, in addition to supporting investigations along the entire spectrum of the nation's strategic research projects, was the development of one of two versions of the "radio proximity fuze," used to detonate explosives, such as bombs and mortars, when at optimal range from their targets, rather than detonating on contact. This turned out to be a massive technological problem, and while the device was used only near the end of the war, its major elements had great consequences for the high technology weaponry of the Cold War, and for the electronics industry generally.

The first postwar director of NBS, Edward Condon, was also the first scientist chosen for that position from outside the established bureau culture. Condon had great ambitions to return NBS to the international preeminence it once enjoyed. He moved it more aggressively into nuclear physics research, and especially into the nascent science of electronic computing. The new Applied Mathematics Division, which included four separate laboratories, designed and built the Standards Eastern Automatic Computer, which was put into operation in 1950. This was the most advanced computer of its day, incorporating many innovations in dedicated hardware as well as overall design architecture. However, Condon was one of the casualties of the security state paranoia of the early postwar period, and although finally cleared of any charges by the House Un-American Affairs Committee, Condon left the bureau at the height of his troubles in 1951 to prevent any collateral damage to the institution.

Condon was succeeded in turn by Allen Astin, a capable veteran of wartime research (proximity fuze), but a conservative and unassuming administrator. Soon after Astin was appointed director, he and NBS were battered in one of the most enigmatic episodes in the history of American federal science, the AD-X2 affair. The essence of this dispute involved an entrepreneur, Jess Ritchie, who had become a millionaire by mail-order marketing a powder which he advertised as having restorative powers for lead-acid electrical batteries, such as automobile batteries. The post office and the Federal Trade Commission both investigated Ritchie's business on the grounds of mail fraud and false advertising, respectively, and asked the NBS electrochemistry laboratory to conduct scientific tests to determine the actual characteristics of the product.

The bureau reported that the concoction, which was a mixture of sodium and potassium salts (epsom and glauber salts) had no such restorative effects, and the best that could be said for the product was that, unlike many such additives that had been tested since the turn of the century, this one was largely inert and not dramatically harmful to batteries. Ritchie insisted he was being prevented from selling a salutary product, but rather than directing a campaign for redress against the regulatory agencies, Ritchie chose to turn his energies upon NBS itself. He moved from California to Washington, D.C., and personally launched a public relations effort in the halls of Congress and in the media to force a Senate Small Business Committee investigation. He succeeded in getting this hearing in 1953, and NBS was effectively put on trial. The focus soon moved from the results of the AD-X2 tests, which were difficult to impugn, to other areas.

The final result was a scolding of the bureau administration and its policies, and a most dramatic change in responsibilities. Since World War II NBS had become a de facto defense laboratory. Approximately 90 percent of its funding was military, and much of that was through the channel known as "transferred funds," or nonstatutory funding from other government agencies. In addition to major work in ordnance electronics (fuze research and development), the bureau also directed one of the first ballistic missile laboratories. In late 1953, as a result of the AD-X2 hearings and the subsequent (Mervin) Kelly/National Academy of Sciences Committee review, the bureau saw its defense work taken and given to the several defense service corps. Its transferred funding was cut by 55 percent and its workforce was nearly cut in half between 1953 and 1954. This reorganization was, in fact, a corrective to the dominance of defense-related work, which was quite distinct from the intent of the enabling legislation. It is evidence of the unbalanced state of affairs at NBS after World War II that this reorganization would be catalyzed by such an unlikely event as the AD-X2 controversy.

By 1966, NBS had moved to a new, larger campus in Gaithersburg, Maryland, and it had also added the Joint Institute for Laboratory Astrophysics (Boulder, Colorado). The bureau was also temporarily reorganized under Assistant Commerce Secretary (for Science and Technology) Herbert Holloman as four thematic institutes, including Basic Standards, Materials Research, Applied Technology, and the Central Radio Propagation Laboratory. Despite these forward-thinking attempts to refit the once illustrious NBS into the large scheme of postwar national science policy, the bureau remained largely anonymous and, as described in one magazine article in 1956, "the agency nobody understands" (*Business Week,* February 11).

Several attempts to develop a more conscious national technology policy appeared and disappeared in the 1970s and 1980s. However, it was the resounding alarm of international economic competitiveness as a perceived national emergency in the late 1980s that finally produced legislation. The Omnibus Trade and Competitiveness Act, first introduced in 1987 by Senator Ernest Hollings, was passed into law in 1988. One section of the new public law selected NBS, now renamed the National Institute of Standards and Technology (NIST), as a central agency in developing, coordinating, and disseminating critical industrial technologies in a host of commercial areas, from biological engineering, to microelectronics, to automated factory operations. The new charter for the former Bureau of Standards has remarkable similarities to the program for civilian science and technology urged by Samuel W. Stratton in 1918. As of the early 1990s, especially under the new presidential science advisor, John Gibbons, NIST funding has been greatly multiplied, particularly for its Advanced Technology Program.

Historically, NBS is significant for the research it conducted and the scientists who worked at its laboratory benches, but also as a measuring rod, of sorts, for the kind and extent of scientific research that the nation would support at different periods in this century. When scientific management and expert information ruled the formation of policy in many areas of government during the Progressive Era, NBS assumed broad responsibilities. When the nation's scientific talent was largely recruited to serve the weaponeering of the Cold War, the bureau, by default, functioned as a defense laboratory. More recently, concerns over international competitiveness in high technology have led the NBS successor agency, NIST, to take on the role of lead government laboratory in those areas of science-based industry that are considered in the national interest.

The primary records of NBS are located at the National Archives, Washington, D.C., Record Group 167. Complete collections of the many publications of the bureau since its establishment are kept at the main library of NIST, Gaithersburg, Maryland. A descriptive history was commissioned by the Commerce Department in 1960 (Cochrane). More recently, the agency has been analyzed in terms of those larger social, political, and scientific dynamics (Kellogg).

BIBLIOGRAPHY

Cahan, David. *An Institute for an Empire: The Physikalisch-Technische Reichsanstalt, 1871–1918.* New York: Cambridge University Press, 1989.

Cochrane, Rexmond C. *Measures for Progress: A History of the National Bureau of Standards.* Washington, DC: Government Printing Office, 1966.

Dupree, A. Hunter. *Science in the Federal Government.* 1957. Reprint, Baltimore: Johns Hopkins University Press, 1986.

N

Forman, Paul. "Behind Quantum Electronics: National Security as Basis for Physical Research in the United States, 1940–1960." *Historical Studies in the Physical Sciences* 18 (1987): 149–229.

Hawley, Ellis W. *The Great War and the Search for Modern Order: A History of the American People and Their Institutions, 1917–1933.* New York: St. Martin's, 1979.

Kellogg, Nelson R. "Gauging the Nation: Samuel Wesley Stratton and the Invention of the National Bureau of Standards." Ph.D. diss., Johns Hopkins University, 1991.

Pursell, Carroll W., Jr. "A Preface to Government Support of Research and Development: Research Legislation and the National Bureau of Standards." *Technology and Culture* 9 (1968): 145–164.

Reich, Leonard S. *The Making of American Industrial Research: Science and Business at GE and Bell, 1876–1926.* New York: Cambridge University Press, 1985.

Rhodes, Richard. *The Making of the Atomic Bomb.* New York: Simon and Schuster, 1986.

Nelson R. Kellogg

National Institutes of Health

The principal agency of the United States government for supporting medical research. The National Institutes of Health (NIH) is one of the agencies in the Public Health Service, which, in turn, is a component of the Department of Health and Human Services. The NIH is comprised of twenty-five institutes and centers. Approximately 80 percent of the NIH budget is awarded as grants-in-aid of research and contracts; 11 percent is allocated for research in laboratories located on its Bethesda, Maryland, campus; and 9 percent is utilized for other obligations. In 1994, the budget exceeded $11 billion.

The NIH traces its roots to a one-room laboratory established in 1887 by Joseph J. Kinyoun, an officer of the Marine Hospital Service (MHS) trained in bacteriological methods. The MHS hoped that the laboratory would prove useful in confirming clinical diagnosis of epidemic diseases among passengers on arriving ships. Initially styled a "laboratory of hygiene" in imitation of German institutions, the facility was moved to Washington, D.C., in 1891 and soon became known by the proper name, Hygienic Laboratory. For more than a decade the laboratory remained tiny, with no official existence in law and with Kinyoun as its only permanent staff member.

In 1901, Congress belatedly provided statutory authority in an appropriations act that authorized funds for a separate building and charged the laboratory to investigate "infectious and contagious diseases and matters pertaining to the public health." The following year, a reorganization act established four research divisions and changed the name of the MHS to Public Health and Marine Hospital Service. Also in 1902, Congress charged the laboratory with regulating the production of vaccines and antitoxins. The laboratory's research mandate was expanded in 1912 to include noncontagious diseases in legislation that also shortened its parent agency's name to Public Health Service. In 1930, the Ransdall Act renamed the Hygienic Laboratory the National Institute of Health. Seven years later, the National Cancer Institute (NCI) was created by Congress, foreshadowing the categorical-disease structure of the agency in the second half of the twentieth century.

The 1944 Public Health Service Act authorized the creation of additional new institutes at NIH, each of which, like NCI, would have authority to make grants to nonfederal scientists. It also permitted NIH to undertake clinical research and, as a corollary, to construct a research hospital known as the Clinical Center on the NIH campus. Congress soon established institutes for research on mental health, dental research, and heart disease, and in 1948 the name of the umbrella agency was made plural: National Institutes of Health. These changes, initiated by supporters of President Franklin D. Roosevelt's activist New Deal policies, marked the advent of large-scale support of medical research by the United States federal government.

Beginning in 1902, when its research program was inaugurated, the NIH and its predecessor laboratories have conducted much of the scientific research in which United States public health policy has been grounded. Between 1902 and 1912, NIH investigators pioneered studies on anaphylaxis, described the toxic effects of methyl and ethyl alcohols, delineated the epidemiology of typhoid fever in the District of Columbia, established the standard units of diphtheria and tetanus antitoxins, and identified rodents as the mammalian reservoir of bubonic plague. With expanded authority in 1912, NIH scientists and physicians demonstrated that pellagra was a nutritional deficiency disease, elucidated the biochemistry of pollution in rivers, contributed to the diagnosis and prevention of rickettsial and viral diseases, conducted epidemiological and biochemical studies on cancer, delineated oxidation-reduction systems in chemical reactions, and developed methods to study addiction in animal models.

The breadth and depth of studies by NIH scientists continued to increase during the 1930s and 1940s, expanding exponentially with the creation of a grants program and many new institutes after World War II. Between the late 1960s and the 1990s, the advent of techniques to study organisms at the molecular level vastly expanded scientific understanding of such varied subjects as viruses, the human immune system, and the structure of the brain. The knowledge produced has had preventative and therapeutic implications for diseases such as cancer and acquired immunodeficiency syndrome (AIDS) and has suggested novel strategies to control previously intractable mental illnesses. More than eighty recipients of the Nobel Prize have been supported by NIH funding; five Nobel laureates have emerged from NIH intramural laboratories.

Between 1946 and the mid 1960s, NIH enjoyed an exceptional period of budgetary expansion and minimal congressional oversight. By 1970, however, thorny social and ethical issues fueled debate over publicly funded research and its oversight. For example, considerable public concern was voiced when the first recombinant DNA experiments were proposed. The conduct of clinical research raised questions about the meaning of informed consent and the composition of research cohorts. More recently, a project to map the human genome has identified the inherited factors responsible for a few diseases and thereby raised legal and ethical issues that may long precede the development of an effective medical intervention for these problems. In addressing these issues, nonfederal advisory panels to NIH have been utilized, thus increasing the level of public oversight of research.

Paralleling increased concern over social issues since the 1970s was a tightening of research budgets. This reflected both the impact of inflation in the U.S. economy and the competition with other worthy public programs in which NIH had to participate. The constriction in funding increased debate over the relative efficacy of unfettered basic research versus goal-directed applied research, the latter most visibly embodied in the so-called war on cancer. The AIDS crisis of the 1980s similarly provided at first an opportunity for goal-directed research to uncover quickly a cure or preventative. As the second decade of AIDS began, however, no quick solution had been found, and many investigators have suggested that increased basic research will be necessary before an efficacious intervention will be discovered.

Physicians, scientists, and political leaders have viewed the NIH as a national treasure, a federal bureaucracy operating on the merit system with minimal political interference and maximum benefit to the taxpayer for the monies expended. Its exceptional status has been reflected in vigorous congressional resistance to members who seek to bypass the scientific peer-review system and to earmark research projects solely on the basis of their location in the states of members. Historians concerned with medical research policy have examined NIH history within the context of the NIH's bureaucratic parent agency, the Public Health Service, and within the goals of emerging scientific research disciplines such as biochemistry and molecular biology. Others have focused on the NIH contribution to the history of particular diseases, scientific concepts, or technologies. Radical scholars have addressed questionable ethical issues in research and have argued for more lay involvement in decisions about specific research proposals.

Although largely neglected in general history texts, medical research has significantly affected the quality of life for people in the twentieth century. Among the documents available about this activity, the records of the National Institutes of Health at the National Archives and Records Administration (NARA) are divided between Record Group 90, Records of the Public Health Service, and Record Group 443, Records of the National Institutes of Health. Additional materials and oral histories with a number of key NIH figures are held in the manuscript collection of the National Library of Medicine (NLM). Prints, photographs, moving pictures, and videotape images can also be found at NARA and NLM. Some historical files from the NIH Office of the Director are retained at the NIH in Bethesda, Maryland. The NIH History Office maintains some reference materials and provides consultations about the location of other materials. Its website (http://www.nih.gov/od/museum) maintains bibliographies and other historical resources.

The National Institutes of Health
Institutes
National Cancer Institute
National Eye Institute
National Heart, Lung, and Blood Institute
National Institute of Allergy and Infectious Diseases
National Institute of Arthritis and Musculoskeletal
and Skin Diseases

N

National Institute of Child Health and Human Development
National Institute of Dental and Craniofacial Research
National Institute of Diabetes and Digestive and Kidney Diseases
National Institute of Environmental Health Sciences
National Institute of General Medical Sciences
National Human Genome Research Institute
National Institute of Mental Health
National Institute of Neurological Disorders and Stroke
National Institute of Nursing Research
National Institute on Aging
National Institute on Alcoholism and Alcohol Abuse
National Institute on Deafness and Other Communication Disorders
National Institute on Drug Abuse
National Library of Medicine

Centers
Center for Information Technology
Center for Scientific Review
John E. Fogarty International Center
National Center for Complementary and Alternative Medicine
National Center for Research Resources
Warren Grant Magnuson Clinical Center

There are also additional components, which are not broken out here, such as the Office of AIDS Research, the Office of Research on Women's Health, and the Office of Minority Health.

BIBLIOGRAPHY

Dickson, David. *The New Politics of Science.* 1984; Reprint ed. Chicago, University of Chicago Press, 1988.

Dyer, R.E. "Medical Research in the United States Public Health Service." *Bulletin of the Society of Medical History of Chicago* 6 (1948): 58–68.

Fox, Daniel M. "The Politics of the NIH Extramural Program, 1937–1950." *Journal of the History of Medicine and Allied Sciences* 42 (1987): 447–466.

Furman, Bess. *A Profile of the United States Public Health Service, 1798–1948.* Washington, DC: Government Printing Office, DHEW Publication No. (NIH) 73–369.

Harden, Victoria A. *Inventing the NIH: Federal Biomedical Research Policy, 1887–1937.* Baltimore: Johns Hopkins University Press, 1986.

Mider, G. Burroughs. "The Federal Impact on Biomedical Research." In *Advances in American Medicine: Essays at the Bicentennial,* edited by John Z. Bowers and Elizabeth F. Purcell. 2 vols. New York: Josiah Macy Jr., Foundation, 1976, 2:806–871.

Shannon, James A. "The Advancement of Medical Research: A Twenty-Year View of the Role of the National Institutes of Health." *Journal of Medical Education* 42 (1967): 97–108.

Stetten, DeWitt, Jr., and William T. Carrigan, eds. *NIH: An Account of Research in Its Laboratories and Clinics.* Orlando, FL: Academic Press, 1984.

Stimson, Arthur H. "A Brief History of Bacteriological Investigations of the U.S. Public Health Service." Supplement No. 141 to *Public Health Reports,* 1938.

Strickland, Stephen P. *Politics, Science, and Dread Disease: A Short History of United States Medical Research Policy.* Cambridge, MA: Harvard University Press, 1972.

———. *The Story of the NIH Grants Program.* Lanham, MD: University Press of America, 1989.

Swain, Donald C. "The Rise of a Research Empire: NIH, 1930–1950." *Science* 138 (1962): 1233–1237.

United States National Library of Medicine. *Notable Contributions to Medical Research by Public Health Service Scientists: A Biobibliography to 1940.* Compiled by Jeanette Barry. Washington, DC: U.S. Department of Health, Education, and Welfare, Public Health Service Publication No. 752, 1960.

Williams, Ralph C. *The United States Public Health Service, 1798–1950.* Washington, DC: Commissioned Officers Association, 1951.

Victoria A. Harden

SEE ALSO
Centers for Disease Control

National Research Council

Operational arm of the National Academy of Sciences (NAS). George Ellery Hale founded the National Research Council (NRC) in April 1916 to mobilize a wide range of American scientists, under the institutional purview and research standards of the conservative and largely honorific NAS, to attack such technical problems of World War I as artillery ranging, sonar detection, and psychological categorization of recruits.

The NRC rechartered itself as a peacetime agency in May 1918. Soon after, the Carnegie Corporation funded the NRC headquarters building in Washington, D.C., and the Rockefeller Foundation used the NRC to administer the first national postdoctoral fellowships for research training. During the 1920s, the NRC functioned as a trade association for American scientists. It promoted and coordinated scientific research on a national level, and mediated between individual scientists and corporations, government agencies and philanthropic foundations. The NRC provided information on funding, trends in research, and methods of organizing science.

NRC members arranged themselves into permanent disciplinary divisions, but did their work through an enormous variety of temporary, problem-oriented, interdisciplinary committees: the Central Petroleum Committee, the Highway Research Board, the Committee on the Effects of Radiation Upon Living Organisms. The Committee for Research on the Problems of Sex, under the entrepreneurial direction of Robert Yerkes, for two decades funded research on the physiology of sex differences. To garner government and industry funding to replace dwindling foundation funding, in 1932, NRC Chairman Isaiah Bowman recast NRC policy to emphasize cooperative committees over the science-divisional structure.

The NRC's self-imposed independence from the federal structure handicapped its efforts to mobilize scientists for World War II. Although under the administrative umbrella of the Office of Scientific Research and Development, the NRC organized committees on medical research, biological warfare, and metallurgy.

Detlev Bronk, then chairman of the NRC, became president of the NAS in June 1950 and gradually merged the two organizations. In the 1950s, the federal government used NAS-NRC committees to advise on research priorities, for funding by government agencies, and to issue reports on matters of international scope like the biological effects of atomic radiation, geophysics, space science (the International Geophysics Year) and oceanography (the Mohole).

In 1973, NRC committees began drawing volunteers only from the membership of the NAS, or the affiliated National Academy of Engineering and the Institute of Medicine, and their research agenda shifted to the environment and health care. Throughout its history, the NRC embodied new ways of applying the committee form of organization to provide advice from a volunteer community of American research scientists to its patrons.

BIBLIOGRAPHY

Acker, Caroline Jean. "Addiction and the Laboratory: The Work of the National Research Council's Committee on Drug Addiction, 1928–1939." *Isis* 86 (1995): 167–193.

Bugos, Glenn E. "Managing Cooperative Research and Borderland Science in the National Research Council, 1922–1942." *Historical Studies in the Physical and Biological Sciences* 20 (1989): 1–32.

Cochrane, Rexmond C. *The National Academy of Sciences: The First Hundred Years, 1863–1963.* Washington, DC: National Academy Press, 1978.

Kevles, Daniel J. "George Ellery Hale, the First World War, and the Advancement of Science in America." *Isis* 59 (1968): 427–437.

Kohler, Robert E. *Partners in Science: Foundations and Natural Scientists, 1900–1945.* Chicago: University of Chicago Press, 1991.

Reingold, Nathan. "The Case of the Disappearing Laboratory." *American Quarterly* 29 (1977) 79–101.

Glenn E. Bugos

SEE ALSO
National Academy of Sciences

National Science Foundation

Established as an independent federal agency in 1950. In 1945, Vannevar Bush, director of the wartime Office of Scientific Research and Development, had recommended the creation of an agency to develop national policy for science and to support basic scientific research and education. Bush's seminal 1945 report, *Science—The Endless Frontier*, became the basis for the National Science Foundation (NSF) legislation.

The subsequent five-year debate over federal support of research and education revolved around several issues: ownership of patents; geographic and institutional distribution of funds; eligibility of the social sciences; basic research versus applied; and control of the agency. The 1950 act sidestepped or compromised most of these issues. It directed NSF to avoid "undue concentration" of its funds. The social sciences were not mentioned, but the act's term "other sciences" allowed their inclusion in NSF's portfolio.

The most important compromise concerned control and direction of the foundation. Backers of the Bush proposal wanted to place control in an independent board which would appoint a director responsible to it. In 1947, President Harry S. Truman vetoed a bill providing such an arrangement. The 1950 law instead created a policymaking Science Board and a full-time director, all appointed by the president and confirmed by the Senate.

The first director, Alan T. Waterman (1951–1963), took care to keep NSF out of politics as well as to avoid

N

the enmity of other federal science agencies. Waterman and the board defined the agency's policy role as one of compiling reliable information on scientific research and manpower, advocating support for basic research, and improving government-university relations. In 1962, President John F. Kennedy issued an executive reorganization plan that transferred the national science policymaking functions from NSF to a permanent Office of Science and Technology located in the Executive Office of the president.

NSF's original charter restricted its support to basic research. Nearly all of the early grants were for "little science" projects, awarded to colleges, universities, and other nonprofit institutions for research by individual investigators. NSF programs—generally organized by discipline (chemistry, physics, etc.) in the mathematical, physical, and engineering sciences, and by function (regulatory, systematic, etc.) in the biological sciences—judged the quality of the unsolicited proposals and the ability of the researchers with the aid of mail reviewers and assembled panels. Competition for the available limited funds has been keen from the beginning.

Emphasis on quality also characterized NSF's first educational program—fellowships for graduate students and postdoctoral scientists. NSF graduate fellows tended to concentrate in a rather small number of graduate schools, causing criticism from "have-not" universities. Later programs of "cooperative" fellowships and traineeships offset most of the criticism by spreading NSF support of graduate education among a larger number of institutions during the 1960s.

Support for precollege science education expanded greatly following the launching of *Sputnik* by the Soviet Union in October 1957. The development of new curricula in physics, biology, chemistry, and mathematics were widely adopted. Some of the new courses came under attack in the 1970s as too difficult for most students. An elementary school social science course—"Man—A Course of Study"—met especially harsh criticism from conservatives.

Since the late 1950s, NSF increasingly sponsored Big Science enterprises. National centers for radio and optical astronomy, and for atmospheric research, required facilities and instruments so costly that only the federal government could build and equip them and pay for their continuing operation. The agency, by law, could not directly operate research laboratories, so universities managed the facilities under contract to the NSF.

NSF sponsorship of other large-scale activities also began in the 1950s and grew greatly in the next two decades. During the 1958–1959 International Geophysical Year, NSF's main interests focused on Antarctica. In 1959, the United States and the eleven other nations engaged in Antarctic operations signed a treaty reserving the continent for peaceful and scientific purposes. NSF continues as the lead federal agency for Antarctic activities. In the 1960s, NSF supported an ambitious attempt to gain knowledge of the earth by drilling through its mantle from an ocean platform (the Mohole project). Escalating costs ended the effort, but a continuing deep-sea drilling program yielded knowledge of such geologic phenomena as plate tectonics, including what is popularly called continental drift. In the 1980s, the agency funded other new research centers in engineering, science and technology, and supercomputing.

A controversial program blossomed and faded between 1971 and 1978. Research Applied to National Needs (RANN) stemmed from a major 1968 amendment to NSF's charter that expanded the agency's authority to include support of applied research. Organized around designated problems rather than science disciplines, the program used criteria and management practices heretofore foreign to the foundation. RANN addressed many of the domestic problems of that time: pollution, energy, transportation, and urban difficulties. It attempted to link industrial enterprises and academic research with the hope that industry eventually would support parts of the program. Criticism came from segments of Congress, other agencies, and particularly from the science community, which feared that RANN would drain funding from NSF's traditional support of basic research. The program began to phase out in 1975 and 1976.

The agency's expanding programs increased its budget. The first large boost—to $40 million—came in 1957. *Sputnik* sparked a series of increases—to $134 million in 1959 and to nearly $500 million by 1968. The budget passed the half-billion dollar mark in 1971 and generally continued to rise thereafter. By the opening of the next decade, the budget reached the billion-dollar level, and by the early 1990s, it stood at nearly $3 billion.

Over the years, foundation reorganizations reflected the changing nature of the research disciplines it supported. Engineering, science and engineering education, computer science, and the social sciences, long supported by the agency but at lesser organizational and budget levels, were given equal stature with the traditional disciplines in mathematics, the physical sciences and the biological sciences. The changes mirror the fact that over its more than forty-year history, the foundation has established itself as the only general-purpose science agency and the United States government's flagship for basic research.

BIBLIOGRAPHY

Dupree, A. Hunter. *Science in the Federal Government: A History of Policies and Activities.* Baltimore: Johns Hopkins University Press, 1986.

England, J. Merton. "Dr. Bush Writes a Report: 'Science—The Endless Frontier.'" *Science* 191 (1976): 41–47.

———. *Patron for Pure Science.* Washington, DC: National Science Foundation, 1982.

———. "The National Science Foundation and Curriculum Reform: A Problem of Stewardship." *The Public Historian* 11 (1989): 23–36.

———. "Investing in Universities: Genesis of the National Science Foundation's Institutional Programs, 1958–63." *Journal of Policy History* 2 (1990): 131–156.

Kevles, Daniel J. "Scientists, the Military, and the Control of Postwar Defense Research: The Case of the Research Board for National Security, 1944–1946." *Technology and Culture* 16 (1975): 20–47.

———. "The National Science Foundation and the Debate over Postwar Research Policy, 1944–1946." *Isis* 68 (1977): 5–26.

———. "Principles and Politics in Federal R&D Policy, 1945–1990: An Appreciation of the Bush Report." New preface in *Vannevar Bush: Science—The Endless Frontier.* Washington, DC: National Science Foundation, 1990, pp. ix–xxx.

Lomask, Milton. *A Minor Miracle: An Informal History of the National Science Foundation.* Washington, DC: National Science Foundation, 1976.

Maddox, Robert F. "The Politics of World War II Science: Senator Harley M. Kilgore and the Legislative Origins of the National Science Foundation." *West Virginia History* 41 (1979): 20–39.

Mazuzan, George T. *NSF: A Brief History.* Washington, DC: National Science Foundation, 1988.

———. "Up, Up, and Away: The Reinvigoration of Meteorology in the United States, 1958–1962." *Bulletin of the American Meteorological Society* 69 (1988): 1152–1163.

———. "'Good Science Gets Funded . . . The Historical Evolution of Grant Making at the National Science Foundation." *Knowledge: Creation, Diffusion, Utilization* 14 (1992): 63–90.

Schaffter, Dorothy. *The National Science Foundation.* New York: Praeger, 1976.

Stine, Jeffrey K. "Scientific Instrumentation as an Element of U.S. Science Policy: National Science Foundation Support of Chemistry Instrumentation." In *Invisible Connections: Instruments, Institutions, and Science,* edited by Robert Bud and Susan E. Cozzens. Bellingham, WA: SPIE Optical Engineering Press, 1992, pp. 238–263.

George T. Mazuzan

National Weather Service, United States

Although weather observations have been made in America since colonial times, the first national service providing daily weather reports and forecasts was established in 1870 in the War Department under the direction of the chief signal officer. Before that, meteorological and climatological observations were collected by a number of federal agencies, including the Surgeon General's Office (1814–1882), the General Land Office (1817–1821), the United States Navy (1834–1837), and the Smithsonian Institution (1849–1874).

In 1814, Surgeon General James Tilton ordered all medical personnel under his command to "keep a diary of the weather" as part of their official duties. Observations were reported in the army *Meteorological Registers* from 1822 to 1854. In 1842, James Espy became in effect the first national meteorologist working under the surgeon general's supervision to chart the course of storms and interpret the data collected by army post surgeons.

Studies of storms and the American climate continued at the Smithsonian Institution under the direction of Joseph Henry. Up to 600 volunteer observers filed their reports monthly. In 1849, the Smithsonian began experiments with the telegraphic transmission of daily weather reports. During the Civil War many volunteer observers stopped reporting and a large amount of data was destroyed.

In 1870, Congress provided funds for a national weather service to provide "telegrams and reports" for the benefit of commerce and agriculture. Colonel Albert J. Myer, founder of the Signal Corps, became its first director. The Signal Office employed civilian scientists Increase A. Lapham and Cleveland Abbe and upward of 500 college-educated observer-sergeants. Its budget increased one hundredfold from 1869 to 1875. The *Monthly Weather Review*, begun in 1872, is still published today. Under the leadership of Brigadier General William B. Hazen (1880–1887) the Signal Office established a scientific study room and defended

N

itself against its critics, notably the Allison Commission, on the issue of whether the military should be supporting a national weather service.

By an act of Congress of 1 October 1890 the United States Weather Bureau was established in the Department of Agriculture, where it remained until 1940. The first chief, Mark W. Harrington (1891–1895), was deposed in a political feud with the secretary of agriculture. The next administrator, Willis L. Moore (1895–1913), was accused of mismanagement and fiscal impropriety. Innovations during this period included the decentralization of forecasting, the use of kites for upper-air observations, and data transmission by cable and telephone.

The administrations of Charles F. Marvin (1913–1934), Willis R. Gregg (1934–1938), and Francis W. Reichelderfer (1938–1963) were less contentious. Marvin supervised American military weather services during World War I, instituted regular upper-air sounding balloons, applied two-way radio communication to meteorological purposes, and developed marine and aviation weather services. Gregg and Reichelderfer brought the Norwegian methods of air-mass and frontal analysis to the United States and standardized the acquisition of upper-air data by the use of balloon-borne radio-meteorographs. In 1940, the Weather Bureau was transferred to the Department of Commerce.

During World War II, the Weather Bureau supported military efforts to establish a worldwide system of weather reports. In the 1950s, the bureau experimented with electronic computers for weather analysis and prediction. In 1960, it established the nation's first meteorological satellite program.

The Weather Bureau was consolidated with the Coast and Geodetic Survey and other agencies to form the Environmental Science Services Administration (ESSA) in 1965. Five years later, a National Weather Service was established within the newly reorganized National Oceanic and Atmospheric Administration (NOAA). Robert M. White served as chief of the Weather Bureau and first director of ESSA and NOAA.

Archival materials are in RG 27 of the National Archives and Records Administration.

BIBLIOGRAPHY

Fleming, James Rodger. *Meteorology in America, 1800–1870.* Baltimore: Johns Hopkins University Press, 1990.

Hartwell, Frank E. *Forty Years of the Weather Bureau, the Transition Years.* Bolton, VT: n.p., 1958.

Hughes, Patrick. *A Century of Weather Service: A History of the Birth and Growth of the National Weather Service, 1870–1970.* New York: Gordon and Breach, 1970.

Popkin, Roy. *The Environmental Science Services Administration.* New York: Praeger, 1967.

Weber, Gustavus A. *The Weather Bureau.* New York: D. Appleton, 1922.

Whitnah, Donald R. *A History of the United States Weather Bureau.* Urbana: University of Illinois Press, 1961.

James Rodger Fleming

SEE ALSO
Meteorology and Atmospheric Science

National Wildlife Federation

The largest private environmental organization in America. The National Wildlife Federation (NWF) was the brainchild of Jay "Ding" Darling, the Pulitzer Prize–winning cartoonist who served briefly as head of the United States Biological Survey (predecessor of the Fish and Wildlife Service) under President Franklin Roosevelt. Early in 1936, Darling convened a National Wildlife Conference attended by two thousand representatives from local, state, and national conservation organizations. At Darling's urging, conference delegates voted to form a new organization, the General Wildlife Federation, which incorporated as the National Wildlife Federation in 1938. Although the new federation attracted affiliates with a variety of agendas, it was long dominated by sportsmen.

Financial problems plagued the fledgling organization throughout its early years. One fund-raising device that eventually proved successful was the sale of stamps depicting wildlife. Darling provided the illustrations for the first stamp series in 1938, one year before resigning from the nearly bankrupt organization. Regular loans from the American Wildlife Institute kept the federation solvent for a number of years thereafter. By 1961, financial prospects had already improved when the NWF began recruiting individuals unaffiliated with other conservation groups to become associate members. One year later, *National Wildlife* was initiated, the first in a series of acclaimed periodicals that eventually included *International Wildlife, Ranger Rick,* and *Your Big Backyard.*

Since its creation, the NWF has served as an information clearinghouse on conservation and wildlife issues as well as an effective lobbyist for state and federal legislation. In the 1970s, the organization also established several wildlife research centers, began sponsoring sessions at scientific meetings, and initiated an active grant program to fund wildlife studies.

After surmounting early financial difficulties, the NWF grew into the largest, wealthiest, and most influential conservation organization in the United States. By 1992, it boasted over 5.5 million members and supporters. Yet despite its size and importance, Allen's uncritical account is the only comprehensive history of the organization thus far. Additional information can be found in most general histories of the American conservation movement.

BIBLIOGRAPHY
Allen, Thomas B. *Guardian of the Wild: The Story of the National Wildlife Federation, 1936–1986.* Bloomington: Indiana University Press in Association with the National Wildlife Federation, 1987.
Fox, Stephen. *John Muir and His Legacy: The American Conservation Movement.* Boston: Little, Brown, and Co., 1981.
Lendt, David L. *Ding: The Life of Jay Norwood Darling.* Ames: Iowa State University Press, 1979.
Trefethen, James B. *An American Crusade for Wildlife.* New York: Winchester Press and the Boone and Crockett Club, 1975.

Mark V. Barrow Jr.

Native Americans—Relations to Natural World

The native populations of what became the United States lived in subsistence economies. Their food, clothing, and shelter came from their environments through their own energy. They did not domesticate animals as major sources of food or as beasts of burden, although the dog was used for both purposes on a very limited scale, and in many areas semidomesticated turkeys lived around Indian villages where they fed on the kitchen middens.

Native Americans saw their environments as manifesting the power of spiritual beings. They controlled their physical surroundings by establishing relationships with those beings, who showed themselves in physical phenomena. The reality of their world lay in beings like Thunderbirds, who brought storms in the Plains and Woodlands, and Kachinas, who, in the form of clouds, brought rain to Pueblo people in the Southwest. Animals were controlled by spirit beings. A hunter on the Great Plains might establish a special relationship with

such a spirit through a vision question, where the spirit appeared to teach special songs or behaviors.

Religious rituals governed their hunting and agricultural practices and often governed the timing of their ceremonies. Ritual activity was equally important with hunting and farming to assure food supplies. Humans must perform their ceremonies to assure that seasons would change or that animals would appear at hunting grounds.

Native Americans also exercised a pragmatic understanding of natural processes based on systematic observation. Ceremonies controlled the turning of the seasons at the summer and winter solstices for some tribes, but their timing depended on observation of the sun's progress across the horizon. The Hopi Soyal ceremony in the Southwest, a marker of the winter solstice, was set by such systematic observation of the path of the sun's rising points. Midwinter ceremonies among the Iroquois in upstate New York, timed by the passage of the Pleiades over their longhouses at midnight, were essential to assure the success of the new cycle of planting. In the Big Horn Mountains, one group of hunters, around 1500 A.D., marked seasonal cycles with a "medicine wheel," whose spokes aligned with solstices and helical risings of certain bright stars that presaged them.

The pragmatic aspects of their control over nature were in such practices as the systematic burning of grasslands and brush to create fresh browse for animals to keep them healthy and productive. Irrigation, as well as Kachinas, made farming possible for Pueblo people along the Rio Grande Valley. Systematic selection of certain kinds of plants for seed and deliberate watering, weeding, and cultivation of soil led to domestication of plants.

The first plants domesticated in the American Midwest were wild sunflowers, chenopodium, marshweed, and squashes, probably about 4000–1000 B.C. Corn and beans were domesticated in northern Mexico by about 7000 B.C. and made their way into the American Southwest, where they were systematically cultivated by about 4000 B.C.

Native American groups throughout the United States have left evidence of systematic observation and recording of seasonal phenomena, and of ability to exercise control over their environments. Since they did not leave written records, this evidence is now being interpreted by anthropologists, biologists, and astronomers, who are attempting to recover their intellectual systems. Their relationships with their environments depended

N

upon ideas of conscious interaction with and control over those environments, and anthropologists have studied the persistence of their ceremonies in contemporary communities.

Native Americans have become part of the history of American science as subjects of study by anthropologists, archaeologists, and biologists. The sophistication of their own systems of knowledge is only now being explored.

BIBLIOGRAPHY

Hallowell, A.I. "Some Empirical Aspects of Northern Saulteaux Religion." *American Anthropologist*, n.s., 36 (1934), 359–384.

Hurt, R. Douglas. *Indian Agriculture in America: Prehistory to the Present.* Lawrence: University Press of Kansas, 1987.

McCluskey, Stephen C. "Historical Archaeoastronomy: The Hopi Example," in *Archaeoastronomy in the New World: American Primitive Astronomy,* edited by A.F. Aveni. Cambridge, U.K.: Cambridge University Press, 1982, pp. 31–57.

Clara Sue Kidwell

SEE ALSO

Archaeoastronomy; Medicine, Native American

Nature Writing

A form or forms of writing especially popular in the United States since at least the late nineteenth century, commonly associated with and perhaps best exemplified by Henry Thoreau's *Walden.* In its Thoreauvian and preeminently American form, nature writing offers an unusual and potentially revealing combination of intensely personal narrative and detailed, impersonal, scientific description and exposition. Close kin historically to the journals and field notebooks of botanists, zoologists, and geologists, it evidences some of the intricate and extensive ties between the initial exploration, discovery, and settlement of the United States (its constitution in fact) and the terminology and methods of the developing modern sciences, particularly systematic and evolutionary biology, geology, and ecology. With its coordinate emphases on the personal and the scientifically impersonal, it illustrates the disposition of many Americans, both early and late, to identify and explain themselves, and to define and appreciate their country, through the disciplined identification, description, and explanation of their nonhuman environments.

American nature writing was born of classical natural history, on the one hand, and of Romantic landscape art and autobiography (perhaps, especially, spiritual autobiography), on the other hand. It provides a particularly rich, if still largely unexamined, set of sources on the interplay among the histories of botanical, zoological, geological, and ecological science, including their increasingly complex institutional histories, and the developing commerce and politics of nature appreciation in the United States, as well as the development of several applied sciences devoted to the management of natural resources.

By now, Thoreau's and *Walden*'s many and various successors number in the thousands, and their readers in the tens of millions. Among some of the most notable in the direct line of descent are John Muir, John Burroughs, Sigurd Olson, Aldo Leopold, Joseph Wood Krutch, Edwin Way Teale, Loren Eiseley, Rachel Carson, John Hay, Edward Abbey, Ann Zwinger, John Janovy, Robert Finch, Barry Lopez, and Annie Dillard. Most are or were serious amateur scientists, and many have otherwise been professionally active scientists. The intensity of their personal engagements in their materials has varied, of course, as has the extent of their commitments to the vocabularies and methods of the professional scientist. All have, however, found a good deal of themselves and their nation in the scientific identification and explanation of their environments. Their works have much potentially to say about the psychohistory of science in the United States, and collectively much to say as well about its historical sociology and even significant portions of its political history, especially in the twentieth century. The impacts these and other writers have had, both in publicizing and popularizing scientific conceptions and methods, and in dramatizing the sense of personal significance provided by them, are without parallel in any other country or culture of the world.

Traditionally, historians have traced the origins of nature writing to the late seventeenth and eighteenth centuries. They find its sources and account for its development, if not its significance, in a classically progressive and cumulative historiography of the rise of modern science, in a coordinate development of several forms of landscape art and nature appreciation, and in the relationships among them. For some of these historiographically classical students of the form, nature writing has been very closely aligned to natural history and to a growing appreciation of nature. For others, nature writing has been a product largely of critical reactions to the impersonality of modern science, an impersonality they have seen as devaluing, if not dehumanizing, the natural world. In either account, the forms of nature writing have been (and continue to be) closely tied to the terms, methods, and persuasions of botanical, zoological, geological, and ecological science.

To date, contemporary developments in the philosophy and historiography of science have had comparatively little impact on the history and criticism of nature writing. A few students of its forms have begun to recast parts of its history in manners consonant with contemporary changes in the history and historiography of science—to find its origins and fundamental functions further back in cultural time, and to try to account for its peculiarly American variants by tying them closely to the particular conditions faced by their authors.

Much remains to be done, however, on the relations among the history of science in America and the developing vocabularies and styles of nature writing, on the scientific educations of nature writers, and on the relations between the biology of ecosystems and the increasingly intricate forms of American nature writing.

BIBLIOGRAPHY

Brooks, Paul. *Speaking for Nature: How Literary Naturalists from Henry Thoreau to Rachel Carson Have Shaped America.* Boston: Houghton Mifflin, 1980.

Buell, Lawrence. *The Environmental Imagination: Thoreau, Nature Writing, and the Formation of American Culture.* Cambridge, MA: Harvard University Press, 1995.

Cooley, John, ed. *Earthly Words: Essays on Contemporary American Nature and Environmental Writers.* Ann Arbor: University of Michigan Press, 1994.

Elder, John, ed. *American Nature Writers.* 2 vols. New York: Scribner's, 1996.

Finch, Robert, and John Elder, eds. *The Norton Book of Nature Writing.* New York: Norton, 1990.

Fritzell, Peter A. *Nature Writing and America: Essays upon a Cultural Type.* Ames: Iowa State University Press, 1990.

Irmscher, Christoph. *The Poetics of Natural History: From John Bartram to William James.* New Brunswick: Rutgers University Press, 1999.

Lyon, Thomas J., ed. *This Incomperable Lande: A Book of American Nature Writing.* Boston: Houghton Mifflin, 1989.

McClintock, James. *Nature's Kindred Spirits: Aldo Leopold, Joseph Wood Krutch, Edward Abbey, Annie Dillard, and Gary Snyder.* Madison: University of Wisconsin Press, 1994.

McIntosh, James. *Thoreau as Romantic Naturalist: His Shifting Stance toward Nature.* Ithaca: Cornell University Press, 1974.

Paul, Sherman. *For Love of the World: Essays on Nature Writers.* Iowa City: University of Iowa Press, 1992.

Regis, Pamela. *Describing Early America: Bartram, Jefferson, Crevecoeur, and the Rhetoric of Natural History.* Dekalb: Northern Illinois University Press, 1992.

Roorda, Randall. *Dramas of Solitude: Narratives of Retreat in American Nature Writing.* Albany: State University of New York Press, 1998.

Scheese, Donald. *Nature Writing: The Pastoral Impulse in America.* New York: Twayne Publishers, 1996.

Slovic, Scott. *Seeking Awareness in American Nature Writing: Henry Thoreau, Annie Dillard, Edward Abbey, Wendell Berry, Barry Lopez.* Salt Lake City: University of Utah Press, 1992.

Stewart, Frank. *A Natural History of Nature Writing.* Washington, D.C.: Island Press, 1995.

Walls, Laura Dassow. *Seeing New Worlds: Henry David Thoreau and Nineteenth-Century Natural Science* Madison: University of Wisconsin Press, 1995.

Peter A. Fritzell

SEE ALSO

Literature—Relations to Science and Technology; Thoreau, Henry David

Naval Observatory, United States

The first national observatory of the United States, comparable to the Greenwich Observatory in England. The observatory began as a Depot of Charts and Instruments in 1830, charged with the functions of rating chronometers and centralizing the navigational charts and instruments of the United States Navy. Because rating the chronometers (determining how fast or slow they ran) required astronomical observations, the navy immediately became involved in astronomy, and under Lieutenant James Melville Gilliss began to expand observations beyond the immediate needs of the navy. In 1842, Gilliss extracted from Congress an appropriation for a new depot, which under its first superintendent, Lieutenant Matthew Fontaine Maury, quickly became a national observatory. Maury pursued hydrographic functions more than astronomical, but after Maury's defection to the Southern cause in the Civil War, Gilliss restored a more proper balance between astronomy and hydrography. In 1866, the Hydrographic Office separated from the Naval Observatory, and in 1893 the Nautical Almanac Office

N

became part of the observatory. Aside from the loss of the chronometer rating function in 1950, the observatory's mission of timekeeping, positional astronomy, and producing almanacs as related to navigation has remained largely the same.

During the latter half of the nineteenth century some of the most famous astronomers of the era spent their their careers at the Naval Observatory, including Simon Newcomb, George W. Hill, Asaph Hall, and William Harkness. They led the observatory to the height of its fame at a time when positional astronomy still played the predominant role in the field. The establishment of privately endowed observatories in the United States eclipsed the Naval Observatory in the early twentieth century, and it was slow to adopt the new techniques of stellar photography and spectroscopy. The observatory gradually modernized over the course of the century, and with the founding of other American national observatories in the 1950s, today remains unique as both a naval and national observatory.

Because it is one of the oldest scientific institutions in the United States government, the United States Naval Observatory offers the opportunity to study the interaction of science, government, and the military over a period of more than 150 years, and is a cornerstone to any history of nineteenth-century astronomy in the United States. As a member of a venerable class of scientific institutions, a comparative study of its programs and problems relative to other national observatories is also desirable. Little has been written on the history of the Naval Observatory, but a detailed history is now in progress.

BIBLIOGRAPHY

Dick, Steven J. "John Quincy Adams, the Smithsonian Bequest, and the Origins of the U. S. Naval Observatory." *Journal for the History of Astronomy* 22 (1991): 31–44.

———. "Centralizing Navigational Technology in America: The U.S. Navy's Depot of Charts and Instruments, 1830–42." *Technology and Culture* 33 (1992): 467–509.

Dick, Steven J., and Leroy Doggett. *Sky with Ocean Joined: Proceedings of the Sesquicentennial Symposia of the U.S. Naval Observatory.* Washington, DC: U.S. Naval Observatory, 1983.

Steven J. Dick

Naval Research Laboratory

Department of the Navy research facility with broad scientific and technical expertise in the physical sciences and engineering. The laboratory serves as the United States Navy's corporate research center and was modeled on the example of large industrial research laboratories, such as established at General Electric, Kodak, and DuPont in the early years of the twentieth century. Based on its staff and scientific accomplishments, the Naval Research Laboratory (NRL) is one of the most successful attempts to create a combination industrial- and academic-type laboratory within the federal government.

The NRL was first proposed in discussions between Thomas Edison and Secretary of the Navy Josephus Daniels in June of 1915. In an interview with the *New York Times Magazine* on May 30, Edison had recommended the establishment of a national laboratory to assist in the development of armaments, as part of a concerted military preparedness effort. Daniels subsequently recruited Edison's assistance as head of what became the Naval Consulting Board. The organization of a Naval Experimental and Research Laboratory became one of the key objectives of the board. Organizational funding was approved by Congress as part of the Navy Department budget in 1916.

However, Edison and other members of the board soon came to loggerheads over the nature of the proposed laboratory. Edison wished to create a civilian-run engineering development center, to a significant degree modeled on his own laboratory at West Orange, New Jersey. Other, younger members of the board, such as Willis Whitney of General Electric and Hudson Maxim of DuPont, hoped to establish a navy-staffed research laboratory comparable to the more scientifically based facilities with which they were professionally associated. The resulting disagreement delayed approval and construction of the laboratory until the waning days of the Wilson administration.

The NRL opened for business in July 1923 with two research divisions, Radio and Sound. Other divisions soon followed, although the laboratory continued to remain best known as a center for research in underwater sound and radio electronics up until World War II. Early collaborative work between A. Hoyt Taylor, superintendent of the Radio Division, and E.O. Hulburt, head of the newly established Division of Heat and Light, explored and mathematically characterized the phenomenon of radio "skip distance," in the mid-1920s. Taylor and Hulburt's work was fundamental in explaining high-frequency radio transmission in the upper atmosphere. Similarly, research in the Sound

Division produced pioneering contributions to the understanding of underwater sound and added the fathometer and sonar to the navy's inventory of instruments for underwater survey and detection.

NRL's expertise in high-frequency radio was central to its most important prewar technical achievement: the development of the United States' first operational radar. The reflection of high frequency radio waves from a moving ship had been observed by navy engineers as early as 1922. A similar observation (this time with an airplane) by NRL engineers Leo Young and Lawrence Hyland in 1930 led to the establishment of a laboratory research project to further explore and exploit the phenomenon.

Progress was initially slow. Researchers encountered significant difficulties when they attempted to produce a shipboard detection system. The need to eliminate operating interference demanded that the receiver be widely separated from the transmitter. This, in turn, appeared to limit the system's fleet-based utility. However, advances in techniques and equipment soon led to the resolution of difficulties. These included a move from continuous to pulsed radio waves in 1933, the addition of new staff, the availability of improved vacuum tubes, and the introduction of the radio duplexer in 1936.

Technical requirements were in place for an operational radar detection system by the end of 1936. Initial sea trials were run in 1937 and later in 1938–1939. The first sets of functional, ship-based radars, the CXAM, were available for deployment on American naval vessels by 1940, in time for World War II.

Wartime saw a rapid expansion of the laboratory. Total civilian employment rose from 234 in 1940 to almost 3,000 by the end of 1945. However, NRL's active research program was largely put on hold as the staff took on testing and troubleshooting tasks connected to new war technologies and materiel.

The postwar years produced new opportunities for broadening and expanding research programs at the laboratory. Gains in staff and funding during the war years were largely held on to in the postwar era. Existing research programs in radio, radar, acoustics, chemistry, metallurgy, and optics were expanded, and new research studies were initiated in nuclear sciences (including studies in radioactivity, nuclear structure, and cosmic rays), in upper-atmospheric sciences (using V-2 and successor rockets as research platforms), in solar and radio astronomy, in electron and X-ray diffraction studies, and in surface chemistry.

NRL's Vanguard rocket project was possibly its most famous postwar research and development program. Between 1946 and 1951, as part of a tri-service program, the laboratory assembled and launched sixty-six V-2s. The missiles served as research platforms for experiments that greatly expanded scientific knowledge of the upper atmosphere, near-earth space, and solar physics. In a successor program, the laboratory developed and instrumented twelve Viking missiles between 1949 and 1954, of which seven reached altitudes of over 100 miles.

The Naval Research Laboratory was subsequently selected to develop and launch the first American satellite for the International Geophysical Year. The launch vehicles, *Vanguard 1* and *2,* proved to be failures. However, *Vanguard 3* was successfully launched on 17 March 1958. It placed into orbit the United States' second satellite, following the United States Army's *Explorer 1,* launched on 31 January 1958. Both satellites, of course, followed in the wake of the Soviet Union's *Sputnik 1,* which achieved orbit on 4 October 1957.

The postwar research program at NRL, as exemplified by its space science and technology efforts, is a clear example of that interpenetration of science, technology, and the military discussed by Everett Mendelsohn, Merritt Roe Smith, Peter Weingart, Stuart Lesley, and other scholars of recent American science. The success of military-scientific cooperation in World War II created both opportunities and infrastructural precedents for postwar science. In the climate of Cold War military mobilization and competition, both the need and the resources were available to fund a massive expansion of American science and engineering. The establishment of military-based research funding agencies, such as the Office of Naval Research (ONR) in 1946, cemented the relationship.

Private universities and research institutes, however, were not the only beneficiaries of military needs and largesse. Intramural military laboratories also profited from the expanded resources. Such was the case with the NRL, which was able to build on prewar strengths and expand as a center of scientific research and development securely within the navy's organizational infrastructure.

NRL administrators had been eager for many years to increase the laboratory's research profile and resources, in simulation of the leading academic and industrial laboratories after which it had been modeled. The conservatism of the navy bureaus and then the funding collapse of the depression had frustrated that aim. However, by 1943, NRL leaders were looking

N

forward to the war's end and the achievement of their goal. The lack of an early national consensus on postwar basic science funding, Cold War needs, and the availability of military funding through ONR subsequently allowed the Naval Research Laboratory the opportunity to establish itself as a significant presence in American science.

BIBLIOGRAPHY

Allison, David K. *New Eye for the Navy: The Origin of Radar at the Naval Research Laboratory.* Washington, DC: Naval Research Laboratory, 1981.

Blumtritt, Oskar, Hartmut Petzold, and William Aspray. *Tracking: The History of Radar.* Piscataway, NJ: Institute of Electrical and Electronics Engineers, 1994.

Hevly, Bruce. "Basic Research Within a Military Context: The Naval Research Laboratory and the Foundations of Extreme Ultraviolet and X-Ray Astronomy, 1923–1960." Ph.D. diss., Johns Hopkins University, 1987.

Lesley, Stuart W. *The Cold War and American Science: The Military-Industrial-Academic Complex at MIT and Stanford.* New York: Columbia University Press, 1993.

Mendelsohn, Everett, Merritt Roe Smith, and Peter Weingart, eds. *Science, Technology, and the Military.* Dordrecht: Kluwer, 1988.

van Keuren, David K. "Science, Progressivism, and Military Preparedness: The Case of the Naval Research Laboratory, 1915–1923." *Technology & Culture* 34 (1992): 710–736.

David K. van Keuren

Nebraska, University of

Throughout its existence, science at the University of Nebraska, in Lincoln, has centered around its dual role as the state university and the state's land-grant institution. The university started in 1871 with one professor of natural sciences, Samuel Aughey. Aughey's contributions included geological surveys, the first catalog of Nebraska plants, and his major study *Sketches of the Physical Geography and Geology of Nebraska* (1880).

With the creation of the Industrial College in 1877, in addition to Aughey the faculty had enlarged to include professors in mathematics, chemistry and physics, chemistry and agricultural chemistry, agriculture, and civil engineering. The physical expansion of the campus during the 1880s illustrated the importance assigned science in the university; the second building on campus was a chemical laboratory and the fourth housed the new Industrial College. Also at this time, with Aughey's departure, his chair of natural sciences gave way to specialization and was divided in 1884 into chairs in chemistry, physics, geology, and botany and horticulture.

During the 1880s and 1890s, the university attracted a number of able scientists who were to provide the foundation for the university's growth and stability that carried well into the twentieth century and provided the basis for claims of leadership among the country's land-grant schools, particularly in the trans-Mississippi West. Outstanding among these newcomers were DeWitt Brace in physics and astronomy, who participated in timely studies on the velocity of light; Lawrence Bruner, an entomologist; Ellery Davis in mathematics; the organic chemist Samuel Avery; and Henry Ward in zoology. Because of the university's dual role, many of the scientists made important contributions in applied research. Examples included Frank Billings and A.T. Peters, both bacteriologists, who conducted pioneering work in germ theory related to such major animal diseases as Texas fever and hog cholera; Rachel Lloyd and H.H. Nicholson, who as part of their chemical investigations helped establish sugar beet production in the region; the pioneering studies of Louis Hicks on irrigation and the underground aquifer that underlay much of Nebraska and the Great Plains; and in a variety of important studies in such areas as plant introduction, insect pests and insecticides, plant and animal diseases, and dry farming, the work of a growing body of agricultural scientists in the university and in the new agricultural experiment station.

Preeminent among these golden-age scientists at the University of Nebraska was Charles Bessey. From 1884 until 1915, Bessey as dean of the Industrial College helped direct the growth of science in the land-grant university and the United States Department of Agriculture, influenced the relationship between agriculture and the basic sciences, and was a leader in the new-botany movement, which shifted emphasis to evolution, physiology, pathology, and ecology. Bessey's most visible role in the "new botany" was as a textbook writer. Active in national efforts to professionalize science, he was botany editor of *American Naturalist and Science,* and included in the rewards for his contributions were the presidency of the Botanical Society of America and the American Association for the Advancement of Science. In botany, his most lasting work was reflected in his summary article "The Phylogenetic Taxonomy of Flowering Plants"; in the numerous botanists, agricultural scientists, and foresters he helped train; and in the foundations he provided, along with Frederic Clements, for the "Nebraska school of grasslands ecology."

Following a period of growth and relative stability, science suffered along with the general university during the 1920s and 1930s. As the golden-age scientists retired or left the university, they were not replaced with persons of equal or greater ability or status. Teaching and research in the sciences remained an important part of the A & S faculty, the colleges of agriculture and engineering expanded, and the agricultural experiment station continued its usual work. Still, the general impression at the university was that Nebraska was slipping from the ranks of the Big Four of midwestern land-grant institutions (with Michigan, Minnesota, and Wisconsin). By the 1930s, only chemistry and botany remained among the leaders in the university's granting of graduate degrees.

Continuing its national influence was the work in grassland ecology led by Raymond Pool and John Weaver. Also attracting national attention was the expansion of the university museum under the leadership of Erwin and Carrie Barbour and C. Bertrand Schultz. Increased exploration under the direction of Schultz of the state's rich fossil resources and a new building to house the prized collection greatly enhanced paleontological investigation.

In the post–World War II years, as the university regained stability and shared in the general student growth of the period, the sciences likewise regained some of their earlier stature. During this recent period, although at least chemistry, geology, bacteriology, physiology, zoology, physics, and particularly a variety of agricultural disciplines produced significant research, little historical study has been done to highlight this work or the individuals involved.

BIBLIOGRAPHY

Manley, Robert N. *Frontier University, 1869–1919.* Vol. 1 of *Centennial History of the University of Nebraska.* Lincoln: University of Nebraska Press, 1969.

Overfield, Richard A. *Science with Practice: Charles E. Bessey and the Maturing of American Botany.* Ames: Iowa State University Press, 1993.

Sawyer, R. McLaran. *The Modern University.* Vol. 2 of *Centennial History of the University of Nebraska.* Lincoln: Centennial Press, 1973.

Tobey, Ronald C. *Saving the Prairies: The Life Cycle of the Founding School of American Plant Ecology, 1895–1955.* Berkeley: University of California Press, 1981.

Richard A. Overfield

Nebular Hypothesis

The concept that the solar system evolved from interstellar matter, or a nebulae. In Europe during the seventeenth century, the idea that the universe consisted of matter and motion, generally referred to as the mechanical philosophy, replaced the belief that the world was an animate being, which we refer to today as Renaissance Naturalism. According to René Descartes, who emerged as the principal spokesman for the mechanical philosophy, a huge vortex of "aether" powered the solar system, constraining the planets in their orbits. Isaac Newton's subsequent discovery of universal gravitation introduced precise relationships among the sun and the planets, and replaced Descartes's vortices with a single force. But if universal gravitation explained why the planets remained in their orbits, it begged the question of how they got there. Moreover, Newton and his contemporaries began to wonder why most of the matter of the solar system resides in a single luminous body in the center while the rest of the matter is divided into opaque planets. They felt compelled to conclude that the solar system resulted from the "council and contrivance of a Voluntary Agent." For the next two centuries the idea that the origin of the solar system required a supernatural explanation existed in tension with a mechanical view of the sun and planets as mere matter and motion, and served as a point of departure for a more general discussion of the role of God in science.

In 1755, Immanuel Kant (in *Universal Natural History*) put forth the idea that "forces of attraction and repulsion" in a diffuse cloud of "elementary matter" would, over immensely long periods of time, give rise to a stable solar system. Problems with his printer and the obscurity of the publication condemned his work to oblivion until its rediscovery in the 1830s. In 1796, Pierre Simon Laplace, responding to Georges Buffon's conjecture that the solar system was born when a comet collided with the sun, developed the most compelling case for a nebular theory. Had cometary impact given rise to the solar system, it would have produced highly eccentric planetary orbits, not the nearly circular, sun-centered orbits that we observe, Laplace pointed out. Further, the common direction of planetary motions could not have arisen as a result of chance. Laplace postulated that the sun had originally extended to the outermost regions of the solar system, and through a process of condensation, abandoned rings of solar matter that later condensed themselves into planets and

N

satellites. As he went through successive editions of his *Exposition du système du monde,* Laplace worked out the details of the hypothesis, explaining why the planets orbits are coplanar and unidirectional.

In the 1830s, Laplace's ideas began entering mainstream intellectual discourse. The hypothesis, originally intended as a plausible alternative to divine creation, ironically found quick acceptance because it bore resemblances to the Mosaic account of creation. Its reconciliation with Scripture, as set forth in the *Bridgewater Treatises,* gained for it widespread acceptance among an increasingly urban, cultivated population, who might otherwise have resisted or disparaged it. In Great Britain, John Pringle Nichol fit it into a more general theory of "progress," and utilized it to justify a political agenda of reform. In the 1840s and 1850s, public lecturers, especially Ormsby MacKnight Mitchel in the United States, incorporated the concept in their popular lectures, utilizing the inspirational value of the hypothesis to excite interest in astronomy. Within this social context came the implication that the universe, solar system, the earth, and, later, man, were not immutable forms, but were subject to change, albeit over millennia. Historians investigating the surprisingly quick acceptance of Darwin's theory of evolution by scientists have pointed out the role of the nebular hypothesis in introducing the concept of evolution.

In the 1840s, Daniel Kirkwood utilized the nebular hypothesis to develop his "analogy," which found a general relationship between hypothetical "sphere of attraction" of a planet in its incipient stage, and the current number of rotations of that planet during its orbit around the sun. Fifteen years later, William Huggins's utilization of spectral analysis offered definitive proof that nebulae were distinct from unresolved clusters of stars, such as remote galaxies, further lending credence to the nebular hypothesis. But the hypothesis has never answered all the questions that the early evolution of the solar system poses. Later in the century, Thomas C. Chamberlin and F.R. Moulton discovered a glaring discrepancy between the momentum retained by the sun, which possesses nearly all the mass of the solar system, and the planets, which retained virtually all the momentum, which seemed to argue against the hypothesis.

With the introduction of astrophysics, however, investigations of the origin of the solar system focused on the chemical composition of the planetary bodies. Although the broad outline of the nebular hypothesis remains the modus operandi for planetary evolution,

the questions now center on what conditions must have existed at the various stages of the solar system to produce the bodies that we now observe.

BIBLIOGRAPHY

Jaki, Stanley L. *Planets and Planetarians, A History of Theories of the Origin of Planetary Systems.* New York: John Wiley and Sons, 1978.

Kant, Immanuel. *Universal Natural History and Theory of the Heavens.* 1755. Reprinted in *Theories of the Universe,* edited by Milton K. Munitz. New York: Free Press, 1957, pp. 231–249.

Numbers, Ronald L. *Creation by Natural Law: Laplace's Nebular Hypothesis in American Thought.* Seattle: University of Washington Press, 1977.

Schaffer, Simon. "The Nebular Hypothesis and the Science of Progress." In *History, Humanity and Evolution: Essays for John C. Greene,* edited by James R. Moore. Cambridge, U.K.: Cambridge University Press, 1989, pp. 131–164.

Whitney, Charles A. *The Discovery of Our Galaxy.* New York: Knopf, 1971.

Philip S. Shoemaker

Neo-Lamarckism (or Neolamarckism)

A branch of evolutionary thought and research that followed the French naturalist Jean Baptiste Lamarck's emphasis on environmentally and behaviorally caused organic variations plus the inheritance of these acquired characters, rather than Darwin's emphasis on natural selection, as the chief cause of evolution. While neo-Lamarckian thinking was present in other fields, such as sociology, this article describes its role in biology.

Neo-Lamarckism flourished in America from 1870 to about 1900. Its chief representatives were the vertebrate paleontologist Edward Cope; the invertebrate paleontologist Alpheus Hyatt: the entomologist Alpheus Packard, Jr.; and the embryologist and fish expert John Ryder. Packard coined the term "neo-Lamarckian" in 1882.

Neo-Lamarckism is usually identified with the now discounted theory of heredity known as the inheritance of acquired characteristics. This identification is due to the fact that heredity became the center of an intense debate from 1887 to about 1895 between the neo-Lamarckians and the neo-Darwinians, led by the German zoologist August Weismann, who argued that the inheritance of acquired characters was wrong.

However, the role of heredity was not uppermost in the early (1870s) evolutionary thinking of these

Americans. Rather, the cause(s) of variation was their focus; so focal that they replaced natural selection with variation as the true cause (*vera causa*, as Packard sometimes said) of evolution.

Beyond this agreement on variation versus natural selection, they differed on what caused variation. Hyatt thought gravitation caused the variations found in fossil shells. Cope thought behavioral actions, guided by intelligence and will responding to environmental conditions, produced movement of muscles and bones, which in turn caused the morphological variations found in fossil vertebrate bones. Initially in agreement with Cope, Ryder eventually concluded that mechanical stresses and pressures, such as found in the movement of teeth, fingers, and toes were enough, without intelligence and will, to explain their evolution. Packard thought that environmental influences, such as climate, moisture, heat, and geologic forces acted directly on gedmetrid moths and cave fauna to cause their evolution.

Regarding heredity, they assumed, as had Lamarck, the inheritance of environmentally and behaviorally caused variations. Until the mid-1880s, little was known about the cellular basis of heredity; and little evidence contradicted this assumption. Even Weismann assumed it until about 1882.

In their evolutionary thinking of the 1870s, Cope and Ryder offered theoretical dynamical, rather than corpuscular, explanations of heredity. Cope adopted Ernst Baeckel's idea of vibratory motion, the "perigenesis of the plastidule." Hyatt said heredity obviously was important but could not explain it. Packard simply said it was a force that strengthened as it acted over time.

Weismann's denial of the inheritance of acquired characters forced these men to think more about heredity. In the 1890s, Ryder countered what he characterized as Weismann's excessively determinist heredity rigorously controlling all embryological development. He offered an epigenetic explanation in terms of the dynamics of forces, such as surface tension, acting around and within developing cells. Cope offered a compromise in his concept of diplogenesis.

All four eventually allowed that the inheritance of acquired characters could not be proved. But they insisted that the neo-Lamarckian causes of variation were obviously acting in nature and so neo-Lamarckian evolution must be right.

Neo-Lamarckism faded from American evolutionary thinking not so much because it was experimentally disproven—not even by Weismann's famous mice tail-cutting experiments; but because its chief supporters died between 1895 and 1905 without strong followers, and because it proved useless in solving questions and fruitless in opening new research areas.

BIBLIOGRAPHY

Bocking, Stephen. "Alpheus Spring Packard and Cave Fauna in the Evolution Debate." *Journal of the History of Biology* 21 (1988): 435–456.

Bowler, Peter. *Eclipse of Darwinism: Anti-Darwinian Evolution Theories in the Decades Around 1900.* Baltimore: Johns Hopkins University Press, 1983.

Burkhardt, Richard W., Jr. "Lamarckism in Britain and the United States." In *The Evolutionary Synthesis,* edited by Ernst Mayr and William B. Provine. Cambridge, MA: Harvard University Press, 1980.

Cope, Edward. *Primary Factors of Organic Evolution.* Chicago: Open Court, 1894.

Fothergill, Phillip. *Historical Aspects of Organic Evolution.* London: Hollis and Carter, 1952.

Greenfield, Theodore. "Variation, Heredity, and Scientific Explanation in the Evolutionary Theories of Four American Neo-Lamarckians, 1867–1897." Ph.D. diss., University of Wisconsin, Madison, 1986.

Joravsky, David. "Inheritance of Acquired Characters." *Dictionary of the History of Ideas.* Edited by P. Weiner. New York: Scribner, 1973.

Pfeifer, Edward J. "The Genesis of American Neo-Lamarckism." *Isis* 56 (1965): 156–167.

Ted Greenfield

Neurobiology

Up through the nineteenth century, the intellectual center of gravity for research into the brain and the rest of the nervous system lay in the European countries, with the United States playing a relatively modest and derivative role. This situation began to change in the early twentieth century as universities in the United States generally began to come of age; it reversed itself decisively during the scientifically assertive years in the United States after World War II.

Prior to World War II, American contributions to neurobiology relied heavily on studies of laboratory animals and focused on behavior mechanisms. Thematically, one sees a marked preoccupation in the early years with the neural organization of affective processes, including instincts, emotions, and bodily regulatory processes. This accent shows an intriguing divergence from the laboratory European tradition that

N

had focused more on the physiology of reflex action (how input to the nervous system leads predictably to output) and on the differential "mapping" of sensory and motor functioning. In the 1920s, Harvard University physiologist Walter Bradford Cannon lay the groundwork for several decades of American neurobiological research in a new, more "affective" key. His work established the global importance of the sympathetic-adrenal system in the arousal processes associated with emotion (especially fear and rage), and ultimately led him to see the nervous system as involved in maintaining a state of physiological balance or "homeostasis" in the organism as a whole.

The 1930s also saw the work of Cornell University anatomist James Papez on a "mechanism of emotion" consisting of certain interconnected subcortical brain structures, especially the hippocampus. This anatomical work served as the basis for the behaviorally grounded studies of Yale physiologist and physician Paul MacLean that established the "limbic system" as the "emotional" center of the brain mediating survival-enhancing behavior, including drives to mate and care for one's young. The themes of feeling and motivation were kept alive into the 1950s by studies on the mechanisms involved in reward and punishment systems in the rat brain (James Olds) and by dramatic demonstration of emotional and behavioral changes in primates following surgical ablation of subcortical regions in the temporal lobes (Heinrich Klüver and Paul Bucy). Beginning in the 1940s, one important and highly contentious direct consequence of this whole direction in neurobiology was the development of the frontal lobectomy operation for agitated or obsessive psychiatric patients. This involved severing connections between the brain's frontal lobes and "lower" systems. Neurologist Walter Freeman explained the operation as an effective intervention for patients suffering from pathological communication between what he characterized as the "thinking" (cortical) and the "feeling" (limbic) parts of their brain; it was widely practiced in state institutions into the late 1950s.

The 1920s in the United States also saw challenges to an older (largely European) view of the cortex as a hard-wired structure in which highly determined nerve connections and brain areas served specific functions. In the 1920s, the failure of psychophysiologist Karl Lashley to find any specific site in the rat cortex where memory ("engram") of a learned behavior could be localized helped usher in a "new view" of the cortex

dominated by principles of functional "equipotentiality" and "mass action." In the 1930s, work on amphibians by Paul Weiss further suggested that when nerve centers to limbs were cut and rearranged, orderly coordination could nevertheless be reestablished. The brain in these years appeared to American neurobiologists to be functionally a marvelously plastic structure. That perspective would only begin to change in the late 1950s with the work of such men as California psychophysiologist Roger Sperry and Harvard neurologist Norman Geschwind—which, in different ways, reasserted the localizability of functions in specific cortical areas, as well as the relative incapacity of the brain to rewire itself after damage.

The swing back toward a localizationist, connectionist model of the brain reached a complex climax of sorts in the 1970s with the explosion of interest in so-called split-brain research and lateralized hemisphere functioning. Also largely pioneered by Sperry and his colleagues, this work studied epileptic patients in which connections between the cerebral hemispheres had been severed for therapeutic reasons. It appeared that each severed hemisphere possessed a more or less independent sphere of consciousness—the left brain literally often did not know what the right was doing. Moreover, the two hemispheres responded to the environment and computed information differently: the left hemisphere was specialized for language and (some began to argue) for analytic, piecemeal thinking in general. The right hemisphere was specialized for visual-spatial information processing and (it was argued) "holistic" (creative, artistic) thinking in general. These studies not only galvanized American research into higher brain function; they also produced a peculiarly American cultural dialog on the relative virtues of what was called "left brain" versus "right brain" thinking.

Otherwise in the postwar era, technological innovation would soon drive neurobiological research as much as theoretical preoccupation. For example, with the development of the microelectrode in the 1940s, much basic neurobiological research went to the cellular level. In the 1960s, Harvard researchers David Hubel and Torsten Wiesel used microelectrodes to record activity in single nerve cells across the cellular columns of the primary visual area of the cortex (the anatomy of which had been worked out by Johns Hopkins neuroanatomist Vernon Mountcastle). They stunned the research community with their conclusions that different individual cells "saw" differently or, more precisely, had different built-in capacities to respond to visual stimuli; what they called "pattern specificity." In other words, it seemed that the specific instructions by which the brain came to know the world were written as far down as the individual cellular level.

In recent years, the dominant molecular focus in basic neurobiological research has been partly overshadowed by excitement over new neuroimaging technologies that promise insights into the contributions made by specific neural structures to more global brain functioning. In the 1940s, Seymour Kety used nitrous oxide to track changes in cerebral blood flow, suggesting that there might be ways to watch the "living brain" in action; this work was one step in a chain of technological developments that ultimately led to the anatomical views created by computer tomography (CT) and the dramatic colored brain pictures produced by positron emission technology (PET), and, more recently, functional magnetic resonance imaging (fMRI). In the 1990s, neurobiologists are hard at work identifying "hot spots" in the human brain that may allow them to understand ways in which different brain regions work together, and how different areas appear to play a special role in various psychological functions, psychiatric disorders, and individual differences in behavior and even personality style.

In the late 1990s, even as American neurobiological research is sustained by considerable optimism, it remains a multidivided and vaguely uneasy soul. For example, notions of hard-wired localization coexist with models of the nervous system as a self-updating system of dynamic "neural nets" (work associated with such names as Gerald Edelman). Research into the neurochemistry of the nervous system—including the discovery in the 1970s of the endorphins, the brain's "natural opiates" (Solomon Snyder, Candace Pert)—has recently begun, for some, to call into question the extent to which the nervous system can be said properly to even exist as an independent entity, and whether it now needs to be reconceived within a much more complex system of interconnected biochemical processes, including those that regulate immune functioning (neuroimmunology). The intellectual stakes of much of American neurobiological research in the past fifty years have been high, and the practical, sociopolitical and existential stakes of the resulting conclusions no less so. Unfortunately, while there is considerable information about the basic conceptual milestones, most available histories are antiquarian or reminiscent in nature. Sophisticated historiographical analysis of neurobiology in American science, especially in the post–World War II era, is in its beginning stages.

BIBLIOGRAPHY

Cannon, Walter Bradford. *The Wisdom of the Body.* New York: W.W. Norton, 1932.

Corsi, Pietro, ed. *The Enchanted Loom: Chapters in the History of Neuroscience.* New York: Oxford University Press, 1991.

Edelman, Gerald M. *Neural Darwinism: The Theory of Neuronal Group Selection.* New York: Basic Books, 1987.

Freeman, Walter E. *Psychosurgery.* Springfield, IL: Charles C. Thomas, 1942.

Harrington, Anne. *Medicine, Mind and the Double Brain.* Princeton: Princeton University Press, 1987.

Haymaker, Webb, and Francis Schiller, eds. *The Founders of Neurology: One Hundred and Forty-Six Biographical Sketches by Eighty-Eight Authors.* 2d ed. Springfield, IL: Charles C. Thomas, 1971.

Hubel, David H. *Eye, Brain, and Vision.* New York: Scientific American Library, 1988.

Kelley, Roger E., ed. *Functional Neuroimaging.* Armonk, NY: Futura Publishing, c1994.

Lashley, Karl S. *Brain Mechanisms and Intelligence: A Quantitative Study of Injuries to the Brain.* Chicago: University of Chicago Press, 1929.

MacLean, Paul D. *A Triune Concept of the Brain and Behaviour.* Toronto and Buffalo: University of Toronto Press, 1973.

Snyder, Solomon H. *Brainstorming: The Science and Politics of Opiate Research.* Cambridge, MA: Harvard University Press, 1989.

Worden, Frederic G., Judith P. Swazey, and George Adelman. *The Neurosciences: Paths of Discovery.* Boston: Birkhauser, 1975.

Anne Harrington

Newcomb, Simon (1835–1909)

North American mathematical astronomer, political economist, science commentator, and science administrator. Born in Wallace, Nova Scotia, he studied under his father, an itinerant school teacher, until becoming apprenticed to an herbal doctor at age sixteen. After two disillusioning years with the herbalist, he made his way to the United States. From 1854 through late 1856, he held a series of teaching and tutoring posts in rural Maryland. Proximity to Washington and the Smithsonian Institution enabled the inquisitive young

N

educator to expand his growing interests in mathematics and astronomy through use of the Smithsonian library and contact with secretary Joseph Henry. One of Henry's colleagues eventually found a suitable position for Newcomb: working as a computational assistant at the Nautical Almanac Office in Cambridge, Massachusetts. A lax work schedule allowed him to enroll as a student of mathematics studying under Benjamin Peirce at Harvard's Lawrence Scientific School. After obtaining his bachelor of science degree in 1858, he remained on the Harvard roles as a "resident graduate" and continued performing calculations at the Almanac Office. He also began independent research in astronomy, mathematics, and physics. In 1861, he launched a lifelong career with the United States Navy, accepting the position of professor of mathematics at the Naval Observatory in Washington. Three years later, he became a naturalized United States citizen. About the same time, he wed Mary C. Hassler, the granddaughter of the founder of the United States Coast Survey.

Although hired as an observational astronomer, Newcomb found time at the Naval Observatory to expand his theoretical studies in mathematical astronomy. In 1877, he parlayed these studies into a position of authority, winning appointment as superintendent of the Nautical Almanac Office, now in Washington, where he would oversee publication of the *American Ephemeris*. Establishing a name for himself as a researcher and administrator, he also served in 1877 as president of the American Association for the Advancement of Science and from 1883 to 1889 as vice president of the National Academy of Sciences. From the 1870s on, he taught in various capacities at the Johns Hopkins University and Columbian (later George Washington) University. In accord with navy retirement policy, he stepped down from the superintendency of the Almanac Office in 1897 at age sixty-two. Receiving support from the Carnegie Institution, he continued to be professionally active, including presiding over the 1904 St. Louis Congress of Arts and Science. When he died, he held the "relative" naval rank of rear admiral and received a state funeral and military burial in Arlington National Cemetery.

To be sure, Newcomb was adept in observational astronomy. He boosted the caliber of work at the Naval Observatory, first by eliminating systematic errors that tainted values of right ascensions of stars and later by directing the observatory's new, refracting telescope. But his true talent and interest centered on theoretical, mathematical astronomy—classical, perturbational analyses of the orbital motions of the planets and the moon in relation to each other and the sun. Initially, while working and studying in Cambridge, he caught the attention of the astronomical community through a convincing demonstration that the asteroids did not result from the breakup of a single planet. After becoming settled at the Naval Observatory, he made more drawn-out analyses of the Uranus-Neptune system and the motion of the moon—the latter evolving into a lifetime focus. Once he gained control of the Almanac Office, he instituted an even more ambitious program of research: a multidecade reevaluation of commonly accepted positions of the planets, moon, and sun coupled with a recalculation of the corresponding perturbational formulae and construction of associated tables. Assisted by George W. Hill and others, he completed the main part of this reevaluation by the mid-1890s and published a component of his research in *The Elements of the Four Inner Planets and the Fundamental Constants of Astronomy*. Building on these foundational studies, he participated in an international campaign to bring uniformity to the world's astronomical ephemerides through standardized constants and data. As the twentieth century opened, many of Newcomb's new astronomical values and theories were becoming the norm in positional astronomy—a status they would hold for decades to come.

Newcomb was the most celebrated and honored American scientist of the late nineteenth century. A flood of major awards began in 1874 when he received the gold medal of London's Royal Astronomical Society. By the 1890s, he held the Copley medal of the Royal Society of London and had become one of eight Foreign Associates of the Paris Academy of Sciences. And his fame reached even to the public, not only because of his research achievements but also because of his many lay writings—including his heavily reprinted and translated *Popular Astronomy* (1878), a successful series of mathematical textbooks (1880s), and even a science fiction novel (1900). His public prominence also reflected his high visibility in areas outside natural science and mathematics. From the 1860s through the 1890s, he wrote extensively on political economy, taking stands in line with the classical, liberal doctrines of particularly John Stuart Mill. Confronting controversial issues on finance, trade, taxation, currency, and labor, he gained a solid reputation through works such as *Principles of Political Economy*

N

(1885). He also added to his visibility through provocative essays and speeches on the failings of the American scientific enterprise and the problems associated with Christian natural theology. And while serving as the first president of the American Society for Psychical Research, he used the opportunity to debunk psychical inquiries. In many of his commentaries dealing with broader social, cultural, and intellectual issues, he buttressed his arguments with appeals to a positivistic vision of scientific method. This rhetorical use of method—influenced by Americans such as Chauncey Wright and Europeans such as Mill—aligned Newcomb with the nation's nascent pragmatic movement and thinkers such as Charles S. Peirce and William James.

The Manuscript Division of the Library of Congress holds the Simon Newcomb Papers. A superb resource for investigating American science and culture, the collection contains approximately 46,200 items. With Newcomb scholarship only beginning to quicken, the collection still contains many untapped documents, some of which, unfortunately, are deteriorating and losing legibility.

BIBLIOGRAPHY

Archibald, Raymond C. "Simon Newcomb." *Science,* n.s., 44 (1916): 871–878.

———. "Simon Newcomb, 1835-1909, Bibliography of His Life and Work." *Biographical Memoirs of the National Academy of Sciences* 17 (1924): 19–69.

Campbell, W.W. "Simon Newcomb." *Biographical Memoirs of the National Academy of Sciences* 17 (1924): 1–18.

Dunphy, Loretta M. "Simon Newcomb: His Contributions to Economic Thought." Ph.D. diss., Catholic University of America, 1956.

Eisele, Carolyn. "The Charles S. Peirce-Simon Newcomb Correspondence." *Proceedings of the American Philosophical Society* 101 (1957): 409–433.

Moyer, Albert E. *A Scientist's Voice in American Culture: Simon Newcomb and the Rhetoric of Scientific Method.* Berkeley: University of California Press, 1992.

Newcomb, Simon. *The Reminiscences of an Astronomer.* Boston: Houghton and Mifflin, 1903.

Norberg, Arthur L. "Simon Newcomb and Nineteenth-Century Positional Astronomy." Ph.D. diss., University of Wisconsin-Madison, 1974.

———. "Simon Newcomb's Early Astronomical Career." *Isis* 69 (1978): 209–225.

———. "Simon Newcomb's Role in the Astronomical Revolution of the Early Nineteen Hundreds." In *Sky with Ocean Joined: Proceedings of the Sesquicentennial Symposia of the U.S. Naval Observatory,* edited by Steven J. Dick and LeRoy E. Doggett. Washington, DC: U.S. Naval Observatory, 1983, pp. 74–88.

Wead, Charles K., et al. "Simon Newcomb: Memorial Addresses. Read Before the Philosophical Society of Washington, December 4, 1909." *Bulletin of the Philosophical Society of Washington* 15 (1910): 133–167.

Winnik, Herbert C. "The Role of Personality in the Science and the Social Attitudes of Five American Men of Science, 1876–1916." Ph.D. diss., University of Wisconsin-Madison, 1968.

Albert E. Moyer

New York Academy of Sciences

Established in 1817 by faculty and students at the College of Physicians and Surgeons, the Lyceum of Natural History (which changed its name to the New York Academy of Sciences in 1876) found its niche in New York cultural life as a general scientific society appealing to an audience of physicians, avocational scientists, and city notables. Its early decades saw the establishment of the *Annals of the Lyceum* in 1823, the creation of a museum collection, agitation by its members for a state geological survey, and the ownership of a meeting-hall on Broadway in 1836. By 1843, the cost of the Broadway building had become too heavy for the lyceum to sustain. In 1866, fire destroyed the lyceum's museum collections stored in New York University Medical College.

In the second half of the nineteenth century, the lyceum was just one of a multitude of New York scientific institutions that included Columbia University, the American Museum of National History, the American Chemical Society, and the New York Botanical Garden. Scientists associated with these institutions saw the academy as a common meeting-ground, a scientific forum for the exchange of ideas across disciplinary boundaries. Thus, the academy was the organizing force for the 1887 meeting of the American Association for the Advancement of Science in New York and, in 1890, helped create the Scientific Alliance of New York, an organization that, in addition to the academy, included societies for mineralogy, botany, microscopy, and mathematics. In 1894, the academy initiated a series of annual exhibitions of scientific progress that drew regular audiences of 4,000 visitors.

The academy as coordinator of New York science received added emphasis with the creation of the Puerto Rico Scientific Survey in 1912 under the leadership of

N

Nathaniel Lord Britton. Financial support from prominent New Yorkers and the Puerto Rico legislature enabled scientists from New York's scientific institutions to catalog and describe the botany, geology, zoology, and anthropology of Puerto Rico and the Virgin Islands. The academy published the results in an extensive series of scientific reports into the 1940s. By 1930, the dominance of the survey in the affairs of the academy had resulted in considerable overlap in membership with the scientific staff of the American Museum of Natural History. Eunice Miner, a research assistant in invertebrate zoology at the museum, became executive secretary of the academy in 1939 and presided over a rapid increase in membership and sales of the *Annals*.

Miner's lasting contribution to the academy's work was to launch a series of conferences on biomedical and pharmaceutical topics. During the 1950s, important meetings were held on antibiotics, the chemotherapy of tuberculosis, oral contraceptives, sulfa compounds, anticoagulents, and dimethyl sulfoxide.

In subsequent decades, the academy sponsored an outreach program to local high schools: the Scientists in Schools Program; and a Junior Academy of Sciences. During the 1970s and 1980s, the number of sections expanded to more than thirty, general membership increased to 44,000, and the series of scientific conferences covered a wide variety of topics.

BIBLIOGRAPHY

Baatz, Simon. *Knowledge, Culture, and Science in the Metropolis: The New York Academy of Sciences, 1817–1970.* New York: Academy of Sciences, 1990.

Fairchild, Herman Le Roy. *A History of the New York Academy of Sciences.* New York: n.p., 1887.

Sloan, Douglas. "Science in New York City, 1867–1907." *Isis* 71 (1980): 35–76.

Simon Baatz

New York Botanical Garden, The

The New York Botanical Garden (NYBG) was founded by an act of the legislature of the state of New York passed in 1891 and amended in 1894 "for the purpose of establishing and maintaining a Botanical Garden and Museum and Arboretum therein, for the collection and culture of plants, flowers, shrubs and trees, the advancement of botanical science and knowledge, and the prosecution of original research therein and in kindred subjects, for affording instruction in the same, for the prosecution and exhibition of ornamental

and decorative horticulture and gardening and for the entertainment, recreation and instruction of the people." Located in the Bronx, in the northern part of New York City, on 250 acres of land, the live plant collections include a pinetum, herbaceous grounds, fruiticetum, deciduous arboretum, and a forty-acre hemlock grove. It was the hemlock grove that attracted the founders to the site because it was the only single patch of natural uncut forest in the region, containing 200–300-year-old specimens.

The Museum Building, built in 1901, was designed by Robert W. Gibson and originally contained a museum of economic botany, systematic botany and paleobotany. Today, it holds a library of 1.26 million items dating from the twelfth to the twentieth centuries and one of the most important herbaria in the world, comprising 6 million specimens, with a focus on plants of the Americas. The Enid A. Haupt Conservatory, renamed in 1978 after this philanthropist funded a major restoration campaign, is the architectural showpiece of the institution. Built in 1900 by William R. Cobb of Lord and Burnham, it is a glass and iron structure covering almost an acre of growing area in which tropical, subtropical, and desert flora are displayed.

The NYBG sent out its first botanical expedition in 1897, to Montana, which initiated a very active program of expeditions around the world—approximately 900 to date. An extensive publication program, begun in 1898, now includes nine scholarly journals and numerous other volumes. The research staff is engaged in advanced scientific work and is particularly noted for its contributions in molecular biology and forest management. The NYBG also administers the Institute for Ecosystem Studies and the Institute for Economic Botany.

BIBLIOGRAPHY

Britton, N.L. "Address on Botanical Gardens." *Bulletin of The New York Botanical Garden* 1 (1896–1900): 75–76.

Johnston, Mea. *A Guide to the New York Botanical Garden.* Bronx: The Garden, 1986.

The New York Botanical Garden, Bronx Park: Descriptive Guide to the Grounds, Buildings and Collections. New York [Lancaster, PA: The New Era Printing Company], 1909.

Tanner, Ogden, and Adele Auchincloss. *The New York Botanical Garden: An Illustrated Chronicle of Plants and People.* New York: Walker, 1991.

Wyman, Donald. "The Arboretum and Botanical Gardens of North America." *Chronica Botanica* 10 (1947): 442–444.

Therese O'Malley

Nott, Josiah Clarke (1804–1873)

Racial theorist and physician. Nott was a South Carolinian who received his initial medical training in New York and Philadelphia. He graduated from the University of Pennsylvania in 1827, practiced in Columbia, South Carolina, and in the mid-1830s furthered his medical studies in Paris. There, he came under the influence of François Broussais's theories of physiological medicine.

In 1836, Nott moved to Mobile, Alabama, became one of the most widely known physicians in the South, achieved a national reputation for his writings on yellow fever, and an international reputation for his writings on race. In writing on yellow fever, he disagreed with those who believed that the disease resulted from morbid atmospheric conditions and argued that it was spread by "animalcules."

Nott began to write on racial matters in 1843, and became one of the members of what later became known as the American School of Ethnology. He ardently defended the idea of innate differences between the races, arguing that blacks were better off under slavery than free and that the American Indians were doomed to extinction. He contended that race mixing brought about national deterioration. Nott wished to free scientific research and writing from clerical and biblical influence, and was an overt and impassioned defender of polygenesis. He was so anxious to defend the position that whites and blacks belonged to different species that he argued that mulattoes were less fertile than either blacks or whites. His racial writings depended less upon scientific methodology than upon an impressionistic discussion of history and contemporary societies.

Nott's *Types of Mankind,* written jointly with George R. Gliddon and published in 1854, elaborately defended the idea of innate racial differences and invited clerical criticism in its determination that God had created different species. This volume was the fullest and most extreme statement of the views of the American School of Ethnology. It was frequently reprinted over the next twenty years.

In the 1850s, Nott was an ardent defender of the institution of slavery, but he also became particularly interested in medical education. He was influential in persuading the Alabama legislature to establish a medical school in Mobile, and was the leading figure in its early history.

Nott served in the Confederate medical service, and after the Civil War moved first to Baltimore and then to New York. In the North, he ceased his writing on racial matters, but established another successful medical practice and wrote on his new speciality of gynecology. He returned to Mobile to die.

BIBLIOGRAPHY

Horsman, Reginald. *Josiah Nott of Mobile: Southerner, Physician, and Racial Theorist.* Baton Rouge: Louisiana State University Press, 1987.

Nott, Josiah C., and George R. Gliddon. *Types of Mankind.* Philadelphia: Lippincott, 1854.

Stanton, William. *The Leopard's Spots: Scientific Attitudes Toward Race in America, 1815–59.* Chicago: University of Chicago Press, 1960.

Reginald Horsman

Noyes, Arthur Amos (1866–1936)

Physical chemist, chemical educator, and institution builder. Noyes was born in Newburyport, Massachusetts, and attended the Massachusetts Institute of Technology (MIT), from which he graduated in 1886. After having obtained a M.Sc. degree for research on organic chemistry, he went to Europe, where he finally managed to work in the research laboratory of Wilhelm Ostwald, one of the leaders of the new field of physical chemistry. He got his Ph.D. in Leipzig in 1890 with a dissertation on the study of deviations of solutions from Van't Hoff's law.

Upon returning to MIT, he established and became director of what he called the Research Laboratory of Physical Chemistry. He remained director from 1903 until 1916 and contributed to its budget. He was the acting president of MIT from 1907 to 1909. During World War I, Noyes was chairman of the National Research Council, an organization created by himself, the astronomer George Ellery Hale, his former student from MIT, and the physicist Robert Andrews Millikan to help the National Academy of Sciences in advising the government on scientific questions. In 1919, he moved to the Throop College in Pasadena. Together with Hale and Millikan, he managed to build the college, which was renamed the California Institute of Technology (Cal Tech), into one of the more important centers of education and research in science and engineering in the United States.

Noyes was president of the American Chemical Society and the American Association for the Advancement of Science. In 1895, he founded the journal *Review of American Chemical Research,* which became in 1907 the *Chemical Abstracts.*

N

Noyes's contributions were threefold: as a scientist, an institution builder, and a teacher. Noyes's research was on the properties of solutions, particularly at high temperatures, the determination of free-energy changes in chemical reactions, the study of the chemical properties of the rarer elements, and the development of a system of chemical analysis including them. In addition, Noyes was instrumental in the introduction and development of research in physical chemistry into the United States. Many of the leading American physical chemists were trained or worked at the Research Laboratory of Physical Chemistry at MIT, or at the Gates Chemical Laboratory at Cal Tech, both founded by Noyes.

As an institution builder, Noyes played a fundamental role in raising to prominence the two institutions he was associated with. He worked toward transforming MIT into an institution where education (both undergraduate and graduate) and research were combined, and was often the inspiration for many of the policies implemented at Cal Tech, but announced by Millikan, such as the emphasis on pure rather than applied science, and the emphasis on humanities' courses as the basis for a broad education for all students.

But according to the Nobel Prize winner Linus Pauling, perhaps Noyes's most famous student, Noyes was above all a great teacher of chemistry, someone with a great intuition to identify potentially great chemists, and then providing all the necessary conditions for their blossoming.

The rising of the United States to scientific leadership in the twentieth century has been recently a topic of election for historians of science. Particular attention has been paid to the development, characteristics, and importance played by universities, research centers, and other institutions, and in this context historians have assessed Noyes's contribution to the building up of MIT and Cal Tech, or the creation of the National Research Council. Concomitantly, his importance in the making of physical chemistry in America has been dealt with in a superb book by John Servos which continues to be the major source of information and reflection on the role of Noyes as an institution builder and a scientific leader.

Noyes's papers are at the Carnegie Institution of Washington.

BIBLIOGRAPHY

Geiger, R.L. *To Advance Knowledge: The Growth of American Research Universities.* New York: Oxford University Press, 1986.

Goodtein, J.R. *Millikan's School: A History of the California Institute of Technology.* New York: Norton, 1991.

Pauling, L. "Arthur Amos Noyes." *Biographical Memoirs of the National Academy of Sciences* 31 (1958): 322–346.

———. "Fifty Years of Physical Chemistry in the California Institute of Technology." *Annals of the Review of Physical Chemistry* 16 (1965): 1–14.

———. "Noyes, Arthur Amos." *Dictionary of Scientific Biography.* Edited by Charles C. Gillispie. New York: Scribner, 1974, 10:156–157.

Servos, J. *Physical Chemistry from Ostwald to Pauling: The Making of a Science in America.* Princeton: Princeton University Press, 1990.

Ana Simões

Nuclear Power

Generation of electrical power from the fission of atomic nuclei. The development of nuclear power for electricity was a by-product of the greatest, or at least the most dramatic, scientific achievement of World War II—the construction of atomic bombs by the release of enormous energy from nuclear fission. In the immediate aftermath of the end of World War II, exaggerated and often fanciful popular accounts of the prospects for peaceful applications of nuclear energy were common. *Newsweek* reported in August 1945, for example, that atomic energy could be used to fuel airplanes, rockets, and automobiles and to provide electricity through small units in individual homes as well as to produce power in large central generating stations. Scientists realized that even the most practical of the hopes for peaceful nuclear power would not come about in the near future, and indeed, the beginning of the Cold War focused the Truman administration's attention on the military rather than the civilian uses of nuclear energy. Nevertheless, the Atomic Energy Commission (AEC), the agency created in 1946 to develop the new technology for both purposes, sponsored some experiments on nonmilitary applications. In December 1951, an experimental breeder reactor at a test site in Idaho generated electricity for the first time from nuclear fission, although only enough to do little more than light the building that housed the reactor.

The development of nuclear power proceeded at a halting pace until the Atomic Energy Act of 1954 became law. The act made possible for the first time the wide use of atomic energy for commercial purposes by ending the government's monopoly of the technology. It assigned the AEC responsibility for both promoting nuclear power and regulating its safety. To fulfill the objective of the new law, the AEC offered incentives to encourage private investment in nuclear power, but the response was tepid. Despite interest in the prospects for nuclear-generated electricity among some leading utilities, many power companies held back because of the abundance of conventional fuels and because of economic uncertainties and unresolved safety questions about nuclear technology.

Research sponsored by both the AEC and private firms provided answers to some key scientific questions about nuclear power safety in the mid- and late 1950s. Perhaps the most important work showed that "inherent mechanisms" would prevent a light-water reactor from surging out of control under unstable conditions. But other issues had to be addressed. By the mid-1960s, the major concern among reactor safety experts, and the focus of research, was a loss-of-coolant accident, which could occur if the circulation of water that cooled the reactor core was disrupted. In the worst imaginable circumstances, this could cause the reactor fuel to melt and lead to a release of large amounts of radioactivity to the environment. Another major scientific issue surrounding nuclear power that defied easy resolution involved the health hazards of radiation. Although scientists agreed on the dangers of exposure to high levels of radiation, they were much less certain about the risks of low levels of exposure from the routine operation of nuclear power plants and from other sources.

Beginning in the mid-1960s, a boom in reactor orders and a rapid growth in the size of individual plants gave those issues greatly increased visibility. The boom came as a result of indications that large nuclear plants could compete economically with coal, the rise of interconnections in electrical grids that encouraged the construction of large plants, and growing concern about the environmental costs of fossil fuels. The nuclear boom took place at virtually the same time as the development of environmentalism as a potent political force. Within a short time, nuclear power became a leading target of environmental activism.

By the early 1970s, a highly visible and increasingly strident debate was raging over nuclear power. Critics claimed that the technology was neither safe nor necessary; supporters argued that it was not only safe but essential for the nation's energy future. At the center of the debate were the unresolved issues of the likelihood and consequences of a loss-of-coolant accident and the effects of low-level radiation. In both cases, nuclear

critics received a great deal of attention in the popular media as well as in scientific journals by charging that the AEC had failed to protect public safety adequately. The AEC and nuclear supporters took sharp exception, but the lack of conclusive scientific evidence on outstanding questions prevented them from proving their case to an increasingly skeptical public. By 1974, the credibility of the AEC on safety issues had deteriorated to a point that Congress abolished the agency and gave its regulatory responsibilities to the newly created Nuclear Regulatory Commission (NRC).

The controversy over nuclear power continued unabated. By the late 1970s, orders for new plants had slowed drastically and public uneasiness about nuclear risks had increased markedly. Those trends were intensified by the most significant event in the history of nuclear power in the United States—the loss-of-coolant accident at the Three Mile Island plant in Pennsylvania in March 1979. The accident occurred as a result of a series of mechanical failures and human errors, and although the amounts of radiation released were very small, the political fallout from the accident was heavy. Ironically, the events at Three Mile Island provided reassuring evidence that safety systems that guarded against a large off-site release of radioactivity from a loss-of-coolant accident worked as designed. Nevertheless, the accident undermined the credibility of the NRC and the nuclear industry while enhancing that of antinuclear critics. Although plants continued to receive operating licenses after the accident, nuclear vendors received no new orders for plants after 1978. Controversy over long-standing issues such as reactor safety, radiation risks, radioactive waste disposal, and the economics of nuclear power keep the technology in the headlines. In addition, newer issues arising from the Three Mile Island accident received increased attention from both supporters and critics of nuclear power. Some, such as "human factors" in reactor safety, probabilistic risk assessment, and estimates of the amount of radiation released by an accident, were scientific questions; others were largely political, legal, or administrative matters. In 1992, 110 nuclear power plants were operating in the United States, providing about 20 percent of the nation's generating capacity.

Nuclear power has not been the subject of a great deal of historical scholarship. Although some accounts have reflected the partisanship of the public debate over the technology, several recent works have taken a more scholarly and more balanced approach.

N

BIBLIOGRAPHY

Balogh, Brian. *Chain Reaction: Expert Debate and Public Participation in American Commercial Nuclear Power, 1945–1975.* New York: Cambridge University Press, 1991.

Hewlett, Richard G., and Jack M. Holl. *Atoms for Peace and War, 1953–1961: Eisenhower and the Atomic Energy Commission.* Berkeley and Los Angeles: University of California Press, 1989.

Mazuzan, George T., and J. Samuel Walker. *Controlling the Atom: The Beginnings of Nuclear Regulation, 1946–1962.* Berkeley and Los Angeles: University of California Press, 1984.

Morone, Joseph G., and Edward J. Woodhouse. *The Demise of Nuclear Energy? Lessons for Democratic Control of Technology.* New Haven: Yale University Press, 1989.

Seaborg, Glenn T., with Benjamin S. Loeb. *The Atomic Energy Commission under Nixon: Adjusting to Troubled Times.* New York: St. Martin's, 1993.

Walker, J. Samuel. *Containing the Atom: Nuclear Regulation in a Changing Environment, 1963–1971.* Berkeley and Los Angeles: University of California Press, 1992.

Weart, Spencer R. *Nuclear Fear: A History of Images.* Cambridge, MA: Harvard University Press, 1988.

Wellock, Thomas Raymond. *Critical Masses: Opposition to Nuclear Power in California, 1958–1978.* Madison: University of Wisconsin Press, 1998.

Winkler, Allan M. *Life under a Cloud: American Anxiety about the Atom.* New York: Oxford University Press, 1993.

J. Samuel Walker

Nuclear Regulatory Commission

Federal agency responsible for assuring safety of nuclear power. The Nuclear Regulatory Commission (NRC), established by the Energy Reorganization Act of 1974, began operations in January 1975. It assumed responsibilities that the Atomic Energy Commission (AEC) had previously exercised for assuring the safety of civilian applications of nuclear energy. In 1954, Congress had assigned the AEC the task of both promoting and regulating the nuclear industry. By the early 1970s, as nuclear power became the focus of intense controversy, the sometimes conflicting mandate of the AEC had generated considerable criticism. The Energy Reorganization Act abolished the AEC and attempted to address the complaints about its dual responsibilities by creating the NRC as an independent regulatory agency.

The NRC sought to separate itself from the legacy of the AEC and to establish its own credibility, but its efforts were soon undercut by a series of events and controversies. These included a major fire at a plant in March 1975, the resignation of two agency employees in 1976 who charged that the NRC was lax in carrying out its mandate, and questions about a variety of unresolved safety issues.

The greatest crisis for the agency and the nuclear industry occurred in March 1979 when a large portion of the core of the Three Mile Island plant in Pennsylvania melted in a loss-of-coolant accident. The plant suffered irreparable damage, and the credibility of the NRC fared almost as badly. Uncertainty about the causes of the accident and confusion about how to deal with it elicited a barrage of criticism and fed public fears of nuclear technology. Despite the fact that the accident released only tiny amounts of radiation to the environment, it showed that serious consequences could arise from unanticipated events. As a result of Three Mile Island, the agency placed much greater emphasis than previously on human errors that could jeopardize plant safety, the performance records of operating plants, and the safety implications of small equipment failures that could lead to large accidents. It also sponsored research on a number of issues regarding the effects of a loss of coolant on the reactor core and the amount of radiation that was likely to be released in an accident. The agency issued a series of new regulations that were designed to improve reactor safety in light of new knowledge acquired.

BIBLIOGRAPHY

Cantelon, Philip L., and Robert C. Williams. *Crisis Contained: The Department of Energy at Three Mile Island.* Carbondale: Southern Illinois University Press, 1982.

Johnson, John W. *Insuring against Disaster: The Nuclear Industry on Trial.* Macon, GA: Mercer University Press, 1986.

Okrent, David. *Nuclear Reactor Safety: On the History of the Regulatory Process.* Madison: University of Wisconsin Press, 1981.

Rees, Joseph V. *Hostages of Each Other: The Transformation of Nuclear Safety since Three Mile Island.* Chicago: University of Chicago Press, 1994.

J. Samuel Walker

SEE ALSO
Atomic Energy Commission

Nuclear Weapons

Nuclear weapons were first developed and used by the United States during World War II in response to the

German discovery of fission and fears that they might develop such a weapon. The two weapons developed at Los Alamos incorporated two different forms of assembly of fissionable materials to produce an explosive chain reaction, in which kilotons of TNT equivalent energy was released. The first, the gun design, fired a fraction of a critical mass of uranium 238 into a target containing another. The second, the implosion technique, used high explosives arranged concentrically around a subcritical mass of plutonium to compress it to a critical mass.

After World War II, the pace of development of nuclear weapons slowed, although Enrico Fermi and Edward Teller had suggested as early as 1942 that a superbomb might be constructed. They suggested fusing light elements of hydrogen with the heat of an exploding fission bomb, in a manner similar to that by which stars produce energy.

Although Teller led a group which studied this process at Los Alamos during and immediately after the war, he returned to the University of Chicago in 1946. The pace of research on the superbomb then slowed. In the view of many Los Alamos scientists, this was due to manpower shortages and the unavailability of sufficient computing resources. However, in Teller's view, and that of Ernest Lawrence and other critics, the cause was the lack of leadership and emphasis from the Atomic Energy Commission (AEC), which replaced the Manhattan District of the Army Corps of Engineers as the custodians of atomic energy research and development.

The Soviet Union discharged its first atomic device in the summer of 1949, leading to an intense debate in the AEC and its General Advisory Committee (GAC), led by J. Robert Oppenheimer, the wartime leader at Los Alamos, over the feasibility of the superbomb. The GAC advised against its development on technical and moral grounds, and this position was sustained by the commission, with significant opposition by Lewis Strauss. A National Security Council panel, including the secretaries of state and defense, and President Harry Truman decided to continue development of the superbomb, and after the treachery of Klaus Fuchs was revealed, to accelerate it.

Critical breakthroughs in the design of the super-weapon and the George test of Operation Greenhouse in 1951 led to a feasible design which was tested in the Mike shot of Operation Ivy on Halloween 1952. Two years later, the Bravo shot of Operation Castle demonstrated a much more powerful and deliverable hydrogen bomb while simultaneously spreading radioactive fallout over a wide area and contaminating ships and islands beyond the restricted zone surrounding the test site.

Partly in response to concerns over the greater destructiveness of nuclear weapons, President Dwight David Eisenhower launched the Atoms for Peace Program in 1953. At a series of Atoms for Peace Conferences in Geneva, the United States, the Soviet Union, Great Britain, and other nations displayed and made available the fruits of their labors in the fields related to atomic physics.

The development of nuclear weapons was continued throughout the 1950s and early 1960s, although testing was interrupted by a moratorium from 1958 to 1961, which was ended by Russian tests and confined to underground tests after the negotiation of the nuclear test-ban treaty in 1963. Subsequent treaties have further restricted the yield of nuclear weapons. The Clinton administration has ended all testing of weapons and has signed the Comprehensive Test Ban Treaty, which prohibits all nuclear weapons test explosions.

In order to produce the nuclear weapons demanded by the military for the stockpile, a vast production complex was created in the early 1950s to supplement the wartime plants at Oak Ridge and Hanford which produced the uranium and plutonium for the first atomic bombs. This massive complex run by industrial and academic contractors in government-owned laboratories and plants made nuclear weapons a major industry. It included a third nuclear weapons laboratory at Livermore, which supplemented the work of the weapons design laboratory at Los Alamos and its spin-off, the weapons engineering laboratory at Sandia base in Albuquerque, the Sandia Laboratory, which was operated by a subsidiary of Bell Laboratories.

The development, use, and policy surrounding nuclear weapons has been controversial among political historians as well as among historians of science who have attempted to explore policy-related issues in the development of nuclear science. Due to unavailability of many of the records of the policy debates, these controversies are likely to continue until those records are declassified. Most controversial have been the fallout effects of nuclear weapons testing in the Pacific and at the Nevada Test Site, which was established during

N

the Korean War to provide a more secure continental test site.

Nuclear weapons are among the most destructive products of science-based technology but because they are cheaper than maintaining a comparable conventional deterrent to aggression, they have been favored by military policymakers as the backbone of the nation's strategic defense. With the dissolution of the principal adversary and competitor in the arms race, it remains to be seen whether nuclear weapons will continue to play an important role in strategic planning.

BIBLIOGRAPHY

Ackland, Len, and Steven McGuire, eds. *Assessing the Nuclear Age.* Chicago: Educational Foundation for Nuclear Science, 1986.

Anders, Roger M., ed. *Forging the Atomic Shield: Excerpts from the Office Diary of Gordon E. Dean.* Chapel Hill: University of North Carolina Press, 1987.

Glasstone, Samuel, ed. *The Effects of Nuclear Weapons.* Washington, DC: Atomic Energy Commission, 1962.

———. *Sourcebook on Atomic Energy.* 3d ed. New York: Van Nostrand Reinhold, 1967.

Herken, Gregg. *The Winning Weapon: The Atomic Bomb in the Cold War 1945–1950.* New York: Knopf, 1980.

Kissinger, Henry A. *Nuclear Weapons and Foreign Policy.* New York: Norton, 1969.

Lawren, William. *The General and the Bomb: A Biography of General Leslie R. Groves, Director of the Manhattan Project.* New York: Dodd Mead, 1988.

McKay, Alwyn. *The Making of the Atomic Age.* New York: Oxford University Press, 1984.

Rhodes, Richard. *The Making of the Atomic Bomb.* New York: Simon and Schuster, 1986.

Robert W. Seidel

Nuttall, Thomas (1786–1859)

Botanist, ornithologist, and explorer. Nuttall was born to modest circumstances in Yorkshire, England, and immigrated to this country in 1808, at the age of twenty-two. He settled in Philadelphia, where he soon came under the influence of the botanist Benjamin Smith Barton. Over the next several years, Barton sponsored his young protégé on several collecting expeditions, including a trip up the Missouri River beyond the Mandan Villages in 1810–1811. After briefly fleeing the United States during the War of 1812, Nuttall returned to explore in the Southeast and the Southwest, traveling along the Arkansas River as far west as present-day Oklahoma. In late 1822, he received an appointment as curator of the botanic garden and lecturer in natural history at Harvard, where he remained for the next eleven years. In 1834, an increasingly restless Nuttall seized the opportunity to accompany Nathaniel Jarvis Wyeth's second expedition to Oregon. He collected specimens along the Pacific Coast and in Hawaii for the next two years before heading back East. In late 1841, Nuttall reluctantly returned to his native England to manage his late uncle's estate.

Nuttall's extensive western explorations became the basis for several important publications. His initial book, *The Genera of North American Plants* (1818), was the "first comprehensive study of American flora" (Thomas, p. 163) and firmly established his scientific reputation. Soon thereafter, Nuttall's friends encouraged him to publish an account of his nearly fatal expedition to the Southwest, *A Journal of Travels into the Arkansa Territory* (1821), which provided an invaluable portrait of frontier life in the region. Before returning to England, he completed the manuscript for a three-volume supplement to François André Michaux's *North American Sylva* (1842–1849), which stressed western species.

In conjunction with his teaching duties at Harvard, Nuttall authored a new textbook, *Introduction to Systematic and Physiological Botany* (1827). He also issued a two-volume *Manual of the Ornithology of the United States and of Canada* (1832, 1834), which combined a review of existing literature with his own field observations of avian habits. Nuttall's inexpensive, reliable, and delightfully written book was still being reprinted at the turn of the century. In 1873, Nuttall was posthumously honored by having the first ornithological club in the United States named after him.

In terms of the discovery and publication of new species, Nuttall was among the most productive naturalists in North American during the first third of the nineteenth century. Although hampered by a lack of surviving personal papers, Graustein has produced a definitive Nuttall biography that corrects numerous errors in earlier sketches. More recent studies by Porter and Greene outline the larger social and intellectual context within which Nuttall labored.

BIBLIOGRAPHY

Graustein, Jeannette E. *Thomas Nuttall, Naturalist: Explorations in America, 1808–1841.* Cambridge, MA: Harvard University Press, 1967.

Greene, John C. *American Science in the Age of Jefferson.* Ames: Iowa State University Press, 1984.

MacPhail, Ian. *Thomas Nuttall.* Sterling Morton Library Bibliographies in Botany and Horticulture 2. Lisle, IL: Morton Arboretum, 1983.

Nuttall, Thomas. *The Genera of North American Plants, and a Catalogue of the Species, to the Year 1817.* Philadelphia: D. Heartt, 1818.

———. *A Journal of Travels into the Arkansa Territory, During the Year 1819.* Philadelphia: Thomas H. Palmer, 1821.

———. *An Introduction to Systematic and Physiological Botany.* Cambridge, MA: Hilliard and Brown, 1827.

———. *A Manual of the Ornithology of the United States and of Canada: The Land Birds.* Cambridge, MA: Hilliard and Brown, 1832.

———. *A Manual of the Ornithology of the United States and of Canada: The Water Birds.* Boston: Hilliard, Gray and Co., 1834.

———. *The North American Sylva; or, A Description of the Forest Trees of the United States, Canada, and Nova Scotia, Not Described in the Work of F. Andrew Michaux.* 3 vols. Philadelphia: Smith and Wistar, 1842–1849.

Porter, Charlotte M. *The Eagle's Nest: Natural History and American Ideas, 1812–1842.* University, AL: University of Alabama Press, 1986.

Thomas, Phillip D. "Nuttall, Thomas." *Dictionary of Scientific Biography.* Edited by Charles C. Gillispie. New York: Scribners, 1974, 10:163–165.

Mark V. Barrow Jr.

Oak Ridge National Laboratory

Oak Ridge National Laboratory is one of ten multipurpose laboratories of the Department of Energy. Founded by the Manhattan Engineer District as Clinton Laboratories, a branch of the Metallurgical Laboratory at the University of Chicago in 1943, it primarily served as a uranium isotope separation and plutonium pilot plant during the war. Since that time, it has been operated by the University of Chicago and a variety of industrial contractors. Oak Ridge developed the electromagnetic, gaseous diffusion, and thermal isotope separation methods which provided the uranium for American nuclear weapons in World War II and produced and chemically separated plutonium on the gram scale to test the feasibility of the Hanford production reactors.

After World War II, the production plants, Y-12 and the Oak Ridge Gaseous Diffusion plant, were separated from the national laboratory, which was so designated by General Leslie R. Groves in 1946.

The X reactor, which served as a pilot plant for plutonium production, was used for isotope production after the war, when operation was transferred to the Monsanto Chemical Company. Oak Ridge also expanded into biomedical research at that time, and, under Eugene Wigner of Princeton, into metallurgy as well. Wigner also redirected the laboratory into reactor development, and built the Materials Testing Reactor and the Daniels Pile.

After the decision was made by the Atomic Energy Commission to consolidate reactor development at Argonne National Laboratory in 1947 and Union Carbide took over its operation in 1948, Oak Ridge became involved in Aircraft Nuclear Propulsion, the homogenous reactor project, and engineering of production technologies related to nuclear weapons.

With the Atomic Energy Act of 1954 transferring the burden of civilian reactor development to the private sector, Argonne diversified its activities into such fields as accelerator development and controlled thermonuclear reaction studies. In addition, it worked in such new fields as ecosystem analysis and radiation biology, and the Oak Ridge Technical Information Center pioneered the rise of information sciences. The act was modified to permit Oak Ridge to work with other federal agencies besides the Atomic Energy Commission, leading to further diversification.

Today, Oak Ridge National Laboratory works in a wide variety of disciplines. Its early work in radiation biology has served as a source of radiation protection practices advised by the International Commission on Radiological Protection (Eckerman and Hawthorne). It has become one of two centers for high-performance computing development in the Department of Energy. It continues a traditional role in reactor development, with an 85-MW High Flux Isotope Reactor producing isotopes for research and therapy, and a Tower Shielding Reactor to develop shielding for liquid metal reactors. It performs research in a variety of newer fields as well, including recombinant DNA research, superconductivity, heavy ion research, materials research, conservation and renewable energy sources, robotics, and intelligent systems.

Manuscripts from the Biology Division, 1955–1988, are in the University of Tennessee Special Collections, MS-1709.

O

BIBLIOGRAPHY

Eckerman, Keith F., and Alan R. Hawthorne. "ORNL's Impact on Radiation Protection Guidance." *Oak Ridge Review* 23:1 (1990): 64–72.

Johnson, Charles W., and Charles O. Jackson. *City behind a Fence; Oak Ridge, Tennessee, 1942–1946.* Knoxville: University of Tennessee Press, 1981.

Seidel, Robert W. "A Home for Big Science: The AEC and Its Laboratory System." *Historical Studies in the Physical and Biological Sciences* 16 (1986): 135–175.

Trivelpiece, Alvin W. "ORNL's Future Missions." *Oak Ridge Review* 23:3 (1990): 36–53.

Robert W. Seidel

Observatory

A building or other edifice that houses instruments used for the observation of celestial bodies. The term is also sometimes used for an institution that carries out astronomical research and teaching, whether or not observations are made on the premises. American observatories range in size from small buildings erected to house the telescopes of amateur astronomers to large tracts of land, often in isolated locations, on which several instruments have been installed.

Several structures built by Native Americans before the European discovery of America show a knowledge of astronomical phenomena, although records of their purpose and actual use are sparse. During the colonial era, particularly at the time of the transit of Venus in 1769, several residents of the Western Hemisphere made observations incorporated into European publications. However, no fixed observatories were erected in the United States until well into the nineteenth century. The observatory at Wesleyan College, founded in 1836, proved the first such observatory in the country to last for some years, although a short-lived observatory at the University of North Carolina preceded it in 1825. Encouraged, in part, by astronomical events such as the comet of 1843, Americans had built some fifteen fixed observatories by 1850. The federal government established the United States Naval Observatory in Washington, D.C., colleges large and small erected buildings to house telescopes, and concerned citizens funded municipal observatories. These new institutions were well suited for instruction, promoted more accurate navigation and timekeeping, and offered tangible symbols of prosperity and improvement. A few, such as the Harvard College Observatory, had instruments that rivaled the largest then available in Europe.

In the late nineteenth and early twentieth century, generous benefactors such as C.T. Yerkes, James Lick, Andrew Carnegie, and the Lowells of Boston made possible the construction of large telescopes in relatively isolated midwestern and western sites. Other funds were used to complement the national observatories of Latin American countries with southern stations of observatories in the United States. Harvard, for example, built the Boyden Station in Peru. The use of photography multiplied the number of observations that could be recorded by a single telescope, and several observatories hired special staff for data reduction. Some observatories became small communities, usually with a strict hierarchy in which separate roles were assigned to men and to women. The rise of astrophysics encouraged the incorporation of physical laboratories into some observatories. Observatories also assumed new roles, editing and publishing research contributions of staff, encouraging publications for both amateur and professional astronomers, hosting professional meetings, and providing both summer seminars and research opportunities for visitors from other institutions and for graduate students.

Buffeted by economic constraints during the depression of the 1930s, American observatories were affected even more severely by World War II. Staff members left to serve in the armed forces, do work as conscientious objectors, or participate in war-related projects. Those who remained found that research programs often gave way to teaching navigation or designing optical equipment. War not only fostered new technologies which would be applied in astronomy, but created new alliances between astronomers and officials of the federal government.

In the wake of World War II, and even more after the U.S.S.R. launched the *Sputnik* satellite in 1957, the American government became the foremost patron of American observatories. Staff of existing institutions negotiated individually with funding agencies such as the National Science Foundation and the National Aeronautics and Space Administration (NASA), rather than following the research program of an observatory director. New observatories carried out studies in planetary astronomy to satisfy the needs of federal patrons. The government also built a new national observatory dedicated to radio astronomy at Green Bank, West Virginia.

Although the vast majority of observatories are located on the ground, from the 1960s there have been a small number of "observatories" launched into space, particularly for the observation of the sun and distant stars, pulsars, and galaxies. In 1962, NASA launched its first "Orbiting Solar Observatory," a satellite laden with instruments for the study of X rays and the solar wind. Two Orbiting Astronomical Observatories were successfully launched, one in 1968 and the other in 1972, both with telescopes sensitive to ultraviolet light. Other observatories in space include the High Energy Astronomical Observatories of the period 1977–1981 and the Gamma Ray Observatory of the 1990s.

There is no single account of the history of observatories in the United States, although such a volume has been written for Canada. Several publications describe the staff, equipment, and research of single institutions, often from the perspective of longtime staff. Accounts of the "observatory movement" of the mid-nineteenth century date from the time of Elias Loomis. Historians have examined the debate about the control of these observatories as part of scientist's assertion of their expertise. There also has been discussion of the way in which astronomers used their skills in politics, navigation, and timekeeping to justify and finance observatories. Literature about Latin American observatories in English includes a discussion of the founding of several national observatories and an examination of the La Plata Observatory in Argentina as an example of cultural imperialism in the exact sciences.

Several articles describe sex roles in late-nineteenth- and early-twentieth-century observatories. Scattered discussions suggest the role of the summer school classes, publications, and social activities sponsored by single observatories. Other articles discuss wartime activities at Yerkes and at Harvard. Detailed studies of the way in which wartime attitudes and acquaintanceships influenced postwar observatories are just beginning. Much has been written about the influence of the space program, both in encouraging renewed interest in planetary astronomy and in financing specific spaceborne observatories.

BIBLIOGRAPHY

Howse, Derek. "The Greenwich List of Observatories: A World List of Astronomical Observatories, Instruments and Clocks, 1670–1850." *Journal for the History of Astronomy* 17 (1986): 1–89.

Hufbauer, Karl. *Exploring the Sun: Solar Science since Galileo.* Baltimore: Johns Hopkins University Press, 1991.

Jarrell, Richard A. *The Cold Light of Dawn: A History of Canadian Astronomy.* Toronto: University of Toronto Press, 1988.

Keenan, Phillip C. "The Earliest National Observatories in Latin America." *Journal for the History of Astronomy* 22 (1991): 21–30.

Lankford, John, and Rickey L. Slavings. "Gender in Science: Women in American Astronomy, 1859–1940." *Physics Today* 43, no. 3 (March 1990): 58–65.

Loomis, Elias. *The Recent Progress of Astronomy.* New York: Harper & Brothers, 1851.

Musto, David F. "A Survey of the American Observatory Movement, 1800–1850." *Vistas in Astronomy* 9 (1967): 87–92.

Needell, Alan. "The Carnegie Institution of Washington and Radio Astronomy: Prelude to an American National Observatory." *Journal for the History of Astronomy* 22 (1991): 55–67.

Pyenson, Lewis. *Cultural Imperialism and Exact Sciences: German Expansion Overseas, 1900–1930.* New York: Lang, 1985.

Rossiter, Margaret W. *Women Scientists in America: Struggles and Strategies to 1940.* Baltimore: Johns Hopkins University Press, 1982.

Rothenberg, Marc. "History of Astronomy." *Osiris*, 2d ser., 1 (1985): 117–131.

Smith, Robert W. *The Space Telescope: A Study of NASA Science, Technology, and Politics.* Cambridge, U.K.: Cambridge University Press, 1989.

Taterewicz, Joseph. *Space Technology and Planetary Astronomy.* Bloomington: Indiana University Press, 1990.

Tucker, Wallace H. *The Star Splitters: The High Energy Astronomy Observatories.* Washington, D.C.: National Aeronautics and Space Administration, 1984.

Warner, Deborah J. and Robert B. Ariail. *Alvan Clark & Sons: Artists in Optics.* Richmond, VA: Willmann-Bell; Washington, DC: National Museum of American History, Smithsonian Institution, 1995.

Peggy Kidwell

SEE ALSO
Astronomy and Astrophysics

Oceanography

The science that studies the ocean, its inhabitants, and its physical and chemical conditions. Since its emergence as a recognized scientific discipline, oceanography has been characterized less by the intellectual cohesiveness of a traditional academic discipline than by large-scale, multidisciplinary investigation of a complex and forbidding place. The term "oceanography" was not applied until the 1880s, at which point it still competed with the alternatives "thassalography" and "oceanology." Before scientists studied the ocean as a geographic

O

place with an integrated ecosystem, they investigated individual biological, physical, and chemical questions that related to the sea. European expansion promoted the study of marine phenomena, initiating a lasting link between commercial interests and oceanography. Institutional interest in the sea flourished briefly from 1660 to 1675, when Royal Society members, including Robert Hooke and Robert Boyle, discussed marine research, developed instruments to make observations at sea, and conducted experiments on seawater to discover its physical and chemical properties. Sailors and travelers continued to make scattered observations at sea, working from the research plan and equipment established by the society. In addition, tidal studies were prosecuted consistently from the late seventeenth century well into the nineteenth.

After decades of quiescence, the mid-eighteenth century saw a renewal of interest in marine phenomena. Participating in the eighteenth-century growth of astronomy, geophysics, chemistry, geology, and meteorology, investigators began making observations at sea as part of their scientific interest in other fields. Observers were initially traveling gentlemen, naturalists, or eclipse-expedition astronomers; later they were explorers. Starting with the voyages of Captain James Cook in the last third of the century, British exploration became characterized by attention to scientific observations. The amount of energy devoted to marine science depended on its significance to expedition members, but, in the last quarter of the century, the volume of experiments and observations made at sea increased. Virtually all ocean investigation during this time focused on temperature and salinity of water, reflecting the growth of chemical sciences. The concept of oceanic circulation sustained by differences in density, which was widely discussed in the early nineteenth century, emerged at this time. The study of waves became more important, while marine natural history continued. The emphasis on physical and chemical studies continued in the early nineteenth century. Curtailed exploration due to the American Revolutionary War and the Napoleonic Wars slowed work in marine science. The years 1815 to 1830 saw, however, another period of rapid expansion. Work focused largely on currents and salinity because marine science became intertwined with the arctic expeditions that searched for sperm whaling grounds and the Northwest Passage. Navigation and arctic exploration fanned curiosity about water temperature and pressure at depths.

Enthusiastic individuals, most frequently ships' captains such as William Scorseby, still carried on observation programs at sea, but the 1830s saw a decrease of interest in marine science by physical scientists, who turned to rival fields of discovery including meteorology and terrestrial magnetism. At this time, however, British zoologists directed particular attention to marine fauna, embarking on small boats and yachts to collect with dredges. Pursuit of new species as well as living relatives of fossilized ones impelled naturalists to reach deeper and deeper into the sea.

Beginning in the 1840s and increasingly during the 1850s, both British and American hydrographic institutions began deep-sea sounding experiments which were inspired by the promise of submarine telegraphy. The decades after 1840 saw the gradual awareness by scientists, sailors, entrepreneurs, and governments that the oceans' depths were commercially and intellectually important places to investigate. Unprecedented increase in popular awareness of the sea accompanied this trend. Prefaced by the rage for seaside vacations that railroad access to beaches initiated, cultural interest in the ocean was characterized by the popularity of marine natural history collecting and the new maritime novels as well as the vogue for yachting and the personal experiences of growing numbers of ocean travelers and emigrants. Submarine telegraphy and public interest in maritime issues helped scientists argue successfully for government funding of oceanographic voyages. Declining fisheries emphasized the need to know more about the biology of the seas.

Until 1840, Britain led marine science, although important work was conducted by investigators in other countries, especially northern ones. American marine science began to threaten British dominance after midcentury. Matthew Fontaine Maury, director of the United States Naval Observatory, was the first investigator to compile wind, current, and whale charts to improve navigation and commerce. He also dispatched the first Atlantic sounding voyages in the early 1850s. The United States Coast Survey began, under Alexander Dallas Bache's tenure, to include alongside routine charting work special studies such as detailed surveys of the Gulf Stream, microscopic examinations of bottom sediments, and dredging cruises with Louis and Alexander Agassiz. Spencer F. Baird, secretary of the Smithsonian Institution and United States Fish Commissioner, oversaw American efforts to study marine fauna. In Britain, in addition to Hydrographic

O

Office routine work and admiralty exploring expeditions, marine science centered around the British Association for the Advancement of Science Dredging Committee from 1839 until the mid-1860s, after which time a Royal Society-admiralty partnership took over the lead and dispatched a series of summer expeditions. These culminated in the four-year circumnavigation of HMS *Challenger* (1872–1876), the first expedition sent out with a mandate to study the world's oceans. Both the United States and Britain quickly followed the example of the Naples Zoological Station and set up coastal marine biological laboratories in the 1880s and 1890s.

In the last quarter of the nineteenth century, many nations sponsored oceanographic voyages modeled after the *Challenger's*. The United States, Russia, Germany, Norway, France, and Italy contributed to the effort to define the limits and contents of the oceans. Late in the nineteenth century, however, leadership in marine science shifted to Scandinavia. Mounting concerns about depleted fisheries inspired national efforts in many countries to study the biology of fish species as well as their migration. Sweden initiated the formation of what became, in 1902, the International Council for the Exploration of the Seas, which coordinated research undertaken by member nations. Although not a member, the United States also continued active biological research. Victor Henson's discovery of plankton and the subsequent realization of how to use physical oceanography to investigate the movements of fish populations gave oceanographers a method with which to study the ocean as an undivided system.

World War I disrupted the international community of oceanographers but provided the impetus for developing echo-sounding technology for submarine detection, which had been pioneered for ice detection, partly in response to the *Titanic* disaster. By the late 1920s, echo sounders revolutionized the study of underwater topography and helped scientists recognize the rift valleys of midocean ridges, showing them to be active, unstable regions. Although government funding of oceanographic research dropped back almost to prewar levels, the late 1920s saw the appearance of the first oceanographic institutions, sponsored mostly by foundations and private individuals. Scripps Institution changed its mission from biological research to oceanography in 1925 and, five years later, the Woods Hole Oceanographic Institution was established on the Atlantic coast. Economic depression affected practical

government science such as fisheries research as well as private projects, so oceanographic work, which was particularly expensive, slowed down dramatically until preparations began for World War II.

As with other sciences, World War II partnerships helped forge a new relationship between governments and oceanography. Oceanographic work during and after the war carried the imprint of wartime government support and policy in both its problem selection and its scale. Physical studies gained and maintained precedence over biological ones. The areas of inquiry promoted by wartime efforts related to submarine and antisubmarine tactics. New research began on underwater acoustics, while ocean floor sediment charts were compiled from existing data. Wave studies also received precedence for their value in predicting surf conditions for landings. After the war, oceanographers and institutions, newly accustomed to generous funding, learned to accept and even encourage government support. Oceanography became characterized by large-scale, expensive research projects such as the 1960s deep-sea drilling by proponents of the theory of seafloor spreading. Oceanography's multifaceted attempt to understand the oceans as integrated biological and physical environments has made it attractive to ecologically and environmentally minded scientists since the 1970s and 1980s, resulting in projects such as Sea-Lab as well as studies of the ocean's role in global warming and weather production. The development of autonomous deep-diving vehicles, an international endeavor, has brought the greatest depths into sharper focus.

BIBLIOGRAPHY
Deacon, Margaret. *Scientists and the Sea, 1650–1900: A Study of Marine Science.* London: Academic Press, 1971.
Mills, Eric. *Biological Oceanography: An Early History, 1870–1960.* Ithaca: Cornell University Press, 1989.
Schlee, Susan. *On the Edge of an Unfamiliar World: A History of Oceanography.* New York: E.P. Dutton, 1973.
Helen M. Rozwadowski

Office of Naval Research, United States

A federal agency created in 1946 to promote scientific research in and out of the navy. As a major source of financial support for academic basic research, especially in its early years, the Office of Naval Research (ONR) played a key role in American science policy in the post–World War II period. The driving personalities

O

behind the establishment of the ONR during World War II included Vice Admiral Harold G. Bowen, former head of the Naval Research Laboratory (NRL), who wanted the ONR to develop nuclear propulsion for the navy, and several reserve naval officers with technical background, known as the "Bird Dogs," who sought to continue the close and fruitful wartime cooperation between the military and university scientists. The Bird Dogs' vision soon dominated the ONR's mission when Bowen lost the battle for nuclear propulsion to the Bureau of Ships. Although formally headed by a naval oficer, civilian scientists administered the ONR, with the help of a Naval Research Advisory Committee composed of prominent scientists outside the navy. What distinguished the ONR from other funding agencies was its liberal support of research projects at universities, other nonprofit institutions, and industrial laboratories, usually through contracts. The great latitude the ONR allowed in the choice of research topics, often without direct military or naval relevance, and in the use of funds, allayed the fear of scientists of undue bureaucratic and military control. The encompassing coverage of all major scientific fields made the ONR into an "Office of National Research" before the founding of the National Science Foundation in 1950. Besides its extramural progams, the ONR also supervised the NRL and other intramural projects and operated several branch offices, including one at London and another at Tokyo.

The ONR's patronage of academic basic research was not without its critics. In the late 1940s, naval officers questioned the necessity of such effort when the navy's budget for research and development was being cut back. Although the Korean War and the *Sputnik* crisis in the 1950s helped the ONR deflect such criticism, the agency became more cautious in its justification for such support. In the 1960s, the ONR's research support programs, like those in many other government agencies, suffered from the deteriorating relationship between the military and the universities caused by the Vietnam War.

Historians have debated whether the ONR's apparent generosity made American scientists feel more autonomous from military control than they actually were during the Cold War. Critics of the postwar science-military relationship argue that such ONR support, with "no strings attached" formed only part of the military design to attract scientists into more practical and military-relevant research. Pure research was also supported, with long-term military applications in mind and with harmful effects on the development of scientific disciplines. In response, other historians have pointed to the diversion toward practical topics as a healthy development of a scientific discipline and to many scientists' willingness to contribute to the American defense effort during the Cold War. More detailed studies of the scientific research sponsored by the ONR, of scientists' attitude toward military patronage, and of the audience-specific rhetoric and justification for military support of science employed by scientists and science administrators are needed for a better understanding and evaluation of the ONR's role in the development of American science.

BIBLIOGRAPHY

Forman, Paul. "Behind Quantum Mechanics: National Security as Basis for Physical Research in the United States, 1940–1960." *Historical Studies in the Physical and Biological Sciences* 18 (1987): 149–229.

Sapolsky, Harvey M. *Science and the Navy: The History of the Office of Naval Research.* Princeton: Princeton University Press, 1990.

Schweber, Samuel S. "The Mutual Embrace of Science and the Miltiary: ONR and the Growth of Physics in the United States after World War II." In *Science, Technology and the Military,* edited by Everett Mendelsohn, M. Roe Smith, and Peter Weingert. Boston: Kluwer Academic, 1988, pp. 3–45.

Zuoyue Wang

Office of Scientific Research and Development

Principal agency for the mobilization of civilian science and engineering in the United States during World War II. By the end of the war, the Office of Scientific Research and Development (OSRD) had spent nearly half a billion dollars and accelerated a revolution in modern warfare. From OSRD-sponsored research in university and industrial laboratories came a host of new and improved weapons, including radar and the proximity fuse that helped create a new electronic combat environment. Other contributions included rockets and high explosives; the Dukw and the Weasel; medical advances such as antimalarial drugs, blood substitutes, and the quantity production of penicillin. OSRD's most notorious involvement was with the atomic bomb, for which the agency bore primary responsibility until its transfer to the army at the end of 1942. By and large, OSRD was a great if somewhat ironic success. For while it helped bring about a new age dominated by federal patronage and preoccupied with military research and development, its creation had been shaped by an older, conservative belief in limited government and the primacy of private enterprise.

The National Defense Research Committee, OSRD's parent organization, was established by presidential order on 27 June 1940. Largely the effort of the Massachusetts Institute of Technology engineer Vannevar Bush, its initial members were Bush himself, Karl Compton, James Conant, Frank Jewett, Conway Coe, Richard Tolman, Rear Admiral Harold Bowen, and Brigadier General George Strong. The committee was reorganized in 1941 with an enlarged mandate which included development and responsibility for medical research. By war's end, OSRD was staffed by more than 1,400 and had let over 2,000 contracts totaling almost $500,000,000. While not the only sponsor of wartime research and development (its share of the R and D budget was approximately 30 percent), it did manage through adroit maneuvering and effective action to dominate scientific mobilization.

OSRD'S work was facilitated by key early decisions. First, in contrast to World War I, Bush determined to rely upon existing private facilities rather than newly built and federally managed laboratories. Second, mobilization was to be managed by civilians familiar with private sector strengths, frequently serving "without compensation" and thus free of political and bureaucratic ties. Third, the agency would operate contractually, in the manner of the marketplace. The contract was doubly crucial to OSRD's achievements, not least of which was the rapid enlistment of private sector leaders and resources. The contract guaranteed centralized control of the agency's programs and funded them in a manner that respected traditional boundaries between the state and private enterprise. Lastly, Bush established close liaison with the military. That partnership was fraught with tension and hindered by bureaucratic jealousies; but by 1945, military men had come to depend on the nation's scientists.

OSRD'S influence on postwar developments was mixed. In November 1944, President Roosevelt asked Bush to report on the requirements of future national science policy: *Science—The Endless Frontier* was delivered to President Truman in July 1945. In the report, Bush argued for the establishment of a new civilian-controlled science agency to manage the massive federal support for civilian and military R and D that

postwar national security implied. While the report quickly became a best-seller, its ambitious hopes for the unified oversight of civilian and military research was attained only in part and with great difficulty. Federal sponsorship, indeed, grew dramatically in the decade after the war, but none of the agencies influenced by OSRD entirely satisfied Bush's requirements. The Atomic Energy Commission, created quickly in 1946, was narrow in focus and tightly constrained by the needs of the military and national defense; the National Science Foundation, finally established in 1950 after five years of political controversy, proved modest in scope, budget, and authority; and attempts to unify military R and D in any manner whatever fell victim to territorial squabbles within the military itself.

OSRD's greatest impact might have come in the realm of political economy, for Bush's agency helped undermine the traditionally antagonistic relationship between the state and the private sector. Indeed, many in the younger and less conservative generation, for whom wartime patronage proved exciting if not addictive, welcomed the new linkage between government, national security, and institutional growth. Furthermore, the cooperation between scientists and military men fostered by OSRD survived the war and contributed to the development of the military-industrial-university complex. Not least, OSRD helped convince the military that future security rested on new and improved weapons. The "Star Wars" defense shield and other federally funded, large-scale, hugely expensive, "high tech" weapons systems like the B-2 Stealth bomber are only recent examples of a military faith in technology encouraged by the success of OSRD.

BIBLIOGRAPHY

Baxter, James Phinney III. *Scientists Against Time.* Boston: Little, Brown and Company, 1946.

Goldberg, Stanley. "Inventing a Climate of Opinion: Vannevar Bush and the Decision to Build the Bomb." *Isis* 83 (1992): 429–452.

Kevles, Daniel. "Principles and Politics in Federal R&D Policy, 1945–1990: An Appreciation of the Bush Report." In *Science—The Endless Frontier. A Report to the President on a Program for Postwar Scientific Research,* edited by Vannevar Bush. 1945. Reprint Washington, DC: National Science Foundation, 1990.

Owens, Larry. "MIT and the Federal 'Angel': Academic R&D and Federal-Private Cooperation before World War II." *Isis* 81 (1990): 189–213.

O

Pursell, Carroll. "Science Agencies in World War Two: The OSRD and Its Challengers." In *The Sciences in the American Context: New Perspectives,* edited by Nathan Reingold. Washington, DC: Smithsonian Institution Press, 1979, pp. 359–399.

Reingold, Nathan. "Vannevar Bush's New Deal for Research: Or the Triumph of the Old Order." *Historical Studies in the Physical and Biological Sciences* 17 (1987): 299–344.

Stewart, Irwin. *Organizing Scientific Research for War: The Administrative History of the Office of Scientific Research and Development.* 1948.

Larry Owens

Oppenheimer, J. Robert (1904–1967)

Theoretical physicist and science administrator. Born in New York City into a well-to-do family, Oppenheimer received his early education at the private Ethical Culture School. Oppenheimer graduated summa cum laude from Harvard College in 1925, after only three years of study. He then studied physics in Europe, receiving his Ph.D. at the University of Göttingen in 1927. After two years of postdoctoral study in the United States and abroad, he joined the faculties of both the University of California at Berkeley and the California Institute of Technology in Pasadena. From 1942 to 1945, he was director of the Los Alamos Laboratory where the atomic bomb was developed. From 1947 until shortly before his death, he was director of the Institute for Advanced Study in Princeton, New Jersey.

Even as young child, Oppenheimer gave evidence of his ability to grasp new ideas quickly and to pursue his own intellectual interests. Before entering Harvard College he had read so extensively in physics that he was allowed to take courses above the normal freshman level. His European studies came just at the time physics was undergoing its quantum mechanical revolution. He stood out among the large number of students from the United States and other countries, impressing Max Born to the extent that Born accepted him as a Ph.D. candidate. Oppenheimer's dissertation used the new quantum mechanics, and he subsequently published a number of additional papers in that field.

Among several offers of a faculty position at American universities, Oppenheimer chose to go to California, where he divided the academic year between Berkeley and Pasadena. A whole new American school of theoretical physics was growing up in California around Oppenheimer. In addition to his teaching duties, he interacted broadly with his students and with other faculty members in various fields, including experimental physics. During the 1930s, Oppenheimer became aware for the first time of social and political problems at home and abroad. He became an active supporter of many left-wing groups and associated with members of the American Communist Party.

In 1942, when the United States decided to actively pursue a program for building an atomic bomb, Leslie Groves, the military commander of the Manhattan Project, chose Oppenheimer to direct the central laboratory for the project. The required isolation and secrecy would be available, Oppenheimer knew, at Los Alamos, New Mexico. Many accounts have been written of the dramatically successful enterprise that brought an end to World War II. All agree that the Los Alamos community was a complex society coping with many physical and social problems and that Oppenheimer did a superb job as director, for which, in 1946, he was awarded the United States Medal for Merit.

Oppenheimer resigned from his directorship in October 1945 to return to teaching for a time before moving to Princeton as director of the Institute for Advanced Study. However, in the postwar years, he was increasingly in demand in Washington to serve as a member of, or consultant to, many committees dealing with domestic and international problems surrounding the further exploitation of atomic energy. For this, he held the highest security clearance. Among those committees was the Atomic Energy Commission (AEC).

In the 1950s, the United States faced pressing questions and concerns associated with the military might of the Soviet Union and the defense measurers appropriate for the United States. Security and loyalty were of prime consideration. Oppenheimer came under scrutiny based on his opposition to the building of the much more powerful hydrogen bomb and on the fact that he had long ago associated with known Communists. As early as 1948, Oppenheimer's security clearance for the AEC was reviewed but continued until suspended in December 1953. In the spring of 1954, Oppenheimer was subjected to a hearing before the Personnel Security Board of the AEC, resulting in a 4–1 vote not to restore his clearance.

Full transcripts and analyses of that hearing have been published showing the strange, quasi-legal nature of the proceedings and the devastating personal effect the ordeal had on Oppenheimer. For the most part, the physics community rallied to his defense. An exception was Edward Teller, a strong proponent of thermo-nuclear energy with whom Oppenheimer had long disagreed on the hydrogen bomb. Further damaging evidence concerned Oppenheimer's having not been completely truthful about a Communist probe made to him by Haakon Chevalier in the early 1940s. After 1954, Oppenheimer was isolated from the United States government until, as a conciliatory gesture, President Lyndon Johnson presented him with the Fermi Medal in 1964.

Oppenheimer's position continued at the Institute for Advanced Study after a vote of confidence by its Board of Trustees. He made the institute an intellectual center for both established scholars and for young aspirants in many fields. Known in his later years as a kind of elder statesman and spokesman in science, Oppenheimer lectured widely on the role of science in human culture.

Much has been written and produced on television about Oppenheimer, the man, and his role in the history of the twentieth century. As yet no full, scholarly biography has been published. George Kennan, an institute fellow, has characterized him in part as follows: "He was one of the few people who could combine in one intellectual and aesthetic personality vast scientific knowledge, impressive erudition in the humanities, and an active, sophisticated interest in the international-political affairs of his own time" (Kennan, p. 18).

BIBLIOGRAPHY

Chevalier, Haakon. *Oppenheimer: The Story of a Friendship.* New York: George Braziller, 1965.

Goodchild, Peter. *J. Robert Oppenheimer: Shatterer of Worlds.* New York: Fromm International, 1985.

Holton, Gerald. "The Trials of J. Robert Oppenheimer." Chap. 10 in *Einstein, History and Other Passions.* New York: American Institute of Physics, 1995, pp. 205–220.

Kennan, George F. *Memoirs 1950–1963.* Vol. 2. Boston: Atlantic Monthly, 1972.

Kunetka, James W. *Oppenheimer: The Years of Risk.* Englewood Cliffs, NJ: Prentice Hall, 1982.

Oppenheimer, J. Robert. *Science and the Common Understanding.* New York: Simon and Schuster, 1953.

———. *Atom and Void: Essays on Science and Community.* Princeton: Princeton University Press, 1989.

Pierls, Rudolf. "Oppenheimer, J. Robert." *Dictionary of Scientific Biography.* Edited by Charles C. Gillispie. New York: Scribner, 1974, 10:213–218.

Rabi, I.I., Robert Serber, Victor F. Weisskopf, Abraham Pais, and Glen T. Seaborg. *Oppenheimer.* New York: Scribner, 1969.

Smith, Alice K., and Charles Weiner, eds. *Robert Oppenheimer, Letters and Recollections.* Cambridge, MA: Harvard University Press, 1980.

Stern, Philip M., with collaboration of Harold P. Green. *The Oppenheimer Case: Security on Trial.* New York: Harper and Row, 1969.

York, Herbert. *The Advisors: Oppenheimer, Teller and the Superbomb.* San Francisco: Freeman, 1976.

Katherine R. Sopka

SEE ALSO

Atomic Energy Commission; Institute for Advanced Study

Ornithology

Until the early twentieth century, determining precisely which avian species resided within the boundaries of the United States was the primary goal of American ornithology. The enterprise generally took the form of amassing skin collections and publishing illustrations, descriptions, and sometimes simply the names of North American species. Explorers, missionaries, and colonists often mentioned birds, especially game species, in travel accounts, local histories, and resource inventories of particular areas. Gradually, this haphazard approach gave way to more systematic study.

As with other cultural pursuits, American natural history was initially dependent on European naturalists, patronage, and traditions. This colonial phase of activity reached its apogee with the work of the British naturalist Mark Catesby, generally considered the "founder of American ornithology." His two-volume *Natural History of Carolina, Florida, and the Bahama Islands* (1731–1743) contained hand-colored engravings and descriptions of 109 North American bird species.

At the end of the eighteenth century, a more indigenous school of American ornithology began to take root around the Philadelphia naturalist William Bartram. His influential *Travels* (1791) included a list of 215 North American birds, and the Bartram homestead became a mecca for naturalists living in or traveling through the area. One frequent visitor was the Scottish immigrant Alexander Wilson, who undertook an ambitious project to illustrate and describe every American bird species at Bartram's persistent urging. Although lacking in formal training either as an artist or a naturalist, Wilson scoured the nation's eastern seaboard to find the material and subscribers needed to complete nine volumes of his *American Ornithology*

O

(1808–1814). Before his premature death, he had treated 264 American species, including 48 that are currently recognized as new to science at the time.

Wilson was soon overshadowed by America's most famous artist-naturalist, John James Audubon. His folio edition of *Birds of America* (1827–1838) contained 435 exquisite, life-sized, color bird portraits. Although brilliant, Audubon was more of an artist than a scientist: he required assistance to complete the technical portions of his *Ornithological Biography* (1831–1839), the text that accompanied the folio plates, and his drawings often sacrificed accuracy for aesthetic effect.

During this period, the first significant bird collections in the United States were initiated. Wilson relied on specimens in Charles Willson Peale's Philadelphia museum, established in 1794, to complete his *American Ornithology*. Between 1812 and 1850, officials at the Academy of Natural Sciences of Philadelphia, the Boston Society of Natural History, the Museum of Comparative Zoology at Harvard, and the Smithsonian Institution in Washington began more enduring ornithological collections. These and later museums became centers of ornithological activity in this country and provided the few paid positions available to ornithologists until the early twentieth century.

During the second half of the nineteenth century, individuals amassed private collections as large as 60,000 specimens, and new urban museums, like the American Museum of Natural History in New York, the Field Museum in Chicago, and the Carnegie Museum in Pittsburgh, were established. Both private and institutionally affiliated collectors tended to stress North American species and both depended on the sale, donation, and exchange of specimens through vast networks of correspondents. These two developments reached their fullest expression with the Smithsonian's Spencer F. Baird, who built an expansive collecting network that included hundreds of naturalists, soldiers, sportsmen, and individuals attached to expeditions throughout the North American continent.

The creation of societies devoted to birds was another important form of institutionalization. The first was the Nuttall Ornithological Club, established in Cambridge, Massachusetts, in 1873. A decade later, three Nuttall Club members created the American Ornithologists' Union (AOU). The new organization was dominated by more technically oriented ornithologists who sought to reform scientific nomenclature,

adopt the American version of the subspecies concept, and carve out professional space for the practice of scientific ornithology. By 1900, there were dozens of ornithological societies in the United States, including the Wilson Ornithological Club and the Cooper Ornithological Club. At the same time, a new kind of organization, the bird club, also came into existence. Bird clubs were closely affiliated with Audubon (bird protection) societies and focused more on observing than collecting birds.

With the advent of graduate programs in ornithology in the early twentieth century, self-training and apprenticeship soon gave way to more broadly based, formal, and systematic education. A pioneering figure in this transformation was Arthur A. Allen, who established one of the first and most productive graduate programs at Cornell in the 1920s. Within a decade Berkeley, Michigan, and Western Reserve also had active programs and the number has continued to rise since that time. University-trained ornithologists were more likely to pursue ecological, behavioral, and physiological studies than the more traditional descriptive taxonomic research that had previously dominated ornithology. After graduation, they typically found employment as museum curators, teachers, and wildlife managers.

Clearly the scope and scale of ornithological activity in the United States has broadened significantly since its modest beginnings in the colonial period. Yet, like natural history more generally, American ornithology has failed to gain the serious historical attention it deserves. There are relatively few studies authored by professionally trained historians and even fewer by historians of science. Developments in ornithology are sometimes discussed in scientific biographies, museum histories, exploration accounts, and more general studies of American science, but very little has been written about twentieth-century trends.

BIBLIOGRAPHY

Allen, Elsa G. "The History of Ornithology before Audubon." *Transactions of the American Philosophical Society,* n.s., 41 (1951): 387–591.

Audubon, John James. *The Birds of America.* 4 vols. Edinburgh, 1827–1838.

Barrow, Mark V., Jr., *A Passion for Birds: American Ornithology after Audubon.* Princeton: Princeton University Press, 1998.

Bartram, William. *Travels thorugh North and South Carolina, Georgia, East and West Florida.* Philadelphia: James and Johnson, 1791.

Catesby, Mark. *The Natural History of Carolina, Florida, and the Bahama Islands.* 2 vols. London, 1731–1743.

Chapman, Frank M., and Theodore S. Palmer, eds. *Fifty Years' Progress in American Ornithology, 1883–1933.* Lancaster, PA: American Ornithologists' Union, 1933.

Cutright, Paul, and Micheal Boardman. *Elliott Coues: Naturalist and Frontier Historian.* Urbana: University of Illinois Press, 1981.

Davis, William E., Jr., and Jerome A. Jackson, eds. *Contributions to the History of North American Ornithology.* Cambridge, MA: Nuttall Ornithological Club, 1995.

Kastner, Joseph. *A World of Watchers: An Informal History of the American Passion for Birds.* New York: Alfred A. Knopf, 1986.

Mayr, Ernst. "Materials for a History of American Ornithology." In *Ornithology from Aristotle to the Present,* edited by Erwin Stresemann; translated. by Hans J. and Cathleen Epstein. Cambridge, MA: Harvard University Press, 1975, pp. 365–396.

Welker, Robert H. *Birds and Men: American Birds in Science, Art, Literature, and Conservation, 1800–1900.* Cambridge, MA: Harvard University Press, 1955.

Wilson, Alexander. *American Ornithology; or, The Natural History of the Birds of the United States.* 9 vols. Philadelphia: Bradford and Inskeep, 1808–1814.

Mark V. Barrow Jr.

Osborn, Henry Fairfield (1857–1935)

Paleontologist and museum administrator. Born in Fairfield, Connecticut, Osborn attended Princeton University from 1873 to 1877. Influenced by Princeton president James McCosh, Osborn pursued a career in science. Following a year of graduate study at Princeton, he did additional course work in biology in England. In 1881, Osborn joined the Princeton faculty and for ten years taught comparative anatomy and embryology. In 1891, he was appointed to positions at Columbia University and the American Museum of Natural History. At Columbia he created the Department of Biology, where he taught until retiring in 1910. At the museum, Osborn, after developing a successful program in vertebrate paleontology, served as president from 1908 to 1933. As president of the New York Zoological Society from 1893 to 1926, he created and administered the Bronx Zoo. In 1928, he was president of the American Association for the Advancement of Science.

Osborn's scientific work focused on paleontology and evolution. At Princeton, he and William Berryman Scott created a small but active research program in vertebrate paleontology. At the American Museum, Osborn and his assistants developed large collections that enabled him to publish extensively on fossil vertebrates. Among his most important works were *The Age of Mammals* (1910), *The Titanotheres of Ancient Wyoming, Dakota, and Nebraska* (1929), and *Proboscidea* (1936, 1942). Osborn also published technical and popular articles on dinosaurs.

Osborn closely examined the causes and patterns of evolution. In the 1880s, he explained evolution in neo-Lamarckian terms, as a result of the use and disuse of parts and the inheritance of acquired characteristics. He later interpreted evolution as a gradual unfolding of characters that proceeded in determinate, linear directions. Applying his ideas to fossils, he described the evolution of horses, elephants, and titanotheres as series of multiple, parallel lines of descent. He rejected genetics and his views exacerbated the differences between paleontology and experimental biology in the early twentieth century.

Osborn explained human evolution not as a branching tree of life, but a series of separate histories and replacements. In *Men of the Old Stone Age* (1915), paleolithic hominids were not ancestors of modern humans, but different species that had gone extinct. In the 1920s, Osborn responded to William Jennings Bryan's fundamentalist attack by separating human from simian evolution. While incorporating data from the fossil record, he interpreted evolution as a progressive, purposeful process that upheld traditional social values and religious beliefs.

Osborn's views influenced his administrative efforts at the museum. By promoting expeditions and developing collections, he established the world's premier program in vertebrate paleontology. His department was a research center as well as a showcase of innovative exhibits that attracted public attention and influenced developments at other institutions. As president, he made the entire museum an extension of his views. The Hall of the Age of Man incorporated Osborn's interpretation of human evolution. His interest in outdoor research justified worldwide explorations as well as massive displays designed to teach the public about nature and nature's laws. Few accepted Osborn's evolutionary interpretations, but through his recognition of important scientific problems and his ability to obtain financial support and orchestrate large projects, he made the American Museum a major center for research and public education.

O

Most studies of Osborn examine only part of his multifarious career. Books on the Cope-Marsh feud discuss his role in that issue. Works on American social and political history refer to his views on eugenics and immigration restriction. Autobiographies by students or associates describe his personality and administrative role, and one history explains how he helped transform the museum but provides little analysis of his scientific work. The most recent study explains Osborn's scientific and institutional work in terms of his social and political commitments and in light of the peripheral role of museums and vertebrate paleontology in early-twentieth-century American science.

BIBLIOGRAPHY

Kennedy, John Michael. "Philanthrophy and Science in New York City: The American Museum of Natural History, 1868–1968." Ph.D. diss., Yale University, 1968.

Osborn, Henry Fairfield. *The Age of Mammals in Europe, Asia, and North America.* New York: Macmillan, 1910.

———. *Men of the Old Stone Age: Their Environment, Life and Art.* New York: Scribners, 1915.

———. *The Earth Speaks to Bryan.* New York: Scribners, 1925.

———. *The Titanotheres of Ancient Wyoming, Dakota, and Nebraska.* 2 vols. Washington, DC: Government Printing Office, 1929.

———. *Proboscidea: A Monograph of the Discovery, Evolution, Migration and Extinction of the Elephants and Mastodonts of the World.* New York: American Museum Press, 1936, 1942.

Rainger, Ronald. *An Agenda for Antiquity: Henry Fairfield Osborn and Vertebrate Paleontology at the American Museum of Natural History. 1890–1935.* Tuscaloosa: University of Alabama Press, 1991.

Ronald Rainger

SEE ALSO

American Museum of Natural History

Owen, David Dale (1807–1860)

Geologist. Born in New Lanark, Scotland, Owen was educated in Hofwyl, Switzerland (1824–1826), where he studied natural history, and Glasgow, where he studied chemistry for a year. He emigrated to the United States in November 1827 and arrived at his destination, New Harmony, Indiana, in January 1828. Although the socialist utopian community established there by his father Robert in 1824 had failed, the town, led by geologist William Maclure's Education Society was still dedicated to social change. However, Owen discovered that because the community had not developed as anticipated, it did not need his services as a chemist. He moved to New York City in 1830 to work as a printer and then traveled to England, where he studied chemistry and geology at the University of London. In 1833, he returned to New Harmony, where he continued his chemical research, in part using homemade equipment and reagents. He delivered a series of popular scientific lectures at New Harmony in 1833–1834. Having become interested in geology, he attended the Medical College of Ohio (1835–1837) to study anatomy and physiology to strengthen his paleontological research. He graduated in 1837 but never practiced medicine.

Owen's career as a geologist began when he was appointed to lead the first geological survey of Indiana in 1837. He then surveyed the mineral lands in parts of Wisconsin, Illinois, and Iowa (1839–1840), and the Chippewa lands in Iowa, Wisconsin, and Minnesota (1847–1852) for the federal government's General Land Office. Later, he served overlapping terms as state geologist for Kentucky (1854–1860), Arkansas (1857–1860), and Indiana (1859–1860). His surveys were characterized by superb organization and attention to matters of economic as well as scientific significance. In the reports (which were his major publications), he accurately described the stratigraphy and structure of the territory he studied and correlated his stratigraphic results with those of European geologists.

Owen was part of a remarkable scientific community at New Harmony, where he trained a generation of geological surveyors. His assistants led geological surveys in seven states and worked for various departments of the federal government, including the United States Coast Survey. His influence as the head of what amounted to a research school for training field geologists deserves to be examined—particularly with reference to its location in a community uniquely dedicated to science and social reform. In this connection, it should be noted that Maclure supported female education and Owen's sister, Jane Dale Owen Fauntleroy, a knowledgeable scientist in her own right, was also an important influence on the New Harmony geologists. For a full list of Owen's publications and the location of his manuscripts, see the biography by Walter B. Hendrickson.

BIBLIOGRAPHY

Friis, Herman R. "The David Dale Owen Map of Southwestern Wisconsin." *Prologue* 1 (1969): 9–21.

O

Hendrickson, Walter Brookfield. *David Dale Owen: Pioneer Geologist of the Middle West.* Indiana Historical Collections 27. Indianapolis: Indiana Historical Bureau, 1943.

Nelson, Katherine G. "Environment for Discovery—The Owen Survey of Wisconsin." *Transactions of the Wisconsin Academy* 64 (1976): 173–179.

Porter, Charlotte M. *The Eagle's Nest: Natural History and American Ideas, 1812–1842.* Tuscaloosa, AL: University of Alabama Press, 1986.

Daniel Goldstein

P

Packard, Alpheus Spring, Jr. (1839–1905)

Zoologist, entomologist, and proponent of neo-Lamarckian evolutionary theory. Packard grew up in Maine and attended Bowdoin College. In 1861, he began the study of entomology at the Lawrence Scientific School under Louis Agassiz. From 1862 to 1864, he was an assistant under Agassiz in the Museum of Comparative Zoology. Packard then worked for several educational institutions and government agencies. He became professor of zoology and geology at Brown University, in 1878, a position he held until his death.

Packard's research extended to insect classification, applied entomology, and invertebrate embryology. Deeply religious, and adhering to the idealist morphology he had learned from Agassiz, Packard was slow to be convinced of evolution. About 1870, however, study of the embryological development of *Limulus* (the horseshoe crab) caused him to follow Edward Drinker Cope and Alpheus Hyatt in accepting a theory of evolution based on the acceleration and retardation of development. Agassiz's principle of recapitulation, whereby the life history of each organism recapitulates the history of life, was recast in evolutionary terms: recapitulation occurs because each stage of an organism's life history results from the inheritance of characteristics acquired in response to conditions present at that stage.

Packard developed his views on evolution through studies of blind fish, crayfish, and other cave fauna, described in a series of papers published from 1871 to 1902. These studies helped convince him that the physical environment was the chief agent of evolution, inducing organisms to become better adapted to their environment. Evolution is therefore progressive, a conclusion consistent with Packard's belief that evolution follows divine guidance. He accordingly drew away, after the 1870s, from the theories of Cope and Hyatt, which postulated nonadaptive evolutionary trends.

Packard linked his evolutionary views to Lamarck, writing a biography of Lamarck, and coining the term "neo-Lamarckism." He thereby helped establish the distinctive identity of this first American school of evolutionary theory. His advocacy of Lamarckian evolution and criticism of neo-Darwinism became increasingly strident, reflecting the polarization between these schools that had developed by the 1890s.

Packard's work therefore reflects several aspects of nineteenth-century American zoological thought. His study of comparative anatomy and embryology places him within a tradition of classical morphology, once significant, but of waning importance by the time of his death. His work illustrates Agassiz's influence on his students' ideas about evolution. His use of cave fauna as evidence for neo-Lamarckian evolution stimulated interest in Lamarck; this interest declined after Packard's death.

BIBLIOGRAPHY

Bocking, Stephen. "Alpheus Spring Packard and Cave Fauna in the Evolution Debate." *Journal of the History of Biology* 21 (1988) 425–456.

Bowler, Peter. *The Eclipse of Darwinism.* Baltimore: Johns Hopkins University Press, 1983.

Cockerell, T.D.A. "Alpheus Spring Packard." *Biographical Memoirs of the National Academy of Sciences* 9 (1920): 180–236.

P

Packard, Alpheus S. "The Cave Fauna of North America, with Remarks on the Anatomy of the Brain and Origin of the Blind Species." *Memoirs of the National Academy of Sciences* 9 (1888): 1–156.

Stephen Bocking

Paleontology

The study of fossils has been an important aspect of American science for over 200 years. Early scientific interest in paleontology was centered in Philadelphia. There, Thomas Jefferson established an important collection of fossil vertebrates, principally mastodon remains found in Kentucky. Jefferson and members of the American Philosophical Society also actively discussed problems of evolution, extinction, and geographical distribution posed by fossil remains. In 1800, Charles Willson Peale excavated mastodon remains in New Jersey and later displayed them in his museum. Philadelphia's Academy of Natural Sciences likewise fostered paleontology. Richard Harlan gained international recognition for his work on extinct mammals and reptiles, and in the 1830s, Samuel George Morton argued persuasively for reliance on fossils, rather than rocks, to determine the age of geological strata. His invertebrate fossil collection made the Philadelphia academy the leading center for the science in the first half of the nineteenth century.

During the antebellum period, geological surveys were an important boon to paleontology. Reconnaissance work by state geologists in Ohio, Indiana, and Wisconsin brought new specimens to light. New York State Geologist James Hall identified hundreds of fossils, promoted other state surveys, and trained many nineteenth-century geologists and paleontologists. Federal surveys sponsored by the army and the General Land Office provided an important training ground for John Strong Newberry, Ferdinand V. Hayden, and Fielding Bradford Meek. Specimens collected on those expeditions went to the Smithsonian Institution's Joseph Henry and Spencer Fullerton Baird, who sent them to specialists, thereby developing scientific networks and further promoting paleontology.

After the Civil War, the creation of national surveys profoundly influenced American paleontology. Meek worked intermittently for Clarence King's Fortieth Parallel Survey, while Hayden's Geological Survey of the Territories provided new opportunities for invertebrate as well as vertebrate paleontologists. Although Joseph Leidy and Edward Drinker Cope had been studying fossil vertebrates since the 1860s, Hayden's expeditions gave them access to fossil deposits in the West. Cope particularly took advantage of that opportunity and by the early 1870s was describing new discoveries with abandon. Yale's Othniel Charles Marsh developed his own expeditions and uncovered equally important remains. The competition between Cope and Marsh resulted in a serious feud, yet they identified hundreds of new specimens and established outstanding fossil collections. The creation of the United States Geological Survey in 1879 provided permanent, full-time career opportunities for paleontologists. Director John Wesley Powell hired over a dozen paleontologists but never effectively managed the survey or established the practical importance of paleontology. His successor, Charles Doolittle Walcott, stabilized and expanded the Geological Society and made work in stratigraphic paleontology an integral component of the agency's activities.

In the twentieth century, vertebrate and invertebrate paleontology followed different patterns of institutional and conceptual development. Vertebrate paleontology, an expensive enterprise that served no practical purpose, became centered at a few major institutions, principally the American Museum of Natural History in New York, the Carnegie Museum of Pittsburgh, and the Field Museum in Chicago. There, prominent philanthropists supported the acquisition and exhibition of mastodons and dinosaurs as a means for promoting personal and civic pride as well as public education. Those museums took the lead in developing innovative displays, and at the American Museum, Henry Fairfield Osborn used fossil vertebrates to study correlation, evolution, and geographical distribution. Osborn and most of his colleagues remained wedded to non-Darwinian interpretations of evolution and at odds with the work of contemporary experimental biologists.

Invertebrate paleontology followed a different path. A number of invertebrate paleontologists, notably Alpheus Hyatt and his disciples, remained interested in biological problems and were outspoken advocates of the doctrine of recapitulation. Others examined evolutionary and ecological questions. But in the early twentieth century, invertebrate paleontology became especially noted for its close ties to industry. Exploration and research pertaining to petroleum influenced all aspects of early-twentieth-century geology, but it transformed invertebrate paleontology. Investigations by Joseph Augustine Cushman and John J. Galloway

P

demonstrated that foraminifera are excellent indicators of petroleum deposits, and made invertebrate paleontology a highly valuable asset to oil companies. By the 1930s, the vast majority of invertebrate paleontologists, trained in geology, were employed in the oil industry, and the rapidly growing Society of Economic Paleontologists and Mineralogists became the principal sponsor of the field's leading periodical, the *Journal of Paleontology.*

Since the 1940s, both fields have undergone important changes. In the 1940s, George Gaylord Simpson, applying the findings of population genetics to the fossil record, brought paleontology into line with the contemporary understanding of evolution and inheritance. Beginning in the 1950s, programs at Columbia University and the University of Chicago emphasized the examination of biological questions pertaining to invertebrate fossils, and that field is central to current interpretations of evolution, ecology, and taphonomy. The theory of punctuated equilibrium and the use of cladistics, both advanced by invertebrate paleontologists, have transformed the understanding of evolution and classification.

Vertebrate paleontology has remained centered in museums and the subject of popular attention. New interpretations of dinosaur anatomy and physiology since the 1970s have sparked tremendous public interest. Extraterrestrial explanations of the demise of the dinosaurs have resulted in detailed investigations of extinction not only by geologists and paleontologists but physicists, astrophysicists, and chemists.

Traditionally studies of the history of paleontology have focused on notable individuals and discoveries. There are useful studies of the contributions of Jefferson, Peale, Morton, and Leidy. However, most biographies of Cope and Marsh focus on personality and their fossil feud. James Hall, the subject of a traditional biography and a recent celebratory volume, certainly merits a full-scale scholarly analysis. Several good studies have been written on state and national geological surveys. While earlier work emphasized the scientific and political aspects of those efforts, more recent studies examine how those agencies provided career and entrepreneurial opportunities for paleontologists and other scientists. Walcott, Osborn and Simpson have been the subjects of recent studies, but no comparable works examine other leading figures or developments in twentieth-century vertebrate or invertebrate paleontology. In the light of recent work on popularization and the social production of scientific knowledge, the role of paleontology and fossil exhibits requires further examination. The analysis of paleontological fieldwork, a rich topic, remains virtually unexplored. Much has been written on the history of petroleum geology, but there exists no extended analysis of the relationship between the oil industry and invertebrate paleontology.

BIBLIOGRAPHY

Eldredge, Niles, and Stephen Jay Gould. "Punctuated Equilibria: An Alternative to Phyletic Gradualism." In *Models in Paleobiology,* edited by T.J.M. Schopf. San Francisco: Freeman, Cooper, 1972, pp. 82–115.

Fakundiny, Robert H., and Ellis L. Yochelson, eds. "Special James Hall Issue." *Earth Sciences History* 6 (1987): 1–133.

Gerstner, Patsy A. "The 'Philadelphia School' of Paleontology, 1820–1845." Ph.D. diss., Case Western Reserve University, 1967.

Glen, William, ed. *Mass Extinction Debates: How Science Works in a Crisis.* Stanford, CA: Stanford University Press, 1994.

Goetzmann, William H. *Exploration and Empire: The Explorer and the Scientist in the Winning of the American West.* New York: Knopf, 1966.

Nelson, Clifford M., and Fritiof M. Fryxell. "The Antebellum Collaboration of Meek and Hayden in Stratigraphy." In *Two Hundred Years of Geology in America,* edited by Cecil J. Schneer. Hanover, NH: University Press of New England, 1979, pp. 187–200.

Rainger, Ronald. *An Agenda for Antiquity: Henry Fairfield Osborn and Vertebrate Paleontology at the American Museum of Natural History, 1890–1935.* Tuscaloosa: University of Alabama Press, 1991.

———. "The Rise and Decline of a Science: Vertebrate Paleontology at Philadelphia's Academy of Natural Sciences, 1820–1900." *Proceedings of the American Philosophical Society* 136 (1992): 1–33.

———. "Biology, Geology or Neither or Both: Vertebrate Paleontology at the University of Chicago, 1892–1950." *Perspectives on Science* 1 (1993): 478–519.

Swetlitz, Marc. "Julian Huxley, George Gaylord Simpson, and the Idea of Progress in Twentieth-Century Evolutionary Biology." Ph.D. diss., University of Chicago, 1991.

Simpson, George Gaylord. *Tempo and Mode in Evolution.* New York: Columbia University Press, 1944.

———. *The Major Features of Evolution.* New York: Columbia University Press, 1953.

Warren, Leonard. *Joseph Leidy: The Last Man Who Knew Everything.* New Haven: Yale University Press, 1998.

Yochelson, Ellis L. *Charles Doolittle Walcott: Paleontologist.* Kent, OH: Kent State University Press, 1998.

Ronald Rainger

P

Paperclip, Project

Secret United States military operation that brought German scientists to America after World War II to work for the defense department and the National Aeronautics and Space Administration. From 1945 to 1970, nearly 1,600 individuals were recruited into Paperclip and given jobs in the United States. One of the most prominent Paperclip recruits was V-2 rocket expert Wernher von Braun.

Paperclip's impact on American science was enormous. Virtually all American moon rockets, jet planes, and postwar chemical weapons owe their development to research conducted by Paperclip scientists in Nazi Germany during the war.

Nevertheless, the project raised serious moral questions. Many Paperclip scientists were avowed Nazis; some were war criminals. One school of thought held that the value of their knowledge and achievements, coupled with the danger of them falling into Soviet hands, outweighed any crimes they many have committed, including murder. The other found it inexcusable for the United States to help the perpetrators of heinous war crimes escape justice.

Until recently, historians regarded Paperclip as a short-term operation that ended in 1950. Documents declassified since 1985 show that it continued for another two decades. The project's later years provide a rich resource for further study, particularly the Paperclip scientists' chemical warfare research in the 1960s.

BIBLIOGRAPHY

Amtmann, Hans H. *The Vanishing Paperclips.* Boylston, MA: Monogram Aviation Publications, 1988.

Hunt, Linda. *Secret Agenda: The United States Government, Nazi Scientists, and Proiect Paperclip, 1945 to 1990.* New York: St. Martin's Press, 1991.

Huzel, Dieter. *From Peenemünde to Canaveral.* Englewood Cliffs, NJ: Prentice Hall, 1962.

Lasby, Clarence. *Project Paperclip.* New York: Atheneum, 1971.

Ordway, Frederick, and Mitchell Sharpe. *The Rocket Team.* Cambridge, MA: MIT Press, 1982.

Linda Hunt

Parapsychology

The word was introduced into English by J.B. Rhine in his monograph, *Extra-Sensory Perception* (1934), to denote the experimental study of purported mental abilities and associated phenomena that appear to be inexplicable to the physical and behavioral sciences. These included "telepathy" (the ability to receive mental information without sensory intermediary), "clairvoyance" (the ability to receive physical information without sensory intermediary), psycho- or telekinesis (the ability to influence physical systems psychically), and "precognition" (the ability to receive future information). The word was intended to have more scientific signification than the then current term, "psychical research."

This latter term, which denoted the study of these phenomena and others, such as hauntings, seances, dowsing, psychic healing, and so forth had become current in the late nineteenth century with the founding, in England, of the Society for Psychical Research (SPR) (1882) and the American Society for Psychical Research (1884). These, in turn, were responses to the popular ascendency in mid-nineteenth century of spiritualism and mediumistic seances.

The [English] SPR was formed by a group of socially and intellectually prominent persons who wished to study these phenomena and the psychical abilities alluded to above by the methods of experimental science. On the whole, this group looked sympathetically on these phenomena. The stance of the group which formed in the United States in 1884 and which included many scientific luminaries, was much more critical, with the exception of William James. However, the American SPR took its work seriously but financial difficulties caused the society to be absorbed into the English SPR in 1889. In 1907, the American SPR was reconstituted, but as a much more spiritualist-oriented society. By this time—and certainly after the death of James—psychical research had become much more marginal vis-à-vis academic science than it had been in the 1880s.

However, in the second decade of the twentieth century, endowments to support psychical research were established at Harvard and Stanford Universities. Harvard proved to be particularly significant in the 1920s under the patronage of William McDougall, the professor of psychology. The young psychologist Gardner Murphy came there to do psychical research in 1922–1925. The young plant physiologist J.B. Rhine and his wife, Louisa, came to study psychical research with McDougall in 1926; although this proved abortive, they followed him to the newly established Duke University in 1927.

From the early 1930s until the 1960s, Rhine and Murphy dominated parapsychology. Rhine was the more visionary; he sought to establish "parapsychology" as a new field of experimental, academic science, most closely allied to psychology. He set out to develop an experimental research program; he trained students; he founded the *Journal of Parapsychology* (1937), and he published popular accounts and textbooks on the subject.

Murphy was more pragmatic; he developed the field through personal patronage (he was chairman of the psychology department at City College of New York) and through cultivation of the American SPR, the traditional psychical research society (also located in New York City), which had sloughed off its extreme spiritualist orientation in 1941.

Rhine's vision was only imperfectly realized. Parapsychology evoked considerable hostility from the scientific and academic communities from the outset of Rhine's bid for establishment, and although there were times when parapsychologists were heartened by what seemed to be victory in confrontation with their scientific opponents (e.g., the session on parapsychology at the 1938 American Psychological Association meeting), such victories never led to any significant advance in institutionalization or acceptance of the field in wider academia. Nevertheless, the field did continue to develop its own professional structures; the most notable was the Parapsychological Association, formed in 1957, and there was sufficient accommodation by established science to enable parapsychology to receive affiliation with the American Association for the Advancement of Science in 1969.

Murphy died in 1979; Rhine in 1980. Although no one with the charisma of Rhine or the professional distinction of Murphy has succeeded them, parapsychology has persevered through such institutions as the American Society for Psychical Research and the Rhine Research Center (the latter in Durham, North Carolina).

The experimental promise of Rhine's original report remained, at best, only fitfully realized in Rhine's own laboratory and in others; moreover, the field has always been plagued by accusations of chicanery. Parapsychological claims continue to be received with skepticism by the general scientific community. New experimental techniques, especially those employing sensory deprivation, and new modes of statistical analysis appear promising to researchers within the field. Whether they will lead to more positive reception of the field remains to be seen.

BIBLIOGRAPHY

Broughton, Richard S. *Parapsychology: The Controversial Science.* New York: Ballantine, 1991.

Collins, Harry M., and Trevor J. Pinch. *Frames of Meaning: The Social Construction of Extraordinary Science.* London: Routledge & Kegan Paul, 1982.

Gauld, Alan. *The Founders of Psychical Research.* London: Routledge & Kegan Paul, 1968.

Grattan-Guinness, Ivor, ed. *Psychical Research: A Guide to Its History, Principles and Practices.* Wellingborough, U.K.: Aquarian Press, 1982.

Mauskopf, Seymour H. "The History of the American Society for Psychical Research: An Interpretation." *Journal of the American Society for Psychical Research* 83 (1989): 7–29.

Mauskopf, Seymour H., and Michael R. McVaugh. *The Elusive Science: Origins of Experimental Psychical Research.* Baltimore: Johns Hopkins University Press, 1980.

McClenon, James. *Deviant Science: The Case of Parapsychology.* Philadelphia: University of Pennsylvania Press, 1984.

Moore, R. Lawrence. *In Search of White Crows: Spiritualism, Parapsychology, and American Culture.* New York: Oxford University Press, 1977.

Taylor, Eugene. "Psychotherapy, Harvard, and the American Society for Psychical Research: 1884–1889." *Proceedings of Presented Papers: The Parapsychological Association 28th Annual Convention.* Vol. 2. Parapsychological Association, Medford, MA (1985), pp. 319–346.

Seymour H. Mauskopf

SEE ALSO
Rhine, Joseph Banks

Pathology

The study of disease. Pathology has traditionally signified the theoretical basis of the practice of medicine; and all healers have always, therefore, been pathologists of a sort. At the end of twentieth century, pathology in the United States manifested itself in a number of specific investigative, didactic, and service activities whose practitioners had little to do with each other. Most Americans who think of themselves as pathologists are not researchers, but rather physicians who specialize in laboratory diagnostic services. On the other hand, many specialists in other areas of medicine involve themselves in clinical investigations whose findings are relevant to pathology; and the field of experimental pathology includes work done by scientists (with or without medical training) in almost any of the basic biomedical disciplines.

P

The nature of the pathologic endeavor has constantly shifted in English-speaking North America. During the eighteenth century, European theorists—looking for alternatives to the humoral pathology inherited from classical antiquity—developed theories of disease based on unitary notions of morbid processes. In terms of this speculative general pathology, the first American pathologist of note was Benjamin Rush, who postulated that all disease was related to tension in the walls of the blood vessels.

By the late eighteenth century, the more empirical pathological anatomy was also maturing, as a means to identify lesions within the body that could be correlated with symptoms experienced by the living patient. Europeans living in North America had sporadically performed autopsies—often for forensic purposes—since the earliest colonial days, but only with the development of hospitals, medical schools, and medical journals in the decades around 1800 was autopsy institutionalized and utilized as a means of advancing medical knowledge.

For American doctors coming of age in the 1820s, 1830s, and 1840s, a visit to the clinics of the great Parisian pathologists was the capstone of their professional training. Back at home, many of the several hundred men who had gone to Paris used their hospital appointments as a means to pursue the study of pathological anatomy. Among the most important of them was the Philadelphian William Wood Gerhard, whose work in the 1830s distinguished typhus from typhoid fever. The first American pathology textbooks also appeared in this period.

In 1847, J.B.S. Jackson acceded to the first chair of pathology in the United States, at Harvard, where he devoted himself to the collection and display of pathological specimens. Most other medical schools established similar positions before the end of the century; but for several decades Harvard's was the only endowed post, and other teachers of pathology remained dependent on income from their medical practices. At the same time, many doctors with no formal appointment in pathology did extensive pathological work and sometimes built private collections of specimens obtained at autopsy or surgery. Pathology societies, founded in a few large cities in the 1840s and 1850s, provided local physicians the opportunity to display gross and microscopic specimens and discuss pathological changes.

As early as the 1820s, often under pressure from their medical staffs, hospital governing boards appointed unpaid pathologists to supervise autopsies, collect specimens, and prepare catalogs of their "cabinets." A particularly significant collection, deriving from the work of military physicians during the Civil War, eventually became the Armed Forces Institute of Pathology. By the 1890s, pathology and its offshoot, bacteriology, had also found a place in the civilian federal bureaucracy, most notably the Department of Agriculture and the Marine Hospital Service (later in U.S. Public Health Service). Municipal, county, and state governments also established laboratories where work was rooted in pathology and allied disciplines.

American doctors were quick to respond to mid-nineteenth-century European innovations in microscopy and the pathology of fluids. In medical schools, optional training in microscopy, hematology, and urine analysis would often be the responsibility of a "demonstrator" serving under the chair of medicine or the chair of pathology. Several leading hospitals appointed microscopists and chemists or expanded the responsibilities of the pathologist. Between 1850 and 1900, the analysis of samples taken from patients gradually overwhelmed the work of collecting and cataloging specimens, and the hospital pathological cabinet was transformed into a clinical laboratory. Doctors working in dissecting rooms, museums, and laboratories did this work voluntarily with no remuneration. The best of them were committed to advancing science and developing their own knowledge of disease. Others were opportunists who used such appointments only to make professional connections. Around 1900 some leading clinicians and pathologists expressed concern about the proliferation of laboratory tests, many of which produced results of no clinical or therapeutic significance.

Through the first two decades of the twentieth century, early unpaid experience in pathology remained almost essential for a clinician to succeed in academic medicine. At the same time, though, hospitals were beginning to appoint full-time, salaried, pathologists. In the hospital context, pathology came to include two different roles (although often combined in the same person): (1) clinical pathology, which used chemical, hematological, and bacteriological techniques; and (2) anatomic pathology, which encompassed gross and microscopic examination of autopsy and surgical specimens. The early hospital laboratories were primarily devoted to routine testing, but the people who worked in them also participated in clinical research and innovation in laboratory practice. In general, hospital laboratories never became important loci for work in experimental pathology, despite the hopes of some clinicians and pathologists in the decades at the turn of the twentieth century. Immediately after World War I, access to diagnostic laboratory services became a requirement for hospital accreditation. By this time, some hospitals had begun charging their paying patients for laboratory procedures, and the laboratory also became a source of revenue.

A late American innovation, dependent on maintaining the traditions of pathological anatomy, was the clinical-pathological conference, begun by the internist Richard C. Cabot at the Massachusetts General Hospital around 1910. At these weekly continuing education meetings (which quickly spread to other leading hospitals), pathologists would effectively function as the physicians' judges, discussing their findings on cases presented and confirming or questioning the original clinical diagnosis.

Just when pathology was maturing as a form of medical practice in America, as a field of scientific research in Europe, it took a new turn toward animal experimentation. Experimental pathology was brought to the United States by one man, William Henry Welch, with the help of his patrons and a few colleagues. Following his first visit to Germany, Welch seized the opportunity in 1878 to open a teaching laboratory at Bellevue Medical College in New York City. In 1886, his innovations won him an appointment as professor of pathology at the recently founded Johns Hopkins University. Best known for his role in medical education reform, Welch was also a productive scientist, having published on circulatory disorders, cirrhosis of the liver, pathogenic fungi, chronic inflammations, and neoplasms.

Welch did not run a Ph.D. program in pathology, but medical graduates who came to Hopkins for training under Welch helped spread his approach around the country. Two Welch protégés who stand out are William T. Councilman, professor of pathology at Harvard, and Simon Flexner, director of laboratories at the Rockefeller Institute. American pathology was not completely dependent on Welch, however. In Chicago, for example, the Danish-born, Vienna-trained Christian Fenger established important teaching and experimental programs.

By 1910, American medical schools had standard pathology courses in which lectures were supplemented by laboratory work. In a sense, experimental pathology is the heir to the traditions of speculative general pathology, with its researches into basic disease processes, such as tumors or inflammation. Modern textbooks of pathology have continued to present this diverse field as a single discipline by presenting it as composed of both general pathology and systemic (or organ) pathology based on pathological anatomy.

The medical specialties of anatomic pathology and clinical pathology were formally recognized in 1936 with the establishment of the American Board of Pathology, and in 1959, a subspecialty board was created for forensic pathology. Clinical and surgical pathology have become lucrative fields, and to most practicing American physicians these now represent all of "pathology." Diagnostic laboratory practice has become much less labor-intensive in recent years, and increased demand for tests has contributed to the overall increase in medical care costs. As opportunities for high income increased, clinical pathologists have generally moved from being hospital employees to owning their own practices.

While American universities and research laboratories began assuming world leadership in experimental pathology during the first half of the twentieth century, in the years following World War II hospitals in this country almost completely abandoned the autopsy, the weekly clinical-pathological conference, and the cabinet or museum of pathological specimens. By the 1970s some pathologists were complaining of a particular lack of identity of the field in the United States, because clinical pathology here encompassed a particularly wide range of techniques increasingly dependent on advanced technological devices and increasingly appropriated by subspecialists in other fields of clinical practice. At the same time, research in what had been called experimental pathology became more and more the province of scientists who identified with other disciplines, such as molecular biology, biochemistry, physiology, pharmacology, microbiology, toxicology, or cancer research.

BIBLIOGRAPHY

Long, Esmond R. *A History of American Pathology.* Springfield, IL: Thomas, 1962.

Maulitz, Russell C. "Pathology." *The Education of American Physicians,* edited by Ronald L. Numbers. Berkeley: University of California Press, 1980, pp. 122–142.

———. "'The Whole Company of Pathology': Pathology as Idea and Work in American Medical Life." In *History of Pathology: Proceedings of the 8th International Symposium on the Comparative History of Medicine—East and West,*

P

September 18–24, 1983, Susono-shi, Japan. Tokyo: Maruzen, 1986, pp. 139–161.

Morman, Edward T. "Clinical Pathology in America, 1865–1915: Philadelphia as a Test Case." *Bulletin of the History of Medicine* 58 (1984): 198–214.

Popper, H., and D.W. King, "The Situation of American Pathology 1975—Education Problems Yesterday, Today and Tomorrow." *Beiträge zur Pathologie* 156 (1975): 85–94.

Wright, James R., Jr. "The Development of the Frozen Section Technique, the Evolution of Surgical Biopsy, and the Origins of Surgical Pathology." *Bulletin of the History of Medicine* 59 (1986): 295–326.

Edward T. Morman

Payne-Gaposchkin, Cecilia (1900–1979)

Astrophysicist. Born in Wendover, England, and the descendent of several scholars, Payne attended Newnham College of Cambridge University. There she studied physics, chemistry, and botany, preparing for a teaching position at an English girl's school. During her first year, she heard a lecture on the theory of relativity by Arthur S. Eddington, and resolved instead to become an astronomer. She continued her studies with Ernst Rutherfurd and other Cambridge physicists, while taking as many astronomy courses as her schedule would allow.

Unable to find a research position in England, Payne pursued graduate work in astronomy under Harlow Shapley at the Harvard College Observatory in Cambridge, Massachusetts. Her doctoral degree, granted by Radcliffe College in 1925, was the first one awarded to a graduate student at the Harvard Observatory. In her dissertation, published as the monograph *Stellar Atmospheres* (1925), she used recent atomic theory and photographs of stellar spectra in the Harvard collections to derive a temperature scale for stellar atmospheres. She also included evidence that these regions of stars were fundamentally different in chemical composition than the earth, consisting primarily of hydrogen and helium. This idea, buttressed by further data, became a basic premise of twentieth-century astrophysics through the work of Princeton astrophysicist Henry Norris Russell. However, when Payne first raised the idea with Russell, he dismissed it as preposterous.

Although her dissertation was widely praised, Payne still was unable to find a position in England. She remained at Harvard, first as a National Research Council Fellow and then as a member of the observatory staff.

In her second book, *The Stars of High Luminosity* (1930), she used Harvard data to describe supergiant stars of diverse spectral types. In later years, she worked increasingly on photometry and the study of variable stars. Drawing on her wide knowledge of the stars, she sought to find order and patterns in vast quantities of data. Her books from this period included *The Galactic Novae* (1957) and a popular book on stellar evolution entitled *Stars in the Making* (1953).

Payne married the Russian-born astronomer Sergei Gaposchkin in 1934. The Gaposchkins worked together at the Harvard College Observatory, and also raised three children.

In 1956, when Harvard University opened its faculty to women, Payne-Gaposchkin was appointed professor of astronomy and chairman of the astronomy department. She was elected to the American Academy of Arts and Sciences and the American Philosophical Society.

BIBLIOGRAPHY

Haramundanis, Katherine, ed. *Cecilia Payne-Gaposchkin: An Autobiography and Other Recollections.* Cambridge, U.K.: Cambridge University Press, 1984.

Kidwell, Peggy A. "Women Astronomers in Britain 1780–1930." *Isis* 75 (1984): 534–546.

———. "Cecilia Payne-Gaposchkin: Astronomy in the Family." In *Uneasy Careers and Intimate Lives: Women in Science, 1789–1979,* edited by P.G. Abir-Am and D. Outram. New Brunswick: Rutgers University Press, 1987, pp. 216–238.

———. "Harvard Astronomers and World War II—Disruption and Opportunity." In *Science at Harvard University: Historical Perspectives,* edited by Clark A. Elliott and Margaret Rossiter. Bethlehem, PA: Lehigh University Press, 1992, pp. 285–302.

Peggy Aldrich Kidwell

Peale, Charles Willson (1741–1827)

Museologist, artist, artisan, and inventor. Born in Queen Anne's County, Maryland, Peale studied with Benjamin West in London, 1767–1769, and returned to paint portraits of the Maryland gentry, with trips to Philadelphia and Virginia, where he painted the first portrait of George Washington. In 1776, Peale moved to Philadelphia and became involved with the city's radical republican organizations. During the Revolution, he was an officer in the Pennsylvania militia who fought at the Battle of Princeton, an agent for the confiscation of Loyalist estates, and a one-term representative in the Pennsylvania

Assembly. Peale continued painting during this time, providing us with many of the only known likenesses of Revolutionary political leaders and military officers. He also utilized his artistic and mechanical skills to orchestrate some of the largest public demonstrations held in America up to that time, such as the Benedict Arnold ceremony of punishment (1780) and the Arch of Triumph celebration of peace (1784).

Peale's greatest scientific achievement and his major contribution to American society and culture was his Philadelphia Museum. Opened in July 1786, it developed from a room with a few "natural curiosities," to the first scientifically organized museum of natural history in the United States. From this point in his life, although he never stopped painting, Peale devoted most of his creative energies to expanding and improving his museum. In 1794, he moved his museum to larger quarters at the American Philosophical Society, of which he had been a member since 1786. The society aided him again in 1801, loaning him money for an expedition to exhume the bones of the "great incognitum," the American mastodon. With his son Rembrandt, Peale reconstructed almost two complete skeletons, and provided descriptions and drawings for European scientists. The hugely successful exhibition of the mastodon made the museum famous in America and to scientists throughout Europe. Popular and scientific notice enabled Peale in 1802 to obtain permission from the Pennsylvania state government to move his museum into Independence Hall, where it remained for more than two decades. In 1816, during the decade of its greatest scientific and popular success, more than 47,000 people may have paid the twenty-five cent admission fee to enter the museum. When the museum closed in the mid-nineteenth century, sales catalogs listed 1,824 birds, 250 quadrupeds, 650 fish, 135 reptiles, lizards, and tortoises, 269 portraits, and 33 cases of shells.

The museum's popularity and prestige can be measured by the range of individuals who exchanged or donated specimens to it. Accession records total some 192 manuscript pages, listing items from local artisans and farmers as well as eminent scientists and collectors in the United States and Europe. While the majority were American citizens, Peale was able to arrange exchanges with collectors in Stockholm, London, Amsterdam, Paris, and Vienna. Peale's relationship with European scientific institutions were not as successful, but after the exhumation of the mastodon, he received respectful recognition from Sir Joseph Banks of the London Museum, and a case of fifty-four birds from Étienne Geoffroy Saint-Hillaire and Georges Cuvier of the Muséum de l'Histoire Naturelle in Paris.

Although Peale failed to make the museum a permanent institution, its collections did have a substantial influence in several fields of natural history. In paleontology, according to Cuvier, classification of the mastodon would have been impossible without the Peales' skeletons and drawings. In ornithology, the museum's great collection of birds was essential to the work of Alexander Wilson and George Ord. The museums collections in minerals and insects appear to have been useful to the work of Gerald Troost and Thomas Say. In zoology, John Godman's four-volume *American Natural History,* the standard work in the field in the mid-nineteenth century, is filled with references to specimens in Peale's museum.

Peale was a man of many interests who contributed in diverse ways to the cultural life of the early Republic. A pivotal figure in the founding of the Pennsylvania Academy of Fine Arts, he was also an inventor and mechanic, holding the first patent for bridge design in America, and winning, with his son Raphaelle, a contest sponsored by the American Philosophical Society for improved fireplaces and stoves. He had a lifelong interest in health and public health reform, patenting a portable steam bath to cure colds and improve public hygiene. Peale helped develop the polygraph, a machine which made copies of documents and which was used by Thomas Jefferson and Benjamin Henry Latrobe to copy their letters. Inclined by his artisan background to an interest in machinery, Peale experimented throughout his life with drawing and perspective devices, and placed a drawing machine, the physiognotrace, in his museum which copied the profiles of hundreds of thousands of museum visitors. And he was a pioneer in American dentistry, one of the first in America to make false teeth out of porcelain.

BIBLIOGRAPHY

Appel, Toby A. "Science, Popular Culture and Profit: Peale's Philadelphia Museum." *Journal of the Society for the Bibliography of Natural History* 9 (1980): 619–634.

Hart, Sidney. "'To encrease the comforts of Life': Charles Willson Peale and the Mechanical Arts." *Pennsylvania Magazine of History and Biography* 110 (1986): 323–357.

Hart, Sidney, and David C. Ward. "The Waning of the Enlightenment Ideal: Charles Willson Peale's Philadelphia

P

Museum, 1790–1820." *Journal of the Early Republic* 8 (1988): 389–418.

Miller, Lillian B., ed. *The Collected Papers of Charles Willson Peale and His Family*. Millwood, NY: Kraus Microform, 1980. Microfiche.

Miller, Lillian B., Sidney Hart, and David C. Ward, eds. *The Selected Papers of Charles Willson Peale and His Family*. New Haven: Yale University Press, 1983–.

Miller, Lillian B., and David C. Ward. *New Perspectives on Charles Willson Peale*. Pittsburgh: University of Pittsburgh Press, 1991.

Schofield, Robert E. "The Science Education of an Enlightened Entrepreneur: Charles Willson Peale and His Philadelphia Museum, 1784–1827." *American Studies* 30 (1989): 21–40.

Sellers, Charles Coleman. *Portraits and Miniatures by Charles Willson Peale. Transactions of the American Philosophical Society* 42, pt. 1 (1952).

———. *Charles Willson Peale*. New York: Charles Scribner's Sons, 1969.

———. *Charles Willson Peale with Patron and Populace. A supplement to Portraits and Minatures by Charles Willson Peale. Transactions of the AmeircanPhilosophical Society* 59, pt. 3 (1969).

———. *Mr. Peale's Museum: Charles Willson Peale and the First Popular Museum of Natural Science and Art*. New York: W.W. Norton, 1980.

Sidney Hart

SEE ALSO
Museums of Natural History and Science

Pearl, Raymond (1879–1940)

Population biologist. Born in New Hampshire, Pearl received an A.B. in 1899 from Dartmouth and a Ph.D. in zoology in 1902 from the University of Michigan, where he remained as instructor until 1905. During the academic year 1905–1906, he worked at the University of Leipzig, the Marine Biological Station at Naples, and the University of London, where he collaborated with the noted biometrician Karl Pearson. After a year as instructor in zoology at the University of Pennsylvania, Pearl in 1907 became head of the Department of Biology at the Maine Agricultural Experiment Station, a position he retained until 1918. From 1917 to 1919, Pearl also served as chief of the statistical division of the United States Food Administration under Herbert Hoover. In 1918, Pearl was named professor of biometry and vital statistics at the Johns Hopkins University School of Hygiene and Public Health. Although his academic title varied, Pearl remained at Hopkins until his death. From 1925 to 1930, he headed the Institute for Biological Research at Hopkins, which was funded by the Rockefeller Foundation.

After his stay at the University of London, Pearl became one of the chief American promoters of biometrical methods for studying statistical variations in populations. While at the Maine Agricultural Experiment Station, Pearl focused on the genetics of domestic fowl, contributing both statistical and experimental studies. During his wartime service with the Food Administration, Pearl examined the relations between food and populations. Thereafter, while connected with Hopkins, Pearl focused on human population biology, although he also carried out breeding experiments on *Drosophila*. Pearl is best known for a series of papers, some coauthored with Lowell J. Reed, in which he proposed that the logistic curve represented the general law for human population growth. While these papers provoked much controversy at the time of their publication, the logistic curve is still used as a starting point in mathematical treatments of population growth. Pearl also contributed numerous other studies to human biology, looking, for example, at the effects of contraception on human populations while arguing in another paper that moderate consumption of alcohol tended to increase human longevity but any consumption of tobacco tended to decrease it.

Historians of science have placed Pearl firmly within the history of population ecology and have also examined his involvement with the eugenics movement. There does not yet exist, however, a detailed biography of Pearl or a comprehensive analysis of his scientific work in its wide range and diversity.

BIBLIOGAPHY

Allen, Garland E. "Old Wine in New Bottles: From Eugenics to Population Control in the Work of Raymond Pearl." In *The Expansion of American Biology*, edited by Keith R. Benson, Jane Maienschein, and Ronald Rainger. New Brunswick: Rutgers University Press, 1991, pp. 231–261.

Fee, Elizabeth. *Disease and Discovery: A History of the Johns Hopkins School of Hygiene and Public Health, 1916–1939*. Baltimore: Johns Hopkins University Press, 1987.

Jennings, H.S. "Raymond Pearl." *Biographical Memoirs of the National Academy of Sciences* 22 (1942): 295–347.

Kingsland, Sharon E. *Modeling Nature: Episodes in the History of Population Ecology*. Chicago: University of Chicago Press, 1985.

Provine, William B. *The Origins of Theoretical Population Genetics.* Chicago: University of Chicago Press, 1971.

Carl-Henry Geschwind

Peck, Charles Horton (1833–1917)

Mycologist and first New York State botanist. Born in Sand Lake, New York, Peck attended the State Normal School at Albany for one year, and graduated from Union College in 1859. He taught at Sand Lake Collegiate Institute and later at Cass's Institute, Albany, also assisting James Hall at the New York State Museum. Peck was an early student of American bryophytes and presented his specimens and "Catalogue of Mosses" to the museum in 1865. Judge George W. Clinton, amateur botanist and member of the New York State Regents, was instrumental in securing temporary and eventually permanent state employment for Peck as botanist from 1868. The New York State Legislature created the position of state botanist in 1883; Peck was appointed and held this position until 1915.

Peck collected vascular plants as well as mosses, lichens, and fungi all over New York State, finding many new species. He published his findings, including many new species collected by himself and others, in his Annual Reports starting in 1868. He continued to specialize in bryophytes until 1870; after that date, Peck worked primarily on fungi. American mycology began with Levis David von Schweinitz and Moses Ashley Curtis, but in 1870 most species of American fungi were as yet undescribed. Peck became the leading nineteenth-century mycologist, describing 2,700 new taxa and collecting about 36,000 specimens, nearly all in New York State. He made field drawings and watercolors of many of these species and even did microscopy in the field.

Peck is important primarily due to his immense legacy in mycology. His main focus was on mushrooms, including agarics and boletes, but he worked with all kinds of fungi, including microfungi. His type specimens and descriptions have been used by all subsequent American mycologists. He also did pioneering work in bryology in New York State and was an important teacher of both mosses and fungi, largely through correspondence. The thousands of letters comprising this correspondence network are largely extant. Over fifty men and women collected bryophytes in New York before 1910, most of whom, including Judge Clinton, received identifications and advice from Peck.

Apart from Peck, only one of these, Elizabeth Britton, held a professional botanical position. Peck's career was also important in terms of both the professionalization and the legitimation of botany in the latter part of the nineteenth century. Letters between Peck and G.W. Clinton as well as legislative records document this process in New York State (Slack). Geology was much earlier considered a science worthy of state support. Although New York temporarily employed the botanist John Torrey to work on a state natural history survey as early as 1835, and yearly appropriation bills usually provided funds for Peck's employment after 1868, the legislature debated the value of botany to the state and only after 1883 created the position of state botanist, equivalent to the state geologist.

Peck was also one of the great botanical explorers of his day, traveling over difficult terrain, including the Adirondack and Catskill Mountains by train, horse-drawn carriage, and largely on foot, sometimes with surveyor-explorer Verplanck Colvin. He was on the first ascents of several Adirondack peaks, including the highest, Mount Marcy, for which he made a catalog of all the plants. He later cataloged the plants of North Elba township, including the alpine flora of several others of New York's highest peaks. His influence, particularly in mycology, was great, despite the fact that due to the provincialism of his New York State botanist position, he rarely left New York State.

BIBLIOGRAPHY

Atkinson, George F. "Charles Horton Peck." *The Botanical Gazette* 65 (1918): 103–108.

Bessey, Charles E. "A Notable Botanical Career." *Science* 40 (1914): 48.

Burnham, Stewart H. "Charles Horton Peck." *Mycologia* 11 (1919): 33–39.

Gilbertson, R.L. "Index to species and varieties of fungi described by C.H. Peck from 1909–1915." *Mycologia* 54 (1962): 460–465.

Haines, John H. "Charles Horton Peck." *McIlvainea* 3 (1978): 3–10.

———. "Charles Peck and His Contributions to American Mycology." *Mycotaxon* 26 (1986): 17–27.

Peck, Charles H. "The Catalogue of the Mosses Presented to the State of New York." In *Eighteenth Annual Report of the Regents of the University of New York on the Condition of the State Cabinet of Natural History.* Albany: New York State, 1865.

———. *Annual Reports of the State Botanist.* 1868–1912. Reprinted, Leiden: Boerhaave Press, 1980.

P

———. "Botany; Plants of the Summit of Mount Marcy." In *Seventh Annual Report on the Progress of the Topographical Survey of the Adirondack Region in New York,* edited by Verplanck Colvin. Albany: Weed, Parsons and Company, Printers for the New York State Legislature, 1880.

———. "Boleti of the United States." *Bulletin of the New York State Museum* 11, no. 8 (1889): 74–166.

———. *Plants of North Elba.* Bulletin, New York State Museum 6 (28). Albany: University of the State of New York, 1899.

Slack, Nancy G. "Charles Horton Peck, Bryologist, and the Legitimation of Botany in New York State." *Memoirs of the New York Botanical Garden* 45: (1987): 28–45.

Nancy G. Slack

Pedersen, Charles John (1904–1989)

Nobel Prize winner in chemistry in 1987 for discovery of crown-shaped large ring ethers. Born in Pusan, Korea, Pedersen came to the United States to study chemical engineering at the University of Dayton, Ohio. After receiving his degree, he studied organic chemistry at the Massachusetts Institute of Technology and received an MS degree in 1927. He then joined the DuPont Company and worked for forty-two years as research chemist for the organic chemicals department. His early work at DuPont concerned problems caused by trace amounts of metals such as copper in petroleum products. Metal ions act as catalysts that accelerate undesirable chemical reactions between oxygen and petroleum products. Pedersen developed organic "de-activators" that formed inactive complexes with metal ions, thus ending their catalytic activity. From 1940 to 1960, he worked on a variety of problems. Over his long career, he published twenty-five papers and received sixty-five patents. In 1960, at the suggestion of his supervisor, Pedersen began a fundamental study of the coordination chemistry of vanadium with the goal of understanding its catalytic activity in oxidation and polymerization reactions. This work was similar to the work he had done with metal deactivators in the 1930s. While attempting to synthesize an organic compound that would form an inactive complex with vanadium ions, Pedersen produced a small quantity of an unusual compound. Pursuing this unexpected result, he determined that he had discovered a straightforward reaction mechanism for creating a new and complex type of organic molecule, which he called crown ethers. These molecules consist of large rings that have ether (oxygen) linkages between every few carbon atoms.

These oxygen atoms in the rings create electronic traps for metal ions which become the head in the crown. Pedersen's original crown ethers were doughnut shaped but other researchers have extended his work to create molecules with complex three-dimensional shapes such as footballs and vases. Recent work by Jean-Marie Lehn and Donald Cram, who shared the Nobel Prize, has led to the creation of synthetic enzymes which mimic the action of powerful and efficient organic catalysts in cells.

BIBLIOGRAPHY

Hounshell, David A., and John Kenly Smith Jr. *Science and Corporate Strategy, Du Pont R&D, 1902–1980.* New York: Cambridge University Press, 1988.

Pedersen, Charles J. "The Discovery of Crown Ethers." *Science* 241 (29 July 1988): 536–540.

Schmeck, Harold, M., Jr. "Chemistry and Physics Nobels Hail Discoveries on Life." *New York Times,* 15 October 1987.

John K. Smith

Penicillin Project

The penicillin project during World War II represents one of the most impressive scientific and medical achievements in the twentieth century. Industrial production of penicillin grew from insignificant levels during the early years of the war to unanticipated mass quantities by 1944. The project featured a cooperative effort between chemical engineers, biochemists, and clinical investigators.

Penicillin remained a laboratory phenomenon from the late 1920s until 1940. Despite Alexander Fleming's discovery of the lytic effect of *Penicillium notatum* on *Staphylococcus aureus,* researchers failed to investigate fully the clinical applications of the substance. International events, however, shifted interest toward the effect of penicillin in vivo as well as in vitro.

Howard Florey and his team of Oxford investigators conducted the first clinical trials of penicillin. By late summer 1941, clinical researchers had demonstrated the in vivo effect of penicillin on certain bacteria. The substance, many in Britain and the United States realized immediately, would prove invaluable to the Allied war effort.

Penicillin presented two interrelated problems, manufacture and clinical investigation. Efficient fermentation methods were developed at the United States Department of Agriculture Research Station at

Peoria, Illinois. There teams of chemical engineers, biochemists, and bacteriologists perfected volumetric production methods for penicillin which replaced the inefficient surface culturing of the mold. American drug manufacturers soon followed with their own penicillin pilot plants.

Clinical investigation represented the other area of the American penicillin project. The National Research Council's Committee on Chemotherapeutic and Other Agents, working in coordination with the Committee on Medical Research of the Office of Scientific Research and Development, oversaw not only the careful clinical investigation of penicillin but its equitable rationing to ill civilians on the American home front. By April 1944, supplies of penicillin had increased to the point that civilian distribution of the drug shifted to the Office of Penicillin Distribution. The Committee on Chemotherapeutic and Other Agents, however, continued its clinical research through the end of the war.

The penicillin project represented an accomplishment similar to the Manhattan Project. Cohorts of the researchers, well funded with federal grants and working in conjunction with military requirements, took Fleming and Florey's findings from laboratory and initial trials to a mass-produced drug in a few short years. Penicillin, like the atomic bomb, became one of the outstanding scientific successes of World War II.

BIBILIOGRAPHY

Adams, David P. *The Greatest Good to the Greatest Number: Penicillin Rationing on the American Home Front, 1940–1945.* New York: Peter Lang, 1991.

Hobby, Gladys L. *Penicillin: Meeting the Challege.* New Haven: Yale University Press, 1985.

Moberg, Carol L., and Zanvil A. Cohn, eds. *Launching the Antibiotic Era: Personal Accounts of the Discovery and Use of the First Antibiotics.* New York: Rockefeller University Press, 1990.

Parascandola, John, ed. *The History of Antibiotics: A Symposium.* Madison, WI: American Institute of the History of Pharmacy, 1980.

Sheehan, John C. *The Enchanted Ring: The Untold Story of Penicillin.* Cambridge, MA: MIT Press, 1982.

Williams. Trevor I. *Howard Florey: Penicillin and After.* Oxford: Oxford University Press, 1984.

David P. Adams Jr.

SEE ALSO

Antibiotics; World War II and Science

Pesticides

Mixtures of chemicals, based on one or more toxic compounds plus auxiliary materials, designed to kill unwanted organisms called "pests." Pesticides from botanical sources and naturally occurring compounds were used in small amounts for thousands of years. In the nineteenth century, an unknown American farmer applied the dyestuff "Paris green" to potato plants infested with Colorado potato beetles. Paris green contained arsenic, which effectively killed the unwanted insects. Subsequent inventions led by scientists in the United States Department of Agriculture produced the compound lead arsenate as an effective pesticide for use against gypsy moth in 1892. Paris green and lead arsenate comprised the vast bulk of pesticides used until after World War I.

Cessation of imports of German-made chemicals into the United States during World War I stimulated the development of a chemical industry in this country. Its first priorities were for explosives and other materials needed in the war, but the by-product paradichlorobenzene was found in 1918 to be effective as a pesticide against the insect, the peach tree borer. Other research developed calcium arsenate and a small number of synthetic organic chemicals into pesticides. By 1939, pesticides were regularly used in agriculture on a limited basis, primarily in fruit and vegetable production.

Two inventions at about the time of World War II transformed the use of pesticides. DDT insecticides, invented in Switzerland, made pesticides so cheap that the science of applied entomology was transformed. 2,4-D herbicides (for killing weeds) created weed science, a new field to study the control of unwanted plants by pesticides. After 1945, the uses of pesticides became numerous and changed many industries dramatically, especially agriculture.

Pesticides were one of the many materials produced by chemical science. Historical studies of chemistry and chemical engineering, however, have not given much attention to the conceptual and technical developments needed to model, synthesize, and mass produce pesticides. Pesticides also had powerful effects on other scientific disciplines. Entomology and weed science were affected strongly in terms of their basic principles and lines of research. After DDT's invention, for example, the science of entomology in the United States was, for over twenty years, completely preoccupied with the use of insecticides as a research line. Older areas of research on insect biology and biological

P

control of insects were discarded. Problems with the effectiveness and social acceptability of insecticides stimulated the development of new lines of inquiries in applied entomology after the 1950s.

Outside of the pest control sciences, pesticides had broad, indirect effects. Applied sciences such as agronomy and forestry reoriented their research lines to projects that presumed the use of pesticides. Ecology acquired both a new tool and a new set of problems. Insecticides, for example, were useful for capturing hard-to-catch insects and for experimental alterations of community structures. Similarly, pollution by pesticides opened up new lines of inquiry about the unintended effects, transport, and metabolic fates of chemicals in the environment. Regulation of pesticides was a stimulus to develop the science of risk assessment, which attempted to quantify the health hazards of factors like pesticides.

BIBLIOGRAPHY

Bosso, Christopher J. *Pesticides & Politics.* Pittsburgh: University of Pittsburgh Press, 1987.

Brooks, Paul. *The House of Life, Rachel Carson at Work.* Greenwich, CT: Fawcett, 1972.

Carson, Rachel. *Silent Spring.* Boston: Houghton Mifflin, 1962.

Debach, Paul, and David Rosen. *Biological Control by Natural Enemies.* 2d ed. Cambridge, U.K.: Cambridge University Press, 1991.

Dunlap, Thomas R. *DDT, Scientists, Citizens, and Public Policy.* Princeton: Princeton University Press, 1981.

Graham, Frank, Jr. *Since Silent Spring.* Greenwich, CT: Fawcett, 1970.

Howard, L.O. *Fighting the Insects, The Story of an Entomologist.* New York: Macmillan, 1933.

Perkins, John H. *Insects, Experts, and the Insecticide Crisis.* New York: Plenum, 1982.

Smith, Ray F., Thomas E. Mittler, and Carroll N. Smith, eds. *History of Entomology.* Palo Alto, CA: Annual Reviews, 1973.

Whorton, James. *Before Silent Spring, Pesticides and Public Health in Pre-DDT America.* Princeton: Princeton University Press, 1974.

Wright, Angus. *The Death of Ramón González, The Modern Agricultural Dilemma.* Austin: University of Texas Press, 1990.

Zimdahl, Robert L. *Weed Science, A Plea for Thought.* United States Department of Agriculture, Cooperative State Research Service, A Symposium Preprint, 1991.

John H. Perkins

Pharmacology

The science involving the study of the interaction of chemicals with living matter. Although the word "pharmacology" goes back to at least the seventeenth century in the English language, the modern science of experimental pharmacology did not emerge until the nineteenth century. Originally the term "pharmacology" was used in a broad sense to refer to the study of drugs in all their aspects, including their origin, composition, physical and chemical properties, physiological effects, therapeutic uses, preparation, and administration. The word is still sometimes used in this older sense, leading to confusion about what the science encompasses. During the course of the nineteenth century, the term "pharmacology" came to be increasingly applied specifically to that portion of the science of drugs that concerned itself with the investigation of their physiological effects. The practitioners of this new science called themselves pharmacologists.

Pharmacology as a discipline may be said to have had its intellectual roots in physiology and its institutional roots in materia medica. The science of experimental pharmacology emerged as an offshoot of physiology. It was the nineteenth-century French pioneers of experimental physiology, such as Francois Magendie and Claude Bernard, who also helped to define the problems to be investigated by pharmacology, such as the site and mode of action of drugs, and developed or refined many of the experimental techniques of the field. It was in the Germanic universities in the second half of the nineteenth century, however, that pharmacology became institutionalized as an independent discipline. It found its niche in the medical schools by replacing the traditional didactic courses in materia medica, which focused on the description of the natural sources of drugs, their composition, preparation, and so forth.

Perhaps no individual did as much to establish pharmacology as a separate discipline as Oswald Schmiedeberg, whose laboratory at the University of Strassburg trained more than 150 pharmacologists. At the time of his death in 1921, some forty chairs of pharmacology were held by his students internationally. It was one of Schmiedeberg's students, John Jacob Abel (1857–1938), who is considered to be the "father of American pharmacology."

After receiving his undergraduate degree at the University of Michigan and doing a year of postgraduate work at Johns Hopkins University, Abel went to Germany to study biomedical science in 1884. He spent six and one-half years studying at universities in Germany, Austria, and Switzerland, perhaps the longest such apprenticeship for an American in that period. Some two years of that time were spent in Strassburg, where he received his M.D. degree and worked in the laboratory of Schmiedeberg.

In 1891, Abel accepted the chair of materia medica and therapeutics at the University of Michigan. Despite the retention of the traditional title for the chair, this appointment represents the first modern chair of pharmacology in the United States. Abel brought with him to Michigan the German tradition of experimental pharmacology as molded by Schmiedeberg and others. He immediately transformed the traditional materia medica course at Michigan into a course in modern pharmacology, which included vivisection demonstrations to illustrate his lectures. He also took steps to establish a laboratory in which he could pursue his research interests.

When Johns Hopkins University opened its medical school in 1893, Abel was called there to be its first professor of pharmacology, a position that he held until his retirement in 1933. Abel's laboratory at Johns Hopkins served as a training ground for a generation of pharmacologists who went on to fill the increasing number of posts that were opening in universities, government agencies, and industrial firms.

By 1910, the year in which the Flexner Report on medical education was issued, the transformation from materia medica to pharmacology had taken place at a significant number of the nation's better medical schools, such as Western Reserve University, the University of Pennsylvania, and the College of Physicians and Surgeons of Columbia University. By that time, certain government agencies, such as the Hygienic Laboratory of the Public Health Service and the Bureau of Chemistry of the Department of Agriculture, has also begun to employ pharmacologists on their staffs. Even a few of the more research-oriented pharmaceutical companies, such as Parke Davis, were beginning to hire pharmacologists. Academic pharmacologists tended to view their industrial colleagues with suspicion, however, and refused to admit them into their national professional society until 1941.

Additional evidence that pharmacology was well on its way to becoming professionalized in the United States by the end of the first decade of the twentieth century may be found in the establishment of a national society and professional journal. On 28 December 1908, eighteen men met at Johns Hopkins University at Abel's invitation to form the American Society for Pharmacology and Experimental Therapeutics. The following year, Abel also took the lead in founding a journal for the field, the *Journal of Pharmacology and Experimental Therapeutics,* a publication which he edited until his retirement in 1933.

Over the course of the twentieth century, American pharmacology has continued to expand its size and influence. Pharmacologists began to be employed by academic health science programs other than medical schools, such as schools of pharmacy and veterinary medicine. Use of pharmacologists in government and industrial laboratories greatly increased. The number of graduate programs in the field has risen dramatically from a handful in the period before 1930 to close to 200 today. Increasingly, pharmacologists are trained by obtaining a specialized Ph.D. in the field rather than an M.D. Subdisciplines such as toxicology, clinical pharmacology, and molecular pharmacology have come into their own in recent decades.

American pharmacology has received relatively little attention from historians of science. One recent book examines the establishment of the discipline in this country, but much remains to be done. There are no full-length biographies, for example, of any of the leaders in the field. Comparative studies with the development of pharmacology in other countries, such as Great Britain and France, would help to establish what was unique about American pharmacology and the circumstances that shaped it. Studies of the relationship of American pharmacology to its sister biomedical disciplines, such as physiology and biochemistry, are also needed. The focus of most of the research to date has been on the institutional development of the subject, with relatively little analysis of the actual scientific work that was carried out in American pharmacological laboratories. The more recent history of the discipline, especially in relation to such developments as the animal rights movement, the rise of molecular biology, and increasing regulation of drugs, also merits attention.

BIBLIOGRAPHY

Chen, K.K., ed. *The American Society for Pharmacology and Experimental Therapeutics, Incorporated: The First Sixty Years, 1908–1969.* Bethesda, MD: American Society for Pharmacology and Experimental Therapeutics, 1969.

Cowen, David. "Materia Medica and Pharmacology." In *The Education of American Physicians,* edited by Ronald

P

L. Numbers. Berkeley: University of California Press, 1980, pp. 95–121.

John Jacob Abel, M.D., Investigator, Teacher, Prophet, 1857–1938: A Collection of Papers by and about the Father of American Pharmacology. Baltimore: Williams and Wilkins, 1957.

Parascandola, John. *The Development of American Pharmacology: John J. Abel and the Shaping of a Discipline.* Baltimore: Johns Hopkins University Press, 1992.

Parascandola, John, and Elizabeth Keeney. *Sources in the History of American Pharmacology.* Madison, WI: American Institute of the History of Pharmacy, 1983.

Rosenberg, Charles E. "Abel John Jacob." *The Dictionary of Scientific Biography.* Edited by Charles Gilliespie. New York, Scribners, 1970, 1:9–12.

Swain, Henry H., E.M.K. Geiling, and Alexander Heingartner. "John Jacob Abel at Michigan: The Introduction of Pharmacology into the Medical Curriculum." *University of Michigan Medical Bulletin* 29 (1963): 1–14.

John Parascandola

Philadelphia Centennial Exhibition

Early in 1876, several months before the opening of the Philadelphia fair, astronomer Simon Newcomb decried the backward state of the theoretical sciences in the United States. Americans, he believed, were accomplished "reasoners" and inventors not given to theorizing. In many respects, the Philadelphia Centennial Exhibition confirmed his worst fears.

Organized to celebrate the centenary of American Independence and to promote sentiments of nationalism in the wake of the Civil War, the Philadelphia Centennial Exhibition included a stunning array of technological innovations: a new and improved Gatling Gun (machine gun), Alexander Graham Bell's telephone, Corliss's towering steam engine, and some seventy-five inventions by women. With many of these displays concentrated in Machinery Hall, the largest building ever constructed to date, the fair certainly gave the impression that technology, not science, represented the soul of America.

Pure, or abstract, science may have been overshadowed by the fair's pulsating engines of change, but it was hardly absent. Central to the exhibition's existence was a taxonomy rooted in contemporary scientific ideas about the nature of human progress, especially the conviction that progress could be measured according to presumed racial differences. This classificatory emphasis was particularly clear in the United States

Government Building, where ethnologists from the Smithsonian Institution organized a major exhibit of Native American cultures that had the effect—especially in the context of George Armstrong Custer's defeat just when the fair was in full swing—of reinforcing prevailing views that Native Americans were closer to "savagery" than "civilization."

For American scientists generally, the centennial exhibition may well have confirmed the perception that in the United States science took a back seat to technology. But for scientists at the Smithsonian Institution, the fair marked a rebirth. In the aftermath of the centennial exhibition, the Smithsonian acquired funds to build a new museum to house exhibits acquired from the fair in Philadelphia and Smithsonian scientists became increasingly committed to educating the public about "applied science." It would remain for a later generation of scientists to seize the offensive on behalf of "pure" scientific research. Their efforts culminated in the Hall of Science at the 1933 Chicago Century of Progress Exposition—a building that initially bore the name The Temple of Science.

BIBLIOGRAPHY

Post, Robert, ed. *1876: A Centennial Exhibition.* Washington, DC: Smithsonian Institution Press, 1976.

Warner, Deborah Jean. "Women Inventors at the Centennial." In *Dynamos and Virgins Revisited: Women and Technological Change in History,* edited by Martha Moore Trescott. Metuchen, NJ: Scarecrow Press, 1979, pp. 102–119.

Robert W. Rydell

SEE ALSO
World's Fairs

Phrenology

The nineteenth-century science of the mind originating in the investigations of European researchers Franz Josef Gall and Johann Gaspar Spurzheim. Gall investigated the anatomy of the brain and proposed a theory of cerebral localization which argued that each of our principal mental traits (e.g., conscientiousness, avarice, self-esteem) is controlled by a specific and determinable area or region of the brain. Gall believed that an examination of the contour of a person's cranium could reveal the size and relative strength of each of these regions of the brain. The sum total of these cranial characteristics would provide a precise index of the individual's intellectual, moral, and emotional character. Spurzheim expanded upon Gall's "discovery" that each of our mental and moral characteristics corresponds to a distinct region of the brain. In particular, Spurzheim maintained that, by engaging in rigorous forms of mental exercise or self-discipline, we can consciously go about the task of strengthening or inhibiting selected character traits. Spurzheim thus gave to phrenology a melioristic quality that made it appealing to the perfectionistic and progressivist spirit of nineteenth-century American culture.

George Combe, a Scottish attorney and founder of the Edinburgh Phrenological Society, and Robert Collyer, a British physician, each conducted lecture tours of the major cities in the eastern portion of the United States between 1838 and 1840. In introducing Americans to Gall's investigations of cerebral physiology, Combe and Collyer hastened its metamorphosis into a fledgling social science with which well-meaning Americans might go about envisioning programs for perfecting the American character. A number of Americans began conducting their own phrenological research and produced phrenological charts mapping out the cranial location of each new mental organ they encountered. Not surprisingly, there was little or no uniformity in their science as independent researchers continued to add such phrenological organs as the love of Bologna sausage, the propensity to kiss women, the tendency to swindle the public out of money, or the urge to enjoy strong drink. Nonetheless, phrenological information was thought to be useful for devising new and scientifically grounded policies for regulating such areas of life as education, moral upbringing, employment decisions, and the treatment of both criminals and the insane. Specific treatment programs ranging from memorization drills to the application of leeches were recommended for the purpose of either strengthening or shrinking the cranial regions associated with specific character traits.

Among the best known of American phrenologists were Lorenzo and Orson Fowler. The Fowlers showed little interest in phrenology's important attempts to further the anatomical study of the brain, but were much taken by its potential for scientifically gauging a person's character. They began publishing a number of books and journals on phrenology that provided information for conducting a "head-reading" with which one might precisely assess another person's mental and moral character. The Fowlers' proselytizing efforts on

behalf of phrenology helped disseminate this early psychological science among the American reading public. And although interest in phrenology dissipated by the late 1850s, phrenological theories found their way into any number of the era's progressivist medical and scientific causes, such as mesmerism, homeopathy, and hydropathy. Most importantly, however, phrenology introduced the American public to the importance of brain physiology for an understanding of the mind and helped forge popular interest in the fledgling field of psychology, which would not appear in American universities until the 1880s.

BIBLIOGRAPHY

Davies, John D. *Phrenology: Fad and Science.* New Haven: Yale University Press, 1955.

Wrobel, Arthur. "Phrenology as Political Science." In *Pseudo-Science and Society in Nineteenth-Century America,* edited by Arthur Wrobel. Lexington: University of Kentucky Press, 1987, pp. 122–143.

Robert C. Fuller

Physics

The practice of physics developed in the United States in four approximate stages. A period of scientific colonialism existed during the early decades of political independence. Next came a mid- through late-nineteenth-century era of increased professionalism and institutional growth. The first half of the twentieth century witnessed a trend toward centralized, Big Science, while the last half saw a resurgence of pluralism within the American community of physicists.

The American Philosophical Society, founded in 1769 in Philadelphia, and the American Academy of Arts and Sciences, organized in Boston in 1780, were regionally important "amateur" societies that reflected both Enlightenment and patriotic spirit. While initiating some internationally respected research in natural philosophy—as physics was then known—the members of these two societies depended heavily on European colleagues for institutional and conceptual support. Furthermore, although these societies were active, natural philosophy in America was not yet a community endeavor, depending more on the strength of a few investigators. Whereas astronomers David Rittenhouse and Nathaniel Bowditch touched on aspects of natural philosophy, their illustrious predecessor Benjamin Franklin carried out the most concerted research program in

P

the field. His midcentury electrical experiments and theories earned him the accolades of his European peers.

The transfer of the seat of government from Philadelphia to Washington in 1800 dampened hopes that the American Philosophical Society might provide a national focus for science. President Thomas Jefferson attempted to foster American scientific excellence around 1800, as did John Quincy Adams around 1825. Reluctant members of Congress, however, often citing constitutional constraints, stifled such plans for federal science programs. Although the colleges that were proliferating during the first half of the nineteenth century offered courses in natural philosophy, the professors and students viewed the courses as providing training in the liberal arts rather than in research. Original investigations in natural philosophy still depended on individual initiatives—particularly initiatives within a European scientific context. Joseph Henry's contributions in electromagnetism in the years around 1830 illustrate the dilemma of the aspiring investigator. Although on the forefront of many important findings—particularly involving electromagnetic induction—Henry repeatedly was constrained by heavy teaching loads, a deficiency of research materials, and limited access to the main international practitioners, societies, and journals.

Near midcentury, the traditional label of "natural philosophy" was giving way to the increasingly popular label of "physics." So, too, amateur organizations were giving way to the more professional American Association for the Advancement of Science (AAAS), started in 1848, and National Academy of Sciences (NAS), founded in 1863. While neither the AAAS nor the NAS provided fully ample institutional support for physicists, the AAAS did establish a division exclusively for physicists. Only in the 1890s, with the organization of their own American Physical Society (APS), however, would physicists obtain a unifying focus for their technical and professional efforts. Similarly, *Silliman's Journal,* an interdisciplinary periodical that ably served investigators such as Henry from the 1820s through the 1860s, gave way after the Civil War to a variety of highly specialized journals. These journals included the *Physical Review,* established by physicists Edward Nichols and Ernest Merritt in 1893 and taken over by the APS in 1912.

As the nineteenth century progressed, government scientific bureaus began to multiply and gave some support for physics, particularly the popular field of geophysics. When Alexander Dallas Bache took control of the Coast Survey in 1843, he soon made it the leading antebellum organization for geophysical research. Meanwhile, after a decade of debate, the government in 1846 finally authorized the Smithsonian Institution, whose board of regents installed Henry as director. By making the Smithsonian a clearinghouse for research in all branches of science, Henry did bring some coherence to the efforts of physics practitioners around the nation.

While antebellum colleges had included natural philosophy as part of the liberal arts curriculum, Harvard's Lawrence Science School, founded in the 1840s, and Yale's Sheffield School, opened in the 1850s, pointed the way to the study of particular technical fields as professional disciplines, including physics. Nevertheless, the more enterprising physics students still felt obliged to study abroad, in the European centers of physics. By the 1880s, however, various American universities, particularly Johns Hopkins University, were further encouraging specialization and professionalism by awarding Ph.D.'s in the sciences. Even high schools and academies reflected and reinforced this trend; in the 1880s and 1890s, educators fostered the transition from the textbook study of natural philosophy to the laboratory study of physics. This professionalizing trend received a further boost at the turn of the century when physicists increasingly found jobs in industry, private foundations, and government. The most visible of these new employers included the National Bureau of Standards and the Carnegie Institute, both opened in 1901, and laboratories at American Telephone and Telegraph and at General Electric.

By the closing decades of the nineteenth century, physicists in the United States were starting to move beyond the era of inadequate colleges and graduate schools, ineffective professional societies, and inconsequential scientific journals. Indeed, the United States had become home to a small but productive group of internationally active research physicists. Most prominent were Henry Rowland, professor at Johns Hopkins University best known for his experiments with diffraction gratings; Josiah Willard Gibbs, Yale mathematical physicist who excelled in thermodynamics and statistical mechanics; and Albert A. Michelson, Annapolis-trained experimenter whose interferometer studies of light waves helped earn him the earliest Nobel Prize awarded to an American scientist.

Beginning about 1900, American academic physicists for the first time matched their counterparts in

France, Germany, and England in level of expenditures, volume of publications, and number of practitioners. Physicists were prospering not only in academic realms, but also in government, industry, and private foundations. The National Research Council—organized during World War I by astrophysicist George Ellery Hale and later directed by physicist Robert A. Millikan, recognized for his measurements of the basic electronic charge—provided the nation's scientists with a persuasive firsthand exposure to the advantages of centralized, large-scale, cooperative research. This positive wartime experience led scientific leaders to endorse this type of coordinated research as the new goal for peacetime science. Although this new image fully matched neither the reality nor the needs of actual scientific endeavor (physics in the United States remained primarily a small-scale, individual enterprise), it did help pave the way for the emergence of Big Science in the 1930s and 1940s. Epitomizing this trend was Ernest O. Lawrence and M. Stanley Livingston's development of successively larger cyclotrons and the use of these particle accelerators in creating radioisotopes (often for medical applications) and, eventually, transuranium elements.

Meanwhile, although the Great Depression caused setbacks, physicists consolidated their gains with new professional organizations, academic programs, and links to industry. In 1931, not only the academic and industrial physicists but also their proliferating professional societies affiliated under the administrative umbrella of the American Institute of Physics. While sharing institutional resources, the affiliated societies insisted on retaining their individual identities: the American Physical Society, the Optical Society of America, the Acoustical Society of America, the Society of Rheology, and the American Association of Physics Teachers. Also, the steadfastness and multiplicity of regional colleges and universities ensured a robust and diverse educational system conducive to the training and employment of physicists.

In the period from about 1919 to 1935, the transmission of quantum mechanics and relativity theory to the United States contributed to the advance of theoretical studies in a community already noted for its experimental investigations. Americans who distinguished themselves in early quantum studies, experimental and theoretical, included Arthur Compton, the team of Clinton Davisson and Lester Germer, and Edward Condon. During the mid-1930s, the influx of European refugee physicists, fleeing political and racial oppression, boosted even further the community's research capabilities. Albert Einstein's emigration to the United States in 1933 symbolized what most observers considered the nation's ascendancy to world leadership in physics.

From 1939 through 1945, with the onset of World War II and the Manhattan Project, many leading native-born and immigrant physicists committed themselves to developing nuclear bombs. Relying on massive, federal funding and working in large, centralized laboratories, these researchers designed bombs that exploited the tremendous energy released from uranium or plutonium atoms undergoing nuclear fission. The crash program to build these weapons fused the relationship in the United States between physics, government, and society. Through organizations such as the Office of Scientific Research and Development and through the actions of physicists such as Lawrence, Enrico Fermi, and J. Robert Oppenheimer, the nation's political and scientific leaders came to embrace the idea of federally funded Big Science. And with the dropping of the first bombs on the Japanese cities of Hiroshima and Nagasaki in August 1945, citizens realized that the interests of society had become inexorably linked to physics.

After the war, the nation's leaders closely scrutinized the relationship between science, government, and society before founding the Atomic Energy Commission in 1946 and the National Science Foundation in 1950. Also after the war, many veterans of Los Alamos and other wartime projects entailing physics became partisans in the political arena. Whereas those physicists who were more critical of the government's nuclear policies participated in postwar political action groups such as the Federation of Atomic Scientists, those who were more supportive served as key presidential and governmental advisors. Some of these physicists—most prominently Oppenheimer in 1954—found themselves entrapped in the loyalty and security quagmire of the era of the Cold War, McCarthyism, and fusion bombs. Fusion or "hydrogen bombs," were the "super" weapons that physicists such as Edward Teller helped bring into production by 1952 to supersede the original fission or "atomic bombs."

Though Big Science projects received the most attention and support in the postwar decades, the physics community never lost its pluralistic character. That is, a variety of institutional, economic, and political principles continued to guide its members as they worked in diverse institutional settings—settings fostered by

P

universities, foundations, industry, the government, and the military. To be sure, the tendency toward centralized Big Science, particularly in nuclear and high-energy physics, persisted. Physicists flourished at major facilities structured around nuclear reactors, magnetic fusion reactors, and particle accelerators. These included Argonne National Laboratory, Brookhaven National Laboratory, Fermi National Accelerator Laboratory, W.K. Kellogg Radiation Laboratory, Lawrence Berkeley Laboratory, Los Alamos National Laboratory, Oak Ridge National Laboratory, Princeton Plasma Physics Laboratory, and the Stanford Linear Accelerator Center. But there remained vigorous, smaller research programs, particularly in academic and industrial settings. Breakthroughs in optical and condensed-matter physics occurred, for example, at industry-sponsored facilities such as Bell Laboratories. Whereas the Big Science efforts allowed for concerted investigations on particular problems, the small-group ventures allowed for a divergence of individual research styles. During the postwar decades, these various initiatives resulted in the development of the transistor and the laser. The initiatives also produced theoretical breakthroughs in quantum electrodynamics and superconductivity. And there were interdisciplinary endeavors: astrophysicists helped detect residual cosmic effects from the big bang; geophysicists participated in the unfolding of plate tectonics; and biophysicists contributed to the advance of molecular biology.

Into the 1960s, veterans of the Manhattan Project still enjoyed a disproportionate level of control over national policies in all fields of science. With the reevaluation of governmental actions sparked by the criticisms of the Vietnam era, however, the aging leadership began to lose its control. This erosion of the physicists' political power was eventually compounded by the erosion of their economic resources, particularly with the end of the Cold War and arms race in the late 1980s. Contending with a less favorable political and economic climate, American physicists witnessed the demise of two predominant federal programs. The Strategic Defense Initiative, a space-weapons program closely tied to the Lawrence Livermore Laboratory and other national physics installations, lost much of its funding in the years bracketing 1990. And the Superconducting Super Collider, a multibillion dollar facility being constructed in Texas for research on quarks and leptons, had its funding withdrawn in the early 1990s. Moreover, within the physics community's own ranks, academic physicists showed signs of becoming an increasingly greying population as fewer students either earned doctoral degrees in physics or took related university positions. And despite repeated corrective efforts, the community achieved only modest improvements in a perennial problem: underrepresentation of women and minorities in physics.

As the twentieth century drew to a close, however, a consensus remained that American physicists still paced the world in most branches of research. Among the achievements of the closing decades was the 1986 isolation of materials that displayed superconductivity at unusually high temperatures. Physicists in the United States further contributed to breakthroughs in quantum chromodynamics, electroweak theory, and renormalization-group theory. Indeed, practitioners' achievements ranged from probing the cosmological concept of an inflationary universe to developing the medically vital technique of magnetic-resonance imaging (MRI). The community's persistent vitality perhaps reflected its continued pluralism. Working in large and small groups and representing a wide spectrum of professional affiliations, the physicists explored a diversity of topics from a variety of perspectives. Their interests extended from classical fields such as optics and acoustic to fields at the frontiers of research: elementary-particle physics; nuclear physics; atomic, molecular, and optical physics; condensed-matter physics; plasmas and fluids; and gravitation, cosmology, and cosmic-ray physics. And their affiliations stretched, as they had for most of the century, from universities and private foundations to the government, the military, and industry.

BIBLIOGRAPHY

Adair, Robert K., Ernest M. Henley, et al. "Special Issue: *Physical Review* Centenary—from Basic Research to High Technology." *Physics Today* 46 (1993): 22–73.

Goodwin, Irwin, et al. "Special Issue: Physics Through the 1990s." *Physics Today* 39 (1986): 22–47.

Kevles, Daniel J. *The Physicists: The History of a Scientific Community in Modern America.* 2d ed. Cambridge, MA: Harvard University Press, 1987.

Moyer, Albert E. "History of Physics." *Osiris,* 2d ser., 1 (1985): 163–182.

Ramsey, Norman F., Spencer R. Weart, A.P. French, et al. "50 Years of Physics in America." [Special issue commemorating the anniversary of the AIP.] *Physics Today* 34 (1981): 13–261.

Rhodes, Richard. *The Making of the Atomic Bomb.* New York: Simon & Schuster, 1986.

Albert E. Moyer

Pickering, Edward Charles (1846–1919)

Astronomer and observatory director. Born in Boston, Pickering graduated from the Lawrence Scientific School in 1865. After teaching there and at the Massachusetts Institute of Technology (MIT), he was appointed director of the Harvard College Observatory (HCO) in 1877, a position he held until his death in Cambridge. From 1903 until his death, he served as president of the American Astronomical Society.

Pickering approached astronomy from the perspective of a physicist. At MIT, he had established the first physical laboratory in the United States specifically designed for student instruction, and later published the first American laboratory manual of physics. At the HCO, he immediately made the new field of astrophysics its main research program.

In all of his astronomical investigations, Pickering was not a speculator or theorizer, but rather a collector of facts. With this Baconian approach, he instituted vast research projects, often of a considerably routine nature, for the future solution of basic stellar problems.

In the early years of his directorship, he initiated several fundamental investigations. These included visual photometric and spectroscopic studies of the stars, a photographic determination of their light and color, and a photographic project to map the entire sky.

The acquisition of two major funds in 1886 and 1887 enabled him to dramatically transform both the nature and scope of the HCO research program. The Henry Draper Fund provided ongoing money to photograph, measure, and classify stellar spectra. The U.A. Boyden bequest enabled him to establish an observatory in Arequipa, Peru. As a result, he was able to carry out his spectroscopic and photometric investigations in both hemispheres.

Around 1902–1903, at the time of the celebration of his twenty-fifth anniversary as director of the HCO and assumption of his duties as president of the American Astronomical Society, Pickering began to see himself in a new, larger role—that of ambassador to the national and international astronomical communities. But his ideas did not always meet with success. He failed, for example, to win support for his plans to secure a multimillion dollar fund which he could use to distribute grants to astronomers in the United States and abroad, and to secure funds for an internationally administered eighty-four-inch telescope to be established in the southern hemisphere.

In the later years of his directorship, he devoted most of his time and energy to secure universal acceptance of the Harvard systems of photographic magnitudes and spectral classification. Pickering achieved brilliant success here; both Harvard systems were adopted by the International Union for Cooperation in Solar Research in 1913.

Pickering ran the HCO like a factory manager, deeply concerned with matters of efficiency and productivity. This entrepreneurial approach led to splendid successes, but also raised some difficult questions. Who deserved credit for the discovery of a star with a peculiar spectra, for example, the assistant at Arequipa who took the photographic plate and first noticed it, or the one in Cambridge who measured and classified it? Pickering straddled the fence on this issue, trying to suggest that both persons should take equal pride in their work.

More difficult was the question of whose name should go on a publication, that of the subordinate who carried out the investigation, or Pickering's, as head of the observatory and organizer of the research? Here, he underwent a change. Although his name appeared as the author of the early Draper catalogs, with the notation that the work was "aided" by one or more assistants, in the later catalogs, he and the chief investigators were listed as coauthors.

A final difficulty centered on the issue of gender. As a resourceful administrator, Pickering was acutely aware that women computers could be hired for considerably lower wages than men. Although most of them performed routine tasks, some assumed roles of greater responsibility. At a time when Mrs. Williamina Paton Fleming held a corporate position as curator of astronomical photographs, she felt compelled to complain to Pickering that she deserved a salary more comparable to those of the male assistants. Along with his economical reasons for hiring women, however, it should be kept in mind that he genuinely took great pride in their work at Harvard, and helped several obtain jobs elsewhere.

During the forty-two years of his directorship of the HCO, Pickering developed a vast network of personal contact and correspondence with astronomers and observatories throughout the world. In many ways, the history of his directorship is the history of the observatory itself; it is next to impossible to separate his achievements from those of the HCO. In the final analysis, his significance lies more in the institutional

P

development of astronomy than in his own scientific accomplishments.

Pickering's personal and official papers, totaling sixty-eight linear feet, are in the Harvard University Archives. To date, there is no full-length biography of him.

BIBLIOGRAPHY

Bailey, Solon I. *The History and Work of Harvard Observatory, 1839 to 1927.* New York: McGraw-Hill, 1931.

———. "Edward Charles Pickering." *Biographical Memoirs of the National Academy of Sciences* 15 (1934): 169–178.

DeVorkin, David H. "A Sense of Community in Astrophysics: Adopting a System of Spectral Classification." *Isis* 72 (1981): 29–49.

Hoffleit, Dorrit. "The Evolution of the Henry Draper Memorial." *Vistas in Astronomy* 34 (1991): 107–162.

Jones, Bessie Zaban, and Lyle Gifford Boyd. *The Harvard College Observatory. The First Four Directorships, 1839–1919.* Cambridge, MA: Harvard University Press, 1971.

Mack, Pamela E. "Strategies and Compromises: Women in Astronomy at Harvard College Observatory, 1870–1920." *Journal for the History of Astronomy* 21 (1990): 65–75.

Pickering, Edward Charles. *Elements of Physical Manipulation.* 2 vols. New York: Hurd & Houghton, 1873–1876.

Plotkin, Howard. "Edward C. Pickering and the Endowment of Scientific Research in America, 1877–1918." *Isis* 69 (1978): 44–57.

———. "Edward C. Pickering, the Henry Draper Memorial, and the Beginnings of Astrophysics in America." *Annals of Science* 35 (1978): 365–377.

———. "Edward C. Pickering." *Journal for the History of Astronomy* 21 (1990): 47–58.

———. "Harvard College Observatory's Boyden Station in Peru: Origin and Formative Years, 1879–1898." In *Mundialización de la ciencia y cultura nacional. Actas del Congreso Internacional "Ciencia, descubrimiento y mundo colonial,"* edited by A. Lafuente, A. Elena, and M.L. Ortega. Madrid: Doce Calles, 1993, pp. 689–705.

Howard Plotkin

SEE ALSO

American Astronomical Society; Harvard University

Pincus, Gregory Goodwin (1903–1967)

Reproductive biologist and endocrinologist. Pincus was born in Woodbine, New Jersey, into a scholarly family of Jewish farmers, grew up in the Bronx, and won a full Regents Scholarship to Cornell University (B.S., 1924). His interest in genetics brought him to Harvard University (M.S. and Sc.D., 1927) where he studied with the geneticist William E. Castle and the physiologist William J. Crozier. The mechanistic biology of Jacques Loeb, Crozier's hero, led Pincus to reproductive biology and endocrinology, where he spent the rest of his career.

After postgraduate work in Germany and England, where his developing interest in mammalian ova was reinforced, he returned to Harvard's Department of General Physiology in 1930. During the 1930s, although he studied diabetes mellitus and steroid hormones (mostly gonadal), his main work was on mammalian egg development. He showed that mammalian (rabbit) eggs could be fertilized in vitro. Like Loeb, who studied parthenogenesis in sea urchins, he also found that the eggs, stimulated parthenogenetically, that is, without a sperm, could develop into full-grown rabbits. This work was controversial—and remains so—because of the low yield (1/200) and doubts as to its reproducibility. Pincus got a national reputation, sometimes unfavorable, as a manipulator of life. Harvard listed his work as one of its "great scientific discoveries" at its tercentenary in 1936, but his department was eliminated by President Conant the next year and Pincus was not given tenure.

Hudson Hoagland, Pincus's fellow graduate student in the 1920s and in 1937 the chairman of Clark University's biology department, raised money to give Pincus a nonacademic position at Clark. Pincus now focused more on steroids and, beginning with World War II, switched mainly to studies of the adrenal cortical response to stress.

Unhappy with Clark, both Hoagland and Pincus left the school in 1944 and founded the Worcester Foundation for Experimental Biology, a research institute run entirely on donated funds. The focus on the adrenal cortex continued, although their junior colleague, M.C. Chang, continued some of the work on ova. Then in 1951, triggered by a visit and money from Margaret Sanger and Katherine McCormick, Pincus and Chang decided to see if some of the newly synthesized analogs of progesterone would prevent conception. Several did so in animals. Another colleague, the physician and gynecologist John Rock, chose one made by the G.D. Searle Co. as best for clinical trials in women. The trials were successful and "the pill," then quite controversial, got approved for marketing from the FDA as an oral contraceptive in 1960.

By now, Pincus was an administrator, fund-raiser, and publicizer; an international figure, his engineering approach to biology had succeeded.

BIBLIOGRAPHY

Ingle, D.J. "Gregory Goodwin Pincus." *Biographical Memoirs of the National Academy of Sciences* 42 (1971): 229–270.

Pincus, G. "Observations on the Living Eggs of the Rabbit." *Proceedings of the Royal Society of London,* B 107 (1930): 132–167.

———. "The Comparative Behavior of Mammalian Eggs in Vivo and in Vitro. IV. The Development of Fertilized and Artificially Activated Eggs." *Journal of Experimental Zoology* 82 (1939): 85–129.

———. *The Control of Fertility.* New York: Academic Press, 1965.

Pincus, G., and E.V. Enzmann. "Can Mammalian Eggs Undergo Normal Development in Vitro?" *Proceedings of the National Academy of Sciences* 20 (1934): 121–122.

Pincus, G., J. Rock, C.-R. Garcia, E. Rice-Wray, M. Paniagua, and I. Rodriquez. "Fertility Control with Oral Medication." *American Journal of Obstetrics and Gynecology* 75 (1958): 1333–1346.

Reed, J. *The Birth Control Movement and American Society: From Private Vice to Public Virtue.* Princeton: Princeton University Press, 1978, 1983.

Werthessen, N.T., and R.C. Johnson. "Pincogenesis-parthenogenesis in Rabbits by Gregory Pincus." *Perspectives in Biology and Medicine* 18 (1974): 86–93.

Clark T. Sawin, M.D.

SEE ALSO
Birth Control

Planetarium

United States astronomy education was transformed in the twentieth century by the introduction of a remarkable teaching tool, the projection planetarium. The word "planetarium" refers to "an optical projection instrument that shows upon the inner surface of a hemispherical dome, the stars, planets, sun, moon, and in most cases, [other] astronomical effects" (Hagar, p. 6). It may also signify the room or building in which the projector is housed.

The individual chiefly responsible for creating the projection planetarium was Oskar von Miller, director of the Deutsches Museum in Munich. As part of his integral approach to exhibit design, Miller wished to secure teaching aids that could provide confirmation of modern scientific theories. Specifically, he sought to demonstrate how apparent (geocentric) motions of celestial objects could be explained according to the Copernican (heliocentric) theory. After mechanical solutions to Miller's proposal were rejected, the projection planetarium was jointly conceived in 1919 by Walther Bauersfeld and Werner Straubel of the Carl Zeiss optical firm, Jena, Germany, and demonstrated publicly in October 1923. Zeiss planetaria were soon erected in a dozen European cities, while efforts were undertaken to bring the device to American audiences.

In the United States, planetaria were established according to three distinct styles of patronage and were responsible for a resurgence of popular interest in astronomy well *before* the first artificial satellites were launched. During the earliest phase, which lasted through 1946, Zeiss projectors were funded by wealthy private donors or foundations and erected in five metropolitan cities (Chicago, 1930; Philadelphia, 1933; Los Angeles, 1935; New York, 1935; and Pittsburgh, 1939). Their introduction was closely linked to construction of the nation's first industrial museums, which emulated Miller's famous Deutsches Museum. Because planetaria could reproduce celestial events, as seen from any location on the earth's surface and at any point in the remote past or distant future, they were readily envisioned as theaters of time and space. Programs initially focused upon the astronomical functions of the projector itself, but more speculative topics were also explored, especially theories concerning the Star of Bethlehem. Many concepts of space travel were first scientifically explained to lay audiences during the 1930s, while viewers witnessed realistic, simulated "trips to the moon." Finding the appropriate balance between education and entertainment has long been an issue among planetarium educators.

During a second phase, which began in 1947, vastly simplified pinhole-projection techniques were introduced by Armand Spitz, a lecturer at Philadelphia's Fels Planetarium. These devices sold for only a fraction of the cost of Zeiss instruments, and brought the planetarium experience to much wider audiences. For the first time, a host of smaller institutions, including public schools, colleges, and museums, could afford to purchase Spitz planetaria and install them in modest facilities everywhere. Spitz's vision of employing the widest possible uses for planetaria further diversified and democratized this growing profession. Concurrently, public interest in space science spread rapidly as

P

plans were formalized to launch an artificial satellite during the International Geophysical Year (1957–1958).

A third and final phase of planetarium development resulted from the "crisis of confidence" caused by launch of the Soviet *Sputnik* satellite. Long-standing resistance to federal support of education was finally broken by this apparent threat to our national security. Passage of the National Defense Education Act of 1958 brought sweeping changes to mathematics, science, and foreign-language instruction. Widespread availability of Title III funds administered under this program created a remarkable era of planetarium building, while the "race to the moon" pushed astronomy and space education to new levels of popularity during the 1960s. The number of American planetaria topped the 500 mark by 1970. Specialized conferences, associations, and internships were organized to meet the demands for a new generation of planetarium instructors. These activities culminated in the formation of the International Society of Planetarium Educators in 1970. On account of these (and other) factors, planetaria are perhaps the longest-lived beneficiaries which emerged from Cold War rhetoric following the aftermath of *Sputnik*.

Through these decades, planetaria were transformed from a handful of "elite" institutions into a national network of professional astronomy education centers. Millions of visitors attend planetarium programs annually to partake in the latest astronomical and space-related information. Planetaria have also been used to train countless military personnel and National Aeronautics and Space Administration astronauts in methods of celestial navigation. Educational research has measured student learning abilities in planetarium versus traditional classroom environments. Even the abilities of migratory birds to recognize celestial cues have been studied under their artificial skies. Once called the greatest teaching aid ever invented, planetaria have far outgrown their original pedagogical purposes and attracted new audiences unimagined by Oskar von Miller.

BIBLIOGRAPHY

Abbatantuono, Brent P. "Armand Neustadter Spitz and His Planetaria, with Historical Notes on the Model A at the University of Florida." Master's thesis, University of Florida, 1994.

Chamberlain, Joseph Miles. "The Administration of a Planetarium as an Educational Institution." Ed.D. diss., Columbia University, 1962.

Hagar, Charles F. *Planetarium: Window to the Universe.* Oberkochen, Ger.: Carl Zeiss, 1980.

King, Henry C. *Geared to the Stars: The Evolution of Planetariums, Orreries, and Astronomical Clocks.* Toronto: University of Toronto Press, 1978.

Lattin, Harriet Pratt. *Star Performance.* Philadelphia: Whitmore Publishing, 1969.

Letsch, Heinz. *Captured Stars.* Jena, Ger.: Gustav Fischer, 1959.

Marché, Jordan Dale, II. "Theaters of Time and Space: The American Planetarium Community, 1930–1970." Ph.D. diss., Indiana University, 1999.

Norton, O. Richard. *The Planetarium and Atmospherium: An Indoor Universe.* Healdsburg, CA: Naturegraph Publishers, 1968.

Werner, Helmut. *From the Aratus Globe to the Zeiss Planetarium.* Stuttgart, Ger.: Gustav Fischer, 1957.

Jordan D. Marché II

SEE ALSO

Astronomy and Astrophysics; Popularization of Science

Plate Tectonics

The term "plate tectonics" was first used by John F. Dewey and John M. Bird in 1970 in a paper entitled "Mountain Belts and the New Global Tectonics," in which they discussed how mountain belts form where crustal plates slide under continental margins. Modern theories of how mantle convection generates new crust along oceanic ridges and consumes equal areas along trenches, moving large plates of the earth's crust around in the process, date from seminal papers by Harry H. Hess in 1960 and 1962, and Robert S. Dietz in 1961. Similar ideas had been proposed previously by Osmond Fisher, Arthur Holmes, Felix Vening-Meinesz and others, but failed to achieve acceptance because supporting evidence was lacking as shown by B.F. Howell, Jr. in 1991. Critical support came from studies of the magnetization of the seafloor by Fred J. Vine and Drummond H. Matthews in 1963 and James R. Heirtzler, Xavier LePichon, and J. Gregory Baron in 1966. In 1965, J. Tuzo Wilson developed the theory of triple junctions, showing how plate motion could be accommodated at places where three plates met. That same year, George Plafker showed how ground displacements produced by the 1964 Alaskan earthquake were consistent with a plate being underthrust under Alaska. During the next few years, Bryan Isacks, Jack Oliver, and Lynn R. Sykes showed how Hess and Dietz's theory was consistent with seismic evidence and explained phenomena not previously understood. W. Jason Morgan showed how the earth's surface could be divided into twenty principal plates and showed that the motion of each could be described as rotation about a fixed pole. X. LePichon computed the relative velocities of the plates in 1968 and related these to the intensity of tectonic activity along the convergent boundaries.

Since the 1960s, plate tectonics has successfully explained a wide variety of current and ancient geologic phenomena and has been accepted as one of the most basic concepts of geoscience.

BIBLIOGRAPHY

Dewey, J.F., and J.M. Bird. "Mountain Belts and the New Global Tectonics." *Journal of Geophysical Research* 75 (1970): 2625–2647.

Dietz, R. S. "Continent and Ocean Basin Evolution by Spreading of the Seafloor." *Nature* 190 (1961): 854–865.

Heirtzler, J.R., X. LePichon, and J.G. Baron. "Magnetic Anomalies over the Reykjanes Ridge." *Deep-Sea Research* 13 (1966): 427–443.

Hess, H.H. "Evolution of Ocean Basins." *Report on Office of Naval Research Contract Nonr, 1958,* (10), 1960.

———. "History of the Ocean Basins," In *Petrologic Studies,* edited by A.E.J. Engel, H.L. James, and B.F. Leonard. Geological Society of America, 1962, pp. 599–620.

Howell, B.F., Jr. "How Misconceptions on Heat Flow May Have Delayed Discovery of Plate Tectonics." *Earth Science History* 10 (1991): 44–50.

Isacks, B.J., J. Oliver, and L.R. Sykes. "Seismology and the New Global Tectonics." *Journal of Geophysical Research* 73 (1968): 5855–5899.

LePichon, X. "Sea-floor Spreading and Continental Drift." *Journal of Geophysical Research* 73 (1968): 3661–3697.

Morgan, W.J. "Rises, Trenches, Great Faults and Crustal Blocks." *Journal of Geophysical Research* 73 (1968): 1659–1682.

Plafker, G. "Tectonic Deformation Associated with the 1964 Alaskan Earthquake." *Science* 148 (1965): 1675–1687.

Sykes, L.R. "Mechanism of Earthquakes and Nature of Faulting on Midocean Ridges." *Journal of Geophysical Research* 72 (1967): 2131–2153.

Vine, F.J., and D.H. Matthews. "Magnetic Anomalies over Ocean Ridges." *Nature* 199 (1963): 947–949.

Wilson, J. T. "A New Class of Faults and Their Bearing on Continental Drift." *Nature* 207 (1965): 243–247.

B.F. Howell Jr.

SEE ALSO
Geology

P

Polio

Paralytic viral disease. Cases of poliomyelitis (infantile paralysis) were rare before the 1890s, when outbreaks began to occur in western Europe and North America. Initially troubling rural communities, epidemic polio became an urban public health problem. In 1916, during the then largest epidemic, New York City alone had 8,900 cases. Physicians were (and remain) unable to provide more than symptomatic therapy, and until the 1950s could neither predict nor prevent the disease.

Polio is a disease of cleanliness. Before 1900, most people were infected by the virus as infants, developed few if any symptoms, and gained lifelong immunity. As improved sanitation and child-care protected young children in industrialized Western countries from natural infection, those infected later in life were more likely to develop paralysis, and the number and ages of paralytic polio cases increased. Thus, children from clean, middle-class homes were more at risk of the paralytic form of the disease than children from poor families.

The polio virus develops in the intestines, and, on occasion, spreads to the nervous system, leading to paralysis. If respiratory muscles are paralyzed, death can occur. In 1905, Swedish clinician Ivar Wickman identified children with limited symptoms, such as a fever and stiff neck, as "abortive" polio cases, and in 1908 and 1909, Karl Landsteiner, Constantin Levaditi, and Simon Flexner established through laboratory studies with experimental animals that polio was a filterable virus. Their view of polio as a neurotropic disease transmitted by droplet infection was not undermined until the 1930s and 1940s, when the work of David Bodian, Dorothy Horstmann, Isabel Morgan, Albert Sabin, John R. Paul, and James Trask suggested that polio entered the body through the mouth, traveled to the intestines via the blood, and only rarely affected the nervous system. In 1948, Boston virologist John Enders, in work that won a Nobel Prize in 1954, grew a strain of the polio virus in nonneurological tissue, pointing the way for the development of a safe vaccine.

Because polio was frightening, unpredictable, and without effective medical treatment, it gained public prominence far beyond its significance as a cause of morbidity and mortality. During the 1930s and 1940s, rehabilitation became a major health concern. The idea that polio could attack any child was promoted by the National Foundation for Infantile Paralysis, a philanthropic organization founded in 1937 as an outgrowth

P

of the interest of President Franklin Delano Roosevelt, whose legs were paralyzed by polio in 1921. The foundation developed sophisticated fund-raising campaigns—its best known, sending a dime to the White House, termed the March of Dimes. It funded a rehabilitation center in Warm Springs, Georgia, and by the late 1940s also supported professional training, hospital beds, crutches, iron lungs, and virological research. In 1940, Elizabeth Kenny, an Australian nurse, arrived in the United States with a new theory of polio that urged active muscle treatment rather than the more common practice of immobilization and splinting. Her relations with the medical establishment were stormy, but by the late 1940s versions of her method were being used in most polio wards.

The foundation funded work by American virologists Jonas Salk and Albert Sabin. By the 1950s, Salk had developed a killed-virus polio vaccine and Sabin a vaccine using an attenuated virus. In 1954, the foundation funded a nationwide double-blind clinical trial of the Salk vaccine, which involved 1.8 million children and established the vaccine as safe and effective. Reports in 1955 that vaccine lots produced by the Cutter Laboratories of Berkeley, California, had led to the paralysis and death of some children threatened public confidence, but the Cutter incident was resolved by greater federal monitoring of vaccine production. In 1961, the United States government licensed Sabin's oral vaccine, which he had tested in Mexico and the Soviet Union. Given in a syrup or sugar cube, unlike the multiple Salk injections, it provides more lasting immunity but holds a predictable risk of paralysis. The oral vaccine has been adopted by the United States and most other industrialized countries, but Sweden, Finland, and the Netherlands continue to use the Salk vaccine.

BIBLIOGRAPHY

Benison, Saul. *Tom Rivers: Reflections on a Life in Medicine and Science.* Cambridge, MA: MIT Press, 1967.

Daniel, Thomas M. and Frederick C. Robbins, eds. *Polio.* Rochester: University of Rochester Press, 1997.

Paul, John R. *A History of Poliomyelitis.* New Haven: Yale University Press, 1971.

Rogers, Naomi. *Dirt and Disease: Polio since FDR.* New Brunswick: Rutgers University Press, 1992.

Sass, Edmund J., ed. *Polio's Legacy: An Oral History.* Lanham, MD: University Press of America, 1996.

Smith, Jane S. *Patenting the Sun: Polio and the Salk Vaccine.* New York: William Morrow, 1990.

Naomi Rogers

Polymers

Long-chain molecules, usually having a carbon atom backbone. Polymers are the basic building materials of living things. In the form of wood, vegetable fibers, and protein, polymers constitute some of the oldest and most basic technologies. Modern polymer science has helped to create the enormous synthetic polymer industry that includes plastics, fibers, films, rubber, and paints. The most important scientific application of the polymer concept has been the elucidation of the storage and transmission of genetic information by the double-helixed DNA polymer; a puzzle first unraveled by James Watson and Francis Crick in 1953.

The scientific understanding of polymers is largely a twentieth-century development. Until modern structural organic chemistry, based on the concept of a carbon atom that forms four covalent chemical bonds to other atoms, was established in the 1860s, chemists did not have the concepts they needed to attack the complexities of large molecules. Earlier chemists had studied natural polymers such as cellulose, silk, and rubber, partly in the hope of discovering synthetic substitutes for these materials. In the 1830s, Jons J. Berzelius had coined the word "polymer" to designate compounds with the same proportionate composition but different number of total atoms. For example, in Great Britain in 1861, Greville Williams discovered that rubber could be decomposed into a single chemical compound, isoprene, suggesting that natural rubber was made of multiple isoprene molecules connected in some manner. Around 1900, the German chemist Emile H. Fischer began to study sugars, starches, and proteins using the new concepts of structural organic chemistry. He argued that these materials were long chains of up to 5,000 molecular weight. At about the same time, however, German physical chemists led by Wolfgang Ostwald, son of the great chemist Wilhelm Ostwald, began to argue that polymers were aggregates of smaller molecules held together by relatively weak colloidal bonds. This view was challenged in 1920 by another German chemist, Hermann Staudinger, who argued that polymers were long-chain molecules held together by ordinary covalent bonds between carbon atoms. Over the next fifteen years, a growing body of evidence validated Staudinger's hypothesis, which was proclaimed triumphant at a Faraday Society symposium in Cambridge, England, in 1935. One of the major paper presenters at the symposium was Wallace H. Carothers, a chemist employed by the DuPont Company in Wilmington, Delaware. Beginning in 1928, Carothers had developed procedures for building very long chain polymers with molecular weights over 10,000 using standard organic chemical reactions. He had synthesized polyesters using the reaction between acids and alcohols to form esters. He built long-chain molecules by using acids and alcohols that had reacting groups on both ends. Thus, the chains grew in a manner analogous to train cars being coupled together. In the course of work on polymer formation, Carothers's associates made polymers that were analogs of rubber and silk, which became the commercial products neoprene and nylon, respectively.

The Faraday Society meeting marked the beginning of polymer science as a discipline, although it grew slowly at first. Because of the growing industrial importance of polymers, much of the early work centered in industry rather than in academia. Future Nobel Prize winner (1974) Paul Flory began his work on the physical chemistry of polymerization and polymers while working with Carothers at DuPont. Academic interest in polymers was stimulated by Carl S. "Speed" Marvel at the University of Illinois and Herman F. Mark at Brooklyn Polytechnic Institute. During the 1930s, industrial polymer technology advanced dramatically with the discovery and/or commercialization of polyvinylchloride, polystyrene, polyethylene, Teflon, nylon, neoprene, synthetic rubber, and acrylic polymers. New production technologies such as emulsion polymerization greatly enhanced control over polymerization reactions and the characteristics of polymers.

An American polymer science community formed during World War II as part of the crash program to develop a synthetic rubber industry. With a solid scientific and technological infrastructure in place, polymers became one of the glamour industries of the postwar era. Important new types of polymers developed included polyesters, polyurethanes, polypropylene, polycarbonates, and many exotic high-technology materials. Polymer science advanced both in the understanding of polymeric materials and in new methods of polymerization. A polymeric substance is not a single chemical compound but a mixture of chains of different lengths which can fold in many ways. Many polymer chains fold in regular patterns creating crystalline regions. Polymer chains can also be branched instead of stringlike. In the postwar era, physical polymer chemists, notably Paul Flory, investigated the relationship between these polymer characteristics and the properties of the

material. In the field of polymerization, there were two significant breakthroughs. The first was solution polymerization developed by Paul Morgan and his associates at DuPont in the 1950s. This method allowed the polymerization of many compounds that resisted other methods. Commercially, Lycra spandex and Kevlar polyaramid fibers resulted from this work. The breakthrough was made in Germany by Karl Ziegler, who discovered a new catalyst system that grew additional polymer chains in an orderly manner. These catalysts allowed chemists to grew very regular polymer chains that exhibited unique properties. In addition, Ziegler's catalysts made the production of new polymers possible, including polypropylene. Ziegler and Italian chemist Gulio Natta shared the 1963 Nobel Prize in chemistry for these discoveries.

Polymer science evolved from the application of scientific concepts from many disciplines to understanding the formation and properties of large molecules.

BIBLIOGRAPHY
Furukawa, Yasu. "Hermann Staudinger and the Emergence of the Macromolecular Concept." *Historia Scientiarum* 22 (1982): 1–18.
Hounshell, David A., and John Kenly Smith Jr. *Science and Corporate Strategy, Du Pont R&D, 1902–1980.* New York: Cambridge University Press, 1988.
Morris, Peter J.T. *Polymer Pioneers.* Philadelphia: Center for History of Chemistry, 1986.

John K. Smith

Popular Science Monthly

Popular science magazine. Founded by the writer and editor Edward L. Youmans, *Popular Science Monthly* (*PSM*) began as an intellectual forum to promote science, especially evolution and the ideas of Herbert Spencer. Highly successful in the late nineteenth century, with a circulation of nearly 20,000, the magazine proselytized for the autonomous authority of science until 1915. Then it became a more prosaic magazine aimed at tinkers and hobbyists. It continues in that vein.

Youmans had no formal training in science, but a fervent belief in the power of rational thought over the conservative forces of mysticism and religion. The magazine championed, vigorously and explicitly, natural explanations for natural events. Youmans and his successors sought out articles arguing that nature was governed by regular laws open to human knowledge. Its authors stressed that the same regular laws applied

P

to both organic and inorganic matter—life itself consisted of nothing supernatural, theological, or metaphysical. Only the scientific method could reveal those natural laws.

From 1900 on, *PSM* was edited by James McKeen Cattell, editor of the technical journal *Science*. Cattell in 1915 sold the *PSM* title to the Modern Publishing Company of New York, which merged the title with *World's Advance,* and boasted that "The Popular Science Monthly now gives the news that comes from those laboratories it helped establish" (Burnham, p. 203). Cattell created a new magazine, *The Scientific Monthly,* dropped the "popular" label, and more explicitly aimed at a scientifically oriented, highbrow audience.

The new *PSM* focused on how-to information for craftsmen and other technically inclined people. After World War II, it added news and feature coverage of science and industry. By the early 1990s, it had a circulation of about 2,000,000.

The original *PSM* has been studied for its importance as a forum for discussions about science. The post-1915 *PSM* has received only passing mention in histories of science and of journalism.

BIBLIOGRAPHY

Burnham, John C. *How Superstition Won and Science Lost: Popularizing Science and Health in the United States.* New Brunswick: Rutgers University Press, 1987.

Haar, Charles M. "E. L. Youmans: A Chapter in the Diffusion of Science in America." *Journal of the History of Ideas* 9 (April 1948): 193–213.

Leverette, William E., Jr. "E. L. Youmans' Crusade for Scientific Autonomy and Respectability." *American Quarterly* 12 (Spring 1965): 12–32.

Peterson, Theodore. *Magazines in the Twentieth Century.* 2d ed. Urbana: University of Illinois Press, 1964.

Bruce V. Lewenstein

Popularization of Science

The European discovery and subsequent settlement of America inspired great interest in the natural history of the continent. Visitors and settlers had an immediate stake in the role that local flora, fauna, geology, and meteorology might play in their survival and prosperity and hence an intense interest. This interest was fostered first by European naturalists and later by homegrown scientists, who provided those willing to collect and observe with the necessary tools, supplies, and sometimes with payment, with little regard to the formal education, occupation, or even in many cases the gender of the observer-collector. Thus, from the start, science was an activity of the people in America.

Communication regarding science in America first took the form of correspondence between those in North America and those in Europe and then among those in North America. This coalesced into a group of American and European naturalists known as the natural history circle who dominated eighteenth-century American science. Their observations and those of others were disseminated to the public through monographs and more commonly through almanacs, newspaper articles on science, and public lectures, all of which addressed issues of science as well as other topics. Heliocentric astronomy, for example, found its way to the America public via the pages of almanacs, which often included astronomical and other scientific and medical information of general interest.

The Revolution disrupted American science and, hence, the popularization of science, which necessarily was viewed as a far lower priority than getting the new nation off to a good start. British support for science, which had been extremely important, was greatly diminished. During the antebellum period, science once more became a subject of interest. Science was seen as having potential utility and, hence, in the national interest. This mood also meant that many individuals perceived science as having potential utility in their own lives. Americans also were by and large strong believers in natural theology and saw science as a potential tool for understanding the work of God by studying the natural world. These two forces—interest in the potential utility of science to individuals and to the nation and belief in natural theology—promoted widespread public interest in science and also shaped the nation's scientific priorities. Fields like natural history found far greater support than theoretical fields.

Jacksonian fervor for education helped to spread this revival. From primary schools through colleges, enrollment was up and science entered the curricula. At the younger levels, primers and readers routinely contained material on science and natural theology. At the secondary level, curricula for both boys and girls incorporated science. Colleges increasingly offered natural history and natural philosophy, as well as natural theology. Less formally, public lecturing also flourished. The lyceum movement brought science lectures to communities big enough to provide an audience.

Science lectures were among the most popular, drawing as many as 2,000 listeners in a city like Boston. Books on science sold well. A field guide and textbook allowed any literate American with a little free time to become a naturalist. Those who preferred to read about other's observations of the natural world have never suffered a shortage of material as writers like Jefferson, Emerson, and Thoreau, and more recently Stephen Jay Gould and Annie Dillard, have been widely published and accessible.

The Republic also spawned a few journals devoted to science and many others that included science in their pages. Benjamin Silliman's *American Journal of Science,* founded in 1818, kept amateurs and professionals alike current on the latest news of science and the scientific community. One Wisconsin land speculator turned naturalist cared so much about his subscription that his biographer uses the periodic lapses in his subscription as an indicator of financial hard times. The *American Naturalist, Scientific American,* and *Popular Science Monthly* all joined in as the century progressed. Science also found space in more general periodicals—for example the *North American Review*—in women's magazines—for example *Godey's Lady's Book*—periodicals for young people—for example the *Youth's Companion*—and agricultural journals—for example the *Country Gentleman.*

Americans with shared interest in science naturally formed groups to share knowledge and experience, equipment, libraries, and the fun of doing science. While some of these groups selected members on the basis of expertise, more were open to enthusiasts. Local groups like the Syracuse Botanical Club, founded in 1878 by a group of female enthusiasts, found that pooling resources improved their scientific experience while comradeship improved the social side. Other groups, for example the Torrey Botanical Club, admitted enthusiasts and experts alike but were led by the experts. As science became more professionalized in America, expert support of amateur participation declined. In the clubs and societies, this took the form of the emergence of professionals-only societies and the decreased participation of experts in groups that included enthusiasts. There are, of course, exceptions to this trend even today, primarily in the fields of ornithology and observational astronomy.

In recent decades, electronic media—first radio, then television, and now the various modes of the information superhighway—have transformed the way we learn about science. From the inception of television, entertainment and education have met in shows like *Mr. Wizard, National Geographic, Nova,* and many others. As more and more Americans have gone on line in recent years, computer bulletin boards, discussion groups, and interactive programs have increased the speed with which we learn of discoveries and have brought the entertainment and education blend to new heights.

BIBLIOGRAPHY

Bode, Carl. *The American Lyceum: Town Meeting of the Mind.* New York: Oxford University Press, 1956.

Burnham, John C. *How Superstition Won and Science Lost: Popularizing Science and Health in the United States.* New Brunswick: Rutgers University Press, 1987.

Hindle, Brook. *Early American Science.* New York: Science History Publications, 1976.

Keeney, Elizabeth B. *The Botanizers: Amateur Scientists in Nineteenth-Century America.* Chapel Hill: University of North Carolina Press, 1992.

Reingold, Nathan, ed. *Science in America Since 1820.* New York: Science History Publications, 1976.

Elizabeth Keeney

Population Council, The

A New York based, nonprofit corporation created by John D. Rockefeller III in 1952 to support demographic and biomedical research on human fertility. Rockefeller was convinced that rapid population growth posed a serious threat to human well-being, and he had long been frustrated by the reluctance of the Rockefeller Foundation and other established corporate philanthropies to become directly associated with birth control. As a student at Princeton in the 1920s and during a long apprenticeship in his father's office, Rockefeller was influenced by scholars and social activists who believed that differential fertility between classes, ethnic groups, and nations might be harmful, and, when he received the resources that made it possible to pursue an independent course, Rockefeller chose population control, along with cultural relations between the United States and Asian nations, as a primary focus for his philanthropy.

The Population Council played a major role in establishing the legitimacy of research on population control, first, by providing research subsidies to distinguished scholars, and then by aggressively promoting contraceptive research and international family-planning programs.

P

The council brought thousands of young professionals from the Third World to the United States for training in both demography and reproductive science, and subsidized the establishment of centers for population research throughout the world. When it became clear in the early 1960s that family-planning programs using conventional barrier methods of contraception were not having an immediate impact on birthrates, the council organized a revival of interest in intrauterine devices (IUDs), sponsored an international clinical testing program, and publicized the successes of population control programs that seemed to work.

A reorganization of the council took place following the World Population Conference in Bucharest (1974). The council's enormous success in institutionalizing population control studies and action programs stimulated criticism of the male-oriented, American managed focus on reducing fertility in the Third World. John D. Rockefeller III proved more sensitive to this criticism than the council's professional managers, who enjoyed considerable autonomy, and he recruited a new executive, George Zeidenstein, a social activist with a background in general development rather than population control, who successfully reorganized the council to reflect changing perceptions of how to promote development. The council continued to realize its founder's vision of an internationally oriented institution dedicated to promoting research on population control and programs to assist economic development.

BIBLIOGRAPHY

Harr, John Enson, and Peter J. Johnson. *The Rockefeller Conscience: An American Family in Public and in Private.* New York: Scribner's, 1991.

The Population Council. *The Population Council: A Chronicle of the First Twenty-Five Years, 1952–1977.* New York: The Population Council, 1978.

Reed, James. *From Private Vice to Public Virtue: The Birth Control Movement and American Society since 1830.* New York: Basic, 1978.

James W. Reed

SEE ALSO
Birth Control

Powell, John Wesley (1834–1902)

Geologist and anthropologist, director of the United States Geological Survey 1881–1894, director of the Smithsonian Bureau of American Ethnology 1879–1902. A self-made product of the American agricultural and scientific frontiers, Powell was born in western New York and raised in farm communities in Ohio, Wisconsin, and Illinois. At eighteen he became a school teacher. An interest in natural history led him to periods of college study and to an energetic promotion of science instruction for Illinois schools. A principal of schools by 1860, Powell served as an artillery officer for the Union Army during the Civil War. He lost an arm to wounds at Shiloh in 1862. After the war Major Powell became professor of geology at Illinois Wesleyan College. He proved an able promoter, earning appointments at Illinois State Normal College and as curator of the state Natural History Society by 1867. He expanded his summer field studies into explorations of the Rocky Mountains in Colorado.

A bold, nationally watched exploration of the canyons of the Colorado River in 1869 won Powell a congressional appropriation. The United States Geographical and Geological Survey of the Rocky Mountain Region operated in the plateau and canyon country of Colorado, Utah, and Arizona from 1870 to 1879. Topographic mapping and physical geology were prominent in the survey's work, the latter featuring Grove K. Gilbert and Clarence E. Dutton as assistants. Powell's personal contribution, *Exploration of the Colorado River of the West* (1875), included a pioneering analysis of the power of erosion in shaping mountain topography. Also notable was Powell's attention to conditions of settlement in the region. His landmark *Report on the Lands of the Arid Region of the United States* (1878) stressed the geographic diversity of western landscapes and called for new, science-based federal land policies.

Powell gave key support to the founding of the United States Geological Survey in 1879. At the same time, he pursued his growing interest in anthropology, seeking and winning federal support for its study. When the Geological Survey was created, Powell moved to the Smithsonian Institution as the first director of the Bureau of American Ethnology. The bureau sponsored collection of a wide assortment of information on Native American peoples. This served Powell's desire to understand the development of human cultures, which he presented in a paper "Human Evolution" (1883). Study of Indian languages was a major theme of the bureau, and a central goal was its landmark *Indian Linguistic Families of America North of Mexico* (1891).

Powell added to his responsibilities in 1881, becoming director of the Geological Survey. He expanded the survey's early focus on mining and minerals geology in the West to a national survey emphasizing topographic mapping and general geology. In 1888, Powell responded to congressional interests with the organization of an Irrigation Survey. Intended to identify irrigable lands and reservoir sites in the West, the work became controversial and was terminated in 1890. Controversy continued to surround Powell's policies, however, forcing his resignation as director in 1894. He continued as director of the Bureau of American Ethnology, but was less active through the remainder of the decade. Powell spent most of his energies in the later years of his life writing educational expositions on geology and geography, and elaborating his views on human evolution.

Each of the major aspects of Powell's scientific life—his geological and anthropological ideas and his direction of two scientific bureaus—has received coverage by historians. However, it is only in his career as an architect of geological surveys that the literature is rich enough to display some diversity of interpretation. This aspect of his career began to draw attention in the 1940s, first from writers interested in federal policies toward the public lands. Powell's preeminent image as a courageous explorer and land law reformer originated in this period, as his canyon adventure and his advocacy of enlightened land policies often were center stage. Excellent biographies of Powell date from this period and include discussions of historical resources.

Historians of science have added attention to Powell's administrative career, primarily in works that focus on the Geological Survey or its antecedents. Powell has received generally favorable treatment in these works, which is consonant with the demonstrable growth of the Geological Survey under Powell and with Powell's image as a trailblazer for Progressive Era conservation. The Geological Survey's centennial history departs from this norm, criticizing Powell's choice of general geology rather than economic geology for the survey's program.

Works displaying the intellectual context of Powell's ideas are rare. This is regrettable, as Powell, through his direction of the Geological Survey and the Bureau of American Ethnology, was among the most prominent figures in nineteenth-century American science. His ideas were influential among his associates in geology and in anthropology. Moreover, Powell lived and worked in a period of great change in science. Studies of his ideas can help to illuminate the disintegration of natural history, the impact of evolution theory, and the paths of development taken by geology, geography, and anthropology in their American settings.

BIBLIOGRAPHY

Chorley, Richard J., Antony J. Dunn, and Robert P. Beckinsale. *History of the Study of Landforms, or the Development of Geomorphology.* London: Methuen, 1964.

Darrah, William Culp. *Powell of the Colorado.* Princeton: Princeton University Press, 1951.

Hinsley, Curtis M., Jr. *Savages and Scientists: The Smithsonian Institution and the Development of American Anthropology, 1846–1910.* Washington, DC: Smithsonian Institution Press, 1981.

Lacey, Michael James. "The Mysteries of Earth-Making Dissolve: A Study of Washington's Intellectual Community and the Origins of American Environmentalism in the Late Nineteenth Century," Ph.D. diss., George Washington University, 1979.

Manning, Thomas G. *Government in Science. The U. S. Geological Survey 1867–1894.* Lexington: University of Kentucky Press, 1967.

Powell, John Wesley. *Exploration of the Colorado River of the West and Its Tributaries. . . .* Washington, DC: Government Printing Office, 1875.

———. *Report on the Lands of the Arid Region of the United States, with a More Detailed Account of the Lands of Utah.* 2d ed. Washington, DC: Government Printing Office, 1878.

———. "Human Evolution." *Transactions of the Anthropoligical Society of Washington* 2 (1883): 176–208.

———. *Indian Linguistic Families of America North of Mexico.* Washington, DC: Government Printing Office, 1891.

Rabbitt, Mary C. *Minerals, Lands, and Geology for the Common Defence and General Welfare.* Vol. 2: *1879–1904.* Washington, DC: Government Printing Office, 1980.

Warman, P.C. "Catalogue of the Published Writings of John Wesley Powell." *Proceedings of the Washington Academy of Sciences* 5 (1903): 131–187.

Zernel, John Joseph. "John Wesley Powell: Science and Reform in a Positive Context." Ph.D. diss., Oregon State University, 1983.

John J. Zernel

President, Scientific Advice to

Recommendations to the president on issues involving science and technology, especially their use and support by the federal government. Presidential science advising initially concentrated on military applications

P

of science and technology, but it has gradually expanded into other areas, such as the support of science, the space program, international relations, and the environment.

As a relatively new part of the system of providing scientific advice to the government, presidential science advising took its shape during World War II, in the form of the Office of Scientific Research and Development (OSRD) under the direction of Vannevar Bush. Earlier attempts at channeling science advice to the government, such as the National Academy of Sciences (founded 1863), the National Research Council (founded 1916), and the Science Advisory Board (1933–1935), were all directed at government agencies, not the presidency. As semiofficial groups, they often acted only in response to requests from the government. Bush and the OSRD broke this tradition by acquiring the authority to take initiatives and to contract with university laboratories and industrial firms. Bush became the de facto science advisor to President Franklin D. Roosevelt during World War II. He provided advice of his own and of other scientists to Roosevelt, especially on the making and using of the first nuclear weapons.

The end of the war brought the dissolution of the OSRD, and Bush left the Executive Office of the President shortly after Harry Truman became president. The Korean conflict led to the formation in 1951 of a Science Advisory Committee in the Office of Defense Mobilization (ODM-SAC), with the chairman reporting to both the ODM director and the president. The group, first chaired by Oliver Buckley, then Lee DuBridge, and finally I.I. Rabi, included many veteran scientists from the wartime Manhattan Project and the Radiation (Radar) Laboratory of the Massachusetts Institute of Technology. It fought for increased federal, and especially military, support of basic research. It also sponsored studies of American defense policy by scientists and engineers. One such project, the Technological Capabilities Panel under James Killian of MIT, resulted in a great acceleration of American missile programs and intelligence capabilities in the mid-1950s. Despite these successes, the ODM-SAC largely languished in the shadow of the H-bomb debate and McCarthyism of this period.

The launching of the Soviet satellite, *Sputnik,* in 1957 marked a turning point in the history of scientific advice to the president. President Dwight D. Eisenhower appointed Killian as his special assistant for science and technology (commonly known as science advisor) and moved the ODM-SAC into the White House as the President's Science Advisory Committee (PSAC). Killian (succeeded in 1959 by George Kistiakowsky) and PSAC advised Eisenhower on missile and space programs, advocated a nuclear test ban, and fought for increased federal funding of science as a way to enhance American national security and international prestige. They also helped establish the subcabinet Federal Council for Science and Technology in 1959. In 1961, when John F. Kennedy moved into the White House, Jerome Wiesner became the new science advisor. A year later, a new statutory Office of Science and Technology (OST), with the science advisor as director, was established in the Executive Office of the President to strengthen science advising. During this period, presidential science advising expanded into health and environmental issues. PSAC's report *The Use of Pesticides* in 1963, for example, was influential in the acceptance of Rachel Carson's warning of the harms of excessive use of pesticides in her book *Silent Spring.* But the effectiveness of the PSAC system of science advising decreased in the Lyndon Johnson and Richard Nixon presidencies, as scientists both in and out of PSAC opposed the administrations' antiballistic missile and supersonic transport programs and the Vietnam War. Nixon abolished PSAC and the OST in 1973.

The National Science Foundation director served as presidential science advisor until 1976, when a congressional act led to the resurrection of the position of science advisor and the creation of the White House Office of Science and Technology Policy. Although a White House Science Council reporting to the science advisor operated in the Ronald Reagan administration, a PSAC-like committee reporting to the president was not reestablished until 1989, in the form of the President's Council of Advisers on Science and Technology (PCAST) reporting to President George Bush and his science advisor, D. Allan Bromley. The major change under President William Clinton was the creation of the National Science and Technology Council, comprised of major cabinet officers and chaired by the president, to coordinate national science policy in the post–Cold War era.

Presidential science advising attracted little attention until after World War II, when the work of Bush and the OSRD became widely known. Interest in the subject rose in the 1950s and 1960s as historians, political scientists, and journalists began to study science in the federal government. These studies tended to focus on the role of presidential science advisors in nuclear weapons policy and arms control negotiations. Supporters and critics of the PSAC-system of science advising debated over whether it was proper for scientists to venture into national policymaking and whether elitism dominated science advising and science policy. The demise of PSAC in the early 1970s brought forth writings, mainly by former science advisors but by others, too, calling for its restoration.

With the recent opening of previously closed government archives and with the rising interest in American science during the Cold War, presidential science advising has become a significant subject of investigation by historians of science. The focus of these works has broadened beyond nuclear policy to explore the science advisors' roles in national and international science policy during the Cold War and in other fields, such as health and environment. Presidential science advising emerges from these studies as a key part of the national security state and of the contract between American science and the government during the Cold War.

Although the presidential libraries and the National Archives have opened a large amount of materials by or on presidential science advisors, a complete picture of presidential science advising will still have to await the declassification of the remaining closed records. Another important aspect that is largely missing in the current literature is an assessment of the significance of informal presidential science advising such as was rendered to the several Republican administrations by the politically conservative physicist Edward Teller. Useful insights to science advising could also come from comparisons with presidential advising in other fields, such as the economy, and with science advising in other countries.

BIBLIOGRAPHY

Bromley, D. Allan. *The President's Scientists: Reminiscences of a White House Science Advisor.* New Haven: Yale University Press, 1994.

Dupree, A. Hunter. *Science in the Federal Government: A History of Policies and Activities to 1940.* Cambridge, MA: Harvard University Press, 1957.

Golden, William T., ed. *Science Advice to the President.* New York: Pergamon Press, 1980.

Herken, Gregg. *Cardinal Choices: Presidential Science Advising from the Bomb to SDI.* New York: Oxford University Press, 1992.

Hewlett, Richard G., and Oscar E. Anderson Jr. *The New World: A History of the United States Atomic Energy Commission.* Vol. 1: *1939–1946.* University Park: Pennsylvania State University Press, 1962.

Kevles, Daniel. "Cold War and Hot Physics: Science, Security, and the American State, 1945–56." *Historical Studies in the Physical and Biological Sciences* 20:2 (1990): 239–264.

Killian, James R., Jr. *Sputnik, Scientists, and Eisenhower: A Memoir of the First Special Assistant to the President for Science and Technology.* Cambridge, MA: MIT Press, 1977.

Kistiakowsky, George B. *A Scientist at the White House: The Private Diary of President Eisenhower's Special Assistant for Science and Technology.* Cambridge, MA: Harvard University Press, 1976.

Lambright, W. Henry. *Presidential Management of Science and Technology: The Johnson Presidency.* Austin: University of Texas Press, 1985.

Smith, Bruce L.R. *The Advisors: Scientists in the Policy Process.* Washington, DC: The Brookings Institution, 1992.

Thompson, Kenneth W, ed. *The Presidency and Science Advising.* Vols. 1–7. Lanham: University Press of America, 1986–1990.

Wells, William G. "Science Advice and the Presidency, 1939–1976." Ph.D. diss., George Washington University, 1976.

Zuoyue Wang

Priestley, Joseph (1733–1804)

English natural philosopher and theologian who emigrated to the United States in 1794. By then Priestly had essentially completed his scientific career. From the publication of his *History of Electricity* in 1767 to that of his last volume of *Experiments and Observations on Air* (1777), he had been a major figure in eighteenth-century science. Then the introduction of Lavoisier's oxidation chemistry made Priestley's phlogistic-mechanical chemistry obsolete. Also his increasing devotion to theological polemics and political agitation would lead to the "Church-and-King Riot" of 1791 in Birmingham and eventually to his seeking asylum for himself and his family.

In spite of the decline of his scientific reputation, Priestley was probably the most prestigious refugee the United States would see in decades. He was not entirely unknown there. He had been a friend of Benjamin Franklin and a vigorous supporter of the colonists' cause before and during the American Revolution. His books, on theology, politics, and education had been read in the United States, where he was perhaps better known for nonscientific work than for science. Twelve

P

editions of seven of his books had been printed in this country before he arrived—none on science. And this pattern continued. Of the fifty-two editions of his books and pamphlets printed in the United States between 1794 and 1806, only six were on science. This mirrors the proportions of his works published in England, where far the greater part were nonscientific.

Although invited to settle in New York City or Philadelphia, he chose Northumberland, Pennsylvania, five days' wagon trip up the Susquehanna. There he prepared to be minister and teacher to an enlightened utopia for liberal Englishmen exiled from a politically and religiously repressive England. This plan failed as emigration from England became difficult and then unnecessary. Priestley, however, stayed in Northumberland. There he attempted to reestablish the life he had been living in Birmingham, England, substituting Philadelphia for London for his annual visits. He declined an invitation to become professor of chemistry at the University of Pennsylvania as he was to decline nomination for the presidency of the American Philosophical Society. He did, however, adopt that society, to which he had been elected in 1785, as replacement for the Royal Society.

Priestley was sixty-one when he sailed and his scientific activities in the United States were inevitably anticlimactic. He published two pamphlets supporting the doctrine of phlogiston and denying the composition of water. He resumed his experiments, reporting the results in more scientific papers than he had published during his years in England: eleven papers in the *Transactions of the American Philosophical Society* and (because the society was slow in publication) more than fifteen in the *New York Medical Repository*. Many of these were reprinted in England in the *Monthly Magazine* or [Nicholson's] *Journal of Natural Philosophy, Science and the Arts*. Most of these papers described repetitions of experiments earlier performed and reported. Still, Priestley's presence and his activities called the attention of citizens and foreigners to science in the United States. His continued attacks on the theory of oxidation were finally noticed and he had the satisfaction of forcing acceptance of some of his criticism, but even this success was minor. His "discovery" of carbon monoxide belongs more to William Cruickshank, who fitted the discovery into the new chemistry of Lavoisier.

The importance of Priestley's presence in the United States is best measured by his influence upon others. He encouraged Benjamin Smith Barton's writing of his *New Views of the Origin of the Tribes and Nations of America* (1797–1798). John Adams and Thomas Jefferson were avid readers of his theology. Jefferson sought advice on college curricula. Priestley's experiments and objections to the theory of oxidation inspired the work and arguments of John Mclean, James Woodhouse, Samuel Latham Mitchill, and the young Robert Hare. Thomas Cooper, Priestley's friend, taught chemistry at Pennsylvania, South Carolina College, and Dickinson College, where he also arranged to donate Priestley's apparatus. And, finally, the American Chemical Society was conceived at a celebration of the centenary of the discovery of oxygen, held at Priestley's grave on 1 August 1874.

BIBLIOGRAPHY

Crook, Ronald E. *A Bibliography of Joseph Priestley 1733–1804.* London: Library Association, 1966.

Priestley, Joseph. *A Scientific Autobiography of Joseph Priestley (1733-1804): Selected Scientific Correspondence,* edited with commentary by Robert E. Schofield. Cambridge: MIT Press, 1966.

Schofield, Robert E. "Joseph Priestley's American Education." In *Early Dickinsoniana; The Boyd Lee Spahr Lectures in Americana, 1957–1961.* Carlisle, PA: Library of Dickinson College, 1961.

———. "Priestley, Joseph." *Dictionary of Scientific Biography.* Edited by Charles C. Gillispie. New York: Charles Scribner's Sons, 1975, 11:139–147.

———. *The Enlightenment of Joseph Priestley: A Study of His Life and Work from 1733 to 1773.* University Park, PA: Pennsylvania State University Press, 1997.

———. *The Enlightened Joseph Priestley, LL.D., F.R.S.: A Study of His Life and Work from 1773 to 1804.* University Park, PA: Pennsylvania State University Press, in press.

Smith, Edgar F. *Priestley in America, 1794–1804.* Philadelphia: Blakiston's, 1920.

Robert E. Schofield

Professionalization and Careers in Science

The historical process by which the practice of science became an activity of a recognized and socially sanctioned occupational group with a significant degree of internal self-governance. The character and significance of the professions is a topic of continuing interest to sociologists and historians and entails parallels and comparisons across many occupational categories (see, e.g., Hatch). Education and employment are two important aspects of the historical development of professions—

that is, the extent to which specific educational preparation was required at any point in time, and whether relevant occupational positions were available. The ministry, law, and medicine are the archetype professions, and consequently there is a historic client-orientation that is part of the traditional definition of a profession. To understand science in the overall context of professionalization, however, consideration of another orientation is required. This other orientation is to the subject matter itself and to methodology, as well as to concerns such as requisite knowledge and standards of conduct and judgment. There are two strands in the historical process of professionalization of science. One was the development of educational and employment opportunities that supported and differentiated the scientist from other groups. Braided with this was the second strand, in which scientists developed ways to judge and to monitor their own activities and at the same time to draw boundaries that protected them and their knowledge conclusions from interference by an external, lay population.

In the colonial period, active involvement with the natural world and knowledge of the physical universe was relatively widespread among educated persons. Natural philosophy—physics and astronomy—was an integral part of a college curriculum. Members of the clergy, physicians, political figures such as Benjamin Franklin and Thomas Jefferson—the class of learned gentlemen—acted as if the study of natural knowledge was part of their social and intellectual definition, even though their primary attention was elsewhere. But even in the colonial period some persons devoted much of their lives to science. John Bartram, from his economic base as a Pennsylvania farmer, explored the colonial wilderness, and developed a paradigmatic role of naturalist-collector for transatlantic botanists. John Winthrop spent all of his adult career as professor of mathematics and natural philosophy at Harvard.

The important growth of supportive institutions (including scientific societies, journals, and college and university programs), and the emergence of an identifiable and self-conscious scientific population, began to accelerate in the first half of the nineteenth century. In this formative period, however, there still were various ways by which one could be involved in science without scientific employment. For example, local natural history and other societies promoted active interest, and the presentation of papers to such bodies could result in publication in their proceedings. During the antebellum period, when natural history studies were so important a part of American science, it was possible to assemble significant collections and resources and to become master of a field (or subfield) by personal exertion and dedication and while earning a living in some other way. Important in this context is the nature of science, or of a particular science, at the time. For example, as botanical and zoological classification became more sophisticated, as resources for study became more demanding, as biological science became more laboratory and experimentally based, personal commitment no longer was sufficient.

The early development of employment opportunities and other signs of professionalization were ad hoc in many ways. Patterns of employment reflect the complex character of science in the antebellum period and into the late nineteenth century. In addition to those outside scientific employment altogether, many contributors to science had medical training, and those who were practicing physicians did their scientific work in leisure hours. Educational and employment opportunities also developed in the colleges, as the range of scientific offerings developed there. Opportunities also existed to work as pharmacists and analytical chemists, botanical, zoological, and geological explorers and collectors, curators and observatory heads, gardeners, school teachers, artists, instrument makers, and inventors. Some also were able to find employment in government science (both state and federal), including natural history and geological surveys, engineering projects and topographical and other surveys of the United States Army, and the work of the United States Coast Survey. Agricultural development and the beginnings of industrialization also offered employment.

From the early decades of the nineteenth century, publishing—and especially of articles in scientific journals—was an important if not an essential part of the definition of a scientist. Initially, a not insignificant percentage of the scientific literature was written by persons with no particular occupational commitment to science, but increasingly through the antebellum period this was less true. As with other aspects of professionalization, the changing nature of publishing reflected communal or planned developments, as well as individual or ad hoc actions. The establishment of the *American Journal of Science* in 1818, and the American Association for the Advancement of Science thirty years later, were institutional events in science that had two effects. On the one hand, they created national forums for science, while, on the other, they presented

P

the scientific leadership with a means to control access and to enforce standards.

The implied network of nineteenth-century scientific listeners and readers, doers of science, and authors of research texts outlined above indicates a layering of interests and involvement. Reingold has presented a three-part hierarchy: those he calls cultivators, who supported and to some degree participated in learned culture in its scientific aspects; practitioners, who made a living in some way from science; and researchers, who came to assume leadership of the scientific community. Reingold's thoughtful analysis and classification helps to deflect discussion away from a simple dichotomy of amateur and professional to consider the more complex mix of status and function in the important transition period of the nineteenth century.

In the period after the Civil War, the development of graduate education, and with it the idea of research as a legitimate function of universities, institutionalized higher education as the locus of science in the United States. This development had two aspects. First, it increased opportunities for full-time employment in science (and it put the professorship at the center of the scientific career structure). Similar to other academic fields, it made the attainment of the Ph.D. degree the primary means of entry for a scientific career. By the early part of the twentieth century, therefore, the attainment of a doctorate and employment in a college or university essentially characterized the "professional" scientist. Whether or not the scientist was also a professor, he or she would have gone through university training and, therefore, would have the academic mark of approval (i.e., the degree).

It would be misleading not to carry the analysis beyond the professionalized scientist as professor, a stage reached by the early twentieth century. The academic scientist has held a central place in American science in this century because the university developed as the locus of "pure" research and the tendency has been to place such activity at the top of the scale of scientific and professional values. If a portrait of the broader scientific population were considered, however, the picture would be quite different. Reingold's characterization of the "practitioner" in the antebellum period suggests that, even in that era, one could be occupationally committed to science without necessarily contributing to the furtherance of knowledge. In the twentieth century, significant numbers of scientists have found employment in industry, and in laboratories or other facilities and programs supported by government and much of their work is not research in the traditional sense; rather, it is applied effort, the development of products based on established knowledge, or routine testing of products and devices.

A systemic difficulty in characterizing the scientific population is to define what is meant by science. The topic has both intellectual and social aspects. In the nineteenth-century development of professionalism, much of the attention focused on science as knowledge, in part because effective means of application had not yet developed. The periphery of the community was characterized, at the outset of that century, by many informed and interested persons, not specially educated nor employed in science, who participated through the scientific societies and publications (as readers and occasionally as contributors). In the twentieth century and with the growth of industrial and governmental applied science, a widespread need for scientific educators at many levels, the complexity of scientific organizations that require informed managers, and other developments have created a structure of science that is activity as well as knowledge. As a consequence, the range of employment possibilities for persons of varying educational levels has greatly expanded. Even for those with the credentials of a doctorate, the definition of "research" has become differentiated (notably along the lines of employment sector). The picture is further complicated by the fact of mobility and individuals with multiple roles (e.g., as professor, consultant to industry, and adviser to government) which tends to blur stereotypical images. While the scientist with the doctorate, engaged in the advance of basic knowledge through publication, still stands as the professional model, there is a great enterprise of science that surrounds this core of the professional ideal.

It is apparent that the study of professionalization and careers in science touches on many other aspects of the organizational, institutional, and social, as well as cognitive areas of science. The definition of a scientist is a continuing problem for study and debate, whether in a particular time frame or through the sweep of American history. Understanding how the central core of scientists related to the many others who have been involved in and who contributed to science is an ongoing problem. Investigating the many beyond the core is a significant need, both as a means of understanding the core professional scientists better, and to see more clearly how scientific interests and activities have pervaded American society.

BIBLIOGRAPHY

Barrow, Mark V. *A Passion for Birds: American Ornithology after Audubon.* Princeton, NJ: Princeton University Press, 1998.

Daniels, George H. "The Process of Professionalization in American Science: The Emergent Period, 1820–1860." *Isis* 58 (1967): 151–166.

Elliott, Clark A. "Models of the American Scientist: A Look at Collective Biography." *Isis* 73 (1982): 77–93.

Goldstein, Daniel. "'Yours for Science': The Smithsonian Institution's Correspondents and the Shape of Scientific Community in 19th-Century America." *Isis* 85 (1994): 573–599.

Hatch, Nathan O., ed. *The Professions in American History.* Notre Dame, IN: University of Notre Dame Press, 1988.

Hirsch, Walter. *Scientists in American Society.* New York: Random House, 1968.

Keeney, Elizabeth. *The Botanizers: Amateur Scientists in Nineteenth-Century America.* Chapel Hill: University of North Carolina Press, 1992.

Lankford, John. *American Astronomy: Community, Careers, and Power, 1859–1940.* Chicago: University of Chicago Press, 1997.

Reingold, Nathan. "Definitions and Speculations: The Professionalization of Science in America in the Nineteenth Century." In *The Pursuit of Knowledge in the Early American Republic: American Scientific and Learned Societies from Colonial Times to the Civil War,* edited by Alexandra Oleson and S.B. Brown. Baltimore: Johns Hopkins University Press, 1976, pp. 33–69.

Clark A. Elliott

Project Paperclip
See Paperclip, Project

Project RAND
See RAND, Project

Psychological Corporation, The

Applied psychology organization founded in 1921. Applied psychology emerged in America quite early in the twentieth century, as American psychologists' Darwinian-based functional concerns—and James McKeen Cattell's 1904 call for an applicable psychol-

ogy—led many of them to approach problems of advertising and personnel management before 1910. During World War I, the army found the efforts of the Committee on the Classification of Personnel in the Army quite useful, and by the early 1920s an appreciable number of psychologists had significant experience with "real world" problems.

In organizing The Psychological Corporation in 1921, however, Cattell ignored this experience and instead sought to involve in its applied efforts all American psychologists, to whom he offered corporation stock. He never asked how they would apply their science, and instead emphasized the corporation's role as a publicity agent, referral service, and supply company for applied psychology. He thought that individuals and firms in need of psychological services would contact the corporation, which would refer them to nearby stockholders, who would perform the required services and share their fees with the corporation. But most stockholders had no applied experience, few firms sought the corporation's help, and during the early 1920s, it derived its minuscule income almost entirely from sales of revised Army Alpha examinations. The corporation reorganized itself late in 1926. Cattell became chairman of the board, seasoned personnel psychologist Walter Van Dyke Bingham became president, and the corporation gradually hired other experienced employees. Its Test Division—which developed, published, and distributed psychological tests—always proved more successful than its consulting divisions, and in the 1940s, it became one of America's leading publishers of psychological tests. The corporation was acquired by publishing conglomerate Harcourt Brace Jovanovich in 1970.

BIBLIOGRAPHY

Achilles, Paul S. "The Role of the Psychological Corporation in Applied Psychology." *American Journal of Psychology* 56 (1937): 229–247.

———. "Commemorative Address on the Twentieth Anniversary of the Psychological Corporation and to Honor Its Founder, James McKeen Cattell." *Journal of Applied Psychology* 25 (1941): 609–618.

Cattell, James McKeen. "The Conceptions and Methods of Psychology." *Popular Science Monthly* 66 (1904): 176–186.

Sokal, Michael M. "The Origins of the Psychological Corporation." *Journal of the History of the Behavioral Sciences* 17 (1981): 54–67.

Michael M. Sokal

P

Psychological and Intelligence Testing

Americans have always used (at times implicit) psychological techniques to understand and evaluate personality and other individual traits, and the early nineteenth century's interest in silhouettes illustrates their use of the folk wisdom of physiognomy to preserve the characters of loved ones. More formal attempts to systematize this folk wisdom include Johann Caspar Lavater's *Physiogomische Fragmente* (1775–1778), which enjoyed some popularity in America, and the "physiognotrace" built by John Isaac Hawkins and exhibited from 1802 at Charles Willson Peale's Philadelphia Museum. After c. 1830, Americans also looked to phrenology, and while many found much of interest (but little of value) in, for example, Johann Gaspar Spurzheim's discussions of the science's philosophical implications, practical phrenologists—like Orson Squire Fowler—provided what might be called individual psychological counseling on personal and professional matters based on detailed character readings performed at his offices in New York, or during tours of other cities.

Even as phrenology gradually lost its authority after the Civil War, American anthropologists adapted its craniometric techniques to characterize the different human races, and soon merged this interest into a generalized physical anthropometry. Meanwhile, other Americans sought other "scientific" techniques for assessing psychological traits, and thus looked hopefully to the laboratory-based "new psychology" that emerged in Germany through the 1870s. In the 1890s, psychologists led by James McKeen Cattell, of Columbia University, combined these interests in a program of self-identified anthropometric "mental tests" that used standard laboratory procedures—which measured (among other traits) short-term memory, reaction times, and the sensitivity of the sense organs under varying conditions—to gather data on how people differ psychologically. But Cattell and his colleagues lacked a functional view of how these traits helped individuals live their lives. Their tests produced results that had no meaning for anyone, and by 1901, most psychologists abandoned these procedures.

But even as Cattell's tests failed, Americans sought psychological expertise more than ever before: to help educators "Americanize" the millions of children of the "new" immigrants from southern and eastern Europe, and to help them deal with the large number of "feebleminded" boys and girls revealed by compulsory education laws; to help corporations select workers for new industries; and (for eugenicists) to determine who should be allowed to enter the country. Psychologists at state schools for the feebleminded most steadily attacked this problem, and in 1908, New Jersey's Henry H. Goddard discovered the tests developed in France in 1905 by Alfred Binet and Theodore Simon, and almost immediately saw their value. These tests called for schoolchildren to perform various "age appropriate" tasks; for example, counting pennies at age four, explaining similarities at age eight, repeating five digits backward at age twelve, and (for "superior adults") explaining stories. In this formulation, the level at which a child performed determined (what the testers called) his or her "mental age," and soon thereafter testers began dividing an individual's mental age by his or her chronological age to calculate his or her "intelligence quotient," or IQ. By 1909, Goddard revised these tests for use in America, and schools like his soon found them extremely useful in determining appropriate programs for the children in their care. (Goddard even developed precise definitions for long-used terms like "idiot" [an adult with a mental age of less than two] and "imbecile" [an adult with a mental age of between three and seven] and coined the term "moron" for adults with a mental age of between eight and twelve.) Through the early part of the second decade of the twentieth century, other Americans developed their own analogous tests, which large urban school systems began using to help deal with the influx of immigrant children. In 1916, Lewis M. Terman and his collaborators at Stanford University published the long-standard first edition of the "Stanford Revision and Extension of the Binet-Simon Intelligence Scale."

While Goddard and Terman developed their tests of intelligence, other psychologists (notably Walter Dill Scott of Northwestern University) developed analogous tests for specific abilities (salesmanship in Scott's case), and these soon supported the new applied specialty of industrial psychology. When the United States entered World War I in 1917, psychologists (led by American Psychological Association president Robert M. Yerkes of the University of Minnesota) mobilized themselves both to aid the war effort and to "put psychology on the map." Efforts led by Scott coalesced around the Committee on the Classification of Personnel in the Army, which produced dozens of "trade tests" and helped the military meet its need for men with specialized training. A more general program, led by Yerkes himself, produced two intelligence tests: the Army Alpha examination, designed for men literate in English; and the Army Beta examination, designed for illiterate men, and for those literate only in another language. Unlike most earlier psychological tests, these called for their subjects to be tested in large groups, to select their answers from the multiple choices offered by the testers, and to indicate these answers on test blanks that psychologists later scored. These "pencil-and-paper" procedures revolutionized psychological testing.

That is, while historians still disagree whether the army found them useful, these tests clearly accomplished the psychologists' goal and "put psychology on the map," and the 1920s saw a boom in group psychological testing. Colleges used modified Army Alpha examinations as admissions tests, schools used other tests to section classes on the basis of (tested) ability, corporations looked to industrial psychologists for highly specialized trade tests, and, perhaps most notably, the College Entrance Examination Board sought to replace its easily-crammed-for essay examinations with a more "objective" (and easily scored) pencil-and-paper Scholastic Aptitude Test. Eugenicists and others also cited army-testing-programs results—which showed that native-born Americans scored higher than immigrants, and that immigrants from northern and western Europe scored higher than those from southern and eastern Europe—to argue (successfully) for immigration restriction. By the end of the decade, however, environmentally based criticisms by cultural anthropologists (led by Columbia University's Franz Boas), statisticians, and other psychologists led testers to downplay (and even retract) some of their earlier overly extravagant claims for the value of their work.

Through the 1930s, however, psychological tests gained notoriety with radio programs like *Dr. IQ*, and schools still used them extensively. Meanwhile, the cultural anthropologists' "environmental" perspective on tests helped shape Gunnar Myrdahl's highly influential Carnegie-supported study *The Negro in America* (1944). (In 1934, however, Raymond Cattell explicitly tried to develop "culture-fair" intelligence tests.) The 1930s' growing interest in personality traits, stimulated in part by the growth of clinical psychology, which in turn derived in part from the growing influence of Freudian ideas, led psychologists to develop personality tests, including many American versions of Hermann Rorschach's "inkblot" tests, the Thematic Apperception Test (in 1936, by Henry A. Murray of the Harvard Psychological Clinic), and the Minnesota Multiphasic

Personality Inventory (in 1943, by Starke Hathaway and J. Charnley McKinley of the University of Minnesota). These tests (and their revisions) proved especially useful in the late 1940s, as clinical psychology expanded to help meet the needs of returning soldiers. But even earlier (in 1939), David Wechsler developed the first version of his adult-oriented Bellevue Intelligence Scale (now the Wechsler Adult Intelligence Scale, Revised, 1981), and in 1938, Oscar K. Buros began to serve both testers and their clients with his first *Mental Measurements Yearbook* (the eleventh edition appeared in 1992).

As the post–World War II baby boom forced schools to deal with an even more diverse population, testing boomed, and psychologists looked to "culture-free" tests. But the call for "equal-opportunity" in the 1960s led radical educators to attack all tests as necessarily reflecting class or race biases, and their historian counterparts found racism and a desire for social control at the root of all testing. Criticisms of tests also grew as competition for college admission became stiffer in the 1960s, and attacks on the cultural biases of the SAT became common. Through the 1970s, psychologists responded both by emphasizing that tests served as "creators of opportunity" that revealed previously hidden ability in individuals of all races (e.g., Lee J. Cronbach, 1970), and by claiming that the tests demonstrated real differences in how individuals of different racial backgrounds function psychologically, and that the American schools had to take these differences into account (e.g., Richard J. Herrnstein, 1971, and especially Arthur R. Jensen, 1969). The critics' point of view gained support with the (recently challenged) charge (by Leon J. Kamin, in 1969; supported by Leslie Hearnshaw, 1979) that mid-twentieth-century English psychologist Cyril Burt apparently based his arguments for inherited differences in intelligence on data he created. But educators still find results of tests useful in dealing with individuals, and the 1990s' call for educational standards and accountability led directly to growing concerns for "educational assessment" of what students know and how they learned it. Most recently, scholars with training in history of science have called for dispassionate analyses of past testing and have argued that, while early-twentieth-century tests clearly do not meet late-twentieth-century standards, many early testers saw themselves as progressive altruists trying to enlarge educational opportunity for those best able to respond. In turn,

P

their critics complain about their subjects' "meritocratic" vision, and the debate continues.

BIBLIOGRAPHY

Fancher, Raymond E. *The Intelligence Men: Makers of the IQ Controversy.* New York: Norton, 1985.

Gould, Stephen Jay. *The Mismeasure of Man.* 1981; 2d ed. New York: Norton, 1996.

Hearnshaw, Leslie S. *Cyril Burt, Psychologist.* Ithaca: Cornell University Press, 1979.

Kamin, Leon J. *The Science and Politics of I.Q.* Potomac, MD: Erlbaum, 1974.

Karrier, Clarence J. "Testing for Order and Control in the Corporate Liberal State." *Educational Theory* 22 (1972): 154–180.

Sokal, Michael M. "Essay Review: Approaches to the History of Psychological Testing." *History of Education Quarterly* 24 (1984): 419–430.

————. "James McKeen Cattell and American Psychology in the 1920s." In *Explorations in the History of Psychology in the United States,* edited by Josef Brozek. Lewisburg, PA: Bucknell University Press, 1984, pp. 273–323.

————, ed. *Psychological Testing and American Society, 1890–1930.* New Brunswick: Rutgers University Press, 1987.

Michael M. Sokal

Public Health

All societies necessarily pay some attention to the collective health of their populations. In the United States, the first organized public health departments were those of the eastern seaboard cities in the late eighteenth century. These were relatively inactive, however, until the mid-nineteenth century, when these rapidly growing cities were threatened by epidemics of cholera, yellow fever, smallpox, and other infectious diseases. Sanitary reformers in New York and other large cities campaigned for more attention to the health and well-being of immigrant populations. These middle-class reformers were motivated in part by humanitarian and religious concerns, and in part by self-interest, fearing the spread of disease from the hovels of the poor to the homes of the respectable classes.

Urban physicians debated the causes of epidemic diseases. Some believed epidemics were imported, others that they arose from decaying organic materials in the unsanitary slums. Similarly, some argued these diseases were spread through the air and others maintained they were transmitted by direct contact with the sick. Such arguments had clear implications for international trade and shipping, immigration, and urban health services of every kind. City councils responsible for making decisions about quarantines and expenditures for street cleaning were often more easily swayed by economic and considerations than by contending medical theories.

In the era before germ theory, both popular and medical conceptions of disease held that personal behavior, and indeed, personal virtue, largely determined one's health or illness. Poverty, immorality, dirt, and disease were clearly associated; wealth, godliness, cleanliness, and health were also natural companions. Given this perspective, most reformers approached public health through public education, moral improvement, and personal hygiene; few, however, advocated the redistribution of wealth.

As urban populations continued to grow, and as the problems of poverty and disease became ever more visible and intractable, the fear of political instability added to the pressures for public health reforms. The American Public Health Association, founded in 1872, brought together sanitary reformers with many physicians and progressive public health officers to shape the social agenda. The most typically enacted measures included tenement house improvements, street cleaning, provision of clean water, public toilets, sewage systems, and inspection of public market places and food-processing industries. Women reformers tended to be especially interested in the care of infants and young children, and the education of mothers in domestic hygiene.

With the growing acceptance of germ theory in the 1880s and 1890s, public health began to take a different, more scientific form. It now married the prestige of scientific discovery to the moral imperative of social reform. In New York City, Hermann Biggs's triumphant introduction of the diphtheria antitoxin brought national attention to the practical promise of laboratory research. City governments began to support bacteriological laboratories, and scientific institutes and technical colleges began research on such useful matters as the purity and pollution of drinking water. Sanitary engineers were increasingly employed by municipalities to construct water supply and sewage systems. Most activities of city health departments were now organized, or at least justified, in terms of their scientific efficiency.

In the early twentieth century, the passion for social improvement based upon scientific principles spread beyond the germ theory into occupational health, nutrition, and maternal and child health. Progressive reformers of every variety promoted public health activities, whether through the abolition of child labor, advocacy of temperance, support for birth control, regulation of workshops, or promotion of public parks. In the southern states, the Rockefeller Sanitary Commission mounted a massive campaign against hookworm and began to cast an imperial eye upon infectious tropical diseases. Success in building the Panama Canal pointed to the vital necessity of controlling malaria and yellow fever. The expanding economic and political interests of the United States made tropical disease and international health matters of concern in the corridors of power.

Given the new enthusiasm for public health, medical leaders, with the financial backing of the Rockefeller Foundation, now began to design the first schools for the education of public health professionals. They were to be trained in the basic biological sciences, including bacteriology and immunology, and also in the newly introduced disciplines of epidemiology and biostatistics. In the professional schools, the older social reform impulse of public health was distinctly subordinated to modern scientific training. Popular health education likewise became more scientific, but still embodied a basic moralism, by emphasizing personal responsibility for health. Eugenic ideas were but an extreme form of the broader conviction that health and disease were an individual matter, more biological than social.

In 1935, the Social Security Act provided the first federal public health funding to the states. The New Deal thus marked an expansion of government responsibility for health. Subsequently, most federal financing supported categorical programs, either for specific diseases or for special population groups. Several commentators have noted that this fiscal approach, together with the relative autonomy of the different states, tended to produce a fragmented public health system.

The public health infrastructure was strengthened during World War II. Mobilization for war directed attention to the problems of infectious diseases. In the South, the program for Malaria Control in the War Areas, the first incarnation of what would later become the Centers for Disease Control (CDC), was founded to eradicate mosquitoes in and around military camps. In the postwar era, the CDC would become the main federal center for controlling infectious diseases, and later, all major health and disease problems. Over the same time frame, the National Institutes of Health were created as the national center for basic research in the biomedical sciences.

The research agenda in the postwar era has emphasized the chronic diseases, especially heart disease and cancer. In prevention research, the chronic disease model has generally focused upon dietary and lifestyle issues in the production of disease. At the same time, public concerns in the 1960s about environmental and occupational hazards led to the creation of the Environmental Protection Agency and the Occupational Safety and Health Administration. Since 1981, AIDS has come to dominate the public health agenda and has drawn new attention to the ways in which public health is intertwined with all aspects of social and political life.

BIBLIOGRAPHY

Brandt, Allen. *No Magic Bullet: A Social History of Venereal Disease in the United States since 1880.* New York: Oxford University Press, 1985.

Carson, Rachel. *Silent Spring.* Boston: Houghton Mifflin, 1962.

Cassedy, James H. *American Medicine and Statistical Thinking, 1800-1860.* Cambridge, MA: Harvard University Press, 1984.

Duffy, John. *The Sanitarians: A History of American Public Health.* Urbana: University of Illinois Press, 1990.

Etheridge, Elizabeth. *Sentinel for Health: A History of the Centers for Disease Control.* Berkeley: University of California Press, 1992.

Ettling, John. *The Germ of Laziness: Rockefeller Philanthropy and Public Health in the New South.* Cambridge, MA: Harvard University Press, 1981.

Fee, Elizabeth. *Disease and Discovery: A History of the Johns Hopkins School of Hygiene and Public Health, 1916–1939.* Baltimore: Johns Hopkins University Press, 1987.

Harden, Victoria. *Inventing the NIH: Federal Biomedical Policy, 1887–1937.* Baltimore: Johns Hopkins University Press, 1986.

Rosen, George. *A History of Public Health.* New York: MD Publications, 1958.

Rosenberg, Charles. *The Cholera Years: The United States in 1832, 1849, and 1866.* Chicago: University of Chicago Press, 1962.

Rosenkrantz, Barbara. *Public Health and the State: Changing Views in Massachusetts.* Cambridge, MA: Harvard University Press, 1972.

P

Rosner, David, and Gerald Markowitz. *Deadly Dust: Silicosis and the Politics of Occupational Disease in Twentieth-Century America.* New Jersey: Princeton University Press, 1991.

Elizabeth Fee
Nancy Krieger

Puritanism and Science

The relationship of Puritanism to the beginnings of modern science has been the subject of ongoing historiographical debate since the late 1930s, when Robert K. Merton published his influential thesis *Science, Technology, and Society.* Merton's thesis argued that Protestant values, especially Puritanism, encouraged scientific progress—much as Max Weber attributed the rise of capitalism in the sixteenth and seventeenth centuries to a dynamic Protestant ethic. Among the values which scholars of the Merton school believe Puritans and contemporary scientists shared were a faith in progress, a concern for social welfare, and a spirit of free inquiry, all of which challenged traditional authoritarian and deductive systems of thought. Men of Puritan backgrounds were to be found among the scientists of the Invisible College of London and the Royal Society in the latter half of the seventeenth century. In New England, John Winthrop Jr., and Cotton Mather were well versed in the new science and corresponded with scientific colleagues overseas. Winthrop experimented with chemical medicines, promoted several industrial projects in Connecticut, and had an interest in astronomy and botany. Mather published his observations on comets, and in 1716 addressed the Royal Society on the topic of smallpox inoculation. Mather's campaign to encourage inoculation placed him at the center of controversy in the 1720s. In the next generation, Ezra Stiles of Connecticut conducted experiments in chemistry, astronomy, and electricity.

However, on both sides of the Atlantic, the relationship between Puritanism and science was complex. While Puritans shared a belief in the supernatural with leading scientists of the time, science was for them a means of discovering God's providential design. Thus, Mather applied Robert Boyle's corpuscularian philoso-phy to the biblical story of creation, while his works on comets, light, and gravity helped to disseminate new scientific discoveries with a Reformed theological context. Yet the accommodation of these two mindsets was problematic. Some historians contend that both the premises and purposes of science and religion were different, if not contradictory. Others have noted that the receptivity of Puritan intellectuals to the new science contributed to the transformation of Puritanism into its eighteenth-century liberal mode. In short, it seems fair to speculate that Puritanism was one expression of a larger social and cultural change that gave rise to early modern science, that this development was both creative and problematic, and that the tension between science and religion continues to shape our contemporary world.

BIBLIOGRAPHY

Cohen, I. Bernard, ed. *Puritanism and the Rise of Modern Science: The Merton Thesis.* New Brunswick: Rutgers University Press, 1990.

Dunn, Richard S. *Puritans and Yankees: The Winthrop Dynasty of New England, 1630–1717.* Princeton: Princeton University Press, 1962.

Greaves, Richard L. "Puritanism and Science: The Anatomy of a Controversy." *Journal of the History of Ideas* 30 (1939): 345–368.

Hall, David D. *Worlds of Wonder, Days of Judgement: Popular Religious Beliefs in Early New England.* New York: Alfred A. Knopf, 1989.

Hill, Christopher. *Intellectual Origins of the English Revolution.* Oxford, U.K.: Clarendon Press, 1965.

Merton, Robert K. *Science, Technology, and Society in Seventeenth-Century England.* 1938. Reprint, New York: Howard Fertig, 1970.

Miller, Perry. *The New England Mind: The Seventeenth Century.* Cambridge, MA: Harvard University Press, 1954.

———. *The New England Mind: From Colony to Province.* Cambridge, MA: Harvard University Press, 1962.

Morgan, Edmund S. *The Gentle Puritan: A Life of Ezra Stiles, 1727–1795.* New Haven: Yale University Press, 1962.

Silverman, Kenneth. *The Life and Times of Cotton Mather.* New York: Harper & Row, 1984.

Webster, Charles. *The Great Instauration: Science, Medicine, and Reform, 1626–1660.* New York: Holmes & Meier, 1976.

Barbara Ritter Dailey

Quantum Theory

Quanta (plural of quantum), tiny bundles of energy, were introduced by Max Planck in 1899 to explain the observed characteristics of black body radiation. Albert Einstein extended quantum theory in 1905 to the photoelectric effect. In 1911, at the first Solvay Congress, European physicists deliberated and accepted the inevitability of quantum theory despite its obvious clash with the older classical physics of Isaac Newton and James Clerk Maxwell.

Niels Bohr used quanta in his model of the hydrogen atom in 1913. Arnold Sommerfeld and others extended the Bohr model with considerable but incomplete success. By the mid-1920s, it became clear that a new quantum mechanics was needed to replace the "old" quantum theory. Werner Heisenberg and Erwin Schrodinger provided the required innovation in matrix and wave form. Further development, known as the Copenhagen Interpretation of Quantum Mechanics evolved. By 1930, physics was altered forever from its classical roots. During the 1930s, there were many successful applications of the new mechanics but fundamental difficulty remained in applying it to electrodynamics that was not successfully overcome until after World War II.

The introduction of quantum theory had a profound effect on the development of physics in the United States in the early decades of the twentieth century. When in 1899, the American physics community formed the American Physical Society (APS), its members were almost all experimentalists working in relative isolation from each other and from the European physics community. Quantum theory was not publicly discussed at an APS meeting until 1912. The transla-tion into English of the second edition of Planck's *Wärmestrahlung* by the American Morton Masius in 1914 encouraged the introduction of quantum theory into the curriculum of universities in the United States.

Soon a whole generation of young American physicists successfully studied and began doing research in quantum theory in the United States and in Europe. In 1918, Edwin C. Kemble at Harvard University wrote the first American Ph.D. thesis to use quantum theory. Later, as a faculty member there, he introduced young, aspiring theoreticians, such as John H. Van Vleck and John C. Slater, to the latest developments occurring in Europe. During the mid-1920s, many young Americans studied theoretical physics at European centers such as Copenhagen, Göttingen, and Munich. Notable among them were Edward U. Condon, J. Robert Oppenheimer, Linus Pauling, I.I. Rabi, and Slater. Upon returning to the United States, they were in demand by universities to teach the new material. In addition, many European physicists, attracted by the emerging activity in physics in the United States, came to lecture and some accepted positions at American universities. Among the visiting lecturers were Max Born, Sommerfeld, Bohr, Schrodinger, Heisenberg and P.A.M. Dirac. Among the permanent émigrés were S.A. Goudsmit, George Uehlenberg, George Gamow, and Eugene Wigner. International groups of theoretical physicists met at the University of Michigan each summer.

American experimentalists contributed to the development and acceptance of quantum theory. For example, Robert A. Millikan determined precisely the value of Planck's constant h. The Compton Effect was discovered by Arthur H. Compton and the wave properties of

Q

electrons were demonstrated by Clinton Davisson and Lester Germer.

Following the advent of quantum mechanics, several American theoreticians played significant roles in exploiting the uses of quantum theory. Van Vleck worked with magnetism and crystal field theory. Condon was a codiscoverer of nuclear barrier penetration. Slater, Pauling, and Robert S. Mulliken focused on the theory of valence bringing quantum theory into chemistry.

American physics "came of age" in the decades prior to World War II, participating fully in mainstream physics, theoretical and experimental. In the postwar years, the young American theoreticians Richard Feynman and Julian Schwinger confronted quantum electrodynamics so successfully that they shared (with Tomanaga) in 1963 the Nobel Prize in physics for their achievement.

BIBLIOGRAPHY

Assmus, Alexi. "The Americanization of Molecular Physics." *Historical Studies in Physical and Biological Sciences* 23 (1992): 1–34.

Holton, Gerald "On the Hesitant Rise of Quantum Physics Research in the United States." Chap. 5 in *Thematic Origins of Scientific Thought: Kepler to Einstein.* Rev. ed. Cambridge, MA: Harvard University Press, 1988.

Schweber, S.S. "The Young John Clarke Slater and the Development of Quantum Chemistry." *Historical Studies in Physical and Biological Sciences* 20 (1990): 339–406.

Slater, John C. "Quantum Physics in America Between the Wars." *Physics Today* 21 (1968): 433–453.

———. *Solid-State and Molecular Theory: A Scientific Biography.* New York: Wiley, 1975.

Sopka. Katherine R. *Quantum Physics in America: The Years through 1935.* New York: American Institute of Physics, 1988.

Stuewer, Roger H. *The Compton Effect: Turning Point in Physics.* New York: Science History Publications, 1975.

Van Vleck, John H. "American Physics Comes of Age." *Physics Today* 17 (1964): 21–26.

Katherine R. Sopka

R

Rafinesque, Constantine Samuel (1783–1840)
Naturalist, archaeologist, botanist, philologist, and zoologist. Born near Constantinople into a French merchant family, Rafinesque had little formal education and was sent to Philadelphia in 1802 to learn his father's profession by apprenticeship. His spare-time exploration of the mid-Atlantic states netted him many botanical specimens and naturalist friends. After three years, he returned to Europe, where, as secretary to the United States consul in Palermo, he quickly became financially independent through trading and could devote his full time to the natural history of the island, sometimes in company with William Swainson. His first publications were issued in Sicily, mostly under the name Rafinesque-Schmaltz, the matronym having been added to allay suspicion of his French ancestry since Sicily was under threat of invasion by the French.

On his return to the United States in 1815, he was shipwrecked in Long Island Sound, losing all of his collections and most of his wealth; thereafter, he supported himself by a variety of means, including dealing in natural history specimens and books. During three years in New York City, where he began a lifelong friendship with John Torrey, he was one of the founders of the Lyceum of Natural History. There, too, he published *Florula Ludoviciana*, which occasioned harsh criticism because in it he described plants he himself had never seen. He remained in the United States the rest of his life, and was naturalized in 1832.

Returning from a collecting trip down the Ohio River in 1818, during which he met John James Audubon, he obtained a professorship at Transylvania University in Lexington, Kentucky. This Ohio River trip resulted in the publication of *Ichthyologia Ohiensis*, a base-line description of the fishes inhabiting the drainage basin of that river, and also marked the beginning of Rafinesque's struggle to devise an acceptable scheme for the classification of unionacean mussels—which has since been seen as his most accomplished taxonomic exercise. Despite his frequent quarrels with colleagues, Rafinesque's Transylvania appointment, which lasted until 1826, was one of his most productive periods. There also began his interest in Indian antiquities and languages, resulting in the publication of such works as *The American Nations*, where the "Walam Olum," the alleged Lenape creation myth, first appeared.

Leaving Transylvania in 1826, he settled permanently in Philadelphia. The forty crates of belongings shipped there from Kentucky provided materials for research the rest of his life, although he also continued to collect in the field and to exchange specimens with other naturalists. For a time, he lectured at the Franklin Institute, marketed a tuberculosis nostrum called Pulmel, and even founded a small workingmen's bank.

Although never rich, he was by no means as poverty-stricken as popularly supposed. At the time of his death he had a whole rented house at his disposal and, thanks to the financial assistance of Charles Wetherill, had been able to publish privately numerous books and pamphlets during the last four years of his life, including *New Flora and Botany of North America;* his autobiography, *A Life of Travels: Flora Telluriana;* a volume of poetry, *The World; Autikon Botanikon;* pamphlets on economics and education, and a linguistic study of the Hebrew Bible. Throughout his career he also launched several unsuccessful magazines, of which the *Atlantic*

R

Journal and Friend of Knowledge is most notable. His only book having any measure of financial success was the two-volume *Medical Flora.*

Rafinesque's interests, which involved most of the branches of natural history including anthropology, focused on fieldwork, classification, and nomenclature. In both botany and zoology, his contributions were principally descriptive. His enthusiasm for the French "natural method" of classification, when most of his American colleagues were confirmed Linneanists, put him at odds with fellow naturalists. His slipshod workmanship and the acerbity of his personality caused his publications to be ignored in his lifetime, a neglect that continued into the twentieth century because of their obscurity, for most were published in such small editions that several have disappeared without leaving a trace.

In the course of his practice, Rafinesque touched on several important considerations in taxonomy, sometimes anticipating his contemporaries, but always he lacked the patience to develop those insights which might have led to significant contributions. Among such larger issues were his pragmatic observations on the impermanence of species (which has caused some to see him as a precursor of Darwin), plant geography and plant succession, the use of organic fossils to date geological strata, and, in linguistics, the crude beginnings of lexicostatistics and some perception of the nature of Mayan glyphs. Although Rafinesque failed to make any theoretical contributions to knowledge, his permanent place in the history of science in America is assured because he published more new plant names than any other botanist who ever lived.

BIBLIOGRAPHY

Boewe, Charles. *Fitzpatrick's Rafinesque: A Sketch of His Life with Bibliography.* Weston: M & S Press, 1982.

Boewe, Charles, Georges Reynaud, and Beverly Seaton, eds. *Précis ou Abrégé des Voyages, Travaux, et Recherches de C. S. Rafinesque (1833), the Original Version of* A Life of Travels *(1836).* Amsterdam: North-Holland Publishing Company, 1987.

Call, Richard Ellsworth. *The Life and Writings of Rafinesque.* Louisville: John P. Morton and Company, 1895.

Dupre, Huntley. *Rafinesque in Lexington, 1819–1826.* Lexington, KY: Bur Press, 1945.

Merrill, Elmer D. *Index Rafinesquianus.* Jamaica Plain, MA: Arnold Arboretum, 1949.

Rafinesque, C.S. *Florula Ludoviciana.* New York: C. Wiley & Co., 1817.

———. *Ichthyologia Ohiensis.* Lexington: The Author, 1820.

———. *Medical Flora.* 2 Vols. Philadelphia: Atkinson & Alexander, 1828; Samuel C. Atkinson, 1830.

———. *The American Nations.* 2 Vols. Philadelphia: The Author, 1836.

———. *New Flora and Botany of North America.* Philadelphia: The Author, 1836–1838.

———. *Flora Telluriana.* Philadelphia: The Author, 1837–1838.

———. *Autikon Botanikon.* Philadelphia: The Author, 1840.

———. *A Life of Travels.* Philadelphia, The Author, 1836.

———. *The World of Instability.* Philadelphia: J. Dobson, 1836.

Charles Boewe

RAND, Project

The first of the military "think tanks" was inaugurated in March 1946 at the Douglas Aircraft Company in Santa Monica, California, under a three-year $10 million contract from the U.S. Army Air Force. In 1948, RAND left Douglas and became a separate, nonprofit corporation, which is still in operation today.

The 1946 contract described RAND's mission as "a program of study and research on the broad subject of intercontinental warfare, other than surface, with the object of recommending to the Army Air Forces preferred techniques and instrumentalities for this purpose." This mission, in part, derived from development of operations research in World War II. More importantly, it resulted from the confluence of two important postwar trends: the political importance of air power and nuclear weapons in the emerging Cold War, and the active involvement of academic and industry experts in military affairs. RAND was an organizational innovation, providing a home for these experts to study the broad military and social ramifications of war fighting with long-range bombers, ballistic missiles, and nuclear weapons.

Reflecting the view that the Cold War embodied a competition between societies, and, hence, that military problems were both technical and social problems, RAND built a professional staff drawing on a wide range of disciplines: engineering, physical sciences, mathematics, economics, political science, sociology, psychology, and others. Consultants from these disciplines also actively contributed to the RAND program, and included such well-known figures as John von Neumann and Kenneth Arrow in the 1950s. An avowed hallmark of RAND research was to join traditionally separate academic disciplines in the study of military problems, the result of which was RAND's signature product, the "systems analysis."

In the late 1960s, RAND broadened its scope of activity to include research on nonmilitary problems, such as education, civil justice, health care, and urban issues.

RAND's history has been probed only in part. Most effort has been directed at RAND's substantial contribution to the development of nuclear-war-fighting doctrine, and the rise of a class of strategy professionals. Still needed are studies on RAND's other research lines, its development as an institution, its relations with its military sponsors, and its relation to the broader pattern of changes between science and the state in the postwar period.

BIBLIOGRAPHY

Davies, Merton E., and William R. Harris. *RAND's Role in the Evolution of Balloon and Satellite Observation Systems and Related U.S. Space Technology.* Santa Monica, CA: The RAND Corporation, 1988.

Herken, Gregg. *Counsels of War.* New York: Knopf, 1985.

Kaplan, Fred. *Wizards of Armageddon.* New York: Simon & Schuster, 1983.

Smith, Bruce L.R. *The RAND Corporation: Case Study of a Nonprofit Advisory Corporation.* Cambridge, MA: Harvard University Press, 1966.

Williams, Barbara R., and Malcolm Palmatier. "The RAND Corporation." In *Organizations for Policy Analysis,* edited by Carol H. Weiss. Newbury Park, CA: Sage Publications, 1992, pp. 48–68.

Martin J. Collins

Redfield, William C. (1789–1857)

Merchant, transportation engineer, and scientist. Redfield was born in South Farms, Connecticut, the eldest of five children of Peleg Redfield, seaman, and Elizabeth Pratt. He was apprenticed to a saddle and harness maker in Cromwell in 1803, following his father's death. Redfield was interested in science and helped establish the local debating society and library. After completing his apprenticeship in 1810, Redfield walked to Ohio to visit his family, who had moved there. He opened a country store and saddle shop in Middletown, Connecticut, in 1811.

In 1823, Redfield became a charter member and New York agent of the Hartford Steam-Boat Company. The following year he became a partner in the Steam Navigation Company, which carried passengers and freight on the Hudson River between New York City and the Erie Canal. He was also active in the development of railroads, publishing a plan for service extending west to the Mississippi River and designing the course of the local Harlem and Hartford-New Haven Railroads.

Redfield's meteorological studies focused on the gales of the North Atlantic. He collected weather information from newspapers, ships' logs, and coastal stations which he used to reconstruct the wind patterns and path of storms. With the support of Denison Olmsted, Redfield published his first paper on Atlantic storms in the *American Journal of Science* in 1831.

Redfield believed that gravitational forces were the source of all atmospheric disturbances and hypothesized that hurricanes were caused when the trade winds were deflected into a circular pattern by the Caribbean islands. He believed that waterspouts, tornadoes, and winter storms were smaller whirlwinds following the same principles. Redfield claimed to be merely describing the phenomena of whirlwind storms, but his theoretical model had practical importance for mariners since the complex motion of a hurricane's winds meant that common weather vanes could not be trusted to indicate a storm's true motion. His meteorological studies, which he pursued until his death, brought him into a heated controversy with two other prominent scientists, James Espy and Robert Hare.

Redfield joined the New York Lyceum of Science in 1837 and later served as its vice president. He explored the sources of the Hudson River and became an expert on fossil fish, naming one genus and seven species of Triassic fish. Redfield served as the first president of the American Association for the Advancement of Science in 1848. His final scientific paper, on the cyclones or typhoons of the north Pacific Ocean, was prepared at the request of Commodore Matthew Perry and published in the report of his expedition.

Redfield's papers, letterbooks, and correspondence with William Reid are in the Beinecke Rare Book and Manuscript Library at Yale University. The Redfield Family Papers are at the Library of Congress Manuscript Division.

BIBLIOGRAPHY

Burstyn, Harold L. "Redfield, William." *Dictionary of Scientific Biography.* Edited by Charles C. Gillispie. New York: Scribner, 1975, 11:340–341.

R

Fleming, James Rodger. *Meteorology in America, 1800–1870.* Baltimore: Johns Hopkins University Press, 1990.

Olmsted, Denison. "Biographical Memoir of William C. Redfield." *American Journal of Science,* 2d ser., 24 (1857): 355–373.

———. "An Address in Commemoration of William C. Redfield, First President of the Association." *Proceedings of the American Association for the Advancement of Science* 11 (1858): 9–34.

Redfield, John Howard. *Recollections of John Howard Redfield.* Philadelphia: Morris, 1900.

Simpson. George G. "The Beginnings of Vertebrate Paleontology in North America." *Proceedings of the American Philosophical Society* 86 (1942): 130–188.

James Rodger Fleming

Reed, Walter (1851–1902)

Physician and microbiologist. Born in Gloucester County, Virginia, Reed obtained his first medical degree from the University of Virginia in 1869 and a second from Bellevue Hospital in 1870. After postgraduate training in several New York hospitals, he served briefly as a board of health inspector for Brooklyn. Reed passed the army's medical examination in 1874 and spent the rest of his career as a United States Army officer. For the next fifteen years, he was posted at multiple sites, many of them on the western frontier. In 1890, he requested opportunities for further medical study, and was accordingly stationed in Baltimore, where he studied bacteriology with William Welch at Johns Hopkins. For the remaining twelve years of his life, the army sponsored his research on a number of infectious diseases, including erysipelas, diphtheria, typhoid, and yellow fever. From 1893, he was professor at the new army medical school and curator of the army medical museum.

Reed was a clever epidemiologist who successfully devised and tested theories using the latest concepts of bacteriology. Along with Victor Vaughan and Edward Shakespeare, he investigated typhoid fever epidemics among Spanish-American War troops stationed along the southern coast in 1898. Although the prevailing doctrine held that the typhoid germ was transmitted primarily through infected water, Reed and his colleagues demonstrated the greater importance of flies in the transport of bacteria from fecal material to food. Reed's work established the fly as a serious target of public health effort.

In 1900, Surgeon-General George Sternberg appointed Reed to head a commission to study yellow fever in Cuba. For years, researchers, including Sternberg, had sought the yellow fever germ. In 1897, an Italian physician named Giuseppe Sanarelli announced he had found it. Reed, and his colleague James Carroll, first took on the yellow fever question by exploring the validity of Sanarelli's claims. Their argument that his germ was a secondary infectious agent and not the cause of yellow fever at all was only widely accepted after their work on the mosquito vector brought them international fame.

Reed is best known as the man who proved that yellow fever is spread by mosquitoes. The chain of priority in the discovery of the yellow fever vector has disputed links, however. Mid-nineteenth century writers had thought the disease was caused by microscopic flying insects, but these claims took on an aura of prescience only when the mosquito vector was established. More importantly, Carlos Finlay of Cuba argued from the early 1880s that the mosquito was involved in yellow fever transmission. Cuban historians have tended to award him laurels while others have noted that his mosquito concept was buried in a number of incorrect arguments about the disease and lacked the important notion of the mosquito as an obligate intermediate host. There is no doubt that the work of Ronald Ross demonstrating the transmission of malaria by mosquitoes and the descriptions of the extrinsic incubation period of yellow fever by Henry Rose Carter, both in the preceding five years, had a seminal effect on the Reed Commission's conclusions.

The Reed Commission not only suggested the mosquito vector, they proved it. Reed and his coworkers devised a human experiment to test whether the mosquito carried the disease, or if it could be caught from external contact with the body fluids of yellow fever patients. Using closely screened huts, volunteer soldiers were exposed to each possibility, and only the mosquito-bitten sickened.

Reed's work was a masterpiece of disease research, which settled a century-old debate in a few months. Public health efforts based on the mosquito doctrine led to the first effective control of the disease. Reed's team also demonstrated that the causative agent was filterable, and hence a virus. This led to the production of an effective vaccine by the 1930s.

BIBLIOGRAPHY

Bean, William. *Walter Reed, A Biography.* Charlottesville: University of Virginia Press, 1982.

Delaporte, Francois. *Yellow Fever: An Essay on the Birth of Tropical Medicine.* Translated from the French by Arthur Goldhammer. Cambridge, MA: MIT Press, 1991.

Warner (Humphreys), Margaret. "Hunting the Yellow Fever Germ: The Principle and Practice of Etiological Proof in Late Nineteenth-Century America." *Bulletin of the History of Medicine* 59 (1985): 361–382.

Yellow Fever, A Compilation of Various Publications, Results of the Work of Major Walter Reed, Medical Corps, United States Army, and the Yellow Fever Commission. 61st Cong., 3d ses., S. Doc. 822 (Washington, DC, 1911).

Margaret Humphreys

SEE ALSO
Yellow Fever

Regional Characteristics and Centers of Science

Science in the United States has been shaped by the absence of a single city that has served simultaneously as the nation's cultural, political, economic, and commercial center. Nineteenth-century American science developed on a regional basis; patterns of scientific activity in different areas were remarkably similar yet displayed important local variations. In 1790, Philadelphia was the scientific capital of the United States. The American Philosophical Society served as a national society and the University of Pennsylvania, largely on account of the success of its medical school, was the center of academic scientific teaching and research. Subsequent decades witnessed the political and economic decline of Philadelphia. In 1800, the federal and state legislatures moved to Washington and Lancaster respectively; in 1825 the opening of the Erie Canal transformed New York City into the nation's leading entrepôt; and the collapse of the Bank of the United States in the 1830s ended Philadelphia's position as the banking and financial center of the United States. In compensation, the city's patriciate promoted scientific and cultural institutions so that by midcentury Philadelphia could boast an array of preeminent scientific and medical organizations: the Academy of Natural Sciences, the Franklin Institute, the College of Physicians of Philadelphia, the medical school at the University of Pennsylvania, and Pennsylvania Hospital.

In the seventy years before the Civil War, Philadelphia set the pattern followed by other cities. Boston scientists and physicians established many institutions similar to those in Philadelphia—the American Academy of Arts and Sciences, the Linnaean Society of New England, the Boston Society of Natural History, and Massachusetts General Hospital—but all were eventually to be dwarfed by science at Harvard University. The Lawrence Scientific School and the Museum of Comparative Zoology were established at the university in 1847 and 1860 respectively, chairs in, inter alia, anatomy, astronomy, botany, natural history, mathematics, and natural philosophy were endowed in the 1840s and 1850s, and the Harvard Medical School caught up with its Philadelphia rivals—the University of Pennsylvania and Jefferson Medical College—in the 1860s. Science and technology also flourished at the Massachusetts Institute of Technology after its creation in 1861 by William Barton Rogers.

In New York City, progress was weak and uncertain largely because, at a time when energy and attention were focused on economic, banking, and commercial ventures, science was felt to be irrelevant to the city's growth and development. Thus, although New York's clerisy established the customary array of institutions, these either collapsed—most notably, the New-York Literary and Philosophical Society and the American Institute—or led a fitful and impoverished existence. The Lyceum of Natural History and the College of Physicians and Surgeons eventually prospered but only after many uncertain years.

In Albany, science depended for its success on a close identification with agricultural improvement and technological advance and the patronage of both by the New York state legislature. The Society for the Promotion of Agriculture, Arts and Manufactures, founded in 1791 in New York City, followed the state legislature to Albany and in 1804 was rechartered as the Society for the Promotion of Useful Arts. The society's gradual decline after 1819 led to a merger with the Albany Lyceum of Natural History to form the Albany Institute in 1824. In the antebellum period, no state legislature exceeded New York in its support for science, yet there was ample room for private initiatives: Rensselaer Polytechnic, Albany Medical College, and Union College were also significant centers of scientific teaching and research in New York state.

Science at Washington was virtually nonexistent until the 1840s. In the early national period, congressional opposition, constitutional limitations, and Federalist antipathy prevented any federal support for permanent scientific institutions. In 1818, the national government provided the Columbian Institute with a charter and five acres of land but the institute had

R

insufficient members to enable it to endure for more than a few years. John Quincy Adams promoted the idea of a national university, a naval academy, and an observatory during his presidency but Congress failed to pass the necessary appropriations. In 1840, the National Institute for the Promotion of Science proposed using the Smithson bequest to provide funding for a museum to house the collections of the Wilkes Expedition, but six years later, Congress instead used the money to create the Smithsonian Institution.

In the antebellum midwestern cities, the creation of scientific societies depended on a critical mass of interested individuals and relied on a combination of private and public patronage for long-term survival. St. Louis could boast the Franklin Society, the Western Academy of Natural Sciences, the Mechanics Institute, and the St. Louis Lyceum; however, only the Academy of Sciences of St. Louis was sufficiently robust to sponsor a journal—the academy's *Transactions* was published continuously from 1856 to 1958. Both the Naturhistorische Verein von Wisconsin and the Chicago Academy of Sciences served as regional organizations, publishing, for example, the research of the state geological surveys of the Midwest. Other cities with the wealth and population to support science included Cincinnati, where Daniel Drake organized medical colleges and scientific societies, most notably, the Western Academy of Natural Sciences of Cincinnati and the Western Museum Society. At Lexington, science and medicine were concentrated at Transylvania University and supported by the medical school faculty, a group that included Charles Caldwell and Samuel Brown.

Science in the southeastern states before the Civil War was pursued most energetically at Charleston, which, with its large medical community and its prosperity as a commercial center, supported a wide variety of societies; the city's scientific standing was acknowledged in 1850 by the decision of the American Association for the Advancement of Science to hold its third annual meeting at Charleston. Although its medical organizations flourished in the 1840s, New Orleans was less successful as a center of science. Thus, not until the establishment of the New Orleans Academy of Sciences in 1853 could the city boast an exclusively scientific society.

The appearance of credible national institutions for science and medicine began with the founding of the Association of American Geologists in Philadelphia in 1840. Scientists who had worked on the various state geological surveys of the 1830s used the association not only to establish common professional goals but also to exchange information and to establish a uniform geological nomenclature. The organization expanded its scope in 1842 to become the Association of American Geologists and Naturalists, and in 1848, the association transcended regional jealousies and attempted to represent all the members of the nation's scientific community as the American Association for the Advancement of Science (AAAS). The American Medical Association (AMA), founded in Philadelphia in 1847, was a consequence of the movement for the reform of medical education and the establishment of professional standards; the AMA also served to distinguish allopaths from their sectarian rivals and to express the career aspirations of marginal medical men.

Despite the establishment of such national institutions as the AMA, the AAAS, and the National Academy of Sciences (1863), and despite the creation of local scientific societies throughout the United States—the California Academy of Sciences was founded in 1853—American science continued to be dominated by the eastern cities at least until 1900. Thus, the early geological and palaeontological surveys of the western territories were led by scientists from the east, most notably Joseph Leidy and Edward Drinker Cope at the University of Pennsylvania and Othniel Marsh at Yale; the results appeared in journals and monographs published by the Smithsonian Institution, the Academy of Natural Sciences, and the American Philosophical Society; and the specimens were deposited in museums in New Haven, Boston, Philadelphia, and Washington. During the Gilded Age, New York City became an important center of science on account of the development of the American Museum of Natural History into a world-class institution and the expansion of science at Columbia University such that Columbia dominated the academic disciplines of anthropology, psychology, ethnology, physics, chemistry, and developmental biology. It has been only in the twentieth century that science in the United States has become truly national, a phenomenon fueled by the enormous growth of science under the aegis of the federal government, the appearance of the industrial research laboratory and the systematic integration of scientific research within industry, the creation of elite universities throughout the United States, and the growth of new high-technology, science-based industries in such fields as computers and biotechnology.

R

BIBLIOGRAPHY

Bruce, Robert V. *The Launching of Modern American Science, 1846–1876*. New York: Knopf, 1987.

Greene, John C. *American Science in the Age of Jefferson*. Ames: Iowa State University Press, 1984.

Hendrickson, Walter B. "Science and Culture in the American Middle West." *Isis* 64 (1973): 326–340

Kohlstedt, Sally Gregory. *The Formation of the American Scientific Community: The American Association for the Advancement of Science, 1848–60*. Urbana: University of Illinois Press, 1976.

Miller, Howard S. *Dollars for Research: Science and Its Patrons in Nineteenth-Century America*. Seattle: University of Washington Press, 1970.

Oleson, Alexandra, and Sanborn C. Brown. *The Pursuit of Knowledge in the Early American Republic: American Scientific and Learned Societies from Colonial Times to the Civil War*. Baltimore: Johns Hopkins University Press, 1976.

Simon Baatz

Revolutionary War and Science

"The disruptive influence of the war upon the whole pattern of science in America," wrote Brooke Hindle, "was much more serious than the limited number of beneficial influences it provided" (Hindle, p. 247). Colonial science had been, as Hindle put it, a "fragile plant" needing constant nourishment. War endangered the natural history circle that once embraced colonial botanists like John Bartram and British patrons like Peter Collinson. It weakened ties with the University of Edinburgh, which had produced so many of the medical men who dominated colonial science. Benjamin Franklin, the one American scientist of international stature, devoted himself to politics and diplomacy during the war. Astronomer and orrery-designer David Rittenhouse performed duties that left little time for the pursuit of science. Stripling organizations such as the Virginia Society for Advancing Useful Knowledge, founded in 1773, atrophied. Even the older, stronger American Philosophical Society all but collapsed.

Revolutionary Americans devised no effective science policy. They had neither the experience nor the funding, the drive or the wherewithal to mobilize the fledgling scientific community. And yet scientific enterprise did not cease from 1775 to 1783, as Hindle was quick to point out. Anglo-American ties may have been weakened, but they were not severed; Franco-American ties strengthened. War opened engineering opportunities, notably with the fortifications along the Hudson highlands and the Delaware River defense system. War also stimulated David Bushnell's ill-fated but important submarine and underwater explosives experiments. Robert Erskine developed his cartographic skills for the Continental army. Seventeen seventy-eight saw both George Washington's attempt to have all of his troops inoculated for smallpox—a public health milestone of sorts—and Dr. Benjamin Rush's helpful (although hardly original) *Directions for Preserving the Health of Soldiers*. If Virginia's scientific society never revived, the American Philosophical Society did, and before the war ended. The scientifically inclined in and around Boston formed the American Academy of Arts and Sciences in 1780. These men committed themselves to the promotion of agriculture, manufactures, and commerce—a utilitarian or "Baconian" emphasis on science as agent of human progress. In Boston as well as Philadelphia, men of science studied nature, not simply to understand it, but with the hope of better controlling it.

Patriot orators, typified by Dr. David Ramsay in his 4 July 1778 address, waxed enthusiastic on the role they envisioned for science in their new nation. They connected the rise of Western civilization to scientific advance; for their Republic to prosper, they urged listeners, science had to be encouraged. That public linking of science and technology to national peace, power, and prosperity is more important than either the interruptions caused by the outbreak of war or the limited innovations made during the conflict. Revolutionary rhetoric helped to underpin the eventual national reality. Revolutionary Americans began scientific societies and introduced federal patent law; they passed tariffs to protect manufacturing, and they sought to promote progressive farming; some even hoped for a national university with science at its curricular core. They failed in that quest, as they did in others. Even so, by joining national greatness to the promotion of scientific inquiry, by defining economic independence—sustained by scientific and technological change—as essential to true political independence, they charted a course that the nation still attempts to follow.

BIBLIOGRAPHY

Bell, Whitfield. "Science and Humanity in Philadelphia, 1775–1790." Ph.D. diss., University of Pennsylvania, 1947.

Cohen, I. Bernard. "Science and the Revolution." *Technology Review* 47 (1945): 367–368, 374, 376, 378.

R

Hindle, Brooke. *The Pursuit of Science in Revolutionary America, 1735–1790.* Chapel Hill: University of North Carolina Press, 1956.

Struik, Dirk. *Yankee Science in the Making.* Rev. ed., 1962. Reprint. New York: Dover, 1991.

York, Neil Longley. *Mechanical Metamorphosis: Technological Change in Revolutionary America.* Westport, CT: Greenwood, 1985.

Neil L. York

Rhine, Joseph Banks (1895–1980)

Parapsychologist. "J.B." Rhine, born in Juaniata County, Pennsylvania, into an itinerant farming family, spent his childhood in central Pennsylvania and Ohio. After a year at Ohio Northern University, Rhine followed his childhood companion, Louisa Weckesser, to the College of Wooster and then, after military service in World War I, to the University of Chicago, where they both completed Ph.D. degrees in plant physiology. The couple married in 1920; Louisa Rhine was to be J.B.'s intellectual partner in parapsychology and to achieve prominence in her own right in that field.

Originally intending a career in the ministry, Rhine never abandoned his concern about the metaphysical implications of scientific materialism. At Chicago, J.B. and Louisa had been attracted to psychical research as a possible bridge between science, religion, and metaphysics. After two years in plant physiology (one at the University of West Virginia), Rhine and his wife went to Harvard to study with the psychologist William McDougall, well known for his interest in psychical research. Although McDougall was on a sabbatical leave, the Rhine's confirmed their new vocational interest in Cambridge and, in 1927, followed McDougall to Duke University, where the latter had become chairman of the newly created psychology department. Although not trained as a psychologist, Rhine eventually joined the department under McDougall's patronage.

Rhine's most significant and famous work was carried out in the period 1930–1933 and was published in 1934 as *Extra-Sensory Perception.* Using Duke students, Rhine attempted to place on an experimental, quantitative basis the study of purported psychic abilities: telepathy and clairvoyance. Subjects were asked to guess sequences of shuffled twenty-five-card decks consisting of equal numbers of five geometrical symbols, and the results were evaluated statistically for "extra-chance" significance (an average of five correct guesses out of twenty-five being that of chance). Eight subjects were reported to have scored at extraordinarily high extra-chance levels. Rhine subsequently extended similar methodologies to the study of precognition and psychokinesis.

Rhine's work attracted national publicity in the 1930s and subsequently, and he worked to develop the study of psychical abilities (to which he had given the name "parapsychology") into an academic discipline allied to psychology. Graduate students were recruited; a research journal, *The Journal of Parapsychology,* was founded in 1937; considerable financial support from private individuals was secured. During this period, Rhine had found a sympathetic ally in the psychologist Gardner Murphy.

Yet Rhine's work also elicited considerable controversy which was never successfully overcome, and Rhine's vision for the institutionalization of parapsychology was not very well realized. In 1948, he was able to establish the Parapsychology Laboratory at Duke University, but, when he retired, the formal connection with Duke was severed. The Foundation for Research on the Nature of Man of Durham, North Carolina (now Rhine Research Center), was founded in 1962 and is the continuation of Rhine's earlier organization.

By general consensus within the field of parapsychology, Rhine has been the most significant figure in this century. His vision of gaining experimental control over psychical abilities and phenomena continues to dominate the field; terms such as "parapsychology" and "ESP" (for "extrasensory perception") have passed into common usage.

BIBLIOGRAPHY

Mauskopf, Seymour H., and Michael R. McVaugh. *The Elusive Science: Origins of Experimental Psychical Research.* Baltimore: Johns Hopkins University Press, 1980.

McVaugh, Michael R., and Seymour H. Mauskopf. "J. B. Rhine's Extra-Sensory Perception and Its Background in Psychical Research." *Isis* 67 (1976): 161–189.

Pratt, J.G. et al. *Extra-Sensory Perception After Sixty Years.* New York: Henry Holt, 1940. Reprint, Boston: Bruce Humphries, 1966.

Rao, K. Ramakrishna, ed. *J. B. Rhine: On the Frontiers of Science.* Jefferson, NC: McFarland Press, 1982.

Rhine, J.B. *Extra-Sensory Perception.* Boston: Boston Society for Psychical Research, 1934. Reprint, Boston: Bruce Humphries, 1964.

Rhine, Louisa E. *Something Hidden.* Jefferson, NC: McFarland Press, 1983.

Seymour H. Mauskopf

Richards, Ellen Henrietta Swallow (1842–1911)

The first woman to receive a degree from the Massachusetts Institute of Technology (MIT), where she taught sanitary chemistry from 1878 to 1911, Richards is best known as a champion of women's scientific education and a pioneer in home economics.

Richards was born on a farm outside of Dunstable, Massachusetts, the only child of two schoolteachers. The family moved to nearby Westford so that Ellen could attend the coeducational Westford Academy. After graduating, she served a brief stint as a country schoolteacher before returning home to nurse her ailing mother. For two years, she suffered from depression or neurasthenia, which quickly subsided when her parents agreed to send her to the newly opened Vassar College for women.

In 1868, at the age of twenty-five, she entered Vassar, where she studied astronomy with Maria Mitchell and chemistry. Upon her graduation in 1870, she sought work, unsuccessfully, as a chemical analyst. One firm suggested she apply to the newly opened MIT. MIT admitted her in December 1870 and waived her tuition, not wishing to have a female student on the official rolls. "Had I realized on what basis I was taken, I would not have gone," she said (Hunt, p. 68).

Richards received her B.S. in 1873 and submitted a thesis to Vassar which earned her an M.A. Because MIT did not wish to grant its first Ph.D. in chemistry to a woman, she never received the doctorate. On 4 June 1875, she married Robert Hallowell Richards, the institute's professor of mining and metallurgy. The couple had no children.

Richards continued her career in chemistry at MIT after her marriage, publishing over seventeen books in the fields of sanitary chemistry and domestic science. Her survey of Massachusetts drinking water undertaken in 1887 stands as a benchmark for current pollution studies. In her spare time, she continued to promote scientific education for women, founding in 1882, along with Marion Talbot, the American Collegiate Association, precursor to the American Association of University Women. In 1876, she set up the Woman's Laboratory at MIT where she taught as a volunteer. In 1883, largely thanks to her efforts, women gained equal admission to the Institute. The Woman's Lab was torn down, and the following year Richards won an appointment as instructor of sanitary chemistry at MIT. Informally, she served as dean of women,

setting up a women's club and helping women students obtain financial aid.

In 1889, in an uncharacteristic moment of self-pity, she complained to a Vassar classmate, "I might have made a name and fame for myself. I have helped five men to positions they would not have held without me" (*Journal of Home Economics* 23 [December 1931]: 1125). Frustrated and seeking an outlet for her prodigious energy, Richards put her talents to work in the service of domestic science, or home economics.

Richards was the guiding spirit behind the Lake Placid conferences (1899–1907), which defined and developed the field of home economics. Richards herself favored the name "euthenics," which she defined as "the science of right living." At its founding in December 1908, the American Home Economics Association elected Richards its first president. Under her leadership, home economics worked to train women in scientific principles and develop careers for women in college and university teaching and in institutional management. Isabel Bevier, professor of household science at the University of Illinois, observed, "It is safe to say no university department has been organized, no important step taken, in which her ideas and her counsels have not had a part" (*Journal of Home Economics* 3 [June 1911]: 215). Smith College awarded Richards an honorary Doctor of Science degree in 1910.

Manuscript collections and depositories with material bearing on Richards's life include the Edward Atkinson Papers, Massachusetts Historical Society; the MIT Archives; Vassar College Archives; Sophia Smith Collection, Smith College; American Home Economics Association Archives; Arthur and Elizabeth Schlesinger Library.

BIBLIOGRAPHY

Clarke, Robert. *Ellen Swallow: The Woman Who Founded Ecology.* Chicago: Follett Publishing, 1973.

Hunt, Caroline. *The Life of Ellen H. Richards.* Boston: Whitcomb & Barrows, 1912.

Richards, Ellen. *Euthenics.* Boston: Whitcomb & Barrows, 1910.

Richards, Robert H. *His Mark.* Boston: Little Brown, 1936.

Rossiter, Margaret. *Women Scientists in America: Struggles and Strategies to 1940.* Baltimore: Johns Hopkins University Press, 1982.

Stage, Sarah, "From Domestic Science to Social Housekeeping: The Career of Ellen Richards." In *Power and Responsibility: Case Studies in American Leadership,* edited by David M. Kennedy and Michael E. Parrish. New York: Harcourt Brace Jovanovich, 1986, pp. 211–225.

R

Stage, Sarah, and Virginia A. Vincente, eds. *Rethinking Home Economics: Women and the History of a Profession.* Ithaca: Cornell University Press, 1997.

Sarah Stage

Richter, Charles Francis (1900–1985)

Seismologist. Born in Hamilton, Ohio, Richter received his A.B. from Stanford in 1920 and his Ph.D. in physics in 1928 from the California Institute of Technology (Cal Tech). He was recruited while a student by the Carnegie Institution to study southern California earthquakes at their Pasadena laboratory. After the laboratory was taken over by Cal Tech in 1936, he became professor of seismology at the institute. His lectures in the introductory seismology course were notable for their richness in anecdotes and details of observational seismology. In 1958, he authored a widely used textbook, *Elementary Seismology*, which includes much of the material in his lectures.

He is best known for his invention of the magnitude scale. With later modifications, this has become the standard measure of the size of earthquakes. His principal area of research was the seismicity of southern California. He compiled a detailed compendium of the locations, magnitudes, times, and reported effects of all of the recorded earthquakes in this area. He also worked with Harry O. Wood and Hugo Benioff on southern California blasting vibrations. Together with Beno Gutenberg, he authored *Seismicity of the Earth,* published first by the Geological Society of America in 1941, and later by Princeton University Press.

Much of his research was reported in papers jointly with Gutenberg, starting with "On Seismic Waves" and "Materials for the Study of Deep-focus Earthquakes." The two routinely examined each day's new seismograms at the California Institute of Technology Observatory. Richter's remarkable photographic memory of older seismograms contributed importantly to the recognition of significant features in the seismograms.

One of his special interests was providing accurate information on seismic hazards to the public. With patience and perseverance, he attempted to educate news reporters who contacted him after each large earthquake in the basics of seismology so that their reports would be meaningful and accurate.

Richter served as president of the Seismological Society of America in 1959–1960 and was the second recipient of the Society Medal in 1977.

BIBLIOGRAPHY

Gutenberg, B. and C.F. Richter. "On Seismic Waves." *Gerlands Beitrage zur Geophys* 43 (1934): 56–133; 45 (1935): 280–360; 47 (1936): 73–131; 54 (1939): 94–136.
———. "Materials for the Study of Deep-focus Earthquakes." *Bulletin of the Seismological Society of America* 26 (1936): 341–390; 27 (1937): 157–183.
———. *Seismicity of the Earth.* 2d ed. Princeton: Princeton University Press, 1954.
Richter, C. F. "An Instrumental Earthquake Magnitude Scale." *Bulletin of the Seismological Society of America* 25 (1935): 1–32.
———. *Elementary Seismology.* San Francisco: Freeman, 1958.

B.F. Howell Jr.

Richtmyer, Floyd Karker (1881–1939)

Experimental physicist and science administrator. Born and raised in Cobleskill, New York, Richtmyer received his A.B. degree (1904) from Cornell University. After two years as an instructor at the Drexel Institute, he returned to Cornell for his Ph.D. (1910). He remained at Cornell for the rest of his life, first as a professor and then as dean of its Graduate School (from 1931). Richtmyer was a competent experimental physicist, but was most influential through his textbook writing and as an administrator.

Richtmyer's experimental work began with studies of photoelectric cells, especially photometric work. The concern with precision would remain one of his scientific passions; one 1932 lecture was titled "The Romance of the Next Decimal Place." After military service during World War I, he shifted his research to X-rays. After some initial work on X-ray absorption, he turned to X-ray lines known as "satellites." He received the Franklin Institute's Levy Medal in 1929 for a theory explaining satellites, but eventually abandoned the theory.

Richtmyer's most important publication was a textbook, *Introduction to Modern Physics,* first published in 1928. One of the first texts to deal comprehensively with quantum mechanics, the book proved so popular that it outlived him by thirty years (sixth edition, 1969).

But more than his own publications, Richtmyer strove to advance the work of others. From 1922 on, he served on the editorial staff of the Optical Society of America. From 1932 to his death, he was editor in chief of both the *Journal of the Optical Society of America* and the *Review of Scientific Instruments.* He was also editor of a textbook series for McGraw-Hill, and associate editor of several other journals. He also applied his managerial skills to scientific societies: he was president of the Optical Society of America (1920), of Sigma Xi (1924–1926), of the American Physical Society (1936), and of the American Association of Physics Teachers (1937–1938). He was a member of the American Philosophical Society and the National Academy of Sciences.

Richtmyer does not loom large as a figure in the historiography of American science. But he represents an important type in twentieth-century science: the yeoman researcher who takes on the administrative, society, and publishing duties needed to maintain the vibrancy of the scientific establishment. Scientists like Richtmyer provided the senior management of the increasingly complex network of scientific institutions.

Much work remains to be done to understand the role of scientific managers such as Richtmyer, either through individual biographies or through collective biography.

BIBLIOGRAPHY

Hirsh, Frederick R. "Richtmyer, Floyd Karker." In *Dictionary of American Biography.* New York: Scribners, 1958, suppl. 2, pp. 556–667.

Ives, Herbert E. "Floyd Karker Richtmyer." *Biographical Memoirs of the National Academy of Sciences* 22 (1941): 71–81.

Lindsay, R.B. "Richtmyer, Floyd Karker." *Dictionary of Scientific Biography.* Edited by Charles C. Gillispie. New York: Scribners, 1975, 11:441–442.

Richtmyer, Floyd. *Introduction to Modern Physics.* New York, 1928.

Bruce V. Lewenstein

Riley, Charles Valentine (1843–1895)

A central personality in the development of the science and technology of entomology. Riley was born in London to estranged middle-class parents. He grew up at Walton-on-Thames and attended schools in England, France, and Germany. His mastery of two foreign cultures and languages had enduring influence on his outlook. In 1860, Riley joined family acquaintances on their livestock farm at Kankakee County, Illinois. Here, he became acquainted with the rigors of frontier life and acquired a spirit of advocacy for farm people. The vicissitudes of farm life and ill health drove Riley to Chicago in January 1863. By pluck and talent, he soon became enmeshed with *The Prairie Farmer,* the leading agricultural journal of the region; the Chicago

Academy of Sciences, the organizational cradle of the city's scientific elite; and the Masonic Order, which provided social and leadership opportunities. There was a brief interlude of military duty in 1864 with the 134th Illinois Volunteer Regiment. In the Chicago setting, Riley became involved in the issues of agriculture, science, and social controversy (slavery).

Riley's success as artist, editor, and entomological advocate with *The Prairie Farmer* won him appointment as the first Missouri State Entomologist. In the period 1868–1876, Riley published the results of his original research on the insects of Missouri in nine reports. These established new standards for artistic quality, comprehensiveness of life histories, and fundamentals of insect control. Using the reports as a vehicle, Riley established a wide collegial network at home and abroad.

In 1877, Riley was appointed chief, United States Entomological Commission, Department of Interior. The following year he became head, Division of Entomology, United States Department of Agriculture, and in 1885, honorary curator, United States National Museum, Smithsonian Institution. In addition to his official duties in these three government agencies, he was active in the informal Washington scientific network represented by the Philosophical Society, Biological Club, Cosmos Club, and Entomological Society.

As an administrative leader, he was a vigorous advocate for federal funding in support of agriculture, hiring of able personnel, flexibility of both funds and personnel for redeployment as needs changed, and public education regarding entomological matters.

Riley's career paralleled a remarkable period of development in science and technology. He personally contributed to the major entomological issues of his time: evolution, the balance of nature, social insects, and control by biological, cultural, and chemical means. The roots of the present controversy surrounding insecticide use and biodiversity can be traced to Riley's work.

Riley's career is clouded by mystique arising from his competitive nature, opposing scientific views, scant attention given the field by historians, and death at an early age which robbed him of time to write his memoirs and to acquire the mellowness which becomes an elder statesman.

BIBLIOGRAPHY

Goode, George B. "A Memorial Appreciation of Charles Valentine Riley." *Science* 3 (1896): 217–225.

R

Henshaw, Samuel, and Nathan Banks. *Bibliography of the More Important Contributions to American Economic Entomology.* Pts 1–6. Washington, DC: Government Printing Office, 1889–1898.

Howard, L.O. *A History of Applied Entomology.* Smithsonian Miscellaneous Collection, Vol. 84. Washington, DC: 1930.

Mallis, Arnold. *American Entomologists.* New Brunswick: Rutgers University Press, 1971, pp. 69–79.

Riley, Charles V. *Annual Reports On the Noxious and Beneficial and Other Insects of the State of Missouri.* (Reports 1–9). Jefferson City, Missouri, 1868–1876.

Edward H. Smith

Rittenhouse, David (1732–1796)

Astronomer, horologist, and patriot. Born in a house which still stands in what is now part of Philadelphia, Rittenhouse spent the first half his life in Norriton township, and the other half in Philadelphia. His early education is obscure. At some point he mastered the new physics and became a disciple of Isaac Newton. He learned clockmaking, crafting some of the finest clocks of his day, and made scientific instruments as well. Rittenhouse earned his living at these trades until 1777, when he became treasurer of Pennsylvania. Rittenhouse played a substantial role as a politician-patriot in the American Revolution, serving on many committees devoted to the cause. Afterward, in 1792 he became, in a curious parallel to Newton, the first director of the United States Mint. He surveyed several state boundaries and was active in the American Philosophical Society, becoming its president in 1791 after the death of Benjamin Franklin. He became a foreign member of the Royal Society in 1795.

In physical appearance, he was tall and slender, with plain features. He suffered from ill-health most of his life—perhaps from ulcers brought on by his painstaking personality. Despite his outward reserve and modesty, those who met him came away deeply impressed; Thomas Jefferson was one of his most ardent admirers. Rittenhouse also had great integrity.

In his day, Rittenhouse was America's second man of science; Franklin, with his momentous discoveries in electricity, ranked first. Rittenhouse is chiefly remembered as an astronomer, particularly for his observations of the transit of Venus in 1769. Transits were important in determining the solar parallax. He built an observatory at Norriton, constructed most of the instruments used in the observations, made many of the calculations, and published his findings in the *Transactions* of the American Philosophical Society. During his career, he also observed comets, meteors, transits of Mercury, and the newly discovered Uranus, as well as making calculations for almanacs and writing some mathematical papers.

Drawing on his clockmaking talent, Rittenhouse crafted two magnificent orreries, or mechanical solar systems. These had vertical faces, like a clock, rather than the usual horizontal arrangement. His orreries are masterpieces of precision.

After the Revolution, Francis Hopkinson looked at a street lamp through his silk handkerchief and saw a diffraction pattern; he asked his friend Rittenhouse for an explanation. In response, Rittenhouse constructed in 1786 a diffraction grating made of parallel hairs set between two brass wires cut with a very fine screw thread. He observed six orders of spectra and correctly ascribed them as being due to diffraction, although Rittenhouse followed Newton's corpuscular theory of light in explaining the phenomenon, rather than Huygens's wave theory.

From other experiments he shrewdly conjectured that iron consisted of many small magnets, which became aligned when magnetized. He rightly explained the cameo-intaglio illusion, in which depressions can appear as mounds and vice versa, as being a psychological effect.

Rittenhouse's output was not prodigious. His important papers in astronomy and physics were published in the *Transactions*. Miscellaneous experiments and observations appeared elsewhere. His experiments with an electric eel, for example, appeared in the *Medical and Physical Journal,* while his speculations on the generation of clouds appeared in the *Columbian Magazine.*

David Rittenhouse's reputation, which had soared during his lifetime, faded in the nineteenth and early twentieth centuries. Despite Henry Cavendish's repetition of his experiment, Rittenhouse's diffraction grating made little impression on European science. Joseph Fraunhofer, who independently rediscovered the diffraction grating years later, is still often credited with its invention. Further, Simon Newcomb, in reexamining the transit of Venus observations from around the world, dismissed Rittenhouse's observations as being too deviant to be useful.

Rittenhouse's reputation started making a slow comeback in 1932 when Thomas D. Cope pointed out that the Pennsylvanian scientist made the first known diffraction grating. Today, some of the newer textbooks in optics give Rittenhouse priority over Fraunhofer. Astronomers now have a better understanding of the uncertainties in timing the contacts during transits, particularly the notorious "black drop" phenomenon caused by irradiance within the telescope. Rittenhouse's explanation of magnetism is still mostly unappreciated. The biographies by Edward Ford and Brooke Hindle have brought considerable attention to Rittenhouse, but his name is still largely unknown to the scientific community and to the general public.

Much of Rittenhouse's handiwork still survives, including many of his clocks, such as the one at Drexel University, and his two orreries, one at the University of Pennsylvania and the other at Princeton University. There are also portraits and a bust of Rittenhouse.

Intriguing questions about Rittenhouse, which may be unanswerable at this remove in time, are Where did he get his education? From whom did he learn clockmaking?

BIBLIOGRAPHY

Barton, William. *Memoirs of the Life of David Rittenhouse.* Philadelphia, 1813.

Bedini, Silvio. *Thinkers and Tinkers.* New York: Scribner's, 1975.

Cope, Thomas D. "The Rittenhouse Diffraction Grating." *Journal of the Franklin Institute* 214 (1932): 99–104.

Ford, Edward. *David Rittenhouse.* Philadelphia: University of Pennsylvania Press, 1946.

Hindle, Brooke. *The Pursuit of Science in Revolutionary America.* Chapel Hill: University of North Carolina Press, 1956.

———. *David Rittenhouse.* Princeton: Princeton University Press, 1964.

———. *The Scientific Writings of David Rittenhouse.* New York: Arno Press, 1980.

———. "Rittenhouse, David." *Dictionary of Scientific Biography.* Edited by Charles C. Gillispie. New York: Scribner, 1981, 9:471–473.

Rice, Howard C., Jr. *The Rittenhouse Orrery.* Princeton: Princeton University Press, 1954.

Rubincam, David, and Milton Rubincam II. "America's Foremost Early Astronomer." *Sky & Telescope* 89, no. 5 (May 1995): 38–41.

David Parry Rubincam

Rockefeller University

Research institute and university. The Rockefeller University was founded in New York City in 1901 as The Rockefeller Institute for Medical Research (RIMR).

Established by John D. Rockefeller Sr. with an initial pledge of $20,000 per annum over ten years, Rockefeller's confidence in this promising institution soon translated into additional gifts of $2.6 million in 1907 and $3.8 million in 1910. With the encouragement of Rockefeller's two chief philanthropic advisors, his son, John D. Rockefeller Jr. and Frederick T. Gates, Rockefeller believed that his philanthropy could create a research institution of international caliber on American soil.

At its inception, the RIMR functioned as a grant-giving body which provided support to investigators at other institutions. Much of the early focus of the RIMR centered on research on the eradication of infectious diseases. The RIMR opened the first laboratory on its present site between York Avenue and the East River in 1906 on land purchased by the Rockefeller family. Committed to developing a full program of biomedical research, the institute defined its mission broadly; from its earliest period, its members represented a wide array of physicians, biologists, and chemists. Established on the model of the major research institutes of Europe, the RIMR was institutionally structured with laboratories as its core. Each laboratory was headed by a chief investigator who set the research agenda for its researchers. The independence of action engendered by this system, enabled investigators to pursue freely avenues of interest without being encumbered by rigid institutional constructs. Thus, as America's first private scientific research institute, the RIMR was considered a paradigm for the pure pursuit of science. It also infused American culture; the RIMR served as a model for scientific institutions in such American literary works as Sinclair Lewis's *Arrowsmith* and the writings of Paul de Kruif. In many ways, the RIMR took a different path than many other scientific institutions in America. Historians of science have noted that, in the twentieth century, scientific research became increasingly bound to the growth of universities. At the institute, the process was somewhat reversed; only in its sixth decade did the institute graft higher educational goals to its research program.

The laboratories of the Rockefeller University were complemented by a clinical research hospital. Dedicated on 17 October 1910, this thirty-bed hospital realized the marriage of clinical research with clinical care. Simon Flexner, the institute's first director (1901–1935), initiated the idea of such a medical laboratory in order simultaneously to treat and study human disease. Physicians, termed "physician-investigators" or "clinical scientists,"

R

have bridged between the laboratory and practical application of treatment. Tuberculosis, poliomyelitis, and yellow fever are a few of the diseases studied in the past. Heart disease, diabetes, leukemia, arthritis, AIDS, alcoholism, parasitic diseases, and growth and genetic disorders are presently being investigated by the Rockefeller University Hospital researchers.

By the 1950s, the RIMR scientists had established the institution as one of the foremost research facilities in the nation. It also maintained some of America's most significant biomedical research journals, such as *The Journal of Experimental Medicine* and *The Journal of General Physiology*. Pioneering research by the scientists of the institute/university included the identification of human blood groups, production of antibiotics, discovery of viral cancers, research on vision, taste, and smell, methadone-based drug rehabilitation, and the discovery of the first effective treatment for African sleeping sickness. With twenty Nobel laureates associated with this institution, The Rockefeller University has secured a prominent role in the history of medicine and science and has attracted notable men and women of science to its campus. Members or associates of the RIMR/university research community have included: Alexis Carrel, Karl Landsteiner, Jacques Loeb, Peyton Rous, Rebecca Lancefield, Hideyo Noguchi, Fritz Lipmann, Louise Pearce, Oswald Avery, Rene Dubos, Joshua Lederberg, and Thorsten Wiesel.

The RIMR became a degree-granting institution on 19 November 1954, graduating its first class of Ph.D.'s in 1959. In 1965, the institute's name was changed to The Rockefeller University, reflecting its new commitment to the academic exploration of science. Unlike the typical university, Rockefeller is dedicated to graduate study conferring only the Ph.D. degree, degrees in the medical sciences, and honorary degrees. Students pay no tuition and receive a yearly stipend. Relying on its traditional configuration, the components of graduate work—courses, discussion groups, tutorials, and research apprenticeships—all revolve around the laboratory headed by a senior professor; there are no academic departments. Striving to fulfill its motto, *pro bono humani generis,* "for the betterment of humanity," university research today encompasses such diverse fields as cell and molecular biology, genetics, biochemistry, neurobiology, immunology, mathematics, physics, chemistry, ecology, and the behaviorial sciences.

As historians explore the development of scientific institutions in American and the role of philanthropy in the growth of research, they will continue to make use of the records of the Rockefeller University. The archives of the Rockefeller University are part of the Rockefeller Archive Center in Sleepy Hollow, New York. Also, the papers of some of the early members of the RIMR are housed at other repositories, especially the American Philosophical Society in Philadelphia.

BIBLIOGRAPHY

Corner, George W. *A History of the Rockefeller Institute, 1901–1953: Origins and Growth.* New York: Rockefeller Institute Press, 1964.

Harr, John Ensor, and Peter J. Johnson. *The Rockefeller Century: Three Generations of America's Greatest Family.* New York: Scribners, 1988.

Jonas, Gerald. *The Circuit Riders: Rockefeller Money and the Rise of Modern Science.* New York: W.W. Norton, 1989.

Kevles, Daniel J. "Foundations, Universities and Trends in Support of the Physical and Biological Sciences, 1900–1992." *Daedalus* 121:4 (Fall 1992): 195–235.

Lee R. Hiltzik

Rogers, Henry Darwin (1808–1866)

Geologist and director of the first state geological surveys of Pennsylvania and New Jersey. He had three brothers: William Barton, James Blythe, and Robert Empie, all distinguished in science. Born in Philadelphia, Henry Rogers was educated in mathematics and chemistry, principally by his father. From 1829 until 1831, he taught these subjects at Dickinson College. In 1832, he went to England to further his studies of science, and while there, his attention was turned to geology. He returned to the United States in 1833 and began to study the geology of the United States, particularly the Appalachian Mountains. He was appointed director of the New Jersey survey in 1835 and the Pennsylvania survey in 1836. Rogers completed a report on the New Jersey survey in 1840, but the Pennsylvania report was not completed until 1858; thus it occupied much of his life. Rogers was instrumental in the founding of the Association of American Geologists in 1840 and active in its transition to the American Association for the Advancement of Science in 1848. He was widely recognized as a lecturer and sought after as a geological consultant in the anthracite coal fields of Pennsylvania. In 1857, he was appointed Regius Professor of Natural History at the University of Glasgow in Scotland where he taught until his death.

R

Rogers's work on the Appalachians resulted in the first theory of mountain elevation by an American. His theory suggested that mountains were formed when the earth's molten interior was set into a wavelike motion, folding and lifting the overlying strata. Most of his work was focused on Paleozoic rocks, the predominant rocks of the Appalachian Mountains. Working with his brother William Barton, who was simultaneously the director of the state geological survey of Virginia, he distinguished and ordered several Paleozoic formations on the basis of their mineral content. He was one of the first persons in the United States to attempt this. Again working with his brother, he also devised a nomenclature for these formations that indicated both their chronological position and mineral content.

Rogers's work met with a mixed reception. His final report on Pennsylvania's geology was praised as a monument to patient observation and detailed study. His theory of elevation was dismissed as insupportable, and his classification was suspect because it was based on mineral characters rather than fossils, which were preferred by his peers. His nomenclature did not gain a significant hearing.

The primary sources of information on Rogers are a collection of family letters at the Massachusetts Institute of Technology, *The Life and Letters of William Barton Rogers* edited by Emma Rogers, and the recent biography by Patsy Gerstner. A 1916 biography by J.W. Gregory provides some personal recollections of Rogers and an overview of his work.

BIBLIOGRAPHY

Gerstner, Patsy A. "A Dynamic Theory of Mountain Building: Henry Darwin Rogers, 1842." *Isis* 66 (1975): 26–37.

———. "Henry Darwin Rogers and William Barton Rogers on the Nomenclature of the American Paleozoic Rocks." In *Two Hundred Years of Geology in America. Proceedings of the New Hampshire Bicentennial Conference on the History of Geology.* Hanover: For the University of New Hampshire by the University Press of New England, 1979, pp. 175–186.

———. *Henry Darwin Rogers (1808–1866): An American Geologist.* Tuscaloosa: University of Alabama Press, 1994.

Gregory, J.W. *Henry Darwin Rogers, An Address to the Glasgow University Geological Society, 20th January, 1916.* Glasgow: James MacLehose and Son, 1916.

Rogers, Emma, ed. *Life and Letters of William Barton Rogers.* 2 vols. Boston and New York: Houghton, Mifflin, 1896.

Patsy Gerstner

Rogers, William Barton (1804–1882)

Geologist, natural philosopher, and educator; founder of the Massachusetts Institute of Technology (MIT). Rogers was born in Philadelphia, the second of four brothers, all of whom distinguished themselves in science. He studied with his father, at private schools, and finally at the College of William and Mary, where his father taught and from which he graduated in 1821. In 1827, he and his brother Henry Darwin Rogers went to Windsor, Maryland, where they opened a private school. The next year, William organized a high school at the Maryland Institute in Baltimore. In both cases, he was interested in providing a practical education for young men that would equip them to find jobs. After his father's sudden death in 1828, Rogers replaced him as professor of natural philosophy and mathematics at William and Mary. In 1835, he accepted a position as professor of natural philosophy and geology at the University of Virginia. He married Emma Savage in 1849. In 1853, he moved to Boston, where efforts that led to the founding of MIT began in 1859.

William and Henry Rogers studied the geology of Virginia together in 1834, concentrating on the Tertiary formations of the state. William became especially interested in the analysis of the Virginia marls which were just then being recognized as important natural fertilizers. He became well known in the state because of these studies, and succeeded in convincing the state to consider a geological survey of the entire state. He was appointed to a committee to study the feasibility of such a survey, and when it was approved in 1835, he was appointed to head it. At the same time, his brother Henry was the director of the state survey of New Jersey and, beginning in 1836, of Pennsylvania. They worked together on the older, or Paleozoic, formations of the Appalachian area. This resulted in a paper in 1842 that elaborated on an earlier theory proposed by Henry Rogers to explain the elevation of mountains. Their work also resulted in a numerical system of numbering the geological formations and eventually in a nomenclature for Paleozoic formations. Neither the theory of elevation nor the classification system met with much success. The Virginia survey ended in 1842, but money was not made available to publish a comprehensive final report. However, in 1884, Rogers's widow arranged for a reprint of his annual reports and other papers on the geology of the state which served in lieu of a final report.

William enjoyed an illustrious career at the University of Virginia, establishing himself as a distinguished

R

and popular educator and scientist. However, when Henry Rogers took up residence in Boston in 1845, William entertained the idea of joining him. Since their early involvement with schools in Maryland, the two brothers had dreamed of opening a polytechnic school emphasizing practical subjects that would give young men an alternative to traditional college education. Boston seemed to them a good place for such a school. However, pleas from administration and students kept William in Virginia until 1853 when he finally moved to Boston. Henry Rogers left Boston for permanent residence in Scotland in 1856, but William continued to pursue the idea of a school. In 1859, a movement was begun in Boston to acquire land in the newly developed Back Bay area for such a school along with other institutions. Rogers was a leader in this move, and in 1861, his dream was finally fulfilled by the establishment of MIT. He served as its first president from 1862 until 1870 and as professor of physics and geology from 1865 until 1870. Although in poor health, he served again as president from 1878 until 1881. He died suddenly as he began his traditional commencement address the following year.

In 1861, he was appointed inspector of gas meters and illuminating gas for the state of Massachusetts. This was a new position created to oversee and to regulate gas meters in the state and to generally improve the standards of measuring gas.

Rogers maintained an active interest in all the sciences, especially geology, throughout his life. He was an early member of the Association of American Geologists, a forerunner of the American Association for the Advancement of Science, and played a critical role in efforts to maintain a broad base of leadership in the organization. Rogers participated in many scientific organizations during his life, and was elected president of the National Academy of Sciences in 1879. One of his favorite organizations was the Boston Society of Natural History, where he engaged in a historically interesting debate on organic evolution in 1860. He took a strong stand in favor of the theory against one of its most vehement opponents in America, Louis Agassiz.

His widow, Emma Savage Rogers, prepared an invaluable two-volume edition of Rogers's letters. These volumes and the collection of Rogers letters in the archives of MIT are the principal sources of information on William Rogers and his brothers.

BIBLIOGRAPHY

Gerstner, Patsy A. "Henry Darwin Rogers and William Barton Rogers on the Nomenclature of the American Paleozoic Rocks." In *Two Hundred Years of Geology in America. Proceedings of the New Hampshire Bicentennial Conference on the History of Geology.* Hanover: For the University of New Hampshire by the University Press of New England, 1979, pp. 175–186.

Kohlstedt, Sally Gregory. *The Formation of the American Scientific Community: The American Association for the Advancement of Science 1848–1860.* Urbana: University of Illinois Press, 1976.

Milici, Robert C., and C.R. Bruce Hobbs Jr. "William Barton Rogers and the First Geological Survey of Virginia 1835–1841." *Earth Sciences History* 6 (1987): 3–13.

[Rogers, Emma]. *A Reprint of Annual Reports and Other Papers on the Geology of the Virginias by the Late William Barton Rogers.* New York: D. Appleton, 1884.

Rogers, Emma. *Life and Letters of William Barton Rogers.* 2 vols. Boston and New York: Houghton, Mifflin, 1896.

Ruffner, W.H. "The Brothers Rogers." In *The Scotch-Irish in America. Proceedings and Addresses of the Seventh Congress at Lexington, Va. June 20–23, 1895.* Nashville, 1895, pp. 123–139. Also published in *The Alumni Bulletin* [University of Virignia], 1898, pp. 1–13.

Ruschenberger, W.S.W. "A Sketch of the Life of Robert E. Rogers, M. D., LL.D., with Biographical Notices of his Father and Brothers." *Proceedings of the American Philosophical Society* 23 (1885): 104–146.

Smallwood, W.M. "The Agassiz-Rogers Debate on Evolution." *Quarterly Review of Biology* 16 (1941): 1–12.

Patsy Gerstner

Rowland, Henry (1848–1901)

Physicist and educator. Rowland was born in Pennsylvania and raised there and in New Jersey. Expected to become a clergyman like three generations of male Rowlands before him, he attended Phillips Academy at Andover, Massachusetts, for one year, but displayed such an aversion to Latin that he was allowed to switch to Rensselaer Polytechnic Institute in Troy, New York. There, his interest in devices and in physics found a more receptive environment. Although Rowland briefly studied at the Sheffield Scientific School at Yale, he graduated from Rensselaer in 1870 as a civil engineer.

After working briefly as a surveyor, and then a science teacher in Ohio, Rowland returned to Rensselaer in 1872 as an instructor in physics. In 1875, Daniel Coit Gilman in Baltimore began organizing the Johns Hopkins University, the first vigorous American research university, based on the German model. President Gilman hired Rowland as the first professor of physics, and enabled him to tour physics laboratories in Europe, and acquire physical apparatus there, before Johns Hopkins opened in 1876.

As well as professor, Rowland became director of the physical laboratory at Johns Hopkins, and late in his career served as the first president of the American Physical Society. He held memberships in many European scientific societies, and participated in international conferences for the establishment of electrical standards, needed by the rapidly growing electrical industry. During Rowland's twenty-five years at Johns Hopkins, his department trained forty-five Ph.D.'s in physics, many of whom became leaders in the new American physics profession. Previously, advanced training was only available in Europe, or more specifically, Germany.

Rowland's own research principally concerned three areas of physics: electricity and magnetism, heat, and light. In each case, he made his mark by devising apparatus that would make new or more accurate measurements possible. His most famous single experiment, conducted in the Berlin laboratory of Hermann von Helmholtz in 1876, measured the magnetic effects of a rotating, electrified disk. It tended to support James Clerk Maxwell's idea that an electric charge in motion produces a magnetic field.

At Johns Hopkins, Rowland directed a series of experiments by Edwin Hall, one of his first graduate students, on the effects of a transverse magnetic field on an electric current. These led to the discovery of the eponymous "Hall effect." With money specially appropriated by the United States Congress, Rowland contributed to the establishment of a definitive, international value of the ohm, the unit of electric resistance. His published works also described a variety of ways of measuring different electrical and magnetic quantities.

His publications on heat were few in number, but included his most lengthy report, on a redetermination of the mechanical equivalent of heat, improving on and extending the work of English brewer James Joule, thirty years earlier. In the process, he cultivated more accurate thermometry and evaluated variations in the specific heat of water with varying temperature.

Rowland entered his third principal area of interest by inventing a new instrument for spreading light out into a spectrum. His concave diffraction gratings made possible bigger, brighter spectra that could be measured with great precision. Specially built engines at Rowland's department took up to five continuous days and nights to produce one grating, but the results were released at cost for many laboratories in Europe, America, and other parts of the world, and they remained unrivaled in quality for decades. They greatly advanced the discipline of spectroscopy, which was then a major branch of physics. Rowland used the instrument himself to measure the wavelengths of 20,000 absorption lines in the solar spectrum, and he and his students used it in many laboratory studies of light from the chemical elements. In Europe, some wavelengths that were measured with the aid of Rowland gratings became important explananda for quantum theories of the atom.

Rowland is most often described in historical accounts as an exponent of "pure science," untainted by commercial interests. However, he also received income from commercial ventures. A past historiographic emphasis on theory may explain Rowland's relative historical obscurity until recent years. Indeed, he corresponded quite closely to the nineteenth-century characterization of American scientists as interested primarily in experiment and measurement, not theory. (For example, he believed that physicists knew almost nothing about the nature of atoms.) Recent accounts explore the ways in which Rowland, as an educator, saw experiment in the physical laboratory as a means to instill personal discipline and clarity of thought in students. In addition, it is becoming clear that, while Rowland saw himself only as a physicist, his laboratory and his instruments produced many results significant to astronomy, especially to the new science of astrophysics, which then relied heavily on spectroscopy.

Only one book-length study of Rowland exists (Miller). The Rowland Papers at Johns Hopkins University include fifty document boxes.

BIBLIOGRAPHY

Beer, Peter, and Richard C. Henry, eds. "Henry Rowland and Astronomical Spectroscopy." *Vistas in Astronomy* 29 (1986): 119–236.

Hentschel, Klaus. "The Discovery of the Redshift of Solar Fraunhofer Lines by Rowland and Jewell in Baltimore around 1890." *Historical Studies in the Physical and Biological Sciences* 23, pt. 2 (1993): 219–277.

Kevles, Daniel. "Rowland, Henry Augustus." *Dictionary of Scientific Biography.* Edited by Charles C. Gillispie. New York: Scribner, 1975, 11:577–579.

Miller, John David. "Henry Augustus Rowland and His Electromagnetic Researches." Ph.D. diss., Oregon State University, 1970.

R

Rowland, Henry A. *The Physical Papers of Henry Augustus Rowland.* Baltimore: Johns Hopkins University Press, 1902.

Sweetnam, George. "Precision Implemented: Henry Rowland, the Concave Diffraction Grating, and the Analysis of Light." In *The Values of Precision,* edited by M. Norton Wise. Princeton: Princeton University Press, 1995, pp. 283–310.

———. "The Command of Light: Rowland's School of Physics and the Spectrum." Ph.D. diss., Princeton University, 1996.

George Sweetnam

Rubber, Synthetic

The synthetic rubber which became the basis of the GR-S (Government Rubber-Styrene) used by the United States during World War II was patented by the German chemical combine IG Farben in July 1929. In June 1940, fears grew about the safety of America's rubber supplies from German U-boat attack and the Japanese threat to the rubber-producing areas of east Asia. The Advisory Committee of the Council for National Defense set up a committee headed by Clarence Francis to establish a synthetic rubber industry. President Roosevelt had created the Rubber Reserve Company (RRC) to stockpile natural rubber, and the RRC took over the functions of the Francis Committee in October 1940.

The RRC was dominated by its chairman, Secretary of Commerce Jesse Jones. Jones was relatively successful stockpiling natural rubber. However, there was considerable dissatisfaction with the progress of the synthetic rubber program. In the summer of 1942, Roosevelt appointed a committee headed by Bernard Baruch to look into the synthetic rubber issue, which recommended an increase in the amount of synthetic rubber to be made from grain alcohol instead of petroleum, and the appointment of a rubber director to oversee the program.

The first rubber director was William Jeffers, president of the Union Pacific Railroad. He was replaced in September 1943 by Colonel Bradley Dewey, the deputy rubber director and a chemical engineer, who resigned the following year, and the position of rubber director was abolished. Most of its functions were taken over by the RRC, which had continued to administer routine production matters. The RRC was replaced in June 1945 by the Office of Rubber Reserve, later the Office of Synthetic Rubber, within the Reconstruction Finance Corporation (RFC).

The synthetic rubber plants came into production with comparative ease and, with one exception, reached or exceeded their planned capacity. The four plants in the original program started up during 1942, and all fifteen plants were in operation by the end of November 1943. Butadiene-from-alcohol plants first came on stream in January 1943. They were soon operating at up to twice their rated capacity. By contrast, the butadiene-from-petroleum plants labored under a shortage of crucial materials needed to construct the plant, competition from the aviation fuel program, and several technical problems. While the alcohol plants also fell short of their 1943 target, they continued to carry the burden during 1944. While this butadiene shortage led to a shortfall of synthetic rubber in 1943 and early 1944, it is uncertain that the rubber processing plants could have easily handled the planned totals. Fortunately for the rubber program, and Allied war effort, the peak military demand for rubber did not occur until the summer of 1944. GR-S production rose from a minuscule 3,721 long tons in 1942 to 182,259 long tons in 1943, and then soared to 670,268 long tons in 1944. GR-S production was running ahead of demand by early 1945, when the problems at the petroleum-based plants had been solved, and production at the more expensive alcohol-based plants was cut back. Total GR-S production in 1945 was 719,404 long tons.

The wartime research, especially within the rubber industry, was concerned with the improvement of the existing processes. While no radical changes took place, this research greatly improved the production and quality of GR-S by the end of the war.

After the war, synthetic rubber production was maintained at 300,000 to 400,000 long tons a year, because of the threat posed by the Soviet Union. Plants were mothballed, rather than scrapped, or sold on condition that they could be reactivated for synthetic rubber production at short notice. Government control of plants and rubber inventories was retained, but the Rubber Act of 1948 called for the disposal of the plants by 1950. Research funds continued to flow at a rate of $3.5 million a year, despite the drop in production, and research groups were now free to pursue long-term goals. The immediate aim was the development of a synthetic rubber that could compete with natural rubber in both quality and price. In October 1948, the RFC announced the introduction of a superior form of GR-S, called "cold" rubber. The original idea had been taken from the German firm IG Farben at the end of the war, but the process adopted by the RFC in 1948 for the standard production of cold rubber was based largely on research by Izaak (Piet) Kolthoff at the University of Minnesota, and by William B. Reynolds and Charles Fryling at Phillips Petroleum. Cold rubber already accounted for 38 percent of all GR-S production by 1950. It was the equal of natural rubber for automobile tires, but it was difficult to process and no cheaper than standard GR-S.

Even before North Korea invaded South Korea in June 1950, initiating the Korean War, the price of natural rubber had been rising sharply because of heavy buying by the Soviet Union. It reached a peak of 73 cents/lb compared with a fixed price of 18.5 cents/lb for GR-S. By September, the synthetic rubber industry had been completely reactivated. GR-S production in 1951 was 697,000 long tons, almost double the previous year's figure. To cover the additional cost of the alcohol-based butadiene from the standby plants, the government raised the price of GR-S to 24.5 cents/lb. In 1952 and 1953, GR-S production remained high. Oil-extended rubber (a 4:1 mixture of cold rubber and selected mineral oils) was introduced independently by General Tire and Goodyear as a way of increasing the volume of synthetic rubber production. The addition of mineral oils also made cold rubber both easier to process and cheaper.

The superior properties of cold rubber and the cheapness of oil-extended rubber made synthetic rubber more competitive with natural rubber. This increased the pressure to privatize the synthetic rubber industry; the 1950 deadline in the Rubber Act of 1948 had been extended to 1954 because of the Korean War. The 1953 Rubber Producing Facilities Disposal Act created an independent commission to take charge of the disposal process. On 15 July 1955, the United States government was out of the synthetic rubber business. The 1953 Disposal Act made provision for the continuation of the research program for a year after the sale of the production facilities, at which point a final decision would be made. After a year's supervision by the National Science Foundation, the research program was allowed to lapse at the end of 1956, and the Government Laboratories in Akron were sold to Firestone.

BIBLIOGRAPHY

Herbert, Vernon, and Attilio Bisio. *Synthetic Rubber: A Project That Had to Succeed.* Westport, CT: Greenwood Press, 1985.

Morris, Peter J.T. *The American Synthetic Rubber Research Program.* Philadelphia: University of Pennsylvania Press, 1989.

———. "Transatlantic Transfer of Buna S Synthetic Rubber Technology, 1932–45." In *The Transfer of International Technology. Europe, Japan and the USA in the Twentieth Century,* edited by David J. Jeremy. Aldershot, U.K.: Edward Elgar, 1992.

Ross, Davies R.B. "Patents and Bureaucrats: US Synthetic Rubber Developments before Pearl Harbor." In *Business and Government,* edited by Joseph R. Frese, S.J., and Jacob Judd. Tarrytown, NY: Sleepy Hollow Press, 1985, pp. 119–155.

Tuttle, William M., Jr. "The Birth of an Industry: The Synthetic Rubber 'Mess' in World War II." *Technology and Culture* 22 (1981): 35–67.

Peter J. T. Morris

Rumford, Benjamin Thompson, Count (1753–1814)

Benjamin Thompson defies twentieth-century political and scientific categories. Born in America, he spent much of his life in Europe, where he gained a reputation as an experimentalist, inventor, and social reformer. He was a mercenary by profession, traveled constantly, and promoted himself and his myriad investigations into heat, light, and the elimination of poverty. Rumford's education was largely informal, although he attended Harvard. He became a schoolteacher before having to flee America when Boston fell. After serving in the Colonial Office he joined the British Army, eventually serving in America (1781–1783) during the Revolutionary War. He then (1784) entered the service of the elector of Bavaria, experimented on gunpowder, the nature of heat, heating and lighting systems, the housing and employment of the poor of Munich, and the clothing of the Bavarian Army. Already knighted by the British (1784), he became a count of the Holy Roman Empire (1791), just at it was officially disappearing. He was elected fellow of the Royal Society of London (1795), followed by the American Academy of Arts and Sciences. At both of these institutions, he established prizes for investigations into the nature of heat. He left the residue of his estate to Harvard for a chair in the applications of science to the useful arts.

The latter indicates Rumford's real interests, the useful ends of science and exemplifies eighteenth-century hopes for the sciences. His earliest work, on gunpowder, was to change the mix of ingredients in the powder

R

and structural elements in the cannon to improve the whole system. Rumford developed tests for the goodness of powder that became standard. Through experiments on boring out and firing empty cannons, he questioned the caloric theories of heat. He became convinced that heat was a vibratory motion of the particles of bodies but was unsuccessful in convincing many of his contemporaries of this. Rumford's experiments challenging caloric theory were ingenious, but his own theory was vague and could not cover the explanatory ground of its rivals.

Rumford then moved into more utilitarian areas, including the loss of heat through various types of cloth and its absorption by different surfaces and colors. He turned his attention to fireplaces, which were smoky and inefficient. Rumford redesigned them, introducing the smoke shelf and damper, and investigated the relationship between the size of the fireplace opening and its throat. He claimed to have invented and installed steam heating systems at the Royal Institution, the Institut de France, private homes, and manufacturing plants for soaps and dyes. Increasing the efficiency of cooking devices led him to put the fire into an insulated box, the beginnings of the modern cooking range.

Efficiency was a key to much of his work, especially in nutrition and illumination. While ridding Munich of its poor by rounding them up and putting them to work in Bavaria's military workshops, Rumford was faced with feeding and housing them without increasing the state's budget. He developed a theory of the nutritional value of water and of soup as a stable diet. He continued experimenting on cheap, mass feeding for the poor and later claimed to have introduced the potato into central Europe. Faced with lighting his military workhouses for the poor, he improved the efficiency of lighting systems and developed instruments to measure illuminations, the shadow photometer and the standard candle.

Rumford's interests coincided with those of a group of landowners in Britain interested in eliminating poverty without increasing costs to local rate payers. The establishment of an institution in London to promote useful knowledge, especially of improved agriculture for the poor, persuaded Rumford to delay his return to America. Despite his own accounts, the Royal Institution was not his idea nor did he really control it. Within months, he was a figurehead, although he was its director from 1799 to 1802. After he left, accusations of embezzlement were again heard—he was previously accused when he served as an officer in the British Army. Critics even questioned his scientific work (Berman).

As a native son, Rumford's place in American science was assured as long as the history of physics was written from the twentieth century backward. Rumford was seen, helped by believing his own pronouncements, as a pioneer in the development of the mechanical theory of heat. He established this theory experimentally which it took others some forty to fifty years to accept. Recent work disputes much of Rumford's narrative, arguing the superiority of caloric theories of the time and the undeveloped state of Rumford's ideas (Brush, Goldfarb). Recently, historians have considered Rumford's place in late-eighteenth-century social-reform movements. These movements were driven by the determination of some members of the elite to preserve social peace and the political status quo.

BIBLIOGRAPHY

Berman, Morris. *Social Change and Scientific Organization: The Royal Institution, 1799–1844.* London: Heinemann, 1978.

Brown, Sanborn C. *Rumford on the Nature of Heat.* New York: Pergamon, 1967.

———. "Benjamin Thompson, Count Rumford." *Dictionary of Scientific Biography.* Edited by Charles C. Gillispie. New York: Scribner, 1971, 13:350–352.

———. *Benjamin Thompson, Count Rumford.* Cambridge, MA: MIT Press, 1979.

———. ed. *The Collected Works of Benjamin Thompson, Count Rumford.* 5 vols. Cambridge, MA: Harvard University Press, 1968–70.

Brush, Stephen G. *The Kind of Motion We Call Heat.* Bk. 1. New York: North Holland, 1976.

Carae, Gwen. *The Royal Institution: An Informal History.* London: John Murray, 1985.

Ellis, George E. *Memoir of Sir Benjamin Thompson, Count Rumford.* Boston, 1871.

Goldfarb, Stephen J. "Rumford's Thought: A Reassessment." *British Journal of the History of Science* 10 (1977): 25–36.

Heller, R.A. "Let Them Eat Soup: Count Rumford and Napoleon Bonaparte." *Journal of Chemical Education* 53 (1976): 499–500.

Martin, John Stephen. "Count Rumford's Munich Workhouse." *Studies on Voltaire and the Eighteenth Century* 263 (1989): 206–208.

Sokolow, Jayne. "Count Rumford and Late Eighteenth-Century Science, Technology and Reform." *Eighteenth Century Studies* 21 (1980): 67–86.

Thompson, Benjamin. *Complete Works*. 4 vols. Boston, 1871–75.

Elizabeth Garber

Rush, Benjamin (1746–1813)

Physician, chemist, and psychiatrist. Rush was born near Philadelphia and graduated from the College of New Jersey (now Princeton University) in 1760. After a five-year medical apprenticeship in Philadelphia, he entered the University of Edinburgh in 1766 and took his medical degree in 1768. He returned to Philadelphia in 1769 and began practicing medicine, while at the same time being appointed professor of chemistry at the College of Philadelphia (now the University of Pennsylvania). During the period of the American Revolution, Rush participated in various social, educational, and political reforms, and signed the Declaration of Independence. After 1789, the year he succeeded John Morgan as professor of medicine at the College of Philadelphia, he turned away from the body politic and more fully toward the body natural. Through a flood of influential writings, inspired teaching, tireless clinical treatment, and prominent positions, including the vice presidency of the American Philosophical Society (1797–1801), he helped shape the medical and scientific thought of the early national age.

Rush's initial scientific contributions were in the area of chemistry, and the post he assumed in 1769 was the first professorship in this subject in the colonies. His approach to the field revealed a great debt to his Edinburgh teacher Joseph Black. Rush, however, was primarily interested in practical applications rather than basic research, and he presented numerous medical, domestic, and military uses of chemical knowledge, most notably for the manufacture of gunpowder during the Revolution.

The medical procedure, and controversy, that indelibly colored Rush's career was the practice of bloodletting. Rush had inherited from William Cullen the idea that the physiological tone of the nervous and vascular systems is responsible for health and disease, and from Cullen's student John Brown the doctrine that either too much or too little nervous stimulation is the root of all disorders. But he singled out a state of convulsion, or "morbid excitement," in the blood vessels, particularly the arteries, as the prime pathological condition. This physiological theory underlay his extensive use of the already common procedure of phlebotomy, which was put to a severe test during the yellow fever epidemics in Philadelphia in the 1790s. His views on a great variety of medical topics were published in the five volumes of *Medical Inquiries and Observations* (1789–1798). He laid out his general physiological ideas in *Three Lectures Upon Animal Life* (1799), which is his most substantial philosophical work.

Rush had an abiding interest in the relation between mind and body, as first revealed in his influential *Enquiry into the Influence of Physical Causes upon the Moral Faculty* (1786). Here, his blend of associational and faculty psychology is infused with his ever-present zeal for personal reformation. He implemented his ideas by reforming the treatment of insane patients at the Pennsylvania Hospital beginning in 1787, introducing more humane methods similar to those instituted contemporaneously in Great Britain and France. This innovative work, along with his *Medical Inquiries and Observations Upon the Diseases of the Mind* (1812), the first significant psychiatric book written by an American, has confirmed his position as the father of American psychiatry.

Within a few years of his death, Rush was dubbed "The Sydenham of America," an epitaph with which the Philadelphian would have been quite pleased. He revered and identified with his English counterpart, and found encouragement in his writings for the use of aggressive purging and bleeding. Rush has come under harsh criticism for this practice from his day onward, and his medical reputation has, to some extent, followed the fortunes of this therapeutic method, which has been out of favor since the mid-nineteenth century. Sensitive historical understanding of his approach has thus sometimes been hindered by presentist preconceptions.

His more general scientific reputation rests securely on his role as a herald of scientific ideas and applications. In this capacity, he embodied Enlightenment ideals, always believing that scientific knowledge is most properly pursued and employed for the alleviation of suffering and the advancement of humankind. Although for a time his faith in reason gave way to a larger hope in divine providence, he continued to administer mechanical and pharmacological cures to ills both physiological and social.

The American Psychiatric Association, which was founded in 1844, memorialized Rush's pioneering contributions to psychiatry by emblazoning his portrait on their official seal. Numerous brief hagiographic accounts of his life and work, as well as a few longer

R

and more balanced studies, appeared during the later nineteenth and early twentieth centuries. It was not until the middle of the twentieth century, however, that serious Rush scholarship truly got underway, led by the work of Lyman Butterfield. The late 1960s and 1970s saw a spate of studies, devoted primarily to his medical, psychiatric, and political endeavors, including two book-length biographies, although one is somewhat unscholarly and the other incomplete. During the 1980s and 1990s, scholars turned more toward the social, religious, and literary aspects of Rush's multifaceted career.

There remains a need for a full-scale scholarly biography, at least for the important and turbulent final twenty-five years of Rush's life, one that is informed by the mass of recent research and that interprets his life and work in an integrated manner against the social and scientific contours of his times.

BIBLIOGRAPHY

Binger, Carl. *Revolutionary Doctor: Benjamin Rush, 1746–1813*. New York: Norton, 1966.

Goodman, Nathan G. *Benjamin Rush, Physician and Citizen, 1746–1813*. Philadelphia: University of Pennsylvania Press, 1934.

Fox, Claire G., Gordon L. Miller, and Jacquelyn C. Miller. *Benjamin Rush: A Bibliographic Guide*. Westport, CT: Greenwood, 1995.

Hawke, David F. *Benjamin Rush: Revolutionary Gadfly*. Indianapolis: Bobbs-Merrill, 1971.

King, Lester. *Transformations in American Medicine: From Benjamin Rush to William Osler*. Baltimore: Johns Hopkins University Press, 1991.

Miles, Wyndham. "Benjamin Rush, Chemist." *Chymia* 4 (1953): 37–77.

Rush, Benjamin. *An Oration, Delivered before the American Philosophical Society, held in Philadelphia on the 27th of February, 1786; Containing An Enquiry into the Influence of Physical Causes upon the Moral Faculty*. Philadelphia: Cist, 1786.

———. *Medical Inquiries and Observations*. 5 vols. Philadelphia: various publishers, 1789–1798. Reprint, New York: Arno, 1972.

———. *Three Lectures Upon Animal Life*. Philadelphia: Dobson, 1799.

———. *Medical Inquiries and Observations Upon the Diseases of the Mind*. Philadelphia: Kimber & Richardson, 1812. Reprint, Birmingham, AL: Classics of Medicine Library, 1979.

Shryock, Richard H. *Medicine and Society in America: 1660–1860*. New York: New York University Press, 1960.

Sullivan, Robert B. "Sanguine Practices: A Historical and Historiographic Reconsideration of Heroic Therapy in the Age of Rush." *Bulletin of the History of Medicine* 68 (1994): 211–234.

Gordon L. Miller

S

Sabin, Florence Rena (1871–1953)

Pathbreaking female scientist, medical researcher, and public health activist. After their mother's untimely death in 1878, Florence Sabin and her sister Mary moved between Denver, Chicago, and rural Vermont. In 1889, Sabin enrolled at Smith College, where she excelled in biology, chemistry, and geology. Having decided to pursue a career in medicine, Sabin selected the newly established program at Johns Hopkins over a traditional women's medical college. Sabin's subsequent career is usually divided into three distinct phases: the Hopkins's years, the Rockefeller years, and the Colorado years.

During the first phase she completed medical school and conducted anatomical research under the guidance of Franklin Mall. With Mall's backing, Sabin became the first woman to join the Hopkins faculty. A dedicated teacher and researcher, Sabin used new staining techniques to elucidate the origin of the lymphatic system and then to study the cellular response provoked by specific diseases. Despite considerable recognition for her work and promotion to full professorship in 1917, Sabin encountered the proverbial glass ceiling when Mall died in 1917 and the more junior George Streeter was asked to head the department of anatomy. Several historians, including Margaret Rossiter, have suggested that this setback compelled Sabin to become more actively involved in the promotion of women's rights.

Sabin herself benefited from contemporary efforts to improve women's access to scientific careers. The Baltimore Association for the Promotion of University Education of Women provided her salary during her first year with Mall. The next year, she received a $1,000

prize from the Association for Promoting Scientific Research by Women. As Sabin's career evolved, she became an important example of what women could accomplish. In 1923, the League of Women Voters identified her as one of the twelve greatest living women, an honor reinforced by her election as the first female member of the National Academy of Science two years later.

Shortly thereafter, Sabin became the first woman to join the Rockefeller Institute when Simon Flexner suggested she establish a new Department of Cellular Studies. There, Sabin and her staff studied the intracellular synthesis of antibodies triggered by various diseases. In 1939, Sabin outlined one of the central tenets of modern immunology when she hypothesized that exposed cells retain a "memory" which permits them to produce antibodies more quickly in response to a second exposure. That same year, the Rockefeller Institute's mandatory retirement policy interrupted her productivity and Florence Sabin went to join her older sister in Denver.

The third phase of Sabin's career began in 1946 when the governor of Colorado asked her to join his Post War Planning Committee. Always the epitome of diligence, Sabin took her new job seriously and soon discovered that public health in Colorado had been woefully neglected despite the state's reputation as a health resort. At first, Sabin's campaign to redress the situation through better control of the milk supply, restructuring the state's Health Division, and increasing aid to counties met with considerable resistance from cattlemen, bureaucrats, and politicians. Sabin effectively circumvented this problem by launching a speaking tour during which she explained proposed reforms to community groups around the state. It was largely through her efforts that health reform became a significant issue in the next gubernatorial election and that a series of important state health laws were approved by the Colorado legislature in 1947.

Sabin received many honors in recognition of the contributions she made during all three phases of her career. Repeatedly cited as a model of female achievement, she became the subject of several biographies directed at school-age children (Downing, Kaye, Kronstadt, Phelan). Scholarly accounts of her career tend to emphasize her status as "the first woman to . . ." without necessarily exploring the full impact of gender on Sabin's activities. Sabin's own perspective on work, family, feminism, teaching, and research are available through papers at Smith College, at the American Philosophical Society (13.5 cubic feet with finding aid), the Schlesinger Library, as well as in the biography of Mall she published in 1934. Additional resources include the papers of Ross Harrison and George Comer as well as other scientists affiliated with Johns Hopkins or the Rockefeller Institute.

BIBLIOGRAPHY

Andriole, Vincent. "Florence Rena Sabin—Teacher, Scientist, Citizen." *Journal of the History of Medicine and Allied Sciences* 13 (1959): 320–350.

Bluemel, Elinor. *Florence Sabin: Colorado Woman of the Century.* Boulder, CO: Johnson, 1959.

Campbell, Robin. *Florence Sabin: Scientist.* New York: Chelsea House, 1995.

Downing, Sybil. *Florence Rena Sabin Pioneer Scientist.* Boulder, CO: Pruett, 1981.

Heidelberger, Michael, and Philip McMaster. "Florence Rena Sabin." *Biographical Memoirs of the National Academy of Sciences* 34 (1960): 271–305.

Kaye, Judith. *The Life of Florence Sabin.* New York: Twenty-First Century Books, 1993.

Kronstadt, Janet. *Florence Sabin.* New York: Chelsea House, 1990.

Kubie, Lawrence. "Florence Rena Sabin, 1871–1953." *Perspectives in Biology and Medicine* 4 (1961): 306–315.

Maisel, Albert. "Dr. Sabin's Second Career." *Survey Graphic* 36 (1947): 138–140.

Phelan, Mary. *Probing the Unknown.* New York: Dell, 1969.

Sabin, Florence. *An Atlas of the Medulla and Midbrain.* Baltimore: Friedenwald, 1901.

———. *Franklin Paine Mall: The Story of a Mind.* Baltimore: Johns Hopkins University Press, 1934.

Deborah Julie Franklin

Sabine, Wallace Clement Ware (1868–1919)

Experimental physicist, educator, and military consultant. Born in Richwood, Ohio, Sabine attended Ohio State University, then undertook graduate study in physics at Harvard University. After receiving his M.A., Sabine remained at Harvard to teach physics, first as an instructor, then as assistant professor (1895), and full professor (1905). Sabine was dean of the Harvard Graduate School of Applied Science from its founding in 1906 until 1915, when the school was dissolved by a brief merger between Harvard and the Massachusetts Institute of Technology. During World War I, Sabine served on the Rockefeller War Relief Commission; he directed the Department of Technical Information of the Bureau of Aircraft Production; and he was also a member of the National Advisory Committee for Aeronautics. Sabine's busy wartime schedule weakened his already fragile health, and he died of complications after surgery to treat a kidney infection.

Wallace Sabine is best known for scientific work in the field of architectural acoustics. In 1895, he was asked by Harvard president Charles Eliot to improve the faulty acoustics of a university lecture hall. Sabine focused his investigation on the sound-absorbing properties of materials and their effect upon reverberation, the rate of decay of residual sound. Sabine's approach differed from earlier attempts to solve this problem; while typical nineteenth-century approaches were geometric in nature and concentrated on manipulating the propagation of sound rays, Sabine characterized sound in a room as a diffuse body of energy. This approach led him to develop a mathematical formula that related the reverberation time of a room to its architectural volume and to the materials that constituted its interior surfaces. This formula enabled him to predict the acoustical quality of rooms in advance of construction, a goal that architects had long sought. Sabine first applied his formula to architect Charles McKim's design for Symphony Hall in Boston, and he subsequently consulted with numerous other architects of the period. He additionally helped develop special sound-absorbing building materials. At the time of his death, Sabine was planning to move his investigations to a laboratory outside of Chicago, built for him by a philanthropist, Colonel George Fabyan.

In the years after Sabine's death, architectural acoustics became a field of expertise for a growing number of scientists and engineers. These men identified Sabine as the founder of their profession, and they have generated a small body of literature on the physicist and his work. A biography, apparently commissioned by Sabine's widow, also exists. A less heroic, more contextualized account of his life and work has more recently begun to appear.

BIBLIOGRAPHY

Beranek, Leo L. "The Notebooks of Wallace C. Sabine." *Journal of the Acoustical Society of America* 61 (1977): 629–639.

———. "Wallace Clement Sabine and Acoustics." *Physics Today* (1985): 44–51.

Beranek, Leo L., and John Kopec. "Wallace C. Sabine, Acoustical Consultant." *Journal of the Acoustical Society of America* 69 (1981): 1–16.

Orcutt, William Dana. *Wallace Clement Sabine: A Study in Achievement.* Norwood, MA: Plimpton Press, 1933.

Sabine, Wallace C. *Collected Papers on Acoustics.* Cambridge, MA: Harvard University Press, 1922.

Thompson, Emily. "'Mysteries of the Acoustic': Architectural Acoustics in America, 1800–1932." Ph.D. diss., Princeton University, 1992.

———. "Dead Rooms and Live Wires: Harvard, Hollywood and the Deconstruction of Architectural Acoustics, 1900–1920." *Isis* 88 (1997): 597–626.

———. "Listening to/for Modernity: Architectural Acoustics and the Development of Modern Spaces in America." In *The Architecture of Science,* edited by Peter Galison and Emily Thompson. Cambridge, MA: MIT Press, 1999, pp. 253–280.

Emily Thompson

SEE ALSO
Acoustics

SAGE (Semi-Automatic Ground Environment) Project

One of the largest computer-based applications undertaken in the 1950s. It was to provide an air-defense system for the United States. SAGE was a massive technological effort involving the development of software, hardware, procedures, radar devices, and communications. The first SAGE center became operational on 1 July 1958, and four were still in use as of the early 1980s.

The concept was to cover all the skies with radar, with radar stations linked by telecommunications controlled by computers to provide nationwide coverage. Work done at the Massachusetts Institute of Technology on the WHIRLWIND computer was integrated into the project. The computer was the first real-time control system which could trap information on radar, transmit it instantaneously to someone to study, and display information either on a terminal or print it out. WHIRLWIND was the fastest computer of its day. The system was upgraded as computer technologies improved throughout the 1950s and 1960s, incorporating, for example, random access computer memory, a massive operating system, and other technologies which made their way into commercial products by the end of the 1950s. Full deployment finally came in 1963 when twenty-three locations became operational, each with a data center responsible for a specific geographical area covered by radar and linked to each other by ground communications, using fifty-four computers. It was the largest computer project of the 1950s, and the most expensive of the period. It was the most dramatic example of United States military investments pushing back the frontiers of technology in communications, computers, and software.

BIBLIOGRAPHY

Astrahan, Morton M., and John F. Jacobs. "History of the Design of the SAGE Computer—The AN/FSQ-7." *Annals of the History of Computing* 5 (1983): 340–349.

James W. Cortada

SANE, the Committee for a Sane Nuclear Policy

Citizen's organization dedicated to nuclear disarmament and peace. SANE was formed in November 1957 by a coalition of pacifist and nonpacifist groups amid growing public concerns about the effects of radioactive fallout from nuclear tests. Its founders included Norman Cousins, former president of the United World Federalists, Clarence Pickett, of the American Friends Service Committee, and Norman Thomas, former president of the Socialist Party. SANE was originally a single-issue group, concentrating on nuclear disarmament. By 1958, it had 25,000 members in 130 chapters across the United States. From the late 1950s to the early 1960s, SANE focused on publicizing the danger posed by radioactive fallout and the need for a nuclear test ban. By the mid-1960s, it turned to protesting American involvement in Vietnam as the most pressing obstacle to peace and disarmament. Opposition to the Vietnam War broadened SANE's agenda beyond its early exclusive attention to nuclear

S

issues, and to reflect its expanded concerns, in 1969 it changed its name from the Committee for a Sane Nuclear Policy to SANE: A Citizens' Organization for a Sane World. During the 1970s, SANE's agenda included nuclear disarmament, economic conversion to redirect military resources toward civilian purposes, peace in the Middle East, and more general efforts to ensure greater international cooperation on world problems. It faced declining membership throughout the early 1970s, but by the early 1980s, it was revived by the nuclear freeze movement. By 1983, it had 75,000 members.

SANE has engaged in a wide variety of activities throughout its history, including making public statements and publishing influential political advertisements, circulating petitions, organizing conferences, mobilizing rallies, and lobbying public officials. By the early 1980s, it began to directly participate in electoral politics, forming a political action committee (SANE-PAC) and attempting to elect candidates dedicated to peace and disarmament to public office.

The papers of SANE are located in the Swarthmore College Peace Collection in Swarthmore, Pennsylvania.

BIBLIOGRAPHY

Katz, Milton S. "Peace Liberals and Vietnam: SANE and the Politics of 'Responsible' Protest." *Peace and Change* 9 (Summer 1983): 21–39.

———. *Ban the Bomb: A History of SANE, the Committee for a Sane Nuclear Policy, 1957–1985.* Westport, CT: Greenwood Press, 1986.

Katz, Milton S., and Neil H. Katz. "Pragmatists and Visionaries in the Post–World War II American Peace Movement: SANE and CNVA." In *Doves and Diplomats: Foreign Officers and Peace Movements in Europe and America in the Twentieth Century,* edited by Solomon Wank. Westport, CT: Greenwood Press, 1978, pp. 265–288.

McCrea, Frances B., and Gerald Markle. *Minutes to Midnight: Nuclear Weapons Protest in America.* Newbury Park, CA: Sage Publications, 1989.

Wittner, Lawrence S. *Rebels Against War: The American Peace Movement, 1933–1983.* Philadelphia: Temple University Press, 1984.

Jessica Wang

Say, Thomas (1787–1834)

Naturalist and explorer who founded the sciences of entomology and conchology in the United States. Born in Philadelphia of Quaker parents, Say attended the Westtown School as a boarder and subsequently took courses at the University of Pennsylvania Medical School. But he was essentially self-taught in natural science.

Say's father was a prominent and affluent physician, who was a colleague of Dr. Benjamin Rush and served in the Pennsylvania Senate and in the United States Congress. His mother, Ann Bonsall Say, was the granddaughter of the botanist John Bartram. Bartram's son, William, an artist/naturalist of note, was inspirational to the young Say, as was Bartram's neighbor and friend, the artist and writer of the first book on American birds, Alexander Wilson. Also strongly influential was Charles Willson Peale and his large collection of fauna in the Philadelphia Museum.

In 1812, Say, with six others, founded the Academy of Natural Sciences of Philadelphia. He served as curator of the new institution and was tireless in arranging its ever-expanding collections and assisting others in their search for natural knowledge. With the financial help of William Maclure, a wealthy Scottish businessman and amateur geologist, Say and his associates published a journal for the society beginning in 1817. The *Journal of the Academy of Natural Sciences of Philadelphia* was sent abroad in exchange for the publications of other scientific organizations and in this way established the international reputation of the institution. Through this medium also, foreign naturalists were encouraged to belong to the academy as "corresponding members."

Say's first expedition occurred in December of 1817 when he accompanied Maclure on a cruise by hired sloop to the sea islands off Georgia and to Spanish-held Florida. Also included in the party were George Ord, vice president of the academy, and Titian Ramsay Peale, the youngest son of Charles Willson Peale, as hunter and artist. The trip was cut short because of Indian hostility, but Say nevertheless collected some insects, and, particularly, a number of interesting mollusks, which he later described in the *Journal*.

During 1819–1820, Say served as zoologist on the United States government-sponsored Long Expedition to the Rocky Mountains. From this journey, he brought back many previously unknown insects, land shells, birds, reptiles, and a few mammals many of which he named and described for science. Among these were the swift, or kit, fox, and the coyote. Say, as part of his official assignment, also studied the habits and manners of the native peoples and compiled vocabularies of their various languages.

Again, in 1823, he joined Major Stephen Long on an expedition to the western United States, this time to the St. Peters (now Minnesota) River, the Lake of the Woods in Canada, and the northern part of Lake Superior.

He published part one of his first major work, *American Entomology, or Descriptions of the Insects of North America*, in 1824, in Philadelphia, with illustrations by Titian R. Peale, Charles Alexandre Lesueur, Hugh Bridport, and William Wood. Two other parts were subsequently published in 1825 and 1828.

Persuaded by Maclure, who for some time had been his patron in natural science, to join him in an educational experiment in Robert Owen's "utopian" town of New Harmony, Indiana, Say moved there permanently at the end of 1825. It was on the journey down the Ohio River on a keelboat that was later called "the boatload of knowledge," because of the many scientists aboard, that Say fell in love with his future wife, Lucy Way Sistare, who had been hired to teach at New Harmony. They were married in January 1827.

At the end of 1827, Say accompanied Maclure on a trip to Mexico, where he added significantly to his insect and shell collections.

Say's second major work, *American Conchology, or Descriptions of the Shells of North America*, with plates from drawings by his wife, who had once studied briefly in Philadelphia with Audubon, and also with Lesueur, appeared in seven parts between 1830 and 1836. It had been mostly printed on a handpress in New Harmony.

Say died in New Harmony. He had named and described approximately 1,500 insects for science, for which he has been called the "father of American entomology," as well as numerous land and freshwater shells, which has given him the same title for the science of conchology (now malacology).

In 1818, Say's article on fossil shells that appeared in Benjamin Silliman's *American Journal of Science and Arts* discussed the pioneering concept that fossils could be used to date rock strata.

Say's scientific articles appeared in many publications of his day, and because of his contributions to the taxonomy of native species, his name has been immortalized in the names of birds—most popularly, Say's Phoebe (*Sayornis saya*), reptiles, mammals, insects, and shells. But his most important contribution to early natural science in America was his insistence that the flora and fauna of the United States be named and described by American scientists and not be sent to Europe for that purpose.

BIBLIOGRAPHY

Evans, Howard Ensign. *The Pleasures of Entomology: Portraits of Insects and the People Who Study Them.* Washington, DC: Smithsonian Institution Press, 1985.

Jaffe, Bernard. *Men of Science in America.* New York: Simon and Schuster, 1944.

James, Edwin, ed. *Account of an Expedition From Pittsburgh to the Rocky Mountains, Performed In the Years 1819, 1820, by Order of the Hon. J. C. Calhoun, Secretary of War, Under the Command of Maj. S. H. Long of the U. S. Top. Engineers. Compiled from the Notes of Major Long, Mr. T. Say, and Other Gentlemen of the Party.* 3 vols. Philadelphia: H.C. Carey and I. Lea, 1823.

Keating, William H., ed. *Narrative of an Expedition to the Source of St. Peter's River, Lake Winnepeek, Lake of the Woods, etc. Performed in the Year 1823, by Order of the Hon. J. C. Calhoun, Secretary of War, Under the Command of Stephen H. Long, U.S.T.E. Compiled from the Notes of Major Long, Messrs. Say, Keating & Calhoun.* 2 vols. Philadelphia: H.C. Carey and I. Lea, 1824.

Mallis, Arnold. *American Entomologists.* New Brunswick: Rutgers University Press, 1971.

Say, Thomas. *American Entomology, or Descriptions of the Insects of North America.* 3 vols. Philadelphia: Samuel Augustus Mitchell, 1824, 1825, 1828.

———. *American Conchology, or Descriptions of the Shells of North America.* Pts. 1–6, New Harmony, IN: School Press, 1830–1834. Pt. 7, Philadelphia, 1836.

Stroud, Patricia Tyson. *Thomas Say: New World Naturalist.* Philadelphia: University of Pennsylvania Press, 1992.

Patricia Tyson Stroud

SEE ALSO
Academy of Natural Sciences of Philadelphia, The

Schoolcraft, Henry Rowe (1793–1864)

Ethnologist, explorer and government agent to the Indians. Born in Albany County, New York, and trained as a glassmaker, Schoolcraft traveled in 1818 down the Ohio River exploring the mineral resources of the Missouri and Arkansas regions. The following year, he was appointed as a geologist on the exploring expedition to the Northwest under Lewis Cass, territorial governor of Michigan, about which he reported in *Narrative Journal of Travels . . . to the Sources of the Mississippi River* (1821). In 1822, he arrived in Sault Ste. Marie, a frontier post, as an Indian agent to the tribes of Lake Superior. He led the 1832 expeditionary party that, with the help of Chippewa (Ojibway) guides, traced the origin of the Mississippi River's primary

S

branch to Lake Itasca—a mock aboriginal name he coined from the Latin, *veritas caput* (true-head). He was later promoted to the position of superintendent of Indian affairs in Michigan (1836). Marrying into a family with Chippewa lineage, he studied local dialects and soon became an important source on Indian life for East Coast ethnologists as well as President Andrew Jackson's administration which was eager to find scientific justification for its Indian removal policy. He later shifted his interest from philology to history and mythology in an effort, culminating in *Algic Researches* (1839), to probe the Indians' "mental characteristics" and thus supposedly account for their reluctance to cooperate with projects aimed at their "civilization." Moving back East in 1841, he attempted to launch a literary-scientific career based on his extensive field experience. In numerous books, such as *Oneóta* (1844–1845), he collected and popularized Indian folklore, in particular legends. He lobbied to secure government patronage for a variety of large-scale projects; proposed a plan of ethnological investigation for the nascent Smithsonian Institution; and then embarked on a statistical and historical survey for the state of New York published as *Notes on the Iroquois* (1847). During the same year, he began soliciting and editing materials for his most ambitious ten-year scientific endeavor, sponsored by Congress and the Bureau of Indian Affairs, *Historical and Statistical Information, Respecting the History, Condition, and Prospects of the Indian Tribes of the United States* (1851–1857). This luxurious six-volume edition included Seth Eastman's famous illustrations but received mixed reviews. Despite the wealth of information it offered, the study represented an eclectic and outmoded style of ethnology. Schoolcraft's attitude toward the Indians, highly informed by his growing religiosity, became with time increasingly pessimistic and paternalistic. Nevertheless, his religious convictions drove Schoolcraft to position himself strongly against Samuel Morton's controversial polygenism.

Schoolcraft's career epitomized the antebellum convergence of ethnology with politics, administration of Indian affairs, and society's fascination with Native American culture. He is viewed today as a transitory figure between the salon ethnology of the Enlightenment and a younger generation of scholars, most notably Lewis Morgan, who combined fieldwork with theoretical sophistication. Declaring himself first and foremost a "fact finder," his main scientific asset was thirty years of direct contact with western tribes.

BIBLIOGRAPHY

Bieder, Robert E. *Science Encounters the Indian, 1820–1880: The Early Years of American Ethnology.* Norman: University of Oklahoma Press, 1986.

Bremer, Richard G. *Indian Agent and Wilderness Scholar: The Life of Henry Rowe Schoolcraft.* Mount Pleasant: Clarke Historical Library, Central Michigan University, 1987.

Schoolcraft, Henry Rowe. *A View of the Lead Mines of Missouri, including Some Observations on the Mineralogy, Geology, Geography, Antiquities, Soil, Climate, Population and Production of Missouri and Arkansaw, and Other Sections of the Western Country.* New York: Charles Wiley, 1819.

——. *Narrative Journal of Travels Through the Northwestern Regions of the United States Extending from Detroit Through the Great Chain of American Lakes, to the Sources of the Mississippi, Performed as a Member of the Expedition Under Governor Cass in the Year 1820.* Albany, NY: E. & E. Hosford, 1821.

——. *Algic Researches, Comprising Inquiries Respecting the Mental Characteristics of Indians.* 2 vols. New York: Harper & Brothers, 1839.

——. *Oneóta, or the Red Race of America: Their History, Traditions, Customs, Poetry, Picture-writing.* 8 numbers. New York: Burgess, Stringer, 1844–1845.

——. *Notes on the Iroquois: or Contributions to American History, Antiquities, and General Ethnology.* Albany, NY: Erastus H. Pease, 1847.

——. *Historical and Statistical Information Respecting the History, Condition and Prospects of the Indian Tribes of the United States; Collected and Prepared Under the Direction of the Bureau of Indian Affairs, per Act of Congress of March 3rd, 1847.* 6 vols. Philadelphia: Lippincott, Grambo, 1851–1857.

Oz Frankel

Science

As the American scientific community grew in the 1860s, its members sought their own journal analogous to their British colleagues' *Nature,* which regularly and rapidly reported news of science and of the institutions that supported it. Several such American periodicals failed in the 1870s, and *Science* first appeared as a weekly magazine in 1880, with financial support initially from Thomas A. Edison, and then from Alexander Graham Bell and his father-in-law, Gardner Greene Hubbard. The journal produced by its editors—successively journalist John Michels, Harvard librarian Samuel H. Scudder, and N.D.C. Hodges—at times served its readers well. But Bell and Gardner gradually withdrew their financial subsidies, and *Science* ceased publication in March 1894. Later that year, Columbia University psychologist James McKeen Cattell assumed control of *Science*.

As both owner and editor, Cattell avoided many of his predecessors' problems. His influential Editorial Committee included representatives of the leading federal scientific agencies (e.g., the Bureau of American Ethnology, the Nautical Almanac Office, and the Biological, the Coast and Geodetic, and the Geological Surveys) and the emerging research universities (e.g., Columbia, Cornell, Harvard, and Johns Hopkins). Cattell often tapped these contacts, and with their help *Science* regularly published unsigned editorials about major policy matters, Current Notes about important developments in many sciences, and letters on controversial subjects. Early in 1896, *Science* reported more on Roentgen's discovery of X-rays than any specialized journal, and its readership multiplied. In 1900, *Science* became the official journal of the American Association for the Advancement of Science (AAAS), even while privately owned. Cattell guaranteed publication of AAAS official papers and AAAS members began to receive *Science* without paying higher dues. This action increased AAAS membership, *Science*'s circulation, and Cattell's advertising revenue dramatically.

American scientists thus read *Science* as it reported news of the institutions that employed them and the latest discoveries in their fields. As editor, Cattell also set the terms and drew participants into major policy debates. Before 1910, these included plans for the Smithsonian Institution's scientific bureaus and for Andrew Carnegie's $10 million endowment for the Carnegie Institution of Washington. After 1910, *Science* emphasized (through articles and letters) serious debates about the governance of higher education and about support for scientific research and both the National Research Council and the AAAS's own Committee of One Hundred on Scientific Research. These concerns attracted additional readers, and as success bred success *Science*'s growing readership attracted significant submissions. After 1920, however, *Science* paid less attention to policy issues than it had—for example, in the 1930s, Cattell tried to avoid discussing the Social Relations of Science Movement—and others thought the journal had grown dull. But *Science* still reached a large audience, and still attracted major submissions.

From Cattell's death in 1944 (when it assumed ownership of *Science*) through 1956 (when Stanford University biologist Graham DuShane became editor), the

AAAS tried various editorial arrangements. None worked well, but its continuing reputation and the post–World War II expansion of American science assured *Science*'s continued growth. As editor, DuShane professionalized the magazine's staff, standardized refereeing procedures, and most notably hired experienced journalists for a new News and Comment section. His successor, Carnegie Institution geophysicist Philip H. Abelson, built on these initiatives, expanded the News and Comment section, instituted one for Research News and, by speeding up refereeing, enabled *Science* to publish significant research results more quickly than ever before. Berkeley molecular biologist Daniel Koshland became editor in 1985; he was succeeded by Floyd Bloom in 1995.

BIBLIOGRAPHY

Kohlstedt, Sally Gregory. "Science: The Struggle for Survival." *Science* 209 (1980): 33–42.
Kohlstedt, Sally Gregory, Michael M. Sokal, and Bruce V. Lewenstein, *The Establishment of American Science: 150 Years of the American Association for the Advancement of Science.* New Brunswick: Rutgers University Press, 1999.
Sokal, Michael M. "Science and James McKeen Cattell, 1894–1945." *Science* 209 (1980): 43–52.
Walsh, John. "Science in Transition, 1946 to 1962." *Science* 209 (1980): 52–57.
Wolfle, Dael. "Science: A Memoir of the 1960's and 1970's." *Science* 209 (1980): 57–60.

Michael M. Sokal

Science for the People (Scientists and Engineers for Social and Political Action)

An organization of scientists, engineers, and other persons dedicated to progressive political action to ensure the responsible use of scientific knowledge. The organization was originally named Scientists and Engineers for Social and Political Action (SESPA), but it eventually became known by its slogan, Science for the People, which was also the title of its magazine. Founded at the 1969 meeting of the American Physical Society, SESPA at first articulated a relatively moderate political program focused on opposition to President Richard Nixon's plans to build an antiballistic missile system. Inspired by the antiwar movement of the Vietnam era, SESPA grew increasingly radical after its inception. It advocated confrontational tactics to protest the militarization of American science (including presentation of the "Dr. Strangelove" award to Edward Teller during his talk at

S

the 1970 American Association for the Advancement of Science meeting), and it initially promoted a radical critique of capitalism. By the mid-1970s, however, Science for the People identified less with long-term radical reform and instead adopted an issue-oriented style, addressing particular matters of concern through direct action, publications, and study groups. In addition to opposing the military use of science, Science for the People addressed health and environmental issues, and through its Genetics and Social Policy Group, it was especially active in considering the ethical implications of genetics research. Science for the People adamantly opposed genetic explanations of human intelligence, criminality, and other areas of human behavior, and it warned of potential misuses of genetic engineering throughout the 1970s and 1980s.

In the early 1970s, Science for the People estimated that it had at least 2,500 members, with chapters in a dozen cities across the United States. It was most active in the Boston area, where it published *Science for the People.* At its height, the magazine had a circulation of 10,000. *Science for the People* ceased publication in 1989, and the organization went out of existence in 1991.

The papers of Science for the People are still in the personal possession of its former members; there is currently no central depository.

BIBLIOGRAPHY

Krimsky, Sheldon. *Genetic Alchemy: The Social History of the Recombinant Controversy.* Cambridge, MA: MIT Press, 1982.

Moore, Kelly. "Doing Good While Doing Science: The Origins and Consequences of Public Interest Science Organizations in America, 1945–1990." Ph.D. diss., University of Arizona, 1993.

Nichols, David. "The Associational Interest Groups of American Science." In *Scientists and Public Affairs,* edited by Albert H. Teich. Cambridge, MA: MIT Press, 1974, pp. 123–170.

Science for the People. 1–21 (1969–1989).

Jessica Wang

Science in the United States during the Colonial Period (to 1789)

It might first appear that there was little interest in Western science in America at the outset of the colonial period. The earliest European explorers were too absorbed in trying to discover a passage to the Orient or too intent on exploiting precious metals and resources; the first settlers were too obsessed with converting Native Americans to Christianity or too busy establishing homesteads and a working economy. Indeed, there were "all thinges to doe, as in ye beginning of ye world," remarked John Winthrop Jr., a son of the governor of the Massachusetts Bay Colony, himself the governor of Connecticut (1662–1676), and a charter member of the Royal Society. It was no surprise, he told Henry Oldenburg, the Royal Society Secretary, in 1668, that there was little time for science (Stearns, p. 133).

And yet Winthrop was able to squeeze time from his busy schedule of diplomacy, farming, and land speculation in order to study alchemy and experimental philosophy, practice medicine, and be an entrepreneur in mining and the manufacture of salt and iron. He offered the Royal Society papers on maize, the making of tar and pitch, and beer brewed from cornbread. He sent New England curiosities to the society as well. On a transatlantic crossing, he performed oceanographic experiments with sounding leads and a water-catching device. He had the first telescope in New England—a ten-foot instrument—and later a three-and-a-half foot one, which he bestowed on Harvard College. In 1664, he observed a comet and believed he had discovered a fifth satellite of Jupiter. The Royal Society was pleased to receive reports from the colonies, and responded to Winthrop's missives with letters and gifts of books.

Working in the wilderness, Winthrop was more assiduous than most in overcoming the obstacles that deterred many from scientific endeavors—namely the lack of time, books, apparatus, and like-minded scholars—but he was not alone in his efforts. Remarks of Winthrop to the contrary, it was not long after Christopher Columbus encountered the Americas that Western science gained its first footholds in the New World. Many early settlers valued astronomy and natural history for their presumed relevance to religion and their applications in the fields of navigation, time finding, land measure, and medicine. With time, they also valued scientific knowledge as evidence of breeding and education.

Historians generally agree that science in the colonies was decidedly provincial when compared to that emanating from the hallowed centers of learning overseas, but they are now giving colonial scholars their due. Thanks to the preservation efforts of nineteenth-century historical societies and recent bibliographers, we learn that the colonists produced modest, but surprisingly numerous scientific publications (numbered in the thousands). Their correspondence also testifies

S

to a substantial traffic in scientific ideas. This survey will sketch colonial accomplishments in the life and physical sciences, science education, and the organization of scientific activities, and will examine both the obstacles that hampered and the assets that promoted colonial undertakings. What follows is largely descriptive, reflecting the rudimentary state of historiography, but is intended to lay the groundwork for the historiographic issues to be highlighted later.

Although more historical research has focused on the "pure" sciences, it is fitting for this survey to begin with the "applied" sciences. Exploration and settlement made much work for mathematical practitioners, who guided ships to port, surveyed boundaries, and mapped the terrain. These tasks employed navigators, astronomers, surveyors, and cartographers. Some of these individuals, such as the eighteenth-century surveyors Charles Mason and Jeremiah Dixon, were professionally trained in England and imported to the colonies; others, such as their contemporarties David and Benjamin Rittenhouse, were self-taught residents of the New World.

Scientific instruments were essential to these assignments, and all were initially imported. Nautical instruments, traditionally made from wood, were among the first to be duplicated in the colonies, since they were relatively easy to produce. Brass instruments, with finely divided scales, were difficult to finish in America, and colonial surveyors, mariners, and cartographers were forced to rely on skilled English and European makers until the nineteenth century for theodolites, sextants, and rules. Production of instruments was also impeded by the scarcity of brass in the colonies, but resourceful instrument makers substituted hardwood for metal when they could. In this way, the wooden surveying compass emerged as an instrument peculiar to America. The most noteworthy colonial innovation, however, was the reflecting quadrant (or octant) devised in 1730 by Thomas Godfrey of Philadelphia; it was nearly identical to one invented independently by John Hadley, an Englishmen for whom the instrument was ultimately named.

Mariners, surveyors, cartographers, and traders were frequently accompanied in their rounds by naturalists, who compiled lists of resources and collected curiosities. The work of naturalists was guided in part by practical considerations such as the search for marketable commodities, medicinal plants, or timber for ships, but their interests were also piqued by the previously unknown animals and plants they encountered.

The exchange of plants and animals between the Old and New Worlds began as early as Columbus's second voyage (1493). As eyewitness observers, three sixteenth-century Spanish authors—Gonzalo Fernandez de Oviedo y Valdés, Nicolás Bautista Monardes, and José d'Acosta—wrote pioneer and influential studies of the natural history of America. Their works raised as many questions as they answered. They sought to incorporate American specimens into preexisting categories used by ancient Greek, Roman, and contemporary European naturalists, but their efforts revealed many inadequacies in the old system. Moreover, the existence of indigenous American animals unlike any in Europe posed problems with respect to Scripture. Since there was no record of these animals on Noah's Ark, was one to assume that the Deluge did not extend to America? Could God have created them separately after the Flood? Or was it possible for antediluvian species to change over time?

More fodder for these debates was to be found in reports of expeditions designed to assess the viability of colonization. In the late sixteenth and early seventeenth centuries, Thomas Harriot, Captain John Smith, William Wood, Samuel de Champlain, and other explorers described the topography, flora, fauna, geology, and native peoples of the New World. Specimens and artifacts were shipped back to Europe to be studied in botanical gardens and museums. Although the collections and publications of explorers were promotional, being designed to attract investors and settlers, they nonetheless helped to disseminate scientific and ethnological discoveries.

Another side of the promotional efforts were early experiments in cultivating English plants in America. In Virginia, for instance, Harriot tried to grow barley, oats, and peas in 1585–1586.

News from the New World surprised Europeans, who encouraged further exploration of the continent and closer study of natural specimens. After 1660, the Royal Society promoted such undertakings. Its archives contain many documents of value to historians, such as a letter circulated in 1669 requesting information about the Virginia plantation; the cultivation and merits of tobacco; experiments in raising rice, coffee, olives, vines, hemp, and silkworms; resources for ship building; the existence of medicinal springs and origins of rivers; Native American skills; magnetic variation; weather; tides; and topography. Also requested were samples of seawater, flora, fauna, minerals, and earths. Farmers, surgeons, and clergymen responded, including

S

John Clayton (1657–1725), a naturalist and experimental philosopher who spent two years in Jamestown. Clayton's contributions, however, were overshadowed by those of John Banister, a field agent whose work was financed by fellows of the Royal Society. Banister cast a trained eye upon mollusks, fossils, insects, and plants of Virginia and sent hundreds of specimens back to England, along with detailed descriptions and sketches. He began to prepare a natural history of Virginia, but died tragically in a shooting accident in 1692 before he could complete it. His writings were appropriated by John Ray and others.

The Temple Coffee House Botany Club, a loose association of naturalists who met from 1689 until about 1720, joined the Royal Society in promoting the study of botany at home and abroad. Hans Sloane, William Sherard, and James Petiver were among the members who corresponded with colonial and continental scholars, frequently putting them in direct touch with each other, thereby expanding the scholarly horizons of colonials. Club members took particular interest in the natural history of the southern mainland colonies. Another promoter was Peter Collinson, a Quaker merchant in London, who used his countinghouse as a clearinghouse for American natural history specimens and letters, which he redirected to Carl Linnaeus and others. Thus, there arose a natural history circle.

Hans Sloane, William Sherard, and Peter Collinson helped to back the expeditions of Mark Catesby (1683–1749), who traveled from Virginia to Florida between 1712 and 1726, forwarding specimens, sketches, and notes back to London. Catesby collected seeds, plants, mosses, nuts, berries, roots, shells, birds, animals, snakes, insects, fish, amphibia, and Indian curios, but his best work was in the field of ornithology. He rejected theories that birds flew to retreats above the atmosphere or hibernated in caves, hollow trees, or beneath pond water. He proposed instead a new theory, based on observation, that birds migrated south to avoid cold weather and seek food. Linnaeus made extensive use of Catesby's works.

Also praised by Linnaeus was John Bartram (1699–1777), a superb field naturalist and collector with a formidable knowledge of American natural history. Backed by Peter Collinson and other English gentlemen, Bartram traveled throughout the colonies from New York to Florida and as far west as Ohio, seeking seeds to send to his patrons. He was appointed King's Botanist in 1765.

Bartram and Catesby were unconcerned about systematic classification and content to send specimens back to Europe for cataloging. Others were not. John Clayton (1694–1773), a distant relative of the earlier namesake, cataloged Virginia plants according to John Ray's system, but forwarded them to Johann Friedrich Gronovius in Holland for identification of species according to the Linnaean method. After Gronovius appropriated Clayton's findings in a treatise on American botany, Clayton decided to master the Linnaean system himself. Working in Virginia at the same time (1735–1746), Dr. John Mitchell pursued taxonomy, suggesting that the classification of species be based on the ability of males and females to have offspring. He discovered new genera and studied the reproductive system of the opossum and pigmentation in humans. Others who mastered the Linnaean system included Dr. Alexander Garden of Charleston, South Carolina, Dr. Cadwallader Colden of New York, and his daughter Jane Colden Farquher.

Female scientists were a novelty in colonial America, as they were elsewhere, and have barely begun to be studied by historians. Those eighteenth-century women who excelled in science, such as Jane Colden Farquher, Martha Laurens Ramsay, Martha Daniell Logan, and Eliza Lucas Pinckney, were engaged in botany, agronomy, or horticulture. They were encouraged by their fathers and husbands, who thought these pursuits were particularly appropriate for women, enabling them to overcome the purportedly female vice of idleness while improving their domestic capabilities.

While interest in natural history was rising to ever higher levels in the southern and middle colonies, it was declining in the northern ones during the eighteenth century. In the previous century, the Royal Society had urged John Winthrop to write a complete history, both civil and natural, of New England, but that task was first undertaken in the 1670s by John Josselyn, the son of the councillor of the province of Maine. After Josselyn, little of value for natural history came out of New England until the early eighteenth century, when Cotton Mather offered the society his *Curiosa Americana*. This collection of eighty-two letters written between 1712 and 1724 covered many topics in the fields of biology, ornithology, zoology, entomology, geology, anthropology, medicine, astronomy, meteorology, and mathematics. He offered the first recorded account of plant hybridization, described the successful but controversial trial in Boston (1721–1722) of inoculating for smallpox, and advanced the theory that diseases were caused by animalcules that invaded the body. He delineated the nesting habits of pigeons, reported medical practices among the Indians, and described a medicine extracted from a rattlesnake's gall bladder. In the 1720s, Paul Dudley also wrote from Boston about deer, bees, and the hybridization of Indian corn. He identified whales as the source of ambergris. Mather and Dudley were elected Fellows of the Royal Society but few in New England followed their leads in the study of natural history.

Whereas natural history was the preferred science of southerners, astronomy and experimental natural philosophy held the interest of northerners throughout the colonial period.

Set up in 1638 in Harvard Yard, the first printing press in the colonies was put to immediate use in publishing almanacs for New England. The Cambridge printer took advantage of his location to tap recent Harvard graduates (usually tutors or fellows) for help in calculating and compiling the astronomical entries. In return, the young Harvard authors were entitled to fill up blank pages with original poems and essays. Many chose to spread word of the new astronomy and introduce scientific debate into the wilderness. Popular topics included Copernican heliocentrism and Keplerian astronomy, telescopic discoveries, comets, and meteorology. Later in the century, almanacs began to be issued in Boston, Philadelphia, and New York, and by the end of the eighteenth century, they were published throughout the colonies. Although later almanacs popularized Newtonian science, they devoted more space to astrology, satire, humor, politics, and practical advice.

In addition to work on almanacs, Harvard tutors got to try their hands at research when John Winthrop Jr. donated his three-and-a-half-foot telescope to the college in 1672. With this instrument, Thomas Brattle studied the path of the comet of 1680–1681 and recognized that the comet had made a hairpin turn around the sun. He transmitted his observations to John Flamsteed, the Astronomer Royal, who shared them with Isaac Newton. The comet became an important test case for Newton's theory of gravitation, and in the *Principia* (1687), he cited Brattle's observations along with those of Arthur Storer of Maryland. Brattle visited Flamsteed at Greenwich in 1689, and continued to correspond with him, sending observations of solar and lunar eclipses. At his death, the Royal Society tried vainly to secure his scientific papers.

Like the comet of 1664, those of 1680–1681 and 1682 attracted much notice in New England. Increase Mather, the esteemed Puritan divine and later president of Harvard College (1685–1701), preached and published on comets, incorporating the latest research into his pronouncements. Although comets were natural bodies according to him, they remained signs of divine anger, portending and possibly causing future calamities. His son, Cotton Mather, parted company with his father's older attitude and suggested that comets were not necessarily harbingers of disaster, yet believed comets to be planets transformed into blazing hells.

In contrast to the Mathers, who viewed astronomical study as an act of piety, astronomers of the eighteenth century surveyed the heavens with a more secular gaze. They revered God's handiwork and were mindful of his powers, but did not scan the skies for divine bulletins of future judgments. This shift in intellectual priorities is evident in the research of Thomas Robie, a Harvard librarian and tutor, and John Winthrop (1714–1779), a descendant of the Connecticut governor of the same name, and the second incumbent of the Hollis Professorship of Mathematics and Natural Philosophy at Harvard (1738–1779). Robie set up a makeshift observatory on the rooftop of a college building, and from this perch observed Jupiter's satellites, eclipses, and the aurora borealis, which he described in wholly natural terms. The essays he prepared for almanacs were equally secular in outlook. The foremost astronomer in the colonies, Winthrop had a long-standing interest in comets, publishing his observations in Boston newspapers, delivering public lectures on the occasion of the return of Halley's comet in 1759, and offering the Royal Society a paper on the masses and densities of comets as deduced from their comas. He carried out observations of transits of Mercury in an effort to determine the longitude of Cambridge, and hoping to shed light on the dimensions of the solar system, he traveled to Newfoundland in order to observe a transit of Venus in 1761.

The transits of Venus in 1761 and 1769 were of international interest, and unlike the first transit, the second was visible throughout the settled colonies. David Rittenhouse, William Smith, and John Ewing in Pennsylvania, Ezra Stiles and Benjamin West in Rhode Island, Samuel Williams in Massachusetts, Owen Biddle in Delaware, William Alexander in New Jersey, and others joined Winthrop in observing the transit. These observations enhanced the reputation of American astronomy at home and abroad.

S

Whereas astronomy was pursued with great zeal in America, other physical sciences were not without their devotees. Thomas Robie chemically analyzed the remains of a scorched oak tree, and Cadwallader Colden claimed he had discovered the cause of gravity. Optics was pursued by David Rittenhouse and James Logan, who also distinguished himself in experiments on the pollination of plants. Benjamin Franklin immersed himself in the study of electricity. In proposing a single-fluid theory of electricity, dubbing charges negative and positive, mapping the flow of current from positive to negative, and suggesting that lightning was electrical, Franklin had a lasting impact on electrical studies and became America's foremost colonial scientist.

Franklin's invention of the lightning rod led studies of electricity to intersect with seismology. Soon after an earthquake leveled Lisbon and shook Boston in 1755, the Reverend Thomas Prince suggested that it was caused by electricity driven into the ground by lightning rods. Winthrop vociferously disagreed and was the first to point out the wave character of tremors.

That Winthrop and Prince carried on their debate in the press exposes the role of periodicals in the diffusion of scientific ideas. Science was also popularized by itinerant lecturers, such as Isaac Greenwood, Ebenezer Kinnersley, and Archibald Spencer, who offered demonstrations of electrical phenomena from Boston to Savannah in the mid-eighteenth century. The broadened base for science depended on the increased urbanization of colonial society and improved communication offered by better roads, a reliable postal system, more printing presses and periodicals, a proliferation of coffeehouses and inns where people could congregate, and accessible libraries and colleges.

Americans had high regard for higher education, and by 1780 there were eight colleges actively teaching science. Listed in the chronological order of classroom instruction, they were Harvard, Yale, William and Mary, Princeton, King's (later Columbia), the College of Philadelphia (later the University of Pennsylvania), Rhode-Island (later Brown), and Dartmouth. In 1638, Harvard students learned natural philosophy, botany, astronomy, and mathematics. These laid the groundwork for surveying, navigation, mensuration, geography, horology, and later Newtonian philosophy. Fluxions (calculus) made a noteworthy appearance first at Harvard and Yale. Botany was dropped, but reappeared along with zoology and chemistry near the end

of the eighteenth century at colleges that had medical schools (namely Philadelphia, King's, and Harvard).

The most original feature of colonial instruction was not the disciplines taught but the method used. Isaac Greenwood brought the scientific instruments and experiments of London lecturers, such as Jean Desaguliers, back home to Harvard in 1727, and colleges scrambled to acquire globes, sundials, barometers, thermometers, microscopes, telescopes, quadrants, air pumps, electrical machines, and orreries. At the close of the colonial period, students spent 20 to 40 percent of their time on science instruction. The aims of these studies were both utilitarian and philosophical. It was expected that scientific knowledge not only would help students to become productive citizens, but also would teach them how wisely God had designed the universe.

Small scientific communities emerged in the neighborhoods of colleges, and many of their members corresponded with the Royal Society. They were cognizant of the advantages of establishing a scientific society closer to home, and tried to set up institutions that would promote the pursuits of local scientists while reaching out to like-minded individuals at a distance. Increase Mather had endeavored to create a philosophical society in Boston in the 1680s, and John Bartram and Benjamin Franklin drew up a proposal for a society in Philadelphia in 1743, but neither survived for long. Plans for an American Philosophical Society were revived in the late 1760s, and in 1769 it joined forces with the American Society for Promoting and Propagating Useful Knowledge, which had its roots in an informal club that had met since 1750. In 1780, the American Academy of Arts and Sciences was established in Boston. At the close of the colonial era, there were enough men of learning to make the societies effective and a widespread belief that these societies not only did the country honor, but also would encourage scientific activities of use to the community.

The utility of science was widely endorsed and exploited by colonial scholars in order to pry funds from mercantile interests and local governments in support of scientific activities. Expeditions to observe the transits of Venus or catalog new plants were frankly of little commercial value, however. As the break with England loomed larger, colonists wanted to be self-sufficient, and they encouraged research that would improve agriculture and navigation, the processing of raw materials, and the production of textiles and goods that could be used at home or exported abroad. Mercantile interests turned their attention to harbor improvements and work on roads, bridges, and riverways. In this context, it comes as no surprise that astronomers found it impossible to raise funds to erect a permanent observatory. The public suspected that lipservice was being paid to the role of astronomy in improving navigation and commerce. Americans were eager to support physical science in general only if, like the steamboat experiments of the 1780s, it smacked of immediate utility.

And yet, "utility" was a marvelously elastic word, which could be made to encompass many things. For instance, colonial scientists got far by suggesting (and wholeheartedly believing in) the usefulness of science to religion. American Puritans believed that there was a correspondence between the natural and spiritual worlds; the Book of Nature was a divine ledger in which the devout were to decipher God's designs. It was for these reasons that Increase and Cotton Mather championed scientific research as an act of religious devotion. Quakers shared many of the values of Puritans, including an empirical and rational approach to knowledge. Scientific study was deemed a wholesome recreation and was to be encouraged with the expectation that it would benefit the material conditions of life, promote a reverent frame of mind, and reveal God's plan. These attitudes pervaded and shaped scientific enquiries in Massachusetts and Pennsylvania, perhaps even after these colonies ceased to be dominated by Puritans and Quakers, and may be responsible for the accelerated growth of science there. Massachusetts, for example, boasted more colonial fellows of the Royal Society than any other mainland colony, and when it came to organizing, Pennsylvania Quakers and their closest friends were represented disproportionately (with respect to the population as a whole) in the American Society for Promoting and Propagating Useful Knowledge and the American Philosophical Society.

In 1776, the Declaration of Independence was first read publicly from the platform of the crude observatory built by the American Philosophical Society to observe the second transit of Venus, but the outbreak of war on 19 April 1775 had a mixed affect on the promotion of science in the colonies. On the negative side, college study was disrupted. American, British, and French troops were garrisoned at many colleges, and patriotic professors, such as Harvard's John Winthrop, turned their attention to the inspection of powder mills and the production of munitions. Tory faculty vacated their posts. Thomas Jefferson and the new president of William and Mary, the Reverend James Madison, saw this as an opportunity to fortify the science curriculum, but they were sidetracked when the college was converted into a hospital. The activities of learned societies were also disrupted, but this was as much due to political infighting as to British occupation.

On the positive side, war focused attention on the need for American engineers and cartographers. It encouraged military-science projects such as the submarine of David Bushnell. And even though colonial scientists loyal to England emigrated, new ties were forged with French, German, and English scientists who fought on American soil during the war.

In fact, the relation of science to politics was remarkably diverse. On one hand, science became a diplomatic tool. Gifts of seeds and curiosities were presented to foreign nobility whom Americans hoped would be powerful allies, and after the war, Jefferson initiated a plan to offer a Rittenhouse orrery to the king of France in order to honor him for his help. On the other hand, there were extraordinary efforts to keep international scientific cooperation above the conflict. In 1779, Benjamin Franklin urged American ship captains to grant safe passage to Captain James Cook on his last expedition. Harvard College and Greenwich Observatory shared astronomical observations during the war, and professor Samuel Williams was permitted to cross enemy lines in 1780 in order to observe a solar eclipse from Penobscot Bay in Maine.

All in all, scientific creativity was not enhanced by the political turmoil, and was perhaps hindered by the withdrawal of financial support from overseas institutions such as the Royal Society. With the war, American scientists had to make it on their own, but had faith that science would advance the wealth, happiness, and honor of the new nation.

The foregoing summary suggests the principal issues of concern to historians: how the European encounter promoted scientific inquiry in the New World; which scientific fields were emphasized by colonists and what contributions were made in those areas; how scientists communicated, congregated, and organized their activities; what role mathematical practitioners played; how practical and philosophical pursuits intersected; whether regional differences existed; how religion affected scientific inquiry; what financial support existed; whether scientific research was hindered by isolation from Europe; which academies offered science instruction; how learning was diffused to the public; whether science and the

S

state interacted; and how the American Revolution affected scientific activities. All these issues need further analysis.

Historiography of the colonial period is very uneven. More research has been done on natural history than natural philosophy; and much of what has been written is biographical or descriptive, and that in a scattershot manner. Benjamin Franklin, Increase and Cotton Mather, John Banister, Mark Catesby, John Clayton, John Bartram, and Alexander Garden have been the subjects of detailed biographies, but others have been treated only tersely in journals or biographical dictionaries. The descriptive materials do little more than lay out before the reader the results of excavations in the archives or collections of historical institutions; there is more show than tell.

A number of books and essays, however, have tried to survey the development of one or more scientific disciplines or communities, and a few authors have attempted to present their findings within an analytical framework. These authors concur that colonial Americans made modest contributions to science when compared to European contemporaries and agree that isolation and inadequate apparatus were real impediments to early investigations. A central question of this historiography is what drove the colonists to try to overcome these obstacles. Some historians have pointed to the role of the Royal Society and individual foreign scientists in promoting science in America, whereas others have emphasized the importance of religious belief or economic imperatives. Each reason by itself is unsatisfactory. Foreign promotions are better at explaining the collecting activities of naturalists than, say, the dedication of astronomers preparing farmers' almanacs. Religion may have galvanized a Mather or a Bartram, but was not the principal force behind Franklin or Rittenhouse. And the colonial economy, dependent on raw materials being traded overseas, may have encouraged interest in navigation and natural resources, but few aspects of Newtonian natural philosophy and Linnaean natural history can honestly be said to reflect the needs of the mercantile classes. But to say that each historiographic position is inadequate is not to say that it is useless. Quests for prestige, revelation, and wealth remain worthy of consideration as stimuli to research in colonial America.

Major resources for the study of colonial science have barely been tapped. These include the archives and collections of colonial colleges, learned societies, museums, and botanical gardens; colonial periodicals; promotional and travel literature; the correspondence and diaries of individual scholars; the business records of instrument makers; and surviving scientific apparatus.

BIBLIOGRAPHY

Batschelet, Margaret W. *Early American Scientific and Technical Literature: An Annotated Bibliography of Books, Pamphlets, and Broadsides.* Metuchen, NJ: Scarecrow Press, 1990.

Bedini, Silvio A. *Thinkers and Tinkers: Early American Men of Science.* New York: Charles Scribner's Sons, 1975.

Bell, Whitfield J., Jr. *Early American Science: Needs and Opportunities for Study.* Williamsburg, VA: Institute of Early American History and Culture, 1955.

Clarke, Larry R. "The Quaker Background of William Bartram's View of Nature." *Journal of the History of Ideas* 46 (1985): 435–448.

Cohen, I. Bernard. *Some Early Tools of American Science: An Account of the Early Scientific Instruments and Mineralogical and Biological Collections in Harvard University.* Cambridge, MA: Harvard University Press, 1950.

———. *Science and the Founding Fathers: Science in the Political Thought of Thomas Jefferson, Benjamin Franklin, John Adams, and James Madison.* New York: W.W. Norton, 1995.

Davis, Richard Beale, "Science and Technology, Including Agriculture." In *Intellectual Life in the Colonial South, 1585–1763.* Knoxville: University of Tennessee Press, 1978, pp. 801–1112.

Hindle, Brooke. *The Pursuit of Science in Revolutionary America, 1735–1789.* Chapel Hill: The University of North Carolina Press, 1956.

———, ed. *Early American Science.* New York: Science History Publications, 1976.

Hornberger, Theodore. *Scientific Thought in the American Colleges, 1638–1800.* Austin: University of Texas Press, 1945.

Rittenhouse: Journal of the American Scientific Instrument Enterprise.

Schechner Genuth, Sara. "From Heaven's Alarm to Public Appeal: Comets and the Rise of Astronomy at Harvard." In *Science at Harvard University: Historical Perspectives,* edited by Clark A. Elliott and Margaret W. Rossiter. Bethlehem, PA: Lehigh University Press, 1992, pp. 28–54.

Stearns, Raymond Phineas. *Science in the British Colonies of America.* Urbana: University of Illinois Press, 1970.

Struik, D.J. "The Influence of Mercantilism on Colonial Science in America." *Organon* 1 (1964): 157–163.

Wilson, Joan Hoff. "Dancing Dogs of the Colonial Period: Women Scientists." *Early American Literature* 7 (1973): 225–235.

Sara Schechner

Science in the United States from 1789 to 1865

In the decades between the inauguration of George Washington as president of the United States and the death of Abraham Lincoln at the close of the Civil War, American science graduated from the status of a colonial adjunct of European, especially British, science to that of an independent, although still a junior, partner in the Western scientific enterprise. It did so on a regional basis, without either the centralized bureaucratic control and patronage typical on the Continent of Europe or the centralizing influence of a great capital city and the extensive private patronage of an aristocratic society, as in England. For a brief period, it seemed that Philadelphia, with its American Philosophical Society, its School of Medicine of the University of Pennsylvania, its botanical gardens, and its privately owned museum of natural history, might develop into a capital city in the European style, but with the removal of the national capital to Washington, D.C. in 1800 that prospect was eclipsed. Science developed regionally in urban centers as the Philadelphia pattern of institutions was copied with varying success in Boston, New York, Charleston, Cincinnati, Lexington, St. Louis, and New Orleans. Only gradually did the state and national governments begin to subsidize scientific research.

In the absence of substantial government or private patronage, the promotion and prosecution of science fell largely on the shoulders of persons engaged in practical callings, professional or otherwise. Of these, the most prominent and numerous were the medical men, many of whom studied in Edinburgh, London, or on the Continent as well as in Philadelphia, New York, Boston, or Charleston. In these schools, they were exposed not only to anatomy, physiology, and therapeutics but also to materia medica and botany, chemistry and its adjuncts mineralogy and geology, comparative anatomy and its offshoots paleontology and physical anthropology, thus acquiring a range of knowledge and interests from which to develop their own specialties of research and teaching. Samuel Latham Mitchill (New York) ranged over chemistry, natural history, mineralogy, geology, anthropology, and ethnology and published a medical journal, the *Medical Repository*, which served as a sort of general scientific journal until the founding of Benjamin Silliman's *American Journal of Science* in 1818. Benjamin Smith Barton (Philadelphia) embraced nearly as wide a field of inquiry, adding comparative linguistics to his repertoire. Archibald Bruce (New York) concentrated on mineral-ogy, John Torrey (New York) on botany, chemistry, and mineralogy, John Collins Warren (Boston) on physical anthropology and paleontology from the standpoint of comparative anatomy.

Second only to the medical professors among academic scientists were the teachers of undergraduate courses in the sciences. Mathematics and natural philosophy (physics and astronomy) had been the only scientific subjects in the traditional college curriculum, but gradually botany, chemistry, mineralogy, geology, and other subjects usually associated with medical schools began to be offered to undergraduates, especially in the New England colleges. Benjamin Silliman led the way at Yale, Parker Cleaveland at Bowdoin, Benjamin Waterhouse and Aaron Dexter at Harvard, and Silliman's students wherever they went to teach after graduation. Research and publication were not part of the official duties of these professors, but they managed to do much of both, and these activities soon became the best qualifications for good academic appointments.

Among the clergy, too, could be found some devotees of the sciences. Henry Muhlenberg, Manasseh Cutler, and Lewis D. von Schweinitz were botanists of considerable ability. John Bachman of Charleston, South Carolina, was a botanist and zoologist who collaborated with John James Audubon in producing *The Viviparous Quadrupeds of North America* (1846–1854). Jedidiah Morse pioneered in North American geography, Samuel Stanhope Smith in physical anthropology. John Heckewelder and David Zeisberger provided essential information to lawyer Peter S. Duponceau in his study of Indian linguistics.

Completing the roster of what might be called the wheelhorses of American science in the period before the establishment of governmentally supported scientific positions (1830 ff.) were various kinds of practical men without college education but with marked talent and interest in the sciences. David Rittenhouse, instrument maker and surveyor, won election to the Royal Society of London for his work in astronomy and experimental physics. Nathaniel Bowditch, seafarer turned businessman, introduced continental mathematical astronomy into the United States with his translation with extended commentary of Pierre Simon Laplace's *Mécanique céleste*. Charles Willson Peale, portrait painter, built up an invaluable museum of natural history, and William Bartam, gardener and naturalist, made his garden on the Schuylkill River a haven for naturalists like Thomas Nuttall, Alexander Wilson, and Thomas Say.

S

Of gentleman scientists with private means, a breed well known in England—men like Charles Lyell and Charles Darwin—there were only a few in the United States, for example George Gibbs of Newport, Rhode Island, Robert Gilmore Jr. of Baltimore, and Benjamin Vaughan of Brunswick, Maine, in mineralogy and geology and, later in the period, Benjamin Apthorp Gould in astronomy. But there was a fascinating assortment of immigrant naturalists from Europe who came to America to study its climate, soil, natural history, geology, and the like. From their researches sprang such important scientific works as William Maclure's "Observations on the Geology of the United States, Explanatory of a Geological Map" (1809), Frederick Pursh's *Flora Americae Septentrionalis* (1814), Thomas Nuttall's *Genera of North American Plants,* Alexander Wilson's *American Ornithology* (1808–1814), and John James Audubon's *Birds of America* (1827–1838).

The task of bringing together these various kinds of scientific workers for mutual stimulation and for publication of their researches fell largely to societies organized in the leading urban centers. Philadelphia led the way with its American Philosophical Society, followed by its Academy of Natural Sciences (1812) and its Franklin Institute of the State of Pennsylvania (1824). Not to be outdone, Boston responded with the American Academy of Arts and Sciences, the Linnaean Society of New England, and its successor the Boston Society of Natural History. Slower to develop as a scientific center, New York made its bid with its Society for the Promotion of Agriculture, Arts, and Manufactures (reorganized in 1804 as the Society for the Promotion of Useful Arts and absorbed eventually into the Albany Institute), its Literary and Philosophical Society, and its Lyceum of Natural History. Charleston had its Library Society, its Literary and Philosophical Society, and, in the 1850s, its Elliott Society of Natural History. Cincinnati could point to its Western Museum Society, Lexington to its Kentucky Institute, St. Louis and New Orleans to their academies of science.

Of these societies, the most vigorous and productive were those in Philadelphia and Boston. The three in Philadelphia were mutually reinforcing, with overlapping memberships, and two of them, the Academy of Natural Sciences and the Franklin Institute, developed ties with agencies of the federal government as these acquired scientific missions (see below). Both the Philadelphia and the Boston societies, and to some extent the Albany Institute and the Lyceum of Natural

History, reached well beyond their own cities in attracting scientific papers and support. Indeed, they may be said to have held together and sustained the American scientific enterprise until it became organized on a national scale, chiefly after the Civil War.

Constitutional scruples, originating in Thomas Jefferson's narrow view of the powers of Congress, inhibited federal support for science for many years. The military, however, was not subject to these inhibitions, and Jefferson himself inaugurated what was to become a long and brilliant series of exploring expeditions under military command, combining political and scientific purposes, when he persuaded Congress to authorize the Lewis and Clark Expedition to the Pacific Ocean. Other expeditions, accompanied by civilian naturalists, followed in rapid succession—to Colorado, to the Red River and Upper Mississippi Valley, to the Rocky Mountains and California, to the territories acquired from Mexico in 1848, to the regions to be traversed by transcontinental railroads. There were also naval expeditions to the Pacific islands, Chile, Japan, and the North Pacific. Meanwhile, the United States Military Academy at West Point, modeling itself on the École Polytechnique, under the leadership of Sylvanus Thayer and brilliant teachers like Denis Hart Mahan, began turning out scientifically trained engineers whose services were invaluable not only to government-sponsored expeditions but to private enterprises in canal and railroad construction as well.

Political animosities prevented the implementation of President John Quincy Adams's proposal for a national observatory, but Lieutenants Charles Wilkes and James Gilliss of the United States Navy developed a small observatory, sub rosa, in the Depot of Charts and Instruments in support of the United States Exploring Expedition, 1838–1842. Congress eventually recognized the fait accompli and authorized the United States Naval Observatory, which concentrated its energies on the study of oceanography under Commander Matthew Fontaine Maury (author in 1855 of *The Physical Geography of the Sea*) while continuing the astronomical observations underlying the publication in 1849 of *The American Ephemeris and Nautical Almanac.*

Meanwhile, the United States Coast Survey, authorized by Congress during Jefferson's presidency and resuscitated under the able leadership of Ferdinand Hassler in 1833, entered on a period of rapid expansion when Alexander Dallas Bache succeeded Hassler in 1843. Under Bache's guidance the survey not only continued its geodetic and hydrographic work on the ever expanding coasts of the United States but also provided support for work in terrestrial magnetism, meteorology, topography, oceanography, astronomy, and the development of standard weights and measures. The Harvard mathematician Benjamin Peirce, the geophysicist William Ferrel, and the astronomers Benjamin A. Gould, Maria Mitchell, Sears Walker, Charles Henry Davis, John D. Runkle were all on the payroll of the Coast Survey at one time or another.

In these same years, federal support for science took another important step forward with the founding in 1846 of the Smithsonian Institution. James Smithson's bequest of a half million dollars to the United States government to establish an institution for the increase and diffusion of knowledge eventuated, after much congressional wrangling, in an establishment which its first secretary, the physicist Joseph Henry, resolved to dedicate to scientific research as well as to the other purposes—a library, a museum, and an art gallery—specified by Congress. Under the leadership of Henry and his energetic assistant Spencer Baird, the Smithsonian became a clearinghouse and publication center for the specimens collected on the numerous government exploring expeditions and written up for the scientific world by leading American scientists. The *Smithsonian Contributions to Knowledge,* launched in 1848 with the publication of *The Aboriginal Monuments of the Mississippi Valley,* a pioneering work by the Ohio archaeologists Ephraim George Squier and Edwin H. Davis, went on to include monographs by Asa Gray, Joseph Leidy, Jeffries Wyman, Sears Walker, Louis Agassiz, John Torrey, Wolcott Gibbs, and other stalwarts of American science. The *Miscellaneous Collections* contained natural history, physical tables, reports on the progress of science, and the like. The *Annual Report* included not only a survey of the institution's activities but translations of important scientific papers and addresses abroad. Henry also organized a national system of weather reporting in collaboration with the surgeon general's office, the regents of the University of the State of New York (with whom Henry had worked during his years in Albany), and the meteorologists associated with the American Philosophical Society and the Franklin Institute.

While the federal government moved gradually toward supporting scientific research, the state governments did likewise, primarily by supporting geological and natural history surveys. North Carolina led the

way in 1823 with a small grant to Denison Olmsted, a Silliman student. The Massachusetts survey, undertaken in 1830 by Edward Hitchcock, was a much more extensive survey, combining economic geology with "scientific geology" but relying too heavily on Abraham Gottlob Werner's classification of strata. More important in the long run was the New York Geological and Natural History Survey, begun in 1836. It served as a training ground for geologists like James Hall, Ebenezer Emmons, and Eben Horsford, all of whom had studied geology under Amos Eaton at the Rensselaer School in Troy. Other members of the survey, like Lardner Vanuxem and Timothy Conrad, had already gained experience in Pennsylvania and New Jersey.

Thanks to the splendid exposures of Cambrian, Silurian, and Devonian rocks in the Genesee Valley and the publications of the chief paleontologist James Hall, the New York survey soon achieved international prominence. Charles Lyell and other European geologists came to see the spectacular exposures and the invaluable collection of fossils at the State Museum in Albany, and Hall emerged as a leading invertebrate paleontologist and champion of the theory of geosynclines in relation to mountain building. The combined work of Hall, Conrad, and Vanuxem enabled the European geologists Edouard de Verneuil and J.J. Bigsby to correlate the New York system, as Hall had named it, with parallel formations in Europe. Meanwhile, Hall was making Albany a clearinghouse for the geology of the regions beyond the Appalachian Mountains. He surveyed the Lake Superior District for the federal government and collaborated with David Dale Owen in Indiana, with Fielding B. Meek and Ferdinand B. Hayden in the Nebraska Territory, with Josiah Whitney in Iowa, with Whitney and others in Wisconsin, and with Sir William Logan on the geology of Canada.

Second only to the New York survey was the Pennsylvania survey (1836 ff.), the groundwork for which had been laid by the researches in the middle states of Lardner Vanuxem, Timothy Conrad, Isaac Lea, Samuel G. Morton, and other members of the Academy of Natural Sciences of Philadelphia and by Henry Darwin Rogers's work on the New Jersey survey the year before he took charge of the Pennsylvania survey. In the ensuing years, Rogers and his brother William Barton Rogers, director of the Virginia survey, worked out the structure of the Appalachian Mountains and developed a theory of their formation by combined undulatory and tangential movements of the earth's crust. Presented before the

S

American and British associations for the advancement of science in 1842, it led George P. Merrill, historian of American geology, to describe H.D. Rogers as "the leading structural geologist of his time" (Merrill, p. 168).

Through the state geological surveys, a cadre of professional geologists took shape. In 1840, under the leadership of Edward Hitchcock and Henry Darwin Rogers, they were organized into the American Association of Geologists, which by 1848 had evolved into the American Association for the Advancement of Science, modeled on the British Association.

The colleges, too, played an important role in the development of American science through their medical faculties and their faculties of arts and sciences and in conjunction with local scientific societies. There was little purely medical research in the United States in this period, with the exception of William Gerhard's work distinguishing typhoid and typhus (1837), Oliver Wendell Holmes's study of puerpal fever, and William Beaumont's contribution to the physiology of digestion (1833). But medical men were active researchers in other fields of science. At the University of Pennsylvania the medical faculty gained distinction in such varied fields as natural history, paleontology, and physical anthropology. Beginning with Dr. Caspar Wistar's collaboration with Thomas Jefferson on the bones of megalonyx and other extinct animals, a series of professors of anatomy—Richard Harlan, Isaac Hays, Samuel G. Morton, and Joseph Leidy—worked through the Academy of Natural Sciences and the American Philosophical Society to make Philadelphia the leading center of vertebrate paleontology in the United States. Morton was best known, however, for his impressive collection of human crania, described in his *Crania Americana* (1839). In chemistry and natural philosophy, Robert Hare, although not a physician himself, trained a generation of medical students, including the future scientists John W. Draper and Oliver Wolcott, using scientific instruments—the oxyhydrogen blowpipe, the calorimotor, the deflagrator, and the electric furnace—which he had invented himself. He also published copiously in the *American Journal of Science.*

Other medical schools followed the lead of the University of Pennsylvania. At New York University, John W. Draper conducted important researches on the photochemical effects of radiant energy, showing that only absorbed rays can produce chemical change (Grotthuss-Draper law) and that given chemical effects are associated with rays of certain wavelengths. He discovered photochemical induction and constructed an instrument for measuring the intensity of light, foreshadowing the development of photometry. He photographed the spectrum, including the infrared regions, and the spectra of incandescent solids, and showed the coincidence of maximum luminosity and maximum heat. Applying photography to science, he experimented with photographs of the moon, spectrographs, photomicrographs, and techniques for enlarging and multiplying.

At Harvard University, Dr. John Collins Warren published the first American book on physical anthropology (1822) and a study of the mastodon, although he became famous primarily for performing the first operation under anesthesia. His colleague Jeffries Wyman published the first scientific description of the gorilla (1847). In South Carolina, the scientific interests of the faculty of the Medical College found outlet in the pages of the *Charleston Medical Journal and Review* and in treatises such as John E. Holbrook's outstanding *North American Herpetology* (1842).

Among the faculties of arts and sciences, the New England colleges led the way in scientific research and teaching. At Yale, Benjamin Silliman introduced chemistry, geology, and mineralogy into the undergraduate curriculum and trained a good many students, including Edward Hitchcock, Amos Eaton, Charles U. Shepard, Denison Olmsted, George F. Bowen, and Oliver Payson Hubbard, who went out to teach in other colleges, conduct geological surveys, and pursue their own researches. Two of Silliman's students, James Dwight Dana and Silliman's son Benjamin, eventually took over the editorship of the *American Journal of Science* and succeeded him at Yale as professors of the subjects he had taught. Silliman also gave public lectures on chemistry and geology throughout the United States, from Boston southward to New York, Baltimore, and Mobile and westward to St. Louis, stimulating a public taste for scientific lectures and enjoying great success wherever he went. He also took the lead in organizing the American Geological Society (1819–1828).

At Harvard College, the science faculty began its rise to prominence in the 1830s and 1840s with the appointment of Benjamin Peirce in mathematics and natural philosophy, William Bond in astronomy, and Asa Gray and Louis Agassiz in botany and zoology-paleontology. Peirce, who had aided Nathaniel Bowditch in his monumental translation with commentary of Laplace's *Mécanique céleste,* established his own reputation in celestial mechanics with his *System of Analytic Mechanics* (1855) and in mathematics with his pioneering work *Linear Associative Algebra* (1870). William Bond and his son George, provided with an endowed chair and a first-rate refracting telescope through the generosity of Boston businessmen and Harvard alumni, soon made the Harvard College Observatory an institution of international importance with their photographs and drawings of nebulae, stars, and comets, including the nebula of Orion and the great comet of Donati (1858), which latter memoir gained George Bond the gold medal of the Royal Astronomical Society. Through the joint activities of the observatory, the Cambridge Astronomical Society, the Boston office of the United States Navy's *American Ephemeris and Nautical Almanac,* the Cambridge office of the Coast Survey, and Benjamin Apthorp Gould's privately funded *Astronomical Journal,* the Cambridge-Boston area became a leading center of astronomical research.

Meanwhile, Asa Gray and Louis Agassiz were doing for natural history what Peirce and the Bonds were accomplishing in mathematics and astronomy. Gray could not match Agassiz's dramatic talents as a teacher and public lecturer, but he did inspire his best students and set out to make the botanical garden at Harvard a focus for North American botany rivaling that which John Torrey had established in New York City. Through his network of correspondents in the south and west, relying especially on Dr. George Engelmann in St. Louis to stimulate and help provision botanical explorers, Gray procured an ever increasing flow of plant specimens which he used for exchanges with European botanists and wrote up for publication by the American Academy of Arts and Sciences or the Boston Society of Natural History. His *Manual of the Botany of the United States* (1848) displayed such a command of that subject that Charles Darwin wrote to him to enlist his aid in comparing the plants of the world and, in 1857, disclosed to Gray his revolutionary theory of evolution by natural selection.

Unlike Gray, Louis Agassiz was a master teacher and lecturer, acquainted with the leaders of European science and capable of winning the hearts and loosening the purse strings of the Boston elite. Within a few years of his appointment as professor of zoology and geology at Harvard's newly established Lawrence Scientific School, he had filled the school buildings, including Engineering Hall, with his specimens, had raised the funds for constructing and staffing a museum of comparative zoology worthy of comparison with European institutions, had introduced European standards of research, had organized a nationwide network of ichthyological enthusiasts for collecting fish specimens, had joined Alexander Dallas Bache and other leaders of American science in pushing for the creation of a National Academy of Sciences, and had laid the groundwork for a multivolume work, *Contributions to the Natural History of the United States.* The first volume, containing Agassiz's major theoretical manifesto entitled "Essay on Classification," appeared in 1857, the year in which Charles Darwin confided to Asa Gray the evolutionary ideas which were to overthrow Agassiz's blend of Cuvierian creationism and German Naturphilosophie and precipitate Agassiz's dogged defense of a position which even his students soon abandoned.

Elsewhere in New England, the various colleges did their best to emulate the examples set by Yale and Harvard. Benjamin Silliman's students introduced his ideas and methods at Amherst, Williams, Dartmouth, and Brown, and Edward Hitchcock, who came under Silliman's tutelage while studying for the ministry at Yale, gained national and international attention for his work on the geological survey of Massachusetts, his studies of the river terraces of the Connecticut River Valley, and his pioneering papers on the mysterious "bird tracks" of that valley, which were later identified as dinosaur tracks by the English paleontologist Richard Owen. At Bowdoin College, Parker Cleaveland introduced chemistry, geology, and mineralogy and brought together the mineral localities of numerous American mineralogists in his *Elementary Treatise on Mineralogy and Geology* (1816 and 1822), a worthy forerunner of James Dwight Dana's *System of Mineralogy* (1837).

Throughout the nation, a college teaching position was often the best means of support for an aspiring scientist. Joseph Henry conducted the researches that led to his discovery of electromagnetic induction in an empty classroom during the one-month summer vacations at the Albany Academy. This great discovery, anticipating a similar one by Michael Faraday several months later, earned Henry an appointment at Princeton College (1832). There, he soon made contact with Alexander Dallas Bache and other Philadelphia scientists at the American Philosophical Society and the Franklin Institute and found avenues of publication for the important experiments he conducted at Princeton. These led him to the discovery of self-induction, noninductive windings, the electromagnetic relay, the principle of the

S

transformer, and the propagation throughout space of wavelike discharges from the Leyden jar—an experimental finding which eventually attained theoretical interpretation in the work of Lord Kelvin, James Clerk Maxwell, and Heinrich Hertz. At the same time, Henry was able to resume his meteorological researches, begun at Albany, in conjunction with James Espy and Elias Loomis at the Franklin Institute.

Americans made original theoretical contributions in the period before the Civil War. In two papers published in the *American Journal of Science* in 1831 and 1833, William C. Redfield, a self-taught engineer from Middletown, Connecticut, expounded a theory of hurricanes and other cyclonic storms as blowing counterclockwise around a center advancing in the direction of the prevailing winds. In 1836 and again in 1841, in his *Philosophy of Storms,* James Espy, working at the Franklin Institute, developed a rival theory to the effect that storm winds blew from all points of the compass toward a central space of lowest pressure, and Espy presented a thermodynamic mechanism for the upward movement of the air in the storm center and the precipitation resulting from its consequent expansion and cooling. The rival theories were presented abroad, British scientists leaning toward Redfield's theory and the French toward Espy's. Meanwhile, Elias Loomis, alternating teaching positions at Yale, Western Reserve College, and New York University, set out to gather data designed to test these two theories. In 1843, in a paper read before the American Philosophical Society, Loomis used a method of presenting the data by drawing lines of equal deviation from the normal average pressure for each locality, which soon became the standard method of graphic illustration in meteorology. Then, in 1856, William Ferrel, a self-taught genius who had managed to get hold of copies of Newton's *Principia Mathematica* and Nathaniel Bowditch's translation of Laplace's *Mécanique céleste* while teaching in Liberty, Missouri, published in Dr. William Bowling's *Nashville Journal of Medicine and Surgery* his "Essay on the Winds and Currents of the Ocean," correcting Matthew Fontaine Maury's ideas on this subject and showing the deflection of these winds and currents by the earth's rotation, thus mediating between the theories of Redfield and Espy. By 1856, Ferrel was invited to join the staff of the *American Ephemeris and Nautical Almanac* in Boston, where he worked out a quantitative version of his theory in an essay "The Motions of Fluids and Solids Relative to the Earth's Surface"

(1859), which remained standard in geophysical fluid dynamics for a century and won him inclusion in the charter membership of the National Academy of Sciences.

Through the energetic efforts of Alexander Dallas Bache and Joseph Henry, geophysical researches found support at the Coast Survey and the Smithsonian Institution. Bache himself achieved international recognition for his researches on terrestrial magnetism, begun in 1840 at the Girard College Observatory in Philadelphia, supported by the War Department, 1843–1845, extended to Key West under the Coast Survey, and published in several volumes of the *Smithsonian Contributions to Knowledge* as well as in the *Proceedings* of the American Association for the Advancement of Science and in the *American Journal of Science.* Of the work of the Coast Survey generally—geodetic, hydrographic, geomagnetic, oceanographic—the president of the Royal Geographic Society, Sir Roderick Murchison, said: "I have studied the question closely, and do not hesitate to pronounce the conviction, that though the Americans were last in the field, they have leaped into the very first rank" (quoted in Merle M. Odgers, *Alexander Dallas Bache: Scientist and Educator, 1806–1867* [Philadelphia: University of Pennsylvania Press, 1947], p. 152).

By the seventh decade of the nineteenth century, American science was nearly ready to enter into full partnership in the Western scientific enterprise. Governments, both federal and state, were increasingly aware of the importance of scientific research for agriculture, public health, and economic development. The scientists themselves were organized and increasingly professionalized, and the newly established National Academy of Sciences provided a means of recognizing scientific achievement and making expert scientific advice available to the national government. At Harvard, Yale, and the University of Pennsylvania, graduate programs had been established, although not fully developed. The founding of the Massachusetts Institute of Technology in 1861–1862, the evolution of the Rensselaer School into the Rensselaer Polytechnic Institute, and the passage of the Morrill Act (1862) providing for agricultural experiment stations and for land-grant colleges of agriculture and mechanic arts pointed the way toward linking science to the practical arts. Americans still looked to Europe for theoretical innovation and leadership—there was as yet no American scientist of the stature of Charles Lyell, Charles Darwin, James Clerk Maxwell, or Claude

Bernard—but American contributions in a few fields, notably astronomy, geology, natural history, and the geophysical sciences, commanded international respect. The Civil War put the development of science on hold for a few years, but the resulting triumph of nationalism and industrialism unloosed forces that were soon to revolutionize American industry, American education, and American science.

BIBLIOGRAPHY

American Association for the Advancement of Science. *Proceedings* 1–3 (1849).

Bruce, Robert V. *The Launching of Modern American Science 1846–1876.* New York: Knopf, 1987.

Daniels, George H. *American Science in the Age of Jackson.* New York and London: Columbia University Press, 1968.

———. ed. *Nineteenth-Century American Science. A Reappraisal.* Evanston, IL: Northwestern University Press, 1972.

Dupree, A. Hunter. *Science in the Federal Government. A History of Policies and Activities to 1940.* Cambridge, MA: Harvard University Press, 1957.

Ewan, Joseph, ed. *A Short History of Botany in the United States.* New York and London: Hafner, 1969.

Goode, George Brown. *The Origins of Natural Science in America.* Edited by Sally Gregory Kohlstedt. Washington, DC: Smithsonian Institution Press, 1991.

Greene, John C. *American Science in the Age of Jefferson.* Ames: Iowa State University Press, 1984.

Kohlstedt, Sally Gregory. *The Formation of the American Scientific Community: The American Association for the Advancement of Science 1848–1860.* Urbana: University of Illinois Press, 1976.

Merrill, George P. *The First One Hundred Years of American Geology.* New York: Hafner, 1964.

Oleson, Alexandra, and Sanborn C. Brown, eds. *The Pursuit of Knowledge in the Early Republic. American Scientific and Learned Societies from Colonial Times to the Civil War.* Baltimore: Johns Hopkins University Press, 1976.

Reingold, Nathan, ed. *Science in America since 1820.* New York: Science History Publications, 1976.

———. *Science in Nineteenth-Century America. A Documentary History.* New York: Hill and Wang, 1964.

Sinclair, Bruce. *Philadelphia's Philosopher Mechanics. A History of the Franklin Institute 1824–1865.* Baltimore: Johns Hopkins University Press, 1974.

John C. Greene

Scientific American

Magazine of science and technology. Founded in 1845, *Scientific American* quickly came under the control of Orson D. Munn, a patent attorney. Weekly until 1921, and monthly thereafter, the illustrated magazine published news about inventions and technology. In 1947, the Munn family sold the magazine to new editors, who put the name on a new magazine that published in-depth articles written by scientists and directed toward "the intelligent layman." The new *Scientific American* was one of the major success stories of postwar publishing, and continues serving the technical elite today, with a circulation of about 750,000.

For its first 103 years, *Scientific American* was published for the mechanics and artisans of the second industrial revolution. Patronized by eminent inventors, it addressed both individual craftsmen and the growing industrial research and development community. Its weekly publication schedule gave it authority as a source of news and information. After 1921, however, the magazine lost focus; by the end of World War II, its circulation had dropped from 100,000 to less than 50,000.

At that time, science journalist Gerard Piel and his colleagues bought the magazine's assets, to jump-start their own new magazine for the technological elite. The new *Scientific American* (first issued in 1948) quickly became a fixture of the postwar scientific community, directing itself to "the scientific professional who is a layman in departments outside his own" (*Scientific American,* December 1947, p. 244). Leaders of the scientific establishment flocked to the magazine, both as readers and as contributors of articles that popularized the major scientific ideas of the time. Although the magazine suffered some financial woes in the 1970s and 1980s, it entered the 1990s in strong editorial and financial position.

Scientific American is used frequently by historians as a primary source, but little analytical work has been done on its role in the history of American science and technology, either before or after 1948.

BIBLIOGRAPHY

Borut, Michael. "The Scientific American in Nineteenth Century America." Ph.D. diss., Columbia University, 1977.

Burnham, John. *How Superstition Won and Science Lost: Popularizing Science and Health in the United States.* New Brunswick: Rutgers University Press, 1987.

Ford, James L.C. *Magazines for Millions: The Story of Specialized Publications.* Carbondale: Southern Illinois University Press, 1969.

Lewenstein, Bruce V. "Magazine Publishing and Popular Science After World War II." *American Journalism* 6 (1989): 218–234.

S

Peterson, Theodore. *Magazines in the Twentieth Century.* 2d ed. Urbana: University of Illinois Press, 1964.

Bruce V. Lewenstein

Scientists and Engineers for Social and Political Action

See Science for the People

Scopes Trial

Instigated in 1925 by the American Civil Liberties Union (ACLU) to challenge a new Tennessee statute outlawing the teaching of human evolution in public schools. The statute represented the first major victory for a intense national campaign against Darwinian evolution launched by Protestant fundamentalists following World War I. Their effort gained momentum during the early 1920s when popular Democratic politician William Jennings Bryan lent his influential voice to the cause. After the statute passed, the ACLU invited teachers to challenge it. Dayton science teacher John Scopes accepted this invitation at the urging of publicity-minded community leaders. Famed litigator Clarence Darrow led a team of prominent attorneys and scientists in defense of Scopes and the broader right to teach evolution, while Bryan joined the prosecution in supporting the state's right to restrict the content of public instruction.

The confrontation produced a show trial that captured the nation's attention. Although widely hailed as a battle royal between science and religion, no clear winner emerged. Despite Scopes's eventual acquittal on a technicality, the statute was upheld and similar restrictions were imposed in other southern states. Publishers responded by deemphasizing evolution in many high school biology textbooks. Protestant fundamentalism was widely ridiculed for its quixotic opposition to modern science, however. Public attacks by fundamentalists against evolution and science largely disappeared for a generation, as did organized political activity by conservative religious groups.

By the time antievolution statutes were overturned in the 1960s, the Scopes trial had entered the nation's folklore as an American equivalent of Galileo's persecution. Later religious opponents of Darwinian evolution distanced themselves from the Scopes legend by stressing the allegedly scientific basis for their theories of creation or design and by promoting the inclusion of their views in the classroom rather than the exclusion of evolution. For supporters of evolutionary teaching, the Scopes trial remained an object lesson in the danger to science posed by popular religion.

BIBLIOGRAPHY

Ginger, Ray. *Six Days or Forever? Tennessee v. John Thomas Scopes.* Boston: Beacon, 1958.

Larson, Edward J. *Trial and Error: The American Controversy Over Creation and Evolution.* New York: Oxford University Press, 1989.

———. *Summer for the Gods: The Scopes Trial and America's Continuing Debate over Science and Religion.* New York: Basic Books, 1997.

Levine, Lawrence W. *Defender of the Faith: William Jennings Bryan, The Last Decade.* New York: Oxford University Press, 1965.

Marsden, George M. *Fundamentalism and American Culture: The Shaping of Twentieth-Century Evangelicalism, 1879–1925.* New York: Oxford University Press, 1980.

Numbers, Ronald L. *The Creationists: The Evolution of Scientific Creationism.* New York: Knopf, 1992.

The World's Most Famous Court Trial: State of Tennessee v. John Thomas Scopes. 1925. Reprint, New York: Da Capo, 1971 [trial transcript].

Edward J. Larson

Scripps Institution of Oceanography

The Scripps Institution grew out of a series of summer seaside marine biological investigations conducted along the California coast by University of California zoologist William Ritter (1856–1944) beginning in 1892. In 1903, Ritter, newspaper magnate E.W. Scripps, his sister Ellen Browning Scripps, and a group of San Diego business and civic leaders formed the Marine Biological Association of San Diego (MBASD) to establish and endow a permanent marine station. The purpose of the station was to conduct a biological and hydrographic survey of the Pacific Ocean adjacent to southern California and to maintain a public aquarium and museum. In 1907, the MBASD purchased land in La Jolla, and built a laboratory and other facilities with funds provided by the Scrippses.

Informally associated with the University of California from its inception, the MBASD transferred its property to the university in 1912. The institution received university and state funding which approximately matched the annual Scripps donations. This income was supplemented by small research grants from industry and, during World War I, from the federal government.

The institution was renamed the Scripps Institution for Biological Research of the University of California in 1912 and became the Scripps Institution of Oceanography (SIO) in 1925. These name changes reflect changes in the research program from marine biology, to biology, to oceanography. While offering graduate instruction, SIO was primarily a research institution that emphasized marine ecological studies, in contrast to the emphasis on teaching, phylogeny, and morphology at the Marine Biological Laboratory at Woods Hole.

Harald Ulrik Sverdrup (1888–1957), Norwegian oceanographer and polar explorer, transformed SIO from a nationally known marine station to an oceanographic institution with an international reputation during his tenure as its third director, 1936–1948. Scripps scientists, funded by the National Defense Research Committee (NDRC) and the United States Navy, conducted research on underwater sound, meteorology, and other topics of vital interest to the federal government during World War II. Much of this work was done at the University of California Division of War Research (UCDWR), a San Diego laboratory established with NDRC funds in 1941. The Normandy and other allied amphibious landing forecasts were based on sea, swell, and surf forecasting methods developed at Scripps by Harald Sverdrup and Walter Munk, and Scripps research on underwater acoustics aided submarine detection and concealment.

Roger Revelle (1909–1991) led SIO during a postwar period of intensive growth. While director of Scripps, 1951–1964, Revelle convinced the federal government to increase support of oceanographic research, including ships provided by the navy, and research contracts provided by federal agencies. The Marine Physical Laboratory (MPL) was created in 1946 to continue research conducted by the UCDWR which was closed at the end of the war. MPL became part of the Scripps Institution in 1948. California and its fisheries industry provided funds in 1948 for a comprehensive study of conditions leading to the depletion of the sardine in California waters. The study was known as CalCOFI (California Cooperative Oceanic Fisheries Investigations) and contributed fundamentally to knowledge of world fisheries and physical oceanography of the Pacific. Studies of the marine environment conducted by Scripps scientists before and after Pacific atomic tests of the 1950s contributed

significantly to the scientific understanding of the biological effects of atomic radiation.

Scripps participation in the International Geophysical Year led to the first continuous measurements of atmospheric carbon dioxide, started by Charles Keeling in 1957. Revelle and other Scripps scientists were among the geophysicists who promoted the ill-fated Project Mohole, and its successful progeny, the Deep Sea Drilling Project was operated at Scripps from 1966 to 1986. While the research program of the institution continued to be focused on oceanography, areas of study were expanded during the postwar decades to include marine and coastal geology, physiology, climate research, geophysics. Revelle headed a successful effort to create a new University of California campus, and in 1959, Scripps became part of the University of California, San Diego (UCSD). During the 1990s, the institution initiated a program of global change research. The instruction program was expanded to include upper division undergraduates in 1992.

BIBLIOGRAPHY

Menard, Henry W. *Anatomy of an Expedition.* New York: McGraw-Hill, 1969.

Raitt, Helen, and Beatrice Moulton. *Scripps Institution of Oceanography: First Fifty Years.* San Diego, CA: Ward Ritchie Press, 1967.

Revelle, Roger. "The Age of Innocence and War in Oceanography." *Oceans* 1 (1969): 6–16.

———. "How I became an Oceanographer and Other Sea Stories." *Annual Review of Earth and Planetary Sciences* 15 (1987): 1–23.

Ritter, William. "The Marine Biological Station of San Diego: Its History, Present Conditions, Achievements and Aims." *University of California Publications in Zoology* 9 (9 March 1912): 137–248.

Shor, Elizabeth N. *Scripps Institution of Oceanography: Probing the Oceans 1936 to 1976.* San Diego: Tofua Press, 1978.

Deborah C. Day

Secret and Classified Research

Secret research has gone on in science since its origins. The formula for Greek fire, one of the most famous ancient products of secret research, remains unknown. Alchemists' search for an elixir of life and the philosopher's stone was conducted in secrecy so formidable as to be impenetrable to scholars even today. Military and proprietary interest remain the principal reasons for

S

classified and secret research today. Although the complexity of security systems have increased with increasing technology, the object—to deny to one's competitors the fruits of one's inquiries—is the same. World War I saw the organization of formal channels whereby science and technology could be conducted secretly. The National Research Council of the National Academy of Sciences, the Naval Consulting Board, and the Chemical Warfare Service made generous use of academic scientists and engineers. From this work grew the National Advisory Committee on Aeronautics and a number of military laboratories, including the Naval Research Laboratory, which carried on secret research. The expansion of industrial research after the war increased the proportion of secret research carried on by the nation's scientists far more than the creation of government laboratories, simply because many more scientists were involved. Although both government and industrial scientists did publish portions of their research, proprietary considerations meant that until patented, major applications were kept secret. Secrecy engulfed nuclear physics when the cavity magnetron and fission were discovered at the onset of World War II. Although self-imposed by Leo Szilard (who had patented the concept of a chain reaction in 1933), the secrecy shrouding research in nuclear physics as well as in radar was enforced by the National Defense Research Committee and the Office of Scientific Research and Development after the war began. Security background checks were required of contractors to the OSRD, and the Espionage Act was required reading. Army and navy classifications of confidential, secret, and top secret were applied to their work. These security regulations were relaxed to allow for the crucial scientific interchanges with the British that led to the expansions of efforts in radar and nuclear physics during the war. Although this greatly advanced research in both fields, it also led to the most serious breaches of security, for example, the treachery of Klaus Fuchs, who was admitted to Los Alamos as part of the British Mission. This fed the postwar debate about the nature of secrecy and security, in which scientists held that secrecy, by retarding research, also impacted security, while their patrons in the military and the Atomic Energy Commission sought to preserve the "secrets" of military technology as a means to staying ahead of the nation's adversaries. In the postwar era, the development of national laboratories by the commission and the Department of Defense increased secret research exponentially. A substantial fraction of

America's scientists and engineers became involved in defense-related research, augmenting the growth of proprietary research in industry. Consequently, it became necessary to establish the rudiments of a scientific community in many fields, for example, nuclear weapons development and military laser research, where classified meetings and even classified journals became common. Concern about the proliferation of nuclear weapons and the loss of trade secrets to industrial competitors continues to fuel secrecy in advanced industrial nations. This secret scientific community has only recently begun to divulge itself to historians through efforts to permit them access to classified materials for the purpose of writing history. Efforts within the Department of Defense and the Department of Energy to prepare histories of classified work, some of which is of high quality, affords a glimpse into the substantial effort carried on in government-owned, contractor-operated laboratories.

BIBLIOGRAPHY

Baxter, James Phinney. *Scientists Against Time.* Cambridge, MA: MIT Press, 1968.

Forman, Paul. "Behind Quantum Electronics: National Security as Basis for Physical Research in the United States, 1940–1960." *Historical Studies in the Physical and Biological Sciences* 18, pt. 1 (1987): 149–229.

Hackman, Willem D. "Sonar Research and Naval Warfare 1914–1954: A Case Study of a Twentieth Century Science." *Historical Studies in the Physical and Biological Sciences* 16, pt. 1 (1986): 83–110.

Hewlett, Richard, and Oscar E. Anderson Jr. *The New World, 1939/1946.* Vol. 1 of *A History of the United States Atomic Energy Commission.* Berkeley: University of California Press, 1990.

Hewlett, Richard, and Francis Duncan. *Nuclear Navy 1945–1962.* Chicago: University of Chicago Press, 1974.

———. *Atomic Shield.* Vol. 2 of *A History of the United States Atomic Energy Commission.* Berkeley: University of California Press, 1990.

Hewlett, Richard, and Jack M. Holl, *Atoms for Peace and War 1953–1961: Eisenhower and the Atomic Energy Commission.* Berkeley: University of California Press, 1989.

Kevles, Daniel J. *The Physicists: The History of a Scientific Community in Modern America.* New York: Knopf, 1978.

Seidel, Robert. "From Glow to Flow: A History of Military Laser R&D." *Historical Studies in the Physical and Biological Sciences* 18, pt. 1 (1987): 111–148.

———. "Clio and the Complex: Recent Historiography of Science and National Security." *Proceedings of the American Philosophical Society* 134 (1990): 420–441.

Shils, Edward A. *The Torment of Secrecy: The Background and Consequences of American Security Policies.* Glencoe, IL: Free Press, 1956.

Robert W. Seidel

Seismological Society of America

Organized in 1906 on the initiative of Alexander McAdie of the United States Weather Bureau at San Francisco, California. It was incorporated in 1910 to promote seismological research, promote public safety, interest practioners in earthquake-resistant building, and educate the public on how to minimize earthquake hazards. Four directors are elected annually from the membership, which numbered 2,025 in 1999. The directors elect a president, a vice president, a secretary, and a treasurer, and appoint the editors of its bimonthly publications, *Bulletin of the Seismological Society of America* and *Seismological Research Letters.* Two annual meetings are held, one usually in the western United States and the other east of the Rocky Mountains, the latter organized by the Eastern Section of the society, which is semi-independent having its own officers (chairman, vice chairman, secretary, and treasurer). The society is managed by an executive committee consisting of the secretary, the president, and a third member, usually the vice president. The western annual meeting is often held with another society such as the American Association for the Advancement of Science (until 1931) or the Geological Society of America (since 1933).

The first president was George Davidson, professor of geography, and the first secretary was George D. Louderbach, professor of geology, both at the University of California, Berkeley. The secretary and treasurer usually serve for as long as they are willing. Sidney D. Townley served as secretary and treasurer from 1910 to 1929, and Perry Byerly as secretary from 1930 to 1956.

The society has sponsored various projects at different times: mapping a row of monuments along the San Andreas Fault in the society's early years, publishing a fault map of California in 1923, and distributing computer programs developed by the International Association of Seismology and Physics of the Earth's Interior in recent years.

BIBLIOGRAPHY

Byerly, Perry. "History of the Seismological Society of America." *Bulletin of the Seismological Society of America* 54 (1964): 1723–1741.

Minutes of the meetings of the Board of Directors of the Seismological Society of America, published annually in the *Bulletin of the Seismological Society of America,* and (since 1994) in *Seismological Research Letters.*

B.F. Howell Jr.

Seismology

The study of earthquakes and other ground vibrations. The history of the study of earthquakes can be divided into four periods: mythology until 1755; descriptive until 1890; timed measurements until 1960; and computerized since then.

Until about 1755, earthquakes were generally considered to be "acts of God" imposed in retribution for sin. After the Lisbon, Portugal, earthquake of 1755, earthquakes were studied as natural phenomena. Detailed studies were made of their effects, and the first maps drawn showing where earthquakes occur. Intensity scales were proposed based on damage and how widely each event was observed.

Toward the end of the nineteenth century, seismometers were developed to record the ground movements during an earthquake. The 1906 San Francisco, California earthquake was the first large United States earthquake to be widely recorded. It greatly stimulated seismology in America. A committee chaired by Andrew C. Lawson (1908) reported on the effects of the earthquake and included a paper by Harry Fielding Reid proposing the elastic rebound theory. This is still the basic theory of how earthquakes occur. Seismology shifted its emphasis to recognizing types of waves (compressional, shear, and a variety of surface waves), and timing their arrivals at different locations. From these times, the velocity structure of the earth was calculated, and the earth divided into layers: a solid crust with sound velocities below eight kilometers per second, a mantle with higher velocities, and a two-layered core, the outer part of which did not transmit shear waves, so was assumed to be liquid. Leading early investigators in the United States included James B. Macelwane at St. Louis University, Perry Byerly at the University of California, Berkeley, and Beno Gutenberg and Charles F. Richter at the California Institute of Technology.

Around 1960, three developments revolutionized seismology. The first was the development of digital computers, which made possible treatment of previously intractable problems, such as the computation of

S

dispersion curves. The second was the increased support of research by the United States government in hopes (ultimately successful) that the seismograms of blasts would be sufficiently different from those of earthquakes that clandestine nuclear explosions could thereby be identified, thus making practical a nuclear test-ban treaty. Standard sets of seismometers were installed worldwide, and the seismograms from these instruments sent to a data center at Boulder, Colorado, from which seismologists could obtain copies. This greatly facilitated exchange of data; and, because the seismographs were identical at all the stations of the network, the seismograms were easier to interpret than had been the case when each observatory had instruments of its own design. In the 1990s, direct digital recording of seismograms became common. Many energetic young investigators were attracted into seismology, with the result that new discoveries quickly followed.

The third development was the rapid acceptance of plate tectonics as the basic cause of earthquakes, leading to an understanding of the worldwide pattern of seismicity. From the rate of plate motions, it became possible to estimate recurrence rates of earthquakes on plate boundaries, leading to the hope that predicting earthquakes might soon be possible. Predicting earthquakes became a goal of several countries including the United States, China, and Japan, and a few earthquakes were successfully predicted.

Using the new standard seismometers to record ground motion accurately, and processing these data on digital computers, improved models of earth's internal structure were developed, and the exact nature of ground movements at the epicenters of earthquakes calculated. Using strong-motion seismograms, engineering seismologists have learned what motions buildings, highways, bridges, dams, and so forth must withstand, with the result that, in California and a few other states, building codes have been rewritten to provide protection against future earthquakes.

BIBLIOGRAPHY

Bates, C.C., T.F. Gaskell, and R.B. Rice. *Geophysics in the Affairs of Man.* New York: Pergamon, 1982.

Dziewonski, A.M., and D.L. Anderson. "Seismic Tomography of the Earth's Interior." *American Scientist* 72 (1984): 483–494.

Howell, B.F., Jr. *Introduction to Seismological Research: History and Development.* Cambridge, UK: Cambridge University Press, 1990.

Lawson, A.C. *The California Earthquake of April 19, 1906.* 2 vols. Washington, DC: Carnegie Institution of Washington, 1908–1910.

B.F. Howell Jr.

Sex and Sexuality

Sex research was what might be called a closet science through the first two decades of the twentieth century. Individual physicians reported cases from their clinical practice and those who attempted larger surveys were more concerned with moral issues than with the science of sex. Although a few individuals were doing serious research, they were generally motivated by the moral issues of sex, particularly the "evils" of prostitution.

It was prostitution that led John D. Rockefeller Jr. to establish the Bureau of Social Hygiene in 1912 and to authorize serious studies, first into prostitution but eventually into human sexuality in general. Under the direction of Katherine Bement Davis (1860–1935), the bureau began to expand its concept of sex research and through her initiative in 1922 the Committee for Research in Problems of Sex (CRPS) was established under the auspices of the National Research Council with Robert M. Yerkes as chair. Davis was a member of the controlling committee along with Yerkes and three others. Initially Rockefeller Jr. provided the funding through the Bureau of Social Hygiene, but later, after Bement's retirement, this was taken over by the Rockefeller Foundation.

Much of the early research was in the biology of sex, including the effects of castration and gonad transplantation, nutritional and glandular factors in relation to the estrous cycle, pubescent boys and the appearance of sperm cells, and most particularly into endocrinology. There was some research into what might be called the norms of sex behavior among students, but in general the research in the early years was not in the areas of social science. This was because such projects seemed too controversial for the committee and the few projects of this nature that appeared in the 1920s and early 1930s were sponsored by the Bureau of Social Hygiene.

Ultimately, however, the committee sponsored the work of Alfred Kinsey, and it was the controversy over his work which caused the Rockefeller Foundation to end the funding of sex research in the 1950s. The individuals sponsored by the committee include many of the most distinguished biologically oriented scientists in the United States. There was a reluctance, however,

S

of the individuals involved to be labeled sexologists, and for the most part they remained outside the circle of European sexologists such as Magnus Hirschfeld and Havelock Ellis. The Americans, with few exceptions, did not regard themselves as sexologists but looked to their own specialties, such as endocrinology, for their identity. They also tried to avoid publicity, something that proved impossible with the Kinsey studies. Kinsey himself, however, was reluctant to be associated with any professional group called sexologists. It was not until after his death that the Society for the Scientific Study of Sex was organized and a journal specifically devoted to sex research, the *Journal of Sex Research,* was established. Interestingly also, the CRPS was reluctant to get involved in contraceptive research per se, and although the endocrine research ultimately led to the oral contraceptive, the specific work on this was funded through different agencies, many of them supported by the Rockefeller Foundation. There were also specialized studies, particularly while Davis was most active, including her own studies on the sexuality of women, the analysis of the Robert Latou Dickinson data on married and single women, and the research of Gilbert V. Hamilton on sex activity in marriage, all of which were published at the end of the 1920s and beginning of the 1930s.

In the post–Kinsey period, when the CRPS was no longer in existence, the more valuable studies into the physiology of sexual response were those of William Masters and Virginia Johnson, and the growth of what is now called psychoendocrinology, which had been pioneered by the CRPS through grants to Adolf Meyer and others.

Generally, however, the various government agencies which since the 1960s have been dominant in supporting science research have not supported studies devoted to sexology per se but to problem areas such as lesbianism and alcoholism, contraceptive usage among poor African-American women, or problems associated with sexually transmitted diseases. Money has also been given to abstinence education but not to any attempt to find out the long-term effectiveness of such efforts.

BIBLIOGRAPHY

Aberle, S.D., and G.W. Corner. *Twenty Five Years of Sex Research: History of the National Research Council Committee for Research in the Problems of Sex.* Philadelphia: W.B. Saunders, 1953.

Bullough, V.L. *Science in the Bedroom: A Brief History of Sex Research.* New York: Basic Books, 1994.

Vern L. Bullough

SEE ALSO
Birth Control

Shaler, Nathaniel Southgate (1841–1906)

Geologist and geographer. Born in Newport, Kentucky, Shaler was the son of Nathaniel Burger Shaler, an army surgeon, and Ann Hinde Southgate, daughter of a prosperous Virginia lawyer. A sickly child, Shaler had little formal schooling, but he knew the plants and animals of the countryside and developed an interest in geology by examining the specimens in his father's mineral cabinet. At age fifteen, he began study with a German tutor to prepare for entrance to Harvard. In 1859, he enrolled in the Lawrence Scientific School and studied paleontology and geology with Louis Agassiz, becoming one of Agassiz's favorite students. He graduated with a B.S. degree in 1862.

After serving briefly as a captain in the Union Army, Shaler returned to Harvard in 1864 as lecturer on paleontology and assistant to Agassiz in the Museum of Comparative Zoology. He was soon one of Harvard's most popular teachers; his stimulating lectures on geology attracted hundreds of students (Theodore Roosevelt was one), who had no intention of becoming geologists but who enjoyed his excursions into the field to study nature at first-hand. In 1872, Shaler suggested to Agassiz the establishment of a permanent summer school for science teachers. The Anderson School of Natural History on Penikese Island in Buzzard's Bay had a short life, but was a prototype for other American summer schools such as that established at Woods Hole in 1882.

In addition to his teaching, Shaler served at various times as government geologist: from 1869 until the mid-1870s with the United States Coast Survey; from 1873 to 1880 as director of the Kentucky Geological Survey; and from 1884 until 1900 as head of the United States Geological Survey's (USGS) Atlantic Coast Division. For the USGS Shaler produced reports on the geology of Cape Cod, Martha's Vineyard, and Cape Ann; surveyed coastal lands for sources of coal, bog ores, and phosphate; studied the geology of harbors; and investigated the possibility of reclaiming swampland. In 1891, he became dean of Harvard's

S

Lawrence Scientific School, remaining there until his death from pneumonia following an appendectomy in 1906. Shaler revitalized the school, which had gone through a period of decline, dramatically increased the enrollment, and opposed a suggested merger with the Massachusetts Institute of Technology.

Shaler's principal contribution to geology and geography was as a teacher, synthesizer, and popularizer of the mainstream theories of his day on such subjects as mountain building, glaciers, isostacy, and changes in sea level. He wrote frequently for popular magazines, and published several books for general audiences, including *Nature and Man in America* (1891), *Sea and Land* (1894), and *Man and the Earth* (1905), the latter a warning about the eventual depletion of earth's natural resources. In 1895, Shaler, as president, addressed the Geological Society of America on one of his favorite subjects: the importance of geology in the curriculum. He thought that a knowledge of the earth's resources was important, but that teaching the history of the earth's development with emphasis on "the appearance and the fate of man" would better stimulate the undergraduate mind (Shaler, "Relations," p. 319). J.E. Wolff, a former student, thought that it was "as one of the great teachers of geology" that Shaler is best remembered (Wolff, p. 599).

David N. Livingstone sees Shaler as one of the great nineteenth-century geographers, who wrote frequently on the influence of the physical environment on human history and on the effect of human activity on the land. Like many of his contemporaries, Shaler believed that mankind had evolved both through interaction with the environment and through a process of Lamarckian inheritance of acquired characteristics; that the Anglo-Saxon race had reached the highest point in evolution, but that other races could be improved through education. Like Frederick Jackson Turner, Shaler saw how the advancing frontier had shaped the history of the United States. For his ideas on the influence of environmental factors such as climate, topography, earthquakes, and soil, Livingstone calls Shaler "a founding father of historical geography" (Livingstone, p. 189).

BIBLIOGRAPHY

Livingstone, David N. *Nathaniel Southgate Shaler and the Culture of American Science.* Tuscaloosa: University of Alabama Press, 1987.

Shaler, Nathaniel S. "Relations of Geologic Science to Education." *Bulletin of the Geological Society of America* 7 (1896): 315–326.

———. *The Autobiography of Nathaniel Southgate Shaler, With a Supplementary Memoir By His Wife.* Boston: Houghton Mifflin, 1909.

Wolff, John E. "Memoir of Nathaniel Southgate Shaler." *Geological Society of America Bulletin* 18 (1907): 592–609.

Peggy Champlin

Sigma Xi, The Scientific Research Society

Twentieth-century America's leading honor society for scientists and engineers. The letters sigma xi stand for the society's Greek motto: Spoudon Xynones, "Companions in Zealous Research." Founded at Cornell University in 1886 as a scientific Phi Beta Kappa to help win recognition for the emerging science-based approach to engineering, by the early 1990s, Sigma Xi evolved into a confederation of over 500 individual chapters and clubs at colleges, universities, and research laboratories throughout the United States. The local groups annually elect to membership more than 5,000 members on the basis of their research achievement (and associate members for their research potential) and some support other programs. The national society (with almost 85,000 members) encourages chapter initiatives and sponsors an award-winning magazine, *American Scientist*, a program of grants-in-aid of research, and other activities.

Although the number of chapters and members grew rapidly from 1886 through the 1960s, this growth paralleled that of the American scientific community, and for many years, most local groups existed primarily to honor research and academic achievement and, perhaps, to hold meetings to discuss scientific subjects. This view of Sigma Xi—as a purely honorary society—contrasts sharply with the one shared (since the society's founding) by many national leaders, who hoped the society would foster scientific activity in other ways.

In 1913, the national society established the *Sigma Xi Quarterly,* designed to create further interest in the Society and increase its usefulness, and its program of small grants-in-aid of research—which still serves the needs of many students in the "field" and "bench" sciences—began in 1927. But the newsletterlike *Quarterly* interested only the most committed Sigma Xi members until the late 1930s, when Yale biologist George Baitsell converted it into the *American Scientist,* and its metamorphosis into an exceptionally well-written and well-illustrated general interest science magazine (whose contents often had little to do with its sponsoring society) finally occurred in the 1970s. Similarly, Sigma Xi began awarding small grants-in-aid only after the National Research Council (with Rockefeller support) co-opted its plans for a more broadly influential program of postdoctoral fellowships. These grants (and the society itself) thus never played a leading role in Big Science, which emerged after World War I and expanded rapidly after World War II. Academic scientists guarding the society's status as an honorary society also opposed post–World War II attempts (led by Harvard astronomer Harlow Shapley and Princeton physical chemist Hugh Taylor) to promote Sigma Xi's growth in industrial and federal research laboratories, and from 1947 they segregated local groups at such organizations into a (supposedly) "separate-but-equal" organization—RESA, the Scientific Research Society of America—which finally merged with Sigma Xi in 1974. In the 1960s, the society began to address science-and-society issues through programs concerned with (among other topics) undergraduate education in science and mathematics and honor in science, and in the 1980s, Sigma Xi tried to capitalize on its confederational structure and draw on the views of its members scattered throughout the United States. Despite efforts of leaders like Georgia Institute of Technology historian of technology Melvin Kranzberg, these initiatives also proved less successful. For example, only about 5 percent of all chapters and clubs answered a late-1980s centennial call for proposals for "A New Agenda for Science," which the leaders of the national society hoped to develop in response to contemporary contractions of the American scientific community.

BIBLIOGRAPHY

Sokal, Michael M. "Companions in Zealous Research, 1886–1986." *American Scientist* 74 (1986): 486–508.

Ward, Henry Baldwin. *Sigma Xi Quarter Century Record and History: 1886–1911.* Urbana-Champaign: University of Illinois, 1911.

Ward, Henry Baldwin, and Edward Ellery. *Sigma Xi Half Century Record and History: 1886–1936.* Schenectady, NY: Union College, 1936.

Michael M. Sokal

Silliman, Benjamin, Jr. (1816–1885)

Chemist. Born in New Haven, he received his early education in science from his father, the professor of chemistry and natural history at Yale College. Silliman graduated from Yale in 1837, and after further studies in his father's laboratory, he earned an M.A. in 1840. His father made him an associate editor of the *American Journal of Science and Arts* in 1838, and Silliman remained an editor in one capacity or another until his death. He began teaching at Yale as assistant to his father in 1838, and by 1842, Silliman was providing laboratory instruction to his father's advanced students. In 1846, he was officially appointed "Professor of Chemistry and the Kindred Sciences as Applied to the Arts," one of two professorships of practical chemistry created by Yale College. The other position was held by John P. Norton who, along with Silliman, established a school of applied chemistry at Yale in 1847. Neither Silliman nor Norton were paid by the college, and they had to rely on student fees and commercial commissions to continue the school. The lack of a salary forced Silliman to accept a professorship in chemistry in the Medical School of the University of Louisville, Kentucky, in 1849. He traveled between Louisville and New Haven (teaching in the science school during the summer) regularly until 1853, when he was appointed to succeed his father as professor of chemistry in Yale College and Yale Medical School.

Silliman pursued a broad range of scientific interests, including chemistry, mineralogy, and geology. He was especially interested in applied science, and through his position as editor of the *American Journal of Science and Arts*, he brought many practical discoveries into print. His diversified approach probably undermined any attempt to establish a strong research program, but it did make him particularly attractive to students. Silliman was an outstanding teacher, and he trained several well-known chemists, including John Norton, George Brush, and T. Sterry Hunt. His two textbooks, *First Principles of Chemistry* (1847) and *First Principles of Physics or Natural Philosophy* (1859), were very popular and went through several editions.

Silliman's ability to explain scientific methods and theories clearly and to seize upon potential commercial applications made him the most highly sought after consulting scientist of his generation. Mining companies frequently sought his advice, and occasionally he served as an expert witness in court cases, an important role in the relations of science and industry that has only recently been investigated by historians. Silliman was active in strengthening the links between

S

science and industry, and his most famous commission was his *Report on the Rock Oil or Petroleum of Venango County* (1855), which served as the spark to the American petroleum industry. In this report, Silliman described the distillation of petroleum and the use of one fraction (later called kerosene) for illumination. The petroleum industry was also the source of Silliman's professional downfall. In 1864, he agreed to undertake several private mining surveys in California, including reports for three petroleum companies in the southern part of the state. Silliman's enthusiastic predictions for California petroleum ran counter to the estimations of Josiah Dwight Whitney, the director of the California Geological Survey, and William Brewer, Whitney's assistant and later professor of agriculture in the Yale Scientific School. Whitney and Brewer launched a vicious attack on Silliman's scientific credibility and tried to oust him from the National Academy of Sciences, of which Silliman had been a founding member. Whitney and Brewer were unsuccessful in removing Silliman from the National Academy, but they made teaching at Yale impossible for him. He resigned from the Yale Scientific School and the college in 1870. Silliman did continue teaching in the medical school. In the late 1870s, petroleum was discovered in southern California, which seemed to reinvigorate Silliman, and he once again began consulting and participating actively in the National Academy. He died of a heart attack while consulting for a western mining company.

BIBLIOGRAPHY

Bruce, Robert V. *The Launching of Modern American Science, 1846–1876.* New York: Knopf, 1987.

[Dana, James D.]. "Benjamin Silliman." *American Journal of Science.* 3d ser., 22 (1885): 85–92.

Kuslan, Louis I. "Benjamin Silliman, Jr.: The Second Silliman." In *Benjamin Silliman and His Circle,* edited by Leonard G. Wilson. New York: Science History Publications, pp. 159–205.

Lucier, Paul. "Commercial Interests and Scientific Disinterestedness: Consulting Geologists in Antebellum America." *Isis* 86 (1995): 245–267.

White, Gerald T. *Scientists in Conflict: The Beginnings of the Oil Industry in California.* San Marino, CA: Huntington Library, 1968.

Wright, Arthur W. "Benjamin Silliman." *Biographical Memoirs of the National Academy of Sciences* 7 (1913): 115–141.

Paul L.M. Lucier

Silliman, Benjamin, Sr. (1779–1864)

Chemist, geologist, educator, and editor. Born in Trumball, Connecticut, Silliman attended Yale (1792–1796), studied law in New Haven, and was admitted to the bar in 1802. He served as a tutor at Yale beginning in 1799. In 1802, Yale president Timothy Dwight appointed him professor of chemistry and natural history on the strength of his character, and he set about learning the science he was to teach. He studied in Philadelphia, Princeton, London, and Edinburgh. Although the name of his professorship changed periodically, he taught at Yale until retiring in 1853. He began giving public lectures in science in 1808 and continued to enjoy great popularity into the early 1850s. In 1818, he founded the *American Journal of Science,* serving as its sole editor for two decades. He was a founding member of the short-lived American Geological Society (1819), president of the Association of American Geologists (1841), and a founding member when that organization became the American Association for the Advancement of Science (1848). He was a charter member of the National Academy of Sciences (1863).

Silliman's scientific investigations in chemistry and geology constituted a relatively minor part of his career and of his contributions to American science. He won acclaim at home and abroad for his investigations of the Weston meteor of 1807. Early in his career, he also conducted a series of experiments on heat fusion of various chemical substances. His geological publications generally resulted from tours of local sites or from investigations undertaken in the employ of private individuals.

Silliman's real impact on the history of American science came from his teaching and his role as advocate and public representative of American science. His courses at Yale and the additional training available to those chosen to serve as his assistants made Yale a national center for training in chemistry, mineralogy, and geology. Among his students were Charles Baker Adams, James Dwight Dana, Chester Dewey, Amos Eaton, Edward Hitchcock Sr., Oliver P. Hubbard, Charles Upham Shepard, and Benjamin Silliman Jr. His ideas in chemistry and geology were available to students far beyond his direct tutelage through textbooks he authored or edited. Among the latter were three editions of Robert Bakewell's *Introduction to Geology,* each of which appeared with an appendix by Silliman designed to reconcile the biblical and geological accounts of earth history. Silliman's emphasis on reconciliation was strongly reflected in the work of two of his students, Hitchcock and Dana.

Silliman was easily the best-known scientist in early-nineteenth-century America. His *American Journal of Science* appealed to a broad audience, and gave him a platform from which to argue for public and private support of science in America. His career as a popular lecturer carried his subjects before the public in communities from Nantucket to St. Louis. When he delivered the inaugural series of Lowell Lectures in Boston in the winter of 1839–1840, the demand for tickets was so great that each lecture had to be repeated before a second audience. Public lectures spread not only the content of his sciences but also the idea of science as an endeavor of interest and value to the citizens of the nation.

Silliman used his position as editor of the *American Journal of Science* to lobby for scientific projects, to editorialize about the proper nature and practice of science in America, and to project an image of progress and maturity for American science and scientists to observers both at home and abroad. The journal made him the hub of an extensive network of correspondents. He often served as counselor to his friends and colleagues and moderator in disputes over priority or due credit. When possible, he preferred that such disputes be settled without ever reaching the pages of the journal, but several lengthy exchanges of charges and countercharges appeared in print during his editorship.

Chandos Brown's excellent biography explores Silliman's early life and career with careful attention to the historical context, but carries the story only to 1818. It is to be hoped, especially by historians of science, that future volumes will carry the story forward. The Silliman Family Papers at Yale provide a rich resource for exploring his life and activities and especially the conduct of the journal. Silliman's letters to his friend, colleague, and student Edward Hitchcock are especially valuable for their unguarded comments and observations and are available in the President Edward Hitchcock Papers at Amherst.

BIBLIOGRAPHY

Brown, Chandos Michael. *Benjamin Silliman: A Life in the Young Republic.* Princeton: Princeton University Press, 1989.

Daniels, George H. *American Science in the Age of Jackson.* New York: Columbia University Press, 1968.

Fisher, George P., ed. *Life of Benjamin Silliman, M.D., LL.D., Late Professor of Chemistry, Mineralogy, and Geology in Yale College.* 2 vols. New York: Charles Scribner, 1866.

Fulton, John F., and Elizabeth H. Thomson. *Benjamin Silliman: Pathfinder in American Science.* New York: Henry Schuman, 1947.

Greene, John C. *American Science in the Age of Jefferson.* Ames: Iowa State University Press, 1984.

Newell, Julie R. "American Geologists and Their Geology: The Formation of the American Geological Community, 1780–1865." Ph.D. diss., University of Wisconsin-Madison, 1993.

Rossiter, Margaret. "Benjamin Silliman and the Lowell Institute: The Popularization of Science in Nineteenth-Century America." *New England Quarterly* 44 (1971): 602–626.

Wilson, Leonard G., ed. *Benjamin Silliman and His Circle: Studies on the Influence of Benjamin Silliman on Science in America.* New York: Science History Publications, 1979.

Julie R. Newell

Simpson, George Gaylord (1902–1984)

Vertebrate paleontologist. Simpson was born in Chicago and raised in Denver, Colorado, where his father was an attorney and his mother active in the Presbyterian church. At age sixteen, Simpson entered the University of Colorado and following his junior year transferred to Yale, where he received his undergraduate and graduate degrees in geology (1923, 1926). For his doctoral dissertation, Simpson studied a large collection of primitive mammals from Mesozoic-age rocks of the American West and then went on to the British Museum (Natural History) in London for a year of postdoctoral research on similar British and Continental fossil specimens. Simpson quickly earned an international reputation as a paleomammalogist that led to his appointment at the American Museum of Natural History in New York City in 1927.

Simpson's continuing research on fossil mammals took him to Patagonia in the 1930s, and his first book, *Attending Marvels* (1934), tells of his travels there. In the late 1930s and early 1940s, Simpson began to address broader issues in evolution theory. In 1939, he published *Quantitative Zoology* in collaboration with his second wife, Anne Roe, a distinguished clinical psychologist, and by the end of 1942, just before Simpson entered military service, he had completed two book-length manuscripts, *Tempo and Mode in Evolution*

S

(1944) and *Principles of Classification and a Classification of Mammals* (1945). In the former work, one of several that helped found the "modern evolutionary synthesis," Simpson brought paleontology into the mainstream of twentieth-century biology by using fossil evidence to expand on contemporary claims by geneticists that natural selection operating upon the inherited variation within living populations could also adequately explain the patterns and rates of evolution within fossils.

In late 1942, Simpson was commissioned as a captain, then major, in U.S. Army military intelligence, where he served for two years in the Mediterranean theater of operations. Simpson returned to the American Museum in late 1944, and in the following year became chairman of the new Department of Geology and Paleontology; at that time he was also appointed professor of vertebrate paleontology at Columbia University. In 1949, Simpson published *The Meaning of Evolution,* a popular and widely read account of modern evolutionary theory, and in 1953, he completed another semitechnical volume, *Evolution and Geography,* which argued for the wide dispersal of animals, particularly mammals, across fixed continents over long spans of geologic time. In so doing, Simpson vigorously challenged the theory of drifting continents as earlier formulated by Alfred Wegener. That same year, Simpson saw the publication of *Major Features of Evolution,* which was a much enlarged revision of the earlier *Tempo and Mode in Evolution.*

In 1958, Simpson resigned as chairman of the Department of Geology and Paleontology at the American Museum, after a dispute with the director, and joined the staff of Harvard's Museum of Comparative Zoology as an Alexander Agassiz Professor of Vertebrate Paleontology. In 1964, Simpson published his "favorite book" (Simpson, *Autobiography,* p. 321), *This View of Life,* a collection of essays on various topics including Darwin and evolution, historical biology, apparent purpose in animate nature, speculations about life beyond the earth, and the human evolutionary future.

In 1967, Simpson left Harvard and joined the faculty at the University of Arizona, where he remained until his death. Simpson did a little teaching, lunched regularly with faculty and graduate students, but mostly continued to publish technical articles and books—on South American mammals, penguins, Darwin, fossils and the history of life, collections of essays, and his autobiography.

As one of the leading authorities in vertebrate paleontology and evolutionary theory during the middle half of the twentieth century, Simpson received many honors during his professional career, including membership in the American Philosophical Society (1936), the National Academy of Sciences (1941), and the Royal Society of London (Foreign Member, 1958), as well as election as president of the Society of Vertebrate Paleontology (1942), the Society for the Study of Evolution (1946), the American Society of Mammalogists (1962), the Society for Systematic Zoology (1962), and the American Society of Zoologists (1964). He also received the National Medal of Science from President Lyndon Johnson (1966) and more than a dozen other medals and prizes from international scientific societies and organizations.

BIBLIOGRAPHY

Laporte, Léo F. *George Gaylord Simpson, Paleontologist and Evolutionist.* New York: Columbia University Press, 2000.

Simpson, George G. *Concession to the Improbable: An Unconventional Autobiography.* New Haven: Yale University Press, 1978.

———. *Simple Curiosity: Letters from George Gaylord Simpson to His Family, 1921–1970.* Edited by Léo F. Laporte. Berkeley and Los Angeles: University of California Press, 1987. [Contains an annotated bibliography of Simpson's major publications.]

Léo F. Laporte

Skinner, B.F. (1904–1990)

Psychologist. B.F. (Burrhus Frederic) Skinner was born in a small, northeastern-Pennsylvania railroad town, originally called Susquehanna Depot. He was the elder son of William A. Skinner, an attorney for the Erie Railroad, and Grace Burrhus, housewife. From 1922 to 1926, he majored in English at Hamilton College; after graduating in 1926, he spent a year at home fruitlessly trying to develop a career as a short-story writer. In 1928, he enrolled for graduate study in psychology at Harvard University and received the doctorate in 1931, with a dissertation on the behavior of rats given reward-training in an apparatus that others would later call the "Skinner box." At Harvard, he enjoyed five years of postdoctoral support of research on what he called operant conditioning, then accepted a position in the psychology department at the University of Minnesota in 1936. In the same year, he married

S

Yvonne Blue of Flossmoor, Illinois, and daughters Julie and Deborah were born in 1938 and 1944. He was involved in a wartime project at General Mills (Minneapolis) to develop the behavioral procedures for a missile-guidance system that would employ a pigeon located in the nose cone and trained to keep the missile on target by pecking at a screen; the proficiency of his pigeons convinced Skinner of the possibility of achieving far more extensive control of behavior than psychologists had hitherto imagined.

He chaired the psychology department at Indiana University from 1945 to 1948; a grassroots Skinnerian psychology slowly began at Indiana and was promoted elsewhere by his students and by converts. In 1948, he accepted the offer of a professorship at Harvard; he maintained a full engagement in lecturing and writing through his retirement and up to his death.

Skinner is classified among "neobehaviorists," behavior-laboratory researchers and theorists (including Clark Hull, Edwin Guthrie, Edward Tolman, and their most prominent students) who succeeded the first generation of American behaviorists (called "early behaviorists" and including John B. Watson). Early behaviorists relied on reflex physiology and Pavlovian conditioning for their philosophical attitudes and for analogies and concepts they used in investigating and explaining human and animal behavior. That was also the intellectual atmosphere of Skinner's laboratory research at Harvard (1928–1936), where an apprenticeship with the physiologist W.J. Crozier and reading in physiology (especially Ivan Pavlov and Charles Sherrington) led him into the study of reflexes in freely moving laboratory animals.

While he was at Harvard in the 1930s, Skinner's machine-shop skills enabled him to turn standard animal-maze equipment into a fully automated apparatus in which a laboratory rat freely executes a designated activity (e.g., pressing a small lever that projects into the box), with rewards ("reinforcers") delivered according to a preestablished plan ("reinforcement schedule"). Instead of using the standard "learning curve," the operant-conditioning enterprise used the "cumulative record," which plots cumulative responses against time, allowing one to see how a number of variables affect momentary response rate (which Skinner came to regard as an indicator of response probability). Thus, in the course of time and in opposition to the neobehaviorist mainstream, a distinctive "Skinnerian psychology" developed its own experimental methods,

apparatus, vocabulary, journals, professional organizations ("Behavior Analysis"), guiding philosophy ("radical behaviorism"), and a strong interest in applying Skinner's ideas in therapy ("behavior therapy") and in other settings (prisons, hospitals, schools, etc.) that manage or modify human behavior. The vigorous creation of an applied behavioral technology reflected Skinner's disenchantment with the traditional goal of finding the laws of learning (in laboratory research) and creating theories to explain them; instead he was drawn to searching for techniques to control behavior and applying them to behavioral difficulties beyond the laboratory.

Skinner's particular genius consisted of a willingness to break with conventions in psychology and boldly to extend, both speculatively and in behavior-technology equipment, the findings of rat (and pigeon, etc.) research in the operant-conditioning laboratory to the problems of humans in everyday life. In contrast to his neobehaviorist contemporaries such as Hull, Skinner courted public notice. *Life* magazine provided photo coverage of his animal-training accomplishments of the 1940s. In a novelistic format (*Walden Two*, 1948), he described a fictional utopia based on behaviorally sophisticated engineering of the environment. In 1971, he followed up with *Beyond Freedom and Dignity,* which argued that Western cultural practices inappropriately aggrandize the individual at the expense of society. He made a spirited defense of radical behaviorism as a scientific-materialistic philosophy of human nature, and was sharply critical of philosophical psychologies which assume that the individual person is a creative agent causally responsible for its own behavior. He believed that the environment is the primary source of influences that "shape" the behavior of the individual during its lifetime and of its species during evolution. He tried out controversial, alternative techniques in the raising of his own children (the "baby tender" in which Deborah spent part of her infancy); he and his students developed behavioral technologies for education (programmed instruction), for the treatment of those who are institutionalized because of intellectual deficiency or serious mental-health problems (token economy), and for personnel management (contingency management). His influence touched even those who opposed him. For example, his *Verbal Behavior* (1957), an operant-conditioning account of language productions, led to a very critical reaction that gave rise, in the 1960s, to the discipline of "psycholinguistics." He was the most

S

visible and influential American psychologist of the period 1950–1990.

BIBLIOGRAPHY

Bjork, Daniel W. *B. F. Skinner: A Life.* New York: Basic-Books, 1993.

Catania, Charles A., and Stevan Harnad, eds. *The Selection of Behavior: The Operant Behaviorism of B. F. Skinner: Comments and Consequences.* Cambridge, UK: Cambridge University Press, 1988.

Skinner, B.F. *Behavior of Organisms: An Experimental Analysis.* New York: Appleton-Century-Crofts, 1938.

———. *Walden Two.* New York: Macmillan, 1948.

———. *Science and Human Behavior.* New York: Macmillan, 1953.

———. *Verbal Behavior.* New York: Appleton-Century-Crofts, 1957.

———. *Beyond Freedom and Dignity.* New York: Knopf, 1971.

———. *Cumulative Record.* 3d ed.; Englewood Cliffs, NJ: Prentice-Hall, 1972.

———. *Particulars of My Life.* New York: Knopf, 1976.

———. *Reflections on Behaviorism and Society.* Englewood Cliffs, NJ: Prentice-Hall, 1978.

———. *Shaping of a Behaviorist.* New York: Knopf, 1979.

———. *A Matter of Consequences.* New York: Knopf, 1983.

———. *Upon Further Reflection.* Englewood Cliffs, NJ: Prentice-Hall, 1987.

S.R. Coleman

Smallpox (variola)

An acute, infectious, and highly contagious viral disease that is characterized by lesions or pockmarks on the skin. There are two clinical types: *Variola major,* which is more virulent, and *Variola minor,* which is milder. In 1980, after an epic ten-year (1967–1977) global campaign, the World Health Organization declared smallpox to be eradicated. However, a small number of the virus are retained for scientific purposes in at least two laboratories in Atlanta, Georgia, and Birmingham, England.

Smallpox first appeared in British North America early in the seventeenth century. It was brought here from England, the West Indies, and Africa. Although the disease was endemic in England, it was always epidemic in the British mainland colonies. This led to the misconception that the colonists were more susceptible to smallpox. In the century before the Revolution, there were only two periods of as long as five years when smallpox was not active somewhere in the region.

Of the many diseases that attacked the colonists, smallpox caused the greatest alarm. It was repulsive, highly contagious, often had a high mortality rate, and could leave a survivor permanently scarred, deaf, or blind. During the colonial period, smallpox had a great economic impact. It disrupted business and resulted in the disabling and loss of much-needed human resources. Because they lacked acquired immunity, smallpox often devastated the Native American population and weakened their resistance to white encroachment.

In the eighteenth century, the two most effective methods for controlling smallpox were isolation and inoculation. Isolation was the older method. When quickly and properly employed, it lessened considerably the chances of the disease getting out of hand. Inoculation involved inserting a small amount of matter from a smallpox lesion into the skin of an individual who had not suffered from the malady in order to induce an acquired immunity. The Reverend Cotton Mather and Dr. Zabdiel Boylston introduced this procedure to America amid great contention during the Boston epidemic of 1721. This was the first large-scale demonstration of inoculation in the Western world.

Because smallpox was a distinctive disease, the preventive efficacy of inoculation was relatively easy to prove. Nonetheless, inoculation remained a highly controversial procedure throughout the rest of the colonial period. There were two major arguments against its use. First, it was costly in time and money and many people could not afford it. Gradually, this objection was met by local governments assuming the costs of inoculating the poor and by doctors donating their services. Secondly, inoculated persons were contagious and could spread, sustain, or intensify the disease. This gradually resulted in strict controls being applied to the procedure. During the Revolution, George Washington adopted a successful policy of general inoculation for the Continental Army.

During the 1790s, Dr. Edward Jenner of England demonstrated that cowpox matter could also induce long-term immunity to smallpox. Because vaccination with cowpox was less expensive, milder, and, most importantly, not contagious in humans, it soon replaced inoculation. Dr. Benjamin Waterhouse, the first professor of medicine at Harvard Medical School, was the leading figure in the introduction and widespread adoption of vaccination in the United States. His efforts were strongly supported by President Thomas Jefferson. Waterhouse has been criticized for initially trying to maintain a monopoly over the use of vaccine in New England. He did this partly out of greed and partly to keep vaccination from being discredited by falling into incompetent or fraudulent hands.

After 1830, complacency, accidents, and growing opposition brought about a decline in the use of vaccination in America. By the 1870s, smallpox was once again a major epidemic disease. When states attempted to enforce their vaccination laws or pass new ones, they met with intense opposition, led by the Anti-Vaccination Society of America. This opposition did not begin to dissipate until the 1930s. By 1962, smallpox had disappeared from North America.

BIBLIOGRAPHY

Blake, John B. "The Inoculation Controversy in Boston, 1721–1722." *The New England Quarterly* 25 (1952): 489–506.

———. *Benjamin Waterhouse and the Introduction of Vaccination: A Reappraisal.* Philadelphia: University of Pennsylvania Press, 1957.

Cohen, I. Bernard, ed. *The Life and Scientific and Medical Career of Benjamin Waterhouse; with Some Account of the Introduction of Vaccination In America.* 2 vols. New York: Arno Press, 1980.

Dixon, C.W. *Smallpox.* London: Churchill, 1962.

Duffy, John. *Epidemics in Colonial America.* Baton Rouge: Louisiana State University Press, 1953.

Hopkins, Donald R. *Princes and Peasants: Smallpox in History.* Chicago: University of Chicago Press, 1983.

Kaufman, Martin. "The American Anti-Vaccinationists and Their Arguments." *Bulletin of the History of Medicine* 41 (1967): 463–478.

Stearns, E.W., and A.E. Stearns. *The Effect of Smallpox on the Destiny of the Amerindians.* Boston: Humphries, 1945.

Waterhouse, G.H. "Descendents of Richard Waterhouse of Portsmouth, N.H." 3 vols. 1934. Typescripts in the Library of Congress, Washington, DC and the New England Historic Genealogical Society, Boston, MA.

Winslow, Ola E. *A Destroying Angel: The Conquest of Smallpox in Colonial Boston.* Boston: Houghton Mifflin. 1974.

Philip Cash

Smithsonian Institution

Largest museum complex in the world. Funded through a bequest of James Smithson (1756–1829), an English scientist, "to the United States of America, to found at Washington, under the name of the Smithsonian Institution, an Establishment for the increase and diffusion of knowledge among men" (Rhees, 1:6), the Smithsonian Institution was established in August 1846 after ten years of sometimes rancorous debate in the United States Congress. The Smithsonian is not part of the federal government, but a charitable trust, with the government serving as trustee. The Smithsonian's governing board—the Board of Regents—has representatives from all three branches of government, as well as private citizens appointed by joint resolution of Congress. Originally financed exclusively through Smithson's bequest, the Smithsonian now receives approximately 70 percent of its operating funds from the federal government. However, unlike federal science bureaus, the mission of the Smithsonian is much more general.

Although there was widespread belief in 1846 that the Smithsonian legislation specified that the institution serve as the national library and museum, this interpretation was not shared by Joseph Henry, the Smithsonian's first secretary (chief administrative officer.) Henry, a physicist, argued that Smithson, as a scientist, had scientific research in mind when he wrote his famous phrase "increase and diffusion of knowledge." He also resisted efforts to localize the Smithsonian's activities. He argued that the Smithsonian's programs must be national and international in scope. The program developed by Henry was a sort of national science foundation. It provided for direct support of research, the publication series Smithsonian Contributions to Knowledge, an international exchange of scientific publications, and coordination of large-scale research projects. Among the latter was the Smithsonian meteorological system, a direct forerunner of the National Weather Service. Henry successfully repelled the effort to make the Smithsonian the national library and was an important player in the evolution of the Library of Congress to that status. He was forced to compromise, however, regarding the national collections, and eventually agreed to take care of the large number of natural history specimens that the various army and navy expeditions and surveys had collected. In 1858, the collections from the Wilkes Expedition were sent to the Smithsonian and the principle of a federally funded national museum confirmed.

Henry's selection had established the precedent that the secretary would be a scientist, and the selection of his successor, the zoologist Spencer F. Baird (1878–1887), who had served as his assistant since 1850, that physical (later social) and natural scientists would alternate as secretary. Baird was much more interested in

S

the support of museum collections than Henry and welcomed the Smithsonian's role as the national museum. Baird oversaw the construction of the first National Museum building, now known as the Arts and Industries Building.

Samuel Pierpont Langley followed Baird, and served as secretary until 1906. Langley was an astrophysicist with a deep interest in aeronautics. During his tenure, the National Zoo and the Smithsonian Astrophysical Observatory were established. Also, construction of a new National Museum building (now the National Museum of Natural History) was begun.

Langley was followed successively by the geologist Charles Doolittle Walcott (1907–1927), the astrophysicist Charles Greeley Abbot (1928–1944), the ornithologist Alexander Wetmore (1944–1952), the psychologist Leonard Carmichael (1952–1964), the ornithologist S. Dillon Ripley (1964–1984), and the anthropologist Robert M. Adams (1984–1994). The selection of I. Michael Heyman, a lawyer, as secretary in 1994 marked the first time a nonscientist was chosen.

Although the museums of the Smithsonian are generally clustered around the Mall in Washington, D.C., by the end of the twentieth century, a great deal of the scientific research generated by the institution was taking place elsewhere. Among the non-Washington facilities are the Conservation and Research Center in Virginia; the Marine Station at Fort Pierce, Florida; the Smithsonian Center for Materials Research and Education in Maryland; the Smithsonian Environmental Research Center in Maryland; the Smithsonian Astrophysical Observatory in Cambridge, Massachusetts; and the Smithsonian Tropical Research Institute in Panama.

There is considerable literature on the history of the Smithsonian, although very little which is broad in scope. Most of the attention of the scholarly community has focused on the nineteenth century, when the Smithsonian was central to the development of American science generally and to individual disciplines such as anthropology and meteorology. The history of the institution through the death of Baird is well understood.

Only very recently has there been much research on the history of the Smithsonian post-1887. The biology practiced in the National Museum of Natural History was not as interesting to historians as that practiced in the universities and elsewhere (e.g., an important history of twentieth-century American biology does not mention the Smithsonian once in its discussions of zoology, paleontology, embryology, human behavior, animal behavior, cytology, and genetics). This is in the process of changing, as interest in conservation and ecology has led to interest in the work of the National Zoological Park and the Smithsonian Tropical Research Institute.

What is lacking in Smithsonian history is an overview history which places the institution within the context of the rise of federal funding for science and the research university. Documentation for such a history would not be a problem. The Smithsonian Institution Archives has the official records (post the January 1865 Smithsonian fire which wiped out earlier material), the papers of the secretaries and major Smithsonian scientists, and the records of many disciplinary societies.

BIBLIOGRAPHY

Bruce, Robert V. *The Launching of American Science 1846–1876*. Ithaca: Cornell University Press, 1987.

Fleming, James Rodger. *Meteorology in America, 1800–1870*. Baltimore: Johns Hopkins University Press, 1990.

Hellman, Geoffrey T. *The Smithsonian: Octopus on the Mall*. Westport, CT: Greenwood Press, 1978.

Hinsley, Curtis M., Jr. *The Smithsonian and the American Indian: Making Moral Anthropology in Victorian America*. Washington, DC: Smithsonian Institution Press, 1994.

Jones, Bessie Z. *Lighthouses of the Skies: The Smithsonian Astrophysical Observatory: Background and History, 1846–1955*. Washington, DC: Smithsonian Institution Press, 1965.

Metgen, Alexa. *From Bison to Biopark: 100 Years of the National Zoo*. Washington, DC: Friends of the National Zoo, 1994.

Oehser, Paul H. *Sons of Science: The Story of the Smithsonian Institution and Its Leaders*. New York: Henry Schuman, 1949.

———. *The Smithsonian Institution*. Boulder, CO: Westview Press, 1983.

Rhees, William Jones, ed. *The Smithsonian Institution: Documents Relative to Its Origin and History*. 2 vols. Washington, DC: Smithsonian Institution, 1901.

Rivinus, Edward F., and Elizabeth M. Youssef. *Spencer F. Baird of the Smithsonian*. Washington, DC: Smithsonian Institution Press, 1994.

Rothenberg, Marc, ed. *The Papers of Joseph Henry*. Vols. 6–8. Washington, DC: Smithsonian Institution Press, 1992–1998.

Washburn, Wilcomb E. "Joseph Henry's Conception of the Purpose of the Smithsonian Institution." In *A Cabinet of Curiosities: Five Episodes in the Evolution of American Museums*. Charlottesville: University Press of Virginia, 1967, pp. 106–166.

Marc Rothenberg

S

SEE ALSO
Baird, Spencer Fullerton; Henry, Joseph; Walcott, Charles Doolittle

Social Darwinism

A broad term used to identify various conservative sociological theories of the late nineteenth century that drew on scientific concepts of biological evolution to explain the development of human individuals and groups. It typically carried pejorative connotations and, from the beginning, was primarily used by opponents of such theories.

The basic doctrines of social Darwinism were articulated by English philosopher Herbert Spencer in the early 1850s, before publication of Charles Darwin's theory of natural selection. The appearance and rapid acceptance of Darwin's scientific explanation for the evolutionary development of plants and animals in nature through a competitive struggle for existence, however, boosted Spencer's view that humans in society advanced through the "survival of the fittest," a phrase originating with Spencer but adopted by Darwin. Applying this view to domestic social policy, Spencer and other social Darwinists promoted an extreme form of laissez-faire capitalism that left persons free to prosper or perish according to their abilities. Society, they maintained, benefited from a natural process of eliminating the unfit and, more importantly, individuals needed the stimulus to initiative and self-help provided by a struggle for survival. In America, these view were principally associated with Yale sociologist William Graham Sumner and industrialist Andrew Carnegie and were seen as justifying cutthroat Gilded Age business practices.

English social Darwinist Walter Bagehot applied these concepts to foreign policy by arguing that stronger nations naturally dominated weaker nations, adding that this process promoted the advance of civilization. Austrian sociologist Ludwig Gumplowicz and German scientist Ernst Haeckel articulated the racist implications of this line of thought by positing a competitive struggle between racial groups, with superior races naturally dominating and, in some instances, supplanting inferior races. At this level, social Darwinism offered a justification for late-nineteenth- and early-twentieth-century practices of imperialism, colonization, and racism.

Recent scholarship has questioned the extent of interest in and support for social Darwinism even among capitalists, imperialists, and others whose practices it allegedly justified. Certainly, Darwin recoiled from the harsh implications of any simplistic application of his biological theories to social institutions. For Spencer and many of his followers, this harshness was minimized by their belief in a Lamarckian version of evolution, which allowed the struggle for survival to serve as a stimulant for self-help through the inheritance of acquired improvements rather than as a death sentence for those born with inherited weaknesses. Identifying these theories with Darwinism instead of Lamarckism emphasized their fatalistic aspects and made them easier to ridicule. Indeed, by exposing their harsh philosophical underpinnings, the articulation of social Darwinist theory may have hurt social Darwinist practices more than it helped them, especially in America where an optimistic, democratic spirit prevailed.

Even if social Darwinism had little impact on actual practices, however, its development reflected a fundamental change in the study of people and social institutions that is worthy of further historical investigation. Social Darwinists equated the development of humans in society with the evolution of animals in nature, and assumed that both were the product of natural laws subject to scientific investigation and exploitation. While academic support for their particular theories quickly waned in the face of mounting criticism from American social scientists, their basic approach of applying scientific methods to the prediction and control of human behavior survived in the emerging disciplines of sociology, psychology, and anthropology.

BIBLIOGRAPHY

Bagehot, Walter. *Physics and Politics.* New York: Appleton, 1873.

Bannister, Robert C. *Social Darwinism: Science and Myth in Anglo-American Social Thought.* Philadelphia: Temple University Press, 1979.

Bowler, Peter J. *Evolution: The History of an Idea.* Berkeley: University of California Press, 1984.

Cravens, Hamilton. *The Triumph of Evolution: American Scientists and the Heredity-Environment Controversy, 1900–1941.* Philadelphia: University of Pennsylvania Press, 1978.

Degler, Carl N. *In Search of Human Nature: The Decline and Revival of Darwinism in American Social Thought.* New York: Oxford University Press, 1991.

Hofsteader, Richard. *Social Darwinism in American Thought.* New York: Braziller, 1959.

Russett, Cynthia Eagle. *Darwin in America: The Intellectual Response, 1865–1912.* San Francisco: Freeman, 1976.

S

Spencer, Herbert. *On Social Evolution: Selected Writings.* Edited by J.D.Y. Peel. Chicago: University of Chicago Press, 1972.

Sumner, William Graham. *Social Darwinism: Selected Essays.* Englewood Cliffs, NJ: Prentice-Hall, 1963.

Wilson, Edward O. *On Human Nature.* Cambridge, MA: Harvard University Press, 1978.

Edward J. Larson

SEE ALSO

Evolution and Darwinism

Social Psychology

The study of human behavior in social or collective interactions. Social psychologists comprise one of the largest professional specialty areas within the American Psychological Association. As a result of the nature of its subject matter and the number of its practitioners, social psychology has throughout its history debated the focus of its research. Much of this debate has centered around whether the focus should be on the individual and how he/she is influenced by the social environment, or the group and its dynamics.

Social psychology had its origins in the writings of nineteenth-century French and German sociologists and cultural anthropologists. It is in the early works that the emphasis on the group is most pronounced. In France, Gabriel Tarde and Gustave LeBon developed theories of crowd behavior based on imitation and suggestion, while in Germany, Wilhelm Wundt advocated the study of cultural products such as language and mythology as the means for investigating higher mental processes. This approach found its major American proponent in the work of George Mead, who theorized that individuals exist only to the extent that they engage in interdependent interaction. Thus, the group and its organized activities form a living system.

An alternative approach traces its origins to British associationistic philosophy in general, and Bentham's utilitarianism in particular. The individual was to be the unit of analysis, with his/her thoughts and actions explained by the laws of association and utility. Floyd Allport was the primary American proponent of this view, directing his work to the study of social influence as a consequence of the association of sensations and ideas.

Of these two approaches, the Allport's model became dominant in American psychology. Despite having a more extensive literature and theoretical base, the group model clashed with the growing behavioral orientation of American psychology. Thus, Allport set the tone for the future of social psychology, while the study of the group became relegated primarily to sociology.

Following this schism, social psychology's development can be divided into three distinct periods. The first covers the period up to the start of World War II. The emphasis of this period was on establishing the credibility of social psychology as an experimental science. Popular topics of research included attitude measurement scales and public opinion polls, as well as studies on the effect of an audience on the behavior of individuals.

The second period comprised the years from the start of World War II up to 1970. Many social psychologists contributed to the war effort by conducting research on persuasive communication, leadership, and group dynamics issues. Research on these issues continued after the war and led to important theoretical advances and many practical applications. Also important was the role played by several German émigré psychologists, most notably the Gestalt psychologist Kurt Lewin. Due to his untimely death in 1947, Lewin's influence was felt largely through the work of his many students, most notably Leon Festinger (cognitive dissonance theory), Harold Kelley and John Thibaut (social exchange theory and attribution theory), and Stanley Schachter (two-factor theory of emotion).

The third, and current, period was ushered in on a wave of professional self-doubt. Growing concerns about the distinction between "pure" and "applied" research, methodological limitations, ethical shortcomings, and a fragmentation of the field into competing subdisciplines led many to conclude that a crisis existed. While many of the conditions that led to this crisis have yet to be addressed, a positive theme has emerged to provide a theoretical thread to tie together the divergent areas of research. This theme is social cognition. Much of the current research on social behavior focuses on how individuals gather and process information about their social environments.

BIBLIOGRAPHY

Allport, Floyd H. *Social Psychology.* Boston: Houghton Mifflin, 1924.

Elms, Allen C. "The Crisis of Confidence in Social Psychology." *American Psychologist* 30 (1975): 967–976.

Festinger, Leon. *A Theory of Cognitive Dissonance.* Evanston, IL: Row, Peterson, 1957.

Fiske, Susan T., and Shelley E. Taylor. *Social Cognition.* 2d ed. New York: McGraw-Hill, 1991.

Hilgard, Ernest R. *Psychology in America: A Historical Survey.* San Diego, CA: Harcourt Brace Jovanovich, 1987.

Kelley, Harold H. "Attribution Theory in Social Psychology." In *Nebraska Symposium of Motivation.* Vol. 15. Lincoln: University of Nebraska Press, 1967.

LeBon, Gustave. *The Crowd: A Study of the Popular Mind.* 1895. Reprint, New York: Viking, 1960.

Mead, George H. *Mind, Self, and Society from the Standpoint of a Social Behaviorist.* Chicago: University of Chicago Press, 1934.

Murchison, Carl, ed. *Handbook of Social Psychology.* Worcester, MA: Clark University Press, 1935.

Murphy, Gardner, and Lois B. Murphy. *Experimental Social Psychology.* New York: Harper, 1931.

Schachter, Stanley, and Jerome L. Singer. "Cognitive, Social and Physiological Determinants of Emotional States." *Psychological Review* 69 (1962): 379–399.

Steiner, Ivan D. "Social Psychology." In *The First Century of Experimental Psychology,* edited by Eliot Hearst. Hillsdale, NJ: Erlbaum, 1979.

Tarde, Gabriel. *Social Laws: An Outline of Sociology.* Translated by H.C. Warren. New York: Macmillan, 1899.

Thibaut, John W., and Harold H. Kelley. *The Social Psychology of Groups.* New York: Wiley, 1959.

Wundt, Wilhelm. *Völkerpsychologie.* Vols. 1–10. Leipzig, Germany: Engelmann, 1900–1920.

Rodney G. Triplet

Social Science Research Council

Founded in 1923 by Charles E. Merram of the University of Chicago, who was serving as head of the committee on research of the American Political Science Association. The political scientists expanded their initiative to include representatives from national associations in economics, sociology, statistics, anthropology, history, and psychology. Three representatives from each of these disciplines have made up the council's board since its incorporation on 27 December 1924.

For its first fifty years, the council focused its energies on training researchers, improving methodology, and on supporting basic and applied research by individual and collaborative groups of social scientists. As the only autonomous international group exclusively committed to the advancement of the social sciences, it operates free from disciplinary boundaries and the constraints of governments and universities. It pursues important efforts without concern for quick or politically correct results. During World War II, the council added a new mission when it entered into a partnership with the American Council of Learned Societies and others to overcome the parochialism of American social science and holistically study the cultures of major foreign areas. These joint committees now support collaborative work in twelve areas including Africa, Latin America, China, the Middle and Near East, and Eastern Europe.

While the Social Science Research Council has maintained an influence disproportionate to its size and program expenditures, it has not been without critics. Historically, social scientists have worried that the council stratifies the disciplines, defines their theoretical, research, and methodological paradigms, and participates in a funding elite that sets future scholarly priorities and concerns. Regardless, the council remains an influential organization among the social sciences.

BIBLIOGRAPHY

Sibley, Elbridge. *The Social Science Research Council: The First Fifty Years.* New York: Social Science Research Council, 1974.

Social Science Research Council. *1996–98 Biennial Report.* New York: Social Science Research Council, New York: 1999.

Barry V. Johnston

Societies and Associations

Voluntary associations are the earliest and most enduring formal scientific organizations in America. The American Philosophical Society, founded by Benjamin Franklin and members of the Philadelphia elite in 1743, and its weaker counterpart, the Boston-based American Academy of Arts and Sciences (organized 1780) were the first permanent scientific institutions in America. Wherever and whenever circumstances have permitted, scientific researchers, educators, and enthusiasts have formed societies to further their interests. No single type of organization could fill all the varied, and sometimes conflicting, roles required of them by their members. Ultimately, scientists created four distinct types of associations to meet their needs, all of which had come into existence by the end of the nineteenth century. Since they were shaped by and for scientists and represented all parts of the scientific community, local and statewide academies, national

S

associations, and disciplinary societies are the key to understanding the changing structure of science and the multiple roles of scientists in American society and culture.

Local Societies and Academies

In the nineteenth century, all parts of a diverse and diffuse community intersected in the local societies. Experts from around the world, novices, enthusiasts with no other scientific contacts, natural history museums, government agencies, and commercial scientific enterprises were all either members or correspondents of local academies. Typically formed by white middle-class men—bankers, businessmen, and doctors, as well as local scientists—these societies were not professional organizations; as a rule, interest in science rather than education or achievement was the principal qualification for membership. However, although scientific expertise was rarely a requirement, academies' membership criteria did reflect local social values and divisions. Eastern societies, for example, tended to admit men of the middle and upper classes, while some southern groups were more elitist. Women were far more likely to join, and on occasion, dominate organizations in the West and especially the Middle West than they were in other regions. Race, ethnicity, and religion were all used at one time or another to restrict admission.

The Philadelphia Academy of Natural Sciences, established in 1812, directly or indirectly provided the inspiration and frequently the prototype for most local societies. Unlike the older patrician American Philosophical Society, the Academy of Natural Sciences welcomed members from a broader spectrum of society. Between 1810 and 1830 innumerable local societies were formed on this model (with variations) throughout the East. Many of these attempts were premature, and these societies failed after a short period because the base of support was too narrow. The most important and enduring societies established during this period tended to be in the northeastern cities—New York (1817), Albany (1823), and Boston (1830) among others.

Basic scientific information became more widely available and the scientifically active population increased during the decades before the Civil War. At that time, scientists and their supporters established successful societies in large cities throughout the country, including Charleston, South Carolina (1853), New Orleans (1853), St. Louis (1856), and Chicago (1856). However, most attempts at forming societies in smaller cities outside the Northeast failed until after the Civil War. Local academies were at the height of their popularity and importance—especially in the West and Middle West—in the 1870s and 1880s when they were founded and flourished in larger numbers than at any other time. These included societies in Davenport, Iowa (1867), San Diego (1874), Peoria, Illinois (1875), and Denver (1882).

Local academies expressed interest in all the sciences. However, they realized that they could make their greatest contributions to the earth and life sciences. Leading scientists, novices, and interested laypeople attended monthly meetings where they either presented formal papers on their research or enjoyed informal discussions in a congenial setting. In addition to the stimulus provided by regular meetings, academies facilitated members' research and education through their journals and museums. Despite their chronic shortage of funds, academies usually struggled to publish their proceedings both to disseminate news of their activities and because a journal, which could be exchanged for other scientific publications, was the key to building a reference library. Similarly, members were spurred to gather natural history specimens to build a museum collection through exchange with naturalists in other parts of the world. Both the journal and the museum—especially if it could be prominently displayed and open to the public—also served to generate public interest in science and raise the social status of local scientists.

National Associations

Both the American Philosophical Society and the American Academy of Arts and Sciences tried to be national societies. But the scientific community was not sufficiently large and travel within the nation too difficult to make a truly national organization feasible until the 1840s. The American Association for the Advancement of Science was founded in 1848 to accomplish on a national scale many of the same objects as local societies sought to achieve in a single community. In addition, it hoped to carry sufficient prestige to be able to both improve the quality and direct the course of the nation's scientific research. In emulation of the British Association for the Advancement of Science, the AAAS sought to reach the greatest number of scientists by holding its annual meetings in a different city each year. Although not explicitly more selective than most local societies, the AAAS membership was weighted heavily toward the most committed members of the scientific community. Dues, the costs in time and money of attending annual meetings, and the prestige of the organization itself all served to keep the most decidedly local scientists (especially women) from joining for more than a year or two if at all.

State Academies of Science

The earliest state academies, including the Connecticut Academy of Arts and Sciences (established 1799) and several efforts in Maryland (beginning in 1797), were essentially local societies. Similarly, the original members of the California Academy of Sciences (1853) were predominantly San Franciscans. These organizations broadened their geographical base after the Civil War at the same time that scientists elsewhere established truly statewide academies (except in the South). These new organizations were frequently modeled on the AAAS or the state agricultural society and like these groups held peripatetic meetings once or twice a year. They sought to stimulate scientific activity within the state, and frequently argued that such activity was the surest route to economic and cultural progress. For this reason, they strongly promoted state geological and natural history surveys. The strongest academies in this period were, like Wisconsin's (established 1870), found in states with a dispersed population and few local societies. State academies generally represented a narrower segment of the scientific community than did local groups. Women for example were less likely to join (and less likely to be permitted to join) state academies than local societies.

National Disciplinary Societies

By the last quarter of the nineteenth century, growing numbers of formally trained, research-oriented scientists found that many of their needs were not being met by general societies with few membership restrictions. Professional scientists (almost all of whom were men) created specialized national organizations which established disciplinary boundaries (especially in the biological sciences) and provided opportunities for the discussion, evaluation, and publication of highly specialized research. Unlike other associations, the disciplinary societies excluded enthusiasts and even (in most cases) advanced students. Membership criteria and degree of specialization of the society varied according to conditions specific to each science. Among the disciplines to found societies at this time were chemistry (1876), physiology (1887), anatomy

(1888), geology (1888), morphology (1890), physics (1899), and botany (1906).

The Twentieth Century

By 1920, most local societies were no longer active as research institutions (the New York Academy of Science is a notable exception); some evolved into natural history museums and emphasized education while others focused on conservation. However, they still offered scientists the companionship and regular opportunity to exchange ideas that was not available elsewhere. Also, because they continued to admit nonscientists, they maintained an important link between professionals and the public.

Statewide and national organizations encouraged the academic scientists who belonged to them by organizing meetings, printing journals, and offering research grants. In addition, they allowed scientists to exchange ideas across disciplinary boundaries. State academies, particularly in the South (most were founded between 1900 and 1940) were important for scientists who could not afford to attend national meetings. They were also a vehicle for some scientists' sense of social obligation as they took up matters of importance to their state—the use and conservation of natural resources in particular.

From the outset, professional societies represented the interests of their members to both the general public and to the government. More recently, during and after the Vietnam War, they discussed the political and social responsibilities of scientists, as well as the need for internal reform in response to changing social realities, including the role of women and minorities in the sciences.

Many scientific societies have left rich and detailed records which they either possess themselves or have deposited in museums, universities, and historical societies around the country. Historians using these materials tend to focus on only one aspect of these multifaceted organizations—their contributions to professionalization. Analysis of membership, geographical distribution, local significance, and functions of these societies will reveal the changing contours, needs, and goals of a remarkably extensive and diverse scientific community.

BIBLIOGRAPHY

Appel, Toby A. "Organizing Biology: The American Society of Naturalists and its 'Affiliated Societies.'" In *The American Development of Biology*, edited by Ronald Rainger, Keith R. Benson, and Jane Maienschein. Philadelphia: University of Pennsylvania Press, 1988, pp. 87–120.

S

Baatz, Simon. "Philadelphia Patronage: The Institutional Structure of Natural History in the New Republic, 1800–1833." *Journal of the Early Republic* 8 (1988): 111–138.

———. *Knowledge, Culture, and Science in the Metropolis: The New York Academy of Sciences, 1817–1970. Annals of the New York Academy of Sciences,* 584 (1990).

Bates, Ralph S. *Scientific Societies in the United States.* 3d ed. Cambridge, MA: MIT Press, 1965.

Bloland, Harland G., and Sue M. Bloland. *American Learned Societies in Transition: The Impact of Dissent and Recession.* New York: McGraw-Hill, 1974.

Goldstein, Daniel. "Midwestern Naturalists: Academies of Science in the Mississippi Valley, 1850–1900." Ph.D. diss., Yale University, 1989.

Hendrickson, Walter B. "Science and Culture in the American Middle West." *Isis* 64 (1973): 326–340.

Kohlstedt, Sally Gregory. *The Formation of the American Scientific Community: The American Association for the Advancement of Science, 1848–1860.* Chicago: University of Illinois Press, 1976.

———. "The Nineteenth-Century Amateur Tradition: The Case of the Boston Society of Natural History." In *Science and Its Public: The Changing Relationship,* edited by G. Holton and W.A. Blanpied. Dordrecht, Holland: D. Reidel, 1976, pp. 173–190.

Midgette, Nancy Smith. *To Foster the Spirit of Professionalism: Southern Scientists and State Academies of Science.* Tuscaloosa and London: University of Alabama Press, 1991.

Oleson, Alexandra, and Sanborn C. Brown, eds. *The Pursuit of Knowledge in the Early American Republic: American Scientific and Learned Societies from Colonial Times to the Civil War.* Baltimore: Johns Hopkins University Press, 1976.

Stephens, Lester D. "Scientific Societies in the Old South: The Elliott Society and the New Orleans Academy of Sciences." In *Science and Medicine in the Old South,* edited by Ronald L. Numbers and Todd L. Savitt. Baton Rouge and London: Louisiana State University Press, 1989, pp. 55–78.

Daniel Goldstein

Society for Integrative and Comparative Biology

See American Society of Zoologists

Society for Social Responsibility in Science

An organization of scientists formed in 1949 and dedicated to the use of scientific knowledge for peaceful purposes. The Society for Social Responsibility in Science (SSRS) was originally a pacifist organization, formed at the instigation of A.J. Muste, co-secretary of the Fellowship of Reconciliation and an articulate proponent of conscientious objection. SSRS required its members to "abstain from destructive work," especially military research, and to dedicate themselves to the constructive application of science. It offered an employment service to assist scientists who felt it necessary to leave their present employment for moral reasons, and it also sponsored general public education programs.

SSRS was concerned primarily with individual conduct, rather than collective political action. It promoted conscientious objection as an expression of the individual's moral judgment about the nature of his or her work, but SSRS did not try to organize large numbers of scientists to engage in collective protests to shut down laboratories engaged in military research. SSRS did not limit itself exclusively to individual expression, however. For example, in 1969, SSRS condemned American involvement in Vietnam and called for a complete withdrawal of American troops. That same year, after the repeated failure of the American Association for the Advancement of Science (AAAS) to agree to undertake a study of the ecological effects of chemical weapons used in Vietnam, SSRS sponsored a team of scientists who conducted a preliminary study. AAAS finally sent its own herbicide assessment commission to Vietnam eighteen months later.

SSRS was a small organization, but it attracted some prominent scientists. Early members included Albert Einstein, E.U. Condon, and Linus Pauling. SSRS had approximately 700 members by the early 1960s. According to David Nichols, its membership was still under a thousand in the early 1970s; its members at that time were spread throughout twenty-four countries, although most lived in the United States. By the mid-1970s, SSRS had become less a pacifist group and more "a typical professional organization" (Robinson, p. 285).

Detailed information about SSRS is difficult to find in the existing historical literature. Most references to SSRS are found in works concerned with either peace movements or social responsibility in science.

BIBLIOGRAPHY

Chalk, Rosemary. "Drawing the Line: An Examination of Concientious Objection in Science." In *Ethical Issues Associated with Scientific and Technological Research for the*

Military. Annals of the New York Academy of Sciences 589 (1989): 61–74.

Nichols, David. "The Associational Interest Groups of American Science." In *Scientists and Public Affairs,* edited by Albert H. Teich. Cambridge, MA: MIT Press, 1974, pp. 123–170.

Primack, Joel, and Frank von Hippel. *Advice and Dissent: Scientists in the Political Arena.* New York: Basic Books, 1974.

Robinson, Jo Ann Ooiman. *Abraham Went Out: A Biography of A. J. Muste.* Philadelphia: Temple University Press, 1981.

Wittner, Lawrence S. *One World or None: A History of the World Nuclear Disarmament Movement through 1953.* Vol. 1 of *The Struggle against the Bomb.* Stanford: Stanford University Press, 1993.

Jessica Wang

Society of Systematic Biology

Formerly the Society of Systematic Zoology, which was founded in 1947 by a small group of systematists who felt that their specialty did not enjoy the priority it should have in scientific circles. They sought to create a regular forum for the exchange of ideas among systematists. The founders felt isolated from other practicing taxonomists and from most of the rest of the scientific community. In part this was due to the fact that a majority of zoologists belonged to taxonomically defined professional societies concerned with particular kinds of organisms. Many members preferred an organization separate from those focusing on the interests of evolutionary biologists, arguing that at least some of their interests and objectives were unique and different. A formal structure was necessary because this would facilitate some members securing research grants from agencies making such subventions. In 1952, publication of a journal, *Systematic Zoology,* was undertaken. One of the charter members of the society, Ernst Mayr of Harvard, together with E. Gorton Linsley and R.L. Usinger, published a pioneering text in 1953, *Methods and Principles of Systematics,* which helped to define the modern parameters of the discipline. Over the years, members have primarily been concerned with elucidating the fundamental principles of classification. The subject has often been heatedly debated at annual meetings and other professional gatherings. From its inception, *Systematic Zoology* has featured a Points of View section in addition to the usual professional articles and book reviews, and this outlet for airing controversies continues to be a prominent feature of the journal. The evolutionary systematics espoused by many of the original members have long been challenged by several competing philosophical approaches. The principal ones have included phenetics, or numerical taxonomy, and cladistics, which is concerned with "sister group" or phylogenetic relationships among organisms. Beginning in the mid-1970s, sociobiology, as espoused by E.O. Wilson at Harvard and others, gained some adherents. Cladists have perhaps predominated among the membership in recent years, but exponents of the various approaches to issues in systematics began forming new professional organizations which reflected their particular philosophical viewpoints in the late 1960s. For nearly a quarter century, *Systematic Zoology* was virtually the only international forum for papers dealing with systematic issues. Since the mid-1970s, however, several other journals, notably *Systematic Botany* (1976), the *Journal of Classification* (1984), and *Cladistics* (1985), have made their appearance. In 1991, the society expanded its focus to include botanists and their concerns, and accordingly became the Society of Systematic Biology. The society's journal was therefore renamed *Systematic Biology* to reflect this change in emphasis.

BIBLIOGRAPHY

Hull, David L. *Science as a Process: An Evolutionary Account of the Social and Conceptual Development of Science.* Chicago: University of Chicago Press, 1988.

Keir B. Sterling

Sociobiology

The study of social behavior as a biological phenomenon. In *The Origin of Species,* published in 1859, Charles Darwin argued that all organisms, including humans, are the end result of a slow evolutionary process, caused by the mechanism of natural selection. Darwin stressed that the key to understanding life lies in its *adapted* nature. We must see all features—eyes, noses, teeth, fur, leaves, shells—as things which aid their possessors in the struggle to survive and reproduce. Moreover, argued Darwin, this applies to behavior, and even more so to *social* behavior. The intricate relationships that one finds in the hymenoptera (ants, bees, and wasps) must be seen as adaptations brought on by selection.

Convinced that selection works ultimately only for the individual, Darwin worried over the paradox that hymenopteran females often spend their whole lives

S

devoted to the welfare of their nest mates. How could this benefit their own reproduction, something often barred in any case through sterility? The solution came only in the 1960s, thanks to the insight of the then-graduate student William Hamilton, who seized on the fact that whereas hymenopteran females (the products of fertilized eggs) have both mothers and fathers, the males (the products of unfertilized eggs) have only mothers. This means that females are more closely related to sisters than to daughters and so, in fact, by helping to raise such sisters, one can serve one's own reproductive ends (selection at the individual level) even though one may never reproduce oneself.

Hamiltonian "kin selection," as the general extension of his mechanism became known, proved a powerful stimulus for the renewed study of social behavior—both at the theoretical level, where new models were devised, and at the empirical level, where more detailed studies of animals acting socially in nature were collected. Important contributions included the work of the American biologist Robert Trivers, who went beyond the scope of kin selection, arguing that even nonrelatives can find cooperation selectively advantageous from the perspective of enlightened self-interest or "reciprocal altruism." As important was the work of the English biologist John Maynard Smith, who applied models of game theory to animal behavior, developing the notion of an "evolutionary stable strategy," where organisms find themselves locked into behavior which cannot really be changed to their advantage since it is balanced by the behavior of others. (These ideas were popularized by Richard Dawkins in his best-selling *The Selfish Gene*.)

By the mid-1970s, the time was ripe for a synthesis of what was now becoming known as "sociobiology," and this major overview came from the pen of the Harvard student of social behavior, Edward O. Wilson. Gathering information from across the animal world, and backed by a deep understanding of evolutionary mechanisms, Wilson produced the new discipline's Bible: *Sociobiology: The New Synthesis*.

Yet, although greeted initially with acclaim, Wilson and his work soon ran into heavy criticism, from social scientists and from radical critics of modern science, including uncomfortably some of the members of his own department (most famously, the geneticist Richard C. Lewontin and the paleontologist Stephen Jay Gould). Had Wilson (and his fellow sociobiologists) simply confined his attentions to the animal world, unrestricted praise would no doubt have come his way. However, like Darwin himself who turned to our species in his *Descent of Man*, Wilson brought *Sociobiology: The New Synthesis* to a climax by considering Homo sapiens from the viewpoint of evolutionary biology.

Hence, the ways in which we behave and interact with each other, whether we be Kalahari bushman or New York business executive, were seen to be the result of natural selection. Cooperation, aggression, language, sexuality were all interpreted in terms of adaptive function. And this inflamed the critics, who argued that Wilson (and his fellow sociobiologists) were simply cloaking their personal prejudices in a thin veneer of biological respectability. Without solid evidence, the sociobiologists were spinning "just so" stories, of the kind that Rudyard Kipling described in his fairy tales, to justify their beliefs that human nature is fixed ("genetically determined") and that, hence, any attempt at social reconstruction is doomed. Black inequality, the oppression of women, the superiority of the traditional family, and homosexual inadequacy were being painted as "natural" and, hence, beyond change or reform.

Expectedly, Wilson and his supporters and coenthusiasts for sociobiology (especially the human kind) counterattacked, arguing that they never claimed that all of human behavior is rigidly determined, merely that biology is a very significant factor; that the evidence for the main claims goes far beyond hearsay and wishful thinking and that it is quite wrong to equate the subject with Kipling's fantasies; and that in any case (what was often true) if real ideology is sought as a basis of supposedly scientific claims, one would do better to look at the critics' motivations. (Lewontin, for instance, is notoriously enamoured with Marxism.)

Scientific controversies rarely end with decisive victory or defeat, and this seems particularly so here. Today, sociobiology thrives, and this applies especially to the human variety (although, as is the case in these circumstances, many prefer a more innocuous name such as "human behavioral ecology"). Much exciting work is being done to tie human activities to their biologies. Typical is the work of a pair of psychologists who (by focusing on the nonbiological relatedness of stepparental relationships) have been able to discern significant, widespread, robust patterns in family violence. At the same time, many of the grandiose and insensitive claims that so infuriated the critics have been shelved or quietly dropped or modified. Indeed, in some areas, for instance in the case of male-female differences, one might almost say that it is the sociobiologists who have taken on the ideology of the critics. (In fairness, one should note that, starting with Alfred Russel Wallace, codiscoverer with Charles Darwin of natural selection, there has been a long history of feminist interpretations of evolutionary biology.)

In conclusion, it is worth stressing the fundamental fact which emerges from the discussion above, namely that sociobiology (including its human extension) is no absolutely new theory or "paradigm" or whatever. It is rather a vital development of the overall world picture produced by traditional Darwinian evolutionary biology. And what must be appreciated is the fact that here, as elsewhere, this biology shows itself to be one of the most powerful tools available to scientists and to all others who would understand the world of which we ourselves are an intimate part.

BIBLIOGRAPHY

Darwin, Charles. *On the Origin of Species.* London: John Murray, 1859.

———. *The Descent of Man.* London: John Murray, 1871.

Dawkins, R. *The Selfish Gene.* Oxford: Oxford University Press, 1976.

Kitcher, P. *Vaulting Ambition.* Cambridge, MA: MIT Press, 1985.

Lewontin, R.C., S. Rose, and L.J. Kamin. *Not in Our Genes.* New York: Pantheon, 1984.

Maynard Smith, J. "Game Theory and the Evolution of Behaviour." *Proceedings of the Royal Society,* B: *Biological Sciences* 205 (1979): 41–54.

Ruse, M. *Sociobiology: Sense or Nonsense?* Dordrecht, Holland: Reidel, 1979.

Trivers, R. "The Evolution of Reciprocal Altruism." *Quarterly Review of Biology* 46 (1971): 35–57.

Wilson, Edward O. *Sociobiology: The New Synthesis.* Cambridge, MA: Harvard University Press, 1975.

———. *On Human Nature.* Cambridge, MA: Harvard University Press, 1978.

Michael Ruse

Sociology

This academic discipline is traced to Auguste Comte, who coined the term in the early nineteenth century and focused attention on the positivistic study of social order and change. However, Comte's works intertwined sociology with social philosophy and blurred it's character. Emile Durkheim later clarified the uniqueness of the discipline, demonstrated that social forces were independent from the psychological and biological forces of life, and convincingly argued that they required separate treatment by analysts of human social behavior.

The broadest view of sociology sees it as a discipline concerned with the entire spectrum of human social action. Various schemes then divide it into subfields that focus on macro and micro sociological units. Others state that the discipline is fundamentally concerned with human interaction and how it is manifested in patterned social relationships, groups, and collective action. These scholars accept the distinction between macro and micro sociological processes, but regard the discipline as a science or study of society. The breadth of the field is liberating yet troublesome. Sociologists value the freedom to study the full range of behavior, but worry that differences in theoretical approaches and methodology make meaningful cumulative observations and theoretical understandings impossible. However, many scholars seek a body of factually based, integrated propositions that explain and allow prediction of human actions in a variety of specified situations. Sociologists have historically questioned the goals of their discipline. Should they seek an all-inclusive social theory that integrates micro and macro sociological processes; a body of theory and methods that can be applied to discrete problems and areas of intimate and large scale collective life; or should the goal be an increased understanding of the epistemological and philosophical concerns of social existence?

Practitioners have regularly debated whether sociology is a science, and nowhere was the dialog more heated than in the United States prior to 1945. From 1920 to 1940, however, American sociologists increasingly linked theory with quantitative research methods and established a paradigm for doing sociological work. The Chicago School of Sociology advanced the paradigm as an important element in their leadership of the discipline from 1915 to 1935. In the 1940s, the rise of research institution and collaborative social science programs intensified the search for a fruitful union of theory and research. Major efforts like those of the Bureau of Applied Social Research at Columbia, the Department and Laboratory of Social Relations at Harvard, the Institute for Survey Research at the University of Michigan, and Chicago's later development of the National Opinion Research Center made Big Science a defining force in American sociology by the 1950s.

Concurrently, sociology was developing as an academic discipline. In the early 1900s, sociology courses

S

moved from economics to independent departments, and sociologists separated from the American Economics Association to form the American Sociological Society. Growth accelerated from the 1940s to the 1960s and sociology increasingly became a freestanding part of the academic landscape in American universities. Academic acceptance was accompanied by increasing professionalization and organization, and sociologists typically belong to regional, national, and international scholarly associations.

The contemporary practice of sociology is characterized by a healthy diversity. European, Asian, and Third World practitioners favor a more abstract, political, and social philosophical approach. Americans have continuously and productively challenged purely empirical social science and developed humanistic, problem oriented, qualitative, philosophical, and historical traditions. Current sociological practice reflects a robust theoretical and methodological pluralism that operates alongside a prevailing commitment to scientific sociology.

BIBLIOGRAPHY

Faris, Robert E.L., ed. *Handbook of Modern Sociology.* Chicago: Rand McNally, 1964.

MacIver, R.M. "Sociology." *The Encyclopedia of the Social Sciences.* Edited by Edward R.A. Seligman and Alvin Johnson. New York: Macmillan, 1934, 14:232–247.

Reiss, Albert J., Schmuel N. Eisenstadt, Bernard Lecuyer, and Anthony R. Oberschall. "Sociology." *The International Encyclopedia of the Social Sciences.* Edited by David Sills. New York: Macmillan and The Free Press, 1968, 15:1–53.

Smelser, Neil J. *Handbook of Sociology.* Newbury Park, CA: Sage Publications, 1988.

Barry V. Johnston

Sociology of Science

Four major lines of research and reflection are evident in the social study of science—the Mertonian approach (named after its founder, Robert K. Merton), the sociology of scientific knowledge, reflexivity, and studies of scientific practice. None of them are very old, dating back as organized fields of research only to the 1960s (Mertonian sociology), 1970s (the sociology of scientific knowledge), and 1980s (reflexivity and studies of practice). As one might expect, the oldest is the most conservative, the two youngest possibly the most radical.

To locate the break between Mertonian sociology of science and later perspectives one needs to think about a distinction that was once central to history and philosophy of science, that between "internal" and "external" factors in scientific development. The former relate to a special rationality or method imputed to science which guarantees the autonomy of scientific knowledge from social influence, the latter to the social character of the scientific community and its relations with the wider society. Only the Mertonian approach has respected this distinction and confined itself to an "external" sociology, with Merton himself arguing in his pioneering *Science, Technology, and Society in Seventeenth Century England* (1938) that religious, political, economic, and military contexts have influenced the choice of scientific research topics and the rate at which scientific knowledge has been produced but *not* the specific content of that knowledge. Merton's perspective has subsequently been elaborated in a series of studies of scientific specialty formation, most notably in Joseph Ben-David's work on the rise of experimental psychology in the nineteenth-century German university system.

Another line of research in this tradition also springs directly from Merton's work and concerns the normative order of the scientific community. Arguing from the structural-functionalist perspective once dominant in sociology, Merton suggested that scientists should subscribe to four behavioral norms—universalism, communism, disinterestedness, and organized skepticism—variously concerned with the ways in which they present their knowledge claims to their community and evaluate the contributions of others. Conformity to these norms, Merton supposed, would optimize the rate of production of reliable scientific knowledge, and many studies have since aimed to explore how well contemporary scientific communities, especially in the United States, measure up to these standards. Closely related investigations have aimed to determine whether social stratification (by age, sex, institutional affiliation, etc.) has any effect on performance in science. Studies by Jonathan and Stephen Cole, Harriet Zuckerman, and others have generally arrived at reassuring results. More recently, fraud has become a key research site for the Mertonian tradition, being understood as a location where the normative order has conspicuously broken down.

The sociology of scientific knowledge approach (SSK for short) departs from the Mertonian picture, and from traditional history and philosophy of science, in rejecting the internal/external dichotomy. SSK denies the existence of any special, nonsocial, scientific method and, as its name suggests, argues that even scientific knowledge needs to be understood as a social product. Often looking for inspiration toward Thomas Kuhn's *The Structure of Scientific Revolutions,* empirical research in SSK has tended to focus upon controversies—in contemporary science, or in the history of science going back to the scientific revolution—for the simple reason that in controversies the lack of any consensually unproblematic method to which scientists can appeal is apparent. In canonical works in the 1970s, Barry Barnes and Steven Shapin developed ideas taken from Marx and Weber in their arguments that scientific knowledge is structured by the social interests of its producers and consumers, David Bloor articulated the Durkheimian argument that social structure imposes significant constraints upon scientific belief, and Harry Collins argued that the resolution of contemporary scientific controversies depends upon contingent "negotiations" between the scientists involved.

As one would expect, through its rejection of the internal/external distinction, SSK has found itself at the center of many controversies in the history, philosophy, and sociology of science. Critics have often charged that it is prey to a self-defeating relativism; in denying to science any nonsocial authority, does not SSK undermine its own claim to authority, too? But there is now widespread agreement that SSK has had an invigorating effect upon science studies. It has served to promote empirical curiosity concerning the historical interweaving of the social and the technical in science. And it has also helped to dislodge the traditional identification of science with scientific theory. Many studies in SSK have focused upon the social construction of scientific *facts,* and this has helped to stimulate historical and philosophical as well as sociological enquiry into the nature of scientific experimentation and observation.

The reflexive and science-as-practice approaches to the sociology of science can in many ways be regarded as continuous extensions of SSK, but they differ from SSK in their relation to mainstream sociology. Whereas SSK (like the Mertonian tradition) draws upon standard sociological repertoires in its interpretations of science, the two younger approaches are sociologically (and philosophically) more quarrelsome. Reflexivity, as it were, folds SSK back upon itself. SSK can be seen as highlighting what Steve Woolgar calls the "methodological horrors" of scientific representation–the fact that any scientific account can be made controversial and deconstructed. This is the move that opens the way for sociological accounts of scientific knowledge. And reflexivity applies this move to SSK and sociology at large, asking how such methodological horrors are managed in SSK. Within the reflexive frame, definitive answers to such questions in the style of the natural or social sciences are ruled out, since such answers are now themselves the objects of analysis. Instead, in the works of Michael Mulkay, Steve Woolgar, and Malcolm Ashmore, one finds writing that interrogates its own construction–"new literary forms," for example, in which multiple and competing voices and representations deconstruct one another within a single text.

Studies of scientific practice focus on the doing of science, on scientific work, rather than upon scientific knowledge per se. They seek to understand the day-to-day performance of science, controversial or not, in laboratories, offices, grant-giving agencies, and so on. The pioneering studies here were ethnographic ones, including book-length studies of laboratory life by Bruno Latour and Steve Woolgar (1979), Karin Knorr-Cetina (1981), and Michael Lynch (1985), although historical reconstructions of scientific practice have also been developed in, for example, Andrew Pickering's work on the history of elementary-particle physics, David Gooding's studies of Michael Faraday, and Bruno Latour's of Louis Pasteur. Again, such studies have been made the basis for critiques of traditional sociology, most notably in the "actor-network" approach developed by Michel Callon and Bruno Latour, who suggest that the entire science-technology-society complex should be conceptualized as a mesh of competing networks composed of human and nonhuman agents which reciprocally and continually redefine one another. Neither science nor society is seen as having any necessary autonomy in this approach. In contrast to SSK and its appeal to the social to explain the technical contents of science, studies of science-as-practice suggest that the technical and the social are coproduced, in one and the same technosocial process. Here, then, the sociology of science dissolves, losing its disciplinary integrity within an all-embracing field of science, technology, and society studies.

BIBLIOGRAPHY

Barnes, Barry. *Interests and the Growth of Knowledge.* Boston: Routledge & Kegan Paul, 1977.

Bloor, David. *Knowledge and Social Imagery.* 2d ed. Chicago: University of Chicago Press, 1991.

S

Collins, Harry M. *Changing Order: Replication and Induction in Scientific Practice.* 2d ed. Chicago: University of Chicago Press, 1992.

Knorr-Cetina, Karin. *The Manufacture of Knowledge: An Essay on the Constructivist and Contextual Nature of Science.* New York: Pergamon, 1981.

Latour, Bruno. *Science in Action: How to Follow Scientists and Engineers through Society.* Cambridge, MA: Harvard University Press, 1987.

Latour, Bruno, and Steve Woolgar. *Laboratory Life: The Construction of Scientific Facts.* 2d ed. Princeton: Princeton University Press, 1986.

Lynch, Michael. *Art and Artifact in Laboratory Science: A Study of Shop Work and Shop Talk in a Research Laboratory.* London: Routledge & Kegan Paul, 1985.

Merton, Robert K. *The Sociology of Science: Theoretical and Empirical Investigations.* Edited by Norman W. Storer. Chicago: University of Chicago Press, 1973.

Mulkey, Michael. *The Word and the World: Explorations in the Form of Sociological Analysis.* London: George Allen and Unwin, 1985.

Pickering, Andrew, ed. *Science as Practice and Culture.* Chicago and London: University of Chicago Press, 1992.

———. *The Mangle of Practice: Time, Agency, and Science.* Chicago: University of Chicago Press, 1995.

Shapin, Steven. "History of Science and Its Sociological Reconstructions." *History of Science* 20 (1982): 157–211.

Woolgar, Steve, ed. *Knowledge and Reflexivity: New Frontiers in the Sociology of Knowledge.* Beverly Hills and London: Sage, 1988.

Andrew Pickering

Soil Science

American soil science has two major branches. The vast majority of soil scientists have studied soil as it related to soil fertility and agricultural production. Another group has studied soils as natural bodies worthy of scientific study. Among the first group, nineteenth-century Americans such as Edmund Ruffin sought the keys to special soil management problems and made significant contributions, such as using lime to correct acidity. The nineteenth-century agricultural scientists imported the ideas of Justus Liebig on soil fertility and crop production as proposed in *Organic Chemistry and Its Application to Agriculture and Physiology.* Geologists and geographers linked geology to agricultural potential of the soils in broad areas.

One major conceptual shift in soil science in the United States, perhaps the major change, was the shift from viewing soils as the residuum of weathered material to recognizing biologic and other influences on soil genesis. Beginning with the *Report on the Geology and Agriculture of the State of Mississippi* (1860), Eugene W. Hilgard, state geologist in Mississippi, contributed the concept of dynamic soils that formed under unique conditions of climate and associations of native plants acting upon weathered material.

While Hilgard's place in the history of soil science is well understood today, his ideas about soil formation had little influence on his contemporaries. A Russian school of soil scientists led by Vasilii V. Dokuchaev in the 1870s and 1880s recognized that each soil had unique layers, or horizons; thus, each soil was a natural body with its own morphology. After World War II, Curtis F. Marbut, head of the soil survey division in the United States Department of Agriculture, made these concepts available to Americans when he translated K.D. Glinka's 1914 treatise on Russian soil science, *Die typen der Bodenbildung.* Since then, the concepts of individual natural soil bodies based on soil genesis have influenced soil classification and soil survey in the United States. Hans Jenny's *Factors of Soil Formation* (1941) provided a highly useful quantitative method of understanding soil through the five soil-forming factors: climate, organisms, relief, parent material, and time.

Out of the myriad important discoveries for the development of soil science, the discovery of the crystalline nature of soil clays merits special mention. Sterling Hendricks of the United States Department of Agriculture used X-ray diffraction to demonstrate the crystalline nature of soil clays. The further understanding of the importance of soil clays to chemical reactions, especially cation exchange reactions, in the soil transformed the static concept of soil to a view more attuned to its truly dynamic nature. This discovery also contributed to a better understanding of the physical attributes of soils. Overall advances in knowledge in particular aspects provided a greater appreciation of the complexity of the biogeochemical nature of the soil.

Much of the institutional support for soil science, soil mapping, and soil classification has historically come from agriculture, through the land-grant universities, and the United States Department of Agriculture. The Department of Agriculture has carried out a soil survey program since 1899 and has developed the soil classification systems to support the surveys. The current system of *Soil Taxonomy,* adopted in 1975 and significantly revised since, made soil classification quantitative. Soil scientists in developing *Soil Taxonomy* either validated or rejected many long-held concepts and ideas heretofore not tested.

One advantage to a more quantifiable soil classification system was the potential for interpretation of soil properties. Besides the long-accepted interpretations for crop production, soil scientists in the 1960s began developing soil survey interpretations for soil conservation, environmental protection, recreation, construction, engineering, wildlife, and other purposes. The work of interpretation drew in other sciences and disciplines, making the effort interdisciplinary.

The current trend in soil science is toward a more environmental view of soil in all of its biogeochemical nature. While it would be incorrect to believe that soil science was exclusively directed toward crop production, most of the institutional support for soil science was linked to agricultural production. The increased public attention to environmental concerns has prodded the soil science profession in the late 1980s to embrace a broader array of concerns under the umbrella of soil quality.

BIBLIOGRAPHY

Cline, Marlin G. *Soil Classification in United States.* Ithaca: Department of Agronomy, Cornell University, 1979.

Factors of Soil Formation: A Fiftieth Anniversary Retrospective. Special Publication Number 33. Madison, WI: Soil Science Society of America, 1994.

Gardner, David R. *The National Cooperative Soil Survey of the United States.* Historical Note Number 7. Washington, DC: Natural Resources Conservation Service, 1998.

Jenny, Hans. *E. W. Hilgard and the Birth of Modern Soil Science.* Pisa, Italy: Collana Della Rivista Agrochimica, 1961.

Kellogg, Charles E. "We Seek; We Learn." *Soil: The Yearbook of Agriculture 1957.* Washington, DC: Government Printing Office, 1957.

Krupenikov, I.A. *History of Soil Science: From Its Inception to the Present.* Translated from the Russian by A.K. Dhote. New Delhi, India: Amerind Publishing, 1992.

McDonald, Peter, ed. *The Literature of Soil Science.* Ithaca: Cornell University, 1994.

Rossiter, Margaret W. *The Emergence of Agricultural Science: Justus Liebig and the Americans, 1840–1880.* New Haven: Yale University Press, 1975.

Simonson, Roy W. *Historical Aspects of Soil Survey and Classification.* Madison, WI: Soil Science Society of America, 1987.

Smith, Guy D. *The Soil Taxonomy: Rationale for Concepts in Soil Taxonomy.* Washington, DC: Soil Conservation Service, 1986.

Soil Science Society of America Proceedings, Silver Anniversary Issue 25 (November-December 1961).

Soil Taxonomy: Achievements and Challenges. Madison, WI: Soil Science Society of America, 1984.

Soil and Water Quality: An Agenda for Agriculture. Washington, DC: National Academy Press, 1993.

J. Douglas Helms

SEE ALSO
Agricultural Chemistry

Space Science and Exploration

An omnibus term referring to the conduct of science beyond the surface of the earth, and to the exploration of the solar system and beyond using rockets, satellites, or spacecraft. The term "space science" did not come into use until shortly after the October 1957 launch of *Sputnik I,* the first artificial satellite. Responding to the perceived challenge, the United States (and other nations to a much lesser degree) joined the Soviet Union in creating vastly expanded programs aimed at exploring what was then called "outer space." Although during the last years of the decade, small scientific sounding rockets and small instrumented satellites and space probes were limited to exploring the upper atmosphere and magnetosphere of the earth and making crude measurements of radiation from brighter celestial objects, much more ambitious craft were on the drawing boards or under development. Some scientists and entrepreneurs thought that the stringent requirements of conducting scientific study using rockets and satellites were so different from previous practice that a new field had been born. Space science(s) to them was a field where the bonds of instrumentation and practice were stronger than traditional disciplinary affiliations. Others disagreed strongly, arguing that disciplines should not be organized according to instrumental techniques or the location of the observer. To them, space technology was just another instrumental tool and did not affect the disciplinary economy of science.

Between the end of World War II and the launch of *Sputnik,* various scientists from many disciplines had experimented with balloons and rockets for lofting instruments. Aeronomy, meteorology, auroral studies, solar physics, cosmic ray research, astronomy, particles and fields, and other areas all benefited from early rocket and balloon instruments. Even researchers from biology and medicine, frequently under military sponsorship,

S

showed some interest in the reaction of organisms to the space environment. Numerous feasibility studies of satellites and space probes were done, and development started on secret satellites for reconaissance of the earth, communications, and meteorology. The International Geophysical Year (IGY), a coordinated effort to study the earth and its environs (1957–1958) from multiple disciplinary perspectives, included many rocket-borne measurements. In addition, the Soviet Union and the United States planned to put the first artificial satellites into earth orbit. The Soviet *Sputnik* satellites of late 1957 were followed by the American *Explorer*s and *Vanguard*s, and concerted efforts to inaugurate a major American space program.

The American response to *Sputnik* included a renewed President's Science Advisory Committee, and the creation of a new agency to oversee all civilian space research, the National Aeronautics and Space Administration (NASA). Science appealed to President Eisenhower, his advisors, and others as a major public justification for the space program. The promotion of scientific research in space became a major component of the legislation creating NASA. NASA was seen in some ways as a parallel agency to the National Science Foundation, which already provided funding and some facilities for scientific research on the ground.

Even before the creation of NASA, the National Academy of Sciences combined its IGY technical committees on rocketry and the Earth Satellite Program into a new Space Science Board. As its first official act, in June 1958, the board solicited and evaluated proposals for scientific experiments to be conducted in space, since it was clear that a dramatic expansion of spaceflight opportunities was imminent. When NASA began operation later that year, with former *Vanguard* scientific director Homer Newell in charge of space science, the board became an advisory body, a role in which it continues to this day. The transition was not without controversy, however, and Newell later described a continuing "love-hate" relationship between the board and NASA (Newell, p. 205). The board organized and arranged to have published an introductory book on space science, designed to introduce the field to scientists and hopefully attract them into participation as well (Berkner and Odishaw, 1961). The board remained a most influential venue, holding several meetings each year where distinguished active researchers from all areas assessed the state of the field and made recommendations concerning NASA and other programs. The numerous reports of the board and its evolving membership provide a chronicle of

the disciplines considered part of space science, their achievements, and their chief outstanding research priorities. As the official United States representative to the Committee on Space Research (COSPAR) of the International Council of Scientific Unions (ICSU), the Space Science Board reports and archives provide entry to understanding space science in an international context.

The dramatic scientific results that ensued from the admittedly crude and preliminary satellites fueled the belief that space technology would be a revolutionary development for science, and that space science would become a new discipline. Simple Geiger counters on the first satellites revealed the so-called Van Allen belts of trapped radiation and the earth's magnetosphere. Analysis of their orbital perturbations revealed the "pear-shaped" earth, a major development for geodesy. These and other first in situ measurements in a previously inaccessible and dynamic region had a profound effect on existing theories and interpretations of the terrestrial environment and its interaction with the sun.

At NASA, a major space science division was created, organized variously according to program, vehicle, or discipline. From the beginning, officials knew they would have to have individuals and offices representing recognized scientific disciplines as points of contact with the university community. Hence, although there might be a labyrinth of functional areas on the NASA organizational chart, there were always "discipline chiefs," accredited scientists who watched over various scientific programs and activities. The titles and affiliations of NASA managers and scientists in the organization charts and telephone directories give a sense of the evolving disciplinary and topical composition of "space science."

While NASA at its headquarters and field centers built up its staff with scientists from many disciplines, it adopted a policy of encouraging and relying on space research by university investigators. The Space Science Board and NASA promoted the programs and encouraged university scientists to develop instruments to be flown on rockets and satellites. They sponsored conferences, wrote articles in leading journals, and published introductory books. During the expansion of the agency in the 1960s, NASA administrator James Webb attempted to persuade universities to establish interdisciplinary space science programs and departments. Grants were made available for buildings that would house space-related academic departments to encourage interaction between disciplines by putting them physically under the same roof. Traditional disciplinary boundaries proved resilient, however, and "space science" at universities remained an omnibus designation usually applied to programs or loosely organized clusters of departments. Sometimes, it was a mere adornment of funding proposals, packaging existing or lightly revamped university departments in a more attractive manner for the facilities grants being offered by NASA.

The precise meaning of "space science" was subject to controversy as academic departments and societies debated whether to gather space-related research into separate divisions. Several scientific journals were founded devoted to "space science," including *Planetary and Space Science* (1959), *Space Science Reviews* (D. Reidel, 1962), and *Space Science Instrumentation* (D. Reidel, 1975). However, the vast majority of journal articles reporting and analyzing research conducted from space continued to be published in disciplinary or topical journals (Newell, 1980, especially Chapter 1, "The Meaning of Space Science").

The meaning of space science proved problematic for scientific societies as well. Within the American Geophysical Union, a vigorous debate ensued in 1959–1962 when proponents, including NASA's Homer Newell and Robert Jastrow, campaigned for establishing a new section on "planetary physics" to serve as a home for space research. Several committees considered a variety of names and divisions, finally settling on a new section called "planetary sciences." This section grew through the 1960s, when it was split into separate planetology and solar-planetary relationships sections. The American Astronomical Society, the Geological Society of America, the American Physical Society, and other professional associations were also the sites of similar discussions, and various separate divisions were created for space-related research within these organizations during the late 1960s and 1970s (Tatarewicz, Chapter 6).

Space technology and space institutions had profound effects on a great many scientific fields and disciplines. Whether space science has a meaning beyond simply conducting science in space is subject to considerable debate.

Textbooks and introductory volumes include those by Berkner, Le Galley, Glasstone, and Haymes. Well-written and reliable memoirs include those by Newell, Naugle, Massey, and others. Thoughtful policy analysis can be found in a report on space science by the United States Congress Office of Technology Assessment (OTA), which discusses the impact of space research on

traditional scientific disciplines and includes historical financial and demographic data. Historical studies include DeVorkin on the early rocket and balloon research, Hetherington on the creation of the Space Science Board, and Tatarewicz on planetary science. The archives of NASA, the Space Science Board at the National Academy of Sciences, the papers of Homer E. Newell at the National Archives, and the papers of Lloyd Berkner at the Library of Congress are large, well-organized collections essential for understanding the phenomenon of space science and exploration.

BIBLIOGRAPHY

Berkner, Lloyd V., and Hugh Odishaw, eds. *Science in Space.* 1961. Reprint, New York: McGraw-Hill, 1967.

DeVorkin, David H. *Science with a Vengeance: How the Military Created US Space Sciences After World War II.* New York: Springer-Verlag, 1992.

Glasstone, Samuel. *Sourcebook on the Space Sciences.* Princeton, NJ: D. Van Nostrand, 1965.

Hanle, Paul A., and Von Del Chamberlain, eds. *Space Science Comes of Age: Perspectives in the History of the Space Sciences.* Washington, DC: Smithsonian Institution Press, 1981.

Haymes, Robert C. *Introduction to Space Science.* Space Science Text Series. New York: Wiley, 1971.

Hetherington, Norriss S. "Winning the Initiative: NASA and the U.S. Space Program." *Prologue* 7 (1975): 99–107.

Le Galley, Donald P., ed. *Space Science.* New York: Wiley, 1963.

Massey, Harrie, Sir. *History of British Space Science.* New York: Cambridge University Press, 1986.

Naugle, John E. *First Among Equals: The Selection of NASA Space Science Experiments.* Washington, DC: Government Printing Office, 1991.

Newell, Homer E. *Beyond the Atmosphere: Early Years of Space Science.* Washington, DC: National Aeronautics and Space Administration, 1980.

Russo, Arturo, ed. *Science Beyond the Atmosphere: The History of Space Science in Europe.* Proceedings of a Symposium Held in Palermo, Italy, 5–7 November 1992. ESA HSR-Special, 1993.

Tatarewicz, Joseph N. *Space Technology and Planetary Astronomy.* Bloomington: Indiana University Press, 1990.

United States Congress Office of Technology Assessment. *Space Science Research in the United States: A Technical Memorandum.* Washington, DC: Government Printing Office, 1982.

Joseph N. Tatarewicz

SEE ALSO

National Aeronautics and Space Administration

S

SRI (Stanford Research Institute)

A nonprofit, revenue-producing research corporation in Menlo Park, California. The institute was founded by the president and trustees of Stanford University in 1946, after extensive consultation with regional businessmen. It was intended to serve and promote postwar regional economic development, to provide research opportunities for Stanford scientists and engineers, and to pay Stanford University a portion of its profits. Providing services under contract to the federal government was a secondary goal. The institute was unsuccessful financially in its early years. It was also criticized by some Stanford professors for undertaking research that was commercial rather than academic in nature.

The institute's fortunes improved with the onset of the Korean War in 1950. It became heavily involved in applied research and development work sponsored by the federal government. The institute continued to expand both in size and in amount of contract revenue in the late 1950s and 1960s. In 1970, Stanford University divested SRI, largely in response to faculty and student criticisms of the institute's deep involvement in military-sponsored, classified research and development projects. Some faculty members continued to provide consulting services to the institute. In 1977, the institute changed its name to SRI International.

Very little has been written about SRI or, more generally, about nonprofit research corporations and their relationship to industry and the government. A two-volume history by one of SRI's first staff members has some useful information but is severely marred by boosterism and a failure to document its sources. Some information relating to the institute's early history is available in the Stanford University Archives, but documentary sources are quite scarce, for reasons that remain unclear. SRI International has not collected or made available to scholars documents relating to its history.

BIBLIOGRAPHY

Gibson, Weldon B. *SRI: The Founding Years.* Los Altos, CA: Publishing Services Center, 1980.
———. *SRI: The Take-Off Days.* Los Altos, CA: Publishing Services Center, 1986.
Ikenberry, Stanley O., and Renee C. Friedman. *Beyond Academic Departments: The Story of Institutes and Centers.* San Francisco: Jossey-Bass, 1972.
Lowen, Rebecca S. *Creating the Cold War University: The Transformation of Stanford.* Berkeley: University of California Press, 1997.
Smith, James A. *The Idea Brokers: Think Tanks and the Rise of a New Policy Elite.* New York: Free Press, 1991.

Rebecca S. Lowen

SEE ALSO
Stanford University

Stallo, Johann Bernhard (John Bernard) (1823–1900)

German-born educator, philosopher, jurist, and scientific commentator. Born in Sierhausen, Olderburg, Germany, into a family long affiliated with school teaching, young Stallo studied at home before enrolling at a Catholic normal school. In 1839, at age sixteen, he emigrated to Cincinnati, Ohio, where he began teaching German in a parish school. The next year he published a successful German spelling and reading book. Beginning in 1841, he taught and studied at the newly organized St. Xavier's College, where he started to shift his area of specialization from German to mathematics, physics, and chemistry. In the fall of 1844, he left Ohio for New York, becoming an ordained Catholic priest and a professor of physics, chemistry, and mathematics at St. John's College (later Fordham University). While at St. John's, he also delved into philosophy, and in 1848 published a book on Hegel and other German thinkers. But about this time, he turned to the study of law, renouncing his ecclesiastical and academic career to return to Cincinnati, where he passed the bar examination in 1849.

A staunch and eloquent defender of human liberties as advocated by his hero Thomas Jefferson, Stallo prospered as a lawyer. Through gubernatorial appointment and then by election, he served as a common pleas judge for two years in the mid-1850s. Then, in 1885, President Grover Cleveland appointed him ambassador to Rome; after four years of service, he retired in Florence. From the time he took the bar examination through his Italian years, Stallo continued to write essays on a wide range of civic, historical, and philosophical topics, many of which he published in an 1893 collection. He also worked out the rudiments of a critique of contemporary physical science and mathematics. These nascent thoughts appeared during 1873–1874 in a series of four articles collectively titled "The Primary Concepts of Modern Physical Science" and published in *Popular Science Monthly*. In 1882, large sections of these articles reappeared in Stallo's most famous book: *The Concepts and Theories of Modern Physics.*

Adopting an empiricist stance tempered by his Hegelian and Kantian roots, Stallo set himself two related goals in this book. Both goals arose from his perception that most physical scientists, to their discredit, shared a "metaphysical" commitment to an "atomo-mechanical" view of nature. First, by examining the detailed workings of mechanical science—physical theories involving unseen atoms that supposedly obeyed established laws of classical mechanics—he wished to show that this approach was neither internally consistent nor capable of explaining certain basic empirical facts. Second, he sought to account for these failings by exposing the shaky, metaphysical foundations of the approach. This latter was, in fact, his primary goal. Physics, chemistry, and some areas of modern mathematics provided a case study to demonstrate the "logical and psychological origin" of metaphysical modes of thought and cognition—modes that were intellectually debilitating but pervasive in nearly all fields of inquiry.

Although it eventually went through various domestic and foreign editions, *The Concepts and Theories of Modern Physics* initially precipitated a spirited exchange between Stallo and American and British reviewers. Positivist Ernst Mach and, later, operationalist Percy Bridgman enhanced the book's long-term impact, however, by reacting favorably to its strong phenomenalistic and antimetaphysical message.

BIBLIOGRAPHY

Drake, Stillman. "J. B. Stallo and the Critique of Classical Physics." In *Men and Moments in the History of Science,* edited by Herbert M. Evans. Seattle: University of Washington Press, 1959, pp. 22–37.

Easton, Loyd D. *Hegel's First American Followers, the Ohio Hegelians: John B. Stallo, Peter Kaufmann, Moncure Conway, and August Willich.* Athens: Ohio University Press, 1966.

McCormack, Thomas J. "John Bernard Stallo: American Citizen, Jurist, and Philosopher." *The Open Court* 14 (1900): 276–283.

Moyer, Albert E. *American Physics in Transition: A History of Conceptual Change in the Late Nineteenth Century.* Los Angeles, CA: Tomash Publishers, 1983.

Rattermann, H.A. "Johann Bernhard Stallo, Deutsch-Amerikanischer Philosoph, Jurist und Staatsmann." In *Gesammelte Werke.* Cincinnati, OH: Selbstverlag der Verfässer, 1911, 12: 11–55.

Stallo, J.B. *Reden, Abhandlungen und Briefe.* New York: E. Steiger, 1893.

———. *The Concepts and Theories of Modern Physics.* Edited by Percy W. Bridgman. 3d ed., 1938. Reprint, Cambridge, MA: The Belknap Press of Harvard University Press, 1960.

Strong, John V. "The 'Erkenntnistheoretiker's' Dilemma: J.B. Stallo's Attack on Atomism in His 'Concepts and Theories of Modern Physics.'" *PSA: Proceedings of the Biennial Meeting of the Philosophy of Science Association, 1974,* pp. 105–123.

Wilkinson, George D. "John B. Stallo's Criticism of Physical Science." Ph.D. diss., Columbia University, 1951.

Albert E. Moyer

Standard Time

Standard time is the civil time of day in any of the world's twenty-four time zones, usually the mean solar time of the zone's central meridian. One time zone usually covers fifteen degrees longitude from pole to pole and differs by one hour from its neighboring zones. This global system of zoned time is based on the equivalence of time and longitude (one hour equals 15 degrees longitude and twenty-four hours equals 360 degrees). Almost all of the countries of the world cooperate to observe this system, but in some places the zone boundaries deviate from the convention to accommodate local time preferences. The starting line for calculating longitude is the prime meridian (zero degrees longitude) running through Greenwich, England.

The division of the globe into twenty-four zones, one hour apart, resulted from the International Meridian Conference held in Washington, D.C., in 1884. Delegates from twenty-five countries in the Americas and Europe attended. The conferees recommended that the nations of the world establish a prime meridian at Greenwich, England; count longitude east and west from the prime meridian up to 180 degrees in each direction; and adopt a universal day beginning at Greenwich at midnight. Although the conference had no authority to enforce its suggestions, the meeting resulted in the gradual worldwide adoption of the time-zone system based on Greenwich as prime meridian in use today.

Organized international support for fixing a common prime meridian had emerged at the International Geographical Congress held at Antwerp, Belgium, in 1870. Scientists, interested in establishing a coordinated time system for their worldwide observations, met throughout

S

the decade to discuss the desirability of a standard time for the world. Cleveland Abbe, first official weather forecaster for the U.S. government, led the effort to gain federal backing for time standardization. Sandford Fleming, engineer in chief of the Canadian Pacific Railway, was the first to publish a systematic scheme for a global system of time zones in *Uniform Non-Local Time (Terrestrial Time)* in 1876.

By the time of the International Meridian Conference in 1884, Sweden (1879) and Great Britain (1880) had each adopted a national standard time, and the railroads of North America had already begun their own experiment with zoned time. In North America, by the 1880s, it had become impractical to operate on a single time because of the enormous differences in longitude from east to west.

On 18 November 1883, Standard Railway Time went into effect in North America. That day, most railroads in the United States and Canada replaced a profusion of nearly fifty local times with five zones—Intercolonial, Eastern, Central, Mountain, and Pacific—each of which had a uniform time within its boundaries. The zones were calculated on meridians, fifteen degrees apart, based on Greenwich as the prime meridian (zero degrees longitude), following North American shipping practice. Fearing government intervention, the railroads voluntarily introduced the new system to help organize the ever-increasing traffic of passengers and freight. The railroads' transition from multiple times to zoned time was orchestrated by William F. Allen, publisher of *Travelers' Official Guide* and secretary of the railroads' two organizations for coordinating timetables, the General Time Convention and the Southern Railway Time Convention.

Although pockets of local resistance to railroad standard time persisted into the twentieth century, most large cities in North America immediately adopted the railroad's artificial time. The Standard Time Act of 1918 made the system federal law in the United States, and Canada adopted similar legislation that same year. In the United States, the Interstate Commerce Commission was responsible for drawing and changing the zone boundaries, which have been adjusted many times since then. The Uniform Time Act of 1966 placed time one matters under the Department of Transportation.

The 100th anniversary of both Standard Railway Time in the United States and the International Meridian Conference prompted a reexamination of the history of time standardization. This recent research has uncovered the role of scientists, especially American scientists, in the global movement, and also has highlighted long-overlooked, but persistent, opposition to national efforts to standardize time.

Modern opposition to standardized time mainly targets extensions of daylight saving time, rather than the zone system on which daylight saving time is based. Daylight saving time provides more hours of daylight in the evening by adjusting the clock one or two hours ahead of standard time. Although Benjamin Franklin facetiously suggested a plan for saving daylight in a 1784 essay, the modern system is credited to English builder William Willett, who proposed it in his 1907 pamphlet "The Waste of Daylight." Germany, the first nation to adopt daylight saving time, advanced its clocks in 1915 during World War I as a measure to save fuel. Great Britain followed in 1916.

The first legislation establishing both standard time and daylight saving time for the United States also came during World War I. On 19 March 1918, in an effort to promote industrial efficiency, Congress approved the division of the country into five zones—Eastern, Central, Mountain, Pacific, and Alaska—measured from the Greenwich meridian and prescribed that the time in each zone was to advance one hour for the seven months beginning the last Sunday in March and ending the last Sunday in October. Canada approved daylight saving time in the same year.

But with the end of World War I, a deluge of protests—many of which came from farmers whose work days were based on sun time rather than clock time—caused Congress in 1919 to repeal the daylight saving provision of the original act. President Wilson vetoed the repeal twice, but was overridden. The Canadian law was in effect only the summer of 1918.

At the outbreak of World War II, the United States and Canada once again adopted extended daylight saving time. In the United States, this "War Time" began 9 February 1942, and continued year-round until 30 September 1945. Canada began on the same date and ended two weeks earlier.

Although many states and localities observed daylight saving time between the wars and after World War II, no national time legislation took effect again in the United States until the Uniform Time Act of 1966. The act provided for eight time zones and required all states choosing to observe daylight saving time to do so uniformly—from the last Sunday in April to the last

Sunday in October. The mnemonic—"spring forward, fall back"—came into common usage as a reminder for altering the nation's clocks.

In response to the energy shortage of 1973, Congress extended daylight saving time. The measure, controversial and short-lived, was observed from 6 January through 27 October 1974 and from 23 February through 26 October 1975. In 1986, Congress once again extended daylight saving time to begin, starting with the 1987 season, on the first Sunday in April rather than the last.

The worldwide observation of daylight saving time, or summer time, varies considerably. Many countries do not advance their clocks in the summer months, and those that do advance them do so on widely different dates.

BIBLIOGRAPHY

Bartky, Ian. "The Adoption of Standard Time." *Technology and Culture* 30 (1989): 25–56.

Howse, Derek. *Greenwich Time and the Discovery of the Longitude.* Oxford: Oxford University Press, 1980.

O'Malley, Michael. *Keeping Watch: A History of American Time.* New York: Viking, 1990.

Thomson, Malcolm. *The Beginning of the Long Dash: A History of Timekeeping in Canada.* Toronto: University of Toronto Press, 1978.

Carlene E. Stephens

Stanford Research Institute

See SRI

Stanford University

An elite, private university in northern California with an international reputation in science and engineering. The university was founded in 1885 by Leland Stanford, a California politician and railroad baron, and his wife, Jane, as a memorial to their son. The university was given 8,800 acres of land and an endowment worth $20 milllion, the largest of any university at that time. The coeducational, tuition-free university opened in 1891, with the aims of advancing scientific research and preparing students for "direct usefulness in life" (Elliott, p. 24).

David Starr Jordan, a prominent ichthyologist, graduate of Cornell University, and former president of Indiana University, was Stanford's first president (1891–1913). He established respected programs in botany, zoology, geology, chemistry, and engineering, and a laboratory on the Pacific coast (later called the Hopkins Marine Station). He also encouraged professors to interact with the local, nonacademic community. Expectations that Stanford would be a "university of high degree" (Mirrielees, p. 21) were not immediately fulfilled, however. Legal problems relating to the endowment, and the disastrous impact of the 1906 earthquake, constrained severely the university's finances in its first two decades. The university's reputation was also marred by Jane Stanford's interference in academic affairs.

Stanford geologist John Caspar Branner served as Stanford's second president (1913–1915); upon retirement, he was replaced by Ray Lyman Wilbur, dean of the university's medical school, who served until 1942. The 1920s was a decade of generous philanthropic support for scientific research, and Stanford's fortunes improved. The university also began charging tuition in order to raise faculty salaries and create a small fund to support faculty research. In these years, research programs in physics, microbiology, aeronautical engineering, radio engineering, and psychological testing were developed and strengthened.

Some of these advances were eroded in the 1930s. Income from endowment and tuition was reduced significantly during the depression. Also, the university's academic reputation was decisively eclipsed by those of other universities more successful in developing patronage for organized scientific research. The profile of the physics department began to rise in these years, however. Theoretician Felix Bloch, a refugee from fascism in Europe, joined the department in 1934. (In 1952, he became Stanford's first Nobel laureate for his work on nuclear magnetic resonance.) Also, in 1937, physicist William Hansen and unpaid researchers Russell and Sigurd Varian, invented the klystron, a microwave tube later used in radar. In 1938, the physics department began a program of research related to the klystron under industrial sponsorship.

During World War II, Stanford University was only marginally involved in the federal research program sponsored by the Office of Scientific Research and Development (OSRD). Many faculty members left Stanford for war work elsewhere. Electrical engineering chairman Frederick Terman directed the OSRD-sponsored Radio Research Laboratory, which developed countermeasures to enemy radar.

After the war, Stanford president Donald Tresidder (1943–1948), a businessman and former president of

S

the university's board of trustees, encouraged the development of industrially sponsored research programs. For this purpose, he established the Stanford Research Institute and a laboratory for research related to microwave devices. The laboratory and the institute, as well as the chemistry, physics, and electrical engineering departments, also began doing some research under contract with the navy after the war. The Korean War produced a tremendous expansion in military support for academic science and engineering at Stanford and other universities. Under military sponsorship, the university established new laboratories for basic and applied research related to electronics, countermeasures, and missile guidance systems. Most of this work was subject to security restrictions.

Through the 1950s and 1960s, Stanford underwent further transformation and expansion. The university's president, J.E. Wallace Sterling (1949-1968), and his provost, Frederick Terman (1954-1965), reshaped the university, raising standards for admission, imposing stringent requirements for tenure, inaugurating new research programs in materials science, artificial intelligence, genetics, solid state physics, and population biology, and raising funds to rebuild the Departments of Biology and Chemistry. They also established the Stanford Industrial Park, leasing university property to high-technology companies whose products, often, were based on research done in departments at Stanford. In the 1960s, Stanford also became the site of the Stanford Linear Accelerator Center, a federally funded, high-energy physics facility housing a two-mile electron accelerator based on the klystron and designed by Stanford physicists.

By the mid-1960s, Stanford's academic reputation had improved considerably; the university was ranked fifth in a comparison with other leading American universities. It also ranked third among universities with the most support from the Department of Defense. This became an issue for some faculty and students who opposed the Vietnam War and questioned the university's involvement in, and dependence on, military sponsorship. Their protests did not change the structure of scientific patronage at Stanford, although, in 1970, university administrators did ban classified research from the campus and divested the university of ownership of SRI. Dissension over the war, on and off campus, led to the resignation of Stanford's sixth president, Kenneth Pitzer (1969–1970), a prominent chemist and former president of Rice University. He

was succeeded by Stanford historian Richard W. Lyman (1970–1979).

During the presidency of Stanford biologist Donald Kennedy (1980–1991), the university's reputation in the sciences and engineering continued to grow, as did financial support from industry and the federal government. At the end of the decade, the university suffered serious setbacks. Structural damage caused by the 1989 earthquake created financial problems. The university's reputation was also damaged when the navy, a chief sponsor of academic research, charged Stanford administrators with improper use of overhead funds from government contracts. President Kennedy resigned, and the federal government began investigating the finances of other leading research universities.

The earliest studies of Stanford University are faithful, if glorified, accounts of the institution's development by nonprofessional historians. In the early 1960s, scholars began looking at Stanford and other universities as a group, seeking to understand the origins and unique characteristics of the "American university" (Veysey, p. vii), and how it became the main locus for scientific research in the late nineteenth century. Attention was also paid to the post–World War II university, an institution seen as distinctly different in structure and function from the Gilded Age university. Studies, mostly by social scientists, agreed that the transformation of the university resulted from an infusion of federal funds for scientific research and undergraduate education.

More recently, historians of science began asking whether federal support for scientific research had shaped the practice and intellectual content of academic science, and if so, how and to what end. The relationship between industrial patronage and academic science also came under scrutiny. In attempting to delineate the way in which material and institutional factors affect scientific production, scholars have begun to examine in depth individual institutions of higher education, including Stanford. Most of this work has focused on developments in physics and electrical engineering.

Documents relating to the history of science and Stanford University may be found in the Stanford University Archives, which holds both the university's administrative records as well as the papers of a number of Stanford scientists and engineers.

BIBLIOGRAPHY

Ben-David, Joseph. *Trends in American Higher Education.* Chicago: Chicago University Press, 1972.

Elliott, Orrin Leslie. *Stanford University: The First Twenty-Five Years.* 1937. Reprint, New York, Arno Press, 1977.

Galison, Peter, Bruce Hevly, and Rebecca Lowen. "Controlling the Monster: Stanford and the Growth of Physics Research, 1935–1962." In *Big Science: The Growth of Large-Scale Research,* edited by Peter Galison and Bruce Hevly. Stanford: Stanford University Press, 1992.

Geiger, Roger. *To Advance Knowledge: The Growth of American Research Universities, 1900–1940.* New York: Oxford University Press, 1986.

Leslie, Stuart W. *The Cold War and American Science.* New York: Columbia University Press, 1992.

Lowen, Rebecca S. "Transforming the University: Administrators, Physicists, and Industrial and Federal Patronage at Stanford." *History of Education Quarterly* 34/3 (Fall 1991): 365–388.

———. *Creating the Cold War University: The Transformation of Stanford.* Berkeley: University of California Press, 1997.

Mirrielees, Edith R. *Stanford: The Story of a University.* New York: Putnam, 1959.

Veysey, Laurence. *The Emergence of the American University.* Chicago: Chicago University Press, 1965.

Rebecca S. Lowen

Stanley, Wendell Meredith (1904–1971)

Biochemist and biomedical administrator. Born and raised in Ridgeville, Indiana, Stanley completed his undergraduate work in 1926 at the nearby Earlham College and planned a career as an athletic coach. A chance visit to the chemistry department at the University of Illinois, Urbana, sparked his lifelong interest in organic chemistry. He received his Ph.D. in 1929 under Roger Adams at Illinois, then spent a postdoctoral year (1930–1931) as a National Research Fellow in Chemistry under Heinrich Wieland in Munich. He joined the department of John V.L. Osterhout at the Rockefeller Institute in New York in 1931, moving the following year to the Institute's newly expanded unit of plant pathology in Princeton. There, he crystallized the tobacco mosaic virus (TMV) in 1935, initiating and developing new approaches to virus research. He received numerous honors and awards, including the Nobel Prize in chemistry in 1946, shared with John H. Northrop and John B. Sumner, for their contributions to enzyme and protein chemistry. He was elected to many scientific societies, including the American Philosophical Society, National Academy of Sciences, American Academy of Arts and Sciences, Sigma Xi,

Harvey Society, Japan Academy, and French Academy of Sciences. In 1948, he became professor of biochemistry at the University of California, Berkeley, and served as director of their new virus laboratory until 1969. He was an effective promoter of cancer research and an influential adviser to the National Institutes of Health and other government agencies.

Stanley's career in biomedicine displayed a meteoric rise. Soon after arriving in the Rockefeller Institute in Princeton, he was assigned to one of the most challenging biochemical projects: the crystallization of the tobacco mosaic virus. Scientists' persistent inability to isolate viruses in pure forms had greatly hampered virus and medical research. Stanley's technical skills in bioorganic chemistry, including his earlier experience with biphenyls and sterols, stood him in good stead; he was also aided by the proximity of biochemists who were leaders in the crystallization of proteins. He succeeded in performing the crystallization of TMV within a couple of years, identified the virus particle as protein, and determined its molecular weight (40,000,000). The availability of highly active and relatively pure preparations ushered in a new era in virus and gene research. On the philosophical level, the chemical transformation of organisms into crystal powder further blurred the distinction between the animate and inanimate realms. From a technical standpoint, viruses, as organisms, molecules, and gene analogs, became amenable to physicochemical analyses and to precise physiological manipulations. With expanding technical and institutional resources, Stanley's research group performed many such analyses on several plant viruses, researches that were on the interface of biochemistry, plant physiology, microbiology, genetics, and medicine. The scientific mobilization during World War II brought him even closer to medicine. His team worked on the influenza virus, obtaining highly purified preparations and effective antiserum vaccine. After his move to Berekely, he became increasingly involved with the administration of the large Virus Laboratory, where his group made important advances in TMV and polio research, contributing to both molecular genetics and medicine. From the mid-1950s on, Stanley became one of the early promoters of virus research as a central feature in the campaign against cancer, thus helping channel massive resources that not only built up this field but molecular biology as a whole (Creager).

Stanley's place in life science and medicine was compared with that of Louis Pasteur. He was instantly seen

S

as a pioneer, his crystallization of TMV has been touted as revolutionary, and in the decades following the discovery, it has been viewed as a symbolic beginning of molecular biology. More recently, Stanley's contributions and his place in the history of molecular biology have been reassessed (Olby, p. 156, Kay, 1986, p. 450). A reexamination of Stanley's chemical accomplishments has spotlighted the serious flaws in his work: he had missed the viral nucleic acids, the preparations were not true crystals, and the virus was not an enzyme. Rather than being a scientific revolutionary, he has been seen as firmly grounded in an older, prestigious research program which regarded viruses as autocatalytic enzymes. His institutional affiliation and commitment to the "protein paradigm" (Kay, *Molecular Vision,* p. 104) had biased both his approach and conclusions. These institutional and disciplinary factors help explain why the objections of his critics in the 1930s in the United State and England had not received serious considerations, and why the protein view of viruses and genes lingered into the 1950s. By then, after his work had been corrected, it was reintegrated in its reinterpreted form into the history of the DNA double helix. The reexamination of Stanley's research has contributed to broader revisions of the history of molecular biology. His career underscores the important role that technological and institutional resources have played in the rise of that powerful hybrid discipline.

The Stanley Papers, have been deposited at the Bancroft Library, University of California, Berkeley. This voluminous collection documents in great detail Stanley's research and administrative activities. These records shed light not only on Stanley, but on his career as a window for viewing major developments in molecular biology, cancer research, and the rise of the biomedical establishment in America.

BIBLIOGRAPHY

Creager, Angela N.H. "Wendell Stanley's Dream of a Free-Standing Biochemistry Department at the University of California, Berkeley." *Journal of the History of Biology* 29 (1996): 331–360.

Edsall, John D. "Wendell Meredith Stanley." *The American Philosophical Society Year Book,* 1971, pp. 184–190.

Kay, Lily E. "W.M. Stanley's Crystallization of the Tobacco Mosaic Virus." *Isis* 77 (1986): 450–472.

———. *The Molecular Vision of Life: Caltech, the Rockefeller Foundation, and the Rise of the New Biology.* New York: Oxford University Press, 1993.

———. "The Intellectual Politics of Laboratory Technology: The Protein Network and the Tiselius Apparatus." In *Center on the Periphery: Historical Aspects of 20th-Century Swedish Physics,* edited by Svante Linquist. Canton, MA: Science History Publications, 1993, pp. 398–423.

Olby, Robert C. *The Path to the Double Helix.* London: Macmillan, 1974.

Lily E. Kay

Stein, William Howard (1911–1980)

Biochemist. Stein was awarded the 1972 Nobel Prize in chemistry together with Stanford Moore, both at Rockefeller University, and jointly with Christian Anfinsen. Stein and Moore's contribution was the elucidation of the chemical structure and the catalytic activity of the active center of the ribonuclease molecule. Stein was born in New York City. He studied at Harvard and obtained his Ph.D. after a study of the amino acid composition of elastin in 1938. He then joined the department of Max Bergmann at the Rockefeller Institute, of which he became a member in 1952.

After World War II, Stein and Stanford Moore developed chromatographic methods for the separation of all of the amino acids in a protein hydrolysate. They applied partition chromatography on starch columns with alcohol/water as the solvents, and developed an automatic fraction collector based on a photoelectric drop-counting technique. They eventually were able to reduce the time of analysis for a single chromatogram to six hours.

In 1949, Stein and Moore started the study of an enzyme, pancreatic ribonuclease, which had first been described in 1920 and had been crystallized by Moses Kunitz in 1940. Ribonuclease was found to be a molecule containing 124 amino acid residues (approximate molecular weight of 14,000) and in 1951, Stein and Moore had obtained finite distribution coefficients of ribonuclease on an ion exchanger comparable to that obtained with a simple amino acid. Stein and Moore published the complete sequence of ribonuclease between 1958 and 1960, the first reported sequence of an enzyme. They used chemical methods to study the conformational structure of ribonuclease and especially the "active site" of the enzyme, their conclusions being corroborated by the results of X-ray analysis. Their research was continued with the study of deoxyribonuclease, a glycoprotein with about twice as many

In the summer of 1969, Stein developed a severe case of Guillain-Barré syndrome and remained a quadriplegic until his death.

BIBLIOGRAPHY

Moore, Stanford. "William Howard Stein [1911–1980]." *Journal of Biological Chemistry* 255 (1980): 9517–9518.

———. "William Howard Stein." *Biographical Memoirs of the National Academy of Sciences* 56 (1987): 414–440.

Moore, Stanford, and William H. Stein. "Chemical Structures of Pancreatic Ribonuclease and Deoxyribonuclease [Nobel Lecture]." *Science* 180 (1973): 458–464.

———. "Stanford Moore and W. H. Stein." In *75 Years of Chromatography: A Historical Dialogue—Journal of Chromatography Library*. Vol. 17. Edited by Leslie S. Ettre and Albert Zlatlds. Amsterdam: Elsevier, 1979, pp. 297–308.

Richards, Frederic M. "The 1972 Nobel Prize for Chemistry." *Science* 178 (1972): 492–493.

Smith, Emil L. "Stanford Moore." *Biographical Memoirs of the National Academy of Sciences* 56 (1987): 354–385.

———. "Stein, William Howard." *Dictionary of Scientific Biography.* Vol. 18, supplement 2. Edited by F. Larry Holmes. New York: Scribner, 1990, pp. 851–855.

Stein, William H., and Stanford Moore. "Chromatography." *Scientific American* 184 (March 1951): 35–41.

———. "The Chemical Structure of Proteins." *Scientific American* 204 (February 1961): 81–92.

Ton van Helvoort

Stevens, Nettie Maria (1861–1912)

Cytologist and embryologist. Born in Cavendish, Vermont, Stevens was educated in the public schools of Westford, Massachusetts, and graduated from the Westfield, Massachusetts, Normal School in 1883. After teaching school for several years to save money for higher education, she saved enough money to go to Stanford University. She began as a special student in September 1896, was awarded regular freshman standing in January 1897, and three months later was admitted to advanced standing. Stevens received her bachelor's degree in 1899 (concentrating in histology) and remained at Stanford to work on her master's degree, which she received in 1900. Her thesis, "Studies on Ciliate Infusoria," was published in the *Proceeding of the California Academy of Sciences* in 1901. Stevens returned to the East to pursue a Ph.D. degree at Bryn Mawr College. Her first work there was with Joseph Weatherland

Warren on the physiology of frog contractions, but very shortly thereafter she began to work with the geneticist Thomas Hunt Morgan. Stevens received the Ph.D. degree in 1903 and her dissertation was published that same year. She retained an affiliation with Bryn Mawr for the rest of her life, beginning as a research fellow in biology from 1902 to 1904 (her research from 1903 to 1904 was funded by a Carnegie Institution Grant). In 1904 to 1905, she was a reader in experimental morphology, and from 1905 to 1912, an associate in experimental morphology. The trustees of Bryn Mawr eventually created a research professorship for her, but she died of breast cancer before she could occupy it.

Stevens published at least thirty-eight papers during the eleven years between 1901, when she published her first paper, and her death. Her most important work was in cytology, when she, as a recipient of a Carnegie Foundation grant, demonstrated that sex is determined by a particular chromosome. During the same period, other investigators were also exploring the relationship between the chromosomes and heredity. Although the behavior of the chromosomes during cell division had been described, speculations about their relation to Mendelian heredity had not been experimentally confirmed. No trait had been traced from the chromosomes of the parent to those of the offspring, nor had a specific chromosome been linked with a specific characteristic even though hints that the inheritance of sex might be related to a morphologically distinct chromosome suggested the possibility of such a connection. If sex were shown to be inherited in a Mendelian fashion, then a chromosomal basis for heredity would be supported.

By 1903, Stevens had become interested in the problem of chromosomes and sex determination. In this year, she applied to the Carnegie Institution for a grant, and described one of her research interests as "the histological side of the problems of heredity connected with Mendel's Law (quoted in Brush, p. 171)." Another important cytologist, Columbia University professor Edmund Beecher Wilson, was working on the same problem at the same time. Since both Wilson and Stevens concluded that sex was determined by a specific chromosome, the question of priority is sometimes raised. Until recently, it was usually Wilson who was credited with the discovery. However, it is apparent that the two arrived at their corresponding discoveries quite independently. The important breakthrough described by Stevens in her paper included her study of the common mealworm, *Tenebrio molitor.* In 1905, she

S

established that male mealworms have nineteen large chromosomes and one small one, and females twenty large ones. She cautiously concluded that this situation represented a case of sex determination by the particular pair of differently sized chromosomes. Postulating that the spermatozoa containing the small chromosome determine the male sex and that those containing ten large chromosomes determine the female sex, she suggested that sex may in some cases be determined by a difference in the amount or quality of the chromatin. Since the results in other species were so variable, Stevens, like Wilson, hesitated to make an unequivocal statement. Yet, she clearly recognized the significance of her discovery and investigated spermatogenesis in a number of different species to try to determine a pattern. Although biologists at the time were skeptical of her theory and she herself constantly questioned her assumption of a Mendelian basis for the inheritance of sex, her work was vitally important in providing observational evidence for the importance of the chromosomes in heredity.

Stevens's accomplishments were recognized by many of her colleagues, yet she remained on a low rung of the academic ladder at Bryn Mawr College, and her achievements still have not yet received full credit, partially because of gender bias. Hans Ris, in an article in *Notable American Women 1607–1950* wrote an early account of Stevens's life and works. Stephen Brush then was intrigued by the fact that Wilson was more often credited with the discovery of sex determination by chromosomes than Stevens. At Brush's suggestion, Marilyn Ogilvie and Cliff Choquette pursued the question and determined that Stevens and Wilson worked independently and simultaneously. Wilson's more frequent attribution is partially because of his more extensive contributions to biology in general and partially because of gender bias.

Stevens is especially important because she was one of the first American women to make a significant theoretical contribution to biology, but materials for a full-length biography are scarce. Those papers that are available can be found chiefly in the archives of the Carnegie Institution of Washington, the American Philosphical Society, and Bryn Mawr College.

BIBLIOGRAPHY

Brush, Stephen. "Nettie M. Stevens and the Discovery of Sex Determination by Chromosomes." *Isis* 69 (1978): 163–172.

Maienschein, Jane. "Stevens, Nettie Maria." *Dictionary of Scientific Biography.* Vol. 18, supplement 2. Edited by Frederic L. Holmes. New York: Scribner, 1990, pp. 867–868.

Morgan, Thomas Hunt. "The Scientific Work of Miss N.M. Stevens." *Science* 36 (1912): 468–470.

Ogilvie, Marilyn Bailey, and Clifford J. Choquette. "Nettie Maria Stevens (1861–1912): Her Life and Contributions to Cytogenetics." *Proceedings of the American Philosophical Society* 125 (1981): 292–311.

Stevens, Nettie Maria. "Further Studies on the Ciliate Infusoria, Licnophora and Boveria." *Archiv für Protistenkunde* 3 (1904): 1–43.

———. *Studies in Spermatogenesis with Especial Reference to the "Accessory Chromosome."* Carnegie Institution of Washington, Publication no. 36, pt. 1. Washington, DC, 1905.

———. "A Study of the Germ Cells of *Aphis rosae* and *Aphis oenetherae.*" *Journal of Experimental Zoology,* 2 (1905): 313–333.

———. *Studies on the Germ Cells of Aphids.* Carnegie Institution of Washington, Publication no. 51. Washington, DC, 1906.

———. *Studies in Spermatogenesis. A Comparative Study of the Heterochromosomes in Certain Species of Coleoptera, Hemiptera and Lepidoptera, with Especial Reference to Sex Determination.* Carnegie Institution of Washington, Publication no. 36, pt. 2. Washington, DC, 1906.

Marilyn Bailey Ogilvie

Strong, Theodore (1790–1869)

Born in South Hadley, Massachusetts, Strong was a leading American mathematician during the middle of the nineteenth century. He is important for the high level of his mathematical work, for the part he played in introducing continental methods to the United States, and as a mathematical educator. At Yale, Strong studied under two leading contemporary American scientists: Benjamin Silliman and Jeremiah Day. Strong distinguished himself in mathematics at Yale, and after graduation in 1812, became the mathematics tutor at newly founded Hamilton College, in Clinton, New York. In 1816, Strong became professor of mathematics and natural philosophy at Hamilton and held this post until 1827, when he accepted the same position at Rutgers College, a position he held for thirty-five years.

Strong's mathematics professor, Day, was a leader in introducing continental ideas into American mathematics textbooks, but whether Day introduced continental mathematics to Strong while he was an undergraduate is unknown. None of Strong's mathematical work published before 1825 reflects this influence. Thereafter, Strong's work shows a strong continental influence, and his papers helped to introduce these ideas to his countrymen.

Although inferior to the best European contributions, Strong's mathematical work is superior to that of most contemporary Americans. Strong published work in virtually every branch of mathematics being investigated in the United States during his lifetime, including the theory of equations, geometry, mechanics, analysis, and number theory.

Unlike many of his contemporaries, Strong did not publish successful mathematical textbooks. His two published books, one on algebra and one on calculus, are a puzzling amalgam of elementary and advanced mathematics; both saw limited circulation. Strong was not a popular teacher with the average student, but he was highly appreciated by those of ability, including his most notable student, the mathematical astronomer George William Hill, who acknowledged his debt to Strong.

Strong received the honorary Doctor of Laws from Rutgers in 1835. He was elected a member of the American Academy of Arts and Sciences in 1832 and the American Philosophical Society in 1844. He became one of the original members of the National Academy of Sciences in 1863.

Some of Strong's correspondence is preserved in the Yale University Libraries; The Library of the American Philosophical Society; The Benjamin Peirce Papers, Houghton Library, Harvard University; and The Charles Gill Papers, John M. Olin Library, Cornell University.

BIBLIOGRAPHY

Bradley, Joseph P. "Theodore Strong." *Biographical Memoirs of the National Academy of Sciences* 2 (1886): 1–28.

Colton, A. S. "Theodore Strong." In *Memorial of Theodore Strong, LL. D.* New York: S.W. Green, 1869, pp. 26–28.

Dwight, B.W. *The History of the Descendants of Elder John Strong.* Vol. 1. Albany, NY: n.p., 1871.

Hogan, Edward R. "Theodore Strong and Ante-Bellum American Mathematics." *Historia Mathematica* 8 (1981): 439–455.

Edward R. Hogan

Surveying

The technique of precisely locating features on the surface of the ground or aligning manufactured structures using measuring instruments and the principles of geometry and trigonometry to calculate distance and elevation. Surveying has been connected to science both through the calculating techniques, which require a knowledge of mathematics beyond arithmetic, and astronomy (to calculate latitude and longitude through celestial observations), and the measuring instruments, which are the products of scientific instrument making because of the precision required to achieve accurate results. Thus, surveying occupies one of the intersections between science and engineering.

In the eighteenth and nineteenth centuries, surveying provided an important entrée into American science. Knowledge of surveying provided an entry into the field for several prominent colonial American scientists, among them Cadwallader Colden and Benjamin Banneker. The most notable example of this pattern was David Rittenhouse, whose career as a watch and instrument maker led him to surveying, as he first constructed and then used transits, the telescopic sites used to determine angles for surveying measurements. Surveying, in turn, led Rittenhouse to astronomy and underlay his successful attempts to build several extremely accurate orreries.

The effort to conduct geodetic surveys (surveys to map large areas) of the United States also provided a link between surveying and science. From the Lewis and Clark Expedition through the United States Coast Survey to the great surveys of the West after the Civil War, the federal government's support of science more often than not was justified by the desire for accurate maps of American territory. Thus, surveys were the most typical example of federally sponsored scientific activity throughout the nineteenth century, and included many smaller, focused projects, such as those conducted by the United States Army. These surveys produced maps using triangulation methods, beginning with the accurate measurement of a baseline from which all subsequent distances and elevations could be calculated. While this painstaking work was proceeding, most government surveys also pursued other scientific collecting and observational missions, significantly advancing the American scientific enterprise.

The act of surveying, however, is primarily an engineering activity. Before a college education provided the normal preparation for entering the field, generations of engineers found surveying the essential tool on which their careers were founded. At the same time, surveying provided their initial introduction to mathematics.

S

Many learned to survey through practical experience in the construction of such early engineering projects as the Erie Canal and the Baltimore & Ohio Railroad. Even after engineers began to emerge from colleges, through the early twentieth century, every engineering student, regardless of specialization, was required to have knowledge of surveying.

After World War II, surveying was no longer so important, and since then, only civil engineering students are exposed to the subject. Yet, recent surveying technologies have continued to demonstrate the interaction of science and engineering in this field. In the 1920s, aerial photography offered new possibilities for mapping, leading to the development of photogrammetry, in which stereo cameras produce images that can be translated easily into highly accurate charts, especially when linked to computers. By harnessing satellites and global positioning systems, surveyors have further automated and computerized mapping techniques. Another recent development is the replacement of older telescopic transits with lasers, permitting highly accurate measurements of distance for vertical controls in photogrammetry and for line and grade measurements in local surveys.

BIBLIOGRAPHY

Bedini, Silvio. *The Life of Benjamin Banneker.* Rancho Cordova, CA: Landmark Enterprises, 1984.

Cazier, Lola. *Surveys and Surveyors of the Public Domain, 1785–1975.* Washington, DC: U.S. Department of the Interior, 1975.

Hindle, Brooke. *The Pursuit of Science in Revolutionary America, 1735–1789.* Chapel Hill: University of North Carolina Press, for the Institute of Early American History and Culture, 1956.

"The History of Surveying in the United States (A Panel Discussion)." *Surveying and Mapping* 18 (April–June 1958): 179–219.

Kirby, Richard S., and F.G. Laurson. *The Early Years of Modern Civil Engineering.* New Haven: Yale University Press, 1932.

Kreisle, William E. "History of Engineering Surveying." *Journal of Surveying Engineering* 114 (August 1988): 102–124.

Stuart, Lowell O. *Public Land Surveys; History, Instruction, Methods.* Ames, IA: Collegiate Press, 1935.

Bruce E. Seely

SEE ALSO
Engineering, Civil and Military

Surveys, Federal Geological and Natural History

From 1804, reconnaissances and surveys sponsored by the Interior, War, and Navy Departments examined physical features and living and nonliving resources while mapping routes through, areas in, and the boundaries of the public domain. The executive branch conducted these expeditions, and those overseas, for their potential economic value as aids to commerce, transportation, settlement, resource development, and defense. Until 1867, these explorations of geographical and intellectual frontiers principally sought increased topographical or hydrographical knowledge. In 1867, geology joined geography as a continuing major objective of federal surveys of the trans-Mississippi West. The government established the United States Geological Survey (USGS) and the Bureau of Ethnology as statutory agencies in 1879. Botany and zoology remained in the federal service through other organizations' work in forestry and in fisheries and surveys of other wildlife.

Scientists primed the early military explorers, but civilians trained academically as physician-naturalists did not accompany federal explorations until 1820. Officers continued to lead military expeditions thereafter, but only a few served in them as geologists and naturalists, or by assignment participated in the civilian-sponsored surveys. Beginning in the 1840s, civilian specialists trained in Europe, the state surveys, and the new scientific schools at Harvard and Yale joined federal reconnaissances or worked up their collections under contract.

Federal sponsorship began when Congress provided $2,500 in 1803 to extend the external commerce of the United States by supporting Meriwether Lewis and William Clark's army-mapping (1804–1806) of the most direct passage by water across the continent. President Thomas Jefferson also asked Lewis to observe enroute the country's native peoples, soils, plants, animals, fossils, minerals, and climate, and to return collections for study by specialists in the East.

Subsequent reconnaissances, sponsored principally by the army's Topographical Bureau and its successor the Corps of Topographical Engineers (CTE), established a successful military-civilian partnership in mapping, assessing, and illustrating the West's lands and resources. Historians have asserted that the CTE contributed to the rapid economic and territorial expansion of the United States before the Civil War (Dupree) by functioning as a public-works bureau (Goetzmann, 1959).

The CTE also helped to institutionalize science within the government and to train the physician-scientists who, doubling as geologist-naturalists on about one-half of its sixty antebellum expeditions, returned collections in botany, ethnology, mineralogy, paleontology, and zoology for further study.

During 1853–1855, the CTE extended its previous ad hoc expeditions with a comprehensive assessment of the West within the search for the best railroad route to the Pacific. The results of this program, and those from the contemporary CTE-Interior Department surveys of the U.S.-Mexican and the Northwest boundaries, and the Interior Department's wagon-road operations, remade the understanding of the West's lands and resources. The navy's United States Exploring Expedition (1838–1842) and subsequent searches for coaling stations and isthmanian canals likewise improved existing knowledge of the world's coasts, islands, and oceans. The civilian geologists employed by the Interior Department's General Land Office (GLO) provided plat- or drainage-based geologic maps and evaluations of public mineral lands in the Mississippi and Missouri Valleys, the Lake Superior region, Oregon Territory, and California as aids to their reasoned disposition and to science. The CTE and Interior Department antebellum surveys gave the nation master maps of the topography and geology of the West and a better comprehension of its living and past biotas.

The federal government resumed its land and maritime explorations after the Civil War, reviving both ad hoc linear reconnaissances and systematic surveys of areas. In 1867, the Corps of Engineers, which absorbed the CTE in 1863, began the United States Geological Exploration of the Fortieth Parallel, led by geologist Clarence King. King's well-planned, well-funded, and civilian-staffed survey (fieldwork, 1867–1872; publications, 1870–1880) used trigonometric-triangulation methods to map and assess the lands and resources that flanked the route of the transcontinental railroad between the Sierras and the Great Plains. King and his staff represented the growing professionalization of science in America; educated in eastern scientific schools (and some in European mining academies), they had gained additional experience in instrument-based federal or state surveys.

King introduced to federal surveys the modern topographical and geological methods he had learned while serving in the 1860s with Josiah Whitney's state-sponsored Geological Survey of California. The three other surveys of areas in the West adopted King's methods and standards in 1872–1873. Ferdinand Hayden's United States Geological and Geographical Survey of the Territories (fieldwork, 1867–1878; publications, 1868–1890) and John Powell's United States Geographical and Geological Survey of the Rocky Mountain Region (fieldwork, 1871–1878; publications, 1872–1893) mapped for the Department of the Interior. The Engineers sponsored Lieutenant George Wheeler's U.S. Geographical Surveys West of the One Hundredth Meridian (fieldwork, 1871–1879; publications, 1872–1889). Through the 1870s, these three surveys increased Hayden and Powell's efforts in land-use classification.

During 1874–1877, the Interior Depatment separated Hayden and Powell's work geographically and (in part) topically. Hayden continued to emphasize paleontology, botany, and zoology, while Powell concentrated on ethnology, but their planned atlas of the West competed with Wheeler's. When these and other internal reforms did not eliminate duplication of work, requests for deficiency appropriations, and topically inappropriate studies by the three organizations, Congress asked the National Academy of Sciences (NAS) in 1878 to plan a system for conducting the surveys of the public lands to yield better results at less cost.

The NAS Committee, advised by King at its request, recommended three Interior Department agencies. The new USGS would scientifically classify the public domain and study its geologic structure, natural resources, and products; its collections would go to the Smithsonian's National Museum. The United States Coast and Geodetic Survey, transferred from the Treasury Department to the Department of the Interior and renamed "Coast and Interior," would conduct cadastral, geodetic, and topographic surveys and produce maps for the USGS and the GLO. The Public Lands Commission (PLC) would codify the land laws and recommend an improved system of land-parceling surveys. GLO, shorn of its surveyors, would conduct and record sales of the public lands.

Congress and President Rutherford Hayes approved a revised plan that established only the USGS and the PLC. The new statute discontinued Hayden's, Powell's, and Wheeler's organizations, confined the Engineers to their regular surveys for transportation and defense, but provided funds for the terminated surveys to publish the remainder of their reports. The USGS continued to map the West, but at larger scales. The agency extended its

S

operations eastward in 1882 and to Alaska in the 1890s, where it replaced army and navy reconnaissances.

Greene (p. 101) rightly called for new histories to provide evaluations of the scientific methods and products of the federal reconnaissances and surveys equivalent to the many works that discuss their societal context and influence. Additional studies of manuscript and published sources in government and nongovernment repositories are required for improved understanding of the field- and laboratory work, technology, and publications of these federal organizations. Their work also should be compared to that of contemporary state surveys and the national and provincial surveys (and their predecessors) of other countries.

BIBLIOGRAPHY

Bartlett, Richard A. *Great Surveys of the American West.* Norman: University of Oklahoma Press, 1962.

Bruce, Robert V. *The Launching of Modern American Science 1846–1876.* New York: Alfred A. Knopf, 1987.

Dupree, A. Hunter. *Science in the Federal Government: A History of Policies and Activities to 1940.* Cambridge, MA: Harvard University Press, 1957.

Goetzmann, William H. *Army Exploration on the American West 1803–1863.* New Haven: Yale University Press, 1959.

———. *Exploration and Empire: The Explorer and the Scientist in the Winning of the American West.* New York: Alfred A. Knopf, 1966.

Goetzmann, William H., and Glyndwr Williams. *Atlas of North American Exploration.* Englewood Cliffs, NJ: Prentice Hall, 1992.

Greene, Mott T. "History of Geology." *Osiris,* 2d ser., 1 (1985): 97–116.

Jackson, W. Turrentine. *Wagon Roads West: A Study of Federal Road Surveys and Constructions in the Trans-Mississippi West, 1846–1869.* New Haven: Yale University Press, 1952.

Manning, Thomas G. *Government in Science: The U.S. Geological Survey 1867–1894.* Lexington: University of Kentucky Press, 1967.

Meisel, Max. *Bibliography of American Natural History: The Pioneer Century 1769–1865.* Brooklyn, NY: Premier, 1924–1929.

Nelson, Clifford M. "Paleontology in the United States Federal Service, 1804–1904." *Earth Sciences History* 1 (1982): 48–57.

Rabbitt, Mary C. *Minerals, Lands, and Geology for the Common Defence and General Welfare.* Vol. 1, *Before 1879*; Vol. 2, *1879–1904.* Washington, DC: Government Printing Office, 1979–1980.

Schubert, Frank N. *Vanguard of Expansion: Army Engineers in the Trans-Mississippi West 1819–1879.* Washington, DC: Government Printing Office, 1980.

Sherwood, Morgan B. *Exploration of Alaska 1865–1900.* New Haven and London: Yale University Press, 1965.

Clifford M. Nelson

SEE ALSO
Geological Survey, United States

T

Tatum, Edward Lawrie (1909–1975)

Biochemist and microbiologist. Born in Boulder, Colorado, Tatum attended the Laboratory School at the University of Chicago. He studied biochemistry and microbiology at the University of Wisconsin (where his father was a professor of pharmacology), earning a bachelor's degree in 1931 and a Ph.D. in 1935. A General Education Board fellowship supported his postdoctoral studies in microbial nutrition in Utrecht, where he forged important links with leaders in this field. The year 1937 marked the beginning of an unusually convoluted professional path. He moved to Stanford as a research associate to George W. Beadle, where together they developed a major program in biochemical genetics. He remained there until 1945, by then an assistant professor. In 1945, he accepted a tenured chair in the botany department at Yale University, developing a biochemically oriented microbiology program that rapidly generated fundamental discoveries in bacterial genetics. In 1948, Tatum was persuaded to return to Stanford in order to assume a full professorship in the biology department. He pursued and supervised diverse projects until 1957, when an outstanding offer brought him to the newly reorganized Rockefeller University in New York; he remained there until his death. Tatum received many honors, among them membership in the National Academy of Sciences, American Philosophical Society, and Harvey Society. He was awarded several prizes, notably the 1958 Nobel Prize for Physiology or Medicine, shared with Beadle and Joshua Lederberg for their contributions to microbial genetics. Beyond his research accomplishments, Tatum also served on editorial boards and advisory committees, notably the National Institutes of Health, National Foundation, and American Cancer Society; this work too contributed significantly to the growth of American life science and medicine.

Tatum's research projects always lay at the interface of several disciplines. At Wisconsin, where strong departments of biochemistry and microbiology flourished through close ties to the region's agricultural concerns and the food and drug industries, his graduate work focused on microbial biochemistry and the role of vitamins in bacterial nutrition; his postdoctoral research dealt with the nutritional significance of growth factors in microorganisms. The concept that microbial nutrition was a marker for evolutionary biochemical change was gaining currency during this time. When he joined Beadle at Stanford, Tatum added yet another dimension to his interdisciplinary research: genetics. This, in the late 1930s, was a professional risk. Indeed, Tatum's convoluted career path reflected the institutional complexities inherent in this novel configuration. Utilizing *Neurospora* as a model system, Beadle and Tatum developed a major program in biochemical genetics. They demonstrated that one gene controlled only a single biochemical reaction governed by its own specific enzyme, a key conceptual and disciplinary development in the history of molecular biology. Tatum also showed that *Neurospora* methods applied to bacteria. In 1946, he and Lederberg discovered genetic recombination in e. coli bacteria, thus bringing these organisms into the realm of genetics and molecular biology. In subsequent years, he became interested in the relation between carcinogenesis and mutagenesis, pursuing and supervising projects in bacteria and

T

Neurospora. Despite his remarkable achievements, Tatum often labored under precarious institutional conditions, seen neither as a conventional biochemist nor as a recognized geneticist. This ambiguous disciplinary status strongly contributed to his geographic mobility. After winning the Nobel Prize, Tatum became deeply involved in scientific organization, promoting life science both nationally and internationally.

The historiographic treatment of Tatum is incomplete and contradictory. On the one hand, he is seen as a principal figure in life science. But perhaps due to his institutional instability, or because his scientifically formative period emerged under the long shadow of Beadle, historians have not treated Tatum's career as an autonomous development. Although his achievements catalyzed the emergence of microbial genetics as a central feature of the new biology, unlike Beadle, he is not viewed as a discipline builder. Historical portrayals of Tatum are rather pale relative to the extraordinary historiographic glamour attached to the "founding fathers" of molecular biology. On the other hand, recent scholarship in the history of genetics (Sapp, Harwood) has challenged the historical novelty and primacy of Beadle's and Tatum's work. These studies show that microbial genetics flourished in Europe before Beadle's and Tatum's entry into the field. These scholars have argued that political and institutional contingencies, especially World War II, handicapped European progress while catapulting the *Neurospora* program to the vanguard. Regardless of approach, in all these histories, Tatum appears as an appendage figure.

The Tatum Papers are deposited at the Rockefeller Archive Center in Tarrytown, New York, but it is a relatively small collection. To date, there is no biography of Tatum, nor major studies of his researches. There is a great need for a historical treatment that would interpret his work outside the reconstructions of the path to the double helix. Whether utilizing a biographical or analytical genre, a close examination of Tatum's scientific trajectory would enrich our understanding of the history of life science in America.

BIBLIOGRAPHY

Harwood, Jonathan. *Styles of Scientific Thought: The German Genetics Community, 1900–1933.* Chicago: University of Chicago Press, 1993.

Kay, Lily E. "Selling Pure Science in Wartime: The Biochemical Genetics of G.W. Beadle." *Journal of the History of Biology* 22 (1989): 73–101.

———. *The Molecular Vision of Life: Caltech, the Rockefeller Foundation, and the Rise of the New Biology.* New York: Oxford University Press, 1993.

Lederberg, Joshua. "Edward Lawrie Tatum." *Biographical Memoirs of the National Academy of Sciences* 59 (1990): 357–385.

Nelson, D.L., and B.C. Soltvedt, eds. *One Hundred Years of Agricultural Chemistry and Biochemistry at Wisconsin.* Madison, WI: Science Tech, 1989.

Olby, Robert C. *The Path to the Double Helix.* London: Macmillan, 1974.

Sapp, Jan. *Beyond the Gene: Cytoplasmic Inheritance and the Struggle for Authority in Genetics.* New York: Oxford University Press, 1987.

———. *Where the Truth Lies: Franz Moewus and the Origins of Molecular Biology.* Cambridge, UK: Cambridge University Press, 1990.

Lily E. Kay

Telegraph Industry

The United States telegraph industry emerged in the 1840s after several decades of research by European and American scientists on electrical phenomena. Early attempts to use electricity for transmitting information grew directly out of scientific experiments on current ("galvanic") electricity and electromagnetism, but only as knowledge of electrical science was combined with the practical design knowledge possessed by a group of skilled mechanics did electric telegraphs evolve as practical instruments of communication in the United States and Europe. In the United States, Samuel Morse turned his rudimentary knowledge of recent electrical research and his artistic design skills to developing a telegraph system in the early 1830s. By 1837, he had designed a crude system using elements from his practical experience—his receiver incorporated the artist's wooden canvas-stretcher and his transmitter employed the printer's type and composing stick. The potential of this elementary telegraph gained Morse the help of two key assistants whom he knew through his university teaching. Chemistry professor Leonard Gale contributed a more sophisticated knowledge of electricity, especially electrochemistry, and also provided access to the important electromagnetic researches of Joseph Henry. Alfred Vail, Morse's student and a skilled mechanic whose father provided funding and machine-shop facilities, designed the more substantial and commercially viable instruments that they demonstrated in early 1838, the same year that commercial service began in Great Britain and Bavaria.

In developing his telegraph, Morse brought together preexisting scientific and technical communities, and in the process, he began the creation of a specialized technical community. As the telegraph industry grew, this community provided the necessary resources of knowledge and skill for telegraph inventors. The knowledge of electrical science that Morse gained through personal contacts with scientists became available to later inventors through industry's technical publications, while skilled mechanics could be found readily in the industry's manufacturing shops. Although telegraph invention usually required some knowledge of electricity, practical experience and knowledge of mechanical movements often proved more valuable than advanced knowledge of the science of electricity. Those operators responsible for maintaining lines, instruments, and batteries could acquire a good practical knowledge of electricity as well as of the mechanical operation of their equipment. The industry's machinists gained their own electrical knowledge through practical experience in building and testing telegraph equipment and in working with inventors. When the problem was essentially mechanical, even mechanics unschooled in electrical science produced important improvements. Nonetheless, inventors and telegraph engineers responsible for major technical improvements also sought deeper understanding of electrical science through reading in works on electrical and chemical science and through their own experimentation. In contrast to Europe, where scientists took the lead in developing many of the early telegraph systems and where the scientific community maintained much stronger ties to the new technology, the United States scientific community contributed little to telegraph technology. This was especially true with respect to Great Britain, where cable telegraphs produced more complex physical phenomena, and prominent scientists such as William Thomson made important contributions to telegraph technology. Only as telephony became the dominant telecommunications system in the second decade of the twentieth century did telegraphy's technical development feel the influence of the science-educated engineers who had begun to solve long-distance transmission problems for the electric light and power and telephone industries in the late nineteenth century.

Telegraphy has been a largely neglected subject of historical investigation. The early heroic histories of the industry provide some information about its technical development, but like the more scholarly histories of the mid-twentieth century, they focus on its business history. The standard nineteenth-century technical manuals are a better source of knowledge about technical developments. Only in the last decade have historians begun to produce scholarly studies of telegraph technology and its relationship to the scientific community, but more work is needed to clarify these connections and to provide necessary comparisons with European telegraphy.

BIBLIOGRAPHY
Hunt, Bruce. "'Practice vs. Theory': The British Electrical Debate, 1888–1891." *Isis* 74 (1983): 341–355.
Israel, Paul. *From the Machine Shop to the Industrial Laboratory: Telegraphy and the Changing Context of American Invention, 1832–1920.* Baltimore: Johns Hopkins University Press, 1992.
Israel, Paul, and Keith A. Nier. "The Transfer of Telegraph Technologies in the Nineteenth Century." In *International Technology Transfer: Europe, Japan and the USA, 1700–1914,* edited by David J. Jeremy. Aldershot, UK.: Edward Elgar, 1991.
Jenkins, Reese, et al. *The Papers of Thomas A. Edison, Volumes 1–3 (1847–1877).* Baltimore: Johns Hopkins University Press, 1989–1994.
Thompson, William. *Wiring a Continent: The History of the Telegraph Industry in the United States, 1832–1866.* Princeton: Princeton University Press, 1947.

Paul B. Israel

Terman, Frederick Emmons (1900–1982)

Electrical engineer, radio scientist, and university administrator. Terman was born in English, Indiana, the first son of Lewis Terman, the psychologist and developer of the Stanford-Binet IQ test, whose faculty appointment brought the family to Stanford University in 1910. Frederick grew up on campus, shaped by the strong influence of his father, and would spend nearly his entire career at Stanford.

After graduating from Stanford in 1920 with a degree in chemistry, he moved to electrical engineering and the laboratory of Harris J. Ryan, one of the leading power engineers in the United States and one of only two research engineers at Stanford. In 1922, Terman completed a master's thesis in Ryan's area of high-voltage engineering. He then pursued doctoral studies in electrical engineering at the Massachusetts Institute of Technology (MIT), where Arthur Kennelly and Vannevar Bush followed his father and Ryan in a line of able mentors. Terman wrote his dissertation on electrical

T

power transmission, but he also expanded his earlier interest in ham radio through the strong communications program at MIT.

Rather than assume an instructorship at MIT in 1924, he returned to Stanford to recuperate from a bout with tuberculosis and took a part-time position as head of Stanford's new communications laboratory. In 1926, he accepted a faculty position in the Department of Electrical Engineering and soon succeeded Ryan as its driving force. The small communications laboratory made strides in radio tube design and long-distance radiowave propagation, with support from the Bell Telephone System and the National Bureau of Standards. In 1932, Terman published *Radio Engineering*, which would become a standard textbook in the field. Five years later, he became executive head of the department.

In 1941, Terman became the first president of the Institute of Radio Engineers from a western state. The honor reinforced Terman's insistence on the importance of topics such as power networks and radio communication for the west, which was his primary justification for building Stanford into a center of research and the "western terminal" of experimental work on radio waves. Terman hoped that in time strong industries standing on a foundation of research could provide opportunities for engineers and scientists educated at Stanford. Fewer of them would then move east to find work, resulting in a concentration of talent that would foster regional industrial development and university-industry linkages like those in radio electronics. The Hewlett-Packard Company, founded by two of Terman's students in 1939, provided the archetype for Terman's model.

Vannevar Bush, by then director of the United States Office of Research and Development, selected Terman late in 1941 to organize and head the Harvard Radio Research Laboratory. Under Terman's guidance, it would develop radar countermeasures, such as radar jammers and "chaff," during World War II. For Terman, this assignment coalesced his ideas and experiences concerned with the organization and management of research. After returning to Stanford in 1946 as dean of engineering, he applied his realization of the significance of federal support for research and his many discussions with Harvard's educational strategists to his central task: the conversion of Stanford University into a top-notch research university. As provost of the university from 1955 until his retirement in 1965, he worked with J.E. Wallace Sterling, the university's president, to reshape departments and laboratories at Stanford and to exploit—as well as define—the role of the university in a growing complex of relationships with federal agencies and industry. After his retirement, he worked as a consultant on higher education policy, engineering curricula, and various university-industry and university-government partnerships. He died at his home on the Stanford campus.

Terman's moniker, "Father of Silicon Valley," expresses one aspect of his legacy. Historical research has focused more intensively, however, on his shaping of the strategy and mechanisms of federally funded university research. The common element is his role as a mover and shaker of research policy in the early Cold War era; Terman has figured in studies of links between federal funding and university research, between Stanford and technology-based companies, and between defense agencies and laboratories. He has loomed large in thematic investigations of postwar science and engineering, but his own contributions to radio science and electrical engineering have not received detailed attention, and he has not been the subject of a full biographical study. The starting point for such a biography would be his voluminous papers in the Department of Special Collections at Stanford, which span his entire career, including the wartime stint in the Radio Research Laboratory.

BIBLIOGRAPHY

Leslie, Stuart W. "Playing the Education Game to Win: The Military and Interdisciplinary Research at Stanford." *Historical Studies in the Physical and Biological Sciences* 18 (1987): 55–88.

Leslie, Stuart W., and Bruce Hevly. "Steeple Building at Stanford: Electrical Engineering, Physics, and Microwave Research." *IEEE Proceedings* 73 (1985): 1169–1180.

Lowen, Rebecca Sue. *Creating the Cold War University: The Transformation of Stanford*. Berkeley: University of California Press, 1997.

Lowood, Henry. *From Steeples of Excellence to Silicon Valley: The Story of Varian Associates and Stanford Industrial Park*. Palo Alto, CA: Varian Associates, 1989.

McMahon, A. Michal. *The Making of a Profession: A Century of Electrical Engineering in America*. New York: IEEE Press, 1984.

Medeiros, Frank A. "The Sterling Years at Stanford: A Study in the Dynamics of Institutional Change." Ph.D. diss., Stanford University, 1979.

Norberg, Arthur L. "The Origins of the Electronics Industry on the Pacific Coast." *IEEE Proceedings* 64 (September 1976): 1314–1322.

Terman, Frederick. *Radio Engineering*. New York: McGraw-Hill, 1932.

———. "A Brief History of Electrical Engineering Education." *IEEE Proceedings* 64 (September 1976): 1399–1407.

Henry Lowood

SEE ALSO
Stanford University

Thermodynamics

Thermodynamics, like evolution, is enmeshed in both the science and culture of the nineteenth century.

The two laws of thermodynamics became the main organizing principles for the physical sciences during the latter half of the nineteenth century. The term "thermodynamics" was coined by William John Macquorn Rankine in 1854 to define the study of the mechanical effects of heat without using any hypotheses regarding the motions that constituted heat. Rankine's cosmos was governed by the conservation of energy, the second law was merely mathematical. The second law was stated by Rudolph Julius Emmanuel Clausius in 1850 as a physical principle, that heat cannot flow from a colder to a hotter body. It was William Thomson (Lord Kelvin) who first exploited it, physically and cosmically (1852). With each cycle of real heat engines, some heat was not converted into work. It became unavailable. Thomson leaped to the conclusion that there was, over time, an absolute decrease in the energy available for useful work. The cosmos was doomed to a heat death. Thomson had struggled mightily to bring his religion and his science together on the issue of conservation. The second law reaffirmed his theological views. While Thomson's theological message was muted that of his contemporaries Balfour Stewart and Peter Guthrie Tait was explicit. Thermodynamic laws led to a belief in the immortality of the soul. This (1873) countered John Tyndall's self-sufficient Nature.

Clausius's focus on heat led to the same cosmic conclusions along a very different path. In a heat engine, heat was transformed into work and into heat at a lower temperature (1854). Plunging into the thermal changes of bodies on a microscopic level, Clausius discerned a quantity, entropy, as a property of bodies that was conserved in reversible heat cycles, yet was always positive for irreversible heat engines (1865).

The thermodynamics of both Thomson and Clausius ended where that of Josiah Willard Gibbs began, in the second law. He generalized Rankine's graphical representation of the thermal behavior of equilibrium systems by centering his analysis on entropy as a property of a thermal system. Gibbs explored homogeneous, then the thermal properties of heterogeneous, substances. His work contained important results for chemistry, such as reaction rates and the phase rule (1873–1879). Gibbs's work was only widely appreciated after Wilhelm Ostwald's research in the 1880s and the latter's efforts to develop a "general" chemistry. Ostwald, together with Svente August Arrenhius and Jacobus Henricus vant' Hoff established the discipline of physical chemistry. That field and its research methods were imported into the United States during the 1890s with the return of young American chemists from their laboratories in Europe. Gibbs thus became known to more than a small coterie of faculty at Yale, where Gibbs had spent his career.

While thermodynamics made no reference to the microscopic structure of matter, physicists believed that matter was made up of particles that behaved as mechanical bodies. Experiments based in kinetic theory indicated that molecular motions were reversible. Yet the irreversibility of the second law also was based upon observation. Efforts were made to make molecular models of matter compatible with the second law. Some depended upon particular molecular models, others on claims of ignorance, and a third on simply exploring the thermal behavior of gases without specifying how its component parts interacted—statistical mechanics. There were two approaches to exploring statistical mechanics, one tracing the approach of a thermal system to equilibrium, initiated by Ludwig Boltzmann. The other, begun by Maxwell, was explored in more depth by Gibbs. The system was already in equilibrium and its behavior was traced from one equilibrium state to the next. In statistical mechanics the second law became one of probabilities, not certainties. To demonstrate this, Maxwell invented his demon, that he considered simply as a valve, which opened or closed a door letting through fast molecules and, hence, separating them from slow ones. The demon could undo entropy.

The probabilistic nature of the second law also produced arguments for religious belief and free will and for skepticism. Thomson elaborated Maxwell's demon only to deny his effects in the physical world. Maxwell regarded mechanical systems as undefined at certain

T

points in their paths and, hence, free will was possible. Boltzmann, however, could use the second law to argue for religious skepticism.

Such discussions by scientists on religious topics were well known, but both Herbert Spencer and Henry Brooks Adams read the original papers and drew their own conclusions. Both assumed physical laws applied to society and history and used thermodynamics to support social theories drawn from other sources. Their uses of thermodynamics led them to diametrical conclusions. Spencer and Adams also enmeshed their own work in contradictions trying to align physical laws with their own ideas.

For Spencer, the second law lent support for his evolutionary mechanism that claimed development went from the homogeneous and simple to the heterogeneous and diverse. Elsewhere, he argued for the heat death of the cosmos.

The second law seemed to lend support to Adams's arguments of decline and moral degradation in Western history since its apogee of the High Middle Ages. Confusing complexity with chaos and the technical usage of phase with historical epochs, Adams could counter the evolutionary progressivism of Auguste Comte and Spencer. He cited and sometimes quoted Thomson, Maxwell, Clausius, Gibbs, and Ostwald, although in the latter case, his work on life and society not his science. Simultaneously, Adams saw Maxwell's demon as reopening the possibility for free will and spirituality. The phase rule gave Adams the language, phases ending in critical points, to explain the discontinuities of history and the beginnings of the modern, "mechanical phase" of history.

The scientific and cultural uses of thermodynamics expanded in the twentieth century to include the development of information theory, science fiction, and economic prophesy.

There is no comprehensive history of thermodynamics tracing its technical development beyond the 1850s, although there are rich sources for parts of that history in monographs and articles. Recently, historians have tried to trace the cultural origins of the basic ideas of thermodynamics in nineteenth-century Britain (Porter, Schweber). This is not easy. How do we fit in Clausius and Boltzmann. Both Maxwell and Gibbs kept their professional work strictly outside any cultural values that may inform that work. Such contextual accounts focus on fundamental ideas, not theories. Thermodynamics as a theory depended on the mathematical properties of functions. Origins become remote.

Adams and Spencer are only two thinkers who explicitly used the theory of heat for guidance in understanding history on a grand scale. Their sources are easy to trace, although the meanings they attached to them may be difficult to fathom. At least in the case of thermodynamics, historians have tried to place physics in its cultural place, not see it merely as a series of technical developments defined by the logical needs of the state of the argument leading, naturally, to the theories of the twentieth century.

BIBLIOGRAPHY

Adams, Henry. *The Degradation of Democratic Dogma.* Edited by Brooks Adams. 1919. Reprint, New York: Capricorn Books, 1958.

———. *The Education of Henry Adams.* Edited by Ernest Samuels. Boston: Houghton Mifflin, 1973.

Brush, Stephen G. *The Temperature of History; Phases of Science and Culture in the Nineteenth Century.* New York: Burt Franklin, 1978.

Daub, E.E. "Probability and Thermodynamics." *Isis* 60 (1969): 318–330.

———. "Maxwell's Demon." *Studies in the History and Philosophy of Science* 1 (1970): 213–227.

Gibbs, Josiah Willard. "Graphical Methods in the Thermodynamics of Fluids." *Transactions of the Connecticut Academy of Sciences* 2 (1873): 309–342.

———. "A Method of Geometrical Representation of the Thermodynamic Properties of Substances by Means of Surfaces." *Transactions of the Connecticut Academy of Sciences* 2 (1873): 362–404.

———. "On the Equilibrium of Heterogeneous Substances." *Transactions of the Connecticut Academy of Sciences* 3 (1878): 108–248, 343–524.

———. *Scientific Papers.* Edited by Henry Andrews Bumstead and Ralph Van Name. 2 vols. New York: Dover, 1961.

Hayles, N. Katherine. *Chaos Bound: Orderly Disorder in Contemporary Literature and Science.* Ithaca: Cornell University Press, 1990.

Hiebert, Erwin. "The Uses and Abuses of Thermodynamics in Religion." *Daedalus* 95 (1966): 1046–1080.

Jordy, William. *Henry Adams, Scientific Historian.* New Haven: Yale University Press, 1952.

Klein, Martin J. "Maxwell, His Demon and the Second Law of Thermodynamics." *American Scientist* 58 (1970): 84–97.

———. "The Early Papers of J. Willard Gibbs: A Transformation of Thermodynamics." *Proceeding of the Fifteenth Congress of the History of Science.* Edinburgh: Edinburgh University Press, 1978, pp. 330–341.

Myers, Gregg. "Nineteenth-Century Popularizations of Thermodynamics and the Rhetoric of Social Prophecy." *Victorian Studies* 29 (1985): 35–66.

Partenheimer, David. "Henry Adams' Scientific History and German Scientists." *English Language Notes* 27 (3) 1990: 44–52.

Porter, Theodor. "A Statistical Survey of Gases: Maxwell's Social Physics." *Historical Studies in the Physical Sciences* 12 (1981): 77–116.

Schweber, Silvan S. "Demons, Angels and Probability: Some Aspects of British Science in the Nineteenth Century." In *Physics as Natural Philosophy*, edited by Abner Shimony and Herman Feshbach. Cambridge, MA: MIT Press, 1982, pp. 319–363.

Servos, John W. *Physical Chemistry from Ostwald to Pauling: The Making of a Science in America.* Princeton: Princeton University Press, 1990.

Smith, Crosbie, and M. Norton Wise. *Energy and Empire: A Biographical Study of Lord Kelvin.* Cambridge, UK: Cambridge University Press, 1989.

Elizabeth Garber

SEE ALSO
Gibbs, Josiah Willard

Thoreau, Henry David (1817–1862)

Writer and philosopher. Thoreau was born and lived his entire life in Concord, Massachusetts, with occasional journeys to Maine, Canada, Cape Cod, and Minnesota. He graduated from Harvard College. His important works include his extensive *Journal*, essays collected under the title *Excursions* and including his influential "Civil Disobedience" (more properly, "Resistance to Civil Government"), *A Week on the Concord and Merrimack Rivers, Walden, Cape Cod*, a series of essays collected together as *The Maine Woods*, and *A Yankee in Canada*.

Thoreau supplemented what he could not learn in Harvard's lecture halls with careful reading. He knew especially Gilbert White's *Natural History of Selborne* (1788), and may perhaps have derived from it a model of the ways in which careful and extended observations of a single, out-of-the-way place can be turned both to scientific and literary advantage. He owned, read, and often referred to Darwin's *The Voyage of the Beagle* (1839).

With his reading, and on his own walks, Thoreau honed his skills as a naturalist. In an entry in his *Journal* from March 5, 1853, he defined himself as "a mystic, a transcendentalist, and a natural philosopher" (today, we would say "field naturalist"). As a transcendentalist, he followed Emerson's famous dictum that "particular natural facts are symbols of particular spiritual facts" (*Nature: 1836*). As a naturalist, he put to work, again and again, the careful observational methods of that science, as a way to "manage," organize, and learn from the nearly incomprehensible richness of data he encountered.

The natural historian works first of all by careful observation and collection of firsthand data; an impulse to be seen in all of Thoreau's longer works. This data functions both as a source of hypothesis and as a test of that hypothesis and of other, less reliable sources of information—especially dusty town histories, of which Thoreau was particularly fond. From these collected data, the natural historian constructs a careful definition of the phenomenon to be explained. Then, and only then, is he ready to propose an explanation, following insofar as is possible the known "laws" of natural process and behavior. The final, all-important step is to corroborate both the initial data and the constructed explanation by direct observation.

While Thoreau learned method from White and the possibilities of literary form from Darwin, he acted in the end not as a natural historian per se, but (as he admitted) as a mystic, too. His goal is not only the proposal of scientific generalizations, but the recognition of metaphor, symbol, and parable, moving beyond pure science to what he called, at one point, that "higher law" visible to the truly attentive eye.

So he can only in part be called a true natural historian. But that part is essential to the shape and content of *Walden* and other books. The method of the scientist allows Thoreau, whether venturing in Maine or navigating the Concord and Merrimack Rivers, or "squatting" on land loaned to him by Emerson, next to Walden Pond, or traveling further west in search of "Wild Apples," to draw not only upon his own scrupulous observations and collections, but also on the widest possible range of materials—maps, guidebooks, rumors, legends, the chatter of old men like the Wellfleet Oysterman—in an effort to see not just what is apparent but what that world of appearances might *mean*, metaphorically and metaphysically considered.

BIBLIOGRAPHY

Dean, Bradley P., ed. *Wild Fruits: Thoreau's Rediscovered Last Manuscript.* New York: W.W. Norton & Company, 1999.

Harding, Walter. *The Days of Henry Thoreau.* Princeton: Princeton University Press, 1962; reprinted, 1982.

Hildebidle, John. *Thoreau: A Naturalist's Liberty.* Cambridge, MA: Harvard University Press, 1983.

Richardson, Robert D. *Henry Thoreau: A Life of the Mind.* Berkeley: University of California Press, 1986.

Sattelmeyer, Robert. *Thoreau's Reading.* Princeton: Princeton University Press, 1988.

T

Thoreau, Henry David. *The Natural History Essays.* Salt Lake City, UT: Peregrine Smith, 1980.

John Hildebidle

SEE ALSO
Nature Writing

Torrey, John (1796–1873)

Botanist. Born in New York City, the son of William Torrey, merchant and civil servant, and Margaret Nichols. John Torrey became interested in botany as a child when the scientist and educator Amos Eaton was incarcerated in a prison of which Torrey's father was the superintendent. Torrey collected specimens for Eaton and was introduced to botany in the process. Following his graduation from the College of Physicians and Surgeons in 1818, Torrey practiced medicine in New York. From 1824 through 1827, Torrey began teaching chemistry, mineralogy, and geology at the United States Military Academy. Returning to New York City, Torrey began a pattern of teaching part time (College of Physicians and Surgeons, Princeton University, College of Pharmacy, New York University, Columbia College) to support his botanical activities that lasted until he became a United States assayer, in 1853, a position he held until his death.

This varied career marks Torrey as a member of the last generation of American botanists to manage to be national leaders in the science with neither specialized training nor professional employment as botanists. Torrey patched together income to support his family and his botanical research by teaching chemistry and mineralogy at Williams College, New York University, and Princeton. After assuming the assayer's position and becoming a trustee of Columbia, he made an arrangement with the college to give it his 40,000-specimen herbarium and 600-volume scientific library in return for housing.

In about 1830, he began a friendship with Asa Gray, that would be the most important of his professional career. Torrey's first major work, *The Flora of the Northern and Middle Sections of the United States* (Volume 1, 1824) was the first attempt (however primitive) at a comprehensive, synthetic American flora. With Gray, who lived with the Torreys off and on from 1834 to 1842, Torrey undertook to modernize the practice of botany in America by introducing the natural system of classification that was already the vogue in Europe. In

1831, Torrey published an American edition of John Lindley's *Introduction to the Natural System of Botany,* which made the work of Antoine Laurent de Jessieu and Alphonse P. De Candolle available to Americans. Torrey planned, and made some modest beginnings toward, a *Flora of North America,* which would have employed the natural system. His helpmate Gray's departure in 1842 for a professorship at Harvard made that too big a project for Torrey, a problem exacerbated by his commitment to helping to process the flood of specimens that the exploration of the American West yielded. In the 1840s, he was occupied with describing and classifying the flora collected by John Charles Frémont during his surveys of the American West. In the 1850s, the plants of the Mexican Boundary Survey came his way. In 1843, Torrey's last major publication, a two volume *Flora of the State of New York,* appeared. In the thirty remaining years of his life, he occupied himself with reports of the western specimens he received.

Torrey's greatest contribution may have been the mentoring relationships he held with a number of the succeeding generation of American botanists, most notably Gray. The years that Gray lived with the Torrey family and worked with John Torrey were critical to both his personal and professional development. In a day when graduate education was by apprenticeship, the import of such contributions must not be overlooked. Torrey's herbaria work is also of significance. His personal herbarium formed the nucleus of the herbarium of the New York Botanical Garden. During the 1860s, so much of the western material was in his possession that Torrey in effect had in his possession the herbarium of the Smithsonian Institution, which bears his mark to this day. The standard sources on Torrey remain Andrew Denny Rodgers's *John Torrey* and many references in A. Hunter Dupree's *Asa Gray.* The most extensive manuscript collection of Torrey material is housed at the New York Botanical Garden along with his herbarium.

BIBLIOGRAPHY

Dupree, A. Hunter. *Asa Gray: American Botanist, Friend of Darwin.* Cambridge, MA: Harvard University Press, 1959.

Robins, Christine Chapman. "John Torrey (1796–1873), His Life and Times." *Bulletin of the Torrey Botanical Club* 95 (1968): 515–645.

Rodgers, Andrew Denny III. *John Torrey: A Story of North American Botany.* Princeton: Princeton University Press, 1942.

Torrey, John. *Flora of the State of New York.* 2 vols. Albany, NY: Carroll and Cook, 1843.

Torrey, John, and Asa Gray. *A Flora of North America. . . . Arranged According to the Natural System.* 2 vols. New York: Wiley and Putnam, 1838–1843.

Elizabeth Keeney

Tuberculosis

A highly contagious infection resulting from confined living and working conditions, poor nutrition, and colonization by a certain bacterial agent; its enormity and persistence indicate its importance in American history, as compared with diseases of a more episodic nature. Thirty percent of the skeletal remains in a seventeenth-century Rhode Island cemetery probably had tuberculosis. By 1830, tuberculosis had become and remained the greatest killer of American adults for at least half a century.

Early tuberculosis treatments ranged across extremes. Benjamin Rush advocated horseback riding for the fresh air. Other nineteenth-century treatments consisted of creosote, gold, cod liver oil, and other concoctions. Bleeding and the avoidance of cold or night air were also practiced. In 1887, Edward Trudeau, a New York physician and tuberculosis victim, went to the Adirondacks to die. Surprisingly, he appeared to recover. Crediting fresh air and rest, he established Saranac Lake, America's first tuberculosis sanatorium.

The sanatorium movement that followed offered hope and optimism, as well as improved nutrition, rest, and a change from unhealthy urban living conditions. In fact, the movement represented a return to the more spacious living of preindustrial life. The healthy members of society approved of this isolation of the tuberculous. While well-to-do sanatorium patients socialized with renowned and obscure art and literary figures, the less prosperous sought relief in more spartan public facilities. Some tuberculosis treatment research, including surgery, was conducted within sanatoriums, the intention of which was to decrease chest wall and lung motion. The popularity of sanatoriums peaked by 1910, but by 1908, certain leaders expressed reservations regarding the efficacy of long-term sanatorium care. Mortality rates of those treated, and not treated, at sanatoriums were equal when measured in decades after discharge.

In 1882, German bacteriologist Robert Koch isolated *Mycobacterium tuberculosis,* a discovery that had few immediate implications for treatment but major ones for prevention. Hermann Biggs, leader of the New York City Health Department from 1892 to 1914, believed in the political and social control of tuberculosis victims. He advocated the methods of case-finding, disinfection of homes, limited employment opportunities for patients, registration of cases, compulsory hospitalization, and isolation of hospitalized patients. In the early twentieth century, the focus of prevention migrated from the environmental to the individual. Charles V. Chapin of Providence, Rhode Island, became instrumental in promoting personal hygiene and medical examinations as the keystones to the improvement in health, forgoing sanitary measures.

Lawrence Flick, Pennsylvania physician and tuberculosis victim, was instrumental in founding the National Association for the Study and Prevention of Tuberculosis in 1904, which evolved into the American Lung Association in 1973. Emphasizing cooperation among physicians, philanthropists, and the public, this was the first large-scale public health campaign, and became the model for campaigns against poliomyelitis and heart disease. In the first decades of the twentieth century, new means of diagnosis were available in the use of tuberculin and chest X ray; the latter were widely used in the screening of recruits during both world wars.

A vaccine of bovine tubercle bacilli, Bacille Calmette-Guerin (BCG) was produced at the Pasteur Institute in 1908. Trials in the United States were carried out at the University of Chicago in the late 1940s with federal approval following in 1950, but the warning by the American Medical Association and others against its widespread use was heeded.

During the 1940s, drugs entered the antituberculosis arsenal. Rutgers researcher Selman Waksman discovered streptomycin in 1944, but its side effects were, for some, intolerable. The great hope embodied in streptomycin was more nearly realized with isoniazid, developed in 1952 in the United States and in Germany.

The combination of screening and drug treatment was thought to have brought an end to the tuberculosis epidemic. But a resurgence of tuberculosis began in 1979, due in part to patients who discontinue treatment. Drug-resistant bacilli develop. The need for vigilance, particularly among the immuno-compromised, remains.

BIBLIOGRAPHY

Bates, Barbara. *Bargaining for Life: A Social History of Tuberculosis 1876–1938.* Philadelphia: University of Pennsylvania Press, 1992.

T

Bonner, Thomas N. *Medicine in Chicago 1850–1950: A Chapter in the Social and Scientific Development of a City.* 2d ed. Urbana/Chicago: University of Illinois Press, 1991.

Caldwell, Mark. *The Last Crusade: The War on Consumption 1862–1954.* New York: Atheneum, 1988.

Dubos, Rene, and Jean Dubos. *The White Plague: Tuberculosis, Man, and Society.* New Brunswick: Rutgers University Press, 1987.

Ellison, David L. *Healing Tuberculosis in the Woods: Medicine and Science at the End of the Nineteenth Century.* Contributions in Medical Studies, no. 41. Westport, CT: Greenwood Press, 1994.

King, Lester S. *Transformations in American Medicine from Benjamin Rush to William Osler.* Baltimore: Johns Hopkins University Press, 1991.

Lowell, Anthony M., Lydia B. Edwards, and Carroll E. Palmer. *Tuberculosis.* American Public Health Association Vital and Health Statistics Monographs. Cambridge, MA: Harvard University Press, 1969.

Ott, Katherine. *Fevered Lives: Tuberculosis in American Culture since 1870.* Cambridge, MA: Harvard University Press, 1996.

Rothman, Sheila M. *Living in the Shadow of Death: Tuberculosis and the Social Experience of Illness in America.* New York: Basic Books, 1994.

Starr, Paul. *The Social Transformation of American Medicine.* New York: Basic Books, 1982.

Teller, Michael. *The Tuberculosis Movement: A Public Health Campaign in the Progressive Era.* New York: Greenwood Press, 1988.

Priscilla Jordan Elliott

Tuve, Merle Antony (1901–1982)

American experimental physicist and research director. Born in Canton, South Dakota, Tuve received his baccalaureate (1922) and his master's degree (1923) at the University of Minnesota. After a year at Princeton University, he entered the graduate program at Johns Hopkins University, where he received his doctorate in 1926. He then accepted a staff position at the Department of Terrestrial Magnetism (DTM), one of the research departments of the Carnegie Institution of Washington, in Washington, D.C.

Working at the DTM with Gregory Breit in 1925, Tuve narrowly missed making the first direct demonstration of the existence of the earth's ionosphere. Priority instead went to Edward V. Appleton and M.A.F. Barnett in England. Nevertheless, the Breit-Tuve technique of using radio-wave pulses quickly became the standard experimental approach for ionospheric studies (and also helped to suggest the possibility of radar).

In the late 1920s and throughout the 1930s, Tuve concentrated on developing particle accelerators for use in the newly emerging field of nuclear physics. Initially, he and his DTM colleagues worked with Tesla coils. But in the early 1930s, they shifted to the electrostatic generator that Robert J. Van de Graaff had recently invented. During the second half of the decade, they used their new equipment to study the scattering of protons by protons. In the process, they determined experimentally how the electrostatic repulsive force between protons is replaced in the nucleus by a strong, charge-independent, attractive force.

With the onset of World War II, Tuve turned his attention to war-related projects. He led the successful American efforts to develop a proximity fuze, a device containing a miniaturized radio transmitter and receiver that triggered an explosive shell as it neared its target. Later, the wartime organization he headed (Section T of the National Defense Research Committee) developed into the Applied Physics Laboratory at Johns Hopkins.

In 1946, Tuve succeeded John Adam Fleming as DTM director, a position he held until his retirement in 1966. Under his leadership, the DTM emphasized geophysics, biophysics, and astrophysics. His personal areas of research after the war included studies of the earth's crust using seismic waves generated by conventional explosives, studies of hydrogen gas in space using radio telescopes, and the development of image tubes for use by optical astronomers.

Tuve was elected to the American Philosophical Society in 1943 and to the National Academy of Sciences (NAS) in 1946. He served the NAS as chairman of the Geophysics Research Board (1960–1969) and as home secretary (1965–1971).

One noteworthy feature of Tuve's early life was his childhood friendship with Ernest O. Lawrence, who later invented the cyclotron and served as the founding director of the Radiation Laboratory at the University of California at Berkeley.

Because his mature years coincided with the period in which the federal government greatly expanded its support for research and because the fields of research to which he contributed were so varied, Tuve's career provides an important window on American science in the mid-twentieth century.

Of particular interest to historians of science has been Tuve's role in postwar science-policy matters. One study (Kevles) has described how Tuve proposed giving civilian researchers considerable autonomy in a successor agency to the wartime Office of Scientific Research and Development. Another study (Needell) has contrasted the opposing plans that Tuve and Lloyd V. Berkner offered in the mid-1950s for a federally funded radio telescope. Regarding John W. Graham's work on paleomagnetism at the DTM, a third study (Le Grand) has argued that Graham's own assessment gave Tuve little choice but to terminate the project in the late 1950s. A fourth study (Forman, pp. 218–219) has critiqued Tuve's oft-expressed view that applied science ought not to be favored to the detriment of basic science.

For a selected listing of Tuve's publications, see Abelson. Tuve's papers are held by the Library of Congress.

BIBLIOGRAPHY

Abelson, Philip H. "Merle Antony Tuve." *Biographical Memoirs of the National Academy of Sciences* 70 (1966): 407–422.

Cornell, Thomas D. "Merle Antony Tuve: Pioneer Nuclear Physicist." *Physics Today* 41 (January 1988): 57–64.

———. "Tuve, Merle Antony." *Dictionary of Scientific Biography.* Edited by Frederic L. Holmes. New York: Scribner, 1990, 18: 936–941.

———. "Merle A. Tuve's Post-War Geophysics: Early Explosion Seismology." In *The Earth, the Heavens and the Carnegie Institution of Washington,* edited by Gregory A. Good. Washington, DC: American Geophysical Union, 1994, pp. 185–214.

Forman, Paul. "Behind Quantum Electronics: National Security as Basis for Physical Research in the United States, 1940–1960." *Historical Studies in the Physical and Biological Sciences* 18 (1987): 149–229.

Kevles, Daniel J. "Scientists, the Military, and the Control of Postwar Defense Research: The Case of the Research Board for National Security, 1944–46." *Technology and Culture* 16 (1975): 20–47.

Le Grand, Homer. "Conflicting Orientations: John Graham, Merle Tuve and Paleomagnetic Research at the DTM 1938–1958." *Earth Sciences History* 8 (1989): 55–65.

Needell, Allan A. "Lloyd Berkner, Merle Tuve, and the Federal Role in Radio Astronomy." *Osiris,* 2d ser., 3 (1987): 261–288.

Thomas David Cornell

U

Unidentified Flying Objects

Reported phenomena that appear as lights, disks, and other forms traveling through the earth's atmosphere, often at high speeds, with motions that appear to defy the known laws of physics. Although such appearances have been reported sporadically throughout history, they are largely a twentieth-century phenomenon. They have been seen worldwide, but their nature and reality have been the subject of intense controversy, especially in the United States. The most widespread explanation for them among the media and public has been the "extraterrestrial hypothesis" that they are spaceships controlled by alien intelligence; for this reason they have become associated with the debate over extraterrestrial life. Most scientists, however, reject the extraterrestrial hypothesis, and separate their belief in intelligent life beyond the earth from the idea that such life has arrived on earth. The majority of cases are explained as astronomical objects, atmospheric phenomena, illusions, and hoaxes, but none of these fully accounts for all cases.

Unidentified Flying Objects (UFOs) have occurred in "waves" in terms of numbers of widespread sightings, the most notable of which were in 1896–1897, 1947, 1952, 1957, 1965–1967, and 1973. The modern era of UFOs is considered to have begun in 1947 when businessman Kenneth Arnold reported nine disk-shaped objects flying at high speed near Mount Ranier in Washington State. His description of the objects led the media to coin the term "flying saucers"; the United States Air Force later named them "unidentified flying objects."

For almost two decades after the Arnold sightings, most scientists ignored UFOs. The United States Air Force, concerned about national security, first began to study the subject, successively with Projects Sign (January 1948), Grudge (December 1948), and Bluebook, the latter running for seventeen years beginning in March 1952. Although a panel of scientists headed by H.P. Robertson briefly considered the UFO phenomenon in 1953, the media was largely left to elaborate its favored extraterrestrial hypothesis. The only exceptions were the astronomers J. Allen Hynek (the official Air Force consultant) and Donald H. Menzel, who, like the Air Force, favored prosaic explanations. Menzel maintained his skeptical attitude throughout his life, while Hynek by the late 1960s had changed his mind and favored nonprosaic explanations, including various forms of the extraterrestrial hypothesis.

Scientific attitudes changed briefly during the latter half of the 1960s, when scientific study of UFOs reached its peak. Congressional hearings were held in the United States following another wave of sightings, and under pressure from the Congress, the Air Force contracted physicist Edward U. Condon to lead an independent university-based study. This gave a certain scientific legitimacy to the subject, and for the first time a broad spectrum of scientific opinion emerged. Despite a number of unexplained cases, the Condon study concluded that further study was unwarranted. Although this conclusion was criticized by many scientists on the grounds of methodology, the publication of the Condon Report in 1969 effectively put a damper on further serious scientific discussion. The Air Force immediately dropped Project Bluebook. Since then, the extraterrestrial hypothesis has been in decline and the entire subject of UFOs has been avoided by most

U

scientists, especially with the advent of "alien abduction" claims.

Because of their elusive and controversial nature, UFOs are an interesting case study of science attempting to function at its limits under popular scrutiny. The debate reveals the varied scientific reaction toward hypotheses of low probability, and demonstrates the existence of many cultures of science, each with its own ideas of problem choice, scientific methodology, the nature of evidence, and rules of inference. Although one scholarly history of the UFO debate has been written (Jacobs), the subject has scarcely been treated at all from the perspective of the history, philosophy, and sociology of science. The archives of Condon and Menzel at the American Philosophical Society Library, and the Air Force Project Bluebook files at the National Archives are a rich source of material for further study.

BIBLIOGRAPHY

Condon, Edward U. (project director) and Daniel S. Gillmore (editor). *Final Report of the Scientific Study of Unidentified Flying Objects*. New York: Bantam Books, 1969.

Hynek, J. Allen. *The UFO Experience: A Scientific Inquiry*. Chicago: Henry Regnery, 1972.

Jacobs, David M. *The UFO Controversy in America*. Bloomington: Indiana University Press, 1975.

Menzel, Donald H., and Ernest H. Taves. *The UFO Enigma. The Definitive Explanation of the UFO Phenomenon*. New York: Doubleday, 1977.

Steven J. Dick

Union of Concerned Scientists

Organization of scientists dedicated to promoting awareness of the misuses of science and ensuring the beneficial application of scientific knowledge. The Union of Concerned Scientists (UCS) was formed in December 1968 from a group of antiwar faculty at the Massachusetts Institute of Technology who helped sponsor the March 4 movement, a one-day work stoppage organized by students which was meant to give scientists an opportunity to consider the social implications of their work. By March 1969, the UCS had approximately 300 members in the Boston area. Among the members were Daniel F. Ford, Richard L. Garwin, Henry W. Kendall, and James MacKenzie.

The UCS sponsors educational and lobbying efforts to publicize the misuse of science, especially with respect to military technology. Members of the organization undertake such activities as conducting and publishing studies of the technologies in question, testifying in public hearings, making public statements, and circulating petitions. Like the Federation of American Scientists, the UCS has paid particular attention to arms control and nuclear energy. It has been especially concerned with educating the public about the technical and political shortcomings of newly proposed strategic weapons systems, the need for arms control agreements, and the technical feasibility of verification procedures for arms control. The UCS was an early opponent of the ABM (antiballistic missile) system and MIRV (multiple independent reentry vehicles), and more recently it has concentrated upon revealing the technical fallacies of SDI (the Strategic Defense Initiative). The UCS has also focused on the implications of chemical and biological weapons, environmental issues, and renewable energy sources, and it has been especially effective in exposing the dangers posed by unsafe nuclear reactors.

Archival materials relating to the UCS are held at the MIT Institute Archives and Special Collections. The collection contains sixty-seven cubic feet of material, consisting primarily of records of UCS's efforts regarding nuclear reactor safety.

BIBLIOGRAPHY

Allen, Jonathan, ed. *March 4: Scientists, Students, and Society*. Cambridge, MA: MIT Press, 1970.

Jasper, James M. *Nuclear Politics: Energy and the State in the United States, Sweden, and France*. Princeton: Princeton University Press, 1990.

Moore, Kelly. "Doing Good While Doing Science: The Origins and Consequences of Public Interest Science Organizations in America, 1945–1990." Ph.D. diss., University of Arizona, 1990.

Nelkin, Dorothy. *The Univeristy and Military Research: Moral Politics at MIT*. Ithaca: Cornell University Press, 1972.

Primack, Joel, and Frank von Hippel. *Advice and Dissent: Scientists in the Political Arena*. New York: Basic Books, 1974.

Prince, Jerome. *The Antinuclear Movement*. Boston: Twayne, 1982.

Jessica Wang

Walcott, Charles Doolittle (1850–1927)

Geologist, paleontologist, conservationist, and science administrator. Walcott was born near Utica, New York, and became interested in fossils by about age ten. During the Civil War, he spent summers assisting on a farm near Trenton Falls and gained a detailed knowledge of the Middle Ordovician fossils and local geology. Formal schooling was ended at age eighteen, and he then worked as a hardware clerk. Disliking that, he moved to the farm of William Rust in Trenton Falls. Walcott assisted on the farm, studied, and collected fossils jointly with Rust for commercial sale. In 1873, they sold a collection to Louis Agassiz. Later, Rust made major sales to Cornell University and to the New York State Museum, and Walcott made a sale to Alexander Agassiz.

Walcott's total college experience consisted of a week in 1873 at the Museum of Comparative Zoology unpacking his collection. Louis Agassiz encouraged him to study trilobites, particularly the appendages. In 1875, Walcott published his first scientific paper, and early in 1876, he discovered the legs of trilobites in material from the Rust farm.

James Hall, state paleontologist of New York, employed Walcott late in 1876 as a special assistant, Walcott's first professional position. This lasted for about eighteen months, but Walcott remained in Albany, studying, writing and publishing. In July 1879, he was suddenly appointed to the just-formed United States Geological Survey as a temporary assistant geologist.

For his first field assignment, Walcott began at the Tertiary Pink Cliffs in southwestern Utah and measured a stratigraphic section some two miles thick into Kanab Creek at the Grand Canyon. During this investigation, he located the Permian-Triassic boundary on the Kanab Plateau. His effort was so impressive that he received a permanent position. Walcott also published in 1881 a fundamental work on trilobite limbs.

Arnold Hague took Walcott west in 1880 to the Eureka, Nevada, mining district, where Walcott studied all the Paleozoic stratigraphy and fauna. He returned to Eureka in 1882 and published his findings in 1887.

During the fall and winter of 1882–1883, Walcott was in the Grand Canyon and was the first geologist to study the Cambrian and Precambrian rocks. In connection with this, he measured a stratigraphic section of more than two miles thickness. Combined with his 1879 study, he had the record for the longest sections measured by one person.

Walcott's next assignment was to investigate the "Taconic problem" in eastern New York and western New England. Since 1842, geologists had argued as to whether the strata exposed in the Taconic Mountains constituted an old, distinct geologic system. By 1887, Walcott collected convincing evidence from fossils that these strata were younger rocks which had been misinterpreted and he removed the Taconic concept from consideration. More or less concurrently during the 1880s, Scandinavian geologists had noted that the sequence of trilobites zones used by them in the Cambrian was reversed in America. In 1888, Walcott determined that the American zonation was incorrect. As another dramatic discovery in 1891, Walcott found the oldest known vertebrate remains, and it was more than half a century before older fish were found.

In 1894, Walcott succeeded John Wesley Powell as the third Director of the Geological Survey. During the thirteen years he held this administrative post, Walcott continued as a working scientist, studying Cambrian rocks and fossils, and extended his investigations to the older, enigmatic, Precambrian strata. Powell had lost the confidence of Congress and the Geological Survey was in dire straits when Walcott took over. He was able to restore the budget to former levels and then increase it. Under Walcott, the Geological Survey flourished, particularly increasing its efforts in topographic mapping and water investigations. For almost a decade, beginning in 1897, the Geological Survey studied and mapped the National Forest Reserves. In addition, the Reclamation Service, formed in 1902, was placed under the Geological Survey; Walcott actively supervising its programs, a politically sensative subject. Walcott laid the foundation for the future Bureau of Mines, and served as a behind-the-scenes advisor on conservation to President Theodore Roosevelt.

Walcott played a key role in the founding of the Carnegie Institution of Washington, late in 1901, shepherding its incorporation and bylaws. He served as the first secretary of the new organization for four years, particularly as a key member of the Executive Committee and continued on that committee for two decades. Walcott overcame the opposition of the board and of Carnegie in order to establish the Geophysical Laboratory, world-renowned for studies of igneous rocks.

Following the death of Samuel Pierpont Langley, Walcott, in 1907, was appointed as the fourth secretary of the Smithsonian Institution. For several months, he also continued to direct the Geological Survey, but he still was able to arrange for fieldwork that summer in western Canada. Cambrian deposits were known from that area but had been little studied. For nearly two decades, Walcott conducted a research program there, measuring sections and collecting fossils. His publications after 1907 fill five entire volumes of *Smithsonian Miscellaneous Collections,* most of which are devoted to rocks and fossils of western Canada.

Walcott's most notable scientific achievement was the discovery of the Burgess Shale fauna in western Canada, the single most important fossil locality in the world. Walcott made a massive collection through several seasons and described a host of bizarre animals, for this fauna contains many soft-bodied organisms not normally preserved in the geologic record. Walcott was able to demonstrate how incomplete is the fossil record when it is based only on organisms which developed hard parts. He was also able to demonstrate that such diverse groups as holothurians and annelid worms have vastly longer records than had ever been suspected.

Another significant investigation during his tenure as secretary was a systematic study of Precambrian algae. In connection with these studies, Walcott found evidence of ancient bacteria.

Walcott and F.C. Cottrell, in 1912, founded the Research Corporation dedicated to providing funds for science. As of 1993, the corporation had funded the early research of twenty-two persons who subsequently received Nobel Prizes.

As acting assistant secretary of the Smithsonian Institution from 1897 to 1898, Walcott was keenly aware of Langley's experiments with heavier than air aircraft. He recognized the need for a greater research effort in aviation, and in 1913, organized the Advisory Committee for Aeronautics. In 1915, the National Advisory Committee for Aeronautics (NACA) was established by Congress through Walcott's efforts. From 1919 until his death, Walcott was chairman of NACA. He was also a member of the Aircraft Production Board during World War I and drafted the first legislation for civilian aerial navigation and regulation.

In 1896, Walcott was elected to the National Academy of Sciences. He served as treasurer, member of the council, and from 1907 to 1917 as vice president. He played a key role in establishing the National Research Council during 1916. Walcott became president of the National Academy in 1917 and served six years in this office. He was simultaneously first vice president of the National Research Council and during World War I was on numerous committees.

Walcott did not neglect his duties as secretary of the Smithsonian Institution, for he is to be credited with convincing Charles Freer to build the Freer Gallery before Freer's death. Walcott obtained an aviation hangar, situated behind the "Castle," for an aircraft museum, and he made strenuous efforts both to have a building constructed for the National Gallery of Art and to increase the Smithsonian endowment. His death effectively ended both of these efforts.

Walcott was a world-class scientist. He was a consummate politician in his dealings with Congress, and he was an outstanding administrator. During his time as first vice president of the National Research Council, he was as close to being a Secretary of Science as the nation has ever had. Despite his manifold accomplishments, Walcott remains a little-known and little-studied individual.

BIBLIOGRAPHY

Darton, N.H. "Memorial of Charles Doolittle Walcott." *Bulletin of the Geological Society of America* 39 (1928): 80–116.

Yochelson, E. L. "Charles Doolitte Walcott." *Biographical Memoirs of the National Academy of Sciences* 39 (1967): 471–540.

———. *Charles Doolittle Walcott, Paleontologist.* Kent, OH: Kent State University Press, 1998.

Ellis L. Yochelson

Walker, Sears Cook (1805–1853)

Astronomer. After graduation from Harvard in 1825, Walker taught in Boston until 1827, and in Philadelphia from 1827 until he became an actuary for the Pennsylvania Company for Insurance of Lives and Granting Annuities in 1836. His position as actuary provided sufficient free time for him to study astronomy, a science he had come to love while at Harvard. He was the unofficial director of the Philadelphia High School Observatory from about 1839 through 1845. In February 1846, he joined the staff of the Naval Observatory, but left after only a year. Walker was then hired by an old friend from Philadelphia, Alexander Dallas Bache, the superintendent of the United States Coast Survey, to conduct longitude observations. Walker remained with the Coast Survey until his death. Early in 1852, he suffered from a mental collapse, and he spent most of that year in various asylums.

Walker was principally a celestial mechanist. His most important publication while in Philadelphia, written with his half-brother, E. Otis Kendall, professor of mathematics and astronomy at the Philadelphia High School, was an effort to prove that the Great Comet of 1843 was identical with one observed in 1618 and 1669. During his years with the Naval Observatory and the Coast Survey, Walker focused on the computation of the elements of the orbit of Neptune. The existence of Neptune had been independently predicted by Urbain J.J. Leverrier in France and John Crouch Adams in England and was first observed by Johann Gottfried Galle on 23 September 1846. Walker began searching for instances when Neptune had been observed earlier but mistaken for a star. Using these observations, Walker computed an orbit for Neptune which differed so much from those of Leverrier and Adams that Benjamin Peirce of Harvard concluded that Galle's discovery was only "a happy accident" (quoted in Hubbell and Smith, p. 270), a controversial conclusion rejected by European astronomers.

His other major contribution was in the application of the telegraph to longitude observations. As the assistant in charge, he oversaw the Coast Survey experiments in what became known as the "American method of observation," which was one of the first important contributions of the American scientific community to astronomical practice.

Although during the 1840s Walker was probably the leading American astronomer, he has attracted little biographical interest. Gould's biographical memoir, written shortly after Walker's death, is still the most reliable account of his life. Harvard University and the University of Pennsylvania have the most important Walker manuscript material.

BIBLIOGRAPHY

Gould, B.A. "An Address in Commemoration of Sears Cook Walker." *Proceedings of the American Association for the Advancement of Science* 8 (1854): 18–45.

Hubbell, John G., and Robert W. Smith, "Neptune in America: Negotiating a Discovery." *Journal for the History of Astronomy* 23 (1992): 261–291.

Walker, Sears Cook. *A Report by the Superintendent of the Coast Survey, on an Application of the Galvanic Circuit to an Astronomical Clock and Telegraph Register in Determining Local Differences of Longitude, and in Astronomical Observations Generally.* House Executive Documents, No. 21 (1849).

———. "Researches Relative to the Planet Neptune." *Smithsonian Contributions to Knowledge* 2 (1851).

Marc Rothenberg

Warner & Swasey Company

Makers of astronomical instruments and machine tools, 1880–1980, Cleveland, Ohio. The Warner & Swasey Company designed and constructed the mechanical components for some of the largest astronomical telescopes in the world, including the refractors at the Naval, Lick, and Yerkes Observatories, and the reflectors at the Dominion Astrophysical Observatory in Canada and the McDonald Telescope in Texas. The company's primary business was machine tool manufacture, especially turret lathes. Following the personal interests of its founders, Worcester Reed Warner (1846–1929) and Ambrose Swasey (1846–1937), the company aggressively sought out contracts for telescope construction and for a short time marketed a complete line of astronomical instruments.

The founders were New England machinists who used profits from contracting at Pratt & Whitney during the 1870s to start their own company in 1880. Warner had a lifelong interest in astronomy and shared this with Swasey. In 1886, after building a series of small telescopes and observatory domes, they were awarded the contract to build the mounting for the world's largest telescope at the new Lick Observatory in California. The success of that work led to international recognition for both their instrument making and machine tools. Their work in precision scientific instruments included apparatus for the famous Michelson-Morley experiments. Their careers as scientific instrument makers can be interpreted in terms of the professionalization of mechanical engineering and the increasing connections between science and engineering during the nineteenth century. Both served terms as president of the American Association of Mechanical Engineers and Swasey was a longtime member of the American Association for the Advancement of Science.

The company, successful in the machine tool business, continued to build astronomical instruments on a limited basis until the early 1960s. The decline of the American machine tool industry affected the company's fortunes in the 1970s. Bendix Corporation bought the company, and in 1980 closed the Warner & Swasey division and discontinued the use of the name.

Manuscript collections for the founders and company records can be found at Case Western Reserve University and the Western Reserve Historical Society in Cleveland, Ohio.

BIBLIOGRAPHY
Hubbard, Guy. "Worcester Reed Warner." *Mechanical Engineering* 8 (1929): 633–635.
Miller, Dayton C. "Ambrose Swasey." *Biographical Memoirs of the National Academy of Sciences* (1943).
Pershey, Edward. "The Early Telescope Work of Warner & Swasey." Ph.D. diss., Case Western Reserve University, 1982.

Edward Jay Pershey

SEE ALSO
Lick Observatory

Weaver, Warren (1894–1978)

Internationally known foundation officer, mathematician, and author. Born in Reedsburg, Wisconsin, Weaver received his formal education at the University of Wisconsin, (B.S., 1916; C.E., 1917; and Ph.D., 1921). Weaver taught mathematics at Throop College (now the California Institute of Technology), 1917–1920, and then joined the mathematics department at the University of Wisconsin, where he was departmental chairman, 1928–1932. His major work was in the theory of probability and communication.

He was a major force in the government and university research communities. During the 1930s, Weaver promoted the development and diffusion of scientific instrumentation, for example, the Van de Graff generator, the Tiselivs apparatus, the ultracentrifuge, and the differential analyzer. Throughout the 1930s and 1940s, Weaver championed the use of physical science techniques in biological research, which prepared the ground for modern genetics. In the 1940s and 1950s, he also participated in the founding of the "Green Revolution."

Weaver worked for the Rockefeller Foundation as director for the natural sciences (1932–1952), director of the division of natural sciences and agriculture (1952–1955), and vice president, natural and medical sciences (1955–1959). At the Alfred P. Sloan Foundation, Weaver was trustee (1956–1967), vice president (1959–1964), and from 1965 until his death, special advisor to the Sloan Foundation's president.

He was a second lieutenant in the Air Service during World War I, and for his work during World War II on bombsights and antiaircraft fire-control devices, Weaver received the United States Medal for Merit, the King's Medal for Service in the Cause of Freedom from Great Britain, and the French Legion of Honor.

As an officer of two of America's major institutions for the support of science, and a member of many committees, boards, and organizations, Weaver was actively and centrally involved in a variety of major scientific endeavors. Affiliations included the National Science Board; the genetics panel for the National Academy of Science's report on the biological effects of radiation; the Applied Mathematics Panel of the Office of Scientific Research and Development; the board of trustees of the Memorial Sloan-Kettering Cancer Center; the Committee on Scientific Policy of the Memorial Sloan-Kettering Cancer Center; and the Public Health Research Institute of the City of New York. Weaver was elected a fellow of the American Association for the Advancement of Science in 1928; a member of the executive committee in 1950, and president in 1954.

He also served as chairman of the board of the Salk Institute for Biological Studies.

A prolific author, Weaver's books include *The Mathematical Theory of Communication* (with Claude E. Shannon), 1949; *Elementary Mathematical Analysis* (with Charles S. Slichter), 1925; *The Electromagnetic Field* (with Max Mason), 1929; *The Scientists Speak* (editor), 1947; *Lady Luck—The Theory of Probability,* 1963; *U.S. Philanthropic Foundations, Their History, Structure, Management and Record,* 1967. An afficionado of Lewis Carroll, Weaver wrote numerous articles on *Alice's Adventures in Wonderland,* as well as a book, *Alice in Many Tongues,* devoted to the translations of *Alice's Adventures in Wonderland* into nearly forty languages.

BIBLIOGRAPHY

Fosdick, Raymond B. *The Story of the Rockefeller Foundation.* New Brunswick, NJ: Transaction Publishers, 1989.
Weaver, Warren. *Scene of Change.* New York: Scribner, 1970.

Erwin Levold

Webster, Arthur Gordon (1863–1923)

Mathematical and experimental physicist. Born in Brookline, Massachusetts, Webster was graduated from Harvard College in 1885, A.B. summa cum laude in physics, with highest honors in mathematics, and was valedictorian of his class. After another year at Harvard as instructor in mathematics, he went abroad in 1886 to study at the universities of Paris, Stockholm, and Berlin. At the latter institution, he studied mathematical physics with Hermann von Helmholtz and experimental physics with August Kundt, under whom he earned the Ph.D. in 1890.

In 1890, Webster was appointed docent in mathematical physics in Albert A. Michelson's graduate program at the recently opened Clark University. After Michelson's resignation in 1892, Webster was made assistant professor and director of the physical laboratories. He was promoted to professor of physics in 1900 and remained at Clark until his death. He was a principal founder of the American Physical Society (1899) and served as its third president (1903–1905). Elected to the National Academy of Sciences at age thirty-nine, he was a member of several scientific organizations here and abroad. During World War I he chaired the physics committee of the Naval Consulting Board.

Webster's research spanned a wide range of topics in classical physics. His early experimental work centered on electricity and magnetism. He was awarded the Elihu Thomson prize in 1895 for his research on electrical oscillations. In this period, too, Webster designed a new drop chronograph and worked out refinements on electrometers and galvanometers. Webster also developed a celebrated two-year cycle of lectures in mathematical physics synthesizing a broad range of the European literature. Out of these lectures grew his *Theory of Electricity and Magnetism* (1897) and the more widely used *The Dynamics of Particles and of Rigid, Elastic, and Fluid Bodies* (1904).

He also made important contributions to acoustics. Webster devised an extremely sensitive portable phonometer for making absolute measures of the intensity of sound. In 1914, he first suggested the concept of acoustical impedance, subsequently verifying it mathematically and experimentally. Webster regularly taught a course in advanced differential equations, and in his final, posthumously published text, *Partial Differential Equations of Mathematical Physics* (1927), he attempted to unify the various branches of classical physics mathematically. An outstanding lecturer and laboratory director, Webster turned out twenty-nine Ph.D.'s in physics, including the rocket pioneer Robert H. Goddard, and played an important role in the training of Clark mathematicians as well.

In 1918, Webster virtually turned the Clark physics department into a ballistics institute on the model of the Ballistisches Institut at Charlottenburg. Out of this came a series of papers on the theory and practice of gunnery.

Although Webster lectured on recent European developments in modern physics, including quantum theory, electron theory, and relativity, he never pursued or directed research in these new areas. Partly for this reason and partly because Clark's laboratory facilities and scale of graduate work had been surpassed by many other centers of learning, no new doctoral candidates in physics enrolled at Clark after 1917. In the post-1920 reorganization of Clark University, Webster was pressured either to retire or to take a short-term research post with no future guarantees. Discouraged over his financial position and prospects, and depressed over his research and the failure of his ballistic institute to attract external visibility and funding, Webster took his own life.

In recent years, Webster has attracted some scholarly interest, less for his research than for his influential teaching and texts and his role in founding the American Physical Society. Manuscript and printed materials relating to his life and career are in the Clark University Archives, which also holds apparatus Webster designed or used. The University of Illinois Archives has some of his professional correspondence.

BIBLIOGRAPHY

Ames, Joseph S. "Arthur Gordon Webster." *Biographical Memoirs of the National Academy of Sciences* 18 (1938): 337–347.

Duff, A. Wilmer. "Arthur Gordon Webster: Physicist, Mathematician, Linguist, and Orator." *American Physics Teacher* 6 (1938): 181–194.

Koelsch, William A. *Clark University, 1887–1987: A Narrative History.* Worcester, MA: Clark University Press, 1987.

———. "The Michelson Era at Clark, 1889–1892." In *The Michelson Era in American Science, 1870–1930,* edited by Stanley Goldberg and Roger H. Stuever. AIP Conference Proceedings, no. 179. New York: American Institute of Physics, 1988, pp. 133–151.

Moyer, Albert E. "Webster, Arthur Gordon." *Dictionary of Scientific Biography.* Edited by Frederick L. Holmes. New York: Scribner, 1990, 18:983–984.

Phillips, Melba. "Arthur Gordon Webster, Founder of the APS." *Physics Today* 40, no. 6 (June 1987): 48–52.

William A. Koelsch

Wheeler, William Morton (1865–1937)

Entomologist, field zoologist, and ethologist. Born in Milwaukee, Wisconsin, and educated there at the German-American Academy, Wheeler spent a year at age nineteen as an assistant at Ward's Natural Science Establishment in Rochester, New York, identifying and labeling specimens. After several years of teaching high school and serving as curator of the Public Museum in Milwaukee, Wheeler in 1890 entered Clark University, from which he received a Ph.D. in zoology in 1892. After sojourns as instructor and assistant professor of embryology at the University of Chicago (1892–1899), professor of zoology at the University of Texas (1899–1903), and curator of invertebrate zoology at the American Museum of Natural History in New York City (1903–1908), Wheeler in 1908 became professor of economic entomology at Harvard University's Bussey Institution. Besides remaining as professor at this institution until his death, Wheeler also served as its dean from 1915 to 1929.

Early in his career, Wheeler worked in a wide variety of zoological fields, contributing to taxonomy, morphology, embryology, developmental biology, marine zoology, and entomology. Beginning around 1900, Wheeler's research focused on the study of ants, culminating in 1910 with the publication of his classic *Ants: Their Structure, Development and Behavior.* In this study, he examined not only the taxonomy, geographical distribution, morphology, and developmental biology of ants, but also their social organization and behavior. As a student of animal behavior (an activity for which he popularized the term "ethology"), Wheeler at first was intrigued by the work of Jacques Loeb on animal tropisms, but eventually he concluded that behavior involved more than just mechanistic responses to stimuli. Throughout his life, Wheeler advocated a comparative, field-oriented natural history approach for the study of animals; he was emphatically opposed to the reductionist tendencies imposed by experimental and quantitative methods and thus, for example, belittled the importance of genetics.

His interest in the behavior of social insects resulted in a number of further monographs during the 1920s, including *Social Life Among the Insects* (1923) and *The Social Insects, Their Origin and Evolution* (1928). In these studies, Wheeler insisted that insect colonies be treated as organisms in their own right possessing characteristic emergent properties. His investigation of the evolution of such organized entities led him to popularize the notion of emergent evolution. A prolific essayist as well as naturalist, Wheeler also drew numerous parallels between insect and human societies.

Wheeler has been the subject of several biographical studies written by fellow scientists, including a book-length biography based in part on privately held manuscript material. Historians of ecology, fascinated by his philosophical musings on organicism, have also touched upon his work. There does not yet exist, though, a fully historical study of Wheeler's life and thought within the disciplinary contexts of ecology and ethology and the institutional context of the Bussey Institution.

BIBLIOGRAPHY

Evans, Mary Alice, and Howard Ensign Evans. *William Morton Wheeler, Biologist.* Cambridge, MA: Harvard University Press, 1970.

Parker, George Howard. "William Morton Wheeler." *Biographical Memoirs of the National Academy of Sciences* 19 (1938): 201–241.

Wheeler, William Morton. *Ants: Their Structure, Development and Behavior.* New York: Columbia University Press, 1910.

———. *Social Life Among the Insects.* New York: Harcourt, Brace, 1923.

———. *The Social Insects, Their Origin and Evolution.* New York: Harcourt, Brace, 1928.

Worster, Donald. *Nature's Economy: A History of Ecological Ideas.* Cambridge, UK: Cambridge University Press, 1977.

Carl-Henry Geschwind

Whitney, Josiah Dwight (1819–1896)

Economic geologist and first state geologist of California. Whitney was born in Northampton, Massachusetts, the eldest of eight children of Sarah (Williston) and Josiah Dwight Whitney, a banker, who sent his son to the best schools hoping he would enter the ministry. Shy, studious, and unsociable, but loved by his family and close friends, Whitney entered Yale in 1836, where he studied chemistry with Benjamin Silliman. In the summer of 1840, he worked under Charles Jackson on the New Hampshire geological survey, and at Jackson's urging he went to Europe in 1842 for advanced study in geology and chemistry. From 1847 to 1850, Whitney conducted a federal survey of the booming iron and copper districts of Northern Michigan with John W. Foster, after which he set himself up as a consulting mining expert. His *Metallic Wealth of the United States* (1854) was an important statistical compilation as well as a contribution to the scientific study of ore deposits. From 1855 to 1858, Whitney surveyed the lead regions of the Midwest for the Iowa, Wisconsin, and Illinois state geological surveys, and from 1860 to 1874 he directed the Geological Survey of California. In 1865, he organized the School of Mining and Practical Geology at Harvard University. Perhaps because he was distracted by his California duties, the mining school closed for lack of students in 1875, but as Sturgis-Hooper Professor of Geology, Whitney lectured to advanced students at Harvard for the rest of his life.

Whitney's work in the Midwest helped to promote mining geology as a science that could put an end to uncontrolled speculation in mines. As California's state geologist Whitney directed the preparation of the state's first accurate topographic maps and issued several volumes of reports, one of them on Yosemite Park, for which he served as a commissioner. The personnel he trained and the methods of topographic mapping by triangulation that he developed in California contributed

to the success of the later federal geological surveys of the West. One of his assistants, Clarence King, became the first director of the United States Geological Survey.

Like survey directors of other states, Whitney had to fight for yearly renewal, aware of the possible loss of research results if money was not provided for continued work and publication. Unfortunately, Whitney, who wanted to include basic science, made the mistake of submitting a report on paleontology before producing the reports on ore deposits that the state had wanted. He was often arrogant in his dealings with the legislature, and he offended oil interests by denying that California had petroleum in commercial quantities. Detesting any hint of corruption, Whitney waged an unrelenting campaign against the otherwise respected mineralogist Benjamin Silliman Jr., who had been accused of salting oil samples, and resigned from the National Academy of Sciences when it refused his request to drop Silliman as a member. Whitney dogmatically upheld his own interpretations on a few other subjects on which he was later proved wrong, insisting that there were no glaciers in the state, for example, and maintaining that the famous Calaveras skull, later revealed as a hoax, was genuine evidence of Tertiary man. In spite of his combative personality, or perhaps because of it, Whitney obtained funding yearly until 1868 and intermittently after that, although he complained that it was never enough. Some of his California work, including *The Auriferous Gravels of the Sierra Nevada*, was published under the auspices of Harvard's Museum of Comparative Zoology.

Robert Block sees the Whitney survey as a transitional link between Humboldtian exploration science and later specialized investigations. Like earlier explorations of the West, it was a comprehensive inventory, covering zoology, botany, and physical geography as well as geology, while, like later surveys, it was the work of professional field scientists and as such was widely praised as one of the best state surveys of its day.

BIBLIOGRAPHY

Block, Robert Harry. "The Whitney Survey of California, 1860–74: A Study of Environmental Science and Exploration." Ph.D. diss., University of California at Los Angeles, 1982.

Brewer, William H. *Up and Down California in 1860–1864: The Journal of William H. Brewer.* 3d ed. Edited by Francis P. Farquhar. Berkeley and Los Angeles: University of California Press, 1966.

Brewster, Edwin Tenney. *Life and Letters of Josiah Dwight Whitney.* Boston: Houghton Mifflin, 1909.

Nash, Gerald D. "Whitney, Josiah Dwight." *Dictionary of Scientific Biography.* Edited by Charles C. Gillispie. New York: Scribners, 1976, 14:315–316.

White, Gerald T. *Scientists in Conflict: The Beginnings of the Oil Industry in California.* San Marino, CA: Huntington Library, 1968.

Whitney, Josiah Dwight. *The Metallic Wealth of the United States.* Philadelphia: Lippincott, Grambo, 1854.

———. *Report of Progress and Synopsis of the Field Work, from 1860–1864.* Vol. 1 of *Geology.* Cambridge, MA: John Wilson and Son, 1865.

———. *The Yosemite Guide-Book.* Cambridge, MA: Harvard University Press, 1869.

———. *The Auriferous Gravels of the Sierra Nevada of California.* Cambridge, MA: Harvard University Press, 1880.

Peggy Champlin

Wiener, Norbert (1894–1964)

Mathematician and intellectual. Wiener was the son of an American-born mother, and a Russian immigrant Jew who had come to America to join a utopian vegetarian community but instead became a Harvard professor in Slavic languages. Norbert Wiener's intellectually demanding father, who was his exemplar, mentor, and disciplinarian, had a powerful impact on him. He attended first Tufts College, then entered Harvard at age fourteen, and received his doctorate in philosophy in 1913 with a dissertation under Josiah Royce. Subsequently, he studied in England with Bertrand Russell, G.E. Moore, and G.H. Hardy, and also in Germany. From 1919 on, he was on the mathematics faculty of the Massachusetts Institute of Technology (MIT). His brilliance and international stature as a mathematician helped to enhance the standing of MIT as a center of science. When he reached retirement age, he was appointed "Institute Professor," honoring his long-standing cross-disciplinary interests. He received the Bocher Prize from the American Mathematical Society in 1933, was elected to the National Academy of Sciences the same year, but resigned from that organization seven years later. In the last year of his life, he received the National Medal of Science from President Lyndon B. Johnson. He traveled widely, was a visiting professor in Peiping, China, in 1935–1936, periodically worked with biologist Arturo Rosenblueth in Mexico City after World War II, and at other times lectured in India, Japan, Norway, Italy, and France. After appearance of his book on cybernetics in 1948, he was also a popular speaker and became widely known in the United States as an original thinker about science, technology, and society.

Wiener's primary professional work was in pure mathematics. The areas of mathematics to which he made major contributions are integration in function space, theory of Fourier integrals, potential theory, Tauberian theorems, and probability theory. His work, especially his sophisticated theory of Brownian motion, extended the domain of applicability of the concept of probability to sets of functionals, rather than only points. He also came to collaborate with electrical engineers on the theory of electrical devices. In the 1930s, he became very interested in physiology, and attended regular seminars at the Harvard Medical School. During World War II, he developed a general statistical theory of prediction, filtering, and communication. In 1943, he wrote a philosophical article together with Harvard physiologist Arturo Rosenblueth and the engineer Julian Bigelow, which laid the foundation for what came to be known as cybernetics. After World War II, Wiener contributed to the research on prosthesis, such as an artificial arm which had tactile sensibilities or devices to replace hearing for the deaf.

Books which Wiener wrote in the latter part of his life stirred wide interest among the generally educated public. *Cybernetics* (1948), a bestseller, combined technical description of new ideas about computers, information technologies, and neurobiology, with discussion of Wiener's concerns about potential misuses of modern technologies. His reflections on atomic bombs and scientists' responsibilities had led him a year earlier to state in print that—unlike most scientists—he planned to no longer work on any topic likely to be useful to the miliary. Some of his colleagues were angered by his moral stance and tried to dismiss it as Wiener's strange quirk. He was a heretic in regarding engineering as applied social and moral philosophy instead of as only applied science. In the second book for the general public, *The Human Use of Human Beings* (1950), he reiterated the ideas of his first book, but left off the technical mathematics. Until Wiener's books only Lewis Mumford had presented a broad philosophy of technology that engaged the American reading public. Wiener contacted labor leader Walter Reuther to advise him of the new inventions that were on the horizon in the late 1940s so that labor could anticipate the danger of large layoffs and de-skilling of workers.

In the 1950s, Wiener's two-volume autobiography appeared. The story of his being shaped by his father, which he likened to a sculptor making a figure out of marble, was a masterpiece in autobiography. It bears a resemblance to the educational experience of John Stuart Mill. In turn, Wiener used "sculptor" as a simile for the modern scientist or engineer creating artifacts. He returned to the issue of the moral philosophy of the engineer-creator in his last book, *God and Golem, Inc.* (1964).

BIBLIOGRAPHY

Heims, Steve Joshua. *John von Neumann and Norbert Wiener.* Cambridge, MA: MIT Press, 1980.

Lee, Y.W., et al., eds. *Selected Papers of Nobert Wiener.* Cambridge, MA: MIT Press, 1964.

Masani, Pesi R. *Norbert Wiener 1894–1964.* Basel: Birkhäuser, 1990.

———, ed. *Norbert Wiener: Collected Works.* 4 vols. Cambridge, MA: MIT Press, 1976–1985.

Wiener, Norbert. *Cybernetics.* Cambridge, MA: MIT Press, 1948.

———. *The Human Use of Human Beings.* Boston: Houghton Mifflin, 1950.

———. *Ex-Prodigy.* New York: Simon and Schuster, 1953.

———. *I Am a Mathematician.* Cambridge, MA: MIT Press, 1956.

———. *God and Golem, Inc.* Cambridge, MA: MIT Press, 1964.

Steve Joshua Heims

SEE ALSO
Cybernetics

Wiley, Harvey Washington (1844–1930)

As chief of the Bureau of Chemistry of the United States Department of Agriculture, Wiley built the coalition whose lobbying was largely responsible for getting Congress to enact the Food and Drugs Act of 1906. He then directed that law's enforcement, amidst considerable controversy, from 1907 to 1912.

Wiley received his M.D. degree from Indiana Medical College in 1871, but he decided not to practice, instead choosing chemistry as a career. He had done so well in his medical school chemistry course that he was picked to fill the chair of chemistry. He wrote a textbook, *The New Chemistry,* for his students. In 1872, he went to Harvard for several months, adding a chemistry B.S. to his M.D. Wiley was appointed professor at newly opening Purdue University in 1874, where he stressed learning through laboratory experiment. In 1878, he visited Europe to attend scientific lectures and to observe Eugen Sell's analysis of food and drink in the German Imperial Health Office. Wiley learned new techniques and brought home new instruments, especially the polariscope. His published research on the chemistry of sugars and the adulteration of cane syrup quickly made him one of the nation's experts in this field. He also exposed frauds in fertilizers. The Indiana legislature designated Wiley state chemist in 1881.

Two years later, Wiley was called to Washington as chief chemist of the Department of Agriculture. For a decade, he directed experiments in the field with sorghum and beet sugar, seeking to make the nation less dependent on imports, but without perceptible success. He shifted his main emphasis to food, especially the detection of adulterants. In 1887, Wiley published the first part of Bulletin 13, *Foods and Food Adulterants,* concerned with butter and oleomargarine. In the next sixteen years, he supervised the publication of nine more parts, ranging across the gamut of foods and drinks. Initially, Wiley deemed adulteration immoral but posing scant danger. In 1902, he began five years of diet tests with human volunteers, mostly young men in his department, to study the effect of the chemical preservatives boric, salicylic, sulphurous, and benzoic acids, and formaldehyde on health. He concluded that the hazards were too great to warrant permitting preservatives in processed foods.

Long before, Wiley had concluded that public morality and safety required enactment of a broad national food and drug statute. Bills had been before the Congress since 1879, and in 1898 Wiley served as key witness and official adviser to a Senate committee that held the first major hearing on the issue. Wiley was active in organizations concerned with chemistry, serving on committees and holding high offices in the Association of Official Agricultural Chemists, the American Chemical Society, and the American Association for the Advancement of Science. He sought recruits for support of a law from his professional associates, and he went further, becoming a chemical evangelist carrying the pure food gospel to the nation's physicians, women's club members, and food processors threatened by adulterating competitors. Wiley continued to work with the cadre of members of congress seeking to enact a law, and he helped the new breed of muckraking journalists who sought to expose to public scrutiny the evils of adulteration and patent medicines. President Theodore Roosevelt, in late 1905, urged Congress to act and then signed the measure in June 1906.

Wiley had been willing to compromise to get the Food and Drugs Act, but as its enforcer, persuaded by his "Poison Squad" results, he took a hard line. He considered chemical preservatives, in the words of the law, added "poisonous" and "deleterious" ingredients "injurious to health." He opposed processors being permitted to call glucose "corn syrup," objected to the use of sulphur dioxide in drying fruit, and sought to ban saccharin as a sweetener in canned fruits and vegetables. These and other decisions, motivated by what has been called Wiley's "chemical fundamentalism," disturbed the affected elements of the food-growing and processing industries who brought pressure on Secretary of Agriculture James Wilson and President Roosevelt. Concerned about Wiley's intransigence and its political consequences and coming to doubt his science, Wilson and Roosevelt hedged in the chief chemist's independence as regulator. The president appointed a five-man Referee Board of Consulting Scientific Experts, chaired by the noted organic chemist Ira Remsen, president of Johns Hopkins University, to reconsider some of Wiley's key decisions. On some points they agreed with the chief chemist, but regarding benzoate of soda and benzoic acid, they determined, after new diet experiments, that a small amount in processed foods would pose no hazard.

Controversy continued, and a frustrated Wiley resigned in 1912. Since enactment of the law, he had been too busy administering and disputing to be a bench chemist. He did, however, manage to publish reference works on the adulteration of foods and beverages. Wiley continued his public pressure on behalf of rigorous law enforcement through the pages of *Good Housekeeping Magazine*. He also presented his apologia in *The History of a Crime Against the Food Law* (1929) and *An Autobiography* (1930).

BIBLIOGRAPHY

Anderson, Oscar E., Jr. *The Health of a Nation: Harvey W. Wiley and the Fight for Pure Food.* Chicago: University of Chicago Press, 1958.

Crunden, Robert M. *Ministers of Reform: The Progressives; Achievement in American Civilization.* New York: Basic Books, 1982.

Young, James Harvey. *Pure Food: Securing the Federal Food and Drugs Act of 1906.* Princeton: Princeton University Press, 1989.

James Harvey Young

Wilkes Expedition (The United States Exploring Expedition to the South Seas)

The first major overseas scientific exploring expedition conducted by the United States Navy. Usually known as the Wilkes Expedition (after its commander, Lieutenant Charles Wilkes), the primary mission of the expedition was to survey and chart the Pacific Ocean in support of American commerce. Among its other missions were the establishment of good relations with the native populations of the region and the conduct of scientific research.

Wilkes set sail in August 1838 with six vessels and a contingent of seven civilian scientists with responsibility for zoology, botany, geology, and anthropology (naval officers were to conduct the investigations in the physical sciences). The civilians were young, either well-educated or experienced, and among the best men available. They included Titian Ramsay Peale (naturalist), James Dwight Dana (geologist), and Horatio E. Hale (philologist). The major exception was botany. When Asa Gray resigned his position, he was replaced by William Rich, who proved to be incompetent.

During the four years the expedition was at sea, it explored both coasts of South America, the Antarctic, the Fiji Islands, the Hawaiian Islands, and the west coast of North America. It arrived in New York in June 1842.

The Wilkes Expedition was a major turning point in the history of American science. For the first time, the federal government was making a major financial contribution to scientific research. The nineteen volumes and supporting atlas published by the expedition scientists, other American scientists using the collections, and Wilkes, were "the grandest production yet to come out of America" (Viola and Margolis, pp. 22–23). Especially significant were Dana's insights on coral, the coral islands, and volcanoes, and the two botanical volumes written by a group of collaborators led by Gray. Although the specimens brought back by the expedition suffered damage at the hands of its temporary custodians—the National Institute, a scientific society in Washington which was attempting to obtain the legacy of James Smithson in order to establish a national museum—the surviving material was still spectacular. More than 50,000 plant specimens, thousands of zoological specimens, and one of the most important ethnographic collections from the Pacific islands and West Coast of the United States have survived. Finally, the expedition also initiated a quarter century of naval exploration and scientific surveying throughout the world.

The literature on the expedition is extensive. Most of the controversy has centered on the character and contributions of Wilkes himself. Contemporaries—both military and civilian—saw him as an egotistical tyrant, but some also credited him with a respect for science uncommon in the navy. Historians have continued the debate. The consensus now is that, although his shortcomings were numerous, Wilkes fought long and hard for the expedition and its science, especially during the long years that the publications were being prepared.

The manuscript sources for the Wilkes expedition are extensive and scattered. Wilkes had ordered that the officers of the expedition keep journals, and many of these survive in the National Archives. Wilkes's papers are in the Library of Congress.

BIBLIOGRAPHY

Bartlett, Harley Harris. "The Reports of the Wilkes Expedition, and the Work of the Specialists in Science." *Proceedings of the American Philosophical Society* 82 (1940): 601–705.

Haskell, Daniel C. *The United States Exploring Expedition, 1838–1842, and Its Publications, 1844–1874*. New York: New York Public Library, 1942.

Hibler, Anita M. "The Publication of the Wilkes Reports, 1842–1877." Ph.D. diss., George Washington University, 1989.

Kazar, John D. "The United States Navy and Scientific Exploration, 1837–1860." Ph.D. diss., University of Massachusetts, 1973.

Stanton, William. *The Great United States Exploring Expedition of 1838–1842*. Berkeley: University of California Press, 1975.

Tyler, David. B. *The Wilkes Expedition: The First United States Exploring Expedition (1838–1842)*. Memoirs of the American Philosophical Society 73. Philadelphia: American Philosophical Society, 1968.

Viola, Herman J., and Carolyn Margolis, eds. *Magnificent Voyagers: The U.S. Exploring Expedition, 1838–1842*. Washington, DC: Smithsonian Institution Press, 1985.

Marc Rothenberg

SEE ALSO
Dana, James Dwight

Wilson, Alexander (1766–1813)

Ornithologist and illustrator. Wilson was born in Paisley, Scotland, the third child and only son of Mary McNab and Alexander Wilson, a reasonably prosperous weaver, smuggler, and illicit distiller. After attending Paisley Grammar School, Wilson tried his hand at weaving, peddling, and writing verse. His literary efforts compared favorably with those of his fellow countryman Robert Burns, and in 1790, Wilson secured publication of his own volume of vernacular poetry. He fled Scotland in 1794 after becoming deeply involved in political reform circles and a scandalous episode in which he was briefly imprisoned for demanding payment to suppress a poem satirizing a local mill owner.

Wilson emigrated to the United States, and within two years after settling near Philadelphia, became schoolmaster at Milestone (1796–1801) and Gray's Ferry (1802–1806). At the latter location, he soon discovered William Bartram, who tutored him in the rudiments of ornithology and encouraged his plan to begin compiling material on the birds of his adopted nation, where Wilson became a citizen in 1804. Once the idea for *American Ornithology* came into focus, Wilson pushed himself mercilessly to bring the ambitious project to completion. In an effort to secure new birds and new subscribers, he traveled extensively as well as made regular visits to the Peale Museum in Philadelphia. Between 1808 and 1813, Wilson published eight volumes and completed the notes and drawings for a ninth before succumbing to dysentery at the age of forty-seven. George Ord, his friend and literary executor, saw the final volume through press and later published two new editions to satisfy the continuing demand for the book.

Although soon eclipsed by the work of John James Audubon, Wilson's *American Ornithology* was a remarkable achievement. With little previous background and few reliable publications to guide him, in less than a decade Wilson had located and painstakingly "drawn from nature" 268 North American species, including 26 that are currently recognized as new to science at the time. The accompanying text included a great deal of new ecological, behavioral, and life history data and was presented in a clear, sympathetic, and engaging style. Although the engraver Alexander Lawson cut the majority of plates, Wilson carefully supervised all of the publication details himself, even taking the place of his colorists when they went out on strike during the War of 1812. In the period of nationalistic fervor that followed the war, Wilson's *American Ornithology* provided the inspiration for a series of similar illustrated volumes depicting American flora and fauna, written by American scientists and published by American presses.

Wilson's achievements as well as his foibles are ably chronicled in two modern biographies by Cantwell and Hunter, although there are still several periods where his movements remain obscure. Hunter also reproduces the extant correspondence. Burtt and Peterson provide a recent assessment of Wilson's scientific accomplishment, while Allen, Blum, Greene, and Porter do a thorough job of placing his life and work into broader context.

BIBLIOGRAPHY

Allen, Elsa G. "The History of American Ornithology before Audubon." *Transactions of the American Philosophical Society,* n.s., 41, pt. 3 (1951): 387–591.

Blum, Ann Shelby. *Picturing Nature: American Nineteenth-Century Zoological Illustration.* Princeton: Princeton University Press, 1993.

Burtt, Edward H., and Alan P. Peterson. "Alexander Wilson and the Founding of North American Ornithology." In *Contributions to the History of North American Ornithology,* edited by William E. Davis Jr., and Jerome Jackson. Cambridge, MA: Nuttall Ornithological Club, 1995, pp. 359–386.

Cantwell, Robert. *Alexander Wilson: Naturalist and Pioneer.* Philadelphia: J. B. Lippincott, 1961.

Greene, John C. *American Science in the Age of Jefferson.* Ames: Iowa State University Press, 1984.

Hunter, Clark. *The Life and Letters of Alexander Wilson.* Philadelphia: American Philosophical Society, 1983.

Porter, Charlotte M. *The Eagle's Nest: Natural History and American Ideas, 1812–1842.* University: University of Alabama Press, 1986.

Wilson, Alexander. *American Ornithology; or, The Natural History of the Birds of the United States.* 9 vols. Philadelphia: Bradford and Inskeep, 1808–1814.

Mark V. Barrow Jr.

SEE ALSO
Ornithology

Wilson, Edmund Beecher (1856–1839)

Leader in American biology. Wilson was born in Geneva, Illinois, the son of Isaac G. Wilson, a lawyer who became circuit court judge and later chief justice of Chicago's Appellate Court, and Caroline Clarke, a descendant of a Mayflower voyager. After a year teaching a one-room school, he resolved to continue his education. Influenced by his cousin Samuel Clarke, he attended Antioch College (1873–1874), Yale University's Sheffield Scientific School (1875–1878) where he received a Ph.B. degree, then on to Johns Hopkins University for graduate work with William Keith Brooks. With the help of fellowships and assistantships, Wilson entered the world of biology and received his Ph.D. in 1881 for embryological study of the coelenterate *Renilla.*

After one more year at Hopkins as Brooks's assistant, Wilson traveled for a year to Cambridge, Leipzig, and settled at the Stazione Zoologica in Naples. In part because of his love for music and culture, expressed in his serious cello playing, the young Wilson became a good friend of the Stazione's director Anton Dohrn, who urged Wilson to remain in Naples to continue his studies. Yet, Wilson felt obliged to return to the United States, where he taught for a year at Williams College to replace his cousin Samuel Clarke while the latter took his own tour to Europe. Wilson was then given a lectureship at the Massachusetts Institute of Technology, where he worked on a new textbook on *General Biology* with fellow Hopkins graduate William Sedgwick. Finally, Wilson received a "real" position at Bryn Mawr College in 1885, as head of the biology program. He taught there until Henry Fairfield Osborn hired him at Columbia University in 1891, where he remained until he retired. As a committed teacher, Wilson gained his students' respect and affection. He introduced them to the basic concepts and theories in biology, but also to research. For Wilson, the driving question concerned the way in which heredity is reflected in the developmental process. To what extent is the developing embryo directed by its own internal (and largely inherited) conditions, and to what extent by external, environmental factors? His first fascination with biology began as an undergraduate when he encountered Harvard zoologist Edward Laurens Mark's careful study of the details of early cell division. Wilson began to explore with meticulous care the precise nature of cell division and cell growth, asking what each part of the nucleus and cytoplasm do at each stage. Comparing his results with studies of cell lineage in other species, he became a central figure in the major debates of the day about the extent to which the cell divisions are determinate or indeterminate of what occurs in later developmental stages.

Exploring a variety of species, Wilson found the polychaetous worm *Nereis* particularly useful for showing determinacy and regularity of cleavage pattern. Yet, the evidence did not fit with a more fully mosaic view, like Wilhelm Roux's, which held that each cell division divides the material into differentiated pieces which act like mosaic tiles in making up the whole while retaining their own individual characters. This view held that cell divisions, therefore, involve carrying out preset steps and serve as a sort of preformation. Embryos are more complex than that, Wilson felt, and they are capable of responding to changing factors in their environment in ways that allow much more regulation, perhaps even regulation by the whole organism as Hans Driesch had suggested.

Wilson continued to pursue the same set of questions, searching for better answers by seeking more reliable and varied approaches. Various experimental manipulations provided new data for Wilson and the community of experimental embryologists and cytologists. It became clear that the subcellular parts, such as spindle fibers, centrosomes, and chromosomes, pass through regular patterns of change that correspond to predictable stages of cell division. This suggested a correlation, the study of which took him deeper into the cell nucleus and back toward heredity, toward chromosomes, and eventually to a Mendelian interpretation of heredity, as laid out in an impressive series of articles.

Most of the key pieces of what made up the Mendelian-chromosome theory of heredity and development came from Wilson, his students, or those closely associated with him. Although Nettie Marie Stevens and Thomas Hunt Morgan are the most famous contributors, there were many others. Wilson inspired them to take up a wide variety of studies of the cell, heredity, and development. Through his influence as a teacher, a scholar, and a leader at Bryn Mawr, Columbia, and at the Marine Biological Laboratory in Woods Hole, Massachusetts, where he spent most of his summers, Wilson taught generations of students to love and respect science. His leadership in most of the major scientific organizations reinforced this message, and the excellence of his own research provided a fine example. He also taught that scientists need not be single-mindedly dedicated to their science. Music was also central in his life—both in his own performance and through the commitment of his cellist daughter Nancy Wilson. As one famous contemporary musician reported, Wilson was "the foremost non-professional player in New York" (Muller, p. 166).

Wilson stands out among early American biologists as an outstanding scientist, a strong leader, and a fine

man. His work in cytology led to his encyclopedic textbook *The Cell in Development and Inheritance* in 1896, which was revised into further editions in 1900 and 1925. That classic work, still cited by modern cell biologists, reflects Wilson's attention to detail and his grasp of the central theoretical and methodological issues of the day. As his friend and colleague Thomas Hunt Morgan wrote of Wilson, "It is given to few men to exert so great an influence in their chosen field of scientific research and also to attract so many friends over a much wider range of interest. The beauty of Wilson's workmanship and the balanced judgments of his decisions are two of his outstanding accomplishments" (Morgan, 1939, p. 258).

BIBLIOGRAPHY

Baxter, Alice Levine. "Edmund Beecher Wilson and the Problem of Development: From the Germ Layer Theory to the Chromosome Theory of Inheritance." Ph.D. diss., Yale University, 1974.

Morgan, Thomas Hunt. "Edmund Beecher Wilson." *Science* 89 (1939): 258–259.

———. "Edmund Beecher Wilson." *Biographical Memoirs of the National Academy of Sciences* 21 (1941): 315–342.

Muller, H.J. "Edmund Beecher Wilson—an Appreciation." *American Naturalist* 77 (1943): 5–37, 142–172.

Sedwick, William T., and Edmund B. Wilson. *General Biology.* New York: Henry Holt, 1886.

Wilson, Edmund Beecher. "The Development of Renilla." *Philosophical Transactions of the Royal Society* 174 (1883): 723–815.

———. *The Cell in Development and Inheritance.* New York: Macmillan, 1896; 2d ed., 1900; 3d ed. as *The Cell in Development and Heredity,* 1925.

———. "Studies of Chromosomes." *Journal of Experimental Zoology* 2 (1905): 371–405, 507–547; 3 (1906): 1–40; 6 (1909): 69–99, 147–205; 9 (1910): 53–78; 12 (1911): 71–110; 13 (1912): 345–448.

Jane Maienschein

Winthrop, John, Jr. (1605/06–1676)

Born in England, he was the first Englishman permanently resident in North America to engage in the systematic study of nature. Winthrop was the son of the first governor of the Massachusetts Bay Colony and was himself the first governor of Connecticut.

Although his close ties to England and English culture make it more nearly correct to classify him as an English natural philosopher than as an American scientist, his position in New England did much to determine the nature of his studies and enterprises. His work can be placed under three modern headings: scientific investigation (but including alchemy), technological enterprise, and medicine. The latter two encompass most of his activity outside politics. His primary role in the colonies was as a politician and promoter.

He studied, as a young man, at Trinity College, Dublin, but was largely self-educated in the sciences and medicine. His interest and research in alchemy dated at least from his residence at the Inner Temple (1624/25 to 1627). (The alchemical works of the pseudonymous "Eirenaeus Philalethes," once argued to be the work of Winthrop, are now known to have been written by the American George Starkey; see the paper by Newman.) After his removal to New England, in 1631, Winthrop acquired a reputation as a medical healer, with inclinations toward iatrochemical remedies, although he also proffered help from herbal and other natural compounds. His medical advice was sought widely by colonists of both Massachusetts and Connecticut. He exhibited greater constancy in his medical and alchemical work than in his other efforts, in which he tended to be less than dogged. He remained in communication with England and the Continent, his familiarity with German facilitating his access to German texts and writers. His correspondence with Samuel Hartlib (c. 1600–1662), a hub of scientific communication and promoter of technological, economic, and scientific enterprise in England, is insufficient to identify him as part of the neo-Baconian enterprise. The colonies having been created as corporations that the founders intended to be economically more than viable, Winthrop's contributions to technological development were, even when unsuccessful, of the essence of the enterprise. Among his several efforts, in which his role was that of entrepreneur, were ironworks in Massachusetts and Connecticut, which came to fruition, and a scheme to mine graphite from a putative "black lead" deposit, which did not. To these, he applied a knowledge of mineralogy.

On an extended visit to England on colonial business, he was almost immediately elected, on 1 January 1661/62, to membership in the Royal Society, only recently established. Considered an "Original Fellow," he was the first North American member, and read numerous papers, some published in the *Transactions*. He acquired a new telescope, 3.5 feet in focal length (and later donated to Harvard), in London, although he had already, at home, used one of 10-foot focal

length. At the society's request, he undertook experiments at sea during his return voyage. He remained in constant communication, and supplied, among other matters, his telescopic observations of the heavens, but mostly his reports were on mineralogy, natural history, and anthropology.

BIBLIOGRAPHY

Birch, Thomas. *The History of the Royal Society for Improving of Natural Knowledge*... Vol. 1. 1756. Reprint, New York: Johnson Reprint, 1968.

Black, Robert C. III. *The Younger John Winthrop.* New York: Columbia University Press, 1966.

Hall, A.R., and M.B. Hall, eds. *The Correspondence of Henry Oldenburg.* Vols. 2–9, 13. Madison: University of Wisconsin Press, 1965–1986.

Newman, William. "Prophecy and Alchemy: The Origin of Eirenaeus Philalethes." *Ambix* 37, pt. 3 (November 1990): 97–115.

Turnbull, G.H., ed. "Some Correspondence of John Winthrop, Jr., and Samuel Hartlib." *Proceedings of the Massachusetts Historical Society* 57 (1963): 36–67.

Wilkinson, Ronald Sterne. "John Winthrop, Jr. and the Origins of American Chemistry." Ph.D. diss., Michigan State University, 1969.

Winthrop Papers. Boston: Massachusetts Historical Society, 1929–. [Only six volumes, covering period up to 1654, have been published.]

Adam Jared Apt

Wistar Institute of Anatomy and Biology

Established in 1892 at the University of Pennsylvania as a semi-independent anatomical institute organized around a neo-Lamarckian research program under the intellectual leadership of Edward Drinker Cope. Isaac Jones Wistar, an executive of the Pennsylvania Railroad, provided financial support for the institute which was named after his great-uncle, Caspar Wistar, a former professor of anatomy at Penn. In 1905, after the resignation of Horace Jayne as director, and with the support of the institute's principal benefactor, Isaac Jones Wistar, the Scientific Advisory Board, consisting of leading members of the American Association of Anatomists, recommended a reorientation to research in experimental biology. Henry H. Donaldson was recruited from the University of Chicago to lead the institute's research in neurology. Shinkishi Hatai, who studied the mychnation of the nervous system, recruited many research scientists to the institute from Japan and established strong links between Wistar and Tohoku Imperial University. Helen Dean King studied the effects of inbreeding on the sex ratio of the albino rat and, together with the director, Milton J. Greenman, produced the Wistar Rat as a standardized laboratory organism of known genetic traits, trademarked in 1942 as WISTARAT. On the deaths of Greenman and Donaldson in 1937 and 1938 respectively, research at Wistar under the director Edmund J. Farris diversified into cytology, chemistry, and microbiology. Hilary Koprowski, director from 1957 to 1991, promoted research in virology and immunology. In 1961, Leonard Hayflick and Paul S. Moorhead discovered the cell line WI-38, with the subsequent development at Wistar of vaccines against rubella and rabies; in 1972 the National Cancer Institute designated Wistar as a federally approved cancer research center, and in 1975 the National Institutes of Health provided $5 million for the construction of a new cancer section. In the 1980s, research in tumor immunology resulted in the development of the monoclonal antibody 17-1A for use against colon cancer and the discovery of the oncogene bcl-2. Under Giovanni Rovera, director since 1991, research on autoimmune diseases (lupus and rheumatoid arthritis) has been carried out at Wistar; federal and private support have funded the construction of the Albert R. Taxin Brain Tumor Research Center.

BIBLIOGRAPHY

Baatz, Simon. "Biology in Nineteenth-Century America: The Wistar Museum of Anatomy." In *Non-Verbal Communication in Science Prior to 1900,* edited by Renato G. Mazzolini. Florence: Instituto e Museo di Storia della Scienza, Biblioteca di Nuncius, Studi e Testi, no. 11, 1993, pp. 449–478.

Brosco, Jeffrey P. "Anatomy and Ambition: The Evolution of a Research Institute." *Transactions & Studies of the College of Physicians of Philadelphia,* 5th ser., 13 (1991): 1–28.

Clause, Bonnie Tocher. "The Wistar Rat as a Right Choice: Establishing Mammalian Standards and the Ideal of a Standardized Mammal." *Journal of the History of Biology* 26 (1993): 329–349.

Simon Baatz

Witchcraft

Witchcraft had several meanings in the period from the fifteenth to the eighteenth centuries. Traditionally, it was believed to be the practice of harmful magic (maleficium), typically by older women. Religious leaders, especially Protestant clergy, regarded all magic as witchcraft, from the "high magic" of astrology and alchemy to the folk remedies and divinations of the village cunning men and women. By the fourteenth century, too, the church had redefined the witch as one who made a covenant with the devil. This diabolical meaning of witchcraft underlay the massive witch-hunts of Europe, and was also encoded in the laws that made witchcraft a capital crime in New England.

Early modern science touched on each of these several meanings of witchcraft. As recent scholarship has shown, the magic of Neoplatonism and hermeticism influenced scientific discoveries. From Paracelsus to Isaac Newton, religious and occult beliefs provided a context for the development of modern socience and medicine. Science also had a controversial role in the history of witch-hunting. The sixteenth-century Protestant physician Jacob Weyer offered humanist and medical arguments against the torture of innocent women, although Weyer himself believed in the devil's magic. Indeed, the majority of early modern scientists believed in witches and apparitions. English philosopher Joseph Glanvill, whose book *Saducismus Triumphatus* (1689) denounced all skeptics as promoters of atheism, was a member of the Royal Society, and corresponded with the English scientist Robert Boyle on the subject of witchcraft. In New England, Boston clergymen Increase and Cotton Mather similarly reconciled their scientific interests with their belief in diabolical witchcraft, and their publications on demonology in part influenced the course of the Salem witch trials of 1692. Both Mathers, however, opposed the use of spectral evidence by the court, not on scientific grounds, but because they believed that the devil could project the aerial shape of innocent persons. Still, historians tend to agree that religion and science together contributed to a process of disenchantment, which made the prosecution of witchcraft anachronistic even by the year 1692. While the educated elite abandoned witchcraft beliefs by the mid-eighteenth century, however, these same beliefs perdured among ordinary people well into the nineteenth century, and to some extent into the twentieth.

BIBLIOGRAPHY

Easlea, Brian. *Witch Hunting, Magic and the New Philosophy: An Introduction to Debates of the Scientific Revolution, 1450–1750.* Brighton, Sussex, UK.: The Harvester Press; Atlantic Highlands, NJ: Humanities Press, 1980.

Glanvill, Joseph. *Saducismus Triumphatus; or, Full and Plain Evidence Concerning Witches and Apparitions.* 1689. Facsimile reproduction by Coleman O. Parsons. Gainsville, FL: Scholars' Facsimiles & Reprints, 1966.

Hall, David D. *Worlds of Wonder, Days of Judgment: Popular Religious Beliefs in Early New England.* New York: Alfred A. Knopf, 1989.

MacDonald, Michael. *Mystical Bedlam: Madness, Anxiety, and Healing in Seventeeth-Century England.* Cambridge, UK: Cambridge University Press, 1981.

Osler, Margaret J., and Paul L. Faber, eds. *Religion, Science, and World View: Essays in Honor of Richard S. Westfall.* Cambridge, UK: Cambridge University Press, 1985.

Prior, Moody E. "Joseph Glanvill, Witchcraft, and Seventeenth-Century Science." *Modern Philology* 30 (1932–33): 167–194.

Silverman, Kenneth. *The Life and Times of Cotton Mather.* New York: Harper & Row, 1984.

Thomas, Keith. *Religion and the Decline of Magic.* New York: Charles Scribners' Sons, 1971.

Webster, Charles. *From Paracelsus to Newton: Magic and the Making of Modern Science.* Cambridge, UK: Cambridge University Press, 1982.

Barbara Ritter Dailey

Women in Science

Women have always been in a minority in American science as they have been in all countries, although both their relative and absolute numbers have increased. Based on figures from *American Men of Science,* only 47 women earned doctorates in the sciences during the entire nineteenth century. However, by the 1921 edition, 323 earned doctorates were reported, and by the 1938 edition, 1,591 women had obtained Ph.D. degrees.

In the early twenty-first century, in spite of the increase, the number of women scientists still lags far behind men. Explanations vary according to different philosophies of the nature of woman. Essentialist explanations stem from the time of Aristotle and assume that something in woman's "essential" nature precludes her from succeeding in science. A variation of the essentialist view, complementarianism, also postulates that woman's nature, although basically different from man's, is not necessarily inferior. Man and woman are complementary to each other, with woman's sphere of influence the home and man's the public arena. Cultural feminists, although they are essentialists in believing that woman's nature is innately different from man's, believe that woman is superior and could direct science away from the desire to control toward a gentler, more humane enterprise. The liberal feminist position, on the other hand, claims that men and women are equally able by nature to do science, but nurture explains woman's relative absence from the field.

It was obvious to those of all philosophical persuasions that education was necessary if women were to be scientists. Those essentialists who believed that educating women was contrary to nature opposed education beyond the basics. There was a fear by others that educated women might neglect household duties, become politically radicalized, or try to usurp men's jobs. In the United States (although girls had long been permitted to attend elementary schools to render them more useful as daughters, wives, and mothers), to progress beyond the rudiments of reading, writing, and arithmetic was considered a luxury for women during most of the eighteenth and nineteenth centuries. The lack of educational opportunities beyond the elementary level during these years put even the exceptional women at a decided disadvantage when it came to competing in scientific fields.

Jane Colden was one of these exceptional women. Colden received a basic education from her mother, Alice, and an interest in botany from her father, Cadwallader (a politician and amateur botanist). Cadwallader corresponded with the chief European botanists of the day, including Carolus Linnaeus, and produced an explication of the principles of botany for Jane. Although she did not learn Latin, she became adept at writing plant descriptions in English and, by 1757, had compiled a catalog of over 300 local plants. Colden's botanical career was cut short by her marriage in 1759, but she remained a pioneer of American women in science.

During the first half of the nineteenth century, several avenues were available for women to get an informal education. Popular lectures, lyceums, and museums (such as Charles Willson Peale's in Philadelphia) welcomed women. Popular science books, many written with women explicitly in mind, were an important source for women's scientific education in the late eighteenth and early nineteenth centuries. For example, the English popularizer Jane Marcet produced a number of introductory science books intended for women and young people that became very popular in the United States. Her *Conversations on Chemistry* (1806), consisted of a dialog between three protagonists—Mrs. B., the teacher, and Caroline and Emily, the students—during which Mrs. B. expounded on current ideas in chemistry. This book went through more than fifteen editions in the United States before 1860, and the approach was so successful that Marcet continued it in several subsequent books.

Postelementary formal education got a boost from Emma Hart Willard who, in 1819, argued effectively for the education of girls before the New York legislature. She carefully appealed to their sense of "woman's place" when she assured them that the study of natural philosophy would increase the girls' "moral taste" by allowing them to better perceive the works of God in the creation. Although Willard emphasized the separate spheres concept, her Troy Female Seminary provided a starting point for educating women in science. Following the pattern established by Willard, in the 1830s through the 1850s, female academies, seminaries, and a few female colleges flourished. Many of these included science in their curricula, but one in particular, Mount Holyoke Seminary (later Mount Holyoke College), is known to have stressed science.

Although the female academies represented a vast improvement over previous opportunities for women to learn scientific subjects, these institutions were still inferior to comparable schools for men. The next step was to upgrade secondary education and to provide collegiate education for women.

Women encountered more resistance when they attempted to penetrate postsecondary education. Oberlin College was the first coeducational college, having allowed women to enter since its founding (1833). Several other institutions, mainly southern, called themselves colleges, with some even offering degrees before the Civil War. The educational situation was much improved by the founding of the women's colleges in the northeastern United States: Vassar (1865), Smith (1875), Wellesley (1875), Radcliffe (1879), Bryn Mawr (1885), and Mount Holyoke (1893; begun as Mount Holyoke Seminary in 1837). These colleges produced numerous contributors to science as well as providing employment for many women on the faculties. The astronomer Maria Mitchell, who was Vassar's first professor of astronomy, advanced knowledge in her discipline and, more importantly, trained a new generation of women astronomers. Cytogeneticist Nettie Stevens received her Ph.D. degree from Bryn Mawr, where she taught for many years. By 1870, many of the state universities, especially the land-grant colleges, accepted women students.

A strategy that proved effective for women who wanted to enter science was to choose a field that seemed to have a relationship to the private sphere of home and

family. Ellen Swallow Richards (1842–1911) established home economics as a science. Her pioneering efforts resulted in the establishment of the Woman's Laboratory at MIT and the eventual acceptance of women in regular courses. Home economics was rapidly institutionalized as an academic field for women after 1910. This strategy resulted in the view that certain sciences (those involved in the health and helping professions) were peculiarly and appropriately related to the feminine sphere. Physics and engineering, on the other hand, were cold, masculine areas and it was the rare woman who entered either field.

At the turn of the century, although much of the world of scholarship had been opened to women, their numbers in scientific disciplines remained low. Even today, women who choose scientific and technological fields often drop out of educational programs and careers. Although formal barriers have been lifted, working conditions and promotion opportunities are often less desirable than for men.

Historians have gone through a number of interpretative stages regarding women in science. The earliest sources tended to be encyclopedia listings of "great women." After Gino Loria (1903) pointed out that, if there were enough great women to fill a book of 300 pages, an equivalent listing of "great men" would fill 3,000 pages, H.J. Mozans (pseudonym of the priest J.A. Zahn) responded by compiling a book, *Woman in Science,* in which he stressed the vicissitudes that scientific women had overcome. The earlier books were written by those outside of both the historical and scientific establishment. Women's scientific achievements were ignored by professional historians. Even after the history of science emerged as a discipline (1920s and 1930s), historians purporting to study the relationship between science and society neglected gender's role while considering other social factors. In the 1970s, the literature on women in science began to swell, and the trend continued in the 1980s. The result was an increased awareness of the role of women scientists through a number of intellectual biographies and biographical and bibliographical dictionaries. Margaret Rossiter (1982) pioneered a new approach by shifting the emphasis from the exceptional woman to a more typical pattern of women working in science.

Two syntheses, the synthesis of social history and the history of science, and feminism and social history, have proved important in current interpretations of the role of women in science. The first synthesis involves locating the development of science within its social and political context. Although such an "externalist" approach is not new, a version of it developed by Thomas S. Kuhn in *The Structure of Scientific Revolutions* (1962) is used to explain the acceptance or rejection of scientific theories. Kuhn postulated that the appearance of a better theory is insufficient to explain so-called revolutions in science, for other factors above and beyond the empirical enter into the scientific community's selection of a theory, implying that different interpretations of the world are possible. The second synthesis applies feminist theory to social history. Carolyn Merchant's *The Death of Nature: Women, Ecology, and the Scientific Revolution* (1979) was a pioneer work in the new kind of history. Feminist Evelyn Fox-Keller (1985) concluded that so-called laws of nature are socially constructed. Rather than depicting an objective reality, the investigator chooses to decide which phenomena are worth studying, which kinds of data are significant, and which theories about these phenomena are satisfying. Since, typically, the decisions have been made by males, one could ask Would science have been different if women had been the decision makers? These feminists do not agree about the form which feminist science would take, but assume that there is a historic conjunction of science and masculinity and a historic disjunction between science and femininity.

The critical theoretical factors necessary to evaluate contributions of women to science are just beginning to be understood. Although there is no unanimity in opinion, a better understanding of the social nature of science and the social construction of theories has made the task less daunting.

BIBLIOGRAPHY

Abir-Am, Pnina G., and Dorinda Outram, eds. *Uneasy Careers and Intimate Lives. Women in Science, 1789–1979.* New Brunswick: Rutgers University Press, 1987.

Brush, Stephen G. "Women in Science and Engineering." *American Scientist* 79 (July-August 1991): 404–419.

Haraway, Donna. *Primate Visions. Gender, Race, and Nature in the World of Modern Science.* New York: Routledge, 1989.

Keller, Evelyn Fox. *Reflections on Gender and Science.* New Haven: Yale University Press, 1985.

Merchant, Carolyn. *The Death of Nature: Women, Ecology, and the Scientific Revolution.* San Francisco: Harper and Row, 1979.

Ogilvie, Marilyn Bailey. *Women in Science: Antiquity through the Nineteenth Century. A Biographical Dictionary with Annotated Bibliography.* Cambridge, MA: MIT Press, 1986.

Rossiter, Margaret W. *Women Scientists in America. Struggles and Strategies to 1940.* Baltimore: Johns Hopkins University Press, 1982.

Schiebinger, Londa. *The Mind Has No Sex? Women in the Origins of Modern Science.* Cambridge, MA: Harvard University Press, 1989.

Marilyn Bailey Ogilvie

SEE ALSO
Gender—in Science

Worcester Foundation for Experimental Biology

Founded in February 1944 in Worcester, Massachusetts, by Gregory Pincus and Hudson Hoagland. Both had Harvard Ph.D.'s (1927) in general physiology, the one focusing on mammalian reproduction and steroid physiology and the other on neurophysiology. Hoagland had directed the department of biology at Clark University from 1931 and brought in Pincus in 1938. Administrative difficulties with Clark's president led them to establish the Worcester Foundation for Experimental Biology (WFEB) as an independent, collegial, self-supporting research institute with no endowment. WFEB, aided by Worcester businessmen, moved to Shrewsbury, Massachusetts, in 1945 after buying a large estate.

The post–World War II expansion of funds for scientific research from both government and industry allowed WFEB to grow rapidly. Pincus and his group were the scientific "drivers," while Hoagland gradually took up administration. The initial focus was on adrenal cortical hormones because of military and commercial interest in hormones and stress. By the early 1950s, one of WFEB's main sponsors, the G.D. Searle Company, hoped to market hydrocortisone, but another company found a cheaper synthetic method. WFEB then switched to studying steroid analogs of progesterone as possible oral contraceptives. With the stimulus of Margaret Sanger, funds donated by Katherine McCormick, the steroids from several companies, and the unstinting labor of Pincus's colleague M.C. Chang, under Pincus's direction WFEB identified several progestins as effective contraceptives in animals. Pincus's gynecologist colleague, John Rock, chose norethynodrel for a large-scale trial in Puerto Rico. It worked strikingly well, and after the purposeful addition of a small amount of mestranol, an estrogen, "The Pill," brought fame but no fortune to WFEB when the United States Food and Drug Administration approved its use as a human contraceptive in 1960.

In its first twenty years, WFEB's annual budget rose from $100,000 to $4,500,000 and it had become world famous. However, after Pincus died in 1967 and Hoagland retired in 1968, WFEB was in parlous times and needed new direction and leadership. These arrived in 1970 with the new director, Mahlon Hoagland, Hudson's son and a well-known biochemist. WFEB permanently shifted its focus to cancer and molecular/cell biology and today continues its long-standing connection with both basic research and the pharmaceutical industry.

BIBLIOGRAPHY

Hoagland, M. "Change, Chance and Challenge." Unpublished manuscript, Worcester Foundation for Experimental Biology, c. 1972.

———. *Toward the Habit of Truth: A Life in Science.* New York: Norton, 1990.

Clark T. Sawin, M.D.

SEE ALSO

Pincus, Gregory Goodwin

World's Fairs

Following London's 1851 Crystal Palace Exhibition, international expositions, known in the United States as world's fairs, occurred throughout the industrial and industrializing world. They introduced hundreds of millions of people to technological and architectural innovations and served as the handmaidens of imperial policies developed by western powers. It is significant that some of the earliest exhibits devoted to highlighting scientific discoveries occurred at expositions intended to promote colonialism. At fairs such as the 1883 Amsterdam and the 1924–1925 Wembley Expositions, scientists, especially botanists, linked the practice of science to the support of national imperial policies. This trend would continue through the 1958 Brussels Universal Exposition, when colonial science was featured as part of the Belgian government's efforts to sustain public support for its African colonial policies.

Anthropologists also played a crucial role in organizing displays for world's fairs and lending the authority of science to expositions. The 1889 Paris Universal Exposition, remembered chiefly for its Eiffel Tower, featured an extensive exhibit of people from the French colonies living in so-called ethnological villages that were authenticated by leading French anthropologists. American anthropologists also relied on the exposition medium to popularize the science of anthropology. Beginning with the 1876 Philadelphia Centennial Exposition, ethnologists from the Smithsonian Institution began an almost forty-year involvement with American fairs. The 1893 Chicago Columbia Exposition featured an anthropology department headed by Harvard ethnologist Frederic W. Putnam and his assistant Franz Boas. At the 1904 St. Louis Louisiana Purchase Exposition, American government anthropologists organized a massive colonial display of Filipinos that, along with other ethnological displays, helped provide the intellectual underwriting for American turn-of-the-century imperial ventures. Through their involvement with fairs, anthropologists helped popularize social Darwinian ideas and provided substantial support for hierarchical ways of thinking about race and culture.

Inspired by the displays developed by anthropologists and especially by British scientists at the Wembley Exposition, American physical scientists determined to use the 1933 Chicago Century of Progress Exposition as a vehicle for launching a counteroffensive against the growing criticism leveled at scientists for their involvement in the chemical warfare practiced during World War I. At the urging of the exposition's management, the National Research Council agreed to provide a "philosophy of science" for the fair, and exposition sponsors agreed to build a Hall of Science dedicated to the proposition that "science finds, industry applies, and mankind conforms."

Throughout the century-long tradition of international expositions, scientists relied on the exposition medium to build public faith in science. Whether the emphasis was on Darwinism and social Darwinism at nineteenth-century fairs or on the physical sciences at twentieth-century expositions, science seemed inseparable from visions of national progress.

BIBLIOGRAPHY

Benedict, Burton, et al. *The Anthropology of World's Fairs: San Francisco's Panama Pacific International Exposition of 1915.* Berkeley, CA: Lowie Museum of Anthropology, 1983.

Rydall, Robert W. *All the World's a Fair: Visions of Empire at America's International Exposition, 1876–1916.* Chicago: University of Chicago Press, 1984.

Robert W. Rydell

SEE ALSO

Philadelphia Centennial Exhibition

World War I and Science

For American science, World War I continued trends which had begun during the Civil War. First, war was becoming increasingly industrial and mechanized. For a nation to engage in war meant that its entire economy had to be committed. Industrial production was an essential element of the war effort. World War I demonstrated the undeniability of this trend. Second, science does have some impact upon the war effort. World War I has frequently been described as a "chemist's war," but psycologists and physicists also contributed to the war effort. Historians have debated whether those contributions were at all significant. Third, war influences the general practice of science. One result of World War I was the expansion of cooperative research. Fourth, and perhaps most importantly, efforts to organize the war effort, which began before the United States actually entered the conflict in 1917, led to the establishment of institutions which either survived the war or at least provided precedents for the later establishment of permanent institutions. An example of the former is the National Research Council (1916). The Naval Consulting Board (1915) is an example of the latter. A board consisting primarily of engineers and industrial scientists, whose task was to provide external technical advice to the navy, the Naval Consulting Board had relatively little importance for the war effort. However, it did lead to the establishment of the Naval Research Laboratory.

The one weapon which is inevitably identified with World War I science is poison gas. First used by the Germans in April 1915, and the Allies five months later, poison gas "was one of the first weapons to result from intensively organized work of professional scientists" (Slotten, pp. 476–477). Chemists had no hesitation in applying their skills to weaponry—just the opposite. Scientists were eager to demonstrate how research could support military efforts. By doing so, they hoped to establish political power and cultural authority.

Chemistry was also the discipline most impacted upon by the war. Historians have argued that World War I accelerated the process of the transformation of chemistry into an industrialized Big Science. It also changed the way research was organized. The project-research method of organizing research—stipulating projects and allotting them to researchers in separate laboratories—was first developed in the United States during World War I for chemical warfare. The model was used after the war in an effort to foster cooperative research.

Physicists also contributed to the war effort. In an example of the direct role of science in combat operations, physicists developed techniques to spot enemy artillery by its flash and sound. These techniques were permanently incorporated into army artillery.

Submarine warfare was another area where physicists were active. They focused on U-boat detection through listening devices. Advocates of the physicists argue that their contributions should receive more attention since submarine warfare was ultimately a more critical aspect of World War I than chemical warfare.

Yet a third discipline which came to the forefront during the war was psychology. Intelligence testing was introduced into the American military during World War I. The psychologists soon clashed with critics who argued that tests were too academically oriented and unpractical. Testing was abandoned in 1919. The army saw the tests as both a threat to the authority of the officer corps and unnecessary in times of peace with greatly reduced manpower needs.

World War I also marked the death of one of the great ideals of science—that it was an international activity which transcended borders, nations, and politics. The postwar scientific community was split between former enemies. George Ellery Hale led the efforts to establish the International Research Council and exclude the Central Powers, especially Germany, from international science. In the words of one historian, the result was a "cold war in science" (Kevles, *Physicists,* p. 139).

BIBLIOGRAPHY

Dupree, A. Hunter. *Science in the Federal Government: A History of Policies and Activities.* 1957. Reprint, Baltimore: Johns Hopkins University Press, 1986.

Jones, Daniel P. "Chemical Warfare Research during World War I: A Model of Cooperative Research." In *Chemistry and Modern Society: Historical Essays in Honor of Aaron J. Ihde,* edited by John Parascandola and James C. Whorton. Washington, DC: American Chemical Society, 1983, pp. 165–185.

Kevles, Daniel J. "Testing the Army's Intelligence: Psychologists and the Military in World War I." *Journal of American History* 55 (1968): 565–581.

———. "Flash and Sound in the AEF: The History of a Technical Service." *Military Affairs* 33 (1969): 374–384.

———. "'Into Hostile Political Camps': The Reorganization of International Science in World War I." *Isis* 62 (1971): 47–60.

———. *The Physicists.* 1978. Reprint, New York: Random House, 1979.

Rhees, David J. "The Chemists' Crusade: The Rise of an Industrial Science in Modern America, 1907–1922." Ph.D. diss., University of Pennsylvania, 1987.

Roland, Alex. "Science and War." *Osiris,* 2d ser., 1 (1985): 247–272.

Slotten, Hugh R. "Humane Chemistry or Scientific Barbarism? American Responses to World War I Poison Gas, 1915–1930." *Journal of American History* 77 (1990): 476–498.

Van Keuren, David K. "Science, Progressivism, and Military Preparedness: The Case of the Naval Research Laboratory, 1915–1923." *Technology and Culture* 33 (1992): 710–736.

Marc Rothenberg

World War II and Science

World War II thrust leading administrators of scientists into policy-making circles and subjected active researchers to governmental management. The same is true for World War I, but unlike World War I, the nation's experiences in World War II gave rise to an ongoing symbiosis between academic scientists and the federal government. The difference is certainly due in part to the longer United States involvement in World War II—scientists had time to turn insights into practices that changed military strategy—but also to the effective arrangements that were made for orienting scientists to military problems.

Vannevar Bush, who became president of the Carnegie Institution of Washington in 1939 after twenty years as professor of electrical engineering and vice president of the Massachusetts Institute of Technology, convinced President Roosevelt in June 1940 to establish a National Defense Research Committee (NDRC) within the White House's Office of Emergency Management. That maneuver won Bush and his chosen collaborators, Karl Compton, president of MIT, James Conant, president of Harvard, Frank Jewett, president of Bell Telephone Laboratories, and Richard Tolman, dean of science at the California Institute of Technology, the power to make research policy without the constraints of a legislative history or an institutional tradition. Drawing on their own experiences and contacts, NDRC's members quickly decided to organize themselves around self-invented categories of military functions rather than either the armed services' missions or the academic community's disciplines. And they decided to contract with extant institutions for research rather than build and staff new government organizations. The result was that research scientists worked in familiar academic surroundings and set their own standards of quality but worked on problems of relevance to military technology and in equitable partnerships with engineers.

Science supported by NDRC, given the current state of historical research, can best be exemplified by the MIT Radiation Laboratory, one of NDRC's earliest contractors and ultimately its largest. In NDRC's initial organizational meetings, Karl Compton assumed responsibility for a Detection Division that would investigate the use of electromagnetic waves in the ten-centimeter wavelength region, which lay beyond the efforts in either the army or navy research laboratories. He formed a "Microwave Committee" whose chairman, the financier and amateur physicist Alfred Loomis, had been supporting MIT's research into the generation and propagation of microwaves, and whose secretary, the MIT electrical engineer Edward Bowles, had directed MIT's research. In the fall of 1940, the Microwave Committee learned that British physicists had invented a powerful generator of microwaves and recommended that NDRC set up a central laboratory at MIT to develop radar components and systems. Compton lined up E.O. Lawrence, the inventor of the cyclotron, to recruit experimental nuclear physicists to join with MIT's researchers to form the core of the Radiation Laboratory's staff. Early success at using microwave radar to detect surfaced submarines from airplanes fueled rapid growth that prompted some physicists and engineers to doubt the administrative rationality of working as interdependent equals under single management. However, Compton and NDRC held firm to its original conception and resisted pressures to split significant responsibilities for microwave radar among more institutions with more homogeneous staffs.

Once the experimental physicists accepted that they were to work principally with engineers on radar systems and secondarily with theorists on the character of microwaves, they found NDRC's structure provided broad latitude to exercise their skills. The central problem to effective microwave radar—synchronizing the motion of charged particles to amplify electromagnetic waves at ever higher frequencies—was the converse of their experimental specialty—synchronizing the application of electric fields to accelerate charged particles to ever higher velocities. They were able to focus on this problem (and its ramifications for other radar components) as a challenge to their creativity without worrying about building a particular system to the specifications of one or another of the armed services. Visits from junior military officers kept the scientists apprised of the tactical conditions faced by radar's users, and NDRC was responsible for goading senior military officers to reconsider military strategy in light of laboratory accomplishments. Toward the end of the war, MIT laid plans for a Research Laboratory of Electronics to continue the Radiation Laboratory in a much reduced state, and after the war, Radiation Laboratory scientists who returned to their original institutions and disciplinary concerns were able to use their highly honed skills in detecting and generating electromagnetic radiation in a host of scientific areas.

While the Radiation Laboratory best represents science in World War II as initiated and directed by NDRC, the ambitions of active researchers and pressures from political quarters pushed NDRC to broaden its scope or created other avenues for scientists to contribute to the war. Scientists worked directly for the military, with the most outstanding example being the Manhattan Project, which Bush wanted the army's Corps of Engineers to administer once the partisans of uranium fission could outline plausible plans for making an atomic bomb. The army harnessed unprecedented industrial resources to achieving the scientists' aspirations while also bringing the army's security concerns directly into the scientists' laboratories. Scientists consulted executive branch agencies on issues of industrial policy, with the most important example being the participation of James Conant and Karl Compton on a panel to evaluate the problems of, and prospects for, the production of synthetic rubber. While the panel was useful in reducing the rhetoric and charting a course for what had been a politically charged program, NDRC shunned institutional involvement in industrial policy and research. Finally, scientists pushed into broader executive-branch politics on the basis of the breadth and depth of their activities. The most important example was Bush's willingness, in 1942, to assume oversight of a Committee on Medical Research to stand alongside NDRC in a new Office of Scientific Research and Development with Bush as director. The added responsibilities and the presidential appointment provided Bush with the bureaucratic muscle to enter discussions of military strategy and international relations when he

thought they bore on the use or availability of scientific resources.

At war's end, Bush pulled together a report, *Science—The Endless Frontier*, to justify legislation creating a National Research Foundation that would permanently institutionalize relations between academic scientists and the federal government. However, the variety of successes achieved by scientists during the war and the revival of partisan politics after the war undermined his efforts. Instead of building a consensus on the importance of a single agency to support university research, legislative hearings attracted a cacophonous string of scientists, public administrators, and representatives of interest groups, who all had conflicting views on what the science agency's goals and means should be. As debate dragged on over a national foundation, other government agencies picked up the support of wartime research programs, and President Truman appointed a science advisor independently of the administration of any scientific research program. Thus, out of political stalemate came the traditions of ad hoc science advice and multiple government sources for the support of extramural research.

World War II left no principal institutional legacy, but NDRC's practice of abstracting scientific challenges from a military context did endure. Until political ferment over the Vietnam War prompted a reconsideration of the scope of the military's activities, the armed services remained liberal patrons of academic science, especially physical scientists whose efforts to improve experimental or computational techniques could serve military as well as scientific ends. The ease with which scientists could obtain financing for such investigations has probably affected the pace and direction of scientific research in ways that are only now becoming discernible.

World War II has become known as "the physicists' war" because of the prominence of physicists in creating the atomic bomb and radar. These projects, especially the bomb project, and the making of policy within the Roosevelt administration have understandably received the overwhelming bulk of historical attention. This essay is obviously captive to that condition. More case studies on the origins, organization, and legacy of other wartime research projects supported by NDRC, the Committee on Medical Research, and the armed services are needed to draw comparisons and form more secure generalizations than is currently possible.

BIBLIOGRAPHY

Baxter, James P. *Scientists Against Time.* Boston: Little, Brown, 1946. Reprint, Cambridge, MA: MIT Press, 1968.

Dupree, A. Hunter. "The Great Instauration of 1940: The Organization of Scientific Research for War." In *The Twentieth-Century Sciences,* edited by Gerald Holton. New York: Norton, 1970, pp. 443–467.

Genuth, Joel. "Microwave Radar, the Atomic Bomb, and the Background to U.S. Research Priorities in World War II." *Science, Technology, & Human Values* 13 (1988): 276–289.

Goldberg, Stanley. "Inventing a Climate of Opinion: Vannevar Bush and the Decision to Build the Bomb." *Isis* 83 (1992): 429–452.

Guerlac, Henry. *Radar in World War II.* New York: American Institute of Physics and Tomash Publishers, 1987.

Hewlett, Richard G., and Oscar E. Anderson Jr. *The New World, 1939–1946.* Vol. 1 of *A History of the United States Atomic Energy Commission.* University Park: Pennsylvania State University Press, 1962.

Hoddeson, Lillian. "Mission Change in the Large Laboratory: The Los Alamos Implosion Program, 1943–1945." In *Big Science, The Growth of Large-Scale Research,* edited by Peter Galison and Bruce Hevly. Stanford, CA: Stanford University Press, 1992, pp. 265–289.

Kevles, Daniel J. *The Physicists: The History of a Scientific Community in Modern America.* New York: Knopf, 1978.

Leslie, Stuart W., and Bruce Hevly. "Steeple Building at Stanford: Electrical Engineering, Physics, and Microwave Research." *Proceedings of the Institute of Electrical and Electronics Engineers* 73 (1985): 1169–1180.

Pursell, Carroll. "Science Agencies in World War II: The O.S.R.D. and Its Challengers." In *The Sciences in the American Context: New Perspectives,* edited by Nathan Reingold. Washington, DC: Smithsonian Institution Press, 1979, pp. 359–378.

Reingold, Nathan. "Vannevar Bush's New Deal for Research: Or the Triumph of the Old Order." *Historical Studies in the Physical and Biological Sciences* 17 (1987): 299–344.

Smyth, Henry D. *Atomic Energy for Military Purposes: The Official Report on the Development of the Atomic Bomb under the Auspices of the United States Government, 1940–1945.* Princeton: Princeton University Press, 1948.

Stewart, Irwin. *Organizing Scientific Research for War.* Boston: Little, Brown, 1948. Reprint, New York: Arno, 1980.

Wildes, Karl L., and Nilo A. Lindgren. *A Century of Electrical Engineering and Computer Science at MIT.* Cambridge, MA: MIT Press, 1985.

Joel Genuth

Y

Yale University

From its founding in 1701, the third oldest "Collegiate School" in the American colonies was established as an institution "wherein Youth may be instructed in the Arts & Sciences who through the blessing of Almighty God may be fitted for Publick employment both in Church and Civil State" (Kelley, p. 7). The first rector, Abraham Pierson, who held the school in his Killingworth, Connecticut, home, filled the void in available physics textbooks by writing one of his own. His most outstanding student was Jared Eliot, class of 1706, who, as a minister, became the first Yale graduate to practice medicine and wrote pamphlets on scientific farming and silkworm cultivation. He, in turn, was the mentor of Samuel Johnson, class of 1714, a student at the college at the time a great donation of books, rich in the works of Isaac Newton and other scientists, was received from England. After the school was removed to New Haven and named Yale College in 1718 in honor of Elihu Yale's donation, Senior Tutor Johnson utilized this scientific library both in teaching the undergraduates and in leading a graduate seminar of faculty and local ministers. An initial step toward laboratory experimentation was taken in 1734 when Yale acquired its first microscope, the university's oldest surviving scientific instrument and perhaps the first of its kind to have been brought to America. Prior to this date, the only scientific equipment at Yale consisted of two pairs of globes, celestial and terrestrial; but a gift by Joseph Thompson of London of a complete set of surveying instruments, motivated Yale to purchase in addition to the microscope, a reflecting telescope, a barometer, and "sundry other Mathematical Instruments." The appointment of Thomas Clap as rector in

1740, expanded Yale's scientific view toward the heavens. A minister by profession, as were all of the early college presidents, he was also a competent astronomer and constructed an orrery, or planetarium, to augment the philosophical apparatus of the college. Benjamin Franklin was awarded an honorary M.A. degree in 1753 for his donation of a frictional electrical machine to the collection.

In 1770, a professorship of natural and experimental philosophy was established, which was first held by Nehemiah Strong, class of 1755. When science enthusiast Ezra Stiles was appointed president of the college in 1778, he had a new planetarium constructed to include recently discovered Uranus, and after the Revolution, he raised enough money to purchase the most modern scientific instruments available in London. His successor, Timothy Dwight the Elder, ushered in the golden age of Yale science in 1799 by appointing as tutors two members of the class of 1796, Benjamin Silliman and Jeremiah Day, who worked together for sixty-five years. Their first project was to remove the library from the upper floor of the chapel and remodel it into a philosophical room, apparatus room, and museum. In 1802, the year following Day's appointment as professor of mathematics and natural philosophy, Dwight offered the newly created professorship of chemistry and natural history to Silliman. Although unprepared, Silliman was selected because Dwight believed that probably no one in America was adequately prepared, and he feared that a foreigner might "not act in harmony with his colleagues," and also that a learned scientist would not share his opinion that "science is a means, and not an end" (Kelley, pp. 129–130). Silliman justified this

Y

fortuitous choice by establishing a reputation for himself as the father of American scientific education and for Yale as its educational center, first in the college, then in the medical school opened in 1813, and in the private school operated in his laboratory by his son Benjamin Silliman Jr., which developed into a graduate school and the Sheffield Scientific School. He also admitted women to his courses, although they were not permitted to matriculate for a Yale degree. In 1805, he traveled to Europe and purchased for the college books and apparatus amounting to $10,000, including a mineralogical cabinet which became the basis for the study of mineralogy at Yale. At the time of Day's appointment as president in 1817, Yale, with 275 students, was the largest college in the United States. He increased the amount of science in the curriculum with required courses in natural philosophy, chemistry, mineralogy, and geology. In 1818, Silliman established the *American Journal of Science,* which became one of the world's great scientific journals and continues to be published at Yale. Scientific textbooks by Yale professors which became classics in their fields extended the university's fame, most notably by geologist and astronomer Denison Olmsted and James Dwight Dana, whose *A System of Mineralogy* appeared in new editions for over a century. Olmsted and professor Elias Loomis were the first Americans to observe Halley's comet in 1835.

During the administration of President Theodore Dwight Woolsey (1846–1871), the number of science courses doubled. In 1846, two professorships were established, a chair in agricultural chemistry and animal and vegetable physiology and one given to Silliman Jr. "to instruct others than members of the undergraduate classes in respect to the application of chemistry" (Chittenden, pp. 37–38). A new department of philosophy and the arts opened in 1847, with five professors offering science courses, and in 1852, the first undergraduate degrees of Bachelor of Philosphy were conferred and instruction in engineering began. In 1861, the Yale Scientific School was named the Sheffield Scientific School. When the first American Doctor of Philosophy degrees were awarded at Yale in 1861, one of the three was in physics. The faculty proposed the degree to enable Yale "to retain in this country many young men, and especially students of science, who now resort to German universities for advantages of study no greater than we are able to afford" (Chittenden, p. 87).

The modern age of Yale science began in 1871 with the appointment of Josiah Willard Gibbs as professor of mathematical physics. His seminal work, "On the Equilibrium of Heterogeneous Substances," published in 1876 and 1878, formed a new branch of science: physical chemistry. Other notable Yale scientists of the later nineteenth century include paleontologist Othniel Charles Marsh, zoologist Addison Emery Verrill, vitamin theorist Lafayette B. Mendel, botanist Daniel Cady Eaton, and Samuel William Johnson, founder of the first state agricultural station. Scientific education for women at Yale became a reality in 1892 when they were admitted to the graduate school. Among the first group of seven women to receive their doctorates in 1894, two received them in science. William Henry Brewer, professor of applied chemistry and agriculture, became a pioneer in the emerging field of environmental sciences at the turn of the century by establishing the Yale Forestry School. In 1907, Ross G. Harrison, eminent tissue culturist, was appointed professor of zoology. During World War I, Yale was the headquarters for the Army Laboratory School, which trained over 1,000 men in bacteriological and chemical techniques, and for the Yale Chemical Warfare Unit, a national center for the study of its medical effects. During World War II, research was performed for the government on the development of the atomic bomb and radar. Through the 1920s and 1930s, the sciences did not progress as significantly at Yale, partly due to the lack of facilities and also to the university's reluctance to take part in the hiring of refugee scholars fleeing Hitler's Germany, which was so actively pursued by other Ivy League universities. Upon taking office in 1950, President A. Whitney Griswold launched a strong campaign to build up the sciences, mainly through the construction of new facilities. The development of the Kline Science Center for chemistry, biology, and geology in the early 1960s and the opening of other laboratories sparked a new vitality in scientific research and instruction, which has been fostered by subsequent administrations. Yale alumni and faculty who have been awarded Nobel Prizes in science, in addition to nine in physiology or medicine, are Ernest O. Lawrence, 1939, in physics; Willis E. Lamb Jr., 1955, in physics; Lars Onsager, 1968, in chemistry; Murray Gell-Mann, 1969, in physics; Sidney Altman, 1989, in biology, and David Lee, 1996, in physics.

BIBLIOGRAPHY

Chittenden, Russell H. *History of the Sheffield Scientific School of Yale University 1846–1922.* 2 vols. New Haven: Yale University Press, 1928.

Kelley, Brooks Mather. *Yale: A History.* New Haven: Yale University Press, 1974.

McKeehan, Louis W. *Yale Science: The First Hundred Years, 1701–1801.* New York: Henry Schuman, 1947.

Stokes, Anson Phelps. *Memorials of Eminent Yale Men.* 2 vols. New Haven: Yale University Press, 1914.

Wilson, Leonard G., ed. *Benjamin Silliman and His Circle: Studies on the Influence of Benjamin Silliman on Science in America.* New York: Science History Publications, 1979.

Judith Ann Schiff

Yellow Fever

A disease of key importance in the history of American science and medicine. It was one of the major foci of the debate over contagionism; it spurred the federal government to spend money on bacteriological research and public health; it inspired the formation of state boards of health in the South; and it was the problem which brought Walter Reed and William Crawford Gorgas international fame at the turn of the twentieth century.

The first yellow fever epidemic to attract widespread scientific attention in the United States occurred in Philadelphia in 1793. Benjamin Rush, probably the premier American physician of his time, used the epidemic to argue both for heroic forms of therapy and, at the same time, for sanitary reform to prevent the disease's ravages. He was an ardent anticontagionist, antiquarantine physician and teacher who conveyed his beliefs to a generation of medical students. It was not until the 1840s that Rush's hold on etiological dogma began to loosen.

While in the federal period, yellow fever was common in the northern seaports, by the mid-nineteenth century it had become predominantly a southern disease. Although physicians in cities like New Orleans and Mobile, which were visited frequently by yellow fever, continued to believe, with Rush, that the disease was generated by the conjunction of foul vapors arising from the cities's streets with peculiar meterological conditions, their colleagues in inland towns more and more began to track first cases to the arrival of ships or persons from infected districts. The fact of the transmissibility of yellow fever gradually gained acceptance; with it came the notion that whatever was transported could be eliminated by means of disinfectants. By the 1880s, as the germs of more and more diseases were demonstrated, it had become standard thinking that yellow fever was spread by a germ and that that germ could be killed by treating fomites or contaminated air with sulphur, chloride, or heat.

The economic and social havoc wrought by yellow fever demanded a solution from southern governments. During the 1870s, state boards of health were established in most southern states in a wave of nationwide public health activity; however, it was those boards most involved with yellow fever that were the most active and best funded. The dramatic yellow fever epidemic of 1878 spurred federal involvement as well, leading directly to the creation of the National Board of Health. This body was superceded in the 1880s by the Marine Hospital Service. The latter manipulated the urgency for yellow fever control into greater and greater public health responsibilities, changing its name to the United States Public Health Service in 1902. The nation's first federally funded bacteriological research was done under the National Board's aegis, and continued to grow with the expanding Public Health Service.

When the Spanish-American War resulted in the United States Army occupation of Cuba, the problem of troop exposure to yellow fever became acute. Yellow fever was endemic there, providing army physicians Walter Reed and James Carroll with an ideal research environment. Reed and Carroll established that the disease was spread by infected mosquitoes, and suggested that the etiological agent was a virus. William Crawford Gorgas used this theory to limit the spread of yellow fever in Cuba, and then went on to make Panama safe for American workers digging the canal. His techniques focused on killing mosquitoes, preventing their exposure to the sick and their movement to the well.

The last yellow fever epidemic in America occurred in New Orleans in 1905. Armed with the mosquito theory, the United States Public Health Service contained the disease and strenghthened the reputation of the federal public health power.

BIBLIOGRAPHY

Coleman, William. *Yellow Fever in the North: The Methods of Early Epidemiology.* Madison: The University of Wisconsin Press, 1987.

Delaporte, Francois. *The History of Yellow Fever: An Essay on the Birth of Tropical Medicine.* Translated from the French by Arthur Goldhammer. Cambridge, MA: MIT Press, 1991.

Ellis, John H. *Yellow Fever and Public Health in the New South.* Lexington: University Press of Kentucky, 1992.

Y

Humphreys, Margaret. *Yellow Fever and the South.* New Brunswick: Rutgers University Press, 1992.

Pernick, Martin S. "Politics, Parties and Pestilence: Epidemic Yellow Fever in Philadelphia and the Rise of the First Party System." In *Sickness and Health in America: Readings in the History of Medicine and Public Health,* edited by Judith Walzer Leavitt and Ronald L. Numbers. 2d ed. Madison: University of Wisconsin Press, 1985, pp. 356–371.

Margaret Humphreys

SEE ALSO
Reed, Walter

Z

Zoological Parks and Aquariums

The earliest New World captive wild animal collections were those the Aztecs and Incas maintained. Precolonial collections are not known to have existed in what was to become the United States, nor were any collections begun during the colonial period. The colonists had little time or need for wild animal collections. However, there was a curiosity about the wild beasts of this new country.

At some point, the popular entertainment of the colonists began to include itinerant animal acts featuring individual native animals. These occurred on occasion when someone would show a bear or some other animal at the local tavern or the village commons. By 1716, these exhibits were featuring individual exotic species. In this year, a lion became the first exotic animal to be exhibited. This was followed by a camel (1721), a polar bear (1733), and a leopard (1768).

After independence, the new Republic began to experience an increasing number of menageries (i.e., multispecies exhibits). Throughout the latter 1700s, these menageries existed in the major cities, exhibiting for the first time an orangutan (1789), tiger (1789), buffalo (1789), ostrich (1794), elephant (1796), monkeys, various other mammals, a variety of birds, and reptiles. By 1813, the menagerie was on the road, traveling to the major cities and visiting many of the smaller towns along the way.

The early 1800s were dominated by traveling menageries and circus menageries. New species were being exhibited, including the zebra (1805), rhinoceros (1826), giraffe (1837), and hippopotamus (1850). The large variety of traveling menageries continued until 1835, when the Zoological Institute, a consortium of menagerie owners, brought together those then in existence. This control ended shortly after, in 1837, and from then until the Civil War, only two major traveling menageries remained. The circus menageries continued to be popular and included trained animals.

The post–Civil War 1800s provided a cultural milieu in which the menagerie was transformed into the zoological park: civic leaders were increasingly aware of European zoological collections and wanted similar institutions in their cities; parks and outdoor recreation were becoming increasingly popular in large urban areas; exploration of the world's wilderness areas was introducing the public to new species; governments were finally considered appropriate funding sources for cultural facilities; and the natural sciences (along with natural history collections) were becoming professionalized.

In 1859, the Zoological Society of Philadelphia was chartered, but the Civil War and the economic condition of the country kept the society from developing its ideas for a zoological park. A second effort was made, and the Philadelphia Zoological Garden opened in 1874 with a collection significantly larger and different from any of the then existing menageries. It opened with permanent buildings to exhibit the animals, a professional staff to care for the animals, and a community-based society to support it.

Other menageries existed, some of which were to become zoological parks. Some twenty-nine zoos existed prior to 1900: Philadelphia Zoological Garden (1859/1874), Central Park Zoo (New York, 1861), Lincoln Park Zoological Gardens (Chicago, 1868), Roger Williams Park Zoo (Providence, Rhode Island, 1872),

Z

Cincinnati Zoo (1873), Buffalo Zoological Gardens (1875), Ross Park Zoo (Binghamton, New York, 1875), Baltimore Zoo (1876), Cleveland Metroparks Zoo (1882), Metro Washington Park Zoo (Portland, Oregon, 1887), Dallas Zoo (1888), National Zoological Park (Washington, D.C., 1889), Zoo Atlanta (1889), San Francisco Zoological Gardens (1889), Dickerson Park Zoo (Springfield, Missouri, 1890), St. Louis Zoological Park (1890), Miller Park Zoo (Bloomington, Illinois, 1891), John Ball Zoological Garden (Grand Rapids, Michigan, 1891), Milwaukee County Zoological Gardens (1892), Prospect Park Zoo (Brooklyn, New York, 1893), St. Augustine Alligator Farm (St. Augustine, Florida, 1893), New Bedford Zoo (New Bedford, Massachusetts, 1894), Seneca Park Zoo (Rochester, New York, 1894), Denver Zoological Gardens (1896), St. Paul's Como Zoo (St. Paul, Minnesota, 1897), Alameda Park Zoo (Alamogordo, New Mexico, 1898), Omaha's Henry Doorly Zoo (1898), Pittsburgh Zoo (1898), and New York Zoological Park (1899). However, prior to the turn of the century the only major collections were those of Philadelphia, Cincinnati, Washington, D.C., and New York.

The earliest public or commercial aquariums were the Aquarial Gardens in Boston (1850s), the P.T. Barnum aquarium in New York (1861), the National Aquarium (Washington, D.C., 1873) and the New York Aquarium (1896). The first oceanarium was Marineland of Florida in St. Augustine (1938). The first zoological park research center was the Penrose Research Laboratory, established at the Philadelphia Zoological Garden in 1901.

By the turn of the century, the modern concept of the zoological park had been established, with programs committed to education, scientific studies, and conservation. After 1900, these programs increased in sophistication as did their counterparts throughout society, and the number of zoological parks increased greatly (until there are now some 250 major collections in the United States).

The American Zoo and Aquarium Association was established in 1924 to promote the professionalization of zoo and aquarium management, captive wildlife management, and wildlife conservation programs.

Although a number of zoological parks received renovations by the Works Progress Administration in the 1930s, most suffered financially during the years of the Great Depression and World War II. Zoological parks bounced back with modern exhibits in the 1950s, significantly increased their conservation efforts in the 1960s and 1970s, and developed more natural habitat exhibits in the 1980s. The 1990s have been dominated by ecosystem exhibits for ex situ conservation and in situ field conservation efforts in order to more effectively educate the public and conserve endangered species.

BIBLIOGRAPHY

Croke, Vicki. *The Modern Ark: The Story of Zoos Past, Present and Future.* New York: Scribner, 1997.

Fisher, James. *Zoos of the World: The Story of Animals in Captivity.* Garden City, NY: Natural History Press, 1967.

Kisling, Vernon N., Jr. "The Origin and Development of American Zoological Parks to 1899." In *New Worlds, New Animals: From Menagerie to Zoological Park in the Nineteehth Century,* edited by R.J. Hoage and William A. Deiss. Baltimore: Johns Hopkins University Press, 1996, pp. 109–125.

Loisel, Gustave. *Histoire des Menageries de l'Antiquite a nos jours.* Paris: Octave Doin et fils and Henri Laurens, 1912.

Norton, Bryan G., Michael Hutchins, Elizabeth F. Stevens, and Terry L. Maple, eds. *Ethics on the Ark: Zoos, Animal Welfare, and Wildlife Conservation.* Washington, DC: Smithsonian Institution Press, 1995.

Stott, R. Jeffrey. "The American Idea of a Zoological Park: An Intellectual History." Ph.D. diss., University of California, Santa Barbara, 1981.

Thayer, Stuart. *The Travelling Menagerie in America.* Seattle, WA: Stuart Thayer, 1989.

Vail, R.W.G. *Random Notes on the History of the Early American Circus.* Barre, MA: Barre Gazette, 1956.

Weemer, Christen M., ed. *The Ark Evolving: Zoos and Aquariums in Transition.* Front Royal, VA: National Zoological Park, 1995.

Vernon N. Kisling Jr.

Index

astroarchaeology, 49–50
astrometry, 58
Astronomical and Astrophysical Society of
America, 29–30
Astronomical Journal, 30, 244
astronomy, 1, 24, 38, 49–50, 56–59,
86, 243–244, 253, 256–257,
292–293, 302–303, 337,
353–354, 355, 387–388, 476,
497, 499, 504–505, 567–568,
581, 589, 590
astrophysics, 58–59, 105–106,
250–251, 271–272, 428,
441–442,
Coast Survey, United States, and, 68,
127
Astrophysical Journal, 30, 251
astrophysics. *See* astronomy, astrophysics
Atanassoff, John Vincent, 135, 284
atomic bomb, 25, 99, 173, 174, 338, 412
Atomic Bomb Casualty Commission, 60,
368
atomic bonding, 116–117, 117
Atomic Energy Act, 293, 400–401, 407
Atomic Energy Commission, 3, 61–62, 99,
138, 168, 192, 208, 209, 219–220,
229, 293, 400–401, 402, 403, 407,
413, 414–415, 439, 510
Atoms for Peace Conference, 403
Atwater, Caleb, 52
Atwater, Wilbur Olin, 14–15, 62–63,
156
Audubon, John James, 5, 53, 63–64, 68,
231, 330, 416, 501, 502, 575
Audubon, John Woodhouse, 64
Audubon, Victor Grifford, 64
Audubon Society, 373
Aughey, Samuel, 390
automobiles, 224–225
Avery, Oswald, 478
Avery, Samuel, 390
Avery, William, 87
Aydelotte, Frank, 279

B
Babcock, E.B., 226, 227
Babcock, Stephen, 15
Babbitt, Bruce, 210–211
Bache, Alexander Dallas, 67–68, 69,
127–128, 181, 190, 205, 218,
262, 310, 337–338, 368, 438
502–503, 505, 506
Bacher, Robert, 102
Bachman, John, 64, 330, 501
bacteriology, 46–47, 468, 591
Bahcall, John, 279
Bailey, Liberty Hyde, 89
Bain, Edgar, 285

Baird, Spencer Fullerton, 64, 68–70, 80,
209–210, 331, 410, 416, 422, 503,
521–522
Baitsell, George, 514
Bakhmeteff, Boris A., 275
Baldwin, James Mark, 112
Ballooning, 70–71, 535
Baltimore & Ohio Railroad, 548
Baltimore Association for the Promotion of
University Education, 487
ballistics, 569
Bamberger, Louis, 279
Banneker, Benjamin, 24, 71–72, 547
Bannister, John, 496, 501
Barbour, Carrie, 391
Barbour, Erwin, 391
Bardeen, John, 277
Barnard, Frederick A.P., 130, 339
Barnes, Barry, 533
Barnum, P.T., 365
Baron, J. Gregory, 444
Barth, Carl, 332–333
Barton, Benjamin Smith, 5, 73, 88, 454,
501
Barton, Edward, 342
Bartram, John, 72, 87, 90, 129, 455, 471,
496, 498, 500
Bartram, William, 5, 72–73, 90, 417, 490,
501, 575
Bateson, Gregory, 148
Battelle Memorial Institute, 343
batteries, 115
Bauer, Louis Agricola, 106, 240
Bazerman, Charles, 322
Beach, Frank, 38
Beach, S.A., 226
Beadle, George W., 82, 227, 228,
229, 551
Beaumont, William, 73–75, 504
beaver, 357
Beck, Lewis, 167
Beckman Institute for Advanced Science
and Technology, 277
Beebe, William, 374
Beecher, Catharine, 121
Beer, Gillian, 322
behaviorists, 75–76, 308, 519
Bell, Alexander Graham, 76–77, 103, 374,
492
Bell, Marian, 203
Bell Telephone Laboratories, 6, 136, 307,
440, 554
Ben-David, Joseph, 4
Bendix Corporation, 568
Benedict, Francis G., 107
Benedict, Ruth, 131
Bentley, Orville, 277
Bergh, Henry, 45–46, 149

Bergmann, Gustav, 75
Berkner, Lloyd V., 282, 561
Berkshire Agricultural Society, 16
Bessey, Charles Edwin, 77–78, 89, 90,
168, 284, 390–391
Bethe, Hans, 59
Bewick, Thomas, 330
Bickmore, Albert, 37
Biddle, Owen, 497
big bang theory, 59, 145, 221
Bigelow, Julien, 147, 572
Biggs, Hermann, 460, 559
Big Science, 15, 78–79, 94–95, 128, 138,
382, 439, 531, 584
Billings, Frank, 390
Billings, John Shaw, 40, 278
Binford, Lewis, 52
Bingham, Hiram, 374
Bingham, Walter Van Dyke, 457
biochemistry, 118, 162, 542–543,
544–545
Biological Resources Division, 211
Biological Sciences Curriculum Study, 82
Biological Society of Washington, 80
Biological Survey, 331
biology, 41–42, 80–82, 125
cell, 576–577
engineering approach to, 442–443
experimental, 139, 324
marine biology, 69
molecular, 154–155, 216
radiation, 62
teaching of, 81, 82, 508
biometrical studies, 430
Bird, John M., 444
Birge, Edward, 318, 319
Birkhoff, George David, 82–83
birth control, 84, 121, 125, 442, 449–450,
513, 582–583
Birth Control Clinical Research Bureau, 84
Bjerknes, Jacob, 347
Black, Lindsay, 277
Blakesless, Albert F., 107
blast furnaces, 249
Blavatsky, Madame, 346
bleaching, 141
Block, Konrad E., 131
Block, Robert, 571
Blodget, Lorin, 275
Bloom, Floyd, 493
Bloor, David, 533
blowpipe, oxyhydrogen, 115
Bluebook, Project, 137, 563
Blum, Ann Shelby, 576
Boas, Franz, 29, 37, 125, 131, 459, 583
Bôcher, Maxime, 83
Bodian, David, 445
Bodley, Rachel Littler, 85

Bogert, Charles M., 38
Bohr, Aage, 131
Bohr, Niels, 209
Bok, Bart, 29
boll weevil, 269
Bond, George, 86, 505
Bond, William Cranch, 85–86, 256, 504, 505
Borman, Frank, 49
Booth, James Curtis, 285
Boss, Benjamin, 163
Boss, Lewis, 58, 106, 163–164
Boston, as center of scientific activity, 469
Boston Philosophical Society, 87
Boston Society of Natural History, 231, 416, 469, 502
Boston Women's Health Book Collective, 122
botanical gardens, 87–89, 95, 96–97, 204, 256, 257, 353, 398
Botanical Society of America, 89
bryology, 95
botany, 80, 85, 89, 89–91, 106–107, 110, 111, 167, 203–204, 245, 323, 404, 431, 465–466, 505, 558, 574
    botanical gardens, 87–89, 95, 96–97, 204, 256, 257, 353, 398
    colonial, 72, 128, 129–130, 496
    new botany, 78–79, 390–391
Botany Club, 89
Boucher de Perthes, Jacques Crèvecoeur de, 51
Bowditch, Henry Pickering, 91–92, 149, 337
Bowditch, Nathaniel, 57, 92–93, 437, 501, 504
Bowen, George F., 504
Bowen, Harold G., 412, 413
Bowen, Ira S., 105
Bowie, William, 30
Bowles, Edward, 585
Bowman, Isaiah, 93–94, 207, 290, 381
Boxer War indemnity, 122, 123
Boyden, Uriah, 275
Boylston, Zabdiel, 520
Brace, DeWitt, 390
Brady, St. Elmo, 116, 270
brain mechanisms, 308
Branner, John Caspar, 541
Brattle, Thomas, 56, 256, 497
breeding research, 226
Breit, Gregory, 560
Brewer, Thomas, M., 69
Brewer, William Henry, 516, 590
Bridges, Calvin B., 227, 358
Bridgman, Percy Williams, 94–95, 539

Bridport, Hugh, 491
Briggs, Lyman J., 161, 275, 376
Brimhall, Dean R., 36
Brink, R.A., 227
British Association for the Advancement of Science, as inspiration for American Association for the Advancement of Science, 27
British engineering, 181
Britton, Elizabeth Gertrude Knight, 89, 95, 96, 431
Britton, J. Blodgett, 285
Britton, Nathaniel Lord, 89, 95, 96–97, 398
Bromley, D. Allan, 452
Brookhaven National Laboratory, 440
Brooks, William Keith, 81, 198, 336
Brown, Chandos, 517
Brown, E.W., 58
Brown, Judge Addison, 96
Brown, Samuel, 470
Browner, Carol, 187
Brown University, 498
Bruce, Archibald, 37
Bruce, Robert V., 206
Brünnow, F.F.E., 1, 57
Brush, George, 515
Bryan, William Jennings, 417, 508
Bryant, William Cullen, 167
Bryn Mawr College, 81, 581
Bryologist, 95
Buckley, Oliver, 452
Bucy, Paul, 394
Buffalo Botanical Garden, 88
Buffon, Georges Louis de, 51
Bulletin of Atomic Scientist, 97–98
Burbank, Luther, 106
Bureau of Air Commerce, 9
Bureau of Aircraft Production, 488
Bureau of American Ethnology, 69, 98, 450–451, 548
Bureau of Animal Industry, 155, 206
Bureau of Chemistry, 206, 435
Bureau of Fisheries, 210
Bureau of Reclamation, 275
Bureau of Social Hygiene, 84, 512
Burford, Ann Gorsuch, 187
Burgess, Ernest W., 119
Burgess Shale, 566
Buros, Oscar K., 459
Burrill, Thomas J., 277
Burroughs, John, 386
Burroughs, Wise, 284
Burt, Cyril, 459
Burtt, E.A., 322
Burtt, Edward H., 576
Bush, George, 452

Bush, Vannevar, 3, 99–100, 105, 134, 207, 216, 381, 413, 452, 553, 554, 585, 586
Bushnell, David, 471, 499
Bussey Institution, 257, 570
Butler, Nicholas M., 112
Byerly, Perry, 511
Byrd, Richard E., 374

C

Cabot, Richard C., 427
Caldwell, Charles, 470
California, University of, 88, 118, 120, 312, 508–509
California Academy of Sciences, 470, 527
California geological survey, 300, 571
California Institute of Technology, 3, 21, 101–102, 82, 106, 216, 292, 297–298, 358, 399–400
Callon, Michel, 533
Calvin, Melvin, 117
Cambria Iron, 285
Campbell, William Wallace, 318
Canada, 103–104
Canadian Space Agency, 104
cancer research, 62, 543, 583
Cannon, Walter Bradford, 29, 394
Cantwell, Robert, 576
carbohydrate metabolism, 143–144
Carlson, Anton J., 29
Carmichael, Leonard, 522
Carnegie, Andrew, 214, 408, 523
Carnegie Corporation, 214
Carnegie Foundation, 334
Carnegie Institute of Technology, 343
Carnegie Institution of Washington, 3, 58, 103, 104–108, 168, 214 334, 438, 493, 566
    Department of Terrestrial Magnetism, 106, 240, 560–561
    Station for Experimental Evolution, 107, 152, 225, 343
Carnegie Mellon University, 343
Carnegie Museum, 416, 422
Carothers, Wallace Hume, 108–110, 165, 446–447
Carpenter, Thorne M., 107
Carr, Emma Perry, 118
Carrel, Alexis, 478
Carroll, James, 590
Carson, Rachel, 185, 186, 192, 386, 452
Carter, Henry Rose, 468
Carver, George Washington, 110–111, 284
Cassin, John, 64, 69
Castle, William Ernest, 42, 226, 227
Catesby, Mark, 111, 330, 415, 496, 500
Catlin, George, 54

Cattell, James McKeen, 27, 36, 111–112, 131, 448, 457, 458, 493
Cattell, Jaques, 36, 112
Cattell, Raymond, 277, 459
celestial mechanics, 57, 58, 92–93, 302, 395–396, 567
celestial photography, 157, 159
cell biology, 576–577
cell-lineage, 139
Census, United States, 43
Centers for Disease Control and Prevention, 19, 113–114, 461
Central High School (Philadelphia), 67, 566, 567
Central Naturalists, 41
cephalosporins, 47
Cernan, Eugene, 49
Chaffee, Roger B., 49
Chaillu, Paul Du, 231
Challenger, HMS, 411
Challenger (space shuttle), 79
Chalmers, Lionel, 342
Chamberlin, Thomas C., 238, 392
Chambers, Robert, 29
Chandler, Charles Frederick, 130
Chandler, Seth, 240
Chang, M.C., 442, 582
Chapin, Charles V., 559
Chariot, Project, 192, 193
Charney, Jule, 347
Chemical Abstracts, 399
chemical engineering, 31, 176–177
Chemical Foundation, 32–33
chemical metallurgy, 285
chemical physics, 118
chemical revolution, 115
Chemical Society of Philadelphia, 115
Chemical Warfare Service, 8, 424, 510
chemistry, 85, 114–118, 140–141, 159, 185, 316–317, 359, 446–447, 454, 515–516, 516–517, 584
   agricultural, 13–14, 62–63, 116
   chemical engineering concerns different from, 31
   food, 573–574
   history of, 140
   industrial, 164–166
   organic, 9, 108–110, 116, 125, 432, 534–535
   physical, 116, 118, 242–243, 314–315, 362–363, 399–400, 555, 590
   polymer, 108–110
   theoretical, 115, 363, 464
chemurgy, 13
Chenea, Paul, 225
Chevalier, Haakon, 415
Chicago, University of, 3, 22, 43, 81, 119, 133, 168, 531

Chicago Century of Progress Exposition, 436, 583
Chicago Columbia Exposition, 268, 583
Chicago Museum of Science and Industry, 366
Chicago School of Sociology, 119, 531
child development studies, 119–121
childbirth and childrearing, 121–122
China, 122–123
China Foundation for the Promotion of Education and Culture, 123
Christian Science, 346
chromosome mapping, 227
Church, Frederic Edwin, 54
Cincinnati, science in, 157, 470
Cincinnati Astronomical Society, 353–354
Cincinnati Female Seminary, 85
Cincinnati Observatory, 1, 57, 353–354
circuses, 593
civil engineering, 41, 177–178, 276
Civilian Conservation Corps, 212, 213
Civil War, 68, 123–124, 205, 311–312, 337, 354
cladistics, 199–200, 423, 529
Cladists, 529
Clap, Thomas, 589
Clapp, Earle H., 212
Clark, Jonas Gilman, 125
Clark University, 81, 124–126, 569
Clarke, Frank W., 270, 352
Clarke, John, 255
Clarke-McNary Act, 212, 213
Claude, Albert, 126
Clay, Lucius B., 8
Clayton, John (1657–1725), 496
Clayton, John (1694–1773), 90, 496, 500
Cleaveland, Parker, 146, 329, 501, 505
Clements, Frederic E., 106, 168, 184, 391
climatic change, 274
Clinton, DeWitt, 274
Clinton, George W., 431
Clinton, William Jefferson, 208, 452
Córdoba Observatory, 244
Coast and Geodetic Survey, United States, 1, 23, 67–68, 86, 127–128, 205, 240, 338, 354, 410, 438, 455, 502–503, 506, 549, 567
COBOL, 135
Coe, Conway, 413
coenzyme A, 319–320
Coffin, James, 190, 346
Colden, Cadwallader, 90, 128–129, 496, 498, 547, 580
Colden, Jane, 129–130, 496, 580
cold fusion, 220
Cold Regions Research and Engineering Laboratory, 183–184
Cold Spring Harbor, 154–155

Cold War, impact on science, 47–49, 59, 61, 100, 113, 191, 193, 204, 207–208, 216, 219, 241, 282, 293, 299, 338, 370, 390, 412, 439, 440, 444, 466
Cole, Jonathan, 532
Cole, Leon J., 226, 228
Cole, Stephen, 532
Coleman, Frank, 270
Coles, Robert, 121
College Entrance Examination Board, 459
College of Physicians and Surgeons, 130
Collins, Arnold, 109
Collinson, Peter, 72, 87, 129, 364, 471
Collyer, Robert, 437
Colorado School of Mines, 352
color-vision theory, 305
Columbia Presbyterian Medical Center, 131
Columbia University, 81, 88, 112, 114, 120, 130–131, 307, 352, 470
Combe, George, 437
Commission of Fish and Fisheries, United States, 69
Committee for a Sane Nuclear Policy, 489–490
Committee for Research in Problems of Sex, 512
Committee for the Study of Animal Societies Under Natural Conditions, 45
Committee on Maternal Health, 84
Committee on Medical Research, 368, 433, 586
Committee on Science and Technology, United States House of Representatives, 132
Commoner, Barry, 185
Commonwealth Fund, 214
Communicable Disease Center, 113
communists, role in American science, 29, 338, 414
Comprehensive Environmental Response, Compensation, and Liability Act, 187
Comprehensive Nuclear Test Ban Treaty, 403
Compton, Arthur Holly, 25, 29, 105, 132–133, 137, 439, 463
Compton, Karl Taylor, 29, 132, 133–134, 207, 216, 413, 585, 586
Compton effect, 133
computers, 10, 99, 134–137, 138, 279, 280–281, 376, 489
Comstock, George C., 30
Comstock, John Henry, 268–269
Comstock Lode, 238
Conant, James B., 207, 413

Drosophila, 227, 229, 358–359, 430
drugs, 160–161
Dryden, Hugh, 161–162
Dryden Flight Research Center, 45, 370
Dubos, René Jules, 162–163, 478
DuBridge, Lee Alvin, 102, 452
Dudley, Paul, 497
Dudley Observatory, 58, 106, 163–164, 243–244
Duke University, 472
Dunglison, Robley, 74
Dunn, L.C., 227
Dunning, John R., 131
Duponceau, Peter S., 501
du Pont, Lammot, 164
du Pont, Pierre S., 164, 224
DuPont Company, 8, 109, 164–166, 224, 432, 446–447
Duran, Fray Diego, 51
Durant, William C., 224
DuShane, Graham, 493
Du Simietere, Pierre Eugene, 365
Dutcher, William, 373
Dutton, Clarence E., 239, 450
Dwight, Timothy, 589
dyes, 164, 166, 206
Dyson, Freemam, 279

E
Eakins, Thomas, 54
earthquakes, 511–512
East, E.M., 226, 227
Eaton, Amos, 116, 167–168, 237, 238, 254, 503, 504, 516, 558
Eaton, Daniel Cady, 590
Ebert, James D., 105, 107
echinoderms, 11
Echo, Project, 370
Eckert, J. Presper, 135
Eckleberry, Don, 64
Ecological Society of America, 45, 168
ecology, 22, 90, 106, 168–169, 184–186, 200, 316, 390–391, 434
Economic Cooperation Administration, 94
economics, 131, 169–171, 396–397
Eddy, Mary Baker, 346
Edelman, Gerald, 395
Edison, Thomas Alva, 27, 171–173, 174–175, 332–333, 344, 388, 492
Edison effect, 172
Edwards, George, 111
Edwards, Jonathan, 321
Eights, James, 266
Ehrlich, Paul, 185
Einstein, Albert, 102, 133, 173–174, 209, 279, 349, 350–351, 439, 528

Einstein, Hans Albert, 275
Eisenhower, Dwight David, 282, 298–299, 403, 452
Eisley, Loren, 386
Eldredge, Niles, 200
electrical engineering, 280, 553–554
electricity, 174–175, 219, 498
electric light bulb, 174–175
electric lighting, 344
electromagnetism, 254, 261–262, 438, 481, 505–506
Electronic Computer Project, 279
Elgin Gardens, 88
Eliot, Charles W., 3, 257
Eliot, Jared, 589
Ellicott, Andrew, 71
Ellicott, George, 71
Elliot, Daniel Giraud, 64
Elliott, James, 328
Elliott Society of Natural History, 502
Ellis, John, 129
embryology, 11, 107, 138–139, 295, 324, 358, 576–577
Emerson, Alfred Emerson, 22
Emerson, R.A., 227
Emerson, Ralph Waldo, 449
Emerson, Sterling, 227, 228
Emma Willard School, 167
Emmons, Ebenezer, 254, 255, 331, 503
Emporium of Arts and Sciences, 140
Enders, John Franklin, 175–176
Energy Reorganization Act, 293, 402
Energy Research and Development Administration, 62
engineering, 99, 257, 326
    British influence on American, 181
    chemical, 31, 176–177
    civil, 41, 177–178, 276
    compared to science and technology, 179–182
    electrical, 553–554
    French influence on American, 181
    societies, academic curricula accredited by, 31
Engineering Council, 28
Engineers Joint Council, 28, 367
Englemann, George, 353
ENIAC, 138
Entomological Society of Pennsylvania, 249
entomology, 249, 310–311, 421, 433–434, 490–491, 570
    applied, 255–256, 268–269, 475
entropy, 555–556
Environmental & Engineering Geoscience, 234
environmental concerns, 184–186

environmentalism, 168–169, 334–335, 373, 384–385
environmental movement, 192
Environmental Protection Agency, United States, 186–188, 461
environmental science, 590
Environmental Science Services Administration, 347, 384
environment versus heredity, 262–264
enzymology, 143–144
ephemeris, 24
Ephrussi, Boris, 228
Epidemic Intelligence Service, 113
Erie Canal, 178–179, 181, 205, 237, 548
Erlanger, Joseph, 189, 222
ESP, 472
Espy, James Pollard, 189–190, 346, 383, 467, 506
ethics in science, 190–193
ethnicity, 194–196
ethnography, 575
ethnology, 98, 268, 316, 399, 436, 491–492
eugenics, 107, 112, 152, 196–197, 227, 274, 293–294, 430
Eugenics Record Office, 107, 152
Evans, Ronald E., 49
Everitt, William L., 277
evolution, 37–38, 139, 247, 293–294, 417, 447, 508
    Darwinian, 11, 69, 150–151, 197–200, 245, 246, 392, 480
    Modern Synthesis, 22, 199, 517–518
    neo-Lamarckism, 142–143, 151, 199, 263, 312, 392–393, 421, 523
    punctuated equilibrium, 423
    punctuational model, 199–200
Ewald, Paul P., 146
Ewing, John, 497
Ewing, Maurice, 31
expeditions, scientific, 37–38
Experiments in Art and Technology, 55
exploration, geographical, 5, 230–232, 315–316, 325–326, 494–496
Exploring Expedition to the South Seas, United States. *See* Wilkes Expedition
explosives, 164
extraterrestrial life, 201

F
Faget, Max, 47
Fairchild, David Grandison, 203–204
Fairchild Tropical Gardens, 88, 204
Fanning, Edmund, 266
farm organizations, 16–17
Farmers' Alliance, 17

Farrar, John, 204, 256
Farris, Edmund J., 579
Fauntleroy, Jane Dale Owen, 418
federal government, science and, 22–23, 132, 204–208
    statistics and, 43–44
    support of research, 127
    See also specific agencies and bureaus
Federated American Engineering Societies, 28
Federation of American Scientists, 191, 192, 209, 564
Federation of American Societies for Experimental Biology, 55, 81
Federation of Atomic Scientists, 439
Feiss, Richard, 332–333
Female Medical College, 85
Fenger, Christian, 427
Fermi, Enrico, 117, 131, 133, 403, 439
Fermi National Accelerator Laboratory, 440
Ferrel, William, 190, 346, 503, 506
fertilizer, artificial, 13
Fessenden, Reginald, 280
Festinger, Leon, 524
Feynman, Richard, 102, 464
Field Museum, 331, 365, 416, 422
Finch, Robert, 386
Finlay, Carlos, 468
Fischer, Edmond, 144
Fish and Wildlife Service, United States, 209–211
Fishbein, Morris, 36
Fish Commission, United States, 210, 294
Fisher, R.A., 43
Fiske, Thomas Scott, 34
Fiske, William F., 269
Fleming, Alexander, 47
Fleming, John Adams, 30, 106
Fleming, Sandford, 540
Fleming, Williamina Paton, 441
Flexner, Abraham, 279
Flexner, Simon, 427, 445, 477
Flick, Lawrence, 559
Florey, Howard, 432
Flory, Paul, 109, 118, 447
fluid mechanics, 276
Food and Drug Act, 206, 210–211, 573, 574
Food and Drug Administration, 84, 211–212, 430
Foote, Don, 192
Forbes, Stephen A., 168, 277, 318
Ford, Henry, 214
Ford Foundation, 216
Forest and Rangeland Renewable Resource Planning Act, 212
Forest Products Laboratory, 212

forestry, 212, 185, 213–214
Forest Service, United States, 107, 155, 206, 212, 235
Fortran, 135
Forry, Samuel, 342
Foster, John W., 238
Foster, Richard, 270
Fothergill, John, 72
foundations, 214–216. *See also* specific foundations
Foundation for Research on the Nature of Man, 472
founder engineering societies, 28, 31
Fowler, Lorenzo Niles, 217, 437
Fowler, Orson Squire, 217–218, 437, 458
Fox-Keller, Evelyn, 582
Fracastoro, 51
Fraenkel, Gottfried, 277
Francis, Clarence, 482
Francis, James B., 181, 275
Frank, Lawrence K., 309
Franklin, Benjamin, 24, 240, 261, 321, 346, 437–438, 455, 471, 498, 499, 500
Franklin Institute of the State of Pennsylvania, 67, 181–182, 189, 218–219, 346, 469, 502, 503, 506
Franz, Shephard Ivory, 308
Freeman, Walter, 394
Freer, Charles, 566
Frémont, John Charles, 231, 558
French engineering style, 181
Freon, 225
Frigidaire, 225
Frosch, Robert, 225
Fuchs, Klaus, 403, 510
Fuertes, Louis Agassiz, 64
Fuld, Caroline Bamberger Frank, 279
fusion research, 219–220
fuze, proximity, 207, 376, 560

G

Gage, Thomas, 51
Gaia hypothesis, 148
Gale, Leonard, 552
Gallo, Robert, 19
Galloway, John J., 422
Galton, Francis, 111, 196
Gamma Ray Observatory, 408
Gamow, George, 145, 221, 463
Gannett, Henrt, 374
Gantt, Henry, 332–333
Garden, Alexander, 129, 496, 500
Gardner, Marshall B., 267
Garrison, William, 233
Gasser, Herbert Spencer, 189, 222
G. D. Searle Company, 442, 582
geiger counter, 25

Gell-Mann, Murray, 102, 590
Gemini, Project, 47, 48, 306, 371
gender in science, 222–224, 546
General Education Board, 214, 334
General Electric, 136, 175, 182, 438
General Land Office, 346, 383, 418, 422, 549
General Motors Corporation, 224–225
genetics, 60, 91, 105, 107, 131, 139, 152, 198, 225–229, 272–273, 358–359, 478
    ethics of research, 493
    statistical, 15
geoarchaeology, 239
geodesy, 30, 240–241
geographical distribution of plants, 168
geographical exploration, 5, 230–232, 315–316, 325–326, 494–496
geography, 93–94, 153, 232–233, 245–247, 273–274, 289–290, 374
Geological Society of America, 233–234
Geological Survey, United States, 23, 127, 142, 234–236, 239, 240, 259, 275, 300, 336, 352, 422, 450–451, 513, 548, 549–550, 565–566
    Biological Resources Division, 211
Geological Survey of Canada, 103
geology, 12–13, 106, 150, 151, 167, 233–234, 234–236, 236–240, 245–247, 254–255, 258–259, 265, 267–268, 287, 313–314, 329, 344, 418, 450–451, 478, 479, 503–504, 513–514, 516–517, 565–566, 571, 574, 590
geomagnetism, 240
Geophysical Research Corporation, 241
geophysics, 30–31, 68, 240–241, 506
Gerard, Ralph, 29
Gerhard, William Wood, 426, 504
Germer, Lester, 439, 464
Geschwind, Norman, 394
Gestalt psychology, 303–304, 308–309
Gibbons, John, 377
Gibbs, George, 502
Gibbs, Josiah Willard, 116, 117, 206, 242–243, 438, 555, 590
Gibbs, Wolcott, 503
Giddings, Franklin, 131
Gilbert, Grove Karl, 239, 267–268, 275, 450
Gilbert, Walter, 272
Gilbreth, Frank, 332–333
Gilliss, James Melville, 205, 388, 502
Gilman, Daniel Coit, 80–81, 104
Gilmore, Robert, Jr., 502
Gilruth, Robert R., 47
Girard College Observatory, 506
glacier theory, 238, 246, 265

Holden, Edward S., 318
Holden, P.G., 284
Hollis, Thomas, 256
hollow-earth, theory of, 266–267
Holmes, Arthur, 444
Holmes, Oliver Wendell, 288, 504
Holmes, William Henry, 267–268
Holyoke, Edward, 342
Homans, George, 260
home economics, 121, 223, 473, 581
Hoover, Herbert, 28
Hoover, J. Edgar, 338
Horn, George H., 310
Horsford, Eben, 503
Horstmann, Dorothy, 445
Horton, Robert E., 275, 276
Hosack, David, 88, 130, 167
Hough, George W., 163
House Committee on Science and
        Astronautics, United States,
        132
House UnAmerican Activities Committee,
        137, 376
Howard University, 270–271, 295
Howard, Leland Ossian, 268–269
Howe, Henry M., 285
Howell, William H., 336
Hubbard, Oliver Payson, 504, 516
Hubble, Edwin Powell, 106, 145,
        271–272
Hubble Space Telescope, 79, 371–372
Hubel, David, 394
Hulburt, E.O., 388
Hull, Clark, 75, 309, 519
Hull, Cordell, 94
Human Genome Project, 79, 104,
        272–273, 327
human immunodeficiency virus, 19–20
Humason, Milton, 145, 271
Humble Oil, 240–241
Humphrey Instruments, 26
Humphreys, Andrew A., 275
Hunt, J. McVicker, 277
Hunt, Robert W., 285
Hunt, T. Sterry, 515
Hunter, Clark, 576
Huntington, Ellsworth, 273–274, 290,
        342
Huntington Botanical Garden, 88
Hutchinson, G. Evelyn, 148, 168, 169,
        319
Hutton, James, 52
Hyatt, Alpheus, 392–393, 421, 422
hybridization, plant, 496
hydraulics, 181, 183
hydrology, 30, 274–276
Hyland, Lawrence, 389
Hynek, J. Allen, 563

I
Ice Age, theory of, 12
ichthyology, 12–13, 69, 293–294
Ickes, Harold L., 207, 212
Ihde, Aaron, 118
Illinois, University of, 8, 118, 277–278
Illinois state geological survey, 277
Immigration Restriction Act, 227
immunology, 487, 579
industrial research, 109–110, 164–166,
        172, 174–175, 224–225, 343,
        344–345, 515–516, 538
inflationary universe model, 145
insanity, 483
insecticides, 475. *See also* pesticides
Institute for Advanced Study, 173,
        278–279, 414–415
Institute for Economic Botany, 398
Institute for Ecosystem Studies, 398
Institute of Electrical and Electronic
        Engineers, 280
Institute of Medicine, 368, 381
Institute of Radio Engineers, 280
institutional economics, 169
insurance, national health, 36
intelligence testing, 120, 194–195, 584
International Association of
        Hydrogeologists, 234
International Association of Hydrological
        Sciences, 276
International Association of Seismology
        and Physics, 511
International Astronomical Union, 252
International Biological Program, 169
International Business Machines
        Corporation, 135, 136, 280–281
International Council for Science, 369
International Council of Scientific Unions,
        369, 536
International Education Board, 82, 214
International Geophysical Year, 31,
        103, 241, 282, 381, 382, 389,
        509, 536
International Meridian Conference, 539
International Polar Years, 103, 241, 282
International Research Council, 584
International Society of Planetarium
        Educators, 444
International Thermonuclear Experimental
        Reactor, 220
International Union for Cooperation in
        Solar Research, 252
International Union of Geodesy and
        Geophysics, 241
International Wildlife, 384
Introduction Garden, United States, 203
ionospheric studies, 560
Iowa, University of, 120

Iowa Agricultural College, 77–78
Iowa Child Welfare Research Station, 120,
        282–283
Iowa State College of Agriculture and
        Mechanics Arts, 120
Iowa State University of Science and
        Technology, 118, 283–284
IQ, 120, 194–195, 283, 458
iron industry, 285
Iroquois society, 357
Irrigation Survey, 235, 451
Irwin, James B., 49
Irwin, M.R., 228
Isacks, Byran, 444
Isherwood, Benjamin Franklin, 181

J
Jackson, Charles Thomas, 287
Jackson, J.B.S., 426
Jackson, Oscar T., 164
Jakob, Max, 181
James, William, 288–289, 397
Janovy, John, 386
Japan, links with research community of,
        578–579
Jastrow, Robert, 537
Javam, Ali, 307
Jayne, Horace, 578
Jeffers, William, 482
Jefferson, Edward, 166
Jefferson, Mark, 93, 289–290
Jefferson, Thomas, 5, 52, 88, 115, 140,
        205, 230, 263, 290–291, 315, 316,
        346, 422, 438, 449, 455, 499, 502,
        504, 520
Jennings, Herbert Spencer, 42, 81, 226,
        227
Jesup, Morris K., 37
jet planes, 9–10
Jet Propulsion Laboratory, 102, 292–293,
        298, 370
Jewett, Frank, 413
Johns Hopkins Applied Physics Research
        Laboratory, 560
Johns Hopkins University, 3, 80–81, 435,
        481, 487
Johnson, Lyndon Baines, 415, 452
Johnson, Samuel, 589
Johnson, Samuel W., 13, 14, 62, 63, 590
Johnson, Virginia, 513
Joint Committee on Atomic Energy, 293
Joint Conference Committee, 28
Joint Institute for Laboratory Astrophysics,
        377
Jones, Jesse, 482
Jones, William B., 86
Jordan, David Starr, 69, 197, 293–294,
        541

Josephson, Matthew, 172
Josselyn, John, 496
Journal of American Folklore, 131
Journal of Applied Hydrogeology, 234
Journal of Applied Physics, 33
Journal of Chemical Physics, The, 33
Journal of Classification, 529
Journal of Paleontology, 423
Journal of Parapsychology, 472
Journal of Pharmacology and Experimental Therapeutics, 435
Journal of Sex Research, 513
Journal of the Acoustical Society of America, 6, 7
Journal of the Optical Society of America, 474
journals, scientific, 33–34, 37
Juday, Chancey, 168, 318, 319
Julian, Percy, 117
Julius Rosenwald Fund, 295
Jungle, The, 206
Just, Ernest Everett, 270, 294–295

K

Kalm, Peter, 90, 129, 330
Kaplan, Joseph, 282
Kármán, Theodore von, 161, 181, 276, 297–298
Kaysen, Carl, 279
Keeler, James E., 29, 318
Keeling, Charles, 509
Kefauver amendments, 210
Keller, Patricia, 144
Kelley, Harold, 524
Kelley, Oliver Hudson, 16
Kellogg, W.K., Radiation Laboratory, 440
Kemble, Edwin C., 463
Kemp, John, 130
Kendall, E. Otis, 567
Kennedy, Donald, 542
Kennedy, John Fitzgerald, 47, 371, 382, 452
Kennelly, Arthur, 553
Kennicott, Robert, 69
Kenwood Observatory, 250–251
Kerst, Donald, 277
Kettering, Charles, 224–225
Kety, Seymour, 395
Keynesian economics, 169
Kidder, Alfred Vincent, 52, 107–108
Killian, James R., Jr., 298–299, 452
King, Clarence Rivers, 231, 235, 238–239, 259, 300–301, 336, 422, 549
King, Helen Dean, 579
King's College. *See* Columbia University
Kinnersley, Ebenezer, 498
Kinsey, Alfred, 512–513
Kinyoun, Joseph J., 378

Kirkwood, Daniel, 302, 378
Kistiakowsky, George, 452
Kitt Peak National Observatory, 302–303
Klüver, Heinrich, 394
Knipling, Edward F., 156
Knorr-Cetina, Karin, 533
Köhler, Wolfgang, 303–304
Komorov, Vladimir, 49
Koprowski, Hilary, 579
Korean War, 452, 484, 538, 542
Korff, Serge Alexander, 317
Koshland, Daniel, 493
Kraus, Charles A., 125
Kreb, Edwin, 144
Krutch, Joseph Wood, 386
Kuhn, Thomas S., 76, 240, 533, 582
Kusch, Polykarp, 131
Kwa, Chunglin, 169

L

Laboratory Animal Welfare Act, 46
Ladd-Franklin, Christine, 305, 356
La Leche League, 122
Lamb, Willis E., Jr., 590
Lamont-Doherty Geological Laboratory, 131
Lancefield, Rebecca, 478
Landsteiner, Karl, 445, 478
Langbein, Walter B., 275
Langley, Samuel Pierpont, 522, 566
Langley Memorial Aeronautical Laboratory, 20, 44, 369
Langley Research Center, 306–307. *See also* Langley Memorial Aeronautical Laboratory
Langmuir, Irving, 117, 175
Lapham, Increase A., 346, 383
Larner, Joseph, 144
Laser, 307–308
Lashley, Karl Spencer, 308–309, 394
Lathroup, Barbour, 203
Latour, Bruno, 533
Latrobe, Benjamin, 178
Laughlin, Harry H., 107
Laura Spelman Rockefeller Memorial, 120, 214, 309
Lavoisier, Antoine, 115
Lawrence, Ernest O., 25, 216, 403, 439, 560, 585, 590
Lawrence Berkeley Laboratory, 440
Lawrence Livermore Laboratory, 440
Lawrence Scientific School, 2, 257, 513–514
Lawson, Alexander, 575
Lawson, Andrew C., 511
Lazarsfeld, Paul, 131
Lazzaroni, 68, 159, 160, 262, 310, 337–338, 368

Lea, Isaac, 503
Leavitt, Henrietta, 145
LeBon, Gustave, 524
LeConte, John, 310, 312
LeConte, John Eatton, 310
LeConte, John Lawrence, 310–311
LeConte, Joseph, 310, 311–312
Lederberg, Joshua, 478, 551
Ledermann, Leon, 131
Lee, David, 590
Lee, Tsung Dao, 122, 131
Legionnaires' Disease, 114
Lehn, Jean-Marie, 432
Leidy, Joseph, 259, 312–313, 331, 422, 423, 470, 503, 504
Leopold, Aldo, 185, 386
Leopold, Luna B., 275
LePichon, Xavier, 444, 445
Lesley, J. Peter, 250, 313–314
Leslie, Stuart, 4
Lesquereux, Leo, 238, 259
Lesueur, Charles, Alexandre, 491
Levaditi, Constintin, 445
Lewin, Kurt, 283, 524
Lewis, Edmund, 332–333
Lewis, Gilbert Newton, 116–117, 314–315
Lewis, Oscar, 277
Lewis, Sinclair, 324, 477
Lewis and Clark expedition, 5, 88, 205, 230, 315–316, 330, 502, 548
Lewis Flight Propulsion Laboratory, 370
Lewis-Langmuir theory, 315
Lewontin, Richard C., 530
Libbey, William, 247
Libby, Willard Frank, 52, 316–317
Library of Congress, 522
Lick Observatory, 317–318, 567, 568
light, chemical effects of, 159
light, velocity of, 348–349, 350–351, 359–360
Light-House Board, United States, 261
lightning, 240, 346, 498
Lilenthal, David E., 208
Lille, Frank Raytray, 42, 216, 226, 295, 333
Limnological Society of America, 318
limnology, 168, 318–319
Lincoln, Abraham, 124
Lindeman, Raymond, 319
Lindstrom, E.W., 227
linguistics, 249
Lining, John, 341, 346
Linnaean Society of New England, 469, 502
Linnaeus, Carl, 90, 128, 129, 130, 364, 496, 580
Linsley, E. Gorton, 529

Lipmann, Fritz, 319–320, 478
Lipscomb, William, 118
Literary and Philosophical Society, New
    York, 356, 469, 502
literature and science, 73, 266–267,
    320–323, 386–387, 557
Little, Arthur D., 31, 177
Livermore Laboratory, 219, 220, 403
Livingston, M. Stanley, 439
Livingstone, David N., 514
Lloyd, John Uri, 267
Lloyd, Rachel, 390
Locke, John, 323–324
Loeb, Jacques, 75, 81, 324, 333, 442, 478
Logan, James, 498
Logan, Martha Daniell, 496
Logan, William, 503
logic, 305,
Long, Stephen Harriman, 5, 53, 325–326,
    330, 490, 491
longitudinal studies of children, 120
Loomis, Alfred, 585
Loomis, Elias, 190, 240, 270, 346, 506,
    590
Loomis, F. Wheeler, 277
Lopez, Barry, 386
Lorain, John, 16
Loria, Gino, 581
Los Alamos National Laboratory,
    326–327, 440
Louderbach, George D., 511
Love, Harry Houser, 226, 228
Love Canal, 187
Lovejoy, A.O., 322
Lovell, James A., Jr., 49
Lovell, Joseph, 74
Low, Seth, 130
Lowell, A. Lawrence, 257
Lowell, Percival, 201, 327, 328
Lowell Institute, 12
Lowell Lectures, 517
Lowell Observatory, 327–328
Lummus, 177
Lunar Orbital Rendezvous, 48
Lunar Orbiter, 48
Luria, Salvador E., 131
Lyceum of Natural History, 231, 356, 397,
    469, 502
Lyell, Charles, 51
Lyman, Richard W., 542
Lynch, Michael, 533
Lynd, Robert, 131

M

McAdie, Alexander, 511
McAllister, Ethel M., 167
MacArthur, Douglas, 8
McBride, James, 266

McCarthyism, 173, 338, 439, 452
McCay, Charles Francis, 92
McClintock, Barbara, 107, 227
McCollum, E.V., 15
McCormick, Katherine, 84, 442, 582
McCulloch, Warren, 147–148
McDade, Joseph, 114
McDonald Observatory, 567
MacDougal, Daniel T., 106
MacDougall, William, 112, 424, 472
Macelwane, James B., 31, 511
Macgillervay, William, 64
McKinley, J.C., 459
McKern, W.C., 52
McLachlan, Dan, Jr., 146
MacLean, Paul, 394
Maclure, William, 5, 237, 329, 490, 491,
    502
McMahon, Brian, 138
McMahon Act, 209
McMillan, Edwin, 117
Madison, James, 499
Magellan, Project, 292
magnetism, terrestrial, 106
Mahan, Dennis Hart, 181
Maiman, Theodore, 307
Malaria Control in War Areas, 113
Mall, Franklin P., 107, 487
Mallett, John William, 116
Malone, Dumas, 141
mammalogy, 64, 330–331
management, scientific, 332–333
Manhattan District Project, 3, 24, 79, 97,
    131, 137, 138, 174, 207, 209,
    326, 414, 439, 586
Marbut, Curtis F., 534
Marcet, Jane, 580–581
Marconi, Guglielmo, 280
Mark, Edward Laurens, 576
Marine Biological Association of San
    Diego, 508
Marine Biological Laboratory, 138, 198,
    210, 295, 333–334, 509, 577
marine embryology, 295
Marine Hospital Service, 206, 378, 426,
    590
Marineland of Florida, 594
Mariner, Project, 292
Mark, Herman F., 447
Mars, 44, 201, 253, 306, 327, 372
Marsh, George Perkins, 184, 213,
    334–335
Marsh, Othniel Charles, 23, 142, 143,
    259, 331, 335–336, 422, 423,
    470, 590
Martin, H. Newell, 81, 92, 149, 336–337
Marvel, Carl S., 447
Marvin, Charles F., 384

Marx, Leo, 322
MASER, 307
Masius, Morton, 463
Mason, Charles, 495
Mason, Max, 241
Massachusetts, University of, 125
Massachusetts Institute of Technology, 2,
    81, 133–134, 136, 176, 177,
    208, 216, 257, 298–299,
    399–400, 469, 473, 480, 506,
    572
    Radiation Laboratory, 25, 585–586
Massachusetts state geological survey, 237,
    503
Masters, William, 513
mathematics, 34–35, 82–83, 92–93, 125,
    243, 546–547, 572
Mather, Cotton, 87, 266, 463, 496–497,
    499, 500, 520, 579
Mather, Increase, 87, 497, 498, 499, 500,
    579
Mather, Nathaniel, 87
Mather, Kirtley, 29
Matthews, Drummond H., 444
Mauchley, John, 135
Maury, Mathew Fontaine, 231, 337–338,
    387, 410, 502
Maxwell's demon, 555–556
Mayor, Alfred F., 107
Mayr, Ernst, 38, 199, 529
Mead, Daniel, 275
Mead, George, 524
Mead, Margaret, 38, 131
measles, 176
measurement, 338–340
Medical Repository, 356, 501
medical schools, 35, 85, 92, 114, 130, 149,
    157, 426–427, 501, 504
Medical Society of South Carolina, 88
Medicare, 36
medicine, 35–36, 485
    iatromechanical, 128
    medicine, Native American, 340
    radiation, 62
    space, 48–49
medicine, unorthodox, 340–341
medicine, weather and, 341–342
Meek, Fielding B., 238, 258, 259, 422,
    503
Meigs, M.C., 23
Meinzer, Oscar E., 275, 276
Mellon Institute of Industrial Research,
    343
Melsheimer, Friedrich Ernst, 311
Melville, Herman, 267
menageries, 593
Menard, Henry William, 343–344
Mendel, Lafayette B., 590

National Defense Education Act, 444
National Defense Research Committee, 8, 99, 105, 134, 413, 585–586
National Environmental Policy Act, 184
National Farmers Organization, 17
National Farmers Union, 17
National Foundation for Infantile Paralysis, 176, 445–446
National Gallery of Art, 268
National Gallery of the Patent Office, 231
National Geographic Magazine, 374, 449
National Geographic Society, 71, 77, 103, 374
National Grange of the Patrons of Husbandry, 16–17
National Hydraulic Laboratory, 275
National Industrial Recovery Act, 134
National Institute for the Promotion of Science, 470, 574
National Institute of Standards and Technology, 375–377
National Institutes of Health, 46, 82, 273, 378–380, 461, 579
National Library of Medicine, 278
National Museum, United States, 69, 80, 98, 331, 365, 521. *See also* Smithsonian Institution
National Ocean Service, 127
National Oceanic and Atmospheric Administration, 347, 384
National Optical Astronomical Observatories, 303
National Origins Act, 196–197
National Park Service, 213
National Research Council, 30, 206–207, 252, 367, 369, 368, 380–381, 399, 439, 452, 510, 566, 583, 584
National Research Fund, 252
National Resources Board, 131
National Science and Technology Council, 452
National Science Foundation, 3, 59, 99, 132, 168, 177, 207, 303, 381–383, 408, 413, 439, 452
National Weather Service, United States, 1, 132, 155, 275, 347, 383–384, 521
National Wilderness Preservation System, 213
National Wildlife Federation, 384–385
Native Americans, 52, 54, 338, 385–386, 436
  agriculture of, 18
  health of, 520
  knowledge of medicinal uses of plants, 130
  medicine of, 340

mounds, 52
science of, 49–50, 384–385
natural history, 80, 111, 231, 557
  illustrations, 53–55, 63–64, 111
Nature Study Movement, 226
nature writing, 72, 73, 386–387, 557
Navy, United States, science and, 383, 502, 574–575
  Depot of Charts and Instruments. *See* Naval Observatory
  Nautical Almanac Office, 58, 387–388, 396
  Naval Consulting Board, 388, 584
  Naval Observatory, 57, 240, 205, 253, 337, 387–388, 396, 408, 502, 567
  Naval Research Laboratory, 388–390, 412, 510, 584
  Office of Naval Research, 3, 168, 389–390, 411–412
  Permanent Commission, 68, 205
navigation, 92–93
Nebraska, University of, 78, 168, 390–391
nebular hypothesis, 302, 391–392
Neel, James V., 60
Nef, John U., 125
Nelson, Nels C., 52
neobehaviorists, 519
neo-Lamarckism. *See* evolution, neo-Larmarckism
neoprene, 109
Neptune, discovery of, 567
neurobiology, 393–395. *See also* neurophysiology
neurophysiology, 189, 222, 308, 393
Neurospora, 228, 551–552
Nevis Laboratories, 131
New American Practical Navigation, The, 92–93
Newberry, John Strong, 259, 422
Newcomb, Simon, 29, 30, 58, 104, 388, 395–397
Newcomer, H. Sidney, 222
Newell, Homer, 536, 537
New Jersey state geological survey, 478
Newmark, Nathan, 277
New York Academy of Sciences, 397–398. *See also* Lyceum of Natural History
New York Botanical Garden, 88, 95, 96–97, 398, 558
New York City, science in, 37–38, 356, 397–398, 469, 470
New York Dada, 55
New York Mathematical Society, 34
New York State Natural History Survey, 167, 237–238, 254–255, 431, 503
Nichols, Edward, 438
Nicholson, H.H., 390
Nicolson, Marjorie Hope, 322

Nixon, Richard M., 186, 452
Noble, G.K., 38
Noguchi, Hideyo, 478
Normandie, John de, 115
North American Review, 449
North Carolina, University of, 118
North Carolina state geological survey, 503
Norton, John Pitkin, 13, 116, 515
Notestein, Frank, 84
Nott, Josiah Clarke, 362, 399
Nova, 449
Noyes, Albert, 368
Noyes, Alfred, 82
Noyes, Arthur Amos, 101, 399–400
Noyes, John Humphrey, 196
Noyes, William A., 118, 277
nuclear disarmament, 489–490
nuclear physics, 61
nuclear power, 400–401
nuclear reactors, 61–62, 401
Nuclear Regulatory Commission, 62, 401, 402
nuclear weapons, 61–62, 326–327, 402–404
nursing, 223
nutrition, 62–63, 107
Nuttall, Thomas, 5, 73, 404, 501, 502
Nuttall Ornithological Club, 416
nylon, 108–109, 165, 447

O

Oak Ridge National Laboratory, 403, 407, 440
observatories, 408–409. *See also* specific observatories
Occupational Safety and Health Administration, 461
oceanarium, 594
oceanography, 11, 30, 241, 333, 337–338, 344, 409–411, 508–509
octant, 495
Odum, Eugene, 185
Office of Defense Mobilization, Science Advisory Committee, 452
Office of Naval Research. *See* Navy, United States, science and, Office of Naval Research
Office of Penicillin Distribution, 433
Office of Population Research, 84
Office of Science and Technology, 452
Office of Scientific Research and Development, 99, 105, 134, 207, 368, 381, 412–413, 439, 452, 510, 586
Office of Technology Assessment, 132
Office of Weights and Measures, 68, 375
oil companies, 422–423
Old Farmer's Almanac, 24

Olds, James, 394
Oliver, Jack, 444
Olmsted, Denison, 503, 504, 590
Olson, Sigurd, 386
Omnibus Trade and Competitiveness Act, 377
Onsager, Lars, 118, 590
operationalism, 94–95
Oppenheimer, J. Robert, 29, 94, 207, 208, 279, 403, 414–415, 449, 463
Optical Society of America, 33
optics, 128–129, 498
Orbital Solar Observatory, 408
Orbiting Astronomical Observatories, 408
Ord, George, 330, 429, 575
organic chemistry, 9, 108–110, 116, 125, 432, 534–535
organization of systems, 260
ornithology, 64, 68–69, 111, 404, 415–416, 575–576
orreries, 476
Orton, William A., 156
Osborn, Henry Fairfield, 37–38, 42, 131, 156, 247, 417–418, 422, 423
Osler, William, 104
Owen, David Dale, 205, 238, 418, 503
Owen, Robert, 329, 418, 491
ozone, 185

P

Pacific railroad surveys, 209, 331
Packard, Alpheus Spring, Jr., 259, 392–393, 421
painting, 53–55
Pais, Abraham, 279
Palache, Charles, 146
paleomagnetism, 561
paleontology, 12–13, 142–143, 237–238, 247, 254–255, 312–313, 335–336, 361, 417, 422–423, 517–518, 565–566
Palladino, Paola, 169
Palmer, Daniel D., 346
Palomar Observatory, 102, 106
Pammel, L.H., 284
Panama Canal, 461
Paperclip, Project, 424
Papez, James, 394
parameter variation, 180
Parapsychological Association, 424
parapsychology, 424–425, 472
Parents Magazine, 120
Park, Robert, 119
Parke Davis, 435
Parker, G.H., 82
Parr, Albert E., 38
Parsons, Talcott, 260
particle physics, 26, 102, 560

Partridge, Alden, 361
Pash, Boris T., 25
Patent Office, United States, 16
pathology, 425–427
Patton, Horace B., 270
Paul, John R., 445
Pauling, Linus, 82, 117, 317, 363, 400, 463, 464, 528
Pavlov, Ivan, 75
Payne-Gaposchkin, Cecilia, 428
Peabody Museum of Natural History, 335
Peale, Albert Charles, 259
Peale, Charles Willson, 53, 330, 365, 422, 428–429, 501
Peale, Titian Ramsey, 5, 490, 491, 574
Peale Museum, 330, 365, 416, 429, 575, 580
Pearce, Louise, 478
Pearl, Raymond, 15, 81, 226, 227, 228, 430
Pearson, Karl, 152
Peary, Robert E., 232, 374
Peck, Charles Horton, 431
Peck, William Dandridge, 147
Pecos Classification, 52
Pecos Pueblo, 52
Pederson, Charles John, 165, 432
Peebles, P.J.E., 145
Pegram, George B., 131
Peirce, Benjamin, 68, 92, 127, 310, 368, 503, 504–505, 567
Peirce, Charles Sanders, 240, 287, 397
Peking Union Medical College, 123
penicillin, 47, 99, 412, 432–433
Pennsylvania, University of, 88, 114, 130, 176, 469, 498, 501
Pennsylvania Hospital, 88
Pennsylvania state geological survey, 237, 313, 478, 503
Penrose, R.A.F., Jr., 234
Penrose Research Laboratory, 594
Penzias, Arno, 145
Pert, Candace, 395
pesticides, 185, 192, 433–434, 452
Peters, A.T., 390
Peters, C.H.F., 57
Peterson, Alan P., 576
Peterson, Roger Tory, 64
petroleum, 240–241, 422–423, 516
Petroleum Research Fund, 8
Petrosky, Henry, 321
pharmacology, 434–435
Phelps, Almira Hart Lincoln, 167
Philadelphia, as leader in science, 330, 501, 502, 504
Philadelphia Biological Society, 80
Philadelphia Centennial Exposition, 268, 436, 583
Philadelphia Columbianum, 53

Philadelphia High School Observatory, 567
Philadelphia Society for Promoting Agriculture, 16
Philadelphia Zoological Garden, 593
philanthropy, private, 104–108. *See also* foundations
Philbrick, George A., 136
Phillips, Melba, 29
philosophy, 94–95, 288–290, 538
photography, 54–55
    celestial, 86
photosynthesis, 106–107
phrenology, 217–218, 436–437, 458
physical chemistry, 116, 118, 242–243, 314–315, 362–363, 399–400, 555, 590
Physical Review, 33, 38, 438
physics, 7, 32–33, 38–39, 125, 131, 132–133, 133–134, 253–254, 437–440, 569, 584
    experimental, 261–262, 474, 481, 560
    high-pressure, 94–95
    Newtonian, 128–129
    nuclear, 25–26, 61, 134
    particle, 26, 102, 560
    solar, 58
    teaching of, 204, 254
    theoretical, 102, 137–138, 173–174, 221, 414, 506
Physics Today, 33
physiology, 73–75, 81, 91–92, 149, 260, 336–337
    plant, 106–107
Pickering, Andrew, 533
Pickering, Edward C., 30, 58, 441–442
Pickering, W.H., 327
Pickett, Clarence, 489
Pickney, Eliza Lucas, 496
Piel, Gerard, 507
Pierson, Abraham, 589
Pike, Zebulon, 330
Pinchot, Gifford, 184, 206, 212, 213, 335
Pincus, Gregory, 84, 125, 324, 442–443, 582–583
Pitzer, Kenneth, 542
Pitts, Walter, 147–148
Plafker, George, 444
planetarium, 443–444
Planetary and Space Science, 537
plant ecology, 78, 106, 184–185, 390–391
plant physiology, 106–107
Plant Science Bulletin, 89
plate tectonics, 240, 241, 344, 382, 444–445
Plough, H.H., 227, 228
Pluto, discovery of, 328
Poe, Edgar Allan, 266–267, 321

poison gas, 207, 584
polio, 175, 445–446, 478, 543
political action by scientists, 29
Pollock, Harry E.R., 108
Pollution Prevention Act, 188
polygenism, 197, 492
polymers, 108–109, 165, 446–447
Pool, Raymond, 391
Popular Science Monthly, 112, 447–448, 449
popularization of science, 24, 221, 337, 353–354, 443–444, 448–449, 517, 582
Population Association of America, 84
population biology, 430
Population Council, The, 84, 449–450
Porter, Thomas C., 259
Porush, David, 321–322
Powell, John Wesley, 23, 80, 231, 235, 239, 259, 300, 301, 336, 374, 422, 450–451, 566
Prairie States Forestry Project, 212
Precisionism, 55
Presbyterian Hospital, 131
president, scientific advice to, 208, 298–299, 451–453, 536
President's Science Advisory Committee, 208, 298–299, 452, 536
Price, Derek J. de Solla, 79
Priestley, Joseph, 115, 140, 453–454
Prince, Thomas, 498
Princeton University, 247, 417, 498
   Office of Population Research, 84
   Plasma Physics Laboratory, 440
professionalization of science, 13, 26, 90–91, 454–457
Progressive Era, model agency, 375
Project Bluebook, 137, 567
Project Chariot, 192, 193
Project Echo, 370
Project Galileo, 292
Project Gemini, 47, 48, 306, 371
Project Magellan, 292
Project Mercury, 47, 48, 306, 370, 371
Project Mohole, 381, 382, 509
Project Paperclip, 424
Project RAND, 466–467
Project Ranger, 48, 292–293, 370
Project Surveyor, 48, 292
Project Viking, 44, 201, 292, 306, 372
Project Voyager, 292, 372
proximity fuze, 207, 376, 560
Pruitt, William, 192
psychical research, 424–425
psychoendrocrinology, 513
psychological and intelligence testing, 380, 457, 458–460
Psychological Corporation, The, 112, 457

Psychological Review, 112
psychology, 39–40, 75–76, 131, 288–290, 305, 308, 437, 518–520, 584
   experimental, 111–112, 125, 303–304
   social, 524
public health, 40–41, 378–379, 460–461, 487–488
Public Health Service, United States, 3, 113–114, 206, 378, 426, 435, 590
publications, scientific, 112. *See also* specific journals
Puerto Rico Scientific Survey, 397–398
Pumpelly, Raphael, 107
Pupin, Michael, 131
Puritanism, 462
Purnell Act, 15
Pursh, Frederick, 502
Putnam, Frederic C., 583

Q

quantum chemistry, 363
quantum theory, 133, 173–174, 414, 439, 463–464
Quimby, Phineas, 345

R

Rabi, I.I., 131, 452, 463
Rabinowitch, Eugene, 209, 277
race, 194–196, 361–362, 399
radar, 99, 389, 489, 585–586
radar astronomy, 292, 561
Radcliff College, 581
radiation, genetic effects of, 60
radiation biology, 62
Radiation Effects Research Foundation, 60
radiation medicine, 62
radio, 182, 241, 280, 388–389, 554
radio astronomy, 408
radiocarbon dating, 52
Radio Corporation of America, 6
Radio Research Laboratory, 257
Rafinesque, Constantine Samuel, 465–466
Rainwater, James, 131
Ramsey, Martha Laurens, 496
RAND, Project, 466–467
Randall, Merle, 314
Ranger, Project, 48, 292–293, 370
Ranger Rick, 384
reactors, nuclear, 61–62, 401
Reagan, Ronald, 452
recombinant DNA, 192–193, 379, 407
Redfield, Robert, 108
Redfield, William C., 190, 346, 467, 506
Redstone rocket, 48
Reed, Lowell J., 430
Reed, Walter, 468, 591
Reese, Charles Lee, 164
reflexive sociology of science, 533

Regge, Tullio, 279
regional characteristics of science, 469–470
Reichelderfer, Francis W., 347, 384
Reid, Henry Fielding, 511
Reighard, Jacob, 168, 318
Reilly, William, 187
Reines, Frederick, 327
Reingold, Nathan, 456
relativity theory, 83, 94, 314, 318, 350–351
religion and science, 139, 140, 150–151, 160, 197–198, 246, 247, 265, 288, 312, 313, 341, 346, 397, 417, 447–448, 448, 462, 472, 500, 508, 516–517
Remington, Frederic, 54
Remsen, Ira, 574
Rensselaer Polytechnic Institute, 167, 237, 469, 506
Renwick, James, 130
RESA, 515
Research Corporation, 134, 566
Reuther, Walter, 572
Revelle, Roger, 509
Review of Scientific Instruments, 33, 474
Reviews of Modern Physics, 39
Revolutionary War, 56, 471, 499
rewards and honors, scientific, 36
Reynolds, Jeremiah N., 266–267
Rhine, Joseph Banks, 424–425, 472
Rhine, Louisa, 424, 472
Rhine Research Center, 425, 472
Rich, William, 574
Richards, Dickinson W., 131
Richards, Ellen Henrietta Swallow, 116, 121, 356, 473
Richards, Theodore W., 117
Richardson, Owen W., 133
Richter, Charles Francis, 106, 474, 511
Ricker, Norman H., 241
Richtmyer, Floyd Karker, 474–475
Ridenour, Louis, 277
Ridgeway, Robert, 69
Riley, Charles Valentine, 80, 475
Ripley, James W., 124
Ripley, S. Dillon, 522
Ritchey, George Willis, 29
Rittenhouse, Benjamin, 495
Rittenhouse, David, 339, 437, 471, 476–477, 495, 498, 501, 547
Ritter, William, 508
Robbins, Frederick C., 175
Roberts, Charlotte Fitch, 116
Robertson, H.P., 563
Robie, Thomas, 497, 498
Robinson, Thomas, 270
Robinson, W. Edward, 270
Rochester code of nomenclature, 96

Rock, John, 442, 582
Rockefeller, John D., 214, 309, 477
Rockefeller, John D., Jr., 84, 512
Rockefeller, John D., III, 84, 449, 450
Rockefeller Brothers Fund, 214
Rockefeller Foundation, 81–82, 106, 122, 123, 154–155, 214, 215, 216, 228, 334, 461, 512, 513, 568
  Bureau of Social Hygiene, 84
Rockefeller Institute for Medical Research, 3, 477–478, 487
Rockefeller Sanitary Commission, 461
Rockefeller University, 477–478
rocketry, 9
Rodgers, Andrew Denny, 558
Roe, Ann, 517
Rogers, Henry D., 237, 238, 249, 313, 478–479, 503
Rogers, William Barton, 197, 238, 479–480, 503
Roosevelt, Franklin D., 94, 133, 173, 585
Roosevelt, Theodore, 212, 573–574
Rose, Wickliffe, 215
Rosenblueth, Arturo, 147, 572
Rosenbluth, Marshall, 279
Ross, Edward, 325
Ross, Ronald, 468
Rossby, Carl G., 347
Rossiter, Margaret, 85, 487, 581
Rous, Peyton, 478
Rous sarcoma virus, 126
Rousseau, G.S., 321, 322
Rovera, Giovanni, 579
Rowland, Henry Augustus, 38, 438, 480–481
Royal Society of London, 56, 87, 114, 462, 494, 495–496, 497, 498, 499, 500, 578
Royce, Josiah, 260
rubber, synthetic, 109, 165, 447, 482–483, 586
Rubber Producing Facilities Disposal Act, 484
Rubber Reserve Company, 482
Ruckelshaus, William, 186, 187
Ruffin, Edmund, 13
Rumford, Count, 483–484
Ruml, Beardsley, 215, 309
Runkle, John D., 503
Rush, Benjamin, 114–115, 342, 471, 485–486, 559, 591
Russell, Henry Norris, 59, 105–106, 428
Russell, J.B., 136
Russell Sage Foundation, 214
Rutherfurd, L. M., 58
Ryan, Harris J., 553
Ryder, John, 392–393

S

Sabin, Albert, 175, 445, 446
Sabin, Florence Rena, 487–488
Sabine, Wallace Clement Ware, 7, 488–489
Sage, Olivia, 214
Sagendorph, Robb, 24
SAGE Project, 489
St. Louis, science in, 470
St. Louis Louisiana Purchase Exposition, 112, 583
St. Martin, Alexis, 74
Salk, Jonas, 175, 176, 446
San Cristobal Pueblo, 52
Sandia Laboratory, 403
SANE, 489–490
San Francisco Earthquake, 239
Sanger, Margaret, 84, 442, 582
Sanitary Commission, United States, 68, 244
Sargent, Charles Sprague, 89, 96
Sarton, George, 260
Sauer, Carl, 233
Sauveur, Albert, 285
Say, Thomas, 5, 73, 311, 429, 490–491, 501
scale insects, 269
Schachter, Stanley, 524
Schamberg, Motron, 54
Schawlow, Arthur L., 307
Scherer, James A.B., 101
Schmidt, Harrison, 47
Schmitt, Jack, 49
Scholastic Aptitude Test, 459
School and Society, 112
Schoolcraft, Henry Rowe, 491–492
Schotte, Oscar, 228
Schultz, C. Bertrand, 391
Schwartz, Melvin, 131
Schweinitz, Lewis D. von, 501
Schwem Technology, 26
Schwinger, Julian, 464
Science, 27, 77, 112, 172, 492–493
science, compared to engineering and technology, 179–182
science, interaction with technology, 172, 552–553, 554
Science Advisory Board, 134, 207, 452
Science for the People, 493–494
Science—The Endless Frontier, 3, 99, 100, 381, 413, 586
Scientific American, 221, 321, 449, 507
Scientific Monthly, The, 112, 221
Scientists and Engineers for Social and Political Action, 192, 493–494
Scopes, John, 508
Scopes trial, 508
Scott, David R., 49

Scott, Walter Dill, 458
Scott, William Berryman, 247, 417
Scripps, E.W., 508
Scripps, Ellen Browning, 508
Scripps Foundation for Research in Population Problems, 84
Scripps Institution of Oceanography, 508–509
Scudder, Samuel Hubbard, 259, 492
sculpture, 54–55
Seaborg, Glenn T., 29, 62, 117
Sea-Lab, 411
Sears, Paul, 184
Sears, Robert R., 282–283
secret and classified research, 509–510
Sedgwick, William T., 336, 576
Seismological Society of America, 511
seismology, 30, 106, 474, 498, 511–512
Seitz, Frederick, 277
Sellers, William, 181, 218–219
Sewall, Henry, 336
Sewall, Samuel, 87
sex and sexuality, 512–513
sex determination, 545–546
Seymour, Samuel, 53
Shakespeare, Edward, 468
Shaler, Nathaniel Southgate, 513–514
Shane, C. Donald, 318
Shannon, E.F., 321
Shapin, Steven, 533
Shapley, Harlow, 29, 145, 182, 428, 515
Shaw's Garden, 88, 353
Sheeler, Charles, 54
Sheffield Scientific School. *See* Yale University
Shelford, Victor Ernest, 22, 168, 277
Shepard, Anna O., 108
Shepard, Charles Upham, 504, 516
Shreve, Forrest, 107
Shreve, Henry, 177
Shull, 227
Sierra Club, 232
Sigma Xi, 514–515
Sign, project, 563
Silicon Valley, 182
Silliman, Benjamin, Jr., 34, 287, 504, 515–516, 571, 590
Silliman, Benjamin, Sr., 115, 150, 167, 237, 238, 351–352, 501, 504, 513, 516–517, 589–590
  as editor of *American Journal of Science*, 33–34, 37, 590
Simpson, George Gaylord, 38, 199, 423, 517–518
Simpson, John A., 209
Sinclair, Upton, 206
Singer, Edgar A., 75
Singer, Maxine, 105

Taube, Henry, 118
Taylor, A. Hoyt, 388
Taylor, Frank B., 239
Taylor, Frederick W., 332–333
Taylor, Henry C., 156
Taylor, Hugh, 515
Taylor, Peter, 169
Taylorism, 191
Teale, Edwin Way, 386
technology, compared to science and
    engineering, 179–182
technology, history of, 363–364
technology-science interaction, 172,
    552–553, 554
technology transfer, 134
tectonophysics, 30
Teed, Cyrus Reed, 267
telegraph, 172, 552–553
    and longitude observations, 86, 323,
    354, 567
telephone, 7, 77
telescopes, building of, 567–568
Teller, Edward, 221, 317, 403, 415, 439,
    493–494
Temple Coffee House Botany Club, 496
Tennessee Valley Authority, 213, 275
Terman, Frederick Emmons, 182, 541,
    542, 553–554
Terman, Lewis M., 120, 195, 458
terrestrial magnetism, 30, 67, 106, 127
testing, psychological
    and intelligence, 112
tetracyclines, 47
Texas, University of, 118
Texaco, 240–241
Thayer, Sylvanus, 181
thermodynamics, 242, 314, 555–556
Thibaut, John, 524
Thimann, Kenneth V., 29
Thomas, Cyrus, 52, 259
Thomas, E. Donnall, 131
Thomas, Lewis, 321
Thomas, Norman, 489
Thomas, W.I., 119
Thompson, Benjamin, 483–484
Thomsen, Christen Juergenson, 51
Thomson, Elihu, 219
Thoreau, Henry David, 184, 335, 386,
    449, 557
Thorkelson, Halston J., 215
Thorndike, Edward L., 131
Three Mile Island nuclear power plant,
    401, 402
Throop Polytechnic Institute, 101
Trowbridge, Augustus, 215
Thurston, Robert, 179
Tilden, William C., 270
Tilton, James, 383

Timoshenko, Stephen, 181
Tiros, 347
Tiselivs apparatus, 568
Titanic, 411
Titan II, 48
tobacco mosaic virus, 543, 544
Tohoku Imperial University, 579
Tolman, Edward C., 57, 519
Tolman, Richard, 272, 413, 585
Tombaugh, Clyde, 328
Torrey, John, 90, 167, 245, 431, 501, 503,
    505, 558
Torrey Botanical Club, 95, 449
Townes, Charles H., 307
Townley, Sidney D., 511
Townsend, John Kirk, 5
Toxic Substances Control Act, 187
toxicology, 185
Train, Russell, 186
transcendentalism, 557
transit of Venus, 56, 339, 408, 476, 497,
    498
Transylvania University, 470
Trask, James, 445
Tresidder, Donald, 541–542
Trichinella spiralis, 312
Trivers, Robert, 530
Troost, Gerard, 5, 429
Troy Female Seminary, 167, 581
Trudeau, Edward, 559
Truman, Harry S., 208, 381, 403
Trumpler, Robert J., 318
tuberculosis, 163, 478, 559
Turner, Jonathan B., 361
Turner, Frederick Jackson, 231, 513–514
Turner, Thomas W., 270
Tuskegee Normal and Industrial Institute,
    110
Tuve, Merle Antony, 106, 560–561
Tykociner, Joseph, 277

U

Udall, Stewart, 335
Uehlenberg, George, 463
UFO, 137, 201, 563–564
ultracentrifugation, 126
Union Carbide Corporation, 343
Union of Concerned Scientists, 192, 564
Union Medical College, 123
United Nations Educational, Scientific,
    and Cultural Organization, 27–28
United States Agricultural Society, 16
United States Steel Corporation, 285
unit operations, 31, 176–177
UNIVAC, 135
Universal Oil Products, 177
universities, chemistry in, 114–118

University of California, 88, 118, 120,
    312, 508–509
University of Chicago, 3, 22, 43, 81, 119,
    133, 168, 531
University of Illinois, 8, 118, 277–278
University of Iowa, 120
University of Massachusetts Medical
    School, 125
University of Michigan, 2, 118, 435
University of Minnesota, 120
University of Nebraska, 78, 168, 390–391
University of North Carolina, 118
University of Pennsylvania, 88, 114, 130,
    176, 469, 498, 501
University of Texas, 118
University of the State of New York, 503
University of Washington, 118
unorthodox medicine, 340–341
Urey, Harold C., 117, 131
Usinger, R.L., 529

V

Vail, Alfred, 552
valence, 116–117, 117
Van Allen, James, 282
Van Allen belts, 241, 536
Vancouver, George, 231
Van de Graaff, Robert J., 134
Van de Graaf generator, 568, 560
van de Kamp, Peter, 201
Vanguard, 389
Van Vleck, John H., 94, 463, 464
Varian, Russell, 541
Varian, Sigurd, 541
Vassar College, 355–356, 581
Vanuxem, Lardner, 503
Vaughan, Victor, 468
Veblen, Oswald, 279
vector analysis, 243
Vening-Meinesz, Felix, 444
Venus, transit of, 56, 339, 408, 476, 497,
    498
Verrill, Addison Emery, 69, 590
Vidal, Gore, 301
Viereck, Les, 192
Vietnam War, 191, 412, 452, 489–490,
    528, 542
Viking, Project, 44, 201, 292, 306, 372
Vincenti, Walter, 180
Vine, Fred J., 444
Virginia state geological survey, 479
virology, 175–176, 579
vision, physiology of, 312
vitamins, 15
vivisection, 45–46
volcanology, 30, 574
von Braun, Werher, 48, 424
von Foerster, Heinz, 277